California

North Coast & Redwoods
p217

Northern Mountains
p272

Gold Country
p337

Lake Tahoe
p362

Napa & Sonoma Wine Country
p161

Yosemite & the Sierra Nevada
p400

San Francisco
p70

Marin County & the Bay Area
p110

Sacramento & Central Valley
p307

Central Coast
p456

Palm Springs & the Deserts
p661

Santa Barbara County
p514

Los Angeles
p555

Disneyland & Orange County
p593

San Diego & Around
p625

D1016522

THIS EDITION WRITTEN AND RESEARCHED BY

Sara Benson,

Andrew Bender, Alison Bing, Celeste Brash, Tienlon Ho, Beth Kohn,

Adam Skolnick, John A Vlahides

Contents

VENICE BOARDWALK P566

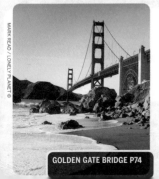

GOLDEN GATE BRIDGE P74

Contents

Contents

ON THE ROAD

YOSEMITE FALLS P404

Contents

UNDERSTAND

SURVIVAL
GUIDE

SPECIAL FEATURES

Welcome to California

From towering redwood forests in foggy Northern California to perfectly sun-kissed surf beaches in Southern California, this Golden State alongside the Pacific is a prize.

Natural Beauty

Don't be fooled by its perpetually fresh outlook and gung-ho attitude: California is older than it seems. Coastal bluffs and snowy peaks were created over millennia of tectonic upheavals that have threatened to shake California right off the continent. After unchecked 19th-century mining, logging and oil-drilling threatened to undermine the state's natural splendors, California's pioneering environmentalists – including John Muir and the Sierra Club – rescued old-growth trees and spurred the creation of national and state parks that still astound visitors today.

Fabulous Food & Drink

Because California produces most of the fresh produce in the US, minor menu decisions here can have nationwide impact. Every time they sit down to eat, Californians take trend-setting stands on mealtime moral dilemmas: certified organic versus spray-free, farm-to-table versus urban-garden-grown, veganism versus grass-fed humanely raised meats. But no matter what you order, it's likely to be local and creative, and it had better be good. For a chaser, California produces over 90% of the nation's wine-making grapes, and has twice as many breweries as any other state.

Creative Arts & Tech

From the Gold Rush to the dot-com bubble, California has survived extreme booms and busts, often getting by on its wits. Hollywood still makes most of the world's movies and TV shows, fed by a vibrant performing arts scene on stages across the state. Trends are kick-started here not by moguls in offices, but by motley crowds of surfers, artists and dreamers concocting the out-there ideas behind anything from skateboarding to biotechnology. If you linger in art galleries, cafes and bars, you may actually see the future coming.

Road Tripping

The wonder about hitting California's highways and byways is that things get more dramatic with every winding mile you detour from the big cities – trees get bigger, picturesque towns cuter and beaches more idyllic. Hug scenic oceanfront cliffs on Hwys 1 and 101 from Mexico to Oregon, or take an equally winding jaunt through historic Gold Country along Hwy 49. Follow pastoral back roads between vineyards in California's many wine countries (it's not just Napa), or take a weekend for a loop drive around Lake Tahoe. It's enough for a lifetime of road trips.

Why I Love California

By Sara Benson, Coordinating Author

Like almost half the people who live here, California is not where I was born, but it's where I've chosen to live. I never get tired of exploring (or more truthfully, eating my way around) my adopted home state, with its vibrant multicultural mix. Summer finds me climbing mountains in the Sierra Nevada and hitting SoCal beaches, while spring is time for wildflower blooms in the desert. Fall brings wine-country festivals and the tasting of new vintages straight from the barrel. In winter, nothing beats skiing at Lake Tahoe or Yosemite National Park.

For more about our authors, see page 784

Above: Big Sur (p481)

California

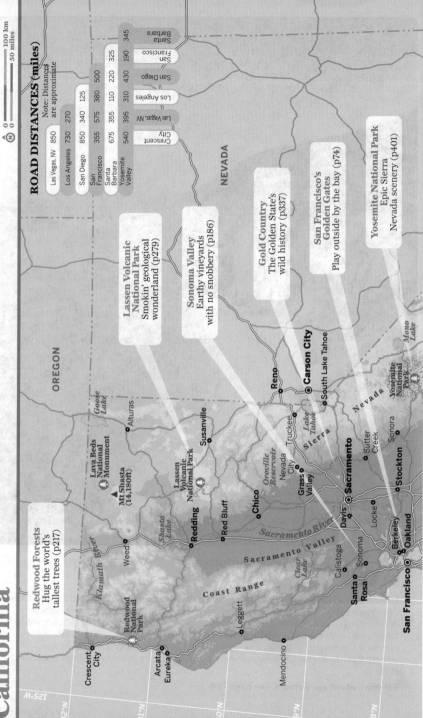

ROAD DISTANCES (miles)

Note: Distances are approximate

	Crescent City	Las Vegas, NV	Los Angeles	San Diego	Santa Barbara	San Francisco
Las Vegas, NV	850					
Los Angeles	730	270				
San Diego	850	340	125			
San Francisco	355	575	380	500		
Santa Barbara	675	355	110	220	325	
Yosemite Valley	540	395	310	430	190	345

Redwood Forests
Hug the world's tallest trees (p217)

Lassen Volcanic National Park
Smokin' geological wonderland (p279)

Sonoma Valley
Earthy vineyards with no snobbery (p186)

Gold Country
The Golden State's wild history (p337)

San Francisco's Golden Gates
Play outside by the bay (p74)

Yosemite National Park
Epic Sierra Nevada scenery (p401)

OREGON

NEVADA

Goose Lake

Lava Beds National Monument

Alturas

Mt Shasta (14,180ft)

Susanville

Lassen Volcanic National Park

Weed

Klamath River

Shasta Lake

Redding

Red Bluff

Chico

Oroville Reservoir

Nevada City

Grass Valley

Truckee

Reno

Carson City

Lake Tahoe

South Lake Tahoe

Sierra

Nevada

Sacramento River

Sacramento

Davis

Locke

Stockton

Sutter Creek

Sonora

Yosemite National Park

Mono Lake

Crescent City

Redwood National Park

Arcata
Eureka

Leggett

Mendocino

Coast Range

Clear Lake

Calistoga

Sonoma

Sacramento Valley

Santa Rosa

Berkeley

Oakland

San Francisco

100 km
50 miles

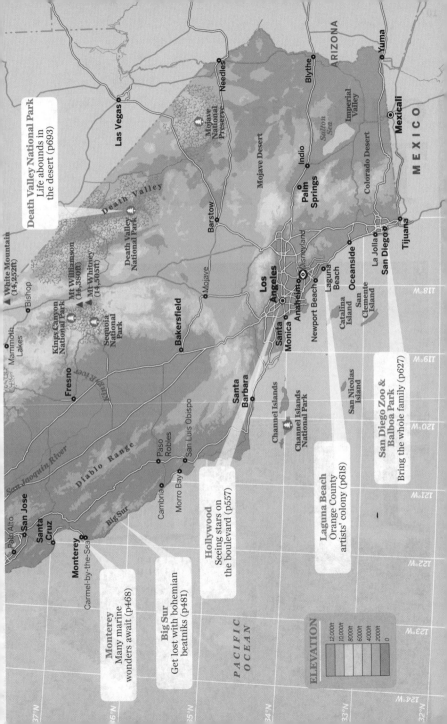

Death Valley National Park
Life abounds in the desert (p693)

Monterey
Many marine wonders await (p468)

Big Sur
Get lost with bohemian beatniks (p481)

Hollywood
Seeing stars on the boulevard (p557)

Laguna Beach
Orange County artists' colony (p618)

San Diego Zoo & Balboa Park
Bring the whole family (p627)

ELEVATION

12,000ft
10,000ft
8000ft
6000ft
4000ft
2000ft
0

PACIFIC OCEAN

MEXICO

ARIZONA

California's
Top 25

San Francisco's Golden Gates

1 Sashay out onto San Francisco's iconic bridge (p74) to spy on cargo ships threading through pylons painted 'International Orange.' Memorize the 360-degree views of the rugged Marin Headlands, downtown skyscrapers and the speck that is Alcatraz (p76). Not too far away, you could spend days getting lost in Golden Gate Park (p97) without uncovering all of its secret haunts, like the paddleboat pond and bison paddock, or fully exploring its innovative science and art museums. Weekend traffic closures make the park even more of a paradise for pedestrians and cyclists.

Redwood Forests

2 Ditch the cellphone and hug a tree, dude. And why not start with the world's tallest trees, redwoods? California's towering giants grow along much of the coast, from Big Sur north to the Oregon border. It's possible to cruise past these trees – or even drive right through them at old-fashioned tourist traps – but nothing compares to the awe you'll feel while walking underneath the ancient ones. Meditate on eternity at Muir Woods National Monument (p125), Humboldt Redwoods State Park (p39) or Redwood National & State Parks (p265).

DANITA DELIMONT / GETTY IMAGES ©

PGIAM / GETTY IMAGES ©

CHRIS MOORE / EXPLORING LIGHT PHOTOGRAPHY / GETTY IMAGES ©

PAUL HIFFMEYER / DISNEY ©

Sonoma Valley

3 As winemaking in the Napa Valley grows ever more dizzyingly upscale, here sun-dappled vineyards are still surrounded by pastoral ranchlands. The uniqueness of terroir is valued in this down-to-earth wine country, where you may taste new vintages straight from the barrel inside a tin-roofed shed while playing with the winemaker's pet dog. Who cares if it's not even noon yet? Relax and enjoy your late-harvest Zinfandel with a scoop of white-chocolate ice cream drizzled with organic olive oil. This is Sonoma (p190): conventions need not apply.

Disneyland Resort

4 Where orange groves and walnut trees once grew, Walt Disney built his dream, throwing open the doors of his 'Magic Kingdom' in 1955. Today, Disneyland (p596) and neighboring Disney California Adventure are SoCal's most-visited tourist attractions. Inside Anaheim's mega-popular theme parks, beloved cartoon characters waltz arm-in-arm down Main Street, U.S.A. and fireworks explode over Sleeping Beauty Castle on hot summer nights. If you're a kid, or just hopelessly young at heart, perhaps this really is 'The Happiest Place on Earth.'

Yosemite National Park

5 Welcome to what conservationist John Muir called his 'high pleasure-ground' and 'great temple.' Everything looks bigger at Yosemite National Park (p401), whether you're getting splashed by thunderous waterfalls that tumble over sheer cliffs, staring up at granite domes or walking in ancient groves of giant sequoias. Meander through valleys carved by glaciers, avalanches and earthquakes. For sublime views, perch at Glacier Point under a full moon or drive the high country's Tioga Rd on a cloudless summer day. Yosemite Valley

Santa Monica & Venice

6 How do you beat LA traffic? Hit the beach instead. Sunny Santa Monica (p565) grants instant happiness: learn to surf, ride a solar-powered Ferris wheel, dance under the stars on an old-fashioned pier, show kids the aquarium's tidal touch pools or just dip your toes in the water and let your troubles float away. Did we mention jaw-dropping sunsets? Then join the parade of New Agers, muscled bodybuilders, goth punks and hippie drummers at nearby Venice Beach, where everyone lets their freak flag fly. Venice Boardwalk (p566)

ARIADNE VAN ZANDBERGEN / GETTY IMAGES ©

MEDIOIMAGES / PHOTODISC / GETTY IMAGES ©

Death Valley National Park

7 Just uttering the name brings up visions of broken-down pioneer wagon trains and parched lost souls crawling across desert sand dunes. But the most surprising thing about Death Valley (p693) is how full of life it is. Spring wildflower blooms explode with a painter's palette of hues across camel-colored hillsides. Twist your way up narrow canyons cluttered with geological oddities, stand atop volcanic craters formed by violent prehistoric explosions, or wander Wild West mining ghost towns where fortunes have been lost – and found.

San Diego Zoo & Balboa Park

8 Beautiful Balboa Park (p629) is where San Diegans come to play – that is, when they're not at the beach. Bring the whole family to spend the day immersed in more than a dozen art, cultural and science museums, or simply marvel at the Spanish colonial and mission revival-style architecture while sunning yourself along El Prado promenade. Glimpse exotic wildlife and ride the 'Skyfari' aerial tram at San Diego's world-famous zoo (p629), or nab tickets for a show at the Old Globe Theaters (p647). Balboa Park

Hollywood

9 The movie and TV studios have all moved away, but Hollywood (p557) and Hollywood Walk of Fame still attract millions of visitors every year. This once-gritty neighborhood in LA is undergoing a rebirth of cool, blossoming with hip hotels, glittering restored movie palaces and glitzy velvet-roped bars and nightclubs. Snap a souvenir photo outside Grauman's Chinese Theatre (p557) or inside Hollywood & Highland's Babylon Court with the iconic Hollywood sign as a backdrop.

California's Missions

10 If you road-trip along the coast between San Diego and Sonoma you'll be following in the footsteps of early Spanish conquistadors and Catholic priests. Franciscan friar Junípero Serra founded many of California's 21 original missions in the late 18th century, including San Juan Capistrano (p622), which has been authentically restored, with gardens, stone arcades and chapels adorned by spiritual frescoes. Others are the haunting ruins of an era long past, where ghosts still pace the cloisters. Mission San Juan Capistrano

Mt Shasta

11 There's no other pile of rock in California that stirs the imagination quite like Mt Shasta (p288), as it suddenly rises from the surrounding flatlands. Native Californians believed that it was home of a sky-spirit chief, John Muir said its beauty made his 'blood turn to wine,' and a late-19th-century explorer reported that survivors of a lost continent were living in tunnels below its surface. Whether it's the 'energy vortex' felt by today's New Age pilgrims or the spine-tingling chills of hikers summiting its wind-blown peak, this mountain is magical.

Laguna Beach

12 In Orange County, Huntington Beach draws the hang-loose surfer crowd, while yachties play in the fantasy-land of Newport Beach. But further south, Laguna Beach (p618) beckons, with its more sophisticated blend of money, culture and natural beauty. Laguna's bohemian past still peeks out in downtown's art galleries, adorable Arts and Crafts bungalows tucked beside multimillion-dollar mansions, and the annual Festival of Arts and dramatic Pageant of the Masters.

LAURA CIAPPONI / GETTY IMAGES ©

JASON TODD / GETTY IMAGES ©

Monterey

13 The peninsular fishing village of Monterey (p468) calls to mind John Steinbeck and his gritty novels of American realism. Hop aboard a whale-watching cruise out into the bay's national marine sanctuary, some of whose aquatic denizens also swim in Cannery Row's eco-conscious, family-friendly aquarium. Soak up more authentic maritime atmosphere at the West Coast's oldest lighthouse in Pacific Grove, then wander downtown Monterey's hidden gardens and historic adobe-walled buildings from California's Spanish, Mexican and early American days. Monterey Bay Aquarium

Coronado

14 Who says you can't turn back time? Speed over the curved bay bridge or board the ferry from San Diego to seaside Coronado, a civilized escape back to a more genteel era. Revel in the late-19th-century socialite atmosphere at the palatial 'Hotel Del' (p639), where royalty and presidents have bedded down, and Marilyn Monroe cavorted in the 1950s screwball classic *Some Like It Hot*. Then pedal past impossibly white beaches all the way down the peninsula's Silver Strand, stopping for ice cream and rainbow-colored cotton candy.
Hotel del Coronado

Big Sur

15 Nestled up against mossy, mysterious-looking redwood forests, the rocky Big Sur (p481) coast is a secretive place. Get to know it like the locals do, especially if you want to find hidden hot springs and beaches where the sand is tinged purple or where giant jade has washed up. Time your visit for May, when waterfalls peak, or after summer vacation crowds have left but sunny skies still rule. Crane your neck skyward to catch sight of endangered California condors taking wing above ocean cliffs.

JOE MCBRIDE / GETTY IMAGES ©

S. GREG PANOSIAN / GETTY IMAGES ©

DAVID PEEVERS / GETTY IMAGES ©

Lake Tahoe

16 High in the Sierra Nevada Mountains, this all-seasons adventure base camp revolves around the USA's second-deepest lake (p362). In summer, startlingly clear blue waters lead to splashing, kayaking or even scuba diving. Meanwhile, mountain bikers career down epic single-track runs and hikers stride along trails threading through thick forests. After dark, retreat to a cozy lakefront cottage and toast s'mores in the firepit. When the lake turns into a winter wonderland, gold-medal ski resorts keep downhill fanatics, snowboarders and Nordic traditionalists more than satisfied.

Santa Barbara

17 Justifiably calling itself the 'American Riviera,' Santa Barbara (p516) is so idyllic, you just have to sigh. Waving palm trees, powdery beaches, fishing boats clanking about in the harbor – it'd be a travel cliché if it wasn't the plain truth. California's 'Queen of the Missions' is a rare beauty, especially with its signature red-roofed, white-washed adobe buildings. In fact, all of downtown was rebuilt harmoniously in Spanish Colonial Revival style after a devastating earthquake in 1925. Come escape just for the day, or maybe a wine-soaked weekend in the country.
Mission Santa Barbara

Surfing

18 Even if you never set foot on a board – and we, like, totally recommend that you do, brah – there's no denying the influence of surfing on all aspects of California beach life, from fashion to street slang. With gnarly local waves, you won't need to jet over to Hawaii to experience it for yourself. Pros ride world-class breaks off Malibu, Huntington Beach (aka 'Surf City USA'), La Jolla and Santa Barbara, while newbies get schooled at 'surfari' camps along the coast from San Diego north to Santa Cruz.

Gold Country

19 'Go west, young man!' could have been the rallying cry of tens of thousands of immigrants who arrived during California's Gold Rush era, which kicked off in 1848. Today, these rough-and-tumble Sierra Nevada foothills are a stronghold of history. Slowly wind past sleepy townships and abandoned mines on Hwy 49, also a gateway to swimming holes, white-water rafting, downhill mountain-biking bomber runs and tasting wine made from some of the state's oldest grapevines. Columbia State Historic Park (p358)

Coastin' on Amtrak

20 Evocatively named routes like *Coast Starlight* and *Pacific Surfliner* will tempt you to leave your car behind and ride the rails in SoCal. South of San Luis Obispo, glimpse remote beaches from Amtrak's panoramic-view observation cars. Blink and you're in Santa Barbara; hop off for a seaside swim at whistle-stop Carpinteria or Ventura, before rolling into LA's grand Union Station. Roll south to historic Mission San Juan Capistrano and North County beach towns before finishing in downtown San Diego. All aboard! Amtrak train, Los Angeles

HOLGER LEUE / GETTY IMAGES ©

HAL BERGMAN PHOTOGRAPHY / GETTY IMAGES ©

Lassen Volcanic National Park

21 Anchoring the southernmost link in the Cascades' chain of volcanoes, this alien landscape bubbles over with roiling mud pots, steamy fumaroles, colorful cinder cones and crater lakes. You won't find the crowds of more famous national parks, but Lassen (p279) still offers peaks to be conquered, azure waters to be paddled, forested campsites for pitching your tent and boardwalks through Bumpass Hell that will leave you awestruck.

Bumpass Hell, Lassen Volcanic National Park

Palm Springs

22 A star-studded oasis in the Mojave ever since the retro days of Frank Sinatra's Rat Pack, 'PS' (p663) is a chic desert resort getaway. Do like A-list stars and hipsters do: lounge by your mid-century modern hotel's swimming pool, go art-gallery hopping or vintage shopping, and drink cocktails from sunset till dawn. Feeling less loungey? Break a sweat on hiking trails that wind through desert canyons, or scramble to a summit in the San Jacinto Mountains, reached via a head-spinning aerial tramway.

JOHN ELK III / GETTY IMAGES ©

PANORAMIC IMAGES / GETTY IMAGES ©

MILES ERTMAN / GETTY IMAGES ©

EMILY RIDDELL / GETTY IMAGES ©

Channel Islands

23 Tossed like so many lost pearls off the coast, the Channel Islands are California's last outpost of civilization. They've been that way for thousands of years, ever since seafaring Chumash tribespeople established villages on these remote rocks. The islands also support an abundance of marine life, from coral reefs to giant elephant seals. Get back to nature in Channel Islands National Park (p551), a wildlife haven with fantastic sea kayaking and snorkeling, or make a posh getaway to Mediterranean-esque Catalina Island, with its harborfront hotels. Kelp forest, Anacapa Island (p552)

Mendocino

24 Mendocino (p543) is the North Coast's salt-washed sandcastle of dreams. Nothing restores the soul like a ramble out onto craggy headland cliffs and among berry brambles. In summer, fragrant bursts of lavender and jasmine drift on fog-laden winds over the town's unique redwood water towers. Churning surf is never out of earshot, and driftwood-littered beaches are potent reminders of the sea's power. Originally a 19th-century port built by New Englanders, Mendo today belongs to bohemians who favor art and nature for their religions.

Point Reyes National Seashore

25 If one park could encapsulate Northern California, Point Reyes (p129) would get our vote. Step across the San Andreas fault, then stand out by the lighthouse at what truly feels like land's end and peer through binoculars at migratory whales. Witness the raucous antics of a seasonal colony of giant elephant seals at Chimney Rock or hike among free-ranging herds of hulking tule elk. Then drive out to wind-swept beaches, where the horizon stretches toward infinity. Point Reyes Lighthouse (p130)

Need to Know

For more information, see Survival Guide (p749)

Currency
US dollars ($)

Language
English

Visas
Generally not required for citizens of Visa Waiver Program (VWP) countries with ESTA approval (apply online at least 72 hours in advance).

Money
ATMs widely available. Credit cards usually required for reservations. Traveler's checks (US dollars) rarely accepted. Tipping is customary, not optional.

Cell Phones
The only foreign phones that will work in the USA are multiband GSM models. Buy prepaid SIM cards locally.

Time
Pacific Standard Time (GMT/UTC minus eight hours)

When to Go

Arcata
GO Apr–Oct

San Francisco
GO Apr–Oct

Yosemite Village
GO Apr–Oct

Los Angeles
GO Apr–Oct

Palm Springs
GO Dec–Apr

Desert, dry climate
Dry climate
Warm to hot summers, mild winters
Warm to hot summers, cold winters

High Season (Jun–Aug)

➡ Accommodation prices up 50% to 100% on average.

➡ Major holidays are even busier and more expensive.

➡ Summer is low season in the desert, where temperatures exceed 100°F (38°C).

Shoulder Season (Apr–May & Sep–Oct)

➡ Crowds and prices drop, especially on the coast and in the mountains.

➡ Mild temperatures and sunny, cloudless days.

➡ Typically wetter in spring, drier in autumn.

Low Season (Nov–Mar)

➡ Accommodation rates lowest along the coast.

➡ Chilly temperatures, frequent rainstorms and heavy snow in the mountains.

➡ Winter is peak season in SoCal's desert regions.

Useful Websites

California Travel & Tourism Commission (www.visitcalifornia.com) Trip-planning guides.

Lonely Planet (www.lonelyplanet.com/usa/california) Destination info, hotel bookings, travelers' forums and more.

LA Times Travel (www.latimes.com/travel) News and blogs.

Sunset (www.sunset.com/travel/california) Travel tips.

California State Parks (www.parks.ca.gov) Activities, camping.

CalTrans (www.dot.ca.gov) Current highway conditions.

Important Numbers

All phone numbers have a three-digit area code followed by a seven-digit local number. For long-distance and toll-free calls, dial 1 plus all 10 digits.

Country code	1
International dialing code	011
Operator	0
Emergency	911
Directory assistance (local)	411

Exchange Rates

Australia	A$1	$0.88
Canada	C$1	$0.90
Euro zone	€1	$1.26
China	Y10	$1.63
Japan	¥100	$0.92
Mexico	MXN10	$0.75
New Zealand	NZ$1	$0.79
UK	£1	$1.62

For current exchange rates see www.xe.com.

Daily Costs

Budget:
Less than $75

➡ Hostel dorm beds: $25–$55

➡ Take-out meal: $6–$12

Midrange:
$75–$200

➡ Two-star motel or hotel double room: $75–$150

➡ Rental car per day, excluding insurance and gas: $30–$75

Top End:
Over $200

➡ Three-star hotel or beach resort room: $150–$300

➡ Three-course meal excluding drinks in top restaurant: $75–$100

Opening Hours

Businesses, restaurants and shops may close earlier and on additional days during the off-season (usually winter, except summer in the deserts). Otherwise, standard opening hours are as follows:

Banks 9am–5pm Monday to Thursday, to 6pm Friday, some 9am–1:30pm Saturday

Bars 5pm–2am daily

Business hours (general) 9am–5pm Monday to Friday

Nightclubs 10pm–4am Thursday to Saturday

Post Offices 8:30am–4:30pm Monday to Friday, some 9am–noon Saturday

Restaurants 7:30am–10:30am, 11:30am–2:30pm and 5:30pm–9pm daily, some later Friday and Saturday

Shops 10am–6pm Monday to Saturday, noon–5pm Sunday (malls open later)

Arriving in California

Los Angeles International Airport (p589) Taxis to most destinations ($30 to $50) take 30 minutes to one hour. Door-to-door shuttles ($16 to $27) operate 24 hours. FlyAway bus ($8) runs to Downtown LA. Free shuttles head to LAX City Bus Center and Metro Rail station.

San Francisco International Airport (p761) Taxis into the city ($35 to $55) take 25 to 50 minutes. Door-to-door shuttles ($16 to $20) operate 24 hours. BART trains ($8.65, 30 minutes) serve the airport from 5:30am to 11:45pm.

Getting Around

Most people drive themselves around California. You can also fly (it's expensive) or save money by taking long-distance buses or scenic trains. When distances are too far to walk in cities, hop aboard buses, trains, streetcars, cable cars or trolleys, or grab a taxi.

Car Traffic in metro areas and along coastal highways can be nightmarish, especially during weekday rush hours (7am to 10am and 3pm to 7pm). City parking is often an expensive hassle.

Train They're the fastest way to get around the San Francisco Bay Area and LA, but lines don't go everywhere. More expensive regional and long-distance Amtrak trains connect some destinations.

Bus Usually the cheapest and slowest option, but with more extensive metro-area networks. Inter-city, regional and long-distance Greyhound routes are limited and cost more.

For much more on **getting around**, see p760

What's New

Bay Bridge & Trail

After years of costly construction delays, the graceful new span of San Francisco's Bay Bridge between Oakland and Yerba Buena Island is finally open – you can drive, cycle or even walk across it. (p131)

Sunnylands

Near Palm Springs, step inside a mid-century modern estate where heads of state, royalty and Hollywood celebrities once stayed, surrounded by desert gardens and a fine-art collection. (p671)

Ace Hotel, Downtown Los Angeles

Portland's hip hotel chain wows with new downtown digs and the restored United Artists Theatre, a glittering 1920s movie palace now showcasing live music and dance. (p584)

Exploratorium

Newly expanded and relocated to the waterfront, San Francisco's Exploratorium – an interactive science museum that delights kids and adults alike – is better than ever. (p75)

SFJAZZ Center

See legendary performers on stage in Hayes Valley at the country's only purpose-built, stand-alone jazz center. (p105)

Paso Robles Wine Country

Gold medal–winning grapes have long grown in these sunny Central Coast vineyards, even before *Wine Enthusiast* magazine named Paso Robles 'wine region of the year' in 2013. (p501)

Santa Barbara's Funk Zone

It's just what this sometimes stuffy seaside city needed: an edgy, creative neighborhood space for art, food, craft beer and regional wines, all just a short walk from the beach. (p528)

Yosemite National Park

In 2014, California's most beloved national park celebrated the 150th anniversary of its original grant, which jump-started the USA's entire national park system. (p401)

Legoland Hotel

Let your kids pretend to be pirates or rule their own castle inside this northern San Diego theme park's super-fun lodgings, a quick drive from the ocean in Carlsbad. (p659)

Anaheim Packing District

Only a couple of miles from Disneyland, downtown Anaheim's early-20th-century citrus-packing house and car dealership have been transformed into a dining, drinking and shopping hot spot. (p602)

Devil's Slide Tunnels & Trail

Above the ocean in Pacifica, south of San Francisco, a perilously landslide-prone stretch of Hwy 1 has been paved over for hikers and cyclists, while drivers zip through nearly mile-long tunnels. (p157)

For more recommendations and reviews, see lonelyplanet.com/california

If You Like...

Fantastic Food

Infused by immigrant cultures for more than 200 years, California cuisine is all about creatively mixing it up, from kim-chi tacos to vegan soul food.

Chez Panisse Chef Alice Waters revolutionized California cuisine back in the '70s with seasonal locavarian cooking. (p145)

French Laundry High-flying kitchen mastered by Thomas Keller is a gastronomic highlight of Napa's wine country. (p175)

LA's food trucks They're everywhere now, but LA sparked the mobile foodie revolution, now with 200 chefs on wheels.

Ferry Building Duck inside San Francisco's waterfront collection of artisanal food vendors, or come for the farmers market. (p101)

Fish tacos Start your search for this tasty Mexicali snack by the beach in San Diego. (p642)

Craft Beer

Barrels from California's vineyards may steal the scene, but what's being brewed in copper vats across the Golden State is just as award-winning.

Lost Coast Brewery Knock back a pint of Downtown Brown while admiring conceptual-art beer labels. (p258)

Anderson Valley Brewing Company Mendocino County's solar-powered brewhouse lets you play disc golf with a bottle of oatmeal stout. (p241)

Stone Brewing Company San Diego upstart makes beers with bold character, like Arrogant Bastard Ale or smoked porter spiked with chipotle. (p645)

Anchor Brewing With 19th-century roots, San Francisco's most historic brewer trademarks its unique 'steam beer.' (p64)

Sierra Nevada Brewing Company This pioneer offers tours and pours its mega-popular pale ale in Chico. (p321)

Theme Parks

If visiting Disney's 'happiest place on earth,' getting a thrill from Hollywood's movie magic or riding a rad roller coaster is on your itinerary, Southern California is the place.

Disneyland Topping almost everyone's must-do fun list is Walt Disney's 'imagineered' theme park, with Disney California Adventure next door. (p596)

Universal Studios Hollywood Cinematic theme park with a studio backlot tram tour, rides and special-effects shows. (p567)

Legoland California Low-key theme park made of those beloved building blocks. (p657)

San Diego Zoo Safari Park Take a safari-style tram tour through an 'open-range' zoo. (p658)

Hiking

Ever since Native Americans made the first footpaths in the wilderness, Californians have been walking. Oceanside rambles, desert palm oases, skyscraping peaks and verdant forest idylls await.

Sierra Nevada Spend a lifetime trekking in national parks and alpine wilderness, or just a day summiting Mt Whitney. (p454)

North Coast Hardy backpackers tackle the Lost Coast Trail, while families ramble in misty redwood forests. (p251)

Marin County Headlands tempt hikers from SF's Golden Gate Bridge to Point Reyes. (p130)

Palm Springs & the Deserts Discover hidden oases, stroll across salt flats or enter Native Californian canyons. (p661)

Small Towns

When California's crowded metropolises get to be too much, make your escape to these beautiful in-between places by the beach, up in the mountains and down the road from vineyards.

Calistoga For Napa Valley's blue-jeans-and-boots crowd, mud-bath spas speckle a quaint downtown. (p181)

Bolinas End-of-the-road hamlet in NorCal's Marin County is no longer a secret. (p127)

Ferndale Charming Victorian-era farm town tucked away on the North Coast. (p254)

Mammoth Lakes Eastern Sierra's jumping-off point for all-seasons outdoor adventures. (p443)

Seal Beach Old-fashioned Orange County surf town with a cute main street and pier. (p608)

National & State Parks

Inland, jagged mountain peaks, high-country meadows and desert sand dunes beckon, while back at the coast, you'll be astonished by the diversity, extending to wind-tossed islands.

Yosemite National Park Ascend into the Sierra Nevada, where waterfalls tumble into glacier-carved valleys and wildflower meadows bloom. (p401)

Redwood National & State Parks Get lost among groves of the world's tallest trees on the foggy North Coast. (p265)

Death Valley National Park Uncover pockets of life in this desert landscape, peppered with geological oddities. (p693)

Lassen Volcanic National Park Camp by alpine lakes and traipse around the boiling mud pots of Bumpass Hell. (p279)

Channel Islands National Park Escape civilization on SoCal's isolated islands, nicknamed 'California's Galapagos.' (p551)

Top: Yosemite Valley, Yosemite National Park (p401)
Bottom: Victorian Inn, Ferndale (p255)

Nightlife

Now is your chance to step out at ultra-chic nightclubs. Not a fan of velvet ropes? No problem. California has plenty of other entertaining, come-as-you-are watering holes.

Los Angeles DJs spin at Hollywood's glam clubs, while nearby 'WeHo' is ground zero for LA's gay scene. (p583)

San Francisco Become a beatnik in North Beach, mingle with Mission hipsters or party with the Castro's rainbow-flag nation. (p103)

San Diego Go on a pub crawl in the Gaslamp Quarter, the historic red-light district, or don flip-fops for surfer bars. (p644)

Las Vegas, Nevada The Strip's high-wattage nightclubs are like a fantasy. (p712)

Film & TV Locations

All California's a sound stage, it sometimes seems. To witness the magic in action, join a live studio audience or tour a movie studio in LA.

Los Angeles Hollywood was born here. You can't throw a director's megaphone without hitting a celluloid sight, from Mulholland Drive to Malibu. (p555)

San Francisco Bay Area Relive classics like The Maltese Falcon and Hitchcock's thrillers Vertigo and The Birds.

Lone Pine Get misty-eyed over old-fashioned Westerns filmed in the Alabama Hills over in the Eastern Sierra. (p454)

Orange County Where soap operas, 'dramedies' and reality TV series have struck pop-culture gold. (p593)

Mendocino For over a century, this tiny North Coast town has starred in dozens of movies, from East of Eden to The Majestic. (p228)

Weird Stuff

SoCal's deserts and the North Coast especially rope in kooks and offbeat souls, but loopy LA and bohemian SF are just as jam-packed with memorable oddities.

Venice Boardwalk Gawk at the human zoo of body builders, chainsaw-jugglers and Speedo-clad snake-charmers. (p566)

Kinetic Grand Championship Outrageously whimsical, artistic and human-powered sculptures race along the North Coast. (p260)

Integratron Allegedly built with aliens' help, this giant rejuvenation and time machine awaits near Joshua Tree. (p678)

Madonna Inn Fantastically campy Central Coast hotel with 110 bizarrely themed rooms, from 'Caveman' to 'Hot Pink'. (p506)

Mystery Spot Santa Cruz's shamelessly kitschy 1940s tourist trap will turn your world upside down. (p462)

Solvang Danish-flavored village in Santa Barbara's wine country spirited out of a Hans Christian Anderson fairytale. (p539)

Las Vegas, Nevada Exploding faux volcanoes, a mock Eiffel Tower and an Egyptian-esque pyramid. (p704)

Museums

Who says California only has pop culture? You could spend most of your trip viewing multimillion-dollar art galleries, high-tech science exhibits, out-of-this-world planetariums and more.

Balboa Park Spend all day in San Diego hopping between top-notch art, history and science museums, including for kids. (p629)

Getty Center & Getty Villa Art museums that are as beautiful as their elevated settings and ocean views in West LA and Malibu. (p563 & p565)

California Academy of Sciences Eco-certified natural history museum in SF's Golden Gate Park breathes 'green' with a four-story rainforest and a living roof. (p97)

LA County Museum of Art More than 150,000 works of art span the ages and cross all borders. (p562)

Griffith Observatory There's no better place to see stars in Hollywood than at this hilltop planetarium. (p561)

MH de Young Museum A copper-skinned temple to art from around the globe in SF's Golden Gate Park. (p97)

Exploratorium Even adults love the zany interactive science learning fun at this indoor/outdoor landmark on San Francisco Bay. (p75)

History

Native American tribes, Spanish colonial presidios (forts) and Catholic missions, Mexican pueblos (towns) and mining ghost towns have all left traces here for you to find.

Mission San Juan Capistrano Painstakingly restored jewel along California's mission trail,

Old Town State Historic Park, San Diego (p631)

stretching from San Diego to Sonoma. (p622)

Gold Country Follow in the tracks of Western pioneers and hard-scrabble miners, or pan for gold yourself. (p337)

Old Town, San Diego Time travel on the site of California's first civilian Spanish colonial *pueblo*. (p631)

Monterey State Historic Park Get a feel for California's Spanish, Mexican and early American days inside adobe buildings. (p469)

Bodie State Historic Park Haunting mining ghost town in the Eastern Sierra, above Mono Lake. (p439)

Manzanar National Historic Site WWII Japanese American internment camp interprets a painful chapter of the USA's past. (p453)

Bringing Your Dog

What fun is it to go on vacation and leave your four-legged family member at home? These outdoorsy destinations welcome them with open arms and paws.

Huntington Beach Southern California's biggest and best dog beach, where Fido can run off-leash for 2 miles. (p609)

Lake Tahoe The Sierra Nevada's top outdoor playground for pups, with hiking trails, beaches, campsites and cabins. (p362)

Carmel-by-the-Sea On the Central Coast, everyone takes their pampered pooches to lunch, then lets them play in the surf. (p479)

Big Bear Lake Bring your canine companions for pet-friendly trails, cottages and camping in the mountains outside LA. (p591)

Shopping

It doesn't matter where you go in California, especially along the coast: there's a rack of haute couture, outlet-mall bargains or vintage finds begging to be stashed in your suitcase.

Los Angeles Forget Beverly Hills. Robertson Blvd has more star-worthy boutiques per block, and youthful Melrose Ave is more fashion-forward. (p586)

San Francisco Elevating thrift-store fashion to a high art, while indie boutiques spread from the Marina to the Mission. (p107)

Orange County Hit Costa Mesa's mini-malls, or browse boutiques with beautiful people in Laguna Beach. (p616)

Palm Springs Heaven for shoppers seeking retro 20th-century gems, with outlet shopping, too. (p673)

Month by Month

TOP EVENTS

Rose Bowl & Parade, January

Fleet Week & Miramar Air Show, September

Cinco de Mayo, May

Coachella Music & Arts Festival, April

California State Fair, July

California's most colorful celebrations happen in San Francisco and LA.

Mere mortals scream from the bleachers nearby when stretch limos arrive.

January

Typically the wettest month, January is a slow time for coastal travel. Mountain ski resorts are busy, as are Southern California's deserts.

☆ Rose Bowl & Parade

Held just before the Tournament of Roses college football game, this famous New Year's parade of flower-festooned floats, marching bands and prancing equestrians draws over 700,000 spectators to the LA suburb of Pasadena. (p568)

🎎 Chinese New Year

Firecrackers, parades, lion dances and street food celebrate the lunar new year, falling in late January or early February. Some of

February

Usually another rainy month for coastal California, but mountain ski resorts stay busy. Wildflowers start blooming. Valentine's Day is booked solid.

🏃 Wildlife-Watching

Don't let winter storms drive you away from the coast. February is prime time for spotting whales offshore, colonies of birthing and mating elephant seals, roosting monarch butterflies and hundreds of migratory bird species.

◉ Modernism Week

Do you dig Palm Springs' retro vibe, baby? Join other mid-century-modern style aficionados in mid-February for more than a week of architectural tours, art shows and swingin' cocktail parties. (p669)

☆ Academy Awards

The red carpet gets rolled out for Hollywood's A-list stars on Oscar night at the Dolby Theatre in late February or early March.

March

Less rainy, so travelers head back to the coast, especially for spring break. Desert tourism peaks as wildflowers keep blooming. Ski season winds down.

🏃 Mendocino Coast Whale Festivals

As the northbound winter migration of gray whales peaks, Mendocino, Fort Bragg and nearby towns celebrate with food and wine tasting, art shows and naturalist-guided walks and talks over three weekends.

🎎 Festival of the Swallows

The swallows famously return to Mission San Juan Capistrano in Orange County around March 19. The historic town celebrates its Spanish and Mexican heritage with events all month long. (p623)

April

Peak wildflower season in the high desert. Shoulder

season in the mountains and along the coast means lower hotel prices, except during spring break.

☆ Coachella Music & Arts Festival

Indie rock bands, cult DJs and superstar rock bands and rappers all converge outside Palm Springs for a three-day musical extravaganza held over two weekends in mid-April. (p669)

☆ San Francisco International Film Festival

One of the Americas' longest-running film festivals has been lighting up San Francisco since 1957, with a slate of over 150 independent-minded films, including premieres from around the globe, in late April and early May. (p92)

May

Weather starts to heat up statewide, although some coastal areas are blanketed by fog (May grey). The Memorial Day holiday weekend is the official start of summer, and one of the year's busiest travel times.

☆ Cinco de Mayo

¡Viva México! Margaritas, music and merriment commemorate the victory of Mexican forces over the French army at the Battle of Puebla on May 5, 1862. LA and San Diego really do it in style.

◉ Jumping Frog Jubilee & Calaveras County Fair

Taking inspiration from Mark Twain's famous short

story, the Gold Rush–era pioneer town of Angels Camp offers good old-fashioned family fun over a long weekend in mid-May, with country-and-western musicians and cowboys.

🏃 Bay to Breakers

On the third Sunday in May, costumed (no nakedness allowed nowadays) joggers and inebriated walkers make the annual pilgrimage from San Francisco's Embarcadero to Ocean Beach. Watch out for participants dressed as salmon, who run 'upstream' from the finish line! (p92)

June

Once school lets out for the summer, almost everywhere in California gets busy, from beaches to mountain resorts. But in the deserts, it's just too darn hot. Some coastal fog lingers (June gloom).

☆ Pride Month

Out and proud, California's gay pride celebrations take place throughout June, with costumed parades, coming-out parties, live music, DJs and more. The biggest, bawdiest festivities are in San Francisco and LA. San Diego celebrates in mid-July.

July

Beach season is in full swing, particularly in SoCal. Theme parks are mobbed by families, as are mountain resorts. July 4 is summer's peak travel weekend.

☆ Reggae on the River

Come party with Rastafarians, treehuggers and other fun freaks during two days of live bands, arts and crafts, food vendors, juggling, unicycling, camping and swimming in late July and early August.

◉ Festival of Arts & Pageant of the Masters

Exhibits by hundreds of working artists and a pageant of paintings 're-created' by costumed actors and accompanied by an orchestra keep Orange County's Laguna Beach plenty busy during July and August. (p619)

◉ California State Fair

A million people come to ride the giant Ferris wheel, cheer on pie-eating contests, browse agricultural and arts-and-crafts exhibits, taste California wines and craft beers, and listen to live bands in Sacramento over two weeks in late July. (p309)

☆ Comic-Con International

The alt-nation's biggest annual convention of comic-book geeks, sci-fi and animation lovers, and pop-culture memorabilia collectors brings out-of-this-world costumed madness to San Diego in late July. (p637)

August

Warm weather and water temperatures keep beaches busy. School summer vacations come to an end, but everywhere except for the deserts stays packed. Travel slows slightly before the Labor Day holiday weekend.

☆ Old Spanish Days Fiesta

Santa Barbara shows off its early Spanish, Mexican and American *rancho* culture with parades, rodeo events, arts-and-crafts exhibits and live music and dance shows in early August.

◉ Perseids

Peaking in mid-August, these annual meteor showers are the best time to catch shooting stars with your naked eye or a digital camera. Head away from urban light pollution to places like Joshua Tree and Death Valley National Parks in the deserts.

September

Summer's last hurrah is the Labor Day holiday weekend, which is extremely busy almost everywhere. After kids go back to school, the beaches and cities start seeing fewer visitors.

☆ Monterey Jazz Festival

Cool trad-jazz cats, fusion inventors and world-beat drummers all line up to play at one of the world's longest-running jazz festivals, held on the Central Coast over a long weekend in mid-September. (p473)

◉ Fleet Week & Miramar Air Show

San Diego's military pride is on display during this

week (or actually, more like a month) of land, air and sea events, including parades, concerts, ship-board tours and the USA's largest air show in late September or early October. (p637)

October

Even with beautifully sunny and balmy weather, things quiet down during the shoulder season. Travel deals abound along the coast and in cities, the mountains and the deserts, as temperatures begin cooling off.

🍷 Vineyard Festivals

All month long under sunny skies, California's wine countries celebrate bringing in the vineyard harvest with gourmet food-and-wine shindigs, grape-stomping 'crush' parties and barrel tastings. Some events start earlier in September.

☆ Hardly Strictly Bluegrass

Over half a million people come for free outdoor concerts in Golden Gate Park during the first weekend in October. Big-name stars like Emmylou Harris and Gillian Welch share multiple stages with folk, blues and jazz musicians. (p95)

☆ Halloween

Hundreds of thousands of revelers come out to play in LA's West Hollywood LGBTQ neighborhood for all-day partying and live entertainment. Over-the-top, often X-rated costumes must be seen to be believed.

November

Temperatures drop everywhere, with scattered rain and snowstorms just beginning. Coastal areas, cities and even the deserts are less busy for travelers, except around the Thanksgiving holiday. Ski season just begins.

◉ Día de los Muertos

Mexican communities honor deceased relatives on November 2 with costumed parades, sugar skulls, graveyard picnics, candlelight processions and fabulous altars, including in San Francisco, LA and San Diego.

◉ Death Valley '49ers

Take a trip back to California's Gold Rush during this annual encampment at Furnace Creek, with campfire singalongs, horseshoe tournaments and a Western art show. (p698)

December

Winter rains start to drench coastal areas, while travel to the typically sunny, dry desert regions picks up. Christmas and New Year's Eve are extremely crowded travel times, with a short dip in tourism between them.

◉ Parades of Lights

Sprucing up the Christmas holiday season with nautical cheer, brightly bedecked and illuminated boats float through many coastal California harbors, notably at Orange County's Newport Beach and San Diego.

Itineraries

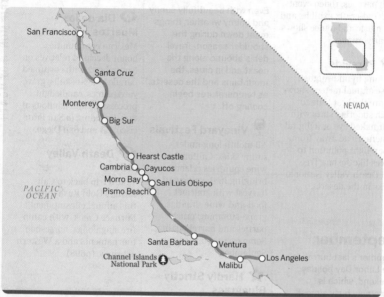

San Francisco

Santa Cruz

Monterey

Big Sur

NEVADA

Hearst Castle

Cambria — Cayucos

Morro Bay — San Luis Obispo

Pismo Beach

PACIFIC
OCEAN

Santa Barbara — Ventura

Channel Islands
National Park — Malibu — Los Angeles

Los Angeles to San Francisco

First-timers can get a taste of both halves of the Golden State – Southern *and* Northern California – on this 450-mile coastal drive, lazily stretching from the 'City of Angels' to the 'City by the Bay,' with astounding ocean panoramas almost all along the way.

Swoop down on **Los Angeles** for stargazing and clubby, cosmopolitan style. Cruise north through celeb-happy **Malibu**, strung with idyllic beaches. Hop aboard a boat to **Channel Islands National Park** from **Ventura**, then slow down for sophisticated seaside **Santa Barbara**, nestled against wine country. North of retro-1950s **Pismo Beach** and the college town of **San Luis Obispo**, Hwy 1 curves past picturesque beach towns like **Morro Bay**, **Cayucos** and **Cambria** reaching hilltop **Hearst Castle**.

Wind north along dizzying cliff edges through soul-stirring **Big Sur**, where redwood forests and waterfalls call. Dive into California's best aquarium in maritime **Monterey**. Next it's time for a bone-rattling roller coaster on the beach boardwalk at **Santa Cruz**.

Snake in the slow lane up Hwy 1, passing lighthouses, wind-tossed beaches and bays, to the counter-cultural capital of **San Francisco** for farm-to-table dining and artisanal cocktails.

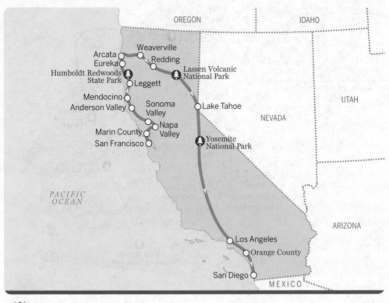

California Classics

Cover almost all of the Golden State's greatest hits on this grand tour, starting up north in foggy San Francisco and finishing over 1400 unforgettable miles later in sunny San Diego, down south by the Mexican border.

Kick off with a dose of big-city culture in **San Francisco**, sitting proudly on its bay. Hop a boat over to infamous Alcatraz prison, aka 'the Rock.' Then it's all aboard a cable car before traipsing through grassy Golden Gate Park. Head north over the arched Golden Gate Bridge into outdoorsy **Marin County**. California's most famous grapes grow just east in down-home **Sonoma Valley** and chichi **Napa Valley**. Detour west through more vineyards and apple orchards in the rural **Anderson Valley**, jumping onto coastal Hwy 1 north to **Mendocino**, a postcard-perfect Victorian seaside town.

Work your way north to rejoin Hwy 101 at **Leggett**, where your magical mystery tour of the Redwood Empire really begins. In **Humboldt Redwoods State Park**, encounter some of the tallest trees on earth. Kick back in historic harborfront **Eureka**, with its candy-colored Victorian architecture, or its radical northern neighbor, **Arcata**. Turn east on Hwy 299 for a long, scenic trip to hidden **Weaverville**, skirting the lake-studded Trinity Alps. Keep trucking east, then south on I-5 to **Redding**, where families throng Turtle Bay Exploration Park. Climb east on Hwy 44 to unearthly **Lassen Volcanic National Park**, a hellishly beautiful world at the southern tip of the Cascades Range.

Head southeast on Hwy 89 to **Lake Tahoe**, a four-seasons outdoor playground in the Sierra Nevada. Roll down the Eastern Sierra's Hwy 395, taking the back-door route via Tioga Rd (open seasonally) into **Yosemite National Park**. Gape at waterfalls tumbling over soaring granite cliffs and wander in groves of giant sequoias, the world's biggest trees.

Zoom south to **Los Angeles**, where cinematic beaches, diverse neighborhoods and cutting-edge cuisine await. Pound the pavement in Hollywood, then sprawl on the sand in chic Santa Monica or quirky Venice. Cruise south past the beautiful beaches of oh-so-stylish **Orange County** to hang-loose **San Diego** for surfing and fish tacos, dude.

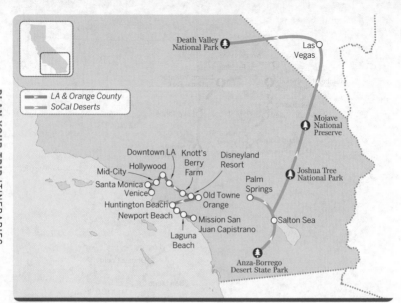

Death Valley
National Park

Las
Vegas

LA & Orange County
SoCal Deserts

Mojave
National
Preserve

Downtown LA
Knott's
Berry
Farm

Disneyland
Resort

Hollywood

Mid-City

Joshua Tree
National Park

Santa Monica

Palm
Springs

Venice

Old Towne
Orange

Huntington Beach

Newport Beach

Mission San
Juan Capistrano

Salton Sea

Laguna
Beach

Anza-Borrego
Desert State Park

5 DAYS LA & Orange County

Top-notch attractions, bodacious beaches and fresh seafood form an irresistible trifecta on this Southern California sojourn, covering 100 miles of sun, sand and surf.

Kick things off in **Los Angeles**. Skate north from oddball **Venice** to oceanfront **Santa Monica**, which beckons with a carnival pier. After you've photographed the star-studded sidewalks of **Hollywood**, dive into the many museums of **Mid-City** and the arts and cultural scenes of **Downtown LA**. Make a date with Mickey at perfectly 'imagineered' Disneyland. Next door, Disney California Adventure celebrates the Golden State. Both theme parks, part of **Disneyland Resort**, are in Anaheim. Not far away is **Knott's Berry Farm**, tempting with more thrill rides, and nostalgic **Old Towne Orange**.

Cruise west toward the Pacific to **Huntington Beach**, aka 'Surf City, USA.' Rent a board, play beach volleyball and build a bonfire. Swing by **Newport Beach** for people-watching by the piers, then roll south to **Laguna Beach**, an artists' colony. Slingshot back toward the I-5, making a quick detour to historic **Mission San Juan Capistrano**.

10 DAYS SoCal Deserts

Southern California's deserts feel like another planet, with giant sand dunes, palm-tree oases, volcanic craters and a rainbow of cinder cones. Go get lost on this 800-mile driving tour.

Start in glam **Palm Springs** resort, a masterpiece of mid-century modern architecture. Sip mojitos poolside, hike to palm-studded canyons and ride a tram into cool pine-scented mountains.

Drive past the Coachella Valley's date farms and along the shores of the mirage-like **Salton Sea**, turning west for wild **Anza-Borrego Desert State Park** to see bighorn sheep and wind-sculpted caves.

Boomerang north to **Joshua Tree National Park**, famous for its giant boulders and twisted namesake trees. Keep motoring north into the **Mojave National Preserve**, which protects 'singing' sand dunes and the world's largest Joshua-tree forest.

Ready for a change of pace? **Las Vegas**, baby. Before you gamble away your life savings at the Strip's casinos, escape west to **Death Valley National Park**, where otherworldly salt flats and marbled canyons amaze.

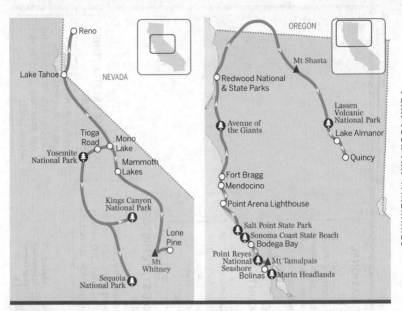

10 DAYS Sierra Nevada Ramble

Nothing can prepare your for the off-the-charts scenery, wildflower meadows and lakes of the Sierra Nevada. Take this 850-mile trip in summer, when all roads are open.

To gaze in awe up at the world's biggest trees and down at a gorge deeper than the Grand Canyon, start in **Sequoia & Kings Canyon National Parks**. Go west, then north to **Yosemite National Park**, where thunderous waterfalls and eroded granite monoliths overhang a verdant valley. Soar over the Sierra Nevada's snowy rooftop on Yosemite's high-elevation **Tioga Rd** (open seasonally). It's a quick trip south on Hwy 395 to **Mammoth Lakes**, an all-seasons adventure base camp, and 100 more miles to **Lone Pine**, in the shadow of mighty **Mt Whitney**.

Backtracking north, gaze out over **Mono Lake** and its odd-looking tufa formations, which you can paddle past in a kayak. Head to **Lake Tahoe**, a deep-blue jewel cradled by jutting peaks endowed with rugged hiking trails, hot springs and the slopes of ski resorts. Roll across the Nevada state line for casino nightlife in **Reno**.

2 WEEKS North Coast & Mountains

North of San Francisco, Hwy 1 skirts rocky shores, secluded coves and wind-whipped beaches before joining Hwy 101. Loop via the majestic Northern Mountains for a memorable 800-mile journey.

Across the Golden Gate Bridge, hike over the **Marin Headlands** or around **Mt Tamalpais**. Uncover **Bolinas** on your way north to ruggedly beautiful **Point Reyes National Seashore**. Beyond **Bodega Bay**, picnic at stunning **Sonoma Coast State Beach** or **Salt Point State Park**. Now the coast gets truly wild; climb to the tippy-top of **Point Arena Lighthouse**, poke around charming **Mendocino** village and ride the Skunk Train at **Fort Bragg**. Hwy 1 curves inland to Hwy 101, running north into hippie Humboldt County. Hike underneath ancient redwood trees on the **Avenue of the Giants** or further north in misty **Redwood National & State Parks**. Cut east through Oregon to the I-5 Fwy southbound to **Mt Shasta**. Pay your respects to that majestic mountain, then dart southeast on Hwy 89 to **Lassen Volcanic National Park**, a geological wonderland. Take a dip in **Lake Almanor**, nearby the amiable mountain town of **Quincy**.

Off the Beaten Track

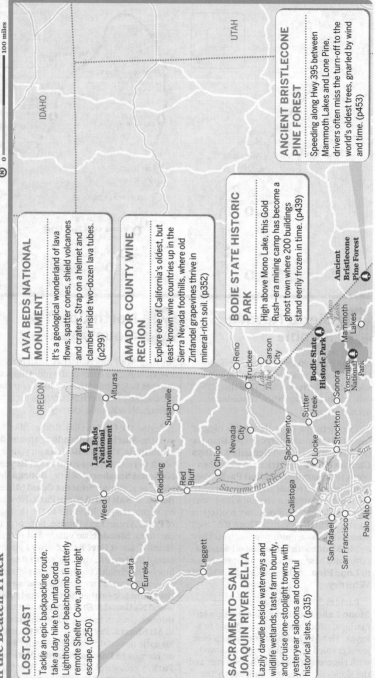

LOST COAST

Tackle an epic backpacking route, take a day hike to Punta Gorda Lighthouse, or beachcomb in utterly remote Shelter Cove, an overnight escape. (p250)

LAVA BEDS NATIONAL MONUMENT

It's a geological wonderland of lava flows, spatter cones, shield volcanoes and craters. Strap on a helmet and clamber inside two-dozen lava tubes. (p299)

AMADOR COUNTY WINE REGION

Explore one of California's oldest, but least-known wine countries up in the Sierra Nevada foothills, where old Zinfandel grapevines thrive in mineral-rich soil. (p352)

BODIE STATE HISTORIC PARK

High above Mono Lake, this Gold Rush–era mining camp has become a ghost town where 200 buildings stand eerily frozen in time. (p439)

ANCIENT BRISTLECONE PINE FOREST

Speeding along Hwy 395 between Mammoth Lakes and Lone Pine, drivers often miss the turn-off to the world's oldest trees, gnarled by wind and time. (p453)

SACRAMENTO–SAN JOAQUIN RIVER DELTA

Lazily dawdle beside waterways and wildlife wetlands, taste farm bounty, and cruise one-stoplight towns with yesteryear saloons and colorful historical sites. (p315)

MOJAVE NATIONAL PRESERVE

More beautifully lonely than Death Valley, this serene desert of volcanic cinder cones, Joshua trees and 'singing' sand dunes is a soul-stirring spot for hikers and campers. (p69)

PINNACLES NATIONAL PARK

On the way to nowhere, petite Pinnacles is worth a big detour for a chance to see endangered California condors soaring above spiring rock formations. (p500)

MINERAL KING VALLEY

Forget overcrowded Yosemite Valley. Head south to Sequoia National Park, where this wildflower-strewn basin shaped by glaciers beckons with hiking trails to unspoiled alpine lakes. (p430)

ANZA-BORREGO DESERT STATE PARK

Just shy of the Mexican border, Anza-Borrego was once an ancient sea. Today this painterly mosaic of Sonoran Desert is home to hot springs, wind caves and rare bighorn sheep. (p682)

Lake Mohave

Needles

ARIZONA

Blythe

Yuma

Mexicali

MEXICO

Tijuana

San Diego

Oceanside

Laguna Beach

Newport Beach

Anaheim

Los Angeles

Santa Monica

Indio

Palm Springs

Anza-Borrego Desert State Park

Salton Sea

Barstow

Mojave National Preserve

Death Valley National Park

Bishop

Mojave

Bakersfield

CALIFORNIA

Sequoia National Park

Kings Canyon National Park

Fresno

San Joaquin River

Paso Robles

San Luis Obispo

Morro Bay

Cambria

Monterey

Santa Cruz

San Jose

Santa Barbara

Pinnacles National Park

Plan Your Trip

Road Trips & Scenic Drives

California is irresistible to road trippers. Gas up and get ready for your jaw to drop, from serpentine coastal drives and sun-washed wine-country vineyards to towering redwood trees, skyscraping Sierra Nevada peaks and dramatic desert landscapes. Just make sure that rental car has unlimited miles – you'll need 'em all.

Tips for Road Trips

Automobile clubs

Consider joining AAA (p764) or Better World Club (p764) to cover emergency towing and roadside assistance service.

Cell (mobile) phones

Talking or texting on a cell phone without a hands-free device while driving is illegal in California.

Gas (fuel)

Readily available at self-service gas stations everywhere, except in national parks and remote desert and mountain areas. Expect to pay more than $4 per US gallon.

Road conditions

The California Department of Transportation (p366) has the latest updates on road closures, construction delays and detours, and winter chain-control requirements.

Speed limits

Unless otherwise posted, 65mph on freeways, 55mph on highways, 35mph on secondary roads.

For more essential driving information, including road rules and hazards, car rental and insurance, driver's licenses and border crossings, see p764.

Pacific Coast Highways

Make your escape from tangled, traffic-jammed freeways and cruise life in the slow lane. Snaking over 1000 miles along dizzying sea cliffs and over landmark bridges, passing ancient redwoods, historic lighthouses and quirky beach towns, California's two-lane coastal highways trace the edge of the continent. Only the stretch of Hwy 1 through Orange and Los Angeles Counties can legally call itself the Pacific Coast Hwy (PCH), but never mind those technicalities because equally bewitching ribbons of Hwy 1 and 101 await all along this shoreline route.

Why Go?

In between the big cities of San Diego, Los Angeles and San Francisco, you'll uncover hidden beaches and surf breaks, rustic seafood shacks dishing up the day's freshest catch, and wooden seaside piers for catching sunsets over boundless Pacific horizons. Lean into the endless curves and pull over for spectacular ocean views, whether brilliantly sunny or partly obscured by dramatic, moody fog. Once you get north of San Francisco, fishing villages are the gateways to wilder beaches and old-growth redwood forests.

When to Go

You can drive this route year-round, but July through September and sometimes into October brings the sunniest skies. Beware of 'May grey' and 'June gloom,' when clouds can blanket the coast almost everywhere south of San Francisco. Winter brings rain and chilly temperatures, especially on the North Coast.

The Route

If you drive the state's entire coastline, you'll get the best of both worlds – sunny SoCal beach life and foggy NorCal forests – with chances to stop and explore cities too. If you only have time to drive part of this coastal route, start with Orange County's beaches on PCH in SoCal; Hwy 1 from hippie Big Sur all the way north to Mendocino, crossing San Francisco's Golden Gate Bridge; or the verdant northern 'Redwood Coast' between Eureka and Crescent City.

Best Detour

Alongside Hwy 101, the incredible 32-mile Avenue of the Giants winds underneath a canopy of the world's tallest trees inside Humboldt Redwoods State Park.

Time & Mileage

Seven to 10 days, 1000 miles

Eastern Sierra Scenic Byway

US Hwy 395 traces the rugged back side of the Sierra Nevada Mountains, passing the otherworldly tufa columns of Mono Lake, thick pine forests, crystal alpine lakes and hot springs galore. Endless outdoor activities – camping, hiking, rock climbing and more – beckon beyond the asphalt.

Why Go?

This road trip is riddled with amazing geological spectacles, like the bizarre volcanic formations at Mono Lake and Devils Postpile, as well as soaring Mt Whitney (14,505ft), the highest peak in the lower 48 states. To unwind, spend an afternoon soaking in one of the area's hot springs.

Also along the way are fascinating historical sites like Bodie, a gold-mining ghost town, and heartbreaking Manzanar, where 10,000 people of Japanese ancestry were unjustly interned during WWII.

When to Go

June to September is peak season, although the shoulder months of May and June may be snow-free at lower elevations. The golden fall foliage of aspen trees is beautiful during October. Driving in winter isn't recommended, because roads can be icy and or even closed by snow.

The Route

If you're coming from SoCal's deserts, pick up Hwy 395 south of Lone Pine. From the north, Reno, Nevada is the closest major access point. Travelers coming from Yosemite National Park via Hwy 120 over Tioga Pass (usually open from May or June to October or November) intersect Hwy 395 at Lee Vining.

Best Detour

The Ancient Bristlecone Pine Forest has some of the oldest living trees on the planet (one named Methuselah has been around for over 4700 years). It's a 22-mile drive east of Big Pine via Hwy 168, then north on White Mountain Rd.

Time & Mileage

Three to five days, 350 miles

Hwy 49 Through Gold Country

That highway number is no coincidence: it commemorates the forty-niners who came to get rich in California's Gold Rush. Today Hwy 49 (Golden Chain Hwy) connects the historic towns and rolling hills of Gold Country up in the Sierra Nevada foothills, a short drive from the state capital of Sacramento.

Why Go?

Get a taste of California's early pioneer days, when hell-raising mine prospectors, railroad workers and ruffians rushed helter-skelter into the Wild West. Ride an antique steam train, try your own hand at panning for gold or be entertained at living-history museums and old-fashioned saloons. Hwy 49 also passes through little-known wine countries such as Amador County, where old-vine Zinfandel grapes grow. When the heat of the blistering summer sun gets to be too much, hop into a swimming hole, go underground and explore a cave or climb aboard a raft for a white-water river-adventure.

When to Go

Sunshine is almost guaranteed from May to October, with daytime highs spiking over 100°F (38°C) during July and August. A few rain showers in April and November shouldn't deter you much.

The Route

Start following Hwy 49 from either its southern end in Jamestown, just down the road from Sonora, or at its northern finish line in Nevada City. Don't count on driving any faster than 35mph along much of this twisting route.

Best Detour

Hwy 49 crosses US Hwy 50 at Placerville and the I-5 Fwy at Auburn; from either place, it's under an hour's drive west to Sacramento. Spend the day at the state capital's museums and riverside historical sites. In July join the crowds at the California State Fair.

Time & Mileage

Three to four days, 200 miles

Route 66

For a classic American road trip, nothing beats Route 66, connecting small-town streets and rural byways. What California novelist John Steinbeck nicknamed the 'Mother Road' triumphantly ends in SoCal, rolling through the Mojave Desert to the Pacific Ocean. You'll know you've finally found this legendary road when you're cruising by neon-lit diners, drive-in movie theaters, 20th-century motor courts and kitschy roadside attractions.

Why Go?

Speed west through eerie ghost towns beside railroad tracks in the Mojave Desert, starting from hot, hot Needles on the Arizona border. Stop into the Route 66 and train museum in the whistle-stop railway town of Barstow. Atop Cajoin Pass, order an ostrich burger and a date shake at the Summit Inn, then sleep inside a faux wigwam outside San Bernardino before getting your final kicks in Pasadena and LA, ending with waving palm trees and a carnival pier in Santa Monica.

When to Go

Springtime in the desert brings wildflower blooms and milder temperatures before the scorching heat of summer hits. Route 66 from Los Angeles to San Bernardino or even Victorville can be driven year-round.

The Route

You need to be an amateur sleuth to follow Route 66 these days. Historical realignments of the highway, dead ends and stretches paved over by the interstate are all par for the course. Getting lost every now and then is inevitable, but you can get turn-by-turn driving directions from the website www.historic66.com. Be prepared for rough, rutted driving conditions in the desert – take it easy on that gas pedal.

Best Detour

From nearby the desert pit stop of Amboy, it's about a 40-mile drive northeast to Kelso in the heart of the vast Mojave National Preserve, strewn with volcanic cinder cones, Joshua trees, sand dunes and hiking trails.

Time & Mileage

Two to three days, 320 miles

Marin County & Wine Country

Loop your way around Northern California's Bay Area, leaving hilly San Francisco behind to drive across the thrilling Golden Gate Bridge over to the tawny headlands and ocean beaches of Marin County before stopping to sip at the world-renowned wineries of Napa and Sonoma Valleys.

Why Go?

Marin County, just across the bay from San Francisco, has untamed beaches, crashing surf and redwood forests for nature lovers. Stop for oysters and to sample locally made cheese on your way out to windy, wild Point Reyes National Seashore. Then steer inland to Northern California's most famous wine country, where star chefs preside over farm-to-table restaurants and dozens of wineries pour out prized vintages, whether inside Sonoma's rustic barns and tin-roofed sheds or Napa's exclusive barrel rooms. Finish with a volcanic mud bath in the hot-springs resort of Calistoga.

When to Go

You can road trip here year-round. Wine-country festivals happen in the balmy spring and fall months. During the busy summer, temperatures are warm by the coast, hotter inland. Winter, when rainstorms and colder temperatures arrive, is great for wildlife-watching along the coast.

The Route

Follow Hwy 1 north over San Francisco's Golden Gate Bridge into Marin County, hugging the coast all the way to Point Reyes. Cut over inland to Hwy 101 flowing north to Santa Rosa. Drop south on Hwy 12 through Sonoma Valley, then take Hwy 29 north from Napa to Calistoga.

Best Detour

Just inland from Hwy 101 in Marin County is the small town of Tiburon, where you catch a ferry over to Angel Island State Park, with its historical sites, hiking and cycling trails, coves and beaches in the middle of San Francisco Bay.

Time & Mileage

Three days, 175 miles

Death Valley

Go where California pioneers and gold miners once rolled their wagons. Ghost towns and abandoned mines are evidence of the human struggle to survive here, yet this national park, the biggest of its kind outside of Alaska, is in fact spectacularly alive with 'singing' sand dunes, water-sculpted canyons, hidden springs and a riot of spring wildflowers.

Why Go?

The can't-miss photo op is in front of the sign for Badwater Basin, the lowest point in North America (282ft below sea level). Panoramas are even more impressive from the Artists Drive, a one-way scenic loop drive, and Zabriskie Point and Dante's View, both east of Furnace Creek. Take time to get out of the car to hike across salt flats and over sand dunes, up narrow slot canyons, atop extinct volcanic craters and into fantastically eroded badlands.

When to Go

February through April is the most popular time to visit for cooler temperatures and wildflower blooms. When temperatures peak over 120°F (49°C) in summer, Death Valley attracts heat-seeking masochists, but that heat can be harmful to your health – not to mention your car's engine.

The Route

Lonely highways crisscross the national park. To minimize doubling back, start in the south near Badwater Basin, then drive north to Furnace Creek, turn west to Stovepipe Wells and Panamint Springs, make a side trip up Emigrant and Wildrose Canyons, and finally end up north by Scotty's Castle.

Best Detour

Just east of the park across the Nevada state line via Hwy 374, the abandoned boomtown of Rhyolite was the queen of Death Valley's mines during its heyday. Next door you'll find the idiosyncratic Goldwell Open Air Museum of trippy outdoor art.

Time & Mileage

Three to four days, 400 miles

California's Best Road Trips & Scenic Drives

0 — 200 km
0 — 100 miles

LASSEN SCENIC BYWAY

Volcanoes, waterfalls & swimming lakes (p283)

FEATHER RIVER SCENIC BYWAY

Lakes, forests & river running (p286)

HWY 49 THROUGH GOLD COUNTRY

Old-timey towns for exploring (p348)

LAKE TAHOE

A lazy weekend loop (p362)

EBBETTS PASS SCENIC BYWAY

Top-of-the-world vistas (p440)

YOSEMITE NATIONAL PARK

Waterfalls, wildlife-watching & peaks (p401)

TRINITY SCENIC BYWAY

Lakes galore, but few tourists (p301)

ANDERSON VALLEY (p241)

Wine tasting & apple orchards

MARIN COUNTY & WINE COUNTRY

From ocean beaches to vineyards (p110 & p161)

OREGON
IDAHO
UTAH

Lava Beds National Monument

Crescent City
Arcata
Eureka
Weed
Redding
Red Bluff
Alturas
Susanville
Chico
Nevada City
Mendocino
Calistoga
Santa Rosa
San Francisco
Palo Alto
Sacramento
Stockton
Locke
Sutter Creek
Sonora
Reno
Truckee
Carson City
Bodie State Historic Park
Yosemite National Park
Mammoth Lakes
Ancient Bristlecone Pine Forest

Sacramento River

Lake Tahoe
Mono Lake

97
395
101
5
5
89
395
80
50
395
80
101

EASTERN SIERRA SCENIC BYWAY
Epic mountains for outdoor fun (p434)

DEATH VALLEY
Dramatic desert panoramas (p693)

ROUTE 66
America's historic 'Mother Road' (p688)

PALMS TO PINES SCENIC BYWAY
Cool off above Palm Springs (p664)

MONTEREY PENINSULA
Famous 17-Mile Drive (p468)

HWY 99
Central Valley farmstands & 'Little Sweden' (p325)

PACIFIC COAST HIGHWAYS
California's ultimate road trip (p456)

SIERRA VISTA SCENIC BYWAY
Mighty mountains, meadows & lakes (p421)

SEQUOIA & KINGS CANYON NATIONAL PARKS
Deep canyons, giant trees (p423)

SANTA BARBARA WINE COUNTRY
Spanish missions, vineyards & country roads (p532)

ANGELES CREST SCENIC BYWAY
Soaring high above LA (p568)

RIM OF THE WORLD SCENIC BYWAY
Escape to Big Bear Lake (p591)

ARIZONA

MEXICO

Needles

Mojave National Preserve (p688)

Barstow

Bishop

Death Valley National Park

Kings Canyon National Park

Sequoia National Park

Fresno

CALIFORNIA

Bakersfield

Mojave

San Jose

Santa Cruz

Monterey

Pinnacles National Park

Paso Robles

San Luis Obispo

Morro Bay

Cambria

Santa Barbara

Los Angeles

Santa Monica

Anaheim

Newport Beach

Laguna Beach

Oceanside

San Diego

Tijuana

Mexicali

Yuma

Blythe

Indio

Palm Springs

Anza-Borrego Desert State Park

Salton Sea

San Joaquin River

MEXICO

Plan Your Trip

Beaches, Swimming & Surfing

Beach life and surf culture are part of California's free-wheeling lifestyle, so play hooky on any day of the week and go hit the waves like locals do. Southern California is where you'll find the sunniest swimming beaches, while Northern California's rockier, often foggy strands beckon to beachcombers.

Best Beaches

San Diego
Coronado, Mission Beach, Pacific Beach, La Jolla

Orange County
Newport Beach, Laguna Beach, Crystal Cove State Park, Doheny State Beach

Los Angeles
Santa Monica, Venice, South Bay, Malibu

Santa Barbara
East Beach, El Capitán State Beach, Refugio State Beach, Carpinteria State Beach

Central Coast
Main Beach (Santa Cruz), Moonstone Beach, Cayucos, Pismo State Beach

San Francisco Bay Area
Stinson Beach, Point Reyes National Seashore, Pacifica State Beach

North Coast
Sonoma Coast State Beach, Lost Coast, Trinidad State Beach

Swimming

If lazing on the beach and taking a dip in the Pacific is what your California dreams are made of, look no further than Southern California (SoCal). With miles and miles of wide, sandy beaches, you will find it easy to get wet and wild almost anywhere between Santa Barbara and San Diego. Ocean temperatures in SoCal become tolerable by May or June, peaking in July and August.

Northern California (NorCal) beaches are generally rocky, with dangerously high swell in some places and windy conditions that make swimming less than inviting. NorCal beaches remain chilly year-round – bring or rent a wetsuit!

Building bonfires on the beach at sunset is a California tradition, but they're no longer permitted at most beaches for environmental reasons. Legally, you can build bonfires only in designated firepits – show up early in the day to snag one and bring your own firewood. Unless otherwise posted, drinking alcohol is usually prohibited on beaches, except at campgrounds.

During the hottest dog days of summer, another way to keep cool is by swimming is at Legoland (p657), in San Diego's

North County; **Soak City Orange County** ([☎]714-220-5200; www.knotts.com; adult/child 3-11yr & senior $27/22; [⊙]mid-May–Sep; [♿]) in Anaheim, near Disneyland; or Wet 'n' Wild Palm Springs (p668) in the desert.

Safety Tips

➡ Most beaches, especially in Southern California, have flags to distinguish between surfer-only sections and sections for swimmers. Flags also alert beachgoers to dangerous water conditions.

➡ Popular beaches (again, mostly in Southern California) have lifeguards, but can still be dangerous places to swim. Obey all posted warning signs and ask about local conditions before venturing out.

➡ Stay out of the ocean for at least three days after a major rainstorm because of dangerously high levels of pollutants flushed out through storm drains.

➡ Water quality varies from beach to beach, and day to day. For current water-safety conditions and beach closures, check the **Beach Report Card** (http://brc.healthebay.org) issued by the nonprofit organization **Heal the Bay** (www.healthebay.org).

Best Family-Friendly Beaches

➡ **Silver Strand State Beach** (p633) Coronado

➡ **Santa Monica State Beach** (p566) Los Angeles

➡ **Leo Carrillo State Beach** Malibu

➡ **Balboa Peninsula** (p612) Newport Beach

➡ **Carpinteria State Beach** (p544) Santa Barbara County

WARNING! RIPTIDES

If you find yourself being carried off-shore by a dangerous ocean current called a riptide, the important thing is to just keep afloat. Don't panic or try to swim against the current, as this will quickly exhaust you and you could drown. Instead, swim parallel to the shoreline and once the current stops pulling you out, swim back to shore.

➡ **Arroyo Burro Beach County Park** (p520) Santa Barbara

➡ **Avila Beach** (p508) San Luis Obispo County

➡ **Natural Bridges State Beach** (p461) Santa Cruz

➡ **Stinson Beach** (p126) Marin County

➡ **Trinidad State Beach** (p263) North Coast

Best Beaches for Bonfires

➡ **Huntington City Beach** (p609) Orange County

➡ **Main Beach** (Corona del Mar State Beach; p617) Orange County

➡ **Mission Beach** San Diego

➡ **Carmel Beach City Park** (p480) Central Coast

➡ **Ocean Beach** (p96) San Francisco

Best Places for Beach Volleyball

➡ **Manhattan Beach** (p563) LA's South Bay

➡ **Hermosa Beach** (p563) LA's South Bay

➡ **Huntington City Beach** (p609) Orange County

➡ **Mission Bay** (p635) San Diego

➡ **East Beach** (p522) Santa Barbara

Books & Maps

The outstanding *California Coastal Access Guide* (University of California Press, 2014) has comprehensive maps of every public beach, reef, harbor, cover, overlook and coastal campground, with valuable information about parking, hiking trails, facilities and wheelchair access. It's especially helpful for finding secret pockets of uncrowded sand.

Surfing

Surf's up! Are you down? Even if you have never set foot on a board, there's no denying the influence of surfing on every aspect of California beach life, from street clothing to slang. Surfing is an obsession up and down the SoCal coast, particularly in San Diego and Orange Counties.

The most powerful ocean swells arrive along California's coast during late fall and winter. May and June are generally the flattest months, although they do bring warmer water. Speaking of temperature, don't believe all those images of hot blonds surfing in skimpy bikinis; without a wetsuit, you'll likely freeze your butt off except at the height of summer, especially in NorCal.

Crowds can be a problem at many surf spots, as can overly territorial surfers. Befriend a local surfer for an introduction before hitting Cali's most famous waves, such as notoriously agro Windansea Beach and Malibu's Surfrider Beach.

Sharks do inhabit California waters but attacks are rare. Most take place in the so-called 'Red Triangle' between Monterey on the Central Coast, Tomales Bay north of San Francisco and the offshore Farallon Islands.

Rentals & Lessons

You'll find board rentals on just about every patch of sand where surfing is possible. Expect to pay about $20 per half day for a board, with wetsuit rental costing another $10 or so.

Two-hour group lessons for beginners start around $100 per person, while private, two-hour instruction easily costs over $125. If you're ready to jump in the deep end, many surf schools offer more expensive weekend surf clinics and weeklong 'surfari' camps.

Stand-up paddleboarding (SUP) is easier than learning to surf, and it's skyrocketing in popularity. You'll find similarly priced board-and-paddle rentals and lessons popping up all along the coast, from San Diego to north of San Francisco Bay.

Top Surf Spots for Pros

California comes fully loaded with easily accessible world-class surf spots, the lion's share of which are in SoCal. If you're already a wave-sliding expert, check out:

➡ **Huntington Beach** (p609) This beach in Orange County may have the West Coast's most consistent waves, with miles of breaks.

➡ **Trestles** (p623) The OC's premier summer spot, with big but forgiving waves, a fast ride and both right and left breaks.

➡ **Windansea Beach** (p652) This San Diego spot has a powerful reef break, while nearby **Big Rock** (p652) churns out gnarly tubes.

➡ **Surfrider Beach** (p565) A clean right break in Malibu that just gets better with bigger waves.

➡ **Rincon Point** (p521) In Carpinteria, this is another legendary point-break that peels forever.

➡ **Steamer Lane** (p460) Glassy point-breaks and rocky reef-breaks below an old lighthouse that houses a small surfing museum in Santa Cruz.

➡ **Mavericks** (p157) Big-wave surfing at Half Moon Bay. Waves top 50ft when the most powerful winter swells arrive (see www.mavericksinvitational.com to learn about the annual surf competition).

Best Surf Breaks for Beginners

The best spots to learn to surf are at the beach breaks of long, shallow bays where waves are small and rolling. Along California's coast, popular places for beginners, and where many surf schools also offer lessons, include the following:

➡ **San Diego** Mission Beach (p635), Pacific Beach (p635), La Jolla (p652), Oceanside (p660)

➡ **Orange County** Seal Beach (p608), Huntington Beach (p609), Newport Beach (p612), Laguna Beach (p618)

➡ **Los Angeles** Santa Monica (p565), Malibu (p565)

➡ **Santa Barbara County** Leadbetter Beach (p522), Carpinteria (p544)

➡ **Central Coast** Santa Cruz (p460), Cayucos (p494)

Online Resources

➡ Browse the atlas, webcams and reports at **Surfline** (www.surfline.com) for the lowdown from San Diego to Humboldt County.

➡ Orange County–based **Surfer** (www.surfermag.com) magazine's website has travel reports, gear reviews, blogs, forums and videos.

➡ Check out **Surfrider Foundation** (www.surfrider.org), a nonprofit organization that works to protect the coastal environment.

➡ Bone up on your surf-speak at the **Riptionary** (www.riptionary.com).

Books & Maps

➡ Water-resistant *Surfer Magazine's Guide to Southern California Surf Spots* (Chronicle Books, 2006) and *Surfer Magazine's Guide to Northern and Central California Surf Spots* (Chronicle Books, 2006) are jam-packed with expert reviews, information, maps and photos.

Plan Your Trip
California Camping & Outdoors

California is an all-seasons outdoor playground. Go hiking among desert wildflowers in spring, swimming in the Pacific under the summer sun, mountain biking among fall foliage and whale-watching in winter. For even bigger thrills, launch a glider off ocean bluffs, climb sheer granite walls or hook a kite onto a surfboard.

Camping

Throughout California, camping is much more than just a cheap way to spend the night. Pitch a tent beside alpine lakes and streams with views of snaggletoothed Sierra Nevada peaks, along gorgeous strands of Southern California sand or take shelter underneath redwoods, the tallest trees on earth, from Big Sur north to Oregon. So-Cal's deserts are magical places to camp next to sand dunes on full-moon nights.

If you didn't bring your own tent, you can buy (and occasionally rent) camping gear at outdoor outfitters and sporting-goods shops in most cities and some towns, especially near national parks.

Campground Types & Amenities

➡ **Primitive campsites** Usually have fire pits, picnic tables and access to drinking water and vault toilets; most common in national forests (USFS) and on Bureau of Land Management (BLM) land.

➡ **Developed campgrounds** Typically found in state and national parks, these offer more

When & Where

Best Times to Go

Cycling & mountain biking Apr-Oct

Hiking Apr-Oct

Kayaking, snorkeling & scuba diving Jul-Oct

Rock climbing Apr-Oct

Skiing & snowboarding Dec-Mar

Whale-watching Jan-Mar

White-water rafting Apr-Oct

Windsurfing Apr-Oct

Top Experiences

Backpacking John Muir Trail

Cycling Pacific Coast Highway

Hiking Redwood National & State Parks

Mountain biking Lake Tahoe

Rock climbing Yosemite National Park

Sea kayaking Channel Islands

Snorkeling & scuba diving La Jolla

White-water rafting Sierra Nevada

California's Best Places to Camp

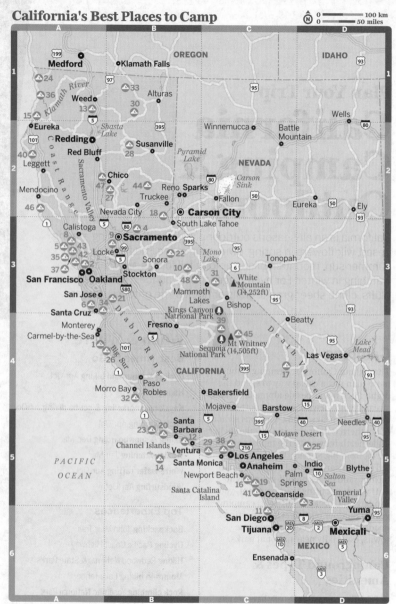

amenities, including flush toilets, barbecue grills and occasionally hot showers.

➡ **Private campgrounds** Often cater to RVs (recreational vehicles) with full electricity and water hookups and dump stations; tent sites may be sparse and uninviting. Hot showers and

coin-op laundry usually available, and possibly a swimming pool, wi-fi and camping cabins.

➡ **Walk-in (environmental) sites** Provide more peace and privacy, and may be significantly cheaper than drive-in sites. A few state-park

California's Best Places to Camp

campgrounds reserve walk-in sites for long-distance hikers and cyclists only.

Seasons, Rates & Reservations

Many campgrounds, especially in the mountains and in Northern California, are closed from late fall through early spring or summer. Opening and closing dates vary each year, depending on weather conditions and the previous winter's snowfall. Private campgrounds are often open year-round, especially those closest to cities, beaches and major highways.

Many public and private campgrounds accept reservations for all or some of their sites, while a few are strictly first-come, first-served. Overnight rates range from free for the most primitive campsites to $60 or more for pull-through RV sites with full hookups.

A few booking services let you search for public and private campground locations and amenities, check availability and

reserve campsites online. They may charge a reservation fee of up to $10.

Recreation.gov (☎877-444-6777, 518-885-3639; www.recreation.gov; most tent & RV sites $10-25) Camping and cabin reservations in national parks, national forests (USFS) and other federal recreational lands (eg BLM).

ReserveAmerica (☎916-638-5883, 800-444-7275; www.reserveamerica.com) Reservations for California state-park campgrounds and cabins that accept advance bookings, as well as East Bay and Orange County regional parks and some private campgrounds.

Kampgrounds of America (KOA; ☎888-562-0000; http://koa.com) National chain of reliable but more expensive private campgrounds offering full facilities, including for RVs.

Good Sam Club (☎866-205-7451; www.goodsamclub.com) Free online search tool for private and public campgrounds popular with RVs. Annual membership (from $25) entitles you to a 10% discount at participating campgrounds.

Cycling & Mountain Biking

Strap on that helmet! California is outstanding cycling territory, no matter whether you're off for a leisurely spin along the beach, an adrenaline-fueled mountain ride or a multiday road-cycling tour along the coast. The cycling season runs year-round in most coastal areas, although coastal fog may rob you of views both in winter and during 'May grey' and 'June gloom.' Avoid the North Coast and the mountains during winter (too much rain and snow at higher elevations) and SoCal's deserts in summer (too dang hot).

Road Rules

➡ In national parks, bicycles are usually limited to paved and dirt roads and are not allowed on trails or in designated wilderness areas.

➡ Most national forests and BLM lands are open to mountain bikers. Stay on already established tracks and always yield to hikers and horseback riders.

➡ At California's state parks, trails are off-limits to bikes unless otherwise posted, while paved and dirt roads are usually open to cyclists and mountain bikers.

Best Places to Cycle

➡ Even heavily trafficked urban areas may have good cycling turf, especially in SoCal. Take, for example, LA's beachside South Bay Trail or shoreline bike paths in beach towns such as Santa Barbara and Newport Beach.

➡ In the Bay Area, cruise through San Francisco's Golden Gate Park (p97) and over the Golden Gate Bridge (p74), then hop on the ferry back across the bay from Sausalito. Angel Island is another great bike-and-ferry combo.

➡ On the Central Coast, the ocean-view Monterey Peninsula Recreational Trail and scenic 17-Mile Drive entice cyclists of all skill levels.

➡ Many of California's wine countries offer beautiful DIY and guided bike tours, including Napa and Sonoma Valleys.

➡ For road cyclists, nothing surpasses winding, coastal Hwy 1, especially the dizzying stretch through Big Sur.

➡ Up north in Humboldt Redwoods State Park (p39), take a gentle ride among the world's tallest trees on the Avenue of the Giants.

➡ In the Sierra Nevada, Yosemite Valley has paved recreational paths that pass by meadows, waterfalls and granite spires.

Best Mountain-Biking Areas

➡ Just north of San Francisco, the Marin Headlands offer a bonanza of trails for fat-tire fans, while Mt Tamalpais lays claim to being the sport's birthplace.

➡ Top-rated single-track rides near Lake Tahoe include Mr Toad's Wild Ride and the Flume Trail. In the neighboring Gold Country, Downieville offers an enormous downhill rush (p346).

➡ Speed freaks sing the praises of the Eastern Sierra's Mammoth Mountain, whose summer bike park beckons with more than 80 miles of single-track. More ski areas that open trails and chairlifts to mountain bikers in summer include Big Bear Lake outside LA and Northstar (p389) at Lake Tahoe.

➡ SoCal's Joshua Tree and Death Valley national parks have miles of backcountry roads for mountain biking. So do Anza-Borrego Desert State Park outside San Diego and the Santa Monica Mountains north of LA.

➡ State parks especially popular with mountain bikers include NorCal's Prairie Creek Redwoods, Montaña de Oro on the Central Coast and Orange County's Crystal Cove.

➡ Inland from Monterey, Fort Ord National Monument has more than 80 miles of dirt single-track and fire roads for mountain bikers.

Maps & Online Resources

Local bike shops and some tourist offices can supply you with more cycling route ideas, maps and advice.

➡ **California Bicycle Coalition** (p763) links to free online cycling maps, bike-sharing programs and community bike shops.

➡ **Adventure Cycling Association** (p763) sells long-distance cycling route guides and touring maps, including for the entire Pacific Coast.

➡ **League of American Bicyclists** (www.bikeleague.org) can help you find bicycle specialty shops and local cycling clubs.

➡ For online forums and reviews of mountain-biking trails in California, search **www.mtbr.com** and **www.socaltrailriders.org**.

Hiking

With epic scenery, California is perfect for exploring on foot. That's true whether you have your heart set on peak-bagging 14,000-footers, trekking to desert oases, rambling among the world's tallest, largest and most ancient trees or simply walking on the beach by booming surf. In spring or early summer, a painter's palette of wildflowers blooms on coastal hillsides, in mountain meadows, on damp forest floors and, most famously, in desert sands.

Best Places to Hike

No matter where you find yourself in California, you're never far from a trail, even in metropolitan areas. Head to national and state parks for a staggering variety of trails, from easy nature walks negotiable by wheelchairs and strollers to multiday backpacking routes through rugged wilderness.

➡ **Sierra Nevada** In Yosemite, Sequoia & Kings Canyon National Parks and around Lake Tahoe, clamber toward waterfalls, wildflower meadows and alpine lakes, tackle mighty granite domes and peaks, or wander in pine-scented forests.

➡ **SoCal's Deserts** Best hiked in spring and fall, Death Valley and Joshua Tree National Parks, Mojave National Preserve and Anza-Borrego Desert State Park lead you to palm-canyon oases and mining ghost towns, up volcanic cinder cones and across sand dunes and salt flats.

➡ **San Francisco Bay Area** Marin Headlands, Muir Woods, Mt Tamalpais and Point Reyes National Seashore, all within a 90-minute drive of San Francisco, are crisscrossed by dozens of superb hiking trails.

➡ **North Coast** Redwood National and State Parks and the Avenue of the Giants offer misty walks through groves of old-growth redwoods, or you can scout out wilder beaches along the challenging Lost Coast Trail (p251).

➡ **Northern Mountains** Summiting Mt Shasta is a spiritually uplifting experience, while Lassen Volcanic National Park is a bizarre landscape of smoking fumaroles, cinder cones and craters.

➡ **Los Angeles** Ditch your car in the Santa Monica Mountains National Recreation Area, where many movies and TV shows were filmed, or head out to the cooler climes of Big Bear Lake.

Fees & Wilderness Permits

➡ Most California state parks charge a daily parking fee of $4 to $15. There's often no charge for pedestrians or cyclists. Don't be a jerk and park your car just outside the gate, then walk in – California's state parks are chronically underfunded and need your support.

➡ National park entry averages $15 to $20 per vehicle for seven consecutive days. Some national parks, including the Channel Islands and Redwood, are free admission.

➡ For unlimited admission to national parks, national forests and other federal recreation lands, buy an 'America the Beautiful' annual pass (p752). They're sold at national park visitor centers and entry stations, as well as at most USFS ranger stations.

➡ If you don't have an 'American the Beautiful' annual pass, you'll need a **National Forest Adventure Pass** (☏909-382-2623, 909-382-2622; www.fs.fed.us/r5/sanbernardino/ap/; per day $5, annual pass $30) to park in some recreational areas of SoCal's national forests. Buy passes from USFS ranger stations and local vendors such as sporting-goods stores (see the website for a complete list).

➡ Often required for overnight backpacking trips and a few extended day hikes, wilderness permits (cost varies, from free to over $20) are issued at ranger stations and park visitor centers. Daily quotas may be in effect during

---

TAKE A (REALLY LONG) HIKE

Famous long-distance trails that wind through California include the 2650-mile **Pacific Crest National Scenic Trail** (PCT; www.pcta.org), which takes hikers from Mexico to Canada. Running mostly along the PCT, the 211-mile **John Muir Trail** (JMT; www.pcta.org) links Yosemite Valley and Mt Whitney via the Sierra Nevada's high country. Enjoy inspirational views of Lake Tahoe while tracing the footsteps of early pioneers and Native Americans along the 165-mile **Tahoe Rim Trail** (www.tahoerimtrail.org). The **California Coastal Trail Association** (www.coastwalk.org) is working to build a 1200-mile trail along California's shoreline that's already over half complete.

peak periods, usually late spring through early fall. Some wilderness permits can be reserved, and the most popular trails (eg Mt Whitney) may sell out several months in advance.

Maps & Online Resources

➡ There are bulletin boards showing basic trail maps and safety information at most major trailheads, some of which also have trail-guide brochure dispensers.

➡ For short, established hikes in national and state parks, free maps handed out at visitor centers or ranger stations are usually sufficient. A more detailed topographical map may be necessary for longer backcountry hikes.

➡ Topo maps are sold at park bookstores, visitor centers, ranger stations and outdoor-gear shops. The **USGS Store** (www.store.usgs.gov) offers its (sometimes outdated) topographic maps as free downloadable PDFs, or you can order print copies online.

➡ Learn how to minimize your impact on the environment while traipsing through the wilderness at the **Leave No Trace Center for Outdoor Ethics** (http://lnt.org) online.

Scuba Diving & Snorkeling

All along California's coast, rock reefs, shipwrecks and kelp beds teem with sea creatures ready for their close-up. Ocean waters are warmest in SoCal, but wetsuits are recommended for divers year-round.

Local dive shops are your best resource for equipment, guides, instructors and boat trips. With PADI certification, you can book one-tank boat dives for $65 to $150; reserve at least a day in advance. To dabble in diving with no previous experience, local outfitters offer beginners' courses that include basic instruction, followed by a shallow beach or boat dive, for around $150.

Snorkelers can rent a mask, snorkel and fins from most dive shops or beach concessionaires for about $20 to $45 per day. If you're going to take the plunge more than once or twice, it's probably worth buying your own mask and fins. Remember not to touch anything while you're out snorkeling, and never snorkel alone.

BUT WAIT, THERE'S MORE!

ACTIVITY	LOCATION	REGION
Bird-watching	Klamath Basin National Wildlife Refuges	Northern Mountains
	Mono Lake	Sierra Nevada
	Salton Se	The Deserts
Caving	Lava Beds National Monument	Northern Mountains
	Crystal Cave	Sierra Nevada
	Pinnacles National Monument	Central Coast
Fishing*	Dana Point	Orange County
	San Diego	San Diego
	Bodega Bay	North Coast
	Trinity Alps	North Coast & Mountains
Golf	Palm Springs & Coachella Valley	The Deserts
	Pebble Beach	Central Coast
	Torrey Pines	San Diego
Hang-gliding & paragliding	Torrey Pines	San Diego
	Santa Barbara	Santa Barbara County
Horseback riding	Yosemite National Park	Sierra Nevada
	Wild Horse Sanctuary	Northern Mountains

* For fishing licenses, regulations and locations, consult the California Department of Fish and Wildlife website (www.wildlife.ca.gov).

Best Scuba Diving & Snorkeling Spots

➡ San Diego–La Jolla Underwater Park Ecological Reserve is a great place for beginning divers, while La Jolla Cove attracts snorkelers.

➡ More experienced divers and snorkelers steer towards Orange County's Crystal Cove State Park and Divers Cove and the shipwrecks off San Diego's Mission Beach.

➡ Offshore from LA and Ventura, Catalina Island and Channel Islands National Park are major diving and snorkeling destinations.

➡ With its national marine sanctuary, Monterey Bay offers world-renowned diving and snorkeling, although you'll need a thick wetsuit.

➡ Just south of Monterey, Point Lobos State Natural Reserve is another gem for scuba divers and snorkelers (permit reservations required).

White-Water Rafting

California has dozens of kick-ass rivers, and feeling their surging power is like taking a thrilling ride on nature's roller coaster. Paddling giant white-water rapids swelled by the snowmelt that rips through sheer canyons, your thoughts are reduced to just two simple words: 'survive' and 'damn!' Myriad opportunities are suited to the abilities of any river rat, even beginning paddlers. Most of the premier river runs are in the Sierra Nevada and Gold Country, but the Northern Mountains also offer some rollicking rides.

White-water trips are not without danger, and it's not unusual for participants to fall out of the raft in rough conditions. Serious injuries are rare, however, and most trips are without incident. No prior experience is needed for guided river trips up to Class III, but for Class IV you want to be an excellent swimmer, in good shape, and with some paddling experience under your life-jacket belt.

Seasons, Rates & Online Resources

The main river-running season is from April to October, although exact months depend on which river you're rafting and

ACTIVITY	LOCATION	REGION
	South Lake Tahoe	Lake Tahoe
Hot-air ballooning	Del Mar	San Diego
	Temecula	San Diego
	Napa Valley	Napa & Sonoma Wine Country
Kiteboarding & windsurfing	San Francisco Bay	San Francisco
	Mission Bay	San Diego
	Donner Lake	Lake Tahoe
Kayaking & canoeing	Channel Islands National Park	Santa Barbara County
	Elkhorn Slough	Central Coast
	Mendocino	North Coast
	Tomales Bay	Marin County
	Russian River	Napa & Sonoma Wine Country
	Morro Bay	Central Coast
	San Diego	San Diego
	Laguna Beach	Orange County
Rock climbing	Yosemite National Park	Sierra Nevada
	Joshua Tree National Park	The Deserts
	Pinnacles National Park	Central Coast
	Bishop	Eastern Sierra
	Truckee	Lake Tahoe

the year's spring snowmelt runoff from the mountains. You'll be hurtling along in either large rafts holding a dozen or more people, or smaller ones seating half a dozen; the latter tend to be more exhilarating because they can tackle rougher rapids and everyone paddles.

The **California Whitewater Rafting website** (www.c-w-r.com) covers all of California's prime river-running spots, with links to outfitters and river conservation groups. Commercial rafting outfitters run a variety of trips, from morning or afternoon floats to overnight and multiday expeditions. Book ahead and expect to pay more than $100 for a one-day trip.

Whale-Watching

During their annual migration, gray whales can be spotted off the California coast from December to April, while blue, humpback and sperm whales pass by in summer and fall. You can try your luck whale-watching (eg from lighthouses) while staying shore-bound – it's free, but you're less likely to see whales and you'll be removed from all the action.

Just about every port town worth its sea salt along the coast offers whale-watching boat excursions, especially during winter. Bring binoculars and dress in warm, waterproof layers. Choppy seas can be nauseating. To avoid seasickness, sit outside on the boat's second level – but not too close to the diesel fumes in back.

Half-day whale-watching cruises cost from $25 to $90 per adult (up to 50% less for children). Make reservations at least a day ahead. Better tour boats limit the number of passengers and have a trained naturalist on board. Some tour companies let you go again for free if you don't spot any whales on your first trip.

Snow Sports

Alpine scenery, luxury mountain cabins, high-speed modern ski lifts, mountains of fresh powder, a cornucopia of trails from easy-peasy 'Sesame Street' to black-diamond 'Death Wish' – they're all hallmarks of a California winter vacation in the snow. The Sierra Nevada Mountains offer the best slopes and trails for skiers and snowboarders, although snow conditions have been unreliable in recent years due to unusually low winter snowfall.

Ski season runs from late November or early December until late March or early April, although this depends on weather conditions and elevation. All resorts have ski schools, rent equipment and offer a variety of lift tickets, including cheaper half-day and multiday versions. Prices vary tremendously, from $45 to $115 per day for adults; discounts for children, teens and seniors are typically available. 'Ski & stay' lodging packages may offer big savings.

Best Places for Snow Sports

➡ **Around Lake Tahoe** For sheer variety, the dozen-plus downhill skiing and snowboarding resorts ringing Lake Tahoe are unbeatable. Alongside world-famous ski resorts such as Squaw Valley (p365), host of the 1960 Winter Olympic Games, you'll find scores of smaller operations, many of them with lower lift-ticket prices, smaller crowds and great runs for beginners and families. Royal Gorge (p367), near Truckee, is North America's largest cross-country ski resort. Family-friendly 'sno-parks' offer sledding hills and snow play.

➡ **Mammoth & June Mountains** Mammoth Mountain (p443) is another darling of downhill devotees and usually has the longest ski and snowboarding season. Beginning and intermediate skiers and snowboarders hit the less-crowded slopes of nearby June Mountain (p442).

➡ **Yosemite National Park** In the glacier-carved winter wonderland of Yosemite National Park, Badger Pass (p411) welcomes families and beginning skiers and snowboarders. California's oldest ski resort, it's also a launch pad for cross-country skiing and snowshoe treks, and kids will love the snow-tubing hill. You can snowshoe or cross-country ski among giant sequoias elsewhere in Yosemite, as well as in Sequoia & Kings Canyon National Parks (p425).

➡ **Northern Mountains** Mt Shasta Board & Ski Park (p289) is popular with families.

➡ **Nearby Los Angeles** Even sunny Southern California gets in on the snow action at Big Bear Lake. Palm Springs' aerial tramway whisks you into the San Jacinto Mountains (p668), where the whole family can rent snowshoes or cross-country skis.

Plan Your Trip

Travel with Children

California is a tailor-made destination for family travel. The kids will be begging to go to theme parks and teens to celebrity hot-spots. Then take 'em into the great outdoors – from sunny beaches shaded by palm trees to four-seasons mountain playgrounds.

California for Kids

There's not too much to worry about when traveling in California with your kids, as long as you keep them covered in sunblock.

Children's discounts are available for everything from museum admission and movie tickets to bus fares and motel stays. The definition of a 'child' varies – from 'under 18' to age six. At theme parks, some rides may have minimum-height require-ments, so let younger kids know about this in advance, to avoid disappointment and tears.

It's fine to bring kids along to most restaurants, except top-end places. Casual restaurants usually have high chairs and children's menus and break out paper placemats and crayons for drawing. At theme parks, pack a cooler in the car and have a picnic in the parking lot to save money. On the road, many supermarkets have wholesome, ready-to-eat takeout dishes.

Baby food, infant formula, disposable diapers (nappies) and other necessities are widely sold at supermarkets and phar-macies. Most women are discreet about breastfeeding in public. Many public toilets have a baby-changing table, while private gender-neutral 'family' bathrooms may be available at airports, museums etc.

Best Regions for Kids

Los Angeles

See stars in Hollywood and get behind the movie magic at Universal Studios, then hit the beaches and Griffith Park for fun in the sun. What, it's raining? Dive into the city's many kid-friendly museums instead.

San Diego, Disneyland & Orange County

Think SoCal theme parks galore: Disneyland, Knott's Berry Farm, the San Diego Zoo & Safari Park, Legoland and more. Oh, and those sandy beaches just couldn't be more beautiful.

San Francisco Bay Area

Explore hands-on, whimsical and 'Wow!' muse-ums, hear the barking sea lions at Pier 39 or Point Reyes National Seashore, traipse through Golden Gate Park and ride San Francisco's famous cable cars.

Yosemite & the Sierra Nevada

Watch your kids gawk at Yosemite's waterfalls and granite domes, then go hiking among groves of giant sequoias, the world's biggest trees. In the Eastern Sierra, Mammoth Lakes is a year-round outdoor-adventure base camp.

Children's Highlights

It's easy to keep kids entertained no matter where you travel in California. At national and state parks, ask at visitor centers about family-friendly, ranger-led activities and self-guided 'Junior Ranger' programs, in which kids earn themselves a badge after completing an activity booklet.

Theme Parks

➡ **Disneyland** (p596) and Disney California Adventure Kids (p602), teens and the young-at-heart – all adore the 'Magic Kingdom

➡ **Knott's Berry Farm** (p605) Near Disney, SoCal's original theme park offers thrills-a-minute, especially on spooky Halloween nights.

➡ **Legoland** (p657) In San Diego's North County, this fantasyland of building blocks is made for tots and youngsters.

➡ **Universal Studios Hollywood** (p567) Enjoy movie-themed action rides, special-effects shows and a working studio backlot tram tour.

Aquariums & Zoos

➡ **Monterey Bay Aquarium** (p468) Meet aquatic denizens of the deep at a national marine sanctuary.

➡ **San Diego Zoo Safari Park** (p629) Go on safari around the world at California's best and biggest zoo.

➡ **Aquarium of the Pacific** (p567) Long Beach's aquarium houses critters from balmy Baja California to the chilly north Pacific, including a shark lagoon.

➡ **Living Desert** (p665) Outside Palm Springs, this educational zoo features a walk-through animal hospital and family camp-outs under the stars.

➡ **Seymour Marine Discovery Center** (p459) Santa Cruz's university-run aquarium makes interactive science fun, with tide pools for exploring nearby at the beach.

Beaches

➡ **Los Angeles** (p555) Carnival fun and an aquarium await on Santa Monica Pier, or hit Malibu's perfect beaches just up Hwy 1.

➡ **Orange County** (p607) Pick from Newport Beach's kiddie-sized rides at Balboa Pier, Laguna Beach's miles of million-dollar sands,

Huntington Beach (aka 'Surf City, USA') or old-fashioned Seal Beach.

➡ **San Diego** (p625) Head over to Coronado's idyllic Silver Strand, play in Mission Bay by SeaWorld, lap up La Jolla or kick back in surf-style North County beach towns.

➡ **Central Coast** (p456) Laze on Santa Barbara's unmatched beaches, then roll all the way north to Santa Cruz's famous boardwalk and pier.

➡ **Lake Tahoe** (p362) In summer, it's California's favorite high-altitude escape: a sparkling diamond tucked in the craggy Sierra Nevada.

The Great Outdoors

➡ **Yosemite National Park** (p401) Get a slice of Sierra Nevada scenery, with gushing waterfalls, alpine lakes, glacier-carved valleys and peaks.

➡ **Redwood National & State Parks** (p265) A string of nature preserves on the North Coast protect magnificent wildlife and the planet's tallest trees.

➡ **Lassen Volcanic National Park** (p279) A peaceful destination in Northern California for otherworldly volcanic scenery and lakeside camping and cabins.

➡ **Griffith Park** (p561) Bigger than NYC's Central Park, this LA greenspace has tons of fun for younger kids, from miniature train rides and a merry-go-round to planetarium shows.

Museums

➡ **San Francisco** (p70) The city is a mind-bending classroom for kids, especially at the interactive Exploratorium, multimedia Children's Creativity Museum and ecofriendly California Academy of Sciences in Golden Gate Park.

➡ **Los Angeles** (p555) See stars (the real ones) at the Griffith Observatory, dinosaur bones at the Natural History Museum of Los Angeles and the Page Museum at the La Brea Tar Pits, then have hands-on fun at the California Science Center.

➡ **San Diego** (p625) Balboa Park is jam-packed with museums and a world-famous zoo, or take younger kids to the engaging New Children's Museum downtown.

➡ **Orange County** (p593) Bring budding lab geeks to the Discovery Science Center and get a pint-sized dose of arts and culture in the Kidseum at the Bowers Museum, all near Disneyland.

➡ **Northern Mountains** (p272) Redding's Turtle Bay Exploration Park combines an ecomuseum, an arboretum and botanical and butterfly gardens beside the Sacramento River.

Planning

A word of advice: don't pack your schedule too tightly. Traveling with kids always takes longer than expected, especially when navigating metro areas such as LA, San Diego and San Francisco, where you'll want to allow extra time for traffic jams and getting lost.

Accommodations

Rule one: if you're traveling with kids, always mention it when making reservations. At a few places, notably B&Bs, you may have a hard time if you show up with little ones. When booking, be sure to request the specific room type you want, although this is often not guaranteed.

Motels and hotels typically have rooms with two beds or an extra sofabed, which are ideal for families. They may also have roll-away beds or cots (also request these when making reservations), typically for a nightly surcharge. Some properties advertise 'kids stay free,' although this may apply only if no extra bedding is required.

Resorts may offer daytime activity programs for kids and child-care services. At other hotels, front desk staff or a concierge might be able to help you make babysitting arrangements. Ask whether babysitters are licensed and bonded, what they charge per hour per child, whether there's a minimum fee and if they charge extra for transportation and meals.

Transportation

Airlines usually allow infants (up to age two) to fly for free – bring proof of age – while older children require a seat of their own and don't usually qualify for reduced fares. Children receive substantial discounts on most trains and buses.

In cars, any child under age six or weighing less than 60lb must be buckled up in the back seat in a child or infant safety seat. Most car-rental agencies offer these for about $10 per day, but you must specifically book them in advance.

On the road, rest stops are few and far between, and gas stations and fast-food bathrooms tend to be icky. However, you're usually never far from a shopping mall, which generally have well-kept restrooms.

What to Pack

Sunscreen. And bringing sunscreen should remind you to bring hats, swimsuits, flip-flops and goggles. If you like beach umbrellas and sand chairs, pails and shovels, you'll probably want to bring your own or buy them at local supermarkets and pharmacies. At many beaches, you can rent bicycles and watersports gear.

For outdoor vacations, bring broken-in hiking shoes and your own camping equipment. Outdoor gear can be purchased or sometimes rented from local outdoor outfitters and sporting-goods shops. But the best time to test out gear is before you take your trip. Murphy's Law dictates that wearing brand-new hiking shoes always results in blisters, and setting up a new tent in the dark ain't easy.

If you forget some critical piece of equipment, **Traveling Baby Company** (www.travelingbaby.com) and **Baby's Away** (www.babysaway.com) rent cribs, strollers, car seats, high chairs, backpacks, beach gear and more.

Books & Online Resources

➡ Lonely Planet's *Travel with Children* is loaded with valuable tips and amusing anecdotes, especially for new parents and kids who haven't traveled before.

➡ **Lonelyplanet.com** (www.lonelyplanet.com): ask questions and get advice from other travelers in the Thorn Tree's 'Kids to Go' and 'USA' forums.

➡ The state's official tourism website, **Visit California** (www.visitcalifornia.com), lists family-friendly attractions, activities and more – just search for 'Family Fun' and 'Events.'

➡ **Travel for Kids** (www.travelforkids.com) has no-nonsense listings of kid-friendly sights, activities, hotels and recommended children's books for all regions of California.

Fruit and vegetable market at Pier 39 (p80), San Francisco

Plan Your Trip

Eat & Drink Like a Local

As you graze the Golden State, you'll often want to compliment the chef – and they're quick to share the spotlight with local farmers, fishers, ranchers and artisanal food producers. Best of all, California cuisine keeps redefining and refining itself – and along with it, the way the rest of the country eats.

Top 10 California Food & Drink Festivals

Asparagus Festival
Central Valley (p327), late April

Arcata Bay Oyster Festival
North Coast (p260), mid-June

California Avocado Festival
Santa Barbara County (p544), early October

Castroville Artichoke Festival
Near Monterey (p472), May/June

Gravenstein Apple Fair
Sonoma County (p202), mid-August

Little Italy Festa
San Diego (p637), mid-October

Mendocino Wine & Mushroom Festival
North Coast (p230), early November

National Date Festival
(www.datefest.org) Outside Palm Springs, February

San Diego Beer Week
(http://sdbw.org) Early November

Strawberry Festival at Monterey Bay
Central Coast (p473), early August

California Cuisine: Then & Now

'Let the ingredients speak for themselves!' is the rallying cry of California cuisine. With fruit, vegetables, seafood and meats this fresh, heavy French sauces and fussy molecular-gastronomy foams aren't required to make meals memorable. That said, California's food fixations are easily exaggerated: not every Californian demands grass-fed burgers with heirloom tomato ketchup.

Even so, when New York chefs David Chang and Anthony Bourdain mocked California cuisine as merely putting an organic fig on a plate, Californian chefs turned the tables, saying that New York needs to get out more often and actually try some Mission figs – one of hundreds of heirloom varietals preserved or developed by California horticulturalists and farmers since the late 18th century.

California's 20th-Century Food Revolution

Seasonal, locavarian eating has become mainstream, but California started the movement more than 40 years ago. As the turbulent 1960s wound down, many disillusioned idealists concluded that the revolution was not about to be delivered on a platter, yet California's pioneering organic farmers weren't about to give up.

In 1971, Alice Waters opened her now legendary restaurant Chez Panisse (p145) in a converted house in Berkeley with the then-radical notion of making the most of California's seasonal, all-natural, sustainably produced food. Waters combined French flourishes with California's natural bounty, and diners tasted the difference.

Today Waters' credo of organic, seasonal, sustainably sourced and locally grown ingredients aligns perfectly with the worldwide Slow Food movement. In California today farmers markets are popular weekly gathering places for local communities, where artisanal producers of foodstuffs, such as honey and cheese, and local farmers come to sell their best, often trucking it in themselves from the fields.

Global Fusion Cooking

Beyond its exceptionally fertile farmland, California has another culinary advantage: an experimental attitude toward food that dates from its Wild West days. Most Gold Rush miners were men not accustomed to cooking for themselves, which resulted in such doomed mining-camp experiments as jelly omelets. But the era also introduced California to the hangtown fry (a scramble of eggs, bacon and deep-fried cornbread-battered oysters), Cantonese dim sum and the USA's first Italian restaurant, which opened in San Francisco in 1886.

Some 150 years later, fusion is not a fad but second nature in California, where chefs can hardly resist adding international twists to local flavors. Menus often infuse ingredients and kitchen craft borrowed from neighbors across the Pacific in Asia, from south of the border and all across Latin America, and from Europe's distant Mediterranean, where the climate and soil are similar to California's.

Keep in mind that California belonged to Mexico before it became a US state in 1850, and Latinos make up almost 40% of the state's population today. It's no surprise that Californicized versions of Mexican classics remain go-to comfort foods, especially for take-out. Culinary cross-pollination has yielded the California burrito – a mega-meal bursting out of a giant flour tortilla – and the Korean taco (grilled marinated beef and spicy, pickled kim chi atop small corn tortillas).

California's Regional Specialties

Calculate the distance between your tomato's origin and your fork: chances are it's shorter than you might think in California. So what are your best bets on local menus? That depends where you are and the time of year; for example, winter can be slim pickings even in the fertile Central Valley, but ideal for Southern California's citrus.

San Francisco Bay Area

For miners converging here for the Gold Rush, San Francisco offered an unrivaled variety of novelties and cuisines, from cheap Chinese street food to French fine dining for those who struck it rich. Today, San Francisco's adventurous eaters support the most restaurants per capita of any US city – five times more than NYC, ahem – and more than two-dozen farmers markets.

Some of San Francisco's novelty dishes have had extraordinary staying power, including ever-popular cioppino (seafood stew), chocolate bars invented by the Ghirardelli family, and sourdough bread, with original Gold Rush–era mother dough still yielding local loaves with a distinctive tang.

Today no star Bay Area chef's tasting menu would be complete without a few foraged ingredients – wild chanterelles found beneath California oaks, miner's lettuce from Berkeley hillsides or stinging nettles from SF backyards.

Cioppino

Napa & Sonoma Wine Country

With international acclaim for local wines in the 1970s came woozy wine-country visitors in need of food, and Sonoma cheesemakers and Napa restaurateurs graciously obliged. In 1994, chef Thomas Keller transformed a 1900s Yountville saloon into an international foodie landmark called the French Laundry (p175), showcasing garden-grown organic produce and casual elegance in multicourse feasts. Other chefs eager to make their names and fortunes among free-spending wine-tasters soon invaded the area. To plug into the locavarian and artisanal food scene, make time for Napa's Oxbow Public Market (p171).

North Coast

San Francisco hippies headed back to the land here in the 1970s to find a more self-sufficient lifestyle, reviving traditions of making breads and cheeses from scratch and growing their own *everything*. Early adopters of pesticide-free farming, these hippie homesteaders innovated hearty,

Fish tacos

organic cuisine that was health-minded yet still satisfied the pot-smoking munchies.

On the North Coast today, you can taste the influence of Ohlone and Miwok traditions. Alongside traditional shellfish collection, sustainable oyster farms have sprung up. Nature has also been kind to this landscape, yielding bonanzas of wildflower honey and berries. Fearless foragers have identified every edible plant from wood sorrel to Mendocino sea vegetables, though key spots for wild mushrooms remain closely guarded local secrets.

Central Valley & Central Coast

Most of California's produce is grown in the hot, irrigated Central Valley south of Sacramento, but road-tripping foodies tend to bolt through the sunny farmlands, if only to make it past stinky cattle feed-lots without losing their appetites. Much of the region remains dedicated to large-scale agribusiness, but valley farms that have converted to organic methods have helped make California the top US producer of organic foods.

Over on the Central Coast, some of California's freshest seafood is harvested from Monterey Bay (click to www.seafoodwatch. org for help choosing the most sustainable catch on restaurant menus). Excellent wine-tasting awaits in the fog-kissed Santa Cruz Mountains, the hot hills around Paso Robles and the sunny valleys north of Santa Barbara. There are farmstand produce pitstops all along the coast, from Watsonville strawberries to Carpinteria avocados. In San Luis Obispo, the weekly farmers market celebrates local farms and Santa Maria–style barbecue.

Southern California

Follow authenticity-seeking Angelenos to Koreatown for flavor-bursting *kalbi* (marinated, grilled beef short ribs), East LA for tacos *al pastor* (marinated, fried pork), Torrance for ramen noodles made fresh daily and the San Gabriel Valley for Chinese dim sum. Further south, San Diego and Orange County surfers cruise from Ocean Beach to Huntington Beach in search of not just epic waves, but also the ultimate Cal-Mex fish taco.

Cocktail hour, Los Angeles

chicken and blue cheese) invented in the 1930s.

Austrian-born chef Wolfgang Puck launched the celebrity-chef trend with his Sunset Strip restaurant Spago in 1982. Reservations at chef's tables are now as sought-after as entry into club VIP rooms. As with Hollywood blockbusters, trendy LA restaurants don't always live up to the hype – for brutally honest opinions, read reviews by respected food critic Jonathan Gold in the *Los Angeles Times*, or follow him on Twitter (@thejgold).

When all else fails, make late-night raids on a cornucopia of local food trucks, especially in LA and San Diego, and Hollywood diners that haven't changed since Technicolor was introduced.

Some say that true immortality isn't achieved with a star in a Michelin guide or on the Hollywood Walk of Fame, but by having a dish named in your honor – Bob Cobb, the celebrity-owner of Hollywood's Brown Derby Restaurant, is remembered as the namesake of the Cobb salad (lettuce, tomato, avocado, egg,

Wine, Beer & Beyond

Powerful drink explains a lot about California. Mission vineyards planted in the 18th century gave California a taste for wine, and the mid-19th-century Gold Rush brought a rush on the bar. By 1850 San Francisco had one woman per 100 men, but 500 saloons shilling hooch. Now California's traditions of wine, beer and cocktails are being reinvented by cult winemakers, craft brewers and microdistillers – and, for the morning after, specialty coffee roasters.

WINE-TASTING TIPS

➡ **Swirl** Before tasting a vintage red, swirl your glass to oxygenate the wine and release the flavors.

➡ **Sniff** Dip your nose (without getting it wet) into the glass for a good whiff.

➡ **Swish** Take a swig, and roll it over the front of your teeth and sides of your tongue to get the full effect of complex flavors and textures. After you swallow, breathe out through your nose to appreciate 'the finish'.

➡ **If you're driving or cycling, don't swallow** Sips are hard to keep track of at tastings, so perfect your graceful arc into the spit bucket.

➡ **You don't have to buy anything** No one expects you to buy, especially if you're paying to taste or take a tour, but it's customary to buy a bottle before winery picnics.

➡ **Take it slow and easy** There's no need for speed. Plan to visit three or four wineries a day maximum.

➡ **Don't smoke** Not in the gardens either. Wait until you're off-property.

Top: Ferry Plaza
Farmers Market (p101),
San Francisco

Bottom: Napa Valley
vineyard (p164)

PIGAM / GETTY IMAGES ©

Weekday lunches may last only 30 minutes for Californians, and every minute counts. Rolling along the streets of many cities, creative food trucks deliver gourmet options on the go, anything from Indian curry-and-naan wraps to Chinese buns packed with roast duck and fresh mango. To find trucks coming soon to a curb near you, search for 'food truck' and your location on Twitter. Come prepared with cash and sunblock: most trucks don't accept plastic cards, and lines can be long.

Lately, dinner has also been popping up in unexpected urban spaces, including art galleries, warehouses and storefronts. Chefs at pop-up restaurants prepare wildly creative meals around a theme, such as street food or winemakers' dinners. Foodies seek out these overnight taste sensations via Twitter and websites like www.eater.com. Bring cash and arrive early, as popular dishes run out fast.

Wine

When imported French wine was slow to arrive in California via Australia during the Gold Rush, three brothers from Bohemia named Korbel started making their own bubbly in 1882. Today, the Russian River winery they founded has become the biggest US maker of traditional sparkling wines.

Some California vines survived federal scrutiny during Prohibition (1920–33) on the grounds that the grapes were needed for sacramental wines back east – a bootlegging bonanza that kept West Coast speakeasies well supplied and saved old vinestock from being torn out by the authorities.

By 1976 California had an established reputation for mass-market plonk and bottled wine spritzers when upstart Napa Valley and Santa Cruz Mountains wineries suddenly gained international status. At a landmark blind tasting by international critics, their Cabernet Sauvignon and Chardonnay beat venerable French wines to take top honors. This event became known as the Judgment of Paris, as amusingly retold in the movie *Bottle Shock* (2008).

During the internet bubble of the late '90s, owning a vineyard became the ultimate Silicon Valley status symbol. It seemed like a comparatively solid investment – until phylloxera insects made a catastrophic comeback and acres of infected vines across the state had to be dug out from the roots. But disaster brought breakthroughs: winemakers rethought their approach, using organic and biodynamic methods to keep the soil healthy and pests at bay.

Beer

In California, which claims almost 400 craft breweries (more than any other US state), beer geeks fuss over their triple Belgians and debate relative hoppiness levels. You won't get attitude for ordering beer with fancy food here, and many sommeliers are happy to suggest beer pairings with your five-star meal.

Any self-respecting California city has at least one brewery or brewpub of note, serving quality small-batch brews you won't find elsewhere. The well-established craft beer scenes in San Diego and on the North Coast are remarkably robust, but you're just as likely to find memorable microbrews on the Central Coast, especially around Santa Cruz and Santa Barbara, and in the San Francisco Bay Area.

California's craft breweries are increasingly canning craft beer to make it cheaper, more ecofriendly and more widely

Blowing off steam took on new meaning during the Gold Rush when entrepreneurs trying to keep up with the demand for drink started brewing beer at higher temperatures. The result was an amber color, rich, malted flavor and such powerful effervescence that when a keg was tapped a mist would rise like steam. San Francisco's Anchor Brewing Company has made its signature Anchor Steam amber ale this way since 1896, using copper distilling equipment.

Anchor Brewing Company, San Francisco

distributable across California. There's nothing as satisfying as popping the tab of a cold one back at your campsite after a hot California day at the beach or on a hiking trail.

Cocktails

Cocktails have been shaken in Northern California since San Francisco's Barbary Coast days, when they were used to sedate sailors and kidnap them onto outbound ships. Now hip bartenders all across the state are researching old recipes and inventing new cocktail traditions. Don't be surprised to see absinthe poured into cordial glasses of Sazerac, or holiday eggnog spiked with tequila and organic orange peel. Originally made in Mexico, margaritas (made with tequila, lime, Cointreau, ice and salt) have refreshed sunny SoCal since the 1940s.

Legend has it that the martini was invented when a boozehound walked into an SF bar and demanded something to tide him over until he reached Martinez across the bay – a likely story, but we'll drink to that. The original was made with vermouth, gin, bitters, lemon, maraschino cherry and ice, although by the days of Sinatra's Rat Pack, the recipe was reduced to gin with vermouth vapors and an olive or two. The tropical mai tai (with rum, Orgeat, Curaçao and lime juice) is another cocktail allegedly invented in the Bay Area at Trader Vic's tiki bar in Oakland during the 1940s.

Coffee

California has become a hub for 'third wave' coffee. Pulitzer Prize–winning critic Jonathan Gold defines this as coffee directly sourced from farms instead of countries and roasted to maximize the bean's unique characteristics. LA's third-wave coffee shops tend not to roast their own, but cherry-pick the best beans from microroasters along the West Coast and Chicago. San Francisco's Blue Bottle Coffee added a 'fourth wave' element of showmanship to coffee geekery, introducing a $20,000 Japanese coffee siphon to filter their brews. Meanwhile, SF's Ritual Coffee Roasters has become the latest object of coffee cult worship with beans roasted in-house in small batches and hand-poured specialty coffees.

Regions at a Glance

California's cities have more flavors than a jar of jellybeans. Start from San Francisco, equal parts earth mother and geek chic, or Los Angeles, where dozens of independent cities are rolled into one multicultural mosaic. Then drift down the coast, past cinematic Southern California beaches to surf-style San Diego. Or escape to the craggy Sierra Nevada mountains, detour to SoCal's soulful deserts and lose yourself in northern redwood forests. On sunny days when the coastal fog lifts, over 1100 miles of ocean beaches await. And no matter where you go, California's vineyards never seem far away.

San Francisco

Food
Culture
Arts

California's 'Left Coast' reputation rests squarely on SF, where DIY self-expression, sustainability and spontaneity are the highest virtues. Free thinkers, techies, foodies and renegade artists are all in the city's creative mix.

p70

Marin County & the Bay Area

Hiking & Cycling
Food
Cities

Outdoors nuts adore Marin County for its beaches, wildlife and hiking and cycling trails. Visit green farms that inspire Bay Area chefs, or keep things urban on the counter-cultural streets of 'Bezerkely' and 'Oaktown.'

p110

Napa & Sonoma Wine Country

Wineries
Food
Cycling & Canoeing

Amid fruit orchards and ranches, these sunny valleys kissed by cool coastal fog have made Napa, Sonoma and the Russian River into California's premier wine-growing region and a showcase for bountiful farm-to-table cuisine.

p161

PLAN YOUR TRIP REGIONS AT A GLANCE

North Coast & the Redwoods

Wildlife
Hiking
Scenic Drives

Primeval redwood forests are prized along NorCal's foggy, rocky and wildly dramatic coastline. Let loose your inner hippy or Rastafarian in Humboldt County or explore bootstrap fishing villages from Bodega Bay to Eureka.

p217

Northern Mountains

Mountains
Lakes
Scenic Drives

Sacred Mt Shasta brings together Native Americans, ice-axe-wielding alpinists and new-age poets. Wilder places also await here, from Lassen's volcanic Bumpass Hell to backcountry byways and lakes.

p272

Sacramento & Central Valley

History
Museums
Farms & Fairs

California's capital is the place to start digging up California's roots – show up in July for the state fair – then cruise the river delta into California's agricultural heartland.

p307

Gold Country

History
Caving & Rafting
Wineries

Wind into the Sierra Nevada foothills to find a rich vein of Wild West history in California's historic gold-mining country. Get more thrills on a river-rafting trip or an underground cave tour, or drop by rustic winery tasting rooms.

p337

Lake Tahoe

Winter Sports
Water Sports
Cabins & Camping

North America's largest alpine lake is a four-seasons outdoor playground. Come for Olympic-worthy skiing in winter, or cool off by the beaches in summer. Nevada's flashy casinos are a bonus attraction.

p362

Yosemite & the Sierra Nevada

Wildlife
Hiking & Climbing
Scenic Drives

Granite peaks, alpine meadows and lakes, natural hot springs, deep canyons and groves of giant sequoias grace California's iconic mountain range. Summer is prime time for all kinds of outdoor adventures.

p400

PLAN YOUR TRIP REGIONS AT A GLANCE

Central Coast

Beaches
Wildlife
Scenic Drives

Surf south from hippy-dippy Santa Cruz to collegiate San Luis Obispo, stopping to hop aboard a whale-watching boat at Monterey Bay and to hike Big Sur's redwood forests, where waterfalls spring to life and California condors soar.

p456

Santa Barbara County

Beaches
Wineries
Outdoor Sports

Spanish colonial Santa Barbara prettily presides over white-sand beaches, with vineyards less than an hour's drive away. Go snorkeling, diving or sea kayaking in treasured Channel Islands National Park just offshore.

p514

Los Angeles

Nightlife
Food
Beaches

There's more to life in La La Land than just sunny beaches and air-kissing celebs. Get a dose of culture downtown, then dive into LA's diverse neighborhoods, from historic Little Tokyo to red-carpet Hollywood.

p555

Disneyland & Orange County

Theme Parks
Beaches
Surfing

The OC's beaches are often packed bronze-shoulder-to-shoulder with surfers, beach-volleyball nuts and soap-opera beauties. Inland, take the kids and grandparents – heck, load up the whole minivan – to Disney's Magic Kingdom.

p593

San Diego & Around

Beaches
Mexican Food
Museums

California's southernmost city, with its nearly perfect year-round climate, lets locals live on permanent vacation. Laze in laid-back beach towns while scarfing down fish tacos, or wander Balboa Park's sunny plazas, gardens and museums.

p625

Palm Springs & the Deserts

Resorts & Spas
Wildflowers
Hiking & Climbing

A retro resort playground, Palm Springs has experienced a rebirth of Rat Pack–era cool. Go get dirty hiking or rock climbing in Joshua Tree, then test your 4WD mettle in Death Valley, where spring wildflowers dazzle.

p661

On the Road

San Francisco

Best Places to Eat

Best Places to Stay

Why Go?

Get to know the world capital of weird from the inside out, from mural-lined alleyways named after poets to clothing-optional beaches on a former military base. But don't be too quick to dismiss San Francisco's wild ideas. Biotech, gay rights, personal computers, cable cars and organic fine dining were once considered outlandish too, before San Francisco introduced these underground ideas into the mainstream decades ago. San Francisco's morning fog erases the boundaries between land and ocean, reality and infinite possibility.

Rules are never strictly followed here. Golden Gate Bridge and Alcatraz are entirely optional – San Franciscans mostly admire them from afar – leaving you free to pursue inspiration through Golden Gate Park, past flamboyantly painted Victorian homes and through Mission galleries. Just don't be late for your sensational, sustainable dinner: in San Francisco, you can find happiness and eat it too.

When to Go
San Francisco

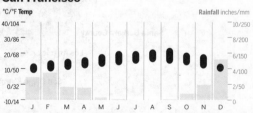

Jan–Mar Low-season rates, brisk but rarely cold days, and Lunar New Year parade fireworks.	May–Aug Farmers markets and festivals make up for high-season rates and chilly afternoon fog.	Sep–Nov Blue skies, free concerts, bargain hotel rates and flavor-bursting harvest cuisine.

Bay Bridge

San Francisco's other landmark bridge was inspired by a madman. Joshua Norton lost his shirt and his mind in the Gold Rush before proclaiming himself 'Emperor of these United States and Protector of Mexico,' and ordering construction of a trans-bay bridge in 1872. Taxpayers took some convincing: the Bay Bridge was completed in 1936. But the eastern span collapsed in the 1989 Loma Prieta earthquake, taking 12 years and $6.4 billion to repair.

Emperor Norton's idea seemed not quite so bright anymore – until artist Leo Villareal installed 25,000 LED lights along the western span, mesmerizing commuters with a 1.8-mile-long light show that shimmers and pulses in never-repeating patterns. The show runs from dusk until 2am nightly until March 2015 – but a crowdfunding campaign may keep the lights twinkling through 2026. For more, see thebaylights.org.

DON'T MISS...

➤ **Saloons** The Barbary Coast is roaring back to life with historically researched whiskey cocktails and staggering gin concoctions in San Francisco's great Western saloon revival (p103).

➤ **Rooftop-garden cuisine** SF chefs are raising the roof on hyperlocal fare with ingredients raised right upstairs: city-bee honey at Jardinière (p102), edible pansies at Coi (p100), herbs at farm:table (p99) and salad greens to feed the homeless at Glide Memorial (p74).

➤ **Green everything** Recent reports rank San Francisco as the greenest city in North America, with its pioneering parklets, citywide composting laws and America's biggest stretch of urban greenery: Golden Gate Park (p97).

SF's Best Free...

➤ **Music** Golden Gate Park hosts free concerts summer through fall, from opera and reggae to Hardly Strictly Bluegrass.

➤ **Speech** City Lights Bookstore (p74) won a landmark free-speech case in 1957 over the publication of Allen Ginsberg's magnificent, incendiary *Howl*; take a seat in the designated Poet's Chair and celebrate your right to read freely.

➤ **Love** Pride fills San Francisco streets with free candy, free condoms and over a million people freely smooching total strangers under rainbow flags.

➤ **Spirits** Anywhere within city limits – and you're free to join in anytime.

DID YOU KNOW?

Despite slacker reputations cultivated at 30 medical marijuana clubs, San Franciscans hold more patents and earn more degrees per capita than residents of any other US city.

Fast Facts

➤ **Population** 839,336
➤ **Area** 47 sq miles
➤ **Telephone area code** 415

Planning Your Trip

➤ **Three weeks before** Book Alcatraz trips and dinner at Coi or Benu.

➤ **Two weeks before** Build stamina for downtown hills, Golden Gate Park adventures and Mission bars.

➤ **One week before** Score tickets to San Francisco Symphony or Opera, and assemble your costume – SF throws parades whenever.

Resources

➤ **SF Bay Guardian** (www.sfbg.com) Hot tips on local entertainment, arts, politics.

➤ **SFGate** (www.sfgate.com) News and event listings.

History

Oysters and acorn bread were prime dinner options in the Mexico-run Ohlone settlement of San Francisco circa 1848 – but a year and some gold nuggets later, Champagne and chow mein were served by the bucket. Gold found in nearby Sierra Nevada foothills turned a sleepy 800-person village into a port city of 100,000 prospectors, con artists, prostitutes and honest folk – good luck telling them apart in the city's 200 saloons.

Panic struck when Australia glutted the market with gold in 1854. Rioters burned waterfront 'Sydney-Town' before turning on SF's Chinese community, who from 1877 to 1945 were restricted to living and working in Chinatown by anti-Chinese exclusion laws. Chinese laborers were left with few employment options besides dangerous work building railroads for San Francisco's robber barons, who dynamited, mined and clear-cut their way across the Golden West, and built Nob Hill mansions above Chinatown.

But the city's grand ambitions came crashing down in 1906, when earthquake and fire reduced the city to rubble. Theater troupes and opera divas performed for free amid smoldering ruins, and reconstruction hummed along at an astounding rate of 15 buildings per day.

During WWII, soldiers accused of insubordination and homosexuality were dismissed in San Francisco, as though that would teach them a lesson. Instead San Francisco's counterculture thrived, with North Beach jazz and Beat poetry. When the Central Intelligence Agency (CIA) tested LSD on the willing volunteer and *One Flew Over the Cuckoo's Nest* author Ken Kesey, he slipped some into Kool-Aid and kicked off the psychedelic '60s.

The Summer of Love brought free food, love and music to the Haight, and pioneering gay activists in the Castro helped elect Harvey Milk as San Francisco supervisor – America's first out gay official. When San Francisco witnessed devastating losses from HIV/AIDS in the 1980s, the city rallied to become a global model for epidemic treatment and prevention.

San Francisco's unconventional thinking spawned the web in the 1990s, until the dotcom bubble burst in 2000. But risk-taking SF continues to float outlandish new ideas –

NEIGHBORHOODS IN A NUTSHELL

North Beach & the Hills Poetry and parrots, top-of-the-world views, Italian gossip and opera on the jukebox.

Embarcadero & the Piers Weird science, sea-lion antics, gourmet treats, and getaways to and from Alcatraz.

Downtown & the Financial District The notorious Barbary Coast has gone legit with banks and boutiques, but shows its wild side in redwood parks and provocative art.

Chinatown Pagoda roofs, mahjong games, revolutionary plots, and fortunes made and lost in historic alleyways.

Hayes Valley, Civic Center & the Tenderloin Grand buildings and great performances, dive bars and cable cars, foodie finds and local designs.

SoMa South of Market; where high technology meets higher art, and everyone gets down and dirty on the dance floor.

Mission A book in one hand, a burrito in the other, and murals all around.

Castro Out and proud with samba whistles, rainbow sidewalks and history-making policy platforms.

Haight Flashbacks and fashion-forwardness, free thinking, free music and pricey skateboards.

Japantown, the Fillmore & Pacific Heights Sushi in the fountains, John Coltrane over the altar, and rock at the Fillmore.

Marina & the Presidio Boutiques, organic dining, peace and public nudity at a former army base.

Golden Gate Park & the Avenues SF's great green streak, surrounded by gourmet hangouts for hungry surfers.

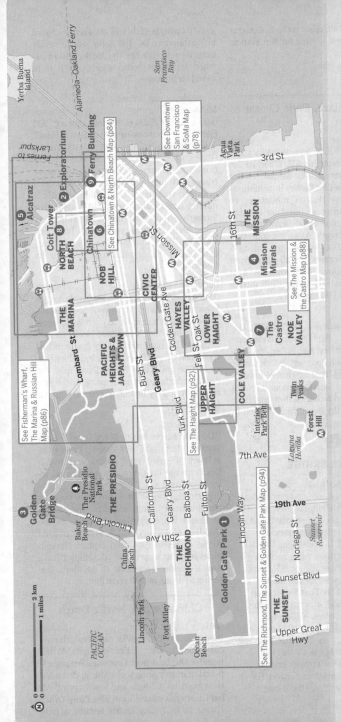

San Francisco Highlights

1 Follow your bliss through SF's mile-wide wild streak: **Golden Gate Park** (p97).

2 See how real life is cooler than science fiction at the **Exploratorium** (p75).

3 Watch fog dance atop the deco towers of the **Golden Gate Bridge** (p74).

4 Explore SF's colorful history, captured in renegade **Mission murals** (p91).

5 Plot your escape from **Alcatraz** (p76), SF's notorious island prison.

6 Wander through 150 years of California history in pagoda-topped **Chinatown** (p74).

7 Come out and celebrate GLBT history in **the Castro** (p87), the center of the gay universe.

8 Get breathless from the climb, freshly restored murals and panoramic views at **Coit Tower** (p81).

9 Graze at the **Ferry Building** (p101), SF's local, sustainable food destination.

social media, mobile apps, biotech. Congratulations: you're just in time for San Francisco's next wild ride.

⊙ Sights

⊙ Union Square, Civic Center & the Tenderloin

★**Asian Art Museum**　　　　MUSEUM
(Map p78; ☏415-581-3500; www.asianart.org; 200 Larkin St; adult/student/child $12/8/free, 1st Sun of month free; ⊗10am-5pm Tue-Sun, to 9pm Thu; 🚼; MCivic Center, BCivic Center) Imaginations race from ancient Persian miniatures to cutting-edge Japanese architecture through three floors spanning 6000 years of Asian arts. Besides the largest Asian art collection outside Asia – 18,000 works – the Asian offers excellent programs for all ages, from shadow-puppet shows and yoga for kids to weeknight Artist's Drawing Club mixers with crosscultural DJ mashups.

City Hall　　　　HISTORIC BUILDING
(Map p78; ☏art exhibit line 415-554-6080, tour info 415-554-6139; http://sfgsa.org/index.aspx?page=1085; 400 Van Ness Ave; ⊗8am-8pm Mon-Fri, tours 10am, noon & 2pm; 🚼; MCivic Center, BCivic Center) FREE That mighty beaux-arts dome has covered San Francisco's greatest civic ambitions and setbacks, from marriage equality to McCarthy hearings. Designed in

---

DON'T MISS

GOLDEN GATE BRIDGE

Hard to believe the Navy almost nixed SF's signature art-deco **landmark** (Map p73; www.goldengatebridge.org/visitors; off Lincoln Blvd; northbound free, southbound toll $6, billed electronically to vehicle's license plate; 🚌28, all Golden Gate Transit buses) by architects Gertrude and Irving Murrow and engineer Joseph B Strauss. Photographers, take your cue from Hitchcock: seen from **Fort Point** (Map p114; ☏415-556-1693; www.nps.gov/fopo; Marine Dr; admission free; ⊗10am-5pm Fri-Sun; P; 🚌28) FREE, the 1937 bridge induces a thrilling case of vertigo. Fog aficionados prefer Marin's Vista Point, watching gusts billow through bridge cables like dry ice at a Kiss concert. For the full effect, hike or bike the 2-mile span.

1915 to outstyle Paris and outsize the capitol in Washington, DC, the dome was unsteady until its retrofit after the 1989 earthquake, when ingenious technology enabled it to swing on its base.

Glide Memorial United Methodist Church　　　　CHURCH
(Map p78; ☏415-674-6090; www.glide.org; 330 Ellis St; ⊗celebrations 9am & 11am Sun; MPowell, BPowell) The rainbow-robed, 100-strong Glide gospel choir kicks off Sunday celebrations with a warm welcome for whomever comes through the door. Between celebrations, volunteers help Glide provide a million free meals a year and housing for formerly homeless families. Thursdays from 10am to 2pm, volunteers head upstairs to Glide's sunny **Graze the Roof** garden, harvesting organic vegetables for its free meals.

Luggage Store Gallery　　　　ART GALLERY
(Map p78; ☏415-255-5971; www.luggagestoregallery.org; 1007 Market St; ⊗noon-5pm Wed-Sat; MCivic Center, BCivic Center) Bringing signs of life to one of SF's toughest blocks for two decades, this nonprofit gallery has launched renowned SF graffiti-art stars including Barry McGee and Clare Rojas. Don't miss the door camouflaged by spray paint, or the new rooftop mural by Brazilian street-art-duo Os Gemeos.

Union Square　　　　SQUARE
(Map p78; intersection of Geary, Powell, Post & Stockton Sts; 🚋Powell-Mason, Powell-Hyde, MPowell, BPowell) Free spirits and socialites converge on Union Square, named after pro-Union Civil War rallies, ringed by department stores and presided over by bare-breasted bronze socialite (and Legion of Honor founder) Alma Spreckels as the Goddess of Victory. Public outcry obliged Apple to revise its Union Square flagship plans in order to preserve SF sculptor Ruth Asawa's beloved Stockton St fountain, featuring SF icons by 250 contributors.

⊙ Chinatown & North Beach

★**City Lights Bookstore**　　　　BUILDING
(Map p84; ☏415-362-8193; www.citylights.com; 261 Columbus Ave; ⊗10am-midnight) When founder and Beat poet Lawrence Ferlinghetti and manager Shigeyoshi Murao defended their right to 'willfully and lewdly print' Allen Ginsberg's magnificent *Howl and Other Poems* in 1957, City Lights became a free-

THREE CHINATOWN ALLEYS THAT MADE HISTORY

➡ **Waverly Place** (Map p84; 🚌 30, 🚋 California St, Powell-Mason) After the 1906 earthquake and fire devastated Chinatown, developers schemed to relocate Chinatown residents left homeless to less-desirable real estate outside the city. But representatives from the Chinese consulate and several gun-toting merchants marched back to Waverly Place, holding temple services amid the rubble at still-smoldering altars. The alley is the namesake of the main character in Amy Tan's bestselling *The Joy Luck Club*.

➡ **Spofford Alley** (Map p84; 🚌 1, 15, 30, 45) Sun Yat-sen plotted the overthrow of China's last emperor at No 36, and the 1920s brought bootleggers' gun battles to this alley – but Spofford has mellowed with age. In the evenings you'll hear shuffling mahjong tiles and *erhu* (two-stringed Chinese fiddle) players warming up at local senior centers.

➡ **Ross Alley** (Map p84; 🚌 1, 30, 45) Alternately known as Manila, Spanish and Mexico St after the working girls who once worked this block, mural-lined Ross Alley is occasionally pimped out for Hollywood productions, including *Karate Kid II* and *Indiana Jones and the Temple of Doom*. Duck into the alley's **Golden Gate Fortune Cookie Factory** (56 Ross Alley; admission free; ⊘ 8am-7pm) for custom cookies hot off the press (50¢ each), and write your own fortune.

speech landmark. Celebrate your freedom to read freely in the designated Poet's Chair upstairs overlooking Jack Kerouac Alley, load up on 'zines on the mezzanine and entertain radical ideas downstairs in the Muckracking and Stolen Continents sections.

Beat Museum   MUSEUM
(Map p84; 📞 1-800-537-6822; www.kerouac.com; 540 Broadway; adult/student $8/5; ⊘ 10am-7pm; 🚌 10, 12, 30, 41, 45, 🚋 Powell-Hyde, Powell-Mason) Grab a ramshackle theater seat redolent with the accumulated odors of literary giants, pets and pot to watch fascinating films about the SF Beat literary scene c 1950–69. Upstairs are shrines to Beat achievements, including *On the Road* and other books that expanded America's outlook to include the margins. Two-hour guided tours at 1pm Wednesday, Saturday and Sunday cover the museum and Beat hangouts (adult/student $30/25).

Chinese Historical Society of America   MUSEUM
(CHSA; Map p84; 📞 415-391-1188; www.chsa.org; 965 Clay St; ⊘ noon-5pm Tue-Fri, 11am-4pm Sat; 🚌 1, 30, 45, 🚋 California St) **FREE** Picture what it was like to be Chinese in America during the gold rush, transcontinental railroad construction or the Beat heyday in this 1932 landmark, built as Chinatown's YWCA by Julia Morgan (also chief architect of Hearst Castle). The nation's largest Chinese American historical institute is a treasury of artifacts and personal stories, tracing journeys from China that made American history.

⊙ Fisherman's Wharf

★ **Exploratorium**   MUSEUM
(Map p86; 📞 415-528-4444; www.exploratorium. edu; Pier 15; adult/child $25/19, Thu evening $15; ⊘ 10am-5pm Tue-Sun, over-18yr only Thu 6-10pm; 🅿 ♿; Ⓜ F) ✎ Is there a science to skateboarding? Do toilets flush conterclockwise in Australia? Find out first-hand with 600-plus fascinating, freaky exhibits. In under an hour you can star in psychedelic fractal music videos, make art from bacteria, and grope your way in total darkness through the Tactile Dome. Founded in 1969 by atom-bomb physicist Frank Oppenheimer, the newly relocated, expanded Exploratorium shows how life is cooler than science fiction.

★ **Musée Mécanique**   AMUSEMENT PARK
(Map p86; 📞 415-346-2000; www.museemechanique.org; Pier 45, Shed A; ⊘ 10am-7pm Mon-Fri, to 8pm Sat & Sun; ♿; 🚌 47, 🚋 Powell-Mason, Powell-Hyde, Ⓜ F) Where else can you guillotine a man for a quarter? Creepy, 19th-century arcade games like the macabre French Execution compete for your spare change with the diabolical Ms Pac-Man.

USS Pampanito   HISTORIC SITE
(Map p86; 📞 415-775-1943; www.maritime.org/ pamphome.htm; Pier 45; adult/child $12/6; ⊘ 9am-8pm Thu-Tue, to 6pm Wed; ♿; 🚌 19, 30, 47, 🚋 Powell-Hyde, Ⓜ F) Explore a restored WWII submarine that survived six tours of duty, while you listen to submariner sailors' tales of stealth mode and sudden attacks in a riveting

Alcatraz

Book a ferry from Pier 33 and ride 1.5 miles across the bay to explore America's most notorious former prison. The trip itself is worth the money, providing stunning views of the city skyline. Once you've landed at the **Ferry Dock & Pier** 1, you begin the 580-yard walk to the top of the island and prison; if you're out of shape, there's a twice-hourly tram.

As you climb toward the **Guardhouse** 2, notice the island's steep slope; before it was a prison, Alcatraz was a fort. In the 1850s, the military quarried the rocky shores into near-vertical cliffs. Ships could then only dock at a single port, separated from the main buildings by a sally port (a drawbridge and moat in what became the guardhouse). Inside, peer through floor grates to see Alcatraz' original prison.

Volunteers tend the brilliant **Officer's Row Gardens** 3 – an orderly counterpoint to the overgrown rose bushes surrounding the burned-out shell of the **Warden's House** 4. At the top of the hill, by the front door of the **Main Cellhouse** 5, beauty shots unfurl all around, including a **view of the Golden Gate Bridge** 6. Above the main door of the administration building, notice the **historic signs & graffiti** 7, before you step inside the dank, cold prison to find the **Frank Morris cell** 8, former home to Alcatraz' most notorious jail-breaker.

TOP TIPS

➡ Book at least two weeks prior for self-guided daytime visits, longer for ranger-led night tours. For info on garden tours, see www.alcatraz gardens.org.

➡ Be prepared to hike; a steep path ascends from the ferry landing to the cell block. Most people spend two to three hours on the island. You need only reserve for the outbound ferry; take any ferry back.

➡ There's no food (just water) but you can bring your own; picnicking is allowed at the ferry dock only. Dress in layers as weather changes fast and it's usually windy.

JOHN A VLAHIDES ©

Historic Signs & Graffiti
During their 1969–71 occupation, Native Americans graffitied the water tower: 'Home of the Free Indian Land.' Above the cellhouse door, examine the eagle-and-flag crest to see how the red-and-white stripes were changed to spell 'Free.'

Warden's House
Fires destroyed the warden's house and other structures during the Indian Occupation. The government blamed the Native Americans; the Native Americans blamed agents provocateurs acting on behalf of the Nixon Administration to undermine public sympathy.

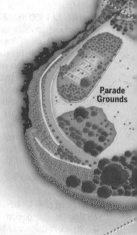

Parade Grounds

DAVID CLAPP / GETTY IMAGES ©

Ferry Dock & Pier
A giant wall map helps you get your bearings. Inside nearby Bldg 64, short films and exhibits provide historical perspective on the prison and details about the Indian

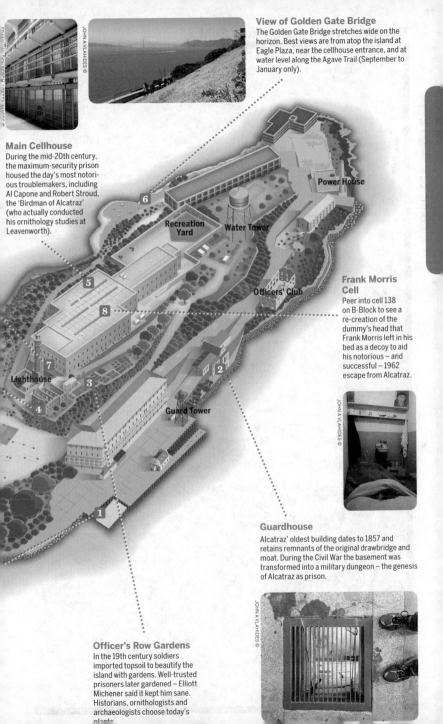

View of Golden Gate Bridge

The Golden Gate Bridge stretches wide on the horizon. Best views are from atop the island at Eagle Plaza, near the cellhouse entrance, and at water level along the Agave Trail (September to January only).

Main Cellhouse

During the mid-20th century, the maximum-security prison housed the day's most notorious troublemakers, including Al Capone and Robert Stroud, the 'Birdman of Alcatraz' (who actually conducted his ornithology studies at Leavenworth).

Power House

Recreation Yard

Water Tower

Officers' Club

Lighthouse

Guard Tower

Frank Morris Cell

Peer into cell 138 on B-Block to see a re-creation of the dummy's head that Frank Morris left in his bed as a decoy to aid his notorious – and successful – 1962 escape from Alcatraz.

Guardhouse

Alcatraz' oldest building dates to 1857 and retains remnants of the original drawbridge and moat. During the Civil War the basement was transformed into a military dungeon – the genesis of Alcatraz as prison.

Officer's Row Gardens

In the 19th century soldiers imported topsoil to beautify the island with gardens. Well-trusted prisoners later gardened – Elliott Michener said it kept him sane. Historians, ornithologists and archaeologists choose today's plants.

Downtown San Francisco & SoMa

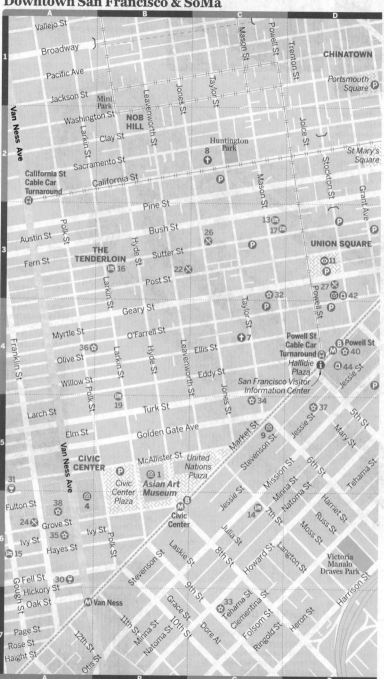

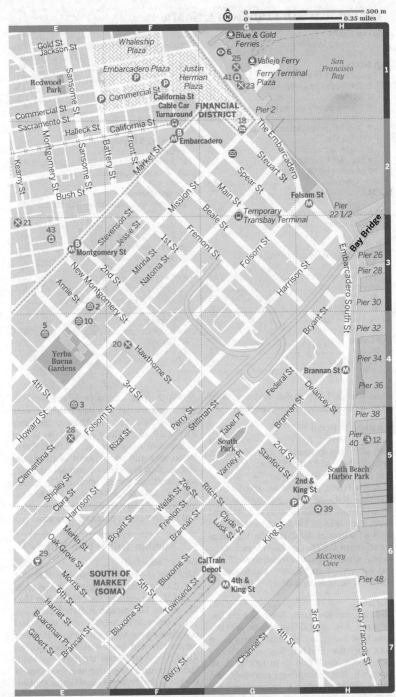

Downtown San Francisco & SoMa

audio tour ($3) that makes surfacing afterwards a relief (caution claustrophobes).

Maritime National
Historical Park   HISTORIC SITE
(Map p86; www.nps.gov/safr; 499 Jefferson St, Hyde St Pier; adult/child $5/free; ⊙9:30am-5pm Oct-May, to 5:30pm Jun-Sep; ⊕; ⊒19, 30, 47, ⬚Powell-Hyde, ⓂF) Historic ships at the Maritime National Historical Park are the Wharf's most authentic attraction. Moored along the Hyde St Pier, standouts include the 1891 schooner *Alma* and the 1895 lumber schooner *CA Thayer*. Also check out the paddle-wheel tugboat *Eppleton Hall* and the iron-hulled *Balclutha*, which hauled coal from Australia and Wales.

Pier 39   PIER
(Map p86; www.pier39.com; Beach St & the Embarcadero; Ⓟ⊕; ⊒47, ⬚Powell-Mason, ⓂF) Sea lions have lived the California dream since 1989, when they first bellyflopped on Pier 39 yacht docks. You'll find up to 1300 of them January to July, sunbathing, canoodling, and setting SF standards for beach-bumming.

Across the pier, sharks circle overhead inside **Aquarium of the Bay** (Map p86; www.aquariumofthebay.com; Pier 39; adult/child/family $21.95/12.95/64; ⊙10am-7pm Mon-Thu, to 8pm Fri-Sun, daily in summer; ⊕; ⊒49, ⬚Powell-Mason, ⓂF), and your chariot awaits at the vintage **San Francisco Carousel** (Map p86; www.pier39.com; Pier 39; admission $3; ⊙11am-7pm; ⊕; ⊒47, ⬚Powell-Mason, ⓂF). The visitors' center rents strollers, stores luggage, and has free phone-charging stations.

◎ Russian Hill & Nob Hill

Grace Cathedral   CHURCH
(Map p78; ☎415-749-6300; www.gracecathedral.org; 1100 California St; suggested donation adult/child $3/2, Sun services free; ⊙8am-6pm Mon-Sat, to 7pm Sun, services 8:30am & 11am Sun; ⊒1, ⬚California St) Rebuilt three times and completed over 40 years, Grace celebrates community and human endeavor with an AIDS memorial chapel altarpiece by Keith Haring, murals honoring the founding of the UN in San Francisco, and Gothic stained-

glass windows featuring Albert Einstein up-lifted in swirling atomic particles. Check the website for choral performances with Grace's splendid acoustics.

San Francisco Art Institute ART GALLERY
(Map p86; www.sfai.edu; 800 Chestnut St; admission free; ⊙Walter & McBean Galleries 11am-7pm Tue, to 6pm Wed-Sat, Diego Rivera Gallery 9am-5pm; 🚇Powell-Mason) **FREE** Founded in the 1870s, SFAI was the vanguard for 1960s Bay Area Abstraction, 1970s conceptual art, and 1990s new-media art – glimpse what's next in contemporary art here at the **Walter & McBean Gallery**. Diego Rivera's 1931 *The Making of a Fresco Showing a Building of a City* sprawls across **Diego Rivera Gallery**, showing the artist pausing to admire the constant work-in-progress that is San Francisco.

Lombard Street STREET
(Map p86; 900 block of Lombard St; 🚇Powell-Hyde) You've seen Lombard's eight downhill switchbacks on postcards, movies *(Vertigo)*, TV *(The Real World)*, even video games (Tony Hawk's *Pro Skater*). Billed incorrectly as 'the world's crookedest street' – SF's Vermont St deserves the honor – scenic Lombard St earns street cred with zigzagging flowerbeds. The street often closes to traffic on busy summer weekends, accommodating pedestrians who brave 250 steps for **Sterling Park** sunsets with Golden Gate Bridge views.

⊙ Japantown

Japan Center BUILDING
(www.sfjapantown.org; 1737 Post St; ⊙10am-midnight; 🚇2, 3, 22, 38, 38L) Welcome to *ka-waii* (cuteness) – this 1968 mall is a vintage gem, with rock gardens, wooden bridges and *maneki-neko* (waving cat) figurines atop sushi-bar counters. Lose track of time in photo-sticker booths, karaoke lounges, *ukiyo-e* (woodblock print) galleries and Japanese video-game arcades – then take a breather under the cherry trees by the Peace Plaza pagoda.

Cottage Row STREET
(off Bush St btwn Webster & Fillmore Sts; 🚇2, 3, 22, 38) Detour to the 1860s and '70s via this National Historic Landmark promenade formerly known as 'Japan Street,' where Japanese Americans lived in clapboard cottages, farmed tiny backyard plots and socialized under plum trees until their forced internment in WWII. Forty-five years later, San Francisco's Japanese American Citizens League won a presidential apology for internees – and today, Cottage Row's public mini-park remains a point of community pride.

⊙ The Marina & Presidio

★ Crissy Field PARK
(Map p86; www.crissyfield.org; 1199 East Beach; 🚇30, PresidioGo Shuttle) The Presidio's army airstrip has been stripped of asphalt and

---

WORTH A TRIP

COIT TOWER

Adding an exclamation mark to San Francisco's landscape, **Coit Tower** (Map p84; 📞415-362-0808; http://sfrecpark.org/destination/telegraph-hill-pioneer-park/coit-tower; Telegraph Hill Blvd; elevator entry (nonresident) adult/child $7/5; ⊙10am-5:30pm Mar-Sep, 9am-4:30pm Oct-Feb; 🚇39) offers views worth shouting about – especially after you climb the giddy, steep Filbert St or Greenwich St steps to the top of Telegraph Hill. This 210ft, peculiar projectile is a monument to San Francisco firefighters financed by eccentric heiress Lillie Hitchcock Coit. Lillie could drink, smoke and play cards as well as any off-duty firefighter, rarely missed a fire or a firefighter's funeral, and even had the firehouse emblem embroidered on her bedsheets.

Even before it opened in 1934, Lillie's tower became a lightning-rod for controversy. Federally funded lobby murals show San Franciscans during the Great Depression at speakeasies, soup kitchens, and dock-workers' unions. Authorities denounced Coit Tower's 25 muralists as communists, but San Franciscans rallied to protect their artwork as a national landmark.

Newly restored in 2014, the bright, bold murals broaden world views just as surely as the 360-degree views from the tower-top viewing platform. To glimpse murals inside Coit Tower's spiral stairwell, join free guided tours at 11am on Saturdays.

Powell-Hyde
Cable Car
Turnaround

5

6

4 Beach St

North Point St

Powell-Mason
Cable Car Turnaround

Bay St

7

Chestnut St

**NORTH
BEACH**

San
Francisco
Bay

The Embarcadero (Herb Caen Way)

Lombard St

Van Ness Ave

Powell-Hyde St Cable Car Line

3

Filbert St

Powell-Mason Cable Car Line

Jones St

8

Grant Ave

Columbus Ave

Stockton St

Sansome St

Battery St

Broadway

Broadway

Jackson St

Washington St

NOB HILL

9 **CHINATOWN**

California St
Cable Car
Turnaround

10 END

B Embarcadero

2

California St Cable Car Line

California St

California St
Cable Car
Turnaround

Pine St

Bush St

NOB HILL

*Powell-Mason &
Powell-Hyde St
Cable Car Lines*

Bush St

Market St

Folsom St M

M B Montgomery St

Powell St

Mason St

Geary Blvd

Geary St

Hyde St

START 1 M B **Powell St**

Brannan St M

0 ——— 1 km
0 ——— 0.5 miles

San Francisco by Cable Car

Carnival rides can't compare to cable cars, San Francisco's vintage public transit. Novices slide into strangers' laps but regular commuters just grip leather hand-straps, lean back and ride downhill slides like pro surfers. On this trip, you'll master the San Francisco stance and conquer SF hills without breaking a sweat.

At the **①Powell St Cable Car Turnaround** operators turn the car atop a revolving wooden platform and a vintage kiosk; buy an all-day Muni Passport for $14 instead of paying $6 per ride. Board the Powell-Hyde cable car and begin your journey up Nob Hill.

As your cable car lurches uphill, you can imagine 19th-century horses struggling up this slippery crag. Inventor Andrew Hallidie's cable cars survived the 1906 earthquake and fire that destroyed 'Snob Hill' mansions, returning the faithful to rebuilt **②Grace Cathedral** (p80).

Back on the Powell-Hyde car, careen past crooked, flower-lined **③Lombard Street** (p81) toward **④Fisherman's Wharf**. The waterfront terminus is named for Friedel Klussman, who saved cable cars from mayoral modernization plans in 1947. She did the math: cable cars brought in more tourism dollars than they cost in upkeep. The mayor demanded a vote – and lost to 'the Cable Car Lady' by a landslide.

At the wharf you can see SF as sailors did as they emerged from the submarine **⑤USS Pampanito** (p75). Witness Western saloon brawls in vintage arcade games at the **⑥Musée Mécanique** (p75) before hitching the Powell-Mason cable car to North Beach.

Hop off to see Diego Rivera's 1934 cityscape at the **⑦San Francisco Art Institute** (p81) or follow your rumbling stomach directly to **⑧Liguria Bakery** (p99). Stroll through North Beach and Chinatown alleyways or take the Powell-Mason line to time-travel through the **⑨Chinese Historical Society of America** (p75). Nearby, catch a ride on the city's oldest line: the California St cable car. The terminus is near the **⑩Ferry Building** (p101), where champagne-and-oyster happy hour awaits.

Top: Cable Car Turnaround; Bottom: Cable car on Hyde St, heading toward Fisherman's Wharf

Chinatown & North Beach

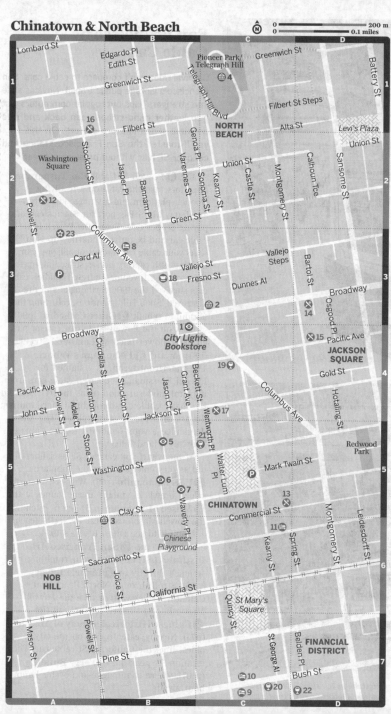

Chinatown & North Beach

reinvented as a haven for coastal birds, kite-fliers and windsurfers enjoying sweeping views of Golden Gate Bridge.

★**Baker Beach**   BEACH
(☉ sunrise-sunset; 🚌 29, PresidiGo Shuttle) Unswimmable waters (except when the tide's coming in) but unbeatable views of the Golden Gate make this former Army beachhead SF's tanning location of choice, especially the clothing-optional north end – at least until the afternoon fog rolls in.

Presidio Visitors Center   TOURIST INFORMATION
(www.presidio.gov; Montgomery St & Lincoln Blvd, Bldg 105; ☉ 10am-4pm Thu-Sun; 🚌 PresidiGo Shuttle) San Francisco's official motto is 'Oro in Paz, Fierro in Guerra' (Gold in Peace, Iron in War), but it hasn't seen much military action since 1776, when its Spanish *presidio* (military post) was built by conscripted Ohlone. Today the revamped **Officers Club** features archaeological displays and California cuisine from celebrity chef Traci des Jardins. Cultural institutions including the **Walt Disney Family Museum** (Map p86; 🕿 415-345-6800; www.waltdisney.org; 104 Montgomery St, Presidio; adult/student/child $20/15/12; ☉ 10am-6pm Wed-Mon, last entry 5pm; P 👶; 🚌 43, PresidiGo Shuttle) line the former **parade grounds**, and a Yoda statue fronts **George Lucas' Letterman Digital Arts Center**.

◉ SoMa

Contemporary Jewish Museum   MUSEUM
(Map p78; 🕿 415-344-8800; www.thecjm.org; 736 Mission St; adult/child $12/free, after 5pm Thu $5, 1st Tue of month free; ☉ 11am-5pm Mon-Tue & Fri-Sun, to 8pm Thu; Ⓜ Montgomery, Ⓑ Montgomery) A blue-steel box balancing on one corner brings signs of life to San Francisco's commercial downtown – literally. Architect Daniel Libeskind based his landmark design for the Contemporary Jewish Museum on the shape of the Hebrew word *l'chaim* – 'to life.' Galleries inside a converted power substation illuminate Jewish life and ideals through artists as diverse as Andy Warhol, Maurice Sendak, Marc Chagall and the Bay Area's own Gertrude Stein.

Cartoon Art Museum   MUSEUM
(Map p78; 🕿 415-227-8666; www.cartoonart.org; 655 Mission St; adult/student $8/6, 1st Tue of month free; ☉ 11am-5pm Tue-Sun; 👶; 🚌 14, 15, 30, 45, Ⓜ Montgomery, Ⓑ Montgomery) Introducing this place to comics fans would be an insult. Of course you know it was funded by *Peanuts'* Charles M Schultz. Naturally you recognize Mike Zeck's *Captain America* covers, own R Crumb's underground classic *Mr Natural,* and can recite Edward Gorey's alphabet ('A is for Amy who fell down the stairs/B is for Basil assaulted by bears...') But even diehard fans learn something new here, from lectures by Pixar animators to celebrations of women cartoonists with SF comics legend Trina Robbins.

Museum of the African Diaspora   MUSEUM
(MoAD; Map p78; 🕿 415-358-7200; www.moadsf.org; 685 Mission St; adult/student/child $10/5/free; ☉ 11am-6pm Wed-Sat, noon-5pm Sun; P 👶; 🚌 14, 15, 30, 45, Ⓜ Montgomery, Ⓑ Montgomery) MoAD tells the epic story of diaspora across three floors with an international cast of artists, writers and historians. Quarterly exhibits

Fisherman's Wharf, The Marina & Russian Hill

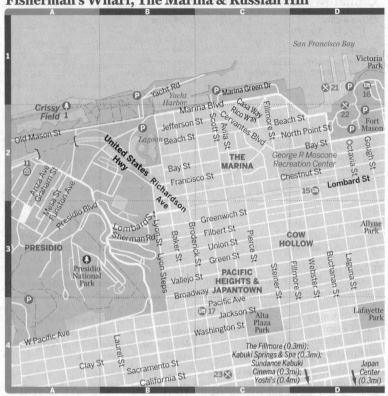

Fisherman's Wharf, The Marina & Russian Hill

have showcased glittering royals by Nigerian British sensation Chris Ofili, Romare Bearden's Harlem jazz portraits, and Siddi family quilts by South Indians descended from African slaves. Don't miss the moving video narrated by Maya Angelou.

The Mission & the Castro

★ 826 Valencia
CULTURAL SITE

(Map p88; ☎ 415-642-5905; www.826valencia.org; 826 Valencia St; ⓧ noon-6pm; ⑅; ⬛ 14, 33, 49, ⒝ 16th St Mission, Ⓜ J) Avast, ye scurvy scala-wags! If ye be shipwrecked without yer eye patch or McSweeney's literary anthology, lay down yer dubloons and claim yer boo-ty at this here nonprofit Pirate Store. Below decks, kids be writing tall tales for dark nights asea, and ye can study making video games and magazines and suchlike, if that be yer dastardly inclination...arrrr!

Mission Dolores
CHURCH

(Misión San Francisco de Asís; Map p88; ☎ 415-621-8203; www.missiondolores.org; 3321 16th St; adult/child $5/3; ⓧ 9am-4pm Nov-Apr, to 4:30pm May-Oct; ⬛ 22, 33, ⒝ 16th St Mission, Ⓜ J) The city's oldest building was founded in 1776 and re-built in 1782 with conscripted Ohlone and Miwok labor – a graveyard memorial hut commemorates 5000 Native laborers who died of hardship and measles epidemics. Today the original adobe is overshadowed by the ornate 1913 Churrigueresque basilica, featuring stained-glass windows of Califor-nia's 21 missions.

GLBT History Museum
MUSEUM

(Map p88; ☎ 415-621-1107; www.glbthistory.org/museum; 4127 18th St; admission $5, 1st Wed of month free; ⓧ 11am-7pm Mon & Wed-Sat, noon-5pm Sun; Ⓜ Castro) America's first gay-history museum captures proud moments and his-toric challenges: Harvey Milk's campaign literature, interviews with trailblazing bisexual author Gore Vidal, matchbooks from long-gone bathhouses and 1950s penal codes banning homosexuality.

Harvey Milk & Jane Warner Plazas
SQUARE

(Market & Castro Sts; Ⓜ Castro) A huge rain-bow flag welcomes arrivals to **Harvey Milk**

The Mission & The Castro

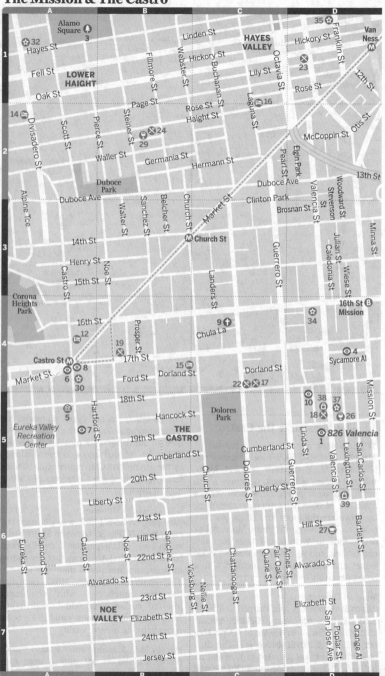

Plaza (Map p88; 🚃 24, 33, F, Castro St), where a display honors the Castro camera-store owner who was assassinated not long after becoming America's first out gay official – but who remains an icon of civil rights and civic pride. By the F-train terminus is Jane Warner Plaza (Map p88), named for the Castro's trailblazing lesbian police officer. The community converges here for sun and local color – including thong-clad protestors of SF's 2013 nudity ban.

Human Rights Campaign Action Center   HISTORIC SITE

(Map p88; 📞 415-431-2200; http://shop.hrc.org/san-francisco-hrc-store; 575 Castro St; ⊙10am-8pm Mon-Sat, to 7pm Sun) You may recognize Harvey Milk's former camera storefront, featured in the Oscar-winning movie *Milk*. Now it's home to the civil rights advocacy group, where supporters converge to sign petitions, shop for 'Equality' wedding rings, and admire the mural featuring Milk's famous words: 'If a bullet should enter my brain, let that bullet shatter every closet door.'

◉ The Haight

Haight & Ashbury   LANDMARK

(Map p92; 🚃 6, 33, 37, 43, 71) This legendary intersection was the epicenter of the psychedelic '60s and remains a counterculture magnet. On average Saturdays here you can sign Green Party petitions, commission a poem, hear Hare Krishna on keyboards and Bob Dylan on banjo. The clock overhead always reads 4:20 – better known in herbal circles as International Bong-Hit Time. A local clockmaker recently fixed it; within a week it was stuck at 4:20.

Alamo Square Park   PARK

(Map p88; Hayes & Scott Sts; 🐾; 🚃5, 21, 22, 24) **FREE** The pastel Painted Ladies of famed Postcard Row on Alamo Square's east side pale in comparison to colorful characters along the park's north side. Here you'll spot Barbary Coast baroque, with facades bedecked with fish-scale shingles and gingerbread trim dripping from peaked roofs. On the northwest corner, the 1889 Westerfield mansion miraculously survived tenancies by czarist Russian bootleggers, Fillmore jazz musicians, and hippie communes – plus watchtower rituals by Church of Satan founder Anton LaVey.

The Mission & The Castro

⊙ The Richmond

Coastal Trail   TRAIL

(Map p94; www.californiacoastaltrail.info; Fort Funston to Lincoln Park; ☉sunrise-sunset; ☐1, 18, 38) Hit your stride on the 9-mile stretch of Coastal Trail starting near former nuclear bunkers at Fort Funston, crossing 4 miles of sandy Ocean Beach, wrapping around the Presidio and ending at the Golden Gate Bridge. Casual strollers can pick up the trail near the ruins of Sutro Baths, head around cliffside Land's End for end-of-the-world views, then duck into the Legion of Honor at Lincoln Park.

**California Palace of the
Legion of Honor**   MUSEUM

(Map p94; ☎415-750-3600; http://legionofhonor. famsf.org; 100 34th Ave; adult/child $10/free, $2 discount with Muni ticket, 1st Tue of month free; ☉9:30am-5:15pm Tue-Sun; P🚼; ☐18) Larger-than-life sculptor's model 'Big Alma' Spreckels gifted this museum to lift San Francisco's spirits and pay tribute to Californians killed in WWI. Featured artworks range from Monet waterlilies to John Cage soundscapes, Iraqi ivories to R Crumb comics – part of the Legion's stellar Achenbach Collection of 90,000 graphic artworks.

🏃 Activities

Cycling & Skating

Blazing Saddles   CYCLING

(Map p86; ☎415-202-8888; www.blazingsaddles. com/san-francisco; 2715 Hyde St; cycle hire per hr $8-15, per day $32-88, electric bikes per day $48-88; ☉8am-7:30pm; 🚼; ☐Powell-Hyde) Cover the waterfront with bikes from the main shop on Hyde St or seven rental stands around Fisherman's Wharf. They also rent electric bikes, offer 24-hour return service and provide extras (bungee cords, packs etc).

Golden Gate Park Bike & Skate   BICYCLING

(Map p94; ☎415-668-1117; www.goldengatepark-bikeandskate.com; 3038 Fulton St; skates per hr $5-6, per day $20-24, bikes per hr $3-5, per day $15-25, tandem bikes per hr/day $15/75, discs $6/25; ☉10am-6pm; 🚼; ☐5, 31, 44) Besides bikes and skates (both quad-wheeled and inline), this little rental shop just outside the park rents disc putters and drivers for the nearby free Frisbee golf course.

Kayaking & Whale-Watching

City Kayak   KAYAKING

(Map p78; ☎415-294-1050; www.citykayak.com; Pier 40, South Beach Harbor; kayak rentals per hr $35-65, 3hr lesson & rental $59, tours $58-98;

Ⓜ Brannan) Newbies to kayaking can take lessons and venture calm waters near the Bay Bridge, and experienced paddlers can brave choppy currents beneath the Golden Gate (conditions permitting) – but romantics prefer calm-water moonlight tours.

Oceanic Society WHALE-WATCHING
(☑ reservations 415-256-9941; www.oceanic-society.org; tours per person $125; ⊙ reservations 8:30am-5pm Mon-Fri, trips Sat & Sun) Whale sightings aren't a fluke on naturalist-led, ocean-going, weekend boat trips during mid-October through December migrations. In the off-season, trips run to the Farallon Islands, 27 miles west of San Francisco.

Spas

★ **Kabuki Springs & Spa** SPA
(☑ 415-922-6000; www.kabukisprings.com; 1750 Geary Blvd; admission $25; ⊙ 10am-9:45pm, co-ed Tue, women-only Wed, Fri & Sun, men-only Mon, Thu & Sat; ☒ 22, 38) Unwind in these elegant Japanese baths. Scrub down with salt in the steam room, soak in the hot pool, take the cold plunge and reheat in the sauna. Most days are clothing-optional, but bathing suits are required on co-ed Tuesdays. Silence is mandatory – if you hear the gong, it means *Shhhh!*

☞ Tours

Day visits to **Alcatraz** (www.nps.gov/alca) include captivating audio tours with pris-

oners and guards recalling cellhouse life, while creepy twilight tours are led by park rangers; book tickets at least two weeks ahead. See also p76.

Alcatraz Cruises BOAT TOUR
(Map p86; ☑ 415-981-7625; www.alcatrazcruises.com; day tours adult/child/family $30/18/92, night adult/child $37/22) Ferries depart Pier 33 half-hourly 9am to 3:55pm, night tours leave at 6:10pm and 6:45pm.

★ **Precita Eyes Mission Mural Tours** TOUR
(Map p88; ☑ 415-285-2287; www.precitaeyes.org; adult $15-20, child $3; ⊙ see website calendar for tour dates; ☑) Muralists lead two-hour tours on foot or bike covering 60 to 70 murals in a six- to 10-block radius of mural-bedecked Balmy Alley; proceeds fund mural upkeep at this community arts nonprofit.

Chinatown Alleyway Tours TOUR
(☑ 415-984-1478; www.chinatownalleywaytours.org; adult/student $18/12; ⊙ 11am Sat; ☑; ☒ 8X, 8AX, 8BX) Neighborhood teens lead two-hour community nonprofit tours for up-close-and-personal peeks into Chinatown's past (weather permitting). Book five days ahead or pay double for Saturday walk-ins; cash only.

Public Library City Guides TOUR
(☑ 415-557-4266; www.sfcityguides.org; donations/tips welcome) **FREE** Volunteer historians lead nonprofit tours organized by neighborhood

---

MISSION MURALS

Inspired by Diego Rivera's San Francisco Works Progress Administration (WPA) murals and outraged by US foreign policy in Central America, Mission *muralistas* set out in the 1970s to transform the political landscape, one alley at a time. Today, 400-plus murals line Mission streets, including:

➡ ★ **Balmy Alley** (Map p88; ☑ 415-285-2287; www.precitaeyes.org; btwn 24th & 25th Sts; ☒ 10, 12, 27, 33, 48, ☐ 24th St Mission) Between Treat Ave and Harrison St, murals spanning 35 years transform garage doors into artistic and political statements, from an early memorial for El Salvador activist Archbishop Òscar Romero to a homage to the golden age of Mexican cinema.

➡ **Clarion Alley** (Map p88; btwn 17th & 18th Sts, off Valencia St; ☒ 14, 22, 33, ☐ 16th St Mission, Ⓜ J) Only the strongest street art survives in Clarion, where lesser works are peed on or painted over. Very few pieces survive for years, such as Megan Wilson's daisy-covered *Capitalism Is Over (If You Want It)* or Jet Martinez' view of Clarion Alley within a man standing in a forest.

➡ **Women's Building** (Map p88; 3543 18th St; ☑; Ⓜ 18th St, ☐ 16th St Mission) San Francisco's biggest mural is the 1994 *MaestraPeace*, a show of female strength painted by 90 *muralistas* that hugs the Women's Building. Featured icons range from ancient Mayan and Chinese goddesses to modern trailblazers, including Nobel Prize–winner Rigoberta Menchu, poet Audre Lorde and artist Georgia O'Keeffe.

The Haight

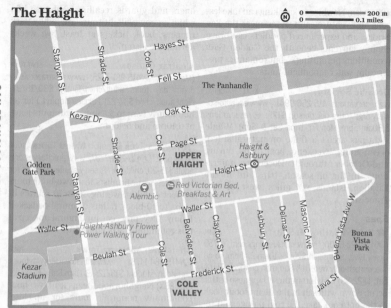

and theme: Art Deco Marina, Gold Rush Downtown, Secrets of Fisherman's Wharf, Telegraph Hill Stairway Hike and more.

Sea Foraging Adventures
TOUR

(www.seaforager.com; tours from $42 per person; ⊙calendar & reservations online) California sealife expert Kirk Lombard leads guided adventures to secret foraging spots around San Francisco's waterfront, finding urban edibles ranging from bullwhip seaweed to eels under the Golden Gate Bridge.

Emperor Norton's Fantastic Time Machine
TOUR

(http://emperornortontour.com/; tours depart from Union Square; tours $20; ⊙tours 11am & 2:30pm Tue & Sun; 2,38, B Powell) Gold Rush through Wild West legends in a 2¾-hour walking tour led by SF's self-proclaimed Emperor Norton, the eccentric schemer and Bay Bridge dreamer reincarnated by SF historian Joseph Amster.

Haight-Ashbury Flower Power Walking Tour
WALKING

(Map p92; ☑415-863-1621; www.haightashburytour. com; adult/child under 9yr $20/free; ⊙10:30am Tue & Sat, 2pm Thu, 11am Fri; 6, 71, MN) Take a long, strange trip through 12 blocks of hippie history in two hours, following the steps of

Jimi, Jerry and Janis – if you have to ask for last names, you totally need this tour. Tours meet at the corner of Stanyan and Waller Sts; reservations required.

★ Festivals & Events

February

Lunar New Year
CULTURAL

(www.chineseparade.com) Firecrackers, legions of tiny-tot martial artists and a 200ft dancing dragon make this parade the highlight of San Francisco winters.

April & May

SF International Film Festival
FILM

(www.sffs.org) Stars align and directors launch premieres each April at the nation's oldest film festival.

Bay to Breakers
SPORT

(www.baytobreakers.com; race registration $58-89.50) Run costumed from Embarcadero to Ocean Beach (7.5 miles) on the third Sunday in May, while joggers dressed as salmon run upstream.

June

SF Pride Celebration
CULTURAL

A day isn't enough to do SF proud: June begins with **International LGBT Film Festival** (www.frameline.org; ⊙mid-Jun) and goes out in

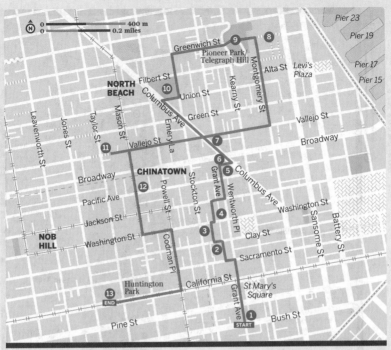

🏃 City Walk
San Francisco Hilltops

START DRAGON GATE
FINISH GRACE CATEHDRAL
LENGTH 2.3 MILES; 2½ HOURS

Conquer San Francisco's three most famous hills – Telegraph, Russian and Nob – for views that are pure poetry.

Enter Chinatown's **❶ Dragon Gate** and walk up dragon-lantern-lined Grant Ave to Sacramento St. Turn left half a block up, then right onto **❷ Waverly Place** (p75), where prayer flags grace painted temple balconies. At Clay St, jog left and right again onto **❸ Spofford Alley** (p75), where Sun Yat-sen plotted revolution. At the end of the block on Washington, take a right and an immediate left onto mural-lined **❹ Ross Alley** (p75), once San Francisco's bordello byway.

Turn right down Jackson to Grant, then turn right onto **❺ Jack Kerouac Alley**, where the pavement echoes Kerouac's ode to San Francisco: 'The air was soft, the stars so fine, and the promise of every cobbled alley so great...' Ahead is literary landmark

❻ City Lights (p74), where you'll pause to read a poem upstairs in the designated Poet's Chair.

Head left up Columbus and veer right up Vallejo to fuel up with an espresso at **❼ Caffe Trieste** (p103), where Francis Ford Coppola drafted his script for *The Godfather*. Continue up Vallejo and scale the steps to Montgomery St. Go left three blocks, and turn left onto cottage-lined **❽ Greenwich Street Steps** to summit Telegraph Hill. Inside **❾ Coit Tower** (p81), enjoy 1934 city views in newly restored murals downstairs and panoramic Bay views up top.

Head downhill, past wild parrots and tai-chi masters at **❿ Washington Square**. Turn left on Columbus, right on Vallejo, and up three blocks to take another picturesque stairway path to flower-lined **⓫ Ina Coolbrith Park**. Any breath you have left will be taken away by sweeping views to Alcatraz. Summit your last hill of the day the easy way: catch the **⓬ Powell-Mason cable car** up Nob Hill to walk the meditation labyrinth at **⓭ Grace Cathedral** (p80).

The Richmond, The Sunset & Golden Gate Park

SAN FRANCISCO

PACIFIC OCEAN

Iris Ave
Cook St
Spruce St
Parker Ave
Commonwealth Ave
Palm Ave
Arguello Blvd
Rossi Playground
Turk Blvd
University of San Francisco
Frederick St
Stanyan St

2nd Ave
3rd Ave
4th Ave
5th Ave
6th Ave
7th Ave
8th Ave
9th Ave
10th Ave
11th Ave
12th Ave

John F Kennedy Dr
Lawn Bowling Club
Children's Playground
Kezar Dr
Carl St
Parnassus Ave
3rd Ave
4th Ave
5th Ave
6th Ave
7th Ave
8th Ave
9th Ave
10th Ave
11th Ave
12th Ave

California Academy of Sciences
Lily Pond
Bowling Green Dr
Lincoln Way
Hugo St

Balboa St
Cabrillo St

MH de Young Museum

Funston Ave
14th Ave
15th Ave
16th Ave
17th Ave
18th Ave

Strawberry Hill
Stow Lake

Park Presidio Blvd

THE RICHMOND

Lake St
California St
Clement St
Anza St
Geary Blvd

Funston Ave
14th Ave
15th Ave
16th Ave
17th Ave
18th Ave
19th Ave
20th Ave
21st Ave

Crossover Dr

Lloyd Lake
Golden Gate Park
Elk Glen Lake
Irving St
24th Ave
25th Ave

22nd Ave
23rd Ave
24th Ave

25th Ave

26th Ave
27th Ave
28th Ave
29th Ave
30th Ave
31st Ave
32nd Ave
33rd Ave
34th Ave
35th Ave
36th Ave
37th Ave
38th Ave

Golden Gate Park
Middle Dr W
Metson Lake
Golden Gate Park Stables
Spreckels Lake

THE SUNSET

Martin Luther King Jr Dr

26th Ave
27th Ave
28th Ave
29th Ave
30th Ave
31st Ave
32nd Ave
33rd Ave
34th Ave
35th Ave

Sunset Blvd
38th Ave

31st Ave
34th Ave
Camino del Mar
Lincoln Park Golf Course

39th Ave
40th Ave
41st Ave
42nd Ave

45th Ave

47th Ave
48th Ave

Balboa St
Cabrillo St
Fulton St

John F Kennedy Dr
North Lake
Middle Lake
South Lake

Lincoln Way
Irving St
Judah St
44th Ave
45th Ave
46th Ave
47th Ave
48th Ave

Point Lobos
Lincoln Park
Fort Miley
Clement St
Point Lobos Ave
Anza St

Windmills
47th Ave
OCEAN BEACH

La Playa St
Great Hwy
Upper Great Hwy

Sutro Heights Park

Seal Rocks

The Richmond, The Sunset & Golden Gate Park

style the last weekend with Pink Saturday's **Dyke March** (www.dykemarch.org) and **Pride Parade** (www.sfpride.org).

August & September

Outside Lands　　　　　　　　　　MUSIC
(www.sfoutsidelands.com/; 1-/3-day $115/375) Three days of major acts – such as Kanye West, Macklemore, The Killers, The Flaming Lips – and outlandish debauchery at Wine Land, Beer Lands and Taste of the Bay.

Folsom Street Fair　　　　　　STREET FAIR
(www.folsomstreetfair.com) Work that leather look and enjoy public spankings for local charities the last weekend of September.

October & November

Litquake　　　　　　　　　　LITERATURE
(www.litquake.org) Score signed books and grab drinks with authors in October.

Hardly Strictly Bluegrass　　　　MUSIC
(www.strictlybluegrass.com) Three days of free Golden Gate Park concerts and headliners ranging from Elvis Costello to Gillian Welch; early October.

Día de los Muertos　　　　　　FESTIVAL
(Day of the Dead; www.dayofthedeadsf.org) Party to wake the dead with a spooky costume parade, sugar skulls and fabulous altars in the Mission on November 2.

🛏 Sleeping

🛏 Union Square & the Tenderloin

Hotel des Arts　　　　　　　　HOTEL $
(Map p84; ☑ 415-956-3232, 800-956-4322; www. sfhoteldesarts.com; 447 Bush St; r with bath $129-

199, without bath $99; 🛜; Ⓜ Montgomery, Ⓑ Montgomery) A budget hotel for art freaks, with jaw-dropping murals by underground artists – it's like sleeping inside a painting. Rooms with private bath require seven-night stays. Bring earplugs.

Pacific Tradewinds Hostel　　　HOSTEL $
(Map p84; ☑ 415-433-7970, 888-734-6783; www. sanfranciscohostel.org; 680 Sacramento St; dm $35; @ 🛜; 🚌 1, 🚋 California St, Ⓑ Montgomery) San Francisco's smartest-looking all-dorm hostel has a blue-and-white nautical theme, fully equipped kitchen, spotless glass-brick showers, no lockout time and great staff. No elevator means hauling bags up three flights.

Hotel Carlton　　　　　　DESIGN HOTEL $$
(Map p78; ☑ 415-673-0242, 800-922-7586; www. hotelcarltonsf.com; 1075 Sutter St; r $175-245; @ 🛜 🛜; 🚌 2, 3, 19, 38, 47, 49) ✔ World travelers fit right into this freshly renovated hotel off the beaten track – a 10-minute walk to Union Square. Spotless rooms have an upbeat, worldly vibe, with colorful bedspreads and tapestry pillows. Rooftop solar panels keep the hotel carbon neutral; downstairs is a top-notch Middle Eastern restaurant.

Phoenix Hotel　　　　　　　MOTEL $$
(Map p78; ☑ 415-776-1380, 800-248-9466; www. thephoenixhotel.com; 601 Eddy St; r $209-244; P 🛜 🛋; 🚌 19, 31, 47, 49) The ultimate rocker crash pad earns street cred with courtyard pool parties (bring earplugs), rooms packed with pop art, and a long list of California rebels (Red Hot Chili Peppers, Joan Jett, Keanu Reeves) who frequent this cool converted midcentury motel in the gritty Tenderloin. Free parking and admission to Kabuki Springs & Spa (p91).

WORTH A TRIP

OCEAN BEACH

Bundle up for strolls along the blustery 4-mile stretch of **Ocean Beach** (Map p94; ☑ 415-561-4323; www.parksconservancy.org; Great Hwy; ☺ sunrise-sunset; ☐ 5, 18, 31, Ⓜ N), where Golden Gate Park greenery ends and the great blue Pacific Ocean begins. Dedicated sand-castle architects dot the water's edge year-round, but only hardcore surfers brave these riptides (casual swimmers beware). Beachcombers may spot sand dollars and 19th-century shipwrecks along the south end – but stick to paths in fragile dunes, where skittish snowy plover shorebirds shelter in winter. Bonfires are permitted in artist-designed fire pits only; no alcohol allowed. For drinks, stop by oceanfront **Beach Chalet** (Map p94; ☑ 415-386-8439; www.beachchalet.com; 1000 Great Hwy; ☺ 9am-10pm Mon-Thu, to 11pm Fri, 8am-11pm Sat, 8am-10pm Sun; ♿; ☐ 5, 18, 31) for house-brewed beer on the heated patio and 1930s lobby murals.

Golden Gate Hotel
HOTEL $$

(Map p78; ☑ 415-392-3702, 800-835-1118; www.goldengatehotel.com; 775 Bush St; r with/without bath $190/135; @ ⑦; ☐ 2, 3, ☐ Powell-Hyde, Powell-Mason) Like an old-fashioned *pensione*, this 1913 Edwardian inn has kindly owners and homey mismatched furniture. Rooms are simple and cozy, most with private baths – request an antique claw-foot tub. Homemade cookies and a resident cat provide comfort after sightseeing.

★ Orchard Garden Hotel
BOUTIQUE HOTEL $$$

(Map p84; ☑ 415-399-9807, 888-717-2881; www.theorchardgardenhotel.com; 466 Bush St; r $295-370; ✳ @ ⑦; ☐ 2, 3, 30, 45, Ⓑ Montgomery) 🍃 San Francisco's first all-green-practices hotel features sustainable wood furnishings, chemical-free cleaning products, and a sunny rooftop terrace. Luxe touches include fluffy down pillows and Egyptian-cotton sheets in soothingly quiet rooms.

Hotel Rex
BOUTIQUE HOTEL $$$

(Map p78; ☑ 415-433-4434, 800-433-4434; www.thehotelrex.com; 562 Sutter St; r $287-309; ✳ @ ⑦ ⌨; ☐ Powell-Hyde, Powell-Mason, Ⓜ Powell, Ⓑ Powell) 🍃 French gramophone music evokes New York's Algonquin in the 1920s, and handsome guestrooms feature hand-painted lampshades, local art and plush beds piled with crisp linens and down pillows. Street-facing rooms are bright but noisy; request air-con.

🛏 North Beach

San Remo Hotel
HOTEL $$

(Map p86; ☑ 415-776-8688, 800-352-7366; www.sanremohotel.com; 2237 Mason St; r with shared bath $99-139; @ ⑦ ⌨; ☐ 30, 47, ☐ Powell-Mason) One of the city's best-value stays, this 1906 inn is an old-fashioned charmer with antique furnishings. Bargain rooms have windows facing the corridor; family suites accommodate up to five. No elevator.

★ Hotel Bohème
BOUTIQUE HOTEL $$$

(Map p84; ☑ 415-433-9111; www.hotelboheme.com; 444 Columbus Ave; r $214-275; @ ⑦; ☐ 10, 12, 30, 41, 45) A love letter to the Beat era, with vintage photos, parasol lights and moody 1950s color schemes. Rooms are smallish and some face noisy Columbus Ave – but the vibrant North Beach neighborhood scene could inspire your next novel.

🛏 Fisherman's Wharf

★ HI San Francisco Fisherman's Wharf
HOSTEL $

(Map p86; ☑ 415-771-7277; www.sfhostels.com; Bldg 240, Fort Mason; dm incl breakfast $30-42, r $75-109; Ⓟ @ ⑦; ☐ 28, 30, 47, 49) A former army hospital building offers bargain-priced private rooms and dorms (some co-ed) with four to 22 beds and a huge kitchen. No curfew, but no heat during the day – bring warm clothes. Limited free parking.

★ Argonaut Hotel
BOUTIQUE HOTEL $$$

(Map p86; ☑ 415-563-0800, 800-790-1415; www.argonauthotel.com; 495 Jefferson St; r $389-449, with view $489-529; ✳ ⑦ ⌨; ☐ 19, 47, 49, ☐ Powell-Hyde) 🍃 Built as a cannery in 1908, Fisherman's Wharf's best inn has century-old wooden beams, exposed brick walls and an over-the-top nautical theme that includes porthole-shaped mirrors. Ultra-comfy beds and iPod docks are standard, though some rooms are small and dark – pay extra for mesmerising bay views.

🛏 The Marina & Pacific Heights

Coventry Motor Inn
MOTEL $$

(Map p86; ☑ 415-567-1200; www.coventrymotorinn.com; 1901 Lombard St; r $155-165; Ⓟ ✳ ⑦;

GOLDEN GATE PARK

When San Franciscans refer to 'the park,' there's only one that gets the definite article. Everything they hold dear is in **Golden Gate Park** (Map p94; http://sfrecpark.org; 🚻 👶; 🚍5, 18, 21, 28, 29, 33, 44, 71, Ⓜ N) 🐾, including free spirits, free music, Frisbee and bison.

At the east end you can join year-round drum circles at **Hippie Hill**, sweater-clad athletes at the historic **Lawn Bowling Club**, toddlers clinging for dear life onto the 100-year-old **carousel** and meditators in the contemplative **AIDS Memorial Grove** (Map p94). To the west, turtles paddle past model yachts at **Spreckels Lake**, offerings are made at pagan altars behind the **baseball diamond** and free concerts are held in the **Polo Fields**, site of 1967's hippie Human Be-In.

This scenery seems far-fetched now, but impossible when proposed in 1866. When New York's Central Park architect Frederick Law Olmsted balked at transforming 1017 acres of dunes into the world's largest developed park, San Francisco's green scheme fell to tenacious young civil engineer William Hammond Hall. He insisted that instead of casinos, resorts, race tracks and an igloo village, park features should include **botanical gardens** (Strybing Arboretum; Map p94; 📞 415-661-1316; www.strybing.org; 1199 9th Ave; adult/child $7/5, 2nd Tue of month free; ⊙9am-6pm Apr-Oct, to 5pm Nov-Mar, bookstore 10am-4pm; 🚻; 🚍6, 43, 44, 71, Ⓜ N) 🐾, a dedicated **bison paddock** (Map p94) and waterfalls at **Stow Lake**.

Today the park offers 7.5 miles of bicycle trails, 12 miles of equestrian trails, an archery range, fly-casting pools, four soccer fields and 21 tennis courts. Sundays, when JFK Dr closes to traffic around 9th Ave, don't miss **roller disco** and **lindy-hopping** in the park. Other times, catch these park highlights:

MH de Young Museum (Map p94; 📞 415-750-3600; http://deyoung.famsf.org/; 50 Hagiwara Tea Garden Dr; adult/child $10/6, discount with Muni ticket $2, 1st Tue of month free, online booking fee $1 per ticket; ⊙9:30am-5:15pm Tue-Sun, to 8:45pm Fri Apr-Nov; 🚍5, 44, 71, Ⓜ N) Follow sculptor Andy Goldsworthy's artificial earthquake fault in the sidewalk into Herzog + de Meuron's faultlessly sleek, copper-clad building that's oxidizing green to blend into the park. Don't be fooled by the de Young's camouflaged exterior: shows here boldly broaden artistic horizons, from Oceanic ceremonial masks and Bulgari jewels to California photographer Anthony Friedkin's 1970s portraits of gay liberation.

California Academy of Sciences (Map p94; 📞 415-379-8000; www.calacademy.org; 55 Music Concourse Dr; adult/child $34.95/24.95, discount with Muni ticket $3; ⊙9:30am-5pm Mon-Sat, 11am-5pm Sun; Ⓟ 🚻; 🚍5, 6, 31, 33, 44, 71, Ⓜ N) Architect Renzo Piano's landmark, LEED-certified green building houses 38,000 weird and wonderful animals, with a four-story rainforest and split-level aquarium under a 'living roof' of California wildflowers. After the penguins nod off to sleep, the wild rumpus starts at kids'-only Academy Sleepovers and over-21 NightLife Thursdays, when rainforest-themed cocktails encourage strange mating rituals among shy first dates.

Japanese Tea Garden (Map p94; 📞 tea ceremony reservations 415-752-1171; www.japaneseteagardensf.com; 75 Hagiwara Tea Garden Dr; adult/child $7/2, before 10am Mon, Wed & Fri free; ⊙9am-6pm Mar-Oct, to 4:45pm Nov-Feb; Ⓟ 🚻; 🚍5, 44, 71, Ⓜ N) Since 1894, this 5-acre garden has blushed with cherry blossoms in spring, turned flaming red with maple leaves in fall, and lost all track of time in the meditative **Zen Garden**. The 100-year-old **bonsai grove** is the legacy of founder Makoto Hagiwara, who tended them until his family's forced deportation to WWII Japanese American internment camps, and spent decades afterwards restoring these priceless miniature evergreens. Don't miss green tea and fortune cookies (invented for the garden's opening) at the **tea pavilion**.

Conservatory of Flowers (Map p94; 📞 info 415-831-2090; www.conservatoryofflowers.org; 100 John F Kennedy Dr; adult/child $7/2, 1st Tue of month free; ⊙10am-4:30pm Tue-Sun; 🚍5, Ⓜ N) Flower power thrives inside this restored 1878 Victorian greenhouse, where orchids dangle from the ceiling like trapeze artists, lilies float contemplatively and creepy carnivorous plants make lunch of passing insects.

ⓘ DEALS & HIDDEN COSTS

San Francisco is the birthplace of the boutique hotel, offering stylish rooms for a price: $150-plus for most midrange rooms, plus 16% hotel tax (hostels exempt) and $35 to $50 for overnight parking. For last-minute vacancies and deals, check **Lonely Planet** (http://hotels.lonelyplanet.com) and San Francisco–based accommodations specialists **HotelTonight** (www.hoteltonight.com), **Airbnb** (www.airbnb.com), **Bed & Breakfast SF** (www.bbsf.com), **Hipmunk** (www.hipmunk.com) and **Hotwire** (www.hotwire.com).

🖵 22, 28, 30, 43) Of the many motels lining Lombard St (Hwy 101), the generic Coventry has the highest quality-to-value ratio with spacious, plain, well-maintained rooms and extras like air-con and covered parking.

★**Hotel Drisco**　BOUTIQUE HOTEL **$$$**
(Map p86; ☎415-346-2880, 800-634-7277; www.hoteldrisco.com; 2901 Pacific Ave; r incl breakfast $375-425; @🖘; 🖵3, 24) A stately apartment-hotel tucked between Pacific Heights mansions, with elegant architecture, attentive service and understated-chic room decor. At this lofty ridgeline location, spring for city-view rooms and taxis.

🛏 SoMa

Hotel Vitale　BOUTIQUE HOTEL **$$$**
(Map p78; ☎415-278-3700, 888-890-8688; www.hotelvitale.com; 8 Mission St; r $419-509; ✳@🖘🐾; Ⓜ Embarcadero, Ⓑ Embarcadero) Behind that tinted glass is a laid-back luxury waterfront hotel. The clever Vitale has thought of everything: 450-thread-count sheets, on-site spa with two rooftop hot tubs and a sleek downstairs lounge. Get bayfront rooms for spectacular Bay Bridge views.

Good Hotel　MOTEL **$$$**
(Map p78; ☎415-621-7001, 800-444-5819; www.thegoodhotel.com; 112 7th St; r $199-279; @🖘🐾; Ⓜ Civic Center, Ⓑ Civic Center) 🗲 SF's hip green motel, with reclaimed-wood headboards, upcycled-bottle chandeliers, and fleece bedspreads made from recycled soda bottles. Drawbacks are the sketchy neighborhood and street noise; book rooms in back.

🛏 The Mission & the Castro

Inn San Francisco　B&B **$$**
(Map p88; ☎800-359-0913, 415-641-0188; www.innsf.com; 943 S Van Ness Ave; r incl breakfast $185-310, with shared bath $135-200; Ⓟ@🖘; 🖵14, 49) 🗲 An impeccably maintained 1872 Italianate-Victorian mansion, this inn has period antiques, fresh-cut flowers, and fluffy featherbeds; some have Jacuzzi tubs. There's also a freestanding garden cottage that sleeps up to six. Outside there's an English garden and redwood hot tub. Limited parking: reserve ahead.

Inn on Castro　GLBT, B&B **$$**
(Map p88; ☎415-861-0321; www.innoncastro.com; 321 Castro St; r incl breakfast $165-185, without bath $125-145, self-catering apt $165-210; 🖘; Ⓜ Castro) Flashback to the Castro's disco heyday inside this Edwardian townhouse with '70s-mod furnishings. Rooms are retro-cool and breakfasts exceptional – the owner is a chef. Ask about nearby apartments also available for rental.

Parker Guest House　B&B **$$$**
(Map p88; ☎415-621-3222, 888-520-7275; www.parkerguesthouse.com; 520 Church St; r incl breakfast $209-259; @🖘; 🖵33, Ⓜ J) Welcome to the Castro's stateliest gay digs, inside twin Edwardian mansions sharing a garden and steam room. Elegant rooms have cushy beds with down duvets; bath fixtures gleam.

🛏 The Haight & Hayes Valley

Metro Hotel　HOTEL **$**
(Map p88; ☎415-861-5364; www.metrohotelsf.com; 319 Divisadero St; r $88-100; @🖘; 🖵6, 24, 71) A central Haight hotel providing cheap, clean rooms with private bath, 24-hour reception, a garden patio and excellent pizza downstairs. No elevator.

Chateau Tivoli　B&B **$$**
(☎415-776-5462, 800-228-1647; www.chateautivoli.com; 1057 Steiner St; r incl breakfast $175-215, with shared bath $115-135; 🖘; 🖵5, 22) This glorious chateau off Alamo Sq once hosted Isadora Duncan and Mark Twain, and shows plenty of character with turrets, carved woodwork and (rumor has it) the ghost of a Victorian opera diva. No elevator, no TV.

Red Victorian Bed, Breakfast & Art　B&B **$$**
(Map p92; ☎415-864-1978; www.redvic.net; 1665 Haight St; r incl breakfast $179-189, without bath $119-149; 🖘; 🖵33, 43, 71) 🗲 The trippy '60s

live on inside this 1904 Victorian, with theme rooms like Sunshine, Flower Children and Summer of Love. Only four of 18 rooms have baths, but all include breakfast in the organic Peace Café downstairs. Reduced rates for longer stays; no elevator.

Hayes Valley Inn
HOTEL $$

(Map p78; ☑ 415-431-9131, 800-930-7999; www.hayesvalleyinn.com; 417 Gough St; d incl breakfast $93-115, queen $103-126; @ 🛜 🛋; 🚇 21, Ⓜ Van Ness) Amid tempting boutiques and bistros, this amazingly reasonable find has simple, small rooms with shared baths, kindly staff and a good-natured resident dog. Bring ear plugs and expect a walk to the nearest bathroom; no elevator.

Parsonage
B&B $$$

(Map p88; ☑ 415-863-3699; www.theparsonage.com; 198 Haight St; r $220-270; @ 🛜; 🚇 6, 71, streetcar F) The charming owners are justly proud of their 23-room Italianate-Victorian's gorgeous original details, including brass chandeliers and Carrara-marble fireplaces. Airy rooms are bedecked with oriental rugs and period antiques. Take breakfast in the formal dining room, and nightcaps of brandy and chocolate by the fire.

✖ Eating

✖ Union Square

farm:table
AMERICAN $

(Map p78; ☑ 415-292-7089; www.farmtablesf.com; 754 Post St; dishes $6-9; ◷ 7:30am-2pm Tue-Fri, 8am-3pm Sat & Sun; 🚇 2, 3, 27, 38) 🍃 A tiny storefront with one wooden communal table inside, two tables and a stand-up outdoor counter, farm:table uses local organics and rooftop-grown herbs in daily menus posted on Twitter (@farmtable). Cash only.

Sweet Woodruff
CAFE, CALIFORNIAN $

(Map p78; ☑ 415-292-9090; www.sweetwoodruffsf.com; 798 Sutter St; dishes $8-14; ◷ 8am-9:30pm Mon-Fri, 9:30am-9:30pm Sat & Sun; 🚇 2, 3, 27) 🍃 Little sister to neighboring Michelin-starred Sons & Daughters, this storefront features top-end, seasonal-regional ingredients in small plates like roasted padron peppers with fromage blanc and sea-urchin baked potatoes with bacon. No waiters, no frills, just tasty.

Cafe Claude
FRENCH $$

(Map p78; ☑ 415-392-3505; www.cafeclaude.com; 7 Claude Lane; mains $15-23; ◷ 11:30am-10:30pm Mon-Sat, 5:30pm-10:30pm Sun; Ⓜ Montgomery,

Ⓑ Montgomery) Hidden in an alleyway, Cafe Claude is a sweet downtown retreat with outdoor tables and effortlessly charming staff. Lunch is served until 5pm, jazz combos play weekends, and coq au vin and a stellar wine list make dream dates.

✖ Chinatown & North Beach

★ Liguria Bakery
BAKERY $

(Map p84; ☑ 415-421-3786; 1700 Stockton St; focaccia $4-5; ◷ 8am-1pm Tue-Fri, from 7am Sat; 🍃 🛗; 🚇 8X, 30, 39, 41, 45, 🚋 Powell-Mason) Bleary-eyed art students and Italian grandmothers line up by 8am for cinnamon-raisin focaccia hot from the 100-year-old oven, leaving 9am dawdlers a choice of tomato or classic rosemary. Take yours in wax paper or boxed for picnics; cash only.

City View
CHINESE $

(Map p84; ☑ 415-398-2838; 662 Commercial St; dishes $3-8; ◷ 11am-2:30pm Mon-Fri, from 10am Sat & Sun; 🚇 8X, 10, 12, 30, 45, 🚋 California St) Order off the menu or hail wait carts loaded with shrimp dumplings, garlicky Chinese broccoli, tangy spare ribs and other tantalizing dim sum. Arrive before noon for first picks from fragrant bamboo steamers.

★ Cotogna
ITALIAN $$

(Map p84; ☑ 415-775-8508; www.cotognasf.com; 490 Pacific Ave; mains $17-29; ◷ 11:30am-11pm Mon-Thu, 11:30am-midnight Fri & Sat, 5-9:30pm Sun; 🍃; 🚇 10, 12) Rustic Italian pastas, wood-fired pizzas and rotisserie meats spiked with rooftop-grown herbs show chef Michael Tusk's finesse with well-chosen, balanced ingredients. Book ahead or plan a late lunch.

Z & Y
CHINESE $$

(Map p84; ☑ 415-981-8988; www.zandyrestaurant.com; 655 Jackson St; mains $9-20; ◷ 11am-9:30pm Mon-Thu, to 10:30pm Fri-Sun; 🚇 8X, 🚋 Powell-Mason, Powell-Hyde) Graduate from so-so sweet-and-sour and middling *mu-shu* pork to sensational Szechuan dishes that go down in a blaze of glory: spicy pork dumplings, heat-blistered string beans, housemade noodles, and fish poached in flaming chili oil. Go early; expect a wait.

Cinecittà
PIZZA $$

(Map p84; ☑ 415-291-8830; www.cinecittarestaurant.com; 663 Union St; pizza $12-15; ◷ noon-10pm Sun-Thu, to 11pm Fri & Sat; 🍃 🛗; 🚇 8X, 30, 39, 41, 45, 🚋 Powell-Mason) Squeeze in at the counter for thin-crust pizza served with local brews on tap and sass by Roman owner Romina.

100

SAN FRANCISCO EATING

ⓘ SF MEALS & DEALS

Hope you're hungry: there are more restaurants per capita in San Francisco than in any other US city. Scan for deals at www.blackboardeats.com and www.opentable.com – and since SF's top restaurants are quite small, reserve now. Some restaurants brazenly tack on a 4% surcharge to cover city-mandated healthcare for SF food workers. Factor in 9.5% tax on top of your meal price, plus 15% to 25% for the tip.

North Beach loyalties are divided between the Roman Travestere (mozzarella, arugula and prosciutto) and Neapolitan O Sole Mio (capers, olives, mozzarella and anchovies).

★**Coi** CALIFORNIAN **$$$**
(Map p84; ☎415-393-9000; www.coirestaurant.com; 373 Broadway; set menu $195; ⊙5:30-10pm Tue-Sat; ☐8X, 30, 41, 45, ☐Powell-Mason) ❧ Chef Daniel Patterson's restlessly imaginative eight-course tasting menu is like licking California's coastline: rooftop-raised pansies grace Sonoma duck's tongue, and wild-caught abalone surfaces in pea-shoot tidepools. Settle in among the shaggy cushions and spot-lit stoneware to enjoy only-in-California wine pairings ($115; generous enough for two).

✕ **Fisherman's Wharf & Russian Hill**

Fisherman's Wharf Crab Stands SEAFOOD **$**
(Map p86; foot of Taylor St; mains $5-15; Ⓜ F) Brawny-armed men stir steaming cauldrons of Dungeness crab at takeaway crab stands at the foot of Taylor St. Crab season runs winter through spring, but you'll find shrimp and seafood year-round. Take your haul to Pier 43 Promenade benches, or duck through glass doors marked 'Passageway to the Boats' at 8/9 Fisherman's Wharf for dockside lunches.

★**Gary Danko** CALIFORNIAN **$$$**
(Map p86; ☎415-749-2060; www.garydanko.com; 800 North Point St; 3-/5-course menu $76/111; ⊙5:30-10pm; ☐19, 30, 47, ☐Powell-Hyde) The true test of SF romance is whether you're willing to share Gary Danko's crèmes brûlée trio. Smoked-glass windows prevent passersby from tripping over their tongues at roast lobster with trumpet mushrooms,

duck breast with rhubarb compote, and the lavish cheese cart. Reservations required.

✕ **The Marina, Japantown & Pacific Heights**

Off the Grid FOOD TRUCK **$**
(Map p86; www.offthegridsf.com; 2 Marina Blvd; dishes $5-10; ⊙5-11pm Fri; ♿; ☐22, 28) Some 30 food trucks converge Fridays for SF's largest mobile-gourmet hootenanny (other nights/locations attract fewer trucks; see website). Arrive before 6:30pm or expect 20-minute waits for Chairman Bao's roast duck buns, Roli Roti's free-range herbed roast chicken, and Crème Brûlée Man desserts. Cash only; enjoy takeout dockside with Golden Gate Bridge sunsets.

★**Greens** VEGETARIAN, CALIFORNIAN **$$**
(Map p86; ☎415-771-6222; www.greensrestaurant.com; Bldg A, Fort Mason Center, cnr Marina Blvd & Laguna St; lunch $15-18, dinner $18-25; ⊙11:45am-2:30pm & 5:30-9pm Tue-Fri, from 11am Sat, 10:30am-2pm & 5:30-9pm Sun, 5:30-9pm Mon; ☎♿; ☐28) ❧ Career carnivores won't realize there's zero meat in hearty roasted-eggplant panini and black-bean chili with crème fraîche and pickled jalapeños – they're packed with flavor-bursting ingredients grown on a Zen farm in Marin. Make reservations on weekends, or get take-out to enjoy on a wharf-side bench.

State Bird Provisions CALIFORNIAN **$$**
(☎415-795-1272; statebirdsf.com; 1529 Fillmore St; ⊙5:30-10pm Sun-Thu, to 11pm Fri & Sat; ☐22, 38) James Beard dubbed State Bird America's best new restaurant in 2013 for its wildly inventive take on dim sum, with esoteric local ingredients like fennel pollen and garum (fish extract). Book ahead, or arrive by 5pm for a coveted walk-in bar spot. Prices are deceptive; all those small plates add up.

Tataki JAPANESE **$$**
(Map p86; ☎415-931-1182; www.tatakisushibar.com; 2815 California St; dishes $12-20; ⊙11:30am-2pm & 5:30-10pm Mon-Thu, 11:30am-2pm & 5:30-10:30pm Fri, 5-10:30pm Sat, 5-9:30pm Sun; ☐1, 24) ❧ Pioneering sustainable sushi chefs Kin Lui, Raymond Ho and Kenny Zhu rescue dinner and the oceans with silky farmed Arctic char with yuzu-citrus and the Golden State Roll – a California dream of spicy, line-caught scallop, Pacific tuna, organic avocado and apple slivers.

SoMa

Zero Zero
PIZZA $$

(Map p78; ☑ 415-348-8800; www.zerozerosf.com; 826 Folsom St; pizzas $12-19; ☻11:30am-2:30pm & 4-10pm Mon-Thu, to 11pm Fri, 11:30am-11pm Sat, 11:30am-10pm Sun; M Powell, B Powell) The name is a throw-down of Neapolitan pizza credentials – '00' flour is used for Naples' famous puffy-edged crust – and these pies deliver on that promise, with inspired SF-themed toppings. The Geary is a crossover hit with Manila clams, bacon and chilies, but the real crowd-pleaser is the Castro, turbo-loaded with housemade sausage.

★ Benu
CALIFORNIAN, FUSION $$$

(Map p78; ☑ 415-685-4860; www.benusf.com; 22 Hawthorne St; tasting menu $195; ☻5:30-8:30pm Tue-Sat; ☐10, 12, 14, 30, 45) SF has refined fusion cuisine over 150 years, but no one rocks it quite like chef/owner Corey Lee (formerly of Napa's French Laundry), who remixes local, sustainable, fine-dining staples and Pacific Rim flavors with a SoMa DJ's finesse. Dungeness crab and truffle bring such outsize flavor to his faux-shark's-fin soup, you'll swear there's Jaws in there.

The Mission & the Castro

★ La Taqueria
MEXICAN $

(Map p88; ☑ 415-285-7117; 2889 Mission St; burritos $6-8; ☻11am-9pm Mon-Sat, to 8pm Sun; ☐; ☐12, 14, 48, 49, B 24th St Mission) SF's definitive burrito has no debatable saffron rice, spinach tortilla or mango salsa – just perfectly grilled meats, slow-cooked beans and classic tomatillo or mesquite salsa wrapped in flour tortillas.

★ Ichi Sushi
SUSHI $$

(☑ 415-525-4750; www.ichisushi.com; 3282 Mission St; sushi $4-8; ☻5:30-10pm Mon-Thu, to 11pm Fri & Sat; ☐14, 49, B 24th St Mission, M J) Ichi Sushi is a sharp cut above other fish joints. Silky, sustainably sourced fish is sliced with a jeweler's precision, balanced atop well-packed rice, and topped with powerfully tangy dabs of gelled yuzu and microscopically diced chili daikon that make soy sauce unthinkable.

★ Namu Gaji
KOREAN, CALIFORNIAN $$

(Map p88; ☑ 415-431-6268; www.namusf.com; 499 Dolores St; small plates $10-21; ☻11:30am-4pm Wed-Fri, from 10:30am Sat & Sun, 5-10pm Tue-Thu & Sun, 5-11pm Fri & Sat; ☐22, 33, M J, B 16th St Mission) ✐ SF's culinary advantages are

---

THE FERRY BUILDING

San Francisco's monument to food, the **Ferry Building** (Map p78; ☑ 415-983-8000; www.ferrybuildingmarketplace.com; Market St & the Embarcadero; ☻10am-6pm Mon-Fri, 9am-6pm Sat, 11am-5pm Sun; P ☐; M Embarcadero, B Embarcadero) still doubles as a trans-bay transit hub – but with dining options like these, you may never leave.

Ferry Plaza Farmers Market (Map p78; ☑ 415-291-3276; www.cuesa.org; Market St & the Embarcadero; ☻10am-2pm Tue & Thu, 8am-2pm Sat; M Embarcadero, B Embarcadero) Star chefs troll farmers-market stalls for rare heirloom varietals, foodie babies blissfully teethe on organic apricots, and organic tamale trucks have rock-star fan bases. Pass time in line exchanging recipe tips, then haul your picnic to Pier 2.

Slanted Door (Map p78; ☑ 415-861-8032; www.slanteddoor.com; 1 Ferry Bldg; lunch $16-36, dinner $18-45; ☻11am-4:30pm & 5:30-10pm Mon-Sat, 11:30am-4:30pm & 5:30-10pm Sun; M Embarcadero, B Embarcadero) Charles Phan earns his 2014 James Beard Outstanding Chef title with California-fresh, Vietnamese-inspired fare that rivals the sparkling Bay views – especially five-spice duck with figs. Reserve ahead or hit the takeout window.

Hog Island Oyster Company (Map p78; ☑ 415-391-7117; www.hogislandoysters.com; 1 Ferry Bldg; 4 oysters $13; ☻11:30am-9pm Mon-Thu, to 10pm Fri, 11am-10pm Sat, 11am-9pm Sun; M Embarcadero, B Embarcadero) ✐ Slurp sustainably farmed Tomales Bay oysters as you please: drizzled with tangy caper buerre blanc, spiked with bacon and paprika, or au naturel with Sonoma bubbly.

Mijita (Map p78; ☑ 415-399-0814; www.mijitasf.com; 1 Ferry Bldg; dishes $4-10; ☻10am-7pm Mon-Thu, to 8pm Fri, 9am-8pm Sat, 8:30am-3pm Sun; ☐ ☐; M Embarcadero, B Embarcadero) Sustainable fish tacos reign supreme and *agua fresca* (fruit punch) is made with fresh juice at chef-owner Traci des Jardin's bayfront Cal-Mex joint.

showcased in Namu's Korean-inspired soul food. Menu standouts include ultra-savory shiitake mushroom dumplings, meltingly tender marinated beef tongue, and a sizzling stone pot of rice with organic vegetables, grass-fed steak and a Sonoma farm egg.

★**Frances** CALIFORNIAN $$$
(Map p88; ☑ 415-621-3870; www.frances-sf.com; 3870 17th St; mains $20-27; ⊙5-10pm Sun-Thu, to 10:30pm Fri & Sat; Ⓜ Castro) Chef/owner Melissa Perello ditched downtown fine dining to start this bistro showcasing bright, seasonal flavors and luxurious textures: cloudlike sheep's-milk ricotta gnocchi with crunchy broccolini, grilled calamari with preserved Meyer lemon, and artisan wine served by the ounce, directly from Wine Country.

🍴 The Haight & Hayes Valley

Second Act FOOD ARTISANS $
(http://secondactsf.com/; 1727 Haight St; dishes $5-12; ⊙8am-6pm, to 8pm Fri) When collectively run Red Vic movie house ended its 30-year run, neighbors demanded an encore – now Second Act Marketplace houses local

food makers and a neighborhood events space. Stop by for dumplings at Anda Piroshki, High Cotton Kitchen soul food, and the cherry-lavender ice cream at Eatwell Farm – and stay for Friday happy hours and indie-movie premieres (see website).

★**Rich Table** CALIFORNIAN $$$
(Map p88; ☑ 415-355-9085; http://richtablesf.com; 199 Gough St; meals $17-30; ⊙5:30-10pm Sun-Thu, to 10:30pm Fri & Sat; ☐5, 6, 21, 47, 49, 71, Ⓜ Van Ness) 🍴 Licking plates is the obvious move after finishing chilled apricot soup with pancetta or rabbit cannelloni with nasturtium cream. Married co-chefs/co-owners Sarah and Evan Rich invent playful, exquisite Californian food like the Dirty Hippie: silky goat-buttermilk pannacotta topped with nutty sunflower seeds and hemp. Book two to four weeks ahead (call the restaurant directly) or arrive early for bar seating.

★**Jardinière** CALIFORNIAN $$$
(Map p78; ☑ 415-861-5555; www.jardiniere.com; 300 Grove St; mains $18-32; ⊙5-10:30pm Tue-Sat, to 10pm Sun & Mon; ☐5, 21, 47, 49, Ⓜ Van Ness) 🍴 *Iron Chef, Top Chef* Master and James Beard Award–winner Traci Des Jardins

TOP SAN FRANCISCO TREATS

Life is sweet in San Francisco, where chocolate bars were invented in the Gold Rush and velvet ropes keep ice-cream lines from getting ugly. Before you dismiss dessert, consider these temptations.

➡ ★**Craftsman & Wolves** (Map p88; ☑ 415-913-7713; http://craftsman-wolves.com; 746 Valencia St; pastries $3-7; ⊙7am-7pm Mon-Thu, to 8pm Fri, 8am-8pm Sat, 8am-7pm Sun; ☐14, 22, 33, 49, Ⓑ16th St Mission, Ⓜ J) A sleek counter fit to showcase diamonds offers something far better: exquisite salted-caramel eclairs and black-sesame checkered cake.

➡ **Bi-Rite Creamery** (Map p88; ☑ 415-626-5600; www.biritecreamery.com; 3692 18th St; ice cream $3-7; ⊙11am-10pm Sun-Thu, to 11pm Fri & Sat; ♿; ☐33, Ⓑ16th St Mission, Ⓜ J) 🍴 Organic ice cream worth the line even in foggy weather – especially salted caramel and balsamic strawberry.

➡ **Tout Sweet** (Map p78; ☑ 415-385-1679; www.toutsweetsf.com; Geary & Stockton Sts, Macy's, 3rd fl; baked goods $2-8; ⊙10am-8pm Mon-Wed, until 9pm Thu-Sat, 11am-7pm Sun; ☐2, 38, 🚋Powell-Mason, Powell-Hyde, Ⓑ Powell St) Bypass sales and head directly to Macy's 3rd floor, where *Top Chef* winner Yigit Pura reinvents French macarons in irreverent SF flavors like sour cherry/bourbon and peanut butter and jelly.

➡ **Benkyodo** (☑ 415-922-1244; www.benkyodocompany.com; 1747 Buchanan St; mochi $1.25-2; ⊙8am-5pm Mon-Sat; ☐2, 3, 22, 38) Legendary *mochi* (rice cakes) made in-house daily – come early for perennially popular green tea, peanut butter, and chocolate-filled strawberry flavors.

➡ **Mission Pie** (Map p88; ☑ 415-282-1500; www.missionpie.com; 2901 Mission St; pie slices $3.50-4; ⊙7am-10pm Mon-Fri, from 8am Sat, from 9am Sun; 📶♿; ☐12, 14, 48, 49, Ⓑ24th St Mission) 🍴 Warm, flaky, heirloom apple pie served with free organic whipped cream in a sunny, certified-green Victorian storefront with toys for kids.

champions sustainable, salacious California cuisine. She lavishes housemade tagliatelle with bone marrow and tops velvety scallops with satiny sea urchin. Go Mondays, when $55 scores three decadent courses with wine pairings.

✖ The Richmond & the Sunset

★ Outerlands
CALIFORNIAN $$

(Map p94; ☎ 415-661-6140; www.outerlandssf.com; 4001 Judah St; sandwiches & small plates $7-14, mains $18-22; ☺ 10am-3pm Tue-Fri, from 9am Sat & Sun, 5:30-10pm Tue-Sun; ; ☐ 18, M N) When windy Ocean Beach leaves you feeling shipwrecked, drift into this beach-shack bistro for organic, seed-to-table California comfort food. Brunch demands Dutch pancakes in iron skillets with housemade ricotta, and lunch brings grilled artisan-cheese combos with farm-inspired soup. Reserve ahead or enjoy wine while you wait.

Nopalito
MEXICAN $$

(Map p94; ☎ 415-233-9966; www.nopalitosf.com; 1224 9th Ave; ☺ 11:30am-10pm; ☐; ☐ 6, 43, 44, 71, M N) ☛ Head south of Golden Gate Park's border for upscale, sustainably sourced Cal-Mex, including tasty *tortas* (flatbread sandwiches), tender *carnitas* (braised pork) tacos and cinnamon-laced Mexican hot chocolate. No reservations; call one to two hours ahead to join the wait list.

★ Aziza
MOROCCAN, CALIFORNIAN $$$

(Map p94; ☎ 415-752-2222; www.aziza-sf.com; 5800 Geary Blvd; mains $19-29; ☺ 5:30-10:30pm Wed-Mon; ☐ 1, 29, 31, 38) *Iron Chef* champ Mourad Lahlou's inspiration is Moroccan and his ingredients organic Californian, but the flavors are out of this world: Sonoma duck confit and caramelized onion fill flaky pastry *basteeya*, and slow-cooked Marin lamb tops saffron-infused barley. Pastry chef Melissa Chou's apricot bavarian is a goodnight kiss.

♟ Drinking & Nightlife

◯ Union Square

★ Rickhouse
BAR

(Map p84; ☎ 415-398-2827; www.rickhouse.com; 246 Kearny St; ☺ 5pm-2am Mon, 3pm-2am Tue-Fri, 6pm-2am Sat; M Montgomery, B Montgomery) Like a shotgun shack plunked downtown, Rickhouse is lined with bourbon casks and shelving from an Ozark Mountains nunnery that once secretly brewed

hooch. The emphasis is on rare bourbon, but groups guzzle authentic Pisco Punch by the garage-sale punchbowl.

Irish Bank
PUB

(Map p84; ☎ 415-788-7152; www.theirishbank.com; 10 Mark Lane; ☺ 11:30am-2am; M Montgomery, B Montgomery) Perfectly pulled pints, thick-cut fries with malt vinegar, and sausages with lashings of mustard are staples at this genuinely friendly Irish pub. Cozy snugs are great for conversation, but tables under alley awnings appeal to smokers.

◯ Chinatown & North Beach

★ Caffe Trieste
CAFE

(Map p84; ☎ 415-392-6739; www.caffetrieste.com; 601 Vallejo St; ☺ 6:30am-11pm Sun-Thu, to midnight Fri & Sat; ☎; ☐ 8X, 10, 12, 30, 41, 45) Poetry on bathroom walls, opera on the jukebox, live accordion jams weekly and sightings of Beat poet laureate Lawrence Ferlinghetti: Trieste has been a North Beach landmark since the 1950s. Sip espresso under the Sicilian mural, where Francis Ford Coppola drafted *The Godfather*. Cash only.

★ Comstock Saloon
BAR

(Map p84; ☎ 415-617-0071; www.comstocksaloon.com; 155 Columbus Ave; ☺ noon to 2am Mon-Fri, from 4pm Sat, 4pm-midnight Sun; ☐ 8X, 10, 12, 30, 45, ☐ Powell-Mason) Cocktails at this Victorian saloon remain period-perfect: Pisco Punch is made with pineapple gum and martini-precursor Martinez features gin, vermouth, bitters and maraschino liqueur. Call ahead for booths or tufted-velvet parlor seating and to get dates when ragtime-jazz bands play.

Specs'
BAR

(☎ 415-421-4112; 12 William Saroyan Pl; ☺ 4:30pm-2am Mon-Fri, from 5pm Sat & Sun) Order pitchers of Anchor Steam, admire walls plastered with merchant-marine memorabilia and join salty old-timers plotting mutinies against last call.

Li Po
BAR

(Map p84; ☎ 415-982-0072; www.lipolounge.com; 916 Grant Ave; ☺ 2pm-2am; ☐ 8X, 30, 45, ☐ Powell-Mason, Powell-Hyde) Beat a hasty retreat to red vinyl booths where Allen Ginsberg and Jack Kerouac debated the meaning of life alongside a bemused golden Buddha. Enter the 1937 faux-grotto doorway and dodge red lanterns to order beer or a sweet, sneaky-strong Chinese mai tai made with *baiju* (rice liquor). Bathrooms and random DJ appearances are in the basement.

Downtown & SoMa

★ Bar Agricole BAR
(Map p88; ☎ 415-355-9400; www.baragricole.com; 355 11th St; ⊗ 6-10pm Tue-Thu & Sun, 5:30-11pm Fri & Sat; ⬚ 9, 12, 27, 47) Drink your way to a history degree with these cocktails: Bellamy Scotch Sour with egg whites passes the test, but Tequila Fix with lime, pineapple gum and hellfire bitters earns honors. Don't miss the sea-urchin deviled eggs.

Blue Bottle Coffee Company CAFE
(www.bluebottlecoffee.net; 66 Mint St; ⊗ 7am-7pm Mon-Fri, 8am-6pm Sat & Sun) The mad-scientist $20,000 coffee siphon yields superior fair-trade, organic drip coffee, rivaled only by bittersweet mochas and an off-menu invention called the Gibraltar.

Local Edition LOUNGE
(☎ 415-795-1375; www.localeditionsf.com; 691 Market st; ⊗ 5pm-2am Mon-Fri, from 7pm Sat) Get the scoop on SF's cocktail scene at this new speakeasy in the historic Hearst newspaper building's basement. Lights are so dim you might bump into typewriters, but all is forgiven when you get the Pulitzer – a scotch-sherry cocktail that goes straight to your head.

DNA Lounge CLUB
(Map p88; www.dnalounge.com; 375 11th St; admission $3-25; ⊗ 9pm-3am Fri & Sat, other nights vary; ⬚ 12, 27, 47) One of SF's last megaclubs hosts live bands, mash-up dance party Bootie, epic drag at Trannyshack, and Monday's 18-plus Goth Death Guild.

The Mission

Ritual Coffee Roasters CAFE
(Map p88; ☎ 415-641-1011; www.ritualroasters.com; 1026 Valencia St; ⊗ 6am-8pm Mon-Thu, to 10pm Fri, 7am-10pm Sat, 7am-8pm Sun; 🛜; ⬚ 14, 49, Ⓑ 24th St Mission) Cults wish they inspired the same devotion as Ritual, where devotees queue for house-roasted espresso drinks and specialty drip coffees with genuinely bizarre flavor profiles – believe descriptions of beans with cashew and grapefruit-peel notes.

GAY/LESBIAN/BI/TRANS SAN FRANCISCO

Singling out the best places to be queer in San Francisco is almost redundant. Though the Castro is a gay hub and the Mission is a magnet for lesbians, dancing queens and party bois head to SoMa for thump-thump clubs. Top GLBT venues include:

➡ **The Stud** (Map p88; www.studsf.com; 399 9th St; admission $5-8; ⊗ noon-2am Tue, from 5pm Wed & Sat, 5pm-3am Thu & Fri, 5pm to midnight Sun; ⬚ 12, 19, 27, 47) Rocking the gay scene since 1966, and branching out beyond leather daddies with rocker-grrrl Mondays, Tuesday drag variety shows, raunchy comedy/karaoke Wednesdays, Friday art-drag dance parties, and performance-art cabaret whenever hostess/DJ Anna Conda gets it together.

➡ **Lexington Club** (Map p88; ☎ 415-863-2052; www.lexingtonclub.com; 3464 19th St; ⊗ 5pm-2am Mon-Thu, from 3pm Fri-Sun; ⬚ 14, 33, 49, Ⓑ 16th St Mission) Odds are eerily high you'll develop a crush on your ex-girlfriend's hot new girlfriend over strong drinks, pinball and tattoo comparisons; live dangerously at SF's most famous/notorious full-time lesbian bar.

➡ **Aunt Charlie's** (Map p78; ☎ 415-441-2922; www.auntcharlieslounge.com; 133 Turk St; admission $2-5; ⊗ noon-2am Mon-Fri, from 10am Sat, 10am-midnight Sun; Ⓜ Powell, Ⓑ Powell) Total dive, with the city's best classic drag show Fridays and Saturdays at 10pm. Thursday nights, art-school boys freak for bathhouse disco at Tubesteak ($5).

➡ **Endup** (Map p78; ☎ 415-646-0999; www.theendup.com; 401 6th St; admission $5-20; ⊗ 10pm Thu-4am Fri, 11pm Fri-11am Sat, 10pm Sat-4am Mon, 10pm Mon-4am Tue; ⬚ 12, 27, 47) Home of Sunday 'tea dances' since 1973, though technically the party starts Saturday, EndUp watching the sunrise Monday over the freeway on-ramp.

➡ **Rickshaw Stop** (Map p78; ☎ 415-861-2011; www.rickshawstop.com; 155 Fell St; admission $5-35; ⊗ variable, check online; Ⓜ Van Ness) Freak beats keep sweaty 18-plus crowds up past their bedtimes at this all-ages, all-orientations, all-fabulous shoebox club; lesbian go-go and bhangra nights rule.

➡ **Sisters of Perpetual Indulgence** (Map p78; www.thesisters.org) For guerrilla antics and wild fundraisers, check the website of the self-described 'leading-edge order of queer nuns,' a charitable organization and San Francisco institution.

El Rio
CLUB

(☑ 415-282-3325; www.elriosf.com; 3158 Mission St; admission $3-8; ⏱ 1pm-2am; ☐ 12, 14, 27, 49, Ⓑ 24th St Mission) The DJ mix takes its cue from El Rio regulars: eclectic, funky and internationally sexy, no matter your orientation. Margaritas get crowds bopping to disco-punk mashups and flirting shamelessly in the back garden. Come for shuffleboard and free oysters Fridays at 5:30pm. Cash only.

🍷 The Haight & Hayes Valley

★ Smuggler's Cove
BAR

(Map p78; ☑ 415-869-1900; www.smugglerscovesf.com; 650 Gough St; ⏱ 5pm-1:15am; ☐ 5, 21, 49, Ⓜ Van Ness) Yo-ho-ho and a bottle of rum...or perhaps a Dead Reckoning with bitters, Nicaraguan rum, tawny port and vanilla liqueur. Pirates be bedeviled by choice at this shipwreck tiki speakeasy – with 400 rums and 70 cocktails, you won't be dry-docked long.

★ Toronado
PUB

(Map p88; ☑ 415-863-2276; www.toronado.com; 547 Haight St; ⏱ 11:30am-2am; ☐ 6, 22, 71, Ⓜ N) Glory hallelujah, beer lovers: your prayers are answered with 50-plus brews on tap and hundreds more bottled. Bring cash and pair seasonal ales with sausages from **Rosamunde** (Map p88; ☑ 415-437-6851; http://rosamundesausagegrill.com; 545 Haight St; sausages $6.50-7; ⏱ 11:30am-10pm Sun-Wed, to 11pm Thu-Sat; ☐ 6, 22, 71, Ⓜ N) next door – it may get too loud to hear your date, but you'll hear angels sing.

Alembic
BAR

(Map p92; ☑ 415-666-0822; www.alembicbar.com; 1725 Haight St; ⏱ 4pm-2am Mon-Fri, from noon Sat & Sun; ☐ 6, 33, 37, 43, 71, Ⓜ N) The floors are well-stomped and the tin ceilings hammered – and you will be too, if you gulp Alembic's potent concoctions made with 250 specialty spirits. Honor the Haight with a Lava Lamp (rosé bubbly with walnut bitters) or be rendered speechless by Charlie Chaplin (sloe gin, lime and apricot liqueur).

☆ Entertainment

Live Music

★ SFJAZZ Center
JAZZ

(Map p88; ☑ 866-920-5299; www.sfjazz.org; 201 Franklin St; ⏱ showtimes vary; ☐ 5, 7, 21, Ⓜ Van Ness) America's newest, largest jazz center draws legendary artists-in-residence like Wynton Marsalis, Regina Carter and Tony Bennett (who left his heart here, after all) – but the real thrills are experimental performances, like pianist Jason Moran's jam session with SF skateboarders pounding a ramp inside the auditorium. Upper-tier cheap seats are more like stools, but offer clear stage views and ledges for drinks.

★ The Chapel
LIVE MUSIC

(Map p88; ☑ 415-551-5157; www.thechapelsf.com; 777 Valencia St; tickets $15-22; ☐ 14, 33, Ⓜ J, Ⓑ 16th St Mission) Musical prayers are answered in a 1914 California Craftsman landmark with heavenly acoustics. The 40ft roof is raised by shows like Preservation Hall Jazz Band jams with Nick Lowe, Polyphonic Spree's full-choir ruckus and Radiohead's *OK Computer* lipsynched by an all-star drag revue. Many shows are all-ages, except when comedians like W Kamau Bell test edgy material.

The Fillmore
CONCERT VENUE

(☑ 415-346-3000; www.thefillmore.com; 1805 Geary Blvd; tickets from $20; ⏱ shows nightly) Hendrix, Zeppelin, Janis – they all played the Fillmore. The legendary venue that launched the psychedelic era has the posters to prove it upstairs, and hosts arena acts in a 1250-seat venue where you can squeeze in next to the stage.

Slim's
LIVE MUSIC

(Map p88; ☑ 415-255-0333; www.slimspresents.com; 333 11th St; tickets $12-30; ⏱ box office 10:30am-6pm Mon-Fri & show nights; ☐ 9, 12, 27, 47) Guaranteed good times by Gogol Bordello, the Expendables and the Mekons fit the bill at this midsized club, where Prince and Elvis Costello have played sets unannounced. Shows are all-ages, though shorties may have a hard time seeing once the floor starts bouncing. Reserve dinner ($25) to score balcony seats.

Great American Music Hall
LIVE MUSIC

(Map p78; ☑ 415-885-0750; www.gamh.com; 859 O'Farrell St; admission $12-35; ⏱ box office 10:30am-6pm Mon-Fri & show nights; ☐ 19, 38, 47, 49) Once a bordello, the Great American Music Hall is full of surprises: Black Rebel Motorcycle Club playing acoustic, hardcore bluegrass jams, and burly bouncers swaying to Vetiver. Arrive early to claim balcony seats, or find standing room near the stage.

Independent
LIVE MUSIC

(Map p88; ☑ 415-771-1421; www.theindependentsf.com; 628 Divisadero St; tickets $12-45; ⏱ box office 11am-6pm Mon-Fri, to 9:30pm show nights; ☐ 5, 6, 21, 71) Shows earn street cred here, featuring indie dreamers (Magnetic Fields, Rogue Wave), rock legends (Courtney Love, Marky Ramone), alterna-pop (Imagine Dragons, Vampire Weekend) and wacky events like the US Air Guitar Championships.

Yoshi's
JAZZ, LIVE MUSIC

(☑ 415-655-5600; www.yoshis.com; 1330 Fillmore St; ⊙ shows 8pm &/or 10pm Tue-Sun, dinner 5:30-9pm Tue & Wed, 5:30-10pm Thu, 5:30-10:30pm Fri & Sat, 5-9pm Sun; ☐ 22, 31) The Fillmore Jazz District was once called 'the Harlem of the West,' and Yoshi's still draws top global talent like guitarist Leon Redbone, singer Nancy Wilson and Sufi electronica artist Niyaz – and it throws Black Panther reunions and serves mean sushi besides.

Mezzanine
LIVE MUSIC

(Map p78; ☑ 415-625-8880; www.mezzaninesf.com; 444 Jessie St; admission $10-40; Ⓜ Powell, Ⓑ Powell) Beats boom off brick walls at shows by Wyclef Jean, Quest Love, Method Man, Nas and Snoop Lion (aka Dogg), plus throwback alt-classics like the Dandy Warhols and Psychedelic Furs.

Theater

★American Conservatory Theater
THEATER

(ACT; Map p78; ☑ 415-749-2228; www.act-sf.org; 415 Geary St; ⊙ box office noon-6pm Mon, to curtain Tue-Sun; ☐ 38, ☐ Powell-Mason, Powell-Hyde) Breakthrough shows destined for Broadway premiere at ACT's Geary Theater, including Tony Kushner's *Angels in America* and Robert Wilson's *Black Rider*, with a libretto by William S Burroughs and music by the Bay Area's Tom Waits.

Beach Blanket Babylon
CABARET

(BBB; Map p84; ☑ 415-421-4222; www.beachblanketbabylon.com; 678 Green St; admission $25-100; ⊙ shows 8pm Wed, Thu & Fri, 6:30pm & 9:30pm Sat, 2pm & 5pm Sun; ☐ 8X, ☐ Powell-Mason) Snow White searches for Prince Charming in San Francisco: what could possibly go wrong? SF's signature musical-comedy cabaret since 1974 stays fresh with topical comedy and

🛈 HOT TICKETS

At **TIX Bay Area** (www.tixbayarea.org), half-price tickets are sold on show day for cash only. For advance tickets to concerts and Broadway shows, check **Ticketmaster** (www.ticketmaster.com) and **SHN** (www.shnsf.com).

wigs big as parade floats. Pop icons and heads of state are spoofed mercilessly – even when President Obama, Queen Elizabeth and the SF Giants attended.

Cobb's Comedy Club
COMEDY

(Map p86; ☑ 415-928-4320; www.cobbscomedyclub.com; 915 Columbus Ave; admission $12.50-45, plus 2-drink minimum; ⊙ showtimes vary; ☐ 8X, 30, 39, 41, 45, ☐ Powell-Mason) Bumper-to-bumper shared tables make an intimate audience for breakthrough talent and big-name acts from Dave Chappelle to Louis CK. Check the website for shows and comically twisted events – Father's Day Burlesque Brunch, anyone?

AsiaSF
DRAG CABARET

(Map p78; ☑ 415-255-2742; www.asiasf.com; 201 9th St; per person from $39; ⊙ 7:15-11pm Wed, Thu & Sun, 7:15pm-2am Fri, 5pm-2am Sat; Ⓜ Civic Center, Ⓑ Civic Center) Cocktails and Asian-inspired dishes are served with surplus sass and one little secret: your servers are drag stars. Hostesses rock the bar/runway hourly, but once drinks kick in, everyone mingles on the downstairs dance floor. Bring cash for tips.

Classical Music, Opera & Dance

★Davies Symphony Hall
CLASSICAL MUSIC

(Map p78; ☑ rush tickets 415-503-5577, 415-864-6000; www.sfsymphony.org; 201 Van Ness Ave; Ⓜ Van Ness, Ⓑ Civic Center) SF Symphony has racked up nine Grammys, and you can see why: conductor Michael Tilson Thomas keeps the audience rapt through Beethoven, Mahler, even Metallica. The season runs September to July; call the rush-ticket hotline for $20 next-day tickets, and don't miss free pre-show talks.

★San Francisco Opera
OPERA

(Map p78; ☑ 415-864-3330; www.sfopera.com; War Memorial Opera House, 301 Van Ness Ave; tickets $10-350; Ⓑ Civic Center, Ⓜ Van Ness) SF Opera rivals New York's Met with original operas like Stephen King's *Dolores Claiborne* and Verdi and Puccini revivals by acclaimed Tuscan director Nicola Luisotti. Book ahead, or score $10 same-day, standing-room tickets at 10am and two hours before curtain.

★ODC Theater
DANCE

(Map p88; ☑ 415-863-9834; www.odctheater.org; 3153 17th St; ⊙ box office noon-3pm Mon-Fri) For 40 years, ODC has redefined dance with risky, raw performances September through December – plus year-round guest performers and 200 dance classes a week.

San Francisco Ballet
DANCE

(Map p78; ☑ 415-861-5600, tickets 415-865-2000; www.sfballet.org; War Memorial Opera House, 301 Van Ness Ave; tickets $10-120; Ⓜ Van Ness, Ⓑ Civic Center) SF Ballet performs 100 gloriously staged shows annually at the War Memorial Opera House January to May; check website for dates and ticket deals.

Cinemas

★ Castro Theatre
CINEMA

(Map p88; ☑ 415-621-6120; www.castrotheatre.com; 429 Castro St; adult/child $11/8.50; ☺ showtimes vary; Ⓜ Castro) The crowd sings along to pre-show Mighty Wurlitzer organ tunes, especially the theme song to the 1936 classic *San Francisco*. Don't miss silver-screen revivals, and cult classics preceded by live re-enactments – in drag. Cash only.

★ Roxie Cinema
CINEMA

(Map p88; ☑ 415-863-1087; www.roxie.com; 3117 16th St; regular screening/matinee $10/7; ☐ 14, 22, 33, 49, Ⓑ 16th St Mission) A little neighborhood nonprofit cinema with major international clout for indie premieres, controversial films and documentaries banned elsewhere. No ads, plus personal introductions to every film.

Sundance Kabuki Cinema
CINEMA

(☑ 415-346-3243; www.sundancecinemas.com; 1881 Post St; adult $9.75-15, child $9.50-12; ☐ 2, 3, 22, 38) ✒ Robert Redford's Sundance Institute runs this innovative green multiplex with first-run flicks, festival premieres and no ads – get comfortable in reserved recycled-fiber seating and booze in 21-plus screenings.

Sports

San Francisco Giants
BASEBALL

(Map p78; ☑ 415-972-2000; www.sfgiants.com; AT&T Park, 24 Willie Mays Plaza; tickets $5-135) Watch and learn how the World Series is won.

🔒 Shopping

San Francisco has big department stores and name-brand boutiques around Union Sq, including Macy's (Map p78; www.macys.com; 170 O'Farrell St; ☺ 10am-9pm Mon-Sat, 11am-7pm Sun; ☐ Powell-Mason, Powell-Hyde, Ⓜ Powell, Ⓑ Powell) and Westfield San Francisco Centre (Map p78; www.westfield.com/sanfrancisco; 865 Market St; ☺ 10am-8:30pm Mon-Sat, to 7pm Sun; ⊞) ☐ Powell-Mason, Powell-Hyde, Ⓜ Powell, Ⓑ Powell) – but only-in-SF scores are found in the Haight, Castro, Mission and Hayes Valley.

SAN FRANCISCO FOR CHILDREN

Imaginations come alive in this story-book city, with wild parrots squawking around Coit Tower (p81) and sunning sea lions gleefully nudging one another off the docks at Pier 39 (p80). For thrills, try rickety, seatbelt-free cable cars. Kids will find playmates at Golden Gate Park (p97) and Crissy Field (p81). The **Children's Creativity Museum** (Map p78; ☑ 415-820-3320; www.zeum.org; 221 4th St; admission $11; ☺ 10am-4pm Wed-Sun Sep-May, Tue-Sun Jun-Aug; ⊞; Ⓜ Powell, Ⓑ Powell) features technology that's too cool for school: robots, live-action video games, and 3D animation workshops.

See also: Exploratorium (p75), California Academy of Sciences (p97), Cartoon Art Museum (p85), Musée Mécanique (p75), Japan Center (p81), and 826 Valencia (p87).

★ Under One Roof
GIFTS

(Map p78; ☑ 415-503-2300; www.underoneroof.org; Crocker Galleria, 50 Post St; ☺ 10am-6pm Mon-Fri) AIDS service organizations receive 100% of the proceeds from goods donated by local designers and retailers, so show volunteer salespeople some love.

★ Gravel & Gold
HOUSEWARES, GIFTS

(Map p88; ☑ 415-552-0112; www.gravelandgold.com; 3266 21st St; ☺ noon-7pm Mon-Sat, to 5pm Sun; Ⓜ 24th St Mission, Ⓑ 24th St Mission) Get back to the land and in touch with California roots with Gravel & Gold's trippy silkscreened totes, hippie homesteader smock-dresses, 1960s Osborne/Woods ecology posters, and rare books on '70s beach-shack architecture.

★ Park Life
ART, GIFTS

(Map p94; ☑ 415-386-7275; www.parklifestore.com; 220 Clement St; ☺ noon-8pm Mon-Thu, from 11am Fri & Sat, 11am-7pm Sun; ☐ 1, 2, 33, 38, 44) Design store, indie publisher and art gallery in one. Park Life presents are too good to wait for birthdays, including Golden State pendants, Sean O'Dell utopia catalogs, and Ian Johnson's portrait of John Coltrane radiating rainbow vibes.

★ Heath Ceramics
HOUSEWARES

(Map p78; ☑ 415-399-9284; www.heathceramics.com; 1 Ferry Bldg; ☺ 10am-7pm Mon-Fri, 8am-6pm Sat, 11am-5pm Sun; Ⓜ Embarcadero,

B Embarcadero) No SF tablescape is complete without handmade modern Heath stoneware, thrown by potters in Heath's Sausalito studio since 1948. Pieces are priced for fine dining except studio seconds, sold on weekends.

★ **Betabrand** CLOTHING
(Map p88; 🖪 800-694-9491; www.betabrand.com; 780 Valencia St; ⊙11am-7pm Mon-Fri, to 8pm Sat, noon-6pm Sun; 🖪 14, 22, 33, 49, **B** 16th St Mission) Experimental designs are put to online votes and winners produced in limited editions. Recent designs include lunch-meat-patterned socks, reversible smoking jackets, and bike-to-work pants with reflective-strip cuffs.

ℹ️ Information

DANGERS & ANNOYANCES

Keep your city smarts and wits sharp, especially at night in SoMa, the Mission and the Haight. Unless you know where you're going, avoid the seedy, depressing Tenderloin (bordered east–west by Powell and Polk Sts and north–south by O'Farrell and Market Sts), Skid Row (6th St between Market and Folsom Sts) and Bayview–Hunters Point. Panhandlers and homeless people are part of San Francisco's community. People will probably ask you for spare change, but donations to local nonprofits stretch further. Don't engage with panhandlers at night or around ATMs. A simple 'I'm sorry,' is a polite response.

EMERGENCY & MEDICAL SERVICES

Haight Ashbury Free Clinic (🖪 415-762-3700; www.healthright360.org; 558 Clayton St; ⊙ by appointment; 🖪 6, 33, 37, 43, 71, **M** N) Provides substance abuse and mental health services by appointment.

San Francisco General Hospital (🖪 emergency 415-206-8111, main hospital 415-206-8000; www.sfdph.org; 1001 Potrero Ave; ⊙24hr; 🖪 9, 10, 33, 48) Provides care to uninsured patients; no documentation required.

Walgreens (🖪 415-861-3136; www.walgreens. com; 498 Castro St, cnr 18th St; ⊙24hr; 🖪 24, 33, 35, **M** F, K, L, M) Pharmacy and over-the-counter meds; locations citywide (see website).

INTERNET ACCESS

SF has free wi-fi hot spots citywide – locate one nearby with www.openwifispots.com.

Apple Store (🖪 415-392-0202; www.apple. com/retail/sanfrancisco; 1 Stockton St; ⊙9am-9pm Mon-Sat, 10am-8pm Sun; 🛜; **M** Powell St) Free wi-fi and internet terminal usage.

San Francisco Main Library (🖪 415-871-4294; www.sfpl.org; 100 Larkin St; ⊙10am-6pm Mon & Sat, 9am-8pm Tue-Thu, noon-6pm Fri, noon-5pm Sun; 🛜; **M** Civic Center) Free 15-minute internet terminal usage; spotty wi-fi access.

MONEY

Bank of America (www.bankamerica.com; 1 Market Plaza; ⊙9am-5pm Mon-Thu, to 6pm Fri)

POST

Rincon Center Post Office (Map p78; www. usps.gov; 180 Steuart St; ⊙7:30am-5pm Mon-Fri, 9am-2pm Sat; **M** Embarcadero, **B** Embarcadero)

US Post Office (Map p78; www.usps.gov; Macy's, 170 O'Farrell St; ⊙10am-5pm Mon-Sat; 🖪 Powell-Mason & Powell-Hyde, **M** Powell St, **B** Powell St) At Macy's department store.

TOURIST INFORMATION

California Welcome Center (Map p86; 🖪 415-981-1280; www.visitcwc.com; Pier 39, Bldg P, Suite 241b; ⊙9am-7pm)

San Francisco Visitor Information Center (Map p78; 🖪 415-391-2000, events hotline 415-391-2001; www.onlyinsanfrancisco.com; lower level, Hallidie Plaza, Market & Powell Sts; ⊙9am-5pm Mon-Fri, to 3pm Sat & Sun; 🖪 Powell-Mason, Powell-Hyde, **M** Powell St, **B** Powell St) Provides practical information and runs a 24-hour events hotline.

USEFUL WEBSITES

Craig's List (http://sfbay.craigslist.org) Events, activities, partners, freebies and dates.

Eater (http://sf.eater.com) Food and bars.

Flavorpill (www.flavorpill.com) Live music, lectures, art openings and movie premieres.

The Bold Italic (www.thebolditalic.com) SF trends, openings and opinions.

Urban Daddy (www.urbandaddy.com) Bars, shops, restaurants and events.

ℹ️ Getting There & Away

AIR

San Francisco is served by three major airports:

➡ **San Francisco International Airport** Most international flights arrive/depart SFO, 14 miles south of downtown SF off Hwy 101.

➡ **Oakland International Airport** Travelers from other US cities may find flights that arrive across the Bay on discount airlines such as JetBlue and Southwest.

➡ **Norman Y Mineta San Jose International Airport** Just 50 miles south of San Francisco along Hwy 101, and accessible via Caltrain.

BUS

Until the new terminal is completed in 2017, SF's intercity hub remains the **Temporary Transbay Terminal** (Map p78; Howard & Main Sts), where you can catch buses on **AC Transit** (www. actransit.org) to the East Bay, **Golden Gate Transit** (http://goldengatetransit.org) north to Marin and Sonoma, and **SamTrans** (www.

samtrans.com) south to Palo Alto and the Pacific coast. **Greyhound** (☎ 800-231-2222; www.greyhound.com) buses leave daily for Los Angeles ($59, eight to 12 hours), Truckee near Lake Tahoe ($31, 5½ hours), and other destinations.

CAR & MOTORCYCLE

Major car-rental operators have offices at airports and downtown.

FERRY

Blue & Gold Ferries (Map p78; ☎ 415-705-8200; www.blueandgoldfleet.com; one-way $6.25) Runs the Alameda–Oakland ferry from Pier 41 and the Ferry Building.

Golden Gate Ferry (☎ 415-455-2000; www.goldengateferry.org; adult/child $9.75/4.75; ☺ 6am-9:30pm Mon-Fri, 10am-6pm Sat & Sun) Ferry service from the Ferry Building to Sausalito and Larkspur.

Vallejo Ferry (Map p78; ☎ 877-643-3779; www.baylinkferry.com; adult/child $13/6.50) Get to Napa car-free via Vallejo Ferry with departures from Ferry Building docks 6:30am to 7pm weekdays and 11am to 7:30pm weekends; bikes permitted. From Vallejo Ferry Terminal, take Napa Valley Vine bus 10.

TRAIN

Amtrak (☎ 800-872-7245; www.amtrakcalifornia.com) Serves San Francisco via Oakland stations, with free shuttle buses to San Francisco. Scenic routes with sleeping cars include the 35-hour Los Angeles–Seattle run via Oakland on the *Coast Starlight*, and the 51-hour Chicago–Oakland journey on the *California Zephyr*.

CalTrain (www.caltrain.com; cnr 4th & King Sts) Links San Francisco to the South Bay, ending in San Jose.

ℹ Getting Around

For Bay Area transit options, departures and arrivals, check ☎ 511 or www.511.org.

TO/FROM THE AIRPORT

➡ **BART** Direct 30-minute ride to/from downtown.

➡ **SuperShuttle** (☎ 800-258-3826; www.supershuttle.com) Door-to-door vans depart baggage-claim areas, taking 45 minutes to most SF locations; $17.

➡ **Taxis** To/from downtown costs $35 to $50.

BART

Bay Area Rapid Transit (Bay Area Rapid Transit; www.bart.gov; one way $8.25) links SFO, the Mission, downtown and the East Bay. Within SF, one-way fares start at $1.75.

BICYCLE

Bicycling is safest in Golden Gate Park and along the waterfront; rentals are readily available.

CAR

Avoid driving in San Francisco: street parking is rare and meter readers ruthless. Convenient downtown parking lots are at 5th and Mission Sts, Union Sq, and Sutter and Stockton Sts. Daily rates run $25 to $50.

If your car is towed for parking violations, retrieve it from **Autoreturn** (☎ 415-865-8200; www.autoreturn.com; 450 7th St, SoMa; ☺ 24hr; Ⓜ 27, 42). Fines run $73, plus towing and storage ($453.75 for the first four hours).

Members of **American Automobile Association** (AAA; ☎ 800-222-4357, 415-773-1900; www.aaa.com; 160 Sutter St; ☺ 8:30am-5:30pm Mon-Fri) can call anytime for emergency service.

MUNI

MUNI (Municipal Transit Agency; www.sfmuni.com) operates bus, streetcar and cable-car lines. The standard fare for buses or streetcars is $2, and tickets are good for transfers for 90 minutes; hang onto your ticket to avoid a $100 fine. The cable-car fare is $6 per ride.

MUNI Passport (1-/3-/7-days $14/22/28) allows unlimited travel on all MUNI transport, including cable cars; it's sold at San Francisco Visitor Information Center and many hotels.

Key routes include:

➡ **California cable car** California St between Market St and Van Ness Ave

➡ **F** Fisherman's Wharf to Castro

➡ **J** Downtown to Mission

➡ **K, L, M** Downtown to Castro

➡ **N** Caltrain to Haight and Ocean Beach

➡ **Powell-Mason** and **Powell-Hyde cable cars** Powell and Market Sts to Fisherman's Wharf

➡ **T** Embarcadero to Caltrain

RIDESHARE & TAXI

SF-based rideshare companies including **Uber** (www.uber.com) and **Lyft** (www.lyft.com) offer rides from mostly non-professional drivers at set rates, starting around $15 for in-city rides. Expect fast dispatch and fares charged to your account; signup and/or app download required.

San Francisco taxi fares run $2.75 per mile, plus 10% tip ($1 minimum); meters start at $3.50. SF taxis have their own app to hail and pay cabs, downloadable at www.flywheel.com. Major cab companies include:

DeSoto Cab (☎ 415-970-1300; www.desotogo.com)

Green Cab (☎ 415-626-4733) Fuel-efficient hybrids; worker-owned collective.

Luxor (☎ 415-282-4141; www.luxorcab.com)

Yellow Cab (☎ 415-333-3333; www.yellow-cabsf.com)

Marin County & the Bay Area

Why Go?

The region surrounding San Francisco encompasses a bonanza of natural vistas and wildlife. Cross the Golden Gate Bridge to Marin and visit wizened ancient redwoods body-blocking the sun and herds of elegant tule elk prancing along the bluffs of Tomales Bay. Gray whales show some fluke off the cape of wind-scoured Point Reyes, and hawks surf the skies in the pristine hills of the Marin Headlands.

On the cutting edge of intellectual thought, Stanford University and the University of California at Berkeley draw academics and students from around the world. The city of Berkeley sparked the locavore food movement and continues to be on the forefront of environmental and left-leaning political causes. South of San Francisco, Hwy 1 traces miles of undeveloped coastline and sandy pocket beaches.

Best Places to Eat

➡ Chez Panisse (p145)

➡ Sushi Ran (p119)

➡ Lake Chalet (p135)

➡ Duarte's Tavern (p159)

➡ Ippuku (p145)

Best Places to Stay

➡ HI Pigeon Point Lighthouse Hostel (p159)

➡ Cavallo Point (p117)

➡ Mountain Home Inn (p123)

➡ Hotel Shattuck Plaza (p145)

When to Go
Berkeley

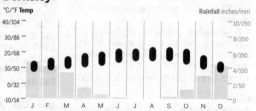

°C/°F Temp — Rainfall inches/mm

Dec–Mar Elephant seal pupping season and the peak of gray whale migrations.

Mar–Apr Wildflowers hit their peak on trails throughout the region.

Jun–Sep Farmers markets overflow with sweet seasonal fruit.

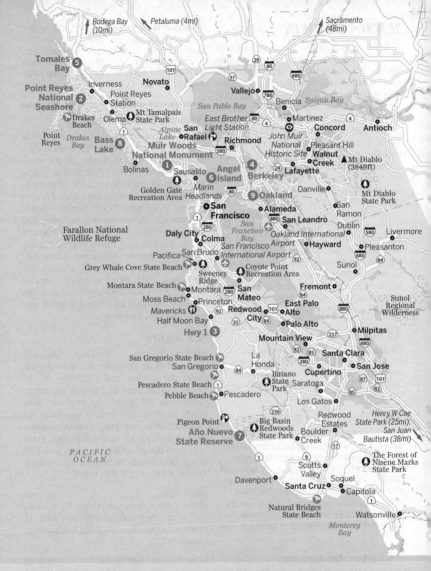

Marin County & the Bay Area Highlights

1 Gazing up at the majestic redwood canopy at **Muir Woods National Monument** (p125).

2 Cavorting with elk and gray whales at the **Point Reyes National Seashore** (p129).

3 Touring the beach-cove coastline along **Hwy 1** from Pacifica to Santa Cruz.

4 Feasting your way through the delectable **Gourmet Ghetto** (p142) in Berkeley.

5 Kayaking **Tomales Bay** (p129) amid harbor seals and splendid shorelines.

6 Hiking or cycling the perimeter of panoramic **Angel Island** (p120).

7 Spying on the elephant seals at **Año Nuevo State Reserve** (p159).

8 Cooling off with a cannonball splash at blissful **Bass Lake** (p127).

9 Heading to Oakland's **Chabot Space & Science Center** (p134) to marvel at the stars.

MARIN COUNTY

If there's a part of the Bay Area that consciously attempts to live up to the California dream, it's Marin County. Just across the Golden Gate Bridge from San Francisco, the region has a wealthy population that cultivates a seemingly laid-back lifestyle. Towns may look like idyllic rural hamlets, but the shops cater to cosmopolitan and expensive tastes. The 'common' folk here eat organic, vote Democrat and drive hybrids.

Geographically, Marin County is a near mirror image of San Francisco. It's a south-pointing peninsula that nearly touches the north-pointing tip of the city, and is surrounded by ocean and bay. But Marin is wilder, greener and more mountainous. Redwoods grow on the coast side of the hills, the surf crashes against cliffs, and hiking and cycling trails crisscross the blessed scenery of Point Reyes, Muir Woods and Mt Tamalpais. Nature is what makes Marin County such an excellent day trip or weekend escape from San Francisco.

ℹ️ Information

The **Marin Convention & Visitors Bureau** (☏ 866-925-2060, 415-925-2060; www.visit-marin.org; 1 Mitchell Blvd, San Rafael; ⊘ 9am-5pm Mon-Fri) provides tourist information for the entire county.

ℹ️ Getting There & Around

Busy Hwy 101 heads north from the Golden Gate Bridge ($7 toll when heading back into San Francisco), spearing through Marin's middle; quiet Hwy 1 winds its way along the sparsely populated coast. In San Rafael, Sir Francis Drake Blvd cuts across west Marin from Hwy 101 to the ocean.

Hwy 580 comes in from the East Bay over the Richmond–San Rafael bridge ($5 toll for westbound traffic) to meet Hwy 101 at Larkspur.

ℹ️ GETTING AROUND

Visitors taking multiple forms of public transportation throughout the Bay Area should note that the regional **Clipper card** (www.clippercard.com) can be used on the Caltrain, BART, SamTrans, VTA, Golden Gate Transit and the Golden Gate Ferry systems. It can be a handy way to avoid buying multiple tickets, and offers some small discounts, plus almost 50% off on the Golden Gate Ferry system.

Frequent **Marin Airporter** (☏ 415-461-4222; www.marinairporter.com; fare $20) buses connect from Marin stops to the San Francisco International Airport (SFO) from 4am until about 10:30pm; SFO–Marin service departs every 30 minutes.

Marin Headlands

The headlands rise majestically out of the water at the north end of the Golden Gate Bridge, their rugged beauty all the more striking given the fact that they're only a few miles from San Francisco's urban core. A few forts and bunkers are left over from a century of US military occupation – which is, ironically, the reason they are protected parklands today and free of development. It's no mystery why this is one of the Bay Area's most popular hiking and cycling destinations. As the trails wind through the headlands, they afford stunning views of the sea, the Golden Gate Bridge and San Francisco, leading to isolated beaches and secluded spots for picnics.

◎ Sights

After crossing the Golden Gate Bridge, exit immediately at Alexander Ave, then dip left under the highway and head out west for the expansive views and hiking trailheads. Conzelman Rd snakes up into the hills, where it eventually forks. Conzelman Rd continues west, becoming a steep, one-lane road as it descends to Point Bonita. From here it continues to Rodeo Beach and Fort Barry. McCullough Rd heads inland, joining Bunker Rd toward Rodeo Beach.

Hawk Hill   HILL
About 2 miles along Conzelman Rd is Hawk Hill, where thousands of migrating birds of prey soar along the cliffs from late summer to early fall.

Point Bonita Lighthouse   LIGHTHOUSE
(www.nps.gov/goga/pobo.htm; off Field Rd; ⊘ 12:30-3:30pm Sat-Mon) **FREE** At the end of Conzelman Rd, this lighthouse is a breathtaking half-mile walk from a small parking area. From the tip of Point Bonita, you can see the distant Golden Gate Bridge and beyond it the San Francisco skyline. It's an uncommon vantage point of the bay-centric city, and harbor seals haul out nearby in season. To reserve a spot on one of the free monthly full-moon tours of the promontory, call ☏ 415-331-1540.

WHY IS IT SO FOGGY?

When the summer sun's rays warm the air over the chilly Pacific, fog forms and hovers offshore; to grasp how it moves inland requires an understanding of California's geography. The vast agricultural region in the state's interior, the Central Valley, is ringed by mountains like a giant bathtub. The only substantial sea-level break in these mountains occurs at the Golden Gate, to the west, which happens to be the direction from which prevailing winds blow. As the inland valley heats up and the warm air rises, it creates a deficit of air at surface level, generating wind that gets sucked through the only opening it can find: the Golden Gate. It happens fast and it's unpredictable. Gusty wind is the only indication that the fog is about to roll in. But even this is inconsistent: there can be fog at the beaches south of the Golden Gate and sun a mile to the north. Hills block fog – especially at times of high atmospheric pressure, as often happens in summer. Because of this, weather forecasters speak of the Bay Area's 'microclimates.' In July it's not uncommon for inland areas to reach 100°F (38°C), while the mercury at the coast barely reaches 70°F (21°C).

Nike Missile Site SF-88   HISTORIC SITE
(🖉 415-331-1453; www.nps.gov/goga/nike-missile-site.htm; off Field Rd; ☺12:30pm-3:30pm Thu-Sat) **FREE** File past guard shacks with uniformed mannequins to witness the area's not-too-distant military history at this fascinating Cold War museum staffed by veterans. Watch them place a now-warhead-free missile into position, then ride a missile elevator to the cavernous underground silo to see the multikeyed launch controls that were thankfully never set in motion.

Marine Mammal Center   ANIMAL RESCUE CENTER
(🖉 415-289-7325; www.marinemammalcenter.org; ☺10am-5pm; 🖈) **FREE** Set on the hill above Rodeo Lagoon, the Marine Mammal Center rehabilitates injured, sick and orphaned sea mammals before returning them to the wild, and has educational exhibits about these animals and the dangers they face. During the spring pupping season the center can have up to several dozen orphaned seal pups on site and you can often see them before they're set free.

Headlands Center for the Arts   GALLERY
(🖉 415-331-2787; www.headlands.org; 944 Simmonds Rd; ☺noon-5pm Sun-Thu) **FREE** In Fort Barry, refurbished barracks converted into artist work spaces host open studios with its artists-in-residence, as well as talks, performances and other events.

🏃 Activities

Hiking

At the end of Bunker Rd sits Rodeo Beach, protected from wind by high cliffs. From here the **Coastal Trail** meanders 3.5 miles inland, past abandoned military bunkers, to the Tennessee Valley Trail. It then continues 6 miles along the blustery headlands all the way to Muir Beach.

All along the coastline you'll find cool old battery sites – abandoned concrete bunkers dug into the ground with fabulous views. Evocative **Battery Townsley**, a half-mile walk or bike ride up from the Fort Cronkite parking lot, opens for free subterranean tours from noon to 4pm on the first Sunday of the month.

Tennessee Valley Trail   HIKING
This trail offers beautiful views of the rugged coastline and is one of the most popular hikes in Marin (expect crowds on weekends), especially for families. It has easy, level access to the cove beach and ocean, and is a short 3.8-mile round trip. From Hwy 101, take the Mill Valley–Stinson Beach–Hwy 1 exit and turn left onto Tennessee Valley Rd from the Shoreline Hwy; follow it to the parking lot and trailhead.

ℹ️ GOLDEN GATE BRIDGE TOLL

The bridge toll ($7) crossing from Marin to San Francisco is now all electronic; drivers can no longer stop to pay. Rental-car drivers may use their car company's toll program or pay in advance online, and motorists in private vehicles are billed by mail if they haven't prepaid online. See www.goldengate.org/tolls/tolltipsforvisitors.php for payment information.

Ross (1mi);
San Anselmo (2mi);
Fairfax (4mi)

Bon
Tempe
Lake

Phoenix
Lake

Alpine
Lake

Marin Municipal
Water District

Lake
Lagunitas

Fairfax Bolinas Rd

Rocky Ridge Rd

Rock Springs Lagunitas Rd

Cataract Creek

Bolinas Ridge Rd

Cataract Trail

Ridgecrest Blvd

Old Railroad Grade

Old Stage Rd

East
Peak
(2571m)

Middle
Peak
(2490m)

7

Mt Tamalpais
State Park

Coastal Trail

West Peak
(2560m)

P
8

3

Mt Tamalpais
Interpretive
Association

Cascade Creek

Old Mill Creek

43

Matt Davis Trail

38

13

Shoreline Hwy

Audubon
Canyon
Ranch (1mi)

STINSON
BEACH

Matt Davis Trail

P
30

Shaver Grade Rd

Alice Eastwood Camp Rd

Redwood Trail

P

18

46

52

14

Cardiac
Hill

P
39

Bootjack Trail

Kent Canyon Creek

Sun Trail

Four
Corners

16

49 **40**

Stinson
Beach **25**

Panoramic Hwy

Webb Creek

Dipsea Trail

Lone Tree Creek

Coastal Trail

Cold Stream

Muir Woods Rd

Redwood Creek

Panoramic Hwy

Diaz Ridge Trail

Shoreline Hwy

Bolinas
Bay

22

Red Rock
Beach
Rocky Point

41

(1)

50

33

Coyote Ridge Trail

Redwood Creek

15

Muir
Beach

Coastal Trail

Tennessee
Beach

Tennessee
Point

2

*Sausalito
Houseboats*

MARIN
CITY

0   1 km
0   0.5 miles

Richardson
Bay

44

47

Bridgeway Blvd

6

28

Oakwood Trail

(1)

Spring St

Redwood Hwy

Caledonia St

51

Sausalito
Visitor Center

i **35**

27

Bobcat Trail

101

SAUSALITO

32

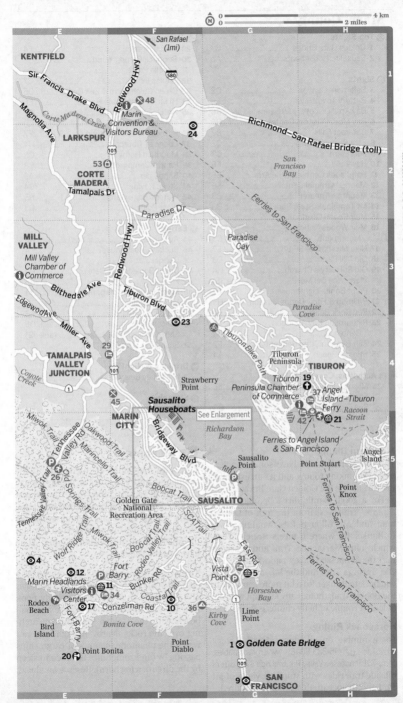

0 — 4 km
0 — 2 miles

San Rafael (1mi)

KENTFIELD

Sir Francis Drake Blvd

Magnolia Ave

Corte Madera Creek

Redwood Hwy

580

⊗48
Marin Convention & Visitors Bureau

◉24

Richmond–San Rafael Bridge (toll)

LARKSPUR

101

53 ⬚

CORTE MADERA
Tamalpais Dr

San Francisco Bay

Paradise Dr

Paradise Cay

Ferries to San Francisco

MILL VALLEY

Mill Valley Chamber of Commerce

Blithedale Ave

Edgewood Ave

Miller Ave

Redwood Hwy

Tiburon Blvd

Paradise Cove

◉23

TAMALPAIS VALLEY JUNCTION

Coyote Creek

29 ⬚

101

1

Tiburon Bike Path

Tiburon Peninsula

TIBURON

◉19

⊗45

Strawberry Point

Tiburon Peninsula Chamber of Commerce

37

Angel Island–Tiburon Ferry

42

21

Racoon Strait

MARIN CITY

Sausalito Houseboats

Bridgeway Blvd

See Enlargement

Richardson Bay

Sausalito Point

Ferries to Angel Island & San Francisco

Angel Island

Point Stuart

Point Knox

Miwok Trail

Tennessee Valley Rd

Oakwood Trail

Marincello Trail

P
26
Old Springs Trail

Tennessee Valley Trail

Wolf Ridge Trail

Miwok Trail

Bobcat Trail

Bobcat Trail

Rodeo Valley Trail

SCA Trail

SAUSALITO

P
Spring

Ferries to San Francisco

Golden Gate National Recreation Area

◉4

◉12

Fort Barry

Bunker Rd

Coastal Trail

East Rd

31

Vista Point
P

5

Horseshoe Bay

Marin Headlands Visitors Center

11

34

17

Conzelman Rd

◉10

36

Kirby Cove

Lime Point

Rodeo Beach

Fort Barry

Bonita Cove

Point Diablo

1 ◉ *Golden Gate Bridge*

Bird Island

20

Point Bonita

101

9 ◉

SAN FRANCISCO

Marin County

◎ Top Sights
1 Golden Gate Bridge	G7
2 Sausalito Houseboats	A6

◎ Sights
3 Baltimore Canyon	D2
4 Battery Townsley	E6
5 Bay Area Discovery Museum	G6
6 Bay Model Visitors Center	B6
7 Cataract Falls	B2
8 East Peak (2571m)	C2
9 Fort Point	G7
10 Hawk Hill	F6
11 Headlands Center for the Arts	E6
12 Marine Mammal Center	E6
13 Mountain Theater	B3
14 Mt Tamalpais State Park	B3
15 Muir Beach Overlook	C5
16 Muir Woods National Monument	C3
17 Nike Missile Site SF-88	E7
18 Old Mill Park	D3
19 Old St Hilary's Church	H4
Plaza Viña Del Mar	(see 35)
20 Point Bonita Lighthouse	E7
21 Railroad & Ferry Depot Museum	H5
22 Red Rock Beach	B4
23 Richardson Bay Audubon Center	F4
24 San Quentin State Penitentiary	F2
25 Stinson Beach	A4

◎ Activities, Courses & Tours
26 Miwok Livery Stables	E5
27 Sausalito Bike Rentals	C7
28 Sea Trek Kayak & SUP	B6

◎ Sleeping
29 Acqua Hotel	E4
30 Bootjack Campground	C3
31 Cavallo Point	G6
32 Gables Inn	C7
33 Green Gulch Farm & Zen Center	D5
34 HI Marin Headlands Hostel	E6
35 Hotel Sausalito	C7
Inn Above Tide	(see 35)
36 Kirby Cove Campground	F7
37 Lodge at Tiburon	H4
38 Mountain Home Inn	C3
39 Pantoll Campground	C3
40 Sandpiper	A3
41 Steep Ravine	B4
42 Water's Edge Hotel	H5
43 West Point Inn	C3

◎ Eating
44 Avatar's	A6
45 Buckeye Roadhouse	F4
Caprice	(see 21)
46 Depot Bookstore & Cafe	D3
47 Fish	B6
48 Marin Brewing Company	F1
Murray Circle	(see 31)
49 Parkside Cafe	A3
50 Pelican Inn	D5
Sam's Anchor Cafe	(see 42)
51 Sushi Ran	B7

◎ Drinking & Nightlife
52 Mill Valley Beerworks	D3

◎ Shopping
53 Book Passage	E2

Mountain Biking

The Marin Headlands have some excellent mountain-biking routes, and it's an exhilarating ride across the Golden Gate Bridge.

For a good 12-mile dirt loop, choose the **Coastal Trail** west from the fork of Conzelman and McCullough Rds, winding down to Bunker Rd where it meets **Bobcat Trail**, which joins **Marincello Trail** and descends into the Tennessee Valley parking area. The **Old Springs Trail** and the **Miwok Trail** take you back to Bunker Rd a bit more gently than the Bobcat Trail, though any attempt to avoid at least a couple of hefty climbs is futile.

Horseback Riding

For a ramble on all fours, **Miwok Livery Stables** (☏ 415-383-8048; www.miwokstables. com; 701 Tennessee Valley Rd; trail ride $75) offers hillside trail rides with stunning views of Mt Tam and the ocean. Reservations required.

🛏 Sleeping

There are four small campgrounds in the headlands, and two involve hiking (or cycling) in at least 1 mile from the nearest parking lot. **Hawk, Bicentennial** and **Haypress** campgrounds are inland, with free camping, but sites must be reserved through the Marin Headlands Visitors Center. None have water available.

Kirby Cove Campground CAMPGROUND $
(☏ 877-444-6777; www.recreation.gov; tent sites $25; ☉ Apr-Oct) In a spectacular shady nook near the entrance to the bay, there's a small beach with the Golden Gate Bridge arching over the rocks nearby. At night you can watch the phantom shadows of cargo ships passing by (and sometimes be lulled to sleep by the dirge of a fog horn). Reserve far ahead.

HI Marin Headlands Hostel   HOSTEL $

(📞 415-331-2777; www.norcalhostels.org/marin; Fort Barry, Bldg 941; dm $26-30, r $72-92, all with shared bath; @) 🖉 Wake up to grazing deer and dew on the ground at this spartan 1907 military compound snuggled in the woods. It has comfortable beds and two well-stocked kitchens, and guests can gather round a fireplace in the common room, shoot pool or play ping-pong. Hiking trails beckon outside.

Cavallo Point   HOTEL $$$

(📞 888-651-2003, 415-339-4700; www.cavallopoint.com; 601 Murray Circle; r from $359; ❄@🛜⚓🐕) 🖉 Spread out over 45 acres of the Bay Area's most scenic parkland, Cavallo Point is a buzz-worthy lodge that flaunts a green focus, a full-service spa and easy access to outdoor activities. Choose from richly renovated rooms in the landmark Fort Baker officers' quarters or more contemporary solar-powered accommodations with exquisite bay views (including a turret of the Golden Gate Bridge).

ℹ️ Information

Information is available from the **Golden Gate National Recreation Area** (GGNRA; 📞 415-561-4700; www.nps.gov/goga) and the **Marin Headlands Visitors Center** (📞 415-331-1540; www.nps.gov/goga/marin-headlands.htm; Fort Barry; 🕐 9:30am-4:30pm), in an old chapel off Bunker Rd near Fort Barry.

ℹ️ Getting There & Away

By car, take the Alexander Ave exit just after the Golden Gate Bridge and dip left under the freeway. Conzelman Rd, to the right, takes you up along the bluffs; you can also take Bunker Rd, which leads to the headlands through a one-way tunnel. It's also a snap to reach these roads from the bridge via bicycle.

On weekdays, **Golden Gate Transit** (📞 415-455-2000, 511; www.goldengatetransit.org) buses 2, 4 and 92 service Sausalito ($4.75) and the eastern Headlands. On Saturday, Sunday and holidays, **MUNI** (📞 511, 415-701-2311; www.sfmta.com) bus 76X runs hourly from San Francisco's Financial District to the Marin Headlands Visitors Center and Rodeo Beach. Both lines are equipped with bicycle racks.

Sausalito

Perfectly arranged on a secure little harbor on the bay, Sausalito is undeniably lovely. Named for the tiny willows that once populated the banks of its creeks, it's a small settlement of pretty houses that tumble neatly down a green hillside into a well-heeled downtown. Much of the town affords the visitor uninterrupted views of San Francisco and Angel Island, and due to the ridgeline at its back, fog generally skips past it.

Sausalito began as a 19,000-acre land grant to an army captain in 1838. When it became the terminus of the train line down the Pacific Coast, it entered a new stage as a busy lumber port with a racy waterfront. Dramatic changes came in WWII when Sausalito became the site of Marinship, a huge shipbuilding yard. After the war a new bohemian period began, with a resident artists' colony living in 'arks' (houseboats moored along

---

HIKING & CYCLING THE GOLDEN GATE BRIDGE

Walking or cycling across the Golden Gate Bridge to Sausalito is a fun way to avoid traffic, get some great ocean views and bask in that refreshing Marin County air. It's a fairly easy journey, mostly flat or downhill when heading north from San Francisco (cycling back to the city involves one big climb out of Sausalito). You can also simply hop on a ferry back to SF.

The trip is about 4 miles from the south end of the bridge and takes less than an hour. Pedestrians have access to the bridge's east walkway between 5am and 9pm daily (until 6pm in winter). Cyclists generally use the west side, except on weekdays between 5am and 3:30pm, when they must share the east side with pedestrians (who have the right-of-way). After 9pm (6pm in winter), cyclists can still cross the bridge on the east side through a security gate. Check the bridge **website** (www.goldengatebridge.org/bikesbridge/bikes.php) for changes.

For more ambitious cyclists, the Cal Park Hill Tunnel is a safe subterranean passage from Larkspur (another ferry terminus) to San Rafael.

More information and resources are available at the websites of the **San Francisco Bicycle Coalition** (www.sfbike.org) and the **Marin County Bicycle Coalition** (www.marinbike.org).

the bay). Hundreds of these floating abodes remain.

Sausalito today is a major tourist haven, jam-packed with souvenir shops and costly boutiques. It's the first town you encounter after crossing the Golden Gate Bridge, so daytime crowds turn up in droves and make parking difficult. Ferrying from San Francisco makes a more relaxing excursion.

⊙ Sights

Sausalito is actually on Richardson Bay, a smaller bay within San Francisco Bay. The commercial district is mainly one street, Bridgeway Blvd, on the waterfront.

★ **Sausalito Houseboats**   ARCHITECTURE
Bohemia still thrives along the shoreline of Richardson Bay, where free spirits inhabit hundreds of quirky homes that bobble in the waves amongst the seabirds and seals. Structures range from psychedelic mural-splashed castles to dilapidated salt-sprayed shacks and immaculate three-story floating mansions. It's a tight-knit community, where residents tend sprawling dockside gardens and stop to chat on the creaky wooden boardwalks as they wheel their groceries home.

You can poke around the houseboat docks located off Bridgeway between Gate 5 and Gate 6½ Rds.

Bay Model Visitors Center   MUSEUM
(☑415-332-3871; www.spn.usace.army.mil/Missions/Recreation/BayModelVisitorCenter.aspx; 2100 Bridgeway Blvd; ⊙9am-4pm Tue-Sat, plus 10am-5pm Sat & Sun in summer; ⊛) One of the coolest things in town, fascinating to both kids and adults, is the Army Corps of Engineers' solar-powered visitor center. Housed in one of the old (and cold!) Marinship warehouses, it's a 1.5-acre hydraulic model of San Francisco Bay and the delta region. Self-guided tours take you over and around it as the water flows.

Bay Area Discovery Museum   MUSEUM
(☑415-339-3900; www.baykidsmuseum.org; 557 McReynolds Rd; admission $11, free 1st Wed each month; ⊙9am-5pm Tue-Sun; ⊛) Just under the north tower of the Golden Gate Bridge, at East Fort Baker, this excellent hands-on activity museum is specifically designed for children. Permanent (multilingual) exhibits include a wave workshop, a small underwater tunnel and a large outdoor play area

with a shipwreck to romp around. A small cafe has healthy nibbles.

Plaza Viña Del Mar   PARK
Near the ferry terminal, the plaza has a fountain flanked by 14ft-tall elephant statues from the 1915 Panama–Pacific Exposition in San Francisco.

🏃 Activities

Sausalito is great for bicycling, whether for a leisurely ride around town, a trip across the Golden Gate Bridge or a longer-haul journey. From the ferry terminal, an easy option is to head south on Bridgeway Blvd, veering left onto East Rd toward the Bay Area Discovery Museum. Another nice route heads north along Bridgeway Blvd, then crosses under Hwy 101 to Mill Valley. At Blithedale Ave, you can veer east to Tiburon; a bike path parallels parts of Tiburon Blvd.

Sea Trek Kayak & SUP   KAYAKING
(☑415-332-8494; www.seatrek.com; Schoonmaker Point Marina; single/double kayaks per hr $20/35) On a nice day, Richardson Bay is irresistible. Kayaks and stand-up paddleboards can be rented here, near the Bay Model Visitor Center. No experience is necessary, and lessons and group outings are also available.

Also on offer are guided kayaking excursions around Angel Island from $75 per person, including overnight camping ($125). Tours include equipment and instructions. May through October is the best time to paddle.

Sausalito Bike Rentals   BICYCLE RENTAL
(☑415-331-2453; www.sausalitobikerentals.com; 34a Princess St; bicycle per hour $10; ⊙10am-6pm) Rent road, mountain, tandems ($25 per hour) and electric ($20 per hour) bicycles to explore the area.

🛏 Sleeping

All of the lodgings below charge an additional $15 to $20 per night for parking.

Hotel Sausalito   HISTORIC HOTEL **$$**
(☑415-332-0700; www.hotelsausalito.com; 16 El Portal; r $180-225, ste $305-320; ⊛🕏) Steps away from the ferry in the middle of downtown, this grand 1915 hotel has loads of period charm, paired with modern touches like MP3-player docking stations. Each guest room is decorated in Mediterranean hues, with sumptuous bathrooms and park or partial bay views.

Inn Above Tide
INN $$$

(☑ 415-332-9535, 800-893-8433; www.innabovetide.com; 30 El Portal; r incl breakfast $345-625, ste $735-1100; ❋ @ 🛜) Next to the ferry terminal, ensconce yourself in one of the 31 modern and spacious rooms – most with private decks and wood-burning fireplaces – that practically levitate over the water. With envy-inducing bay views from your window, scan the horizon with the in-room binoculars. Free loaner bicycles available.

Gables Inn
INN $$$

(☑ 415-289-1100; www.gablesinnsausalito.com; 62 Princess St; r incl breakfast $199-545; @ 🛜) Tranquil and inviting, this inn has nine guest rooms in a historic 1869 home, and six in a newer building. The more expensive rooms have spa baths, fireplaces and balconies with spectacular views, but even the smaller, cheaper rooms are stylish and tranquil. Evening wine and cheese is included.

✖ Eating

Bridgeway Blvd is packed with moderately priced cafes, a few budget ethnic food options and some more expensive bay-view restaurants.

Avatar's
INDIAN $$

(www.enjoyavatars.com; 2656 Bridgeway Blvd; mains $10-17; ⏲ 11am-3pm & 5-9:30pm Mon-Sat; ☑ 🍴) Boasting a cuisine of 'ethnic confusion,' the Indian fusion dishes here incorporate Mexican, Italian and Caribbean ingredients and will bowl you over with their flavor and creativity. Think Punjabi enchilada with curried sweet potato or spinach and mushroom ravioli with mango and rose petal alfredo sauce. All diets (vegan, gluten-free, etc) are graciously accommodated.

Fish
SEAFOOD $$

(☑ 415-331-3474; www.fish311.com; 350 Harbor Dr; mains $14-28; ⏲ 11:30am-8:30pm; 🍴) 🍃 Chow down on seafood sandwiches, oysters and Dungeness crab roll with organic local butter at redwood picnic tables facing Richardson Bay. A local leader in promoting fresh and sustainably caught fish, this place has wonderful wild salmon in season, and refuses to serve the farmed stuff. Cash only.

Sushi Ran
JAPANESE $$$

(☑ 415-332-3620; www.sushiran.com; 107 Caledonia St; sushi $4-33; ⏲ 11:45am-2:30pm Mon-Fri, 5-10pm Sun-Thu, to 11pm Fri & Sat; ☑) Many Bay Area residents claim this place is the best sushi spot around. If you didn't reserve ahead, the wine and sake bar next door eases the pain of the long wait for a table.

Murray Circle
MODERN AMERICAN $$$

(☑ 415-339-4750; www.cavallopoint.com/dine.html; 601 Murray Circle, Fort Baker; dinner mains $23-34; ⏲ 7-11am & 11:30am-2pm Mon-Fri, to 2:30pm Sat & Sun, 5:30-10pm Sun-Thu, to 11pm Fri & Sat) At the Cavallo Point lodge, dine on locally sourced meats, seafood and produce, like grass-fed organic beef burgers or Dungeness crab BLT, in a clubby dining room topped by a pressed-tin ceiling. Reservations recommended for dinner.

🛈 Information

The **Sausalito Visitors Center** (☑ 415-332-0505; www.sausalito.org; 780 Bridgeway Blvd; ⏲ 11:30am-4pm Tue-Sun) has local information. There's also an information kiosk at the ferry terminal.

🛈 Getting There & Away

Driving to Sausalito from San Francisco, take the Alexander Ave exit (the first exit after the Golden Gate Bridge) and follow the signs into Sausalito. There are five municipal parking lots in town, and street parking is difficult to find.

Golden Gate Transit (☑ 415-455-2000; www.goldengatetransit.org) bus 10 runs daily to Sausalito from downtown San Francisco ($4.75). On weekends and holidays from late May through early September, the **West Marin Stagecoach** (☑ 415-526-3239; www.marintransit.org/stage.html) bus 61 extends to Sausalito and Fort Baker, with six daily departures for Mt Tamalpais State Park, Stinson Beach and Bolinas.

The ferry is a fun and easy way to travel to Sausalito. **Golden Gate Ferry** (☑ 415-455-2000; www.goldengateferry.org; one-way $10.25) operates to and from the San Francisco Ferry Building six to nine times daily and takes 30 minutes. The **Blue & Gold Fleet** (☑ 415-705-8200; www.blueandgoldfleet.com; Pier 41, Fisherman's Wharf; one-way $11) sails to Sausalito four to five times daily from the Fisherman's Wharf area in San Francisco. Both ferries operate year-round and transport bicycles for free.

Tiburon

At the end of a small peninsula pointing out into the center of the bay, Tiburon is blessed with gorgeous views. The name comes from the Spanish *Punta de Tiburon* (Shark Point). Take the ferry from San Francisco, browse the shops on Main St, grab a bite to eat and you've seen Tiburon. The town

ANGEL ISLAND

Angel Island (☎ 415-435-5390; www.parks.ca.gov/?page_id=468), in San Francisco Bay, has a mild climate with fresh bay breezes, which makes it pleasant for hiking and cycling. For a unique treat, picnic in a protected cove overlooking the close but distant urban surroundings. The island's varied history – it was a hunting and fishing ground for the Miwok people, served as a military base, an immigration station, a WWII Japanese internment camp and a Nike missile site – has left it with some evocative old forts and bunkers to poke around in. There are 12 miles of roads and trails around the island, including a hike to the summit of 781ft **Mt Livermore** (no bicycles) and a 5-mile perimeter trail.

The **Immigration Station** (☎ 415-435-5537; www.aiisf.org/visit; ⊘ 11am-3pm Mon-Fri, 11am-4pm Sat & Sun), which operated from 1910 to 1940, was the Ellis Island of the West Coast. But this facility was primarily a screening and detention center for Chinese immigrants, who were at that time restricted from entering the US under the Chinese Exclusion Act. Many detainees were held here for long periods before ultimately being returned home, and one of the most unusual sights on the island is the sad and longing Chinese poetry etched into the barrack walls. The site is now a museum with excellent interpretive exhibits; more extensive **tours** (adult/child $7/5) include admission fees and can be reserved ahead or purchased first-come first-served on-site.

Sea Trek (www.seatrek.com) runs **kayaking** excursions around the island. You can rent **bicycles** at Ayala Cove (per hour/day $12.50/40), and there are **tram tours** ($15) around the island. Two-hour tours on Segway scooters ($68) and electric scooters ($50) are another option, and should be booked in advance. Tour schedules vary seasonally; go to www.angelisland.com for more information.

You can camp on the island, and when the last ferry sails off for the night, the place is your own – except for the very persistent raccoons. The dozen hike-, bicycle- or kayak-in **campsites** (☎ 800-444-7275; www.reserveamerica.com; tent sites $30) are usually reserved months in advance. Near the ferry dock, there's a **cafe** serving sandwiches and snacks.

Getting There & Away

From San Francisco, take a **Blue & Gold Fleet ferry** (Map p86; ☎ 415-773-1188; www.blueandgoldfleet.com; round-trip adult/child $17/9.50) from Pier 41. From May to September there are three ferries a day on weekends and two on weekdays; during the rest of the year the schedule is reduced.

From Tiburon, take the **Angel Island–Tiburon** (☎ 415-435-2131; www.angelislandferry.com; round-trip adult/child/bike $13.50/11.50/1) ferry.

From Oakland, **San Francisco Bay Ferry** (☎ 415-705-8291; www.sanfranciscobayferry.com; round-trip adult/child $14.50/8.50) has one round-trip on summer weekends.

---

is also a jumping-off point for nearby Angel Island.

⊙ Sights & Activities

The central part of town is comprised of Tiburon Blvd, with Juanita Lane and charming Main St arcing off. Main St, which is also known as Ark Row, is where the old houseboats have taken root on dry land and metamorphosed into classy shops and boutiques.

Railroad & Ferry Depot Museum   MUSEUM
(www.landmarkssociety.com; 1920 Paradise Dr; suggested donation $5; ⊘ 1-4pm Wed-Sun Apr-Oct) Formerly the terminus for a 3000-person ferry to San Francisco and a railroad that once reached north to Ukiah, this late-19th-century building showcases a scale model of Tiburon's commercial hub, circa 1909. The restored stationmaster's quarters can be visited upstairs.

Old St Hilary's Church   CHURCH
(201 Esperanza; ⊘ 1-4pm Sun Apr-Oct) There are great views from the lovely hillside surrounding this fine 19th-century example of Carpenter Gothic.

Richardson Bay
Audubon Center   NATURE RESERVE
(☎ 415-388-2524; http://richardsonbay.audubon.org/; 376 Greenwood Beach Rd; ⊘ 9am-5pm Mon-Sat; 🅿) Off Tiburon Blvd, this center is home to a huge variety of water birds.

Angel Island–Tiburon Ferry   BOAT TOUR
(☑ 415-435-2131; www.angelislandferry.com; round-trip adult/child/bike $13.50/11.50/1, sunset cruise adult/child 6-12/child 3-5 $20/10/5) Also runs sunset cruises on Friday and Saturday evenings from May through October. Reservations recommended.

🛏 Sleeping

Lodge at Tiburon   HOTEL $$
(☑ 415-435-3133; www.lodgeattiburon.com; 1651 Tiburon Blvd; r from $179; ❄ @ 🛜 🏊) 🅿 Now a stylish and comfortable contemporary hotel with a grill restaurant, the concrete hallways and staircases testify to the more basic motel it once was. The best value in town, it's a short stroll to anywhere – including the ferry – and there's a pool, DVD library, rental bikes, free parking and a rooftop deck with fireplace and heady Mt Tamalpais views.

Water's Edge Hotel   HOTEL $$$
(☑ 415-789-5999; www.watersedgehotel.com; 25 Main St; r incl breakfast $249-539; ❄ @ 🛜) 🅿 This hotel, with its deck extending over the bay, is exemplary for its tasteful modernity. Rooms have an elegant minimalism that combines comfort and style, and all afford an immediate view of the bay. The rooms with rustic, high wood ceilings are quite romantic. Perks include complimentary bicycles and evening wine and cheese.

🍴 Eating

Sam's Anchor Cafe   SEAFOOD $$
(☑ 415-435-4527; www.samscafe.com; 27 Main St; mains $14-32; ⏱ 11am-9:30pm Mon-Fri, 9:30am-10pm Sat & Sun; 🚸) Sam's has been slinging seafood and burgers since 1920, and though the entrance looks like a shambling little shack, the area out back has unbeatable views. On a warm afternoon, you can't beat a cocktail or a tasty plate of sautéed prawns on the deck.

Caprice   AMERICAN $$$
(☑ 415-435-3400; www.thecaprice.com; 2000 Paradise Dr; mains $17-58; ⏱ 5-10pm Tue-Sun, plus 11am-3pm Sun) Splurge-worthy and romantic, book a table here at sunset for riveting views of Angel Island, the Golden Gate Bridge and San Francisco. Caprice mostly features seafood, though other standouts include the artichoke bisque and the filet mignon. Take a peek at the fireplace downstairs – it's constructed into the coast bedrock. A three-course midweek dinner ($30) is easier on the wallet.

ℹ Information

The **Tiburon Peninsula Chamber of Commerce** (☑ 415-435-5633; www.tiburonchamber.org; 96b Main St) can provide information about the area.

ℹ Getting There & Away

Golden Gate Transit (☑ 415-455-2000; www.goldengatetransit.org) commute bus 8 runs directly between San Francisco and Tiburon ($4.75) during the week.

On Hwy 101, look for the off-ramp for Tiburon Blvd, E Blithedale Ave and Hwy 131; driving east, it leads into town and intersects with Juanita Lane and Main St.

Blue & Gold Fleet (☑ 415-705-8200; one-way $11) sails daily from Pier 41 or the Ferry Building (weekdays commute times only) in San Francisco to Tiburon. You can transport bicycles for free. From Tiburon, ferries also connect regularly to Angel Island.

Sir Francis Drake Blvd & Around

The towns along and nearby the Sir Francis Drake Blvd corridor – including Larkspur, Corte Madera, Ross, San Anselmo and Fairfax – evoke charmed small-town life, even though things get busy around Hwy 101.

Starting from the eastern section in **Larkspur**, window-shop along Magnolia Ave or explore the redwoods in nearby **Baltimore Canyon**. On the east side of the freeway is the hulking mass of **San Quentin State Penitentiary**, California's oldest and most notorious prison, founded in 1852. Johnny Cash recorded an album here in 1969 after scoring a big hit with his live *At Folsom Prison* album a few years earlier.

Take the bicycle and pedestrian bridge from the ferry terminal across the road to the **Marin Country Mart**, a shopping center with a dozen excellent eateries and comfortable outdoor seating. One favorite is the **Marin Brewing Company** (www.marinbrewing.com; 1809 Larkspur Landing Cir, Marin Country Mart, Bldg 2, Larkspur; mains $12-19; ⏱ 11:30am-midnight Sun-Thu, to 1am Fri & Sat; 🛜) brewpub, where you can see the glassed-in kettles behind the bar. The head brewer, Arne Johnson, has won many awards, and the Mt Tam Pale Ale complements the menu of pizza, burgers and hearty sandwiches.

Just south, **Corte Madera** is home to one of the Bay Area's best bookstores, **Book Passage** (☑ 415-927-0960; www.bookpassage.com;

51 Tamal Vista Blvd; ⊙9am-9pm), in the Marketplace shopping center. It has a strong travel section, plus frequent author appearances.

Continuing west along Sir Francis Drake, **San Anselmo** has a cute, small downtown area along San Anselmo Ave, including several antique shops. The attractive center of neighboring **Fairfax** has ample dining and shopping options, and cyclists congregate at **Gestalt Haus Fairfax** (28 Bolinas Rd, Fairfax; ⊙11:30am-11pm Sun & Mon, 11:30am-midnight Tue & Wed, 11:30am-2am Thu-Sat) for the indoor bicycle parking, board games, European draft beers and sausages of the meaty or vegan persuasion.

Arti (www.articafe.com; 7282 Sir Francis Drake Blvd, Lagunitas; mains $10-14; ⊙noon-9pm; 🖉) 🖉, between Hwys 1 and 101 in the tiny hamlet of **Lagunitas**, is a tempting stop for organic Indian fare. There's a cozy, casual dining room and an outdoor patio for warm days, and folks from miles around adore its sizzling chicken tikka platter.

Six miles east of Olema on Sir Francis Drake Blvd, **Samuel P Taylor State Park** (📞415-488-9897; www.parks.ca.gov/?page_id= 469; parking $8, tent & RV sites $35, cabin $100) has beautiful, secluded campsites in redwood groves and a coveted handful of new five-person cabins with electricity and wood stoves. The park's also located on the paved **Cross Marin Trail**, with miles of creekside landscape to explore along a former railroad grade.

❶ Getting There & Around

Golden Gate Ferry (📞415-455-2000; www.goldengateferry.org) runs a daily ferry service ($9.50, 50 minutes) from the Ferry Building in San Francisco to Sir Francis Drake Blvd in Larkspur, directly east of Hwy 101. You can take bicycles on the ferry.

San Rafael

The oldest and largest town in Marin, San Rafael is slightly less upscale than most of its neighbors but doesn't lack atmosphere. It's a common stop for travelers on their way to Point Reyes. Just north of San Rafael, Lucas Valley Rd heads west to Point Reyes Station, passing George Lucas' Skywalker Ranch. Fourth St, San Rafael's main drag, is lined with cafes and shops. If you follow it west out of downtown San Rafael, it meets Sir Francis Drake Blvd and continues west to the coast.

◉ Sights

China Camp State Park PARK
(📞415-456-0766; www.parks.ca.gov/?page_id= 466; per car $5) About 4 miles east of San Rafael, this is a pleasant place to stop for a picnic or short hike. From Hwy 101, take the N San Pedro Rd exit and continue 3 miles east. A Chinese fishing village once stood here, and a small museum exhibits interesting artifacts from the settlement.

Mission San Rafael Arcángel MISSION
(www.saintraphael.com; 1104 5th Ave) The town began with this mission, founded in 1817, which served as a sanatorium for Native Americans suffering from European diseases. The present building is a replica from 1949.

🛏 Sleeping & Eating

China Camp State Park CAMPGROUND $
(📞800-444-7275; www.reserveamerica.com; tent sites $35) The park has 30 walk-in campsites with showers and pleasant shade.

Panama Hotel B&B $$
(📞415-457-3993; www.panamahotel.com; 4 Bayview St; s/d with shared bath $75/90, r $120-195; ❄🛜🐾) The 10 artsy rooms at this B&B, in a building dating from 1910, each have their own unique style and charming decor – such as crazy quilts and vibrant accent walls. The hotel restaurant has an inviting courtyard patio.

★Sol Food Puerto Rican Cuisine PUERTO RICAN $$
(📞415-451-4765; www.solfoodrestaurant.com; cnr Lincoln Ave & 3rd St; mains $7.50-16; ⊙7am-midnight Mon-Thu, to 2am Fri, 8am-2am Sat, to midnight Sun) 🖉 Lazy ceiling fans, a profusion of tropical plants and the pulse of Latin rhythms create a soothing atmosphere for delicious dishes such as a *jíbaro* sandwich and other meals concocted with plantains, organic veggies and free-range meats.

☆ Entertainment

Rafael Film Center CINEMA
(📞415-454-1222; www.cafilm.org/rfc; 1118 4th St) A restored downtown cinema offering innovative art-house programming on three screens in state-of-the-art surroundings.

❶ Getting There & Away

Numerous **Golden Gate Transit** (📞415-455-2000, 511; www.goldengatetransit.org) buses operate between San Francisco and the San Rafael Transit Center at 3rd and Hetherton Sts ($5.75, one hour).

Mill Valley

Nestled under the redwoods at the base of Mt Tamalpais, tiny Mill Valley is one of the Bay Area's most picturesque hamlets. Mill Valley was originally a logging town, its name stemming from an 1830s sawmill – the first in the Bay Area to provide lumber. Though the 1892 Mill Valley Lumber Company still greets motorists on Miller Ave, the town's a vastly different place today, packed with wildly expensive homes, fancy cars and pricey boutiques.

Mill Valley also served as the starting point for the scenic railway that carried visitors up Mt Tamalpais. The tracks were removed in 1940, and today the Depot Bookstore & Cafe occupies the space of the former station.

◉ Sights & Activities

Old Mill Park   PARK

Several blocks west of downtown along Throckmorton Ave is Old Mill Park, perfect for a picnic. Here you'll also find a replica of the town's namesake sawmill. Just past the bridge at Old Mill Creek, the **Dipsea Steps** mark the start of the Dipsea Trail.

★ Dipsea Trail   HIKING

A beloved though demanding hike is the 7-mile Dipsea Trail, which climbs over the coastal range and down to Stinson Beach, cutting through a corner of Muir Woods. This classic trail starts at Old Mill Park with a climb up 676 steps in three separate flights, and includes a few more ups and downs before reaching the ocean. **West Marin Stagecoach** (www.marintransit.org/stage.html) route 61 runs from Stinson Beach to Mill Valley, making it a doable one-way day hike.

The few slaloms between staircases aren't well-signed, but locals can point the way.

✦ Festivals & Events

Mill Valley Film Festival   FILM

(www.mvff.com; ◷Oct) Each October the Mill Valley Film Festival presents an innovative, internationally regarded program of independent films.

⌸ Sleeping

Acqua Hotel   BOUTIQUE HOTEL $$

(☏415-380-0400, 888-662-9555; www.marinhotels.com; 555 Redwood Hwy; r incl breakfast from $159; ✸@❀) ∅ With views of the bay and Mt Tamalpais, and a lobby with a soothing fireplace and fountain, the Acqua doesn't lack for pleasant eye candy. Contemporary rooms are sleekly designed with beautiful fabrics.

Mountain Home Inn   INN $$$

(☏415-381-9000; www.mtnhomeinn.com; 810 Panoramic Hwy; r incl breakfast $195-345; ❀) Set amid redwood, spruce and pine trees on a ridge of Mt Tamalpais, this retreat is both modern and rustic. The larger (more expensive) rooms are rugged beauties, with unfinished timbers forming columns from floor to ceiling, as though the forest is shooting up through the floor. Smaller rooms are cozy dens for two. The positioning of a good local trail map on the dresser makes it clear that it's a place to breathe and unwind.

✗ Eating & Drinking

Depot Bookstore & Cafe   CAFE $

(www.depotbookstore.com; 87 Throckmorton Ave; mains under $10; ◷7am-7pm; ❀) Smack in the town center, Depot serves cappuccinos, sandwiches and light meals. The bookstore sells lots of local publications, including trail guides.

Buckeye Roadhouse   AMERICAN $$

(☏415-331-2600; www.buckeyeroadhouse.com; 15 Shoreline Hwy; mains $18-37; ◷11:30am-10:30pm Mon-Sat, 10:30am-10pm Sun) Originally opened as a roadside stop in 1932, the Buckeye is a Marin County gem, and its upscale American cuisine is in no danger of being compared to truck-stop fare. Stop off for chili-lime 'brick' chicken, baby back ribs or oysters Bingo and a devilish wedge of s'more pie before getting back on Hwy 101.

Mill Valley Beerworks   PUB

(www.millvalleybeerworks.com; 173 Throckmorton Ave; mains $18-32; ◷5:30-10:30pm Mon-Fri, 11:30am-10:30pm Sat & Sun, kitchen closed 3-5:30pm) ∅ With 60 bottled varieties of brew and a few of its own (from the Fort Point Brewing Company in San Francisco) amongst the dozen or so on tap, beer lovers can pair their favorites with the kitchen's delicious farm-to-table cuisine. The unsigned setting is stark and stylish, with unfinished wood tables and a pressed-tin wall.

ⓘ Information

Visitor information is available from the **Mill Valley Chamber of Commerce** (☏415-388-9700; www.millvalley.org; 85 Throckmorton Ave; ◷10am-4pm Tue-Fri).

ℹ️ Getting There & Away

From San Francisco or Sausalito, take Hwy 101 north to the Mill Valley–Stinson Beach–Hwy 1 exit. Follow Hwy 1 (also called the Shoreline Hwy) to Almonte Blvd (which becomes Miller Ave), then follow Miller Ave into downtown Mill Valley.

From the north, take the E Blithedale Ave exit from Hwy 101, then head west into Mill Valley.

Golden Gate Transit (📞 415-455-2000; www.goldengatetransit.org) bus 4 runs directly from San Francisco to Mill Valley ($4.75) on weekdays; route 17 ($2) runs between there from the Sausalito ferry terminal daily.

Mt Tamalpais State Park

Standing guard over Marin County, majestic Mt Tamalpais (Mt Tam) has breathtaking 360-degree views of ocean, bay and hills rolling into the distance. The rich, natural beauty of the 2571ft mountain and its surrounding area is inspiring – especially considering it lies within an hour's drive from one of the state's largest metropolitan areas.

Mt Tamalpais State Park (📞 415-388-2070; www.parks.ca.gov/mttamalpais; parking $8) was formed in 1930, partly from land donated by congressman and naturalist William Kent (who also donated the land that became Muir Woods National Monument in 1907). Its 6300 acres are home to deer, foxes, bobcats and many miles of hiking and cycling trails.

Mt Tam was a sacred place to the coastal Miwok people for thousands of years before the arrival of European and American settlers. By the late 19th century, San Franciscans were escaping the bustle of the city with all-day outings on the mountain, and in 1896 the 'world's crookedest railroad' (281 turns) was completed from Mill Valley to the summit. Though the railroad was closed in 1930, Old Railroad Grade is today one of Mt Tam's most popular and scenic hiking and cycling paths.

◎ Sights

Panoramic Hwy climbs from Mill Valley through the park to Stinson Beach. From Pantoll Station, it's 4.2 miles by car to **East Peak Summit**; take Pantoll Rd and then panoramic Ridgecrest Blvd to the top. A 10-minute hike leads to a fire lookout at the very top and awesome sea-to-bay views.

Mountain Theater   THEATER
(📞 415-383-1100; www.mountainplay.org; adult/child $40/20) The park's natural-stone, 4000-seat theater hosts the annual 'Mountain Play' series on a half dozen weekend afternoons between mid-May and late June. Free shuttles are provided from Mill Valley. Free monthly **astronomy programs** (www.friendsofmttam.org/astronomy.html; ☽ Apr-Oct) also take place here on Saturday nights around the new moon.

🏃 Activities

Hiking

The park map is a smart investment, as there are a dozen worthwhile hiking trails in the area. From Pantoll Station, the **Steep Ravine Trail** follows a wooded creek on to the coast (about 2.1 miles each way). For a longer hike, veer right (northwest) after 1.5 miles onto the **Dipsea Trail**, which meanders through trees for 1 mile before ending at Stinson Beach. Grab some lunch, then walk north through town and follow signs for the **Matt Davis Trail**, which leads 2.7 miles back to Pantoll Station, making a good loop. The Matt Davis Trail continues on beyond Pantoll Station, wrapping gently around the mountain with superb views.

Another worthy option is **Cataract Trail**, which runs along Cataract Creek from the end of Pantoll Rd; it's approximately 3 miles to Alpine Lake. The last mile is a spectacular rooty staircase as the trail descends alongside **Cataract Falls**.

Mountain Biking

Cyclists must stay on the fire roads (and off the single-track trails) and keep to speeds under 15mph. Rangers are prickly about these rules, and a ticket can result in a steep fine.

The most popular ride is the **Old Railroad Grade**. For a sweaty, 6-mile, 2280ft climb, start in Mill Valley at the end of W Blithedale Ave and cycle up to East Peak. It takes about an hour to reach the West Point Inn from Mill Valley. For an easier start, begin part way up at the Mountain Home Inn and follow the **Gravity Car Grade** to the Old Railroad Grade and the West Point Inn. From the inn, it's an easy half-hour ride to the summit.

From just west of Pantoll Station, cyclists can either take the **Deer Park fire road**, which runs close to the Dipsea Trail, through giant redwoods to the main entrance of Muir Woods, or the southeastern extension of the **Coastal Trail**, which has breathtaking views of the coast before joining Hwy 1 about 2 miles north of Muir

Beach. Either option requires a return to Mill Valley via Frank Valley/Muir Woods Rd, which climbs steadily (800ft) to Panoramic Hwy and then becomes Sequoia Valley Rd as it drops toward Mill Valley. A left turn on Wildomar and two right turns at Mill Creek Park lead to the center of Mill Valley.

For further information on bicycle routes and rules, contact the Marin County Bicycle Coalition (p117), whose Marin Bicycle Map is the gold standard for local cycling.

🛏 Sleeping & Eating

⭐ Steep Ravine   CAMPGROUND, CABIN **$**
(Map p48; ☎800-444-7275; www.reserveamerica.com; Nov-Sep; tent site $25, cabin $100) Just off Hwy 1, about 1 mile south of Stinson Beach, this jewel has seven beachfront campsites and nine rustic five-person cabins with wood stoves overlooking the ocean. Both options are booked out months in advance and reservations can be made up to seven months ahead.

Bootjack Campground   CAMPGROUND **$**
(Panoramic Hwy; tent sites $25) Recently re-opened after decades of closure, its 15 first-come, first-served walk-in sites are right on two of the park's best hiking trails and adjacent to Redwood Creek, with open vistas to the south. It's a half-mile northeast of Pantoll Station.

Pantoll Campground   CAMPGROUND **$**
(Panoramic Hwy; tent sites $25) From the parking lot it's a 100yd walk or bicycle ride to the campground, with 16 first-come, first-served tent sites but no showers.

West Point Inn   LODGE, CABIN **$**
(☎info 415-388-9955, reservations 415-646-0702; www.westpointinn.com; 100 Old Railroad Grade Fire Rd, Mill Valley; r per adult/child $50/25) Load up your sleeping bag and hike in to this rustic 1904 hilltop hideaway built as a stopover for the Mill Valley and Mt Tamalpais Scenic Railway. It also hosts monthly pancake breakfasts ($10) on Sundays during the summer.

ℹ Information

Pantoll Station (☎415-388-2070; www.parks.ca.gov/?page_id=471; 801 Panoramic Hwy; ⊙variable hours; 🛜) is the park headquarters. Detailed park maps are sold here. The **Mt Tamalpais Interpretative Association** (www.mttam.net; ⊙11am-4pm Sat & Sun) staffs a small visitor center at East Peak.

ℹ Getting There & Away

To reach Pantoll Station by car, take Hwy 1 to the Panoramic Hwy and look for the Pantoll signs. **West Marin Stagecoach** (☎415-526-3239; www.marintransit.org/stage.html) route 61 runs daily minibuses ($2) from Marin City (via Mill Valley; plus weekend and holiday service from the Sausalito ferry) to both the Pantoll Station and Mountain Home Inn.

Muir Woods National Monument

Walking through an awesome stand of the world's tallest trees is an experience to be had only in Northern California and a small part of southern Oregon. The old-growth redwoods at Muir Woods (☎415-388-2595; www.nps.gov/muwo; Muir Woods Rd, Mill Valley; adult/child $7/free; ⊙8am-sunset), just 12 miles north of the Golden Gate Bridge, is the closest redwood stand to San Francisco. The trees were initially eyed by loggers, and Redwood Creek, as the area was known, seemed ideal for a dam. Those plans were halted when congressman and naturalist William Kent bought a section of Redwood Creek and, in 1907, donated 295 acres to the federal government. President Theodore Roosevelt made the site a national monument in 1908, the name honoring John Muir, naturalist and founder of environmental organization the Sierra Club.

Muir Woods can become quite crowded, especially on weekends. Try to come mid-week, early in the morning or late in the afternoon, when tour buses are less of a problem. Even at busy times, a short hike will get you out of the densest crowds and onto trails with huge trees and stunning vistas. A lovely cafe serves local and organic goodies and hot drinks that hit the spot on foggy days.

🚶 Activities

The 1-mile Main Trail Loop is a gentle walk alongside Redwood Creek to the 1000-year-old trees at Cathedral Grove; it returns via Bohemian Grove, where the tallest tree in the park stands 254ft high. The Dipsea Trail is a good 2-mile hike up to the top of aptly named Cardiac Hill.

You can also walk down into Muir Woods by taking trails from the Panoramic Hwy, such as the Bootjack Trail from the Bootjack picnic area, or from Mt Tamalpais' Pantoll Station campground, along the Ben Johnson Trail.

ⓘ Getting There & Away

The parking lot is insanely full during busy periods, so consider taking the seasonal **Muir Woods Shuttle** (Route 66F; www.marintransit. org; round trip adult/child $5/free; ⊘ weekends & holidays late-Mar–Oct). The 40-minute shuttle connects with Sausalito ferries arriving from San Francisco before 3pm.

To get there by car, drive north on Hwy 101, exit at Hwy 1 and continue north along Hwy 1/ Shoreline Hwy to the Panoramic Hwy (a right-hand fork). Follow that for about 1 mile to Four Corners, where you turn left onto Muir Woods Rd (there are plenty of signs).

Muir Beach

The turnoff to Muir Beach from Hwy 1 is marked by the longest row of mailboxes on the north coast. Muir Beach is a quiet little town with a nice beach, but it has no direct bus service. Just north of Muir Beach there are superb views up and down the coast from the Muir Beach Overlook; during WWII, watch was kept from the surrounding concrete lookouts for invading Japanese ships.

⫶ Sleeping & Eating

Green Gulch Farm & Zen Center LODGE **$$**
(☑ 415-383-3134; www.sfzc.org; 1601 Shoreline Hwy; s $90-155, d $160-225, d cottage $350-400, all with 3 meals; @ 🕏) 🍴 Green Gulch Farm & Zen Center is a Buddhist retreat in the hills above Muir Beach. The center's accommodations are elegant, restful and modern, and delicious buffet-style vegetarian meals are included. A hilltop retreat cottage is 25 minutes away by foot.

Pelican Inn PUB **$$$**
(☑ 415-383-6000; www.pelicaninn.com; 10 Pacific Way; mains $14-34; 🍴) The oh-so-English Tudor-style Pelican Inn is Muir Beach's only commercial establishment. Hikers, cyclists and families come for pub lunches inside its timbered restaurant and cozy bar, perfect for a pint, a game of darts and warming up beside the open fire. The British fare is respectable, but it's the setting that's magical. Upstairs are seven luxe rooms (from $206) with cushy half-canopy beds.

Stinson Beach

Just 5 miles north of Muir Beach, Stinson Beach is positively buzzing on warm weekends. The town flanks Hwy 1 for about three blocks and is densely packed with galleries, shops, eateries and B&Bs. The beach itself is often blanketed with fog, and when the sun's shining it's blanketed with surfers, families and gawkers. There are views of Point Reyes and San Francisco on clear days, and the beach is long enough for a vigorous stroll.

◉ Sights

Stinson Beach BEACH
Three-mile-long Stinson Beach is a popular surf spot, but swimming is advised from late May to mid-September only; for updated weather and surf conditions call ☑ 415-868-1922. The beach is one block west of Hwy 1.

Red Rock Beach BEACH
Around 1 mile south of Stinson Beach is Red Rock Beach. It's a clothing-optional beach that attracts smaller crowds, probably because it can only be accessed by a steep trail from Hwy 1.

★ Audubon Canyon Ranch WILDLIFE RESERVE
(☑ 415-868-9244; www.egret.org; donations requested; ⊘ usually 10am-4pm Sat, Sun & holidays mid-Mar–mid-Jul) Audubon Canyon Ranch is about 3.5 miles north of Stinson Beach on Hwy 1, in the hills above the Bolinas Lagoon. A major nesting ground for great blue herons and great egrets, viewing scopes are set up on hillside blinds where you can watch these magnificent birds congregate to nest and hatch their chicks in tall redwoods. At low tide, harbor seals often doze on sand bars in the lagoon. Confirm hours, as a recent nesting failure may alter future public access.

⫶ Sleeping & Eating

Sandpiper MOTEL, CABINS **$$**
(☑ 415-868-1632; www.sandpiperstinsonbeach. com; 1 Marine Way; r $145-225; 🕏) Just off Hwy 1 and a quick stroll to the beach, the ten comfortable rooms and cabins of the Sandpiper have gas fireplaces and kitchenettes, and are ensconced in a lush garden and picnic area. Prices dip from November through March; two-night minimum stay on weekends.

Parkside Cafe AMERICAN **$$**
(☑ 415-868-1272; www.parksidecafe.com; 43 Arenal Ave; mains $9-25; ⊘ 7:30am-9pm, coffee from 6am) 🍴 Parkside Cafe is famous for its hearty breakfasts and lunches, and noted far and wide for its excellent coastal cuisine. Reservations are recommended for dinner.

ⓘ Getting There & Away

West Marin Stagecoach (☎ 415-526-3239; www.marintransit.org/stage.html) route 61 runs daily minibuses ($2) from Marin City, and weekend and holiday services to the Sausalito ferry. By car from San Francisco, it's nearly an hour's drive, though on weekends plan for toe-tapping traffic delays.

Bolinas

For a town that is so famously unexcited about tourism, Bolinas offers some fairly tempting attractions for the visitor. Known as Jugville during the Gold Rush days, the sleepy beachside community is home to writers, musicians and fisherfolk, and deliberately hard to find. The highway department used to put signs up at the turnoff from Hwy 1; locals kept taking them down, so the highway department finally gave up.

⊙ Sights & Activities

★ Point Blue

Conservation Science   BIRD OBSERVATORY
(☎ 415-868-0655; www.pointblue.org) Off Mesa Rd west of downtown and formerly known as the Point Reyes Bird Observatory, its Palomarin Field Station has bird-banding and netting demonstrations, a visitors center and nature trail. Banding demonstrations are held in the morning every Tuesday to Sunday from May to late November, and on Wednesday, Saturday and Sunday the rest of the year.

Bolinas Museum   MUSEUM
(☎ 415-868-0330; www.bolinasmuseum.org; 48 Wharf Rd; ⊙ 1-5pm Fri, noon-5pm Sat & Sun) **FREE**
This courtyard complex of five galleries exhibits local artists and showcases the region's history. Look for the weathered Bolinas highway sign affixed to the wall, since you certainly didn't see one on your way into town.

Agate Beach   BEACH
There are tide pools along some 2 miles of coastline at Agate Beach, around the end of Duxbury Point.

2 Mile Surf Shop   SURFING
(☎ 415-868-0264; www.2milesurf.com; 22 Brighton Ave; ⊙ 9am-6pm May-Oct, 10am-5pm Nov-Apr) Surfing's popular in these parts, and this shop behind the post office rents boards and wetsuits and also gives lessons. Call ☎ 415-868-2412 for the surf report.

Hiking

Beyond the observatory is the Palomarin parking lot and access to various **walking trails** in the southern part of the Point Reyes National Seashore, including the easy (and popular) 3-mile trail to lovely **Bass Lake**. A sweet inland spot buffered by tall trees, this small lake is perfect for a pastoral swim on a toasty day. You can dive in wearing your birthday suit (or not), bring an inner tube to float about, or do a long lap all the way across.

If you continue 1.5 miles northwest, you'll reach the unmaintained trail to **Alamere Falls**, a fantastic flume plunging 50ft off a cliff and down to the beach. But sketchy beach access makes it more enjoyable to walk another 1.5 miles to **Wildcat Beach** and then backtrack a mile on sand.

🛏 Sleeping & Eating

Smiley's Schooner Saloon & Hotel MOTEL **$$**
(☎ 415-868-1311; www.smileyssaloon.com; 41 Wharf Rd; r $104-124; 🛜🐾) A crusty old place dating back to 1851, Smiley's has simple but decent rooms, and last-minute weekday rates can be a bargain. The bar, which serves some food, has live bands Thursday through Saturday and is frequented by plenty of salty dogs and grizzled deadheads.

Bolinas People's Store   CAFE, MARKET **$**
(14 Wharf Rd; ⊙ 8:30am-6:30pm; 🐾) 🍃 An awesome little co-op grocery store hidden behind the community center, the People's Store serves Fair Trade coffee and sells organic produce, fresh soup and excellent tamales. Eat at the tables in the shady courtyard, and have a rummage through the Free Box, a shed full of clothes and other waiting-to-be-reused items.

Coast Café   AMERICAN **$$**
(www.bolinascoastcafe.com; 46 Wharf Rd; mains $10-22; ⊙ 11:30am-3pm & 5-8pm Tue-Thu, to 9pm Fri, 8am-3pm & 5-9pm Sat, to 8pm Sun; 🐾🖼) 🍃 The only 'real' restaurant in town, everyone jockeys for outdoor seats among the flowerboxes for fish and chips, barbecued oysters, or buttermilk pancakes with damn good coffee. Live music Thursday and Sunday nights.

ⓘ Getting There & Away

Route 61 of the **West Marin Stagecoach** (☎ 415-526-3239; www.marintransit.org/stage.html) goes daily ($2) from the Marin City transit hub (weekend and holiday service from the Sausalito ferry) to downtown Bolinas. By car, follow Hwy

1 north from Stinson Beach and turn west for Bolinas at the first road north of the lagoon. At the first stop sign, take another left onto Olema–Bolinas Rd and follow it 2 miles to town.

Olema & Nicasio

About 10 miles north of Stinson Beach near the junction of Hwy 1 and Sir Francis Drake Blvd, Olema was the main settlement in west Marin in the 1860s. Back then, there was a stagecoach service to San Rafael and there were *six* saloons. In 1875, when the railroad was built through Point Reyes Station instead of Olema, the town's importance began to fade. In 1906 it gained distinction once again as the epicenter of the Great Quake.

The **Bolinas Ridge Trail**, a 12-mile series of ups and downs for hikers or bikers, starts about 1 mile west of Olema, on Sir Francis Drake Blvd. It has great views.

In the former Olema Inn, a creaky 1876 building, hyper-local **Sir & Star** (☑415-663-1034; www.sirandstar.com; cnr Sir Francis Drake Blvd & Hwy 1; mains $20, prix fixe Sat/other nights $75/48; ☺5-9pm Wed-Sun, plus earlier hours in summer; ☎) ✐ restaurant delights with Marin-sourced seasonal bounty such as Tomales Bay oysters, Dungeness crab and duck 'faux' gras. Reservations recommended.

About a 15-minute drive inland from Olema, at the geographic center of Marin County, is Nicasio, a tiny town with a low-key rural flavor. In the town center, its music venue, **Rancho Nicasio** (☑415-662-2219; www.ranchonicasio.com; 1 Old Rancheria Rd; ☺11:30am-3pm & 5-9pm Mon-Thu, to 10pm Fri, 11am-3pm & 5-10pm Sat, to 9pm Sun), is a rustic saloon that regularly attracts local and national blues, rock and country performers.

❶ Getting There & Away

Route 68 of the **West Marin Stagecoach** (☑415-526-3239; www.marintransit.org/stage. html) runs daily to Olema and Samuel P Taylor State Park from the San Rafael Transit Center ($2).

Nicasio is located at the west end of Lucas Valley Rd, 10 miles from Hwy 101.

Point Reyes Station

Though the railroad stopped coming through in 1933 and the town is small, Point Reyes Station is nevertheless the hub of west Marin. Dominated by dairies and

ranches, the region was invaded by artists in the 1960s. Today it's an interesting blend of art galleries and tourist shops. The town has a rowdy saloon and the occasional smell of cattle on the afternoon breeze.

🛏 Sleeping & Eating

Cute little cottages, cabins and B&Bs are plentiful in and around Point Reyes. The **West Marin Chamber of Commerce** (☑415-663-9232; www.pointreyes.org) has numerous listings, as does the **Point Reyes Lodging Association** (☑415-663-1872, 800-539-1872; www.ptreyes.com).

Windsong Cottage Guest Yurt   YURT **$$**
(☑415-663-9695;   www.windsongcottage.com; 25 McDonald Lane; d yurt $185-210; ☎) A wood-burning stove, private outdoor hot tub, comfy king bed and kitchen stocked with breakfast supplies make this round sky-lighted abode a cozy slice of heaven.

Bovine Bakery   BAKERY **$**
(www.thebovinebakery.com; 11315 Hwy 1; pastry $3; ☺6:30am-5pm Mon-Fri, 7am-5pm Sat & Sun) ✐ Don't leave town without sampling something buttery from possibly the best bakery in Marin. A sweet bear-claw pastry and an organic coffee are a good way to kick off your morning.

Tomales Bay Foods & Cowgirl Creamery   DELI, MARKET **$**
(www.cowgirlcreamery.com; 80 4th St; sandwiches $6-12; ☺10am-6pm Wed-Sun; ☑) ✐ A market in an old barn selling picnic items, including gourmet cheeses and organic produce. Reserve a spot in advance for the small-scale artisanal cheesemaker's demonstration and tasting ($5); watch the curd-making and cutting, then sample a half dozen of the fresh and aged cheeses. All of the milk is local and organic, with vegetarian rennet in the soft cheeses.

Osteria Stellina   ITALIAN **$$**
(☑415-663-9988; www.osteriastellina.com; 11285 Hwy 1; mains $15-24; ☺11:30am-2:30pm & 5-9pm; ☑) ✐ This place specializes in rustic Italian cuisine made from locally sourced produce, including pizza and pasta dishes and Niman Ranch meats. For dessert, the water-buffalo-milk gelato is the way to go.

Pine Cone Diner   DINER **$$**
(www.pineconediner.com; 60 4th St; mains $9-13; ☺8am-2:30pm; ☑) ✐ The Pine Cone serves big breakfasts and lunches inside a cute

retro dining room and at shaded al fresco picnic tables. Try the buttermilk biscuits, the chorizo or tofu scramble, or the fried oyster sandwich.

☆ Entertainment

Old Western Saloon LIVE MUSIC, BAR
(☑415-663-1661; cnr Shoreline Hwy & 2nd St; ⊙10am-midnight or 2am) A rustic 1906 saloon with live bands and cool tables emblazoned with horseshoes. Prince Charles stopped in here for an impromptu pint during a local visit in 2006.

ℹ Getting There & Away

Hwy 1 becomes Main St in town, running right through the center. Route 68 of the **West Marin Stagecoach** (☑415-526-3239; www.marintransit.org/stage.html) runs here daily from the San Rafael Transit Center ($2).

Inverness

This tiny town, the last outpost on your journey westward, is spread along the west side of Tomales Bay. It's got good places to eat and, among the surrounding hills and picturesque shoreline, multiple rental cottages and quaint B&Bs. Several great beaches are only a short drive north.

🏃 Activities

Blue Waters Kayaking KAYAKING
(☑415-669-2600; www.bluewaterskayaking.com; rentals/tours from $50/68; 🛶) At the Tomales Bay Resort and across the bay in Marshall (on Hwy 1, eight miles north of Point Reyes Station), this outfit offers various Tomales Bay tours, or you can rent a kayak and paddle around secluded beaches and rocky crevices on your own; no experience necessary.

🛏 Sleeping

Cottages at Point Reyes Seashore BUNGALOW $$
(☑800-416-0405, 415-669-7250; www.invernessvalleyinn.com; 13275 Sir Francis Drake Blvd; r $139-219; 🐾🎦) 🐾 Cottages at Point Reyes Seashore is a family-friendly place hidden away in the woods, just a mile from town. It offers clean, modern kitchenette rooms in A-frame structures, and has a tennis court, hot tub, horseshoe pitches, barbecue pits and in-room DVD players. There's also a large garden and private nature trail. It's

past the town, on the way down the Point Reyes peninsula.

Tomales Bay Resort MOTEL $$
(☑415-669-1389; www.tomalesbayresort.com; 12938 Sir Francis Drake Blvd; r $125-275; 🎦🎦) The bayside Tomales Bay Resort has 36 motel rooms and a pool (unheated). When rates drop – Sunday through Thursday and in the winter – it's one of the best bargains around.

Dancing Coyote Beach Cottages BUNGALOW $$$
(☑415-669-7200; www.dancingcoyotebeach.com; 12794 Sir Francis Drake Blvd; cottages $200-260; 🎦🎦) Serene and comfortable, these four modern cottages back right onto Tomales Bay, with skylights and decks extending the views in all directions. Full kitchens contain tasty breakfast foods and fireplaces are stocked with firewood for foggy nights.

ℹ Getting There & Away

From Hwy 1, Sir Francis Drake Blvd leads straight into Inverness. Route 68 of the **West Marin Stagecoach** (☑415-526-3239; www.marintransit.org/stage.html) makes daily stops here from San Rafael ($2).

Point Reyes National Seashore

The windswept peninsula Point Reyes (Map p48; www.nps.gov/pore) **FREE** is a rough-hewn beauty that has always lured marine mammals and migratory birds as well as scores of shipwrecks. It was here in 1579 that Sir Francis Drake landed to repair his ship, the *Golden Hind*. During his five-week stay he mounted a brass plaque near the shore claiming this land for England. Historians believe this occurred at Drakes Beach and there is a marker there today. In 1595 the first of scores of ships lost in these waters, the *San Augustine,* went down. She was a Spanish treasure ship out of Manila laden with luxury goods, and to this day bits of her cargo wash up on shore. Despite modern navigation, the dangerous waters here continue to claim the odd boat.

Point Reyes National Seashore has 110 sq miles of pristine ocean beaches, and the peninsula offers excellent hiking and camping opportunities. Be sure to bring warm clothing, as even the sunniest days can quickly turn cold and foggy.

ⓘ POINT REYES SHUTTLE

On good-weather weekends and holidays from late December through mid-April, the road to Chimney Rock and the lighthouse is closed to private vehicles. Instead you must take a shuttle ($5, children under 17 free) from Drakes Beach.

◉ Sights & Activities

For an awe-inspiring view, follow the **Earthquake Trail** from the park headquarters at Bear Valley. The trail reaches a 16ft gap between the two halves of a once-connected fence line, a lasting testimonial to the power of the 1906 earthquake that was centered in this area. Another trail leads from the visitors center a short way to **Kule Loklo**, a reproduction of a Miwok village.

Limantour Rd, off Bear Valley Rd about 1 mile north of Bear Valley Visitor Center, leads to the Point Reyes Hostel and **Limantour Beach**, where a trail runs along Limantour Spit with Estero de Limantour on one side and Drakes Bay on the other. The **Inverness Ridge Trail** heads from Limantour Rd up to Mt Vision (1282ft), from where there are spectacular views of the entire national seashore. You can drive almost to the top of Mt Vision from the other side.

About 2 miles past Inverness, Pierce Point Rd splits off to the right from Sir Francis Drake Blvd. From here you can get to two nice swimming beaches on the bay: Marshall Beach requires a mile-long hike from the parking area, while Hearts Desire, in **Tomales Bay State Park**, is accessible by car.

Pierce Point Rd continues to the huge windswept sand dunes at **Abbotts Lagoon**, full of peeping killdeer and other shorebirds. At the end of the road is Pierce Point Ranch, the trailhead for the 3.5-mile **Tomales Point Trail** through the **Tule Elk Reserve**. The plentiful elk are an amazing sight, standing with their big horns against the backdrop of Tomales Point, with Bodega Bay to the north, Tomales Bay to the east and the Pacific Ocean to the west.

★ Point Reyes Lighthouse   LIGHTHOUSE
(☺ lighthouse 10am-4:30pm Fri-Mon, lens room 2:30-4pm Fri-Mon) **FREE** At the very end of Sir Francis Drake Blvd, with wild terrain and ferocious winds, this spot feels like the end of the earth and offers the best whale-watching along the coast. The lighthouse sits below the headlands; to reach it requires descending more than 300 stairs. Nearby **Chimney Rock** is a fine short hike, especially in spring when the wildflowers are blossoming. A nearby viewing area allows you to spy on the park's **elephant seal colony**.

Keep back from the water's edge at the exposed North Beach and South Beach, as people have been dragged in and drowned by frequent rogue waves.

Five Brooks Stables   HORSEBACK RIDING
(☎ 415-663-1570; www.fivebrooks.com; trail rides from $40; 🐎) Explore the landscape on horseback with a trail ride. Take a slow amble through a pasture or ascend more than 1000ft to Inverness Ridge for views of the Olema Valley. If you can stay in the saddle for six hours, ride along the coastline to Alamere Falls via Wildcat Beach.

🛏 Sleeping

Wake up to deer nibbling under a blanket of fog at one of Point Reyes' four very popular hike-in **campgrounds** (☎ 877-444-6777; www.recreation.gov; tent sites $20), each with pit toilets, water and tables. Reservations are accepted up to six months in advance, and weekends go fast. Reaching the campgrounds requires a 2- to 6-mile hike or bicycle ride, or you can try for a permit to camp on the beach in Tomales Bay. Check with the Bear Valley Visitor Center for same-day permits.

★ HI Point Reyes Hostel   HOSTEL $
(☎ 415-663-8811; www.norcalhostels.org/reyes; 1390 Limantour Spit Rd; dm $25, r $82-120, all with shared bath; @) 🖉 Just off Limantour Rd, this rustic HI property has bunkhouses with warm and cozy front rooms, big-view windows and outdoor areas with hill vistas, and a newer LEED-certified building with four private rooms (two-night minimum stay on weekends) and a stunning modern kitchen. It's in a secluded valley 2 miles from the ocean and surrounded by lovely hiking trails.

ⓘ Information

The park headquarters, **Bear Valley Visitor Center** (☎ 415-464-5100; www.nps.gov/pore; ☺ 10am-5pm Mon-Fri, from 9am Sat & Sun), is near Olema and has information and maps. You can also get information at the Point Reyes Lighthouse and the **Kenneth Patrick Center** (☎ 415-669-1250; ☺ 9:30am-4:30pm Sat, Sun & holidays) at Drakes Beach. All visitor centers have slightly longer hours in summer.

HIKING & CYCLING THE BAY BRIDGE

Why should the Golden Gate get all the outdoor action? Inaugurated in 2013, the **Bay Bridge Trail** (www.baybridgeinfo.org/path) is a separated pedestrian and bicycle path along the new Bay Bridge span between Oakland and Yerba Buena Island. The path has two access points: from outside the Ikea store on Shellmound St in Emeryville (1.5 miles from the MacArthur BART station), and from the corner of Maritime St and Burma Rd in West Oakland. One-way distances are about 5 miles from Emeryville and 3.5 miles from West Oakland, and a number of benches line the trail so you can drink in the open vistas.

Steps from the ferry in Jack London Square, **Bay Area Bikes** (☑510-836-2311; www. bayareabikerentals.net; 427 Water St; rentals per day from $25; ☉10am-5pm Mon-Fri, 9am-6pm Sat & Sun) rents bikes with helmets and locks.

ⓘ Getting There & Away

By car you can get to Point Reyes a few different ways. The curviest is along Hwy 1, through Stinson Beach and Olema. More direct is to exit Hwy 101 in San Rafael and follow Sir Francis Drake Blvd all the way to the tip of Point Reyes. For the latter route, take the central San Rafael exit and head west on 4th St, which turns into Sir Francis Drake Blvd. By either route, it's about 1½ hours to Olema from San Francisco.

Just north of Olema, where Hwy 1 and Sir Francis Drake Blvd come together, is Bear Valley Rd; turn left to reach the Bear Valley Visitor Center. If you're heading to the further reaches of Point Reyes, follow Sir Francis Drake Blvd through Point Reyes Station and out onto the peninsula (about an hour's drive).

West Marin Stagecoach (www.marintransit. org/stage.html) route 68 makes daily stops at the Bear Valley Visitor Center from San Rafael ($2).

EAST BAY

Berkeley and Oakland are what most San Franciscans think of as the East Bay, though the area includes numerous other suburbs that swoop up from the bayside flats into exclusive enclaves in the hills. While many residents of the 'West Bay' would like to think they needn't ever cross the Bay Bridge or take a BART train under water, a wealth of museums, universities, excellent restaurants, woodsy parklands and better weather are just some of attractions that lure travelers from San Francisco.

Oakland

Named for the grand oak trees that once lined its streets, Oakland is to San Francisco what Brooklyn is to Manhattan. To some degree a less expensive alternative to the nearby city of hills, it's often where people have fled to escape pricey San Francisco housing costs. An ethnically diverse city, Oakland has a strong African American community and a long labor union history. Urban farmers raise chickens in their backyard or occupy abandoned lots to start community gardens, families find more room to stretch out, and self-satisfied residents thumb their noses at San Francisco's fog while basking in a sunnier Mediterranean climate.

⊙ Sights & Activities

Broadway is the backbone of downtown Oakland, running from Jack London Sq at the waterfront all the way north to Piedmont and Rockridge. Telegraph Ave branches off Broadway at 15th St and heads north straight to Berkeley via the Temescal neighborhood (located between 40th St and 51st St). San Pablo Ave also heads north from downtown into Berkeley. Running east from Broadway is Grand Ave, leading to the Lake Merritt commercial district.

Downtown BART stations are on Broadway at both 12th and 19th Sts; other stations are near Lake Merritt, Rockridge and Temescal (MacArthur station).

⊙ Downtown

Oakland's downtown is full of historic buildings and a growing number of colorful local businesses. With such easy access from San Francisco via BART and the ferry, it's worth spending part of a day exploring here – and nearby Chinatown and Jack London Sq – on foot or by bicycle.

The pedestrianized **City Center**, between Broadway and Clay St, 12th and 14th Sts, forms the heart of downtown Oakland. The twin towers of the **Ronald Dellums Federal Building** are on Clay St, just behind it.

Oakland

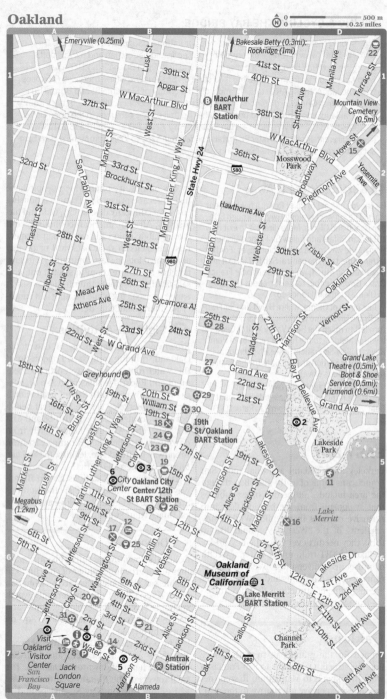

Oakland

◎ Top Sights
1 Oakland Museum of California.............. C6

◎ Sights
2 Children's Fairyland............................ D5
3 City Hall.. B5
4 Farmers Market...................................A7
5 Jack London's Yukon Cabin................. B7
6 Ronald Dellums Federal Building.......... B5
7 USS Potomac.......................................A7

◎ Activities, Courses & Tours
8 Bay Area Bikes.....................................A7
9 California Canoe & Kayak.....................A7
10 Great Western Power Company........... B4
11 Lake Merritt Boating Center D5

◎ Sleeping
12 Washington Inn..................................... B6
13 Waterfront Hotel...................................A7

◎ Eating
14 Bocanova.. B7

15 Commis...D2
16 Lake Chalet...C6
17 Ratto's...B6
18 Rudy's Can't Fail Cafe...........................B5

◎ Drinking & Nightlife
19 Awaken Cafe..B5
20 Beer Revolution....................................A6
21 Blue Bottle Coffee Company.................B7
22 Blue Bottle Coffee Company.................D1
23 Café Van Kleef.......................................B5
   Heinold's First & Last Chance ....(see 5)
24 Make Westing B5
25 Trappist...B6
26 Tribune Tavern......................................B5

◎ Entertainment
   Fox Theater...................................(see 18)
27 Luka's Taproom & Lounge....................C4
28 New Parkway Theater C4
29 Paramount Theatre...............................C4
30 Uptown..B4
31 Yoshi's...A7

MARIN COUNTY & THE BAY AREA OAKLAND

City Hall, at 14th & Clay Sts, is a beautifully refurbished 1914 beaux arts hall.

Old Oakland, along Washington St between 8th and 10th Sts, is lined with historic buildings dating from the 1860s to the 1880s. The buildings have been restored and the area has a lively restaurant and after-work scene. The area also hosts a lively **farmers market** every Friday morning.

East of Broadway and bustling with commerce, **Chinatown** centers on Franklin and Webster Sts, as it has since the 1870s. It's much smaller than the San Francisco version.

◎ Uptown

Continuing north of Oakland's City Center, the Uptown district contains many of the city's art-deco beauties and a proliferating arts and restaurant scene. The area stretches roughly between Telegraph and Broadway, bounded by Grand Ave to the north.

Great Western Power Company CLIMBING, GYM
(☑510-452-2022; www.touchstoneclimbing.com; 520 20th St; day pass $15-20; ☉6am-10pm Mon-Thu, to 11pm Tue & Thu, 10am-6pm Sat & Sun) Work up a sweat in the belly of this former power plant – you can't miss the smokestack – where climbers can scale a 48-foot-high wall (full gear rental $5), conquer their problems in the 1500-square-foot bouldering area, take yoga classes or use the gym.

◎ Jack London Square

The area where writer and adventurer Jack London once raised hell now bears his name, and recent spasms of redevelopment have added a new cinema complex, condo development, excellent restaurants and some eclectic watering holes. The pretty waterfront location is worth a stroll, especially when the Sunday **farmers market** (☉10am-2pm) takes over, or get off your feet and kayak around the harbor. Catch a ferry from San Francisco – a worthwhile excursion in and of itself – and you'll land just paces away.

Jack London's Yukon Cabin LANDMARK
A replica of Jack London's Yukon cabin stands at the eastern end of the square. It's partially built from the timbers of a cabin London lived in during the Yukon Gold Rush. Oddly, people throw coins inside as if it's a fountain. Another interesting stop, adjacent to the tiny cabin, is Heinold's First & Last Chance Saloon.

USS Potomac HISTORIC SITE
(☑510-627-1215; www.usspotomac.org; admission $10; ☉11am-3pm Wed, Fri & Sun) Franklin D Roosevelt's 'floating White House,' the 165ft USS *Potomac*, is moored at Clay and Water Sts by the ferry dock, and is open for dockside tours. Two-hour history cruises (adult/child $55/35) are also held several times a month from May through October.

◎ Lake Merritt

An urban respite, Lake Merritt is a popular place to stroll or go running (a 3.5-mile track circles the lake). The two main commercial streets skirting Lake Merritt are Lakeshore Ave on the eastern edge of the lake and Grand Ave, running along the north shore.

★**Oakland Museum of California** MUSEUM (OMCA; ☑ 888-625-6873, 510-318-8400; www.museumca.org; 1000 Oak St; adult/child 9-17yr $15/6, 1st Sun each month free; ⊙ 11am-5pm Wed-Sun, to 9pm Fri; ⑆) Near the southern end of the lake and one block from the Lake Merritt BART station, this museum has rotating exhibitions on artistic and scientific themes, and excellent permanent galleries dedicated to the state's diverse ecology and history, as well as California art. Admission is half-off on Friday nights, when DJs, food trucks and free kids' art workshops made it a fun hangout spot.

Children's Fairyland AMUSEMENT PARK (☑ 510-452-2259; www.fairyland.org; 699 Bellevue Ave; admission $8; ⊙ 10am-4pm Mon-Fri, to 5pm Sat & Sun Jun-Aug, off-season hours vary; ⑆) Lakeside Park, at the northern end of the saltwater lake, includes this 10-acre attraction, which dates from 1950 and has charming fairy-tale-themed train, carousel and mini Ferris-wheel rides.

Lake Merritt Boating Center WATER SPORTS (☑ 510-238-2196; www2.oaklandnet.com; 568 Bellevue Ave; boat rentals per hour $12-24; ⊙ daily Mar-Oct, Sat & Sun only Nov-Feb) Rents canoes, rowboats, kayaks, pedal boats and sailboats.

◎ Piedmont Ave & Rockridge

North of downtown Oakland, Broadway becomes a lengthy strip of car dealerships called Broadway Auto Row. Just past that is **Piedmont Ave**, wall-to-wall with antique stores, coffeehouses, fine restaurants and an art cinema.

One of Oakland's most popular shopping areas is **Rockridge**, a lively, upscale neighborhood. It is centered on College Ave, which runs from Broadway all the way to the UC Berkeley Campus. College Ave is lined with clothing boutiques, good bookstores, several pubs and cafes, and quite a few upscale restaurants – maybe the largest concentration in the Bay Area. BART at the Rockridge station puts you in the thick of things.

Mountain View Cemetery CEMETERY (www.mountainviewcemetery.org; 5000 Piedmont Ave; ⊙ 6:30am-7pm) At the end of Piedmont Ave, this is perhaps the most serene and lovely artificial landscape in all the East Bay. Designed by Frederick Law Olmstead, the architect of New York City's Central Park, it's great for walking and the views are stupendous.

◎ Oakland Hills

The large parks of the Oakland Hills are ideal for day hiking and challenging cycling, and the **East Bay Regional Parks District** (www.ebparks.org) manages more than 1200 miles of trails in 65 regional parks, preserves and recreation areas in the Alameda and Contra Costa counties.

Off Hwy 24, **Robert Sibley Volcanic Regional Preserve** is the northernmost of the Oakland Hills parks. It has great views of the Bay Area from its Round Top Peak (1761ft). From Sibley, Skyline Blvd runs south past **Redwood Regional Park** and adjacent **Joaquin Miller Park** to **Anthony Chabot Regional Park**. A hike or mountain-bike ride through the groves and along the hilltops of any of these sizable parks will make you forget you're in an urban area. At the southern end of Chabot Park is the enormous **Lake Chabot**, with an easy trail along its shore and canoes, kayaks and other boats for rent from the **Lake Chabot marina** (☑ 510-247-2526; www.norcalfishing.com/chabot).

Chabot Space & Science Center SCIENCE CENTER (☑ 510-336-7300; www.chabotspace.org; 10000 Skyline Blvd; adult/child $16/12; ⊙ 10am-5pm Wed & Thu, to 10pm Fri & Sat, 10am-5pm Sun, plus 10am-5pm Tue summer; ⑆) Stargazers will go gaga over this science and technology center in the Oakland Hills with loads of exhibits on subjects such as space travel and eclipses, as well as cool planetarium shows. When the weather's good, check out the free Friday and Saturday evening viewings (7:30pm to 10:30pm) using a 20in refractor telescope.

🛏 Sleeping

If you like B&Bs, the **Berkeley and Oakland Bed & Breakfast Network** (www.bbonline.com/ca/berkeley-oakland) lists private homes that rent rooms, suites and cottages; prices start from $100 per night and many have a two-night-minimum stay. Reservations recommended.

Anthony Chabot Regional Park
CAMPGROUND $

(☑ 510-639-4751, reservations 888-327-2757; www.ebparks.org/parks/anthony_chabot; tent sites $25, RV sites with hookups $25-35; ☀) This 5000-acre park has 75 campsites open year-round and hot showers. Reservations ($8 service charge) at www.reserveamerica.com.

Waterfront Hotel
BOUTIQUE HOTEL $$

(☑ 510-836-3800; www.waterfronthoteloakland.com; 10 Washington St; r $149-279; ❄@🔊🏊☀) Paddle-printed wallpaper and lamps fashioned from faux lanterns round out the playful nautical theme of this bright, cheerful harborside hotel. A huge brass-topped fireplace warms the foyer, and comfy rooms include MP3-players and coffeemakers, plus microwaves and fridges. Unless you're an avid trainspotter, water-view rooms are preferred, as trains rattle by on the city side.

Washington Inn
HISTORIC HOTEL $$

(☑ 510-452-1776; www.thewashingtoninn.com; 495 10th St; r incl breakfast $99-140; ❄@🔊) Small and modern with a boutique feel, this historic downtown lodging offers guest rooms with character and efficient sophistication. The dramatic high-ceilinged lobby is a wasted opportunity, outfitted with random chairs instead of velvet divans. Still, the carved lobby bar is perfect for a predinner cocktail, and you're spoiled for choice with several fine restaurants within a few blocks' radius.

Claremont Resort & Spa
RESORT $$$

(☑ 800-551-7266, 510-843-3000; www.claremontresort.com; 41 Tunnel Rd; r $215-309, plus $26 nightly resort fee; ❄@🔊🏊☀) Oakland's classy crème de la crème, the Claremont is a glamorous white 1915 building with elegant restaurants, a fitness center, swimming pools, tennis courts and a full-service spa (room/spa packages are available). The bay view rooms are superb. It's located at the foot of the Oakland Hills, off Hwy 13 (Tunnel Rd) near Claremont Ave on the Berkeley border.

✖ Eating

Oakland's fun and sophisticated eateries rival those of its neighbor San Francisco.

✖ Uptown, Downtown & Jack London Square

Ratto's
DELI $

(www.rattos.com; 821 Washington St; sandwiches from $6; ⏱8:30am-4:30pm Mon-Fri, 9:30am-3:30pm Sat; ✍) If you want to eat outside on a sunny day, grab a sandwich from Ratto's, a vintage Oakland grocery (since 1897) with a deli counter (and a few sidewalk tables) that attracts a devoted lunch crowd.

Rudy's Can't Fail Cafe
AMERICAN $$

(www.iamrudy.com; 1805 Telegraph Ave; mains $9-13; ⏱7am-1am; ✍🍴) A modern diner with tables crafted from board games and strange toys under glass, it has a goofy punk rock feel, possibly because an owner is the bassist from Green Day. Show up for huevos or tofu rancheros all day, or just chow down on a big burger under the gaze of an army of Barbie dolls. Right next to the Fox Theater.

Bocanova
LATIN AMERICAN $$

(☑ 510-444-1233; www.bocanova.com; 55 Webster St; mains $12-28; ⏱11:30am-9:30pm Mon-Thu, 11am-10:30pm Fri & Sat, to 9:30pm Sun) Facing the water at sun-drenched Jack London Sq, you can people-watch from the outdoor patio or eat inside the chic industrial dining room lit by hanging glass lamps. The focus here is Pan-American cuisine, and standouts include the Dungeness crab deviled eggs and scallops in Brazilian curry sauce. Reservations recommended on Wednesday – when wine bottles are half-price – and weekends.

✖ Lake Merritt

Arizmendi
BAKERY $

(http://lakeshore.arizmendi.coop; 3265 Lakeshore Ave; pizza slices $2.50; ⏱7am-7pm Tue-Sat, to 6pm Sun, to 3pm Mon; ✍) Great for breakfast or lunch but beware – this bakery co-op is not for the weak-willed. The gourmet vegetarian pizza, yummy fresh breads and amazing scones are mouthwateringly addictive.

Boot & Shoe Service
PIZZERIA $$

(☑ 510-763-2668; www.bootandshoeservice.com; 3308 Grand Ave; pizza from $10; ⏱5:30-10pm Tue-Thu, 5-10:30pm Fri & Sat, to 10pm Sun) 🍃 The name plays off its former identity as a cobbler shop, but the current patrons pack this brick-walled place for its wood-fired pizzas, original cocktails and creative antipasti made from sustainably sourced fresh ingredients.

Lake Chalet
SEAFOOD $$$

(☑ 510-208-5253; www.thelakechalet.com; 1520 Lakeside Dr; mains $17-36; ⏱11am-10pm Mon-Thu, to 11pm Fri, 10am-11pm Sat, 10am-10pm Sun) Whether you stop by the long pump house

BAY AREA BACKPACKING

For an overnight experience in the wilds just outside the city, grab your gear and set off to one of these local jewels. **Sports Basement** (http://community.sportsbasement.com/rentals/camping) and **REI** (www.rei.com) rent all gear.

➜ **Point Reyes National Seashore** (☑877-444-6777; www.recreation.gov; tent sites $20) Established hike- and bike-in campgrounds near the ocean; toilets and potable water.

➜ **Henry W Coe State Park** (p154) Where local backpackers set out when snow engulfs the Sierra, this enormous park has miles of hilly backcountry with seasonal ponds and creeks.

➜ **Hawk Camp** (www.nps.gov/goga/planyourvisit/outdooractivities.htm) Remote Marin Headlands' campsite with the requisite bird's-eye views; toilets but no water.

➜ **Angel Island** (p120) So close to the city and yet so far, you can watch the cargo ships thread under the Golden Gate Bridge.

➜ **Ohlone Wilderness Trail** (www.ebparks.org/parks/ohlone) A 28-mile adventure through mountains and canyons in the East Bay.

view bar for a martini and oysters during the buzzing happy hour (3pm to 6pm and 9pm to close), feast on a whole roasted crab by a window seat in the formal dining room, or cruise Lake Merritt on a Venetian-style **gondola** (www.gondolaservizio.com; per couple from $60), this 100-year-old former park office and boathouse is an enjoyable destination restaurant. Weekend reservations recommended.

Piedmont Ave & Rockridge

À Côté   MEDITERRANEAN $$
(☑510-655-6469; www.acoterestaurant.com; 5478 College Ave; dishes $8-20; ☺5:30-10pm Sun-Tue, to 11pm Wed & Thu, to midnight Fri & Sat) This small-plates eatery with individual and friendly communal tables is one of the best restaurants along College Ave. What the menu calls 'flatbread' is actually pizza for the gods. Mussels with Pernod is a signature dish.

Commis   CALIFORNIAN $$$
(☑510-653-3902; www.commisrestaurant.com; 3859 Piedmont Ave; 8-course dinner $95; ☺from 5:30pm Wed-Sat, from 5pm Sun; ☑) The only Michelin-starred restaurant in the East Bay, the signless and discreet dining room counts a minimalist decor and some coveted counter real estate (reservable by phone only) where patrons can watch chef James Syhabout and his team piece together creative and innovative dishes. Reservations highly recommended.

Temescal & Emeryville

Emeryville is a separate bite-sized city, wedged between Oakland and south Berkeley on I-80.

Bakesale Betty   SANDWICHES, BAKERY $
(www.bakesalebetty.com; 5098 Telegraph Ave; sandwiches $8; ☺11am-2pm Tue-Sat; ☑) An Aussie expat and Chez Panisse alum, Betty Barakat (in signature blue wig) has patrons licking their lips and lining up out the door for her heavenly strawberry shortcake and scrumptious fried-chicken sandwiches. Rolling pins dangle from the ceiling, and blissed-out locals sit down at ironing-board sidewalk tables.

Emeryville Public Market   INTERNATIONAL $
(www.publicmarketemeryville.com; 5959 Shellmound St, Emeryville; mains under $10; ☺7am-9pm Mon-Sat, 7am-8pm Sun; ☎) To satisfy a group of finicky eaters, cross the Amtrak tracks to the indoor area and choose from dozens of ethnic food stalls dishing out a huge range of international cuisines.

Homeroom   AMERICAN $$
(☑510-597-0400; www.homeroom510.com; 400 40th St; mains $9-16; ☺11am-10pm Tue-Sun; ☑🍴) 🍃 Mac-n-cheese, the ultimate in American comfort food, gets a long-overdue ovation at this quirky restaurant modeled after a school. A menu of regionally focused options – including the Ivy Leaguer Truffle, Dungeness crab, vegan and the spicy Exchange Student Sriracha – are more gour-

met than anything Mom packed for your lunchbox. Six rotating beers on tap.

🍷 Drinking & Nightlife

★ Café Van Kleef   BAR

(📞 510-763-7711; www.cafevankleef.com; 1621 Telegraph Ave; ⏰ noon-2am Tue-Fri, 4pm-2am Sat-Mon) Order a greyhound (with fresh-squeezed grapefruit juice) and take a gander at the profusion of antique musical instruments, fake taxidermy heads, sprawling formal chandeliers and bizarro ephemera clinging to every surface possible here. Quirky, kitschy and evocative even *before* you get lit, it features live blues, jazz and the occasional rock band on weekends plus DJs and a drag show other nights.

Awaken Cafe   CAFE

(www.awakencafe.com; 1429 Broadway; ⏰ 7:30am-10pm Mon-Thu, to midnight Fri, 8:30am-midnight Sat, to 7pm Sun; 🛜) The laptop brigade camps out at this central downtown cafe by day, munching wood-fired bagels and drinking fairly traded Four Barrel coffee. But they get sidelined at 5pm, with live Afro-Cuban, folk, R&B and other events (cover free to $15) taking center stage after 7pm.

Beer Revolution   BEER HALL

(www.beer-revolution.com; 464 3rd St; ⏰ noon-11pm Mon-Sat, to 9pm Sun) Go ahead and drool. With almost 50 beers on tap, and more than 500 in the bottle, there's a lifetime of discovery ahead, so kick back on the sunny deck or park yourself at that barrel table embedded with bottle caps. Bonuses include no distracting TVs and a punk soundtrack played at conversation-friendly levels. Check Facebook for meet-the-brewer sessions and Sunday barbecues.

Blue Bottle Coffee Company   CAFE

(www.bluebottlecoffee.com; 300 Webster St; ⏰ 7am-5:30pm Mon-Fri, from 8am Sat & Sun) 🍃 The java gourmands queue up here for single-origin espressos and what some consider the best coffee in the country, and the very origin-specific beans are roasted on site. Its newer cafe (4270 Broadway; ⏰ 7am-6pm Mon-Fri, 8am-6pm Sat & Sun) in the historic WC Morse Building (a 1920s truck showroom) has two communal tables, lofty ceilings and a minimalist white decor for drinking an espresso or an Oji cold-drip coffee.

Trappist   PUB

(www.thetrappist.com; 460 8th St; ⏰ noon-12:30am Sun-Thu, noon-1:30am Fri & Sat) So popular that it busted out of its original brick-and-wood-paneled shoebox and expanded into a second storefront and back terrace, the specialty here is Belgian ales. More than two dozen drafts rotate through the taps, and tasty stews and sandwiches, and seasonal beer-friendly cuisine ($8.50 to $12) make it easy to linger.

Make Westing   COCKTAIL BAR

(www.makewesting.com; 1741 Telegraph Ave; ⏰ 4pm-2am) Named for a Jack London story, the free indoor bocce ball courts and eclectic cocktails pack this Uptown hotspot on weekends. Toss back a garden gimlet and satiate the munchies with some cilantro and habañero-infused popcorn.

Heinold's First & Last Chance   BAR

(www.heinolds.com; 48 Webster St; ⏰ 3-11pm Mon, noon-11pm Tue-Sun, to midnight Fri & Sat) An 1883 bar constructed from wood scavenged from an old whaling ship, you really have to hold on to your beer here. Keeled to a severe slant during the 1906 earthquake, the building's 20% grade might make you feel self-conscious about stumbling before you even order. Its big claim to fame is that author Jack London was a regular patron.

Tribune Tavern   BAR

(www.tribunetavern.com; 401 13th St; ⏰ 11:30am-10pm Mon-Fri, 10:30am-11pm Sat & Sun) For sophisticated downtown drinks under a pressed-tin ceiling and Edison lights, head to the 1923 Tribune Tower, an Oakland icon with a red-neon clock and former home of the *Oakland Tribune* newspaper.

PINBALL WIZARDS, UNITE!

Put down that video game console, cast aside your latest phone app, and return to the bygone days of pinball play. Lose yourself in bells and flashing lights at **Pacific Pinball Museum** (📞 510-769-1349; www.pacificpinball.org; 1510 Webster St, Alameda; adult/child under 16 $15/7.50; ⏰ 2-9pm Tue-Thu, to midnight Fri, 11am-midnight Sat, to 9pm Sun; ♿), a pinball parlor with almost 100 games dating from the 1930s to the present, and vintage jukeboxes playing hits from the past. Take AC Transit bus 51A from downtown Oakland.

☆ Entertainment

A monthly street festival, **Oakland First Fridays** (www.oaklandfirstfridays.org) takes place between 5pm and 9pm on the first Friday of the month. Telegraph Ave between 27th St and W Grand Ave closes to car traffic, with thousands turning out for food vendors, live music and performances. There's a concurrent gallery-hop called **Oakland Art Murmur** (www.oaklandartmurmur.com; ☺6-9pm), which also coordinates a more low-key Saturday Stroll in the afternoons every week.

Music

Uptown   LIVE MUSIC
(☑510-451-8100; www.uptownnightclub.com; 1928 Telegraph Ave; admission free-$20; ☺Tue-Sun) For an eclectic calendar of indie, punk and experimental sounds, burlesque shows and fun DJ dance parties, this club hits the spot. Come for a good mix of national acts and local talent, and the easy two-block walk to BART.

Yoshi's   JAZZ
(☑510-238-9200; www.yoshis.com/oakland; 510 Embarcadero West; admission $15-49) Yoshi's has a solid jazz calendar, with talent from around the world passing through on a near-nightly basis. Often, touring artists will stop in for a stand of two or three nights. It's also a Japanese restaurant, so you might enjoy a sushi plate before the show. Some events have half-price tickets for students and seniors.

Luka's Taproom & Lounge   DJ
(www.lukasoakland.com; 2221 Broadway; ☺DJs Wed-Sun) Go Uptown to get down. DJs spin nightly at this popular restaurant and lounge, with a soulful mix of hip-hop, reggae, funk and house. There's generally a $10 cover on Fridays and Saturdays after 11pm.

Theaters & Cinemas

The Fox Theater is the nucleus of evening activity in the Uptown district, with hip restaurants and bars clustered nearby.

Fox Theater   THEATER
(www.thefoxoakland.com; 1807 Telegraph Ave) A phoenix arisen from the urban ashes, this restored 1928 art-deco stunner adds dazzle to downtown and is a cornerstone of the happening Uptown theater district. It's a popular concert venue for national and international acts.

Paramount Theatre   THEATER
(☑510-465-6400; www.paramounttheatre.com; 2025 Broadway) This massive 1931 art-deco masterpiece shows classic films a few times each month and is also home to the **Oakland East Bay Symphony** (www.oebs.org) and **Oakland Ballet** (www.oaklandballet.org). It periodically books big-name concerts. Tours ($5) are given at 10am on the first and third Saturdays of the month.

Grand Lake Theatre   CINEMA
(☑510-452-3556; www.renaissancerialto.com; 3200 Grand Ave) In Lake Merritt, this 1926 beauty lures you in with its huge corner marquee (which sometimes displays left-leaning political messages) and keeps you coming back with a fun balcony and a Wurlitzer organ playing the pipes on weekends.

New Parkway Theater   CINEMA
(☑510-658-7900; www.thenewparkway.com; 474 24th St) This great, laid-back moviehouse shows quality second-run films in a comfy couch setting, and serves reasonably priced beer, wine, sandwiches and pizza, with delivery to your seat.

Sports

Sports teams play at the (insert most recent and ever-changing corporate branding) **Coliseum** or the **Oracle Arena** off I-880 (Coliseum/Oakland Airport BART station). Cheer on the Golden State Warriors, the Bay Area's NBA basketball team, the Oakland A's, the Bay Area's American League baseball team, and the Raiders, Oakland's NFL team; see www.coliseum.com for listings of upcoming events.

ℹ Information

Oakland's daily newspaper is the *Oakland Tribune* (www.insidebayarea.com/oakland-tribune). The free weekly *East Bay Express* (www.eastbay-express.com) has good Oakland and Berkeley listings.

Visit Oakland Visitor Center (☑510-839-9000; www.visitoakland.org; 481 Water St; ☺9:30am-4pm Tue-Sun) At Jack London Sq.

ℹ Getting There & Away

AIR

Oakland International Airport (p761) is directly across the bay from San Francisco International Airport, and it's usually less crowded and less expensive to fly here. Southwest Airlines has a large presence.

BART

Within the Bay Area, the most convenient way to get to Oakland and back is by BART (☑ 510-465-2278, 511; www.bart.gov). Trains run on a set schedule from 4am to midnight on weekdays, 6am to midnight on Saturday and 8am to midnight on Sunday, and operate at 15- or 20-minute intervals on average.

To get to downtown Oakland, catch a Richmond or Pittsburg/Bay Point train. Fares to the 12th or 19th St stations from downtown San Francisco are $3.30. From San Francisco to Lake Merritt or the Oakland Coliseum/Airport station, catch a BART train that is heading for Fremont or Dublin/Pleasanton. Rockridge is on the Pittsburg/Bay Point line. Between Oakland and downtown Berkeley you can catch a Fremont-Richmond train.

For AC Transit bus connections, take a transfer from the white AC Transit machines in the BART station to save 25¢ off the bus fare.

BUS

Regional company **AC Transit** (☑ 511, 510-817-1717; www.actransit.org; day pass $5) runs convenient buses from San Francisco's Transbay Temporary Terminal at Howard and Main Streets to downtown Oakland and Berkeley, and between the two East Bay cities. Scores of buses go to Oakland from San Francisco during commute hours ($4.20), but only the 'O' line runs both ways all day and on weekends; you can catch the 'O' line at the corner of 5th and Washington Sts in downtown Oakland.

After BART trains stop, late-night transportation between San Francisco and Oakland is with the 800 line, which runs hourly from downtown Market St and the Transbay Temporary Terminal in San Francisco to the corner of 14th St and Broadway.

Between Berkeley and downtown Oakland ($2.10) on weekdays, take the fast and frequent 1R bus along Telegraph Ave between the two city centers. Alternatively, take bus 18 that runs via Martin Luther King Jr Way daily.

Greyhound (☑ 510-832-4730; www.greyhound.com; 2103 San Pablo Ave) operates direct buses from Oakland to Vallejo, San Jose, Santa Rosa and Sacramento. The station is pretty seedy. Discount carrier **Megabus** (across from the south entrance to W Oakland BART station) has daily service to Los Angeles (seven hours), departing from opposite the south entrance to W Oakland BART station.

CAR & MOTORCYCLE

From San Francisco by car, cross the Bay Bridge and enter Oakland via one of two ways: I-580, which leads to I-980 and drops you near the City Center; or I-880, which curves through West Oakland and lets you off near the south end of Broadway. I-880 then continues to the Coliseum, the Oakland International Airport and, eventually, San Jose.

Driving to San Francisco, the bridge toll is $4 to $6, depending on the time and day of the week.

FERRY

With splendid bay views, ferries are the most enjoyable way of traveling between San Francisco and Oakland, though also the slowest and most expensive. From San Francisco's Ferry Building, the **Alameda–Oakland ferry** (☑ 510-522-3300; www.sanfranciscobayferry.com) sails to Jack London Sq (one-way $6.25, 30 minutes, about a dozen times a day, and also departing from Pier 41 on weekends). Ferry tickets include a free transfer, which you can use on AC Transit buses from Jack London Sq.

TRAIN

Oakland is a regular stop for Amtrak trains operating up and down the coast. From Oakland's **Amtrak station** (☑ 800-872-7245; www.amtrak.com; 245 2nd St) in Jack London Sq, you can catch AC Transit bus 72 to downtown Oakland (and the free Broadway Shuttle on weekdays and Saturday night), or take a ferry across the bay to San Francisco.

Amtrak passengers with reservations on to San Francisco need to disembark at the Emeryville Amtrak station, one stop away from Oakland. From there, an Amtrak bus shuttles you to San Francisco's Ferry Building stop. The free **Emery Go Round** (www.emerygoround.com) shuttle runs a circuit that includes the **Emeryville Amtrak station** (☑ 800-872-7245; www.amtrak.com; 5885 Horton St) and MacArthur BART. Emeryville is also the terminus for the California Zephyr (9:10am, one daily departure) to Chicago via Reno, Salt Lake City and Denver.

ⓘ Getting Around

TO/FROM THE AIRPORT

BART is the cheapest and easiest transportation option. From the Coliseum/Oakland Airport BART, the new Oakland Airport Connector train ($6, 15 minutes) runs directly to the airport every five minutes during BART hours.

SuperShuttle (☑ 800-258-3826; www.supershuttle.com) is one of many door-to-door shuttle services operating out of Oakland International Airport. One-way service to San Francisco destinations costs about $27 for the first person and $15 for the second. East Bay service destinations are also served. Reserve ahead.

A taxi from Oakland International Airport to downtown Oakland costs about $30; to downtown San Francisco about $60.

BUS

AC Transit (p139) has a comprehensive bus network within Oakland. Fares are $2.10 and exact change is required.

The free **Broadway Shuttle** (www.meetdowntownoak.com/shuttle.php; ☺7am-7pm Mon-Fri, to 1am Fri, 6pm-1am Sat) runs down Broadway between Jack London Sq and Lake Merritt, stopping at Old Oakland/Chinatown, the downtown BART stations and the Uptown district. The lime-green buses arrive every 10 to 15 minutes.

Berkeley

As the birthplace of the free speech and disability rights movements, and the home of the hallowed halls of the University of California, Berkeley is no bashful wallflower. A national hotspot of (mostly left-of-center) intellectual discourse and one of the most vocal activist populations in the country, this infamous college town has an interesting mix of graying progressives and idealistic undergrads. It's easy to stereotype 'Beserkeley' for some of its recycle-or-else PC crankiness, but the city is often on the forefront of environmental and political issues that eventually go mainstream.

Berkeley is also home to a large South Asian community, as evidenced by an abundance of sari shops on University Ave and a large number of excellent Indian restaurants.

◉ Sights & Activities

Approximately 13 miles east of San Francisco, Berkeley is bordered by the bay to the west, the hills to the east and Oakland to the south. I-80 runs along the town's western edge, next to the marina; from here University Ave heads east to downtown and the campus.

Shattuck Ave crosses University Ave one block west of campus, forming the main crossroads of the downtown area. Immediately to the south is the downtown shopping strip and the downtown Berkeley BART station.

◉ University of California, Berkeley

The Berkeley campus of the University of California (UCB, called 'Cal' by both students and locals) is the oldest university in the state. The decision to found the college was made in 1866, and the first students arrived in 1873. Today UCB has more than 35,000 students, more than 1500 professors and more Nobel laureates than you could point a particle accelerator at.

From Telegraph Ave, enter the campus via Sproul Plaza and Sather Gate, a center for people-watching, soapbox oration and pseudotribal drumming. Or you can enter from Center St and Oxford Lane, near the downtown BART station.

★**UC Berkeley Art Museum**   MUSEUM
(☎510-642-0808;   www.bampfa.berkeley.edu;
2626 Bancroft Way; adult/child $10/7; ☺11am-5pm Wed-Sun) The museum has 11 galleries showcasing a huge range of works, from ancient Chinese to cutting-edge contemporary. The complex also houses a bookstore, cafe and sculpture garden. The museum and the much-loved Pacific Film Archive are scheduled to move to a new home on Oxford St between Addison and Center Streets in 2016.

★**Campanile**   LANDMARK
(Sather Tower; adult/child $3/2; ☺10am-3:45pm Mon-Fri, to 4:45pm Sat, 10am-1:30pm & 3-4:45pm Sun; ♿) Officially called Sather Tower, the Campanile was modeled on St Mark's Basilica in Venice. The 328ft spire offers fine views of the Bay Area, and at the top you can stare up into the carillon of 61 bells, ranging from the size of a cereal bowl to that of a Volkswagen. Recitals take place daily at 7:50am, noon and 6pm, with a longer piece performed at 2pm on Sunday.

Museum of Paleontology   MUSEUM
(☎510-642-1821; www.ucmp.berkeley.edu; ☺8am-10pm Mon-Thu, to 5pm Fri, 10am-5pm Sat, 1-10pm Sun) FREE Housed in the ornate Valley Life Sciences Building (and primarily a research facility that's closed to the public), you can see a number of fossil exhibits in the atrium, including a *Tyrannosaurus rex* skeleton.

Bancroft Library   LIBRARY
(☎510-642-3781;   www.bancroft.berkeley.edu;
☺10am-5pm Mon-Fri) The Bancroft houses, among other gems, the papers of Mark Twain, a copy of Shakespeare's First Folio and the records of the Donner Party. Its small public exhibits of historical Californiana include the surprisingly small gold nugget that sparked the 1849 Gold Rush. To register to use the library, you must be 18 years or older (or a high school graduate) and present two forms of identification (one with a photo). The registration desk is on your way in.

Phoebe A Hearst Museum of Anthropology
MUSEUM

(☎ 510-643-7648; http://hearstmuseum.berkeley.edu; Kroeber Hall) South of the Campanile in Kroeber Hall, this museum includes exhibits from indigenous cultures around the world, including ancient Peruvian, Egyptian and African items. There's also a large collection highlighting native Californian cultures. Closed for renovations until 2015.

◉ South of Campus

Telegraph Ave
STREET

Telegraph Ave has traditionally been the throbbing heart of studentville in Berkeley, the sidewalks crowded with undergrads, postdocs and youthful shoppers squeezing their way past throngs of vendors, buskers and homeless people. Numerous cafes and budget food options cater to students, and most of them are very good.

The frenetic energy buzzing from the university's Sather Gate on any given day is a mixture of youthful posthippies reminiscing about days before their time and young hipsters and punk rockers who sneer at tie-dyed nostalgia. Panhandlers press you for change, and street stalls hawk everything from crystals to bumper stickers to self-published tracts.

People's Park
PARK

This park, just east of Telegraph, between Haste St and Dwight Way, is a marker in local history as a political battleground between residents and the city and state government in the late 1960s. The park has since served mostly as a gathering spot for Berkeley's homeless. A publicly funded restoration spruced it up a bit, and occasional festivals do still happen here, but it's rather run-down.

Elmwood District
NEIGHBORHOOD

South along College Ave is the Elmwood District, a charming nook of shops and restaurants that offers a calming alternative to the frenetic buzz around Telegraph Ave. Continue further south and you'll be in Rockridge.

First Church of Christ Scientist
CHURCH

(www.friendsoffirstchurch.org; 2619 Dwight Way; ⊙ services Sun) Bernard Maybeck's impressive 1910 church uses concrete and wood in its blend of Arts and Crafts, Asian and Gothic influences. Maybeck was a professor of architecture at UC Berkeley and designed San Francisco's Palace of Fine Arts, plus many landmark homes in the Berkeley Hills. Free tours happen the first Sunday of every month at 12:15pm.

Julia Morgan Theatre
THEATER

(☎ 510-845-8542; 2640 College Ave) To the southeast of People's Park is this beautifully understated, redwood-infused 1910 theater, a performance space (formerly a church) created by Bay Area architect Julia Morgan. She designed numerous Bay Area buildings and, most famously, the Hearst Castle.

◉ Downtown

Berkeley's downtown, centered on Shattuck Ave between University Ave and Dwight Way, has far fewer traces of the city's tie-

---

WATERSPORTS ON THE BAY

The San Francisco Bay makes a lovely postcard or snapshot, and there are myriad outfits to help you play in it.

California Canoe & Kayak (☎ 510-893-7833; www.calkayak.com; 409 Water St, Oakland; rental per hour single/double kayak $20/30, canoe $30, stand-up paddleboard $20; ⊙ 10am-6pm) Rents kayaks, canoes and stand-up paddleboards at Oakland's Jack London Sq.

Cal Adventures (☎ 510-642-4000; www.recsports.berkeley.edu; 124 University Ave, Berkeley; ⊞) Run by the UC Berkeley Aquatic Center and located at the Berkeley Marina, Cal offers sailing, windsurfing and sea-kayaking classes and rentals for adults and youth.

Cal Sailing Club (www.cal-sailing.org; Berkeley Marina) An affordable membership-based and volunteer-run nonprofit with sailing and windsurfing programs, based at the Berkeley Marina.

Boardsports School & Shop (www.boardsportsschool.com) Offers lessons and rentals for kiteboarding, windsurfing and stand-up paddleboarding from its three locations in San Francisco, Alameda (East Bay) and Coyote Point.

Sea Trek Kayak & SUP (p118) Located in Sausalito, it has kayaking and stand-up paddleboards, and a fabulous full moon paddle tour.

Central Berkeley

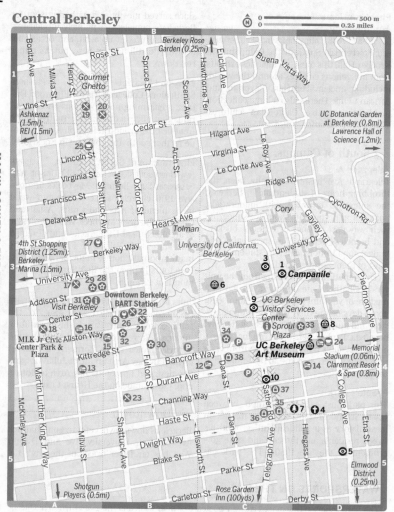

dyed reputation. The area has emerged as an exciting arts district with numerous shops and restaurants and restored public buildings. At the center are the acclaimed thespian stomping grounds of the Berkeley Repertory Theatre and the Aurora Theatre Company and live music at the Freight & Salvage Coffeehouse; a few good movie houses are also nearby.

◉ North Berkeley

Not too far north of campus is a neighborhood filled with lovely garden-front homes,

parks and some of the best restaurants in California. The popular **Gourmet Ghetto** stretches along Shattuck Ave north of University Ave for several blocks, anchored by Chez Panisse. Northwest of here, **Solano Ave**, which crosses from Berkeley into Albany, is lined with lots of funky shops and more good restaurants.

On Euclid Ave just south of Eunice St is the **Berkeley Rose Garden** and its eight terraces of colorful explosions. Here you'll find quiet benches and a plethora of almost perpetually blooming roses arranged by hue. Across the street is a picturesque park with a

Central Berkeley

children's playground (including a very fun concrete slide, about 100ft long).

◉ The Berkeley Hills

Tilden Regional Park   PARK
(www.ebparks.org/parks/tilden) This 2079-acre park, in the hills east of town, is Berkeley's crown jewel. It has more than 30 miles of trails of varying difficulty, from paved paths to hilly scrambles, including part of the magnificent Bay Area Ridge Trail. There's also a miniature steam train ($3), a children's farm, a wonderfully wild-looking botanical garden, an 18-hole **golf course** (☏510-848-7373) and environmental education center. **Lake Anza** is good for picnics, and from spring through late fall you can swim ($3.50).

AC Transit bus 67 runs to the park on weekends and holidays from the downtown BART station, but only stops at the entrances on weekdays.

UC Botanical Garden at Berkeley   GARDENS
(☏510-643-2755; www.botanicalgarden.berkeley.edu; 200 Centennial Dr; adult/child $10/2; ⊙9am-5pm, closed 1st Tue each month) With 34 acres and more than 12,000 species of plants in the Strawberry Canyon hills, the garden is one of the most varied collections in the USA.

A fire trail is a woodsy walking loop around Strawberry Canyon that has great views of town and the off-limits Lawrence Berkeley National Laboratory. Enter at the trailhead at the parking lot on Centennial Dr just southwest of the Botanical Garden; you'll emerge near the Lawrence Hall of Science.

The garden can be reached via the Bear Transit shuttle H line.

Lawrence Hall of Science   SCIENCE CENTER
(☏510-642-5132; www.lawrencehallofscience.org; Centennial Dr; adult/senior & child 7-8/child 3-6 $12/9/6; ⊙10am-5pm daily; 👶) Near Grizzly Peak Blvd, the science hall is named after Ernest Lawrence, who won the Nobel Prize for his invention of the cyclotron particle accelerator. He was a key member of the WWII Manhattan Project, and he's also the name behind the Lawrence Berkeley and Lawrence Livermore laboratories. The Hall of Science has interactive exhibits for kids and adults (many closed on weekdays) on subjects ranging from earthquakes to nanotechnology, and outside there's a 60ft model of a DNA molecule.

AC Transit bus 65 runs to the hall from the downtown BART station. You can also catch the university's Bear Transit shuttle (H line) from the Hearst Mining Circle.

West Berkeley

Berkeley Marina MARINA

At the west end of University Ave is the marina, frequented by squawking seagulls, silent types fishing from the pier, unleashed dogs and, especially on windy weekends, lots of colorful kites. First construction began in 1936, though the pier has much older origins. It was originally built in the 1870s, then replaced by a 3-mile-long ferry pier in 1920 (its length dictated by the bay's extreme shallowness). Part of the original pier is now rebuilt, affording visitors sweeping bay views.

Adventure Playground PLAYGROUND

(☎510-981-6720; www.cityofberkeley.info/adventureplayground; ⏲11am-5pm Sat & Sun & daily mid-Jun–mid-Aug, closed last week of year; 👪) At the Berkeley Marina, this is one of the coolest play spaces in the country – a free outdoor park encouraging creativity and cooperation where supervised kids of any age can help build and paint their own structures. There's an awesome zip line too. Dress the tykes in play clothes, because they *will* get dirty.

San Pablo Ave STREET

Formerly US Rte 40, this was the main thoroughfare from the east before I-80 came along. The area north of University Ave is still lined with a few older motels, diners and atmospheric dive bars with neon signs. South of University Ave are pockets of trendiness, such as the short stretch of gift shops and cafes around Dwight Way.

4th St Shopping District NEIGHBORHOOD

Hidden within an industrial area near I-80 lies a three-block area offering shaded sidewalks for upscale shopping or just strolling, and a few good restaurants.

Takara Sake MUSEUM

(www.takarasake.com; 708 Addison St; ⏲noon-6pm) FREE Stop in to see the traditional wooden tools used for making sake and a short video of the brewing process. Tours of the factory aren't offered, but you can view elements of modern production and bottling through a window. Flights ($5) are available in a spacious tasting room constructed with reclaimed wood and floor tiles fashioned from recycled glass.

Sleeping

Lodging rates spike during special university events such as graduation (mid-May) and home football games. A number of older motels along University Ave can be handy during peak demand. For B&B options, look up the **Berkeley & Oakland Bed & Breakfast Network** (www.bbonline.com).

YMCA HOSTEL $

(☎510-848-6800; www.ymca-cba.org/locations/downtown-berkeley-hotel; 2001 Allston Way; s/d with shared bath from $49/81; @☎≋) The 100-year-old downtown Y building is still the best budget option in town. Rates for the austere private rooms (all with shared bathroom) include use of the sauna, pool and fitness center, and kitchen facilities, and wheelchair-accessible rooms are available as well. Corner rooms 310 and 410 boast enviable bay views. Entrance on Milvia St.

Berkeley City Club HISTORIC HOTEL $$

(☎510-848-7800; www.berkeleycityclub.com; 2315 Durant Ave; r/ste incl breakfast from $165; @☎≋) Designed by Julia Morgan, the architect of Hearst Castle, the 35 rooms and dazzling common areas of this refurbished 1929 historic landmark building (which is also a private club) feel like a glorious time warp into a more refined era. The hotel contains lush and serene Italianate courtyards, gardens and terraces, and a stunning indoor pool.

Elegant Old World rooms contain no TVs, and those with numbers ending in 4 and 8 have to-die-for views of the bay and the Golden Gate Bridge.

Bancroft Hotel HISTORIC HOTEL $$

(☎800-549-1002, 510-549-1000; www.bancrofthotel.com; 2680 Bancroft Way; r incl breakfast $135-179; @☎) 🍃 A gorgeous 1928 Arts and Crafts building that was originally a women's club, the Bancroft is just across the street from campus and two blocks from Telegraph Ave. It has 22 comfortable, beautifully furnished rooms (number 302 boasts a lovely balcony) and a spectacular bay-view rooftop, though no elevator.

Rose Garden Inn INN $$

(☎800-922-9005, 510-549-2145; www.rosegardeninn.com; 2740 Telegraph Ave; r incl breakfast from $138; @☎) The decor flirting with flowery, this cute place is a few blocks south from the Telegraph Ave action and very peaceful, with two old houses surrounded by pretty gardens.

Downtown Berkeley Inn MOTEL $$
(📞 510-843-4043; www.downtownberkeleyinn. com; 2001 Bancroft Way; r $79-129; ✳🅿🛜) A 27-room budget boutique-style motel with good-sized rooms and correspondingly ample flat-screen TVs.

★ Hotel Shattuck Plaza HOTEL $$$
(📞 510-845-7300; www.hotelshattuckplaza.com; 2086 Allston Way; r from $195; ✳@🛜) Peace is quite posh following a $15-million renovation and greening of this 100-year-old downtown jewel. A foyer of red Italian glass lighting, flocked Victorian-style wallpaper – and yes, a peace sign tiled into the floor – leads to comfortable rooms with down comforters, and an airy, columned restaurant serving all meals. Accommodations off Shattuck are quietest; cityscape rooms boast bay views.

Hotel Durant BOUTIQUE HOTEL $$$
(📞 510-845-8981; www.hoteldurant.com; 2600 Durant Ave; r from $209; @🅿) 🍽 Located a block from campus, this classic 1928 hotel has been cheekily renovated to highlight the connection to the university. The lobby is adorned with embarrassing yearbook photos and a ceiling mobile of exam books, and smallish rooms have dictionary-covered shower curtains and bongs repurposed into bedside lamps.

🍴 Eating

Telegraph Ave is packed with cafes, pizza counters and cheap restaurants, and Berkeley's Little India runs along the University Ave corridor. Many more restaurants can be found downtown along Shattuck Ave near the BART station. The section of Shattuck Ave north of University Ave is the 'Gourmet Ghetto,' with lots of excellent eating.

🍴 Downtown & Around Campus

Berkeley Farmers Market MARKET $
(cnr Center St & MLK Way; ⊙10am-3pm Sat) Pick up some organic produce or tasty prepared food at the downtown farmers market, operating year-round, and sit down to munch at MLK Park across from city hall.

Au Coquelet Café CAFE $
(www.aucoquelet.com; 2000 University Ave; mains $7-13; ⊙6am-1:30am Sun-Thu, to 2am Fri & Sat; 🛜) Open till late, Au Coquelet is a popular stop for postmovie meals or late-night studying. The front section serves coffee and pastries while the skylit and spacious back room does a big range of omelets, pastas, sandwiches, burgers and salads.

★ Ippuku JAPANESE $$
(📞510-665-1969; www.ippukuberkeley.com; 2130 Center St; small plates $5-18; ⊙Sun-Thu 5-10pm, to 11pm Fri & Sat) Specializing in *shochu* (flights $12), a distilled alcohol made from rice, barley or sweet potato, Japanese expats gush that Ippuku reminds them of *izakayas* (pub-style restaurants) back in Tokyo. Choose from a menu of skewered meats and settle in at one of the traditional wood platform tables (no shoes, please) or cozy booth perches. Reservations essential.

Gather CALIFORNIAN $$
(📞510-809-0400; www.gatherrestaurant.com; 2200 Oxford St; mains lunch $11-19, dinner $15-25; ⊙11:30am-2pm Mon-Fri, from 10am Sat & Sun, & 5-10pm daily; 🍽) 🌿 When vegan foodies and passionate farm-to-table types dine out together, they often end up here. Inside a salvaged wood interior punctuated by green vines streaking down over an open kitchen, patrons swoon over dishes created from locally sourced ingredients and sustainably raised meats. Reserve for dinner.

La Note FRENCH $$
(📞510-843-1535; www.lanoterestaurant.com; 2377 Shattuck Ave; breakfast mains $10-14, dinner $15-20; ⊙8am-2:30pm Mon-Fri, to 3pm Sat & Sun, & 6-10pm Thu-Sat) A rustic country-French bistro downtown, La Note serves excellent breakfasts. Wake up to a big bowl of café au lait, paired with oatmeal raspberry pancakes or lemon gingerbread pancakes with poached pears. Anticipate a wait on weekends.

🍴 North Berkeley

Cheese Board Pizza PIZZERIA $
(www.cheeseboardcollective.coop; 1512 Shattuck Ave; slice/half-pizza $2.50/10; ⊙7am-8pm Tue-Sat; 🍽) Stop in to take stock of the more than 300 cheeses available at this worker-owned business, and scoop up some fresh bread to make a picnic lunch. Or sit down for a slice of the fabulously crispy one-option-per-day veggie pizza just next door, where live music's often featured.

★ Chez Panisse CALIFORNIAN $$$
(📞cafe 510-548-5049, restaurant 510-548-5525; www.chezpanisse.com; 1517 Shattuck Ave; cafe

dinner mains $22-30, restaurant prix-fixe dinner $65-100; ☺cafe 11:30am-2:45pm & 5-10:30pm Mon-Thu, to 3pm & to 11:30pm Fri & Sat; restaurant seatings 5:30-6pm & 8-8:45pm Mon-Thu & half hour later Fri & Sat) 🖋 Foodies come to worship here at the church of Alice Waters, the inventor of California cuisine. It's in a lovely Arts and Crafts house in the Gourmet Ghetto, and you can choose to pull all the stops with a prix-fixe meal downstairs, or go less expensive and a tad less formal in the cafe upstairs. Reservations accepted one month ahead.

The restaurant is as good and popular as it ever was, and despite its fame, the place has retained a welcoming atmosphere.

✕ West Berkeley

Vik's Chaat Corner INDIAN $
(📞644 4432; www.vikschaatcorner.com; 2390 4th St, at Channing Way; dishes $5-8; ☺11am-6pm Mon-Thu, to 8pm Fri-Sun; 🖋) 🖋 This longtime and very popular *chaat* house has moved to a larger space but still gets mobbed at lunchtime by regulars that include an equal number of hungry office workers and Indian families. Try a *cholle* (spicy garbanzo curry) or one of the many filling *dosas* (savory crepes) on the weekend menu. It's one block east of the waterfront.

Bette's Oceanview Diner DINER $$
(www.bettesdiner.com; 1807 4th St; mains $6-13; ☺6:30am-2:30pm Mon-Fri, to 4pm Sat & Sun) A buzzing breakfast spot, especially on the weekends, serving yummy baked soufflé pancakes and German-style potato pancakes with applesauce, plus eggs and sandwiches. Superfresh food and a nifty diner interior make it worth the wait. It's about a block north of University Ave.

🍸 Drinking & Nightlife

Caffe Strada CAFE
(2300 College Ave; ☺6am-midnight; 🛜) A popular, student-saturated hangout with an inviting shaded patio and strong espressos. Try the signature white-chocolate mocha.

Torpedo Room BEER HALL
(www.sierranevada.com/brewery/california/torpedoroom; 2031 4th St; ☺11am-8pm Tue-Sat, noon-5pm Sun) Sample a flight of 4 oz pours ($2 each) from the sixteen rotating drafts on tap at Sierra Nevada brewery's new tasting room. No pints are served, but growlers are available to go, and a small selection of

bar snacks helps keep you fortified. It's one block south of University Ave.

Jupiter PUB
(www.jupiterbeer.com; 2181 Shattuck Ave; ☺11:30am-1am Mon-Thu, 11:30am-1:30am Fri, noon-1:30am Sat, noon-midnight Sun) This downtown pub has loads of regional microbrews, a beer garden, good pizza and live bands most nights. Sit upstairs for a bird's-eye view of bustling Shattuck Ave.

Albatross PUB
(www.albatrosspub.com; 1822 San Pablo Ave; ☺6pm-2am Sun-Tue, 4:30pm-2am Wed-Sat) A block north of University Ave, Berkeley's oldest pub is one of the most inviting and friendly in the entire Bay Area. Some serious darts are played here, and boardgames will be going on around many of the worn-out tables. Sunday is Pub Quiz night.

Triple Rock Brewery & Ale House BREWERY
(www.triplerock.com; 1920 Shattuck Ave; ☺11:30am-1am Mon-Wed, to 2am Thu-Sat, to midnight Sun) Opened in 1986, Triple Rock was one of the country's first brewpubs. The house beers and pub grub are quite good, and the antique wooden bar and rooftop sun deck are delightful.

Guerilla Café CAFE
(📞510-845-2233; www.guerillacafe.com; 1620 Shattuck Ave; ☺7am-2pm Mon, 7am-4:30pm Tue-Fri, 8am-4:30pm Sat & Sun) 🖋 Exuding a 1970s flavor, this small and sparkling cafe has a creative political vibe, with polka-dot tiles on the counter handmade by one of the artist-owners, and order numbers spotlighting guerillas and liberation revolutionaries. Organic and Fair Trade ingredients feature in the breakfasts and panini sandwiches, and locally roasted Blue Bottle coffee is served.

☆ Entertainment

The arts corridor on Addison St between Milvia and Shattuck Sts anchors a lively downtown entertainment scene.

Live Music

Berkeley has plenty of intimate live-music venues. Cover charges range from $5 to $20, and a number of venues are all-ages or 18-and-over.

Freight & Salvage Coffeehouse FOLK, WORLD
(📞510-644-2020; www.thefreight.org; 2020 Addison St; ♿) This legendary club has almost 50 years of history and is conveniently located

in the downtown arts district. It features great traditional folk and world music and welcomes all ages, with half-price tickets for patrons under 21.

La Peña Cultural Center   WORLD

(☎ 510-849-2568; www.lapena.org; 3105 Shattuck Ave) A few blocks east of the Ashby BART station, this cultural center and Chilean cafe presents dynamic musical and visual arts programming with a peace and justice bent. Look for the vibrant mural on its facade.

Ashkenaz   FOLK, WORLD

(☎ 510-525-5054; www.ashkenaz.com; 1317 San Pablo Ave; 🎵) Ashkenaz is a 'music and dance community center' attracting activists, hippies and fans of folk, swing and world music who love to dance (lessons offered).

924 Gilman   PUNK ROCK

(www.924gilman.org; 924 Gilman St; ⊙ Fri-Sun) This volunteer-run and booze-free all-ages space is a West Coast punk rock institution. From Berkeley BART, take AC Transit bus 25 to Gilman and 8th Sts.

Cinemas

Pacific Film Archive   CINEMA

(PFA; ☎ 510-642-5249; www.bampfa.berkeley.edu; 2575 Bancroft Way; adult/child $9.50/6.50) A renowned film center with an ever-changing schedule of international and classic films, cineasts should seek this place out. The spacious theater has seats that are comfy enough for hours-long movie marathons.

Theater & Dance

Zellerbach Hall   PERFORMING ARTS

(☎ 510-642-9988;   http://tickets.berkeley.edu) On the south end of campus near Bancroft

Way and Dana St, Zellerbach Hall features dance events, concerts and performances of all types by national and international artists. The on-site **Cal Performances Ticket Office** sells tickets without a handling fee.

Berkeley Repertory Theatre   THEATER

(☎ 510-647-2949; www.berkeleyrep.org; 2025 Addison St; tickets $35-100) This highly respected company has produced bold versions of classical and modern plays since 1968. Most shows have half-price tickets for patrons under 30.

California Shakespeare Theater   THEATER

(☎ 510-548-9666; www.calshakes.org; box office 701 Heinz Ave) Headquartered in Berkeley, with a fantastic outdoor amphitheater further east in Orinda, 'Cal Shakes' is a warm-weather tradition of al fresco Shakespeare (and other classic) productions, with a season that lasts from about June through September.

Aurora Theatre Company   THEATER

(☎ 510-843-4822; www.auroratheatre.org; 2081 Addison St) An intimate downtown theater, it performs contemporary and thought-provoking plays staged with a subtle chamber-theater aesthetic.

Marsh   PERFORMING ARTS

(☎ 510-704-8291; www.themarsh.org; 2120 Allston Way) The 'breeding ground for new performance' in Berkeley has eclectic solo and comedy acts.

Shotgun Players   THEATER

(☎ 510-841-6500; www.shotgunplayers.org; 1901 Ashby Avenue) ✍ The country's first all-solar-powered theater company stages exciting

---

WHERE THE EARTH MOVED

Curious to find a few places where the earth shook? Visit these notorious spots in and around the Bay Area:

➡ **Earthquake Trail**, at Point Reyes National Seashore, shows the effects of the big one in 1906.

➡ **Cypress Freeway Memorial Park**, at 14th St and Mandela Parkway, commemorates the forty-two people that died and those who helped rescue survivors when the Cypress Freeway collapsed in West Oakland, one of the most horrifying and enduring images of the 1989 Loma Prieta quake.

➡ In the **Forest of Nisene Marks State Park** (☎ 831-763-7062; www.parks.ca.gov/?page_id=666; parking $8), near Aptos in Santa Cruz County, a sign on the Aptos Creek Trail marks the actual epicenter of the Loma Prieta quake, and on the Big Slide Trail a number of fissures can be spotted.

➡ At UC Berkeley, the Hayward Fault runs just beneath **Memorial Stadium**.

and provocative work in an intimate space. Across from the Ashby BART station.

Sports

Memorial Stadium, which dates from 1923, is the university's 63,000-seat sporting venue, and the Hayward Fault runs just beneath it. On alternate years, it's the site of the famous football frenzy between the UC Berkeley and Stanford teams.

The **Cal Athletic Ticket Office** (☑800-462-3277; www.calbears.com; 2223 Fulton St) on campus has ticket information on all UC Berkeley sports events. Keep in mind that some sell out weeks in advance.

🛍 Shopping

Branching off the UC campus, Telegraph Ave caters mostly to students, hawking a steady dose of urban hippie gear, handmade jewelry and head-shop paraphernalia. Audiophiles will swoon over the music stores. Other shopping corridors include College Ave in the Elmwood District, 4th St (north of University Ave) and Solano Ave.

Amoeba Music   MUSIC
(☑510-549-1125; 2455 Telegraph Ave; ⊙10:30am-8pm Mon-Thu, to 10pm Fri & Sat, 11am-8pm Sun) If you're a music junkie, you might plan on spending a few hours at the original Berkeley branch of Amoeba Music, packed with massive quantities of new and used CDs, DVDs, tapes and records (yes, lots of vinyl).

Moe's   BOOKS
(☑510-849-2087; 2476 Telegraph Ave; ⊙10am-10pm) A longstanding local favorite, Moe's offers four floors of new, used and remaindered books for hours of browsing.

University Press Books   BOOKS
(☑510-548-0585; 2430 Bancroft Way; ⊙10am-8pm Mon-Fri, to 6pm Sat, noon-5pm Sun) Across

the street from campus, this academic and scholarly bookstore stocks works by UC Berkeley professors and other academic and museum publishers.

Down Home Music   MUSIC
(☑510-525-2129; www.downhomemusic.com; 10341 San Pablo Ave, El Cerrito; ⊙11am-7pm Thu-Sun) North of Berkeley in El Cerrito, this world-class store for roots, blues, folk, Latin and world music is affiliated with the Arhoolie record label, which has been issuing landmark recordings since the early 1960s.

Rasputin   MUSIC
(☑800-350-8700; www.rasputinmusic.com; 2401 Telegraph Ave; ⊙11am-7pm Mon-Thu, to 8pm Sat, noon-7pm Sun) A large music store full of new and used releases.

North Face Outlet   OUTDOOR EQUIPMENT
(☑510-526-3530; cnr 5th & Gilman Sts; ⊙10am-7pm Mon-Sat, 11am-5pm Sun) Discount store for the well-respected Bay Area-based brand of outdoor gear. It's a few blocks west of San Pablo Ave.

REI   OUTDOOR EQUIPMENT
(☑510-527-4140; 1338 San Pablo Ave; ⊙10am-9pm Mon-Fri, to 8pm Sat, to 7pm Sun) This large and busy co-op lures in active folks for camping and mountaineering rentals, sports clothing and all kinds of nifty outdoor gear.

❶ Information

Alta Bates Summit Medical Center (☑510-204-4444; www.altabatessummit.org; 2450 Ashby Ave) 24-hour emergency services.
Visit Berkeley (☑800-847-4823, 510-549-7040; www.visitberkeley.com; 2030 Addison St; ⊙9am-1pm & 2-5pm Mon-Fri, 10am-1pm & 2-4pm Sat) The helpful Berkeley Convention & Visitors Bureau has a free visitors guide.
UC Berkeley Visitor Services Center (☑510-642-5215; http://visitors.berkeley.edu; 101

WORTH A TRIP

EAST BROTHER LIGHT STATION

East Brother Light Station (☑510-233-2385; www.ebls.org; d incl breakfast & dinner $295-415; ⊙Thu-Sun) Most Bay Area residents have never heard of this speck of an island off the East Bay city of Richmond, and even fewer know that the East Brother Light Station is an extraordinary five-room Victorian B&B. Spend the night in the romantic lighthouse or fog signal building (the foghorn is used from October through March), where every window has stupendous bay views and harbor seals frolic in the frigid currents.

Resident innkeepers serve afternoon hors d'oeuvres and champagne, and between gourmet meals you can stroll around the breezy one-acre islet and rummage through historical photos and artifacts.

Sproul Hall; ☺ tours usually 10am Mon-Sat & 1pm Sun) Campus maps and information available. Free 90-minute campus tours are given at 10am Monday to Saturday and 1pm Sunday; reservations required.

ⓘ Getting There & Away

BART

The easiest way to travel between San Francisco, Berkeley, Oakland and other East Bay points is on **BART** (☎ 511, 510-465-2278; www.bart. gov). Trains run approximately every 10 minutes from 4am to midnight on weekdays, with limited service from 6am on Saturday and from 8am on Sunday.

To get to Berkeley, catch a Richmond-bound train to one of three BART stations: Ashby (Adeline St and Ashby Ave), Downtown Berkeley (Shattuck Ave and Center St) or North Berkeley (Sacramento and Delaware Sts). The fare ranges from $3.75 to $4 between Berkeley and San Francisco; $1.85 between Berkeley and downtown Oakland. After 8pm on weekdays, 7pm on Saturday and all day Sunday, there is no direct service operating from San Francisco to Berkeley; instead, catch a Pittsburg/Bay Point train and transfer at 19th St station in Oakland.

A **BART-to-Bus** transfer ticket, available from white AC Transit machines near the BART turnstiles, reduces the connecting bus fare by 25¢.

BUS

The regional company **AC Transit** (☎ 511, 510-817-1717; www.actransit.org) operates a number of buses from San Francisco's Transbay Temporary Terminal to the East Bay. The F line leaves from the Transbay Temporary Terminal to the corner of University and Shattuck Aves approximately every half-hour ($4.20, 30 minutes).

Between Berkeley and downtown Oakland ($2.10) on weekdays, take the fast and frequent 1R bus along Telegraph Ave between the two city centers, or bus 18 that runs daily via Martin Luther King Jr Way. Bus 51B travels along University Ave from Berkeley BART to the Berkeley Marina.

CAR & MOTORCYCLE

With your own wheels you can approach Berkeley from San Francisco by taking the Bay Bridge and then following either I-80 (for University Ave, downtown Berkeley and the UCB campus) or Hwy 24 (for College Ave and the Berkeley Hills).

Driving to San Francisco, the bridge toll is $4 to $6, depending on the time and day of the week.

TRAIN

Amtrak does stop in Berkeley, but the shelter is not staffed and direct connections are few. More convenient is the nearby **Emeryville Amtrak**

station (☎ 800-872-7245; www.amtrak.com; 5885 Horton St), a few miles south.

To reach the Emeryville station from downtown Berkeley, take a Transbay F bus or ride BART to the MacArthur station and then take the free Emery Go Round bus (Hollis route) to Amtrak.

ⓘ Getting Around

Public transportation, cycling and walking are the best options for getting around central Berkeley.

BICYCLE

Cycling is a popular means of transportation, and safe and well-marked 'bicycle boulevards' with signed distance information to landmarks make crosstown journeys very easy. Just north of Berkeley, **Wheels of Justice** (☎ 510-524-1094; www.wheelsofjustice.com; 1554 Solano Ave, Albany; ☺ 11am-7pm Thu, 10am-6pm Fri-Wed, to 5pm Sun) has 24-hour mountain-bike rentals for $35.

BUS

AC Transit operates public buses in and around Berkeley, and UC Berkeley's **Bear Transit** (http://pt.berkeley.edu/around/beartransit) runs a shuttle from the downtown BART station to various points on campus ($1). From its stop at the Hearst Mining Circle, the H Line runs along Centennial Dr to the higher parts of the campus.

CAR & MOTORCYCLE

Drivers should note that numerous barriers have been set up to prevent car traffic from traversing residential streets at high speeds, so zigzagging is necessary in some neighborhoods.

Mt Diablo State Park

ⓞ Sights

Mt Diablo State Park   PARK
(☎ 925-837-2525; www.mdia.org; per vehicle $6-10; ☺ 8am-sunset) Collecting a light dusting of snowflakes on the coldest days of winter, at 3849ft Mt Diablo is more than 1000ft higher than Mt Tamalpais in Marin County. On a clear day (early on a winter morning is a good bet) the views from Diablo's summit are vast and sweeping. To the west you can see over the bay and out to the Farallon Islands; to the east you can see over the Central Valley to the Sierra Nevada.

The park has more than 50 miles of hiking trails, and can be reached from Walnut Creek, Danville or Clayton. You can also drive to the top, where there's a visitors center.

🛏 Sleeping

Mt Diablo Campgrounds CAMPGROUND $
(📞 800-444-7275; www.reserveamerica.com; tent & RV sites $30) Of the three campgrounds, Juniper and Live Oak have showers, though the campgrounds can be closed during high fire danger and water may be turned off throughout the park if water restrictions are in effect.

ℹ Information

Mt Diablo State Park Visitors Center
(🕙 10am-4pm) The park office is at the junction of the two entry roads.

John Muir National Historic Site

John Muir Residence HISTORIC SITE
(📞 925-228-8860; www.nps.gov/jomu; 4202 Alhambra Ave, Martinez; 🕙 10am-5pm Wed-Sun) **FREE** Just 15 miles north of Walnut Creek, the John Muir residence sits in a pastoral patch of farmland in bustling, modern Martinez. Though Muir wrote of sauntering the High Sierra with a sack of tea and bread, it may be a shock for those familiar with the iconic Sierra Club founder's ascetic weather-beaten appearance that the house (built by his father-in-law) is a model of Victorian Italianate refinement, with a tower cupola, a daintily upholstered parlor and splashes of white lace.

Muir's 'scribble den' has been left as it was during his life, with crumpled papers over-flowing from wire wastebaskets and dried bread balls – his preferred snack – resting on the mantelpiece.

Acres of his fruit orchard still stand, and visitors can enjoy seasonal samples. The grounds include the 1849 **Martinez Adobe**, part of the rancho on which the house was built, and the oak-speckled hiking trails on nearby **Mt Wanda**.

ℹ Getting There & Away

The park is just north of Hwy 4, and accessible by **County Connection** (www.cccta.org) buses from Amtrak and BART.

Vallejo

For one week in 1852 Vallejo was officially the California state capital – but the fickle legislature changed its mind. It tried Vallejo a second time in 1853, but after a month moved on again (to Benicia). That same year, Vallejo became the site of the first US naval installation on the West Coast (Mare Island Naval Shipyard, now closed).

⊙ Sights

Six Flags Discovery Kingdom AMUSEMENT PARK
(📞 707-643-6722; www.sixflags.com/discovery-kingdom; adult/child under 4ft $63/43; 🕙 approx 10:30am-6pm Fri-Sun spring & fall, to 8pm or 9pm daily summer, variable weekend & holiday hours Dec) The town's biggest tourist draw, this modern wildlife and theme park offers mighty coasters and other rides alongside animal shows featuring sharks and a killer whale. Significant discounts are available on the park's website. Exit I-80 at Hwy 37 westbound, 5 miles north of downtown Vallejo. Parking is $20.

Vallejo Naval & Historical Museum MUSEUM
(📞 707-643-0077; www.vallejomuseum.org; 734 Marin St; admission $5; 🕙 noon-4pm Tue-Sat) This museum tells the story of Vallejo's shortlived history as California's state capital and West Coast naval site.

ℹ Getting There & Away

San Francisco Bay Ferry (📞 415-705-8291; www.sanfranciscobayferry.com; one way adult/child $13/6.50) runs ferries from San Francisco's Pier 41 at Fisherman's Wharf and the Ferry Building to Vallejo; the journey takes one hour. Discount admission and transportation packages for Six Flags are available from San Francisco. The ferry is also a gateway to the Wine Country, with connections via the **Napa Valley Vine** (www.ridethevine.com) buses and the **Napa Valley Wine Train** (www.winetrain.com/ferry).

THE PENINSULA

South of San Francisco, squeezed tightly between the bay and the coastal foothills, a vast swath of suburbia continues to San Jose and beyond. Dotted within this area are Palo Alto, Stanford University and Silicon Valley, the center of the Bay Area's immense tech industry. West of the foothills, Hwy 1 runs down the Pacific Coast via Half Moon Bay and a string of beaches to Santa Cruz. Hwy 101 and I-280 both run to San Jose, where they connect with Hwy 17, the quickest route to Santa Cruz. Any of these routes can be combined into an interesting loop or extended to the Monterey Peninsula.

And don't bother looking for Silicon Valley on the map – you won't find it. Because silicon chips form the basis of modern microcomputers, and the Santa Clara Valley – stretching from Palo Alto down through Mountain View, Sunnyvale, Cupertino and Santa Clara to San Jose – is thought of as the birthplace of the microcomputer, it's been dubbed 'Silicon Valley.' The Santa Clara Valley is wide and flat, and its towns are essentially a string of shopping centers and industrial parks linked by a maze of freeways. It's hard to imagine that even after WWII this area was still a wide expanse of orchards and farms.

San Francisco to San Jose

South of the San Francisco peninsula, I-280 is the dividing line between the densely populated South Bay area and the rugged and lightly populated Pacific Coast. With sweeping views of hills and reservoirs, I-280 is a more scenic choice than crowded Hwy 101, which runs through miles of boring business parks. Unfortunately, these parallel north–south arteries are both clogged with traffic during commute times and often on weekends.

A historic site where European explorers first set eyes on San Francisco Bay, **Sweeney Ridge** (www.nps.gov/goga/planyourvisit/upload/sb-sweeney-2008.pdf) straddles a prime spot between Pacifica and San Bruno, and offers hikers unparalleled ocean and bay views. From I-280, exit at Sneath Lane and follow it 2 miles west until it dead ends at the trailhead.

Right on the bay at the northern edge of San Mateo, 4 miles south of San Francisco International Airport, is **Coyote Point Recreation Area** (parking $6;), a popular park (its playground sports a huge castle) and windsurfing destination. The main attraction – formerly known as the Coyote Point Museum – is **CuriOdyssey** (650-342-7755; www.curiodyssey.org; adult/child $9/7; 10am-5pm Tue-Sat, noon-5pm Sun;), with innovative exhibits for kids and adults highlighting science and wildlife. Exit Hwy 101 at Coyote Point Dr.

Stanford University

Sprawled over 8200 leafy acres in Palo Alto, **Stanford University** (www.stanford.edu) was founded by Leland Stanford, one of the Central Pacific Railroad's 'Big Four' founders and a former governor of California. When the Stanfords' only child died of typhoid during a European tour in 1884, they decided to build a university in his memory. Stanford University was opened in 1891, just two years before Leland Stanford's death, but the university grew to become a prestigious and

---

NERDS' NIRVANA

Touted as the largest computer history exhibition in the world, the **Computer History Museum** (650-810-1010; www.computerhistory.org; 1401 N Shoreline Blvd, Mountain View; adult/student & senior $15/12; 10am-5pm Wed-Sun) has rotating exhibits drawn from its 100,000-item collection. Artifacts range from the abacus to the iPod, including Cray-1 supercomputers, a Babbage Difference Engine (a Victorian-era automatic computing engine) and the first Google server.

Don't come looking to ogle the latest iPhone or get a Genius Bar consultation. At **Apple Headquarters** (www.apple.com/companystore; 1 Infinite Loop, Cupertino; 10am-5:30pm Mon-Fri), hardcore fans can load up on Apple-branded clothing and ephemera from its company store and commiserate that, yes, Steve Jobs has left the building.

Though there are no official tours of the **Googleplex** (www.google.com/about/company/facts/locations; 1600 Amphitheatre Pkwy, Mountain View), visitors can stroll the campus and gawk at the public art on the leafy grounds, where scads of Googlers zoom about on primary-colored bicycles. Don't miss the 'dessert yard' outside Building 44, with lawn sculptures of Android operating systems (a cupcake! a donut! a robot!), and across the street, a toothy T-Rex festooned in pink flamingos next to the volleyball court.

At the company's headquarters, the **Intel Museum** (408-765-5050; www.intel.com/museum; 2200 Mission College Blvd, Santa Clara; 9am-6pm Mon-Fri, 10am-5pm Sat) FREE has displays on the birth and growth of the computer industry with special emphasis, not surprisingly, on microchips and Intel's involvement. Reserve ahead if you want to schedule a guided tour.

wealthy institution. The campus was built on the site of the Stanfords' horse-breeding farm and, as a result, Stanford is still known as 'The Farm.'

⊙ Sights

Main Quad
PLAZA

Auguste Rodin's *Burghers of Calais* bronze sculpture marks the entrance to the university's Main Quad, an open plaza where the original 12 campus buildings, a mix of Romanesque and Mission revival styles, were joined by the Memorial Church (also called MemChu) in 1903. The church is noted for its beautiful mosaic-tiled frontage, stained-glass windows and four organs with more than 8000 pipes.

Hoover Tower
TOWER

(adult/child $2/1; ⊙10am-4pm, closed during final exams, breaks btwn sessions & some holidays) A campus landmark at the east of the Main Quad, the 285ft-high Hoover Tower offers superb views. The tower houses the university library, offices and part of the right-wing Hoover Institution on War, Revolution & Peace (where Donald Rumsfeld caused a university-wide stir by accepting a position after he resigned as Secretary of Defense).

Cantor Center for Visual Arts
MUSEUM

(http://museum.stanford.edu; 328 Lomita Dr; ⊙11am-5pm Wed & Fri-Sun, to 8pm Thu) FREE The Cantor Center for Visual Arts is a large museum originally dating from 1894. Its collection spans works from ancient civilizations to contemporary art, sculpture and photography, and rotating exhibits are eclectic in scope.

Rodin Sculpture Garden
SCULPTURE GARDEN

Immediately south of the Cantor Center is the open-air Rodin Sculpture Garden, which boasts the largest collection of bronze sculptures by Auguste Rodin outside of Paris, including reproductions of his towering *Gates of Hell*. More sculpture can be found around campus, including pieces by Andy Goldsworthy and Maya Lin.

ⓘ Information

Stanford Visitor Center (www.stanford.edu/dept/visitorinfo; 295 Galvez St) The Stanford Visitor Center offers free one-hour walking tours of the campus daily at 11am and 3:15pm, except during the winter break (mid-December through early January) and some holidays. Specialized tours are also available.

ⓘ Getting There & Away

Stanford University's free public shuttle, **Marguerite** (http://transportation.stanford.edu/marguerite), provides service from Caltrain's Palo Alto and California Ave stations to the campus, and has bicycle racks. Parking on campus is expensive and trying.

San Jose

Though culturally diverse and historic, San Jose has always been in San Francisco's shadow, awash in Silicon Valley's suburbia. Founded in 1777 as El Pueblo de San José de Guadalupe, San Jose is California's oldest Spanish civilian settlement. Its downtown is small and scarcely used for a city of its size, though it does bustle with 20-something clubgoers on the weekends. Industrial parks, high-tech computer firms and look-alike

---

WINCHESTER MYSTERY HOUSE

Winchester Mystery House (☎408-247-2101; www.winchestermysteryhouse.com; 525 S Winchester Blvd; adult/senior/child 6-12 $33/30/25; ⊙9am-5pm Oct-Mar, 9am-7pm Apr-Sep) An odd structure purposefully commissioned to be so by the heir to the Winchester rifle fortune, the Winchester Mystery House is a ridiculous Victorian mansion with 160 rooms of various sizes and little utility, with dead-end hallways and a staircase that runs up to a ceiling all jammed together like a toddler playing architect. Apparently, Sarah Winchester spent 38 years constructing this mammoth white elephant because the spirits of the people killed by Winchester rifles told her to.

No expense was spared in the construction and the extreme results sprawl over 4 acres. Tours start every 30 minutes, and the standard hour-long guided mansion tour includes a self-guided romp through the gardens as well as entry to an exhibition of guns and rifles.

It's west of central San Jose and just north of I-280, across the street from Santana Row.

housing developments have sprawled across the city's landscape, taking over where farms, ranches and open spaces once spread between the bay and the surrounding hills.

⊙ Sights

Downtown San Jose is at the junction of Hwy 87 and I-280. Hwy 101 and I-880 complete the box. Running roughly north–south along the length of the city, from the old port town of Alviso on the San Francisco Bay all the way downtown, is 1st St; south of I-280, its name changes to Monterey Hwy.

San Jose State University is immediately east of downtown, and the SoFA district, with numerous nightclubs, restaurants and galleries, is on a stretch of S 1st St south of San Carlos St.

★ **History Park**   PARK
(☑ 408-287-2290; www.historysanjose.org; cnr Senter Rd & Phelan Ave; ⊙ 11am-5pm Tue-Sun, closed 1st Mon of month) Historic buildings from all over San Jose have been brought together in this open-air history museum, southeast of the city center in Kelley Park. The centerpiece is a dramatic half-scale replica of the 237ft-high 1881 Electric Light Tower. The original tower was a pioneering attempt at street lighting, intended to illuminate the entire town center. It was a complete failure but was left standing as a central landmark until it toppled over in 1915 because of rust and wind. Other buildings include an 1888 Chinese temple and the Pacific Hotel, which has rotating exhibits inside. The Trolley Restoration Barn restores historic trolley cars to operate on San Jose's light-rail line, and on weekends you can ride a trolley along the park's own short line.

Tech Museum of Innovation   MUSEUM
(The Tech; ☑ 408-294-8324; www.thetech.org; 201 S Market St; adult/child 3-17 $15/10; ⊙ 10am-5pm; ⊛) This excellent technology museum, opposite Plaza de Cesar Chavez, examines subjects from robotics to space exploration to genetics. The museum also includes an IMAX dome theater (additional $5 admission), which screens different films throughout the day.

San Jose Museum of Art   MUSEUM
(☑ 408-271-6840; www.sjmusart.org; 110 S Market St; adult/student & senior $8/5; ⊙ 11am-5pm Tue-Sun) With a strong permanent collection of 20th-century works and a variety of imaginative changing exhibits, the city's central art museum is one of the Bay Area's finest. The main building started life as the post office in 1892, was damaged by the 1906 earthquake and became an art gallery in 1933. A modern wing was added in 1991.

Rosicrucian Egyptian Museum   MUSEUM
(☑ 408-947-3635; www.egyptianmuseum.org; 1342 Naglee Ave; adult/child/student $9/5/7; ⊙ 9am-5pm Wed-Fri, 10am-6pm Sat & Sun) West of downtown, this unusual and educational Egyptian Museum is one of San Jose's more interesting attractions, with an extensive collection that includes statues, household items and mummies. There's even a two-room, walk-through reproduction of an ancient subterranean tomb. The museum is the centerpiece of Rosicrucian Park (cnr Naglee & Park Aves), west of downtown San Jose.

MACLA   GALLERY
(Movimiento de Arte y Cultura Latino Americana; ☑ 408-998-2783; www.maclaarte.org; 510 S 1st St; ⊙ noon-7pm Wed & Thu, noon-5pm Fri & Sat) FREE A cutting-edge gallery highlighting themes by both established and emerging Latino artists, MACLA is one of the best community arts spaces in the Bay Area, with open-mic performances, hip-hop and other live-music shows, experimental theater and well-curated and thought-provoking visual arts exhibits. It's also a hub for the popular South First Fridays (www.southfirstfridays.com) art walk and street fair.

Plaza de Cesar Chavez   PLAZA
This leafy square in the center of downtown, which was part of the original plaza of El Pueblo de San José de Guadalupe, is the oldest public space in the city. It's named after Cesar Chavez – founder of the United Farm Workers, who lived part of his life in San Jose – and is surrounded by museums, theaters and hotels.

Cathedral Basilica of St Joseph   CHURCH
(80 S Market St) At the top of the Plaza de Cesar Chavez, the pueblo's first church. Originally constructed of adobe brick in 1803, it was replaced three times due to earthquakes and fire; the present building dates from 1877.

Santana Row   MALL
(www.santanarow.com; Stevens Creek & Winchester Blvds) An upscale Main St-style mall, Santana Row is a mixed-use space west of downtown with shopping, dining and entertainment

SAN JOSE FOR CHILDREN

Children's Discovery Museum (☎408-298-5437; www.cdm.org; 180 Woz Way; admission $12; ☉10am-5pm Tue-Sat, from noon Sun; ⊛) Downtown, this science and creativity museum has hands-on displays incorporating art, technology and the environment, with plenty of toys, and very cool play-and-learn areas. The museum is on Woz Way, which is named after Steve Wozniak, the cofounder of Apple.

Great America (☎408-986-5886; www.cagreatamerica.com; 4701 Great America Pkwy, Santa Clara; adult/child under 4ft $60/40; ☉Apr-Oct; ⊛) If you can handle the shameful product placements, kids love the roller coasters and other thrill rides. Note that online tickets cost much less than walk-up prices; parking costs $15 but it's also accessible by public transportation.

Raging Waters (☎408-238-9900; www.rwsplash.com; 2333 South White Rd; adult/child under 4ft $39/29, parking $6; ☉May-Sep; ⊛) A water park inside Lake Cunningham Regional Park, Raging Waters has fast water slides, a tidal pool and a nifty water fort. Online discounts.

along with a boutique hotel, lofts and apartments. Restaurants spill out onto sidewalk terraces, and public spaces have been designed to invite loitering and promenading. On warm evenings, the Mediterranean-style area swarms with an energetic crowd.

🛏 Sleeping

Conventions and trade shows keep the downtown hotels busy year-round, and midweek rates are usually higher than weekends.

Henry W Coe State Park CAMPGROUND $
(☎408-779-2728, reservations 800-444-7275; www.reserveamerica.com; sites $20; ⊛) Southeast of San Jose near Morgan Hill, this huge state park has 20 drive-in campsites at the top of an open ridge overlooking the hills and canyons of the park's backcountry. There are no showers. You can't make reservations less than two days in advance, though it rarely fills up except on spring and summer holidays and weekends.

Hikers (permit $5) can overnight in the park's vast wilderness.

Westin San Jose HISTORIC HOTEL $$
(☎866-870-0726, 408-295-2000; www.thesainte-claire.com; 302 S Market St; r weekend/midweek from $129/179; ⊛⊛@⊛⊛) Formerly the Sainte Claire, this atmospheric 1926 landmark hotel overlooking Plaza de Cesar Chavez has a drop-dead beautiful lobby with stretched leather ceilings. Guest rooms are smallish, and were being completely remodeled at research time.

Hotel De Anza HOTEL $$
(☎800-843-3700, 408-286-1000; www.hoteldean-za.com; 233 W Santa Clara St; r Sun-Thu/Fri & Sat $149/239; ⊛@⊛⊛) This downtown hotel is a restored art-deco landmark, although contemporary stylings overwhelm the place's history. Guest rooms offer plush comforts (the ones facing south are a tad larger) and full concierge service is available.

Hotel Valencia BOUTIQUE HOTEL $$$
(☎866-842-0100, 408-551-0010; www.hotelva-lencia-santanarow.com; 355 Santana Row; r incl breakfast $199-309; ⊛@⊛⊛) A burbly lobby fountain and deep-red corridor carpeting set the tone for this tranquil 212-room contemporary hotel in the Santana Row shopping complex. In-room minibars and bathrobes and a pool and hot tub create an oasis of luxury with European and Asian design accents.

🍴 Eating

Tofoo Com Chay VEGETARIAN, VIETNAMESE $
(☎408-286-6335; 388 E Santa Clara St; mains $6.50; ☉9am-9pm Mon-Fri, 10am-6pm Sat; ⊛) Conveniently located on the border of the San Jose State University campus, students and vegetarians queue up for the Vietnamese dishes such as the fake-meat *pho* and the heaped combo plates.

Original Joe's ITALIAN $$
(www.originaljoes.com; 301 S 1st St; mains $15-37; ☉11am-11pm Sun-Thu, 11am-midnight Fri & Sat) Waiters flit about this busy 1950s San Jose landmark, serving standard Italian dishes to locals and conventioneers. The dining room is a curious but tasteful hodgepodge of '50s

brick, contemporary wood paneling and 5ft-tall Asian vases. Expect a wait.

Arcadia
STEAK $$$

(✓408-278-4555; www.michaelmina.net/restaurants; 100 W San Carlos St; mains lunch $12-19, dinner $28-50; ⊘6:30am-2pm daily, 5:30-10pm Mon-Sat) This fine New American steakhouse restaurant in the Marriott Hotel is run by Chef Michael Mina, one of San Francisco's biggest celebrity chefs. It's not the daring, cutting-edge style Mina is known for, but it's slick, expensive and, of course, very good.

🍷 Drinking & Nightlife

The biggest conglomeration of clubs is on S 1st St, aka SoFA, and around S 2nd at San Fernando. Raucous young clubgoers pack the streets on Friday and Saturday nights.

★ Singlebarrel
COCKTAIL BAR

(www.singlebarrelsj.com; 43 W San Salvador St; ⊘5pm-midnight Sun & Tue, 5pm-1:30am Wed-Sat) A speakeasy-style lounge, where bartenders sheathed in tweed vests artfully mix custom cocktails ($12) tailored to customer's preferences, with some recipes dating back to before Prohibition. There's often a line out the door, but you'll be whisked downstairs as soon as they're ready to craft you a drink.

Caffe Frascati
CAFE

(www.caffefrascati.com; 315 S 1st St; ⊘7am-10pm Mon-Thu, to midnight Fri, 8am-midnight Sat, to 9pm Sun; 🛜) Photos of local theater folks line the walls at this high-ceilinged hangout a few doors down from the California Theatre. Linger over a cappuccino with a pastry or panini, and stop by for live music on Friday and Saturday nights. Opera performances rattle the cups the first Friday of each month.

Trials Pub
PUB

(www.trialspub.com; 265 N 1st St; ⊘from 5pm) If you seek a well-poured pint in a supremely comfortable atmosphere, Trials Pub, north of San Pedro Sq, has many excellent ales on tap (try a Fat Lip), all served in a warm and friendly room with no TVs. There's good pub food and a fireplace in the back room.

Hedley Club
LOUNGE

(www.hoteldeanza.com/hedley_club.asp; 233 W Santa Clara St) Inside the elegant 1931 Hotel De Anza, the Hedley Club is a good place for a quiet drink in swanky art-deco surroundings. Jazz combos play Thursday through Saturday night.

South First Billiards
BAR, POOL HALL

(www.facebook.com/420southfirst; 420 S 1st St; ⊘4pm-midnight Mon-Thu, 4pm-2am Fri & Sat) It's a great place to shoot some stick, and a welcoming club to boot. Check its Facebook page for live music and DJ nights.

☆ Entertainment

Live Music

Blank Club
LIVE MUSIC

(www.theblankclub.com; 44 S Almaden; ⊘Tue-Sat) A small club near the Greyhound station and off the main party streets. Live bands jam on a stage cascading with silver tinsel, and a glittering disco ball presides over fun retro dance parties.

Theaters

California Theatre
THEATER

(✓408-792-4111; www.sanjosetheaters.org/theaters/california-theatre; 345 S 1st St) The absolutely stunning Spanish interior of this landmark entertainment venue is cathedral-worthy. The theater is home to Opera San José, Symphony Silicon Valley, and is a venue for the city's annual film festival, Cinequest (www.cinequest.org), held in late February or early March.

Sports

SAP Center
STADIUM

(✓408-287-9200; www.sapcenteratsanjose.com; cnr Santa Clara & N Autumn Sts) Formerly the HP Pavilion, the fanatically popular San Jose Sharks, the city's NHL (National Hockey League) team, plays at this massive glass-

---

PSYCHO DONUTS? QU'EST QUE C'EST?

Who knew that a sugary confection with a hole could induce such devious giggles and fiendish delight? Saunter on over to **Psycho Donuts** (www.psycho-donuts.com; 288 S 2nd St; ⊘7am-10pm Mon-Thu, to midnight Fri, 8am-midnight Sat, to 10pm Sun; ✓), where counter staff dressed in saucy medical garb hand out bubble wrap to pop as patrons choose from twisted flavors such as Cereal Killer (topped with marshmallows and Cap'n Crunch breakfast cereal), Headbanger (death-metal visage oozing red jelly) and the tantalizing square S'mores (campfire not included).

and-metal stadium. The NHL season runs from September to April.

San Jose Earthquakes SOCCER
(www.sjearthquakes.com) San Jose's Major League Soccer team plays from February through October. Until 2015, when the Quakes' new stadium opens nearby just west of San Jose airport, catch the action at Santa Clara University's **Buck Shaw Stadium** (500 El Camino Real, Santa Clara).

ℹ️ Information

To find out what's happening and where, check out the free weekly *Metro* (www.metroactive. com) newspaper or the Friday 'eye' section of the daily *San Jose Mercury News* (www.mercurynews.com).

San Jose Convention & Visitors Bureau (☑ 800-726-5673, 408-295-9600; www. sanjose.org)

Santa Clara Valley Medical Center (☑ 408-885-5000; 751 S Bascom Ave; ⏱ 24hr)

ℹ️ Getting There & Away

AIR

Two miles north of downtown, between Hwy 101 and I-880, Mineta San José International Airport (p761) has free wi-fi and numerous domestic flights from two terminals.

BART

To access the BART system in the East Bay, **VTA** (☑ 408-321-2300; www.vta.org) bus 181 runs daily between the Fremont BART station and downtown ($4).

BUS

Greyhound buses to Los Angeles ($22 to $59, seven to 10 hours) leave from the **Greyhound station** (☑ 408-295-4151; www.greyhound.com; 70 Almaden Ave). The super-cheap new carrier **Megabus** (us.megabus.com) boasts electrical outlets and free wi-fi, with fares to Los Angeles averaging $10 to $40; departures from Diridon Station.

The VTA Hwy 17 Express bus (route 970) plies a handy daily route between Diridon Station and Santa Cruz ($5, one hour).

CAR & MOTORCYCLE

San Jose is right at the bottom end of the San Francisco Bay, about 40 miles from Oakland (via I-880) or San Francisco (via Hwy 101 or I-280). Expect lots of traffic at all times of the day on Hwy 101. Although I-280 is slightly longer, it's much prettier and usually less congested. Heading south, Hwy 17 leads over the hill to Santa Cruz.

Many downtown retailers offer two-hour parking validation, and on weekends until 6pm parking is free in city-owned lots and garages downtown. Check www.sjdowntownparking.com for details.

TRAIN

A double-decker commuter rail service that operates up and down the Peninsula between San Jose and San Francisco, **Caltrain** (☑ 800-660-4287; www.caltrain.com) makes more than three dozen trips daily (fewer on weekends); the 60-minute (on the Baby Bullet commuter trains) to 90-minute journey costs $9 each way and bicycles can be brought on designated cars. It's definitely your best bet, as traffic can be crazy any day of the week. San Jose's terminal, **Diridon Station** (off 65 Cahill St), is just south of the Alameda.

Diridon Station also serves as the terminal for **Amtrak** (☑ 408-287-7462; www.amtrak.com), serving Seattle, Los Angeles and Sacramento, and **Altamont Commuter Express** (www. acerail.com), which runs to Great America, Livermore and Stockton.

VTA runs a free weekday shuttle (known as the Downtown Area Shuttle or DASH) from the station to downtown.

ℹ️ Getting Around

VTA buses run all over Silicon Valley. From the airport, free VTA Airport Flyer shuttles (route 10) run every 10 to 15 minutes to the Metro/Airport Light Rail station, where you can catch the San Jose light rail to downtown San Jose. The route also goes to the Santa Clara Caltrain station. Fares for buses (except express lines) and light-rail trains are $2 for a single ride and $6 for a day pass.

The main San Jose light-rail line runs 20 miles north–south from the city center. Heading south gets you as far as Almaden and Santa Teresa. The northern route runs to the Civic Center, the airport and Tasman, where it connects with another line that heads west past Great America to downtown Mountain View.

San Francisco to Half Moon Bay

One of the real surprises of the Bay Area is how fast the urban landscape disappears along the rugged and largely undeveloped coast. The 70-mile stretch of coastal Hwy 1 from San Francisco to Santa Cruz is one of the most beautiful motorways anywhere. For the most part a winding two-lane blacktop, it passes small farmstands and beach after beach, many of them little sandy coves hidden from the highway. Most beaches along Hwy 1 are buffeted by wild and unpredictable surf, making them more suitable for sunbathing (weather permitting) than swimming. The state beaches along the coast don't charge an access fee, but parking can cost a few dollars.

A cluster of isolated and supremely scenic HI hostels, at Point Montara (22 miles south of San Francisco) and Pigeon Point (36 miles), make this an interesting route for cyclists, though narrow Hwy 1 itself can be stressful, if not downright dangerous, for the inexperienced.

Pacifica & Devil's Slide

Pacifica and Point San Pedro, 15 miles from downtown San Francisco, signal the end of the urban sprawl. South of Pacifica is Devil's Slide, a gorgeous coastal cliff area now bypassed by a car tunnel, though hikers and cyclists can sightsee on the adjacent Devil's Slide Coastal Trail, a paved 1.3-mile section of old Hwy 1.

In Pacifica, the main attractions are Rockaway Beach and the more popular Pacifica State Beach (also known as Linda Mar Beach; per car $3), where the nearby Nor-Cal Surf Shop (☑650-738-9283; 5440 Coast Hwy; ☺9am-6pm Sun-Fri, 8am-6pm Sat) rents surfboards ($19 per day) and wetsuits ($16.50).

Gray Whale Cove to Half Moon Bay

One of the coast's popular 'clothing-optional' beaches is Gray Whale Cove State Beach, just south of Point San Pedro. Park across the road and cross Hwy 1 to the beach *very* carefully. Montara State Beach is just a half-mile south. From the town of Montara, 22 miles from San Francisco, trails climb up from the Martini Creek parking lot into McNee Ranch, which has hiking and cycling trails aplenty, including a strenuous ascent to the panoramic viewpoint of Montara Mountain, and access to the new 4000-acre park of Ranch Corral de Tierra (www.nps.gov/goga/rcdt.htm).

Starting life as a fog station in 1875, the Point Montara Lighthouse Hostel (☑650-728-7177; www.norcalhostels.org/montara; cnr Hwy 1 & 16th St; dm $27, r $75; @🌐) 🍴 is adjacent to the current lighthouse, which dates from 1928. This very popular hostel has a living room, kitchen facilities and an international clientele. There are a few private rooms for couples or families. Reservations are a good idea, especially on weekends during summer. SamTrans bus 17 stops outside.

The Fitzgerald Marine Reserve (☑650-728-3584; www.fitzgeraldreserve.org; ♿), south of the lighthouse at Moss Beach, is an extensive area of natural tidal pools and a habitat for harbor seals. Walk out among the pools at low tide – wearing shoes that you can get wet – and explore the myriad crabs, sea stars, mollusks and rainbow-colored sea anemone. Note that it's illegal to remove any creatures, shells or even rocks from the marine reserve. From Hwy 1 in Moss Beach, turn west onto California Ave and drive to the end. SamTrans bus 17 stops along Hwy 1.

Overlooking the ocean, the Moss Beach Distillery (☑650-728-5595; www.mossbeach-distillery.com; cnr Beach Way & Ocean Blvd; mains $15-36; ☺noon-9pm Mon-Sat, from 11am Sun; ☎) is a 1927 landmark. In fair weather the restaurant's deck is the best place for miles around to have a leisurely cocktail or glass of vino. Reservations recommended.

South of here is a hamlet named Princeton, with a stretch of coast called Pillar Point. Fishing boats bring in their catch at the Pillar Point Harbor, some of which gets cooked up in a bevy of seafront restaurants. In the harbor, Half Moon Bay Kayak (☑650-773-6101; www.hmbkayak.com; ☺10am-4pm Wed-Mon) rents kayaks and offers guided trips of Pillar Point and the Fitzgerald Marine Reserve. Half Moon Bay Brewing Company (www.hmbbrewingco.com; 390 Capistrano Rd; mains $15-23; ☺11:30am-9pm Mon-Thu, to 10pm Fri, 9:30am-10pm Sat & Sun; ☎) 🍴 serves seafood, burgers and a tantalizing menu of local brews from a sheltered and heated outdoor patio looking out over the bay, complemented by live music on the weekends.

At the western end of Pillar Point is Mavericks, a serious surf break that attracts the world's top big-wave riders to battle its huge, steep and very dangerous waves. The annual Mavericks surf contest, called on a few days' notice when the swells get huge, is usually held between December and March.

Half Moon Bay

Developed as a beach resort back in the Victorian era, Half Moon Bay is the main coastal town between San Francisco (28 miles north) and Santa Cruz (40 miles south). Its long stretches of beach still attract rambling weekenders and hearty surfers. Half Moon Bay spreads out along Hwy 1 (called Cabrillo Hwy in town), but despite the development, it's

SCENIC DRIVE: HIGHWAY 84

Inland, large stretches of the hills are protected in a patchwork of parks that, just like the coast, remain relatively untouched despite the huge urban populations only a short drive to the north and east. Heading east toward Palo Alto, Hwy 84 winds its way through thick stands of redwood trees and several local parks with mountain biking and hiking opportunities.

A mile in from **San Gregorio State Beach** (per car $8) on Hwy 1, kick off your shoes and stomp your feet to live bluegrass, Celtic and folk music on the weekends at the landmark **San Gregorio General Store** (www.sangregoriostore.com), and check out the wooden bar singed by area branding irons.

Eight miles east is the tiny township of **La Honda**, former home to *One Flew Over the Cuckoo's Nest* author Ken Kesey, and the launching spot for his 1964 psychedelic bus trip immortalized in Tom Wolfe's *The Electric Kool-Aid Acid Test*. Housed in an old blacksmith's shop, **Apple Jack's** (☑ 650-747-0331) is a rustic, down-home bar with lots of local color.

To stretch your legs in the redwoods, **Sam McDonald Park** (☑ 650-879-0238; http:// parks.smcgov.org/sam-mcdonald-park; ⊘ parking $6), two miles south of La Honda on Pescadero Rd, has a number of worthy trails and a secluded **hike-to cabin** (http://lp.sierra-club.org/hikers_hut/hikers_hut.asp; ⊘ adult $25-30, child 2-10 $10) available for rent.

still relatively small. The main drag is a five-block stretch called Main St lined with shops, cafes, restaurants and a few upscale B&Bs. Visitor information is available from the **Half Moon Bay Coastside Visitors Bureau** (☑ 650-726-8380; www.halfmoonbaychamber.org).

Pumpkins are a major deal around Half Moon Bay, and the pre-Halloween harvest is celebrated in the annual **Art & Pumpkin Festival** (www.pumpkinfest.miramarevents.com). The mid-October event kicks off with the World Championship Pumpkin Weigh-Off, where the bulbous beasts can bust the scales at more than 1000lb.

Around 1 mile north of the Hwy 92 junction, **Sea Horse Ranch** (☑ 650-726-9903; www.seahorseranch.org) offers daily horseback rides along the beach. A two-hour ride is $75; an early-bird special leaves at 8am and costs just $50.

SamTrans (☑ 800-660-4287; www.samtrans.com) bus 294 operates from the Hillsdale Caltrain station in San Mateo to Half Moon Bay; bus 17 connects up the coast to Moss Beach and Pacifica and has very limited weekday service to Pescadero.

Half Moon Bay to Santa Cruz

With its long coastline, mild weather and abundant fresh water, this area has always been prime real estate. When Spanish missionaries set up shop along the California coast in the late 1700s, it had been Ohlone Native American territory for thousands of years. Pescadero was formally established in 1856, when it was mostly a farming and dairy settlement, although its location along the stagecoach route – now called Stage Rd – transformed it into a popular vacation destination. The Pigeon Point promontory was an active whaling station until 1900, when Prohibition-era bootleggers favored the isolated regional beaches for smuggling booze.

Pescadero

A foggy speck of coastside crossroads between the cities of San Francisco and Santa Cruz, 150-year-old Pescadero is a close-knit rural town of sugar-lending neighbors and community pancake breakfasts. But on weekends the tiny downtown strains its seams with long-distance cyclists panting for carbohydrates and day trippers dive-bombing in from the ocean-front highway. They're all drawn to the winter vistas of emerald-green hills parched to burlap brown in summer, the wild Pacific beaches populated by seals and pelicans, and the food at a revered destination restaurant. With its cornucopia of tide-pool coves and parks of sky-blotting redwood canopy, city dwellers come here to slow down and smell the sea breeze wafting over fields of bushy artichokes.

◉ Sights & Activities

A number of pretty sand beaches speckle the coast, though one of the most interesting places to stop is **Pebble Beach**, a tide-pool jewel a mile and a half south of Pescadero Creek Rd (and part of Bean Hollow State Beach). As the name implies, the shore is awash in bite-sized eye candy of agate, jade and carnelians, and sandstone troughs are pockmarked by groovy honeycombed formations called tafoni. Bird-watchers enjoy **Pescadero Marsh Reserve**, across the highway from Pescadero State Beach, where numerous species feed year-round.

★ **Pigeon Point Light Station**   LIGHTHOUSE
(☑650-879-2120;   www.parks.ca.gov/?page_id=533) Five miles south along the coast, the 115ft Light Station is one of the tallest lighthouses on the West Coast. The 1872 landmark had to close access to the upper tower when chunks of its cornice began to rain from the sky (restoration is in progress), but the beam still flashes brightly and the bluff is a prime though blustery spot to scan for breaching gray whales. The hostel here is one of the best in the state.

Butano State Park   PARK
(☑650-879-2040; per car $10, camping $35 Apr-Nov) About 5 miles south of Pescadero, bobcats and full-throated coyotes reside discreetly in 2800 acres of dense redwood canyon. From Hwy 1, take Gazos Creek Rd.

🛏 Sleeping & Eating

★ **HI Pigeon Point Lighthouse Hostel**   HOSTEL $
(☑650-879-0633;   www.norcalhostels.org/pigeon; 210 Pigeon Point Rd; dm $26-27, r/t/6-bed $75/101/162, all with shared bath; @🤖) 🅿 Not your workaday HI outpost, this highly coveted coastside hostel is all about location. Check in early to snag a spot in the outdoor hot tub, and contemplate roaring waves as the lighthouse beacon races through a starburst sky.

Costanoa   CABIN, CAMPGROUND $$
(☑877-262-7848, 650-879-1100; www.costanoa.com; 2001 Rossi Rd; tent/cabin with shared bath from $89/179, lodge r $203-291; 🤖) Even though the resort includes a **campground** (☑800-562-9867; www.koa.com/campgrounds/santacruz-north; tent site $30-34, RV site from $69; 🤖🐾), no one can pull a straight face to declare they're actually roughing it here. Down bedding swaddles guests in cushy canvas tent cabins, and chill-averse tent campers can use communal 'comfort stations' with 24-hour dry saunas, fireside patio seating, heated floors and hot showers.

Lodge rooms with private fireplaces and hot tub access fulfill the whims of those without such spartan delusions. There's a **restaurant** (dinner mains $17 to $36) and spa on site; bicycle rentals and horseback riding are available as well.

Pescadero Creek Inn B&B   INN $$
(☑888-307-1898;   www.pescaderocreekinn.com; 393 Stage Rd; r $155-225; 🤖) 🅿 Unwind in the private two-room cottage or one of the spotless Victorian rooms in a restored 100-year-old farmhouse with a tranquil creekside garden.

★ **Duarte's Tavern**   AMERICAN $$
(☑650-879-0464; www.duartestavern.com; 202 Stage Rd; mains $11-45; ⊙7am-9pm) You'll rub shoulders with fancy-pants foodies, spandex-swathed cyclists and dusty cowboys at this casual, surprisingly unpretentious fourth-generation family restaurant. Duarte's is the culinary magnet of Pescadero – for many the town and eatery are synonymous. Feast on crab cioppino and a half-and-half split of the cream of artichoke and green chili soups, and bring it home with a wedge of olallieberry pie.

Except for the unfortunate lull of Prohibition, the wood-paneled bar has been hosting the locals and their honored guests since 1894. Reservations recommended.

ℹ Getting There & Away

By car, the town is 3 miles east from Hwy 1 on Pescadero Creek Rd, south of San Gregorio State Beach. On weekdays, **SamTrans** (www.samtrans.com) bus 17 runs once a day to/from Half Moon Bay.

Año Nuevo State Reserve

More raucous than a full-moon beach rave, thousands of boisterous elephant seals party down year-round on the dunes of Año Nuevo point, their squeals and barks reaching fever pitch during the winter pupping season. The beach is 5 miles south of Pigeon Point and 27 miles north of Santa Cruz.

Elephant seals were just as fearless two centuries ago as they are today, but unfortunately, club-toting seal trappers were not in the same seal-friendly category as camera-toting tourists. Between 1800 and

THE CULINARY COAST

Pescadero is renowned for Duarte's Tavern, but loads of other tidbits are very close by.

Arcangeli Grocery/Norm's Market (Norm's Market; www.normsmarket.com; 287 Stage Rd, Pescadero; sandwiches $6.50-8.75; ◷10am-6pm Mon-Thu, 9am-6pm Sat & Sun) Create a picnic with made-to-order deli sandwiches, homemade artichoke salsa and a chilled bottle of California wine. And don't go breezing out the door without nabbing a crusty loaf of the famous artichoke garlic herb bread, fresh-baked almost hourly.

Harley Farms Cheese Shop (☑650-879-0480; www.harleyfarms.com; 250 North St, Pescadero; ◷10am-5pm Wed-Sun; ♠) Follow the cool wooden cut-outs of the goat and the Wellington-shod girl with the faraway eyes. Another local food treasure with creamy artisanal goat cheeses festooned with fruit, nuts and a rainbow of edible flowers. Weekend farm tours by reservation, and a new shop selling goat-milk body products and non-toxic paint. Splurge for a seat at one of the monthly five-course farm dinners in the restored barn's airy hayloft.

Pie Ranch (www.pieranch.org; 2080 Cabrillo Hwy, Pescadero; ◷noon-6pm Thu & Fri, 10am-6pm Sat & Sun; ♠) ✿ Hit the brakes for this roadside farmstand in a wooden barn, and pick up fresh produce, eggs and coffee, plus amazing pies made with the fruit grown here. The historic pie-slice-shaped farm is a nonprofit dedicated to leadership development and food education for urban youth. Check the website for details on its monthly farm tours and barn dances. Located 11 miles south of Pescadero Creek Rd.

Swanton Berry Farm (☑650-469-8804; www.swantonberryfarm.com; Coastways Ranch, 640 Cabrillo Hwy, Pescadero; ◷10am-4pm Fri-Sun) To get a better appreciation of the rigors and rewards of farm life, smoosh up your shirtsleeves and harvest some fruit at this organic pick-your-own farm near Año Nuevo. It's a union outfit (operated by Cesar Chavez's United Farm Workers), with buckets of seasonal kiwis and olallieberries ripe for the plucking. Its **farm stand and strawberry u-pick** (◷8am-5pm) is 8.5 miles further south near Davenport.

Bonnie Doon Vineyard (☑831-471-8031; www.bonnydoonvineyard.com; 450 Hwy 1, Davenport; ◷11am-5pm Thu-Mon) Round out your palate with a flight ($10 to $20) at the new roadside tasting room of Randall Grahm's acclaimed winery, where Edison lights and rough-hewed wooden tables entice you to sample a Cigare Volant (yes, that's a flying cigar) and other bottles made with lesser-known varietals.

1850, the elephant seal was driven to the edge of extinction. Only a handful survived around the Guadalupe Islands off the Mexican state of Baja California. With the availability of substitutes for seal oil and the conservationist attitudes of more recent times, the elephant seal has made a comeback, reappearing on the Southern California coast from around 1920. In 1955 they returned to Año Nuevo Beach.

In the midwinter peak season, during the mating and birthing time from December 15 to the end of March, you must plan well ahead if you want to visit the reserve, because visitors are only permitted access through heavily booked guided tours. For the busiest period, mid-January to mid-February, it's recommended you book eight weeks ahead. If you haven't booked, bad weather can sometimes lead to last-minute cancellations.

The rest of the year, advance reservations aren't necessary, but visitor permits from the entrance station are required; arrive before 3pm from September through November and by 3:30pm from April through August.

Although the **park office** (☑650-879-2025, recorded information 650-879-0227; www.parks.ca.gov/?page_id=523) can answer general questions, high-season tour bookings must be made at ☑800-444-4445 or http://anonuevo.reserveamerica.com. When required, these tours cost $7, and entry is $10 per car year-round. From the ranger station it's a 3- to 5-mile round-trip hike on sand, and a visit takes two to three hours. No dogs are allowed on-site, and visitors aren't permitted for the first two weeks of December.

There's another, more convenient viewing site further south in Piedras Blancas.

Napa & Sonoma Wine Country

Includes ➡

Why Go?

America's premier viticulture region has earned its reputation among the world's best. Despite hype about Wine Country style, it's from the land that all Wine Country lore springs. Rolling hills, dotted with century-old oaks, turn the color of lion's fur under the summer sun and swaths of vineyards carpet hillsides as far as the eye can see. Where they end, lush redwood forests follow serpentine rivers to the sea.

There are over 600 wineries in Napa and Sonoma Counties, but it's quality, not quantity, that sets the region apart – especially in Napa, which competes with France and doubles as an outpost of San Francisco's top-end culinary scene. Sonoma prides itself on agricultural diversity, with goat-cheese farms, you-pick-'em orchards and roadside fruit stands. Plan to get lost on back roads, and, as you picnic atop sun-dappled hillsides, grab a hunk of earth and know firsthand the thing of greatest meaning in Wine Country.

Best Places to Eat

➡ The Shed (p214)

➡ Oxbow Public Market (p171)

➡ Fremont Diner (p193)

➡ Madrona Manor (p215)

Best Places to Stay

➡ Beltane Ranch (p196)

➡ Cottages of Napa Valley (p170)

➡ Mountain Home Ranch (p183)

➡ El Bonita (p177)

When to Go

Napa

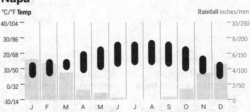

| **Jan** Bright-yellow flowers carpet the valleys during the off-season; room rates plummet. | **Apr–May** Before summer holidays is perfect for touring, with long days and warm sun. | **Sep–Oct** 'Crush' time is peak season, when wine-making operations are in full force. |

ℹ Getting There & Away

Napa and Sonoma counties each have an eponymous city and valley. So, the town of Sonoma is in Sonoma County, at the southern end of Sonoma Valley. The same goes for the city, county and valley of Napa.

From San Francisco, public transportation gets you to the valleys, but it's insufficient for vineyard-hopping. For public-transit information, ☑ dial 511 from Bay Area telephones, or look online at www.transit.511.org.

Both valleys are 90 minutes' drive from San Francisco. Napa, the further inland, has over 400 wineries and attracts the most visitors (expect heavy traffic on summer weekends). Sonoma County has 260 wineries, 40 in Sonoma Valley, which is less commercial and less congested than Napa. If you have time to visit only one, for ease choose Sonoma.

Napa & Sonoma Wine Country Highlights

❶ Sample California's greatest red wines in **Napa Valley** (p164).

❷ Picnic in sun-dappled shade on the state's largest town square, **Sonoma Plaza** (p190).

❸ Bite into the artisanal food scene at Napa's **Oxbow Public Market** (p171).

❹ Get lost on West County Sonoma back roads, like **Coleman Valley Road** (p204).

❺ Submerge yourself in a volcanic-ash mud bath in **Calistoga** (p181).

❻ Meet kooky locals at the **Occidental Farmers Market** (p204).

❼ Pedal between wineries along pastoral **West Dry Creek Road** (p200), in the Dry Creek Valley.

❽ Float in a canoe or kayak down the **Russian River** (p197).

BUS

Evans Transportation (☎707-255-1559; www.evanstransportation.com) Shuttles ($29) to Napa from San Francisco and Oakland Airports.

Golden Gate Transit (☎415-923-2000; www.goldengate.org) Bus 70/80 from San Francisco to Petaluma ($10.25) and Santa Rosa ($11.25); board at 1st and Mission Sts. Connects with Sonoma County Transit buses.

Greyhound Buses (☎800-231-2222; www.greyhound.com) San Francisco to Santa Rosa ($22 to $30); transfer to local buses.

Napa Valley Vine (☎707-251-2800, 800-696-6443; www.nctpa.net) Operates local bus 10 daily from downtown Napa to Calistoga ($1.50); express bus 29 Monday to Friday from the Vallejo Ferry Terminal ($3.25) and El Cerrito del Norte BART station ($5.50), via Napa, to Calistoga; and local bus 11 daily from the Vallejo Ferry Terminal to downtown Napa ($1.50).

Sonoma County Airport Express (☎800-327-2024, 707-837-8700; www.airportexpressinc.com) Shuttles ($34) between Sonoma County Airport (Santa Rosa) and San Francisco and Oakland Airports.

CAR

From San Francisco, take Hwy 101 north over the Golden Gate Bridge, then Hwy 37 east to Hwy 121 north; continue to the junction of Hwy 12/121. For Sonoma Valley, take Hwy 12 north; for Napa Valley, take Hwy 12/121 east. Plan 70 minutes in light traffic, two hours during the weekday commute.

Hwy 12/121 splits south of Napa: Hwy 121 turns north and joins with Hwy 29 (aka St Helena Hwy); Hwy 12 merges with southbound Hwy 29 toward Vallejo. Hwy 29 backs up weekdays 3pm to 7pm, slowing returns to San Francisco.

From the East Bay (or downtown San Francisco), take I-80 east to Hwy 37 west (north of Vallejo), then northbound Hwy 29.

From Santa Rosa, take Hwy 12 east to access the northern end of Sonoma Valley. From Petaluma and Hwy 101, take Hwy 116 east.

FERRY

Baylink Ferry (☎877-643-3779; sanfranciscobayferry.com) Downtown San Francisco to Vallejo (adult/child $13/6.50, 60 minutes); connect with Napa Valley Vine bus 29 (weekdays) or bus 11 (daily).

TRAIN

Amtrak (☎800-872-7245; www.amtrak.com) Trains travel to Martinez (south of Vallejo), with connecting buses to Napa (45 minutes), Santa Rosa (1¼ hours) and Healdsburg (1¾ hours).

BART trains (☎415 989-2278; www.bart.gov) Run from San Francisco to El Cerrito del Norte ($4.40, 30 minutes). Napa Valley Vine bus 29 runs weekdays from BART to Calistoga, via Napa; on Saturdays take **SolTrans** (☎707-648-4666; www.soltransride.com) from BART to Vallejo ($5, 30 minutes), then connect with Napa Valley Vine bus 11 to Napa and Calistoga; on Sundays there's no connecting bus service from BART.

❶ Getting Around

You'll need a car or bike to winery-hop. Alternatively visit tasting rooms in downtown Napa or downtown Sonoma.

BICYCLE

Touring Wine Country by bicycle is unforgettable. Stick to back roads. We most love pastoral West Dry Creek Rd, northwest of Healdsburg, in Sonoma County. Through Sonoma Valley, take Arnold Dr instead of Hwy 12; through Napa Valley, take the Silverado Trail instead of Hwy 29.

Cycling between wineries isn't demanding – the valleys are mostly flat – but crossing between the Napa and Sonoma Valleys is intense, particularly via steep Oakville Grade and Trinity Rd (between Oakville and Glen Ellen).

Bicycles, in boxes, can be checked on Greyhound buses for $30 to $40; bike boxes cost $10 (call ahead). You can transport bicycles on Golden Gate Transit buses, which usually have free racks available (first-come, first-served).

CAR

Napa Valley is 30 miles long and 5 miles across at its widest point (city of Napa), 1 mile at its narrowest (Calistoga). Two roads run north–south: Hwy 29 (St Helena Hwy) and the more scenic Silverado Trail, a mile east. Drive up one, down the other.

The American Automobile Association ranks Napa Valley among America's most congested rural vacation destinations. Summer and fall weekend traffic is unbearable, especially on Hwy 29 between Napa and St Helena. Plan accordingly.

Cross-valley roads linking Silverado Trail with Hwy 29 – including Yountville, Oakville and Rutherford crossroads – are bucolic and get less traffic. For scenery, the Oakville Grade and rural Trinity Rd (which leads southwest to Hwy 12 in Sonoma Valley) are narrow, curvy and beautiful – but treacherous in rainstorms. Mt Veeder Rd leads through pristine countryside west of Yountville.

Note: Police watch like hawks for traffic violators. *Don't drink and drive.*

There are a number of shortcuts between the Napa and Sonoma Valleys: from Oakville, take Oakville Grade to Trinity Rd; from St Helena, take Spring Mountain Rd into Calistoga Rd; from Calistoga, take Petrified Forest Rd to Calistoga Rd.

PUBLIC TRANSPORTATION

Napa Valley Vine (☑707-251-2800, 800-696-6443; www.nctpa.net) Bus 10 runs daily from downtown Napa to Calistoga ($1.50, 1¼ hours).

Sonoma County Transit (☑800-345-7433, 707-576-7433; www.sctransit.com) Buses from Santa Rosa to Petaluma ($2.45, 70 minutes), Sonoma ($3.05, 1¼ hours) and western Sonoma County, including Russian River Valley towns ($3.05, 30 minutes).

NAPA VALLEY

The birthplace of modern-day Wine Country is famous for regal Cabernet Sauvignons, château-like wineries and fabulous food, attracting more than four million visitors a year, many planning to wine and dine themselves into a stupor, maybe get a massage, and sleep somewhere swell with fine linens and a pool.

A few decades ago, this 5-by-35-mile strip of former stagecoach stops seemed forgotten by time, a quiet agricultural valley dense with orchards. Grapes had grown here since the Gold Rush, but grape-sucking phylloxera bugs, Prohibition and the Great Depression reduced 140 wineries in the 1890s, to around 25 by the 1960s.

In 1968, Napa was declared the 'Napa Valley Agricultural Preserve,' effectively blocking future valley development for non-ag purposes. The law stipulated no subdivision of valley-floor land under 40 acres. This succeeded in preserving the valley's natural beauty, but when Napa wines earned top honors at a 1976 blind tasting in Paris, the wine-drinking world noticed and land values skyrocketed. Only the very rich could afford to build. Hence, so many architecturally jaw-dropping wineries. Independent, family-owned wineries still exist – we highlight a number of them – but much of Napa Valley is now owned by global conglomerates.

The city of Napa anchors the valley, but the real work happens up-valley. Napa isn't as pretty as other towns, but has some noteworthy sights, among them Oxbow Public Market. Scenic towns include St Helena, Yountville and Calistoga – the latter more famous for water than wine.

Napa Valley Wineries

Cab is king in Napa. No varietal captures imaginations like the fruit of the Cabernet Sauvignon vine – Bordeaux is the French equivalent – and no wine fetches a higher price. Napa farmers can't afford *not* to grow Cabernet. Other heat-loving varietals, such as Sangiovese and Merlot, also thrive here.

Napa's wines merit their reputation among the world's finest – complex, with luxurious finishes. Napa wineries sell many 'buy-and-hold' wines, versus Sonoma's 'drink-now' wines.

Artesa Vineyards & Winery   WINERY
(☑707-254-2126; www.artesawinery.com; 1345 Henry Rd, Napa; glass $12, tasting $15-20, incl tour $30; ☉10am-4:30pm) Begin or end the day with a glass of bubbly or Pinot at Artesa, southwest of Napa. Built into a mountainside, the ultra-modern Barcelona-style architecture is stunning, and you can't beat the top-of-the-world vistas over San Pablo Bay. Tours run at 11am and 2pm. Bottles cost $20 to $60.

Vintners' Collective   TASTING ROOM
(Map p169; ☑707-255-7150; www.vintnerscollective.com; 1245 Main St, Napa; tasting $10-30; ☉11am-6pm) Ditch the car and chill in downtown Napa at this tasting bar, inside a former 19th-century brothel, representing 20 high-end boutique wineries too small to have their own tasting rooms.

Twenty Rows   WINERY
(☑707-265-7750; www.twentyrows.com; 880 Vallejo St, Napa; tasting $10; ☉11am-5pm Tue-Sat, by appointment Sun & Mon) Downtown Napa's only working winery crafts light-on-the-palate Cabernet Sauvignon for just $20 a bottle. Taste in a chilly garage, on plastic furniture, with fun dudes who know their wines. Good Sauvignon Blanc, too.

★**Hess Collection**   WINERY, GALLERY
(☑707-255-1144; www.hesscollection.com; 4411 Redwood Rd, Napa; tasting $15, gallery free; ☉10am-5:30pm) 🖉 Art lovers: don't miss **Hess Collection**, whose galleries display mixed-media and large-canvas works, including pieces by Francis Bacon and Louis Soutter. In the cave-like tasting room, find well-known Cabernet and Chardonnay, but also try the Viognier. Hess overlooks the valley: be prepared to drive a winding road. Reservations recommended. Bottles: $20 to $60. (NB: Don't confuse Hess Collection with Hess Select, the grocery-store brand.)

Darioush   WINERY
(☑707-257-2345; www.darioush.com; 4240 Silverado Trail, Napa; tasting $18-40; ☉10:30am-5pm)

TOURING NAPA & SONOMA WINE COUNTRY

You have the most flexibility by driving your own vehicle, but to drink and not drive, here are some tour options. Note that some wineries do not allow limousines (because the people in them are often obnoxious and don't buy anything); and limousine companies have set itineraries with little flexibility (ie, you'll have few choices about which wineries you visit).

Bicycle Tours & Rentals

Guided tours start around $90 per day including bikes, tastings and lunch. Daily rentals cost $25 to $85; make reservations.

Backroads (☎800-462-2848; www.backroads.com) All-inclusive guided biking and walking.

Calistoga Bike Shop (☎707-942-9687; www.calistogabikeshop.com; 1318 Lincoln Ave, Calistoga; ☺10am-6pm) Wine-tour rental package ($90) includes wine pickup.

Getaway Adventures (☎800-499-2453, 707-568-3040; http://getawayadventures.com; tours $149) Great guided tours, some combined with kayaking, of Napa, Sonoma, Calistoga, Healdsburg and Russian River. Single- and multiday trips.

Good Time Touring (☎888-525-0453, 707-938-0453; www.goodtimetouring.com) Tours of Sonoma Valley, Dry Creek and West County Sonoma.

Napa River Velo (Map p169; ☎707-258-8729; www.naparivervelo.com; 680 Main St, Napa; ☺10am-7pm Mon-Fri, 9am-6pm Sat, 10am-5pm Sun) Daily rentals and weekend tours with wine pickup.

Napa Valley Adventure Tours (☎707-224-9080, 707-259-1833; www.napavalleyadventuretours.com; 1147 1st St, Napa) Guides tours between wineries, off-road trips, hiking and kayaking. Daily rentals.

Napa Valley Bike Tours (☎707-944-2953; www.napavalleybiketours.com; 6500 Washington St, Yountville; ☺8:30am-5pm) Daily rentals; easy and moderately difficult tours.

Spoke Folk Cyclery (☎707-433-7171; www.spokefolk.com; 201 Center St, Healdsburg; ☺10am-6pm Mon-Fri, to 5pm Sat & Sun) Rents touring, racing and tandem bicycles.

Wine Country Bikes (☎707-473-0610, toll free 866-922-4537; www.winecountrybikes.com; 61 Front St, Healdsburg; rentals per day from $39, multiday guided tours from $595; ☺9am-5pm) Rents bikes in downtown Healdsburg and guides multiday Sonoma County tours.

Other Tours

Wine Country Jeep Tours (☎800-539-5337, 707-546-1822; www.jeeptours.com; 3hr tour $75) Tour Wine Country's back roads and boutique wineries by Jeep, year-round at 10am and 1pm. Also operates tours of Sonoma Coast.

Antique Tours Limousine (☎707-761-3949; www.antiquetours.net) Drive in style in a 1947 Packard convertible; tours cost $120 to $170 per hour.

Beau Wine Tours (☎800-387-2328, 707-938-8001; www.beauwinetours.com) Winery tours in sedans and stretch limos; charges $60 to $95 per hour (four- to six-hour minimum).

Beyond the Label (☎707-363-4023; www.btlnv.com; per couple $995) Personalized tours, including lunch at home with a vintner, guided by a Napa native.

Flying Horse Carriage Company (☎707-849-8989; www.flyinghorse.org; 4hr tour per person $150; ☺Fri-Mon) Trot through Alexander Valley by horse-drawn carriage. Includes picnic.

Magnum Tours (☎707-753-0088; www.magnumwinetours.com) Sedans and specialty limousines from $65 to $125 per hour (four-hour minimum, five hours Saturdays). Exceptional service.

Like a modern-day Persian palace, Darioush ranks high on the fabulosity scale, with towering columns, Le Corbusier furniture, Persian rugs and travertine walls. Though known for Cabernet, Darioush also bottles Chardonnay, Merlot and Shiraz, all made with 100% of their respective varietals. Call about wine-and-cheese pairings. Bottles cost $40 to $95.

Regusci
WINERY

(☎707-254-0403; www.regusciwinery.com; 5584 Silverado Trail, Napa; tasting $25-30, incl tour $30-60; ⊙10am-5pm) One of Napa's oldest, unfussy Regusci dates to the late 1800s, with 173 acres of vineyards unfurling around a century-old stone winery that makes Bordeaux-style blends on the valley's quieter eastern side – good when traffic up-valley is bad. No appointment necessary; lovely oak-shaded picnic area. Bottles cost $36 to $140.

★ Robert Sinskey
WINERY

(☎707-944-9090; www.robertsinskey.com; 6320 Silverado Trail, Napa; tasting $25, incl tour $50-75; ⊙10am-4:30pm) 🍴 Chef-owned Robert Sinskey's dramatic hilltop tasting room, constructed of stone, redwood and teak, resembles a small cathedral – fitting, given the sacred status bestowed upon food and wine here. Sinskey specializes in bright-acid organic Pinot, Merlot and Cabernet, and exceptional Alsatian varietals, Vin Gris, Cabernet Franc and dry Rosé, specifically designed to pair well with food. Tasting fee waived with two-bottle purchase – a rarity. Small bites accompany tastings. Call about culinary tours. Bottles cost $28 to $100.

Robert Mondavi
WINERY

(☎888-766-6328; www.robertmondaviwinery.com; 7801 Hwy 29, Oakville; tasting & tour $20-55; ⊙10am-5pm; 🚻) Tour buses flock to this corporate-owned winery, but if you know nothing about wine and can cope with crowds, the worthwhile tours provide excellent insight into winemaking. Otherwise, skip it unless you're considering one of its glorious outdoor summer **concerts**; call for schedules. Bottles cost $25 to $150.

Elizabeth Spencer
TASTING ROOM

(☎707-963-6067; www.elizabethspencerwines.com; 1165 Rutherford Rd, Rutherford; tasting $20; ⊙10am-5:30pm) Taste inside an 1872 railroad depot or the outdoor garden at this inviting small winery, featuring monster-sized Pinot Noir, grapefruity Sauvignon Blanc, structured light-body Grenache, and signature Cabernet. Bottles cost $30 to $95.

Mumm Napa
WINERY, GALLERY

(☎800-686-6272; www.mummnapa.com; 8445 Silverado Trail, Rutherford; glass $8; tasting $18-40, tour $25; ⊙10am-4:45pm) Valley views are spectacular at Mumm, which makes respectable sparkling wines you can sample while seated on a vineyard-view terrace – ideal when you want to impress conservative parents-in-law. Dodge crowds by coming early, or paying $40 for the reserve-tasting Oak Terrace (reservations advised).

★ Frog's Leap
WINERY

(☎707-963-4704; www.frogsleap.com; 8815 Conn Creek Rd, Rutherford; tasting $15, incl tour $20; ⊙by appointment; 🚻 🌞) 🍴 Meandering paths wind through magical gardens and

---

NAPA OR SONOMA?

Napa and Sonoma Valleys run parallel, separated by the narrow, imposing Mayacamas Mountains. The two couldn't be more different. It's easy to mock aggressively sophisticated Napa, its monuments to ego, trophy homes and trophy wives, $1000-a-night inns, $50-plus tastings and wine-snob visitors, but Napa makes some of the world's best wines. Constrained by its geography, it stretches along a single valley, making it easy to visit. Drawbacks are high prices and heavy traffic, but there are 400 nearly side-by-side wineries. And the valley is gorgeous.

There are three Sonomas: the town of Sonoma, which is in Sonoma Valley, which is in Sonoma County. Think of them as Russian dolls. Sonoma County is much more down-to-earth and politically left-leaning. Though it's becoming gentrified, Sonoma lacks Napa's chic factor (Healdsburg notwithstanding), and locals like it that way. The wines are more approachable, but the county's 260 wineries are spread out. If you're here on a weekend, head to Sonoma (County or Valley), which gets less traffic, but on a weekday, see Napa, too. Ideally schedule two to four days: one for each valley, and one or two additional for western Sonoma County.

Spring and fall are the best times to visit. Summers are hot, dusty and crowded. Fall brings fine weather, harvest time and the 'crush,' the pressing of the grapes, but lodging prices skyrocket.

fruit-bearing orchards – pick peaches in July – surrounding an 1884 barn and farmstead with cats and chickens. The vibe is casual and down-to-earth, with a major emphasis on *fun*. Sauvignon Blanc is its best-known wine, but the Merlot merits attention. There's also a dry, restrained Cabernet, atypical of Napa.

All are organic. Appointments required. Bottles cost $22 to $42.

★ **Tres Sabores** WINERY
(☎707-967-8027; www.tressabores.com; 1620 South Whitehall Lane, St Helena; tour & tasting $20; ⊙by appointment; ☎) ✦ At the valley's westernmost edge, where sloping vineyards meet wooded hillsides, Tres Sabores is a portal to old Napa – no fancy tasting room, no snobbery, just great wine in a spectacular setting. Bucking the Cabernet custom, Tres Sabores crafts elegantly structured, Burgundian-style Zinfandel, and spritely Sauvignon Blanc, which the *New York Times* dubbed a top 10 of its kind in California. Reservations essential.

Guinea fowl and sheep control pests on the 35-acre estate, while golden labs chase butterflies through gnarled old vines. After your tour, linger at olive-shaded picnic tables and drink in gorgeous valley views. Bottles cost $22 to $80.

Hall WINERY
(Map p178; ☎707-967-2626; www.hallwines.com; 401 St Helena Hwy, St Helena; tasting $30, tour $50; ⊙10am-5:30pm; ☎) Owned by Bill Clinton's former ambassador to Austria, Hall specializes in Sauvignon Blanc, Merlot and Cabernet Sauvignon, crafted in big-fruit California style. Its dramatic tasting room has a stand-up bar with 180-degree views of vineyards and mountains through floor-to-ceiling glass, and the glorious art collection includes a giant chrome rabbit leaping over the vines. Bottles cost $22 to $80.

Long Meadow Ranch TASTING ROOM
(Map p178; ☎707-963-4555; www.longmeadowranch.com; 738 Main St, St Helena; tasting $15-25; ⊙11am-6pm) ✦ Long Meadow stands out for olive-oil tastings (free), plus good estate-grown Cabernet, Sauvignon Blanc, Chardonnay and Pinot noir (bottles $20 to $47), served inside an 1874 farmhouse surrounded by lovely gardens.

Pride Mountain WINERY
(Map p178; ☎707-963-4949; www.pridewines.com; 3000 Summit Trail, St Helena; tasting incl tour

ⓘ **BOOKING APPOINTMENTS AT WINERIES**

Because of strict county zoning laws, many Napa wineries cannot legally receive drop-in visitors; unless you've come strictly to buy, you'll have to call ahead. This is *not* the case with all wineries. We recommend booking one appointment, plus a lunch or dinner reservation, and planning your day around them.

$20-25; ⊙by appointment) High atop Spring Mountain, cult-favorite Pride straddles the Napa–Sonoma border and bottles vintages under both appellations. The well-structured Cabernet and heavy-hitting Merlot are the best-known but there's also an elegant Viognier (perfect with oysters) and standout Cab Franc, available only here. Picnicking here is spectacular: choose Viewpoint for drop-dead vistas or Ghost Winery for shade and the historic ruins of a 19th-century winery, but you must first reserve a tasting. Bottles cost $38 to $70.

Titus WINERY
(Map p178; ☎707-963-3235; www.titusvineyards.com; 2971 Silverado Trail North, St Helena; tasting $20; ⊙by appointment; ☎☎) Unfussy Titus occupies a tiny oak-shaded 1910 farmhouse, surrounded by white-picket fence and roses. Call ahead to sample good-value, fruit-forward Cabernet Sauvignon and old-vine Zinfandel, which you taste in an old-fashioned kitchen overlooking the vineyards. Afterward, take your glass outside and wander the vineyards. The tasting fee is waived with a purchase and bottles are $20 to $70.

Casa Nuestra WINERY
(Map p178; ☎866-844-9463; www.casanuestra.com; 3451 Silverado Trail North, St Helena; tasting $10; ⊙by appointment) ✦ A peace flag and portrait of Elvis greet you at this old-school, mom-and-pop winery, which produces unusual blends and interesting varietals (including good Chenin Blanc) and 100% Cabernet Franc. Vineyards are all-organic; the sun provides power. Picnic free (call ahead and buy a bottle) beneath weeping willows shading happy goats. Bottles are $20 to $60.

Cade WINERY
(Map p178; ☎707-965-2746; www.cadewinery.com; 360 Howell Mountain Rd S, Angwin; tasting $40-70; ⊙by appointment) ✦ Ascend Mt Veeder for

NAPA & SONOMA WINE COUNTRY NAPA VALLEY WINERIES

drop-dead vistas, 1800ft above the valley, at Napa's oh-so-swank, first-ever organically farmed, LEED-gold-certified winery, partly owned by former San Francisco mayor Gavin Newsom. Hawks ride thermals at eye level as you sample bright Sauvignon Blanc and luscious Cabernet Sauvignon that's more Bordelaise in style than Californian. Reservations required. Bottles cost $44 to $80.

Ladera WINERY
(Map p178; ☎ 707-965-2445, 866-523-3728; www.laderavineyards.com; 150 White Cottage Rd S, Angwin; tasting $25; ☺ by appointment) 🖉 High atop Howell Mountain, Ladera makes wonderful, little-known, estate-grown Cabernet Sauvignon and Sauvignon Blanc in a well-off-the-beaten-path, 1886, stone-walled winery, one of Napa's oldest – ideal when you want to escape the crowds. Bottle are $28 to $85.

Schramsberg WINERY
(Map p178; ☎ 707-942-2414; www.schramsberg.com; 1400 Schramsberg Rd, off Peterson Dr; tour & tasting $50; ☺ by appointment 10am, 11:30am, 12:30pm, 1:30pm & 2:30pm) Napa's second-oldest winery, Schramsberg makes some of California's best brut sparkling wines, and in 1972 was the first domestic wine served at the White House. Blanc de Blancs is the signature. The appointment-only tasting and tour (book well ahead) is expensive, but you'll sample all the *tête de cuvées*, not just the low-end wines. Tours include a walk through the caves; bring a sweater. Bottles cost $22 to $100.

Castello di Amorosa WINERY, CASTLE
(Map p178; ☎ 707-967-6272; www.castellodiamorosa.com; 4045 Hwy 29, Calistoga; admission & tasting $19-29, incl guided tour $34-75; ☺ 9:30am-6pm, to 5pm Nov-Feb) It took 14 years to build this perfectly replicated, 12th-century Italian castle, complete with moat, hand-cut stone walls, ceiling frescoes by Italian artisans, Roman-style cross-vault brick catacombs, and a torture chamber with period equipment. You can taste without an appointment, but this is one tour worth taking. Oh, the wine? Some respectable Italian varietals, including a velvety Tuscan blend, and a Merlot blend that goes great with pizza. Bottles are $20 to $125.

Lava Vine WINERY
(Map p178; ☎ 707-942-9500; www.lavavine.com; 965 Silverado Trail; tasting $10; ☺ 10am-5pm; 🚻🐾) 🖉 Breaking ranks with Napa snobbery, the party kids at Lava Vine take a light-hearted approach to their seriously good

wines – don't be surprised if they bust out musical instruments and start jamming. Children and dogs play outside, while you tap your toe to uptempo tunes in the tiny tasting room. Picnicking allowed. Reservations recommended. Bottles cost $25 to $55.

Vincent Arroyo WINERY
(Map p178; ☎ 707-942-6995; www.vincentarroyo.com; 2361 Greenwood Ave, Calistoga; ☺ by appointment) **FREE** The tasting room is a garage, where you may even meet Mr Arroyo, known for his all-estate-grown petite Syrah and Cabernet Sauvignon. They're distributed nowhere else and are so consistently good that 75% of production is sold before it's bottled. Tastings are free, but appointments are required. Bottles are $22 to $45.

Napa

The valley's workaday hub was once a nothing-special city of storefronts, Victorian cottages and riverfront warehouses, but booming real-estate values caused an influx of new money that's transforming downtown into a hub of arts and food.

◉ Sights

Napa lies between Silverado Trail and St Helena Hwy/Hwy 29. For downtown, exit Hwy 29 at 1st St and drive east. Napa's main drag, 1st St, is lined with shops and restaurants.

★**Oxbow Public Market** MARKET
(Map p169; ☎ 707-226-6529; www.oxbowpublicmarket.com; 610 1st St; ☺ 9am-7pm Mon, Wed & Thu, to 8pm Tue, Fri & Sat, 10am-6pm Sun; 🚻) 🖉 Produce stalls, kitchen shops, and everywhere something to taste – Oxbow is foodie central, with emphasis on seasonal eating and sustainability. Come hungry.

★**di Rosa Art + Nature Preserve** GALLERY, GARDENS
(☎ 707-226-5991; www.dirosaart.org; 5200 Hwy 121; admission $5, tours $12-15; ☺ 10am-4pm Wed-Sun) West of downtown, scrap-metal sheep graze Carneros vineyards at 217-acre di Rosa Preserve, a stunning collection of Northern California art, displayed indoors in galleries and outdoors in sculpture gardens. Reservations recommended for tours.

☞ Tours

Napa Valley Wine Train TRAIN TOUR
(☎ 800-427-4124, 707-253-2111; www.winetrain.com; adult/child from $109/74) A cushy, if tour-

Napa

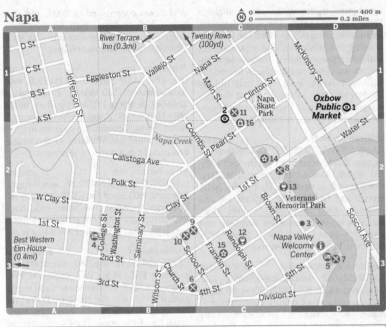

Napa

◎ Top Sights
1 Oxbow Public Market D1

◎ Sights
2 Vintners' Collective C1

✛ Activities, Courses & Tours
3 Napa River Velo D3

🛏 Sleeping
4 Blackbird Inn A3
5 Napa River Inn D3

✦ Eating
6 Alexis Baking Co B3
7 Angèle D3
8 Bounty Hunter Wine Bar &
   Smokin' BBQ C2

9 Norman Rose Tavern B3
10 Oenotri B3
11 Pizza Azzuro C1

🍷 Drinking & Nightlife
12 Billco's Billiards & Darts C3
13 Downtown Joe's C2

✪ Entertainment
14 City Winery at Napa Valley
   Opera House C2
Silo's Jazz Club .... (see 5)
15 Uptown Theatre C3

🛍 Shopping
16 Betty's Girl C2
Napa General Store .... (see 5)

isty, way to see Wine Country, the Wine Train offers three-hour daily trips in vintage Pullman dining cars, from Napa to St Helena and back, with an optional winery tour. Trains depart from McKinstry St, near 1st St.

🛏 Sleeping

Summer demand exceeds supply. Weekend rates skyrocket. Also consider staying in Calistoga.

Chablis Inn   MOTEL $$
(☏707-257-1944; www.chablisinn.com; 3360 Solano Ave; r Mon-Fri $89-109, Sat & Sun $169-189; ✳@🔌🛜🏊) Good-value, well-kept motel near Napa's only stretch of freeway. Hot tub.

★Carneros Inn   RESORT $$$
(☏707-299-4900; www.thecarnerosinn.com; 4048 Sonoma Hwy; r Mon-Fri $485-570, Sat & Sun $650-900; ✳@🔌🛜🏊) Carneros Inn's contemporary aesthetic and retro, small-town

agricultural theme shatter the predictable Wine Country mold. The semi-detached, corrugated-metal cottages look like itinerant housing, but inside they're snappy and chic, with cherry-wood floors, ultrasuede headboards, wood-burning fireplaces, heated-tile bathroom floors, giant tubs and indoor-outdoor showers. Linger by day at the hilltop pool, by night at the outdoor fireplaces. Two excellent on-site restaurants.

Milliken Creek Inn   INN **$$$**
(☑ 888-622-5775, 707-255-1197; www.millikencreek-inn.com; 1815 Silverado Trail; r incl breakfast $295-750; ❋@❅❒) Understatedly elegant Milliken Creek combines small-inn charm, fine-hotel service and B&B intimacy. Rooms are impeccably styled in English-Colonial style, and have top-flight amenities, fireplaces and ultra-high-thread-count linens. Breakfast is delivered. Book a river-view room.

Cottages of Napa Valley   BUNGALOW **$$$**
(☑ 707-252-7810; www.napacottages.com; 1012 Darns Lane; d $395-500, q $475-575; ❋❅) Eight pristine cottages of quality construction – made for romantic hideaways, with extra-long soaking tubs, indoor gas fireplaces and outdoor campfire pits – surround a big garden shaded by towering pines. Cottages 4 and 8 have private porches and swinging chairs. The only drawback is white noise from traffic, but interiors are silent.

Andaz Hotel   HOTEL **$$$**
(☑ 707-224-3900; napa.andaz.hyatt.com; 1450 1st St; r $289-389; ❋@❅) Smack downtown, the Andaz was constructed in 2009, and feels like a big-city hotel, with business-class-fancy rooms, styled in sexy retro-70s style. Walkable to restaurants and bars.

Napa River Inn   HOTEL **$$$**
(Map p169; ☑ 877-251-8500, 707-251-8500; www.napariverinn.com; 500 Main St; r incl breakfast $249-549; ❋@❅❒) Beside the river, in the 1884 Hatt Building, the inn has upper-mid-range rooms, Victoriana to modern, in three satellite buildings. Walkable to restaurants and bars. Dogs get special treatment.

River Terrace Inn   HOTEL **$$$**
(☑ 707-320-9000, 866-627-2386; www.riverterraceinn.com; 1600 Soscol Ave; r $189-360; ❋❅❒) Upmarket, business-class, chain-style hotel with shopping-mall-bland architecture fronting on the Napa River. Heated outdoor pool.

Casita Bonita   BUNGALOW **$$$**
(☑ 707-321-4853, 707-259-1980; www.lacasitabonita.com; q $395; ❋❅) Well decorated two-bedroom cottage with full kitchen and veggie garden – kids love the chickens. Perfect for two couples or a family. Two-night minimum. Check the website for location details.

Best Western Ivy Hotel   HOTEL **$$$**
(☑ 800-253-6272, 707-253-9300; www.ivyhotelnapa.com; 4195 Solano Ave; r $180-295; ❋@❅❒) Redone in 2011, this colorful, smart-looking, two-story hotel, on the suburban strip north of Napa, has extras like fridge, microwave and on-site laundry. Good value when under $250.

Napa Winery Inn   HOTEL **$$$**
(☑ 800-522-8999, 707-257-7220; www.napawineryinn.com; 1998 Trower Ave; r incl breakfast Mon-Fri $179-279, Sat & Sun $229-339; ❋@❅❒❒) Request a remodeled room at this good-value hotel, north of downtown, decorated with generic. Hot tub, good service.

Blackbird Inn   B&B **$$$**
(Map p169; ☑ 888-567-9811, 707-226-2450; www.blackbirdinnnapa.com; 1775 1st St; r incl breakfast $185-300; ❋❅) Gorgeous, eight-room Arts and Crafts–style B&B, but anticipate street noise.

Best Western Elm House   INN **$$$**
(☑ 707-255-1831; www.bestwesternelmhouseinn.com; 800 California Blvd; r incl breakfast $199-299; ❋@❅) Impeccably kept rooms with generic furnishings in soft pastels. Ideal for conservative travelers. Fifteen-minute walk to downtown; easy highway access. Hot tub.

ℹ CUTTING COSTS IN NAPA

To avoid overspending on tasting fees, it's perfectly acceptable to pay for one tasting to share between two people. Ask in advance if fees are applicable to purchase (they usually aren't).

Tour fees cannot be split. Ask at your hotel, or at visitors centers, for free- or discounted-tasting coupons, or download from napatouristguide.com. If you can't afford the hotels, try western Sonoma County, but if you want to be nearer Napa, try the suburban towns of Vallejo and American Canyon, about 20 minutes from downtown Napa. Both have motels for $75 to $125 in high season. Also find chains 30 minutes away in Fairfield, off I-80 exits 41 (Pittman Rd) and 45 (Travis Blvd).

✗ Eating

Make reservations whenever possible. July to mid-August, look for the peach stand at Deer Park Rd and Silverado Trail (across Deer Park Rd from Stewart's farmstand) for juicy-delicious heirloom varieties.

★ Oxbow Public Market   MARKET $
(☎707-226-6529; www.oxbowpublicmarket.com; 644 1st St; dishes from $3; ⏱9am-7pm Mon, Wed & Thu-Sat, to 8pm Tue, 10am-5pm Sun) 🍽 Graze this gourmet market and plug into the Northern California food scene. Standouts: **Hog Island** oysters (six for $16); comfort cooking at celeb-chef Todd Humphries' **Kitchen Door** (mains $14 to $24); Venezuelan cornbread sandwiches ($9) at **Pica Pica**; great Cal-Mexican at **C Casa** (tacos $5 to $9); pastries at **Ca'Momi** ($2); and **Three Twins** certified-organic ice cream ($3.75 for a single cone).

Tuesday is locals' night (5pm to 8pm), with many discounts. Tuesday and Saturday mornings, there's a farmers market. Some stalls remain open till 9pm, even on Sundays, but many close earlier.

Alexis Baking Co   CAFE $
(Map p169; ☎707-258-1827; www.alexisbakingcompany.com; 1517 3rd St; dishes $7-13; ⏱7am-3pm Mon-Fri, 7:30am-3pm Sat, 8am-2pm Sun; 🖉🖥) Our fave spot for quality scrambles, granola, focaccia, big cups of joe and boxed lunches to go.

Taqueria Maria   MEXICAN $
(☎707-257-6925; www.taqueriamaria.com; 640 3rd St; mains $8-13; ⏱9am-8:30pm Sun-Thu, to 9pm Fri & Sat; 🖉🖥) Reliably good Mexican cooking that won't break the bank. Also serves breakfast.

Buttercream Bakery   DINER $
(☎707-255-6700; www.buttercreambakery.com; 2297 Jefferson St; breakfast $5; ⏱5:30am-3pm) For a retro-flashback: this pink-striped diner, favored by Napa's little old ladies, has all-day breakfasts and white-bread lunches, served by matrons in heavy eye shadow.

Soda Canyon Store   DELI $
(☎707-252-0285; www.sodacanyonstore.com; 4006 Silverado Trail; ⏱6am-5:30pm Mon-Sat, 7:30am-5pm Sun) This roadside deli, with shaded picnic area, makes an easy stop while winery-hopping north of town.

Oenotri   ITALIAN $$
(Map p169; ☎707-252-1022; www.oenotri.com; 1425 1st St; dinner mains $17-29, lunch $13-15;

⏱11:30am-2:30pm & 5:30-9pm Sun-Thu, to 10pm Fri & Sat) 🍽 Housemade salumi and pastas, and wood-fired Naples-style pizzas are the stars at always-busy Oenotri, which draws crowds for daily-changing, locally sourced, rustic-Italian cooking, served in a cavernous brick-walled space.

Carpe Diem Wine Bar   CALIFORNIAN $$
(☎707-224-0800; www.carpediemwinebar.com; 1001 2nd St; mains $17-19; ⏱4-9pm Mon-Thu, to 10pm Fri & Sat) This busy storefront wine bar and restaurant makes inventive, flavorful small plates, from simple skewers and flatbreads, to elaborate ostrich burgers, salumi platters and – wait for it – duck confit 'quack and cheese.'

Pearl Restaurant   NEW AMERICAN $$
(☎707-224-9161; www.therestaurantpearl.com; 1339 Pearl St; mains $15-23; ⏱11:30am-2pm & 5:30-9pm Tue-Sat; 🖼) Meet locals at this dog-friendly bistro with pinewood tables and open-rafter ceilings, whose winning down-to-earth cooking includes double-cut pork chops, chicken-verde polenta, steak tacos, and oysters – the specialty.

Pizza Azzuro   PIZZA $$
(Map p169; ☎707-255-5552; www.azzurropizzeria.com; 1260 Main St; mains $13-16; ⏱11:30am-9pm Sun-Thu, to 9:30pm Fri & Sat; 🖉🖥) This Napa classic gets deafeningly loud, but it's worth bearing for tender-crusted pizzas, salad-topped 'manciata' bread, good Caeser salads and pastas.

Norman Rose Tavern   PUB FOOD $$
(Map p169; ☎707-258-1516; www.normanrosenapa.com; 1401 1st St; mains $10-24; ⏱11:30am-9pm Sun-Thu, to 10pm Fri & Sat; 🖥) This happening gastropub, styled with reclaimed wood and tufted-leather banquettes, is good for a burger and beer. Great fries. Beer and wine only.

Bounty Hunter Wine Bar & Smokin' BBQ

BARBECUE $$

(Map p169; ☏ 707-226-3976; www.bountyhunter-winebar.com; 975 1st St; mains $13-24; ⊙ 11am-10pm Sun-Thu, to midnight Fri & Sat; 🐾) Inside an 1888 grocery store, Bounty Hunter has an Old West vibe and superb barbecue, made with house-smoked meats. The standout whole chicken is roasted over a can of Tecate. Ten local beers and 40 wines by the glass.

Torc

CALIFORNIAN $$$

(☏ 707-252-3292; www.torcnapa.com; 1140 Main St; mains $26-29; ⊙ 5-9:30pm daily, 10:30am-2:30pm Sat & Sun) Wildly popular Torc plays off the seasons with dynamic combinations of farm-fresh ingredients, such as springtime white asparagus with black-truffle toasts, and squab with artichoke and licorice. Well-arranged for people-watching, the big stone dining room has an open-truss ceiling, and exposed pinewood tables that downplay formality. Reservations essential.

Bistro Don Giovanni

ITALIAN $$$

(☏ 707-224-3300; www.bistrodongiovanni.com; 4110 Howard Lane; mains $16-28; ⊙ 11:30am-10pm Sun-Thu, to 11pm Fri & Sat) This long-running favorite roadhouse serves modern-Italian pastas, crispy pizzas and wood-roasted meats. Reservations essential. Weekends get packed – and loud. Request a vineyard-view table (good luck).

Angèle

FRENCH $$$

(Map p169; ☏ 707-252-8115; www.angelerestaurant.com; 540 Main St; lunch mains $14-27, dinner $26-34; ⊙ 11:30am-10pm) Stalwart Angèle serves reliable provincial-French cooking –

A LOVELY SPOT FOR A PICNIC

Unlike Sonoma, there aren't many places to picnic legally in Napa. Here's a short list, in south-to-north order, but call ahead and remember to buy a bottle (or glass, if available) of your host's wine. If you don't finish it, California law forbids driving with an uncorked bottle in the car (keep it in the trunk).

➡ Regusci (p166)

➡ Napa Valley Museum (p173)

➡ Pride Mountain (p167)

➡ Casa Nuestra (p167)

➡ Lava Vine (p168)

Niçoise salads and *croques messieurs* at lunch, duck confit and beef Bourguignon at dinner – on a river-view deck or cozy dining room, both perfect for lingering with a good bottle of wine.

 Drinking & Nightlife

Empire

LOUNGE

(☏ 707-254-8888; www.empirenapa.com; 1400 1st St; ⊙ 5:30pm-midnight Tue-Thu, to 2am Fri & Sat) Moody and dark, with candlelight and a jellyfish tank, Empire mimics big-city lounges, with good cocktails and uptempo music. Alas, no dance floor.

Billco's Billiards & Darts

SPORTS BAR

(Map p169; www.billcos.com; 1234 3rd St; ⊙ noon-midnight) Dudes in khakis swill craft beers and throw darts inside this polite pool hall.

Downtown Joe's

SPORTS BAR, BREWERY

(Map p169; www.downtownjoes.com; 902 Main St at 2nd St; 🐾) Live music Thursday to Sunday, TV-sports nightly. Often packed, usually messy.

 Entertainment

Silo's Jazz Club

LIVE MUSIC

(Map p169; ☏ 707-251-5833; www.silosjazzclub.com; 530 Main St; cover varies; ⊙ 6-10pm Wed-Thu, 7pm-midnight Fri & Sat, varied hrs Sun) A cabaret-style wine-and-beer bar, Silo's hosts jazz and rock acts Friday and Saturday nights; Wednesday and Thursday it's good for drinks. Reservations recommended weekends.

City Winery at Napa Valley Opera House

THEATER

(Map p169; ☏ 707-260-1600; www.citywinery.com/napa; 1030 Main St) Napa's vintage-1880s opera theater houses a happening wine bar and restaurant downstairs, and 300-seat cabaret upstairs, hosting acts like Ginger Baker and Graham Nash. Opening hours vary, though it's usually open Thursday to Sunday evenings.

Uptown Theatre

THEATER

(Map p169; ☏ 707-259-0333; www.uptowntheatrenapa.com; 1350 3rd St) Big-name acts play this restored 1937 theater.

 Shopping

Betty's Girl

WOMEN'S CLOTHING, VINTAGE

(Map p169; ☏ 707-254-7560; www.bettysgirlnapa.com; 968 Pearl St; ⊙ 11am-6pm Thu & Fri, 10am-2pm Sat) Expert couturier Kim Northrup fits women with fabulous vintage cocktail dresses and custom-made designs, altering and shipping for no additional charge. Open extra hours by appointment.

Napa Valley Olive Oil Mfg Co   FOOD
(nvoliveoil.com; 1331 1st St; ⊙10am-5:30pm) Sample 30 varieties of fine olive oil and vinegar at this downtown specialty-food boutique, which also carries fancy salts and local jam.

Napa General Store   GIFTS
(Map p169; ☑707-259-0762; www.napageneral-store.com; 540 Main St; ⊙8am-6pm) Finally, cutesy Wine Country souvenirs reasonably priced. The on-site wine bar is convenient for non-shopping spouses.

ℹ Information

Napa Library (☑707-253-4241; www.county-ofnapa.org/Library; 580 Coombs St; ⊙10am-9pm Mon-Thu, to 6pm Fri & Sat; 🕾) Free internet access.

Napa Valley Welcome Center (Map p169; ☑707-251-5895, lodging assistance 707-251-9188, toll free 855-847-6272; www.visitnapaval-ley.com; 600 Main St; ⊙9am-5pm; 🖵) Lodging assistance, wine-tasting passes, spa deals and comprehensive winery maps.

Queen of the Valley Medical Center (☑707-252-4411; www.thequeen.org; 1000 Trancas St; ⊙24hr) Emergency medical.

ℹ Getting Around

Pedi cabs park outside downtown restaurants – especially at the foot of Main St, near the Napa Valley Welcome Center – in summertime. The car-sharing service **Uber** (www.uber.com) also operates in Napa.

Yountville

This onetime stagecoach stop, 9 miles north of Napa, is now a fine-food destination playing to the haute bourgeoisie, with more Michelin stars per capita than any other American town. There are some good inns here, but it's deathly boring by night. You stay in Yountville to drink at dinner without having to drive afterward. Napa, St Helena and Calistoga are more interesting bases. Most businesses are on Washington St.

⊙ Sights

Ma(i)sonry   GALLERY, TASTING ROOM
(☑707-944-0889; www.maisonry.com; 6711 Washington St; ⊙10am-6pm Sun-Thu, to 7pm Fri & Sat) Ma(i)sonry occupies a free-to-browse 1904

stone house and garden, transformed into a fussy winery-collective and gallery of over-priced rustic-modern *meubles* and art, some quite cool. Wine-tasting (by reservation) ranges from $25 to $45.

Napa Valley Museum   MUSEUM
(☑707-944-0500; www.napavalleymuseum.org; 55 Presidents Circle, off California Drive; adult/child $5/2.50; ⊙10am-5pm Wed-Mon) Yountville's modernist 40,000-sq-ft museum chronicles cultural history and showcases local paintings. From town, it's across Hwy 29.

🛏 Sleeping

Napa Valley Railway Inn   INN $$
(☑707-944-2000; www.napavalleyrailwayinn. com; 6523 Washington St; r $125-260; ❋@🕾≋) Sleep in a converted railroad car, part of two short trains parked at a central platform. They've little privacy, but come moderately priced. Bring earplugs.

Maison Fleurie   B&B $$$
(☑800-788-0369, 707-944-2056; www.maison-fleurienapa.com; 6529 Yount St; r incl breakfast $160-295; ❋@🕾≋) Rooms at this ivy-covered country inn are in a century-old home and carriage house, decorated in French-provincial style. Big breakfasts, afternoon wine and *hors d'oeuvres*, hot tub.

Bardessono   LUXURY HOTEL $$$
(☑877-932-5333, 707-204-6000; www.bardes-sono.com; 6524 Yount St; r $600-800, ste from $800; ❋@🕾≋) 🐾 The outdoors flows indoors at California's first-ever (for what it's worth) LEED-platinum-certified green hotel, made of recycled everything, styled in Japanese-led austerity, with neutral tones and hard angles that are exceptionally

urban for farm country. Glam pool deck and on-site spa. Tops for a splurge.

Poetry Inn
INN $$$

(☎707-944-0646; www.poetryinn.com; 6380 Silverado Trail; r incl breakfast $650-1400; ❄️🛜🏊) There's no better valley view than from this contemporary three-room inn, high on the hills east of Yountville. Decorated with posh restraint, rooms have private balconies, wood-burning fireplaces, 1000-thread-count linens and enormous baths with indoor-outdoor showers. Bring a ring.

Napa Valley Lodge
HOTEL $$$

(☎707-944-2468, 888-944-3545; www.napavalley-lodge.com; 2230 Madison St; r $300-475; ❄️🛜🏊) It looks like a condo complex, but rooms are spacious and modern; some have fireplaces. Hot tub, sauna and exercise room.

Petit Logis
INN $$$

(☎707-944-2332, 877-944-2332; www.petitlogis.com; 6527 Yount St; r Mon-Fri $195-285, Sat & Sun $265-295; ❄️🛜) Simple, cozy and comfortable, this cedar-sided inn has five correct rooms, each with jetted tub and gas fireplace.

✖ Eating

Make reservations or you may not eat. **Yountville Park** (cnr Washington & Madison Sts) has picnic tables and barbecue grills. Find groceries across from the post office. There's a great **taco truck** (6764 Washington St) parked in town.

Bouchon Bakery
BAKERY $

(☎707-944-2253; http://bouchonbakery.com; 6528 Washington St; items from $3; ⊙7am-7pm) Bouchon makes as-good-as-in-Paris French pastries and strong coffee. There's always a line and rarely a seat: get it to go.

Napa Style Paninoteca
CAFE $

(☎707-945-1229; www.napastyle.com; 6525 Washington St; dishes $8-10; ⊙11am-3pm) TV-chef Michael Chiarello's cafe (inside his store, Napa Style) makes camera-ready salads and paninos – try the slow-roasted pork – that pair nicely with his organic wines.

Redd Wood
ITALIAN $$

(☎707-299-5030; www.redd-wood.com; 6755 Washington St; pizzas $12-16, mains $24-28; ⊙11:30am-3pm & 5-10pm, to 11pm Fri & Sat) Celeb-chef Richard Reddington's casual Italian trattoria serves outstanding homemade

Napa Valley South

Napa Valley South

◎ **Top Sights**
1 Frog's Leap B1
2 Robert Sinskey B4
3 Tres Sabores A1

◎ **Sights**
4 Darioush B5
  Elizabeth Spencer .... (see 31)
5 Ma(i)sonry B6
6 Mumm Napa B1
7 Napa Valley Museum A3
8 Regusci B3
9 Robert Mondavi A2
10 Twenty Rows A6

◎ **Sleeping**
11 Auberge du Soleil B1
12 Bardessono B7
13 Best Western Elm House A6
14 Best Western Ivy Hotel A5
15 Chablis Inn A6
16 Cottages of Napa Valley A5
17 Maison Fleurie B7
18 Milliken Creek Inn A6
19 Napa Valley Lodge B5
20 Napa Valley Railway Inn B7
21 Napa Winery Inn A5
  Petit Logis .... (see 17)
22 Poetry Inn B3
23 Rancho Caymus A1

24 River Terrace Inn A7

◎ **Eating**
25 Ad Hoc B7
26 Bistro Don Giovanni A5
27 Bistro Jeanty B7
  Bouchon .... (see 17)
  Bouchon Bakery .... (see 17)
28 Buttercream Bakery A6
29 Étoile A3
30 French Laundry B6
31 La Luna Market &
  Taqueria A1
32 Mustards Grill A3
  Napa Style Paninoteca .... (see 40)
33 Oakville Grocery A2
34 Redd Wood B6
35 Rutherford Grill A1
36 Soda Canyon Store B5
37 Taqueria Maria A7

◎ **Drinking & Nightlife**
38 Pancha's B6

◎ **Entertainment**
  Lincoln Theater .... (see 7)

◎ **Shopping**
39 Napa Premium Outlets A6
40 Napa Style B7

pastas, salumi, and tender-to-the-tooth pizzas from a wood-fired oven.

★ **French Laundry** CALIFORNIAN **$$$**
(☑707-944-2380; www.frenchlaundry.com; 6640 Washington St; prix-fixe dinner $295; ⊗seatings 11am-1pm Fri-Sun, 5:30pm-9:15pm daily) The pinnacle of California dining, Thomas Keller's French Laundry is epic, a high-wattage culinary experience on par with the world's best. Book two months ahead at 10am sharp, or log onto OpenTable.com precisely at midnight. Avoid tables before 7pm; first-service seating moves a touch quickly.

Ad Hoc CALIFORNIAN **$$$**
(☑707-944-2487; www.adhocrestaurant.com; 6476 Washington St; prix-fixe dinner from $52; ⊗5-10pm Mon & Thu-Sat, 10am-1pm & 5-10pm Sun) A winning formula by Yountville's culinary patriarch, Thomas Keller, Ad Hoc serves the master's favorite American home cooking in four-course family-style menus, with no variations (dietary restrictions notwithstanding). Monday is fried-chicken night, which you can also sample weekend lunchtime, takeout only, behind the restaurant at Keller's latest venture, **Addendum** (⊗11am-

2pm Thu-Sat), which serves to-go boxed-lunch barbecue (order ahead).

Bouchon FRENCH **$$$**
(☑707-944-8037; www.bouchonbistro.com; 6354 Washington St; mains $19-45; ⊗11am-midnight Mon-Fri, from 10am Sat & Sun) Details at celeb-chef Thomas Keller's French brasserie are so impeccable you'd swear you were in Paris. Only the Bermuda-shorts-clad Americans look out of place. On the menu: oysters, onion soup, roasted chicken, leg of lamb, trout with almonds, runny cheeses and perfect profiteroles.

Bistro Jeanty FRENCH **$$$**
(☑707-944-0103; www.bistrojeanty.com; 6510 Washington St; mains $19-30; ⊗11:30am-10:30pm) French bistros by classical definition serve comfort food to weary travelers, and that's what French-born chef-owner Philippe Jeanty does, with succulent cassoulet, coq au vin, *steak-frites*, braised pork with lentils, and scrumptious tomato soup.

Mustards Grill CALIFORNIAN **$$$**
(☑707-944-2424; www.mustardsgrill.com; 7399 St Helena Hwy; mains $25-30; ⊗11:30am-9pm

Mon-Thu & Sun, to 10pm Fri & Sat; 🚻) The valley's original and always-packed roadhouse makes platters of crowd-pleasing, wood-fired, California comfort food – roasted meats, lamb shanks, pork chops, hearty salads and sandwiches.

Étoile   CALIFORNIAN $$$
(☎707-944-8844; www.chandon.com; 1 California Dr, Chandon Winery; lunch mains $28-36, dinner mains $29-39; ⊗11:30am-2:30pm & 6-9pm Thu-Mon) At Chandon winery, Étoile is perfect for a top-shelf lunch, an ideal one-stop destination when you want to visit a winery, eat a good meal and minimize driving.

🍷 Drinking & Entertainment

Pancha's   DIVE BAR
(6764 Washington St; ⊗noon-2am) Swill tequila with vineyard-workers early, waiters later.

Lincoln Theater   THEATER
(☎box office 707-949-9900; www.lincolntheater.org; 100 California Dr) Various artists, including Napa Valley Symphony, play this theater.

🛍 Shopping

Napa Style   FOOD
(☎707-945-1229; www.napastyle.com; 6525 Washington St; ⊗10am-6pm) The only worthwhile store at Yountville's V Martketplace is this fancy cookware shop by celeb-chef Michael Chiarello.

Oakville & Rutherford

But for its famous grocery, you'd drive through Oakville (pop 71) and never know you'd missed it. Vineyards sprawl everywhere. Rutherford (pop 164) is more conspicuous.

🛏 Sleeping & Eating

There's no budget lodging.

★ Auberge du Soleil   LUXURY HOTEL $$$
(☎800-348-5406, 707-963-1211; www.aubergedusoleil.com; 180 Rutherford Hill Rd, Rutherford; r $850-1200, ste $1500-4000; ❈ 🐾 ≋) The top splurge for a no-holds-barred romantic weekend. A meal in its **dining room** (breakfast mains $16 to $19, lunch $31 to $42, three-/four-/six-course prix-fixe dinner $105/125/150) is an iconic Napa experience: come for a fancy breakfast, lazy lunch or will-you-wear-my-ring dinner; valley views are mesmerizing – *don't* sit inside. Make reservations; arrive before sunset.

Rancho Caymus   HOTEL $$$
(☎800-845-1777, 707-963-1777; www.ranchocaymus.com; 1140 Rutherford Rd, Rutherford; r $179-299; ❈ @ 🐾 🖥) Styled after California's missions, this hacienda-like inn scores high marks for its fountain courtyard, kiva fireplaces, oak-beamed ceilings, and comparitively great rates.

La Luna Market & Taqueria   MARKET $
(☎707-963-3211; 1153 Rutherford Rd, Rutherford; dishes $4-6; ⊗9am-5pm May-Nov) Vineyard workers flock here for burrito lunches and homemade hot sauce.

Oakville Grocery   DELI, MARKET $$
(☎707-944-8802; www.oakvillegrocery.com; 7856 Hwy 29, Oakville; sandwiches $9-15; ⊗6:30am-5pm) The definitive Wine Country deli: excellent cheeses, charcuterie, bread, olives and wine – however pricy. Find tables outside or ask where to picnic nearby.

Rutherford Grill   AMERICAN $$
(☎707-963-1792; www.rutherfordgrill.com; 1180 Rutherford Rd, Rutherford; mains $15-30) Yes, it's a chain, but its bar provides a chance to rub shoulders with winemakers at lunchtime. The food is consistent – ribs, rotisserie chicken, grilled artichokes – and there's no corkage, so bring that bottle you just bought.

FLYING & BALLOONING

Wine Country is stunning from the air – a multihued tapestry of undulating hills, deep valleys and rambling vineyards. Make reservations.

The **Vintage Aircraft Company** (Map p188; ☎707-938-2444; www.vintageaircraft.com; 23982 Arnold Dr, Sonoma) flies over Sonoma in a vintage biplane with an awesome pilot who'll do loop-de-loops on request (add $50). Twenty-minute tours cost $175/260 for one/two adults.

Napa Valley's signature hot-air balloon flights leave early, around 6am or 7am, when the air is coolest; they usually include a champagne breakfast on landing. Adults pay about $200 to $250, and kids $150 to $175. Call **Balloons above the Valley** (☎800-464-6824, 707-253-2222; www.balloonrides.com) or **Napa Valley Balloons** (☎800-253-2224, 707-944-0228; www.napavalleyballoons.com), both in Yountville.

WINE TASTING

The best way to discover the real Wine Country is to avoid factory wineries and visit family-owned boutique houses (producing fewer than 20,000 annual cases) and mid-sized houses (20,000 to 60,000 annual cases). Why does it matter? Think of it. If you were to attend two dinner parties, one for 10 people, one for 1000, which would have the better food? Small wineries maintain tighter control. Also, you won't easily find these wines elsewhere.

Tastings are called 'flights' and include four to six different wines. Napa wineries charge $10 to $50. In Sonoma Valley, tastings cost $5 to $20, often refundable with purchase. In Sonoma County, tastings are free or $5 to $10. You must be 21 to taste.

Do not drink and drive. The curvy roads are dangerous, and police monitor traffic, especially on Napa's Hwy 29.

To avoid burnout, visit no more than three wineries per day. Most open daily 10am or 11am to 4pm or 5pm, but call ahead if your heart's set, or you absolutely want a tour, especially in Napa, where law requires that some wineries accept visitors only by appointment. If you're buying, ask if there's a wine club, which is free to join and provides discounts, but you'll have to agree to buy a certain amount annually.

St Helena

You'll know you're here when traffic halts. St Helena (ha-*lee*-na) is the Rodeo Dr of Napa. Fancy boutiques line the historic downtown's Main St (Hwy 29) and provide excellent window-shopping. Parking, however, is next-to-impossible summer weekends (tip: look behind the visitors center).

◉ Sights

Silverado Museum MUSEUM
(Map p178; ☑ 707-963-3757; www.silveradomuseum. org; 1490 Library Lane; ⊙ noon-4pm Tue-Sat) **FREE**
Contains a fascinating collection of Robert Louis Stevenson memorabilia. In 1880, the author – then sick, penniless and unknown – stayed in an abandoned bunkhouse at the old Silverado Mine on Mt St Helena with his wife, Fanny Osbourne; his novel *The Silverado Squatters* is based on his time there. Turn east off Hwy 29 at the Adams St traffic light and cross the railroad tracks.

Farmers Market MARKET
(Map p178; www.sthelenafarmersmkt.org; ⊙ 7:30am-noon Fri May-Oct) Meets at Crane Park, half a mile south of downtown.

🍴 Courses

Culinary Institute of America at Greystone COOKING COURSE
(Map p178; ☑ 707-967-2320; www.ciachef.edu/california; 2555 Main St; mains $25-29, cooking demonstration $20; ⊙ restaurant 11:30am-9pm, cooking demonstrations 1:30pm Sat & Sun) Inside an 1889 stone chateau, now a cooking school, there's a gadget- and cookbook-filled **culinary shop**; fine **restaurant**; weekend **cooking demonstrations**; and **wine-tasting classes** by luminaries including Karen MacNeil, author of *The Wine Bible*.

🛏 Sleeping

El Bonita MOTEL $$
(Map p178; ☑ 707-963-3216; www.elbonita.com; 195 Main St; r $169-239; ❋ @ 🛜 🌊 🐕) Book in advance to secure this sought-after motel, with up-to-date rooms (quietest are in back), attractive grounds, hot tub and sauna.

Wydown Hotel BOUTIQUE HOTEL $$$
(Map p178; ☑ 707-963-5100; www.wydownhotel.com; 1424 Main St; r Mon-Fri $269-380, Sat & Sun $379-475; ❋ 🛜) Opened 2012, this fashion-forward boutique hotel, with good service, sits smack downtown, its 12 over-sized rooms smartly decorated with tufted-velvet, distressed leather, subway-tile baths, and California-king beds with white-on-white high-thread-count linens.

Harvest Inn INN $$$
(Map p178; ☑ 707-963-9463, 800-950-8466; www.harvestinn.com; 1 Main St; r incl breakfast $369-569; ❋ @ 🛜 🌊 🐕) 🌱 A former estate, this 74-room resort has rooms in satellite buildings on sprawling manicured grounds. The newest building's generic; choose the vineyard-view rooms, which have private hot tubs.

Meadowood RESORT $$$
(Map p178; ☑ 800-458-8080, 707-963-3646; www.meadowood.com; 900 Meadowood Lane; r from

Napa Valley North

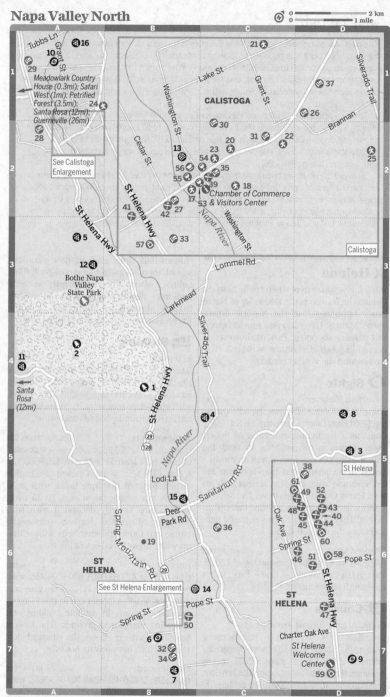

0   2 km
0   1 mile

Tubbs Ln
Grant St
16
10
29
Meadowlark Country
House (0.3mi); Safari
West (1mi); Petrified
Forest (3.5mi);
Santa Rosa (12mi);
Guerneville (26mi)
24
28

See Calistoga
Enlargement

21
Lake St
Grant St
37
Silverado Trail
CALISTOGA
Washington St
30
26
Brannan
Cedar St
13
20
31
22
23
54
25
56
35
55
St Helena Hwy
39
18
17
Chamber of Commerce
53 & Visitors Center
41
Washington St
42 27
Napa River
5
57
33
Calistoga

12
Bothe Napa
Valley
State Park
Lommel Rd
Larkmead
Silverado Trail

11
2
Santa
Rosa
(12mi)

1
4
8

29
128
Napa River
3
38
St Helena
Lodi La
Sanitarium Rd
61
49 52
15
Oak Ave
48 43
40
Deer
Park Rd
45 44
36
60
Spring St
51 58
19
46
Pope St
ST
HELENA
See St Helena Enlargement
14
ST
HELENA
Spring St
Pope St
47
50
Charter Oak Ave
6
St Helena
32
Welcome
34
Center
9
7
59

Napa Valley North

$600; ❄@🛜🌊) Hidden in a wooded dell with towering pines and miles of hiking, Napa's grandest resort has cottages and rooms in satellite buildings surrounding a croquet lawn. We most like the hillside fireplace cottages; lawn-view rooms lack privacy but are good for families. The vibe is Republican country club: wear linen and play *Great Gatsby*. Kids love the mammoth pool.

✗ Eating

Make reservations where possible.

Napa Valley Olive Oil Mfg Co MARKET **$**
(Map p178; ☎707-963-4173; www.oliveoilsainthelena.com; 835 Charter Oak Ave; ⊙8am-5:30pm) Before the advent of fancy-food stores, this ramshackle market introduced Napa to Italian delicacies – real prosciutto and salami, meaty olives, fresh bread, nutty cheeses and, of course, olive oil. Ask nicely and the owner

will lend you a knife and a board to picnic at the rickety tables in the grass outside. Cash only.

Sunshine Foods
MARKET, DELI $
(Map p178; www.sunshinefoodsmarket.com; 1115 Main St; ⊗7:30am-8:30pm) Town's best grocery store; excellent deli.

Model Bakery
CAFE $
(Map p178; ☑707-963-8192; www.themodelbakery. com; 1357 Main St; dishes $5-10; ⊗6:30am-6pm Mon-Sat, 7am-5pm Sun) Good bakery with scones, muffins, salads, pizzas, sandwiches and exceptional coffee.

Gillwood's Cafe
AMERICAN $
(Map p178; www.gillwoodscafe.com; 1313 Main St; dishes $8-13; ⊗7am-3pm; 🖶) Convenient for breakfast and lunch, Gillwood's serves good diner fare – scrambles, pancakes, sandwiches, burgers and salads. Beer and wine, too.

Gott's Roadside
AMERICAN $$
(Map p178; ☑707-963-3486; http://gotts.com; 933 Main St; mains $10-15; ⊗7am-9pm, to 10pm May-Sep; 🖶) 🍴 Wiggle your toes in the grass and feast on quality burgers – of beef or ahi tuna – plus Cobb salads and fish tacos at this classic roadside drive-in, whose original name, 'Taylor's Auto Refresher,' remains on the sign. Avoid weekend waits by phoning ahead or ordering online. There's another at Oxbow Public Market (p171).

Cindy's Backstreet Kitchen
NEW AMERICAN $$
(Map p178; ☑707-963-1200; www.cindysback-streetkitchen.com; 1327 Railroad Ave; mains $16-28; ⊗11:30am-9:30pm) 🍴 The inviting retro-homey decor complements the Cal-American comfort food, such as avocado-and-papaya salad, wood-fired duck, steak with French fries and burgers. The bar makes mean mojitos.

Cook
CAL-ITALIAN $$
(Map p178; ☑707-963-7088; www.cooksthelena. com; 1310 Main St; lunch $14-23, dinner $16-28; ⊗11:30am-10pm Mon-Sat, 10am-9pm Sun) Locals crowd this tiny storefront bistro, beloved for its earthy Cal-Italian cooking – homemade pasta and risotto, melt-off-the-bone ribs and simple-delicious burgers. Expect a wait, even with reservations.

Armadillo's
MEXICAN $$
(Map p178; www.armadillosnv.com; 1304 Main St; mains $8-12; ⊗11am-9pm Sun-Thu, to 10pm Fri & Sat) Respectable, reasonably priced Mexican cooking.

Restaurant at Meadowood
CALIFORNIAN $$$
(Map p178; ☑707-967-1205; www.meadowood. com; 900 Meadowood Lane; 9-course menu $225; ⊗5:30-10pm Mon-Sat) If you couldn't score reservations at French Laundry (p175), fear not: Meadowood – the valley's only other Michelin-three-star restaurant – has a slightly more sensibly priced menu, elegantly unfussy dining room, and lavish haute cuisine that's not too esoteric. Auberge (p176) has better views, but Meadowood's food and service far surpass it.

Terra
CALIFORNIAN $$$
(Map p178; ☑707-963-8931; www.terrarestaurant. com; 1345 Railroad Ave; 4-/5-/6-course menus $78/93/105; ⊗6-9pm Wed-Sun) Seamlessly blending Japanese, French and Italian culinary styles, Terra is one of Wine Country's top tables – the signature is broiled sake-marinated black cod with shrimp dumplings in shiso broth. The adjoining bar serves small bites without reservations, but the dining room's the thing.

Goose & Gander
NEW AMERICAN $$$
(Map p178; ☑707-967-8779; www.goosegander. com; 1245 Spring St; mains $23-32; ⊗5-10pm Sun-Thu, noon-midnight Fri & Sat) Inside a converted Craftsman house, with cathedral ceiling and gorgeous woodwork, Goose & Gander has a clubby vibe conducive to drinking, excellent craft cocktails, and an imaginative (sometimes heavy) menu with some standouts, like the summertime-only shrimp-and-watermelon salad. Consider the garden. Boozy locals favor the basement pub.

Farmstead
NEW AMERICAN $$$
(Map p178; ☑707-963-9181; www.farmsteadnapa. com; 738 Main St; mains $16-27; ⊗11:30am-9pm) 🍴 An enormous open-truss barn with big leather booths and rocking-chair porch, Farmstead draws a youthful crowd and grows many of its own ingredients – including grass-fed beef – for an earthy menu highlighting wood-fired cooking.

Market
NEW AMERICAN $$$
(Map p178; ☑707-963-3799; www.marketsthelena. com; 1347 Main St; mains $18-27; ⊗11:30am-9pm) 🍴 We love Market's big portions of simple, fresh American cooking, including hearty salads of local produce, and soul-satisfying mains like buttermilk fried chicken. The stone-walled dining room dates to the 19th century, as does the ornate backbar, where cocktails get muddled to order. Free corkage.

🛍 Shopping

Main St is lined with high-end boutiques (think $100 socks), but some mom-and-pop shops remain.

Woodhouse Chocolates   FOOD
(Map p178; www.woodhousechocolate.com; 1367 Main St; ☉10:30am-5:30pm) Woodhouse looks more like Tiffany than a candy shop, with housemade chocolates similarly priced, but their quality is beyond reproach.

Napa Soap Company   BEAUTY
(Map p178; www.napasoap.com; 651 Main St; ☉10am-5:30pm) 🌿 Eco-friendly bath products, locally produced.

Baksheesh   HOMEWARES
(Map p178; www.baksheeshfairtrade.com; 1327 Main St; ☉10am-6pm) 🌿 Handcrafted fairtrade home decor from 38 countries.

Lolo's Consignment   VINTAGE
(Map p178; www.lolosconsignment.com; 1120 Main St; ☉10:30am-4pm Mon, to 5:30pm Tue-Sat, 11am-4pm Sun) Groovy cheap dresses and cast-off cashmere.

Vintage Trunk   VINTAGE
(Map p178; http://vintagetrunkonline.com; 1210 Main St; ☉10:30am-5:30pm) High-end women's designer consignment; prices from $90.

Main Street Books   BOOKS
(Map p178; 1315 Main St; ☉10am-5:30pm Mon-Sat, 11am-3pm Sun) Good used books.

ℹ Information

St Helena Welcome Center (Map p178; ☎707-963-4456; www.sthelena.com; 657 Main St; ☉9am-5pm Mon-Fri, plus 10am-4pm Sat-Sun May-Nov) The visitor center has information and lodging assistance.

Calistoga & Around

The least gentrified town in Napa Valley feels refreshingly simple, with an old-fashioned main street lined with shops, not boutiques, and diverse characters wandering the sidewalks. Bad hair? No problem. Fancy-pants St Helena couldn't feel further away. Many don't go this far north. You should.

Famed 19th-century author Robert Louis Stevenson said of Calistoga: 'the whole neighborhood of Mt St Helena is full of sulfur and boiling springs...Calistoga itself seems to repose on a mere film above a boiling, subterranean lake.'

Indeed, it does. Calistoga is synonymous with mineral water bearing its name, bottled here since 1924. Its springs and geysers have earned it the nickname the 'hot springs of the West.' Plan to visit a spa to indulge in the local specialty: hot-mud baths, made with volcanic ash from nearby Mt St Helena.

The town's odd name comes from Sam Brannan, who founded Calistoga in 1859, believing it would develop like the New York spa town of Saratoga. Apparently Sam liked his drink and at the founding ceremony tripped on his tongue, proclaiming it the 'Cali-stoga' of 'Sara-fornia.' The name stuck.

⦿ Sights

Hwys 128 and 29 run together from Rutherford through St Helena; in Calistoga, they split. Hwy 29 turns east and becomes Lincoln Ave, continuing across Silverado Trail, toward Clear Lake. Hwy 128 continues north as Foothill Blvd (not St Helena Hwy). Calistoga's shops and restaurants line Lincoln Ave.

Sharpsteen Museum   MUSEUM
(Map p178; ☎707-942-5911; www.sharpsteen-museum.org; 1311 Washington St; suggested donation $3; ☉11am-4pm; 👪) **FREE** Across from the picturesque 1902 City Hall (originally an opera house), the Sharpsteen Museum was created by an ex-Disney animator (whose Oscar is on display) and houses a fantastic diorama of town in the 1860s, big Victorian dollhouse, full-size horse-drawn carriage, cool taxidermy and a restored cottage from Brannan's original resort. (The only Brannan cottage still at its original site is at 106 Wappo Ave).

**Bale Grist Mill & Bothe-
Napa Valley State Parks**   HISTORIC PARK
(☎707-942-4575; parks.ca.gov; 👪) Both these parks have picnic areas and admission to one includes the other. **Bale Grist Mill State Historic Park** (Map p178; ☎707-963-2236; adult/child $5/2; 👪) features a 36ft-high **water-powered mill wheel** dating to 1846 – the largest still operating in North America; Saturdays and Sundays (and sometimes Fridays and Mondays) from 10am to 4pm, it grinds flour. A mile-long trail leads to adjacent **Bothe-Napa Valley State Park** (Map p178; ☎707-942-4575; parking $8; ☉8am-sunset; 👪), where there's a **swimming pool** ($5), and camping (p183), plus hiking through redwood groves.

If you're two or more adults, go first to Bothe and pay $8, instead of the per-head charge at Bale Grist. The mill and both parks are on Hwy 29/128, midway between St Helena and Calistoga. In early October, look for living-history festival **Old Mill Days.**

Old Faithful Geyser
GEYSER

(Map p178; ☎ 707-942-6463; www.oldfaithfulgeyser.com; 1299 Tubbs Lane; adult/child/under 5yr $14/8/free; ⊙9am-6pm, to 5pm Nov-Mar; ⊛) Calistoga's mini-version of Yellowstone's Old Faithful shoots boiling water 60ft to 100ft into the air, every 30 minutes. The vibe is pure roadside Americana, with folksy hand-painted interpretive exhibits, picnicking and a little petting zoo, where you can come nose-to-nose with llamas. It's 2 miles north of town, off Silverado Trail. Find discount coupons online.

Petrified Forest
FOREST

(☎707-942-6667; www.petrifiedforest.org; 4100 Petrified Forest Rd; adult/child $10/5; ⊙9am-7pm summer, to 5pm winter) Three million years ago at this now roadside-Americana attraction, a volcanic eruption at Mt St Helena blew down a stand of redwoods. The trees fell in the same direction, away from the blast, and over the millennia the mighty giants' trunks turned to stone. Discover them on a short interpretive trail through the woods. The first stumps were discovered in 1870. A monument marks Robert Louis Stevenson's 1880 visit, which he described in *The Silverado Squatters.*

It's 5 miles northwest of town, off Hwy 128.

Safari West
WILDLIFE RESERVE

(☎707-579-2551; www.safariwest.com; 3115 Porter Creek Rd; adult $70-80, child 3-12yr $32; ⊛) Giraffes in Wine Country? Whadya know. Safari West sprawls over 400 acres and protects zebras, cheetahs and other exotic animals, which mostly roam free. See them on a guided two-and-a-half-hour safari in open-sided jeeps; reservations required, no kids under three. If you're feeling adventurous, stay overnight in nifty canvas-sided **tent cabins** (cabin including breakfast $225 to $305) inside the preserve.

Robert Louis Stevenson State Park
PARK

(☎707-942-4575; www.parks.ca.gov; Hwy 29; ⊙sunrise-sunset) FREE At this undeveloped state park 8 miles north of Calistoga, the long-extinct volcanic cone of Mt St Helena marks Napa Valley's end and often gets snow

---

TOP KID-FRIENDLY WINERIES

➡ Kaz (p189) Play-Doh, playground and grape juice.

➡ Benziger (p189) Open-air tram rides.

➡ Frog's Leap (p166) Cats, chickens and croquet.

➡ Casa Nuestra (p167) Playful goats.

➡ Castello di Amorosa (p168) Bona-fide castle.

➡ Lava Vine (p168) Mellow vibe, grassy play area.

---

in winter. It's a strenuous 5-mile climb to the peak's 4343ft summit, but what a view – 200 miles on a clear winter's day. Check conditions before setting out. Also consider 2.2-mile one-way **Table Rock Trail** (go south from the summit parking area) for drop-dead valley views.

Temperatures are best in wildflower season, February to May; fall is prettiest, when the vineyards change colors. The park includes the site of the **Silverado Mine** where Stevenson and his wife honeymooned in 1880.

🏃 Activities

Oat Hill Mine Trail
CYCLING, HIKING

(Map p178) One of Northern California's most technically challenging trails, OHM Trail draws hardcore mountain bikers and hikers. Softcore walkers, take heart: a moderately strenuous half-mile up from town, there's a bench with incredible valley views. The trailhead is at the intersection of Hwy 29 and Silverado Trail.

Calistoga Bike Shop
BICYCLE RENTAL

(Map p178; ☎707-942-9687, 866-942-2453; www.calistogabikeshop.com; 1318 Lincoln Ave; ⊙10am-6pm) Rents full-suspension mountain bikes ($75 per day) and hybrids ($12/39 per hour/day), and provides reliable trail information. Wine-touring packages ($90 per day) include wine-rack baskets and free wine pickup.

Spas

Calistoga is famous for hot-spring spas and mud-bath emporiums, where you're buried in hot mud and emerge feeling supple, detoxified and enlivened. (The mud is made with volcanic ash and peat; the higher the ash content, the better the bath.)

Packages take 60 to 90 minutes and cost $70 to $90. You start semi-submerged in hot mud, then soak in hot mineral water. A steam bath and blanket-wrap follow. A massage increases the cost to $130 and up.

Baths can be taken solo or, at some spas, as couples. Variations include thin, painted-on clay-mud wraps (called 'fango' baths, good for those uncomfortable sitting in mud), herbal wraps, seaweed baths and various massage treatments. Discount coupons are sometimes available from the visitors center. Book ahead, especially on summer weekends. Reservations are essential everywhere.

Most spas offer multi-treatment packages. Some offer discounted spa-lodging packages.

★ Indian Springs Spa SPA
(Map p178; ☑ 707-942-4913; www.indiansprings-calistoga.com; 1712 Lincoln Ave; ☺ by appointment 9am-8pm) California's longest continually operating spa, and original Calistoga resort, has concrete mud tubs and mines its own ash. Treatments include use of the huge, hot-spring-fed pool. Great cucumber body lotion.

Spa Solage SPA
(Map p178; ☑ 707-226-0825; www.solagecalistoga.com/spa; 755 Silverado Trail; ☺ by appointment 8am-8pm) Chichi, austere, top-end spa, with couples' rooms and a fango-mud bar for DIY paint-on treatments. Also has zero-gravity chairs for blanket wraps, and a clothing-optional pool.

Dr Wilkinson's Hot Springs Resort SPA
(Map p178; ☑ 707-942-4102; www.drwilkinson.com; 1507 Lincoln Ave; ☺ by appointment 10am-3:30pm) Fifty years running; 'the doc' uses more peat in its mud.

Mount View Spa SPA
(Map p178; ☑ 707-942-5789, 800-816-6877; www.mountviewhotel.com; 1457 Lincoln Ave; ☺ by appointment 9am-9pm) Traditional full-service, eight-room spa, good for clean-hands people who prefer painted-on mud to submersion.

Lavender Hill Spa SPA
(Map p178; ☑ 707-341-6002, 800-528-4772, 707-942-4495; http://lavenderhillspa.com; 1015 Foothill Blvd; ☺ by appointment 9am-9pm Thu-Mon, to 7pm Tue & Wed) Small, cute spa that uses much-lighter, less-icky lavender-infused mud; offers couples' treatments.

Golden Haven Hot Springs SPA
(Map p178; ☑ 707-942-8000; www.goldenhaven.com; 1713 Lake St; ☺ by appointment 8am-8pm) Old-school and unfussy; offers couples' mud baths and couples' massage.

Calistoga Spa Hot Springs SPA, SWIMMING
(Map p178; ☑ 866-822-5772, 707-942-6269; www.calistogaspa.com; 1006 Washington St; ☺ by appointment 8:30am-4:30pm Tue-Thu, to 9pm Fri-Mon, swimming pools 10am-9pm; ⛹) Traditional mud baths and massage at a motel complex with two huge swimming pools where kids can play while you soak (pool passes $25).

🛏 Sleeping

Bothe-Napa Valley State Park Campground CAMPGROUND $
(Map p48; ☑ 800-444-7275; www.reserveamerica.com; 3801 Hwy 128; camping & RV sites $35; ⛺🐕) Three miles south, Bothe has shady camping near redwoods, coin-operated showers, and gorgeous hiking (p181). Sites 28 to 36 are most secluded.

★ Mountain Home Ranch RESORT $$
(☑ 707-942-6616; www.mountainhomeranch.com; 3400 Mountain Home Ranch Rd; r $111-121, cabins $71-156; @🛜🏊) 🍴 In continuous operation since 1913, this 340-acre homestead outside town is a flashback to old California. Doubling as a retreat center, the ranch has simple lodge rooms and rustic freestanding cabins, some with kitchens and fireplaces, ideal for families, but you may be here during someone else's family reunion or spiritual quest.

No matter. With miles of oak-woodland trails, a hilltop swimming pool, private lake with canoeing and fishing, and a hike to warm springs in a magical fault-line canyon, you may hardly notice – and you may never make it to a single winery. Breakfast is included, but you'll have to drive 15 minutes to town for dinner. Pack hiking boots, not high heels.

Dr Wilkinson's Motel & Hideaway Cottages MOTEL, COTTAGES $$
(Map p178; ☑ 707-942-4102; www.drwilkinson.com; 1507 Lincoln Ave; r $149-255, cottages $165-270; ⛹@🛜🏊) This good-value vintage-1950s motel has well-kept rooms facing a swimming-pool courtyard with hot tub, three pools (one indoors), and mud baths. Also rents simple, great-value stand-alone cottages with kitchens at the affiliated Hideaway Cottages, also with pool and hot tub.

EuroSpa & Inn
MOTEL $$

(Map p178; ☎707-942-6829; www.eurospa.com; 1202 Pine St; r incl breakfast $145-199; ❋❀☀) Immaculate single-story motel on a quiet side street, with extras like gas-burning fireplaces, afternoon wine and small on-site spa. Excellent service, but tiny pool.

Golden Haven Hot Springs
MOTEL $$

(Map p178; ☎707-942-8000; www.goldenhaven. com; 1713 Lake St; r $165-239; ❋❀☀) This motel-spa has mudbath-lodging packages and good-value well-kept rooms, some with Jacuzzis.

Best Western Stevenson Manor
HOTEL $$

(Map p178; ☎800-528-1238, 707-942-1112; www. stevensonmanor.com; 1830 Lincoln Ave; r weekday $159-189, weekend $249-289; ❋@❀☀) This entry-level business-class hotel feels generic, but has good extras, including full hot breakfast. Upstairs rooms are quietest. No elevator.

Calistoga Spa Hot Springs
MOTEL $$

(Map p178; ☎707-942-6269, 866-822-5772; www. calistogaspa.com; 1006 Washington St; r $187-235; ❋❀☀) Great for families, who jam the place weekends, this motel-resort has slightly scuffed generic rooms (request one that's been remodeled) with kitchenettes, and fantastic pools – two full-size, a kiddie-pool with miniwaterfall and a huge adults-only Jacuzzi. Outside are barbecues and snack bar. Wi-fi in lobby.

Calistoga Inn
INN $$

(Map p178; ☎707-942-4101; www.calistogainn.com; 1250 Lincoln Ave; r with shared bath incl breakfast $129-169; ❀) Upstairs from a busy bar, this inn has 18 clean, basic rooms with shared bath, ideal for no-fuss bargain-hunters. No TVs, no elevator. Bring earplugs.

Solage
RESORT $$$

(Map p178; ☎866-942-7442, 707-226-0800; www. solagecalistoga.com; 755 Silverado Trail; r $530-675; ❋❀☀☀) 🍴 Calistoga's top spa-hotel ups the style factor, with Cali-chic semidetached cottages and a glam palm-tree-lined pool. Rooms are austere, with vaulted ceilings, zillion-thread-count linens and pebble-floor showers. Cruiser bikes included.

Indian Springs Resort
RESORT $$$

(Map p178; ☎707-942-4913; www.indiansprings-calistoga.com; 1712 Lincoln Ave; lodge r $229-359, cottage $259-429, 2-bedroom cottage $359-499; ❋❀☀) The definitive old-school Calistoga resort, Indian Springs has cottages facing a central lawn with palm trees, shuffleboard, bocce, hammocks and Weber grills – not unlike a vintage Florida resort. Some sleep six. There are also top-end, motel-style lodge rooms (adults only). Huge hot-springs-fed swimming pool.

Chateau De Vie
B&B $$$

(Map p178; ☎877-558-2513, 707-942-6446; www. cdvnapavalley.com; 3250 Hwy 128; r incl breakfast $229-429; ❋❀☀☀) Surrounded by vineyards, with gorgeous views of Mt St Helena, CDV has five modern, elegantly decorated B&B rooms with top-end amenities and zero froufrou. Charming owners serve wine on the sun-dappled patio, then leave you alone. Hot tub, big pool. Gay-friendly.

Meadowlark Country House
B&B $$$

(☎800-942-5651, 707-942-5651; www.meadow-larkinn.com; 601 Petrified Forest Rd; r incl breakfast $210-265, ste $285; ❋❀☀☀) On 20 acres west of town, Meadowlark has homey rooms decorated in contemporary style, most with decks and Jacuzzis. Outside there's a hot tub, sauna and clothing-optional pool. The truth-telling innkeeper lives elsewhere, offers helpful advice, then vanishes when you want privacy. There's a fabulous cottage for $465. Gay-friendly.

Mount View Hotel & Spa
HISTORIC HOTEL $$$

(Map p178; ☎707-942-6877, 800-816-6877; www. mountviewhotel.com; 1457 Lincoln Ave; r Mon-Fri $209-429, Sat & Sun $279-459; ❋❀☀) Smack in the middle of town, this 1917 Mission Revival hotel is decorated in vaguely mod-Italian style at odds with the vintage building, but rooms are clean and fresh-looking nonetheless. Gleaming bathrooms, on-site spa, year-round heated pool. No elevator.

Chanric
B&B $$$

(Map p178; ☎707-942-4535; www.thechanric. com; 1805 Foothill Blvd; r incl breakfast $249-439; ❋❀☀) A converted Victorian near the road, this cushy B&B has small, but smartly furnished rooms, plus many free extras including champagne on arrival and lavish three-course breakfasts. Gay-friendly. No elevator.

Hotel d'Amici
HOTEL $$$

(Map p178; ☎707-942-1007; www.hoteldamici. com; 1436 Lincoln Ave; r incl breakfast $200-300; ❋@❀) All four rooms at this 2nd-floor hotel are remarkably spacious and include continental breakfast, but they're up two flights of stairs (no elevator) and there's no on-site staff.

Cottage Grove Inn BUNGALOW $$$
(Map p178; ☎707-942-8400, 800-799-2284; www.cottagegrove.com; 1711 Lincoln Ave; cottages $315-450; ❄📶) Romantic cottages for over-40s, with wood-burning fireplaces, two-person tubs and rocking-chair front porches.

Aurora Park Cottages COTTAGES $$$
(Map p178; ☎877-942-7700, 707-942-6733; www.aurorapark.com; 1807 Foothill Blvd; cottages incl breakfast $269-299; ❄📶) Six immaculately kept, sunny-yellow cottages – with polished-wood floors, featherbeds and sundeck – stand in a row beside flowering gardens. Though close to the road, they're quiet by night. The innkeeper couldn't be nicer.

Sunburst Calistoga MOTEL $$$
(Map p178; ☎707-942-0991; www.thesunburstcalistoga.com; 1880 Lincoln Ave; r $229-289; @📶🏊) This single-story 1950s motor lodge got a makeover in 2013, with mid-century-modern-led aesthetics, but it's basically still a drive-to-the-door motel, only with nicer-than-average furnishings and thin walls.

Chelsea Garden Inn B&B $$$
(Map p178; ☎707-942-0948; www.chelseagardeninn.com; 1443 2nd St; r incl breakfast $195-350; ❄📶🏊) On a quiet sidestreet, this single-story inn has five floral-print rooms, with private entrances, facing pretty gardens. Never mind the pool's rust spots.

Wine Way Inn B&B $$$
(Map p178; ☎800-572-0679, 707-942-0680; www.winewayinn.com; 1019 Foothill Blvd; r $189-299; ❄📶) A small B&B, in a 1910-era house, close to the road; friendly owners.

Eating

Buster's Southern BBQ BARBECUE $
(Map p178; ☎707-942-5605; www.busterssouthernbbq.com; 1207 Foothill Blvd; dishes $8-12; ⏲10am-7:30pm Mon-Sat, 10:30am-6pm Sun; 👪) The sheriff dines at this indoor-outdoor barbecue joint, which serves smoky ribs, chicken, tri-tip steak and burgers, but closes early at dinnertime. Beer and wine.

Calistoga Inn & Brewery AMERICAN $$
(Map p178; ☎707-942-4101; www.calistogainn.com; 1250 Lincoln Ave; lunch mains $11-15, dinner $15-30; ⏲11:30am-3pm & 5:30-9pm) Locals crowd the outdoor beer garden Sundays. Midweek we prefer the country dining room's big oak-wood tables – a homey spot for simple American cooking. Live music summer weekends.

Solbar CALIFORNIAN $$$
(☎707-226-0850; www.solagecalistoga.com; 755 Silverado Trail; lunch mains $17-20, dinner $24-34; ⏲7am-11am, 11:30am-3pm & 5:30-9pm) 🍃 We like the spartan ag-chic look of this Michelin-starred resort restaurant, whose menu maximizes seasonal produce in elegant dishes, playfully composed. And this being a spa (p183), too, the menu is split for calorie-counters into light and hearty dishes. Reservations essential.

JoLé CALIFORNIAN $$$
(Map p178; ☎707-942-5938; www.jolerestaurant.com; 1457 Lincoln Ave; mains $25-30; ⏲5-9pm) The inventive farm-to-table plates at chef-owned Jolé evolve seasonally, and may include such dishes as local sole with tangy miniature Napa grapes, caramelized brussels sprouts with capers, and organic Baldwin apple strudel with burnt-caramel ice cream. Four courses cost $55. Reservations essential.

Calistoga Kitchen CALIFORNIAN $$$
(Map p178; ☎707-942-6500; www.calistogakitchen.com; 1107 Cedar St; lunch mains $12-18, dinner $18-29; ⏲5:30-9pm Thu, 11:30am-3pm & 5:30-9pm Fri & Sat, 9:30am-3pm Sun) A sparsely decorated cottage surrounded by a white-picket fence, Calistoga Kitchen is especially good for lunch in the garden. The chef-owner favors simplicity, focusing on quality ingredients in a half-dozen changing dishes, such as a delicious lamb stew. Reservations advised.

All Seasons Bistro NEW AMERICAN $$$
(Map p178; ☎707-942-9111; www.allseasonsnapavalley.net; 1400 Lincoln Ave; lunch mains $12-18, dinner $18-27; ⏲noon-2pm & 5:30-8:30pm Tue-Sun) 🍃 It looks like a white-tablecloth soda fountain, but All Seasons makes very fine meals, from simple *steak-frites* to composed dishes like cornmeal-crusted scallops with summer succotash.

Drinking & Nightlife

Yo El Rey CAFE
(Map p178; ☎707-942-1180; www.yoelreyroasting.com; 1217 Washington St; ⏲6:30am-6pm) 🍃 Hip kids favor this micro-roastery, which serves stellar small-batch, fair-trade coffee.

Hydro Grill BAR
(Map p178; ☎707-942-9777; 1403 Lincoln Ave; ⏲8:30am-midnight Sun-Thu, to 2am Fri & Sat)

OUTLET SHOPPING

Max out your credit cards on last season's close-outs.

Napa Premium Outlets ([📞]707-226-9876; www.premiumoutlets.com; 629 Factory Stores Dr, Napa; ⊙10am-9pm Mon-Sat, to 7pm Sun) Fifty stores.

Petaluma Village Premium Outlets ([📞]707-778-9300; www.premiumoutlets.com; 2200 Petaluma Blvd North, Petaluma; ⊙10am-9pm Mon-Sat, to 7pm Sun) Sixty stores, Sonoma County.

Vacaville Premium Outlets ([📞]707-447-5755; www.premiumoutlets.com/vacaville; 321 Nut Tree Rd, Vacaville; ⊙10am-9pm Mon-Sat, to 7pm Sun) 120 stores, northeast of the Wine Country on I-80.

Live music plays weekend evenings at this hoppin' corner bar-restaurant.

Solbar BAR
(Map p178; [📞]707-226-0850; www.solagecalistoga.com; 755 Silverado Trail; ⊙11am-9pm) Sip craft cocktails beside outdoor fireplaces and a palm-lined pool at this swank resort bar.

Brannan's Grill BAR
(Map p178; [📞]707-942-2233; www.brannanscalistoga.com; 1374 Lincoln Ave; ⊙11am-11pm) The mahogany bar at Calistoga's handsomest restaurant is great for martinis and microbrews, especially weekends when jazz combos play.

Susie's Bar DIVE BAR
(Map p178; [📞]707-942-6710; 1365 Lincoln Ave) Turn your baseball cap sideways, swill beer and shoot pool to a soundtrack of classic rock.

🛍 Shopping

Calistoga Pottery CERAMICS
(Map p178; [📞]707-942-0216; www.calistogapottery.com; 1001 Foothill Blvd; ⊙9am-5pm) Artisanal pottery, hand-thrown on site.

Coperfield's Bookshop BOOKS
(Map p178; [📞]707-942-1616; 1330 Lincoln Ave; ⊙10am-7pm Mon-Sat, 10am-6pm Sun) Indie bookshop, with local maps and guides.

ℹ Information

Chamber of Commerce & Visitors Center
(Map p178; [📞]707-942-6333, 866-306-5588; www.calistogavisitors.com; 1133 Washington St; ⊙9am-5pm)

SONOMA VALLEY

We have a soft spot for Sonoma's folksy ways. Unlike in fancy Napa, nobody cares if you drive a clunker and vote Green. Locals call it 'Slow-noma.' Anchoring the bucolic 17-mile-long Sonoma Valley, the town of Sonoma makes a great jumping-off point for exploring Wine Country – it's an hour from San Francisco – and has a marvelous sense of place, with storied 19th-century historical sights surrounding the state's largest town square. Halfway up-valley, tiny Glen Ellen is straight from a Norman Rockwell painting – in stark contrast to the valley's northernmost town, Santa Rosa, the workaday urban center best known for traffic. If you have more than a day, explore Sonoma's quiet, rustic western side, along the Russian River Valley, and continue to the sea.

Sonoma Hwy/Hwy 12 is lined with wineries, and runs from Sonoma to Santa Rosa, to western Sonoma County; Arnold Dr has less traffic (but few wineries) and runs parallel, up the valley's western side, to Glen Ellen.

Sonoma Valley Wineries

Rolling grass-covered hills rise from 17-mile-long Sonoma Valley. Its 40-some wineries get less attention than Napa's, but many are equally good. If you love Zinfandel and Syrah, you're in for a treat.

Picnicking is allowed at Sonoma wineries. Get maps and discount coupons in the town of Sonoma or, if you're approaching from the south, the Sonoma Valley Visitors Bureau (p192) at Cornerstone Gardens.

Plan at least five hours to visit the valley from bottom to top.

Homewood WINERY
(Map p188; [📞]707-996-6353; www.homewoodwinery.com; 23120 Burndale Rd, at Hwy 121/12; tasting $5; ⊙10am-4pm; 🐾) Barn cats dart about at this down-home winery, where the tasting room is a garage, and the winemaker crafts standout ports and Rhône-style Grenache, Mourvèdre and Syrah – 'Da redder, da better' – plus some late-harvest dessert wines, including excellent Viognier and Albariño. Bottles are $22 to $42, the tasting fee is waived with a purchase.

Robledo WINERY
(Map p188; [📞]707-939-6903; www.robledofamilywinery.com; 21901 Bonness Rd, off Hwy 116; tasting $10-15; ⊙by appointment 10am-5pm Mon-Sat,

11am-4pm Sun) Sonoma Valley's feel-good winery, Robledo was founded by a former grape-picker from Mexico who worked his way up to vineyard manager, then land owner, now vintner. His kids run the place. The wines – served at hand-carved furniture in a garage – include a no-oak Sauvignon Blanc, jammy Syrah, spicy Cabernet, and bright-fruit Pinot Noir. Bottles cost $18 to $60.

Gundlach-Bundschu Winery WINERY
(Map p188; ☎ 707-939-3015; www.gunbun.com; 2000 Denmark St, Sonoma; tasting $10-15, incl tour $20-50; ☺11am-4:30pm, to 5:30pm Jun–mid-Oct; ☎) ✎ California's oldest family-run winery looks like a castle, but has a down-to-earth vibe. Founded 1858 by a Bavarian immigrant, its signatures are Gewürztraminer

and Pinot Noir, but 'Gun-Bun' was the first American winery to produce 100% Merlot. Down a winding lane, it's a terrific bike-to winery, with picnicking, hiking and a lake. Tour the 2000-barrel cave ($20) by reservation only. Bottles are $22 to $45.

★ **Bartholomew Park Winery** WINERY
(☎ 707-939-3026; www.bartpark.com; 1000 Vineyard Lane, Sonoma; tasting $10, incl tour $20; ☺11am-4:30pm) ✎ A great bike-to winery, Bartholomew Park occupies a 375-acre preserve, with oak-shaded picnicking and valley-view hiking. The vineyards were originally cultivated in 1857 and now yield certified-organic Sauvignon Blanc, Cabernet Sauvignon softer in style than Napa, and lush Zinfandel. Tours (reservations

NAPA & SONOMA WINE COUNTRY SONOMA VALLEY WINERIES

A WINE COUNTRY PRIMER

When people talk about Sonoma, they're referring to the *whole* county which, unlike Napa, is huge. It extends all the way from the coast, up the Russian River Valley, into Sonoma Valley and eastward to Napa Valley; in the south it stretches from San Pablo Bay (an extension of San Francisco Bay) to Healdsburg in the north. It's essential to break Sonoma down by district.

West County refers to everything west of Hwy 101 and includes the Russian River Valley and the coast. Sonoma Valley stretches north–south along Hwy 12. In northern Sonoma County, Alexander Valley lies east of Healdsburg, and Dry Creek Valley lies north of Healdsburg. In the south, Carneros straddles the Sonoma–Napa border, north of San Pablo Bay. Each region has its own particular wines; what grows where depends upon the weather.

Inland valleys get hot; coastal regions stay cool. In West County and Carneros, nighttime fog blankets the vineyards. Burgundy-style wines do best, particularly Pinot Noir and Chardonnay. Further inland, Alexander, Sonoma and much of Dry Creek Valleys (as well as Napa Valley) are fog-protected. Here, Bordeaux-style wines thrive, especially Cabernet Sauvignon, Sauvignon Blanc, Merlot and other heat-loving varieties. For California's famous cabernets, head to Napa. Zinfandel and Rhône-style varieties, such as Syrah and Viognier, grow in both regions, warm and cool. In cooler climes, wines are lighter and more elegant; in warmer areas they are heavier and more rustic. As you explore, notice the bases of grapevines: the fatter they are, the older. 'Old vine' grapes yield color and complexity not found in grapes from younger vines.

Some basics: wineries and vineyards aren't the same. Grapes grow in a vineyard, then get fermented at a winery. Wineries that grow their own grapes are called estates, as in 'estate-grown' or 'estate-bottled,' but estates, too, ferment grapes from other vineyards. When vintners speak of 'single-vineyard' or 'vineyard-designate' wines, they mean the grapes all originated from the same vineyard; this allows for tighter quality-control. 'Single varietal' means all the grapes are the same variety (such as 100% merlot), but may come from different vineyards. Reserves are the vintner's limited-production wines; they're usually available only at the winery.

Don't be afraid to ask questions. Vintners love to talk. If you don't know how to taste wine, or what to look for, ask the person behind the counter to help you discover what you like. Just remember to spit out the wine; the slightest buzz will diminish your capacity to taste.

For a handy-dandy reference on the road, pick up a copy of Karen MacNeil's *The Wine Bible* (2001, Workman Publishing) or Jancis Robinson's *The Oxford Companion to Wine* (2006, Oxford University Press) to carry in the car.

required) Friday to Sunday. Bottles are $22 to $45.

Hawkes
TASTING ROOM

(Map p191; ☑707-938-7620; www.hawkeswine. com; 383 1st St W, Sonoma; tasting $10; ⊙11am-6pm) When you're in downtown Sonoma and don't feel like fighting traffic, Hawke's refreshingly unfussy tasting room showcases meaty Merlot and Cabernet Sauvignon, never blended with other varietals. Bottles are $30 to $70, the tasting fee is waived with a purchase over $30.

Little Vineyards
WINERY

(Map p188; ☑707-996-2750; www.littlevineyards. com; 15188 Sonoma Hwy, Glen Ellen; tasting $15; ⊙11am-4:30pm Thu-Mon; 🚶🐾) The name fits at this family-owned small-scale winery surrounded by grapes, with a lazy dog to greet you and a weathered, cigarette-burned tasting bar, at which Jack London formerly drank (before it came here). The big reds include Syrah, petite Syrah, Zin, Cab and several delish blends. Good picnicking on the vineyard-view terrace. Also rents a cottage in the vines. Bottles cost $20 to $45.

BR Cohn
WINERY

(Map p188; ☑800-330-4064, 707-938-4064; www. brcohn.com; 15000 Sonoma Hwy, Glen Ellen; tasting $10; ⊙10am-5pm) Picnic like a rock star at always-busy BR Cohn, whose founder managed '70s-superband the Doobie Brothers before moving on to make outstanding organic olive oils and fine wines – including excellent Cabernet Sauvignon, atypical in Sonoma. The little gourmet shop offers lots to taste, plus limited picnic supplies. In autumn, benefit concerts showcase bands like Skynyrd and the Doobies. Bottles are $16 to $56.

Arrowood
WINERY

(Map p188; ☑707-935-2600; www.arrowood-vineyards.com; 14347 Sonoma Hwy; tasting $20; ⊙10am-4:30pm) 🌿 Arrowood's hilltop tasting room has postcard-perfect valley views and a bourgeois vibe, fussy for Sonoma, but the excellent Chardonnay and Cabernet Sauvignon merit the hype. Tasting fee refunded with two-bottle purchase. Bottles are $25 to $90.

Imagery Estate
WINERY

(Map p188; ☑707-935-4515; www.imagerywinery.com; 14335 Sonoma Hwy; tasting $10-20; ⊙10am-4:30pm; 🚶🐾) 🌿 Imagery produces lesser-known varietals, biodynamically

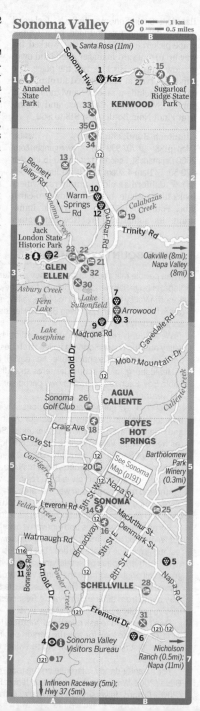

Sonoma Valley

grown, that you can't buy anywhere else – Cabernet Franc and Sangiovese are standouts. Each bottle sports an artist-designed label, with originals on display in the on-site gallery. Lovely gardens include a grassy picnic area with horseshoes and bocce. Limited picnic supplies available. Bottles are $24 to $45.

Benziger WINERY
(Map p188; ☎707-935-4527, 888-490-2739; www. benziger.com; 1883 London Ranch Rd, Glen Ellen; tasting $15-20, tram tour adult/under 21yr $25/10; ☉10am-5pm, tram tours 11:30am-3:30pm; 🅿🎒) 🍷 If you're new to wine, make Benziger your first stop for Sonoma's best crash course in winemaking. The worthwhile, non-reservable tour includes an open-air tram ride (weather permitting) through biodynamic vineyards, and a five-wine tasting. Great picnicking, plus a playground, make it tops for families. The large-production wine's OK (head for the reserves); the tour's the thing. Bottles are $15 to $80.

Wellington WINERY
(Map p188; ☎800-816-9463; www.wellingtonvineyards.com; 11600 Dunbar Rd, Glen Ellen; tasting $10; ☉10:30am-4:30pm) 🍷 Known for port (including a white) and meaty reds, Welling-ton makes great Zinfandel, one from vines planted in 1892 – wow, what color! The noir de noir is a cult favorite. Alas, servers have vineyard views, while you face the warehouse. Bottles are $15 to $30 and the tasting fee is refundable with a purchase.

Loxton WINERY
(Map p188; ☎707-935-7221; www.loxtonwines.com; 11466 Dunbar Rd, Glen Ellen; ☉11am-5pm) **FREE** Say g'day to Chris the Aussie winemaker at Loxton, a no-frills winery with million-dollar views and free tastings. The 'tasting room' is actually a small warehouse, where you can taste wonderful Syrah and Zinfandel; non-oaky, fruit-forward Chardonnay; and good port. Bottles cost $16 to $30.

⭐**Kaz** WINERY
(Map p188; ☎707-833-2536; www.kazwinery. com; 233 Adobe Canyon Rd, Kenwood; tasting $5; ☉11am-5pm Fri-Mon; 🅿🎒) 🍷 Sonoma's cult favorite, supercool Kaz is about blends: whatever's in the organic vineyards goes into the wine – and they're blended at crush, not during fermentation. Expect lesser-known varietals like Alicante Bouschet and Lenoir, and a worthwhile Cabernet-Merlot blend. Kids can sample grape juice, then run

around the playground outside. Bottles cost $20 to $48.

Sonoma & Around

Fancy boutiques may be replacing hardware stores lately, but Sonoma still retains an old-fashioned charm, thanks to the plaza and its surrounding frozen-in-time historic buildings. You can legally drink on the plaza – a rarity in California parks – but only between 11:30am and sunset.

Sonoma has rich history. In 1846 it was the site of a second American revolution, this time against Mexico, when General Mariano Guadalupe Vallejo deported all foreigners from California, prompting outraged frontiersmen to occupy the Sonoma Presidio and declare independence. They dubbed California the Bear Flag Republic after the battle flag they'd fashioned.

The republic was short-lived. The Mexican-American War broke out a month later, and California was annexed by the US. The revolt gave California its flag, which remains emblazoned with the words 'California Republic' beneath a muscular brown bear. Vallejo was initially imprisoned, but ultimately returned to Sonoma and played a major role in its development.

Sonoma Hwy (Hwy 12) runs through town. Sonoma Plaza, laid out by Vallejo in 1834, is the heart of downtown, lined with hotels, restaurants, tasting rooms and shops. The visitors bureau has a walking-tour brochure. Immediately north along Hwy 12, expect a brief suburban landscape before the valley's pastoral gorgeousness begins.

◎ Sights

★ Sonoma Plaza   SQUARE
(Map p191; btwn Napa, Spain & 1st Sts) Smack in the center of the plaza, the Mission-revival-style **city hall**, built between 1906 and 1908, has identical facades on four sides, reportedly because plaza businesses all demanded City Hall face their direction. At the plaza's northeast corner, the **Bear Flag Monument** marks Sonoma's moment of revolutionary glory. The weekly **farmers market** (5:30pm to 8pm Tuesday, April to October) showcases Sonoma's incredible produce.

Sonoma State Historic Park   HISTORIC SITE
(☑707-938-9560; www.parks.ca.gov; adult/child $3/2; ☉10am-5pm) The park is comprised of multiple sites, most side-by-side. The 1823

Mission San Francisco Solano de Sonoma anchors the plaza, and was the final California mission. Sonoma Barracks houses exhibits on 19th-century life. The 1886 Toscano Hotel lobby is beautifully preserved – peek inside. The 1852 Vallejo Home lies a half-mile northwest. One ticket allows admission to all, including **Petaluma Adobe** (☑707-762-4871; www.petalumaadobe.com; 3325 Adobe Rd, Petaluma; ☉10am-5pm Sat & Sun), Vallejo's ranch, 15 miles away.

➜ Mission San Francisco Solano de Sonoma
(Map p191; ☑707-938-9560; 114 E Spain St) At the plaza's northeast corner, the mission was built in 1823, partly to forestall Russians at Fort Ross from moving inland. This was the 21st and final California mission – the northernmost point on El Camino Real – and the only one built during the Mexican period (the rest were founded by the Spanish). Five original rooms remain. The not-to-be-missed chapel dates to 1841.

➜ Sonoma Barracks
(Map p191; ☑707-939-9420; parks.ca.gov; 20 E Spain St; adult/child $3/2; ☉10am-5pm) The adobe Sonoma Barracks was built by Vallejo between 1836 and 1840 to house Mexican troops. Today, interpretive displays describe life during the Mexican and American periods. The Barracks became the capital of a rogue nation on June 14, 1846, when American settlers, of varying sobriety, surprised guards and declared an independent 'California Republc' [sic] with a homemade flag featuring a blotchy bear.

The US took over a month later, but abandoned the barracks during the Gold Rush, leaving Vallejo to turn them into (what else?) a winery, in 1860.

➜ Toscano Hotel
(Map p191; ☑707-938-9560; 20 E Spain St) FREE Toscano Hotel opened as a store and library in the 1850s, then became a hotel in 1886. Peek into the lobby from 10am to 5pm; except for the traffic outside, you'd swear you were peering back in time. There are free tours 1pm through 4pm Saturdays and Sundays.

➜ General Vallejo Home
(☑707-938-9559; 363 3rd St W) A half-mile from the plaza, the lovely Vallejo Home, aka Lachryma Montis (Latin for 'Tears of the Mountain'), was built between 1851 and 1852 for General Vallejo and named for the on-site spring; the Vallejo family made good

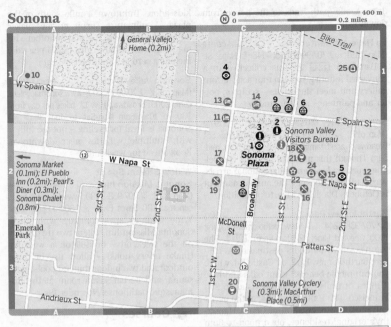

Sonoma

◉ Top Sights
1 Sonoma Plaza C2

◉ Sights
2 Bear Flag Monument............................. C2
3 City Hall C2
4 Hawkes C1
5 La Haye Art Center D2
6 Mission San Francisco Solano de
   Sonoma... D1
7 Sonoma Barracks C1
8 Sonoma Valley Museum of Art C2
9 Toscano Hotel C1

⊕ Activities, Courses & Tours
10 Ramekins Sonoma Valley
   Culinary School A1

🛏 Sleeping
11 El Dorado Hotel.................................... C1
12 Hidden Oak Inn D2
13 Sonoma Hotel C1
14 Swiss Hotel C1

🍴 Eating
15 Cafe La Haye D2
16 Della Santina's D2

El Dorado Kitchen........................... (see 11)
17 Harvest Moon Cafe C2
18 La Salette..D2
19 Red Grape...C2
Sunflower Caffé & Wine Bar .... (see 11)
Taste of the Himalayas ....(see 21)
the girl & the fig ....(see 13)

🍷 Drinking & Nightlife
Enoteca Della Santina...................(see 16)
20 Hopmonk Tavern...................................C3
21 Murphy's Irish Pub...............................D2
Steiner's...(see 17)
Swiss Hotel ....(see 14)

🎭 Entertainment
22 Sebastiani Theatre D2

🛍 Shopping
23 Chateau Sonoma....................................B2
24 Readers' Books......................................D2
Sign of the Bear ....(see 17)
Tiddle E Winks..................................(see 16)
25 Vella Cheese Co D1

money piping water to town. The property remained in the family until 1933, when the state of California purchased it, along with its original furnishings. Docents lead tours Saturdays and Sundays at 1pm, 2pm and

3pm. A bike path leads to the house from downtown.

La Haye Art Center
ARTS CENTER

(Map p191; 707-996-9665; 148 E Napa St; 11am-5pm) FREE At this collective in a converted foundry, you can tour a storefront gallery and meet the artists – sculptor, potter and painters – in their studios.

Sonoma Valley Museum of Art
MUSEUM

(Map p191; 707-939-7862; www.svma.org; 551 Broadway; adult/family $5/8; 11am-5pm Wed-Sun) Though this museum presents compelling work by local and international artists, such as David Hockney, the annual standout is October's Día de los Muertos exhibition.

Bartholomew Park
PARK

(707-938-2244; www.bartholomewpark.org; 1000 Vineyard Lane; 10am-6pm) FREE The top near-town outdoors destination is 375-acre Bartholomew Park, off Castle Rd, where you can picnic beneath giant oaks and hike 2 miles of trails, with hilltop vistas to San Francisco. The Palladian Villa, at the park's entrance, is a re-creation of Count Haraszthy's original residence, open noon to 3pm Saturdays and Sundays. There's also a good winery, independently operated.

Cornerstone Sonoma
GARDENS

(Map p188; 707-933-3010; www.cornerstonegardens.com; 23570 Arnold Dr, Hwy 121; 10am-4pm;) FREE There's nothing traditional about Cornerstone Gardens, which showcases 25 walk-through gardens by renowned avant-garde landscape designers who explore the intersection of art and nature. Let the kids run free while you explore top-notch garden shops, taste wine and gather information from the on-site Sonoma Valley Visitors Bureau (Map p188; 707-935-4747; www.sonomavalley.com; Cornerstone Gardens, 23570 Hwy 121; 10am-4pm); there's also a good, if pricy, on-site cafe. Look for the enormous blue Adirondack chair at road's edge.

We especially love Pamela Burton's 'Earth Walk,' which descends into the ground; and Planet Horticulture's 'Rise,' which exaggerates space.

🏃 Activities

Many local inns provide bicycles.

Traintown
AMUSEMENT PARK

(Map p188; 707-938-3912; www.traintown.com; 20264 Broadway; 10am-5pm daily late May–mid-Sep, Fri-Sun mid-Sep–late May;) Little kids adore Traintown, 1 mile south of the plaza. A miniature steam engine makes 20-minute loops ($5.75), and six other vintage amusement-park rides ($2.75 per ride) include a carousel and Ferris wheel.

Sonoma Valley Cyclery
BICYCLE RENTAL

(Map p188; 707-935-3377; www.sonomacyclery.com; 20091 Broadway/Hwy 12; bikes per day from $30; 10am-6pm Mon-Sat, to 4pm Sun;) Sonoma is ideal for cycling – not too hilly – with multiple wineries near downtown. Book ahead for weekends.

Willow Stream Spa at Sonoma Mission Inn
SPA

(Map p188; 707-938-9000; www.fairmont.com/sonoma; 100 Boyes Blvd; 7:30am-8pm) Few Wine Country spas compare with glitzy Sonoma Mission Inn, where two treatments on the weekend – or $89 on a weekday (make reservations) – allow use of three outdoor and two indoor mineral pools, gym, sauna, and herbal steam room at the Romanesque bathhouse. No under 18s.

🎓 Courses

Ramekins Sonoma Valley Culinary School
COOKING COURSE

(Map p191; 707-933-0450; www.ramekins.com; 450 W Spain St;) Offers demonstrations and hands-on classes for home chefs. Also runs weekend 'culinary camps' for adults and kids.

🛏 Sleeping

Off-season rates plummet. Reserve ahead. Ask about parking; some historic inns have no lots. Also consider Glen Ellen and, if counting pennies, Santa Rosa.

Sonoma Chalet
B&B $$

(800-938-3129, 707-938-3129; www.sonomachalet.com; 18935 5th St W; r $160-180, with shared bath $140, cottages $195-225;) A historic farmstead surrounded by rolling hills, Sonoma Chalet has rooms in a Swiss chalet–style house adorned with little balconies and country-style bric-a-brac. We love the free-standing cottages; Laura's has a wood-burning fireplace. All rooms come with breakfast, which is served on a deck overlooking a nature preserve. No air-con in rooms with shared bath. No phones, no internet.

Sonoma Hotel
HISTORIC HOTEL $$

(Map p191; 800-468-6016, 707-996-2996; www.sonomahotel.com; 110 W Spain St; r incl breakfast $170-200, ste $250;) Long on charm, this good-value, vintage-1880s hotel, decorated with country-style willow-wood furnishings, sits right on the plaza. Double-pane glass blocks the noise, but there's no elevator or parking lot.

Swiss Hotel
HISTORIC HOTEL **$$**

(Map p191; ☎707-938-2884; www.swisshotelsonoma.com; 18 W Spain St; r incl breakfast Mon-Fri $150-170, Sat & Sun $200-240; ❄️🅿️) It opened in 1905, so you'll forgive the wavy floors. The floral prints are likewise dated, but rooms are large, good value and share a plaza-view balcony. Downstairs there's a raucous bar and restaurant. No parking lot or elevator.

Windhaven Cottage
COTTAGE **$$**

(Map p188; ☎707-483-1856, 707-938-2175; www.windhavencottage.com; 21700 Pearson Ave; cottage $155-165; ❄️🅿️) Great-bargain Windhaven has two units: a hideaway cottage with vaulted wooden ceilings and a fireplace, and a handsome 800-sq-ft studio. We prefer the romantic cottage. Both have hot tubs. Tennis facilities, bicycles and barbecues sweeten the deal.

Sonoma Creek Inn
MOTEL **$$**

(Map p188; ☎888-712-1289, 707-939-9463; www.sonomacreekinn.com; 239 Boyes Blvd; r $116-225; ❄️🅿️📶) This cute-as-a-button motel has spotless, cheery, retro-Americana rooms, but it's not downtown. Valley wineries are a short drive. When available, last-minute bookings cost just $89.

El Dorado Hotel
BOUTIQUE HOTEL **$$$**

(Map p191; ☎707-996-3220; www.eldoradosonoma.com; 405 1st St W; r Mon-Fri $165-265, Sat & Sun $245-325; 🅿️❄️🅿️📶) Stylish touches, such as high-end linens, justify rates and compensate for the rooms' compact size, as do private balconies, which overlook the plaza or rear courtyard (we prefer the plaza view, despite noise). No elevator.

El Pueblo Inn
MOTEL **$$$**

(Map p188; ☎707-996-3651, 800-900-8844; www.elpuebloinn.com; 896 W Napa St; r incl breakfast $189-239; ❄️@🅿️📶) One mile west of downtown, family-owned El Pueblo has surprisingly cushy rooms with great beds. The big lawns and the heated pool are perfect for kids; parents appreciate the 24-hour hot tub.

Sonoma's Best Guest Cottages
COTTAGES **$$$**

(Map p188; ☎800-291-8962, 707-933-0340; www.sonomasbestcottages.com; 1190 E Napa St; cottages $199-349, q $279-395; ❄️🅿️) Each of these four colorful, inviting cottages has a bed-

room, living room, kitchen and barbecue, with comfy furniture, stereos, DVDs and bicycles. One mile east of the plaza.

Hidden Oak Inn
B&B **$$$**

(Map p191; ☎707-996-9863; www.hiddenoakinn.com; 214 E Napa St; r incl breakfast $195-245; ❄️📶🅿️) Three-room, 1914 Craftsman B&B with lovely service.

MacArthur Place
INN **$$$**

(☎800-722-1866, 707-938-2929; www.macarthurplace.com; 29 E MacArthur St; r from $350, ste from $499; ❄️@📶🅿️) Sonoma's top full-service inn occupies a former estate with century-old gardens.

✕ Eating

There's creek-side picnicking, with barbecue grills, up-valley at Sugarloaf Ridge State Park (p195). Find late-night taco trucks on Hwy 12, between Boyes Blvd and Aqua Caliente.

Angelo's Wine Country Deli
DELI **$**

(Map p188; ☎707-938-3688; 23400 Arnold Dr; sandwiches $7; ⏱9am-5:30pm) Look for the cow on the roof of this roadside deli, south of town, a fave for fat sandwiches and homemade jerky. In springtime, little lambs graze outside.

Pearl's Diner
DINER **$**

(☎707-996-1783; 561 5th St W; mains $7-10; ⏱7am-2:30pm; 🚼) Across from Safeway's west-facing wall, greasy-spoon Pearl's serves giant American breakfasts, including standout bacon and waffles with batter enriched by melted vanilla ice cream.

Sonoma Market
DELI, MARKET **$**

(☎707-996-3411; www.sonoma-glenellenmkt.com; 500 W Napa St; sandwiches from $6; ⏱5:30am-10pm) Sonoma's best groceries and deli sandwiches.

★ Fremont Diner
AMERICAN **$$**

(Map p188; ☎707-938-7370; http://thefremontdiner.com; 2698 Fremont Dr; mains $10-16; ⏱8am-3pm Mon-Wed, to 9pm Thu-Sun; 🚼) 🍴 Lines snake out the door peak times at this farm-to-table roadside diner. We prefer the indoor tables, but will happily accept a picnic table in the big outdoor tent to feast on ricotta pancakes with real maple syrup, chicken and waffles, oyster po' boys, finger-licking barbecue and skillet-baked cornbread. Arrive early, or late, to beat queues.

Sunflower Caffé & Wine Bar
CAFE **$$**

(Map p191; ☑707-996-6845; www.sonomasunflower.com; 421 1st St W; dishes $8-15; ⊗7am-4pm; 🐾) The big back garden at this local hangout is a great spot for breakfast, a no-fuss lunch or afternoon wine.

Red Grape
ITALIAN **$$**

(Map p191; ☑707-996-4103; http://theredgrape.com; 529 1st St W; mains $10-20; ⊗11:30am-10pm; 🐾) A reliable spot for an easy meal, Red Grape serves good thin-crust pizzas and big salads in a cavernous, echoey space. Good for takeout, too.

Della Santina's
ITALIAN **$$**

(Map p191; ☑707-935-0576; www.dellasantinas.com; 135 E Napa St; mains $14-24; ⊗11:30am-3pm & 5-9:30pm) The waiters have been here forever, and the 'specials' rarely change, but Della Santina's American-Italian cooking – linguini pesto, veal parmigiana, rotisserie chickens – is consistently good, and the brick courtyard is inviting on warm evenings.

Taste of the Himalayas
INDIAN, NEPALESE **$$**

(Map p191; ☑707-996-1161; 464 1st St E; mains $10-20; ⊗11am-2:30 Tue-Sun, 5-10pm daily) Spicy curries, luscious lentil soup and sizzle-platter meats make a refreshing break from the usual French-Italian Wine Country fare.

★ Cafe La Haye
CALIFORNIAN **$$$**

(Map p191; ☑707-935-5994; www.cafelahaye.com; 140 E Napa St; mains $20-32; ⊗5:30-9pm Tue-Sat) 🐾 One of Sonoma's top tables for earthy New American cooking, La Haye only uses produce sourced from within 60 miles. Its dining room gets packed cheek-by-jowl and service can border on perfunctory, but clean simplicity and flavor-packed cooking make it many foodies' first choice. Reserve well ahead.

the girl & the fig
FRENCH **$$$**

(Map p191; ☑707-938-3634; www.thegirlandthefig.com; 11 W Spain St; mains $20-27; ⊗11:30am-10pm Mon-Fri, 11am-11pm Sat, 10am-10pm Sun) For a festive evening, book a garden table at this French-provincial bistro, with good small plates ($12 to $14) including steamed mussels with matchstick fries, and duck confit with lentils. Weekday three-course prix-fixe costs $36, add $12 for wine. Stellar cheeses. Reservations essential.

El Dorado Kitchen
CALIFORNIAN **$$$**

(Map p191; ☑707-996-3030; www.eldorado-sonoma.com; 405 1st St W; lunch mains $12-17, dinner $24-31; ⊗8-11am, 11:30am-2:30pm & 5:30-9:30pm) 🐾 The swank plaza-side choice for contemporary California-Mediterranean cooking, El Dorado showcases seasonal-regional ingredients in dishes like duck-confit salad and housemade ravioli, served in a see-and-be-seen dining room with a big community table at its center. The happening lounge serves good small plates ($9 to $15) and craft cocktails. Make reservations.

La Salette
PORTUGUESE **$$$**

(Map p191; ☑707-938-1927; www.lasalette-restaurant.com; 452 1st St E; lunch mains $12-25, dinner $19-25; ⊗11:30am-2pm & 5:30-9pm) 🐾 Contemporary Portuguese cuisine is the focus at this restaurant that serves excellent-value, proper sit-down meals, including a standout seafood stew. Make reservations.

Harvest Moon Cafe
NEW AMERICAN **$$$**

(Map p191; ☑707-933-8160; www.harvestmooncafesonoma.com; 487 1st St W; mains $19-29; ⊗5:30-9pm Wed-Mon) 🐾 Inside a cozy 1836 adobe, this casual bistro uses local ingredients in its changing menu, with simple soul-satisfying dishes like duck risotto with Bellwether Farms ricotta. Book the patio in warm weather.

🍷 Drinking & Entertainment

Free jazz concerts happen on the plaza every second Tuesday, June to September, 6pm to 8:30pm; arrive early, bring a picnic.

Murphy's Irish Pub
PUB

(Map p191; ☑707-935-0660; www.sonomapub.com; 464 1st St E; ⊗noon-11pm) Don't ask for Bud – there're only *real* brews here. Good hand-cut fries and shepherd's pie, too. Live music Thursday through Sunday evenings.

Swiss Hotel
BAR

(Map p191; www.swisshotelsonoma.com; 18 W Spain St; ⊗11:30am-midnight) Locals and tourists crowd the 1909 Swiss Hotel for cocktails. There's OK food, but the bar's the thing.

Hopmonk Tavern
BREWERY

(Map p191; ☑707-935-9100; www.hopmonk.com; 691 Broadway; ⊗11:30am-10pm) This happening gastro-pub (dishes $10 to $20) and beer garden takes its brews seriously, with 16 on tap, served in type-appropriate glassware. Live music Friday through Sunday.

Enoteca Della Santina
WINE BAR

(Map p191; www.enotecadellasantina.com; 127 E Napa St; ⊗4-10pm Mon-Thu, to 11pm Fri, 2-11pm Sat, 2-10pm Sun) Thirty global vintages by the glass let you compare what you're tasting in California with the rest of the world's wines.

Steiner's
BAR

(Map p191; www.steinerstavern.com; 465 1st St W; ⏰6am-2am; 🛜) Sonoma's oldest bar gets crowded Sunday afternoons with cyclists and motorcyclists.

Sebastiani Theatre
CINEMA

(Map p191; ☑707-996-2020; sebastianitheatre. com; 476 1st St E) The plaza's gorgeous 1934 Mission-revival cinema screens art-house and revival films, and sometimes live theater.

🔒 Shopping

Vella Cheese Co
FOOD

(Map p191; ☑707-938-3232; www.vellacheese.com; 315 2nd St E; ⏰9:30am-6pm Mon-Sat) Known for its dry-jack cheeses (made here since the 1930s), Vella also makes good Mezzo Secco with cocoa powder–dusted rind. Staff will vacuum-pack for shipping.

Tiddle E Winks
TOYS

(Map p191; ☑707-939-6933; www.tiddleewinks. com; 115 E Napa St; ⏰10:30am-5:30pm Mon-Sat, 11am-5pm Sun; 👣) Vintage five-and-dime, with classic, mid-20th-century toys.

Sign of the Bear
HOMEWARES

(Map p191; ☑707-996-3722; 435 1st St W; ⏰10am-6pm) Kitchen-gadget freaks: make a beeline to this indie cookware store.

Chateau Sonoma
HOMEWARES, GIFTS

(Map p191; ☑707-935-8553; www.chateausonoma. com; 153 W Napa St; ⏰10:30am-6pm Mon-Sat, 11am-5pm Sun) France meets Sonoma in one-of-a-kind gifts and arty home decor.

Readers' Books
BOOKS

(Map p191; ☑707-939-1779; readers.indiebound. com; 130 E Napa St; ⏰10am-7pm Mon-Sat, to 6pm Sun) Independent bookseller.

ℹ️ Information

Sonoma Post Office (Map p191; ☑800-275-8777; www.usps.com; 617 Broadway; ⏰9am-5pm Mon-Fri)

Sonoma Valley Hospital (☑707-935-5000; www.svh.com; 347 Andrieux St) Twenty-four-hour emergency room.

Sonoma Valley Visitors Bureau (Map p191; ☑707-996-1090; www.sonomavalley.com; 453 1st E; ⏰9am-5pm Mon-Sat, 10am-5pm Sun) Arranges accommodations; has a good walking-tour pamphlet and events information. There's another at Cornerstone Gardens (p192).

Glen Ellen & Kenwood

Sleepy Glen Ellen is a snapshot of old Sonoma, with white-picket fences and tiny cottages beside a poplar-lined creek. When downtown Sonoma is jammed, you can wander quiet Glen Ellen and feel far away. It's ideal for a leg-stretching stopover between wineries or a romantic overnight – the nighttime sky blazes with stars. Arnold Dr is the main drag and the valley's back-way route. Kenwood lies just north, along Hwy 12, but has no town center like Glen Ellen's. For services, drive 8 miles south to Sonoma. Glen Ellen's biggest draws are Jack London State Historic Park and Benziger winery (p189).

🔘 Sights & Activities

Jack London State Historic Park
PARK

(Map p188; ☑707-938-5216; www.jacklondon-park.com; 2400 London Ranch Rd, Glen Ellen; per car $10, tour adult/child $4/2; ⏰9:30am-5pm) Napa has Robert Louis Stevenson, but Sonoma's got Jack London. This 1400-acre park frames the author's last years; don't miss the excellent on-site museum. Miles of hiking trails (some open to mountain bikes) weave through oak-dotted woodlands, between 600ft and 2300ft elevations; an easy 2-mile loop meanders to a lake, great for picnicking. Watch for poison oak.

Changing occupations from Oakland fisherman to Alaska gold prospector to Pacific yachtsman – and novelist on the side – London (1876–1916) ultimately took up farming. He bought 'Beauty Ranch' in 1905 and moved here in 1910. With his second wife, Charmian, he lived and wrote in a small cottage while his mansion, **Wolf House**, was under construction. On the eve of its completion in 1913, it burned down. The disaster devastated London, and although he toyed with rebuilding, he died before construction got underway. His widow, Charmian, built the **House of Happy Walls**, which has been preserved as a museum. It's a half-mile walk from there to the remains of Wolf House, passing London's grave along the way. Other paths wind around the farm to the cottage where he lived and worked.

Sugarloaf Ridge State Park
HIKING

(Map p188; ☑707-833-5712; www.parks.ca.gov; 2605 Adobe Canyon Rd, Kenwood; per car $8) There's fantastic hiking – when it's not blazingly hot. On clear days, **Bald Mountain** has drop-dead views to the sea; **Bushy Peak**

ⓘ WHAT'S CRUSH?

Crush is autumn harvest, the most atmospheric time of year, when the vine's leaves turn brilliant colors and you can smell fermenting fruit on the breeze. Farmers throw big parties for the vineyard workers to celebrate their work. Everyone wants to be here. That's why room rates skyrocket. If you can afford it, come during autumn. To score party invitations, join your favorite winery's wine club.

Trail peers into Napa Valley. Both are moderately strenuous; plan four hours round-trip.

Morton's Warm Springs　SWIMMING
(Map p188; ☎707-833-5511; www.mortonswarmsprings.com; 1651 Warm Springs Rd, Glen Ellen; adult/child $15/5; ⏰10am-6pm Sat, Sun & holidays May & Sep, Tue-Sun Jun-Aug; 👪) This old-fashioned family swim club has two mineral pools, limited hiking, volleyball and BBQ facilities. No credit cards Tuesday to Friday: exact change required. From Sonoma Hwy in Kenwood, turn west on Warm Springs Rd.

Triple Creek Horse Outfit　HORSEBACK RIDING
(☎707-887-8700; www.triplecreekhorseoutfit.com; 60/90min rides $75/95; ⏰Wed-Mon) Explore Jack London State Park by horseback for stunning vistas over Sonoma Valley. Reservations required.

🛏 Sleeping

Sugarloaf Ridge State Park　CAMPGROUND $
(Map p188; ☎800-444-7275; www.reserveamerica.com; 2605 Adobe Canyon Rd, Kenwood; tent & RV sites $35; 👪) Sonoma's nearest camping is north of Kenwood at this lovely hilltop park, with 50 drive-in sites, clean coin-operated showers and great hiking.

Jack London Lodge　MOTEL $$
(Map p188; ☎707-938-8510; www.jacklondonlodge.com; 13740 Arnold Dr, Glen Ellen; r Mon-Fri $124, Sat & Sun $189; ❄🐾🌐) An old-fashioned wood-sided motel, with well-kept rooms decorated with antique repros, this is a weekday bargain – and the manager will sometimes negotiate rates. Outside there's a hot tub; next door, a saloon.

Glen Ellen Cottages　BUNGALOW $$
(Map p188; ☎707-996-1174; www.glenelleninn.com; 13670 Arnold Dr, Glen Ellen; cottage Mon-Fri $139-159, Sat & Sun $209-249; ❄🐾) Hidden behind

Glen Ellen Inn, these five creek-side cottages are designed for romance, with oversized jetted tubs, steam showers and gas fireplaces.

★Beltane Ranch　B&B $$$
(Map p188; ☎707-996-6501; www.beltaneranch.com; 11775 Hwy 12, Glen Ellen; d incl breakfast $160-285; 🐾🌿) Surrounded by horse pastures and vineyards, Beltane is a throwback to 19th-century Sonoma. The cheerful, lemon-yellow, 1890s ranch house has double porches, lined with swinging chairs and white wicker. Though it's technically a B&B, each country-Americana-style room has a private entrance – nobody will make you pet the cat. Breakfast in bed. No phones or TVs mean zero distraction from pastoral bliss.

Gaige House Inn　B&B $$$
(Map p188; ☎707-935-0237, 800-935-0237; www.gaige.com; 13540 Arnold Dr, Glen Ellen; d incl breakfast from $275, ste from $425; @🐾🌐🌿) Among the valley's most chic inns, Gaige has 23 rooms, five inside an 1890 house decked out in Euro-Asian style. Best are the Japanese-style 'Zen suites,' with requisite high-end bells and whistles, including freestanding tubs made from hollowed-out granite boulders. Fabulous.

Kenwood Inn & Spa　INN $$$
(Map p188; ☎800-353-6966, 707-833-1293; www.kenwoodinn.com; 10400 Sonoma Hwy, Kenwood; r incl breakfast $450-825; ❄@🐾🌿) Lush gardens surround ivy-covered bungalows at this sexy 25-room inn, designed to resemble a Mediterranean château. Two hot tubs (one with a waterfall) and an on-site spa make it ideal for lovers, boring for singles. No kids. Book an upstairs balcony room.

🍴 Eating

Glen Ellen Village Market　DELI, MARKET $
(Map p188; www.sonoma-glenellenmkt.com; 13751 Arnold Dr, Glen Ellen; ⏰6am-8pm) Fantastic market with huge deli, ideal for picnickers.

Garden Court Cafe　CAFE $
(Map p188; ☎707-935-1565; www.gardencourtcafe.com; 13647 Arnold Dr, Glen Ellen; mains $9-12; ⏰8:30am-2pm Wed-Mon) Basic breakfasts, sandwiches and salads.

fig cafe & winebar　FRENCH, CALIFORNIAN $$
(Map p188; ☎707-938-2130; www.thefigcafe.com; 13690 Arnold Dr, Glen Ellen; mains $18-22; ⏰10am-3pm Sat & Sun, 5:30-9pm daily) The fig's earthy California–Provençal comfort food includes flash-fried calamari with spicy-lemon aioli,

duck confit and *moules-frites* (mussels and French fries). Good wine prices and weekend brunch give reason to return.

Yeti
INDIAN $$
(Map p188; ☑707-996-9930; www.yetirestaurant.com; 14301 Arnold Dr, Glen Ellen; mains $12-22; ☺11:30am-2:30pm & 5-9pm) Surprisingly good Indian and Nepalese cooking, served on a creek-side patio at a converted mill, make Yeti worth seeking out. Great value.

Glen Ellen Inn
AMERICAN $$
(Map p188; ☑707-996-6409; www.glenelleninn.com; 13670 Arnold Dr, Glen Ellen; mains $16-25; ☺11:30am-9pm Thu-Tue, 5:30-9pm Wed) Oysters, martinis and grilled steaks. Lovely garden, full bar.

Mayo Winery Reserve
WINERY $$
(Map p188; ☑707-833-5504; www.mayofamilywinery.com; 9200 Sonoma Hwy, Kenwood; 7-course menu $35; ☺by appointment 11am-5pm) Feast on a seven-course small-plates menu, paired with seven wines, for just $35 at this unatmospheric roadside wine-tasting room.

Cafe Citti
ITALIAN $$
(Map p188; ☑707-833-2690; www.cafecitti.com; 9049 Sonoma Hwy, Kenwood; mains $8-15; ☺11am-3:30pm & 5-9pm; 🐾) Locals favor this order-at-the-counter Italian-American deli, with standout roasted chicken, homemade gnocchi and ravioli; lunchtime, there's pizza and house-baked focaccia-bread sandwiches.

Kenwood Restaurant & Bar
CALIFORNIAN $$$
(Map p188; ☑707-833-6326; www.kenwoodrestaurant.com; 9900 Sonoma Hwy, Kenwood; mains $22-30; ☺11:30am-8:30pm Wed-Sun) 🍴 A stone patio flanks vineyards and flowering gardens at this roadhouse restaurant, lovely for a lingering lunch. The chef showcases quality ingredients by local producers in simple-delicious dishes like pork chops with bacon or roasted chicken. The small-plates menu ($10 to $16) is ideal for a quick bite between wineries. Reservations advised.

Aventine
ITALIAN $$$
(Map p188; ☑707-934-8911; http://glenellen.aventinehospitality.com; 14301 Arnold Dr, Glen Ellen; mains $14-28; ☺4:30-10pm Tue-Fri, 11am-10pm Sat & Sun) The Sonoma outpost of the popular San Francisco and Hollywood restaurants occupies an atmospheric former grist mill with a sun-dappled outdoor patio, and serves Italian-derived dishes, including mozzarella-stuffed meatball with pesto over polenta. Make reservations.

Olive & Vine
NEW AMERICAN $$$
(Map p188; ☑707-996-9152; oliveandvinerestaurant.com; 14301 Arnold Dr, Glen Ellen; mains $23-36; ☺5:30-9pm Wed-Sun) 🍴 Inside a repurposed grist mill with mismatched shabby-chic furniture, Olive & Vine showcases seasonal flavors in its cooking. Reservations essential.

🔒 Shopping

Wine Country Chocolates Tasting Bar
FOOD
(Map p188; ☑707-996-1010; www.winecountrychocolates.com; 14301 Arnold Dr, Glen Ellen; ☺10am-5pm) Sample fine chocolates of varying degrees of cacao.

Figone's Olive Oil
FOOD
(Map p188; ☑707-282-9092; www.figoneoliveoil.com; 9580 Sonoma Hwy, Kenwood; ☺11am-5pm) Figone's presses its own extra-virgin olive oil, and infuses some with flavors like Meyer-lemon, all free to sample.

RUSSIAN RIVER AREA

Lesser-known western Sonoma County was formerly famous for its apple farms and vacation cottages. Lately vineyards are replacing orchards, and the Russian River has taken its place among California's important wine appellations, especially for pinot noir.

'The River,' as locals call it, has long been a summertime-weekend destination for Northern Californians, who come to canoe, wander country lanes, taste wine, hike redwood forests and live at a lazy pace. In winter the river floods, and nobody's here.

The Russian River begins in the mountains north of Ukiah, in Mendocino County, but the most-known sections lie southwest of Healdsburg, where the river cuts a serpentine course toward the sea. Just north of Santa Rosa, River Rd, the lower valley's main artery, connects Hwy 101 with coastal Hwy 1 at Jenner. Hwy 116 heads northwest from Cotati through Sebastopol, then at Guerneville joins River Rd and cuts west to the sea. Westside Rd connects Guerneville and Healdsburg. West County's winding roads get confusing and there's limited cell service; carry a proper map.

Russian River Area Wineries

Sonoma County's wine-growing regions encompass several diverse areas, each famous

Russian River Area

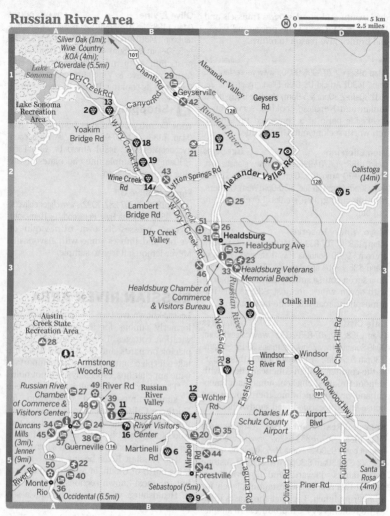

for different reasons (p187). Pick up the free, useful *Russian River Wine Road* map (www.wineroad.com) in tourist-brochure racks.

Russian River Valley

Nighttime coastal fog drifts up the Russian River Valley, then usually clears by midday. Pinot Noir does beautifully, as does Chardonnay, which also grows in hotter regions, but prefers the longer 'hang time' of cooler climes. The highest concentration of wineries is along Westside Rd, between Guerneville and Healdsburg.

Hartford Family Winery   WINERY
(☎707-887-8030; www.hartfordwines.com; 8075 Martinelli Rd, Forestville; tasting $15; ☉10am-4:30pm) 🌿 Surprisingly upscale for West County, Hartford sits in a pastoral valley surrounded by redwood-forested hills, on one of the area's prettiest back roads. It specializes in fine single-vineyard Pinot (12 kinds), Chardonnay and Zinfandel from old-vine fruit. Umbrella-shaded picnic tables dot the garden. Bottles are $38 to $90 and the tasting fee is waived with purchase.

Russian River Area

Korbel

WINERY

(☎707-824-7000, 707-824-7316; www.korbel.com; 13250 River Rd, Guerneville; ⏱10am-5pm; 📷) **FREE** Gorgeous rose gardens (April to October) and an on-site deli make Korbel worth a stop for free tasting; the sparking wine's just OK.

Iron Horse Vineyards

WINERY

(☎707-887-1507; www.ironhorsevineyards.com; 9786 Ross Station Rd, Sebastopol; tasting $20; ⏱10am-4:30pm) Atop a hill with drop-dead views over the county, Iron Horse is known for Pinot Noir and sparkling wines, which the White House often pours. The outdoor tasting room is refreshingly unfussy; when you're done with your wine, pour it in the grass. Sunday noon to 4pm, April to October, they serve oysters ($3). Located off Hwy 116. Bottles cost $27 to $85.

Marimar

WINERY

(☎707-823-4365; www.marimarestate.com; 11400 Graton Rd, Sebastopol; tasting $10-15; ⏱11am-4pm; 📷) 🍷 Middle-of-nowhere Marimar specializes in all-organic Pinot – seven different kinds – and Spanish varietals. The hacienda-style hilltop tasting room has a knockout vineyard-view terrace, good for picnics. Also consider tapas-and-wine pairings ($45). Bottles are $29 to $57.

Gary Farrell

WINERY

(☎707-473-2900; www.garyfarrellwines.com; 10701 Westside Rd, Healdsburg; tasting $15-25; ⏱10:30am-4:30pm; 📷) High on a hilltop, overlooking the Russian River, Gary Farrell's tasting room sits perched among second-growth redwoods. The elegant Chardonnay and long-finish Pinot, made by a big-name winemaker, score high marks for consistency. Bottles are $32 to $60.

Porter Creek

WINERY

(☎707-433-6321; www.portercreekvineyards.com; 8735 Westside Rd, Healdsburg; ⏱10:30am-4:30pm; 📷) 🍷 **FREE** Inside a vintage-1920s garage, Porter Creek's tasting bar is a former bowling-alley lane, plunked atop barrels. Porter is old-school Northern California, an early pioneer in biodynamic farming. High-acid, food-friendly Pinot Noir and Chardonnay are specialties, but there's silky Zinfandel and other Burgundian- and Rhône-style wines, too. Check out the aviary. Bottles cost $20 to $72 and tastings are free.

Hop Kiln Winery

WINERY

(☎707-433-6491; www.hopkilnwinery.com; 6050 Westside Rd, Healdsburg; tasting $7; ⏱10am-5pm) This photogenic, historic landmark, has a busy tasting room inside a former hop kiln; we especially like the flavored vinegars, which make great $10 gifts.

De La Montanya

WINERY

(☎707-433-3711; www.dlmwine.com; 999 Foreman Lane, Healdsburg; tasting $10; ⏱by appointment Mon-Thu, 11am-4:30pm Fri-Sun; 📷) This tiny winery, tucked amid vineyards, is known for 17 small-batch varieties made with estate-grown fruit. Viognier, Primitivo, Pinot and Cabernet are signatures; the 'summer white' and Gewürtztraminer are great back-porch wines. Apple-shaded picnic area, bocce ball and horseshoes add to the fun. Bottles are $20 to $60 and the tasting fee is refundable with a purchase.

J Winery

WINERY

(☎707-431-3646; www.jwine.com; 11447 Old Redwood Hwy, Healdsburg; tasting $20, tour $30; ⏱11am-5pm) 🍷 J crafts crisp sparkling wines, among Sonoma's best, but it's pricy. Splurge on seated food-and-wine pairings ($45; Friday to Sunday, May to October, call ahead). Bottles cost $20 to $90.

Dry Creek Valley

Hemmed in by 2000ft-high mountains, Dry Creek Valley is relatively warm, ideal for Sauvignon Blanc and Zinfandel, and in some places Cabernet Sauvignon. It's west of Hwy 101, between Healdsburg and Lake Sonoma. Dry Creek Rd is the fast-moving main thoroughfare. Parallel-running West Dry Creek Rd is an undulating country lane with no center stripe – one of Sonoma's great back roads, ideal for cycling.

Quivira

WINERY

(☎707-431-8333; www.quivirawine.com; 4900 West Dry Creek Rd; tasting $10; ⏱11am-5pm; 🚻📷) 🍷 Sunflowers, lavender and crowing roosters greet your arrival at this winery and biodynamic farm, with self-guided garden tours and a picnic grove beside the vines. Kids can giggle with pigs and chickens, while you sample Rhône varietals, unusual blends, and lip-smacking Sauvignon Blanc. Bottles are $22 to $45; the tasting fee is refundable with purchase.

Unti Vineyards

WINERY

(☎707-433-5590; www.untivineyards.com; 4202 Dry Creek Rd; tasting $5; ⏱by appointment 10am-4pm; 📷) 🍷 Inside a vineyard-view tasting room, Unti pours all estate-grown reds –

Châteauneuf-du-Pape-style grenache, compelling Syrah, and superb Sangiovese – favored by oenophiles for their structured tannins and concentrated fruit. If you love small-batch wines, don't miss Unti. Bottles are $23 to $40 and the tasting fee is refundable with a purchase.

Family Wineries   WINERY
(☎ 707-433-0100; familywines.com; 4791 Dry Creek Rd; tasting $10; ⏱ 10:30am-4:30pm) Sample multiple varietals at this cooperative, which showcases six boutique wineries too small to have their own tasting rooms. Tasting fee is refundable with a purchase.

Truett Hurst Vineyards   WINERY
(☎ 707-433-9545; www.truetthurst.com; 5610 Dry Creek Rd; tasting $5-10; ⏱ 10am-5pm) ⚑ Pull up an Adirondack chair and picnic creekside at Truett Hurst, Dry Creek's newest biodynamic winery. Sample terrific old-vine zins, standout petite Syrah and Russian River Pinots at the handsome contemporary tasting room, then meander through fragrant butterfly gardens to the creek, where salmon spawn in autumn. Saturdays there are snacks, Sundays **live music** (1pm to 4:30pm). Bottles are $18 to $50.

Bella Vineyards   WINERY
(☎ 707-473-9171; www.bellawinery.com; 9711 West Dry Creek Rd; tasting $10; ⏱ 11am-4:30pm) Atop the valley's north end, always-fun Bella has caves built into the hillside. The estate-grown grapes include 110-year-old vines from Alexander Valley. The focus is on big reds – Zin and Syrah – but there's terrific rosé (good for barbecues), and late-harvest Zin (great with brownies). The wonderful vibe and dynamic staff make Bella special. Bottles are $25 to $42.

Preston Vineyards   WINERY
(www.prestonvineyards.com; 9282 West Dry Creek Rd; tasting $5; ⏱ 11am-4:30pm; 🖼) ⚑ An early leader in organics, Lou Preston's 19th-century farm is old Sonoma. Weathered picket fencing frames the 19th-century farmhouse-turned-tasting room, with candy-colored walls and tongue-in-groove ceilings setting a country mood. The signature is citrusy Sauvignon Blanc, but try the Rhône varietals and small-lot wines: Mourvèdre, Viognier, Cinsault and cult-favorite Barbera. Preston also bakes good bread; picnic in the shade of a walnut tree. Monday to Friday, there's bocce ball. Bottles are $24 to

$38, and the tasting fee is refundable with a purchase.

Alexander Valley

Bucolic Alexander Valley flanks the Mayacamas Mountains, with postcard-perfect vistas and wide-open vineyards. Summers are hot, ideal for Cabernet Sauvignon, Merlot and warm-weather Chardonnays, but there's also fine Sauvignon Blanc and Zinfandel. For events info, visit www.alexandervalley.org.

Hanna   WINERY
(☎ 800-854-3987, 707-431-4310; http://hannawinery.com; 9280 Hwy 128, Healdsburg; tasting $10-20; ⏱ 10am-4pm; 🖼) Abutting oak-studded hills, Hanna's tasting room has lovely vineyard views and good picnicking. At the bar, find estate-grown Merlot and Cabernet, and big-fruit Zins and Syrah. Sit-down wine-and-cheese tastings are available ($25). Bottles cost $18 to $56.

Hawkes   TASTING ROOM
(☎ 707-433-4295; www.hawkeswine.com; 6734 Hwy 128, Healdsburg; tasting $10; ⏱ 10am-5pm; 🖼) Friendly Hawkes' makes an easy stopover while you're exploring the valley. The single-vineyard Cab is damn good, as is the blend; there's also a clean-and-crisp, non-malolactic Chardonnay. Bottles are $30 to $70 and the tasting fee is refundable with a purchase.

Stryker Sonoma   WINERY
(☎ 707-433-1944; www.strykersonoma.com; 5110 Hwy 128, Geyserville; tasting $10; ⏱ 10:30am-5pm; 🖼) ⚑ Wow, what a view from the hilltop concrete-and-glass tasting room at Stryker Sonoma. The standouts are fruit-forward Zinfandel and Sangiovese, which you can't buy anywhere else. Good picnicking. Bottles are $20 to $50; tasting fee is refundable with purchase.

Trentadue   WINERY
(☎ 888-332-3032, 707-433-3104; www.trentadue.com; 19170 Geyserville Ave, Geyserville; tasting $5-10; ⏱ 10am-5pm; 🖼) Specializes in ports (ruby, not tawny); the chocolate port makes a great gift.

Sebastopol

Grapes have replaced apples as the new cash crop, but Sebastopol's farm-town identity remains rooted in the apple – evidence the much-heralded summertime Gravenstein

Apple Fair. The town center feels suburban because of traffic, but a hippie tinge gives it color. This is the refreshingly unfussy side of Wine Country, and makes a good-value base for exploring the area.

Hwy 116 splits downtown; southbound traffic uses Main St, northbound traffic Petaluma Ave. North of town, it's called Gravenstein Hwy N and continues toward Guerneville; south of downtown, it's Gravenstein Hwy S, which heads toward Hwy 101 and Sonoma.

◉ Sights

Around Sebastopol, look for family-friendly farms, gardens, animal sanctuaries and pick-your-own orchards. For a countywide list, check out the **Sonoma County Farm Trails Guide** (www.farmtrails.org).

★ The Barlow   MARKET
(☑707-824-5600; thebarlow.net; 6770 McKinley St; ☺8:30am-9:30pm; ⊞) The Barlow occupies a former apple processing plant, covering 12 acres, re-purposed into a village of food producers, artists, winemakers, coffee roasters, spirits distillers and indie restaurateurs, who showcase West County's culinary and artistic diversity. Wander shed to shed, sample everything from house-brewed beer to nitrogen flash-frozen ice cream, and meet artisanal producers in their workshops. Thursdays 4pm to 8pm, mid-June to mid-October, the Barlow hosts a 'street fair,' with live music and local vendors.

Spirit Works Distillery   DISTILLERY
(☑707-634-4793; www.spiritworksdistillery.com; 6790 McKinley St, 100, The Barlow; tasting $5, tour $15; ☺11am-4pm Thu-Sun) ✿ A bracing alternative to wine-tasting, Spirit Works crafts superb small-batch spirits – vodka, gin, sloe gin and (soon) whiskey – of organic California red-winter wheat. Sample and buy in the warehouse. Tours (by reservation) happen Friday to Sunday at 4pm. Bottles are $27 to $36.

California Carnivores   GARDENS
(☑707-824-0433; www.californiacarnivores.com; 2833 Old Gravenstein Hwy S; ☺10am-4pm Thu-Mon) Even vegans can't help admiring these incredible carnivorous plants – the largest collection in the US – including specimens from around the globe.

Farmers Market   MARKET
(www.sebastopolfarmmarket.org; cnr Petaluma & McKinley Aves; ☺10am-1:30pm Sun) Meets at the downtown plaza.

✸✸ Festivals & Events

Apple Blossom Festival   CULTURAL
(appleblossomfest.com) Live music, food, drink, wine, a parade and exhibits in April.

Gravenstein Apple Fair   FOOD
(www.gravensteinapplefair.com) Arts, crafts, food, wines and brews, games, live entertainment and farm-life activities in August.

⊨ Sleeping

Staying in Sebastopol is convenient to Russian River Valley, the coast, and Sonoma Valley.

Sebastopol Inn   MOTEL $$
(☑800-653-1082, 707-829-2500; www.sebastopolinn.com; 6751 Sebastopol Ave; r $119-209; ❉ 🐾 ≋) We like this independent, *non*-cookie-cutter motel for its quiet, off-street location, usually reasonable rates and good-looking if basic rooms. Outside are grassy areas for kids and a hot tub.

Fairfield Inn & Suites   HOTEL $$
(☑800-465-4329, 707-829-6677; www.winecountryhi.com; 1101 Gravenstein Hwy S; r $134-249; ❉@🐾≋) Generic but modern, this hotel has little extras, such as in-room refrigerators and coffee makers, plus a hot tub.

✕ Eating

Fiesta Market   MARKET $
(Pacific Market; ☑707-823-9735; fiestamkt.com; 550 Gravenstein Hwy N; ☺8am-8pm) Excellent for groceries and picnics; north of downtown.

East-West Cafe   MEDITERRANEAN $
(☑707-829-2822; www.eastwestcafesebastopol.com; 128 N Main St; meals $9-13; ☺8am-9pm Mon-Sat, to 8pm Sun; ✎⊞) ✿ This unfussy cafe serves everything from grass-fed burgers to macrobiotic wraps, stir-fries to *huevos rancheros* (corn tortilla with fried egg and chili-tomato sauce). Good blue-corn pancakes at breakfast.

Slice of Life   VEGETARIAN $
(☑707-829-6627; www.thesliceoflife.com; 6970 McKinley St; mains under $10; ☺11am-9pm Tue-Fri, 9am-9pm Sat & Sun; ✎) ✿ This vegan-vegetarian kitchen doubles as a pizzeria. Breakfast all day. Great smoothies and date shakes.

Screamin' Mimi   ICE CREAM $
(☑707-823-5902; www.screaminmimisicecream.com; 6902 Sebastopol Ave; ☺11am-10pm) Delish homemade ice cream.

Mom's Apple Pie
DESSERTS $

(☑707-823-8330; www.momsapplepieusa.com; 4550 Gravenstein Hwy N; whole pies $7-17; ☉10am-6pm; 🚗♿) Pie's the thing at this roadside bakery – and yum, that flaky crust. Apple is predictably good, especially in autumn, but the blueberry is our fave, made better with vanilla ice cream.

Forchetta Bastoni
ITALIAN, SOUTHEAST ASIAN $$

(☑707-829-9500; www.forchettabastoni.com; 6948 Sebastopol Ave; mains $10-16; ☉11am-9pm Sun-Thu, to 10pm Fri & Sat; 🚗) Inside a converted brick-walled warehouse, Forchetta Bastoni has two kitchens that make wildly different food – Southeast Asian and Italian. Pick a cuisine, then be seated on one side or the other for wood-fired pizzas, pastas and roasted meats; or noodles, rice bowls and curries. If you can't decide, sit at the happening bar.

Red's Apple Roadhouse
AMERICAN $$

(☑707-861-9338; www.redsappleroadhouse.com; 4550 Gravenstein Hwy N; mains $9-15; ☉8am-9:30pm Tue-Sat, to 5pm Sun) 🚗 A rustic roadhouse and tavern north of downtown (next door to Mom's Apple Pie), Red's smokes its own bacon and pastrami, bakes its own bread and serves simple, quality American cooking, using locally sourced ingredients in dishes like fried chicken and waffles, pulled-pork sandwiches, biscuits and gravy, and classic mac-n-cheese. Local beer and wine. Live music Wednesday and Friday evenings.

Hopmonk Tavern
PUB FOOD $$

(☑707-829-9300; www.hopmonk.com; 230 Petaluma Ave; mains $12-23; ☉11:30am-9pm Sun-Wed, to 9:30pm Thu-Sat, bar to 1:30am; 🛜) Inside a converted 1903 railroad station, Hopmonk's serves 76 varieties of beer – served in type-specific glassware – that pair with a good menu of burgers, fried calamari, charcuterie platters and salads.

K&L Bistro
FRENCH $$$

(☑707-823-6614; www.klbistro.com; 119 S Main St; lunch $14-20, dinner $19-29; ☉11am-9pm) K&L serves earthy provincial Cal-French bistro cooking in a convivial bar-and-grill space with sidewalk patio. Expect classics like mussels and French fries, and grilled steaks with red-wine reduction. Reservations essential.

Zazu Kitchen & Farm
ITALIAN, NEW AMERICAN $$$

(☑707-523-4814; zazukitchen.com; 6770 McKinley St, 150, The Barlow; lunch mains $13-18, dinner $24-29; ☉11:30am-10pm Wed & Thu, to midnight Fri, from 9am Sat & Sun, from 5pm Mon) 🚗 We love the farm-to-table ethos of Zazu – they raise their own pigs and source everything locally – but some dishes miss, and the industrial-style space gets crazy loud. Still, we love their pizzas, salads, housemade salumi and bacon. Good breakfasts, too.

🍷 Drinking & Entertainment

Woodfour Brewing Co.
BREWERY

(☑707-823-3144; www.woodfourbrewing.com; 6780 Depot St, The Barlow; ☉11am-9pm Sun-Thu, to 11pm Fri & Sat) 🚗 Woodfour's solar-powered brewery serves 12 housemade beers, light on alcohol and hops, plus several sours (high-acid beer). It has an exceptionally good menu of small plates, designed to pair with beer, from simple snacks to refined, technique-driven dishes better than any we've had at a California brewery.

Taylor Maid Farms
CAFE

(☑707-634-7129; www.taylormaidfarms.com; 6790 Depot St, The Barlow; ☉6am-7pm Sun-Thu, to 9pm Fri & Sat) 🚗 Choose your brew method (drip, press, etc) at this third-wave coffeehouse that roasts its own organic beans. Exceptional seasonal drinks include lavender lattes.

Hardcore Espresso
CAFE

(☑707-823-7588; 1798 Gravenstein Hwy S; ☉6am-7pm; 🛜) 🚗 Meet local hippies and art freaks over coffee and smoothies at this classic Nor-Cal, off-the-grid, indoor-outdoor coffeehouse, south of downtown, that's essentially a corrugated-metal-roofed shack surrounded by umbrella tables.

Jasper O'Farrell's
BAR

(☑707-823-1389; 6957 Sebastopol Ave; ☉noon-2am) Busy bar with billiards and live music most nights; good drink specials.

Hopmonk Tavern
LIVE MUSIC

(☑707-829-7300; www.hopmonk.com; 230 Petaluma Ave; ☉11:30am-11pm Sun-Wed, to midnight Thu-Sat) This always-busy tavern and beer garden has town's most diverse live-music calendar, and sometimes hosts the likes of Jonathan Richman.

🛍 Shopping

Antique shops line Gravenstein Hwy S toward Hwy 101.

Aubergine
VINTAGE

(☑707-827-3460; 755 Petaluma Ave; ☉10am-6pm) Vast vintage emporium, specializing in cast-off European thrift-shop clothing.

Sumbody
BEAUTY

(☎ 707-823-2053; www.sumbody.com; 118 N Main St; ☺ 10am-7pm Mon-Wed, to 8pm Thu-Sat, to 6pm Sun) Eco-friendly bath products made with all-natural ingredients. Also offers well-priced facials ($49) and massages ($85) at its small on-site spa.

Toyworks
TOYS

(☎ 707-829-2003; www.sonomatoyworks.com; 6940 Sebastopol Ave; ☺ 10am-6pm Mon-Sat, 11am-5pm Sun; ⚑) Indie toy-seller with phenomenal selection of quality games for kids.

Funk & Flash
CLOTHING

(☎ 707-829-1142; www.funkandflash.com; 228 S Main St; ☺ 11am-7pm) Disco-glam party clothes, inspired by Burning Man.

Antique Society
ANTIQUES

(☎ 707-829-1733; www.antiquesociety.com; 2661 Gravenstein Hwy S; ☺ 10am-5pm) One-hundred-and-twenty-five antiques vendors under one roof.

Beekind
FOOD, HOMEWARES

(☎ 707-824-2905; www.beekind.com; 921 Gravenstein Hwy S; ☺ 10am-6pm Mon-Sat, to 4pm Sun) ⚑ Local honey and beeswax candles.

Copperfield's Books
BOOKS

(☎ 707-823-2618; www.copperfields.net; 138 N Main St; ☺ 10am-7pm Mon-Sat, to 6pm Sun) Indie bookshop with literary events.

Midgley's Country Flea Market
MARKET

(☎ 707-823-7874; mfleamarket.com; 2200 Gravenstein Hwy S; ☺ 6:30am-4:30pm Sat & Sun) The region's largest flea market.

❶ Information

Sebastopol Area Chamber of Commerce & Visitors Center (☎ 877-828-4748, 707-823-3032; www.visitsebastopol.org; 265 S Main St; ☺ 10am-4pm Mon-Fri) Maps, information and exhibits.

Occidental & Around

Our favorite West County town is a haven of artists, back-to-the-landers and counter-culturalists. Historic 19th-century buildings line a single main street, easy to explore in an hour; continue north by car and you'll hit the Russian River, in Monte Rio. At Christmastime, Bay Area families flock to Occidental to buy trees. The town decorates to the nines, and there's weekend cookie-decorating and caroling at the Union Hotel's Bocce Ballroom.

◉ Sights & Activities

Occidental Farmers Market
MARKET

(www.occidentalfarmersmarket.com; ☺ 4pm-dusk Fri Jun-Oct) Meet the whole community at Occidental's detour-worthy farmers market, with musicians, craftspeople and – the star attraction – **Gerard's Paella** (www.gerardspaella.com) of TV-cooking-show fame.

Sonoma Canopy Tours
OUTDOORS

(☎ 888-494-7868; www.sonomacanopytours.com; 6250 Bohemian Hwy; adult $99-109, child $69) North of town, fly through the redwood canopy on seven interconnected ziplines, ending with an 80ft-rappel descent; reservations required.

Osmosis
SPA

(☎ 707-823-8231; www.osmosis.com; 209 Bohemian Hwy, Freestone; ☺ by appointment) Three miles south in Freestone, tranquility prevails at this Japanese-inspired spa, which indulges patrons with dry-enzyme baths of aromatic cedar fibers (bath-and-blanket wrap $89

WORTH A TRIP

SCENIC DRIVE: COLEMAN VALLEY ROAD

Wine Country's most scenic drive isn't through the grapes, but along these 10 miles of winding West County byway, from Occidental to the sea. It's best late morning, after the fog has cleared. Drive west, not east, with the sun behind you and the ocean ahead. First you'll pass through redwood forests and lush valleys where Douglas firs stand draped in sphagnum moss – an eerie sight in the fog. The real beauty shots lie further ahead, when the road ascends 1000ft hills, dotted with gnarled oaks and craggy rock formations, with the vast blue Pacific unfurling below. The road ends at coastal Hwy 1, where you can explore Sonoma Coast State Beach (p222), then turn left and find your way to the tiny town of Bodega (not Bodega Bay) to see locales where Hitchcock shot his 1963 classic, *The Birds*.

to $99), lovely tea-and-meditation gardens, plus outdoor massages. Make reservations.

🛏 Sleeping

Occidental Hotel
MOTEL $$
(☎877-867-6084, 707-874-3623; www.occidentalhotel.com; 3610 Bohemian Hwy; r $120-160, 2-bedroom q $200-240; ✺❀✵✤) Rates are sometimes negotiable for these well-kept motel rooms

Valley Ford Hotel
INN $$
(☎707-876-1983; www.vfordhotel.com; r $115-175) Surrounded by pastureland 8 miles south in Valley Ford, this 19th-century, six-room inn has good beds, great rates and a terrific roadhouse restaurant.

Inn at Occidental
INN $$$
(☎707-874-1047, 800-522-6324; www.innatoccidental.com; 3657 Church St; r incl breakfast $249-339; ✤) One of Sonoma's finest, this beautifully restored 18-room Victorian inn is filled with collectible antiques; rooms have gas fireplaces and cozy feather beds.

✗ Eating

Howard Station Cafe
AMERICAN $
(☎707-874-2838; www.howardstationcafe.com; 3811 Bohemian Hwy; mains $6-12; ⊘7am-2:30pm Mon-Fri, to 3pm Sat & Sun; ✦✤) Big plates of comfort cooking and fresh-squeezed juices. Cash only.

Wild Flour Bread
BAKERY $
(www.wildflourbread.com; 140 Bohemian Hwy, Freestone; items from $3; ⊘8:30am-6:30pm Fri-Mon) Organic brick-oven sourdough breads, giant sticky buns and good coffee.

Bohemian Market
DELI $
(☎707-874-3312; 3633 Main St; ⊘8am-9pm) Occidental's best grocery store has an OK deli.

Rocker Oysterfeller's
NEW AMERICAN $$
(☎707-876-1983; www.rockeroysterfellers.com; 14415 Hwy 1, Valley Ford; mains $13-24; ⊘5pm-8:30pm Thu & Fri, from 3pm Sat, from 10am Sun) We love the flavor-rich cooking at this Valley Ford roadhouse, which features barbecued oysters, local crab cakes, steaks and fried chicken. Great wine bar, too. Sundays there's brunch.

Barley & Hops
PUB FOOD $$
(☎707-874-9037; www.barleynhops.com; 3688 Bohemian Hwy; mains $10-15; ⊘4-9:30pm Mon-Thu, from 11am Fri-Sun) Serves over 100 beers, sandwiches, giant salads and shepherd's pie.

Union Hotel
ITALIAN $$
(☎707-874-3555; www.unionhoteloccidental.com; 3703 Bohemian Hwy; meals $15-25; ⊘11am-9pm; ✦) Occidental has two old-school American-Italian restaurants that serve family-style meals. The Union is slightly better (neither is great), and has a hard-to-beat lunch special in its 1869 saloon – whole pizza, salad and soda for $12. At dinner, sit in the fabulous Bocce Ballroom.

Bistro des Copains
FRENCH-CALIFORNIAN $$$
(☎707-874-2436; www.bistrodescopains.com; 3728 Bohemian Hwy; mains $24-26, 3-course menu $40-45; ⊘5-9pm Wed-Mon) ✔ Worth a special trip, this convivial bistro draws bon vivants for Cal-French country cooking, like *steak-frites* and roast duck. Great wines; $10 corkage for Sonoma vintages. Make reservations.

🔒 Shopping

Verdigris
HOMEWARES
(☎707-874-9018; www.1lightartlamps.com; 72 Main St; ⊘11am-6pm Thu-Mon) Crafts gorgeous art lamps.

Hand Goods
CERAMICS
(☎707-874-2161; www.handgoods.net; 3627 Main St; ⊘10am-6pm) Collective of ceramicists and potters.

Guerneville & Around

The Russian River's biggest vacation-resort town, Guerneville gets busy summer weekends with party-hardy gay boys, sun-worshipping lesbians and long-haired, beer-drinking Harley riders, earning it the nickname 'Groin-ville.' Though the town is slowly gentrifying, it hasn't lost its honky-tonk vibe – fun-seeking crowds still come to canoe, hike redwoods and hammer cocktails poolside.

Downriver, some areas are sketchy (due to drugs). The local chamber of commerce has chased most of the tweakers from Main St in Guerneville, but if some off-the-beaten-path areas feel creepy – especially campgrounds – they probably are.

Four miles downriver, tiny Monte Rio has a sign over Hwy 116 declaring it 'Vacation Wonderland' – an overstatement, but the dog-friendly beach is a hit with families. Further west, idyllic Duncans Mills is home to a few dozen souls and has picture-ready historic buildings, now converted into cute shops. Upriver, east of Guerneville, Forestville is where agricultural country resumes.

⊙ Sights & Activities

Look for sandy beaches and swimming holes along the river; there's good river access east of town at **Sunset Beach** (www.sonoma-county.org/parks; 11060 River Rd, Forestville; per car $7; ⊙7am-sunset). Fishing and watercraft outfitters operate mid-May to early October, after which winter rains dangerously swell the river. A **farmers market** meets downtown on Wednesdays, June through September, from 3pm to 7pm. On summer Saturdays, there's also one at Monte Rio Beach, 11am to 2pm.

Armstrong Redwoods State Natural Reserve
FOREST

(⊘information 707-869-2015, office 707-869-9177, visitor center 707-869-2958; www.parks.ca.gov; 17000 Armstrong Woods Rd; per car $8; ⊙8am-sunset; 🖫) A magnificent redwood forest 2 miles north of Guerneville, the 805-acre Armstrong Redwoods State Reserve was saved from the saw by a 19th-century lumber magnate. Short interpretive trails lead into magical forests, with trees 30-stories high. Beyond lie 20 miles of backcountry trails, through oak woodlands, in adjoining **Austin Creek State Recreation Area**, one of Sonoma County's last-remaining wilderness areas. Walk or cycle in for free; pay only to park.

Burke's Canoe Trips
CANOEING

(⊘707-887-1222; www.burkescanoetrips.com; 8600 River Rd, Forestville; canoe/kayak rental incl shuttle $65/45; ⊙10am-6pm Mon-Fri, 9am-6pm Sat & Sun) You can't beat Burke's for a day on the river. Self-guided canoe and kayak trips include shuttle back to your car. Make reservations; plan four hours. Camping in its riverside redwood grove costs $10 per person.

R3 Hotel Pool
SWIMMING

(Triple R; ⊘707-869-8399; www.ther3hotel.com; 16390 4th St, Guerneville; ⊙9am-midnight) FREE The gay, adults-only, party-scene swimming pool at the Triple R is free, provided you buy drinks. Bring your own towel. Bathing suits mandatory, but only because state liquor-license laws require them.

Pee Wee Golf & Arcade
GOLF, CYCLING

(⊘707-869-9321; 16155 Drake Rd at Hwy 116, Guerneville; 18/36 holes $8/12; ⊙11am-10pm Jun-Aug, to 5pm Sat & Sun May & Sep; 🖫) Flashback to 1948 at this impeccably kept, retro-kitsch, 36-hole miniature golf course, just south of the Hwy 116 bridge, with brilliantly painted obstacles, including T Rex and Yogi Bear.

Bring your own cocktails; also rents gas barbecue grills ($20).

King's Sport & Tackle
FISHING, KAYAKING, CANOEING

(⊘707-869-2156; www.kingsrussianriver.com; 16258 Main St, Guerneville; ⊙8am-6pm) *The* local source for fishing and river-condition information. Also rents kayaks ($35 to $55), canoes ($55) and fishing gear.

River Rider
BICYCLE RENTAL

(⊘707-483-2897; www.riverridersrentals.com; half-/full-day rental $25/45; ⊙7am-7pm) Delivers bicycles, along with wine-tasting passes on request; discounts for multiday rentals.

Johnson's Beach
WATER SPORTS

(⊘707-869-2022; www.johnsonsbeach.com; 16241 First St, Guerneville; kayak & canoe per hr/day $10/30; ⊙10am-6pm May-Sep; 🖫) Canoe, paddleboat and watercraft rental (from $30). Beach admission free, and you can camp here.

Northwood Golf Course
GOLF

(⊘707-865-1116; www.northwoodgolf.com; 19400 Hwy 116, Monte Rio; walking $25-27, riding $33-35, 9 holes $25-35, 18 holes $35-53; ⊙7:30am-sunset) Vintage-1920s Alistair MacKenzie–designed, par-36, nine-hole course.

🎉 Festivals & Events

Monte Rio Variety Show
MUSIC

(www.monterioshow.org) Members of the elite, secretive Bohemian Grove (Google it) perform publicly, sometimes showcasing unannounced celebrities, in July.

Lazy Bear Weekend
CULTURAL

(www.lazybearweekend.com) Read: heavy, furry gay men; August.

Russian River Jazz & Blues Festival
MUSIC

(www.russianriverfestivals.com) A day of jazz, followed by a day of blues in September, with occasional luminaries like BB King.

🛏 Sleeping

Russian River has few budget sleeps; prices drop midweek. For weekends and holidays, book ahead. Many places have no TVs. Because the river sometimes floods, some lodgings have cold linoleum floors: pack slippers.

🏠 Guerneville

Staying downtown means you can walk to restaurants and bars.

Guerneville Lodge CAMPGROUND $
(☑707-869-0102; www.guernevillelodge.com; 15905 River Rd; tent sites $40) The prettiest place to camp in downtown Guerneville is behind this retreat-center lodge, on sprawling grassy lawns fronting on the river. Amenities: hot clean showers, big campsites, refrigerator access, fire pits with grills. When available, lodge rooms cost $189 to $229.

Bullfrog Pond Campground CAMPGROUND $
(☑Mon-Fri reservations & information 707-869-9177, Sat & Sun ranger kiosk 707-869-2015; www.stewardscr.org; sites reserved/non-reserved $35/25; 🐾) Reached via a steep road from Armstrong Redwoods State Natural Reserve, 4 miles from the entrance kiosk, Bullfrog Pond has forested campsites, with cold water, and primitive hike-in and equestrian backcountry campsites. Reserve via www.hipcamp.com or by phone.

Schoolhouse Canyon Campground CAMPGROUND $
(☑707-869-2311; www.schoolhousecanyon.com; 12600 River Rd; tent sites $30; 🐾) Two miles east of Guerneville, Schoolhouse's well-tended sites lie beneath tall trees, across the main road from the river. Coin-operated hot showers, clean bathrooms, quiet by night.

Johnson's Beach Resort CABIN, CAMPGROUND $
(☑707-869-2022; www.johnsonsbeach.com; 16241 1st St; tent sites $25, RV sites $25-35, cabins $75, per week $400) On the river in Guerneville, Johnson's has rustic, but clean, thin-walled cabins on stilts; all have kitchens. Bring earplugs. There's camping, too, but it's loud. No credit cards.

Fern Grove Cottages CABIN $$
(☑707-869-8105; www.ferngrove.com; 16650 River Rd; cabins incl breakfast $159-219, with kitchen $199-269; @🛜🐾🐾) Downtown Guerneville's cheeriest resort, Fern Grove has vintage-1930s pine-paneled cabins, tucked beneath redwoods and surrounded by lush flowering gardens. Some have Jacuzzis and fireplaces. The pool uses salt, not chlorine; the lovely English innkeeper provides concierge services; and breakfast includes homemade scones.

Highlands Resort CABIN, CAMPGROUND $$
(☑707-869-0333; www.highlandsresort.com; 14000 Woodland Dr; tent sites $20-30, r with bath $90-100, without $70-80, cabins $120-205; 🛜🐾🐾) Guerneville's mellowest all-gay resort sits on a wooded hillside, walkable to

town, and has simply furnished rooms, little cottages with porches and good camping. The large pool and hot tub are clothing-optional (weekday/weekend day use $10/15).

R3 Hotel RESORT $$
(Triple R; ☑707-869-8399; www.ther3hotel.com; 16390 4th St; r Mon-Fri $80-150, Sat & Sun $105-215; 🛜🐾) Ground zero for party-hardy gay lads and lesbians, Triple-R (as it's known) has plain-Jane, motel-style rooms surrounding a bar and pool deck that get so crowded summer weekends, management won't allow guests to bring pets because 'they get hurt' (actual quote). Come for the scene, not for quiet (light sleepers: bring ear plugs). Midweek it's mellow, wintertime dead.

Riverlane Resort CABIN $$
(☑707-869-2323, 800-201-2324; www.riverlaneresort.com; 16320 1st St; cabins $90-140; 🛜🐾) Right downtown, Riverlane has basic cabins with kitchens, decorated with mismatched furniture, but they're very clean and have decks with barbecues. Best for no-frills travelers or campers wanting an upgrade. Heated pool, private beach and hot tub.

Applewood Inn INN $$$
(☑800-555-8509, 707-869-9093; www.applewoodinn.com; 13555 Hwy 116; r incl breakfast $215-345; 🛇@🛜🐾) A hideaway estate on a wooded hilltop south of town, cushy Applewood has marvelous 1920s-era detail, with dark wood and heavy furniture that echo the forest. Rooms have Jacuzzis, couples' showers and top-end linens; some have fireplaces. Small on-site spa.

Boon Hotel + Spa BOUTIQUE HOTEL $$$
(☑707-869-2721; www.boonhotels.com; 14711 Armstrong Woods Rd; r $165-275; 🛜🐾🐾) 🔏 Rooms surround a swimming-pool courtyard (with Jacuzzi) at this mid-century-modern, 14-room motel-resort, gussied up in minimalist style. The look is austere but fresh, with organic-cotton linens and spacious rooms; most have wood-burning fireplaces. Drive to town, or ride the free bicycles.

Santa Nella House B&B $$$
(☑707-869-9488; www.santanellahouse.com; 12130 Hwy 116; r incl breakfast $199-219; @🛜🐾) All four spotless rooms at this 1871 Victorian, south of town, have wood-burning fireplaces and frilly Victorian furnishings. Upstairs rooms are biggest. Outside there's a hot tub and sauna. Best for travelers who appreciate the B&B aesthetic.

Forestville

Raford Inn
B&B **$$$**

(☑800-887-9503, 707-887-9573; http://rafordinn.com; 10630 Wohler Rd, Healdsburg; r $185-270; ❄@🛜) 🏊 We love this 1880 Victorian B&B's secluded hilltop location, surrounded by tall palms and rambling vineyards. Rooms are big and airy, done with lace and antiques; some have fireplaces. And wow, those sunset views.

Farmhouse Inn
INN **$$$**

(☑800-464-6642, 707-887-3300; www.farmhouseinn.com; 7871 River Rd; r $445-795; ❄@🛜🏊) Think love nest. The area's premier inn has spacious rooms and cottages, styled with cushy amenities like saunas, steam-showers and wood-burning fireplaces. Small on-site spa and top-notch restaurant. Check in early to maximize time.

Monte Rio

Village Inn
INN **$$**

(☑707-865-2304; www.villageinn-ca.com; 20822 River Blvd; r $145-235; 🛜) 🏊 A retired concierge owns this cute, old-fashioned, 11-room inn, beneath towering trees, right on the river. Some rooms have river views; all have fridge and microwave. No elevator.

Rio Villa Beach Resort
INN **$$**

(☑877-746-8455, 707-865-1143; www.riovilla.com; 20292 Hwy 116; r with kitchen $149-209, without $139-189; ❄🛜🏊) Landscaping is lush at this small riverside resort with excellent sun exposure (you see redwoods, but you're not under them). Rooms are well kept but simple (request a quiet room, not by the road); the emphasis is on the outdoors, evident by the large riverside terrace, outdoor fireplace and barbecues. Some air-con.

Highland Dell
INN **$$**

(☑707-865-2300; highlanddell.com; 21050 River Blvd; r $109-179; ⊗Apr-Nov; ❄🛜) 🏊 Built in 1906 in grand lodge style, redone in 2007, the inn fronts right on the river. Above the giant dining room are 12 bright, fresh-looking rooms with comfy beds. No elevator.

Duncans Mills

Casini Ranch
CAMPGROUND **$**

(☑800-451-8400, 707-865-2255; www.casiniranch.com; 22855 Moscow Rd; tent sites $45-52, RV sites partial hookups $47-58, full hookups $53-56; 🛜🏊) In quiet Duncans Mills, beautifully set on riverfront ranchlands, Casini is an enormous, well-run campground. Amenities include kayaks and paddleboats (day use $5 to $10); bathrooms are spotless.

 Eating

Guerneville

There's a good **taco truck**, in the Safeway parking lot at 16451 Main St.

Big Bottom Market
MARKET, CAFE **$**

(☑707-604-7295; www.bigbottommarket.com; 16228 Main St; sandwiches $7-10; ⊗8am-5pm Sun-Thu, to 6pm Fri & Sat) 🏊 Gourmet deli and wine shop with scrumptious pastries and grab-and-go picnic supplies.

Coffee Bazaar
CAFE **$**

(☑707-869-9706; www.mycoffeeb.com; 14045 Armstrong Woods Rd; dishes $5-9; ⊗6am-8pm; 🛜) Happening cafe with salads, sandwiches and all-day breakfasts; adjoins a good used bookstore.

Taqueria La Tapatia
MEXICAN **$**

(☑707-869-1821; 16632 Main St; mains $7-14; ⊗11am-9pm) Reasonable choice for traditional Mexican.

Garden Grill
BARBECUE **$**

(☑707-869-3922; www.gardengrillbbq.com; 17132 Hwy 116, Guernewood Park; mains $6-12; ⊗8am-8pm) One mile west of Guerneville, this roadhouse barbecue joint, with redwood-shaded patio, serves good house-smoked meats, but the fries could be better. Breakfast till 3pm.

Food for Humans
MARKET **$**

(☑707-869-3612; 16385 1st St; ⊗9am-8pm; 🏊) 🏊 Organic groceries; better alternative than neighboring Safeway, but no meat.

Seaside Metal Oyster Bar
SEAFOOD **$$**

(☑707-604-7250; seasidemetal.com; 16222 Main St; dishes $11-16; ⊗5-10pm Wed-Sun) Unexpectedly urban for Guerneville, this storefront raw bar is an offshoot of San Francisco's Bar Crudo – one of the city's best – and showcases oysters, clams, lobster and exquisitely prepared raw-fish dishes. There's limited hot food, but it's overwrought: stick to raw.

Dick Blomster's Korean Diner
KOREAN, AMERICAN **$$**

(☑707-896-8006; 16236 Main St; mains $15-20; ⊗5-10pm Sun-Thu, to 2am Fri & Sat Jun-Aug, to 11pm Fri & Sat Sep-May) By day a vintage-1940s coffee shop, by night a Korean-American diner with full bar, Dick Blomster's serves playfully tongue-in-cheek dishes, including fried PB&J sandwiches and 'the other KFC – Korean fried crack' – fried chicken with sugary-sweet brown sauce, which sure hits the spot after a night's drinking.

Boon Eat + Drink   CALIFORNIAN $$$

(☑707-869-0780; http://eatatboon.com; 16248 Main St; lunch mains $14-18, dinner $15-26; ⊙11am-3pm Mon, Tue, Thu & Fri, 5-9pm Mon-Fri, 10am-3pm & 5-10pm Sat & Sun) Locally sourced ingredients inform the seasonal, Cali-smart cooking at this tiny, always-packed, New American bistro, with cheek-by-jowl tables that fill every night. Make reservations or expect to wait.

Applewood Inn Restaurant   CALIFORNIAN $$$

(☑707-869-9093; www.applewoodinn.com; 13555 Hwy 116; mains $20-28; ⊙5:30-8:30pm Wed-Sun) Cozy up by the fire in the treetop-level dining room and sup on quality Euro-Cal cooking that maximizes seasonal produce, with dishes like rack of lamb with minted *chimichuri* (garlic-parsley vinaigrette) and smoked trout with corn and crayfish. Sunday nights there's a $35 prix-fixe menu. Reservations essential.

✕ Forestville

Canneti Roadhouse   ITALIAN $$

(☑707-887-2232; http://cannetirestaurant.com; 6675 Front St; lunch mains $12-24, dinner $15-28; ⊙11:30am-3pm Wed-Sat, to 5pm Sun, 5:30-9pm Tue-Sun) 🍴 A Tuscan-born chef makes bona fide *cucina Italiana*, using quality ingredients from local farms, at this austere restaurant in downtown Forestville, worth the 15-minute drive from Guerneville. The menu ranges from simple brick-oven pizzas to an all-Tuscan, five-course tasting menu ($55, dinner only). When it's warm, sit on the patio beneath a giant redwood. Make reservations.

Farmhouse Inn   NEW AMERICAN $$$

(☑707-887-3300; www.farmhouseinn.com; 7871 River Rd; 3-/4-course dinner $69/84; ⊙from 5.30pm Thu-Mon) 🍴 Special-occasion worthy, Michelin-starred Farmhouse changes its seasonal Euro-Cal menu daily using locally raised, organic ingredients like Sonoma lamb, wild salmon and rabbit – the latter is the house specialty. Details are impeccable, from aperitifs in the garden to tableside cheese service, but detractors call it precious. Make reservations.

✕ Monte Rio

Don's Dogs   FAST FOOD $

(☑707-865-4190; cnr Bohemian Hwy & Hwy 116; sandwiches $4-12; ⊙9am-4pm Thu-Mon Oct-May, to 7pm daily Jun-Sep; 🅿) Gourmet hot dogs, wine, beer, simple breakfasts and coffee, behind the Rio Theater.

Highland Dell   GERMAN $$$

(☑707-865-2300; http://highlanddell.com; 21050 River Blvd; mains $20-22; ⊙4-10pm Fri-Tue Apr-Nov) A dramatic, three-story-high, chalet-style dining room with a river-view deck, Highland Dell makes pretty good German-inspired cooking, including steaks and schnitzel. Full bar.

Village Inn   AMERICAN $$$

(☑707-865-2304; www.villageinn-ca.com; 20822 River Blvd; mains $19-26; ⊙5-8pm Wed-Sun) The straightforward steaks-and-seafood menu is basic American and doesn't distract from the wonderful river views. Great local wine list, full bar.

✕ Duncans Mills

Cape Fear Cafe   AMERICAN $$

(☑707-865-9246; 25191 Main St; lunch mains $9-15, dinner $15-25; ⊙10am-8pm Mon & Thu, to 3pm Tue & Wed, to 9pm Fri-Sun) A country-Americana diner in a 19th-century grange, Cape Fear is visually charming, but it's erratic – except at weekend brunch, when the kitchen makes excellent Benedicts. Good stopover en route to the coast.

🍷 Drinking & Nightlife

Stumptown Brewery   BREWERY

(www.stumptown.com; 15045 River Rd, Guerneville; ⊙11am-midnight Sun-Thu, to 2am Fri & Sat) Guerneville's best straight bar, 1 mile east of downtown, is gay-friendly and has a foot-stompin' jukebox, billiards, riverside beer garden, and several homemade brews. Pretty-good pub grub includes house-smoked barbecue.

Rainbow Cattle Company   GAY

(www.queersteer.com; 16220 Main St, Guerneville; ⊙noon-midnight Sun-Thu, to 2am Fri & Sat) The stalwart gay watering hole has pinball and shuffleboard.

Sophie's Cellars   WINE BAR

(☑707-865-1122; www.sophiescellars.com; 25179 Main St/Hwy 116, Duncans Mills; glasses $7-15; ⊙11am-5pm Mon, Thu, Sat & Sun, to 7pm Fri) The perfect stopover between river and coast, Sophie's rural wine bar, in Duncans Mills, pours glasses and tastes of local wine, and carries cheese, salami and a well-curated selection of bottles. Friday's 'locals happy hour' (4pm to 7pm) brings hors d'oeuvres, drink specials and a big crowd.

☆ Entertainment

Rio Theater
CINEMA
(☑707-865-0913; www.riotheater.com; cnr Bohemian Hwy & Hwy 116, Monte Rio; adult/child $8/5; ♠) Dinner and a movie take on new meaning at this vintage-WWII Quonset hut converted to a cinema in 1950, with a concession stand serving gourmet hot dogs with a drink and chips for just $7. In 2014 they finally added heating, but still supply blankets. Only in Monte Rio. Shows nightly (and sometimes Sunday afternoons), but call ahead, especially off-season.

Main Street Station
CABARET
(☑707-869-0501; www.mainststation.com; 16280 Main St, Guerneville; ⊙7-10pm or 11pm; ♠) FREE Hosts live acoustic-only jazz, blues and cabaret nightly in summer (weekends in winter), and families are welcome because the cabaret doubles as an American-Italian restaurant (stick to pizza).

Rio Nido Roadhouse
LIVE MUSIC
(☑707-869-0821; www.rionidoroadhouse.com; 14540 Canyon Two, Rio Nido) Raucous roadhouse bar, off River Rd, 4 miles east of Guerneville, with eclectic lineup of live bands. Shows start 6pm Saturday and sometimes Friday and Sunday, too; check website.

🛍 Shopping

Eight miles west of Guerneville, tiny Duncans Mills (pop 85) has good shopping in a handful of side-by-side businesses within weathered 19th-century cottages.

Mr Trombly's Tea & Table
FOOD & DRINK
(www.mrtromblystea.com; 25185 Main St, Duncans Mills; ⊙10am-5pm Sun-Thu, to 6pm Sat & Sun) Different kinds of tea and teapots, plus quality kitchen gadgets and well-priced tableware.

Pig Alley
JEWELRY
(☑707-865-2698; www.pigalleyshop.com; 25193 Main St, Duncans Mills; ⊙10:30am-5:30pm) Vast selection of handcrafted American-made jewelry, notable for gorgeous earrings.

ℹ Information

Russian River Chamber of Commerce & Visitors Center (☑707-869-9000, 877-644-9001; www.russianriver.com; 16209 1st St, Guerneville; ⊙10am-4:45pm Mon-Sat, plus 10am-3pm Sun May-Sep) For information and lodging referrals.

Russian River Visitors Center (☑707-869-4096; ⊙10am-3pm Oct-Apr, to 4pm May-Sep) At Korbel Cellars.

Santa Rosa

Wine Country's biggest city and the Sonoma County seat, Santa Rosa claims two famous native sons – a world-renowned cartoonist and a celebrated horticulturalist – whose legacies include museums and gardens enough to keep you busy for an afternoon. Otherwise, there ain't much to do, unless you need your car fixed or you're here in July during the **Sonoma County Fair** (www.sonomacountyfair.com), at the fairgrounds on Bennett Valley Rd. Santa Rosa is mostly known for traffic and suburban sprawl. It generally lacks charm (except downtown, where redwood trees serve as landscaping and tower over buildings), but has reasonably priced accommodations and easy access to Sonoma County and Valley.

◉ Sights & Activities

The main shopping stretch is 4th St, which abruptly ends at Hwy 101, but re-emerges across the freeway at historic Railroad Sq. Downtown parking garages (75¢ hour, $8 max) are cheaper than street parking. East of town, 4th St becomes Hwy 12 into Sonoma Valley.

Luther Burbank Home & Gardens GARDENS
(☑707-524-5445; www.lutherburbank.org; cnr Santa Rosa & Sonoma Aves; ⊙8am-dusk) FREE Pioneering horticulturist Luther Burbank (1849–1926) developed many hybrid plant species, including the Shasta daisy, here at his 19th-century, Greek-revival home. The extensive gardens are lovely. The house and adjacent **Carriage Museum** (guided tour adult/child $7/free; ⊙10am-3:30pm Tue-Sun Apr-Oct) have displays on Burbank's life and work, you can take a self-guided cell phone tour for free. Across the street from Burbank's home, **Julliard Park** has a playground.

Charles M Schulz Museum · MUSEUM

(☑ 707-579-4452; www.schulzmuseum.org; 2301 Hardies Lane; adult/child $10/5; ☺ 11am-5pm Mon & Wed-Fri, 10am-5pm Sat & Sun; ⓙ) Charles Schulz, Santa Rosa resident and creator of *Peanuts* cartoons, was born in 1922, published his first drawing in 1937, introduced Snoopy and Charlie Brown in 1950, and produced *Peanuts* cartoons until his death in 2000. This modern museum honors his legacy with a Snoopy labyrinth, *Peanuts*-related art, and a re-creation of Schulz's studio. Skip Snoopy's Gallery gift shop; the museum has the good stuff.

Farmers Markets · MARKET

(4th & B Sts; ☺ 5-8:30pm Wed mid-May–Aug) Sonoma County's largest farmers market. Another year-round market meets 8:30am to 1pm Saturdays at Santa Rosa Veterans Building, 1351 Maple Ave.

Redwood Empire Ice Arena · SKATING

(☑ 707-546-7147; www.snoopyshomeice.com; 1667 West Steele Lane; adult incl skates $9-12, child $7-10; ⓙ) This skating rink was formerly owned and deeply loved by Schulz. It's open most afternoons (call for schedules). Bring a sweater.

Children's Museum of Sonoma County · SCIENCE CENTER

(☑ 707-546-4069; www.cmosc.org; 1835 Steele Lane; admission $7; ☺ 9am-4pm Tue-Sat, noon-4pm Sun; ⓙ) Geared to little children 10 and under, this happy learning center inspires discovery, exploration and creativity with hands-on exhibits, most outdoors, focused on nature and science. Picnicking welcome. No adults without kids.

🛏 Sleeping

Find chain hotels near Railroad Sq. Nothing-special motels line Cleveland Ave, fronting Hwy 101's western side, between the Steele Lane and Bicentennial Lane exits; skip Motel 6. Nearby Windsor has two chain hotels (Hampton Inn and Holiday Inn) off Hwy 101 at exit 'Central Windsor.'

Spring Lake Park · CAMPGROUND $

(☑ 707-539-8092, reservations 707-565-2267; www.sonomacountyparks.org; 5585 Newanga Ave; sites $32; ⛟) 🍃 Lovely lakeside park, 4 miles from downtown; make reservations ($8.50 fee) online or 10am to 3pm weekdays by phone. The park is open year-round, with lake swimming in summer; the campground operates May to September, weekends Oc-

OLIVE-OIL TASTING

When you weary of wine-tasting, pop by one of the following olive-oil makers and dip some crusty bread – it's free. Harvest and pressing happen in November.

➡ BR Cohn (p188)

➡ Napa Valley Olive Oil Mfg Co (p173)

➡ Long Meadow Ranch (p167)

➡ Figone's Olive Oil (p197)

tober to April. Take 4th St eastbound, turn right on Farmer's Lane, pass the first Hoen St and turn left on the second Hoen St, then left on Newanga Ave.

Hillside Inn · MOTEL $

(☑ 707-546-9353; www.hillside-inn.com; 2901 4th St; s/d Nov-Mar $70/82, Apr-Oct $74/86; ☏ 🖥) Santa Rosa's best-value motel, Hillside is close to Sonoma Valley; add $4 for kitchens. Furnishings are dated and service peculiar, but everything is scrupulously maintained. Adjoins an excellent breakfast cafe.

Hotel La Rose · HISTORIC HOTEL $$

(☑ 707-579-3200; www.hotellarose.com; 308 Wilson St; r Mon-Fri $139-199, Sat & Sun $159-229; ❄🖥) 🍃 At Railroad Sq, Hotel La Rose has rooms in a well-kept historic 1907 brick hotel, and across the street in a 1980s-built 'carriage house,' which feels like a small condo complex with boxy, spacious rooms. All are decorated in out-of-fashion pastels, but have excellent beds with quality linens and down duvets; some have jetted tubs.

Flamingo Resort Hotel · HOTEL $$

(☑ 800-848-8300, 707-545-8530; www.flamingoresort.com; 2777 4th St; r $159-269; ❄@🖥⛟🏋) 🍃 Sprawling over 11 acres, this mid-century modern hotel doubles as a conference center. Rooms are business-class-generic, but the pool is gigantic – and kept 82°F year-round. Kids love it. On-site health-club and gym. Prices double summer weekends.

Best Western Garden Inn · MOTEL $$

(☑ 888-256-8004, 707-546-4031; www.thegardeninn.com; 1500 Santa Rosa Ave; r Mon-Fri $119-139, Sat & Sun $199-229; ❄@🖥⛟🏋) Well-kept motel, south of downtown, with two pools. Rear rooms open to grassy gardens, but you may hear kids in the pool; book up front for

NAPA & SONOMA WINE COUNTRY SANTA ROSA

quiet. The street gets seedy by night, but the hotel is secure, clean and comfortable.

Vintners Inn
INN $$$

(☑ 800-421-2584, 707-575-7350; www.vintnersinn. com; 4350 Barnes Rd; r $245-495; ❈ @ ☜) ✦ Surrounded by vineyards north of town (near River Rd), Vintner's Inn caters to the gated-community crowd with business-classy amenities. Jacuzzi, no pool. Check for last-minute specials.

✕ Eating

Jeffrey's Hillside Cafe
AMERICAN $

(www.jeffreyshillsidecafe.com; 2901 4th St; dishes $8-12; ☻ 7am-2pm; ✦) ✦ East of downtown, near Sonoma Valley, chef-owned Jeffrey's is excellent for breakfast or brunch before wine-tasting.

Rosso Pizzeria & Wine Bar
PIZZA $$

(☑ 707-544-3221; www.rossopizzeria.com; 53 Montgomery St, Creekside Shopping Centre; pizzas $13-17; ☻ 11am-10pm; ✦) ✦ Fantastic wood-fired pizzas, inventive salads and standout wines make Rosso worth seeking out.

Naked Pig
CAFE $$

(☑ 707-978-3231; 435 Santa Rosa Ave; mains $11-14; ☻ 8am-3pm Wed-Sun) ✦ This tiny cafe in a former bus depot makes everything from scratch and serves simple-delicious, farm-to-table breakfasts and lunches at communal tables.

El Coqui
CARIBBEAN $$

(☑ 707-542-8868; http://elcoqui2eat.com; 400 Mendocino Ave; lunch mains $10-14, dinner $14-19; ☻ 11am-10pm Mon-Sat, noon-9pm Sun) Unique in Wine Country, El Coqui serves yummy Puerto Rican food, including stuffed plantains. Beer and wine.

Spinster Sisters
CALIFORNIAN $$$

(☑ 707-528-7100; www.thespinstersisters.com; 401 South A St; lunch mains $10-16, dinner $23-26; ☻ 8am-3pm Mon, to 10pm Tue-Fri, 9am-10pm Sat & Sun) ✦ At Santa Rosa's culinary vanguard, this casual market-driven restaurant makes its own bagels, cheese and charcuterie meats. The diverse tapas-like small plates ($7 to $14) pair well with the extensive wine list.

☕ Drinking & Nightlife

★ Russian River Brewing Co
BREWERY

(www.russianriverbrewing.com; 729 4th St; ☻ 11am-midnight Sun-Thu, to 1am Fri & Sat) Santa Rosa's justly famous brewery crafts outstanding double IPA, called Pliny the Elder, plus top-grade sour beer aged in wine barrels. Good pizza and pub grub, too.

ⓘ Information

California Welcome Center & Santa Rosa Visitors Bureau (☑ 800-404-7673, 707-577-8674; www.visitsantarosa.com; 9 4th St; ☻ 9am-5pm Mon-Sat, 10am-5pm Sun) Same-day lodging assistance. At Railroad Sq, west of Hwy 101; take downtown exit from Hwy 12 or 101.

Santa Rosa Memorial Hospital (☑ 707-546-3210; 1165 Montgomery St)

Healdsburg & Around

Once a sleepy ag town best known for its Future Farmers of America parade, Healdsburg has emerged as northern Sonoma County's culinary capital. Foodie-scenester restaurants and cafes, wine-tasting rooms and fancy boutiques line Healdsburg Plaza, the town's sun-dappled central square (bordered by Healdsburg Ave and Center, Matheson and Plaza Sts). Traffic grinds to a halt summer weekends, when second-home-owners and tourists jam downtown. Old-timers aren't happy with the Napa-style gentrification, but at least Healdsburg retains its historic look, if not its once-quiet summers. It's best visited weekdays – stroll tree-lined streets, sample locavore cooking and soak up the NorCal flavor.

◉ Sights

Tasting rooms surround the plaza. Free summer concerts play Tuesday afternoons.

Healdsburg Museum
MUSEUM

(☑ 707-431-3325; www.healdsburgmuseum.org; 221 Matheson St, Healdsburg; donation requested; ☻ 11am-4pm Wed-Sun) Exhibits include compelling installations on northern Sonoma County history, with an emphasis on Healdsburg. Pick up the walking-tour pamphlet.

Healdsburg Public Library
LIBRARY

(☑ 707-433-3772; sonomalibrary.org; cnr Piper & Center Sts; ☻ 10am-6pm Tue, Thu & Fri, to 8pm Wed, to 4pm Sat) Wine Country's leading oenology-reference library.

Healdsburg Veterans Memorial Beach
BEACH

(☑ 707-433-1625; www.sonomacountyparks.org; 13839 Healdsburg Ave, Healdsburg; parking $7; ☻ 7am-sunset; ✦) You can swim at this beach – lifeguards are on duty summer weekends –

but if you're squeamish, confirm current water quality online (www.sonoma-county.org/health/services/freshwater.asp).

Locals Tasting Room TASTING ROOM
(707-857-4900; www.tastelocalwines.com; Geyserville Ave & Hwy 128, Geyserville; 11am-6pm) FREE Eight miles north of Healdsburg, tiny Geyserville is home to this indie tasting room, which represents 12 small-production wineries with free tastings.

Farmers Markets MARKET
(www.healdsburgfarmersmarket.org; Healdsburg) Discover Healdsburg's agricultural abundance at the **Tuesday market** (cnr Vine & North Sts; 3:30pm-6pm Wed Jun-Oct) and **Saturday market** (9am-noon Sat May-Nov), the latter held one block west of the plaza.

Activities

After you've walked around the plaza, there isn't much to do in town. Go wine-tasting in Dry Creek Valley or Russian River Valley (p197). Bicycling on winding West Dry Creek Rd is brilliant, as is paddling the Russian River, which runs through town. Rent bikes from Spoke Folk Cyclery (p165).

Coppola Winery Swimming Pool SWIMMING, WINERY
(707-857-1400, 877-590-3329; www.francisfordcoppolawinery.com; 300 Via Archimedes, Geyserville; adult/child $30/15; 11am-6pm daily Jun-Sep, Fri-Sun Apr, May & Oct;) The two huge interconnected pools at Francis Ford Coppola Winery are a glam way to spend a hot day with kids. To ensure admission, reserve in advance a cabine ($135), which includes chairs for four and wine-tasting passes; day passes include towel and lawn seating, not chairs; summer weekends sell out immediately – arrive before 10:45am.

Russian River Adventures CANOEING
(707-433-5599; russianriveradventures.com; 20 Healdsburg Ave, Healdsburg; adult/child $50/25;) Paddle a secluded stretch of river in quiet inflatable canoes, stopping for rope swings, swimming holes, beaches and bird-watching. This ecotourism outfit points you in the right direction and shuttles you back at day's end. Or they'll guide your kids downriver while you go wine-tasting (guides $125 per day). Reservations required.

Getaway Adventures CYCLING, KAYAKING
(800-499-2453, 707-763-3040; www.getawayadventures.com) Guides spectacular morning vineyard cycling in Dry Creek Valley, followed by lunch and optional kayaking on Russian River ($150 to $175).

River's Edge Kayak & Canoe Trips BOATING
(707-433-7247; www.riversedgekayakandcanoe.com; 13840 Healdsburg Ave, Healdsburg) Rents hard-sided canoes ($90/110 per half/full day) and kayaks ($40/55). Self-guided rentals include shuttle.

Courses

The Shed COURSE
(707-431-7433; healdsburgshed.com; 25 North St, Healdsburg) Healdsburg's culinary center (p214) leads classes and workshop on topics related to food and sustainability, from seed-saving and bee-keeping, to home-brewing and kombucha-fermenting. Also hosts important lecturers, such as Michael Pollan.

Relish Culinary Adventures COOKING COURSE
(707-431-9999, 877-759-1004; www.relishculinary.com; 14 Matheson St, Healdsburg; by appointment) Plug into the locavore food scene with culinary day trips, demo-kitchen classes or winemaker dinners.

Festivals & Events

Russian River Wine Road Barrel Tasting WINE
(www.wineroad.com) Sample wine, directly from the cask, before it's bottled or released for sale, in March.

Future Farmers Parade CULTURAL
(www.healdsburgfair.org) The whole town shows up for this classic-Americana farm parade in May.

Wine & Food Affair FOOD
(www.wineroad.com/events) Special food and wine pairings at over 100 wineries in November.

Sleeping

Healdsburg is expensive: demand exceeds supply. Rates drop winter to spring, but not significantly. Guerneville is much less expensive, and just 20 minutes away. Most Healdsburg inns are within walking distance of the plaza; several B&Bs are in surrounding countryside. Find motels at Hwy 101's Dry Creek exit.

Cloverdale Wine Country KOA CAMPGROUND $
(800-368-4558, 707-894-3337; www.winecountrykoa.com; 1166 Asti Ridge Rd, Cloverdale; tent/RV sites from $50/65, 1-/2-bedroom cabins $85/95;

🐕 🏊 ♿) Six miles from central Cloverdale (exit 520) off Hwy 101; hot showers, pool, hot tub, laundry, paddleboats and bicycles.

L&M Motel
MOTEL $$

(☎707-433-6528; www.landmmotel.com; 70 Healdsburg Ave, Healdsburg; r $150-180; ❄ 🛜 ♿ 🐕) Simple, clean, old-fashioned motel, with big lawns and barbecue grills, great for families. Dry sauna and Jacuzzi. Winter rates plummet.

Geyserville Inn
MOTEL $$

(☎877-857-4343, 707-857-4343; www.geyservilleinn.com; 21714 Geyserville Ave, Geyserville; r Mon-Fri $129-169, Sat & Sun $269-289; ❄ 🛜 ♿ 🐕) Eight miles north of Healdsburg, this immaculately kept upmarket motel is surrounded by vineyards. Rooms have unexpectedly smart furnishings and quality extras, like feather pillows. Request a remodeled room. Hot tub.

Best Western Dry Creek
MOTEL $$

(☎707-433-0300; www.drycreekinn.com; 198 Dry Creek Rd, Healdsburg; r Mon-Fri $109-149, Sat & Sun $219-319; ❄ @ ♿) This generic midrange motel has good service and an outdoor hot tub. New rooms have jetted tubs and gas fireplaces.

Hotel Healdsburg
HOTEL $$$

(☎707-431-2800, 800-889-7188; www.hotelhealdsburg.com; 25 Matheson St, Healdsburg; r incl breakfast from $450; ❄ @ 🛜 ♿) Smack on the plaza, the fashion-forward HH has a coolly minimalist style of concrete and velvet, with requisite top-end amenities, including sumptuous beds and extra-deep tubs. Full-service spa.

H2 Hotel
HOTEL $$$

(☎707-431-2202, 707-922-5251; www.h2hotel.com; 219 Healdsburg Ave, Healdsburg; r incl breakfast Mon-Fri $289-389, Sat & Sun $409-509; ❄ @ 🛜 ♿) 🖋 Little sister to Hotel Healdsburg, H2 has the same angular concrete style, but was built LEED-gold-certified from the ground up, with a living roof, reclaimed everything, and fresh-looking rooms with cush organic linens. Tiny pool, free bikes.

Madrona Manor
HISTORIC HOTEL $$$

(☎800-258-4003, 707-433-4231; www.madronamanor.com; 1001 Westside Rd, Healdsburg; r incl breakfast Mon-Fri $260-305, Sat & Sun $385-515; ❄ 🛜 ♿) The first choice of lovers of country inns and stately manor homes, the regal 1881 Madrona Manor exudes Victorian elegance. Surrounded by 8 acres of woods and gorgeous century-old gardens, the hilltop mansion is decked out with many original furnishings. A mile west of downtown, it's convenient to Westside Rd wineries.

Belle de Jour Inn
B&B $$$

(☎707-431-9777; www.belledejourinn.com; 16276 Healdsburg Ave, Healdsburg; r $225-295, ste $355; ❄ 🛜) Charming Belle de Jour's sunny, uncluttered rooms have American-country furnishings, with extras like private entrances, sun-dried sheets and jetted tubs. The manicured gardens are ready-made for a moonlight tryst.

Healdsburg Inn on the Plaza
INN $$$

(☎800-431-8663, 707-433-6991; www.healdsburginn.com; 110 Matheson St, Healdsburg; r $295-375; ❄ 🛜 ♿) The spiffy, clean-lined rooms, conservatively styled in khaki and beige, feel bourgeois summer-house casual, with fine linens and gas fireplaces; some have jetted double tubs. The plaza-front location explains the price.

Honor Mansion
INN $$$

(☎707-433-4277, 800-554-4667; www.honormansion.com; 891 Grove St, Healdsburg; r incl breakfast $330-595; ❄ 🛜 ♿) Elegant 1883 Victorian mansion with spectacular resort-like grounds, cushy rooms and great service.

Camellia Inn
B&B $$$

(☎707-433-8182, 800-727-8182; www.camelliainn.com; 211 North St, Healdsburg; r $139-395; ❄ 🛜 ♿) Elegantly furnished 1869 mansion, with (among others) one budget room ($139), plus a two-bed family room ($259).

Haydon Street Inn
B&B $$$

(☎707-433-5228, 800-528-3703; www.haydon.com; 321 Haydon St, Healdsburg; r $195-325, cottage $425; ❄ 🛜) Two-story Queen Anne with big front porch and separate cottage.

Piper Street Inn
INN $$$

(☎707-433-8721, 877-703-0370; www.piperstreetinn.com; 402 Piper St, Healdsburg; r $295; ❄ 🛜 ♿) Cozy garden cottage.

🍴 Eating

Healdsburg is the gastronomic capital of Sonoma County. Your hardest decision will be choosing where to eat. Reservations essential.

★ The Shed
CAFE, MARKET $

(☎707-431-7433; healdsburgshed.com; 25 North St, Healdsburg; dishes $3-15; ⏰8am-7pm Wed-Mon; 🚗) 🖋 At the vanguard of locavore eating, the Shed integrates food at all stages of production, milling its own locally sourced flours, pressing olive oils, fermenting vinegars and kombucha from local fruit, and growing its own produce. It comprises a cafe with wood-fired dishes, fermentation bar with housemade shrubs, coffee bar with stellar pastries, and a market with prepared to-go foods.

Healdsburg Bar & Grill
PUB FOOD $$

(☑707-433-3333; www.healdsburgbarandgrill.com; 245 Healdsburg Ave, Healdsburg; mains $9-15; ⊙8am-9pm) 'Top Chef Masters' winner Doug Keane's gastropub is perfect when you're famished, but don't want to fuss. Expect simple classics – mac-n-cheese, pulled-pork sandwiches, top-end burgers and truffle-parmesan fries. At breakfast, look for homemade bagels and waffles. Sit in the garden.

Oakville Grocery
DELI $$

(☑707-433-3200; www.oakvillegrocery.com; 124 Matheson St, Healdsburg; sandwiches $10; ⊙8am-7pm) Luxurious smoked fish and caviar, fancy sandwiches and grab-and-go gourmet picnics. It's overpriced, but the plaza-view fireside terrace is ever-fun for scouting Botox blonds, while nibbling cheese and sipping vino.

Scopa
ITALIAN $$

(☑707-433-5282; www.scopahealdsburg.com; 109A Plaza St, Healdsburg; mains $15-24; ⊙5:30-10pm Tue-Sun) Space is tight inside this converted barbershop, but it's worth cramming in for perfect thin-crust pizza and rustic Italian home cooking, like Nonna's slow-braised chicken, with sautéed greens, melting into toasty polenta. A lively crowd and good wine prices create a convivial atmosphere.

Diavola
ITALIAN $$

(☑707-814-0111; www.diavolapizzeria.com; 21021 Geyserville Ave, Geyserville; pizzas $15-18; ⊙11:30am-9pm; 📶) 🔗 Ideal for lunch while wine-tasting in Alexander Valley, Diavola makes oustanding salumi and thin-crust pizzas, served in an Old West, brick-walled space, loud enough to drown out the kids.

Ravenous
NEW AMERICAN $$

(☑707-431-1302; 117 North St, Healdsburg; lunch mains $12-17, dinner $20-24) Chalkboard-scrawled menu, with California comfort cooking and excellent burgers, served in a tiny eight-table dining room inside a former theater lobby.

Costeaux French Bakery & Cafe
CAFE $$

(☑707-433-1913; www.costeaux.com; 417 Healdsburg Ave, Healdsburg; mains $10-13; ⊙7am-3pm Mon-Sat, to 1pm Sun; 📶) This cavernous bakery-cafe is good for an easy lunch of salads and sandwiches on house-baked bread, plus all-day breakfast dishes including omelets and scrambles.

★Madrona Manor
CALIFORNIAN $$$

(☑800-258-4003, 707-433-4231; www.madronamanor.com; 1001 Westside Rd, Healdsburg; 6-/11-course menu $106/$129; ⊙6-9pm Wed-Sun) 🔗 You'd be hard-pressed to find a lovelier place to propose than this retro-formal Victorian mansion's garden-view verandah – though there's nothing old-fashioned about the artful haute cuisine: the kitchen churns its own butter, each course comes with a different variety of just-baked bread, lamb and cheese originate down the road, and desserts include ice cream flash-frozen tableside. Reserve a pre-sunset table on the verandah.

Mateo's Cucina Latina
MEXICAN $$$

(☑707-433-1520; www.mateoscocinalatina.com; 214 Healdsburg Ave, Healdsburg; small plates $11-15, mains $21-25; ⊙11:30am-9pm Thu-Tue, 4-9pm Wed, closed Tue Nov-Apr) 🔗 This is not Mexican food as you may know it. Here the upmarket Yucatan-inspired cooking integrates fine technique and all-local ingredients for standout small plates, such as wild-nettle empanadas and slow-roasted suckling pig, whose subtle flavors shine through the spice. The full bar showcases rare tequilas and mescals. Make reservations; request a garden table.

Barndiva
CALIFORNIAN $$$

(☑707-431-0100; www.barndiva.com; 231 Center St, Healdsburg; lunch mains $15-22, dinner $28-38; ⊙noon-2:15 & 5:30pm-9pm Wed-Sat, from 11am Sun) 🔗 Impeccable seasonal-regional cooking, happening bar, beautiful garden, but service sometimes misses.

Self-Catering

Dry Creek General Store
DELI $

(☑707-433-4171; www.drycreekgeneralstore1881.com; 3495 Dry Creek Rd, Healdsburg; sandwiches $8-10; ⊙6:30am-6pm) Stop at this vintage general store, where locals and cyclists gather for coffee on the creaky front porch. Perfect picnic supplies include Toscano-salami-and-manchego sandwiches on chewy-dense ciabatta.

NAPA & SONOMA WINE COUNTRY HEALDSBURG & AROUND

Cheese Shop FOOD $
(☎707-433-4998; www.sharpandnutty.com; 423 Center St, Healdsburg; ⊙11am-6pm Mon-Sat) Top-notch imported and local cheeses.

Shelton's Natural Foods MARKET, DELI $
(☎707-431-0530; www.sheltonsmarket.com; 428 Center St, Healdsburg; ⊙8am-8pm) Indie alternative for groceries and picnic supplies; reasonably priced.

Moustache Baked Goods BAKERY $
(☎707-395-4111; moustachebakedgoods.com; 381 Healdsburg Ave, Healdsburg; cupcakes $3; ⊙11am-7pm) Incredible locavore small-batch sweets (some gluten-free), including scrumptious cupcakes in unusual combos like maple-bacon.

Noble Folk Ice Cream & Pie Bar DESSERTS $
(☎707-395-4426; 116 Matheson St, Healdsburg; slice $5.25, single cone $3.25; ⊙noon-9pm) Handcrafted ice cream and classic American pie, made with top-quality, all-local ingredients.

Downtown Bakery & Creamery BAKERY $
(☎707-431-2719; www.downtownbakery.net; 308A Center St, Healdsburg; ⊙7am-5:30pm) Healdsburg's classic bakery makes perfect breakfast pastries and specialty breads.

Jimtown Store DELI, MARKET $$
(☎707-433-1212; www.jimtown.com; 6706 Hwy 128; sandwiches $6-14; ⊙7:30am-3pm Mon, Wed & Thu, to 5pm Fri-Sun) One of our favorite Alexander Valley stopovers, Jimtown is great for picnic supplies and sandwiches made with housemade condiment spreads.

Drinking & Entertainment

Flying Goat Coffee CAFE
(www.flyinggoatcoffee.com; 324 Center St, Healdsburg; ⊙7am-7pm) See ya later, Starbucks. Flying Goat is what coffee should be – fairtrade and house-roasted – and locals line up for it every morning.

Bear Republic Brewing Company BREWERY
(☎707-433-2337; www.bearrepublic.com; 345 Healdsburg Ave, Healdsburg; ⊙11am-9:30pm Sun-Thu, to 11pm Fri & Sat) Bear Republic features handcrafted award-winning ales, non-award-winning pub grub, and live music weekends.

Alexander Valley Bar COCKTAIL BAR
(AVB; ☎707-431-1904; 3487 Alexander Valley Rd, Medlock Ames Winery; ⊙5-9pm Sun-Thu, to 11pm Fri & Sat) Vineyard sunsets are incredible at this speakeasy-style bar in Alexander Valley, which crafts cocktails ($10) using whatever's growing in the garden outside.

Raven Theater & Film Center THEATER
(☎707-433-5448; www.raventheater.com; 115 N Main St, Healdsburg) Hosts concerts, events and first-run art-house films.

Shopping

The Shed GARDEN, CULINARY
(☎707-431-7433; healdsburgshed.com; 25 North St, Healdsburg; ⊙8am-7pm Wed-Mon) 'Tools and supplies for growing, preparing and sharing food,' including heritage seeds by local farmers, house-milled California flour, and practical cookware.

Jimtown Store GIFTS
(☎707-433-1212; www.jimtown.com; 6706 Hwy 128) Forage antique bric-a-brac, candles and Mexican oilcloths at this roadside deli and store in Alexander Valley.

Gardener GARDENS
(☎707-431-1063; www.thegardener.com; 516 Dry Creek Rd, Healdsburg) Garden-shop lovers: don't miss this rural beauty.

One World GIFTS, HOMEWARES
(☎707-473-0880; www.oneworldfairtrade.net; 104 Matheson St, Healdsburg; ⊙10am-6pm Mon-Sat, to 5:30pm Sun) Household goods from fairtrade collectives.

Options Gallery CRAFTS, JEWELRY
(☎707-431-8861; www.optionsgallery.com; 126 Matheson St, Healdsburg; ⊙10:30am-5:30pm Mon-Sat, 11am-4pm Sun) Gifts, crafts and jewelry by local artists, including lovely earrings.

Copperfield's Books BOOKS
(☎707-433-9270; copperfieldsbooks.com; 104 Matheson St, Healdsburg; ⊙9am-6pm Sun-Thu, to 7pm Fri & Sat) Good general-interest books.

Levin & Company BOOKS, MUSIC
(☎707-433-1118; 306 Center St, Healdsburg; ⊙9am-9pm Mon-Sat, 10am-6pm Sun) Fiction and CDs; co-op art gallery.

Information

Healdsburg Chamber of Commerce & Visitors Bureau (☎707-433-6935, 800-648-9922; www.healdsburg.com; 217 Healdsburg Ave, Healdsburg; ⊙9am-5pm Mon-Fri, to 3pm Sat, 10am-2pm Sun) A block south of the plaza. Has winery maps and information on ballooning, golf, tennis, spas and nearby farms (get the *Farm Trails* brochure); 24-hour walk-up booth.

North Coast & Redwoods

Best Places to Eat

➡ Café Beaujolais (p232)

➡ Brick & Fire (p258)

➡ Café Aquatica (p223)

➡ Mario's Lost Coast Cafe (p255)

➡ Table 128 (p242)

Best Places to Stay

➡ Mar Vista Cottages (p226)

➡ Philo Apple Farm (p242)

➡ Benbow Inn (p249)

➡ Alegria (p231)

➡ Gold Bluffs Beach (p267)

Why Go?

There's a stretch of the coast with no road access called the 'Lost Coast,' but even the rest of the region, reached by a circuitous two-lane blacktop, feels far from the world's radar. The North Coast is no Beach Boys' song; there are no bikinis and few surfboards. The jagged edge of the continent is wild, scenic and even slightly foreboding, where spectral fog and an outsider spirit have fostered the world's tallest trees, most potent weed and a string of idiosyncratic two-stoplight towns. Explore hidden coves with a blanket and a bottle of local wine, scan the horizon for migrating whales and retreat at night to fire-warmed Victorians. As you travel further north, find valleys of redwood, wide rivers and mossy, overgrown forests. Befitting this dramatic clash of land and water are its unlikely mélange of residents: timber barons and tree huggers, pot farmers and political radicals of every stripe.

When to Go
Eureka

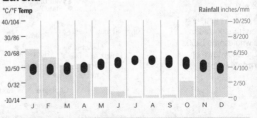

Jun–Jul The driest season in the Redwoods is spectacular for day hikes and big views.

Aug–Oct Warm weather and clear (or clearer) skies are the best for hiking the Lost Coast.

Dec–Apr Whales migrate off the coast. In early spring look for mothers and calves.

North Coast & Redwoods Highlights

1 Explore the gargantuan forests and dramatic coast of **Redwood National & State Parks** (p265).

2 Feel small amongst the standing and fallen giants in **Humboldt Redwoods State Park** (p252).

3 Hike the lush, remote and wild **Lost Coast** (p250).

4 Find a hidden cove on the **Sonoma Coast** (p222).

5 Get pampered at the B&Bs of **Mendocino** (p228).

6 Drink the sampler at McKinleyville's **Six Rivers Brewery** (p262), NorCal's best brewpub.

7 Climb to the top of **Point Arena Lighthouse** (p226) for views over the jagged coast.

8 Tour the laid-back vineyards of the **Anderson Valley** (p241).

9 Indulge in some all-American roadside kitsch along Hwy 101 like **Trees of Mystery** (p269).

10 Feel like you've been transported to the wholesome 1950s in the dairy town of **Ferndale** (p254).

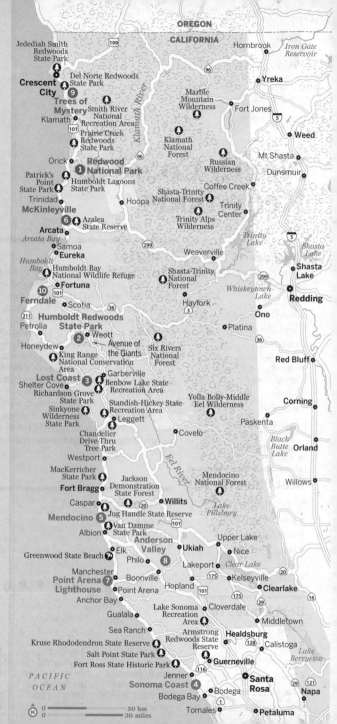

ⓘ Getting Around

Although Hwy 1 is popular with cyclists and there are bus connections, you will almost certainly need a car to explore this region. Those headed to the far north and on a schedule should take Hwy 101, the faster, inland route and then cut over to the coast. Windy Hwy 1 hugs the coast, then cuts inland and ends at Leggett, where it joins Hwy 101. Neither Amtrak nor Greyhound serve cities on coastal Hwy 1.

Amtrak (☑ 800-872-7245; www.amtrakcalifornia.com) operates the *Coast Starlight* between Los Angeles and Seattle. From LA, Amtrak buses connect to several North Coast towns including Leggett ($85, 11 hours, two daily) and Garberville ($87, 11½ hours, two daily).

Brave souls willing to piece together bus travel through the region will face a time-consuming headache, but connections are possible to almost every town in the region. **Greyhound** (☑ 800-231-2222; www.greyhound.com) runs buses between San Francisco and Ukiah, ($44, three hours, one daily) Willits ($44, 3½ hours, one daily), Rio Dell (near Fortuna, $57, six hours, one daily), Eureka ($57, 6¾ hours, one daily) and Arcata ($57, seven hours, one daily).

The **Mendocino Transit Authority** (MTA; ☑ 800-696-4682, 707-462-1422; www.4mta. org; fares $3.25-7.75) operates bus 65, which travels between Mendocino, Fort Bragg, Willits, Ukiah and Santa Rosa daily, with an afternoon return. Bus 95 runs between Point Arena and Santa Rosa, via Jenner, Bodega Bay and Sebastopol. Bus 75 heads north every weekday from Gualala to the Navarro River junction at Hwy 128, then runs inland through the Anderson Valley to Ukiah, returning in the afternoon. The North Coast route goes north between Navarro River junction and Albion, Little River, Mendocino and Fort Bragg, Monday to Friday. The best long-distance option is a daily ride between Fort Bragg and Santa Rosa via Willits and Ukiah ($21, three hours).

North of Mendocino County, the **Redwood Transit System** (☑ 707-443-0826; www.hta. org) operates buses ($3) Monday through Saturday between Scotia and Trinidad (2½ hours), stopping en route at Eureka (1¼ hours) and Arcata (1½ hours). **Redwood Coast Transit** (☑ 707-464-9314; www.redwoodcoasttransit. org) runs buses Monday to Saturday between Crescent City, Klamath ($1.50, one hour, five daily) and Arcata ($30, two hours, three daily), with numerous stops along the way.

COASTAL HIGHWAY 1

Down south it's called the 'PCH,' or Pacific Coast Hwy, but North Coast locals simply call it 'Hwy 1.' However you label it, get ready for a fabulous coastal drive, which cuts a winding course on isolated cliffs high above the crashing surf. Compared to the famous Big Sur coast, the serpentine stretch of Hwy 1 up the North Coast is more challenging, more remote and more *real*; passing farms, fishing towns and hidden beaches. Drivers use roadside pull-outs to scan the hazy Pacific horizon for migrating whales and explore a coastline dotted with rock formations that are relentlessly pounded by the surf. The drive between Bodega Bay and Fort Bragg takes four hours of daylight driving without stops. At night in the fog, it takes steely nerves and much, much longer. The most popular destination is the cliffside charmer of Mendocino.

Considering their proximity to the Bay Area, Sonoma and Mendocino counties remain unspoiled, and the austere coastal bluffs are some of the most spectacular in the country. But the trip north gets more rewarding and remote with every mile. By the time Hwy 1 cuts inland to join Hwy 101, the land along the Pacific – called the Lost Coast – the highway disappears and offers the state's best-preserved natural gifts.

Coastal accommodations (including campgrounds) can fill from Memorial Day to Labor Day (late May to early September) and on fall weekends, and often require two-night stays, so reserve ahead. Try to visit during spring or fall, especially in September and October; when the fog lifts, the ocean sparkles and most other visitors have gone home.

Bodega Bay

Bodega Bay is the first pearl in a string of sleepy fishing towns that line the North Coast and was the setting of Hitchcock's terrifying 1963 avian psycho-horror flick *The Birds*. The skies are free from bloodthirsty gulls today (though you best keep an eye on the picnic); it's Bay Area weekenders who descend en masse for extraordinary beaches, tide pools, whale-watching, fishing, surfing and seafood. Mostly a few restaurants, hotels and shops on both sides of Hwy 1, the downtown is not made for strolling, but it is a great base for exploring the endless nearby coves of the Sonoma Coast State Beach (p222).

Originally inhabited by the Pomo people, the bay takes its name from Juan Francisco de la Bodega y Quadra, captain of the Spanish sloop *Sonora*, which entered the bay in 1775. The area was then settled by Russians in the early 19th century, and farms were established to grow wheat for the Russian fur-trapping empire, which stretched from Alaska all the way down the coast to Fort Ross. The Russians pulled out in 1842, abandoning fort and farms, and American settlers moved in.

Hwy 1 runs through town and along the east side of Bodega Bay. On the west side, a peninsula juts out to sea, forming the entrance to Bodega Harbor.

◉ Sights & Activities

Surfing, beach combing and sportfishing are the main activities here – the latter requires advance booking. From December to April, the fishing boats host whale-watching trips, which are also good to book ahead. Just about everyone in town sells kites which are great for flying at Bodega Head. The excellent *Farm Trails* (www.farmtrails.org) guide at the Sonoma Coast Visitor Center (p222) has suggestions for tours of local ranches, orchards, farms and apiaries.

Bodega Head LOOKOUT
At the peninsula's tip, Bodega Head rises 265ft above sea level. To get there (and see the open ocean), head west from Hwy 1 onto Eastshore Rd, then turn right at the stop sign onto Bay Flat Rd. It's great for whale-watching. Landlubbers enjoy hiking above the surf, where several good trails include a 3.75-mile trek to Bodega Dunes Campground and a 2.2-mile walk to Salmon Creek Ranch.

Bodega Marine Laboratory & Reserve SCIENCE CENTER
(☑707-875-2211; www.bml.ucdavis.edu; 2099 Westside Rd; ☺2-4pm Fri) FREE Run by University of California (UC) Davis, this spectacularly diverse teaching and research reserve surrounds the research lab, which has studied Bodega Bay since the 1920s. The 263-acre reserve hosts many marine environments, including rocky intertidal coastal areas, mudflats and sandflats, salt marsh, sand dunes and freshwater wetlands. On most Friday afternoons docents give tours of the lab and surrounds.

Ren Brown Collection Gallery GALLERY
(www.renbrown.com; 1781 Hwy 1; ☺10am-5pm Wed-Sun) The renowned collection of modern Japanese prints and California works at this small gallery is a tranquil escape from the elements. Check out the Japanese garden at the back.

Chanslor Ranch HORSEBACK RIDING
(☑707-785-8849; www.chanslorranch.com; 2660 N Hwy 1; rides from $40) Just north of town, this friendly outfit leads horseback expeditions along the coastline and the rolling inland hills. Ron, the trip leader, is an amiable, sun-weathered cowboy straight from central casting; he recommends taking the Salmon Creek ride or calling ahead for weather-permitting moonlight rides. The 90-minute beach rides are donation based, and support a horse-rescue program.

Overnight trips in simple platform tents, which are excellent for families, can also be arranged. If you book a ride, you can park your RV at the ranch for free.

BLOODTHIRSTY BIRDS OF BODEGA BAY

Bodega Bay has the enduring claim to fame as the setting for Alfred Hitchcock's *The Birds*. Although special effects radically altered the actual layout of the town, you still get a good feel for the supposed site of the farm owned by Mitch Brenner (played by Rod Taylor). The once-cozy Tides Restaurant, where much avian-caused havoc occurs in the movie, is still there but since 1962 it has been transformed into a vast restaurant complex. Venture 5 miles inland to the tiny town of Bodega and you'll find two icons from the film: the schoolhouse and the church. Both stand just as they did in the movie – a crow overhead may make the hair rise on your neck. The **Bodega Country Store** (☺8am-8pm) claims to have more *The Birds* artifacts than anywhere else in the world.

The movie's star Tipi Hedren, now in her 80s, visits Bodega Bay at least once a year to help with local events and fundraisers. She also was in town for the movie's 50th anniversary festival in 2013 and there are hopes that the event will become annual.

Coincidentally, right after production of *The Birds* began, a real-life bird attack occurred in Capitola, the sleepy seaside town south of Santa Cruz. Thousands of seagulls ran amok, destroying property and attacking people.

Bodega Bay

Sportfishing Center   FISHING, WHALE-WATCHING
(📞707-875-3344; www.bodegacharters.com; 1410
Bay Flat Rd) Beside the Sandpiper Cafe, this
outfit organizes full-day fishing trips ($135)
and whale-watching excursions (three hours
adult/child $50/35). It also sells bait, tackle
and fishing licenses. Call ahead to ask about
recent sightings.

Bodega Bay Surf Shack   SURFING
(📞707-875-3944; http://bodegabaysurf.com; 1400
N Hwy 1; surfboard/wetsuit/kayak rentals from
$17/17/45) If you want to get on the water,
this easygoing one-stop shop has all kinds of
rentals, lessons and good local information.

Festivals & Events

**Bodega Seafood, Art &
Wine Festival**   FOOD, WINE
(www.winecountryfestivals.com; 📅) In late August, this festival of food and drink brings
together the best beer- and wine-makers of
the area, tons of seafood and activities for
kids. It takes place in the town of Bodega.

Bodega Bay Fishermen's Festival   CULTURAL
(www.bbfishfest.org) At the end of April, this
festival culminates in a blessing of the fleet,
a flamboyant parade of vessels, an arts-and-
crafts fair, kite-flying and feasting.

Sleeping

There's a wide spread of options – RV and
tent camping, quaint motels and fancy hotels. All fill up early during peak seasons.
Campers should consider heading just north
of town to the state-operated sites.

**Sonoma County
Regional Parks**   CAMPGROUND $
(📞707-565-2267;   www.parks.sonomacounty.
ca.gov; tent sties $7, RV sites without hookups $32)
There are a few walk-in sites at the **Doran
Regional Park** (201 Doran Beach Rd), at the
quiet Miwok Tent Campground, and **Westside Regional Park** (2400 Westshore Rd),
which is best for RVs. It caters primarily to
boaters and has windy exposures, beaches,
hot showers, fishing and boat ramps. Both
are heavily used. Excellent camping is also
available at the Sonoma Coast State Beach
(p222).

Bodega Harbor Inn   MOTEL $$
(📞707-875-3594;   www.bodegaharborinn.com;
1345 Bodega Ave; r $80-155, cottages $135-175;
📶🐾) Half a block inland from Hwy 1, sur-
rounded by grassy lawns and furnished with
both real and faux antiques, this modest yet
adorable blue-and-white shingled motel is
the town's most economical option. Pets are
allowed in some rooms for a fee of $15 plus
a security deposit of $50. They also offer a
variety of cottages and rentals around town.

Chanslor Guest Ranch   RANCH $$
(📞707-875-2721;   www.chanslorranch.com;   2660
Hwy 1; campsites $40, furnished tents from $80, r
from $175) A mile north of town, this working
horse ranch has rooms and options for upscale camping. Wildlife programs and guided horse tours make this one sweet place,
with sweeping vistas across open grasslands
to the sea.

Bodega Bay Lodge & Spa   LODGE $$$
(📞888-875-2250, 707-875-3525; www.bodegabay-
lodge.com; 103 Hwy 1; r $190-470; @📶🐾) Bode-
ga's plushest option, this small oceanfront
resort has an ocean-view swimming pool,
golf course, a Jacuzzi and a state-of-the-art
fitness club. In the evenings it hosts wine
tastings. The more expensive rooms have
commanding views, but all have balconies.
The other pluses on-site include Bodega
Bay's best spa and the **Duck Club** (📞707-
875-3525; mains $16-37; ⏰7:30-11am & 6-9pm),
which is the fanciest dining in town.

Bay Hill Mansion   B&B $$$
(📞877-468-1588; www.bayhillmansion.com; 3919
Bay Hill Rd; d $279-299; 📶🐾) A luxe B&B in
a spacious, modern mansion. The decor is
tasteful without much imagination but the
cleanliness and comfort standards here are
some of the best we've ever seen. Get a private yoga class or massage then the helpful
hosts can direct you to the area's best spots.
Views overlook trees with just a peek at the
bay.

Eating & Drinking

For the old-fashioned thrill of seafood by the
docks there are two options: **Tides Wharf &
Restaurant** (835 Hwy 1; breakfast $8-22, lunch
$13-28, dinner $16-28; ⏰7:30am-9:30pm Mon-
Thu, 7:30am-10pm Fri, 7am-10pm Sat, 7am-9:30pm
Sun; 📅) and **Lucas Wharf Restaurant &
Bar** (595 Hwy 1; mains $9-28; ⏰11:30am-9pm
Mon-Fri, 11am-10pm Sat; 📅). Both have views
and similar menus of clam chowder, fried
fish and coleslaw, and markets for picnic
supplies. Tides boasts a great fish market,
though Lucas Wharf feels less like a factory.
Don't be surprised if a bus pulls up outside
either of them.

Spud Point Crab Company SEAFOOD $
(www.spudpointcrab.com; 1910 Westshore Rd; dishes $4-11; ⊙9am-5pm; 🅿) In the classic tradition of dockside crab shacks, Spud Point serves salty-sweet crab cocktails and *real* clam chowder, served at picnic tables overlooking the marina. Take Bay Flat Rd to get here.

The Birds Cafe MEXICAN, AMERICAN $
(1407 Hwy 1; meals $6-14; ⊙11:30am-5pm) The menu consists of just a few things – usually fish tacos, fish 'n' chips, chowder and a few salads. Barbecued oysters are available seasonally. Order at the bar then take it to an outdoor picnic table overlooking the harbor. There's beer and wine available. Bliss.

Terrapin Creek Cafe & Restaurant CALIFORNIAN $$
(☑707-875-2700; www.terrapincreekcafe.com; 1580 Eastshore Dr; lunch mains $12-19, dinner mains $23-30; ⊙11am-2:30pm & 4:30-9pm Thu-Sun; 🖉) 🍃 Bodega Bay's most exciting upscale restaurant is run by a husband-wife team who espouse the slow food movement and serve local dishes sourced from the surrounding area. Comfort-food offerings like black cod roasted in lemon grass and coconut broth are artfully executed, while the Dungeness crab salad is fresh, briny and perfect. Jazz and warm light complete the atmosphere.

Gourmet Au Bay WINE BAR
(913 Hwy 1; ⊙11am-6pm Thu-Tue) The back deck of this wine bar offers a salty breeze with wine tasting.

❶ Information

Sonoma Coast Visitor Center (☑707-875-3866; www.bodegabay.com; 850 Hwy 1; ⊙9am-5pm Mon-Thu & Sat, to 6pm Fri, 10am-5pm Sun) Opposite the Tides Wharf. Stop by for the best help on the coast and for a copy of the *North Coaster*, a small-press indie newspaper of essays and brilliant insights on local culture.

Sonoma Coast State Beach

Stretching 17 miles north from Bodega Head to Vista Trail, the glorious **Sonoma Coast State Beach** (☑707-875-3483) is actually a series of beaches separated by several beautiful rocky headlands. Some beaches are tiny, hidden in little coves, while others stretch far and wide. Most of the beaches are connected by vista-studded coastal **hiking trails** that wind along the bluffs. Exploring this area makes an excellent day-long adventure, so bring a picnic. Be advised however: the surf is often too treacherous to wade, so keep an eye on children. While this system of beaches and parks has some camping, you can't just pitch a tent anywhere; most are for day-use only.

◉ Sights & Activities

Beaches

Salmon Creek Beach BEACH
Situated around a lagoon, this has 2 miles of hiking and good waves for surfing.

Portuguese Beach & Schoolhouse Beach BEACHES
Both are very easy to access and have sheltered coves between rocky outcroppings.

Duncan's Landing BEACH
Small boats unload near this rocky headland in the morning. A good place to spot wildflowers in the spring.

Shell Beach BEACH
A boardwalk and trail leads out to a stretch perfect for tide-pooling and beachcombing.

Goat Rock BEACH
Famous for its colony of harbor seals, lazing in the sun at the mouth of the Russian River.

🛌 Sleeping

Bodega Dunes CAMPGROUND $
(☑800-444-7275; www.reserveamerica.com; 3095 Hwy 1, Bodega Bay; tent & RV sites $35, day use $8) The largest campground in the Sonoma Coast State Beach system of parks, it is also closest to Bodega Bay. It gets a lot of use. Sites are in high dunes and have hot showers but be warned – the fog horn sounds all night.

Wright's Beach Campground CAMPGROUND $
(☑800-444-7275; www.reserveamerica.com; tent & RV sites $35, day use $8) Of the few parks that allow camping along Sonoma Coast State Beach, this is the best, even though sites lack privacy. Sites can be booked six months in advance, and numbers 1–12 are right on the beach. There are BBQ pits for day use and it's a perfect launch for sea kayakers.

Everyone else, stay out of the water; according to camp hosts the treacherous rip tides claim a life every season.

Jenner

Perched on the hills looking out to the Pacific and above the mouth of the Russian River, tiny Jenner offers access to the coast and the Russian River wine region. A **harbor-seal colony** sits at the river's mouth and pups are born here from March to August. There are restrictions about getting too close to the chubby, adorable pups – handling them can be dangerous and cause the pups to be abandoned by their mothers. Volunteers answer questions along the roped-off area where day trippers can look on at a distance. The best way to see them is by kayak and most of the year you will find **Water Treks Ecotours** (☎707-865-2249; 2hr rental from $25; ⊙10am-3pm) renting kayaks on the highway. Heading north on Hwy 1 you will begin driving on one of the most beautiful, windy stretches of California highway. You'll also probably lose cell-phone service – possibly a blessing.

🛏 Sleeping & Eating

Jenner Inn & Cottages INN $$
(☎707-865-2377; www.jennerinn.com; 10400 Hwy 1; r incl breakfast creekside $118-278, cottages $228-298; @) It's difficult to sum up this collection of properties dispersed throughout Jenner – some are in fairly deluxe ocean-view cottages with kitchen and ready-to-light fireplaces, others are small and upland near a creek. All have the furnishings of a stylish auntie from the early 1990s.

★ Café Aquatica CAFE $
(www.cafeaquatica.com; 10439 Hwy 1; sandwiches $10-13; 🛜) This is the kind of North Coast coffee shop you've been dreaming of: fresh pastries, organic coffee and chatty locals. The view of the Russian River from the patio and gypsy sea-hut decor make it hard to leave.

★ River's End CALIFORNIAN $$$
(☎707-865-2484; www.rivers-end.com; 11048 Hwy 1; lunch mains $14-26, dinner mains $25-39; ⊙noon-3pm & 5-8:30pm Thu-Mon; 🖊) Unwind in style at this picture-perfect restaurant that overlooks the river's mouth and the grand sweep of the Pacific Ocean. It serves world-class meals at world-class prices, but the real reward is the view. Its ocean-view **cottages** (rooms and cottages $159 to $229) are wood paneled and have no TVs, wi-fi or phones. Children under 12 are not recommended.

Fort Ross State Historic Park

A curious glimpse into Tsarist Russia's exploration of the California coast, the salt-washed buildings of **Fort Ross State Historic Park** (☎707-847-3286; www.fortrossstatepark.org; 19005 Hwy 1; per car $8; ⊙10:30am-4pm Sat & Sun) offer a fascinating insight into the pre-American Wild West. It's a quiet, picturesque place with a riveting past.

In March 1812, a group of 25 Russians and 80 Alaskans (including members of the Kodiak and Aleutian tribes) built a wooden fort here, near a Kashaya Pomo village. The southernmost outpost of the 19th-century Russian fur trade on America's Pacific Coast, Fort Ross was established as a base for sea-otter hunting operations and trade with Alta California, and for growing crops for Russian settlements in Alaska. The Russians dedicated the fort in August 1812 and occupied it until 1842, when it was abandoned because the sea otter population had been decimated and agricultural production had never taken off.

Fort Ross State Historic Park, an accurate reconstruction of the fort, is 11 miles north of Jenner on a beautiful point. The original buildings were sold, dismantled and carried off to Sutter's Fort during the Gold Rush. The **visitor center** (☎707-847-3437) has a great museum with historical displays and an excellent bookshop on Californian and Russian history. Ask about hikes to the Russian cemetery.

On **Fort Ross Heritage Day**, the last Saturday in July, costumed volunteers bring the fort's history to life; check the website www.parks.ca.gov or call the visitor center for other special events.

If you pass by on a weekday when the fort is closed (due to budget cuts), you still may be able to walk down and have a peek inside if a school group is there.

🛏 Sleeping

Stillwater Cove Regional Park CAMPGROUND $
(☎reservations 707-565-2267; www.sonoma-county.org/parks; 22455 N Hwy 1; tent & RV sites $28) Two miles north of Timber Cove, this park has hot showers and hiking under Monterey pines. Sites 1, 2, 4, 6, 9 and 10 have ocean views.

Timber Cove Inn INN $$
(☎800-987-8319, 707-847-3231; www.timbercoveinn.com; 21780 N Hwy 1; r from $155, ocean view from $183) A dramatic and quirky '60s-modern seaside inn that was once a top-of-the-line luxury lodge. Though the price remains high, it has slipped a bit. The rustic architectural

shell is still stunning, though, and a duet of tinkling piano and crackling fire fills the lobby. The quirky rooms facing the ocean have a treehouse feel, with rustic redwood details, balconies, fireplaces and lofted beds. Even those who don't bunk here should wander agape in the shadow of Benny Bufano's 93ft peace statue, a spectacular totem on the edge of the sea. The expensive restaurant on-site is nothing to write home about and the staff were grumpy when we passed by.

Salt Point State Park

Stunning 6000-acre **Salt Point State Park** (☑707-847-3321; per car $8; ☺visitor center 10am-3pm Sat & Sun Apr-Oct) has sandstone cliffs that drop dramatically into the kelp-strewn sea and hiking trails that crisscross windswept prairies and wooded hills, connecting pygmy forests and coastal coves rich with tidepools. The 6-mile-wide park is bisected by the San Andreas Fault – the rock on the east side is vastly different from that on the west. Check out the eerily beautiful *tafonis*, honeycombed-sandstone formations, near Gerstle Cove. For a good roadside photo op, there's a pullout at mile-marker 45, with views of decaying redwood shacks, grazing goats and headlands jutting out to the sea.

Though many of the day use areas have been closed off due to budget cuts, trails lead off Hwy 1 pull-outs to views of the pristine coastline. The platform overlooking **Sentinel Rock** is just a short stroll from the Fisk Mill Cove parking lot at the park's north end. Further south, seals laze at **Gerstle Cove Marine Reserve**, one of California's first underwater parks. Tread lightly around tidepools and don't lift the rocks: even a glimpse of sunlight can kill some critters. If you're here between April and June, you *must* see **Kruse Rhododendron State Reserve**. Growing abundantly in the forest's filtered light, magnificent, pink rhododendrons reach heights of over 30ft, making them the tallest species in the world; turn east from Hwy 1 onto Kruse Ranch Rd and follow the signs. Be sure to walk the short **Rododendron Loop Trail**.

🛏 Sleeping

Woodside & Gerstle Cove Campgrounds   CAMPGROUND $
(☑800-444-7275; www.reserveamerica.com; tent & RV sites $35; ☺Woodside Apr-Sep) Two campgrounds, Woodside and Gerstle Cove, both signposted off Hwy 1, have campsites with cold water. Inland Woodside is well protected by Monterey pines. Gerstle Cove's trees burned over a decade ago and have only grown halfway back, giving the gnarled, blackened trunks a ghostly look when the fog twirls between the branches.

Ocean Cove Lodge Bar & Grill   MOTEL $
(☑707-847-3158; www.oceancovelodge.com; 23255 Hwy 1; r from $69; ❋🛜) Just a few minutes south of Salt Point State Park is Ocean Cove Lodge Bar & Grill, a godsend for those on a budget. It's just a basic motel but the location is fabulous, there's a hot tub and a surprisingly good American-style restaurant on the premises.

Stuart Point Store & Retreat   TENT CABINS, GROCERY $$
(32000 Hwy 1; d tents Mon-Fri $155, Sat & Sun $225-250; ☺8am-5pm) For snacks, coffee and photo ops, don't miss a stop at Stuart Point Store just north of Salt Point State Park. This may be the oldest continuously family-run business west of the Mississippi (it opened in 1868), and while the decor has stayed true to its heritage, the gourmet fare on offer is deliciously modern. The owner's house is in the antique-looking ranch next door and about a quarter of a mile south down Hwy 1 are the eerie remains of the old schoolhouse.

'Glamping' is now available on the wild, 1200-acre property with canvas tents perched 400ft over stunning sea cliffs, all equipped with queen-sized beds and luxury linens. It's a bit pricey considering there's no electricity (tents are lit by battery-powered lanterns) and showers are outdoors, but the setting is unparalleled.

Sea Ranch

Though not without its fans, the exclusive community of Sea Ranch is a sort of weather-beaten Stepford-by-the-Sea. The ritzy subdivision that sprawls 10 miles along the coast is connected with a well-watched network of private roads. Approved for construction prior to the existence of the watchdog Coastal Commission, the community was a precursor to the concept of 'slow growth,' with strict zoning laws requiring that houses be constructed of weathered wood only. According to *The Sea Ranch Design Manual*: 'This is not a place for the grand architectural statement; it's a place to explore the subtle nuances of fitting in...'. Indeed. Though there are some lovely and recommended short-term rentals here, don't break any community rules – like throwing wild parties – or security will come knockin'. For supplies and gasoline, go to Gualala.

After years of litigation, public throughways onto private beaches have been legally mandated and are now well marked. Hiking trails lead from roadside parking lots to the sea and along the bluffs, but don't dare trespass on adjacent lands. **Stengel Beach** (Hwy 1, Mile 53.96) has a beach-access staircase, **Walk-On Beach** (Hwy 1, Mile 56.53) provides wheelchair access and **Shell Beach** (Hwy 1, Mile 55.24) also has beach-access stairs; parking at all three areas costs $6. For hiking details, including maps, contact the **Sea Ranch Association** (www.tsra.org).

Sea Ranch Lodge (☑707-785-2371; www.searanchlodge.com; 60 Sea Walk Dr; r incl breakfast $199-369; ☎) ⌖, a marvel of '60s-modern California architecture, has spacious, luxurious, minimalist rooms, many with dramatic views to the ocean; some have hot tubs and fireplaces. The fine contemporary **restaurant** (lunch mains $12-18, dinner mains $22-38; ☺8am-9pm) has a menu for discerning guests; expect everything from duck breast to local fish tacos. North of the lodge you'll see Sea Ranch's iconic nondenominational **chapel**; it's on the inland side of Hwy 1, mileage marker 55.66. For those short on time or on a budget, this is the best reason to pull over in Sea Ranch.

Depending on the season, it can be surprisingly affordable to rent a house in Sea Ranch; contact **Rams Head Realty** (www.ramshead-realty.com), **Sea Ranch Rentals** (www.searanchrentals.com), or **Sea Ranch Escape** (www.searanchescape.com).

Gualala & Anchor Bay

At just 2½ hours north of San Francisco, Gualala – pronounced by most locals as 'Wah-*la*-la' – is northern Sonoma coast's hub for a weekend getaway as it sits square in the middle of the 'Banana Belt,' a stretch of coast known for unusually sunny weather. Founded as a lumber town in the 1860s, the downtown stretches along Hwy 1 with a bustling commercial district that has a great grocery store and some cute, slightly upscale shops.

Just north, quiet Anchor Bay has several inns, a tiny shopping center and, heading north, a string of secluded, hard-to-find

ANNAPOLIS WINERY

Just south of Sea Ranch on Hwy 1, you'll see signs for **Annapolis Winery** (☑707-886-5460; www.annapoliswinery.com; 26055 Soda Springs Rd; tasting fee $5; ☺12-5pm daily). Swing a right onto Annapolis Rd and drive a winding, scenic 7½ miles to this small, remote, yet utterly charming winery. This super-friendly, mom-and-pop place produces highly regarded small-batch wines. The Gewürztraminer, Pinot Noir and Zinfandel Port get the most raves but all the varieties are worth sampling. A few picnic supplies are available or bring your own to enjoy the views over the vines and coastal mountains.

beaches. Both are excellent jumping-off points for exploring the area.

◉ Sights & Activities

Seven miles north of Anchor Bay, pull off at mile-marker 11.41 for **Schooner Gulch**. A trail into the forest leads down cliffs to a sandy beach with tidepools. Bear right at the fork in the trail to reach iconic **Bowling Ball Beach**, where low tide reveals rows of big, round rocks resembling bowling balls. Consult tide tables for Arena Cove. The forecast low tide must be lower than +1.5ft on the tide chart for the rocks to be visible.

Gualala Arts Center   ARTS CENTER
(☑707-884-1138; www.gualalaarts.org; ☺9am-4pm Mon-Fri, noon-4pm Sat & Sun) Inland along Old State Rd, at the south end of town and beautifully built entirely by volunteers, this center hosts changing exhibitions, organizes the **Art in the Redwoods Festival** in late August and has loads of info on local art.

Adventure Rents   KAYAKING
(☑888-881-4386, 707-884-4386; www.adventurerents.com) In the summer, a sand spit forms at the mouth of the river, cutting it off from the ocean and turning it into a warm-water lake. This outfit rents **canoes** (two hours/half-day/full day $70/80/90) and **kayaks** (two hours/half-day/full day $35/40/45) out of a van and provides instruction.

🛏 Sleeping & Eating

Of the two towns, Gualala has more services and is a more practical hub for exploring –

there are a bunch of good motels and a pair of nice grocery stores. Get fresh veggies at the **farmers market** (Gualala Community Center; ⊙10am-12:30pm Sat Jun-Oct) and organic supplies and local wine at the **Anchor Bay Village Market** (35513 S Hwy 1).

Gualala Point Regional Park CAMPGROUND $
(http://parks.sonomacounty.ca.gov; 42401 Highway 1, Gualala; campsites $32) Shaded by a stand of redwoods and fragrant California Bay laurel trees, a short trail connects this creekside campground to the windswept beach. The quality of sites, including several secluded hike-in spots, makes it the best drive-in camping on this part of the coast.

Gualala River Redwood Park CAMPGROUND $
(☑707-884-3533; www.gualalapark.com; day use $6, tent & RV sites $42-49) Another excellent Sonoma County Park. Inland along Old State Rd, you can camp and do short hikes along the river.

★St Orres Inn INN $$
(☑707-884-3303; www.saintorres.com; 36601 Hwy 1, Gualala; B&B $95-135, cottages $140-445; 🐾🐕) Famous for its striking Russian-inspired architecture: dramatic rough-hewn timbers, stained glass and burnished copper domes, there's no place quite like St Orres. On the property's fairytale-like, wild-mushroom-strewn 90 acres, hand-built cottages range from rustic to luxurious. The inn's fine **restaurant** (☑707-884-3335; dinner mains $40-50) serves worth-the-splurge, inspired Californian cuisine in one of the coast's most romantic rooms.

North Coast Country Inn B&B $$
(☑800-959-4537, 707-884-4537; www.northcoastcountryinn.com; 34591 S Hwy 1, Gualala; r incl breakfast $185-235; 🐾🐕) Perched on an inland hillside beneath towering trees, surrounded by lovely gardens, the perks of this adorable place begin with the gregarious owner and a hot tub. The six spacious, country-style rooms are decorated with lovely prints and boast exposed beams, fireplaces, board games and private entrances.

★Mar Vista Cottages CABIN $$$
(☑877-855-3522, 707-884-3522; www.marvistamendocino.com; 35101 S Hwy 1, Gualala; cottages $175-305; 🐾🐕) 🐾 The elegantly renovated 1930s fishing cabins offer a simple, stylish seaside escape with a vanguard commitment to sustainability. The harmonious environment is the result of pitch-perfect details: linens are line-dried over lavender, guests browse the organic vegetable garden to harvest their own dinner and chickens cluck around the grounds laying the next morning's breakfast. It often requires two-night stays.

Laura's Bakery & Taqueria MEXICAN $
(☑707-884-3175; 38411 Robinson Reef Rd, at Hwy 1, Gualala; mains $7-12; ⊙7am-7pm Mon-Sat; 🐾) Laura's is a refreshing, low-key break from Hwy 1 upscale dining. The menu's taqueria staples are fantastic (the Baja-style fish tacos are a steal) but the fresh *mole* dishes and distant ocean view are the real surprises.

Bones Roadhouse BARBECUE $$
(www.bonesroadhouse.com; 39350 S Hwy 1, Gualala; mains $9-20; ⊙11:30am-9pm Sun-Thu, to 10pm Fri & Sat) Savory smoked meats and a busy biker bar vibe make this Gualala's most fun lunch stop. On weekends a codgerly blues outfit may be growling out 'Mustang Sally.'

ⓘ Information

Redwood Coast Visitors Center (www.redwoodcoastchamber.com; 39150 Hwy 1, Gualala; ⊙12-5pm Thu-Sat) Has local information.

Point Arena

This laid-back little town combines creature comforts with relaxed, eclectic California living and is the first town up the coast where the majority of residents don't seem to be retired Bay Area refugees. Sit by the docks a mile west of town at **Arena Cove** and watch surfers mingle with fishermen and hippies.

⊙ Sights

Point Arena Lighthouse LIGHTHOUSE
(☑707-882-2777; www.pointarenalighthouse.com; 45500 Lighthouse Rd; adult/child $7.50/1; ⊙10am-3:30pm, to 4:30pm late May-early Sep) Two miles north of town, this 1908 lighthouse (the tallest on the US West Coast) stands 10 stories high and is the only lighthouse in California you can ascend. Check in at the museum, then climb the 145 steps to the top and see the Fresnel lens and the jaw-dropping view. You an stay on-site (p227).

Stornetta Public Lands NATURE RESERVE
For fabulous bird-watching, hiking on terraced rock past sea caves and access to hidden coves, head 1 mile down Lighthouse Rd from Hwy 1 and look for the Bureau of Land Management (BLM) signs on the left

indicating these 1132-acre public lands. The best, most dramatic walking trail leads along the coast and also begins on Lighthouse Rd from a small parking area about a quarter-mile before the Lighthouse parking area.

Sleeping & Eating

Wharf Master's Inn
HOTEL **$$**

(☎800-932-4031, 707-882-3171; www.wharfmasters.com; 785 Iversen Ave; r $100-195; ☎❋) This is a cluster of small, modern rooms on a cliff overlooking fishing boats and a stilt pier. Tidy and very clean, rooms have the character of a chain hotel.

Coast Guard House Inn
INN **$$**

(☎707-882-2442; www.coastguardhouse.com; 695 Arena Cove; r $165-265; ☎) Come here if you want to soak up old-world oceanside charm and are willing to deal with historic plumbing. It's a 1901 Cape Cod–style house and cottage, with water-view rooms.

Coast Guard Homes
VACATION RENTAL **$$**

(☎877-725-4448; 45500 Lighthouse Rd; houses $135-235) True lighthouse buffs should look into staying at the plain three-bedroom, kitchen-equipped former Coast Guard homes at the Lighthouse. They're quiet, wind-swept retreats.

Franny's Cup & Saucer
BAKERY **$**

(www.frannyscupandsaucer.com; 213 Main St; items from $2; ☉8am-4pm Wed-Sat) The cutest patisserie on this stretch of coast is run by Franny and her mother, Barbara (a veteran of Chez Panisse). The fresh berry tarts and creative housemade chocolates seem too beautiful to eat, until you take the first bite and immediately want to order another. Several times a year they pull out all the stops for a Sunday garden brunch ($25).

Arena Market
ORGANIC, DELI **$**

(www.arenaorganics.org; 183 Main St; ☉7:30am-7pm Mon-Sat, 8:30am-6pm Sun; ☎❋) ✿ The deli in front of this fully stocked organic grocer makes excellent to-go veg and gluten-free options, often sourced from local farms. The serve-yourself soup is delish.

Pizzas N Cream
PIZZA **$$**

(www.pizzasandcream.com; 790 Port Rd; pizzas $10-18; ☉11:30am-9pm; ☎❋) In Arena Cove, this friendly place whips up exquisite pizzas and fresh salads, and serves beer and ice cream.

🍷 Drinking & Entertainment

215 Main
BAR

(www.facebook.com/215Main; 215 Main St; ☉2pm-2am Tue-Sun) Head to this open, renovated historic building to drink local beer and wine. There's jazz on the weekends.

Arena Cinema
CINEMA

(www.arenatheater.org; 214 Main St) Shows mainstream, foreign and art films in a beautifully restored movie house. Sue, the ticket seller, has been in that booth for 40 years. Got a question about Point Arena? Ask Sue.

Manchester

Follow Hwy 1 for about 7 miles north of Point Arena, through gorgeous rolling fields dropping down from the hills to the blue ocean, and a turnoff leads to **Manchester State Beach**, a long, wild stretch of sand. The area around here is remote and beautiful (only one grocery store), but it's a quick drive to Point Arena for more elaborate provisions.

Ross Ranch (☎707-877-1834; www.rossranch.biz) at Irish Beach, another 5 miles to the north, arranges two-hour horseback beach ($60) and mountain ($50) rides; reservations recommended.

Mendocino Coast KOA (☎707-882-2375; www.manchesterbeachkoa.com; tent/RV sites from $29/49, cabins $64-78; ☎❋) is an impressive private campground with tightly packed campsites beneath enormous Monterey pines, a cooking pavilion, hot showers, a hot tub and bicycles. The cabins are a great

TOP WHALE-WATCHING SPOTS

Watch for spouts, sounding and breaching whales and pods. Anywhere coastal will do, but the following are some of the north coast's best:

➡ Bodega Head (p220)

➡ Mendocino Headlands State Park (p229)

➡ Jug Handle State Reserve (p233)

➡ MacKerricher State Park (p237)

➡ Shelter Cove & Lost Coast (p250)

➡ Trinidad Head Trail (p263)

➡ Klamath River Overlook (p268)

option for families who want to get the camping experience without roughing it.

A quarter-mile west, the sunny, exposed campground at **Manchester State Park** (www.parks.gov.ca; tent & RV sites $29-39) has cold water and quiet sites right by the ocean. Sites are nonreservable. Budget cuts have all but eliminated ranger service.

Elk

Thirty minutes north of Point Arena, itty-bitty Elk is famous for its stunning cliff-top views of 'sea stacks,' towering rock formations jutting out of the water. Otherwise, it's one of the cutest yet gentrified-looking villages before Mendocino. There is *nothing* to do after dinner, so bring a book if you're a night owl. And you can forget about the cell phone, too; reception here is nonexistent. Elk's **visitor center** (5980 Hwy 1; ⊙11am-1pm Sat & Sun mid-Mar–Oct) has exhibits on the town's logging past. At the southern end of town, **Greenwood State Beach** sits where Greenwood Creek meets the sea.

Tucked into a tiny house looking across the road to the ocean, the **Elk Studio Gallery & Artist's Collective** (www.artists-collective.net; 6031 S Hwy 1; ⊙10am-5pm) is cluttered with local art – everything from carvings and pottery to photography and jewelry.

🛏 Sleeping & Eating

Griffin House   INN $$
(☑707-877-3422; www.griffinn.com; 5910 S Hwy 1; cottages incl breakfast $138-260; 🐾🐱) This is the most affordable choice, with an adorable cluster of simple, powder-blue bluffside cottages with wood-burning stoves.

Elk Cove Inn & Spa   INN $$$
(☑800-725-2967; www.elkcoveinn.com; 6300 S Hwy 1; r $100-375, cottages $275-355; 🐾🐱) Several upmarket B&Bs take advantage of the views. You simply can't beat those from Elk Cove Inn & Spa, located on a bluff with steps leading down to the driftwood-strewn beach below. Prices in the wide selection of rooms and cottages include breakfast, wine, champagne and cocktails plus you can relax even further at their deluxe spa.

Harbor House Inn   INN $$$
(☑800-720-7474, 707-877-3203; www.theharborhouseinn.com; 5600 S Hwy 1; r & cottages incl breakfast & dinner $360-490; 🐾) Harbor House Inn, located in a 1915 Arts and Crafts–style mansion (closed for renovations when we passed), has gorgeous cliff-top gardens and a private beach. Rates include a superb four-course dinner for two in the ocean-view room with a lauded wine list.

Queenie's Roadhouse Cafe   CAFE $
(☑707-877-3285; 6061 S Hwy 1; dishes $6-10; ⊙8am-3pm Thu-Mon; 🍴) Everyone swears by excellent, retro-chic Queenie's Roadhouse Cafe for a creative range of breakfast (try the wild-rice waffles) and lunch treats.

Bridget Dolan's   AMERICAN $$
(☑707-877-1820; 5910 S Hwy 1; mains $10-15; ⊙4:30-8pm) Sweet, little Bridget Dolan's serves straight-forward cookin' like pot pies, and bangers and mash.

Van Damme State Park

Three miles south of Mendocino, this gorgeous 1831-acre **park** (☑707-937-5804; www.parks.ca.gov; per car $8) draws divers, beachcombers and kayakers to its easy-access beach. It's also known for its **pygmy forest**, where the acidic soil and an impenetrable layer of hardpan just below the surface create a bonsai forest with decades-old trees growing only several feet high. A wheelchair-accessible boardwalk provides access to the forest. Turn east off Hwy 1 onto Little River Airport Rd, a half-mile south of Van Damme State Park, and drive for 3 miles. Alternatively, hike or bike up from the campground on the 3.5-mile **Fern Canyon Scenic Trail**, which crosses back and forth over Little River.

The **visitor center** (☑707-937-4016; ⊙10am-3pm Fri-Sun) has nature exhibits, videos and programs; a half-hour **Marsh Loop Trail** starts nearby.

Two pretty **campgrounds** (☑800-444-7275; www.reserveamerica.com; tent & RV sites $35; 🐾) are excellent for family car camping. They both have hot showers: one is just off Hwy 1, the other is in a highland meadow, which has lots of space for kids to run around. Nine **environmental campsites** (tent sites $25) lie just a 1¼-mile hike up Fern Canyon; there's untreated creek water.

For sea-cave kayaking tours ($60), contact **Kayak Mendocino** (☑707-937-0700; www.kayakmendocino.com).

Mendocino

Leading out to a gorgeous headland, Mendocino is the North Coast's salt-washed perfect village, with B&Bs surrounded by rose gardens, white-picket fences and New England–style redwood water towers. Bay Area weekenders walk along the headland among berry bramble and wildflowers, where cypress trees stand over dizzying cliffs. Nature's power is evident everywhere, from driftwood-littered fields and cave tunnels to the raging surf. The town itself is full of cute shops – no chains – and has earned the nickname 'Spendocino,' for its upscale goods. In summer, fragrant bursts of lavender and jasmine permeate the foggy wind, tempered by salt air from the churning surf, which is never out of earshot.

Built by transplanted New Englanders in the 1850s, Mendocino thrived late into the 19th century, with ships transporting redwood timber from here to San Francisco. The mills shut down in the 1930s, and the town fell into disrepair until it was rediscovered in the 1950s by artists and bohemians. Today the culturally savvy, politically aware, well-traveled citizens welcome visitors, but eschew corporate interlopers – don't look for a Big Mac or Starbucks. To avoid crowds, come midweek or in the low season, when the vibe is mellower – and prices more reasonable.

⊙ Sights

Mendocino is lined with all kinds of interesting galleries, which hold openings on the second Saturday of each month from 5pm to 8pm.

Mendocino Art Center   GALLERY
(☏ 707-937-5818, 800 653 3328; www.mendocinoartcenter.org; 45200 Little Lake St; ⊙ 10am-5pm Apr-Oct, to 4pm Tue-Sat Nov-Mar) Behind a yard of twisting iron sculpture, the city's art center takes up a whole tree-filled block, hosting exhibitions, the 81-seat **Helen Schoeni Theatre** and nationally renowned art classes. This is also where to pick up the *Mendocino Arts Showcase* brochure, a quarterly publication listing all the happenings and festivals in town.

Kelley House Museum   MUSEUM
(www.mendocinohistory.org; 45007 Albion St; admission $2; ⊙ 11am-3pm Thu-Tue Jun-Sep, Fri-Mon Oct-May) With a research library and changing exhibits on early California and Mendocino, the 1861 museum hosts seasonal, two-hour **walking tours** for $10; call for times.

Kwan Tai Temple   TEMPLE
(www.kwantaitemple.org; 45160 Albion St) Peering in the window of this 1852 temple reveals an old altar dedicated to the Chinese god of war. Tours are available by appointment.

Point Cabrillo Lighthouse   LIGHTHOUSE
(www.pointcabrillo.org; Point Cabrillo Dr; ⊙ 11am-4pm Sat & Sun Jan & Feb, daily Mar-Oct, Fri-Mon Nov & Dec) FREE Restored in 1909, this stout lighthouse stands on a 300-acre wildlife preserve north of town, between Russian Gulch and Caspar Beach. **Guided walks** of the preserve leave at 11am on Sundays from May to September. You can also stay in the lighthouse keeper's house and cottages which are now vacation rentals (p231).

🏃 Activities

Wine tours, whale-watching, shopping, hiking, cycling: there's more to do in the area than a thousand long weekends could accomplish. For navigable river and ocean kayaking, launch from tiny Albion, which hugs the north side of the Albion River mouth, 5 miles south of Mendocino.

Catch A Canoe & Bicycles Too!   CANOEING, KAYAKING
(☏ 707-937-0273; www.catchacanoe.com; Stanford Inn by the Sea, 44850 Comptche-Ukiah Rd; kayak & canoe rental adult/child from $28/14; ⊙ 9am-5pm) This friendly outfit at the Stanford Inn south of town rents bikes, kayaks and stable outrigger canoes for trips up the 8-mile Big River tidal estuary, the longest undeveloped estuary in Northern California. No highways or buildings, only beaches, forests, marshes, streams, abundant wildlife and historic logging sites. Bring a picnic and a camera to enjoy the ramshackle remnants of century-old train trestles and majestic blue herons.

Mendocino Headlands State Park OUTDOORS
A spectacular park surrounds the village, with trails crisscrossing the bluffs and rocky coves. Ask at the visitor center about guided weekend walks, including spring wildflower walks and whale-watching.

✪ Festivals & Events

For a complete list of Mendocino's many festivals, check with the visitor center or www.gomendo.com.

Mendocino Whale Festival   WILDLIFE
(www.mendowhale.com) Early March, with wine and chowder tastings, whale-watching and music.

Mendocino

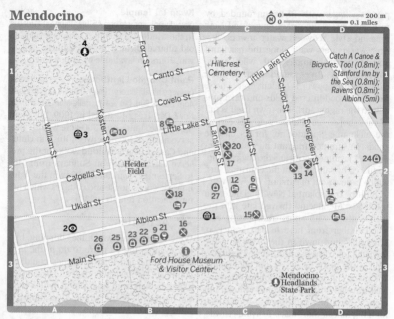

Mendocino

⊙ Sights

🛏 Sleeping

⊗ Eating

⊙ Drinking & Nightlife

🛍 Shopping

Mendocino Music Festival　　MUSIC
(www.mendocinomusic.com; 🎵) Mid-July, with orchestral and chamber music concerts on the headlands, children's matinees and open rehearsals.

Mendocino Wine & Mushroom Festival　　FOOD, WINE
(www.mendocino.com) Early November, guided mushroom tours and symposia.

🛏 Sleeping

Standards are high and so are prices; two-day minimums often crop up on weekends. Fort Bragg, 10 miles north, has cheaper lodgings. All B&B rates include breakfast; only a few places have TVs. For a range of cottages and B&Bs, contact **Mendocino Coast Reservations** (📞800-262-7801, 707-937-5033; www.mendocinovacations.com; 45084 Little Lake St; ⊙9am-5pm).

Russian Gulch State Park CAMPGROUND $
(🖱reservations 800-444-7275; www.reserveameri-ca.com; tent & RV sites $35) In a wooded canyon 2 miles north of town, with secluded drive-in sites, hot showers, a small waterfall and the Devil's Punch Bowl (a collapsed sea arch).

Andiron CABIN $$
(🖱800-955-6478, 707-937-1543; http://theand-iron.com; 6051 N Hwy 1, Little River; most cabins $109-299; 📶🛜🐾) 🖋 Styled with hip vintage decor, this cluster of 1950s roadside cottages is a refreshingly playful option amid the cabbage-rose and lace aesthetic of Mendocino. Each cabin houses two rooms with complementing themes: 'Read' has old books, comfy vintage chairs and hip retro eyeglasses, while the adjoining 'Write' features a huge chalk board and a ribbon typewriter.

A favorite for travelers? 'Here' and 'There,' themed with old maps, 1960s airline paraphernalia and collectables from North Coast's yesteryear.

MacCallum House Inn B&B $$
(🖱800-609-0492, 707-937-0289; www.maccallum-house.com; 45020 Albion St; r & cottages from $149, water tower from $225; @📶🛜🐾) 🖋 The finest B&B option in town with gardens in a riot of color. There are cheerful cottages, and a modern luxury home, but the most memorable space is within one of Mendocino's iconic historic water towers – living quarters fill the ground floor, a sauna is on the 2nd floor and there's a view of the coast from the top.

All accommodations have cushy extras like robes, DVD players, stereos and plush linens.

Packard House B&B $$
(🖱888-453-2677, 707-937-2677; www.packard-house.com; 45170 Little Lake St; r $175-225; 📶) Decked out in contemporary style, this place is Mendocino's most chic and sleek B&B choice, with beautiful fabrics, colorful minimalist paintings and limestone bathrooms.

Headlands Inn B&B $$
(🖱707-937-4431; www.headlandsinn.com; cnr Albion & Howard Sts; r $139-249; 📶) Homey saltbox with featherbeds, English gardens and fireplaces. Quiet rooms have sea views and staff will bring you the gourmet breakfast in bed.

Sea Gull Inn B&B $$
(🖱888-937-5204, 707-937-5204; www.seagullbb.com; 44960 Albion St; r $130-198, barn $200; 📶) With pristine white bedspreads, organic breakfasts and a flowering garden, this cute, converted motel is extremely comfortable, fairly priced, and right in the thick of the action.

Lighthouse Inn at Point Cabrillo HISTORIC B&B $$
(🖱866-937-6124, 707-937-6124; www.pointcabril-lo.org; Point Cabrillo Dr; lightkeeper's house from $461, cottages from $132; 📶) On 300 acres, in the shadow of Point Cabrillo Lighthouse, the stately lightkeeper's house and the staff's two turn-of-the-century cottages have been turned into vacation rentals. All options have verandahs and lush period decor but are not very private.

★ Alegria B&B $$$
(🖱800-780-7905, 707-937-5150; www.ocean-frontmagic.com; 44781 Main St; r $239-299; 📶) A perfect romantic hideaway, beds have views over the coast, decks have ocean views and all rooms have wood-burning fireplaces. Outside a gorgeous path leads to a big, amber-grey beach. Ever-so-friendly innkeepers whip up amazing breakfasts served in the sea-view dining area. Less expensive rooms are available across the street at bright and simple Raku House (www.raku-house.com; r from $159).

Glendeven B&B $$$
(🖱707-937-0083; www.glendeven.com; 8205 N Hwy 1; r $165-320; 📶) 🖋 This elegant estate 2 miles south of town has organic gardens, grazing llamas (with daily feedings at dusk), forest and oceanside trails, and a wine bar serving only Mendocino wines – and that's just the start. Romantic rooms have neutral-toned, soothing decor, fireplaces and top-notch linens. Farm-to-table dinners are available at the bistro.

Brewery Gulch Inn B&B $$$
(🖱800-578-4454, 707-937-4752; www.brewer-ygulchinn.com; 9401 N Hwy 1; d incl breakfast $245-495; 📶) 🖋 Just south of Mendocino, this bright, woodsy place has 10 modern rooms (all with flat-screen televisions, gas fireplaces and spa bathtubs), and guests enjoy touches like feather beds and leather reading chairs. The hosts pour heavily at the complimentary wine hour and leave out sweets for midnight snacking. Made-to-order breakfast is served in a small dining room overlooking the distant water.

Stanford Inn by the Sea INN $$$
(🖱800-331-8884, 707-937-5615; www.stanfordinn.com; cnr Hwy 1 & Comptche-Ukiah Rd; r $211-299;

NORTH COAST & REDWOODS MENDOCINO

@🛜🖥️🐾) 🐾 This masterpiece of a lodge standing on 10 lush acres has wood-burning fireplaces, knotty pine walls, original art, stereos and top-quality mattresses in every room. Figure in a stroll in the organic gardens, where they harvest food for the excellent on-site restaurant Ravens (p232), the solarium-enclosed pool and the hot tub, and it's a sublime getaway.

Mendocino Hotel HISTORIC HOTEL $$$
(📞800-548-0513, 707-937-0511; www.mendocinohotel.com; 45080 Main St; r with/without bath from $261/186, ste $475; 🅿🛜) Built in 1878 as the town's first hotel, this is like a piece of the Old West. The modern garden suites sit behind the main building and don't have a shade of old-school class, but are modern and serviceable. As gorgeous as it is, the prices are inflated, especially for the rooms with shared bathrooms.

🍴 Eating

With quality to rival Napa Valley, the influx of Bay Area weekenders have fostered an excellent dining scene that enthusiastically espouses organic, sustainable principles. Make reservations. Gathering picnic supplies is easy at **Mendosa's** (📞8am-9pm; www.harvestmarket.com; 10501 Lansing St) 🐾 organic grocery store (with deli) and the **farmers market** (cnr Howard & Main St; ⊙noon-2pm Fri May-Oct).

GoodLife Cafe & Bakery CAFE $
(http://goodlifecafemendo.com; 10485 Lansing St; light meals $6-10; ⊙8am-4pm) 🐾 Here's where locals and tourists mingle in an unpretentious, noisy and cozy cafe setting. Get bakery goods and fair-trade coffee for breakfast and comfort food like mac and cheese or curry bowls at lunch. Lots of gluten-free options are available.

Mendocino Market DELI $
(45051 Ukiah St; sandwiches $6-9; ⊙11am-5pm Mon-Fri, to 4pm Sat & Sun; 🛜) Pick up huge deli sandwiches and picnics here.

Mendocino Cafe CALIFORNIAN, FUSION $$
(www.mendocinocafe.com; 10451 Lansing St; lunch mains $12-16, dinner mains $21-33; ⊙11:30am-8pm; 🐾) One of Mendocino's few fine dinner spots that also serves lovely alfresco lunches on its ocean-view deck surrounded by roses. Try the fish tacos or the 'Healing Bowl' of soba noodles, miso, shitake mushrooms and choice of meat or seafood. At dinner there's grilled steak and seafood.

Ledford House MEDITERRANEAN $$
(📞707-937-0282; www.ledfordhouse.com; 3000 N Hwy 1, Albion; mains $14-30; ⊙5-8pm Wed-Sun; 🐾) Watch the water pound the rocks and the sun set out of the Mendocino hubbub (8 miles south) at this friendly Cal-Med bistro. Try the cassoulet or the gnocchi. It's a local hangout and gets hoppin' with live jazz most nights.

Flow CALIFORNIAN $$
(45040 Main St; mains $10-25; ⊙8am-10pm; 🛜🐾) Run by the Mendocino Cafe, this new, very busy place has the best views of the ocean in town from its 2nd-story perch. Brunch is a specialty as are Mexican-inspired small plates, artisanal pizzas and a sublime local dungeness crab chowder. Gluten-free and vegan options are available.

Patterson's Pub PUB FOOD $$
(www.pattersonspub.com; 10485 Lansing St; mains $13-16; ⊙food till 11pm) If you pull into town late and hungry, you'll thank your lucky stars for this place; it serves quality pub grub – fish and chips, burgers and dinner salads – with cold beer. The only traditional Irish pub ambience spoiler is the plethora of flat-screen TVs. A busy brunch is served on Saturday and Sunday mornings from 10am to 2pm.

★ Café Beaujolais CALIFORNIAN $$$
(📞707-937-5614; www.cafebeaujolais.com; 961 Ukiah St; dinner mains $23-35; ⊙11:30am-2:30pm Wed-Sun, dinner from 5:30pm daily) 🐾 Mendocino's iconic, beloved country-Cal-French restaurant occupies an 1896 house restyled into a monochromatic urban-chic dining room, perfect for holding hands by candlelight. The refined, inspired cooking draws diners from San Francisco, who make this the centerpiece of their trip. The locally sourced menu changes with the seasons, but the Petaluma duck breast served with crispy skin is a gourmand's delight.

Ravens CALIFORNIAN $$$
(📞707-937-5615; www.ravensrestaurant.com; Stanford Inn, Comptche-Ukiah Rd; breakfast $11-15, mains $24-30; ⊙8-10:30am Mon-Sat, to noon Sun, dinner 5:30-10pm; 🐾) 🐾 Ravens brings haute-contemporary concepts to a completely vegetarian and vegan menu. Produce comes from the idyllic organic gardens of the Stanford Inn (p231), and the bold menu takes on everything from sea-palm strudel and portabella sliders to decadent (guilt-free) desserts.

MacCallum House Restaurant
CALIFORNIAN $$$

(☑707-937-0289; www.maccallumhouse.com; 45020 Albion St; cafe dishes $12-18, mains $25-42; ⊙8:15-10am Mon-Fri, to 11am Sat & Sun, 5:30-9pm daily; 🖉) 🍴 Sit on the verandah or fireside for a romantic dinner of all-organic game, fish or risotto primavera. Chef Alan Kantor makes *everything* from scratch and his commitment to sustainability and organic ingredients is nearly as visionary as his menu. The cafe menu, served at the **Grey Whale Bar**, is one of Mendocino's few four-star bargains.

955 Ukiah Street
CALIFORNIAN $$$

(☑707-937-1955; www.955restaurant.com; 955 Ukiah St; mains $18-37; ⊙from 6pm Thu-Sun) One of those semi-secret institutions, the menu here changes with what's available locally. When we passed that meant wonderous things like yogurt and scallion marinated wild jumbo prawns. The dimly lit, bohemian setting overlooks rambling gardens. Check the website for the excellent-value, three-course meal with wine for $25 and other events.

🍷 Drinking & Nightlife

Have cocktails at the Mendocino Hotel or the Grey Whale Bar at the MacCallum House Restaurant. For boisterousness and beer head straight to Patterson's Pub.

Dick's Place
DIVE BAR

(45080 Main St) A bit out of place among the fancy-pants shops downtown, but an excellent spot to check out the *other* Mendocino and do shots with rowdy locals.

🛍 Shopping

Mendocino's walkable streets are great for shopping, and the ban on chain stores ensures unique, often upscale gifts. There are many small galleries in town where one-of-a-kind artwork is for sale.

Compass Rose Leather
LEATHER GOODS

(45150 Main St) From hand-tooled belts and leather-bound journals to purses and peg-secured storage boxes, the craftsmanship here is unquestionable.

Out Of This World
OUTDOOR EQUIPMENT

(45100 Main St) Birders, astronomy buffs and science geeks head directly to this telescope, binocular and science-toy shop.

Village Toy Store
TOYS

(10450 Lansing St) Get a kite or browse the old-world selection of wooden toys and games that you won't find in the chains – hardly anything requires batteries.

Gallery Bookshop
BOOKS

(www.gallerybookshop.com; 319 Kasten St) Stocks a great selection of books on local topics, titles from California's small presses and specialized outdoor guides.

Twist
CLOTHING

(45140 Main St) 🍴 Twist stocks ecofriendly, natural-fiber clothing and lots of locally made clothing and toys.

Moore Used Books
BOOKS

(990 Main St) An excellent bad-weather hideout, the stacks here have over 10,000 used titles. The shop is in an old house at the far east end of Main St.

❶ Information

Ford House Museum & Visitor Center (☑707-537-5397; http://mendoparks.org; 735 Main St; ⊙11am-4pm) Maps, books, information and exhibits, including a scale model of 1890 Mendocino.

Jug Handle State Reserve

Between Mendocino and Fort Bragg, Jug Handle preserves an **ecological staircase** that you can view on a 5-mile (round-trip) self-guided **nature trail**. Five wave-cut terraces ascend in steps from the seashore, each 100ft and 100,000 years removed from the previous one, and each with its own distinct geology and vegetation. One of the terraces has a **pygmy forest**, similar to the better-known example at Van Damme State Park. Pick up a printed guide detailing the area's geology, flora and fauna from the parking lot. The reserve is also a good spot to stroll the headlands, whale-watch or lounge on the beach. It's easy to miss the entrance; watch for the turnoff, just north of Caspar.

Jug Handle Creek Farm & Nature Center (☑707-964-4630; www.jughandlecreekfarm.com; tent sites $14, r & cabins adult $45, student $38; 🖐) is a nonprofit 39-acre farm with rustic cabins and hostel rooms in a 19th-century farmhouse. Call ahead about work-stay discounts. Drive 5 miles north of Mendocino to Caspar; the farm is on the east side of

NORTH COAST & REDWOODS JUG HANDLE STATE RESERVE

Hwy 1. Take the second driveway after Fern Creek Rd.

Fort Bragg

In the past, Fort Bragg was Mendocino's ugly stepsister, home to a lumber mill, a scrappy downtown and blue-collar locals who gave a cold welcome to outsiders. Since the mill closure in 2002, the town has started to reinvent itself, slowly warming to a tourism-based economy. What to do with the seaside mill site is the talk of the town, running the gamut from ideas like a marine research center or university to commercial ones like a condo development. The town itself has little say since, including projected acquisitions, it will hold under 100 acres of the 415-acre site; the rest is owned by Georgia Pacific, which is owned by Koch Industries, which is majority owned by the Koch brothers.

In the meantime, Fort Bragg's downtown continues to develop as a wonderfully unpretentious alternative to Mendocino, even if the southern end of town is hideous. Unlike the *entire* franchise-free 180-mile stretch of Coastal Hwy 1 between here and the Golden Gate, in Fort Bragg you can get a Big Mac, grande latte or any of a number of chain store products whose buildings blight the landscape. Don't fret. In downtown you'll find better hamburgers and coffee, old-school architecture and residents eager to show off their little town.

Twisting Hwy 20 provides the main access to Fort Bragg from the east, and most facilities are near Main St, a 2-mile stretch of Hwy 1. Franklin St runs parallel, one block east.

◎ Sights & Activities

Fort Bragg has the same banner North Coast activities as Mendocino – beach combing, surfing, hiking – but basing yourself here is much cheaper and arguably less quaint and pretentious. The wharf lies at Noyo Harbor – the mouth of the Noyo River – south of downtown where you can find **whale-watching cruises** and **deep-sea fishing trips**.

Mendocino Coast Botanical Gardens
GARDENS

(☑707-964-4352; www.gardenbythesea.org; 18220 N Hwy 1; adult/child/senior \$14/5/10; ☉9am-5pm Mar-Oct, to 4pm Nov-Feb) 🍃 This gem of Northern California displays native flora, rhododendrons and heritage roses. The succulent display alone is amazing and the organic garden is harvested by volunteers to feed area residents in need. The serpentine paths wander along 47 seafront acres south of town. Primary trails are wheelchair-accessible.

Glass Beach
BEACH

Named for (what's left of) the sea-polished glass in the sand, remnants of its days as a city dump, this beach is now part of MacKerricher State Park (p237) where visitors comb the sand for multicolored glass. Take the headlands trail from Elm St, off Main St, but leave the glass; as a part of the park system, visitors are not supposed to pocket souvenirs.

Northcoast Artists Gallery
GALLERY

(www.northcoastartists.org; 362 N Main St; ☉10am-6pm) An excellent local arts cooperative that has the useful *Fort Bragg Gallery & Exhibition Guide*, which directs you to other galleries around town. Openings are the first Fridays of the month. Antique and book stores line Franklin St, one block east.

Triangle Tattoo & Museum
MUSEUM

(www.triangletattoo.com; 356B N Main St; ☉noon-7pm) FREE Shows multicultural, international tattoo art.

Guest House Museum
MUSEUM

(☑707-964-4251; www.fortbragghistory.org; 343 N Main St; admission \$2; ☉1-3pm Mon, 11am-2pm Tue-Fri, 10am-4pm Sat & Sun May-Oct, 11am-2pm Thu-Sun) A majestic Victorian structure built in 1892 displays historical photos and relics of Fort Bragg's history. As hours vary, call ahead.

★ Skunk Train
HISTORIC TRAIN

(☑866-866-1690, 707-964-6371; www.skunktrain.com; adult/child \$54/34; 🐾) Fort Bragg's pride and joy, the vintage train got its nickname in 1925 for its stinky gas-powered steam engines, but today the historic steam and diesel locomotives are odorless. Passing through redwood-forested mountains, along rivers, over bridges and through deep mountain tunnels, the trains run from both Fort Bragg and Willits (p245) to the midway point of Northspur, where they turn around.

If you want to go to Willits, plan to spend the night. The rain depot is downtown at the foot of Laurel St, one block west of Main St.

All-Aboard Adventures　FISHING, WHALE-WATCHING
(☎707-964-1881; www.allaboardadventures.com; 32400 N Harbor Dr) Captain Tim leads crabbing and salmon-fishing trips (five hours, $80) and whale-watching during the whale migration (two hours, $35).

Pudding Creek Trestle　BOARDWALK
(🚶) The walk along the Pudding Creek Trestle, north of downtown, is fun for the whole family.

🎉 Festivals & Events

Fort Bragg Whale Festival　WILDLIFE
(www.mendowhale.com) Held on the third weekend in March, with microbrew tastings, crafts fairs and whale-watching trips.

Paul Bunyan Days　CARNIVAL
(www.paulbunyandays.com) Held on Labor Day weekend in September, celebrate California's logging history with a logging show, square dancing, parade and fair.

🛏 Sleeping

Fort Bragg's lodging is cheaper than Mendocino's, but most of the motels along noisy Hwy 1 don't have air-conditioning, so you'll hear traffic through your windows. Most B&Bs do not have TVs and they all include breakfast. The usual chains abound. The best-value bland motel is **Colombi Motel** (☎707-964-5773; www.colombimotel.com; 647 Oak St; 1-/2-bedroom units with kitchenette from $60/70; 🛜) which is in town, not on the highway.

Country Inn　B&B $
(☎707-964-3737; www.beourguests.com; 632 N Main St; r $80-220; 🛜♨) This cute-as-a-button, gingerbread-trimmed B&B is right in the middle of town and is an excellent way to dodge the chain motels for a good-value stay. The lovely family hosts are welcoming and easygoing, and can offer good local tips. Breakfast can be delivered to your room and at night you can soak in a hot tub out back.

California Department of Forestry　CAMPGROUND $
(☎707-964-5674; 802 N Main St; ⊙8am-4:30pm Mon, to noon Tue-Thu) Come here for maps, permits and camping information for the **Jackson State Forest**, east of Fort Bragg, where camping is free – which attracts all sorts so this isn't recommended for families or solo women.

NORTH COAST BEER TOUR

The craft breweries of the North Coast don't mess around – bold hop profiles, Belgian-style ales and smooth lagers are regional specialties, and they're produced with flair. Some breweries are better than others, but the following tour makes for an excellent long weekend of beer tasting in the region.

➡ Ukiah Brewing Co (p244), Ukiah

➡ Anderson Valley Brewing Company (p241), Boonville

➡ North Coast Brewing Company (p236), Fort Bragg

➡ Six Rivers Brewery (p262), McKinleyville

➡ Eel River Brewing (p254), Fortuna

Shoreline Cottages　MOTEL, COTTAGE $$
(☎707-964-2977; www.shoreline-cottage.com; 18725 Shoreline Hwy, Fort Bragg; d $95-165; 🛜🐾) Low-key, four-person rooms and cottages with kitchens surround a central, tree-filled lawn. The family rooms are a good bargain, and suites feature modern artwork and clean sight lines. All rooms have docks for your iPod, snacks and access to a library of DVDs and there's a communal hot tub.

Grey Whale Inn　B&B $$
(☎800-382-7244, 707-964-0640; www.greywhaleinn.com; 615 N Main St; r $110-195; 🛜) Situated in a historic building on the north side of town (walking distance from downtown and Glass Beach), this comfortable, family-run inn has simple, straightforward rooms that are good value – especially for families.

Weller House Inn　B&B $$$
(☎877-893-5537, 707-964-4415; www.wellerhouse.com; 524 Stewart St; r $200-310; 🛜) Rooms in this beautifully restored 1886 mansion have down comforters, good mattresses and fine linens. The water tower is the tallest structure in town – and it has a hot tub at the top! Breakfast is in the massive redwood ballroom.

🍴 Eating

Similar to the lodging scene, the food in Fort Bragg is less spendy than Mendocino, but there are a number of truly excellent options. Self-caterers should try the **farmers market** (cnr Laurel & Franklin Sts; ⊙3:30-6pm

Wed May–Oct) downtown or the **Harvest Market** (☑707-964-7000; cnr Hwys 1 & 20; ⊙5am–11pm) for the best groceries.

Cowlick's Handmade Ice Cream
ICE CREAM $

(250B N Main St; scoops from $1.85; ⊙11am–9pm) Just great ice cream in fun flavors from classics like mocha almond fudge to the very unusual like candy cap mushroom (tastes like maple syrup but better), ginger or blackberry chocolate chunk. The sorbets (try the grapefruit Campari) are also delish.

Los Gallitos
MEXICAN $

(130 S Main St; burritos $5.25-6.25; ⊙11am–8pm Mon-Sat, from 10am Sun) A packed hole-in-the-wall that serves the best Mexican on the coast. Chips are homemade, the guacamole is chunky and the dishes, from the fresh fish tacos to homemade pork tamales and generous *sopas*, are consistently flavorful and well beyond the standard glob of refried beans. It's located across the parking lot from the CVS.

Living Light Café
VEGAN $

(☑707-964-2420; 301 N Main St; mains $5-11; ⊙8am-5:30pm Mon-Sat, to 4pm Sun; ☑) ☑ As an extension of the renowned Living Light Culinary Institute, one of the nation's leading raw food schools, this bright cafe serves a tasty to-go menu that can rival cooked food at even some of the better restaurants. Try the Sicilian-style pizza on a sprouted-seed crust, raw desserts (the brownies are amazing), salads and fresh juices.

Headlands Coffeehouse
CAFE $

(www.headlandscoffeehouse.com; 120 E Laurel St; dishes $4-8; ⊙7am-10pm Mon-Sat, to 7pm Sun; ☎☑) The town's best cafe is in the middle of the historic downtown, with high ceilings and lots of atmosphere. The menu gets raves for the Belgian waffles, homemade soups, veggie-friendly salads, panini and lasagna.

Eggheads
BREAKFAST $

(www.eggheadsrestaurant.com; 326 N Main St; mains $8-15; ⊙7am-2pm) Enjoy the *Wizard of Oz* theme as you tuck into one of 50 varieties of omelet, crepe or burrito, some with local Dungeness crab.

★ Piaci Pub & Pizzeria
ITALIAN $$

(www.piacipizza.com; 120 W Redwood Ave; mains $8-18; ⊙11am-9:30pm Mon-Thu, to 10pm Fri & Sat, 4-9:30pm Sun) Fort Bragg's must-visit pizzeria is known for its sophisticated wood-fired, brick-oven pies as much as for its long list of microbrews. Try the 'Gustoso' – with chèvre, pesto and seasonal pears – all carefully orchestrated on a thin crust. It's tiny, loud and fun, with much more of a bar atmosphere than a restaurant. Expect to wait at peak times.

Mendo Bistro
AMERICAN $$

(☑707-964-4974; www.mendobistro.com; 301 N Main St; mains $14-28; ⊙5-9pm; ☑) This dining option gets packed with a young crowd on the weekend, offering a choose-your-own-adventure menu, where you select a meat, a preparation and an accompanying sauce from a litany of options. The loud, bustling 2nd-story room is big enough for kids to run around and nobody will notice.

North Coast Brewing Company
BREWERY $$

(www.northcoastbrewing.com; 455 N Main St; mains $8-25; ⊙7am-9:30pm Sun-Thu, to 10pm Fri & Sat) Though thick, rare slabs of steak and a list of specials demonstrate that they take the food as seriously as the bevvies, it's burgers and garlic fries that soak up the fantastic selection of handcrafted brews. A great stop for serious beer lovers.

☆ Entertainment

Gloriana Opera Company
THEATER

(www.gloriana.org; 721 N Franklin St) Stages musical theater and operettas.

🛍 Shopping

There's plenty of window-shopping in Fort Bragg's compact downtown, including a string of antique shops along Franklin St.

Outdoor Store
OUTDOOR EQUIPMENT

(www.mendooutdoors.com; 247 N Main St) If you're planning on camping on the coast or exploring the Lost Coast, this is the best outfitter in the region, stocking detailed maps of the region's wilderness areas, fuel for stoves and high-quality gear.

Mendocino Vintage
ANTIQUES

(www.mendocinovintage.com; 344 N Franklin St) Of the antique shops on Franklin, this is the hippest by a long shot, with a case full of vintage estate jewelry, antique glassware and old local oddities.

ⓘ Information

Fort Bragg-Mendocino Coast Chamber of Commerce (www.fortbragg.com; 332 N Main St; per 15min $1; ⊙9am-5pm Mon-Fri, to 3pm Sat) Internet access.

Mendocino Coast District Hospital (☏707-961-1234; 700 River Dr; ⊙24hr) Emergency room.

ⓘ Getting There & Around

Fort Bragg Cyclery (☏707-964-3509; www.fortbraggcyclery.com; 221a N Main St; bike rental per day from $32) Rents bicycles.

Mendocino Transit Authority (MTA; ☏800-696-4682, 707-462-1422; www.mendocinotransit.org) Runs local route 5 'BraggAbout' buses between Noyo Harbor and Elm St, north of downtown ($2). Service runs throughout the day.

MacKerricher State Park

Three miles north of Fort Bragg, the **MacKerricher State Park** (☏707-964-9112; www.parks.ca.gov) preserves 9 miles of pristine rocky headlands, sandy beaches, dunes and tidepools.

The **visitor center** (⊙10am-4pm Mon-Fri, 9am-6pm Sat & Sun Jun-Aug, 9am-3pm Sep-May) sits next to the whale skeleton at the park entrance. Hike the **Coastal Trail** along dark-sand beaches and see rare and endangered plant species (tread lightly). **Lake Cleone** is a 30-acre freshwater lake stocked with trout and visited by over 90 species of birds. At nearby **Laguna Point** an interpretive disabled-accessible boardwalk overlooks harbor seals and, from December to April, migrating whales. **Ricochet Ridge Ranch** (☏707-964-7669; www.horse-vacation.com; 24201 N Hwy 1) offers horseback-riding trips through redwoods or along the beach ($50 for 90 minutes).

Just north of the park is **Pacific Star Winery** (33000 Hwy 1; tastings $5; ⊙11am-5pm), in a dramatic, rub-your-eyes-in-disbelief-beautiful location on a bluff over the sea. The wines don't get pros excited but they are very drinkable, the owners are supremely friendly and you're encouraged to picnic at one of the many coast-side tables, stroll some of the short coastal trails along the cliffs and generally enjoy yourself (which isn't hard).

Popular **campgrounds** (☏800-444-2725; www.reserveamerica.com; tent & RV sites $35), nestled in pine forest, have hot showers and water; the first-choice reservable tent sites are numbers 21 to 59. Ten superb, secluded walk-in tent sites (numbers 1 to 10) are first-come, first-served.

Westport

If sleepy Westport feels like the peaceful edge of nowhere, that's because it is. The last hamlet before the Lost Coast, on a twisting 15-mile drive north of Fort Bragg, it is the last town before Hwy 1 veers inland on the 22-mile ascent to meet Hwy 101 in Leggett.

Head 1.5 miles north of town for the ruggedly beautiful **Westport-Union Landing State Beach** (☏707-937-5804; tent sites $25), which extends for 3 miles on coastal bluffs. A rough **hiking trail** leaves the primitive campground and passes by tidepools and streams, accessible at low tide. Bring your own water.

🛏 Sleeping & Eating

Westport Inn INN $
(☏707-964-5135; www.westportinnca.com; 37040 N Hwy 1; r incl breakfast from $70; 🐾) Simple accommodations in town include the blue-and-red, plastic-flower-festooned Westport Inn.

★**Westport Hotel & Old Abalone Pub** INN $$
(☏877-964-3688; www.westporthotel.us; Hwy 1; r $150-225; 🐾) Westport Hotel & Old Abalone Pub is quiet enough to have a motto which brags 'You've finally found nowhere.' The rooms are bright and beautiful – feather duvets, hardwood furniture, simple patterns – and enjoy excellent views. The classy historic pub downstairs is the only option for dinner, so be thankful it's a delicious sampling of whimsical California fusions (like turduken sausage and buttermilk potatoes, and rock shrimp mac and cheese) and hearty, expertly presented pub food.

Howard Creek Ranch RANCH $$
(☏707-964-6725; www.howardcreekranch.com; 40501 N Hwy 1; r $90-198, cabins $105-198; 🐾🐾) Howard Creek Ranch, sitting on 60 stunning acres of forest and farmland abutting the wilderness, has accommodations in an 1880s farmhouse or a few cabins including a carriage barn, whose way-cool redwood rooms have been expertly handcrafted by the owner. Rates include full breakfast. Bring hiking boots, not high heels.

ALONG HIGHWAY 101

To get into the most remote and wild parts of the North Coast on the quick, eschew winding Hwy 1 for inland Hwy 101, which runs north from San Francisco as a freeway, then as a two- or four-lane highway north of Sonoma County, occasionally pausing under the traffic lights of small towns.

Know that escaping the Bay Area at rush hour (weekdays between 4pm and 7pm) ain't easy. You might sit bumper-to-bumper through Santa Rosa or Willits, where trucks bound for the coast turn onto Hwy 20.

Although Hwy 101 may not look as enticing as the coastal route, it's faster and less winding, leaving you time along the way to detour into Sonoma and Mendocino counties' wine regions (Mendocino claims to be the greenest wine region in the country), explore pastoral Anderson Valley, splash about Clear Lake or soak at hot-springs resorts outside Ukiah – time well spent indeed!

Hopland

Cute Hopland is the gateway to Mendocino County's wine country and flaunts its eco-minded, green-living ways at every turn. Hops were first grown here in 1866, but Prohibition brought the industry temporarily to a halt. Today, booze drives the local economy again with wine tasting as the primary draw.

⊙ Sights

For an excellent weekend trip, use Hopland as a base for exploring the regional wineries. More information about the constantly growing roster of wineries is available at www.destinationhopland.com. Find a map to the wine region at www.visitmendocino.com.

Real Goods Solar Living Center
ENVIRONMENT CENTER
(www.solarliving.org; 13771 S Hwy 101; ⊙9am-6pm; 🅟) 🌿 This progressive, futuristic 12-acre campus is largely responsible for the area's bold green initiates. The Real Goods Store, which sold the first solar panel in the US, is an impressive straw-bale house showroom that also has free Frey Wine tastings. The suggested donation for tours of the center (11am and 3pm Friday to Sunday, April through October) is $3 to $5.

Sip! Mendocino
WINERY
(www.sipmendocino.com; 13420 S Hwy 101; tastings $5; ⊙11am-6pm) In central Hopland, this is a friendly place to get your bearings, pick up a map to the region and taste several wines without navigating all the back roads.

Amiable proprietors guide you through a tour of 18 wines with delectable appetizer pairings and a blossom-filled courtyard.

Saracina
WINERY
(www.saracina.com; 11684 S Hwy 101; ⊙10am-5pm) 🌿 The highlight of a tour here is the descent into the cool caves. Sensuous whites are all biodynamcially and sustainably farmed.

Fetzer Vineyards Organic Gardens
WINERY
(www.fetzer.com; 13601 Eastside Rd; ⊙9am-5pm) 🌿 Fetzer's sustainable practices have raised the bar, and their gardens are lovely. The wines are excellent value.

Brutocao Schoolhouse Plaza
TASTING ROOM
(www.brutocaoschoolhouseplaza.com; 13500 S Hwy 101; ⊙10am-5pm) In central Hopland, this place has bocce courts and bold reds – a perfect combo.

Graziano Family of Wines
WINERY
(www.grazianofamilyofwines.com; 13251 S Hwy 101; ⊙10am-5pm) Specializes in 'Cal-Ital' wines – nebbiolo, dolcetto, barbera and Sangiovese – at some great prices.

🍴 Sleeping & Eating

Piazza de Campovida
INN $$$
(📞707-744-1977; www.piazzadecampovida.com; 13441 S Hwy 101; ste $250-285; 🛜) Modern Californian meets Italian at this very comfortable spot where all the spacious suites have Jacuzzi tubs, fireplaces and private balconies. The homey pizzeria in front has big tables for communal dining and fantastic artisanal pizzas – there's no corkage fee either so bring your wine find of the day.

Hopland Tap House
PUB FOOD $
(13351 S Hwy 101; mains $6-9; ⊙11:30am-9pm Wed-Mon) Friendly locals, good sandwiches and selection of local beers all served in a bright brick building (plus shuffleboard). What more could you want?

Bluebird Cafe
AMERICAN $
(📞707-744-1633; 13340 S Hwy 101; breakfast & lunch $5-15, dinner $12-22; ⊙7am-2pm Mon-Thu, to 7pm Fri-Sun; 📶) For conservative tastes, this classic American diner serves hearty breakfasts, giant burgers and homemade pie (the summer selection of peach-blueberry pie is dreamy). For a more exciting culinary adventure, try the wild game burgers, including boar with apple chutney and elk with a bite of horseradish.

Clear Lake

With over 100 miles of shoreline, Clear Lake is the largest naturally occurring freshwater lake in California (Tahoe is bigger, but crosses the Nevada state line). In summer the warm water thrives with algae, giving it a murky green appearance and creating a fabulous habitat for fish – especially bass – and tens of thousands of birds. Mt Konocti, a 4200ft-tall dormant volcano, lords over the scene. Alas, the human settlements don't always live up to the grandeur and thousands of acres near the lake remain scarred from wildfires in 2008.

⊙ Sights & Activities

Locals refer to the northwest portion as 'upper lake' and the southeast portion as 'lower lake.' Likeable and well-serviced Lakeport (population 4695) sits on the northwest shore, a 45-minute drive east of Hopland along Hwy 175 (off Hwy 101); tiny, Old West style Kelseyville (population 3353) is 7 miles south. Clearlake, off the southeastern shore, is the biggest (and ugliest) town.

Hwy 20 links the relatively bland northshore hamlets of Nice (the northernmost town) and Lucerne, 4 miles southeast. Middletown, a cute village, lies 20 miles south of Clearlake at the junction of Hwys 175 and 29, 40 minutes north of Calistoga.

Clear Lake State Park STATE PARK
(☑707-279-4293; 5300 Soda Bay Rd, Kelseyville; per car $8) Six miles from Lakeport, on the lake's west shore, the park is idyllic and gorgeous, with hiking trails, fishing, boating and camping. The bird-watching is extraor-

dinary. The visitor center has geological and historical exhibits.

Redbud Audubon Society BIRD WATCHING
(www.redbudaudubon.org) In lower lake, this conservation group leads birding walks.

🛏 Sleeping & Eating

Make reservations on weekends and during summer, when people flock to the cool water.

🛏 Lakeport & Kelseyville

There are a number of motels along the main drag in Keleysville and Lakeport, but if you want fresh air, Clear Lake State Park has four campgrounds (☑800-444-7275; www.reserveamerica.com; tent & RV sites $35) with showers. The weekly farmers market (Hwy 29 & Thomas Rd; ⊙8:30am-noon Sat May-Oct) is in Kelseyville.

Mallard House MOTEL $
(☑707-262-1601; www.mallardhouse.com; 970 N Main St, Lakeport; r with kitchen $69-149, without $55-99; ❀🐾🛜) Waterfront motels with boat slips include this good-value, cottage-style place. There's a tiny beach in front half covered with reeds.

★**Lakeport English Inn** B&B $$
(☑707-263-4317; www.lakeportenglishinn.com; 675 N Main St, Lakeport; r $185-210, cottages $210; ❀🛜) The finest B&B at Clear Lake is an 1875 Carpenter Gothic with 10 impeccably furnished rooms, styled with a nod to the English countryside. Weekends take high tea (nonguests welcome by reservation) – with real Devonshire cream.

NORTH COAST & REDWOODS CLEAR LAKE

TOP CLEAR LAKE WINERIES

From north to south, the following four wineries are the best; some offer tours by appointment. Tastings generally cost $5 to $10.

Ceago Vinegarden (www.ceago.com; 5115 E Hwy 20, Nice; ⊙noon-5pm) Ceago (cee-*ay*-go) occupies a spectacular spot on the north shore, and pours biodynamic, fruit-forward wines.

Brassfield Estate (www.brassfieldestate.com; 10915 High Valley Rd, Clearlake Oaks; ⊙11am-5pm Mar-Nov, from noon Dec-Apr) A stunning, unique property in the remote High Valley appellation, try the Eruption and Serenity blends.

Wildhurst Vineyards (www.wildhurst.com; 3855 Main St, Kelseyville; ⊙10am-5pm) The best wine on the lake, but the place lacks atmosphere. Try the Sauvignon Blanc.

Langtry Estate Vineyards (21000 Butts Canyon Rd, Middletown; ⊙11am-5pm) The most beautiful vineyard. Try the port.

Skylark Shores Resort INN $$

(🖰 800-675-6151; www.lakeportskylarkshores. com; 1120 N Main St, Lakeport; r $84-145; ❄️ 🖥️ 🏊) There's a 1960s holiday-camp feel here with a sprawl of well-maintained older units, many of which overlook the lakeside full of wading ducks and splashing kids and a big lawn dotted with smoking barbecues. Some units also have kitchens and there's a public launch boat dock.

Park Place AMERICAN $

(50 3rd St, Lakeport; mains $7-11; 🕐 11am-9pm Tue-Sun, to 3pm Mon) 🍴 Simple but right on the waterfront, come to this bright and completely unpretentious eatery for basics like pasta, burgers and pizza made from sustainable, local produce at great prices. A local favorite.

Studebaker's Coffee House DELI $

(3990 Main St, Kelseyville; sandwiches from $6; 🕐 6am-4pm Mon-Fri, 7am-4pm Sat, 7am-2pm Sun) A friendly, old-style diner/fountain place with plenty of character from black-and-white checker linoleum floors to old photos on the wall. Great sandwiches including vegetarian options and the coffee's good too.

★ Saw Shop Gallery Bistro CALIFORNIAN $$$

(🖰 707-278-0129; www.sawshopbistro.com; 3825 Main St, Kelseyville; small plates $10-16, mains $15-26; 🕐 from 3pm Tue-Sat) The best restaurant in Lake County serves a Californian-cuisine menu of wild salmon and rack of lamb, as well as a small plates menu of sushi, lobster tacos, Kobe-beef burgers and flatbread pizzas. Laid-back atmosphere, too.

🏠 North Shore

Tallman Hotel HISTORIC HOTEL $$

(🖰 888-880-5253, 707-274-0200; www.tallmanhotel.com; 9550 Main St, Nice; cottages $169-274; ❄️ 🖥️ 🏊 🐕) 🍴 The centerpiece may be the smartly renovated historic hotel – tile bathrooms, warm lighting, thick linens – but the rest of the property's lodging, including several modern, sustainably built cottages, are equally peaceful. The shaded garden, walled-in swimming pool, brick patios and porches exude timeless elegance. Garden rooms come with Japanese soaking tubs heated by an energy-efficient geothermal-solar system.

Featherbed Railroad Co HOTEL $$

(🖰 800-966-6322, 707-274-8378; www.featherbedrailroad.com; 2870 Lakeshore Blvd, Nice; cabooses incl breakfast $175-220; ❄️ 🏊) A treat for train buffs and kids, Featherbed has 10 comfy, real cabooses on a grassy lawn. Some of the cabooses straddle the border between kitschy and tacky (the 'Easy Rider' has a Harley Davidson headboard and a mirrored ceiling), but they're great fun if you keep a sense of humor. There's a tiny beach across the road.

Sea Breeze Resort COTTAGES $$

(🖰 707-998-3327; www.seabreezeresort.net; 9595 Harbor Dr, Glenhaven; cottages $125-180; 🕐 Apr-Oct; ❄️ 🖥️) Just south of Lucerne on a small peninsula, gardens surround seven spotless lakeside cottages. All have barbecues.

🏠 Middletown

★ Harbin Hot Springs SPA $$

(🖰 800-622-2477, 707-987-2377; www.harbin.org; Harbin Hot Springs Rd; tent & RV sites midweek/weekend $30/40, dm $40/60, s $50-75, d $100-190) Harbin is classic Northern California. Originally a 19th-century health spa and resort, it now has a retreat-center vibe and people come to unwind in silent, clothing-optional hot- and cold-spring pools. This is the birthplace of Watsu (floating massage) and there are wonderful body therapies as well as yoga, holistic-health workshops and 1160 acres of hiking.

Accommodations are in Victorian buildings (which could use sprucing up) and share a common vegetarian-only kitchen. Food is available at the market, cafe and restaurant. Day-trippers are welcome Monday through Thursday only; day rates are $20.

The springs are 3 miles off Hwy 175. From Middletown, take Barnes St, which becomes Big Canyon Rd, and head left at the fork.

🍷 Drinking & Entertainment

Library Park, in Lakeport, has free lakeside Friday-evening **summer concerts**, with blues and rockabilly tunes to appeal to middle-aged roadtrippers. Harbin Hot Springs presents a surprising line-up of world music and dances.

Kelsey Creek Brewing BREWERY

(3945 Main St, Kelseyville; 🕐 2-8pm Tue-Fri, noon-8pm Sat, noon-5pm Sun) A 'hop'-ping fun local's scene with excellent craft beer, peanut shells on the floor and a bring-your-own-food, bring-your-dog kind of laid-back vibe.

Lakeport Auto Movies CINEMA

(www.lakeportautomovies.com; 52 Soda Bay Rd, Lakeport; 1/2/3 people per car $10/18/25)

Lakeport is home to one of the few surviving drive-in movie theaters, with showings on Friday and Saturday nights.

❶ Information

Lake County Visitor Information Center (www.lakecounty.com; 6110 E Hwy 120, Lucerne; ⊙9am-5pm Mon-Sat, noon-4pm Sun) Has complete information and an excellent website, which allows potential visitors to narrow their focus by interests.

❶ Getting Around

Lake Transit (☑707-994-3334, 707-263-3334; www.laketransit.org) operates weekday routes between Middletown and Calistoga ($3, 35 minutes, three daily); on Thursday it connects through to Santa Rosa. Buses serve Ukiah ($5, two hours, four daily), from Clearlake via Lakeport ($3, 1¼ hours, seven daily). Since piecing together routes and times can be difficult, it's best to phone ahead.

Anderson Valley

Rolling hills surround rural Anderson Valley, famous for apple orchards, vineyards, pastures and quiet. Visitors come primarily to winery-hop, but there's good hiking and bicycling in the hills, and the chance to escape civilization. Traveling through the valley is the most common route to Mendocino from San Francisco.

❍ Sights & Activities

Boonville (population 1488) and **Philo** (population 349) are the valley's principal towns. From Ukiah, winding Hwy 253 heads 20 miles south to Boonville. Equally scenic Hwy 128 twists and turns 60 miles between Cloverdale on Hwy 101, south of Hopland, and Albion on coastal Hwy 1.

Philo Apple Farm FARM (www.philoapplefarm.com; 18501 Greenwood Rd, Philo; ⊙dawn-dusk) For the best fruit, skip the obvious roadside stands and head to this gorgeous farm for organic preserves, chutneys, heirloom apples and pears. It also hosts **cooking classes** with some of the Wine Country's best chefs. You can make a weekend out of it by staying in one of the orchard cottages (p242).

Anderson Valley Brewing Company BREWERY (☑707-895-2337; www.avbc.com; 17700 Hwy 253; ⊙11am-6pm) 🚲 East of the Hwy 128 crossroads, this solar-powered brewery crafts

> ### BOONTLING
>
> Boonville is famous for its unique language, 'Boontling,' which evolved about the turn of the 20th century when Boonville was very remote. Locals developed the language to *shark* (stump) outsiders and amuse themselves. You may hear *codgie kimmies* (old men) asking for a horn of *zeese* (a cup of coffee) or some *bahl gorms* (good food). If you are really lucky, you'll spot the tow truck called Boont Region De-arkin' Moshe (literally 'Anderson Valley Un-wrecking Machine'). Find a fun dictionary at www.andersonvalleymuseum.org.

award-winning beers in a Bavarian-style brewhouse. You can also toss around a disc on the **Frisbee-golf course** while enjoying the brews, but, be warned, the sun can take its toll. Tours leave at 1:30pm and 3pm daily (only Tuesday and Wednesday in winter); call ahead.

Anderson Valley Historical Society Museum MUSEUM (www.andersonvalleymuseum.org; 12340 Hwy 128; ⊙1-4pm Sat & Sun Feb-Nov) In a recently renovated little red schoolhouse west of Boonville, this museum displays historical artifacts.

❋ Festivals & Events

Pinot Noir Festival WINE (www.avwines.com) One of Anderson Valley's many wine celebrations; held in May.

Sierra Nevada World Music Festival MUSIC (www.snwmf.com) In June, the sounds of reggae and roots fill the air, co-mingling with the scent of Mendocino County's *other* cash crop.

Mendocino County Fair FAIR (www.mendocountyfair.com) A county classic in mid-September.

🛏 Sleeping

Accommodations fill on weekends.

Hendy Woods State Park CAMPGROUND $ (☑707-937-5804, reservations 800-444-7275; www.reserveamerica.com; tent & RV sites $40, cabins $60) Bordered by the Navarro River on Hwy 128, west of Philo, the park has hiking,

TOP ANDERSON VALLEY WINERIES

The valley's cool nights yield high-acid, fruit-forward, food-friendly wines. Pinot Noir, Chardonnay and dry Gewürtztraminer flourish. Most **wineries** (www.avwines.com) sit outside Philo. Many are family-owned and offer free tastings, some give tours. The following are particularly noteworthy:

Navarro (www.navarrowine.com; 5601 Hwy 128; ⊙10am-6pm) The best option with award-winning Pinot Noir and a delicious Riesling, picnicking is encouraged.

Esterlina (www.esterlinavineyards.com) For big reds, pack a picnic and head high up the rolling hills; call ahead.

Husch (www.huschvineyards.com; 4400 Hwy 128; ⊙10am-5pm) The oldest vineyard in the valley serves exquisite tastings inside a rose-covered cottage.

Bink (9000 Hwy 128; ⊙11am-5pm Wed-Mon) Small-batch artisanal wines that get rave reviews are served in the Madrones complex.

NORTH COAST & REDWOODS ANDERSON VALLEY

picnicking and a forested campground with hot showers.

The Other Place   COTTAGES $$
(☑707-895-3979; www.sheepdung.com; Boonville; cottages $150-350; �hⓖ) Outside of town, 500 acres of ranch land surrounds private, fully equipped hilltop cottages.

★**Philo Apple Farm**   COTTAGES $$$
(☑707-895-2333; www.philoapplefarm.com; 18501 Greenwood Rd, Philo; r Mon-Thu $200, Fri-Sun $275) Set within the orchard (p241), guests of Philo's bucolic apple Farm choose from four exquisite cottages, each built with reclaimed materials. With bright, airy spaces, polished plank floors, simple furnishings and views of the surrounding trees, each one is an absolute dream.

Red Door cottage is a favorite because of the bathroom – you can soak in the slipper tub, or shower on the private deck under the open sky. The cottages often get booked with participants of the farm's cooking classes, so book well in advance. For a swim, the Navarro River is within walking distance.

Boonville Hotel   BOUTIQUE HOTEL $$$
(☑707-895-2210; www.boonvillehotel.com; 14050 Hwy 128, Boonville; r $150-360; ⓖ) Decked out in a contemporary American-country style with sea-grass flooring, pastel colors and fine linens that would make Martha Stewart proud, this historic hotel's rooms are safe for urbanites who refuse to abandon style just because they've gone to the country.

The Madrones   HOTEL $$$
(www.themadrones.com; 9000 Hwy 28, Philo; r $160-325; ⓖ) Tucked off the back of the Madrones Mediterranean-inspired complex

that includes a restaurant and the wonderful Bink Wines tasting room (p242), the spacious 'guest quarters' here are as modern-country-luxe, with a tinge of Tuscany, as you'd hope they'd be.

✖ Eating

Boonville restaurants seem to open and close as they please, so expect hours to vary based on season and whimsy. There are several places along Hwy 128 which can supply a picnic with fancy local cheese and fresh bread.

Paysenne   ICE CREAM $
(14111 Hwy 128, Boonville; cone $2; ⊙10am-3pm Thu-Mon) Booneville's fantastic ice-cream shop serves the innovative flavors of Three Twins Ice Cream, whose delightful choices include Lemon Cookie and Strawberry Je Ne Sais Quoi (which has a hint of balsamic vinegar).

Boonville General Store   DELI $
(17810 Farrer Lane, Boonville; dishes $5-12; ⊙7:30am-3pm Mon-Thu, 7:30am-3pm & 5:30-8pm Fri, 8:30am-3pm Sat & Sun) Opposite the Boonville Hotel, this deli is good to stock up for picnics, offering sandwiches on homemade bread, thin-crust pizzas and organic cheeses.

★**Table 128**   CALIFORNIAN $$
(14050 Hwy 128, Boonville; lunch mains $10-14, dinner mains $19-31; ⊙6:30-8:15pm Fri-Sun) Food-savvy travelers love the constantly changing New American menu here, featuring simple dishes done well, like roasted chicken, grilled local lamb, and cheesecake. The family-style service makes dinner here a freewheeling, elegant social affair, with big

farm tables and soft lighting. It also has great wines, craft beers, fine scotch and cocktails.

Lauren's
AMERICAN $$

(www.laurensgoodfood.com; 14211 Hwy 128, Boonville; mains $13-16; ⊗5-9pm Tue-Sat; 🅿🛉) Locals pack Lauren's for eclectic homemade cookin' and a good wine list. Musicians sometimes jam on the stage by the front window.

ⓘ Information

Anderson Valley Chamber of Commerce
(☑707-895-2379; www.andersonvalleychamber. com; 9800 Hwy 128, Boonville) Has tourist information and a complete schedule of annual events.

Ukiah

As the county seat and Mendocino's largest city, Ukiah is mostly a utilitarian stop for travelers to refuel the car and get a bite. But, if you have to stop here for the night, you could do much worse: the town is a friendly place that's gentrifying. There are a plethora of cookie-cutter hotel chains, some cheaper midcentury motels and a handful of very good dining options. The coolest attractions, thermal springs and a sprawling campus for Buddhist studies, lie outside the city limits. Ukiah has a pleasant, walkable shopping district along School St near the courthouse.

◉ Sights

Germain-Robin
DISTILLERY

(☑707-462-0314; unit 35, 3001 S State St; ⊗by appointment) Makes some of the world's best brandy, which is handcrafted by a fifth-generation brandy-maker from the Cognac region of France. It's by appointment only, but if you're into cognac, you gotta come.

Grace Hudson Museum & Sun House
MUSEUM

(www.gracehudsonmuseum.org; 431 S Main St; admission $4; ⊗10am-4:30pm Wed-Sat, from noon Sun) One block east of State St, the collection's mainstays are paintings by Grace Hudson (1865–1937). Her sensitive depictions of Pomo people complement the ethnological work and Native American baskets collected by her husband, John Hudson.

🎋 Festivals & Events

Redwood Empire Fairs
FAIR

(www.redwoodempirefair.com) At the end of July through early August.

Ukiah Country PumpkinFest
CULTURAL

(www.cityofukiah.com; 🛉) In late October, with an arts-and-crafts fair, children's carnival and fiddle contest.

🛏 Sleeping

Every imaginable chain resort is here, just off the highway – the best of these is the **Hampton Inn** (☑707-462-6555; hamptoninn3. hilton.com; 1160 Airport Blvd; r $143-209; 🕸🛜🌊). For something with more personality, hot-spring resorts and campgrounds cluster around Ukiah.

Discovery Inn Motel
MOTEL $

(☑707-462-8873; www.discoveryinnukiahca.com; 1340 N State St; r $51-95; 🕸🛜🌊) Clean, but dated with a 75ft pool and several Jacuzzis.

🍴 Eating

It'd be a crime to eat the fast-food junk located off the highway; Ukiah has a burgeoning food scene that pairs nicely with the surrounding wine country.

★ Schat's Courthouse Bakery & Cafe
CAFE $

(www.schats.com; 113 W Perkins St; lunch mains $3-7, dinner mains $8-14; ⊗5:30am-6pm Mon-Fri, to 5pm Sat) Founded by Dutch bakers, Schat's makes a dazzling array of chewy, dense breads, sandwiches, wraps, big salads, delish hot mains, full breakfasts and homemade pastries.

Ukiah Farmers Market
MARKET $

(cnr School & Clay Sts; ⊗9am-noon Sat) The market offers farm-fresh produce, crafts and entertainment.

Kilkenny Kitchen
CAFE $

(www.kilkennykitchen.com; 1093 S Dora St; sandwiches $8; ⊗10am-3pm Mon-Fri; 🅿🛉) Tucked into a neighborhood south of downtown, county workers love this chipper yellow place for the fresh rotation of daily soups and sandwich specials (a recent visit on a blazing-hot day found a heavenly, cold cucumber dill soup). The salads – like the pear, walnut and blue cheese – are also fantastic, and there's a kid's menu.

★ Saucy
PIZZA $$

(☑707-462-7007; 108 W Satandley St; pizzas $11-19; ⊗11:30am-9pm Mon-Thu, to 10pm Fri, noon-10pm Sat) Yes there are arty pizzas with toppings like Calabrian love sausage (really), fennel pollen and almond basil pesto but there are also amazing soups, salads, pastas and starters – Nana's meatballs are to die for and the 'kicking' minestrone lives up to its name. The small-town ambience is slightly chic but also boistrous at the same time.

Oco Time
JAPANESE $$

(☏707-462-2422; www.ocotime.com; 111 W Church St; lunch mains $7-10, dinner mains $8-19; ⏱11:15am-2:30pm Tue-Fri, 5:30-8:30pm Mon-Sat; ☑) Shoulder your way through the locals to get Ukiah's best sushi, noodle bowls and *oco* (a delicious mess of seaweed, grilled cabbage, egg and noodles). The 'Peace Café' has a great vibe, friendly staff and interesting special rolls. Downside? The place gets mobbed, so reservations are a good idea.

Patrona
NEW AMERICAN $$

(☏707-462-9181; www.patronarestaurant.com; 130 W Standley St; lunch mains $10-16, dinner mains $15-34; ⏱11am-9pm; ☑) ✤ Foodies flock to excellent Patrona for earthy, flavor-packed, seasonal and regional organic cooking. The unfussy menu includes dishes like roasted chicken, brined-and-roasted pork chops, housemade pasta and local wines. Make reservations and ask about the prix fixe.

Himalayan Cafe
HIMALAYAN $$

(www.thehimalayancafe.com; 1639 S State St; curries $15; ☑) South of downtown, find delicately spiced Nepalese cooking – tandoori breads and curries. Some Sundays there's a Nepalese buffet at 4pm.

Drinking & Entertainment

Ask at the chamber of commerce about cultural events, including **Sunday summer concerts** at Todd Grove Park, which have a delightfully festive atmosphere, and local **square dances**.

Dive bars and scruffy cocktail lounges line State St.

Ukiah Brewing Co
BREWERY

(www.ukiahbrewingco.com; 102 S State St; ☎) ✤ A great place to drink, this local brewpub makes organic beer and draws weekend crowds.

Black Oak Coffee Roasters
CAFE

(476 N State St; lavender lattes from $4; ⏱6:30am-6pm) A big modern coffeehouse with interesting and delicious choices like a local lavender latte or a matcha chia milkshake. Light breakfasts and lunches are also on offer.

ℹ Information

Running north–south, west of Hwy 101, State St is Ukiah's main drag. School St, near Perkins St, is also good for strolling.

Bureau of Land Management (☏707-468-4000; 2550 N State St) Maps and information on backcountry camping, hiking and biking in wilderness areas.

Greater Ukiah Chamber of Commerce (☏707-462-4705; www.gomendo.com; 200 S School St; ⏱9am-5pm Mon-Fri) One block west of State St; information on Ukiah, Hopland and Anderson Valley.

Around Ukiah

Ukiah Wineries

You'll notice the acres of grapes stretching out in every direction on your way into town. Winemakers around Ukiah enjoy much of the same climatic conditions that made Napa so famous. Pick up a wineries map from the Ukiah chamber of commerce. Tasting fees are generally around $5.

Parducci Wine Cellars
WINERY

(www.parducci.com; 501 Parducci Rd, Ukiah; ⏱10am-5pm) ✤ Sustainably grown, harvested and produced, 'America's Greenest Winery' produces affordable, bold, earthy reds. The tasting room, lined in brick and soft light, is a perfect little cave-like environment to get out of the summer heat, sip wine and chat about sustainability practices.

Nelson Family Vineyards
WINERY

(www.nelsonfamilyvineyards.com; 550 Nelson Ranch Rd, Ukiah; ⏱10am-5pm; 🎿) Just north of Ukiah, this winery, vineyard, pear, olive and Christmas-tree farm with wondrous views over the valley is a great place to picnic (in a redwood grove), make friends and sip not-too-sweet Chardonnay and luscious red blends.

Vichy Hot Springs Resort

Opened in 1854, Vichy is the oldest continuously operating mineral-springs spa in California. The water's composition perfectly matches that of its famous namesake in Vichy, France. A century ago, Mark Twain, Jack London and Robert Louis Stevenson traveled here for the water's restorative properties, which ameliorate everything from arthritis to poison oak.

Today, the beautifully maintained historic **resort** (☏707-462-9515; www.vichysprings.com; 2605 Vichy Springs Rd, Ukiah; lodge s/d $145/205, creekside r $205/255, cottages from $295; ❄ 🖥 🐕) has the only warm-water, naturally carbonated mineral baths in North America. Unlike others, Vichy requires swimsuits (rentals $2). Day use costs $30 for two hours, $50 for a full day.

Facilities include a swimming pool, outdoor mineral hot tub, 10 indoor and outdoor tubs with natural 100°F (38°C) waters, and a grotto for sipping the effervescent waters. Massages and facials are available. Entry includes use of the 700-acre grounds, abutting Bureau of Land Management (BLM) lands; hiking trails lead to a 40ft waterfall, an old cinnabar mine and 1100ft peaks – great for sunset views.

The resort's suite and two cottages, built in 1854, are Mendocino County's three oldest structures. The cozy rooms have wooden floors, top-quality beds, breakfast and spa privileges, and no TVs.

From Hwy 101, exit at Vichy Springs Rd and follow the state-landmark signs east for 3 miles. Ukiah is five minutes, but a world, away.

Orr Hot Springs

A clothing-optional resort that's beloved by locals, back-to-the-land hipsters, backpackers and liberal-minded tourists, **springs** (☏707-462-6277; tent sites $50-60, d $150-180, cottages $215-250; 🐕) has private tubs, a sauna, spring-fed rock-bottomed swimming pool, steam, massage and magical gardens. Day use costs $30.

Accommodation includes use of the spa and communal kitchen; some of the rustic cottages have kitchens. Reservations are essential.

To get there from Hwy 101, take the N State St exit, go north a quarter of a mile to Orr Springs Rd, then 9 miles west. The steep, winding mountain road takes 30 minutes to drive.

Montgomery Woods State Reserve

Two miles west of Orr, this 1140-acre **reserve** (Orr Springs Rd) protects five old-growth redwood groves, and some of the best groves within a day's drive from San Francisco. A 2-mile loop trail crosses the creek, winding through the serene groves, starting near the picnic tables and toilets. It's out of the way, so visitors are likely to have it mostly to themselves. Day use only; no camping.

Lake Mendocino

Amid rolling hills, 5 miles northeast of Ukiah, this tranquil 1822-acre artificial lake fills a valley, once the ancestral home of the Pomo people. On the lake's north side, **Pomo Visitor Center** (☏707-467-4200) is modeled after a Pomo roundhouse, with exhibits on tribal culture and the dam. The center was closed indefinitely for upgrades at the time of update, but was still offering information via phone about camping.

Coyote Dam, 3500ft long and 160ft high, marks the lake's southwest corner; the lake's eastern part is a 689-acre protected wildlife habitat. The **Army Corps of Engineers** (www.spn.usace.army.mil/mendocino; 1160 Lake Mendocino Dr; ⏰8am-4pm Mon-Fri) built the dam, manages the lake and provides recreation information. Its office is inconveniently located on the lower lake.

There are 300 **tent and RV sites** (☏877-444-6777; www.reserveusa.com; sites $25-30), most with hot showers and primitive boat-in sites ($8).

City of Ten Thousand Buddhas

Three miles east of Ukiah, via Talmage Rd, the **site** (☏707-462-0939; www.cttbusa.org; 2001 Talmage Rd; ⏰8am-6pm) used to be a state mental hospital. Since 1976 it has been a lush, quiet 488-acre Chinese-Buddhist community. Don't miss the temple hall, which really does have 10,000 Buddhas. As this is a place of worship, please be respectful of those who use the grounds for meditating. Stay for lunch in the vegetarian Chinese **restaurant** (4951 Bodhi Way; mains $8-12; ⏰noon-3pm; 🅿).

Willits

Twenty miles north of Ukiah, Willits mixes NorCal dropouts with loggers and ranchers (the high school has a bull-riding team). Lamp posts of the main drag are decorated with bucking broncos and cowboys, but the heart of the place is just as boho. Though ranching, timber and manufacturing may be its mainstays, tie-dye is de rigueur. For visitors, Willits' greatest claim to fame is as the eastern terminus of the Skunk Train. Fort

Bragg is 35 miles away on the coast; allow an hour to navigate twisty Hwy 20.

◉ Sights & Activities

Ten miles north of Willits, Hwy 162/Covelo Rd makes for a superb drive following the route of the Northwestern Pacific Railroad along the Eel River and through the **Mendocino National Forest**. The trip is only about 30 miles, but plan on taking at least an hour on the winding road, passing exquisite river canyons and rolling hills. Eventually, you'll reach **Covelo**, known for its unusual round valley.

Mendocino County Museum   MUSEUM
(www.mendocinomuseum.org; 400 E Commercial St; adult/child $4/1; ⏲ 10am-4:30pm Wed-Sun) Among the best community museums in this half of the state, this puts the lives of early settlers in excellent historical context – much drawn from old letters – and there's an entire 1920s soda fountain and barber shop inside. You could spend an hour perusing Pomo and Yuki basketry and artifacts, or reading about local scandals and countercultural movements.

Outside, the **Roots of Motive Power** (www.rootsofmotivepower.com) exhibit occasionally demonstrates steam logging and machinery.

Ridgewood Ranch   HISTORIC SITE
(☑ reservations 707-459-7910; www.seabiscuitheritage.com; 16200 N Hwy 101; tours $20) Willits' most famous resident was the horse Seabiscuit, which grew up here. Ninety-minute tours operate on Monday, Wednesday and Friday (June to September) at 9:30am; three-hour tours for eight or more people are available by reservation and there are other events listed on the website. Reserve-in-advance, docent-led nature tours of the surrounding natural area are free.

Skunk Train   HISTORIC TRAIN
(☑ 866-866-1690, 707-964-6371; www.skunktrain.com; adult/child $54/34) The depot is on E Commercial St, three blocks east of Hwy 101. Trains run between Willits and Fort Bragg (p234).

Jackson Demonstration State Forest   HIKING
Fifteen miles west of Willits on Hwy 20, the forest offers day-use recreational activities, including educational hiking trails and mountain biking. You can also camp here.

★ Festivals & Events

Willits Frontier Days & Rodeo   RODEO
(www.willitsfrontierdays.com) Dating from 1926, Willits has the oldest continuous rodeo in California, occurring in the first week in July.

🛏 Sleeping

Some of the in-town motels – and there seems to be about a hundred of them – are dumps, so absolutely check out the room before checking in. Ask about Skunk Train packages. There are a couple crowded, loud RV parks on the edges of town for only the most desperate campers.

Old West Inn   MOTEL $
(☑ 707-459-4201; www.theoldwestinn.com; 1221 S Main St; r $79; ✲ 🛜) The facade looks like a mock up of an Old West main street and each room has a theme from the 'Stable' to the 'Barber Shop.' The decor is simple and comfy with just enough imagination to make it interesting. Besides that this is the cleanest, friendliest and most highly recommended place in town.

Jackson Demonstration State Forest   CAMPGROUND $
(☑ 707-964-5674; campsites $15) Campsites have barbecue pits and pit toilets, but no water. Get a permit from the on-site host, or from a self-registration kiosk.

Baechtel Creek Inn & Spa   BOUTIQUE HOTEL $$
(☑ 800-459-9911, 707-459-9063; www.baechtelcreekinn.com; 101 Gregory Lane; d incl breakfast $119-159; ✲ 🛜 ☒ ☒) As Willits' only upscale option, this place draws an interesting mix: Japanese bus tours, business travelers and wine trippers. The standard rooms are nothing too flashy, but they have top-notch linens, iPod docks and tasteful art. Custom rooms come with local wine and more space. The immaculate pool and lovely egg breakfast on the patio are perks.

✕ Eating

Loose Caboose Cafe   SANDWICHES $
(10 Woods St; sandwiches $7-11; ⏲ 7:30am-3pm) People tend to get a bit flushed when talking about the sandwiches at the Loose Caboose, which gets jammed at lunch. The Reuben and Sante Fe Chicken sandwiches are two savory delights.

Aztec Grill   MEXICAN $
(781 S Main St; burritos $5-8; ⏲ 5am-9pm) Yes this is in the Chevron Gas Station but the

unanimous vote from locals is that this is, hands down, the best Mexican food in town. Cheap too.

Mariposa Market GROCERIES $
(600 S Main St) Willits' natural food outlet.

Ardella's Kitchen AMERICAN $
(35 E Commercial St; mains $5-11; ☺6am-noon Tue-Sat) For quick eats, this tiny place is tops for breakfast – and is *the* place for gossip. Prices are great, portions are big and fresh and there's an infectious, cheery vibe.

Adam's Restaurant MEDITERRANEAN $$$
(☏707-456-9226; 50 S Main St; mains $22-27) Willits' swankiest address is known for its crab cakes and special occasion-worthy mains like big New York steaks, lamb osso boco or bouillabaisse, perhaps finished off with a blueberry crème brûlée. The ambiance is simple and service stellar.

🍸 Drinking & Entertainment

Shanachie Pub BAR
(50 S Main St; ☺Mon-Sat) This is a friendly little garden-side dive with tons on tap.

Willits Community Theatre THEATER
(www.willitstheatre.org; 37 W Van Lane) Stages award-winning plays, readings and comedy.

🛍 Shopping

JD Redhouse & Co CLOTHING, HOMEWARES
(212 S Main St; ☺10am-6pm) Family-owned and operated, this central mercantile is a good reflection of Willits itself, balancing cowboy essentials – boots and grain, tools and denim – with treats for the weekend tourist. The Cowlick's counter (with excellent Mendocino-made ice cream) is a good place to cool off when the heat on the sidewalk gets intense.

Book Juggler BOOKS
(182 S Main St; ☺10am-7pm Mon-Thu, to 8pm Fri, to 6pm Sat, noon-5pm Sun) Has dense rows of new and used books, music books and local papers (pick up the weird, locally printed *Anderson Valley Advertiser* here).

SOUTHERN REDWOOD COAST

There's some real magic in the loamy soil and misty air 'beyond the redwood curtain'; it yields the tallest trees and most potent herb on the planet. North of Fort Bragg, Bay Area weekenders and antique-stuffed B&Bs give way to lumber wars, pot farmers and an army of carved bears. The 'growing' culture here is palpable and the huge profit it brings to the region has evident cultural side effects – an omnipresent population of transients who work the harvests, a chilling respect for 'No Trespassing' signs and a political culture that is an uneasy balance between gun-toting libertarians, ultra-left progressives and typical college-town chaos. Nevertheless, the reason to visit is to soak in the magnificent landscape, which runs through a number of pristine, ancient redwood forests.

ⓘ Information

Redwood Coast Heritage Trails (www.redwoods.info) Gives a nuanced slant on the region with itineraries based around lighthouses, Native American culture, the timber and rail industries, and maritime life.

Leggett

Leggett marks the redwood country's beginning and Hwy 1's end. There ain't much but a creepy and expensive gas station (cash only), pizza joint and two markets (not always open).

Visit 1000-acre **Standish-Hickey State Recreation Area** (☏707-925-6482; www.parks. ca.gov; 69350 Hwy 101; per car $8;), 1.5 miles to the north, for picnicking, swimming and fishing in the Eel River and hiking trails among virgin and second-growth redwoods. Year-round **campgrounds** (☏800-444-7275; www.reserveamerica.com; tent & RV sites $35) with hot showers book up in summer. Avoid highway-side sites.

Chandelier Drive-Thru Tree Park (www.drivethrutree.com; 67402 Drive Thru Tree Road, Leggett; per car $5; ☺8:30am-9pm; 🚗) has 200 private acres of virgin redwoods with picnicking and nature walks. And yes, there's a redwood with a hole carved out, which cars can drive through. Only in America.

The 1949 tourist trap of **Confusion Hill** (www.confusionhill.com; 75001 N Hwy 101; adult/child Gravity House $5/4, train rides $8.50/6.50; ☺9am-6pm May-Sep, 10am-5pm Oct-Apr; 🚗) is an enduring curiosity and the most elaborate of the old-fashioned stops that line the route north. The Gravity House challenges queasy visitors to keep their balance while standing at a 40-degree angle (a rad photo

Southern Redwood Coast

PACIFIC OCEAN

Trinidad

McKinleyville

Lanphere Dunes Preserve

Arcata

Samoa Peninsula
Arcata Bay

Samoa

Eureka
Arcata Marsh & Wildlife Sanctuary

Humboldt Bay

Humboldt Bay National Wildlife Refuge

Centerville Beach

Ferndale

Fortuna

Cape Mendocino

Rio Dell

Scotia

Pepperwood

Punta Gorda Lighthouse

Petrolia

Redcrest

Mattole Campground

Humboldt Redwoods State Park

Weott

King Range National Conservation Area

Honeydew

Rockefeller Forest

Myers Flat

Big Flat

King Peak

Miranda

Lost Coast
Black Sands Beach

Lost Coast Trail

Avenue of the Giants

Phillipsville

Redway

Shelter Cove

Benbow Lake State Recreation Area

Garberville

Wailaki & Nadelos Campgrounds

Richardson Grove State Park

Sinkyone Wilderness State Park

Standish-Hickey State Recreation Area

Usal Beach Campground

Leggett

(☎707-925-6444; 69501 Hwy 101; ☺8am-9pm) north of Leggett on Hwy 101.

Richardson Grove State Park

Fifteen miles to the north of Leggett, and bisected by the Eel River, serene **Richardson Grove** (☎707-247-3318; www.parks.ca.gov; per car $8) occupies 1400 acres of virgin forest. Many trees are over 1000 years old and 300ft tall, but there aren't many hiking trails. In winter, there's good fishing for silver and king salmon. For the last few years, CalTrans has been considering widening the road through Richardson Grove, which has sparked an intense protest.

The **visitor center** (☺9am-2pm) sells books inside a 1930s lodge, which often has a fire going during cool weather. The park is primarily a **campground** (☎reservations 800-444-7275; www.reserveamerica.com; tent & RV sites $35) with three separate areas with hot showers; some remain open year-round. Summer-only Oak Flat on the east side of the river is shady and has a sandy beach.

Benbow Lake

On the Eel River, 2 miles south of Garberville, the 1200-acre **Benbow Lake State Recreation Area** (☎summer 707-923-3238, winter 707-923-3168; per car $8) exists when a seasonal dam forms the 26-acre Benbow Lake, mid-June to mid-September. In mid-August avoid swimming in the lake or river until two weeks after the **Reggae on the River** festival, when 25,000 people use the river as a bathtub. The water is cleanest in early summer. You can avoid the day use fee by parking near the bridge and walking down to the river. According to a ranger, you can float from here all the way through the redwood groves along the Avenue of the Giants.

🛏 Sleeping

Campground CAMPGROUND $
(☎reservations 800-444-7275; www.reserveamerica.com; tent & RV sites $35) The year-round riverside campground is subject to wintertime bridge closures due to flooding. This part of the Eel River has wide banks and is also excellent for swimming and sunbathing.

op). Kids and fans of kitsch go nuts for the playhouse quality of the space and the narrow-gauge train rides are exciting for toddlers.

For basic supplies, a burger and some good Americana visit **Price's Peg House**

★**Benbow Inn** HISTORIC HOTEL **$$$**
(☑707-923-2124, 800-355-3301; www.benbowinn.
com; 445 Lake Benbow Dr, Garberville; r $99-315,
cottage $230-315; ❋☎❋❋) This inn is a
monument to 1920s rustic elegance; the
Redwood Empire's first luxury resort is a na-
tional historic landmark. Hollywood's elite
once frolicked in the Tudor-style resort's lob-
by, where you can play chess by the crackling
fire, and enjoy complimentary afternoon tea
and evening hors d'oeuvres.

Rooms have top-quality beds, antique
furniture and crystal sherry decanters
(including complimentary sherry). The
window-lined **dining room** (breakfast and
lunch $10 to $15, dinner mains $22 to $32)
serves excellent meals and the rib eye earns
raves.

Garberville

The main supply center for southern Hum-
boldt County is the primary jumping-off
point for both the Lost Coast, to the west,
and the Avenue of the Giants, to the north.
There's an uneasy relationship between the
old-guard loggers and the hippies, many
of whom came in the 1970s to grow sin-
semilla (potent, seedless marijuana) after
the feds chased them out of Santa Cruz. At
last count, the hippies were winning the
culture wars, but it rages on: a sign on the
door of a local bar reads simply: 'Absolute-
ly NO patchouli oil!!!' Two miles west, Gar-
berville's ragtag sister, Redway, has fewer
services. Garberville is about four hours
north of San Francisco, one hour south of
Eureka.

✵ Festivals & Events

The **Mateel Community Center** (www.
mateel.org), in Redway, is the nerve center
for many of the area's long-running annual
festivals, which celebrate everything from
hemp to miming.

Reggae on the River MUSIC
(www.reggaeontheriver.com) In mid-July, this
fest draws huge crowds for reggae, world
music, arts and craft fairs, camping and
swimming in the river.

Avenue of the Giants Marathon MARATHON
(www.theave.org) Among the nation's most
picturesque marathons, held in May.

**Harley-Davidson
Redwood Run** MOTORCYCLE RALLY
(www.redwoodrun.com) The redwoods rumble
with the sound of hundreds of shiny bikes
in June.

🛏 Sleeping

Garberville is lined with motels and many
of them, although serviceable, rent out long-
term and can house questionable charac-
ters. South of town, Benbow Inn blows away
the competition. For cheaper lodging try
Humboldt Redwoods Inn (☑707-923-2451;
www.humboldtredwoodsinn.com; 987 Redwood Dr;
r $65-110; ❋☎❋), the least dodgy of the low-
budget places.

Riverwood Inn INN **$**
(☑707-943-1766; www.riverwoodinn.info; 2828 Av-
enue of the Giants, Phillipsville; r $80-98; ❋) Six
miles north of Garberville is this rockin', vin-
tage 1937, all-American roadhouse with a big
bar at the front, an OK Mexican restaurant
at the back and simple lodge rooms (some
with lovely terraces) downstairs. There's live
music most weekend nights when you can
get rowdy with the locals and traveling mo-
torbikers then sleep it off downstairs.

✕ Eating & Drinking

Woodrose Café BREAKFAST **$$**
(www.woodrosecafe.com; 911 Redwood Dr; meals
$9-16; ☺8am-12pm; ☑❋) Garberville's be-
loved cafe serves organic omelets, veggie
scrambles and buckwheat pancakes with
real maple syrup in a cozy room. Lunch
brings crunchy salads, sandwiches with
all-natural meats and good burritos. Plenty
of gluten-free options.

Cecil's New Orleans Bistro CAJUN **$$$**
(www.cecilsgarberville.com; 733 Redwood Dr;
dinner mains $18-28; ☺5-9pm Thu-Mon) This
2nd-story eatery overlooks Main St and
serves ambitious dishes that may have mint-
ed the California-Cajun style. Start with
fried green tomatoes before launching into
the smoked boar gumbo. Check the website
for music events.

Branding Iron Saloon BAR
(744 Redwood Dr) Craft beer, nice locals and a
hopping pool table. We'll forgive the stripper
pole in the middle of the room.

ℹ Information

Find out what's really happening by tuning in to
community radio **KMUD FM91** (www.kmud.org).

Garberville-Redway Area Chamber of Commerce (www.garberville.org; 784 Redwood Dr; ⊙10am-4pm May-Aug, Mon-Fri Sep-Apr) Inside the Redwood Drive Center.

Lost Coast

The North Coast's superlative backpacking destination is a rugged, mystifying stretch of coast where narrow dirt trails ascend rugged coastal peaks. Here you'll find volcanic beaches of black sand and ethereal mist hovering above the roaring surf as majestic Roosevelt elk graze the forests. The rugged King Range boldly rises 4000ft within 3 miles of the coast between where Hwy 1 cuts inland north of Westport to just south of Ferndale. The coast became 'lost' when the state's highway system deemed the region impassable in the early 20th century.

The best hiking and camping is within the King Range National Conservation Area and the Sinkyone Wilderness State Park, which make up the central and southern stretch of the region. The area north of the King Range is more accessible, if less dramatic.

In autumn, the weather is clear and cool. Wildflowers bloom from April through May and gray whales migrate from December through April. The warmest, driest months are June to August, but days are foggy. Note that the weather can quickly change.

❶ Information

Aside from a few one-horse villages, Shelter Cove, the isolated unincorporated town 25 long miles west of Garberville, is the only option for services. Get supplies in Garberville, Fort Bragg, Eureka or Arcata. The area is a patchwork of government-owned land and private property; visit the Bureau of Land Management office for information, permits and maps. There are few circuitous routes for hikers, and rangers can advise on reliable (if expensive) shuttle services in the area.

A few words of caution: lots of weed is grown around here and it's wise to stay on trail and respect no trespassing signs, lest you find yourself at the business end of someone's right to bear arms. And pot farmers don't pose the only threat: you'll want to check for ticks (Lyme disease is common) and keep food in bear-proof containers, which are required for camping.

Bureau of Land Management (BLM; ☑707-825-2300, 707-986-5400; 768 Shelter Cove Rd; ⊙8am-4:30pm Mon-Sat Sep-May, 8am-4:30pm Mon-Fri Jun-Aug) Nine miles east of Shelter Cove, the Bureau of Land Management has maps and directions for trails and campsites; they're posted outside after hours.

Sinkyone Wilderness State Park

Named for the Sinkyone people who once lived here, this 7367-acre wilderness extends south of Shelter Cove along pristine coastline. The Lost Coast Trail passes through here for 22 miles, from Whale Gulch south to Usal Beach Campground, taking at least three days to walk as it meanders along high ridges, providing bird's-eye views down to deserted beaches and the crashing surf (side trails descend to water level). Near the park's northern end, you can register at the (haunted!) Needle Rock Ranch (☑707-986-7711; tent sites $35) for the adjacent campsites. This is the only source of potable water. For information on when the ranch is closed (most of the time), call Richardson Grove State Park (p248).

To get to Sinkyone, drive west from Garberville and Redway on Briceland-Thorn Rd, 21 miles through Whitethorn to Four Corners. Turn left (south) and continue for 3.5 miles down a very rugged road to the ranch house; it takes 1½ hours.

There's access to the Usal Beach Campground (tent sites $25) at the south end of the park from Hwy 1 (you can't make reservations). North of Westport, take the unpaved County Rd 431 beginning from Hwy 1's Mile 90.88 and travel 6 miles up the coast to the campground. The road is graded yearly in late spring and is passable in summer via 2WD vehicles. Most sites are past the message board by the beach. Use bear canisters or keep food in your trunk. Look for giant elk feeding on the tall grass – they live behind sites No 1 and 2 – and osprey by the creek's mouth.

North of the campground, Usal Rd (County Rd 431) is much rougher and recommended only if you have a high-clearance 4WD and a chainsaw. Seriously.

King Range National Conservation Area

Stretching over 35 miles of virgin coastline, with ridge after ridge of mountainous terrain plunging to the surf, the 60,000-acre area tops out at namesake King's Peak (4087ft). The wettest spot in California, the range receives over 120in – and sometimes as much as 240in – of annual rainfall, causing frequent landslides; in winter, snow falls

HIKING THE LOST COAST

The best way to see the Lost Coast is to hike, and the best hiking is through the southern regions within the Sinkyone and Kings Range Wilderness areas. Some of the best trails start from Mattole Campground, just south Petrolia, which is on the northern border of the Kings Range. It's at the ocean end of Lighthouse Rd, 4 miles from Mattole Rd (sometimes marked as Hwy 211), southeast of Petrolia.

Both Wailaki and Nadelos have developed **campgrounds** (tent sites $8) with toilets and water. There are another four developed campgrounds around the range, with toilets but no water (except Honeydew, which has purifiable creek water). There are multiple primitive walk-in sites. You'll need a bear canister and backcountry permit, both available from Bureau of Land Management (BLM) offices.

Lost Coast Trail The Lost Coast Trail follows 24.7 miles of coastline from Mattole Campground in the north to Black Sands Beach at Shelter Cove in the south. The prevailing northerly winds make it best to hike from north to south; plan for three or four days. In October and November, and April and May, the weather is iffy and winds can blow south to north, depending on whether there's a low-pressure system overhead. The best times to come are summer weekdays in early June, at the end of August, September and October. The trail is 'discovered' and will often have hikers; busiest times are Memorial Day, Labor Day and summer weekends. The only reliable shuttle with permits to transport backpackers through the area is pricey **Lost Coast Shuttle** (☑ 707-223-1547; www. lostcoastshuttle.com; 2 people $200-450, extra passenger $25). Transport prices depend on the distance you want to travel.

Highlights include an abandoned lighthouse at Punta Gorda, remnants of early shipwrecks, tidepools and abundant wildlife including sea lions, seals and some 300 bird species. The trail is mostly level, passing beaches and crossing over rocky outcrops. Along the Lost Coast Trail, **Big Flat** is the most popular backcountry destination. Carry a tide table, lest you get trapped: from Buck Creek to Miller Creek, you can only hike during an outgoing tide.

Punta Gorda Lighthouse Hike A good day hike starts at the Mattole Campground trailhead and travels 3 miles south along the coast to the Punta Gorda lighthouse (return against the wind).

Ridgeline Trails To ditch the crowds, take any of the (strenuous) upland trails off the beach toward the ridgeline. For a satisfying, hard, 21-mile-long hike originating at the Lost Coast Trail, take Buck Creek Trail to King Crest Trail to Rattlesnake Ridge Trail. The 360-degree views from **King Peak** are stupendous, particularly with a full moon or during a meteor shower. Note that if you hike up, it can be hellishly hot on the ridges, though the coast remains cool and foggy; wear removable layers. Carry a topographical map and a compass: signage is limited.

on the ridges. (By contrast, nearby sea-level Shelter Cove gets only 69in of rain and no snow.) Two-thirds of the area is awaiting wilderness designation.

See the Bureau of Land Management (BLM; p250) for information. For overnight hikes, you'll need a backcountry-use permit. Don't turn left onto Briceland-Thorn Rd to try to find the 'town' of Whitethorn; it doesn't exist. Whitethorn is the BLM's name for the general area. To reach the BLM office from Garberville/Redway, follow signs to Shelter Cove; look for the roadside information panel, a quarter mile past the post office. Information and permits are also available from the BLM in Arcata (p262).

Fire restrictions begin July 1 and last until the first soaking rain, usually in November. During this time, there are no campfires allowed outside developed campgrounds.

North of the King Range

Though it's less of an adventure, you can reach the Lost Coast's northern section year-round via paved, narrow Mattole Rd. Plan on three hours to navigate the sinuous 68 miles from Ferndale in the north to the coast at Cape Mendocino, then inland to Humboldt

Redwoods State Park (p252) and Hwy 101. Don't expect redwoods; the vegetation is grassland and pasture. It's beautiful in spots – lined with sweeping vistas and wildflowers that are prettiest in spring.

You'll pass two tiny settlements, both 19th-century stage-coach stops. **Petrolia** has an all-in-one **store** (☎707-629-3455; ◷9am-5pm) which rents bear canisters and sells supplies for the trail, good beer and gasoline. **Honeydew** also has a **general store**. The drive is enjoyable, but the Lost Coast's wild, spectacular scenery lies further south in the more remote regions.

Shelter Cove

The only sizable community on the Lost Coast, Shelter Cove is surrounded by the King Range National Conservation Area and abuts a large south-facing cove. It's a tiny seaside subdivision with an airstrip in the middle – indeed, many visitors are private pilots. Fifty years ago, Southern California swindlers subdivided the land, built the airstrip and flew in potential investors, fast-talking them into buying seaside land for retirement. But they didn't tell buyers that a steep, winding, one-lane dirt road provided the *only* access and that the seaside plots were eroding into the sea.

Today, there's still only one route, but now it's paved. Cell phones don't work here: this is a good place to disappear. The town, though sleepy and bland, offers surfing (beginners to advanced), sea kayaking, fishing, whale-watching from the shore and fantastic tide pooling; a short drive brings you to the stunning **Black Sands Beach** stretching for miles northward. You can rent surf boards, kayaks, wetsuits and more at the **Lost Coast Surf Shack** (surfboards $25 per day, kayaks half/full-day $45/70; ◷10:30am-4:30pm).

🛏 Sleeping

Shelter Cove RV Park, Campground & Deli CAMPGROUND $
(☎707-986-7474; 492 Machi Rd; tent/RV sites $33/43) The services may be basic, but the fresh gusts of ocean air can't be beat – the deli has good fish and chips.

Oceanfront Inn & Lighthouse INN $$
(☎707-986-7002; www.sheltercoveoceanfrontinn. com; 10 Seal Court; r $150-250; ⊜) It looks funky on the outside but the big, bright rooms have phenomenal sea views and are tidy and modern with microwaves, refrigerators and balconies. Plus **Cove Restaurant** downstairs is the best place to eat in town.

Tides Inn HOTEL $$
(☎707-986-7900; www.sheltercovetidesinn.com; 59 Surf Pt; r $165, ste with kitchen $190-380; ⊜) Perched above tidepools teeming with starfish and sea urchins, the squeaky-clean rooms here offer excellent views (go for the mini-suites on the 3rd floor). The suite options are good for families, and kids are greeted warmly by the innkeeper with an activity kit.

Inn of the Lost Coast INN $$
(☎888-570-9676, 707-986-7521; www.innofthelostcoast.com; 205 Wave Dr; r $160-250; ⊜⊛) This is the most family-friendly hotel in town with clean rooms with basic cooking facilities, breathtaking ocean views and fireplaces. Downstairs there's a serviceable take-out pizza place and **coffeehouse** as well as ping pong and a hot tub.

Spy Glass Inn INN $$$
(☎707-986-4030; www.spyglassinnsheltercove. com; 118 Dolphin Dr; ste $295-335; ⊜) Up on a hill a short walk from town, the relatively new, luxurious suites here all have sea-view Jacuzzi tubs, full kitchens and windows lit up by the expansive shoreline beyond.

✗ Eating

Shelter Cove General Store GROCERIES $
(☎707-986-7733; 7272 Shelter Cove Rd) For those who are self-catering, Shelter Cove General Store is 2 miles beyond town. Get groceries and gasoline here.

Cove Restaurant AMERICAN $$
(☎707-986-1197; 10 Seal Ct; mains $8-25; ◷10am-2pm & 5-9pm Thu-Sun) The first-choice place to eat, Cove has everything from veggie stir-fries to New York steaks.

Humboldt Redwoods State Park & Avenue of the Giants

Don't miss this magical drive through California's largest redwood park, **Humboldt Redwoods State Park** (www.humboldtredwoods.org), which covers 53,000 acres – 17,000 of which are old-growth – and contains some of the world's most magnificent trees. It also boasts three-quarters of the world's tallest 100 trees. Tree huggers take note: these groves rival (and some say surpass) those in Redwood National Park (p265), which is a long drive further north, although the landscapes here are less diverse.

Exit Hwy 101 when you see the 'Avenue of the Giants' sign, take this smaller alternative to the interstate; it's an incredible, 32-mile, two-lane stretch. You'll find free driving guides at roadside signboards at both the avenue's southern entrance, 6 miles north of Garberville, near Phillipsville, and at the northern entrance, south of Scotia, at Pepperwood; there are access points off Hwy 101.

Three miles north, the **California Federation of Women's Clubs Grove** is home to an interesting four-sided hearth designed by renowned San Franciscan architect Julia Morgan in 1931 to commemorate 'the untouched nature of the forest.'

Primeval **Rockefeller Forest**, 4.5 miles west of the avenue via Mattole Rd, appears as it did a century ago. It's the world's largest contiguous old-growth redwood forest, and contains about 20% of all such remaining trees. Walk the 2.5-mile **Big Trees Loop** (note that at the time of research a footbridge had been taken out and you'll have to walk across a fallen tree to cross the river where the trail starts). You quickly walk out of sight of cars and feel like you have fallen into the time of dinosaurs.

In **Founders Grove**, north of the visitor center, the **Dyerville Giant** was knocked over in 1991 by another falling tree. A walk along its gargantuan 370ft length, with its wide trunk towering above, helps you appreciate how huge these ancient trees are.

The park has over 100 miles of trails for hiking, mountain biking and horseback riding. Easy walks include short nature trails in Founders Grove and Rockefeller Forest and **Drury-Chaney Loop Trail** (with berry picking in summer). Challenging treks include popular **Grasshopper Peak Trail**, south of the visitor center, which climbs to the 3379ft fire lookout.

🛏 Sleeping & Eating

If you want to stay along the avenue, several towns have simple lodgings of varying calibers and levels of hospitality, but camping at Humboldt Redwoods is by far the best option.

Humboldt Redwoods State Park Campgrounds　CAMPGROUND $
(☎800-444-7275;　www.reserveamerica.com; campsites from $35) The park runs three

---

DRIVE-THRU TREES

Three carved-out (but living) redwoods await along Hwy 101, a bizarre holdover from a yesteryear road trip.

➡ **Chandelier Drive-Thru Tree** (p247) Fold in your mirrors and inch forward, then cool off in the über-kitschy gift shop; in Leggett and arguably the best one.

➡ **Shrine Drive-Thru Tree** (13078 Avenue of the Giants, Myers Flat; walk/drive through $3/6; ☉ sunrise-sunset; 🚗) Look up to the sky as you roll through. The least impressive of the three.

➡ **Tour Thru Tree** (430 Highway 169, Klamath; ☉ sunrise-sunset; 🚗) Take exit 769 in Klamath, squeeze through a tree and check out an emu.

---

campgrounds, with hot showers, two environmental camps, five trail camps, a hike/bike camp and an equestrian camp. Of the developed spots, **Burlington Campground** is open year-round beside the visitor center and near a number of trailheads. **Hidden Springs Campground**, 5 miles south, and **Albee Creek Campground**, on Mattole Rd past Rockefeller Forest, are open mid-May to early fall.

Miranda Gardens Resort　RESORT $$
(☎707-943-3011; www.mirandagardens.com; 6766 Avenue of the Giants, Miranda; cottages with kitchen $165-300, without kitchen $115-200; ✴🐾) The best indoor stay along the avenue. The slightly rustic cottages have redwood paneling, some with fireplaces, and are spotlessly clean. The grounds – replete with outdoor ping pong and a play area for kids and swaying redwoods – have wholesome appeal for families.

Chimney Tree　AMERICAN $
(1111 Avenue of the Giants, Phillipsville; burgers $7-11; ☉10am-7pm May-Sep) If you're just passing through and want something quick, come here. It raises its own grass-fed beef. Alas, the fries are frozen, but those burgers... mmm-mmm!

Riverbend Cellars　WINERY $$
(www.riverbendcellars.com; 12990 Avenue of the Giants, Myers Flat; ☉11am-5pm) For something a bit posh, pull over here. The El Centauro red – named for Pancho Villa – is an excellent estate-grown blend.

ℹ Information

Visitor Center (☑707-946-2263; ⊗9am-5pm May-Sep, 10am-4pm Oct-Apr) South of Weott, a volunteer-staffed visitor center shows videos and sells maps.

Scotia

For years, Scotia was California's last 'company town,' entirely owned and operated by the Pacific Lumber Company, which built cookie-cut houses and had an open contempt for long-haired outsiders who liked to get between their saws and the big trees. The company went belly up in 2006, sold the mill to another redwood company and, though the town still has a creepy *Twilight Zone* vibe, you no longer have to operate by the company's posted 'Code of Conduct.'

A history of the town awaits at the **Scotia Museum & Visitor Center** (www.townofscotia.com; cnr Main & Bridge Sts; ⊗8am-4:30pm Mon-Fri Jun-Sep), at the town's south end. The museum's **fisheries center** (admission free) is remarkably informative – ironic, considering that logging destroys fish habitats – and houses the largest freshwater aquarium on the North Coast.

There are dingy motels and diners in **Rio Dell** (aka 'Real Dull'), across the river but the best place to stay is Scotia itself at the historic but rather plain **Scotia Inn** (☑707-764-5338; www.thescotiainn.com; 100 Main St; r $75-150; ☎☀) with rooms that look like Grandma's house, with lace curtains and flowery wallpaper. Back in the day, Rio Dell is where the debauchery happened: because it wasn't a company town, Rio Dell had bars and hookers. In 1969, the freeway bypassed the town and it withered.

As you drive along Hwy 101 and see what appears to be a never-ending redwood forest, understand that this 'forest' sometimes consists of trees only a few rows deep – called a 'beauty strip' – a carefully crafted illusion for tourists. Most old-growth trees have been cut. **Bay Area Coalition for Headwaters Forest** (www.headwaterspreserve.org) helped preserve over 7000 acres of land with public funds through provisions in a long-negotiated agreement between the Pacific Lumber Company and state and federal agencies.

Up Hwy 101 there's a great pit stop at **Eel River Brewing** (www.eelriverbrewing.com; 1777 Alamar Way; ⊗11am-11pm Mon-Sun) where a breezy beer garden and excellent burgers accompany all-organic brews.

Ferndale

The North Coast's most charming town is stuffed with impeccable Victorians – known locally as 'butterfat palaces' because of the dairy wealth that built them. There are so many, in fact, that the entire place is a state and federal historical landmark. Dairy farmers built the town in the 19th century and it's still run by the 'milk mafia': you're not a local till you've lived here 40 years. A stroll down Main St offers a taste of super wholesome, small-town America from galleries to old-world emporiums and soda fountains. Although Ferndale relies on tourism, it has avoided becoming a tourist trap – and has no chain stores. Though a lovely place to spend a summer night, it's dead as a doornail in winter.

⊙ Sights

Half a mile from downtown via Bluff St, enjoy short tramps through fields of wildflowers, beside ponds, past redwood groves and eucalyptus trees at 110-acre **Russ Park**. The **cemetery**, also on Bluff St, is amazingly cool with graves dating to the 1800s and expansive views to the ocean. Five miles down Centerville Rd, **Centerville Beach** is one of the few off-leash dog beaches in Humboldt County.

Kinetic Sculpture Museum   MUSEUM
(580 Main St; ⊗10am-5pm Mon-Sat, noon-4pm Sun; ⊕) This warehouse holds the fanciful, astounding, human-powered contraptions used in the town's annual Kinetic Grand Championship (p260). Shaped like giant fish and UFOs, these colorful piles of junk propel racers over roads, water and marsh in the May event.

Fern Cottage   HISTORIC BUILDING
(☑707-786-4835; www.ferncottage.org; Centerville Rd; group tours per person $10; ⊗by appointment) This 1866 Carpenter Gothic grew to a 32-room mansion. Only one family ever lived here, so the interior is completely preserved.

✷ Festivals & Events

This wee town has a packed social calendar, especially in the summer. If you're planning a visit, check the events page at www.victorianferndale.com.

Tour of the Unknown Coast BICYCLE RACE
(www.tuccycle.org) A challenging event in May, in which participants in the 100-mile race climb nearly 10,000ft.

Humboldt County Fair FAIR
(www.humboldtcountyfair.org) Held mid-August, the longest-running county fair in California.

🛏 Sleeping

Francis Creek Inn MOTEL $
(☏707-786-9611; www.franciscreekinn.com; 577 Main St; r from $85; 🖃) White picket balconies stand in front of this downtown motel, which is family owned and operated (check in at the Red Front convenience store, right around the corner). Rooms are basic, clean and furnished simply; the value is outstanding.

Humboldt County Fairgrounds CAMPGROUND $
(☏707-786-9511; www.humboldtcountyfair.org; 1250 5th St; tent/RV sites $10/20) Turn west onto Van Ness St and go a few blocks for lawn camping with showers.

Hotel Ivanhoe HISTORIC HOTEL $$
(☏707-786-9000; www.ivanhoe-hotel.com; 315 Main St; r $95-145; 🖃) Ferndale's oldest hostelry opened in 1875. It has four antique-laden rooms and an Old West–style, 2nd-floor gallery, perfect for morning coffee. The adjoining saloon, with dark wood and lots of brass, is an atmospheric place for a nightcap.

Shaw House B&B $$
(☏800-557-7429, 707-786-9958; www.shawhouse.com; 703 Main St; r $110-159, ste $200-250; 🖃🖃) Shaw House, an emblematic 'butterfat palace,' was the first permanent structure in Ferndale, completed by founding father Seth Shaw in 1866. Today, it's California's oldest B&B, set back on extensive grounds. Original details remain, including painted wooden ceilings. Most of the rooms have private entrances, and three have private balconies over a large garden.

Victorian Inn HISTORIC HOTEL $$
(☏888-589-1808, 707-786-4949; www.victorianvillageinn.com; 400 Ocean Ave; r $105-225; 🖃) The bright, sunny rooms inside this venerable, two-story former bank building (1890), are comfortably furnished with thick carpeting, good linens and antiques.

⭐**Gingerbread Mansion** HISTORIC B&B $$$
(☏707-786-4000; www.gingerbread-mansion.com; 400 Berding St; r $175-495; 🖃) This is the cream of dairyland elegance, an 1898 Queen Anne–Eastlake that's unsurprisingly the town's most photographed building. And the inside is no less extravagant with each room having its own unique (and complex) mix of floral wallpaper, patterned carpeting, grand antique furniture and perhaps a fireplace, wall fresco, stained glass window or Greek statue thrown in for kicks.

🍴 Eating

There is an abundance of great places to eat in Ferndale (mostly along Main St) – from pie shops and ice cream to a butcher/deli and chocolate shop – so take this list as a starting point only. A **farmers market** (400 Ocean Ave; ⏱10:30am-2pm Sat May-Oct) has locally grown veggies and locally produced dairy – including the freshest cheese you'll find anywhere.

⭐**Mario's Lost Coast Cafe** VEGETARIAN, VEGAN $
(468 Main St; sandwiches $7.25; ⏱10am-3:30pm; 🖃🖃) Step into Mario's homey kitchen and be blown away. This guy mills his own flour, bakes his own bread and is so passionate and well-versed in all things food that it's no wonder the soups, sandwiches, salads and baked goods are easily the best vegetarian choices north of Fort Bragg. Coffee is on the house. Cash only.

No Brand Burger Stand BURGERS $
(989 Milton St; burgers $7; ⏱11am-5pm) Hiding near the entrance to town by an industrial building, this hole-in-the-wall turns out a juicy jalapeño double cheese burger that ranks easily as the North Coast's best burger. The shakes – so thick your cheeks hurt from pulling on the straw – are about the only other thing on the menu.

Poppa Joe's AMERICAN $
(409 Main St; mains $5-7; ⏱11am-8:30pm Mon-Fri, 6am-noon Sat & Sun) You can't beat the atmosphere at this diner, where trophy heads hang from the wall, the floors slant at a precarious angle and old men play poker all day. The American-style breakfasts are good, too – especially the pancakes.

☆ Entertainment

Ferndale Repertory Theatre THEATER
(☏707-786-5483; www.ferndale-rep.org; 447 Main St) This top-shelf community company produces excellent contemporary theater in the historic Hart Theatre Building.

🔒 Shopping

Main St is a great place to shop. Look for the handful of secondhand stores selling vintage cowboy boots and used designer jeans at reasonable prices.

Blacksmith Shop & Gallery METAL GOODS
(📞707-786-4216; www.ferndaleblacksmith.com; 455 & 491 Main St) From wrought-iron art to hand-forged furniture, this is the largest collection of contemporary blacksmithing in America.

Abraxas Jewelry & Leather Goods JEWELRY
(505 Main St) The pieces of locally forged jewelry here are extremely cool and moderately priced. The back room is filled with tons of hats.

Humboldt Bay National Wildlife Refuge

This pristine **wildlife refuge** (www.fws.gov/humboldtbay) protects wetland habitats for more than 200 species of birds migrating annually along the Pacific Flyway. Between the fall and early spring, when Aleutian geese descend en masse to the area, more than 25,000 geese might be seen in a cackling gaggle outside the visitor center.

The peak season for waterbirds and raptors runs September to March; for black brant geese and migratory shorebirds mid-March to late April. Gulls, terns, cormorants, pelicans, egrets and herons come year-round. Look for harbor seals offshore; bring binoculars. If it's open, drive out South Jetty Rd to the mouth of Humboldt Bay for a stunning perspective.

Pick up a map from the **visitor center** (1020 Ranch Rd; ⏲8am-5pm). Exit Hwy 101 at Hookton Rd, 11 miles south of Eureka, turn north along the frontage road, on the freeway's west side. In April look for the **Godwit Days** festival, a celebration of the spring bird migration.

Eureka

One hour north of Garberville, on the edge of the giant Humboldt Bay, lies Eureka, the largest bay north of San Francisco. With strip-mall sprawl surrounding a lovely historic downtown, it wears its role as the county seat a bit clumsily. Despite a diverse and interesting community of artists, writers, pagans and other free-thinkers, Eureka's wild side slips out only occasionally – the **Redwood Coast Dixieland Jazz Festival** (www.redwoodcoastmusicfestivals.org) is a rollicking festival with events all over town, and **summer concerts** rock out the F Street Pier – but mostly, Eureka goes to bed early. Make for Old Town, a small district with colorful Victorians, good shopping and a revitalized waterfront. For night life head to Eureka's trippy sister up the road, Arcata.

👁 Sights

The free *Eureka Visitors Map*, available at tourist offices, details walking tours and scenic drives, focusing on architecture and history. **Old Town**, along 2nd and 3rd Sts from C St to M St, was once down-and-out, but has been refurbished into a buzzing pedestrian district. The F Street Plaza and Boardwalk run along the waterfront at the foot of F St. **Gallery openings** fall on the first Saturday of every month.

Blue Ox Millworks & Historic Park HISTORIC BUILDING
(www.blueoxmill.com; adult/child 6-12yr $10/5; ⏲9am-4pm Mon-Sat; 🚼) One of only seven of its kind in America, antique tools and mills are used to produce authentic gingerbread trim for Victorian buildings; one-hour self-guided tours take you through the mill and historical buildings, including a blacksmith shop and 19th-century skid camp. Kids love the oxen.

Romano Gabriel Wooden Sculpture Garden GARDENS
(315 2nd St) The coolest thing to gawk at downtown is this collection of whimsical outsider art that's enclosed by aging glass. For 30 years, wooden characters in Gabriel's front yard delighted locals. After he died in 1977, the city moved the collection here.

Clarke Historical Museum MUSEUM
(www.clarkemuseum.org; 240 E St; suggested donation $3; ⏲11am-4pm Wed-Sat) The best community historical museum on this stretch of the coast houses a set of typically musty relics – needlework hankies and paintings of the area's history-making notables (in this case Ulysses Grant, who was once dismissed from his post at Fort Humboldt for drunkenness). Its best collection is that of intricately woven baskets from local tribes.

Carson Mansion HISTORIC BUILDING
(143 M St) Of Eureka's fine Victorian buildings the most famous is the ornate 1880s

home of lumber baron William Carson. It took 100 men a full year to build. Today it's a private men's club. The **pink house** opposite, at 202 M St, is an 1884 Queen Anne Victorian designed by the same architects and built as a wedding gift for Carson's son.

Sequoia Park   PARK
(www.sequoiaparkzoo.net; 3414 W St; park free, zoo adult/child $5/3; ⊙zoo 10am-5pm May-Sep, Tue-Sun Oct-Apr; ▣) A 77-acre old-growth redwood grove is a surprising green gem in the middle of a residential neighborhood. It has biking and hiking trails, a children's playground and picnic areas, and a small **zoo**.

Morris Graves Museum of Art   MUSEUM
(www.humboldtarts.org; 636 F St; admission $5; ⊙noon-5pm Thu-Sun) Across Hwy 101, the excellent museum shows rotating Californian artists and hosts performances inside the 1904 **Carnegie library**, the state's first public library.

Discovery Museum   MUSEUM
(www.discovery-museum.org; 517 3rd St; admission $4; ⊙10am-4pm Tue-Sat, from noon Sun; ▣) A hands-on kids' museum.

🏃 Activities

Harbor Cruise   CRUISE
(www.humboldtbaymaritimemuseum.com; narrated cruise adult/child $18/10) Board the 1910 *Madaket*, America's oldest continuously operating passenger vessel, and learn the history of Humboldt Bay. Located at the foot of C St, it originally ferried mill workers and passengers until the Samoa Bridge was built in 1972. The $10 sunset cocktail cruise serves from the smallest licensed bar in the state; there's also a 75-minute narrated cruise.

Hum-Boats Sail, Canoe &
Kayak Center   BOAT RENTAL
(www.humboats.com; Startare Dr; ⊙9am-5pm Mon-Fri, to 6pm Sat & Sun Apr-Oct, to 2:30pm Nov-Mar) At Woodley Island Marina, this outfit rents kayaks and sailboats, offering lessons, tours, charters, sunset sails and full-moon paddles.

🛏 Sleeping

Every brand of chain hotel is along Hwy 101. Room rates run high midsummer; you can sometimes find cheaper in Arcata, to the north, or Fortuna, to the south. There are also a handful of motels which cost from $55 to $100 and have no air-conditioning; choose places set back from the road. The cheapest are south of downtown on the suburban strip.

Abigail's Elegant Victorian Mansion INN $$
(☑707-444-3144; www.eureka-california.com; 1406 C St; r $115-145; 🖥) Inside this National Historic Landmark that's practically a living-history museum, the sweet-as-could-be innkeepers lavish guests with warm hospitality.

Eureka Inn   HISTORIC HOTEL $$
(☑877-552-3985, 707-497-6903; www.eurekainn. com; cnr 7th & F Sts; r from $109; 🖥) This magestic and enormous historic hotel is slowly being renovated. The style is cozy, in an early-20th-century-lodger, vagely Wild West sort of way. The staff are extremely friendly and there's a decent bar and restaurant on the premises.

Bayview Motel   MOTEL $$
(☑866-725-6813, 707-442-1673; www.bayviewmotel.com; 2844 Fairfield St; r $94-175; 🖥🐾) Spotless rooms are of the chain-motel standard; some have patios overlooking Humboldt Bay.

Eagle House Inn   HISTORIC INN $$
(☑707-444-3344; www.eaglehouseinn.com; 139 2nd St; r $105-250; 🖥) This hulking Victorian hotel in Old Town has 24 rooms above a turn-of-the-century ballroom that's used for everything from theater and movie performances to special events. Rooms and common areas are tastefully done with precious period decor. The coolest rooms are in the corner and have sitting areas in turrets looking over the street.

Daly Inn   B&B $$
(☑800-321-9656, 707-445-3638; www.dalyinn. com; 1125 H St; r with bath $170-185, without bath $130) This impeccably maintained 1905 Colonial Revival mansion has individually decorated rooms with turn-of-the-20th-century European and American antiques. Guest parlors are trimmed with rare woods; outside are century-old flowering trees.

Carter House Inns   B&B $$$
(☑800-404-1390, 707-444-8062; http://carter-house.com; 301 L St, Eureka; r incl breakfast $179-385; 🖥🐾) Recently constructed in period style, this hotel is a Victorian lookalike, holding rooms with top-quality linens and modern amenities; suites have in-room Jacuzzis and marble fireplaces. The same owners operate three sumptuously decorated houses: a single-level 1900 house, a honeymoon-

hideaway cottage and a replica of an 1880s San Francisco mansion, which the owner built himself, entirely by hand.

Unlike elsewhere, you won't see the innkeeper unless you want to. Guests have an in-room breakfast or can eat at the understated, elegant **restaurant**.

✖ Eating

Eureka is blessed with two excellent natural food grocery stores – **Eureka Co-op** (cnr 5th & L Sts) and **Eureka Natural Foods** (1626 Broadway) – and two weekly **farmers markets** (cnr 2nd & F Sts; ⊙10am-1pm Tue Jun-Oct) and the **Henderson Center** (⊙10am-1pm Thu Jun-Oct). The vibrant dining scene is focused in the Old Town district.

Ramone's　　　　　　　　BAKERY, DELI $
(2223 Harrison St; mains $6-10; ⊙7am-6pm Mon-Sat, 8am-4pm Sun) For grab-and-go sandwiches, fresh soups and wraps.

★ Brick & Fire　　　　　CALIFORNIAN $$
(☑707-268-8959; 1630 F St; pizzas from $14, mains $15-25; ⊙11:30am-8:30pm Mon, Wed & Thu, 11:30am-9pm Fri, 5-9pm Sat & Sun) Eureka's best restaurant is in an intimate, warm-hued, bohemian-tinged setting that is almost always busy. Choose from thin-crust pizzas, delicious salads (try the pear and blue cheese) and an ever-changing selection of appetizers and mains that highlight local produce and wild mushrooms. There's a weighty wine list and servers are well-versed in pairings.

Kyoto　　　　　　　　　　JAPANESE $$
(☑707-443-7777; 320 F St; sushi $4-6, sushi $15-27; ⊙11:30am-3pm & 5:30-9:30pm Wed-Sat) Renowned as the best sushi in Humboldt County, dine in a tiny, packed room, where conversation with the neighboring table is inevitable. A menu of sushi and sashimi is rounded out by grilled scallops and fern-tip salad. North Coast travelers who absolutely need sushi should phone ahead for a reservation.

Waterfront Café Oyster Bar　　SEAFOOD $$
(102 F St; lunch $8-17, dinner $15-24; ⊙9am-9pm) With a nice bay view and baskets of steamed clams, fish and chips, oysters and chowder, this is a solid bayside lunch for the atmosphere more than anything. A top spot for Sunday brunch, with jazz and Ramos fizzes.

Restaurant 301　　　　　CALIFORNIAN $$$
(☑800-404-1390; www.carterhouse.com; 301 L St; dinner mains $23-32; ⊙6-9pm) Eureka's top

table, romantic, sophisticated 301 serves a contemporary Californian menu, using produce from its organic gardens (tours available). Mains are pricey, but the prix-fixe menu is a good way to taste local food in its finest presentation. The eight-course Chef's Grand Menu ($96) is only worthy of *really* special occasions.

🍷 Drinking & Nightlife

Lost Coast Brewery　　　　　BREWERY
(☑707-445-4480; 617 4th St; 10 tasters for $12; ⊙11am-10pm Sun-Thu, to 11pm Fri & Sat; 🛜) The roster of the regular brews at Eureka's colorful brewery might not knock the socks off a serious beer snob (and can't hold a candle to some of the others on the coast), but highlights include the Downtown Brown Ale, Great White and Lost Coast Pale Ale. After downing a few pints, the fried pub grub starts to look pretty tasty.

2 Doors Down　　　　　　WINE BAR
(1626 F St; glass/bottle from $5/19; ⊙4:40-9:30pm Wed-Mon) Wonderfully cozy and inviting, this Victorian-feeling wine bar lets you create your own flights and will open any bottle on their list of 80 plus wines if you're getting two or more glasses from it. Plenty of snacks are available or order from Brick & Fire (p258) next door.

Shanty　　　　　　　　　DIVE BAR
(213 2nd St; ⊙noon-2am; 🛜) The coolest spot in town is grungy and fun. Play pool, Donkey Kong, Ms Pac Man or ping pong, or kick it on the back patio with local 20- and 30-something hipsters.

Old Town Coffee & Chocolates　　CAFE
(211 F St; ⊙7am-9pm) You'll smell roasting coffee blocks before you see this place. It's a local hang out with plenty of tables, baked goods and a board where you can give a cup of whatever to your favorite regular.

☆ Entertainment

For gay events, log onto www.queerhumboldt.com.

Morris Graves
Museum of Art　　　　　PERFORMING ARTS
(www.humboldtarts.org; 636 F St; suggested donation $4; ⊙noon-5pm Thu-Sun) Hosts performing-arts events between September and May, usually on Saturday evenings and Sunday afternoons.

The Alibi CLUB
(www.thealibi.com; 744 9th St) Live music on Wednesdays and Saturdays.

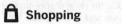 Shopping

Eureka's streets lie on a grid; numbered streets cross lettered streets. For the best window shopping, head to the 300, 400 and 500 blocks of 2nd St, between D and G Sts. The town's low rents and cool old spaces harbor lots of indie boutiques.

Shipwreck VINTAGE
(430 3rd St; ⊙ 10am-6pm Mon-Fri, noon-5pm Sun) The quality of vintage goods here – *genuinely* distressed jeans and leather jackets, 1940s housedresses and hats – is complimented by handmade local jewelry and paper products.

Going Places BOOKS
(328 2nd St; ⊙ 10:30am-5:30pm Mon-Sat, 11am-5pm Sun) Guidebooks, travel gear and international goods are certain to give a thrill to any vagabond. It's one of three excellent bookshops in Old Town.

ⓘ Information

Eureka Chamber of Commerce (☑ 800-356-6381, 707-442-3738; www.eurekachamber.com; 2112 Broadway; ⊙ 8:30am-5pm Mon-Fri; �͡) The main visitor information center is on Hwy 101.

Six Rivers National Forest Headquarters (☑ 707-442-1721; 1330 Bayshore Way; ⊙ 8am-4:30pm Mon-Fri) Maps and information.

ⓘ Getting There & Around

The Arcata/Eureka Airport (ACV) is a small, expensive airport which connects regionally. The Greyhound station is in Arcata.

Eureka Transit Service (☑ 707-443-0826; www.eurekatransit.org) operates local buses ($1.70), Monday to Saturday.

Samoa Peninsula

Grassy dunes and windswept beaches extend along the half-mile-wide, 7-mile long Samoa Peninsula, Humboldt Bay's western boundary. Stretches of it are spectacular, particularly the dunes, which are part of a 34-mile-long dune system – the largest in Northern California – and the wildlife viewing is excellent. The shoreline road (Hwy 255) is a backdoor route between Arcata and Eureka.

At the peninsula's south end, **Samoa Dunes Recreation Area** (⊙ sunrise-sunset) is good for picnicking and fishing. For wildlife, head to **Mad River Slough & Dunes**; from Arcata, take Samoa Blvd west for 3 miles, then turn right at Young St, the Manila turnoff. Park at the community center lot, from where a trail passes mudflats, salt marsh and tidal channels. There are over 200 species of birds: migrating waterfowl in spring and fall, songbirds in spring and summer, shorebirds in fall and winter, and waders year-round.

These undisturbed dunes reach heights of over 80ft. Because of the environment's fragility, access is by guided tour only. **Friends of the Dunes** (www.friendsofthedunes.org) leads free guided walks; register via email through the website and check online for departure locations and information.

The lunch place on the peninsula is the **Samoa Cookhouse** (☑ 707-442-1659; www.samoacookhouse.net; 908 Vance Ave; breakfast $12, lunch $13, dinner $16; ⊙ 7am-3pm & 5-8pm; ⎙), the last surviving lumber camp cookhouse in the West, where you can shovel down all-you-can-eat meals at long red-checkered tables. Kids eat for half-price. The cookhouse is five minutes northwest of Eureka, across the Samoa Bridge; follow the signs. From Arcata, take Samoa Blvd (Hwy 255).

Arcata

The North Coast's most progressive town, Arcata surrounds a tidy central square that fills with college students, campers, transients and tourists. Sure, it occasionally reeks of patchouli and its politics lean far left, but its earnest embrace of sustainability has fostered some of the most progressive civic action in America. Here, garbage trucks run on biodiesel, recycling gets picked up by tandem bicycle, wastewater gets filtered clean in marshlands and almost every street has a bike lane.

Founded in 1850 as a base for lumber camps, today Arcata is defined as a magnet for 20-somethings looking to expand their minds: either at Humboldt State University (HSU), and/or on the highly potent marijuana which grows around here like, um, weeds. After a 1996 state proposition legalized marijuana for medical purposes, Arcata became what one *New Yorker* article referred to as the 'heartland of high grade marijuana.' The economy of the regions has become inexorably tied to the crop since.

Roads run on a grid, with numbered streets traveling east–west and lettered streets going north–south. G and H Sts run north and south (respectively) to HSU and Hwy 101. The plaza is bordered by G and H and 8th and 9th Sts.

⦿ Sights

Around Arcata Plaza are two National Historic Landmarks: the 1857 Jacoby's Storehouse (cnr H & 8th Sts) and the 1915 Hotel Arcata (cnr G & 9th Sts). Another great historic building is the 1914 Minor Theatre (1013 10th St), which some local historians claim is the oldest theater in the US built specifically for showing films.

Humboldt State University UNIVERSITY
(HSU; www.humboldt.edu; 1 Harpst St) The University on the northeastern side of town holds the Campus Center for Appropriate Technology (CCAT), a world leader in developing sustainable technologies; on Fridays at 2pm you can take a self-guided tour of the CCAT House, a converted residence that uses only 4% of the energy of a comparably sized dwelling.

Arcata Marsh & Wildlife Sanctuary WILDLIFE RESERVE
On the shores of Humboldt Bay, this has 5 miles of walking trails and outstanding birding. The Redwood Region Audubon Society (✆826 7031; www.rras.org; donation welcome) offers guided walks Saturdays at 8:30am, rain or shine, from the parking lot at I St's south end. Friends of Arcata Marsh offer guided tours Saturdays at 2pm from the Arcata Marsh Interpretive Center (✆707-826-2359; 569 South G St; tours free; ☻9am-5pm).

🏃 Activities

Finnish Country Sauna & Tubs DAY SPA, MASSAGE
(✆707-822-2228; http://cafemokkaarcata.com; cnr 5th & J Sts; 30min per adult/child $9.50/2; ☻noon-11pm Sun-Thu, to 1am Fri & Sat) Like some kind of Euro-crunchy bohemian dream, these private, open-air redwood hot tubs (half-hour/hour $9/17) and sauna are situated around a small frog pond. The staff is easygoing, and the facility is relaxing, simple and clean. Reserve ahead, especially on weekends.

HSU Center Activities OUTDOORS
(www.humboldt.edu/centeractivities) An office on the 2nd floor of the University Center, beside the campus clock tower, sponsors myriad workshops, outings and sporting-gear rentals; nonstudents welcome.

Arcata Community Pool SWIMMING
(ww.arcatapool.com; 1150 16th St; adult/child $7/4.50; ☻5:30am-9pm Mon-Fri, 9am-6pm Sat, 1-4pm Sun; ♿) Has a co-ed hot tub, sauna and exercise room.

Adventure's Edge OUTDOORS
(www.adventuresedge.com; 650 10th St; ☻9am-6pm Mon-Sat, 10am-5pm Sun) Rents, sells and services outdoor equipment.

🎉 Festivals & Events

Kinetic Grand Championship RACE
(www.kineticgrandchampionship.com) Arcata's most famous event is held Memorial Day weekend: people on amazing self-propelled contraptions travel 38 miles from Arcata to Ferndale.

Arcata Bay Oyster Festival FOOD
(www.oysterfestival.net) A magical celebration of oysters and beer happens in June.

North Country Fair FAIR
(www.sameoldpeopl.org) A fun September street fair, where bands with names like the Fickle Hillbillies jam.

🛌 Sleeping

Arcata has affordable but limited lodgings. A cluster of hotels – Comfort Inn, Hampton Inn, etc – is just north of town, off Hwy 101's Giuntoli Lane. There's cheap camping further north at Clam Beach.

Fairwinds Motel MOTEL $
(✆707-822-4824; www.fairwindsmotelarcata.com; 1674 G St; s $70-75, d $80-90; ☜) Serviceable rooms in a standard-issue motel, with some noise from Hwy 101. It's more expensive than the chain motels but has the advantage of being in town.

Hotel Arcata HISTORIC HOTEL $$
(✆707-826-0217; www.hotelarcata.com; 708 9th St; r $89-156; ☜) Anchoring the plaza, this renovated 1915 brick landmark has friendly staff, high ceilings and comfortable, old-world rooms of mixed quality. The rooms in front are an excellent perch for people-watching on the square, but the quietest face the back.

Lady Anne Inn
B&B $$

(☎707-822-2797; www.ladyanneinn.com; 902 14th St; r $115-140) Roses line the walkway to this 1888 mansion full of Victorian bric-a-brac. The frilly rooms are pretty, but there's no breakfast.

Arcata Stay
VACATION RENTALS $$

(☎877-822-0935, 707-822-0935; www.arcatastay.com; apt from $169) A network of excellent apartment and cottage rentals. There is a two-night minimum and prices go down the longer you stay.

✗ Eating

Great food abounds in restaurants throughout Arcata, almost all casual.

There are fantastic **farmers markets** at the **Arcata Plaza** (⊘9am-2pm Sat Apr-Nov) and in the parking lot of Wildberries Market. Just a few blocks north of downtown, there is a cluster of the town's best restaurants on G St.

Wildberries Marketplace
MARKET, DELI $

(www.wildberries.com; 747 13th St, Arcata; sandwiches $4-10; ⊘6am-midnight; 🖉) Wildberries Marketplace is Arcata's best grocery, with natural foods, a good deli, bakery and juice bar.

North Coast Co-op
GROCERIES $

(cnr 8th & I Sts; ⊘6am-9pm) The gigantic North Coast Co-op carries organic foods and is a community staple; check the kiosk out front.

Japhy's Soup & Noodles
NOODLES $

(1563 G St; mains $5-9; ⊘11:30am-8pm Mon-Fri) Big salads, tasty coconut curry, cold noodle salads and homemade soups – and cheap!

Stars Hamburgers
BURGERS $

(1535 G St; burgers $3-6; ⊘11am-8pm Mon-Thu, to 9pm Fri, to 7pm Sat, noon-6pm Sun; 🖬) Uses grass-fed beef to make fantastic burgers.

Los Bagels
BAGELS $

(1061 I St; bagels from $3.75; ⊘6:30am-5pm Mon-Fri, 7am-5pm Sat, 7am-3pm Sun) Mixing 'traditional Jewish food with the taste of Mexico.' Get all kinds of creative spreads and toppings on fresh bagels. Locals swear the Swedish dill sauce served here (from Trinidad's Larrapin Restaurant) is one of the best things on earth.

Don's Donuts
FAST FOOD $

(933 H St; donuts 80¢-$1.35, sandwiches from $6; ⊘24hr) Tasty Southeast Asian sandwiches and doughnuts, even at 3am.

Arcata Scoop
ICE CREAM $

(1068 I St; cones from $3.50; ⊘12-10:30pm) Creamy and wonderful flavors inspired by seasonal ingredients. Try the honey vanilla lavender. These are the same folks who run the ever-popular Fairfax Scoop in Marin County, California.

★ 3 Foods Cafe
FUSION $$

(www.cafeattheendoftheuniverse.com; 835 J St; dishes $4-14; ⊘5:30am-10pm Tue-Thu, to 11pm Fri & Sat, to 9pm Sun; 🖉) A perfect fit with the Arcata dining scene: whimsical, creative, worldly small plates (think Thai-style tacos or buttermilk fried chicken) at moderate prices (a prix fixe is sometimes available for $20). The lavender-infused cocktails start things off on the right foot. The 'uber' mac and cheese is the crowd favorite.

Wildflower Cafe & Bakery
CAFE $$

(☎707-822-0360; 1604 G St; breakfast & lunch $5-8, dinner mains $15-16; ⊘8am-8pm Sun-Wed; 🖉) Tops for vegetarians, this tiny storefront serves fab frittatas, pancakes and curries, and big crunchy salads.

Machine Works
CALIFORNIAN $$

(937 10th St; mains $10-20; ⊘5-10pm Mon-Sun, 10am-2pm Sat & Sun) Inside the Robert Goodman Winery, this place gets raves from locals for its brunch (think: crab Benedict or

---

DON'T LEGALIZE IT: ECONOMICS OF HUMBOLDT HERB

With an estimated one-fifth of Humboldt County's population farming its world-famous weed, a good chunk of the economy here has run, for decades, as bank-less, tax-evading and cash only – but it's also been prosperous enough to strongly support many local businesses. Back in the 1990s farmers could expect to get around $6000 a pound for their crops but since medical marijauna has become legal the price has dropped radically, to just above $1000 per pound. So what happens if pot is legalized as it's expected to by 2016? Prices may plummet even further and everything from local restaurants to clothing stores will suffer for it. So yeah, those 'Save Humboldt County Keep Pot Illegal' bumper stickers you may see around town, are serious.

eggs baked in chèvre mousse) and dinner fare from a killer French onion soup to burgers and hoisin-braised short ribs. It's also a fab spot for creative cocktails.

Folie Douce MODERN AMERICAN **$$$**
(☑707-822-1042; www.foliedoucearcata.com; 1551 G St; dinner mains $24-37; ☺5:30-9pm Tue-Thu, to 10pm Fri & Sat; ☑) ☑ Just a slip of a place, but with an enormous reputation. The short but inventive menu features seasonally inspired bistro cooking, from Asian to Mediterranean, with an emphasis on local organics. Wood-fired pizzas ($16 to $22) are renowned. Sunday brunch, too. Reservations essential.

🍷 Drinking & Nightlife

Dive bars and cocktail lounges line the plaza's northern side. Arcata is awash in coffeehouses and brewpubs.

★ Six Rivers Brewery BREWERY
(www.sixriversbrewery.com; 1300 Central Ave, McKinleyville; ☺11:30am-midnight Tue-Sun, from 4pm Mon) One of the first female-owned breweries in California, the 'brew with a view' kills it in every category: great beer, amazing community vibe, occasional live music and delicious hot wings. The spicy chili-pepper ale is amazing. At first glance the menu might seem like ho-hum pub grub (mains $11 to $18), but portions are fresh and huge. They also make a helluva pizza.

Redwood Curtain Brewery BREWERY
(550 S G St, suite 6; ☺3-11pm Mon-Fri, 12-11pm Sat & Sun) A newer brewery (started in 2010), this tiny gem has a varied collection of rave-worthy craft ales and live music most Thursdays and Saturdays. Plus they offer free wheat thins and goldfish crackers to munch on.

Humboldt Brews BAR
(www.humbrews.com; 856 10th St) This popular beer house has been elegantly remodeled and has a huge selection of carefully selected beer taps, fish tacos and buffalo wings (pub grub $5 to $10). Live music nightly.

Cafe Mokka CAFE
(www.cafemokkaarcata.com; cnr 5th & J Sts) Bohos head to this cafe at Finnish Country Sauna & Tubs (p260) for a mellow, old-world vibe, good coffee drinks and homemade cookies (snacks $4).

☆ Entertainment

Arcata Theatre CINEMA
(www.arcatatheater.com; 1036 G St) An exquisite remodeling has revived this classic movie house, which shows art films, rock documentaries, silent films and more. Serves beer.

Center Arts PERFORMING ARTS
(☑tickets 707-826-3928; www.humboldt.edu/centerarts) Hosts events on campus and you'd be amazed at who shows up: from Diana Krall and Dave Brubeck to Ani DiFranco. The place to buy tickets is at the University Ticket Office in the HSU Bookstore on the 3rd floor of the University Center.

🛍 Shopping

Tin Can Mailman BOOKS
(www.tincanbooks.com; 1000 H St) Used volumes on two floors; excellent for hard-to-find books.

ℹ Information

Arcata Eye (www.arcataeye.com) Free newspaper listing local events; the 'Police Log' column is hysterical.

Bureau of Land Management (BLM; ☑707-825-2300; 1695 Heindon Rd) Has information on the Lost Coast.

California Welcome Center (☑707-822-3619; www.arcatachamber.com; ☺9am-5pm) At the junction of Hwys 299 and 101 is a California Welcome Center, with area info.

ℹ Getting There & Around

United (www.united.com) makes regional connections (which are predictably expensive) to the Arcata/Eureka Airport.

Greyhound (www.greyhound.com) serves Arcata; from San Francisco budget $57 and seven hours. **Redwood Transit buses** (www.hta.org) serve Arcata and Eureka on the Trinidad–Scotia routes ($3, 2½ hours), which don't run on Sunday.

Arcata city buses (☑707-822-3775; ☺Mon-Sat) stop at the **Arcata Transit Center** (☑707-825-8934; 925 E St at 9th St). For shared rides, read the bulletin board at the North Coast Co-op (p261).

Revolution Bicycle (www.revolutionbicycle.com; 1360 G St) and **Life Cycle Bike Shop** (www.lifecyclearcata.com; 1593 G St; ☺Mon-Sat) rent, service and sell bicycles.

Only in Arcata: borrow a bike from **Library Bike** (www.arcata.com/greenbikes; 865 8th St) for a $20 deposit, which gets refunded when you return the bike – up to six months later! They're beaters, but they ride.

NORTHERN REDWOOD COAST

Congratulations, traveler, you've reached the middle of nowhere, or at least the top of the middle of nowhere. Here, the trees are so large that the tiny towns along the road seem even smaller. The scenery is pure drama: cliffs and rocks, native lore, legendary salmon runs, mammoth trees, redneck towns and RVing retirees. It's certainly the *weirdest* part of the California Coast. Leave time to dawdle and bask in the haunting grandeur of it all and, even though there are scores of mid-century motels, you simply must make an effort to sleep outdoors if possible.

Trinidad

Cheery, tiny Trinidad perches prettily on the side of the ocean, combining upscale homes with a mellow surfer vibe. Somehow it feels a bit off-the-beaten-path even though tourism augments fishing to keep the economy going. Trinidad gained its name when Spanish sea captains arrived on Trinity Sunday in 1775 and named the area La Santisima Trinidad (the Holy Trinity). It didn't boom, though, until the 1850s, when it became an important port for miners.

◉ Sights & Activities

Trinidad is small: approach via Hwy 101 or from the north via Patrick's Point Dr (which becomes Scenic Dr further south). To reach town, take Main St.

The free town map at the information kiosk (p265) shows several fantastic hiking trails, most notably the **Trinidad Head Trail** with superb coastal views; excellent for whale-watching (December to April). Stroll along an exceptionally beautiful cove at **Trinidad State Beach**; take Main St and bear right at Stagecoach, then take the second turn left (the first is a picnic area) into the small lot.

Scenic Dr twists south along coastal bluffs, passing tiny coves with views back toward the bay. It peters out before reaching the broad expanses of **Luffenholtz Beach** (accessible via the staircase) and serene white-sand **Moonstone Beach**. Exit Hwy 101 at 6th Ave/Westhaven to get there. Further south Moonstone becomes **Clam Beach County Park**.

Surfing is good year-round, but potentially dangerous: unless you know how to judge conditions and get yourself out of trouble – there are no lifeguards here – surf in better-protected Crescent City.

HSU Telonicher Marine Laboratory   AQUARIUM

(☑707-826-3671; www.humboldt.edu/marinelab; 570 Ewing St; self-guided tours $1; ⊙9am-4:30pm Mon-Fri, 10am-5pm Sat & Sun mid-Sep–mid-May; ⓓ) Near Edwards St, this marine lab has a touch tank, several aquariums (look for the giant Pacific octopus), an enormous whale jaw and a cool 3D map of the ocean floor. You can also join a naturalist on **tidepooling expeditions** (90 minutes, $3). All tours are by appointment only so call ahead and be sure to ask about conditions.

🛏 Sleeping

Many of the inns line Patrick's Point Dr, north of town. **Trinidad Retreats** (www.trinidadretreats.com) and **Redwood Coast Vacation Rentals** (www.redwoodcoastvacationrentals.com) handle local property rentals.

Clam Beach   CAMPGROUND $

(tent sites per car $15) South of town off Hwy 101, this beach has excellent camping, but can get very crowded and it's a favorite with traveling homeless folks. Pitch your tent in the dunes (look for natural windbreaks). Facilities include pit toilets, cold water, picnic tables and fire rings.

View Crest Lodge   LODGE $$

(☑707-677-3393; www.viewcrestlodge.com; 3415 Patrick's Point Dr; sites $27, 1-bedroom cottages $95-240; ��) On a hill above the ocean on the inland side, some of the well-maintained, modern and terrific-value cottages have views and Jacuzzis; most have kitchens. There's also a good campground.

Trinidad Inn   INN $$

(☑707-677-3349; www.trinidadinn.com; 1170 Patrick's Point Dr; r $75-195; ⓦⓩ) Sparklingly clean and attractively decorated rooms (many with kitchens) fill this upmarket, gray-shingled motel under tall trees. Most rooms have fully equipped kitchens.

★ Trinidad Bay B&B   B&B $$$

(☑707-677-0840; www.trinidadbaybnb.com; 560 Edwards St; r incl breakfast $200-300; ⓦ) Opposite the lighthouse, this gorgeous light-filled Cape Cod–style place overlooks the harbor

Northern Redwood Coast

0 ——— 10 km
0 ——— 5 miles

Oregon
California

Pelican State Beach
Smith River
Smith River National Recreation Area
Tolowa Dunes State Park
Six Rivers National Forest Headquarters
Partick Creek Lodge (3.5mi)
Lake Earl Wildlife Area
Gasquet
Lake Tolowa
Lake Earl
Ruby Van Deventer
Simpson-Reed Grove
Crescent City
Hiouchi
Jedediah Smith Redwoods State Park
Stout Grove
Battery Point Lighthouse
Crescent Beach
Crescent Beach Overlook
Mill Creek Campground
Enderts Beach
Del Norte Coast Redwoods State Park
South Fork Rd
False Klamath Cove
Hidden Beach
Trees of Mystery
Turwar Ck
Klamath River Overlook
Historic Requa Inn
Klamath
Flint Ridge
PACIFIC OCEAN
Six Rivers National Forest
Klamath Glen
Newton B Drury Scenic Parkway
Yurok Indian Reservation
Prairie Creek Redwoods State Park
Fern Canyon
Klamath River
Gold Bluffs Beach
Big Tree
Elk Prairie
Prairie Creek Visitors Center
Davison Rd
Lady Bird Johnson Grove
Thomas H Kuchel Visitor Center
Orick
Redwood Creek Trail
Stone Lagoon
Stone Lagoon Boat-in
Dry Lagoon
Redwood Creek Overlook
Humboldt Lagoons State Park
Tall Trees Grove
Big Lagoon
Bald Hills Rd
Redwood National Park
Partick's Point State Park
Trinidad State Beach
Trinidad
Trinidad Head
Clam Beach
Redwood Creek

Hwy 299 (10mi);
Arcata (12mi);
Eureka (18mi)

and Trinidad Head. Breakfast is delivered to your uniquely styled room and in the afternoon the house fills with the scent of freshly baked cookies. The Trinity Alps room has a kitchenette and is well-set up for families.

Lost Whale Inn
B&B $$$

(707-677-3425; www.lostwhaleinn.com; 3452 Patrick's Point Dr; r incl breakfast $199-325, ste $408-750;) Perched atop a grassy cliff, high above crashing waves and braying sea lions, this spacious, modern, light-filled B&B has jaw-dropping views out to the sea. The lovely gardens have a 24-hour hot tub. Kids under seven are not permitted.

Turtle Rocks Oceanfront Inn
B&B $$$

(707-677-3707; www.turtlerocksinn.com; 3392 Patrick's Point Dr; r incl breakfast $195-335) Enjoy truly stunning sea vistas from every room at this plush, modern place on three peaceful, windswept acres.

Eating & Drinking

Lighthouse Café
FAST FOOD $

(707-677-0390; 355 Main St; mains $6-9; 11am-7pm Tue-Sun;) Across from the Chevron, this fun little arty joint makes good food fast, using mostly organic ingredients – try the creative soups, fish and chips with hand-cut fries, local grass-fed beef burgers and homemade ice creams. Order at the counter and then sit inside or out.

Katy's Smokehouse & Fishmarket
SEAFOOD $

(www.katyssmokehouse.com; 740 Edwards St; 9am-6pm) Makes its own chemical-free and amazingly delicious smoked and canned fish, using line-caught sushi-grade seafood. There's no restaurant, just grab some for a picnic.

The Seascape
SEAFOOD $$

(1 Bay St; mains $12-35; 7am-8:30pm) Go to this old-school, diner-type place for a panoramic view of the sea more than the food. It's a lovely spot to watch the daily catch come in over a slice of pie or a bowl of yummy clam chowder.

Larrupin Cafe
CALIFORNIAN $$$

(707-677-0230; www.larrupin.com; 1658 Patrick's Point Dr; mains $20-37; 5-9pm) Everybody loves Larrupin, where Moroccan rugs, chocolate-brown walls, gravity-defying floral arrangements and deep-burgundy Oriental carpets create a moody atmosphere perfect for a lovers' tryst. On the menu expect consistently good mesquite-grilled seafood and

NORTH COAST & REDWOODS TRINIDAD

meats – the smoked beef brisket is amazing. In the summer book a table on the garden patio for live music Wednesday and Friday nights.

Moonstone Grill SEAFOOD $$$
(Moonstone Beach; mains $20-90; ⊘5:30-8:30pm Wed-Sun) Enjoy drop-dead sunset views over a picture-perfect beach while supping on the likes of oysters on the half-shell, Pacific wild king salmon or spice-rubbed rib eye. If the high price tag is a bit out-of-budget, drop in for a glass of wine.

Beachcomber Café CAFE
(☑707-677-0106; 363 Trinity St; ⊘7am-4pm Mon-Fri, 8am-4pm Sat & Sun) Head here for the best homemade cookies and to meet locals. Bring your own cup if you want a drink to go. Friday rocks live music and beer's on tap.

❶ Information

Information Kiosk (cnr Patrick's Point Dr & Main St) Just west of the freeway. The pamphlet *Discover Trinidad* has an excellent map.

Trinidad Chamber of Commerce (☑707-667-1610; www.trinidadcalif.com) Information on the web, but no visitor center.

Patrick's Point State Park

Coastal bluffs jut out to sea at 640-acre **Patrick's Point** (☑707-677-3570; www.parks.ca.gov; 4150 Patrick's Point Dr; per car $8), where sandy beaches abut rocky headlands. Five miles north of Trinidad, with supereasy access to dramatic coastal bluffs, it's a best-bet for families. Stroll scenic overlooks, climb giant rock formations, watch whales breach, gaze into tidepools, or listen to barking sea lions and singing birds from this manicured park.

Sumêg (⊘daily) **FREE** is an authentic reproduction of a Yurok village, with hand-hewn redwood buildings where Native Americans gather for traditional ceremonies. In the native plant garden you'll find species for making traditional baskets and medicines.

On **Agate Beach** look for stray bits of jade and sea-polished agate. Follow the signs to tidepools, but tread lightly and obey regulations. The 2-mile **Rim Trail**, a old Yurok trail around the bluffs, circles the point with access to huge rocky outcroppings. Don't miss **Wedding Rock**, one of the park's most romantic spots. Other trails lead around unusual formations like **Ceremonial Rock** and **Lookout Rock**.

The park's three well-tended **campgrounds** (☑reservations 800-444-7275; www.reserveamerica.com; tent & RV sites $35) have coin-operated hot showers and very clean bathrooms. Penn Creek and Abalone campgrounds are more sheltered than Agate Beach.

Humboldt Lagoons State Park

Stretching out for miles along the coast, Humboldt Lagoons has long, sandy beaches and a string of coastal lagoons. **Big Lagoon** and the even prettier **Stone Lagoon** are both excellent for kayaking and bird-watching. Sunsets are spectacular, with no artificial structures in sight. Picnic at Stone Lagoon's north end. The Stone Lagoon Visitor Center, on Hwy 101, has closed due to staffing shortages, but there's a toilet and a bulletin board displaying information.

A mile north, **Freshwater Lagoon** is also great for birding. South of Stone Lagoon, tiny **Dry Lagoon** (a freshwater marsh) has a fantastic day hike and good agate hunting. Park at Dry Lagoon's picnic area and hike north on the unmarked trail to Stone Lagoon; the trail skirts the southwestern shore and ends up at the ocean, passing through woods and marshland rich with wildlife. Mostly flat, it's about 2.5 miles one way – and nobody takes it because it's unmarked.

All campsites are first-come, first-served. The park runs two **environmental campgrounds** (tent sites $20; ⊘Apr-Oct); bring water. Stone Lagoon has six boat-in environmental campsites. Check in at Patrick's Point State Park, at least 30 minutes before sunset.

Humboldt County Parks (☑707-445-7651; tent sites $20) operates a lovely cypress-grove picnic area and campground beside Big Lagoon, a mile off Hwy 101, with flush toilets and cold water, but no showers.

Redwood National & State Parks

A patchwork of public lands jointly administered by the state and federal governments, the Redwood National & State Parks include Redwood National Park, Prairie Creek Redwoods State Park, Del Norte Coast Redwoods State Park and Jedediah Smith Redwoods State Park. A smattering

THE ENDANGERED MARBLED MURRELET: KEEPER OF THE FORESTS

Notice how undeveloped the Redwood National & State Parks have remained? Thank the marbled murrelet, a small white and brown-black auk that nests in old-growth conifers. Loss of nesting territory due to logging has severly depleted the bird's numbers but Redwood National Park scientists have discovered that corvid predators (ravens, jays etc) are also to blame. Because corvids are attracted to food scraps left by visitors, the number of snacking, picnicking or camping humans in the park greatly affects predation on the marbled murrelet. Restrictions on development to prevent food scraps and thus protect the birds are so strict that it's nearly impossible to build anything new.

of small towns break up the forested area, making it a bit confusing to get a sense of the parks as a whole. Prairie Creek and Jedediah Smith parks were originally land slated for clear-cutting, but in the '60s activists successfully protected them and today all these parks are an International Biosphere Reserve and World Heritage Site. At one time the national park was to absorb at least two of the state parks, but that did not happen, and so the cooperative structure remains.

Little-visited compared to their southern brethren, the world's tallest living trees have been standing here for time immemorial, predating the Roman Empire by over 500 years. Prepare to be impressed.

The small town of **Orick** (population 650), at the southern tip of the park, in a lush valley, is barely more than a few storefronts, the only gas station between Trinidad and Klamath, and a vast conglomeration of woodcarving.

Redwood National Park

Just north of the southern visitor center, turn east onto Bald Hills Rd and travel 2 miles to **Lady Bird Johnson Grove**, one of the park's most spectacular groves, and also one of the busiest, accessible via a gentle 1-mile loop trail. Continue for another 5 miles up Bald Hills Rd to **Redwood Creek**

Overlook. On the top of the ridgeline, at 2100ft, get views over the forest and the entire watershed – provided it's not foggy. Just past the overlook lies the gated turnoff for **Tall Trees Grove**, the location of several of the world's tallest trees. Rangers issue 50 vehicle permits. Pick one up, along with the gate-lock combination, from the visitor centers. Allow four hours for the round-trip, which includes a 6-mile drive down a rough dirt road (speed limit 15mph) and a steep 1.3-mile one-way hike, which descends 800ft to the grove.

Several longer trails include the awe-inspiring **Redwood Creek Trail**, which also reaches Tall Trees Grove. You'll need a free backcountry permit to hike and camp (highly recommended, as the best backcountry camping on the North Coast), but the area is most accessible from Memorial Day to Labor Day, when summer footbridges are up. Otherwise, getting across the creek can be perilous or impossible.

For hikes, kayaking, fishing or a slew of other tours, book with **Redwood Adventures** (☑ 866-733-9637; www.redwoodadventures.com; 7 Valley Green Camp Rd, Orick) whose guides know the area better than anyone and will get you to places you may not otherwise find on your own. For horseback riding from May to November call the **Redwood Creek Bukarettes** (☑ 707-499-2943; www.redwoodcreekbukarettes.com; 1000 Drydens Rd, Orick; 1½hr trail rides from $60).

🛏 Sleeping

Elk Meadow Cabins   CABINS $$$
(☑ 866-733-9637; www.redwoodadventures.com; 7 Valley Green Camp Rd, Orick; cabins $179-279; 🛜🐾) These spotless and bright cabins with equipped kitchens and all the mod-cons are in a perfect mid-parks location – they're great if you're traveling in a group and the most comfy choice even if you're not. Expect to see elk on the lawn in the mornings. Cabins sleep six to eight people and there's an additional $45 cleaning fee.

❶ Information

Unlike most national parks, there are no fees and no highway entrance stations at Redwood National Park, so it's imperative to pick up the free map at the park headquarters in Crescent City (p271) or at the infomation center in Orick. Rangers here issue permits to visit Tall Trees Grove and loan bear-proof containers for backpackers.

For in-depth redwood ecology, buy the excellent official park handbook. The **Redwood Parks Association** (www.redwoodparksassociation.org) provides good information on its website, including detailed descriptions of all the parks hikes.

Redwood Information Center (Kuchel Visitor Center; ☑ 707-464-6101; www.nps.gov/redw; Hwy 101; ☺ 9am-6pm June-Aug, to 5pm Sep-Oct & Mar-May, to 4pm Nov-Feb) On Hwy 101, a mile south of tiny Orick.

Prairie Creek Redwoods State Park

Famous for some of the world's best virgin redwood groves and unspoiled coastline, this 14,000-acre section of Redwood National & State Parks has spectacular scenic drives and 70 miles of hiking trails, many of which are excellent for children. Pick up maps and information and sit by the river-rock fireplace at **Prairie Creek Visitor Center** (☑ 707-464-6101; ☺ 9am-5pm Mar-Oct, 10am-4pm Nov-Feb; ♿). Kids will love the taxidermy dioramas with push-button, light-up displays. Outside, elk roam grassy flats.

🏃 Activities

There are 28 mountain-biking and hiking trails through the park, from simple to strenuous. Only a few of these will appeal to hard-core hikers, who should take on the Del Norte Coast Redwoods State Park. Those tight on time or with mobility impairments should stop at **Big Tree**, an easy 100yd walk from the car park. Several other easy nature trails start near the visitor center, including **Revelation Trail** and **Elk Prairie Trail**. Stroll the recently reforested logging road on the **Ah-Pah Interpretive Trail** at the park's north end. The most challenging hike in this corner of the park is the truly spectacular 11.5-mile **Coastal Trail** which goes through primordial redwoods.

Just past the Gold Bluffs Beach Campground the road dead ends at **Fern Canyon**, the second busiest spot in the parks, where 60ft fern-covered sheer-rock walls can be seen from Steven Spielberg's *Jurassic Park 2: The Lost World*. This is one of the most photographed spots on the North Coast – damp and lush, all emerald green – and *totally* worth getting your toes wet to see.

Newton B Drury Scenic Parkway DRIVING
Just north of Orick is the turn off for the 8-mile parkway, which runs parallel to Hwy 101 through untouched ancient redwood forests. This is a not-to-miss short detour off the freeway where you can view the magnificence of these trees. Numerous trails branch off from roadside pullouts, including family-friendly options and trails that fit ADA (American Disabilities Act) requirements, including Big Tree and Revelation Trail.

🛌 Sleeping

Welcome to the great outdoors: without any motels or cabins, the only choice here is to pitch a tent in the campgrounds at the southern end of the park.

★**Gold Bluffs Beach** CAMPGROUND $
(tent sites $35) This gorgeous campground sits between 100ft cliffs and wide-open ocean, but there are some windbreaks and solar-heated showers. Look for sites up the cliff under the trees. No reservations.

Elk Prairie Campground CAMPGROUND $
(☑ reservations 800-444-7275; www.reserveamerica.com; tent & RV sites $35) Elk roam this popular campground, where you can sleep under redwoods or at the prairie's edge. There are hot showers, some hike-in sites and a shallow creek to splash in. Sites 1–7 and 69–76 are on grassy prairies and get full sun; sites 8–68 are wooded. To camp in a mixed redwood forest, book sites 20–27.

Del Norte Coast Redwoods State Park

Marked by steep canyons and dense woods north of Klamath, half the 6400 acres of this park (☑ 707-464-6101, ext 5120; per car day-use $8) are virgin redwood forest, crisscrossed by 15 miles of hiking trails. Even the most cynical of redwood-watchers can't help but be moved.

Pick up maps and inquire about guided walks at the Redwood National & State Parks Headquarters (p271) in Crescent City or the Redwood Information Center in Orick.

Hwy 1 winds in from the coast at rugged, dramatic **Wilson Beach**, and traverses the dense forest, with groves stretching off as far as you can see.

Picnic on the sand at **False Klamath Cove**. Heading north, tall trees cling precipitously to canyon walls that drop to the rocky, timber-strewn coastline, and it's almost impossible to get to the water, except via the

SMITH RIVER NATIONAL RECREATION AREA

West of Jedediah Smith Redwoods State Park, the Smith River, the state's last remaining undammed waterway, runs right beside Hwy 199. Originating high in the Siskiyou Mountains, its serpentine course cuts through deep canyons beneath thick forests. Chinook salmon (October to December) and steelhead trout (December to April) annually migrate up its clear waters. Camp (there are four developed campgrounds), hike (75 miles of trails), raft (145 miles of navigable white water) and kayak here, but check regulations if you want to fish. Stop by the **Six Rivers National Forest Headquarters** (☑707-457-3131; www.fs.fed.us/r5/sixrivers; 10600 Hwy 199, Gasquet; ☺8am-4:30pm daily May-Sep, Mon-Fri Oct-Apr) to get your bearings. Pick up pamphlets for the **Darlingtonia Trail** and **Myrtle Creek Botanical Area**, both easy jaunts into the woods, where you can see rare plants and learn about the area's geology.

gorgeous but steep **Damnation Creek Trail** or **Footsteps Rock Trail**.

Between these two, serious hikers will be most greatly rewarded by the Damnation Creek Trail. It's only 4 miles long, but the 1100-ft elevation change and cliff-side redwood makes it the park's best hike. The unmarked trailhead starts from a parking area off Hwy 101 at Mile 16.

Crescent Beach Overlook and picnic area has superb wintertime whale-watching. At the park's north end, watch the surf pound at **Crescent Beach**, just south of Crescent City via Enderts Beach Rd.

Mill Creek Campground (☑800-444-7275; www.reserveamerica.com; tent & RV sites $35) has hot showers and 145 sites in a redwood grove, 2 miles east of Hwy 101 and 7 miles south of Crescent City. Sites 1-74 are woodsier; sites 75-145 sunnier. Hike-in sites are prettiest.

Jedediah Smith Redwoods State Park

The northernmost park in the system of Redwood National & State Parks, the dense stands at **Jedediah Smith** (☑707-464-6101, ext 5112; day use $8) are 10 miles northeast of Crescent City (via Hwy 101 east to Hwy 197). The redwood stands are so thick that few trails penetrate the park, but the outstanding 11-mile **Howland Hill scenic drive** cuts through otherwise inaccessible areas (take Hwy 199 to South Fork Rd; turn right after crossing two bridges). It's a rough road, impassable for RVs, but if you can't hike, it's the best way to see the forest.

Stop for a stroll under enormous trees in **Simpson-Reed Grove**. If it's foggy at the coast it may be sunny here. There's a swimming hole and picnic area near the park entrance. An easy half-mile trail, departing from the far side of the campground, crosses the **Smith River** via a summer-only footbridge, leading to **Stout Grove**, the park's most famous grove. The **visitor center** (☑707-464-6101; ☺10am-4pm daily Jun-Aug, Sat & Sun Sep-Oct & Apr-May) sells hiking maps and nature guides. If you wade in the river, be careful in the spring when currents are swift and the water cold.

🛏 Sleeping

Campground   CAMPGROUND $
(☑reservations 800-444-7275; www.reserveamerica.com; tent & RV sites $35) The popular campground has gorgeous sites tucked through the redwoods beside the Smith River.

Hiouchi Motel   MOTEL $
(☑888-881-0819, 707-458-3041; www.hiouchimotel.com; 2097 Hwy 199; s $50, d $65-71; @🐾🤶) If you don't camp, try the renovated Hiouchi Motel offering clean, straightforward motel rooms.

Klamath

Giant metal-cast golden bears stand sentry at the bridge across the Klamath River announcing Klamath, one of the tiny settlements that break up Redwood National & State Parks between Prairie Creek Redwoods State Park and Del Norte Coast Redwoods State Park. With a gas station/market, diner and a casino, Klamath is basically a wide spot in the road with some seriously great roadside kitsch at its edges. The **Yurok Tribal Headquarters** is in the town center and the entire settlement and much of the surrounding area is the tribe's ancestral land. Klamath is roughly an hour north of Eureka.

⊙ Sights & Activities

The mouth of the **Klamath River** is a dramatic sight. Marine, riparian, forest and meadow ecological zones all converge and the **birding** is exceptional. For the best views, head north of town to Requa Rd and the **Klamath River Overlook** and picnic on high bluffs above driftwood-strewn beaches. On a clear day, this is one of the most spectacular viewpoints on the North Coast, and one of the best whale-watching spots in California (this is one of the mammal's first feeding stops as they come south from Alaska). For a good hike, head north along the **Coastal Trail**. You'll have the sand to yourself at **Hidden Beach**; access the trail at the northern end of Motel Trees.

Just south of the river, on Hwy 101, the scenic **Coastal Drive**, a narrow, winding country road traces extremely high cliffs over the ocean. Due to erosion a 3.3 mile section of the 9.5 mile loop (between Carruther's Cove trailhead and the intersection of the Coastal Drive with Alder Camp Rd) has been closed to motor traffic since 2011 but it's still walkable and bikeable. Though technically in Redwood National Park, this drive is much closer to Klamath.

Klamath Jet Boat Tours   BOAT TOURS
(www.jetboattours.com; 17635 US 101; 2hr tours adult/child $45/25) Book jet-boat excursions and fishing trips run by the Yukon Tribe.

🛏 Sleeping & Eating

Woodsy Klamath is cheaper than Crescent City, but there aren't as many places to eat or buy groceries, and there's nothing to do at night but play cards. There are ample private RV parks in the area.

Flint Ridge Campground   CAMPGROUND
(☎707-464-6101) **FREE** Four miles from the Klamath River Bridge via Coastal Drive, this tent-only, hike-in campground sits among a wild, overgrown meadow of ferns and moss. It's a 10-minute walk (half a mile) east, uphill from the parking area. There's no water, plenty of bear sightings (bear boxes on site) and you have to pack out trash. But, hey, it's free.

Ravenwood Motel   MOTEL $
(☎866-520-9875, 707-482-5911; www.ravenwoodmotel.com; 131 Klamath Blvd; r/ste with kitchen $75/125; ☎) The spotlessly clean rooms are better than anything in Crescent City and individually decorated with furnishings and flair you'd expect in a city hotel, not a small-town motel.

★**Historic Requa Inn**   HISTORIC HOTEL $$
(☎707-482-1425; www.requainn.com; 451 Requa Rd, Klamath; r $119-199; ☎) 🐾 A woodsy country lodge on bluffs overlooking the mouth of the Klamath, the creaky and bright 1914 Requa Inn is a North Coast favorite and – even better – it's a carbon-neutral facility. Many of the charming old-time-America–style rooms have mesmerizing views over the misty river, as does the dining room, which serves new Native American, organic cuisine.

Crescent City

Though Crescent City was founded as a thriving 1853 seaport and supply center for inland gold mines, the town's history was quite literally washed away in 1964, when half the town was swallowed by a tsunami. Of course, it was rebuilt (though mostly with the utilitarian ugliness of ticky-tacky buildings), but its marina was devastated by the 2011 Japan earthquake and tsunami, when the city was evacuated. Crescent City remains California's last big town north of Arcata, though the constant fog (and sounding fog horn) and damp, '60s sprawl makes it about as charming as a wet bag of dirty laundry. The economy depends heavily on shrimp and crab fishing, hotel tax and on Pelican Bay maximum-security prison, just

---

TREES OF MYSTERY

It's hard to miss the giant statues of Paul Bunyan and Babe the Blue Ox towering over the parking lot at **Trees of Mystery** (☎707-482-2251; www.treesofmystery.net; 15500 Hwy 101; adult/child & senior $14/7; ⊘8am-7pm Jun-Aug, 9am-4pm Sep-May; ♿), a shameless tourist trap with a gondola running through the redwood canopy and a fun 'Tall Tales Forest' where chainsaw sculptures tell the tale of Paul Bunyan. It's perfect for families, anyone unable to take a strenuous hike or lovers of kitsch. The surprisingly wonderful **End of the Trail Museum** located behind the Trees of Mystery gift shop has an outstanding collection of Native American arts and artifacts, and it's *free*.

north of town, which adds tension to the air and lots of cops to the streets.

Hwy 101 splits into two parallel one-way streets, with the southbound traffic on L St, northbound on M St. To see the major sights, turn west on Front St toward the lighthouse. Downtown is along 3rd St.

Sights & Activities

If you're in town in August, the **Del Norte County Fair** features a rodeo, and lots of characters. Jedediah Smith Redwoods State Park (p268) is 10 miles inland.

North Coast Marine Mammal Center   SCIENCE CENTER

(707-465-6265; www.northcoastmmc.org; 424 Howe Dr; admission by donation; 10am-5pm;) Just east of Battery Point, this is the ecologically minded foil to the garish Ocean World: the clinic treats injured seals, sea lions and dolphins and releases them back into the wild (donation requested).

Battery Point Lighthouse   LIGHTHOUSE

(707-467-3089; www.delnortehistory.org; adult/child $3/1; 10am-4pm Wed-Sun Apr-Oct) The 1856 lighthouse, at the south end of A St, still operates on a tiny, rocky island that you can easily reach at low tide. You can also get a tour of the on-site **museum** for $3. Note that the listed hours are subject to change due to tides and weather.

Beachfront Park   PARK

(Howe Dr;) Between B and H Sts, this park has a harborside beach with no large waves, making it perfect for little ones. Further east on Howe Dr, near J St, you'll come to **Kidtown**, with slides and swings and a make-believe castle.

Sleeping

Most people stop here for one night while traveling; motels are overpriced, but you'll pass a slew of hotels on the main arteries leading into and out of town. The county operates two excellent first-come, first-served campgrounds just outside of town.

★ Curly Redwood Lodge   MOTEL $

(707-464-2137; www.curlyredwoodlodge.com; 701 Hwy 101 S; r $56-98;) The Redwood Lodge is a marvel: it's entirely built and paneled from a single curly redwood tree which measured over 18in thick in diameter. Progressively restored and polished into a gem of mid-century kitsch, the inn is a delight

for retro junkies. Rooms are clean, large and comfortable (request one away from the road). For truly modern accommodations, look elsewhere.

Bay View Inn   HOTEL $

(800-742-8439; www.ccbvi.com; 2844 Fairfield; r $55-135;) Bright, modern, updated rooms with microwaves and refrigerators fill this centrally located independent hotel. It may seem a bit like a better-than-average highway exit chain, but colorful bedspreads and warm hosts add necessary homespun appeal. The rooms upstairs in the back have views of the lighthouse and the harbor.

Crescent Beach Motel   MOTEL $

(707-464-5436; www.crescentbeachmotel.com; 1455 Hwy 101 S; r $84-136;) Just south of town, this basic, old-fashioned motel is the only place in town to stay right on the beach, offering views that distract you from the somewhat plain indoor environs. Skip rooms without a view.

Florence Keller Park   CAMPGROUND $

(707-464-7230; http://www.co.del-norte.ca.us; 3400 Cunningham Lane; sites $10) County-run Florence Keller Park has 50 sites in a beautiful grove of young redwoods (take Hwy 101 north to Elk Valley Cross Rd and follow the signs).

Ruby Van Deventer Park   CAMPGROUND $

(4705 N Bank Rd; sites $15;) The county's Ruby Van Deventer Park has 18 sites along the Smith River, off Hwy 197.

Eating

Good Harvest Café   AMERICAN $

(575 Hwy 101 S; mains $7-14; 7am-9pm Mon-Sat, from 8am Sun;) This popular local cafe is in a spacious location across from the harbor. It's got a bit of everything – all pretty good – from soups and sandwiches to full meals and smoothies. Good beers, a crackling fire and loads of vegetarian options make this the best dining spot in town.

Tomasini's Enoteca   ITALIAN, AMERICAN $

(960 3rd St; mains $4-11; 7:30am-2pm;) Stop in for salads, sandwiches or jazz on weekend nights. Hands down the most happening place downtown.

Chart Room   SEAFOOD $$

(130 Anchor Way; dinner mains $10-28; 6:30am-7pm Sun-Thu, to 8pm Fri & Sat;) At the tip of the South Harbor pier, this joint is

renowned far and wide for its fish and chips: batter-caked golden beauties which deliver on their reputation. It's often a hive of families, retirees, Harley riders and local businessmen, so grab a beer at the small bar and wait for a table.

ℹ Information

Crescent City-Del Norte Chamber of Commerce (✆800-343-8300, 707-464-3174; www.northerncalifornia.net; 1001 Front St; ⊙9am-5pm May-Aug, Mon-Fri Sep-Apr) Local information.

Redwood National & State Parks Headquarters (✆707-464-6101; 1111 2nd St; ⊙9am-5pm Oct-May, to 6pm Jun-Sep) On the corner of K St; you'll find rangers here and information about all four parks under its jurisdiction.

ℹ Getting There & Around

United Express (✆800-241-6522) flies into tiny **Crescent City Airport** (CEC), north of town. **Redwood Coast Transit** (www.redwoodcoast-transit.org) serves Crescent City with local buses ($1), and runs buses Monday to Saturday to Klamath ($1.50, one hour, two daily) and Arcata ($30, two hours, two daily) with stops in between.

Tolowa Dunes State Park & Lake Earl Wildlife Area

Two miles north of Crescent City, this **state park and wildlife area** (✆707-464-6101, ext 5112; ⊙sunrise-sunset) encompasses 10,000 acres of wetlands, dunes, meadows and two lakes, **Lake Earl** and **Lake Tolowa**. This major stopover on the Pacific Flyway route brings over 250 species of birds here. Listen for the whistling, warbling chorus. On land, look for coyotes and deer, angle for trout, or hike or ride 20 miles of trails; at sea, spot whales, seals and sea lions.

The park and wildlife area are a patchwork of lands administered by California State Parks and the Department of Fish and Game (DFG). The DFG focuses on single-species management, hunting and fishing; the State Parks' focus is on ecodiversity and recreation. You might be hiking a vast expanse of pristine dunes, then suddenly hear a shotgun or a whining 4WD. Strict regulations limit where and when you can hunt and drive; trails are clearly marked.

Register for two primitive, nonreservable **campgrounds** (tent sites $20) at Jedediah Smith (p268) or Del Norte Coast Redwoods State Park (p267) campgrounds. The mosquitoes are plentiful in the spring and early summer.

Pelican State Beach

Never-crowded **Pelican State Beach** (✆707-464-6101, ext 5151) occupies five coastal acres on the Oregon border. There are no facilities, but it's great for kite flying; pick one up at the shop just over the border in Oregon.

🛏 Sleeping

Clifford Kamph Memorial Park CAMPGROUND $
(✆707-464-7230; 15100 Hwy 101; tent sites $10) Pitch a tent by the ocean (no windbreaks) at Clifford Kamph Memorial Park; no RVs. It's a steal for the beachside location and, even though sites are exposed in a grassy area and there isn't much privacy, all have BBQs.

Casa Rubio BOUTIQUE HOTEL $$
(✆707-487-4313; www.casarubio.com; 17285 Crissey Rd; r $98-178; 🐾🍴) The best reason to visit Pelican State Beach is to stay at secluded, charming Casa Rubio, where three of the four ocean-view rooms have kitchens.

Northern Mountains

Best Places to Eat

➜ Red Onion Grill (p284)

➜ Trinity Café (p293)

➜ Café Maddalena (p296)

➜ La Grange Café (p303)

➜ Pangaea Café & Pub (p287)

Best Places to Stay

➜ McCloud River Mercantile Hotel (p298)

➜ Houseboat on Shasta Lake (p278)

➜ Quincy Courtyard Suites (p286)

➜ Weaverville Hotel (p302)

➜ Feather River Canyon Campgrounds (p286)

Why Go?

'Hidden California' gets bandied around fairly casually, but here you have an entire corner of the state that does seem forgotten. The coast and foggy redwood groves are far away, so prepare yourself for something completely different: vast expanses of wilderness – some 24,000 protected acres – divided by rivers and streams, dotted with cobalt lakes, horse ranches and alpine peaks; further east is a stretch of shrubby, high desert cut with amber gorges, caves and dramatic light that is a photographer's dream. Much of it doesn't look the way people envision California – the topography more resembles the older mountains of the Rockies than the relatively young granite Yosemite. The towns are hospitable but tiny, with few comforts; come to get lost in vast remoteness. Even the two principal attractions, Mt Shasta and Lassen Volcanic National Park, remain uncrowded (and sometimes snow-covered) at the peak of the summer.

When to Go
Lassen Volcanic National Park

Jul–Sep Warm weather and snow-free passes are ideal for backcountry camping.

Oct–Nov & Apr–May Shoulder seasons; scattered showers and snow at the high elevations.

Nov–Jan Skiing Mt Shasta is the main draw. Prices drop outside ski areas.

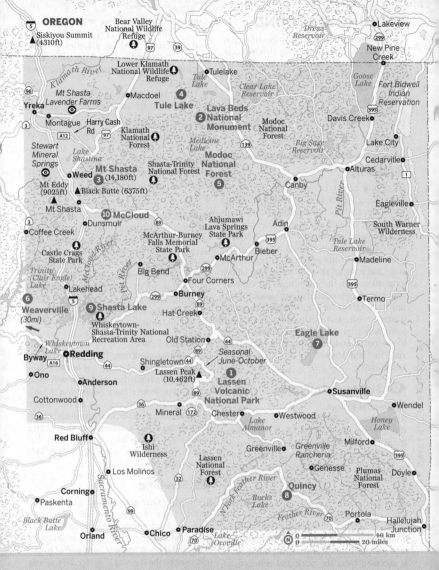

Northern Mountains Highlights

1 Gaping at geothermal spectacles in **Lassen Volcanic National Park** (p279).

2 Exploring the many caves of **Lava Beds National Monument** (p299).

3 Hiking and skiing **Mt Shasta** (p288).

4 Looking overhead at the bird superhighway at **Tule Lake** (p300).

5 Getting lost in **Modoc National Forest** (p300).

6 Hiding out in **Weaverville** and wading in the trout-filled water nearby (p302).

7 Camping along the shores of **Eagle Lake** (p285).

8 Chilling out in the mountain town of **Quincy** (p285).

9 Floating with a dozen pals on a **Shasta Lake houseboat** (p278).

10 Kicking up your heels at **McCloud's famous dance hall** (p298).

REDDING & AROUND

North of Red Bluff the dusty central corridor along I-5 starts to give way to panoramic mountain ranges on either side. Redding is the last major outpost before the small towns of the far north, and the surrounding lakes make for easy day trips or overnight camps. If you get off the highway – way off – this can be an exceptionally rewarding area of the state to explore.

Redding

Originally called Poverty Flats during the Gold Rush for its lack of wealth, Redding today has a whole lot of tasteless new money – malls, big-box stores and large housing developments surround its core. A tourist destination it is not, though it is the major gateway city to the northeast corner of the state and a useful spot for restocking before long jaunts into the wilderness. Recent constructions like the Sundial Bridge and Turtle Bay Exploration Park are enticing lures and worth a visit...but not a long one. Downtown is bordered by the Sacramento River to the north and east. Major thoroughfares are Pine and Market Sts and there's often lots of traffic.

◉ Sights & Activities

★ Sundial Bridge   BRIDGE
Resembling a beached cruise ship, the shimmering-white 2004 Sundial Bridge spans the river and is one of Redding's marquee attractions, providing an excellent photo op. The glass-deck pedestrian overpass connects the Turtle Bay Exploration Park to the north bank of the Sacramento River and was designed by renowned Spanish architect Santiago Calatrava.

The bridge/sundial attracts visitors from around the world who come to marvel at this unique feat of engineering artistry. It is accessed from the park and connects to the Sacramento River Trail system. The surrounding river scenery is beautiful.

Turtle Bay Exploration Park MUSEUM, GARDENS
(☑ 800-887-8532; www.turtlebay.org; 844 Sundial Bridge Dr; adult/child $14/10, after 3:30pm $9/5; ☺ 9am-5pm Mon-Sat & 10am-5pm Sun, closing 1hr earlier Oct-Mar; ♣) Situated on 300 meandering acres, this is an artistic, cultural and scientific center for visitors of all ages, with an emphasis on the Sacramento River watershed. The complex houses art and natural-science museums, with fun interactive exhibits for kids. There are also extensive arboretum gardens, a butterfly house and a 22,000-gallon, walk-through river aquarium full of regional aquatic life (yes, including turtles).

The on-site **Café at Turtle Bay** (meals $12) serves good coffee and decent light meals.

Cascade Theatre   HISTORIC BUILDING
(www.cascadetheatre.org; 1733 Market St) Try to catch some live music downtown at this refurbished 1935 art-deco theater. Usually it hosts second-tier national acts, but if nothing else, take a peek inside; this is a neon-lit gem.

Redding Trails   HIKING, CYCLING
Eighty miles of trails loop through parks, along rivers and up hills for strolling, hiking and mountain biking. Check out www.reddingtrails.com for maps or pick up the pamphlet at almost any hotel. The star is the Sacramento River Trail, which meanders along the river all the way to Shasta Dam. There are several access points, including the Sundial Bridge.

Waterworks Park   WATER PARK
(www.watersorkspark.com; 151 N Boulder Dr; day passes adult/child $20/16; ☺ late-May–Sep) Redding gets really hot, and although most hotels and motels have pools, you'll have more fun splashing around at this water park, including on the four-story-high, cliff-steep Avalanche, a simulated white-water river, giant waterslides, plus a 'Lazy Lagoon' and kiddie pool. Great for kids or kid-like adults.

🛏 Sleeping

Redding's many motels and hotels (most major chains are represented and many have small swimming pools) huddle around noisy thoroughfares. A couple of rows lie close to the I-5 at the southern end of town: just west of the freeway close to the Cypress Ave exit on Bechelli Lane, and on the east side of the freeway on Hilltop Dr. But aim for the ones on less-busy N Market St. The best tent camping is just up the road at Whiskeytown Lake or Shasta Lake.

Apples' Riverhouse B&B   B&B $$
(☑ 530-243-8440; www.applesriverhouse.com; 201 Mora Ct; r $99-115; 🖥) Just steps from the Sacramento River Trail, this modern, ranch-style home has three comfortable upstairs rooms, two with decks. It's a bit suburban, but it's

Redding

the best independent stay in Redding. In the evening the sociable hosts invite you for cheese and wine. Bikes are yours to borrow and the proximity to the trail is inviting.

Tiffany House B&B Inn　　　B&B $$

(☑530-244-3225; www.tiffanyhousebb.com; 1510 Barbara Rd; r $125-170; ☎☀) In a quiet cul-de-sac, a mile north of the river, this Victorian cottage has an expansive garden with sweeping views. Cozy rooms are packed with antiques, rosebuds and ruffles. Affable hosts make a big yummy to-do over breakfast.

✖ Eating & Drinking

If you want Redding's best food, it's essential that you get off the highway and into the downtown area.

Grilla Bites　　　SANDWICHES $

(www.grillabites.com; 1427 Market St; meals $5-11; ☉11am-8pm Mon-Thu, to 9pm Fri & Sat, to 4pm

Redding

◎ Top Sights
1 Sundial Bridge D2

◎ Sights
2 Cascade Theatre C3
3 Turtle Bay Exploration Park D2

▣ Sleeping
4 Apples' Riverhouse B&B A1

✖ Eating
Café at Turtle Bay .... (see 3)
5 Cafe Paradisio C3
6 Grilla Bites C3
7 Jack's Grill C3
8 Wilda's Grill B3

Sun; ☎☀) ✦ It doesn't get much simpler than this menu of grilled sandwiches and pay-by-the-pound salad bar, but the food is fresh, locally sourced and the sandwiches are punched up with fresh herbs and global fusions. The Thai Tuna is a local favorite. The restaurant was getting a full remodel when we passed.

Wilda's Grill
HOT DOGS, VEGETARIAN **$**

(1718 Placer St; mains $4.75-6; ⏲11am-4pm Mon-Fri; 🖉) The combo sounds weird but it works: Choose from big, excellent hot dogs with toppings from roasted garlic to homemade chili or blue cheese – or go vegetarian with falafal, breaded eggplant or the much-lauded Buddha Bowl, made from rice, veggies and yummy, spicy sauces. Expect a line at peak hours.

Cafe Paradisio
MEDITERRANEAN **$$**

(🖉530-215-3499; 1270 Yuba St; lunch mains $6-10, dinner $8-25; ⏲11am-2pm Mon-Sat, 5-10pm Mon-Wed, 5pm-1am Thu-Sat; 🖉) Take Mediterranean food and give it a bit of Asian flair and you have the comforting fare of this casual and friendly little nook. Start with the baked brie platter then continue with salmon with coconut curry or three-cheese lasagne. The portions are huge and there are lots of vegetarian choices.

Moonstone Bistro
CALIFORNIAN **$$$**

(www.moonstonebistro.com; 3425 Placer St; lunch mains $13-18, dinner $24-36; ⏲11am-2pm & 5pm-late Tue-Sat, 10am-2pm Sun) 🌱 Organic, local, free range, line-caught, you name it, if the word is associated with sustainable food, you can use it to describe this place. Try the fish tacos at lunch and the hickory-smoked pork chops with mustard herb reduction for dinner, but don't skip dessert – the chocolate souffle in particular is to die for. Top it off with a microbrew.

Jack's Grill
STEAK **$$$**

(🖉530 241 9705; www.jacksgrillredding.com; 1743 California St; mains $15-36; ⏲5-11pm, bar from 4pm Mon-Sat) This funky little old-time place doesn't look so inviting – the windows are blacked out and it's dark as a crypt inside – but the popularity with locals starts with its stubborn ain't-broke-don't-fix-it ethos and ends with its steak – a big, thick, charbroiled decadence.

Regulars start lining up for dinner at 4pm, when cocktail hour begins. There are no reservations, so it easily takes an hour to get a seat.

Alehouse Pub
BAR

(www.reddingalehouse.com; 2181 Hilltop Dr; mains $8-16; ⏲3pm-midnight Mon-Thu, to 1:30am Fri & Sat) Too bad for fans of the cheap stuff, this local pub keeps a selection of highly hopped beers on tap and sells T-shirts emblazoned with 'No Crap on Tap.' It's a fun local place that gets packed after Redding's young professionals get out of work.

ℹ Information

California Welcome Center (🖉530-365-1180; www.shastacascade.org; 1699 Hwy 273, Anderson; ⏲9am-6pm Mon-Sat, from 10am Sun) About 10 miles south of Redding, in Anderson's Prime Outlets Mall. It's an easy stop for northbound travelers, who are likely to pass it on the I-5 approach. It stocks maps for hiking and guides to outdoor activities, and the website has an excellent trip-planning section for the region.

Redding Convention & Visitor Center (🖉530-225-4100; www.visitredding.com; 777 Auditorium Dr; ⏲9am-6pm Mon-Fri, 10am-5pm Sat) Near Turtle Bay Exploration Park.

Shasta-Trinity National Forest Headquarters (🖉530-226-2500; 3644 Avtech Pkwy; ⏲8am-4:30pm Mon-Fri) South of town, in the USDA Service Center near the airport. Has maps and free camping permits for all seven national forests in Northern California.

ℹ Getting There & Around

Redding Municipal Airport (RDD; http://ci.redding.ca.us/transeng/airports/rma.htm; 6751 Woodrum Circle, Redding) is 9.5 miles southeast of the city, just off Airport Rd. United Express flies to San Francisco.

The **Amtrak station** (www.amtrak.com; 1620 Yuba St), one block west of the Downtown Redding Mall, is not staffed. For the *Coast Starlight* service, make advance reservations by phone or via the website, then pay the conductor when you board the train. Amtrak travels once daily to Oakland ($48, six hours), Sacramento ($26, four hours) and Dunsmuir ($28, 1¾ hours).

The **Greyhound bus station** (1321 Butte St), adjacent to the Downtown Redding Mall, never closes. Destinations include San Francisco ($42, 8½ hours, four daily) and Weed ($23, 1½ hours, three daily). The **Redding Area Bus Authority** (RABA; www.rabaride.com) has a dozen city routes operating until around 6pm Monday to Saturday. Fares start at $1.50 (exact change only).

Around Redding

Shasta State Historic Park

On Hwy 299, 6 miles west of Redding, this **state historic park** (🖉520-243-8194; www.parks.ca.gov; ⏲10am-5pm Fri-Sun) preserves the ruins of an 1850s Gold Rush mining town called Shasta – not to be confused with Mt Shasta City. When the Gold Rush was at its heady height, everything and everyone passed through this Shasta. But when the railroad bypassed it to set up in Poverty Flats (present-day Redding), poor Shasta lost its raison d'être. Shopkeepers packed up shingle and moved to Redding – literally. They moved many of Shasta's businesses brick by brick.

An 1861 courthouse contains the excellent **museum** (☏530-243-8194; admission $2; ☺10am-5pm Thu-Sun; ♿), the best in this part of the state. With its amazing gun collection, spooky holograms in the basement and a gallows out back, it's a thrill ride. Pick up walking-tour pamphlets from the information desk and follow trails to the beautiful Catholic cemetery, brewery ruins and many other historic sites.

Whiskeytown Lake

Two miles further west on Hwy 299, sparkling **Whiskeytown Lake** (☏530-242-3400; www.nps.gov/whis; day use per vehicle $5) takes its name from an old mining camp. When the lake was created in the 1960s by the construction of a 263ft dam, designed for power generation and Central Valley irrigation, the few remaining buildings of old Whiskeytown were moved and the camp was submerged. John F Kennedy was present at the dedication ceremony, less than two months before his assassination. Today folks descend on the lake's serene 36 miles of forested shoreline to camp, swim, sail, mountain bike and pan for gold.

The **visitors center** (☏530-246-1225; ☺9am-6pm May-Sep, 10am-4pm Oct-Apr), on the northeast point of the lake, just off Hwy 299, provides free maps and information on Whiskeytown and Whiskeytown-Shasta-Trinity National Recreation Area from knowledgeable and agreeable staff. Look for ranger-led interpretive programs and guided walks. The hike from the visitors center to roaring **Whiskeytown Falls** (3.4 miles round-trip) follows a former logging road and is a good quick trip.

On the southern shore of the lake, **Brandy Creek** is ideal for swimming. Just off Hwy 299, on the northern edge of the lake, **Oak Bottom Marina** (☏530-359-2269; boat rental 2/8hr from $50/180) rents boats. On the western side of the lake, the **Tower House Historic District** contains the El Dorado

① DETOUR AROUND THE I-5 DOLDRUMS

A good alternative for travelers heading north and south on I-5 is to drive along Hwy 3 through the Scott Valley, which rewards with world-class views of the Trinity Alps. Compared to rushing along the dull highway, this scenic detour will add an additional half a day of driving.

mine ruins and the pioneer Camden House, open for summer tours. In winter, when the trees are bare, it's an atmospheric, quiet place to explore.

Oak Bottom Campground (☏800-365-2267; tent/RV sites $20/22) is a privately run place with RV and tent camping. It's a bit tight, but nicer than most private campgrounds, with lots of manzanita shade. Most attractive are the walk-in sites right on the shore. **Primitive campsites** (summer/winter $10/5) surround the lake. The most accessible of these is the one at **Crystal Creek**, which doesn't have water, but has nice views.

Shasta Lake

About 15 minutes north of Redding, **Shasta Lake** (www.shastalake.com) was created in the 1940s when Shasta Dam flooded towns, railways and 90% of the local Wintu tribal lands to make the largest reservoir in California. Today it's home to the state's biggest population of nesting bald eagles. Surrounded by hiking trails and campgrounds, the lake gets packed in summer. The lake is also home to more than 20 different kinds of fish, including rainbow trout.

The **ranger station** (☏530-275-1589; 14250 Holiday Rd; ☺8am-4:30pm daily May-Sep, Mon-Fri Oct-Apr) offers free maps and information about fishing, boating and hiking. To get here, take the Mountaingate Wonderland Blvd exit off I-5, about 9 miles north of Redding, and turn right.

◎ Sights & Activities

The lake is known as the 'houseboat capital of the world,' and is very popular with boaters of all kinds. **Packer's Bay** is the best area for leg-stretcher hikes with easy access off the I-5 (follow the Packer's Bay signs), but the prettiest trail (outside of summer months when the lack of shade can make it intensely hot) is the 7.5-mile loop of the **Clikapudi Trail**, which is also popular with mountain bikers and horse-back riders. To get there, follow Bear Mountain Rd several miles till it dead ends.

Shasta Dam DAM

(☑ 530-275-4463; www.usbr.gov/mp/ncao/shasta/; 16349 Shasta Dam Blvd; ☉ visitor center 8am-5pm, tours 9am-3pm) **FREE** On scale with the enormous natural features of the area, this colossal, 15-million-ton dam is second only in size to Grand Coolie Dam in Washington state (Hoover Dam in Nevada is the fourth biggest – but the tallest in the country). The dam is found at the south end of the lake on Shasta Dam Blvd.

Built between 1938 and 1945, its 487ft spillway is as high as a 60-story building – three times higher than Niagara Falls. Woody Guthrie wrote 'This Land Is Your Land' while he was here entertaining dam workers. The **Shasta Dam visitors center** (☑ 530-275-4463; ☉ 8:30am-4:30pm) offers fascinating free guided tours at 9am, 11am, 1pm and 3pm daily of the structure's rumbling interior – but skip the movie.

Lake Shasta Caverns CAVE TOUR

(www.lakeshastacaverns.com; adult/child 3-11yr $22/13; ☉ tours 9am-4pm; 👪) High in the limestone megaliths at the north end of the lake hide these prehistoric caves. Tours of the crystalline caves operate daily and include a boat ride across Lake Shasta, and the office has a spacious play area for kids. The Cathedral Room is particularly stunning. Bring a sweater as the temperature inside is 58°F (14°C) year-round.

To get there, take the Shasta Caverns Rd exit from I-5, about 15 miles north of Redding, and follow the signs for 1.5 miles.

🛏 Sleeping & Eating

Hike-in camping and RV parks are sprinkled around the shores of the lake, and houseboats are a wildly popular option. Most houseboats require a two-night minimum stay. Make reservations as far in advance as possible, especially in the summer months. Houseboats usually sleep 10 to 16 adults and cost around $1600 to $8400 per week. The RV parks are often crowded and lack shade, but they have on-site restaurants. If you want to explore the area on a day trip, stay in Redding.

US Forest Service (USFS)
Campgrounds 'CAMPGROUND $

(☑ 877-444-6777; www.reserveusa.com; tent sites $10-20) About half of the campgrounds

around the lake are open year-round. The lake's many fingers have a huge range of camping, with lake and mountain views, and some of them are very remote. Free boat-in sites are first-come, first-served – sites without boat launches will be far less busy.

Camping outside organized campgrounds requires a campfire permit, available free from any USFS office.

Holiday Harbor
Resort HOUSEBOATS, CAMPGROUND $

(☑ 530-238-2383; www.lakeshasta.com; Holiday Harbor Rd; tent & RV sites $38.50, houseboat for 2 nights from $920; 🛜) Primarily an RV campground, it also rents houseboats (note that off-season rates are almost 50% lower) and the busy marina offers parasailing and fishing-boat rentals. A little **cafe** (☉ 8am-3pm) sits lakefront. It's off Shasta Caverns Rd, next to the lake.

Antlers RV Park &
Campground CAMPGROUND, CABINS $

(☑ 530-238-2322; www.shastalakevacations.com; 20679 Antlers Rd; tent & RV sites $18-42, trailer rentals $88-105; 🛜🐕🏊) East of I-5 in Lakehead, at the north end of the lake, this very popular, family-oriented campground has cabins, a country store and a marina renting watercraft and houseboats.

Lakeshore Inn & RV CAMPGROUND $

(☑ 530-238-2003; www.shastacamping.com; 20483 Lakeshore Dr; RV sites $20-37, cabins from $95; 🛜🏊) On the western side of I-5, this lakeside vacation park has a restaurant and tavern, horseshoes and basic cabins.

MT LASSEN & AROUND

The dramatic crags, volcanic formations and alpine lakes of Lassen Volcanic National Park seem surprisingly untrammeled when you consider they are only a few hours from the Bay Area. Snowed in through most of winter, the park blossoms in late spring. While it is only 50 miles from Redding, and thus close enough to be enjoyed on a day trip, to really do it justice you'll want to invest a few days exploring the area along its scenic, winding roads. From Lassen Volcanic National Park you can take one of two very picturesque routes: Hwy 36, which heads east past Chester, Lake Almanor and historic Susanville; or Hwy 89, which leads southeast to the cozy mountain town of Quincy.

Lassen Volcanic National Park

The dry, smoldering, treeless terrain within this 106,000-acre **national park** (☑ 530-595-4444; www.nps.gov/lavo; 7-day entry per car $10) stands in stunning contrast to the cool, green conifer forest that surrounds it. That's the summer; in winter tons of snow ensures you won't get too far inside its borders. Still, entering the park from the southwest entrance is to suddenly step into another world. The lavascape offers a fascinating glimpse into the earth's fiery core. In a fuming display the terrain is marked by roiling hot springs, steamy mud pots, noxious sulfur vents, fumaroles, lava flows, cinder cones, craters and crater lakes.

In earlier times the region was a summer encampment and meeting point for Native American tribes – namely the Atsugewi, Yana, Yahi and Maidu. They hunted deer and gathered plants for basket-making here. Some indigenous people still live nearby and work closely with the park to help educate visitors on their ancient history and contemporary culture.

⊙ Sights & Activities

Lassen Peak, the world's largest plug-dome volcano, rises 2000ft over the surrounding landscape to 10,457ft above sea level. Classified as an active volcano, its most recent eruption was in 1917, when it spewed a giant cloud of smoke, steam and ash 7 miles into the atmosphere. The national park was created the following year to protect the newly formed landscape. Some areas destroyed by the blast, including the aptly named **Devastated Area** northeast of the peak, are recovering impressively.

Hwy 89, the road through the park, wraps around Lassen Peak on three sides and provides access to dramatic geothermal formations, pure lakes, gorgeous picnic areas and remote hiking trails.

In total, the park has 150 miles of **hiking trails**, including a 17-mile section of the Pacific Crest Trail. Experienced hikers can attack the **Lassen Peak Trail**; it takes at least 4½ hours to make the 5-mile round trip but the first 1.3 miles up to the Grandview viewpoint are suitable for families. The 360-degree view from the top is stunning, even if the weather is a bit hazy. Early in the season you'll need snow and ice-climbing equipment to reach the summit. Near the Kom Yah-mah-nee visitor facility, a gentler 2.3-mile trail leads through meadows and forest to **Mill Creek Falls**. Further north on Hwy 89 you'll recognize the roadside **sulfur works** by its bubbling mud pots, hissing steam vent, fountains and fumaroles. At **Bumpass Hell** a moderate 1.5-mile trail and boardwalk lead to an active geothermal area, with bizarrely colored pools and billowing clouds of steam.

The road and trails wind through cinder cones, lava and lush alpine glades, with views of Juniper Lake, Snag Lake and the plains beyond. Most of the lakes at higher elevations remain partially and beautifully frozen in summer. Leave time to fish, swim or boat on **Manzanita Lake**, a slightly lower emerald gem near the northern entrance.

🛏 Sleeping & Eating

If you're coming to Lassen Volcanic National Park from the north on Hwy 89, you won't see many gas/food/lodgings signs after Mt Shasta City. Your best option is to stock up en route and camp.

The park has eight developed **campgrounds** (☑ 877-444-6777; www.recreation.gov; tent & RV sites $10-18), and there are many more in the surrounding Lassen National Forest. Campgrounds in the park are open from late May to late October, depending on snow conditions. Manzanita Lake is the only one with hot showers, but the two Summit Lake campgrounds, in the middle of the park, are also popular. Reservations are permitted at Butte Lake in the northeast corner of the park, Manzanita Lake in the

---

ⓘ KNOW ABOUT THE SNOW

Rangers tell rueful stories about people who drive across the country in their RVs to find the roads of Lassen Volcanic National Park impassable; don't let it happen to you. The road through the park is usually only open from June to October, though it has been closed due to snow (as much as 40ft of it) well into July at times. Travelers need to call ahead or check the park website (www.nps.gov/lavo; click 'Current Conditions') to get weather conditions before considering a visit during all but a couple of months of the year – the only safe bets are August and September. A slow melt or freak storm can close major parts of the park at any other time of year.

Lassen Volcanic National Park

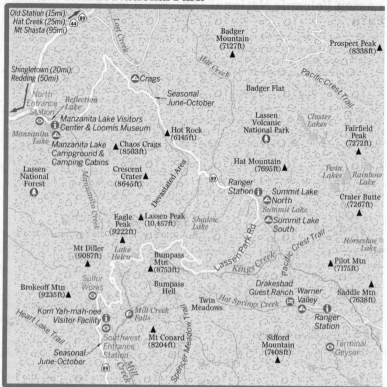

Old Station (15mi);
Hat Creek (25mi);
Mt Shasta (95mi) 44 89

Lost Creek

Badger Mountain (7127ft)

Prospect Peak (8338ft)

Hat Creek

Pacific Crest Trail

Shingletown (20mi);
Redding (50mi)

Crags

Badger Flat

Seasonal June-October

North Entrance Station

Reflection Lake

Manzanita Lake Visitors Center & Loomis Museum

Hot Rock (6145ft)

Lassen Volcanic National Park

Cluster Lakes

Fairfield Peak (7272ft)

Manzanita Lake

Manzanita Lake Campground & Camping Cabins

Chaos Crags (8503ft)

Hat Mountain (7695ft)

Twin Lakes

Rainbow Lake

Lassen National Forest

Crescent Crater (8645ft)

Devastated Area

89

Ranger Station

Summit Lake North

Crater Butte (7267ft)

Manzanita Creek

Eagle Peak (9222ft)

Lassen Peak (10,457ft)

Shadow Lake

Summit Lake

Summit Lake South

Horseshoe Lake

Mt Diller (9087ft)

Lake Helen

Bumpass Mtn (8753ft)

Lassen Park Rd

Kings Creek

Pacific Crest Trail

Pilot Mtn (7175ft)

Brokeoff Mtn (9235ft)

Sulfur Works

Bumpass Hell

Drakesbad Guest Ranch

Warner Valley

Saddle Mtn (7638ft)

Heart Lake Trail

Kom Yah-mah-nee Visitor Facility

Mill Creek Falls

Twin Meadows

Hot Springs Creek

Ranger Station

Spencer Meadow Trail

Southwest Entrance Station

Mt Conard (8204ft)

Sifford Mountain (7408ft)

Terminal Geyser

Seasonal June-October

89

Mill Creek

northwest, Summit Lake North and Summit Lake South.

If you don't want to camp, the nearest place to stay is Chester, which accesses the south entrance of the park. There are some basic services near the split of Hwy 89 and Hwy 44, in the north.

North Entrance of the Park

**Manzanita Lake
Camping Cabins**   CABINS, CAMPGROUND $
(☑ summer 530-335-7557, winter 530-200-4578; www.lassenrecreation.com; Hwy 89, near Manzanita Lake; cabins $63-89; 🛜) These recently built log cabins enjoy a lovely position on one of Lassen's lakes, and they come in one- and two-bedroom options and slightly more basic eight-bunk configurations, which are a bargain for groups. They all have bear boxes, propane heaters and fire rings, but no bedding, electricity or running water.

Those who want to get a small taste of Lassen's more rustic comforts can call ahead to arrange a 'Camper Package,' which includes basic supplies for a night under the stars (starting at $100, it includes a s'mores kit).

**Manzanita Lake
Campground**   CAMPGROUND, CABINS $
(☑ 877-444-6777; www.recreation.gov; campsites $10-18; 🐾) The biggest camping area in these parts has lake access, views of Lassen and 179 sites with fire rings, picnic tables and bear boxes. It has a store, hot showers and kayak rentals here as well.

**Hat Creek Resort &
RV Park**   CABINS, CAMPGROUND $
(☑ 800-568-0109; www.hatcreekresortrv.com; 12533 Hwy 44/89; tent sites from $15, RV sites with/without hookups from $26/15, r $54-209, yurts $54-119; 🛜🐾) Outside the park, Old Station makes a decent stop before entering and is

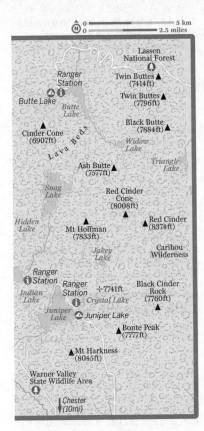

a good second choice after Manzanita Lake Camping Cabins. It sits along a fast-moving, trout-stocked creek. Some simple motel rooms and cabins have full kitchens. Stock up at the convenience store and deli, then eat on a picnic table by the river.

South Entrance of the Park

Mt Lassen/Shingletown KOA CAMPGROUND $
(☎530-474-3133; www.koa.com; 7749 KOA Rd; tent sites $29, RV sites from $42, cabins $67-160; ⊙mid-Mar–Nov; 🛜🐾🏊) Enjoy all the standard KOA amenities: a playground, a deli and laundry facilities. It's off Hwy 44 in Shingletown, about 20 miles west of the park.

Childs Meadow Resort CABINS $
(☎530-595-3383; www.childsmeadowresort.com; 41500 E Hwy 36, Mill Creek; d $60-70, cabins $75-150) Rustic, run-down cabins – some of them more like permanently parked RV trailers – sit at the edge of a spectacularly lush mountain meadow 9 miles outside the park's southwest entrance. Don't expect the Ritz; it's an old-fashioned, fittingly grungy, mountain-resort experience, but it's very close to the park.

Drakesbad Guest Ranch RANCH $$$
(☎530-529-1512, ext 120; www.drakesbad.com; Warner Valley Rd; r per person $140-190; ⊙Jun–early Oct; 🏊) Seventeen miles northwest of Chester, this fabulously secluded place lies inside the park's boundary. Guests, many of whom are repeat visitors, use the hot-springs-fed swimming pool or go horseback riding. Except in the main lodge, there's no electricity (the kerosene lamps and campfires give things a lovely glow). Rates include country-style meals (vegetarian options available) and campfire barbecues every Wednesday.

This is one of the few places in the region to book up solidly, so make advance reservations as soon as possible.

🛈 Information

Whether you enter at the north or southwest entrance, you'll be given a free map with general information.

Kom Yah-mah-nee Visitor Facility (☎530-595-4480; ⊙9am-6pm Jun-Sep, hours vary Oct-May) About half a mile north of the park's southwest entrance, this handsome center is certified at the highest standard by the US Green Building Council. Inside there are educational exhibits (including a cool topographical volcano), a bookstore, an auditorium, a gift shop and a restaurant. Visitor information and maps available.

Manzanita Lake Visitors Center & Loomis Museum (☎530-595-4480; ⊙9am-5pm Jun-Sep) Just past the entrance-fee station at the park's northern boundary, you can see exhibits and an orientation video inside this museum. During summer, rangers and volunteers lead programs on geology, wildlife, astronomy and local culture. Visitor information and maps available.

Park Headquarters (☎530-595-4444; www.nps.gov/lavo; 38050 Hwy 36; ⊙8am-4:30pm daily Jun-Sep, 8am-4:30pm Mon-Fri Oct-May) About a mile west of the tiny town of Mineral, it's the nearest stop for refueling and supplies.

🛈 Getting There & Away

There's virtually no way to visit this park without a car, though all the two-lane roads around the park and the ample free national-forest camping options make for excellent, if fairly serious, cycle touring.

The park has two entrances. The northern entrance, at Manzanita Lake, is 50 miles east of

WORTH A TRIP

WILD HORSE SANCTUARY

Since 1978 the **Wild Horse Sanctuary** (☑ 530-335-2241; www.wildhorsesanctuary.com; Shingletown; admission free; ⊙ 9am-4pm Wed & Sat) **FREE** has been sheltering horses and burros that would otherwise have been destroyed. You can visit its humble visitors center on Wednesdays and Saturdays to see these lovely animals or even volunteer for a day, with advance arrangement. To see them on the open plains, take a two- to three-day weekend pack trip in spring or summer (from $435 per person). Shingletown lies 20 miles to the west of Lassen Volcanic National Park.

Redding via Hwy 44. The southwest entrance is on Hwy 89, about 5 miles north of the junction with Hwy 36. From this junction it is 5 miles west on Hwy 36 to Mineral and 44 miles west to Red Bluff. Heading east on Hwy 36, Chester is 25 miles away and Susanville about 60 miles. Quincy is 65 miles southeast from the junction on Hwy 89.

Lassen National Forest

The vast **Lassen National Forest** (www.fs.fed.us/r5/lassen), surrounding Lassen Peak and Lassen Volcanic National Park, is so big that it's hard to comprehend: it covers 1.2 million acres (1875 sq miles) of wilderness in an area called the Crossroads, where the granite Sierra, volcanic Cascades, Modoc Plateau and Central Valley meet. It's largely unspoiled land, though if you wander too far off the byways surrounding the park, you'll certainly see evidence of logging and mining operations that still happen within its borders.

The forest has some serious hikes, with 460 miles of **trails**, ranging from the brutally challenging (120 miles of the Pacific Crest Trail) to ambitious day hikes (the 12-mile Spencer Meadows National Recreation Trail), to just-want-to-stretch-the-legs-a-little trails (the 3.5-mile Heart Lake National Recreation Trail). Near the intersection of Hwys 44 and 89, visitors to the area will find one of the most spectacular features of the forest, the pitch-black 600yd **Subway Cave** lava tube. Other points of interest include the 1.5-mile volcanic **Spattercone Crest Trail**, **Willow Lake** and **Crater Lake**,

7684ft **Antelope Peak**, and the 900ft-high, 14-mile-long **Hat Creek Rim** escarpment.

For those seeking to get far off the beaten trail, the forest has three wilderness areas. Two high-elevation wilderness areas are the **Caribou Wilderness** and the **Thousand Lakes Wilderness**, best visited from mid-June to mid-October. The **Ishi Wilderness**, at a much lower elevation in the Central Valley foothills east of Red Bluff, is more comfortable in spring and fall, as summer temperatures often exceed 100°F (37°C). It harbors California's largest migratory deer herd, which can be upwards of 20,000 head.

The Lassen National Forest supervisor's office is in Susanville. Other ranger offices include **Eagle Lake Ranger District** (☑ 530-257-4188; 477-050 Eagle Lake Rd, Susanville), **Hat Creek Ranger District** (☑ 530-336-5521; 43225 E Hwy 299, Fall River Mills) and **Almanor Ranger District** (☑ 530-258-2141; 900 E Hwy 36, Chester), about a mile west of Chester.

Lake Almanor Area

Calm, turquoise Lake Almanor lies south of Lassen Volcanic National Park via Hwys 89 and 36. This man-made lake is a crystalline example of California's sometimes awkward conservation and land-management policy: the lake was created by the now-defunct Great Western Power Company and is now ostensibly owned by the Pacific Gas & Electric Company. The lake is surrounded by lush meadows and tall evergreens and was once little-visited. Now, a 3000-acre ski resort sits on the hills above, with properties continually being developed near its shore and power boats zipping across its surface. The northeastern section in particular has become particularly ritzy and there are even a few gated communities. On the rugged southern end you'll find miles with nothing but pine trees.

The main town near the lake, Chester (population 2500, elevation 4528ft), isn't a looker. Though you could whiz right by and dismiss it as a few blocks of nondescript roadside storefronts, this little community, while outwardly drab, has a fledgling art scene hidden along the backroads for those willing to explore. It also offers some comfy places to stay but none as exciting or woodsy as you'll find along the lake.

🏃 Activities

Rent boats and water-sports equipment at many places around the lake.

Bodfish Bicycles & Quiet
Mountain Sports
CYCLING, OUTDOORS

(☑ 530-258-2338; www.bodfishbicycles.com; 152 Main St, Chester; ⊙ 10am-5pm Tue-Sat, noon-4pm Sun) This outfit rents bicycles ($33 per day), cross-country skis and snowshoes, and sells canoes and kayaks. It's a great source of mountain-biking and bicycle-touring advice. If you want just a taste of the lovely rides possible in this part of the state, make this a priority stop.

🛏 Sleeping & Eating

The best sleeping options for campers are in the surrounding national forest.

🛏 Chester

Along Chester's main drag you'll find a scattering of '50s-style inns and a few chain lodgings (the nicest of which is the fairly overpriced Best Western Rose Quartz Inn). Many of these places keep seasonal hours, and when you live in a place where it can snow in mid-June, the season is short. Restaurants are of the burger-and-fries or momn-pop-diner variety – the best dining options are found a few miles out of town along the northeast shores of the lake.

St Bernard Lodge
B&B $$

(☑ 530-258-3382; www.stbernardlodge.com; 44801 E Hwy 36, Mill Creek; d with shared bath from $99; 🐾) Located 10 miles west of Chester, this old-world charmer has seven B&B rooms with views to the mountains and forest. All have knotty-pine paneling and quilted bedspreads. There are stables where those traveling with a horse can board them and have access to the nearby network of Lassen's trails. The tavern is good too – serving meaty American-style fare.

Bidwell House B&B
B&B $$

(☑ 530-258-3338; www.bidwellhouse.com; 1 Main St; r with shared bath $80-115, r with private bath $125-260, cottage $185-285; 🐾) Set back from the street, this historic summer home of pioneers John and Annie Bidwell is packed with antiques. The classic accommodations come with all the modern amenities (including a spa in some rooms) – no roughing it here. Enjoy goodies like a three-course breakfast, home-baked cookies and afternoon sherry.

Knotbumper Restaurant
AMERICAN $

(274 Main St; meals $8-12; ⊙ 11am-8pm Tue-Sat) The Knotbumper is unlikely to dish up your most memorable meal, but it has a generous deli menu, including tamale pies, shrimp salad sandwiches and other eclectic selections. On summer days, eat on the lively front porch and watch the trucks rumble by. This place virtually closes down in winter.

Around the Lake

Book ahead for lakefront lodgings in summer. There are restaurants at the resorts.

PG&E Recreational Area
Campgrounds
CAMPGROUND $

(☑ 916-386-5164; http://recreation.pge.com/Reserve-a-Campsite/; tent sites $16-22; 🐾) A favorite for tents and RVs, Rocky Point Campground is right on the lake, with some sites

---

SCENIC DRIVE: LASSEN SCENIC BYWAY

Even in the peak of summer, you'll have the Lassen Scenic Byway mostly to yourself. The long loop though Northern California wilderness skirts the edge of Lassen Volcanic National Park and circles Lassen Peak, one of the largest dormant volcanoes on the planet. It mostly covers the big green patches on the map: expansive areas perfect for hiking, fishing, camping or just getting lost. This is a place where few people venture, and those who do come back with stories.

The launching point for this big loop could be either Redding or Sacramento, but there are few comforts for travelers along this course. The only cities in this neck of the woods – little places like Chester and Susanville – aren't all that exciting on their own; they're mostly just places to gas up, buy some beef jerky and enjoy the week's only hot meal. But the banner attractions are visible in every direction – the ominous, dormant volcanic peak of Lassen, the windswept high plains and the seemingly endless wilderness of the Lassen and Plumas National Forests.

This loop is formed by Hwy 36, Hwy 44 and Hwy 89. (You can see the map and some of the highlights at www.byways.org/explore/byways/2195.) Its best to do the drive between late June through mid-October. Other times of the year some of these roads close due to snow.

WESTWOOD & THE BIZZ JOHNSON TRAIL

A few miles east of Chester is Westwood, a tiny speck of a town that marks the beginning of the Bizz Johnson Trail, an extremely picturesque route that runs the remote 25.5 miles from Westwood to Susanville. Once part of the old Southern Pacific right-of-way, the wooden bridges and serenely crossing-free trail are traversable by foot, mountain bike, horseback or cross-country skis (no motorized vehicles allowed!). Do the trail in the Westwood–Susanville direction, as it's mostly downhill that way. Get trail guides at the chamber of commerce in Chester or at the Susanville Railroad Depot.

basically on the beach. For something more remote, try the Cool Springs Campground at the Butt Reservoir (try to say that with a straight face!). It's at the south end of the lake, at the end of Prattville Butt Reservoir Rd.

These campgrounds lie within the surrounding Lassen and Plumas National Forests on the lake's southwest shore. Sites tend to be more tranquil than the RV-centric private campgrounds that are right on the water.

North Shore Campground
CABINS, CAMPGROUND $

(☑ 530-258-3376; www.northshorecampground. com; tent sites $40, RV sites $45-56, cabins $119-269, pop-up trailer $89; ☏) Two miles east of Chester on Hwy 36, these expansive, forested grounds stretch for a mile along the water, and get filled up with mostly RVs. Ranch-style cabins have kitchens and are great for families. This place is fine if you want to spend all your time waterskiing on the lake, but those seeking the solitude of nature should look elsewhere.

Knotty Pine Resort & Marina
CABINS $$

(☑ 530-596-3348; www.knottypine.net; 430 Peninsula Dr; weekly RV sites $175, 2-bedroom cabins with kitchen $165, r $145; ☒) This lakeside option, 7 miles east of Chester, has simple cabins and rents boats, kayaks and canoes.

Tantardino's
ITALIAN $$

(☑ 530-596-3902; 401 Ponderosa Dr, Lake Almanor Peninsula; mains $9-19; ☉11:30am-9pm Tue-Sat) This is the locals' favorite place to eat in the

region hands down – even folks from Susanville drive the 32 miles to get here, with pleasure, for the excellent Sicillian-style lasagne, yummy pizzas and meatball or caprese sandwiches at lunch time. It's lively, friendly and you can eat and imbibe outside in summer. Reserve ahead for dinner.

★ Red Onion Grill MODERN AMERICAN $$$
(www.redoniongrill.com; 384 Main St; meals $16-29; ☉11am-9pm) Head here for the finest dining on the lake with upscale Modern American, Italian-influenced cuisine (like the simply prepared rock shrimp and crab alfredo), and bar food that's executed with real panache. The setting is casual and fun – wall lanterns and a crackling fire – made all the more warm by the best wine list in town.

ℹ Information

Chester & Lake Almanor Chamber of Commerce (☑ 530-258-2426; www.chester-lakealmanor.com; 529 Main St, Chester; ☉9am-4pm Mon-Fri) Get information about lodging and recreation around the lake, in Lassen National Forest and in Lassen Volcanic National Park.

Lassen National Forest Almanor Ranger Station (☑ 530-258-2141; 900 E Hwy 36; ☉8am-4:30pm Mon-Fri) About a mile west of Chester, with similar information to the chamber of commerce.

Susanville

Though it sits on a lovely high desert plateau, the Lassen County seat (population 16,616) isn't much of a charmer; it's a resupply post with a Wal-Mart, a few stop lights and two prisons. Although not a tourist destination in itself, it does provide good services for travelers passing through. It lies 35 miles east of Lake Almanor and 85 miles northwest of Reno – and is home to a couple of modest historic sites. The best event in town is the Lassen County Fair (☑ 530-251-8900; www.lassencountyfair.org), which swings into gear in July.

For local information about the town visit the Lassen County Chamber of Commerce (☑ 530-257-4323; www.lassencountychamber.org; 84 N Lassen St; ☉9am-4pm Mon-Fri), while the Lassen National Forest supervisor's office (☑ 530-257-2151; 2550 Riverside Dr; ☉8am-4:30pm Mon-Fri) has maps and recreation information for getting into the surrounding wilds.

The restored Susanville Railroad Depot, south of Main St, off Weatherlow St, sits beside the terminus of the Bizz Johnson Trail (p284). The **visitors center** (☑530-257-3252; 601 Richmond Rd; ⊙10am-4pm May-Oct) rents bicycles and has brochures on mountain-biking trails in the area.

The town's oldest building, **Roop's Fort** (1853), is named after Susanville's founder, Isaac Roop. The fort was a trading post on the Nobles Trail, a California emigrant route. The town itself was named after Roop's daughter, Susan. Beside the fort is the freshly built **Lassen Historical Museum** (75 N Weatherlow St; admission by donation; ⊙10am-4pm Mon-Fri May-Oct), which has well-presented displays of clothing and memorabilia from the area, which are worth a 20-minute visit.

Motels along Main St average $65 to $90 per night, **High Country Inn** (☑530-257-3450; www.high-country-inn.com; 3015 Riverside Dr; r $87-159; ☎☀) is the best of these. Try **Roseberry House B&B** (☑530-257-5675; www.roseberryhouse.com; 609 North St; r/ste $110/135; ☎) for more character. This sweet 1902 Victorian house is two blocks north of Main St. Striking dark-wood antique headboards and armoires combine with rosebuds and frill. There are nice little touches, like bath salts and candy dishes. In the morning, expect homemade muffins and jam as part of the full breakfast.

To eat, head directly to the relatively new **Lassen Ale Works** (724 Main St; mains $9-21; ⊙11am-10pm Mon-Thu, 11am-11pm Fri & Sat, 9am-10pm Sun) in the beautifully renovated circa 1862 Pioneer Saloon. It's known for its fish and chips, but everything from steaks to the Reuben are fresh and as good as the service. Try one of the seven signature brews like the Pioneer Porter or Almanor Amber. Unfortunately for those traveling with kids, you must be 21 years old or over to eat here.

Sage Stage (☑530-233-6410; www.sage-stage.com) runs buses to Redding via Alturas ($18) and south to Reno ($22). **Susanville City Buses** (☑530-252-7433) makes a circuit around town (fare $2).

Eagle Lake

Those who have the time to get all the way out to Eagle Lake, California's second-largest natural lake, are rewarded with one of the most striking sites in the region: a stunningly blue jewel on the high plateau. From late spring until fall this lovely lake, about 15 miles northwest of Susanville, attracts a smattering of visitors who come to cool off, swim, fish, boat and camp. On the south shore, you'll find a pristine 5-mile **recreational trail** and several busy **campgrounds** (☑reservations 877-444-6777; www.recreation.gov; tent sites $20, RV sites $30-60) administered by Lassen National Forest and the **Bureau of Land Management** (BLM; ☑530-257-5381). Campgrounds for tent camping include Merrill, Aspen, Christie and Eagle. Most of them are fairly scrubby, considering how lovely the lake is, though there are some highly sought-after lakeside sites in Merrill. Merrill and Eagle also have RV sites. Nearby **Eagle Lake Marina** (www.eaglelakerecreation-area.com) offers hot showers, laundry and boat rentals. It also can help you get out onto the lake with a fishing license.

Eagle Lake RV Park (☑530-825-3133; www.eaglelakeandrv.com; 687-125 Palmetto Way; tent/RV sites $25/36.50, cabins $37-100; ☎☀), on the western shore, and **Mariners Resort** (☑530-825-3333; Stones Landing; RV sites $37-40, cabins $110-190), on the quieter northern shore, both rent boats.

Quincy

Idyllic Quincy (population 1728) is one of the northern mountains' three mountain communities, which teeter on the edge of becoming an incorporated town (the other two are Burney, in Shasta County, and Weaverville). It's no metropolis, but it does have a large grocery store and even a Subway franchise. In 2013 *Budget Travel* named it one of the 'Coolest Small Towns in America,' and we have to agree. Nestled in a high valley in the northern Sierra, southeast of both Lassen Volcanic National Park and Lake Almanor via Hwy 89, it is a lovely little place, endowed with just enough edge by the student population of the local Feather River College. Nearby Feather River, Plumas National Forest, Tahoe National Forest and their oodles of open space make Quincy an excellent base from which to explore.

Once in town Hwy 70/89 splits into two one-way streets, with traffic on Main St heading east, and traffic on Lawrence St heading west. Jackson St runs parallel to Main St, one block south, and is another main artery. Just about everything you need is on, near or between these three streets, making up Quincy's low-key commercial district.

⊙ Sights & Activities

Pick up free walking and driving tour pamphlets from the visitors center to guide you through the gorgeous surrounding **American Valley**. The **Feather River Scenic Byway** (Hwy 70) leads into the Sierra. In summer the icy waters of county namesake **Feather River** (*plumas* is Spanish for feathers) are excellent for swimming, kayaking, fishing and floating in old inner tubes. The area is also a wonderland of winter activities, especially at Bucks Lake.

Plumas County Museum MUSEUM
(☎ 530-283-6320; www.plumasmuseum.org; 500 Jackson St, at Coburn St; adult/child $2/1; ⏰ 9am-4:30pm Tue-Sat, 10am-3pm Sun; ♿) In the block behind the courthouse, this multifloor county museum has flowering gardens, as well as hundreds of historical photos and relics from the county's pioneer and Maidu days, its early mining and timber industries, and construction of the Western Pacific Railroad. For the price, it's definitely worth the stop.

Plumas County Courthouse HISTORIC BUILDING
(Main St) Pop into the 1921 Plumas County Courthouse, at the west end of Main St, to see enormous marble posts and staircases, and a bronze-and-glass chandelier in the lobby.

Sierra Mountain Sports OUTDOORS
(www.sierramountainsports.net; 501 W Main St) Across from the courthouse, rent cross-country ski gear and snowshoes here.

Big Daddy's Guide Service FISHING
(☎ 530-283-4103; www.bigdaddyfishing.com) Captain Bryan Roccucci is Big Daddy, the only fishing guide in Northeast California. He knows the lakes well and leads trips for all levels (starting at $175 per person).

✸ Festivals & Events

★ **High Sierra Music Festival** MUSIC
(www.highsierramusic.com) On the first weekend in July, quiet Quincy is host to this blowout festival, renowned statewide. The four-day extravaganza brings a five-stage smorgasbord of art and music from a spectrum of cultural corners (indie rock, classic blues, folk and jazz). Past acts include Thievery Corporation, Lauryn Hill, Primus, Ben Harper and Neko Case.

Sure, a curmudgeonly local might call it the Hippie Fest, but it's pretty tame in comparison to some of Northern California's fringe festivals. If you plan to attend, reserve a room or campsite a couple of months in advance. For those who don't want to camp in nearby national forest land, Susanville, one hour away, has the largest number of rooms.

🛏 Sleeping

Ranchito Motel MOTEL **$**
(☎ 530-286-2265; www.ranchitomotel.com; 2020 E Main St; r from $79; 📶) With antique timber pillars, white-painted brick walls, old barn-style doors and the occasional wagon wheel for decoration, this friendly motel (in the eastern half of town) definitely has a Mexican ranch feel. Inside, rooms are modern, freshly painted and very comfortable for the price. The motel offers plenty more choices on the wooded land that extends back a few acres.

Pine Hill Motel MOTEL **$**
(☎ 530-283-1670; www.pinehillmotel.com; 42075 Hwy 70; s/d/cabin from $69/75/150; ❄📶🍴) A mile west of downtown Quincy, this little hotel is protected by an army of statues and surrounded by a big lawn. The units are nothing fancy, but they're clean and in a constant state of renovation. Each is equipped with microwave, coffeemaker and refrigerator; some cabins have full kitchens.

Feather River Canyon Campgrounds CAMPGROUND **$**
(☎ reservations 877-444-6777; www.fs.usda.gov; tent & RV sites $23) Area campgrounds are administered through the Mt Hough Ranger District Office. They are in a cluster along the north fork of the Feather River west of Quincy – five are no-fee, but also have no piped water. All are first come, first served.

★ **Quincy Courtyard Suites** APARTMENT **$$**
(☎ 530-283-1401; www.quincycourtyardsuites.com; 436 Main St; apt $129-169; 📶) Staying in this beautifully renovated 1908 Clinch building, overlooking the small main drag of Quincy's downtown, feels just right, like renting the village's cutest apartment. The warmly decorated rooms are modern – no fussy clutter – and apartments have spacious, modern kitchens, claw-foot tubs and gas fireplaces.

Ada's Place B&B **$$**
(☎ 530-283-1954; www.adasplace.com; 562 Jackson St; cottages $100-145; 📶) Even though it has the feel of a B&B, it's a bit of a misnomer. Without breakfast, Ada's is just an excellent B. No problem, as each of the three brightly painted garden units has a full kitchen. Ada's Cottage is worth the slight extra charge, as

its skylights offer an open feel. It's very quiet and private, yet right in town.

Greenhorn Guest Ranch
RANCH $$$

(☏800-334-6939; www.greenhornranch.com; 2116 Greenhorn Ranch Rd; per person per day incl trail rides from $258; ⊙May-Oct; 🐾🐕🐎) Not a 'dude' ranch but rather a 'guest' ranch: instead of shoveling stalls, guests are pampered with mountain-trail rides, riding lessons, even rodeo practice. Or you can just fish, hike, square dance and attend evening bonfires, cookouts and frog races – think of it like a cowboy version of the getaway resort in *Dirty Dancing*. Meals and riding included.

✖ Eating & Drinking

Quincy is a good supply point for those headed into or out of the wilderness. There are some good restaurants, a big grocery store, and a sprawling **farmers market** (cnr Church & Main Sts; ⊙5-8pm Thu mid-Jul–mid-Sep).

★ Pangaea Café & Pub
CAFE $$

(www.pangaeapub.com; 461 W Main St; mains $9-13; ⊙11am-8pm Mon-Wed, 11am-9pm Thu & Fri; 🐾🔊🚶🐕) 🍴 Like a stranger you feel you've met before, this earthy spot feels warmly familiar, all the more lovable when you consider its commitment to serving local produce. Choose from regional beef burgers, salmon sushi, a slew of panini (many veggie) and rice bowls. It's hopping with locals drinking craft brews, kids running around and lots of hugging.

Morning Thunder Café
BREAKFAST $$

(557 Lawrence St; meals $9-16; ⊙7am-2pm; 🚶) Homey and hip, this is the best place in town for breakfast, and the vine-shaded patio is a lovely way to start the day. The menu is mainly, though not exclusively, vegetarian. Try the vegetaters: roasted veg and potatoes smothered in cheese, the chicken avocado 'thunder melt,' or the 'drunken pig,' which brilliantly balances savory pork and pineapple.

Moon's
ITALIAN $$

(☏530-283-0765; 497 Lawrence St; mains $13-24; ⊙5-9pm Tue-Sun) Follow the aroma of garlic to this welcoming little chalet with a charming ambience. Dig into choice steaks and Italian-American classics, including excellent pizza and rich lasagne.

Sweet Lorraine's
CALIFORNIAN $$

(384 Main St; meals $12-28; ⊙lunch Mon-Fri, dinner Mon-Sat) On a warm day – or, better yet, evening – the patio here is especially sweet. The menu features light Californian cuisine (fish, poultry, soups and salads), but it's also known for its award-winning St Louis ribs. Finish things off with the whiskey bread pudding.

Drunk Brush
WINE BAR

(www.facebook.com/TheDrunkBrush; 438 Main St; ⊙2-7pm Mon-Wed, 2-10pm Thu & Fri, 2-8pm Sat) A sweet little courtyard wine bar that pours 25 wines and a few beers. Sample delicious appetizer pairings in a welcoming, arty atmosphere.

ℹ Information

Mt Hough Ranger District Office (☏530-283-0555; 39696 Hwy 70; ⊙8am-4:30pm Mon-Fri) Five miles west of town. Has maps and outdoors information.

Plumas County Visitors Center (☏530-283-6345; www.plumascounty.org; 550 Crescent St; ⊙8am-5pm Mon-Sat) Half a mile west of town.

Plumas National Forest Headquarters (☏530-283-2050; 159 Lawrence St; ⊙8am-4:30pm Mon-Fri) For maps and outdoors information.

Bucks Lake

This clear mountain lake is cherished by locals in the know. Surrounded by pine forests, it's excellent for swimming, fishing and boating. It's about 17 miles southwest of Quincy, via the white-knuckle roads of Bucks Lake Rd (Hwy 119). The region is lined with beautiful **hiking trails**, including the Pacific Crest Trail, which passes through the adjoining 21,000-acre Bucks Lake Wilderness in the northwestern part of Plumas National Forest. In winter, the last 3 miles of Bucks Lake Rd are closed by snow, making it ideal for cross-country skiers.

Bucks Lake Lodge (☏530-283-2262; www.buckslakelodge.com; 16525 Bucks Lake Rd; d $99-109, cabins $145-195; 🔊🐕) is right on the lakeshore and rents boats and fishing tackle in summer and cross-country skis in winter. The **restaurant** (mains $8 to $16) is popular with locals. **Haskins Valley Inn** (☏530-283-9667; www.haskinsvalleyinn.com; 1305 Haskins Circle; r $129-149; 🔊) is actually a B&B across the street from the lake, with cozily overstuffed furnishings, woodsy paintings, Jacuzzis, fireplaces and a deck. The bold southwestern rugs and heavy rough timber bed posts of the Cowboy Room is a favorite.

Five first-come, first-served **campgrounds** (sites $20-25) are open from June to September. Get a map at the Plumas National Forest Headquarters (p287) or the Mt Hough Ranger District Office (p287), both in Quincy.

MT SHASTA & AROUND

'Lonely as God, and white as a winter moon, Mount Shasta starts up sudden and solitary from the heart of the great black forests of Northern California,' wrote poet Joaquin Miller on the sight of this lovely mountain. A sight of it is so awe-inspiring that the new age prattle about its power as an 'energy vortex' begins to sound plausible even after a first glimpse.

There are a million ways to explore the mountain and surrounding Shasta-Trinity National Forest, depending on the season – you can take scenic drives or get out and hike, mountain bike, raft, ski or snowshoe. At Mt Shasta's base sit three excellent little towns: Dunsmuir, Mt Shasta City and McCloud. Each community has a distinct personality, but all share a wild-mountain sensibility and first-rate restaurants and places to stay. In the same dramatic vicinity rise the snaggle-toothed peaks of Castle Crags, just 6 miles west of Dunsmuir.

Northeast of Mt Shasta, a long drive and a world away, is remote, eerily beautiful Lava Beds National Monument, a blistered badland of petrified fire. The contrasting cool wetlands of Klamath Basin National Wildlife Refuges are just west of Lava Beds.

Further east, high desert plateaus give way to the mountains of the northern Sierra. Folks in this remote area are genuinely happy to greet a traveler, even if they're a bit uncertain why you've come.

Mt Shasta

'When I first caught sight of it I was 50 miles away and afoot, alone and weary. Yet all my blood turned to wine, and I have not been weary since,' wrote naturalist John Muir of Mt Shasta in 1874. Mt Shasta's beauty is intoxicating, and the closer you get to her the headier you begin to feel. Dominating the landscape, the mountain is visible for more than 100 miles from many parts of Northern California and southern Oregon. Though not California's highest peak (at 14,162ft it ranks fifth), Mt Shasta is especially magnificent because it rises alone on the horizon, unrivaled by other mountains.

Mt Shasta is part of the vast volcanic Cascade chain that includes Lassen Peak to the south and Mt St Helens and Mt Rainier to the north in Washington state. The presence of thermal hot springs indicates that Mt Shasta is dormant, not extinct. Smoke was seen puffing out of the crater on the summit in the 1850s, though the last eruption was about 200 years ago. The mountain has two cones: the main cone has a crater about 200yd across; the younger, shorter cone on the western flank, called Shastina, has a crater about half a mile wide.

The mountain and surrounding **Shasta-Trinity National Forest** (www.fs.fed.us/r5/shastatrinity) are crisscrossed by trails and dotted with alpine lakes. It's easy to spend days or weeks here, camping, hiking, river rafting, skiing, mountain biking and boating.

The story of the first settlers here is a sadly familiar one: European fur trappers arrived in the area in the 1820s, encountering several Native American tribes, including the Shasta, Karuk, Klamath, Modoc, Wintu and Pit River people. By 1851, hordes of Gold Rush miners had arrived and steamrolled the place, destroying the tribes' traditional life and nearly causing their extinction. Later, the newly completed railroad began to import workers and export timber for the booming lumber industry. And since Mt Shasta City (called Sisson at the time) was the only non-dry town around, it became *the* bawdy, good-time hangout for lumberjacks.

The lumberjacks have now been replaced by middle-aged mystics and outdoor-sports enthusiasts. While the slopes have immediate appeal for explorers, spiritual seekers are attracted to the peak's reported cosmic properties. In 1987, about 5000 believers from around the world convened here for the Harmonic Convergence, a communal meditation for peace. Reverence for the mountain is nothing new; for centuries Native Americans have honored the mountain as sacred, considering it to be no less than the Great Spirit's wigwam.

Many use Redding as a base since there are plenty of chain options along the highway, but Mt Shasta City is the best balance of convenience, value and personality. For food, there are satisfying restaurants at all the mountain towns, though consider having snacks on hand in the car, as the winding drives from the woods to the lunch counter are time-consuming.

◉ Sights & Activities

The Mountain

You can drive almost the whole way up the mountain via the Everitt Memorial Hwy (Hwy A10) and see exquisite views at any time of year. Simply head east on Lake St from downtown Mt Shasta City, then turn left onto Washington Dr and keep going. **Bunny Flat** (6860ft), which has a trailhead for Horse Camp and the Avalanche Gulch summit route, is a busy place with parking spaces, information signboards and a toilet. The section of highway beyond Bunny Flat is only open from about mid-June to October, depending on snow, but if it's clear, it's worth the trouble. This road leads to **Lower Panther Meadow**, where trails connect the campground to a Wintu sacred spring, in the upper meadows near the **Old Ski Bowl** (7800ft) parking area. Shortly thereafter is the highlight of the drive, **Everitt Vista Point** (7900ft), where a short interpretive walk from the parking lot leads to a stone-walled outcrop affording exceptional views of Lassen Peak to the south, the Mt Eddy and Marble Mountains to the west and the whole Strawberry Valley below.

Climbing the summit is best done between May and September, preferably in spring and early summer, when there's still enough soft snow on the southern flank to make footholds easier on the nontechnical route. Although the elements are occasionally volatile and the winds are incredibly strong, the round-trip could conceivably be done in one day with 12 or more hours of solid hiking. A more enjoyable trip takes at least two days with one night on the mountain. How long it actually takes depends on the route selected, the physical condition of the climbers and weather conditions (for weather information call the recorded message of the Forest Service Mt Shasta climbing advisory on ☎530-926-9613).

The hike to the summit from Bunny Flat follows the **Avalanche Gulch Route**. Although it is only about 7 miles, the vertical climb is more than 7000ft, so acclimatizing to the elevation is important – even hearty hikers will be short of breath. Additionally this route requires crampons, an ice ax and a helmet, all of which can be rented locally. Rock slides, while rare, are also a hazard. If

Mt Shasta Area

you want to make the climb without gear, the only option is the **Clear Creek Route** to the top, which leaves from the east side of the mountain. In late summer, this route is usually manageable in hiking boots, though there's still loose scree, and it should be done as an overnight hike. Novices should contact the Mt Shasta ranger station (p294) for a list of available guides.

There's a charge to climb beyond 10,000ft: a three-day summit pass costs $20, an annual pass is $30. Contact the ranger station for details. You must obtain a free wilderness permit any time you go into the wilderness, whether on the mountain or in the surrounding area.

Mt Shasta Board & Ski Park   SNOW SPORTS (☎ snow reports 530-926-8686; www.skipark.com; full-day lift tickets adult/child $44/25; ⏱ 9am-9pm Thu-Sat, to 4pm Sun-Tue) On the south slope of Mt Shasta, off Hwy 89 heading toward McCloud, this winter skiing and snowboarding park opens depending on snowfall. The park has a 1435ft vertical drop, 32 alpine runs and 18 miles of cross-country trails. These are all good for beginner and intermediate skiers, and are a less-crowded alternative to the slopes around Lake Tahoe.

Rentals, instruction and weekly specials are available. It's Northern California's largest night-skiing operation. There are lots of inexpensive options for skiing half a day or just at night, when hitting the slopes and taking in a full moon can be enchanting.

In summer, the park occasionally hosts mountain-biking events.

The Lakes

There are a number of pristine mountain lakes near Mt Shasta. Some of them are accessible only by dirt roads or hiking trails and are great for getting away from it all.

The closest lake to Mt Shasta City is lovely **Lake Siskiyou** (also the largest), 2.5 miles southwest on Old Stage Rd, where you can peer into **Box Canyon Dam**, a 200ft-deep chasm. Another 7 miles up in the mountains, southwest of Lake Siskiyou on Castle Lake Rd, lies **Castle Lake**, an unspoiled gem surrounded by granite formations and pine forest. Swimming, fishing, picnicking and free camping are popular in summer; in winter folks ice-skate on the lake. **Lake Shastina**, about 15 miles northwest of town, off Hwy 97, is another beauty.

❶ Information

Peak tourist season is from Memorial Day through Labor Day and weekends during ski season (late November to mid-April depending on snow fall). The ranger station (p294) and visitors center (p294) are in Mt Shasta City.

Mt Shasta City

Comfortable and practical Mt Shasta City (population 3330) glows in the shadow of the white pyramid of Mt Shasta. The downtown is charming; you can spend hours poking around bookstores, galleries and boutiques. Orienting yourself is easy with the mountain looming over the east side of town and you may get a kink in your neck from admiring it. The downtown area is a few blocks east of I-5. Take the Central Mt Shasta exit, then drive east on Lake St past the visitors center, up to the town's main intersection at Mt Shasta Blvd, the principal drag.

◉ Sights & Activities

To head out hiking on your own, first stop by the ranger station or the visitors center for excellent free trail guides, including several access points along the **Pacific Crest Trail**. Gorgeous **Black Butte**, a striking, treeless, black volcanic cone, rises almost 3000ft. The 2.5-mile trail to the top takes at least 2½ hours for the round-trip. It's steep and rocky in many places, and there is no shade or water, so don't hike on a hot summer day. Wear good, thick-soled shoes or hiking boots and bring plenty of water. If you want an easier amble, try the 10-mile **Sisson-Callahan National Recreation Trail**, a partially paved trail that affords great views of Mt Shasta and the jagged Castle Crags, following a historic route established in the mid-1800s by prospectors, trappers and cattle ranchers to connect the mining town of Callahan with the town of Sisson, now called Mt Shasta City.

Mt Shasta City Park & Sacramento River Headwaters   PARK
(Nixon Rd) Off Mt Shasta Blvd, about a mile north of downtown, the headwaters of the Sacramento River gurgle up from the ground in a large, cool spring. It's about as pure as water can get – so bring a bottle and have a drink. The park also has walking trails, picnic spots, sports fields and courts, and a children's playground.

Sisson Museum   MUSEUM
(www.mountshastasissonmuseum.org; 1 Old Stage Rd; suggested donation $1; ⊙10am-4pm Mon-Sat, 1-4pm Sun Jun-Sep, 1-4pm Fri-Sun Oct-Dec, 1-4pm daily Apr & May) A half-mile west of the freeway, this former hatchery headquarters is full of curious mountaineering artifacts and old pictures. The changing exhibitions highlight history – geological and human – but also occasionally showcase local artists. Next door, the oldest operating hatchery in the West maintains outdoor ponds teeming with rainbow trout that will eventually be released into lakes and rivers.

Shastice Park   SKATING
(www.msrec.org; cnr Rockfellow & Adams Drs; adult/child $10/5; ⊙10am-5pm Mon-Thu, to 9pm Fri & Sat, 1:30-5pm Sun) East of downtown, the immense outdoor skating rink is open to ice-skaters in winter and in-line skaters on summer weekends.

River Dancers Rafting & Kayaking   RAFTING
(☑530-926-3517; www.riverdancers.com; 302 Terry Lynn Ave) Excellent outfit run by active

environmentalists who guide one- to five-day white-water-rafting excursions down the area's rivers: the Klamath, Sacramento, Salmon, Trinity and Scott. Prices start with a half-day on the nearby Sacramento River for $75.

Shasta Mountain Guides OUTDOORS
(☏530-926-3117; http://shastaguides.com) Offers two-day guided climbs of Mt Shasta between April and September, with all gear and meals included, for $650 per person. The experienced mountaineers have operated in Shasta for 30 years.

🐚 Courses

Osprey Outdoors Kayak School KAYAKING
(www.ospreykayak.com; 2925 Cantara Loop Rd) Owner and instructor Michael Kirwin has a reputation for quality classes on high mountain lakes and rivers. Expect to pay around $175 per adult per day.

Mt Shasta Mountaineering School ADVENTURE SPORTS
(www.swsmtns.com; 210a E Lake St) Conducts clinics and courses for serious climbers, or those looking to get serious. A two-day summit climb of Mt Shasta costs $525.

👉 Tours

Note that hiking Mt Shasta doesn't require an operator, but those wanting one have plenty of options; ask at the visitor center.

Shasta Vortex Adventures OUTDOORS, MEDITATION
(www.shastavortex.com; 400 Chestnut St) For a uniquely Mt Shasta outdoor experience, Shasta Vortex offers low-impact trips accented with the spiritual quest as much as the physical journey. The focus of the trips includes guided meditation and an exploration of the mountain's metaphysical power. Full-day tours for two people cost $474; larger groups get a slight discount.

🛏 Sleeping

Shasta really has it all – from free rustic camping to plush boutique B&Bs. If you are intent on staying at the upper end of the spectrum, you should make reservations well in advance, especially on weekends and holidays and during ski season.

Camping in the area is excellent and the visitors center has details on over two dozen campgrounds around Mt Shasta. Check with the Mt Shasta and McCloud ranger stations

about USFS campgrounds in the area. As long as you set up camp at least 200ft from the water and get a free campfire permit from a ranger station, you can camp near many mountain lakes. Castle Lake (6450ft) and Gumboot Lake (6000ft) have free tent camping (purify your own drinking water), but are closed in winter. Lovely Toad Lake (7060ft), 18 miles from Mt Shasta City, isn't a designated camping area, but you may camp there if you follow regulations. To get there go down the 11-mile gravel road (4WD advised) and walk the last quarter-mile.

Many modest motels stretch along S Mt Shasta Blvd. All have hot tubs and wi-fi, and rooms cost between $60 and $140 in peak season. As many of them were built in the '50s, the cost difference is basically based on how recently they were remodeled. Many motels offer discount ski packages in winter and lower midweek rates year-round.

★ Historic Lookout & Cabin Rentals CABIN $
(☏530-994-2184; www.fs.fed.us/r5/shastatrinity; r up to 4 people from $75) What better way to rough it in style than to bunk down in a fire lookout on forested slopes? Built from the 1920s to '40s, cabins come with cots, tables and chairs, have panoramic views and can accommodate four people. Details about Hirz Mountain, Little Mt Hoffman and Post Creek Lookouts can all be found on the national forest website.

Panther Meadows CAMPGROUND $
(tent sites free; ⊙usually Jul-Nov) Ten walk-in tent sites (no drinking water) sit at the timberline, right at the base of the mountain. They're a few miles up the mountain from other options, but are still easily accessible from Everitt Memorial Hwy. No reservations; arrive early to secure a site.

Lake Siskiyou Camp-Resort CAMPGROUND $
(☏530-926-2618; www.lakesis.com; 4239 WA Barr Rd; tent/RV sites from $20/29, cabins $107-152; 🛜🐕) Tucked away on the shore of Lake Siskiyou, this sprawling place has a summer-camp feel (there's an arcade and an ice-cream stand). Hardly rustic, it has a swimming beach, and kayak, canoe, fishing boat and paddle-boat rentals. Lots of amenities make it a good option for families on an RV trip.

Swiss Holiday Lodge MOTEL $
(☏530-926-3446; www.swissholidaylodge.com; 2400 S Mt Shasta Blvd; d from $60; 🌀🛜🐕🏊)

WEED & STEWART MINERAL SPRINGS

Just outside Weed, **Stewart Mineral Springs** (☑530-938-2222; www.stewartmineral-springs.com; 4617 Stewart Springs Rd; mineral baths $28, sauna $18; ☺10am-6pm Sun-Wed, to 7pm Thu-Sat) is a popular alternative (read clothing-optional) hangout on the banks of a clear mountain stream. Locals come for the day and visitors from afar come for weeks. Henry Stewart founded these springs in 1875 after Native Americans revived him from a near-death experience. He attributed his recovery to the healthful properties of the mineral waters, said to draw toxins out of the body.

Today you can soak in a private claw-foot tub or steam in the dry-wood sauna. Other perks include massage, body wraps, meditation, a Native American sweat lodge and a riverside sunbathing deck. You'll want to call ahead to be sure there is space in the steam and soaking rooms, especially on busy weekends. Dining and **accommodations** (tent & RV sites $35, tipis $50-55, r $70, cabins $90-100) are available. To reach the springs, go 10 miles north of Mt Shasta City on I-5, past Weed to the Edgewood exit, then turn left at Stewart Springs Rd and follow the signs.

While in the area, tickle your other senses at the **Mt Shasta Lavender Farms** (www.mtshastalavenderfarms.com; Harry Cash Rd, off Hwy A12; 100 stems $4; ☺9am-4pm mid-Jun–early Aug), 16 miles northwest of Weed. You can harvest your own sweet French lavender in the June and July blooming season. Or drink up the tasty porter at the **Weed Mt Shasta Brewing Company** (www.weedales.com; 360 College Ave, Weed). The rich, amber-colored Mountain High IPA is delicious, but watch out – at 7% ABV it has real kick.

Run by a friendly family and a small, energetic dog, you get a peek of the mountain from the back windows of these clean, well-priced rooms.

Horse Camp   HUT $

(www.sierraclubfoundation.org; per person with/without tent $5/3) This 1923 alpine lodge run by the Sierra Club is a 2-mile hike uphill from Bunny Flat, at 8000ft. The stone construction and natural setting are lovely. Caretakers staff the hut from May to September only.

McBride Springs   CAMPGROUND $

(tent sites $10; ☺Memorial Day-late Oct, depending on weather) Easily accessible from Everitt Memorial Hwy, this campground has running water and pit toilets, but no showers. It's near mile-marker 4, at an elevation of 5000ft. It's no beauty – a recent root disease killed many of the white fir trees that shaded the sites – but it's convenient. Arrive early in the morning to secure a spot (no reservations).

★ Shasta MountInn   B&B $$

(☑530-926-1810; www.shastamountinn.com; 203 Birch St; r with/without fireplace $185/135; 🛜) Only antique on the outside, this bright Victorian 1904 farmhouse is all relaxed minimalism, bold colors and graceful decor on the inside. Each airy room has a great bed and exquisite views of the luminous mountain.

Enjoy the expansive garden, wraparound deck, outdoor sauna and a complimentary foot massage. Not relaxed enough yet? Chill on the perfectly placed porch swings.

Dream Inn   B&B $$

(☑530-926-1536; www.dreaminnmtshastacity.com; 326 Chestnut St; r with shared bath $80-160, ste $120-160; 🛜❄) Made up of two houses in the center of town: one is a meticulously kept Victorian cottage stuffed with fussy knickknacks; the other a Spanish-style two-story with chunky, raw-wood furniture and no clutter. A rose garden with a koi pond joins the two properties. A hefty breakfast is included.

Finlandia Motel   MOTEL $$

(☑530-926-5596; www.finlandiamotel.com; 1612 S Mt Shasta Blvd; r $65-120, with kitchen $115-200) An excellent deal, the standard rooms are... standard – clean and simple. The suites get a little chalet flair with vaulted pine ceilings and mountain views. There's an outdoor hot tub and the Finnish sauna is available by appointment.

Strawberry Valley Inn   B&B $$

(☑530-926-2052; 1142 S Mt Shasta Blvd; d $99-159; 🛜) The understated rooms surround a garden courtyard, allowing you to enjoy the intimate feel of a B&B without the pressure of having to chat with the darling newlyweds around the breakfast table. A continental breakfast is included, guests can use the kitchen and the new owners are keen to please.

Mt Shasta Resort   RESORT $$

(☑ 530-926-3030; www.mountshastaresort.com; 1000 Siskiyou Lake Blvd; r from $109, 1-/2-bedroom chalets from $169/229; 🖲 🖳) Divinely situated away from town, this upscale golf resort and spa has Arts and Crafts–style chalets nestled in the woods around the shores of Lake Siskiyou. They're a bit soulless, but they're immaculate, and each has a kitchen and gas fireplace. Basic lodge rooms are near the golf course, which boasts some challenging greens and amazing views of the mountain.

The restaurant has excellent views as well and serves Californian cuisine with a large selection of steaks.

✕ Eating

Trendy restaurants and cafes here come and go with the snowmelt, but there are still some tried-and-true places, favored by locals and visitors alike. For more options head 6 miles south to Dunsmuir, an unexpected hotspot for great food. A **farmers market** (⊙ 3:30-6pm Mon) sets up on Mt Shasta Blvd during summer.

Mount Shasta Pastry   BAKERY $

(610 S Mt Shasta Blvd; pastries from $1.95; ⊙ 6am-2:30pm Mon-Sat, 7am-1pm Sun) Walk in hungry and you'll be plagued with an existential breakfast crisis: the feta spinach quiche or the Tuscan scramble? The flaky croissants or a divine apricot turnover? It also serves terrific sandwiches, gourmet pizza and Peet's Coffee.

Poncho & Lefkowitz   MEXICAN, INTERNATIONAL $

(401 S Mt Shasta Blvd; meals $4-12; ⊙ 11am-4pm Tue-Sat; 🖋) Surrounded by picnic tables, this classy, wood-sided food cart – sort of a cafe on wheels – turns out juicy Polish sausage, big plates of nachos and veggie burritos. It's a good bet for food on the go.

Berryvale Grocery & Deli   MARKET $

(www.berryvale.com; 305 S Mt Shasta Blvd; mains $9; ⊙ 8:30am-7pm Mon-Sat, 10am-6pm Sun; 🖋) 🌿 This market sells groceries and organic produce to the health conscious. The excellent deli cafe serves good coffee and an array of tasty – mostly veggie – salads, sandwiches and burritos.

★ Trinity Café   CALIFORNIAN $$

(☑ 530-926-6200; 622 N Mt Shasta Blvd; mains $17-28; ⊙ 5-9pm Tue-Sat) Trinity has long ri-

valed the Bay Area's best. The owners, who hail from Napa, infuse the bistro with a Wine Country feel and an extensive, excellent wine selection. The organic menu ranges from delectable, perfectly cooked steaks, savory roast game hen to creamy-on-the-inside, crispy-on-the-outside polenta. The warm, mellow mood makes for an overall delicious experience.

Lily's   CALIFORNIAN $$

(www.lilysrestaurant.com; 1013 S Mt Shasta Blvd; breakfast & lunch mains $9-17, dinner mains $14-25; ⊙ 8am-4pm Mon-Fri, 4-10pm Sat & Sun; 🖋 🖳) Enjoy quality Californian cuisine – Asian- and Mediterranean-touched salads, fresh sandwiches and all kinds of veg options – in a cute, white, clapboard house. Outdoor tables overhung by flowering trellises are almost always full, especially for breakfast. After closing and re-opening in a few variations, the old management is back, keeping this a Shasta classic.

Andaman Healthy Thai Cuisine   THAI $$

(313 N Shasta Blvd; mains $12-23; ⊙ 11am-9pm Mon, Tue, Thu & Fri, from 4pm Sat & Sun) The food is great, but the kitchen and the staff can't keep up with the crowds. It also serves burgers if you're traveling with fussy folk.

☕ Drinking & Nightlife

Goats Tavern   BAR

(www.thegoatmountshasta.com; 107 Chestnut St; ⊙ 7am-6pm; 🖲) Come here first to drink – it has 12 taps rotating some of the best microbrewed beer in the country – and then tuck into a 'wino burger,' which comes topped with peppered goat cheese, thick sliced bacon and a red-wine reduction sauce. It's a friendly place with an affable staff, surly regulars and a great summer patio.

Seven Suns Coffee & Cafe   CAFE

(1011 S Mt Shasta Blvd; light meals from $6.75; ⊙ 5:30am-7pm; 🖲) This snug little hangout serves organic, locally roasted coffee and is consistently busy. There's live acoustic music some evenings.

🔒 Shopping

Looking for an imported African hand drum, some prayer flags or a nice crystal? You've come to the right place. The downtown shopping district has a handful of cute little boutiques to indulge a little shopping for the spiritual seeker.

Village Books BOOKS
(320 N Mt Shasta Blvd; ⊘10am-6pm Mon-Sat, 11am-4pm Sun) Carries fascinating volumes about Mt Shasta, on topics ranging from geology and hiking to folklore and mysticism.

Fifth Season Sports SPORTS
(☑530-926-3606; http://thefifthseason.com; 300 N Mt Shasta Blvd; ⊘8am-5pm) A favorite outdoor store in Shasta, this place rents camping, mountain-climbing and backpacking gear and has staff familiar with the mountain. It also rents skis, snowshoes and snowboards.

ⓘ Information

Mt Shasta Ranger Station (☑530-926-4511; www.fs.usda.gov/stnf; 204 W Alma St; ⊘8am-4:30pm Mon-Fri) One block west of Mt Shasta Blvd. Issues wilderness and mountain-climbing permits, good advice, weather reports and all you need for exploring the area. It also sells topographic maps.

Mt Shasta Visitors Center (☑530-926-4865; www.mtshastachamber.com; 300 Pine St; ⊘9am-5:30pm Mon-Sat, to 4:30pm Sun summer, 10am-4pm daily winter) Detailed information on recreation and lodging across Siskiyou County.

ⓘ Getting There & Around

Greyhound (www.greyhound.com) buses heading north and south on I-5 stop opposite the Vet's Club (406 N Mt Shasta Blvd) and at the **depot** (628 S Weed Blvd) in Weed, 8 miles north on I-5. Services include Redding ($23, one hour and 20 minutes, three daily), Sacramento ($55, 5½ hours, three daily) and San Francisco ($68, 10½ hours, two or three times daily).

The **STAGE bus** (☑530-842-8295; www.co.siskiyou.ca.us) includes Mt Shasta City in its local I-5 corridor route (fares $1.75 to $8, depending on distance), which also serves McCloud, Dunsmuir, Weed and Yreka several times each weekday. Other buses connect at Yreka.

Dunsmuir

If you love railroad towns, stop here. Built by Central Pacific Railroad, Dunsmuir (population 1650) was originally named Pusher, for the auxiliary 'pusher' engines that muscled the heavy steam engines up the steep mountain grade. In 1886 Canadian coal baron Alexander Dunsmuir came to Pusher and was so enchanted that he promised the people a fountain if they would name the town after him. The fountain stands in the park today.

Stop there to quench your thirst; it could easily be – as locals claim – 'the best water on earth.'

Dunsmuir might have aptly been named Phoenix. Rising from the ashes, this town has survived one cataclysmic disaster after another – avalanche, fire, flood, even a toxic railroad spill in 1991. Long since cleaned up, the river has been restored to pristine levels and the community has a notably plucky spirit, though today a number of empty storefronts attest to the community's greatest challenge: the Global Economic Crisis.

Still, it's home to a spirited set of artists, naturalists, urban refugees and native Dunsmuirians, who are rightly proud of the fish-stocked rivers (yes, the fishing is great) around their little community. Its downtown streets – once a bawdy Gold Rush district of five saloons and three brothels – hold cafes, restaurants and galleries, and the town's reputation is still inseparable from the trains.

Split in two by the I-5, the southern half is where you'll find the bright and pleasant historic downtown.

◉ Sights & Activities

The chamber of commerce stocks maps of **cycling trails** and **swimming holes** on the Upper Sacramento River.

Ruddle Cottage GALLERY
(www.ruddlecottage.net; 5815 Sacramento Ave; ⊘10am-4pm May-Oct, 11am-4pm Nov-Apr) Behind a shaded garden, cluttered with eclectic sculptures, Jayne Bruck-Fryer's colorful gallery feels a bit like something from a fairy tale. Fryer makes each and every ingenious creation – from sculptures to jewelry – from recycled materials. The pretty fish hanging in the window? Dryer lint!

California Theater HISTORIC BUILDING
(5741 Dunsmuir Ave) At downtown's north end stands what was once the town's pride. In a community effort, this once-glamorous venue is being restored to its original glory. First opened in 1926, the theater hosted stars such as Clark Gable, Carole Lombard and the Marx Brothers. Today the lineup includes second-run films, musical performances and yoga classes.

Dunsmuir City Park & Botanical Gardens PARK
(www.dunsmuirparks.org; ⊘dawn-dusk) FREE
As you follow winding Dunsmuir Ave north

over the freeway, look for this park with its local native gardens and a **vintage steam engine** in front. A forest path from the riverside gardens leads to a small waterfall, but **Mossbrae Falls** are the larger and more spectacular of Dunsmuir's waterfalls.

To reach the falls, park by the railroad tracks (there's no sign), then walk north along the right-hand side of the tracks for a half-hour until you reach a railroad bridge built in 1901. Backtracking slightly from the bridge, you'll find a little path going down through the trees to the river and the falls. Be extremely careful of trains as you walk by the tracks – the river's sound can make it impossible to hear them coming.

Shasta Valley Balloons   BALLOONING
(☑530-926-3612; www.hot-airballoons.com; 5304 Dunsmuir Ave, Dunsmuir; rides $200) Live a dream by seeing the area from a hot-air balloon. The office is in Dunsmuir but flights leave from Montague Municipal Airport, 6 miles east of Yreka.

🛌 Sleeping

Dunsmuir Lodge   MOTEL $
(☑530-235-2884; www.dunsmuirlodge.net; 6604 Dunsmuir Ave; r $79-153; 🛜🐾) Toward the south entrance of town, the simple but tastefully renovated rooms have hardwood floors, big chunky blond-wood bed frames and tiled baths. A grassy communal picnic area overlooks the canyon slope. It's a peaceful little place and very good value.

Cave Springs   MOTEL, CABIN $
(☑530-235-2721; www.cavesprings.com; 4727 Dunsmuir Ave; cabins from $76, r from $99; ❄🛜🐾) These creekside cabins seem unchanged since the 1920s even though the interiors were recently updated. They are rustic – *very* rustic – but their location, nestled on a piney crag above the Sacramento River, is lovely and ideal for anglers. At night the sound of rushing water mingles with the haunting whistle of trains.

The motel rooms are bland, but they're up to modern standards and have amenities.

Dunsmuir Inn & Suites   MOTEL $
(☑530-235-4395; www.dunsmuirinn.com; 5400 Dunsmuir Ave; r $79-159; 🛜) Straightforward, immaculately clean motel rooms make a good, no-fuss option.

Railroad Park Resort   INN, CAMPGROUND $$
(☑530-235-4440, 800-974-7245; www.rrpark.com; 100 Railroad Park Rd; tent/RV sites from $29/37, d

$105-130; ❄🛜🐾🐾) About a mile south of town, off I-5, visitors can spend the night inside refitted vintage railroad cars and cabooses. The grounds are fun for kids, who can run around the engines and plunge in a centrally situated pool. The deluxe boxcars are furnished with antiques and claw-foot tubs, although the cabooses are simpler and a bit less expensive.

You get tremendous views of Castle Crags, a peaceful creekside setting and tall pines shading the adjoining campground.

🍴 Eating & Drinking

There's an impressive number of really good eating options for such a small town.

Cornerstone Bakery & Café   CAFE $
(5759 Dunsmuir Ave; mains $8-9; ⏰8am-2pm Thu-Mon; 🍴) Smack in the middle of town, it serves smooth, strong coffee, espresso and chai. All the baked goods – including thick, gooey cinnamon rolls – are warm from the oven. Creative omelets include cactus. The wine list is extensive, as is the dessert selection.

★ Dunsmuir Brewery Works   PUB FOOD $$
(☑530-235-1900; www.dunsmuirbreweryworks. info; 5701 Dunsmuir Ave; mains $11-20; ⏰11am-9pm Tue-Sun; 🛜) It's hard to describe this little microbrew pub without veering into hyperbole. Start with the beer: the crisp ales and chocolate porter are perfectly balanced, and the IPA is apparently pretty good, too, because patrons are always drinking it dry. Soak it up with awesome bar food – a warm potato salad, bratwurst or a thick Angus burger.

The atmosphere, with a buzzing patio and aw-shucks staff, completes a perfect picture.

Brown Trout Gallery & Dogwood Diner   CAFE $$
(☑530-235-0754; 5841 Sacramento Ave; mains $10; ⏰11am-8pm Mon, Tue & Fri, 8am-9pm Sat & Sun; 🛜🍴) This casual, high-ceilinged, brick-walled hangout (formerly the town mercantile) serves creative, internationally inspired dishes from burgers and salads to pasta and wild-caught salmon. Weekend breakfasts are a treat with mains like poached eggs and butter beans, pineapple French toast or peanut-butter-stuffed cinnamon rolls.

Railroad Park Dinner House   CALIFORNIAN $$
(☑530-235-4440; Railroad Park Resort, 100 Railroad Park Rd; mains $15-28; ⏰5-9pm Fri & Sat Apr, 5-9pm Wed-Sun May-Oct) Set inside a vintage

railroad car with views of Castle Crags, this popular restaurant-bar offers trainloads of dining-car ambience and Californian cuisine. Prime rib specials are on Friday and Saturdays.

YAKs AMERICAN $$
(4917 Dunsmuir Ave; mains around $12; ◷7:30am-7pm Mon-Sat, 7:30am-5pm Sun; ◈) Hiding under the Hitching Post sign just off I-5, come here to blow your diet. Breakfast means Cuban peppersteak hash or perhaps home-baked cinnamon roll French toast with choice of house syrups like Baileys bourbon-butter. Lunch offers a huge range of burgers (try the one with the house-roasted coffee rub). There's also a take-out counter.

Sengthongs THAI, VIETNAMESE $$
(☑530-235-4770; http://sengthongs.com; 5855 Dunsmuir Ave; mains $17-27; ◷usually 5-8:30pm Thu-Sun) This funky joint serves up sizzling Thai, Lao and Vietnamese food and books first-rate jazz, reggae, salsa or blues most nights. Many dishes are simply heaping bowls of noodles, though the meat dishes – flavored with ginger, scallions and spices – are more complex and uniformly delicious.

★**Café Maddalena** EUROPEAN, NORTH AFRICAN $$$
(☑530-235-2725; www.cafemaddalena.com; 5801 Sacramento Ave; mains $22-25; ◷5-10pm Thu-Sun Feb-Nov) Simple and elegant, this cafe put Dunsmuir on the foodie map. The menu was designed by chef Bret LaMott (of Trinity Café fame) and changes weekly to feature dishes from southern Europe and north Africa. Some highlights include pan-roasted king salmon with basil cream, or sauteed rabbit with carrots and morel sauce.

The wine bar is stocked with rare Mediterranean labels, including a great selection of Spanish varietals.

ℹ️ Information

Dunsmuir Chamber of Commerce (☑530-235-2177; www.dunsmuir.com; Suite 100, 5915 Dunsmuir Ave; ◷10am-3:30pm Tue-Sat) Free maps, walking-guide pamphlets and excellent information on outdoor activities.

ℹ️ Getting There & Away

Amtrak Station (www.amtrak.com; 5750 Sacramento Ave) Dunsmuir's Amtrak station is the only train stop in Siskiyou County and it is not staffed. Buy tickets for the north–south Coast Starlight on board the train, but only after making reservations by phone or via the website. The Coast Starlight runs once daily to Redding ($28, 1¾ hours), Sacramento ($38, 5¾ hours) and Oakland ($42, eight hours).

STAGE Bus (☑530-842-8295) The STAGE bus includes Dunsmuir in its local I-5 corridor route, which also serves Mt Shasta City ($2.50, 20 minutes), Weed ($4, 30 minutes) and Yreka ($6, 1¼ hours) several times each weekday. The bus runs on Dunsmuir Ave.

Castle Crags State Park

The stars of this glorious state park alongside Castle Crags Wilderness Area are its soaring spires of ancient granite formed some 225 million years ago, with elevations ranging from 2000ft along the Sacramento River to more than 6500ft at the peaks. The crags are similar to the granite formations of the eastern Sierra, and Castle Dome resembles Yosemite's famous Half Dome.

Rangers at the **park entrance station** (☑530-235-2684; per car $8) have information and maps covering nearly 28 miles of **hiking trails**. There's also **fishing** in the Sacramento River at the picnic area on the opposite side of I-5.

If you drive past the campground, you'll reach **Vista Point**, near the start of the strenuous 2.7-mile **Crags Trail**, which rises through the forest past the Indian Springs spur trail, then clambers up to the base of **Castle Dome**. You're rewarded with unsurpassed views of Mt Shasta, especially if you scramble the last 100yd or so up into the rocky saddle gap. The park also has gentle **nature trails** and 8 miles of the **Pacific Crest Trail**, which passes through the park at the base of the crags.

The **campground** (☑reservations 800-444-7275; www.reserveamerica.com; tent & RV sites $35) is one of the nicer public campgrounds in this area, and very easily accessible from the highway. It has running water, hot showers, and three spots that can accommodate RVs but have no hookups. Sites are shady, but suffer from traffic noise. You can camp anywhere in the Shasta-Trinity National Forest surrounding the park if you get a free campfire permit, issued at park offices. At the time of writing, the future of this state park was uncertain because of budget issues.

McCloud

This tiny, historic mill town (population 1101) sits at the foot of the south slope of Mt Shasta, and is an alternative to staying in Mt Shasta City. Quiet streets retain a simple, easygoing charm. It's the closest settlement to Mt Shasta Board & Ski Park and is surrounded by abundant natural beauty. Hidden in the woods upriver are woodsy getaways for the Western aristocracy, including mansions owned by the Hearst and Levi Strauss estates.

The town made some press during a recent battle against the Nestlé corporation, which announced a plan for a water bottling facility on the site of the defunct mill. Fearing the damage to the local watershed, a cadre of residents organized to oppose the factory. By 2009 they had succeeded in entangling the multinational giant in red tape and bad publicity, and Nestlé scuttled the project.

◉ Sights & Activities

The **McCloud River Loop**, a gorgeous, 6-mile, partially paved road along the Upper McCloud River, begins at Fowlers Camp, 5.5 miles east of town on Hwy 89, and re-emerges about 11 miles east of McCloud. Along the loop, turn off at **Three Falls** for a pretty trail that passes...yep, three lovely falls and a riparian habitat for bird-watching in the Bigelow Meadow. The loop can easily be done by car, bicycle or on foot, and has five first-come, first-served campgrounds.

Other good hiking trails include the **Squaw Valley Creek Trail** (not to be confused with the ski area near Lake Tahoe), an easy 5-mile loop trail south of town, with options for swimming, fishing and picnicking. Also south of town, **Ah-Di-Na** is the remains of a Native American settlement and historic homestead once owned by the William Randolph Hearst family. Sections of the **Pacific Crest Trail** are accessible from Ah-Di-Na Campground, off Squaw Valley Rd, and also up near Bartle Gap, offering head-spinning views.

Fishing and swimming are popular on remote **Lake McCloud** reservoir, 9 miles south of town on Squaw Valley Rd, which is signposted in town as Southern. You can also go fishing on the Upper McCloud River (stocked with trout) and at the Squaw Valley Creek.

The huge **McCloud Mercantile** anchors the downtown. There's a hotel upstairs and it hosts a couple of restaurants that warrant a longer stay, but those just passing though can get a bag of licorice at the old-world candy counter or browse the main floor. The collection of dry goods is very woodsy and very NorCal: Woolrich blankets, handmade soap and interesting gifts for the gardener, outdoors person or chef.

A tiny **historical museum** (⊙11am-3pm Mon-Sat, 1-3pm Sun) FREE sits opposite the depot and could use a bit of organization – it has the feel of a cluttered, messy thrift store – but tucked in the nooks and crannies are plenty of worthwhile curiosities from the town's past.

🛏 Sleeping

Lodging in McCloud is taken seriously – all are excellent and reservations are recommended. For camping go to the McCloud ranger district office for information on the

---

SKIING THE NORTHERN MOUNTAINS

Tahoe it ain't, but visitors in winter months will find a few small ski areas that lack the crowds and attitude of elsewhere in the state. These are also places for snowshoeing, sledding, cross-country skiing and general fun in the snow. **Lassen Volcanic National Park** (p279) doesn't have lifts or lodges but it does have over 150 miles of marked and unmarked trails for unmotorized winter sports. Through spring you'll see plenty of folks taking to the woods on skis.

Try the area's ski 'resorts':

Mt Shasta Board & Ski Park (p289) The biggest in this region, although some winters it doesn't snow enough for it to open at all.

Coppervale Ski Hill (Westwood; day passes $20-25; ⊙12:30-4:30pm Tue & Thu, 9:30am-4pm Sat & Sun) There's not even a website for this place (15 miles from Chester near Lake Almanor), but it does have one poma lift, a rope tow and a half pipe. Kids under six ski for free.

Cedar Pass Snow Park (p301) Way over in the Modoc National Forest, 20 minutes from Alturas, this tiny, community-run place has a rope tow, a T-bar and nice family vibe. Find specials and changing opening hours on its Facebook page: https://www.facebook.com/NCCPSP.

half-dozen campgrounds nearby. Fowlers Camp is the most popular. The campgrounds have a range of facilities, from primitive (no running water and no fee) to developed (hot showers and fees of up to $15 per site). Ask about nearby fire-lookout cabins for rent – they give amazing, remote views of the area.

Stoney Brook Inn
HOTEL $

(🕿 530-964-2300; www.stoneybrookinn.com; 309 W Colombero Dr; s/d with shared bath $53/79, d with private bath $94, ste with kitchen $99-156; 🛜🍽) Smack in the middle of town, under a stand of pines, this alternative B&B also sponsors group retreats. Creature comforts include an outdoor hot tub, a sauna, a Native American sweat lodge and massage by appointment. Downstairs rooms are nicest. Vegetarian breakfast available.

McCloud Dance Country RV Park
CAMPGROUND $

(🕿 530-964-2252; www.mccloudrvpark.com; 480 Hwy 89, at Southern Ave; tent sites $28, RV sites $36-45, cabins $140-175; 🛜🍽) Chock-full of RVs, with sites under the trees and a small creek, this is a good option for families. The view of the mountain is breathtaking and there's a large, grassy picnic ground. Cabins are basic but clean.

★ McCloud River Mercantile Hotel
INN $$

(🕿 530-964-2330; www.mccloudmercantile.com; 241 Main St; r incl breakfast $129-250; 🛜) Stoll up the stairs to the 2nd floor of McCloud's central Mercantile and try not to fall in love; it's all high ceilings, exposed brick and a perfect marriage of preservationist class and modern panache. The rooms are situated within open floor plans, and guests are greeted with fresh flowers and can drift to sleep on feather beds after soaking in claw-foot tubs.

McCloud Hotel
HISTORIC HOTEL $$

(🕿 530-964-2822; www.mccloudhotel.com; 408 Main St; r $128-199; 🌐🛜) Regal, butter-yellow and a whole block long, the grand hotel opened in 1916 and has been a destination for Shasta's visitors ever since. The elegant historic landmark has been restored to a luxurious standard, and the included breakfast has gourmet flair. One room is accessible for travelers with disabilities.

McCloud River Inn
B&B $$

(🕿 530-964-2130; www.mccloudriverinn.com; 325 Lawndale Ct; r incl breakfast $99-199; 🌐) Rooms in this rambling Victorian are fabulously big – the bathrooms alone could sleep two.

In the morning look out for the frittatas; in the evening enjoy a couple of glasses of wine in the cute downstairs wine bar. The atmosphere guarantees that it books up quickly.

✖ Eating

McCloud's eating options are few. For more variety, make the trip over to Mt Shasta City.

Mountain Star Cafe
VEGETARIAN $

(241 Main St; mains $7-9; ⏲8am-3pm; 🌿) 🍃 Deep within the creaking Mercantile, this sweet lunch counter is a surprise, serving vegetarian specials made from locally sourced, organic produce. Some options on the menu during a recent visit included morale biscuits and gravy, a garlicky tempeh Ruben, roast vegetable salad and a homemade oat and veggie burger.

White Mountain Fountain Cafe
AMERICAN $

(241 Main St; mains $8; ⏲8am-4pm) In the window-lined corner of the Mercantile, this old-fashioned little soda fountain serves burgers and shakes. The one coyly called 'Not the Dolly Varden' is an excellent vegetarian sandwich with roasted zucchini, red peppers and garlic aioli.

🍷 Drinking & Nightlife

McCloud Dance Country
DANCE

(www.mcclouddancecountry.com; cnr Broadway & Pine Sts; per couple $20; ⏲7pm Fri & Sat) Dust it up on the 5000-sq-ft maple dance floor in the 1906 Broadway Ballroom. Square dancing, round dancing, ballroom dancing – they do it all. Starting at $299 per couple, multiday packages include lessons and evening dances. It's a worthwhile centerpiece to a weekend getaway. Visit the website to see what's on and whether you need a reservation for the event.

ℹ Information

McCloud Chamber of Commerce (🕿530-964-3113; www.mccloudchamber.com; 205 Quincy St; ⏲10am-4pm Mon-Fri)

McCloud Ranger District Office (🕿530-964-2184; Hwy 89; ⏲8am-4:30pm Mon-Sat summer, 8am-4:30pm Mon-Fri rest of year) A quarter-mile east of town. Detailed information on camping, hiking and recreation.

McArthur-Burney Falls Memorial State Park

This beautiful **state park** (🕿530-335-2777, summer reservations 800-444-7275; www.parks.

ca.gov; day-use/campsites $8/25; 🚻) lies southeast of McCloud, near the crossroads of Hwys 89 and 299 from Redding. The 129ft falls cascade with the same volume of water – 100 million gallons per day – and at the same temperature – 42°F (5°C) – year-round. Clear, lava-filtered water surges over the top and also from springs in the waterfall's face. Teddy Roosevelt loved this place; he called it the 'Eighth Wonder of the World.'

A lookout point beside the parking lot also has trails going up and down the creek from the falls. (Be careful of your footing here; in 2011 there was a fatality in the park when someone slipped on the rocks.) The nature trail heading downstream leads to Lake Britton; other hiking trails include a portion of the Pacific Crest Trail. The scenes in the film *Stand By Me* (1986) where the boys dodge the train were shot on the Lake Britton Bridge trestle in the park.

The park's **campgrounds** (☎530-335-2777, summer reservations 800-444-7275; www.reserveamerica.com; tent & RV sites $35) have hot showers and are open year-round.

About 10 miles northeast of McArthur-Burney Falls, the 6000-acre **Ahjumawi Lava Springs State Park** is known for its abundant springs, aquamarine bays, islets, and jagged flows of black basalt lava. It can only be reached by boats that are launched from Rat Farm, 3 miles north of the town of McArthur along a graded dirt road. Arrangements for primitive camping can be made by calling McArthur-Burney Falls Memorial State Park.

Lava Beds National Monument

A wild landscape of charred volcanic rock and rolling hills, this remote **national monument** (☎530-667-8113; www.nps.gov/labe; 7-day entry per car $10) is reason enough to visit the region. Off Hwy 139, immediately south of Tule Lake National Wildlife Refuge, it's a truly remarkable 72-sq-mile landscape of volcanic features – lava flows, craters, cinder cones, spatter cones, shield volcanoes and amazing lava tubes.

Lava tubes are formed when the surface of hot, spreading lava cools and hardens upon exposure to cold air. The lava inside is thus insulated and stays molten, flowing away to leave an empty tube of solidified lava. Nearly 400 such tubular caves have been found in the monument, and many

more are expected to be discovered. About two dozen or so are currently open for exploration by visitors.

On the south side of the park, the **visitors center** (☎530-667-2282, ext 230; ⊙8am-6pm, shorter hours in winter) has free maps, activity books for kids and information about the monument and its volcanic features and history. Rangers loan mediocre flashlights (and rent helmets and kneepads in the summer season only) for cave exploration and lead summer interpretive programs, including campfire talks and guided cave walks. To explore the caves it's essential you use a high-powered flashlight, wear good shoes and long sleeves (lava is sharp), and do not go alone.

Near the visitors center, a short, one-way **Cave Loop** drive provides access to many lava-tube caves. **Mushpot Cave**, the one nearest the visitors center, has lighting and information signs and is beautiful, besides being a good introductory hike. There are a number of caves that are a bit more challenging, including Labyrinth, Hercules Leg, Golden Dome and Blue Grotto. Each one of these caves has an interesting history – visitors used to ice-skate by lantern light in the bottom of Merrill Cave, and when Ovls Cave was discovered, it was littered with bighorn sheep skulls. There are good brochures with details about each cave available from the visitors center. We found Sunshine Cave and Symbol Bridge caves (the latter is reached via an easy 0.8-mile hike) to be particularly interesting. Rangers are stern with their warnings for new cavers, though, so be sure to check in with the visitors center before exploring to avoid harming the fragile geological and biological resources in the park.

The tall black cone of **Schonchin Butte** (5253ft) has a magnificent outlook accessed via a steep 1-mile hiking trail. Once you reach the top, you can visit the fire-lookout staff between June and September. **Mammoth Crater** is the source of most of the area's lava flows.

The weathered Modoc **petroglyphs** at the base of a high cliff at the far northeastern end of the monument, called Petroglyph Point, are thousands of years old, but unfortunately the short interpretive trail has been closed due to vandalism – the rest is worth checking out anyway. At the visitors center, be sure to take the leaflet explaining the origin of the petroglyphs and their probable meaning. Look for the hundreds of nests in holes high up in the cliff face, which provide shelter for birds that sojourn at the wildlife refuges nearby.

Also at the north end of the monument, be sure to go to the labyrinthine landscape of **Captain Jack's Stronghold**, the Modoc Indians' very effective ancient wartime defense area. A brochure will guide you through the breathtaking Stronghold Trail.

Indian Well Campground (tent & RV sites $10), near the visitors center at the south end of the park, has water and flush toilets, but no showers. The campsites are lovely and have broad views of the surrounding valleys. The nearest place to buy food and camping supplies is on Hwy 139 in the nearby town of Tulelake, but the place is pretty bleak and rugged – just a couple of bars, a bunch of boarded-up buildings and a pair of gas stations. Don't count on finding food out of peak times besides the grocery store.

Klamath Basin National Wildlife Refuges

Of the six stunning national wildlife refuges in this group, Tule Lake and Clear Lake refuges are wholly within California, Lower Klamath refuge straddles the California–Oregon border, and the Upper Klamath, Klamath Marsh and Bear Valley refuges are across the border in Oregon. Bear Valley and Clear Lake (not to be confused with the Clear Lake just east of Ukiah) are closed to the public to protect their delicate habitats, but the rest are open during daylight hours.

These refuges provide habitats for a stunning array of birds migrating along the Pacific Flyway. Some stop over only briefly; others stay longer to mate, make nests and raise their young. The refuges are always packed with birds, but during the spring and fall migrations, populations can rise into the hundreds of thousands.

The **Klamath Basin National Wildlife Refuges visitors center** (530-667-2231; http://klamathbasinrefuges.fws.gov; 4009 Hill Rd, Tulelake; 8am-4:30pm Mon-Fri, 10am-4pm Sat & Sun) sits on the west side of the Tule Lake refuge, about 5 miles west of Hwy 139, near the town of Tule Lake. Follow the signs from Hwy 139 or from Lava Beds National Monument. The center has a bookstore and an interesting video program, as well as maps, information on recent bird sightings and updates on road conditions. It rents photo blinds. Be sure to pick up the excellent, free *Klamath Basin Birding Trail* brochure for detailed lookouts, maps, color photos and a species checklist.

The spring migration peaks during March, and in some years more than a million birds fill the skies. In April and May the songbirds, waterfowl and shorebirds arrive, some to stay and nest, others to build up their energy before they continue north. In summer, ducks, Canada geese and many other waterbirds are raised here. The fall migration peaks in early November. In cold weather the area hosts the largest wintering concentration of bald eagles in the lower 48 states, with 1000 in residence at times from December to February. The Tule Lake and Lower Klamath refuges are the best places to see eagles and other raptors.

The Lower Klamath and Tule Lake refuges attract the largest numbers of birds year-round, and **auto trails** (driving routes) have been set up. Here, a free pamphlet from the visitors center shows the routes. Self-guided **canoe trails** have been established in three of the refuges. Those in the Tule Lake and Klamath Marsh refuges are usually open from July 1 to September 30; no canoe rentals are available. Canoe trails in the Upper Klamath refuge are open year-round. Here, canoes can be rented at **Rocky Point Resort** (541-356-2287; 28121 Rocky Point Rd, Klamath Falls, OR; canoe, kayak & paddle boat rental per hr/half-day/day $15/30/40), on the west side of Upper Klamath Lake.

Camp at nearby Lava Beds National Monument. Alternatively, a couple of RV parks and budget motels cluster along Hwy 139 near the tiny town of Tulelake (4035ft), including the friendly, brightly painted **Ellis Motel** (530-667-5242; 2238 Hwy 139; d with/without kitchen $95/75) about a mile north of town. Comfortable **Fe's B&B** (877-478-0184; www.fesbandb.com; 660 Main St; s/d with shared bath $60/70) has four simple rooms right in 'downtown,' with a big breakfast included. There may or may not be restaurants open (everything was shut at 5pm on a Sunday when we passed). Another option is to drive 9 miles north to Merrill, OR, and stay at the backcountry-cute, good-value **Wild Goose Lodge** (541-331-2701; www.wild-gooselodge.webs.com; 105 E Court Dr, Merrill, OR; r $60, cabins $120;). The closest real town is Klamath Falls, OR, 29 miles from Tulelake.

Modoc National Forest

It's nearly impossible to get your head around this enormous **national forest**

THE AVIAN SUPERHIGHWAY

California is on the Pacific Flyway, a migratory route for hundreds of species of birds heading south in winter and north in summer. There are birds to see year-round, but the best viewing opportunities are during the spring and fall migrations. Flyway regulars include everything from tiny finches, hummingbirds, swallows and woodpeckers to eagles, hawks, swans, geese, ducks, cranes and herons. Much of the flyway route corresponds with I-5 (or Fly-5 in the birds' case), so a drive up the interstate in spring or fall is a show: great Vs of geese undulate in the sky and noble hawks stare from roadside perches.

In Northern California, established wildlife refuges safeguard wetlands used by migrating waterfowl. The Klamath Basin National Wildlife Refuges offer extraordinary year-round bird-watching.

(www.fs.usda.gov/modoc) – it covers almost two million spectacular, remote acres of California's northeastern corner. Travelers through the remote northeast of the state will be passing in and out of its borders constantly. Fourteen miles south of Lava Beds National Monument, on the western edge of the forest, **Medicine Lake** is a stunning crater lake in a caldera (collapsed volcano), surrounded by pine forest, volcanic formations and campgrounds. The enormous volcano that formed the lake is the largest in area in California. When it erupted it ejected pumice followed by flows of obsidian, as can be seen at **Little Glass Mountain**, east of the lake.

Pick up the *Medicine Lake Highlands: Self-Guided Roadside Geology Tour* pamphlet from the McCloud ranger district office to find and learn about the glass flows, pumice deposits, lava tubes and cinder cones throughout the area. Roads are closed by snow from around mid-November to mid-June, but the area is still popular for winter sports, and accessible by cross-country skiing and snowshoeing.

Congratulations are in order for travelers who make it all the way to the **Warner Mountains**. This spur of the Cascade Range in the east of the Modoc National Forest is probably the least-visited range in California. With extremely changeable weather, it's also not so hospitable; there have been snowstorms here in every season of the year. The range divides into the North Warners and South Warners at **Cedar Pass** (elevation 6305ft), east of Alturas. Remote **Cedar Pass Snow Park** (☑ 530-233-3323; all day T-bar adult/child under 6yr-18yr $15/5/12, all-day rope tow $5; ☻ 10am-4pm Sat, Sun & holidays during ski season) offers downhill and cross-country skiing. The majestic **South Warner Wilderness** contains 77 miles of hiking and riding

trails. The best time to use them is from July to mid-October.

Maps, campfire permits and information are all available at the **Modoc National Forest supervisor's headquarters** (☑ 530-233-5811; 800 W 12th St; ☻ 8am-5pm Mon-Fri) in Alturas.

If you are heading east into Nevada from the forest, you'll pass through **Alturas**, the fairly uninspiring seat of Modoc County. The town was founded by the Dorris family in 1874 as a supply point for travelers, and it serves the same function today, providing basic services, motels and family-style restaurants. The best place to stay in town (which won't cost much more than the motels) is the newly re-opened, turn-of-the-century and beautifully period-decorated **Niles Hotel** (☑ 530-233-3773; www.nileshotel.com; 304 S Main St, Alturas; r from $80; ☻), which also has a restaurant where the tables are lit by oil lamps.

WEST OF I-5

The wilderness west of I-5 is right in the sweet spot: here are some of the most rugged towns and seductive wilderness areas in the entire state of California – just difficult enough to reach to discourage big crowds.

The **Trinity Scenic Byway** (Hwy 299) winds spectacularly along the Trinity River and beneath towering cliffs as it makes its way from the plains of Redding to the coastal redwood forests around Arcata. It provides a chance to cut through some of the northern mountains' most pristine wilderness and passes through the vibrant Gold Rush town of Weaverville.

Heavenly Hwy 3 (a highly recommended – although slower and windier – alternative route to I-5) heads north from Weaverville.

This mountain byway transports you through the Trinity Alps – a stunning granite range dotted with azure alpine lakes – past the shores of Lewiston and Trinity Lakes, over the Scott Mountains and finally into emerald, mountain-rimmed Scott Valley. Rough-and-ready Yreka awaits you at the end of the line.

Weaverville

In 1941 a reporter interviewed James Hilton, the British author of *Lost Horizon*. 'In all your wanderings,' the journalist asked, 'what's the closest you've found to a real-life Shangri-La?' Hilton's response? 'A little town in northern California. A little town called Weaverville.'

Cute as a button, Weaverville's streets are lined with flower boxes in the summer and banks of snow in the winter. The seat of Trinity County, it sits amid an endless tract of mountain and forest that's 75% federally owned. With its almost 3300 sq miles, the county is roughly the size of Delaware and Rhode Island together, yet has a total population of only 13,700 and not one freeway or parking meter.

Weaverville (population 3600) is a small gem of a town on the National Register of Historic Places and has a laid-back, gentle bohemian feel (thanks in part to the young back-to-landers and marijuana-growing subculture). You can easily spend a day here just strolling around the quaint storefronts and visiting art galleries, museums and historic structures. If you've got more time, there are 40 miles of hiking and mountain-biking trails in the Weaverville Basin Trail System, or you can cast a line along the Trinity River, Trinity Lake or Lewiston Lake for steelhead, salmon and trout.

⊙ Sights & Activities

★ **Weaverville Joss House State Historic Park**   HISTORIC BUILDING
(☑ 530-623-5284; www.parks.ca.gov; cnr Hwy 299 & Oregon St; tour adult/child $4/2; ⊙ 10am-5pm Thu-Sun, hourly tours until 4pm) The walls here actually talk – they're papered inside with 150-year-old donation ledgers from the once-thriving Chinese community, the immigrants who built Northern California's infrastructure, a rich culture that has all but disappeared. It's a surprise that the oldest continuously used Chinese temple in Cali-

fornia (and an exceptionally beautiful one at that), dating to the 1870s, is in Weaverville.

The blue-and-gold Taoist shrine contains an ornate altar, more than 3000 years old, which was brought here from China. The adjoining schoolhouse was the first to teach Chinese students in California. Even in Asia (let alone California) it's rare to see a Chinese temple with the all the ancient features so well preserved.

JJ Jackson Memorial Museum & Trinity County Historical Park   MUSEUM
(www.trinitymuseum.org; 508 Main St; donation requested; ⊙ 10am-5pm daily May-Oct, noon-4pm daily Apr & Nov-Dec 24, noon-4pm Tue & Sat Dec 26-Mar) Next door to the Joss House you'll find gold-mining and cultural exhibits, plus vintage machinery, memorabilia, an old miner's cabin and a blacksmith shop.

Highland Art Center   GALLERY
(www.highlandartcenter.org; 691 Main St; ⊙ 10am-5pm Mon-Sat, 11am-4pm Sun) Stroll through galleries showcasing local artists.

Coffee Creek Ranch   FISHING, HIKING
(☑ 530-266-3343; www.coffeecreekranch.com) In Trinity Center, these guys lead fishing and fully outfitted pack trips into the Trinity Alps Wilderness and week-long fishing excursions.

🛏 Sleeping

The ranger station (p303) has information on many USFS campgrounds in the area, especially around Trinity Lake. Commercial RV parks, some with tent sites, dot Hwy 299.

Red Hill Motel & Cabins   MOTEL $
(☑ 530-623-4331; www.redhillresorts.com; 116 Red Hill Rd; d $48, cabins with/without kitchen $64/52; ☎ 🐾) This very quiet and rustic motel is tucked under ponderosa pines at the west end of town, just off Main St, next to the library. It's a set of red wooden cabins built in the 1940s and they're equipped with kitchenettes and mini-fridges. The rooms are simple and good value. It sometimes fills with visiting groups, so book ahead.

Weaverville Hotel   HISTORIC HOTEL $$
(☑ 800-750-8957; www.weavervillehotel.com; 203 Main St; r $99-260; ❈ ☎) Play like you're in the Old West at this upscale hotel and historic landmark, refurbished in grand Victorian style. It's luxurious but not stuffy, and the very gracious owners take great care in looking after you. Guests may use the local

gym, and $10 credit at local restaurants is included in the rates. Kids under 12 are not allowed.

Whitmore Inn HISTORIC HOTEL $$
(☎ 530-623-2509; www.whitmoreinn.com; 761 Main St; r $100-165; ❋ ☎) Settle into plush, cozy rooms in this downtown Victorian with a wraparound deck and abundant gardens. One room is accessible for travelers with disabilities. Only kids over five years old are welcome.

✖ Eating

Downtown Weaverville is ready to feed hungry hikers – in the summer the main drag has many cheap, filling options. There's also a fantastic **farmers market** (⊘ 4:30-7:30pm Wed May-Oct), which takes over Main St in the warmer months. In winter the tourist season dries up and opening hours get very short.

Trinideli DELI $
(201 Trinity Lakes Blvd, at Center St; sandwiches $5-9; ⊘ 6am-4pm Mon-Fri) Cheerful staff prepare decadent sandwiches stuffed with fresh goodness. The one-and-a-half-pound 'Trinideli' with four types of meat and three types of cheese will fill the ravenous, while simple turkey and ham standards explode with fresh veggies and tons of flavor. The suite of breakfast burritos is perfect for a quick pre-hike fill up.

Mountain Marketplace MARKET $
(222 S Main St; ⊘ 9am-6pm Mon-Fri, 10am-5pm Sat; ☝) Stock up on natural foods or hit its juice bar and vegetarian deli.

Johnny's Pizza PIZZA $$
(227 Main St; pizzas $9-26; ⊘ 11am-8pm) A small-town pizza joint with a good vibe, rock and roll on the stereo and friendly staff.

★ **La Grange Café** CALIFORNIAN $$
(☎ 530-623-5325; 315 N Main St; mains $15-28; ⊘ 11:30am-9pm Mon-Thu, to 10pm Fri-Sun, with seasonal variations) Spacious yet intimate, this celebrated multistar restaurant serves exceptional light, fresh and satisfying fare. Chef and owner Sharon Heryford knows how to do dining without a whiff of pretention: apple-stuffed red cabbage in the fall, and brightly flavored chicken enchiladas in the summer, plus game dishes and seasonal vegetables.

Exposed brick and open sight lines complement the exceedingly friendly atmos-

WHAT THE...?

Willow Creek China Flat Museum
(☎ 530-629-2653; www.bigfootcountry.net; Hwy 299, Willow Creek; donations accepted; ⊘ 10am-4pm Wed-Sun May-Sep, 11am-4pm Fri & Sat, noon-4pm Sun Oct-Apr) Pop over to this museum to take in its persuasive Bigfoot collection. Footprints, handprints, hair...it has all kinds of goodies to substantiate the ole boy's existence. In fact, namesake Bigfoot Scenic Byway (Hwy 96) starts here and heads north, winding through breathtaking mountain and river country.

phere. A seat at the bar is great when the tables are full, which they often are. The all-you-can-eat soup and salad is a stroke of genius.

🍷 Drinking & Entertainment

Mamma Llama CAFE
(www.mammallama.com; 490 Main St; breakfasts & sandwiches $4.50-10; ⊘ 6am-6pm Mon-Fri, 7am-6pm Sat, 7am-3pm Sun; ☎) A local institution, this coffeehouse is a roomy and relaxed chill spot. The espresso is well made, there's a selection of books and CDs, and there are couches for lounging. The small menu does breakfasts, wraps and sandwiches and there's microbrew beer available by the bottle. Live folk music (often including a hand drum) takes over occasionally.

Red House CAFE
(www.vivalaredhouse.com; 218 S Miner St; soup from $3; ⊘ 6:30am-5:30pm Mon-Fri, 7:30am-1pm Sun) ☕ This airy, light and bamboo-bedecked spot serves a wide selection of teas, light snacks and organic, fair-trade, shade-grown coffee. The daily food specials include a delicious chicken-and-rice soup on Mondays. If you're in a hurry (rare in Weaverville), there's a drive-through window.

Trinity Theatre CINEMA
(310 Main St) Plays first-run movies.

ℹ Information

Trinity County Chamber of Commerce
(☎ 530-623-6101; www.trinitycounty.com; 215 Main St; ⊘ 10am-4pm) Knowledgeable staff with lots of useful information.

Weaverville Ranger Station (☎ 530-623-2121; www.fs.usda.gov/stnf; 360 Main St;

⊘ 8am-4:30pm Mon-Fri) Maps, information and permits for all lakes, national forests and wilderness areas in and near Trinity County.

ℹ Getting There & Away

A local **Trinity Transit** (☑ 530-623-5438; www.trinitytransit.org; fares from $1.50) bus makes a Weaverville–Lewiston loop via Hwy 299 and Hwy 3 from Monday to Friday. Another one runs between Weaverville and Hayfork, a small town about 30 miles to the southwest on Hwy 3.

Lewiston Lake

Pleasant little **Lewiston** is little more than a collection of buildings beside a crossroad, 26 miles west of Redding, around 5 miles off Hwy 299 on Trinity Dam Blvd and a few miles south of Lewiston Lake. It's right beside the Trinity River, and the locals here are in tune with the environment – they know fishing spots on the rivers and lakes, where to hike and how to get around.

The lake is about 1.5 miles north of town and is a serene alternative to the other area lakes because of its 10mph boat speed limit. The water is kept at a constant level, providing a nurturing habitat for fish and waterfowl. Migrating bird species sojourn here – early in the evening you may see ospreys and bald eagles diving for fish. The **Trinity River Fish Hatchery** (⊘ 7am-3pm) FREE traps juvenile salmon and steelhead and holds them until they are ready to be released into the river. The only marina on the lake, **Pine Cove Marina** (www.pine-cove-marina.com; 9435 Trinity Dam Blvd), has free information about the lake and its wildlife, boat and canoe rentals, potluck dinners and guided off-road tours.

If you're just passing through town, make a stop at the **Country Peddler** (4 Deadwood Rd), a drafty old barn that sits behind a field of red poppies and is filled with cool antiques, rusting road signs and antique collectibles that seem like they were pulled out of some long-lost uncle's hunting cabin. The owners, avid outdoor enthusiasts, know the area like the back of their hand. It's often closed outside summer.

🛏 Sleeping & Eating

Several commercial campgrounds dot the rim of the lake. For information on USFS campgrounds, contact the ranger station in Weaverville. Two of these campgrounds are right on the lake: the wooded **Mary**

Smith (☑ 877-444-6777; tent sites $11; ⊘ May-Sep), which is more private; and the sunny **Ackerman** (sites $11), which has more grassy space for families. If there's no host, both have self-registration options. There are all kinds of RV parks, cabins for rent and motels in Lewiston.

★ **Lewiston Hotel** HISTORIC HOTEL $
(☑ 530-778-3823; 125 Deadwood Rd; r $60; 🖲) This 1862 rambling, ramshackle hotel has small, rustic rooms with quilts, historic photos and river views – all have tons of character but none have attached bathrooms. Ask (or don't ask) for the room haunted by George. Explore the building to find giant stuffed moose heads, old girly calendars, old rusty saws and so much more.

On-site are a friendly locals' bar, a dancehall, and a restaurant (with sporadic opening hours especially in winter) that specializes in prime rib.

Lakeview Terrace Resort CABIN, CAMPGROUND $
(☑ 530-778-3803; www.lakeviewterraceresort.com; RV sites $30, cabins $80-155; 🖲🖲🖲🖲) Five miles north of Lewiston, this is a woodsy Club Med, and rents boats.

Old Lewiston Bridge RV Resort CAMPGROUND $
(☑ 530-778-3894; www.lewistonbridgerv.com; 8460 Rush Creek Rd, at Turnpike Rd; tent/RV sites $15/28, trailer $65; 🖲) A pleasant place to park your RV, with campsites beside the river bridge. This place also rents travel trailers that sleep four people (bed linens not included).

Old Lewiston Inn B&B B&B $$
(☑ 530-778-3385; www.theoldlewistoninn.com; Deadwood Rd; r/ste $110/200; 🖲🖲🖲) The prettiest place in town and right beside the river, this B&B is in an 1875 house and serves country-style breakfasts. Enjoy the hot tub, or ask about all-inclusive fly-fishing packages. There's one two-bedroom suite, which is great for families.

Trinity (Clair Engle) Lake

Placid Trinity Lake, California's third-largest reservoir, sits beneath dramatic snow-capped alps north of Lewiston Lake. In the off season it is serenely quiet, but it attracts multitudes in the summer, who come for swimming, fishing and other water sports.

Most of the campgrounds, RV parks, motels, boat rentals and restaurants line the west side of the lake.

The **Pinewood Cove Resort** (☑530-286-2201; www.pinewoodcove.com; 45110 Hwy 3; tent/RV sites $29/46, cabins $98-158; ❄), on the waterfront, is a popular place to stay, but doesn't provide bed linens.

The east side of the lake is quieter, with more secluded campgrounds, some accessible only by boat. The Weaverville ranger station (p303) has information on USFS campgrounds.

Klamath & Siskiyou Mountains

A dense conglomeration of rugged coastal mountains gives this region the nickname 'the Klamath Knot.' Coastal, temperate rainforest gives way to moist inland forest, creating an immense diversity of habitats for many species, some found nowhere else in the world. Around 3500 native plants live here. Local fauna includes the northern spotted owl, the bald eagle, the tailed frog, several species of Pacific salmon and carnivores like the wolverine and the mountain lion. One theory for the extraordinary biodiversity of this area is that it escaped extensive glaciation during recent ice ages. This may have given species refuge and longer stretches of relatively favorable conditions during which to adapt.

The region also includes the largest concentration of wild and scenic rivers in the US: the Salmon, Smith, Trinity, Eel and Klamath, to name a few. The fall color change is magnificent.

Five main wilderness areas dot the Klamath Knot. The **Marble Mountain Wilderness** in the north is marked by high rugged mountains, valleys and lakes, all sprinkled with colorful geological formations of marble and granite, and a huge array of flora. The **Russian Wilderness** is 8000 acres of high peaks and isolated, beautiful mountain lakes. The **Trinity Alps Wilderness**, west of Hwy 3, is one of the area's most lovely regions for hiking and backcountry camping, and has more than 600 miles of trails that cross passes over its granite peaks and head along its deep alpine lakes. The **Yolla Bolly-Middle Eel Wilderness** in the south is less visited, despite its proximity to the Bay Area, and so affords spectacular, secluded backcountry experiences. The **Siskiyou Wilderness**, closest to the coast, rises to heights of 7300ft, from where you can see the ocean. An extensive trail system crisscrosses the wilderness, but it is difficult to make loops.

The **Trinity Scenic Byway** (Hwy 299) follows the rushing **Trinity River** to the Pacific coast and is dotted with lodges, RV parks and blink-and-you'll-miss-'em burgs. There's river rafting at Willow Creek, 55 miles west of Weaverville. **Bigfoot Rafting Company** (☑530-629-2263; www.bigfootrafting.com; half/full-day trips per person $69/89) leads guided trips and also rents rafts and kayaks (from $40 per day).

Scott Valley

North of Trinity Lake, Hwy 3 climbs along the gorgeous eastern flank of the Trinity Alps Wilderness to Scott Mountain Summit (5401ft) and then drops gracefully down into verdant Scott Valley, a bucolic agricultural area nestled between towering mountains. There are good opportunities for hiking, cycling and mountain biking, or taking horse trips to mountain lakes. For a bit of history, pick up the *Trinity Heritage Scenic Byway* brochure from the Weaverville ranger station (p303) before taking this world-class drive.

Etna (population 737), toward the north end of the valley, is known by its residents as 'California's Last Great Place,' and they might be right. It hosts a fantastic **Bluegrass Festival** at the end of July and the tiny **Etna Brewing Company** (www.etnabrew.net; 131 Callahan St; brewery tours free; ☺pub 11am-4pm Tue, to 8pm Wed & Thu, to 9pm Fri & Sat, to 7pm Sun, tours by appointment) offers delicious beers and pub grub. If you're sticking around, try the immaculate 10-room **Motel Etna** (☑530-467-5338; 317 Collier Way; s/d $50/60). **Scott Valley Drug** (www.scottvalleydrug.com; 511 Main St; ☺Mon-Sat) serves up old-fashioned ice-cream sodas. If you're in town in summer and see lots of dirty people with backpacks, these are folks taking a break from hiking the nearby Pacific Crest Trail – Etna is a favorite pit stop.

Beyond Etna **Fort Jones** (population 839) is just 18 miles from Yreka. The **visitors center** (☑530-468-5442; 11943 Main St; ☺10am-5pm Tue-Sat, noon-4pm Sun) sits at the back of the Guild Shop mercantile. Down the street, a small **museum** (www.fortjonesmuseum.com; 11913 Main St; donation requested;

⊙ Mon-Sat Memorial Day-Labor Day) houses Native American artifacts.

Yreka

Inland California's northernmost town, Yreka (wy-*ree*-kah; population 7400) was once a booming Gold Rush settlement and has the gorgeous turn-of-the-century architecture to prove it. Most travelers only pass through en route to Oregon, but the new-age-tinged yet authentically Wild West–feeling historic downtown makes a good spot to stretch, eat and refuel before heading out into the hinterlands of the Scott Valley or the northeastern California wilderness.

⊙ Sights & Activities

About 25 miles north of Yreka, on I-5, just across the Oregon border, Siskiyou Summit (elevation 4310ft) often closes in winter – even when the weather is just fine on either side. Call ✆ 530-842-4438 to check.

Siskiyou County Museum MUSEUM
(www.siskiyoucountyhistoricalsociety.org; 910 S Main St; admission $3; ⊙ 9am-3pm Tue-Sat) Several blocks south of the downtown grid, this exceptionally well-curated museum brings together pioneer and Native American history. An outdoor section contains historic buildings brought from around the county.

Siskiyou County Courthouse HISTORIC BUILDING
(311 4th St) This hulking downtown building was built in 1857 and has a collection of gold nuggets, flakes and dust in the foyer.

Blue Goose Steam Excursion Train RAILWAY
(www.yrekawesternrr.com; adult/child 2-12yr $20/12) This train hisses and chugs along a 100-year-old track. The schedule is sporadic; look at the website for current information. It's one of the last remaining railroads of California's quickly vanishing historic rail network.

Yreka Creek Greenway WALKING, CYCLING
(www.yrekagreenway.org) Behind the museum, the Yreka Creek Greenway has walking and cycling paths winding through the trees.

🛌 Sleeping & Eating

Motels, motels and more motels: budget travelers can do lots of comparison shopping along Yreka's Main St for mid-century motels galore. Klamath National Forest runs several campgrounds; the supervisor's office has information. RV parks cluster on the edge of town. Wander down W Miner St for more quirky places to eat.

Klamath Motor Lodge MOTEL $
(✆ 530-842-2751; www.klamathmotorlodge.net; 1111 S Main St; d from $45; 🛜 ⊛) Folks at this motor court are especially friendly, the rooms are clean and – bonus for those headed in from the wilderness – it has an on-site laundry. Of all the motels in Yreka, this is tops.

Klander's Deli DELI $
(211 S Oregon St; sandwiches $6; ⊙ 8am-2pm Mon-Fri) Local to the core, this deli's long list of yummy sandwiches is named after regulars. Bob is a favorite, named for the first owner and stacked with ham, turkey, roast beef and Swiss.

Nature's Kitchen HEALTH FOOD, BAKERY $
(✆ 530-842-1136; 412 S Main St; dishes $7; ⊙ 8am-5pm Mon-Sat; 🖋) Friendly natural-foods store and bakery, serving healthy and tasty vegetarian dishes, fresh juices and good espresso. The adjoining store has all kinds of fairies, herbal supplements and new-agey trinkets.

ⓘ Information

Klamath National Forest Supervisor's Office
(✆ 530-842-6131; 1312 Fairlane Rd, at Oberlin Rd; ⊙ 8am-4:30pm Mon-Fri) At the south edge of town, with the lowdown on recreation and camping. This place is enormous; you can see it from the highway.

Yreka Chamber of Commerce (✆ 530-842-1649; www.yrekachamber.com; 117 W Miner St; ⊙ 9am-5pm, with seasonal variations; 🛜)

ⓘ Getting There & Away

STAGE (✆ 530-842-8295; fares from $1.75) buses run throughout the region from a few different stops in Yreka. There are several daily services on weekdays along the I-5 corridor to Weed, Mt Shasta, McCloud and Dunsmuir. Other buses depart daily for Fort Jones (25 minutes), Greenview (35 minutes) and Etna (45 minutes) in the Scott Valley. On Monday and Friday only, buses go out to Klamath River (40 minutes) and Happy Camp (two hours).

Sacramento & Central Valley

Why Go?

The Central Valley is a vast swath of golden fields, rolling hills and scenic waterways that span 400 miles from Chico to Bakersfield. Its rich soil feeds the nation. Half the produce in the US — and nearly every carrot, almond and asparagus spear — was grown here.

In spring, the rivers swell and the orchards bloom. In summer, vast vineyards thrive under the relentless sunshine, and produce comes to market still warm from the fields. By fall and winter, the skies mellow and migratory ducks and geese fly in for a visit. The birds stay longer than most travelers, who tend to zip through on their way to more popular parts, but the shady streets and stately mansions of the region's Victorian-era towns and the uniquely scenic communities dotting the Sacramento Delta and Hwy 99, warrant more than a glimpse through the window.

Best Places to Eat

➜ Noriega's (p334)

➜ Kitchen Restaurant (p314)

➜ Peeve's Public House & Local Market (p330)

➜ Diane's Village Bakery & Cafe (p334)

Best Places to Stay

➜ Padre Hotel (p333)

➜ Citizen Hotel (p313)

➜ Lake Oroville State Recreation Area (p320)

When to Go
Sacramento

Feb–Mar Stop for pie and hot cider in the valley's technicolor Blossom Trail orchards.

Nov–Feb Catch the spectacular return of millions of migratory waterfowl in Sacramento.

May–Sep The peak of harvest time brings farmers markets and food festivals aplenty.

Sacramento & Central Valley Highlights

❶ Tubing the cool rivers of **Chico** (p320).

❷ Uncorking the emerging wine scene in **Lodi** (p325).

❸ Tasting the Valley's produce in Sacramento's **farmers markets** (p312).

❹ Discovering the legacy of people who built the Chinese Temple and lake at **Oroville** (p318).

❺ Grooving in a **Bakersfield** (p332) honkytonk to the sounds of musical icons.

❻ Bumping down world-class rapids on **Kern River** (p335).

❼ Circling the maypole during Kingsburg's **Swedish festival** (p334).

❽ Exploring the levees and farms of the **Sacramento River Delta** (p315).

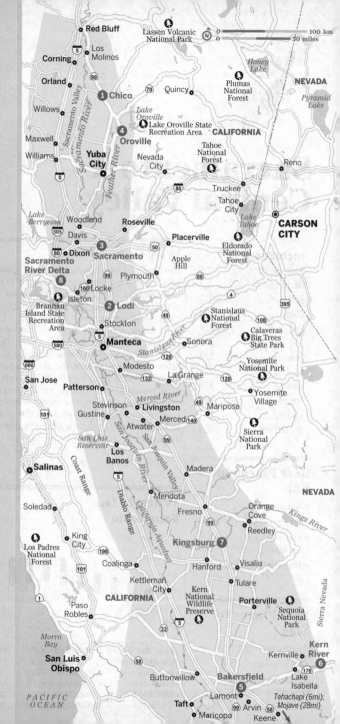

SACRAMENTO VALLEY

The labyrinth of waterways that makes up the Sacramento–San Joaquin River Delta feeds the San Francisco Bay and divides the Central Valley in half, with the Sacramento Valley in the north and the San Joaquin Valley in the south.

The Sacramento River, California's largest, rushes out of the northern mountains from Shasta Lake before hitting the Sacramento Valley basin above Red Bluff. It then snakes south across grassy plains and orchards before lazily skirting the state capital, fanning across the Delta and draining into the San Francisco Bay. The valley is at its most beautiful in the bloom of spring. The shaded gardens and stately homes of Sacramento, the state capital, and its progressive neighbor, the college town of Davis, offer friendly respites from the sun in the summer.

Sacramento

Sacramento is a city of contrasts. It's a former cow town where state legislators' SUVs go bumper-to-bumper with farmers' muddy, half-ton pickups at rush hour. It has sprawling suburbs, but also new lofts and upscale boutiques squeezed between aging mid-century storefronts.

The people of 'Sac' are a resourceful lot that have fostered small but thriving food, art and nightlife scenes. They rightfully crow about **Second Saturday**, the monthly Midtown gallery hop that is the symbol of the city's cultural awakening. Their ubiquitous farmers markets, farm-to-fork fare and craft beers are another point of pride.

History

The history of the state is contained in this city. Paleo-era peoples fished the rivers and thrived before colonists and the scourge of smallpox arrived in the 1800s. Control changed from Spanish to Mexican to finally American hands, when in 1847, a Swiss named John Sutter came seeking fortune. Recognizing the strategic importance of controlling the major rivers, Sutter built an outpost at a confluence and raised a private militia. Soon the outpost became a safe haven for traders, and Sutter expanded his business operations in all directions.

It was at his lumber mill near Coloma that something glittered in the river in 1848. Eureka! Gold rushers stampeded to the trading post, which was eventually christened the newly sprung town 'Sacramento.' Though plagued by fires and relentless flooding, the riverfront settlement prospered and became the state capital in 1850.

The Transcontinental Railroad was soon after conceived in Sacramento by the 'Big Four' – Leland Stanford, Mark Hopkins, Collis P Huntington and Charles Crocker. A fresco of them hangs in Sac's Amtrak station. They founded Central Pacific Railroad, which began construction here in 1863, and connected to the Union Pacific in Promontory, Utah, in 1869.

⊙ Sights

Sacramento is roughly halfway between San Francisco and Lake Tahoe. The city is boxed in by four main highways: Hwy 99, which is the best route through the Central Valley, and I-5, which runs along its west side; I-80 skirts downtown on the city's northern edge, heading west to the Bay Area and east to Reno; and Hwy 50 runs along downtown's southern edge (where it's also called Business Route 80) before heading east to Tahoe.

In the middle is the Grid, where numbered streets run north–south and lettered streets run east–west (Capitol Ave replaces M). One-way J St is a main drag east from Downtown to Midtown.

⊙ The Grid

It's easy finding sights along the Grid, but everything is spread out.

DON'T MISS

CALIFORNIA STATE FAIR

For two weeks in late July, the **California State Fair** (☏916-263-3247; www.bigfun.org; 1600 Exposition Blvd; adult/child $12/8) fills the Cal Expo, east of I-80 on the north side of the American River, with a small city of cows and carnival rides. It's likely the only place on earth where you can plant a redwood tree, watch a pig give birth, ride a roller coaster, catch some barrel racing and taste exquisite Napa vintages within one (exhausting) afternoon. Make time to see some of the auctions ($500 for a dozen eggs!) and the interactive ag-exhibits run by the University of California Davis. Hotels near Cal Expo run regular shuttles to the event.

Downtown Sacramento

★ **California Museum** MUSEUM
(www.californiamuseum.org; 1020 O St; adult/child $9/6.50; ⊙10am-5pm Mon-Sat, from noon Sun) This modern museum is home to the California Hall Of Fame and so the only place to simultaneously encounter César Chávez, Mark Zuckerberg and Amelia Earhart. The *California Indians* exhibit is a highlight, with artifacts and oral histories of more than 100 distinct tribes.

★ **California State Capitol** HISTORIC BUILDING
(capitolmuseum.ca.gov; 1315 10th St; ⊙8am-5pm Mon-Fri, from 9am Sat & Sun) FREE The gleaming dome of the California State Capitol is Sacramento's most recognizable structure. A painting of the Terminator in a suit hangs in the west wing with the other governors' portraits. Some will find **Capitol Park**, the 40 acres of gardens and memorials surrounding the building, more interesting than what's inside. Tours run hourly until 4pm.

Sutter's Fort State Historic Park HISTORIC SITE
(www.suttersfort.org; 2701 L St; adult/child $5/3; ⊙10am-5pm) Originally built by John Sutter, this park was once the only trace of white settlement for hundreds of miles. Reserve a couple hours to stroll within its walls, where furniture, medical equipment and a blacksmith shop are straight out of the 1850s.

State Indian Museum MUSEUM
(www.parks.ca.gov; 2618 K St; adult/child $3/2; ⊙10am-5pm) It's with some irony that the Indian Museum sits in the shadow of Sutter's Fort. The excellent exhibits and tribal handicrafts on display are traces of cultures nearly stamped out by the fervor Sutter ignited.

⦿ Old Sacramento

This historic river port by Downtown remains the city's stalwart tourist draw. The pervasive aroma of salt-water taffy and

pean masters. The contemporary collection is most enthusiastically presented.

California State Railroad Museum MUSEUM
(www.csrmf.org; 125 I St; adult/child $10/5, incl train ride $20/10; ⊙10am-5pm; ⊕) At Old Sac's north end is this impressive collection of railcars and locomotives from miniature to true scale. While the candy-coated recounting of the struggles of those who laid the track is unsettling, the fully outfitted Pullman sleeper and vintage diner cars will thrill rail fans. Board a restored passenger train (adult/child $10/5) from the Sacramento Southern Railroad ticket office, across the plaza on Front St, for a 40-minute jaunt along the river. Train rides run hourly on weekends from April to September.

Sacramento History Museum MUSEUM
(www.historicoldsac.org/museum; 101 I St; adult/child $6/4, Underground Tour Mar-Dec $15/10; ⊙10am-5pm; ⊕) Exhibits stories and artifacts of some of Sacramento's most fascinating citizens, though much of the information is focused on the Gold Rush. Get tickets here for the **Underground Tour**, a 45-minute look at what's under Old Sac's streets.

⊙ Tower District

South of Midtown, at the corner of Broadway and 16th St, the Tower District is dominated by Tower Theatre (p315), a beautiful 1938 art-deco movie palace easy to spot on the way into town. From the theater, head east on Broadway to a stretch of the city's most eclectic and affordable ethnic eateries. The **Tower Records** chain started here in 1960 and closed in 2006, a digital music casualty, but the original neon sign survives.

🏃 Activities

The **American River Parkway** (north bank of American River), a 4600-acre river system, is surely Sacramento's most appealing natural feature. It's one of the most extensive riparian habitats in the continental US, scored by a network of trails and picnic areas. It's accessible from Old Sac by taking Front St north until it becomes Jiboom St and crosses the river, or by the Jiboom St exit off I-5/Hwy 99. The lovely, paved **Jedediah Smith Memorial Trail** (American River Bike Trail), stretches over 30 miles from Old Sac to Folsom Reservoir. Rent wheels from **City Bicycle Works** (www.citybicycleworks.com; 2419 K

somewhat garish restoration give Old Sac the vibe of a second-rate Frontierland, but it's good for a stroll on summer evenings, when boomers on Harleys rumble through the brick streets, and tourists and natty legislative aides stroll the promenade. California's largest concentration of buildings on the National Register of Historic Places is here. Most now peddle Gold Rush trinkets and fudge. There are a few quality attractions, but the restaurant scene is a bust – head to Midtown.

Crocker Art Museum MUSEUM
(https://crockerartmuseum.org; 216 O St; adult/child $10/5; ⊙10am-5pm Tue, Wed & Fri-Sun, to 9pm Thu) Housed in the Crocker family's ornate Victorian mansion (and sprawling additions), this museum is stunning as much for its striking architecture (old and new) as its collections. There are some very fine works by both California painters and Euro-

Downtown Sacramento

St; per hr/day from $5/20; ⊙10am-7pm Mon-Fri, to 6pm Sat, 11am-5pm Sun).

⭐ Festivals & Events

Sacramento Central Farmers Market
MARKET
(www.california-grown.com; cnr 8th & W St, under Hwy 80 overpass; ⊙8am-noon Sun; 🖭) Sacramento has excellent farmers markets, with food trucks and often live music, year-round, and every day in the summer and fall.

Second Saturday
CULTURE
(www.2ndsaturdaysacramento.com) Every second Saturday the galleries and shops in Midtown draw people of all ages to the streets, with open-air music and cultural events.

Sacramento Music Festival & Jubilee
MUSIC
(www.sacmusicfest.com) Forty years old and running strong, this festival of jazz, rockabilly, Latin, swing, blues, zydeco, and anything with a beat takes over Memorial Day weekend (late May).

Gold Rush Days
CULTURE
(www.sacramentogoldrushdays.com; 🖭) Horse races, period costumes, music and kids' events make Old Sacramento particularly festive on Labor Day weekend (early September).

🛏 Sleeping

The capital is a magnet for business travelers, so Sacramento doesn't lack in hotels. Many have good deals during legislative recesses. Unless you're in town for something at Cal Expo, stay Downtown or Midtown, where there's plenty to do within walking distance. If you're into kitschy motor lodges from the 1950s, cross the river into West Sac for the last-standing members of **Motel Row** on Rte 40.

HI Sacramento Hostel
HOSTEL **$**
(📞916-443-1691; http://norcalhostels.org/sac; 925 H St; dm $29-33, r with shared/private bath from $58/99; ⊙check-in 2-10pm; @🛜) In a grand Victorian mansion, this hostel offers impressive trimmings at rock-bottom prices. It's within walking distance of the capitol, Old Sac and the train station and has a piano in the parlor and large dining room. It attracts an international crowd often open to sharing a ride to San Francisco or Lake Tahoe.

Folsom Lake State Recreation Area
CAMPGROUND **$**
(📞916-988-0205; www.parks.ca.gov; 7806 Folsom-Auburn Rd; tent & RV sites without/with hookups $33/58; ⊙office 6am-9pm summer, 7am-6pm winter) Sacramento is a good place for a final gear check before heading into the Sierras. This campground is not ideal – the lake

can be overrun by powerboats – but the only camping is a KOA west of town on I-80.

Delta King
B&B $$

(☎800-825-5464, 916-444-5464; www.deltaking.com; 1000 Front St; d incl breakfast from $139; ✳🕸) It's a treat to sleep aboard the *Delta King*, a 1927 paddlewheeler docked in Old Sac that lights up like a Christmas tree at night.

★Citizen Hotel
BOUTIQUE HOTEL $$$

(☎916-492-4460; www.jdvhotels.com; 926 J St; r/ste $169/269; ✳@🕸✳) With an elegant, ultra-hip upgrade by the Joie de Vivre group, the long-vacant Citizen has suddenly become one of the coolest stays in these parts. Rooms are sleek, with luxe linen and bold-patterned decor. The front desk has loaner bikes. There's an upscale farm-to-fork **restaurant** on the ground floor (mains from $28).

Amber House
B&B $$$

(☎800-755-6526, 916-444-8085; www.amber-house.com; 1315 22nd St; r $199-279; ✳@🕸) This Dutch Colonial home in Midtown has been transformed into an elegant bed and breakfast, where rooms have spa baths and fireplaces. The Mozart and Vivaldi rooms have private balconies perfect for enjoying breakfast.

Eating

Skip the overpriced fare in Old Sacramento or by the capitol and head Midtown or to the Tower District. A cruise up J St or Broadway passes a number of hip, affordable restaurants where tables spill onto the sidewalks in the summer. Many source farm-fresh ingredients, even when they don't advertise.

Shoki II Ramen House
JAPANESE $

(☎916-441-0011; 1201 R St; meals $8-16; ☉11am-10pm Mon-Fri, from noon Sat, 11am-8pm Sun) In their tiny original location on 24th St, diners cram in cheek-to-jowl, but this newer Midtown location offers elbow room and the same amazing housemade noodles. The fresh spinach and shiitake adorning your bowl are, of course, organic and local.

Gunther's
ICE CREAM $

(www.gunthersicecream.com; 2801 Franklin Blvd; sundaes $4; ☉10am-10pm) A popular vintage soda fountain that makes its own ice cream.

Plum Cafe
VEGAN $

(www.plumcafebakery.com; 2315 K St; dishes $8-12; ☉8am-8pm Mon-Thu, to 9pm Fri & Sat, 10am-8pm Sun; 🖋) 🖋 This brunch hotspot and bakery serves vegan and gluten-free fare in a restored Victorian with a tented back garden. Savory options are straightforward. The surprising desserts, such as the Entertainer (styled after a Hostess Cup-Cake) will satisfy sugar fiends.

La Bonne Soupe Cafe
DELI $

(☎916-492-9506; 920 8th St; items $5-8; ☉11am-3pm Mon-Wed, to 8pm Thu & Fri) Divine soup and sandwiches assembled with such care that the line of downtown lunchers snakes out the door. If you're in a hurry, skip it. This humble lunch counter is focused on quality that predates drive-through haste.

DON'T MISS

THE GREAT MIGRATION

The Sacramento Valley serves as a rest stop for countless migrating species that arrive in such great numbers, they are a spectacle even without binoculars.

October to February Four million waterbirds winter in the warm tules (marshes) on their way along the Great Pacific Flyway. Tours at Sacramento National Wildlife Refuge (p319).

October to January Endangered chinook and steelhead fight their way upstream to spawn. Spot them along the American River Parkway (p311) and the **Nimbus Fish Hatchery** (☎916-358-2884; www.dfg.ca.gov; 2001 Nimbus Rd, Gold River; ☉8am-3pm Mon-Fri, from 9am Sat-Sun) FREE.

March to June Cabbage white, painted lady, and Western tiger swallowtail butterflies come to party. Their offspring will gorge and then grow wings to fly north. Sacramento National Wildlife Refuge (p319) has details.

June to August Hundreds of thousands of Mexican free-tailed bats shelter under the Yolo Causeway. Tours (www.yolobasin.org) catch them alighting at twilight.

Tank House BBQ and Bar
BARBECUE $$

(tankhousebbq.com; 1925 J St; pork butt sando $10; ⏱ 11:30am-2am Mon-Fri, from 11am Sat & Sun) The overwhelming hipster vibe – from the greasy 'dos to canned beer (six for $10) – may be hard to swallow, but the legit BBQ is not. Sidle up to the bar to order and start a tab. The smoker goes all day, so if you sit outside, position upwind.

Pizza Rock
PIZZERIA $$

(www.pizzarocksacramento.com; 1020 K St; pizzas $14-30; ⏱ 11am-10pm Sun-Thu, to 3am Fri & Sat; 🛜) An anchor of the K St Mall area, this loud, enormous pizza joint has a great Margherita, a rock 'n' roll theme and a well-tattooed staff.

Andy Nguyen's
VIETNAMESE, VEGETARIAN $$

(www.andynguyenvegetarian.com; 2007 Broadway; meals $9-16; ⏱ 11:30am-9pm Sun & Mon, to 9:30pm Tue-Thu, to 10pm Fri & Sat; 🚗) 🍃 Great meat-free fare is served at this tranquil Buddhist diner. Try the steaming claypots and artful fake meat dishes (the 'chicken' leg has a little wooden bone).

Waterboy
CALIFORNIAN $$

(☎ 916-498-9891; www.waterboyrestaurant.com; 2000 Capitol Ave; mains $13-29; ⏱ 11:30am-2:30pm Mon-Fri, 5-9:30pm Sun-Thu, to 10:30pm Fri & Sat) The wicker and palm in the windowed dining room offer a preview of the chef's style – a French-Italian spin on Central Valley ingredients. The ambitious menu soars from the start. The day's catch is always stellar.

Lucca
ITALIAN $$

(luccarestaurant.com; 1615 J St; meals $13-20; ⏱ 11:30am-10pm Mon-Thu, to 11pm Fri, noon-11pm Sat, 4-9pm Sun) Within a stroll of the convention center is this quality Italian eatery. Parmesan frites with truffle aioli are the way to start.

★ Kitchen Restaurant
CALIFORNIAN $$$

(www.thekitchenrestaurant.com; No 101, 2225 Hurley Way; prix-fixe dinner $125; ⏱ 5-10pm Wed-Sun) Husband-and-wife team Randall Selland and Nancy Zimmer's cozy dining room in the northeast 'burbs is the pinnacle of Sacramento's food experience. Their demonstration dinners focus on – what else? – local, seasonal, organic food, immaculately prepared before your eyes. Reservations are essential.

Mulvaney's B&L
MODERN AMERICAN $$$

(☎ 916-441-6022; mulvaneysbl.com; 1215 19th St; mains $32-40; ⏱ 11:30am-2:30pm Tue-Fri, 5-10pm Tue-Sun) 🍃 With an obsessive commitment to seasonality, the menu at this swank, converted firehouse includes delicate pastas and grilled meats that change every day.

Drinking & Nightlife

Sacramento has a split personality when it comes to drinking – upscale joints where mustachioed bartenders shake cocktails, and sans-bullshit dive bars with vintage neons and menus that begin and end with a-shot-ana-beer. Both options dot the Grid.

Temple Coffee Roasters
COFFEE SHOP

(www.templecoffee.com; 1010 9th St; ⏱ 6am-11pm; 🛜) 🍃 Hip young patrons nurse organic free-trade coffee and chai morning to night in this steel and concrete space.

Mercantile Saloon
GAY

(☎ 916-447-0792; 1928 L St; ⏱ 10am-2am) Down an alley in a yellow Victorian, stiff drinks go for less than $4. Personal space is nil in this rowdy dive. Start here before touring the four-block radius of gay bars and clubs that locals call 'Lavender Heights.'

Pour House
PUB

(www.pourhousesacramento.com; 1910 Q St; ⏱ 11am-11pm Tue-Wed, to 12:30am Thu, to 1am Fri, 10am-1:30am Sat, 9am-10pm Sun) If the walls shake in this upscale watering hole, it's probably a train – not the whiskey or moonshine you've downed. But if your booth starts feeling like a soft bed, it's definitely the beer you've been pulling from the tap, so conveniently built into your table.

Rubicon Brewing Company
BREWERY

(www.rubiconbrewing.com; 2004 Capitol Ave; ⏱ 11am-11:30pm Mon-Thu, to 12:30am Fri & Sat, to 10pm Sun) These people take their hops *seriously*. Their heady selection is brewed on-site. Monkey Knife Fight Pale Ale is ideal for washing back platters of hot wings ($12.49 per dozen).

Old Tavern Bar & Grill
PUB

(1510 20th St; ⏱ 6pm-2am) This friendly dive stands out from Sac's many workaday joints with its huge beer selection, tall pours and '80s-loaded jukebox.

58 Degrees and Holding Co
WINE BAR

(www.58degrees.com; 1217 18th St; ⏱ 11am-10pm Mon, Wed & Thu, to 11pm Fri & Sat, to 9pm Sun) A wide selection of California and European reds and a refined bistro menu make this a favorite for young professionals on the prowl.

☆ Entertainment

Pick up a copy of the free weekly *Sacramento News & Review* (www.newsandreview.com) for a list of current happenings around town.

Harlow's   LIVE MUSIC
(www.harlows.com; 2708 J St) Quality jazz, R&B and the occasional salsa or indie act in a classy joint...if you don't go crazy with the potent martinis.

Old Ironsides   LIVE MUSIC
(www.theoldironsides.com; 1901 10th St; cover $5-10; ☉8am-2am Tue-Fri & Sun, from 6pm Sat) The tiny back room of this cool, somewhat crusty, venue hosts some of the best indie bands that come through town.

California Musical Theatre   PERFORMING ARTS
(www.californiamusicaltheatre.com; 1419 H St) This top-notch company holds court at the Community Center Theater and the Wells Fargo Pavilion in town.

Sacramento River Cats   SPORTS
(www.milb.com; Raley Field, 400 Ballpark Dr; tickets $8-60; ☉Apr-Sep) Sacramento's minor-league baseball team plays across the river at Raley Field, with views of the art-deco Tower Bridge.

Tower Theatre   CINEMA
(☎916-442-4700; www.ReadingCinemasUS.com; 2508 Landpark Dr) Classic, foreign and indie films screen at this historic movie house with a digital upgrade.

Crest Theatre   CINEMA
(www.thecrest.com; 1013 K St) A classic old movie house that's been restored to its 1949 splendor. Hosts indie and foreign films and the annual Trash Film Orgy (trashfilmorgy.com) on Saturdays in July and August.

❶ Information

Convention & Visitors Bureau (www.visitsacramento.com; 1608 I St; ☉8am-5pm Mon-Fri) Local information, including event and bus schedules. The helpful folks at the Visitor Center (☎916.442.7644; www.visitsacramento.com; 1002 2nd St; ☉10am-5pm) in Old Sacramento can also point you in the right direction.

❶ Getting There & Away

Amtrak Station (☎877-974-3322; www.capitolcorridor.org; 401 I St at 5th St) This station between downtown and Old Sac is the major hub for connecting trains to all points east and west, as well as regional bus lines serving the Central Valley. One way to San Francisco is very convenient ($32, two hours).

Greyhound (www.greyhound.com; 420 Richards Blvd) The station is 2 miles north of Downtown off I-5 or N 7th St. Services run to Colfax in Gold Country ($30, 1½ hours), San Francisco ($24, two hours), Bakersfield ($51, 6½ hours), Los Angeles ($86, nine hours) and other major towns.

Sacramento International Airport (SMF; www.sacairports.org; 6900 Airport Blvd) Twelve miles north of Downtown off I-5; SMF is served by major US airlines and has flights to Mexico.

❶ Getting Around

The regional **Yolobus** (☎530-666-2877; www.yolobus.com) route 42B costs $2 and runs hourly between the airport and Downtown and also goes to West Sacramento, Woodland and Davis. Local **Sacramento Regional Transit** (RT; www.sacrt.com; fare/day pass $2.50/6) buses run around town and RT also runs a trolley between Old Sacramento and Downtown, as well as Sacramento's light-rail system, which is best for commuting from outlying communities. Sacramento is also a fantastic city to cruise around by bike, rent them from City Bicycle Works (p311).

Sacramento–San Joaquin River Delta

The Sacramento Delta is a sprawling web of waterways and one-stoplight towns plucked out of the 1930s. On weekends, locals gun powerboats on glassy waterways and cruise the winding levy roads. This wetland area encompasses a huge swath of the state – from the San Francisco Bay to Sacramento, and all the way south to Stockton. Here the Sacramento and San Joaquin Rivers converge to drain into the San Francisco Bay. If you have the time to smell the grassy Delta breezes on the slow route between San Francisco and Sacramento, travel the iron bridges of winding Hwy 160, which lazily makes its way past rice fields, vast orchards, sandy swimming banks and little towns with long histories.

The town of Locke is the most fascinating, built by the Chinese who also built the

ⓘ GETTING AROUND THE CENTRAL VALLEY

Although the Central Valley's main artery is connected by bus and Amtrak, much of the region is best traveled by car. The main routes through are Hwy 99 and I-5. I-80 meets Hwy 99 in Sacramento, and I-5 meets Hwy 99 south of Bakersfield. Amtrak (p315) also intersects the state with two lines – the *San Joaquin* route through the Central Valley and the *Pacific Surfliner* between the Central Coast and San Diego. The *San Joaquin* service stops in just about every tourist destination. Greyhound (p315) stops in most Central Valley towns and cities.

The Central Valley has lots of long, straight byways for those making the trip on bikes, and the American River Parkway (p311) is a veritable human-powered expressway for commuters between Downtown Sacramento and Auburn.

Still, the transportation talk in the Central Valley these days is all about the high-speed rail. California voters gave the green light to build a network of super-fast trains connecting San Francisco and Los Angeles at speeds of up to 220 miles per hour (making the trip just over 2½ hours) by 2029.

The total price tag is a whopping $68 billion, and there are legal hurdles yet, but if everything clears, the first stage will be very humble – a 29-mile track connecting two tiny farm towns on either side of Fresno by 2017.

levees that ended perpetual flooding and allowed agriculture to flourish here. After a malicious fire wiped out the settlement in 1912, a group approached land baron George Locke for a leasehold (California barred Chinese from owning property). Locke became the only freestanding town built and managed by Chinese in the US; its unincorporated status kept it free of pesky lawmen, allowing for gambling houses and bootleg gin joints. Tucked below the highway and the levee, Locke's main street still has a few residents though the feel is of a ghost town, with weather-beaten buildings protected on the National Register of Historic Places that take an afternoon to explore.

The colorful **Dai Loy Museum** (www. locketown.com/museum.htm; 5 Main St, Locke; admission $1.25; ⊙noon-4pm Fri-Sun; ♿), an old gambling hall filled with photos and relics of gaming operations, including *pai gow* tables and an antique safe, is a great stop. Nearby is **Al the Wop's** (☎916-776-1800; 13943 Main St, Locke; mains $8-15; ⊙11am-9pm), a saloon that's been pouring since 1915 and serves peanut-butter-slathered Texas toast. Below are creaking floorboards; above, the ceiling's covered in crusty dollar bills and more than one pair of erstwhile undies. Check in at the **visitors center** (☎916-776-1661; www.locketown.com; 13920 Main St, Walnut Grove; tours adult/student $5/3; ⊙visitors center noon-4pm Tue & Fri, 11am-3pm Sat-Sun) for maps and tours.

Hwy 160 also passes through **Isleton**, so-called Crawdad Town USA, whose main street has more shops, restaurants, bars and buildings hinting at the region's Chinese heritage. Isleton's **Cajun Festival**, at the end of June, draws folks from across the state, but you can get very lively crawdads year-round at **Bob's Bait Shop** (www.isletonjoes. com; 212 Second St, Isleton; mains $5-17; ⊙8am-9pm).

Further west on Hwy 160 you'll see signs for the **Delta Loop**, a drive that passes boater bars and marinas where you can rent something to take on the water. At the end is the **Brannan Island State Recreation Area** (☎916-777-6671; www.parks.ca.gov; 17645 California 160; campsites $28; 🅿🛜), a tidy facility with boat-in, drive-in and walk-in campsites and picnic facilities.

In the 1930s the Bureau of Reclamation issued an aggressive water-redirection program – the Central Valley and California State Water Projects – that dammed California's major rivers and directed 75% of their supply through the Central Valley for agriculture and Southern California. The siphoning affected the Delta, its wetlands and estuaries, and kicked off neverending debate. Learn about the area's unique legacy by bus or on a self-guided tour with **Delta Heartbeat Tours** (☎916-776-4010; http:// deltaheartbeattours.com; Deckhands Marina, 14090 Hwy 160, Walnut Grove), which also has leads on boat rides. If you have a car, taste the fruits of the delta on the **Delta Grown Farm Trail** (☎916-775-1166; http://sacriverdelta-grown.org) FREE.

Davis

Davis, home to a University of California school with the nation's leading viticulture department, is a sunny town where bikes outnumber cars two-to-one (it has more bikes per capita than any other American city). With students comprising about half of the population, it's a progressive outpost amid the conservative towns of Sacramento Valley that comes alive during the school year.

Dodging the bikes on a walk through downtown Davis you will pass a number of cute small businesses (city council has forbidden any store over 50,000 sq ft – sorry, Wal-Mart).

I-80 skirts the south edge of town, and you can reach downtown via the Richards Blvd exit. University of California, Davis (UCD) is southwest of downtown, bordered by A St, 1st St and Russell Blvd.

◉ Sights & Activities

Everyone rides here in 'Bike City USA,' probably because the only hill around is the bridge that crosses over the freeway. **Lake Berryessa**, 30 miles west, is a favorite destination.

UC Davis Arboretum   PARK
(http://arboretum.ucdavis.edu; 1 Shields Ave) FREE Stroll through the peaceful 'Arb' along the paved 3.5-mile loop. It follows one of the state's oldest reservoirs, dug in the 1860s.

Pence Gallery   GALLERY
(www.pencegallery.org; 212 D St; ☉11:30am-5pm Tue-Sun) This community-centric gallery exhibits contemporary California art and hosts classes, lectures and art films. It hosts a free reception 7pm to 9pm on the second Friday of each month.

Davis Transmedia Art Walk   WALKING TOUR
(http://davisartwalk.com) FREE This two-hour walking tour winds through Davis' public art collection, mostly clustered on D and G Sts. Some works interact with your phone – you can hear an audio tour or record your own impressions for others after you. Maps at the Yolo County Visitors Bureau (p318) or **John Natsoulas Center for the Arts** (www.natsoulas.com; 521 1st St; ☉11am-5pm Wed & Thu, to 10pm Fri, noon-5pm Sat & Sun) FREE.

⌂ Sleeping

As with most university towns, Davis' hotel rates are stable until graduation or special campus events, when they skyrocket and sell out fast. Worse, the trains that roll though the middle of town will infuriate a light sleeper. For a utilitarian (if bland) stay, look for chains along the highway.

University Park Inn & Suites   HOTEL $$
(☏530-756-0910; www.universityparkinn.com; 1111 Richards Blvd; r $90-140; P❄@🛜⛱) Right off the highway and a short walk from campus and downtown, this independently operated hotel is not the Ritz but is clean, has spacious suites, and serves waffles for breakfast.

Aggie Inn   HOTEL $$
(☏530-756-0352; www.aggieinn.com; 245 1st St; r from $139; ❄🛜) Across from UCD's east entrance, the Aggie is neat, modern and unassuming. Cottages are not much more than regular rooms and have kitchenettes and spa baths.

✗ Eating & Drinking

College students love to eat and drink cheap, and downtown has no short supply of lively ethnic eateries gunning for the student dollar. The **Davis farmers market** (www.davisfarmersmarket.org; cnr 4th & C Sts; ☉8am-1pm Sat year-round, 2-6pm Wed winter) features food vendors, street performers and live bands. There are a number of good options for self-catering including the **Co-op** (http://davisfood.coop; 620 G St; ☉7am-10pm).

Sam's Mediterranean Cuisine   MIDDLE EASTERN $
(☏530-758-2855; 247 3rd St; shawarma $6.39; ☉11am-8pm Mon-Fri, from noon Sat) Delicious and cheap shawarma and falafel made this little house with a green awning a university institution.

Woodstock's   PIZZERIA $
(www.woodstocksdavis.com; 219 G St; slice $2.50, pizzas $7-25; ☉11am-1am Mon-Wed, to 2am Thu-Sat, 9:30-midnight Sun; 🖉) Woodstock's has Davis' most popular pizza, which is also sold by the slice for lunch. Besides the usual, the toppings get a touch more sophisticated with a variety of gourmet and veggie options all on a chewy wheat crust.

Delta of Venus Cafe & Pub   CAFE $
(www.deltaofvenus.org; 122b St; mains $7-11; ☉7:30am-10pm Mon-Wed, to midnight Thu & Fri, to 2am Sat & Sun; 🖉) This converted Arts and Crafts bungalow has a very social, shaded front patio. The breakfast items, salads, soups and sandwiches include vegetarian

and vegan options. Dinner time you can order jerk-seasoned Caribbean dishes and enjoy the hip folk scene.

Davis Noodle City ASIAN $

(129 E St; mains $7-10; ⊙ 11am-9:30pm Mon-Sat, to 8:30pm Sun) A starving student favorite, the best offerings involve the homemade noodles and scallion pancakes.

Redrum BURGERS $

(☑ 530-756-2142; 978 Olive Dr; burgers $6.25; ⊙ 10am-11pm Mon-Thu, to midnight Fri-Sun) Formerly known as Murder Burger, Redrum serves made-to-order beef and turkey burgers, thick espresso shakes and crispy curly fries. The ZOOM – a gnarled, deep-fried pile of zucchini, onion rings and mushrooms – is to die for.

Davis Beer Shop BEER HALL

(Bottle Shop; ☑ 530-756-5212; 211 G St; bottle from $3; ⊙ 11am-11pm Mon-Wed, to 12:30am Thu-Sat, to 9pm Sun) This mellow beer hall and shop stocks 650 varieties of craft beer, bottled and on tap, import and brewed down the block. Pull any bottle from the back, or order one of their daily changing draft flights. BYO food.

☆ Entertainment

For tickets and information to UC Davis' arts events, call the Mondavi Center. For athletic events, call the **UC Davis Ticket office** (☑ 530-752-2471; http://campusrecreation.ucdavis.edu; Aggie Stadium, off La Rue Rd).

ⓘ TULE FOG

As thick as the proverbial pea soup, tule (too-lee) fog causes chain collisions each year on area roads. In 2007, more than 100 cars and big-rigs collided on a stretch of Hwy 99. At its worst, these dense, immobile clouds can limit visibility to a foot.

Tule fog, named after a marsh grass common here, is thickest from November to March, when cold mountain air settles on the warm valley floor and condenses. The fog burns off for a few afternoon hours, just long enough for the ground to warm again and perpetuate the cycle.

If you find yourself driving in fog, turn on your low beams, give other cars extra distance, and maintain an easy, constant speed. Avoid passing.

Mondavi Center for the Performing Arts CONCERT VENUE

(www.mondaviarts.org; 1 Shields Ave) Major theater, music, dance and other performances take place at this state-of-the-art venue on the UCD campus.

Varsity Theatre CONCERT VENUE

(www.davisvarsity.net; 616 2nd St) Davis' beloved arthouse movie theater began as a performance stage back in 1950.

Palms Playhouse PERFORMING ARTS

(www.palmsplayhouse.com; 13 Main St, Winters) For rhythm 'n' blues and cover bands, just up the road in Winters.

ⓘ Information

The exhaustive www.daviswiki.org is fascinating reading.

Yolo County Visitors Bureau (☑ 530-297-1900; www.yolocvb.net; suite 200, 132 E St; ⊙ 8:30am-4:30pm Mon-Fri) Free bike maps, travel brochures and transit info.

ⓘ Getting There & Away

Amtrak (☑ 530-758-4220; 840 2nd St) Davis' station is on the southern edge of downtown. There are trains bound for Sacramento ($9, 26 minutes) or San Francisco ($30, two hours) throughout the day.

Yolobus (☑ 530-666-2877; ⊙ 5am-11pm) Routes 42A and B ($2) loop between Davis and the Sacramento airport. The route also connects Davis with Woodland and Downtown Sacramento.

ⓘ Getting Around

Be aware of bike traffic when driving (especially backing out of a parking space or opening your door). Two wheels are the primary mode of transportation here.

Ken's Bike, Ski, Board (www.kensbikeski.com; 650 G St; ⊙ 9am-8pm Mon-Fri, to 7pm Sat, noon-5pm Sun) Rents basic bikes (from $19 per day) as well as serious road and mountain bikes.

Unitrans (☑ 530-752-2877; http://unitrans.ucdavis.edu; one-way $1) If you're not biking, this student-run outfit shuttles people around town and campus in red double-deckers.

Oroville

North of Sacramento's bustle, the quiet town of Oroville has seen quite a reversal. Then: the lust for gold brought a crush of white settlers, who drove out the native

WORTH A TRIP

LAKE OROVILLE

Lake Oroville (www.parks.ca.gov; 917 Kelly Ridge Rd; ⊙ 8am–night), a popular summer-time destination, sits 9 miles northeast of town behind **Oroville Dam**, the largest earthen dam in the US. The surrounding **Lake Oroville State Recreation Area** attracts campers, boaters, and fishing folk. The lake's **visitor center** (☑ 530-538-2219; www.parks.ca.gov; 917 Kelly Ridge Rd; ⊙ 9am–5pm) has exhibits on the California State Water Project and local tribe history, plus a **viewing tower** and loads of recreational information.

The area surrounding Lake Oroville is also full of hiking trails, and a favorite is the 7-mile round-trip walk to 640ft **Feather Falls**. To get off your feet, **Lazy T Trailrides** (☑ 530-518-4052; http://lazyttrailrides.com; Saddle Dam parking lot, opp 283 Kelly Ridge Rd; per person $75; ⊙ rides at 10am & 5pm) offers four-hour horseback rides on dedicated trails around the lake. The **Brad Freeman Bicycle Trail** is a 41-mile, off-road loop that takes cyclists to the top of 770ft Oroville Dam, then follows the Feather River back to the Thermalito Forebay and Afterbay storage reservoirs, east of Hwy 70. The ride is mostly flat, but the dam ascent is steep. Get a free map of the ride from the **Oroville Area Chamber of Commerce** (www.orovillechamber.net; 1789 Montgomery St). The **Forebay Aquatic Center** (www.forebayaquaticcenter.com; 930 Garden Dr; kayaks per day from $35; ⊙ 10am–6pm Wed–Sun May–Sep) rents non-motorized watercraft to get out on the water.

Stay overnight in rustic campsites (p320) on land or even on water.

tribes. Now: crowds flock to the thriving tribal casinos, on the outskirts of town, seeking riches. Aside from the slots, the economy leans on the local hospital, the tourists who mill though the throng of antique stores around Montgomery St, and an annual **festival** to celebrate the salmon run in September.

Oroville's most enduring attraction, aside from the nearby lake, is an excellent museum established by the descendants of a long-dispersed Chinese community. Its other preserved legacies relate to the pioneers who arrived after gold was discovered near here in 1848 by John Bidwell, and to a mysterious man who stumbled into town in 1911, and came to be known as the 'last wild Indian' (p320). Oroville is also a gateway to the rugged northern reaches of the Sierra Nevada.

Hwys 162 and 70 head northeast from Oroville into the mountains and on to Quincy. Hwy 70 snakes along the magnificent **Feather River Canyon**, an especially captivating drive in fall.

◉ Sights & Activities

Chinese Temple   MUSEUM
(☑ 530-538-2496; 1500 Broderick St; adult/child $3/free; ⊙ noon–4pm) This restored temple and museum offers a fascinating glimpse into Oroville's Chinese legacy well worth exploring. Built in 1863, it served the Chinese

community, which built the area's levees and at its peak numbered 10,000. Inside is an unrivaled collection of 19th-century stage finery, religious shrines and a small garden with fine Qing-era relics throughout.

This temple's fascinating history includes its role as the last stop for touring Cantonese theater troupes. To lighten the shipload back across the Pacific, they left behind elaborate sets, costumes, and puppets, which are on rotating display.

**Sacramento National
Wildlife Refuge**   BIRD-WATCHING
(www.fws.gov; admission $6; ⊙ 1hr before sunset–1hr after sunset) Serious bird-watchers sojourn here in winter, when millions of migratory waterfowl make a spectacular sight. The **visitor center** (☑ 530-934-2801; 752 County Rd, Willows; ⊙ 9am–4pm, closed Mon Nov–Feb, closed Sat & Sun Mar–Oct) is off I-5 near Willows; a splendid 6-mile driving trail and walking trails are open daily. The peak season to see birds is between October and late February, with the largest skein of geese arriving in December and January.

🛌 Sleeping & Eating

Oroville is a launch pad for outdoorsy trips and there's plenty of camping in the area, which you can arrange through the Chamber of Commerce, the USFS office (p320), or the Lake Oroville visitor center. A strip of decent budget motels – mostly chains and some humble mid-century cheapies – are clustered on Feather River Blvd, between Hwy 162 to the south and Montgomery St to the north.

In terms of dining options, there's not much chance you'll be thrilled, but aside from the fast-food chains, there is decent pub grub and Vietnamese in the small downtown.

★ **Lake Oroville State Recreation Area** CAMPING $
(☎ 800-444-7275, 530-538-2219; www.parks. ca.gov; 917 Kelly Ridge Rd; tent/RV sites $25/45; ☎) The wi-fi might be the first clue that this isn't the most rustic choice, but there are good primitive sites if you're willing to hike, and – perhaps the coolest feature of the park – boat. There's a cove of floating platform campsites ($175 per night).

❶ Information

The office of the **Feather River Ranger District** (US Forest Service Office; ☎ 530-534-6500; 875 Mitchell Ave; ⊙ 8am-4:30pm Mon-Fri) has maps and brochures. For road conditions, phone ☎ 800-427-7623.

❶ Getting There & Away

Although Greyhound (p315) buses stop near the **Valero gas station** (☎ 530-533-2328; 555 Oro Dam Blvd E) a few blocks east of Hwy 70, a car is far and away the simplest and most cost effective way to reach the area. There are two buses daily between Oroville and Sacramento ($35, 1½ hours).

Chico

With its huge population of students, Chico has the devil-may-care energy of a college kegger during the school year, and a lazy, lethargic hangover during the summertime. Its oak-shaded downtown and university attractions makes it one of Sacramento Valley's more attractive social hubs, where easygoing folks mingle late in the restaurants and bars, which open onto patios in the balmy summer evenings.

Though Chico wilts in the heat of the summer, the swimming holes in Bidwell Park take the edge off, as does floating down the gentle Sacramento River. The fine pale ales produced at the Sierra Nevada Brewing Company, near downtown, are another of Chico's refreshing blessings.

There's a bit of irony in the fact a town so widely celebrated for its brews was founded by John Bidwell, the illustrious California pioneer who made a bid for US president with the Prohibitionist party. In 1868, Bidwell and his philanthropist wife, Annie Ellicott Kennedy, moved to the new mansion

---

ISHI, THE 'LAST WILD INDIAN'

At daybreak on August 28, 1911, frantic dogs woke the workers sleeping inside a slaughterhouse outside Oroville. The dogs were holding a man at bay – a Native American, disoriented and clad in a loincloth.

The 'wild man' became a media sensation, and soon Berkeley anthropologists traveled to Oroville to meet him. Testing out snippets of nearly lost vocabulary from native languages, they determined the man belonged to the Yahi, the southernmost tribe of the Yana (also known as the Deer Creek tribe), believed to be extinct.

The man never revealed his true name but adopted the name 'Ishi,' meaning 'man' in the Yana language. The anthropologists took Ishi to the museum at the university, where he was installed as a living exhibit, sharing his story and culture until he died from tuberculosis on March 25, 1916, just five years after he was 'discovered.'

By Ishi's accounts, in 1870, when he was a child, there had been only 12 or 15 Yahi people left, hiding in remote areas in the foothills near Red Bluff. By 1908 Ishi, his mother, sister and uncle were all who were left. His family died that last year, leaving Ishi alone. With Ishi's death, newspapers pronounced the Yahi gone forever.

Anthropologists recently postulated that while Ishi's tribe had been virtually exterminated by settlers by the time he was born, a few found refuge with other tribes, so some of Ishi's kin do live on.

The site where Ishi was captured is east of Oroville along Oro-Quincy Hwy at Oak Ave, marked by a small monument. Part of the Lassen National Forest where Ishi and the Yahi people lived, is now called the Ishi Wilderness.

he had built, now the Bidwell Mansion State Historic Park.

⊙ Sights

Nearly all the sights are downtown, west of Hwy 99, easily reached via Hwy 32 (8th St). Main St and Broadway are the central downtown streets; from there, Park Ave stretches southward and the tree-lined Esplanade heads north.

Sierra Nevada Brewing Company   BREWERY
(☏530-899-4776; www.sierranevada.com; 1075 E 20th St; Brewery tour free, Beer Geek tour $25; ⊙tours 11am-4pm Sun-Thu, to 5:30pm Fri & Sat) 🍺 Hordes of beer snobs gather at the birthplace of the internationally distributed Sierra Nevada Pale Ale and Schwarber, a Chico-only black ale. Also for sale are the 'Beer Camp' collaborations (www.beercamp. sierranevada.com), short-run craft beers brewed by uber-beer nerds at invitation-only summer seminars. Free brewhouse tours are given regularly. True beerheads will want to book the three-hour tour ($25).

There's also a tour of the brewery's cutting-edge sustainable practices – their rooftop solar fields are among the largest privately owned solar fields in the US, and they extended a spur of local railroad to increase transportation efficiency. Recharge in the pub and restaurant (p322).

Chico Creek Nature Center   SCIENCE CENTER
(www.bidwellpark.org; 1968 East 8th St; suggested donation adult/child $4/2; ⊙11am-4pm Wed-Sun; 👶) If you plan on spending the afternoon in Bidwell Park, first stop at this sparkling nature center, with displays on local plants and animals and excellent hands-on science programs for families. The exhibit hall is closed on Wednesday.

Chico State University   UNIVERSITY
Ask for a free map of the Chico State University campus, or about campus events and tours at the **CSU Information Center** (☏530-898-4636; www.csuchico.edu; cnr 2nd & Normal Sts; ⊙7am-11pm Mon-Thu, to 10pm Fri, 11am-10pm Sat, noon-11pm Sun school year), on the main floor of Bell Memorial Union. The attractive campus is infused with sweet floral fragrances in spring, and there's a rose garden at its center.

**Bidwell Mansion State
Historic Park**   HISTORIC BUILDING
(☏530-895-6144; parks.ca.gov; 525 Esplanade; adult/child $6/3; ⊙noon-5pm Mon, 11am-5pm Sat & Sun) Chico's most prominent landmark, the opulent Victorian home was built for Chico's founders John and Annie Bidwell. The 26-room mansion was built between 1865 and 1868 and hosted many US presidents. Tours start every hour from 11am to 4pm.

Honey Run Covered Bridge   HISTORIC SITE
(www.honeyruncoveredbridge.com; parking $3) The historic 1894 bridge is an unusual style this side of the country and a favorite spot for engagement photos. Take the Skyway exit off Hwy 99 on the southern outskirts of Chico, head east and go left on Honey Run-Humbug Rd; the bridge is 5 miles along, in a small park.

🏃 Activities

In summer you'll want to cool off by **tubing** the Sacramento. Inner tubes can be rented at grocery stores and other shops along Nord Ave (Hwy 32) for $7 to $10. Tubers enter at the Irvine Finch Launch Ramp on Hwy 32, a few miles west of Chico, and come out at Washout Beach, off River Rd.

Bidwell Park   PARK
(www.bidwellpark.org) Growing out of downtown, the 3670-acre Bidwell Park is the nation's third-largest municipal park. It stretches 10 miles northwest along Chico Creek with lush groves and miles of **trails**. The upper part of the park is fairly untamed, rather refreshing to find smack in the middle of a city. Several classic movies have been shot here, including parts of *Gone with the Wind* and *The Adventures of Robin Hood*.

The park is full of **swimming spots**. You'll find pools at One-Mile and Five-Mile recreation areas and swimming holes (including Bear Hole, Salmon Hole and Brown Hole) in Upper Bidwell Park, north of Manzanita Ave (don't be surprised if some opt for birthday – rather than swim – suits).

Adventure Outing   OUTDOORS
(☏530-898-4011; www.aschico.com/adventure-outings; 2nd & Chestnut Sts, Bell Memorial Union basement; life jackets $4-8; ⊙9am-5pm Mon-Fri) The CSU-student run outfitter rents equipment such as life jackets, rafts, and even coolers at very reasonable prices by the weekend or week. They also lead popular trips further afield.

🎪 Festivals & Events

With the students out of town, family-friendly outdoor events take over the town each summer. The **Thursday Night Market** fills several blocks of Broadway from April to September. At City Plaza (Main and W 4th Sts), you'll find free **Friday Night Concerts** starting in May.

🛏 Sleeping

There's an abundance of decent independent motels with sparkling swimming pools, some of them along the shaded Esplanade north of downtown. Be aware that Chico State's graduation and homecoming mania (May and October, respectively) send prices skyward.

Woodson Bridge State
Recreation Area   CAMPGROUND $
(☑ 530-839-2112; www.parks.ca.gov; South Ave; tent sites $25) This shaded campground on the banks of the Sacramento is popular with anglers. Its surrounded by a dense riparian forest preserve home to bald eagles and rare birds. The drive-in tent sites are first-come, first-served fall through spring – call for availability. Book online in summer.

The Grateful Bed   B&B $$
(☑ 530-342-2464; www.thegratefulbed.net; 1462 Arcadian Ave; r incl breakfast $140-180; ❄ @) Well, obviously you're a bedhead if you stay here. Tucked in a residential neighborhood near downtown, it's a stately 1905 Victorian home with four sweetly decorated rooms and warm hosts.

★ Hotel Diamond   HISTORIC HOTEL $$$
(☑ 866-993-3100; www.hoteldiamondchico.com; 220 W 4th St; r $120-349; ❄ @ ➛) This white-washed 1904 building is the most luxurious place to lay your head in Chico, with high-thread counts and responsive room service. The Diamond Suite, with its balcony, original furnishings and spacious top-floor balcony, is a-*maz*-ing.

🍴 Eating

Downtown Chico is packed with fun places to eat, many of them catering to a student budget. The outdoor **farmers market** (☑ 530-893-3276; www.chicofarmersmarket.com; 305 Wall St, Chico Municipal parking lot; ⊙ 7:30am-1pm Sat May-Sep) draws from the plentiful surrounding valley.

Nobby's   BURGERS $
(☑ 530-342-2285; 1444 Park Ave; burgers $4.25-6.25; ⊙ 10:30am-9pm Tue-Sat) Simply put, the Nobby Burger, topped with a crispy fried

blanket of cheese and crispier, thick bacon, is a heart attack. Worth it? Probably. This place is so tiny, you'll likely have to stand. Cash only.

Celestino's Live from
New York Pizza   PIZZERIA $
(101 Salem St; pizzas from $14; ⊙ 10:30am-10pm Sun-Thu, to 11pm Fri & Sat) One of the best imitations of 'real' New York pizza in Northern California, they serve thin-crust pies and playfully themed variations such as the meaty Godfather. The slice-n-a-soda lunch special for $4 is a good deal.

Sin of Cortez   CAFE $
(www.sinofcortez.com; 2290 Esplanade; mains $6-16; ⊙ 7am-2pm; 🌱) The service won't win awards for speed, but this local favorite draws both vegetarian and omnivorous mobs with its burly breakfast plates. Order anything with the soy chorizo.

Shubert's Ice Cream & Candy   ICE CREAM $
(www.shuberts.com; 178 E 7th St; ⊙ 9:30am-10pm Mon-Fri, from 11am Sat & Sun) Five generations of Shuberts have produced delicious home-made ice cream and chocolates for more than 75 years at this beloved Chico landmark.

El Paisa Taco Truck   MEXICAN $
(cnr 8th & Pine Sts; mains $1.50-5; ⊙ 11am-8pm) Debate about which of Chico's taco trucks is best can quickly lead to fisticuffs, but the smoky *carnitas* (braised pork) tacos are most certainly a broke college kid's dream.

Sierra Nevada Taproom &
Restaurant   BREWPUB $$
(www.sierranevada.com; 1075 E 20th St; mains $10-32; ⊙ 11am-9pm Sun-Thu, to 10pm Fri & Sat; 🌱) What's on tap is the main draw at the on-site restaurant of the Sierra Nevada Brewery (p321). This genuine Chico destination is great for downing brews but lacks ambience – the huge, loud dining room is basically a factory cafeteria. Still, it has better-than-average pub food and superbly fresh ales and lagers, some not available elsewhere.

Leon Bistro   CALIFORNIAN $$$
(http://leonbistro.com; 817 Main St; mains $18-35; ⊙ from 5pm Wed-Sat) When the most ordinary thing on the menu is a wagyu beef burger with bacon-onion marmalade, you know you're in for something nice. Chef Ann Leon cooked in several fine kitchens before opening her namesake restaurant, a go-to among

Chico tastemakers. She regularly shares her skills in cooking classes.

5th Street Steakhouse AMERICAN $$$
(www.5thstreetsteakhouse.com; 345 W 5th St; steaks from $26; ⊙11:30am-2:30pm Fri, from 4:30pm daily) This is the joint where college kids take their visiting parents. It features crisp white tablecloths, steaks tender enough to cut with a reproachful look, and occasional live jazz loud enough to drown out any disapproval.

Red Tavern AMERICAN $$$
(www.redtavern.com; 1250 Esplanade; mains $17-28; ⊙from 5pm Tue-Sat, 10am-2pm Sun) 🌿 Slightly swanky, the Red Tavern is one of Chico's favorite fine-dining experiences, with a sophisticated menu that uses local, seasonal and organic ingredients, naturally.

🍷 Drinking & Nightlife

As you might have guessed from Chico's party-school rep, you're unlikely to go thirsty. There's a strip of bars on Main St if you want to go hopping.

Empire Coffee CAFE
(http://empirecoffeechico.com; 434 Orange St; ⊙7am-7pm; 🛜) It's not just that this coffee shop is housed in an orange-and-blue 1947 Empire Builder train car or that the baristas draw elaborate images in the foam and host Sunday crochet nights. It's all the fair-trade, organic coffees and creative specials such as macca root and matcha that make this the hippest stop in Chico.

Madison Bear Garden BAR
(www.madisonbeargarden.com; 316 W 2nd St; ⊙11am-1:45am Mon-Sat, from 10am Sun; 🛜) This whimsically decorated campus hangout is housed in a spacious brick building. It's the place to chat with students over thick burgers and cold drafts. The boozy action happens late night in the big beer garden.

Panama Bar & Cafe BAR
(http://panamabarcafeinchico.com; 177 E 2nd St; from $3; ⊙11:30am-1:30am Tue-Sat, 11am-9pm Sun) The house specializes in 31 variations of Long Island iced teas (most of which are around $3), so brace yourself. The only way to take in alcohol any faster would be by IV drip.

LaSalle's CLUB
(www.lasallesbar.com; 229 Broadway; patio cover $5; ⊙7pm-2am Wed-Sun) This venue puts on hip-hop, Top 40 and retro dance nights, and hosts live bands that play anything to pack people in – from reggae to hard rock.

☆ Entertainment

For entertainment options, pick up the free weekly *Chico News & Review* (www.newsandreview.com). For theater, films, concerts, art exhibits and other cultural events at the CSU campus, contact the **CSU Box Office** (📞530-898-6333; http://www.csuchico.edu; cnr 3rd & Chestnut, Sierra Hall; ⊙11am-6pm Mon-Fri) or the CSU Information Center (p321).

Pageant Theatre CINEMA
(www.pageantchico.com; 351 E 6th St; tickets $7.50) Screens international and alternative films. Monday is 'cheap skate night,' with all seats just $3.

1078 Gallery PERFORMING ARTS
(📞530-343-1973; www.1078gallery.org; 820 Broadway; ⊙12:30pm-5:30pm) Chico's contemporary gallery exhibits artworks, and hosts boundary-pushing literary readings, music and theater.

ℹ Information

Chico Chamber of Commerce & Visitor Center (📞800-852-8570, 530-891-5556; www.chicochamber.com; 441 Main St; ⊙10am-4pm Mon-Fri) Local information including bike maps.

ℹ Getting There & Around

Greyhound (www.greyhound.com) buses stop at 11.20am and 7.15pm at the **Amtrak station** (www.amtrak.com; 450 Orange St) heading to San Francisco ($60, five hours 40 minutes), Reno ($74, 10 hours), Los Angeles ($109, 11 hours) and cities in between. The platform is unattended so purchase tickets in advance or on board from the driver. Amtrak trains on the *Coast Starlight* line depart Chico at very inconvenient hours – at 1:47am for Redding ($20, one hour) and at 3:50am for Sacramento ($26, 2½ hours). Amtrak's connecting buses head to Oroville, Sacramento, Stockton, Fresno and Bakersfield, departing at reasonable hours four times daily, but require booking a connecting train.

B-Line (Butte Regional Transit; 📞530-342-0221; www.blinetransit.com; 326 Huss Lane; adult/child $1.40/1) handles all buses throughout Butte County, and can get you around Chico and down to Oroville in 50 minutes.

Car is the easiest way to get around, but Chico is one of the best biking towns in the country.

Rent from **Campus Bicycles** (www.campusbicycles.com; 330 Main St; half/full day $20/35).

Red Bluff

The smoldering streets of Red Bluff – one of California's hottest towns due to the hot-air trap of the Shasta Cascades – are of marginal interest in themselves, but a glimpse towards the mountain-dominated horizon reveals what brings most travelers this way.

Peter Lassen laid out the town site in 1847 and it grew into a key port along the Sacramento River. Now it's a pit stop on the way to the national park that bears his name.

Cowboy culture is alive and well here. Catch it in action the third weekend of April at the **Red Bluff Round-Up** (www.redbluffroundup.com; tickets $10-27), a major rodeo event dating back to 1918, or in any of the dive bars where the jukeboxes are stocked with Nashville, and plenty of big-buckled cowboys belly up to the bar. Or stock up on your own Western wear from one of several historic storefronts in the business district.

◎ Sights & Activities

Red Bluff Recreation Area   PARK
(www.fs.usda.gov) On the east bank of the Sacramento River this sprawling park of meadows has interpretive trails, bicycle paths, boat ramps, a wildlife-viewing area with excellent bird-watching, and a salmon and steelhead ladder (most active July to September).

William B Ide Adobe
State Historic Park   HISTORIC SITE
(☑530-529-8599; 21659 Adobe Rd; per car $6; ☉10am-4pm Fri-Sun) Set on a beautiful, shaded piece of land overlooking a languorous section of the Sacramento River, this park preserves the original one-room adobe house, old forge, and grounds of pioneer William B Ide, who 'fought' in the 1846 Bear Flag Revolt at Sonoma and became president of the California Bear Republic (it lasted 25 days).

Head about a mile north on Main St, turn east onto Adobe Rd and go another mile, following the signs.

Sacramento River
Discovery Center   SCIENCE CENTER
(www.srdc.tehama.k12.ca.us; 1000 Sale Lane; admission by donation; ☉11am-4pm Tue-Sat; ♿) This kid-friendly center has exhibits on the river and the Diversion Dam just outside its doors, which has been permanently opened to allow endangered chinook and green and white sturgeon to migrate. Though the fish aren't visible, 120 species of birds are. Bird walks along the 4.2 miles of wheelchair-accessible trails start the first Saturday of each month at 8am.

◱ Sleeping & Eating

More than a dozen motels are by I-5 and south of town along Main St. The historic residential neighborhood has some bed and breakfasts. The restaurant scene isn't thrilling – a lot of cheap take-out, pizza and stick-to-the-ribs grub straight from a can.

Sycamore Grove
Camping Area   CAMPGROUND $
(☑530-824-5196; www.recreation.gov; tent sites $16-25, RV sites $32.50) Beside the river in the Red Bluff Recreation Area is this quiet USFS campground. Campsites for tents and RVs are first-come, first-served, and offer new, shared showers and flush toilets. You can reserve a large group campground, Camp Discovery, with cabins you must book as a block ($175 for all 11 cabins per night).

Los Mariachis   MEXICAN $
(www.redblufflosmariachis.com; 604 S Main St; mains $5-14; ☉9am-9pm Mon-Fri, to 9:30 Sat & Sun; ♿) This bright, family-run Mexican spot overlooks the central junction of Red Bluff. They have great salsa and *molcajetes* (meat or seafood stew, served in a stone bowl) big enough to satisfy hungry campers.

Thai House   THAI $
(www.newthaihouse.com; 248 S Main St; mains $5-14; ☉11am-3pm & 4-8:30pm Mon-Fri, 11am-8:30pm Sat, from noon Sun; ♿✿✱) ✎ A solid Thai restaurant with excellent curries and soups.

Palomino Room   AMERICAN, BARBECUE $$
(http://palominoroom.com; 723 Main St; mains from $11; ☉from 11am Tue-Fri, from 4pm Sat; ♿) Genuine Texas BBQ in a saloon that's been operating since 1946. Previously known for bar brawls, it's been overhauled and dressed up with signs dating back to Red Bluff's pioneer days. Go for the brisket or ribs with a side of green beans, wrapped in bacon and drizzled with maple glaze. And maybe a salad? Kids eat free on Tuesday.

ⓘ Information

Red Bluff Chamber of Commerce (☑530-527-6220; www.redbluffchamber.com; 100 Main St; ☉8:30am-4pm Mon, to 5pm Tue-Thu, to 4:30pm Fri) To get your bearings and a stack of brochures, find this white building just south of downtown.

ⓘ Getting There & Away

Most visitors pull into Red Bluff to take a break from the busy I-5. By highway, the town is three hours north of San Francisco and 15 minutes north of Sacramento. **Amtrak** (amtrak.com; cnr Rio & Walnut Sts) and **Greyhound** (www.greyhound.com; 22700 Antelope Blvd) connect it with other California cities via bus.

SAN JOAQUIN VALLEY

The southern half of California's Central Valley – named for the San Joaquin River – sprawls from Stockton to the turbine-covered Tehachapi Mountains, southeast of Bakersfield. Everything stretches to the horizon in straight lines – railroad tracks, two-lane blacktop and long irrigation channels.

Through the elaborate politics and machinery of water management, this once-arid region ranks among the most agriculturally productive places in the world, though the profits often go to agribusiness shareholders, not the increasingly disenfranchised family farmer. Some of the tiny towns scattering the region, such as Gustine and Reedley, retain their Main Street Americana appeal while slowly embracing the influence of the Latino labor force that work these fields.

This is a place of seismic, often contentious, development. Arrivals from the coastal cities have resulted in unchecked eastward sprawl – some half a million acres of prime farmland have been paved over as subdivisions in the last decade. What were once actual cattle ranches and vineyards are now nostalgically named developments: a big-box shopping complex named Indian Ranch, a tidy row of McMansions named Vineyard Estates. More green lawns appear as the irrigation systems drain dry. Water rights is *the* issue on everyone's minds.

To really see the region, skip I-5 and travel on Hwy 99 – a road with nearly as long a history as the famous Route 66. It'll be hot – very hot – so roll the windows down and crank up the twangy country or the booming *norteño* (an accordion-driven genre of Mexican folk music). If you have the time, exit often for bushels of the freshest produce on earth and brushes with California's nearly forgotten past.

Many San Joaquin Valley towns are excellent launching points for Yosemite National Park, and Hwy 99 is lined with classic, affordable motor lodges and hotel chains.

Lodi

Although Lodi was once the 'Watermelon capital of the world,' today, full-bodied wine rules this patch of the valley. Breezes from the Sacramento River Delta soothe the area's hot vineyards, where some of the world's oldest Zinfandel vines grow. Lodi's diverse soil is sometimes rocky, sometimes fine sandy loam, giving its grapes a range of distinctive characteristics that allow for experimentation with some less common varietals.

Lodi also hosts a slew of festivals dedicated to their famous export, including the **Wine & Chocolate Weekend** in February and **ZinFest** in May.

⊙ Sights

Lodi Wine & Visitor Center   TASTING ROOM
(www.lodiwine.com; 2545 W Turner Rd; tasting $5; ☉10am-5pm) Get your first taste of Lodi's powerful, sun-soaked Zins and Petite Sirahs at the Lodi Wine & Visitor Center, where 100 local vintages are sold by the glass at the wood–tasting bar. They also provide maps to wineries of the region. Find them on the grounds of Wine & Roses hotel.

Micke Grove Regional Park and Zoo   ZOO
(☑209-331-2010; www.mgzoo.com; 11793 N Micke Grove Rd; adult/child $5/3, parking $5; ☉10am-5pm; 🚼) For the seriously underage, Lodi's Micke Grove Regional Park and Zoo is a good stop, with a water play area, hissing cockroaches and some barking sea lions. There are also kiddie rides in a section called Fun Town. The park also houses an exceptional **Japanese Garden** (www.sjparks.com; 11793 N Micke Grove Rd; ☉9am-2pm Mon-Thu, to 1pm Fri-Sun) FREE.

🛏 Sleeping & Eating

Along Hwy 99, Lodi hosts a string of budget chain hotels. Though the rooms are bland, the competition ensures that they are all very clean, often at a real bargain.

Wine & Roses   B&B $$$
(☑209-334-6988; www.winerose.com; 2505 W Turner Rd; r $179-240, ste from $335; 🕾) Surrounded by a vast rose garden, this is the most luxurious offering to spring up amid

Lodi's vineyards. Tasteful and romantic, the rooms have slate bathrooms, high-quality toiletries and lots of square footage. The suites are grand, some open to private terraces, but there are significant discounts for long-term stays. There's an acclaimed spa and restaurant too.

Cheese Central
MARKET $

(cheesecentrallodi.com; 11 N School St; ⊙10am-6pm Mon-Sat, 1pm to 5pm Sun) Ask Cindy the cheesemonger for thoughtful pairings with Lodi wines. If you want to make a weekend out of Lodi's wine region, the cooking classes here get raves.

Crush Kitchen & Bar
ITALIAN $$

(☏209-369-5400; www.crushkitchen.com; 115 S School St, Woolworth bldg; mains $18-27; ⊙from 11:30am Thu-Mon, 5-9pm Wed) With an excellent, extremely long wine list of Lodi and imported wines plus an Italian-leaning menu to match, Crush is several notches of sophistication ahead of anything else in town. The

plates of fresh tomato salad, gnocchi and duck confit are expert, simple and rustic.

Dancing Fox Winery & Bakery
AMERICAN, BAKERY $$

(☏209-366-2634; www.dancingfoxwinery.com; 203 S School St; mains from $11; ⊙7:30am-9pm Tue-Sat, 9am-3pm Sun) Everything here celebrates grapes — from the Lewis Family Estate's own wines to the bread cultures created from the vineyard's Petite Sirah grapes. The best selections from the overly broad menu involve the wood-burning oven.

Stockton

Stockton has had more than its share of ups and downs. Hit hard by housing foreclosures and almost a billion dollars in debt, in 2012, it became the largest US city to file for bankruptcy.

What remains of its proud past as a major inland port, the main supply hub for gold rushers, and a leading player in shipbuilding

---

TOP LODI WINERIES

Lodi's underrated wineries make an easy escape from the Bay Area, and the quality of grapes will delight true oenophiles. This is the source of many master blenders' secret weapons.

The region is easily accessed from I-5 or Hwy 99 and just as easy to navigate, as roads are well marked. For maps, check the Lodi Wine & Visitor Center (p325).

Jesse's Grove (www.jessiesgrovewinery.com; 1973 W Turner Rd; ⊙noon-5pm) With its summer concert series and very long history, this is an anchor of Lodi wine producers. There's a new tasting room downtown on E Locust St.

Harney Lane (www.harneylane.com; 9010 E Harney Lane; tasting $5; ⊙11am-5pm Thu-Mon) A sweet family outfit that's been around Lodi forever; their Tempranillo is an overachiever. Tasting fee refunded with purchase.

d'Art (www.dartwines.com; 13299 N Curry Ave; tasting $5; ⊙noon-5pm Thu-Mon) Helen and Dave Dart's bold Cab is as fun and inviting as the tasting room. Tasting fee refunded with purchase.

LangeTwins (www.langetwins.com; 1525 East Jahant Rd, Acampo; tasting $5-10; ⊙11am-4pm Thu-Sun) The Viognier and reserve blends are worth the 7-mile drive north of town to this state-of-the-art steel-and-redwood winery.

Riaza Wines (www.riazawines.com; 20 W Elm; ⊙1-6pm Fri-Sat, to 5pm Sun) The downtown tasting room pours Spanish varietals that only recently were discovered to grow like mad in the Lodi sun.

Jeremy Wine Co (www.jeremywineco.com; 6 W Pine St; ⊙1-5pm Wed-Sun) Friendly folk in this brass- and wood-fitted tasting room downtown pour a bright fruit-forward Sangiovese.

Michael David (www.michaeldavidwinery.com; 4580 W Hwy 12; tasting $5; ⊙10am-5pm) These brothers built an enthusiastic following with their oaky, fruity wines. Their renowned Zinfandel, 7 Deadly Zins, is a standout. The cafe and old-timey dry goods store make this tasting room a perfect lunch stop. Tasting fee refunded with purchase.

and modern transport, is today blighted by crime-ridden streets and crumbling facades. Still, the downtown and waterfront redevelopment is one of the valley's more promising grassroots efforts and warrants a brief detour.

A block east of Weber Point, the **Department of Tourism** (209-938-1555; www.visitstockton.org; 125 Bridge Pl; ⊙9am-5pm Mon-Fri) has complete information about the goings-on in town.

◉ Sights & Activities

Weber Point Events Center LANDMARK
(www.stocktongov.com; 221 N Center St) Downtown on the McLeod Lake waterfront, the modern white edifice standing in the middle of a grassy park looking rather like a pile of sailboats is the Weber Point Events Center and marks the center of the action. This is also the site of the huge April Asparagus Festival, a series of open-air concerts, and fountains where squealing kids cool off.

Banner Island Ballpark BASEBALL
(209-644-1900; www.stocktonports.com; 404 W Fremont St) The beautiful Banner Island Ballpark is where the minor-league Stockton Ports play ball April to September.

Haggin Museum MUSEUM
(www.hagginmuseum.org; 1201 N Pershing Ave; adult/child $8/5; ⊙1:30-5pm Wed-Fri, noon-5pm Sat-Sun) This city gem houses a 26ft boat by Stockton's own Stephens Bros company, and an excellent collection of American landscape and 'Golden Age' paintings.

Opportunity Cruises BOAT TOUR
(http://opportunitycruises.com; 445 W Weber Ave, Stockton Marina; cruises without/with meal $37/$55) Cruises around the Sacramento Delta in open-sided river boats depart from the Marina.

🛏 Sleeping & Eating

University Plaza Waterfront Hotel HOTEL $$
(209-944-1140; www.universityplazawaterfronthotel.com; 110 W Fremont St; r from $125; 🛜) If you're spending the night here, a nice option is the University Plaza Waterfront Hotel, a place where business travelers mingle with University of the Pacific students and the mayor, who all live in the lofts on the upper floors. The very modern building overlooking the harbor and historic park, unlike the highway chains, is walkable from other locations in the city center.

STOCKTON ASPARAGUS FESTIVAL

Of all the Central Valley food celebrations, perhaps none pay such creative respect to the main ingredient as the **Stockton Asparagus Festival** (http://asparagusfest.com; N Center St btwn Oak St & W Weber Av; adult/child $13/free), which brings together more than 500 vendors to serve these green stalks – more than 10 tons of them! – every way imaginable. It sprouts along the waterfront at the end of April.

Manny's California Fresh Café AMERICAN $
(209-463-6415; www.mannyscaliforniafresh.com; 1612 Pacific Ave; mains $4.95-7.95; ⊙10am-9:45pm) Get lunch at Manny's, which serves flavorful rotisserie meats and fried-chicken sandwiches. It's at the edge of the Miracle Mile district, a developing shopping stretch on Pacific Ave, north of downtown.

On Lok Sam CANTONESE $
(http://newonlocksam.com; 333 S Sutter St; ⊙11am-9pm) Venture south of the Crosstown Freeway (Hwy 4) to (New) On Lok Sam, established in 1895 in the center of Stockton's lively Chinese settlement.

Modesto

Cruising was banned in Modesto in 1993, but the town still touts itself as the 'cruising capital of the world.' The past time's notoriety stems mostly from homegrown George Lucas' 1973 film *American Graffiti*. You'll still see hot rods and flashy wheels around town, but they no longer clog thoroughfares on Friday nights.

This is a good spot for getting off the dusty highway. Old oaks arch over the city's streets and you can eat well in the compact downtown. The **Ernest & Julio Gallo Winery**, makers of America's best-selling jug wines, is among the town's biggest businesses.

Downtown sits just east of Hwy 99 (avoid the area west of the freeway), centering on 10th and J Sts. From downtown, Yosemite Blvd (Hwy 132) runs east toward Yosemite National Park.

Many historic buildings have survived revitalization, including the 1934 **State Theatre** (www.thestate.org; 1307 J St), which hosts films and live music, and the **Southern**

Pacific depot, a Mission-style beauty at J and 9th Sts that still serves as the transit hub. The famous Modesto Arch, on the corner of 9th and I Sts, stands at what was once the city's main entry point. The town's slogan on it, 'Water, Wealth, Contentment, Health,' came from a 1912 contest and remains as relevant today as when it went up. Ironically, the pithy little poem didn't actually win the contest. Judges chose the folksy, if less eloquent, 'Nobody's Got Modesto's Goat' but were overruled by the city government.

Classic car shows and rock 'n' roll fill the streets every June for Graffiti Summer (http://visitmodesto.com). Amid all the '50s charm, the sparkling Gallo Center for the Arts (☎209-338-2100; www.galloarts.org; 1000 I St; ⊗10am-6pm Mon-Fri, from noon Sat) brings huge acts to the Valley. For details, check the Convention & Visitors Bureau (☎888-640-8467; http://visitmodesto.com; 1150 9th St).

✖ Eating

Brighter Side
SANDWICHES $
(www.brighter-side.com; 1125 K St, cnr 13th & K Sts; mains $5-6; ⊗11am-3:30pm Mon-Fri; ☑) An earthy little sandwich shop housed in a wood-shingled, former gas station, serves up sandwiches including the Larry (polish sausage, mushrooms, green onions on rye) and the veggie Christine on the sunny patio.

A&W Drive-In
AMERICAN $
(www.awrestaurants.com; 1404 G St, cnr 14th & G Sts; cheeseburger $3, float $4; ⊗10am-9pm, to 8pm Oct-Mar) A vintage burger stand (part of a chain founded in nearby Lodi), where roller-skating carhops and classic cars on display move a lot of root beer floats. George Lucas supposedly cruised here as a youth.

Minnie's
CHINESE $
(http://minnies.58-s.com; 107 McHenry Ave; mains from $7.50) On the north end of town, Minnie's is a mid-century Polynesian pop institution, one of the last-standing tiki restaurants of its era. Opened in 1954, the Mah family has kept the original carvings, rattan, and menu favorites including chow mein and deep-fried asparagus. Look for the oil-on-velvet paintings of nippled beauties by the celebrated Ralph Burke Tyree.

Merced

You can jog over to Yosemite from many of the small towns in this part of the valley, but this is a convenient staging area, right on Hwy 140. The machine of progress has not been kind to Merced, as it suffers more than its share of strip malls, but at its core are still tree-lined streets, historic Victorian homes and a magnificent 1875 courthouse. The downtown business district is a work-in-progress, with 1930s movie theaters, antique stores and a few casual eateries undergoing constant renovation.

Merced is right in the midst of a population makeover, thanks to the newest University of California campus, opened in 2005. UC Merced's first freshman class numbered just 1000 students, but the school continues to grow with a diverse student body and has begun to dramatically shape the city.

Downtown Merced is east of Hwy 99 along Main St, between R St and Martin Luther King Jr Way. The California Welcome Center (☎209-724-8104; http://visitmerced.travel; 710 W 16th St; ⊗8:30am-5pm Mon-Sat, 10am-4pm Sun), adjacent to the bus depot, has local maps and information on Merced and Yosemite.

The big attraction is the Castle Air Museum (☎209-723-2178; www.castleairmuseum.org; 5050 Santa Fe Dr, Atwater; adult/child $10/8; ⊗9am-5pm Apr-Sep, 10am-4pm Oct-Mar) in Atwater, about 6 miles northwest. A squadron of restored military aircrafts from WWII, the Korean War and the Vietnam War sit in repose across from a large hangar. Even the most conscientious of objectors will stand agape at these feats of engineering.

🛏 Sleeping & Eating

HI Merced Home Hostel
HOSTEL $
(☎209-725-0407; www.hiusa.org; dm $20-23; ⊗reception 5:30-10pm) A night in this six-bed homestay in the northeast part of town feels like staying with your long-lost Aunt Jan and Uncle Larry, the kind of folks happy to lend advice about Yosemite at the kitchen table. Beds fill quickly and must be reserved in advance (call between 5:30pm and 10pm). They can shuttle you to/from the bus and train stations.

Hooper House Bear Creek Inn
B&B $$
(☎209-723-3991; www.hooperhouse.com; 575 W North Bear Creek Dr; r $139-169; ❉🐾) In a grand old Colonial-style mansion, Hooper House Bear Creek Inn is a leisurely retreat. Rooms are large and beautifully furnished with hardwood furniture, soft beds and tiled bathrooms. A full breakfast is included, which you can have sent to your room.

Branding Iron   STEAKHOUSE **$$**
(www.thebrandingiron-merced.com; 640 W 16th
St; lunch mains $9-11, dinner $10-27; ⊙11:30am-
2pm Mon-Fri, 5-10pm Sun-Thu, to 9:30 Fri & Sat)
The Branding Iron roadhouse, a favorite of
ranchers in the area, has been spruced up
a bit for the tour buses, but locals still dig
the hearty steak platters and Western at-
mosphere. Presiding over the dining room is
'Old Blue,' a massive stuffed bull's head from
a local dairy farm.

❶ Getting There & Away

YARTS (Yosemite Area Regional Transportation
System; ☑209-388-9589; www.yarts.com) bus-
es depart three (winter) to five (summer) times
daily for Yosemite Valley from several Merced
locations, including the **Merced Transpo Center**
(www.mercedthebus.com; cnr 16th & N Sts) and
the **Amtrak station** (www.amtrak.com; 324 W
24th St, cnr 24th & K Sts). The trip takes about
2½ hours and stops include Mariposa, Midpines
and the Yosemite Bug Lodge & Hostel. Round-
trip adult/child costs $25/18 and includes park
entry (quite a bargain!). There's limited space for
bicycles, so show up early.

Greyhound (710 W 16th St) also operates from
the Transpo Center (Los Angeles four times
daily, 6½ hours, $43).

Fresno

Smack in the arid center of the state, Fresno
is the biggest city in the Central Valley. It may
not be scenic (it's a testing ground for every
new chain store), but it is beautifully situated,
an hour's drive from four national parks (Yo-
semite, Sierra, Kings Canyon and Sequoia),
making it an ideal last stop for expeditions.

Unfortunately, in recent years, Fresno's
agriculture-based economy has been hit
hard by catastrophic droughts and plum-
meting food prices, while unemployment
has risen. A local farm movement to regain
footing seeks to revolutionize food produc-
tion through organic, sustainable practices
and fair wages. Fresno's proximity to these
progressive farms means it's experiencing a
food and cultural renaissance. The produce
and meat is the freshest you'll find any-
where. Fresno? Oh, Fresyes.

Like many valley towns, Fresno is home to
diverse Mexican, Chinese and Basque com-
munities, which arrived in successive waves.
More recently thousands of Hmong people
have put down roots in the area. The long-
standing Armenian community is famously
represented by author and playwright Wil-
liam Saroyan, who was born, lived and died
in this city he loved dearly.

◉ Sights & Activities

One hopping side of town is the Tower
District, north of downtown, an oasis of
gay-friendly, alterna-culture, book and
record stores, music clubs and a handful
of stylish restaurants. Many of the histor-
ic buildings are along the Sante Fe rail-
road tracks and downtown, including the
1894 **Fresno Water Tower** and the 1928
Pantages (Warnors) Theatre. The crowds
gather at the sprawling **Convention Center**
and **Chukchansi Park**, home of Fresno's
Triple-A baseball team, the Grizzlies.

Downtown lies between Divisadero St,
Hwy 41 and Hwy 99. Two miles north, the
Tower District sits around the corner of E
Olive Ave and N Fulton Ave.

Forestiere Underground
Gardens   GARDENS
(☑559-271-0734; www.undergroundgardens.info;
5021 W Shaw Ave; adult/child $15/7; ⊙tours 10am-
4pm hourly Wed-Sun May-Sep, reduced hr Oct-Apr)
If you see only one thing in Fresno, make it
this intriguing historic landmark, two blocks
east of Hwy 99. The gardens are the singular
result of Sicilian immigrant Baldassare For-
estiere, who dug out some 70 acres beneath
the hardpan soil to plant citrus trees, start-
ing in 1906. This utterly fantastical accom-
plishment took him 40 years to complete.

With a unique skylight system, Forestiere
created a beautiful subterranean space for
commercial crops and his own living quar-
ters. The tunnel system includes bedrooms,
a library, patios, grottos and a fish pond.
Check the website for tour times.

Tower Theatre   HISTORIC BUILDING
(☑559-485-9050; www.towertheaterfresno.com;
815 E Olive Ave) Fresno's **Tower District** began
as a shopping mecca during the 1920s, gain-
ing its name from the Tower Theatre, a beau-
tiful 1939 art-deco movie house. The theater
is now a center for the performing arts. Sur-
rounding it are bookstores, boutiques, trendy
restaurants and coffeehouses, and hipsters.

Fresno Art Museum   MUSEUM
(☑559-441-4221; www.fresnoartmuseum.org;
2233 N 1st St; admission $5; ⊙11am-5pm Fri-Sun,
to 8pm Thu) This museum has rotating exhib-
its of contemporary art – including work by
local artists – that are among the most in-
triguing in the valley.

BLOODLESS BULLFIGHTS

Bullfighting has been illegal in the US since 1957, but there are exceptions to the rule. Portuguese communities in the Central Valley are permitted to stage bloodless bullfights at *festas*, huge cultural events that draw as many as 25,000 to honor St Anthony or Our Lady of Fátima. Portuguese fishermen and farmers, mostly from the Azores, began settling in California during the late 19th century.

Candlelight processions, folk dancing, blessing of the cows, *pezinho* singing (melodies accompanied by violin) and unbridled eating are all part of the experience. Major events happen in summer in Hanford, Gustine and Stevinson. They're not well publicized. Search 'festas california' and see what comes up in English.

Woodward Park
PARK

(www.fresno.gov; 7775 Friant Rd; per vehicle $5; ◷6am-10pm Apr-Oct, to 7pm Nov-Mar) The city's largest park has 300 acres of barbecue facilities, lakes and ponds, a **Japanese garden** (adult/child $3/50¢) and a huge amphitheater for Shakespeare and other performances. A 6-mile network of bike trails connects to the **Lewis S Eaton Trail**, which runs 22 miles from the northeast corner along Friant Rd to Friant Dam.

Roeding Park
PARK

(www.fresno.gov; 890 Belmont Ave; per vehicle $5; ◷6am-10pm Apr-Oct, to 7pm Nov-Mar) Just east of Hwy 99, this large and shady park is home to the small **Chaffee Zoological Gardens** (☑559-498-2671; www.fresnochaffeezoo.com; adult/child $7/3.50; ◷9am-5pm Mon-Fri, to 6pm Sat & Sun; ▣). Adjacent to it are **Storyland** (☑559-264-2235; storylandplayland.com; 890 W Belmont Ave; adult/child $5/3.50; ◷10am-4pm Sat & Sun; ▣), a kitschy children's fairytale world dating from 1962, and **Playland** (storylandplayland.com; 890 W Belmont Ave; adult/child $5/3.50; ◷10am-4pm Sat & Sun; ▣), which has kiddie rides and games.

🛏 Sleeping & Eating

Fresno has room to grow when it comes to world-class accommodations, but those using it as a launch pad for visiting Sequoia and Kings Canyon National Parks have plenty of options in the cluster of chains near the airport or a couple of high-rise offerings downtown.

For food, the best stuff is scattered around town – making this, most definitely, a driving town. Trendy eateries and breweries are in the Tower District and hidden among abandoned storefronts downtown. **Food trucks** (carthopfresno.com; Fulton Mall; ◷10am-2pm Thu) circle up every Thursday accompanied by live music in front of Fresno Brewing Company. For fantastic raw ingredients, Fresno's excellent **farmers markets** (playfresno.org) are abundant year-round.

Piccadilly Inn Shaw
HOTEL $$

(☑559-348-5520; www.picadillyinn.com; 2305 W Shaw Ave; r $89-159; ▣@▣) This is Fresno's nicest option, with a lovely pool, big rooms and tons of amenities. Ask for a room with a fireplace to cuddle by in winter. If they are full, try one of the other properties, both by the airport: the Piccadilly Inn Express and the Piccadilly Inn Airport.

Dusty Buns Bistro
AMERICAN $

(www.dustybuns.com; 608 E Weldon Ave; mains $6-7; ◷11am-9pm Mon-Sat) This restaurant began as a food truck dishing out sandwiches on buns, made from local ingredients, single handedly actualizing Fresno's modern foodie culture. The young couple in the drivers' seat still makes the rounds in the truck. Try the Dusty Bun, a brilliant little number of chipotle roast chicken and slaw.

Sam's Italian Deli & Market
DELI $

(www.samsitaliandeli.com; 2415 N First St; mains $5-9; ◷9am-6pm Mon-Sat) This Italian market and deli is the real deal, stacking up the 'New Yorker' pastrami and some mean prosciutto and mozzarella.

Chicken Pie Shop
AMERICAN $

(Grandmarie's Chicken Pie Shop; ☑559-237-5042; 861 E Olive Ave; mains $7-8.45; ◷7am-7pm Mon-Fri, 8am-2pm Sat & Sun) With a ladle of gravy and a flaky crust, the beautiful chicken-stuffed pies at this Tower District institution bear no resemblance to the frozen, soggy mess of your childhood, though the nostalgic decor might.

★Peeve's Public House & Local Market
AMERICAN $$

(peevespub.com; 1243 Fulton Mall; mains $10; ◷11am-11pm Mon-Thu, to 1am Fri, 9am-1am Sat, 9am-9pm Sun) Located in the desolate Fulton

Mall in downtown, Peeve's is leading Fresno's new wave of urban-rural revitalization by celebrating hyper-local food. Every ingredient in their three daily offerings (burgers and salads, usually), the dozen microbrews ($5 to $6), and the extensive wine list are pure Fresno County. A small market next door offers some local producers' best.

☆ Entertainment

Check the **Fresno Bee** (http://calendar.fresnobee.com) for what's happening when.

Tower Theatre for the Performing Arts PERFORMING ARTS
(www.towertheatrefresno.com; 815 E Olive Ave) In the center of Fresno's hippest neighborhood, it's hard to miss the neon deco palace that opens its stage to touring rock and jazz acts and seasonal cultural events.

ℹ Information

Fresno/Clovis Convention & Visitors Bureau (☏ 559-981-5500, 800-788-0836; www.playfresno.org; 1550 E Shaw Ave, suite 101; ⊙8am-5pm Mon-Fri) Visitor information in a non-descript office complex. Brochures are also stocked in the Water Tower and airport.

ℹ Getting There & Around

Amtrak (Sante Fe station; ☏ 559-486-7651; 2650 Tulare St; ⊙5:30am-9:45pm) The most scenic way to travel these parts, the San Joaquin service stops in a white Mission building smack in downtown Fresno on its way to other tourist destinations including Yosemite ($40, four hours, twice daily) and San Francisco ($55, four hours).

Fresno Area Express (FAX; ☏ 559-621-7433; www.fresno.gov; one-way $1.25) The local service that has daily bus services to the Tower District (bus 22 or 28) and Forestiere Underground Gardens (bus 20) from the downtown transit center at Van Ness Ave and Fresno St.

Fresno Yosemite International Airport (FAT; www.flyfresno.com; 5175 E Clinton Way) In the Central Valley.

Greyhound (☏ 559-268-1829; 1033 H St) Stops downtown near the Chukchansi ballpark. Multiple regular/express rides daily to Los Angeles ($31/32.50, five/four hours) and San Francisco ($45/47, six/four hours).

Visalia

Its agricultural prosperity and well-maintained downtown make Visalia one of the valley's convenient stops en route to Sequoia and Kings Canyon National Parks or

---

DOWN ON THE FARM

There's no better way to get a taste of this agricultural region than on its farms. Many offer tours and seasonal opportunities to pick your own. Central Valley visitor's bureaus can point you to popular stops. Here are a few family farms paving the way with progressive practices.

Riverdance Farm (☏ 209-394-1420; http://riverdancefarms.com; 12230 Livingston-Cressey Rd, Livingston) Permaculture farming produces delectable blueberries and cherries May to June at this fruit and nut farm, which also hosts a **pick-and-gather festival** the weekend after Memorial Day (late May).

Squaw Valley Herb Garden (www.squawvalleyherbgardens.com; 31765 E Kings Canyon Rd, Squaw Valley; tours Apr-Oct from $15) Pick your way through aromatic herb beds and fields of lavender on this stunning farm in the Sierra foothills.

T&D Willey Farm (http://tdwilleyfarms.com; 13886 Road 20, Madera) In between their work running a popular CSA (community-sourced agriculture program) and leading the regional small-farm movement, Tom and Denesse grow everything from organic arugula to rutabagas. Tours in October.

Page River Bottom Farms (17780 E Vino Ave, Reedley; ⊙8am-5pm Mon-Sat) Heritage chickens and pasture-raised cattle, sheep and pigs roam this happy farm. Call for open house dates.

Organic Pastures (www.organicpastures.com; 7221 S Jameson Ave, Fresno; ⊙8am-5pm Mon-Fri) This dairy offers raw milk and raw milk products – sweet, creamy and totally unlike anything in the supermarket. Regular tours and a chance to camp with the cows every Memorial Day weekend.

WORTH A TRIP

SCENIC DRIVE: THE BLOSSOM TRAIL

When the Central Valley fruit and nut trees are in bloom, the winding roads around Visalia make for a lovely, leisurely afternoon drive (just pack your antihistamines). The 62-mile **Fresno County Blossom Trail** (www.gofresnocounty. com) is especially stunning between February and March, when the orchards are awash in the pastel petals of apricot, almond, peach, nectarine, apple and citrus. Come back starting in May to taste the results.

Route maps are available online and at the Fresno/Clovis Convention & Visitors Bureau (p331), though DIY is possible if you don't mind taking occasional detours on the back roads between Sanger, Reedley, Orange Cove, Selma, Fowler and Kingsburg.

the Sierra Peaks. Bypassed a century ago by the railroad, the city is 5 miles east of Hwy 99, along Hwy 198. Its downtown has old-town charm and makes for a nice stroll.

The original Victorian and Arts and Crafts–style homes in Visalia are architectural gems worth viewing on foot. Maps for many interesting self-guided tours are available via the website of the **Visalia Convention and Visitor's Bureau** (☑ 559-334-0141; www.visitvisalia.org; 303 E Acequia Av; ⊙8:30am-5pm Mon-Fri).

The main draw in the area is the **Kaweah Oak Preserve** (www.sequoiariverlands.org; 29979 Rd 182, Exeter; donation adult/child $3/1; ⊙8am-sunset), about 7 miles east of town. With 324 acres of majestic oak trees, the kind that once stretched from the Sierras to (long-gone) Tulare Lake in the valley, it is a gorgeous setting for easy hikes. From Hwy 198, turn north onto Rd 182; the park is about a half-mile along on your left.

🛏 Sleeping & Eating

If you stay for grub, there are plenty of choices, including a spread of ethnic food, down Main St between Floral and Bridge Sts.

Spalding House B&B $
(☑ 559-739-7877; www.thespaldinghouse.com; 631 N Encina St; s/d $85/95; ❀) Spalding House offers a charming B&B experience for overnights.

★**Brewbaker's Brewing Company** BREWPUB $
(www.brewbakersbrewingco.com; 219 E Main St; mains from $8; ⊙11:30am-10pm; 🛜) Brewbaker's Brewing Company serves up good pub grub and microbrews such as its smooth Sequoia Red for the crowds.

❶ Getting There & Around

Visalia's transit options, including direct access to Sequoia National Park (p429), all funnel through the **Transit Center** (www.ci.visalia. ca.us; 425 E Oak Ave; ⊙6am-9:30pm Mon-Fri, 8am-6:30pm Sat & Sun). **Amtrak** (www.amtrak. com; 425 E Oak Ave) shuttles run between the Transit Center and Hanford station a half hour away by reservation only (use local buses as an alternative). From Hanford, you can connect to all other Amtrak routes in the state, including the *San Joaquin*, which travels north to Sacramento ($32, four hours, two direct daily) or south to Bakersfield ($22.50, 1½ hours, six daily).

The convenient, bike-rack equipped **Sequoia Shuttle** (☑ 877-287-4453; www.sequoiashuttle. com; 425 E Oak Ave; adult/child return incl park entry $15/7; ⊙ late May-Sep) picks up from major hotels and takes two hours to reach the Giant Forest Museum (p429) in Sequoia National Park. The **Visalia Towne Trolley** (425 East Oak Ave; ticket 25¢; ⊙7:30am-5:30pm Mon-Thu, to 11pm Fri, 9:30am-11pm Sat) hits most downtown sights over two circuits and costs just a quarter.

Bakersfield

Nearing Bakersfield, the landscape has evidence of California's *other* gold rush: rusting rigs alongside the route burrow into Southern California's vast oil fields. Black gold was discovered here in the late 1800s, and Kern County, the southernmost along Hwy 99, still pumps more than some OPEC countries.

This is the setting of Upton Sinclair's *Oil!*, which was adapted into the 2007 Academy Award–winning film, *There Will Be Blood*. In the 1930s the oil attracted a stream of 'Okies' – farmers who migrated out of the dusty Great Plains – to work the derricks. The children of these tough-as-nails roughnecks put the 'western' in country western by creating the 'Bakersfield Sound' in the mid-1950s, with heroes Buck Owens and Merle Haggard giving a defiant middle finger at the silky Nashville establishment.

Bakersfield is making moves to fancy-up like some of its valley neighbors, but downtown holds some real surprises in its upbeat mix of restored buildings and new restaurants, theaters and clubs.

Sights

The Kern River flows along Bakersfield's northern edge, separating it from its blue-collar neighbor, Oildale, and a host of oil fields. Truxtun and Chester Aves are the main downtown thoroughfares. Though currently suffering from some neglect, Old Town Kern, located east of downtown around Baker and Sumner Sts, still has character underneath the decay. **Bakersfield Historic Preservation Commission** (www.bakersfieldcity.us/edcd/historic) has downloadable maps of walking tours covering Old Town Kern and Bakersfield's historic downtown.

Five & Dime Antique Mall LANDMARK
(☎ 661-321-0061; 1400 19th St, Woolworth bldg; ☉ 10am-5pm Mon-Sat, from noon Sun) Three stories hold vintage wares that date back to at least the same era as the Woolworth building they're housed in. Try to go when the diner (p334) is open.

Kern County Museum & Lori Brock Children's Discovery Center MUSEUM
(www.kcmuseum.org; 3801 Chester Ave; adult/child $10/$7-9; ☉ 10am-5pm Tue-Sat, from noon Sun; P ⊞) ⊘ This museum covers black and yellow gold with a pioneer village of more than 50 restored and replicated buildings. The musty main structure has a large (and fairly disturbing) display of taxidermied local wildlife. On the 2nd floor waits a collection of pristine memorabilia from Bakersfield's musical heyday.

California Living Museum ZOO
(www.calmzoo.org; 10500 Alfred Harrell Hwy; adult/child $9/5; ☉ 9am-4pm; ⊞) The zoo and botanical gardens have a menagerie of native animals and a rattlesnake house, which has every type of rattler in the state. It's about a 20-minute drive northeast from downtown Bakersfield.

Cesar E Chavez National Monument HISTORIC SITE
(☎ 661-823-6134; http://chavezfoundation.org; 29700 Woodford-Tehachapi Rd, Keene; admission $3; ☉ 10am-4pm) This newly designated national monument, Nuestra Señora Reina de la Paz, is the national headquarters of the United Farmworkers of America and was the home of civil rights leader César Chávez from 1971 until his death in 1993. On view are exhibits on Chávez's work, his office, and grave. Keene is 27 miles southeast of Bakersfield down Hwy 58.

Chávez was born near Yuma, Arizona in 1927, and was 11 when his family lost their farm and became migrant farm workers in California. At 14, he left school to labor in the fields. Eventually, he became a champion of nonviolent social change, negotiating for better wages and access to water and bathrooms in the fields. His work resulted in numerous precedents including the first union contracts requiring safe use of pesticides and the abolition of short-handled tools that had crippled generations of farm workers.

Sleeping & Eating

Chain motels sprout like weeds off the highways near Bakersfield. Old-school budget motels, starting from about $47, line Union Ave south heading south from Hwy 178, but can be shady. Great meals though are easy to find. Bakersfield is blessed with a Basque culinary tradition, where food is served family-style in a procession of courses including soup, salad, beans, thin slices of tangy beef tongue and cottage cheese, which all come *before* the main course.

★ **Padre Hotel** BOUTIQUE HOTEL $$
(☎ 661-427-4900; www.thepadrehotel.com; 1702 18th St; r $119-229, ste from $459) After standing vacant for years, this historic tower

---

KINGS & QUEENS OF THE BAKERSFIELD SOUND

Driving south on Hwy 99 requires getting on a first-name basis with Bakersfield's drawling titans: Merle, Buck and other masters of twanging Telecasters and hayseed heartbreak:

➡ 'I'm Gonna Break Every Heart I Can,' 'Okie from Muskogee,' 'The Bottle Let Me Down,' 'Swinging Doors' – Merle Haggard

➡ 'I've Got A Tiger by the Tail,' 'Second Fiddle,' 'Under Your Spell Again,' 'The Streets of Bakersfield' (with Dwight Yoakam) – Buck Owens

➡ 'A Dear John Letter' (with Ferlin Husky), 'Pitty, Pitty, Patter,' '(I've Got A) Happy Heart' – Jean Shepard

➡ 'LA International Airport,' 'The Great White Horse' (with Buck Owens) — Susan Raye

KINGSBURG: A LITTLE SWEDEN IN THE VALLEY

The quiet hamlet of Kingsburg has a vibrant ethnic heritage. Around 1873, when it was established as a rail stop called 'Kings River Switch,' two Swedes arrived. Their country-men soon followed, and by 1921, 94% of Kingsburg's residents, as it had become known, were of Swedish heritage.

Draper St, the main drag, is decked out in vibrant Swedish Dala horses, a holy symbol. Inside the cutesy Tudor buildings are gift shops and little bakeries stocked with buttery pastries. The restaurants serve Swedish pancakes, Swedish meatballs and Swedish lingonberry soda, just eat early, because many close after lunch. Diane at **Diane's Village Bakery & Cafe** (☑ 559-897-7460; 1332 Draper St, Kingsburg Village Mall; mains less than $8.25; ☺ 8am-2:30pm Mon-Sat) in the back of the Village Mall cooks with her grandmother's recipes. **Dala Horse** (☑ 559-897-7762; 1531 Draper St; mains $7.25-10.25; ☺ 6am-2:30pm, to 2pm Sat, to 2pm Sun) is liberal with their lingonberry jam. Pick up Nordic decor and insight on the town from June, town icon and proprietor of **Svensk Butik**. Sure the town plays up its heritage for the crowds, but there is genuine pride in every 'Valkommen!'

The town has also gone through pains to preserve its oldest structures. Under the coffee-pot water tower, the **city jail** (http://www.kingsburghistoricalpark.org; 1400 Marion St; ☺ 24hr) **FREE** is a quick stop. On the east end of town, a general store, schoolhouse and windmill, as well as artifacts and farm equipment make up **Kingsburg Historical Park** (www.kingsburghistoricalpark.org; 2321 Sierra St; ☺ 1-4pm Fri).

Good times to visit are during the holiday explosion that is the **Santa Lucia Festival** (first Saturday of December) and the **Swedish Festival** (parades, maypole dancing, and a real smorgasbord) in May. The **Chamber of Commerce** (☑ 559-897-1111; www.kingsburg-chamber-of-commerce.org; 1475 Draper St; ☺ 9am-5pm) keeps a calendar.

reopened after a stylish facelift that added an upscale restaurant and two bars that instantly became *the* places for cocktails in Bakersfield. The standard rooms have lavish details: thick mattresses, plush sheets and designer furniture. The two themed suites – the 'Oil Baron' and 'Farmer's Daughter' – have sexy showers for two.

Woolworth Diner   DINER $
(☑ 661-321-0061; 1400 19th St, Five & Dime Antique Mall; burgers $5.95; ☺ 11am-4pm Mon-Sat, noon-4pm Sun) The white capped soda jerks flip fantastic cheeseburgers and pour great shakes at the store's original soda counter, buffed to its former glory.

Wool Growers   BASQUE $
(☑ 661-327-9584; www.woolgrowers.net; 620 E 19th St; lunch $12.50, dinner mains $16.40-27; ☺ 11:30am-2pm & 6-9pm Mon-Sat) A simple Basque eating hall loaded with character. You can order the nine – yes nine – sides without the main, or loosen your belt and get it all.

Luigi's   ITALIAN $
(www.shopluigis.com; 725 E 19th St; mains $7.75-11.95; ☺ 11am-2:30pm Tue-Sat; ☑) Lined with black-and-white photos of sporting legends, this amazing lunch spot has been around

more than 100 years. The stuffed chicken melts in your mouth and the excellent bakery turns out soft, buttery rolls and an exceedingly rich Butterfinger Pie. The adjacent bar and deli stay open until 4pm.

Dewar's Candy Shop   ICE CREAM $
(☑ 661-322-0933; 1120 Eye St; sundaes from $4.50; ☺ 10am-9pm Mon-Sun; ☺) Perched on the pink stools at the counter, families dig into homemade ice cream with ingredients sourced from surrounding farms since 1930. Dreamy flavors such as lemon flake and cotton candy change seasonally.

Jake's Original Tex Mex Cafe SOUTHWESTERN $
(www.jakestexmex.com; 1710 Oak E St; mains $7.95-13.29; ☺ 11am-8pm Mon-Sat) More Tex than Mex, this excellent cafeteria packs in city workers for smoky, slow-roasted pit beef. The chili fries are a messy delight, and the combination plates decadent.

★ **Noriega's**   BASQUE $$
(☑ 661-322-8419; www.noriegahotel.com; 525 Sumner St; breakfast $10, lunch $17, dinner $22; ☺ 7am-9am, from noon, from 7pm Tue-Sun) Surly Basque gentlemen still pass the communal wine carafes at Bakersfield's last family-style Basque institution. Join them at a commu-

nal table for a procession of dishes leading to silky oxtail stew, ribs and every other possible protein (check online for the day's main course). The magical ambience and the food earned a prestigious James Beard award. Reserve in advance, seating hours are strict.

The Mark   AMERICAN **$$**
(atthemark.com; 1623 19th St; mains from $17; ⊙11am-10pm Mon-Fri, 4-11.30pm Sat, 7:30-11:30pm Sun) One of downtown Bakersfield's swanky new additions has red banquettes and big city classics such as cioppino and pistachio-crusted lamb chops.

☆ Entertainment

★ **Buck Owens' Crystal Palace**   LIVE MUSIC
(☑ 661-328-7560; www.buckowens.com; 2800 Buck Owens Blvd) For fans of the city's plucky musical heritage, this is the first stop – hard to miss thanks to the huge neon homage to Buck's famous red, white and blue guitar. Part music museum (gift shop open from 11am), honky-tonk, and steakhouse (dinner from 5pm, brunch 9:30pm to 2pm Sunday), the Palace has top-drawer country acts nearly nightly. Locals in sharp, snap-button shirts, shiny boots and pressed jeans tear up the dance floor.

Trout's & the Blackboard Stage   LIVE MUSIC
(therockwellopry.webs.com; 805 N Chester Ave at Decatur St, Oildale; ⊙11am-late Mon-Sat) The legendary Trout's, north of town, is the only remaining honky-tonk in these parts, hobbling along after half a century as a testament to hell-raisin' days past. This ain't no disco – the only thing glistening is broken glass – but the live music comes from Bakersfield legends and their disciples.

Fox Theater   CONCERT VENUE
(www.foxtheateronline.com; 2001 H St) This gorgeous Gilded Age theater hosts artists of today – from Merle Haggard to the Pixies.

❶ Information

Greater Bakersfield Convention & Visitors Bureau (☑ 661-852-7282; www.bakersfieldcvb.org; 515 Truxtun Ave; ⊙8am-5pm Mon-Fri) A spacious building with maps and brochures.

❶ Getting There & Around

Airport Valet Express (☑ 661-363-5000; www.airportvaletexpress.com; 201 New Stine, suite 120; one way/roundtrip $49/89; ⊙to LAX 3am, 8am, 3pm, 8pm) Large orange and white buses run between Bakersfield (from the north side of the San Joaquin Valley College campus) and LAX (2½ hours, eight daily).

Amtrak Station (☑ 800-872-7245; 601 Truxtun Ave at S St) Trains head north from here to Sacramento ($45 to $65, five hours, two direct trains). Buses head to LA, but tickets must be purchased in combination with a train ticket.

Golden Empire Transit (GET; www.getbus.org; 1830 Golden State Ave, Transit Center; fares from $1.25) The efficient local bus system's Route 22 runs north on Chester Ave to the Kern County Museum (p333) and Oildale (22 minutes).

Greyhound (☑ 661-327-5617; 1820 18th St at G St) Cheap rides from downtown Bakersfield to Los Angeles ($9, two hours).

Kern River Area

A half-century ago the Kern River originated on the slopes of Mt Whitney and journeyed close to 170 miles before finally settling into Buena Vista Lake in the Central Valley. The lake is long dry. Now, after its wild descent from the high country – 60ft per mile – the Kern is dammed in several places and almost entirely tapped for agricultural use.

Its pristine upper reaches, declared wild and scenic by the Secretary of the Interior, is nicknamed the 'Killer Kern' for its occasionally lethal force and makes for world-class rafting.

Hwy 178 follows the dramatic **Kern River Canyon** and offers a stunning drive through the lower reaches of Sequoia National Forest. East of the lake, Hwy 178 winds another 50 miles through a picturesque mixture of pine and Joshua trees before reaching Hwy 395.

There are two **USFS Ranger Stations** in the area, one in **Kernville** (☑ 760-376-3781; www.fs.usda.gov; ⊙8am-4:30pm Mon-Fri) and another in **Lake Isabella** (☑ 760-379-5646; ⊙8am-4:30pm Mon-Fri). Both have hiking and camping information, maps and wilderness permits.

✇ Activities

This part of the state is all about white water, and rafting is the banner attraction. The town of **Lake Isabella** is a dreary strip of local businesses on the south end of the lake, but Hwy 155 runs north to **Kernville**, a cute little town straddling the Kern River that is *the* hub for local water sports. While the lake is popular for cooling off, note that the river's currents can be extremely dangerous.

The Upper Kern and Forks of the Kern (both sections of the river north of Kernville)

WORTH A TRIP

WEEDPATCH CAMP

In the Depression era, more than a million poor, white laborers from the Dust Bowl states in the South and the Great Plains arrived in the Central Valley with dreams of opportunity. Branded 'Okies' by the locals (whether from Oklahoma or not), the majority found only more hardship in the Golden State.

Weedpatch Camp (Arvin Farm Labor Camp; ☑ 661-832-1299; www.weedpatchcamp.com; 8701 Sunset Blvd, Bakersfield; ⊘ by appointment) is one of about 16 Farm Security Administration camps built in the US during the 1930s to aid migrant workers, and today it is the only one with original buildings still standing (as of press time, they were undergoing renovation). A reporter named John Steinbeck researched the people in this camp and their lives inspired *The Grapes of Wrath*. Nearby tract housing still shelters migrant workers for the six-month grape harvest.

From Bakersfield, take Hwy 58 east to Weedpatch Hwy; head south for about 7 miles, past Lamont; then turn left on Sunset Blvd, driving another half mile. Look for the 'Arvin Farm Labor Center' sign on your right. The **Dust Bowl Festival** is a free celebration of Okie history held here the third Saturday of October.

yield Class IV and V rapids during spring runoff and offer some of the most awe-inspiring white-water trips in the country. You'll need experience before tackling these sections, though there are still opportunities for novices. Below Lake Isabella, the Kern is tamer and steadier.

Currently seven rafting companies are licensed to operate out of Kernville; all offer competitive prices and run trips from May to August, depending on conditions. Excursions include popular one-hour runs (from $37) and day-long Lower Kern trips (from $119) and multiday Wild Forks of the Kern experiences (from $600). Walk-ins are welcome and experience is not necessary. Kids ages six and up can usually participate.

Kern River Outfitters　　　　RAFTING
(☑ 800-323-4234; http://kernrafting.com; 6602 Wofford Heights Blvd; ⊘ 8:30am-5:30pm Mon-Fri) Offers the staple menu of trips plus an adults-only Pub & Grub trip, which includes beer tastings from the Kern River Brewery.

**Mountain & River
Adventures**　　　　RAFTING, OUTDOORS
(☑ 760-376-6553, 800-861-6553; www.mtnriver. com; 11113 Kernville Rd) Besides rafting, this outfit offers combo-kayak and rafting, mountain biking and winter excursions.

Sierra South　　　　RAFTING
(☑ 800-457-2082, 760-376-3745; www.sierra-south.com; 11300 Kernville Rd) Rafting or for

something calmer, paddleboarding on Lake Isabella.

Whitewater Voyages　　　　RAFTING
(☑ 660-376-8806, 800-400-7238; www.whitewatervoyages.com; 11006 Kernville Rd) The first outfitter to dare to guide clients down the entire Wild and Scenic Forks of the Kern back in 1980.

🛏 Sleeping

Lake Isabella has motels, but Kernville is a nicer location with still reasonable rates. Many require two-day minimum stays on weekends.

USFS Campgrounds　　　　CAMPGROUND $
(☑ 877-444-6777; www.fs.usda.gov; developed/undeveloped sites $24/20) These campgrounds line the 10-mile stretch between Lake Isabella and Kernville, and several more lie north of Kernville on Mountain Hwy 99. Rangers recommend the Fairview and Limestone sites for their seclusion. Campgrounds without running water and electricity are free.

Whispering Pines Lodge　　　　B&B $$$
(☑ 760-376-3733; http://pineskernville.com; 13745 Sierra Way; r $189-219, house incl breakfast $359; ☳) This secluded B&B, blending rustic character with luxurious comfort, is just north of town. Rooms with kitchens book up quickly in the summer.

Gold Country

Best Places to Eat

➡ New Moon Café (p344)

➡ Big Springs Gardens (p347)

➡ Argonaut Farm to Fork
Cafe (p349)

➡ La Cocina de Oro Taqueria
(p346)

➡ Taste (p352)

Best Places to Stay

➡ Outside Inn (p343)

➡ Lure Resort (p346)

➡ Camino Hotel (p355)

➡ Imperial Hotel (p352)

Why Go?

Hollywood draws the dreamers and Silicon Valley its fortune-hunters, but this isn't the first time droves of young folk looking to hit paydirt streamed into the Golden State. After a sparkle in the American River caught James Marshall's eye in 1848, more than 300,000 prospectors from America and abroad started digging for gold in the Sierra foothills. Soon California entered statehood with the official motto, 'Eureka', solidifying its place as the land of discovery and opportunity.

The miner forty-niners are gone, but a ride along the aptly named Hwy 49 through sleepy hill towns, past clapboard saloons and oak-lined byways, is a journey back to modern California's founding. Between the quaint antique stores and sprawling wineries, historical markers still tell tales of Gold Rush violence and banditry. Many travelers hardly stop while rushing between California's coasts and mountains, but those who slow down will be rewarded with a taste of the helter-skelter era that first kick-started the heartbeat of this state.

When to Go
Nevada City

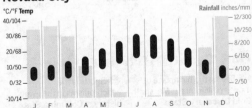

Apr–May Pan for gold after the snowmelt washes the treasure into Jamestown's hills.

Jul When temperatures are scorching, plunge into a refreshing South Yuba swimming hole.

Sep–Nov When crisp apples are ripe for the picking, head to Apple Hill's ranch lands.

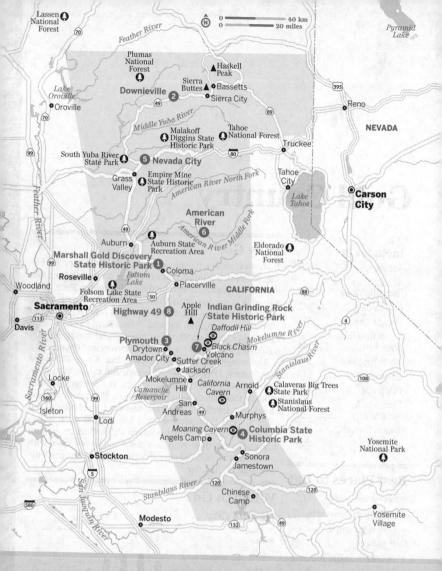

Gold Country Highlights

① Seeing the birthplace of modern California at **Marshall Gold Discovery State Historic Park** (p348).

② Rumbling down the premier single-track bike trails above **Downieville** (p345).

③ Tasting the wines made from grapes grown in the **Plymouth** (p351) hills.

④ Spotting the anachronisms in the living history of **Columbia State Historic Park** (p358).

⑤ Wandering the historic streets of **Nevada City** (p342), Gold Country's relaxing jewel of a town.

⑥ Riding the white water **American River** (p348).

⑦ Discovering traces left by the Miwoks who once thrived near **Indian Grinding Rock State Historic Park** (p354).

⑧ Driving down **Highway 49** (p348) through El Dorado & Amador Counties in pursuit of antiques and ice cream.

NEVADA COUNTY & NORTHERN GOLD COUNTRY

The forty-niners hit it big in Nevada County – the richest score in the region known as the Mother Lode – and their wealth built one of the most picturesque and well-preserved boomtowns, Nevada City. Get out of town and you'll find lovely, remote wilderness areas, a clutch of historic parks and rusting relics of the long-gone miners. This is also a magnet for adrenaline junkies looking to race down single-tracks on mountain bikes or plunge into icy swimming holes that are remote enough for skinny-dipping.

Auburn

Look for the big man: a 45-ton effigy of French gold panner Claude Chana marks your arrival in Placer County's Gold Country. Its hallmarks are all here – ice-cream shops, strollable historic districts and antiques. A major stop on the Central Pacific's transcontinental route, Auburn still welcomes trains on the Union Pacific's main line to the east and is a popular stop for those rushing along I-80 between the Bay Area and Lake Tahoe. You'll have to venture along Hwy 49 for a deeper taste of Gold Country, but those who want just a sample will enjoy this accessible town.

⊙ Sights & Activities

The fact that Auburn minted itself the 'Endurance Sport Capital of the World' will give you a sense of how good the area is for cycling, trail running and other heart-pounding activities. See www.auburnendurancecapital.com for events.

Placer County Museum   MUSEUM
(www.placer.ca.gov; 101 Maple St; ⊙10am-4pm) FREE The 1st floor of the domed 1898 Placer County Courthouse (⊙8am-5pm) has Native American artifacts and displays of Auburn's transportation heritage. It's the easiest museum to visit and gives a good overview of area history; there's also the glitter of the museum's gold collection.

Bernhard Museum Complex   MUSEUM
(291 Auburn-Folsom Rd; entry by donation; ⊙11am-4pm Tue-Sun) This museum, built in 1851 as the Traveler's Rest Hotel, exhibits depictions of typical 19th-century-farm family life. Volunteers in period garb ham it up.

Gold Country Museum   MUSEUM
(1273 High St; ⊙11am-4pm Tue-Sun) FREE Toward the back of the fairgrounds, the Gold Rush history includes a reconstructed mine and gold panning, all great for kids.

Joss House   MUSEUM
(☑530-823-0373; 200 Sacramento St; entry by donation; ⊙10am-3pm 1st Sat of month) Built by the Yue family in the 1920s, this clapboard residence stands on what was known as Chinese Hill, one of many small-town Chinese communities established during the Gold Rush. After a 'mysterious' fire ripped through the Chinese settlement, the family converted their home into a public space for worship, seasonal boarders and a school. Grandson Richard is on hand to tell the full story.

🛏 Sleeping & Eating

Lincoln Way toward the chamber of commerce has several restaurants popular with locals, but there's plenty of sunny outdoor eating right off the highway around Sacramento St. For a place to sleep look to the highway exits where there's every brand of chain hotel.

Ikedas   MARKET $
(www.ikedas.com; 13500 Lincoln Way; sandwiches $6-9; ⊙8am-7pm Mon-Thu, to 8pm Fri-Sun; 🅿) If you're cruising this part of the state without time to explore, the best pit stop is this expanded farm stand off I-80 a few miles north of Auburn. Thick, grass-fed beef or veggie burgers, homemade pies and the seasonal fresh peach shake are deliriously good.

Tsuda   DELI $
(www.tsudabylina.com; 103 Sacramento St; mains $9; ⊙7am-5pm Mon-Thu, to 7pm Fri & Sat, 8am-6pm Sun; 🛜🅿♿🧒) A bakery with crepes, a salad bar and something for every dietary consideration (gluten-free, veg, toddler etc). Eat outside on the adjacent public patio, which is open to pets.

Auburn Alehouse   BREWPUB $$
(www.auburnalehouse.com; 289 Washington; mains $8-21; ⊙11am-10pm Mon-Tue, to 11pm Wed-Thu, to midnight Fri, 9am-midnight Sat, 9am-10pm Sun) One of those rare brewpubs with both excellent craft beer *and* food; patrons dig into burgers, sweet potato fries, 'adult mac and cheese' and sweet-and-savory salads. The beer sampler is a great deal, as Auburn brings home tons of medals for their ales and pilsners. Hand over the keys before trying the PU240 Imperial

IPA, a 'weapons grade hop bomb.' Kitchen closes one hour before the bar.

Awful Annie's AMERICAN $$
(www.awfulannies.com; 160 Sacramento St; mains $9-13; ⏰8am-3pm) Huge breakfast scrambles and a sunny patio keep Annie's packed. Worth the wait.

Katrina's BREAKFAST $$
(www.katrinascafe.com; 456 Grass Valley Hwy; mains $10-15; ⏰7am-2:30pm Wed-Sat, to 2pm Sun) Lemon yogurt pancakes and all manner of sandwiches in a homey atmosphere; this place is legit.

🛍 Shopping

Pioneer Mining Supply OUTDOOR EQUIPMENT
(www.pioneermining.com; 878 High St; ⏰9am-6pm Mon-Fri, 10am-4pm Sat) Your one-stop prospecting shop. Don't mind the gruff salesfolk. They actually are happy to get you started, set up guided tours (from $100 per person), or if you're a pro, showcase the latest in sluicing technology.

ⓘ Information

Auburn Area Chamber of Commerce
(☑530-885-5616; www.auburnchamber.net; 601 Lincoln Way; ⏰10am-4pm Tue-Fri) In the Southern Pacific railroad depot at the north end of Lincoln Way, it has lots of useful local info and a monument to the Transcontinental Railroad nearby.

California Welcome Center (Placer County Visitors Center; ☑530-887-2111; www.visitplacer.com; 1103 High St; ⏰9am-4:30pm Mon-Sat, 11am-4pm Sun) Great information on Gold Country and eastward.

ⓘ Getting There & Away

Amtrak (☑800-872-7245; www.amtrak.com; 277 Nevada St) runs one bus a day along the Capital Corridor route (http://capitolcorridor.org) linking Auburn with Sacramento ($16, one hour), the rest require connecting to Bay Area and Central Valley trains. There is also one bus-train daily east to Reno ($61, six hours).

The **Gold Country Stage** (☑888-660-7433; www.goldcountrystage.com; adult$1.50-3, child free) links Auburn, including its Amtrak station, with Grass Valley and Nevada City five times a day on weekdays, no service weekends. It takes 30 to 50 minutes and kids and bikes ride free.

Amtrak's *California Zephyr* stops in Auburn on its daily run between the Bay Area and Chicago via Reno and Denver (to San Francisco takes three hours and costs $35).

Auburn State Recreation Area

This is a **park** (☑530-885-4527; www.parks.ca.gov; per car $10; ⏰8am-sunset) of deep gorges cut by the rushing waters of the North and Middle Forks of the American River that converge below a bridge on Hwy 49, about 4 miles south of Auburn. In the early spring, when waters are high, this is immensely popular for white-water rafting, as the rivers are class II to V runs. Late summer, calmer waters allow for sunning and swimming, especially around the confluence. Numerous trails are shared by hikers, mountain bikers and horses.

🏃 Activities

One of the most popular hikes is the **Western States Trail**, which connects Auburn State Recreation Area to **Folsom Lake State Recreation Area** and Folsom Lake. It's the site of the **Western States 100-Mile Endurance Run** (www.wser.org) and the **Tevis Cup** (www.teviscup.org), an endurance race on horseback. The **Quarry Trail** takes a level path from Hwy 49, just south of the bridge, along the Middle Fork of the American River. Several side trails reach the river.

All-Outdoors California Whitewater Rafting RAFTING
(☑800-247-2387; www.aorafting.com; from $139/person; ⏰9am-5pm Mon-Fri (seasonal)) The best tours of the American, Tuolumne and Stanislaus rivers are offered spring through fall by this family-run outfit. Their single- and multiday wilderness rafting excursions include breaks for hiking among the boulders and historically significant sights in the canyons. Plus they cook for you (the burrito

---

SUCTION DREDGING FOR GOLD

Floating down Gold Country's waterways, you may see someone trying to strike it rich with a suction dredge – a vacuum that sucks up the river bed and the gold in it. This method of prospecting was banned in California in 2009 for its destructive side effects, including disturbing riparian habitat and stirring up toxic quicksilver, the mercury that the forty-niners used to extract gold from ore.

lunch might be worth the trip alone). Check online for discounts.

⌘ Sleeping

Auburn State Recreation Area CAMPGROUND $
(sites $25-35) There are basic sites on a sweeping bend of the Middle Fork at the blackberry-dotted Ford's Bar that are accessible only by a 2-mile hike from Rucky-A-Chucky Rd, or a half-day raft. Required permits for these sites are available from the **Ranger Office** (☑530-885-4527; 501 El Dorado St; ☉9am-4pm Mon-Fri).

Grass Valley

From the margins, Grass Valley is the ugly utilitarian sister to Nevada City, a place to stock up on supplies and get an oil change, not necessarily vacation, but there are treasures if you dig.

Historic Mill and W Main Sts mark the town center. E Main St leads north to modern shopping centers and mini-malls and into Nevada City. On Thursday nights in late-June through August, Mill St closes to traffic to serve up farmstead food, arts and crafts, and music. In the town's outskirts are some of the state's oldest shaft mines. Being the first to exploit lode-mining (tunneling to find veins of gold in hard rock) rather than placer techniques (sifting debris carried by waterways), these were among the most profitable claims.

⊙ Sights

Empire Mine State Historic Park HISTORIC SITE
(www.empiremine.org; 10791 E Empire St; adult/child $7/3; ☉10am-5pm) Atop 400 miles of mine shafts tunneling 11,000ft below Gold Country's best-preserved gold quartz–mining operation – worth a solid half-day's exploration. The mine yard is littered with mining equipment and buildings constructed from waste rock. You can view main shaft's claustrophobic entry, next to the head frame (a tall structure used to haul ore and people from underground). By the visitor center are the country club–like manor home, gardener's cottage and rose garden of the Bourn family, who ran the mine.

From 1850 to 1956 the miners here, mostly Cornish, produced six million ounces of gold (worth about $4 billion today). Even if you don't have that kind of dough, hiking the trails that meander past abandoned

TRIBAL HISTORY IN GOLD COUNTRY

A few dedicated museums tell part of the stories of the Miwok, Maidu, Konkow, Monache, Nisenan, Tubatulabal, Washoe and Foothill Yokuts – the people who called this region home, even before the gold.

Maidu Museum & Historical Sight
(www.roseville.ca.us; 1970 Johnson Ranch Dr, Roseville; adult/child $4.50/4; ☉9am-4pm Mon-Fri, to 1pm Sat (extended hours every third Sat)) is built on the edge of an ancient Maidu village, where families thrived for over 3000 years.

The roundhouse-shaped museum in **Indian Grinding Rock State Historic Park** (p354) has a variety of artifacts representing different tribes of the area. Outside are more relics.

California State Indian Museum (p310) in Sacramento has the most extensive collections and regularly rotating exhibits on California's tribes.

mines and equipment is free. Trailheads are at the parking lots behind the visitor center and Penn Gate to its west. The visitors center leads guided tours (11am to 2pm) and has maps.

North Star Mining Museum MUSEUM
(Powerhouse and Pelton Wheel Museum; nevadacountyhistory.org; 10933 Allison Ranch Rd; entry by donation; ☉11am-5pm Tue-Sat, noon-4pm Sun May-Oct) A museum for those who ache when they see machinery set aside to rust. The engineering-minded docents here have polished and oiled their extensive collection of 19th-century mining equipment to a shine. See stamp mills, dredges, dynamite packing machines, Cornish pumps and the largest Pelton wheel ever constructed in action. The grassy banks of the creek that once powered the North Star mine are perfect for a picnic.

⌘ Sleeping & Eating

The menus around here don't vary much but the quality is good. There are several good brunch spots and bars around downtown, and every imaginable chain among the strip malls by the highway.

Holbrooke Hotel
HISTORIC HOTEL **$$**

(✆530-273-1353, 800-933-7077; www.holbrooke. com; 212 W Main St; r $129-179, ste incl breakfast $249; ❋🐾🛜) The register in this 1862 hotel boasts the signatures of Mark Twain and Ulysses Grant. The rooms are aging but neat. The **restaurant and saloon** (mains $11 to $22) serves casual fare in the ornate dining room or on the shaded patio, but the best tables overlook the Main St action. Weekday rates drop by 15% to 30%.

Cousin Jack Pasties
BAKERY **$**

(100 S Auburn St; meals $5.25-9; ⏱10:30am-6pm Mon-Sat, 11am-5pm Sun; 🖉) Cousin Jack and his kin have been serving flaky pasties – a meat-and-potato-stuffed pastry beloved by Cornish miners – for five generations. The pies – Basque lamb, pot roast and several vegetarian options – are all made from local ingredients.

Lazy Dog Ice Cream
ICE CREAM **$**

(www.spotlazydog.com; 111 Mill St; ice-cream bars $4; ⏱10am-9pm Sun-Thu, to 10pm Fri & Sat) This colorful ice-cream and candy shop explodes with sugar in all its forms. Besides scoops, there are hand-dipped bars, chocolates and old-timey candies from 'juicy wax sticks' to swirly suckers.

Tofanelli's
ITALIAN **$$**

(www.tofanellis.com; 302 W Main St; mains $8-23; ⏱8am-9pm Mon-Thu, to 10pm Fri & Sat) Hugely popular with locals in the know, this creative restaurant has everything from salads to hearty steaks with seasonal specials like summer squash ravioli. Portions are burly, prices low and the patio a treat.

❶ Information

Greater Grass Valley Visitor Center (✆530-273-4667; www.grassvalleychamber.com; 128 Main St; ⏱10am-5pm Mon-Fri, to 3pm Sat & Sun; ❋) In the thick of the historical sights stands this brick livery stable, which is stocked with maps and brochures covering the county and more. There's a very comprehensive walking-tour map.

❶ Getting There & Away

Transit in Grass Valley is by **Gold Country Stage** (✆888-660-7433; www.goldcountrystage. com), which links to Nevada City hourly from 7am to 6pm weekdays, 8am to 4pm Saturday. Fares are $1.50 to $3 for adults. Kids and bikes ride free. Check the website for connections to Auburn and schedule changes.

Amtrak (p340) bus connections are in Colfax, 12 miles south.

Nevada City

Nevada City knows it's charming, but it doesn't like to brag. Everything here is about balance. In the shops, there are prayer flags, chia smoothies and new-agey tchotchkes, while the drinking holes sling all manner of liquid enlightenment. The person browsing the local history museum with you is just as liable to be a crusty old-timer, a road-weary backpacker or a mystical folk artist. In the midst of all that are the requisite Victorian and Gold Rush tourist attractions – an elegantly restored town center and frilly B&Bs by the dozen.

This is the gateway to Tahoe National Forest, but linger a few days, and you'll experience a distinctly inviting NorCal culture. The theater companies, alternative film houses, bookstores and live music venues put on shows almost every night.

Nevada City's streets, best navigated on foot, are especially lively in the summer. In December the blankets of snow and twinkling lights are something out of a storybook. Broad St is the main drag and the hypotenuse of the Hwy 49 and Hwy 20 junction.

⊙ Sights

The main attraction is the town itself – its restored buildings, all brick and wrought-iron trimmings, wear their history proudly. There are intriguing (if pricey) boutiques, galleries and places for food and drink everywhere, all with exhaustive posted histories.

Firehouse No. 1 Museum
MUSEUM

(www.nevadacountyhistory.org; 214 Main St; admission by donation; ⏱1-4pm Tue-Sun May-Oct) This small, painstakingly curated museum is run by the Nevada County Historical Society. From stunning Nisenan baskets to preserved Victorian bridal wear, its collections tell the story of the local people. The prize exhibit is relics from the Chinese settlers who often built but seldom profited from the mines. By 1880, miners of Chinese origin constituted more than a fifth of all engaged in the industry and were nearly exclusively subject to a hefty Foreign Miners Tax.

The altar was saved by a local merchant who hid the pieces around town to keep it from marauders. Open extra hours by appointment.

Nevada City Winery
WINERY

(✆530-265-9463; ncwinery.com; 321 Spring St; ⏱tasting room noon-5pm Sun-Thu, to 6pm Fri &

Sat) This popular winery excels with Syrah and Zinfandel varietals, which you can savor while touring the production facility in the old Miners Foundry Garage. It's a good place to get information on touring all of the surrounding wine region.

Sleeping

On weekends Nevada City fills up with urban refugees who inevitably weigh themselves down with real-estate brochures. There are B&Bs everywhere. The cheapest options are the National Forest campgrounds, just outside town in any direction.

★ Outside Inn
MOTEL, CABIN $$
(☎ 530-265-2233; www.outsideinn.com; 575 E Broad St; r $79-104, ste $129-145, cottage $155-200; ❈ 🕸 🏊 🐾) The best option for active explorers, this is an unusually friendly and fun motel, with 12 rooms and three cottages maintained by staff that loves the outdoors and has excellent information about area hiking. Some rooms have a patio overlooking a small creek; all have nice quilts and access to BBQ grills. It's a 10-minute walk from downtown.

Broad Street Inn
INN $$
(☎ 530-265-2239; www.broadstreetinn.com; 517 W Broad St; r incl breakfast $115-125; ❈ 🕸 🐾) 🍃 This six-room inn is a favorite because it keeps things simple. (No weird old dolls, no yellowing lace doilies.) The rooms are modern, brightly furnished and elegant. A good value.

Red Castle Historic Lodgings
B&B $$
(☎ 530-265-5135; www.redcastleinn.com; 109 Prospect St; r $155-210; ❈ 🐾) In a city of B&Bs this is the granddaddy – the first in Nevada City and one of the oldest in the state. The red-brick building sits atop a hill a short walk from town. Inside the Gothic Revival exterior are well-appointed Victorian details down to the elevated beds and the breakfast selection. Most private is the Garden Room.

Northern Queen Inn
MOTEL, CABINS $$
(☎ 530-265-5824; www.northernqueeninn.com; 400 Railroad Ave; r $90-140; ❈ 🕸 🏊) With a wide range of options – from basic queen rooms to two-story chalets – this hotel might be a bit dated, but the cabins, with small kitchens, are a good deal for small groups and families.

Eating

In a town of holistic thinkers, it's no surprise most menus emphasize organic and seasonal ingredients. The options are mostly clustered in a three-block radius on Commercial and Broad Sts.

Café Mekka
CAFE $
(☎ 530-478-1517; 237 Commercial St; meals $5-15; ⊙ 7am-10pm Mon-Thu, to midnight Fri, 8am-midnight Sat, to 10pm Sun) Decorated in a style best described as 'whorehouse baroque,' this charmer serves coffee and beer through the day, along with sandwiches, pizzas and delectable desserts. Listen for live folk music some nights.

Treats
DESSERT $
(http://treatsnevadacity.com; 110 York St; items $3.50-5; ⊙ 1-5pm Mon-Thu, 1-9pm Fri, noon-9pm Sat, noon-5pm Sun; 🖐) It's a crowded contest for Gold Country's best ice-cream shop, but this cute little spot – the brilliant second career of avuncular scooper Bob Wright – wins in a walk. Many flavors are sourced from ripe local produce like the River Hill Red sorbet (sweet red peppers and strawberry), mint chip and pear ginger.

Ike's Quarter Cafe
CAJUN, BREAKFAST $$
(www.ikesquartercafe.com; 401 Commercial St; mains $11-23; ⊙ 8am-3pm, closed Tue; 🖐) Ike's serves splendid brunch fare with a sassy charm that delights the blue hairs. There's banana and pecan flapjacks, jambalaya, Creole tempeh and more. It's an excellent place to get 'Hangtown Fry' – a cornmeal-crusted mess of oysters, bacon, caramelized onions and spinach. Right out of New Orleans' Garden District but with vegetarian options.

Fix for Foodies
CAFE $$
(www.superfoodfix.com; 205 York St; mains $8-14; ⊙ 11am-8pm Tue-Sat, 12:30-4:30pm Sun; 🕸🖐) You can't miss this old stable covered in corrugated steel. A favorite of raw, vegan enthusiasts and the generally health obsessed, it's the kind of place that makes its own almond milk, durian shakes, and sprouted breads.

Sopa Thai
THAI $$
(www.sopathai.net; 312 Commercial St; mains $10-15; ⊙ 11am-3pm & 5-9:30pm Mon-Fri, noon-9:30pm Sat & Sun) Mango red curry, steamed mussels and springs rolls are all excellent in the region's best and most popular Thai restaurant. The interior is furnished with imported carvings and silk, and the patio seating

in back is a busy scene midday. The $10.95 lunch special is a good value.

★ **New Moon Café** CALIFORNIAN $$$
(www.thenewmooncafe.com; 203 York St; mains $21-29.50; ⊙11:30-2pm Tue-Fri, 5-8:30pm Tue-Sun) ✐ Pure elegance, Peter Selaya's organic and local ingredient menu changes with the seasons. If you visit during the peak of the summer, go for the line-caught fish or their housemade, moon-shaped fresh ravioli.

☆ Entertainment

This little village has a vibrant art scene. The entertainment section of the *Union* newspaper (www.theunion.com) comes out on Thursday, and lists what's going on throughout the county.

Magic Theatre CINEMA
(www.themagictheatren.com; 107 Argall Way) This beloved theater screens a matchless line-up of unusual films and is about a mile south of downtown Nevada City. Plus bowls of fresh popcorn, coffee in real mugs and hot brownies.

Nevada Theatre THEATRE, CINEMA
(www.nevadatheatre.com; 401 Broad St) This brick fortress is one of California's first theaters (1865) and has welcomed the likes of Jack London, Emma Nevada, and Mark Twain to its stage. Now it's home to a number of small, top-notch theater companies and an off-beat film series.

ⓘ Information

Nevada City Chamber of Commerce (☑530-265-2692; www.nevadacitychamber.com; 132 Main St; ⊙9am-5pm Mon-Fri, 11am-4pm Sat, 11am-3pm Sun) Ideally located at the east end of Commercial St, this has two welcome traveler comforts – expert local advice and public toilets right next door.

Tahoe National Forest Headquarters (☑530-265-4531; www.fs.usda.gov/tahoe; 631 Coyote St; ⊙8am-4:30pm Mon-Fri) A useful and friendly resource for trail and campground information, covering the area from here to Lake Tahoe. They sell topographical maps.

ⓘ Getting There & Away

Nevada City is served by the **Gold Country Stage** (☑530-477-0103; www.goldcountrystage.com), which links it with Grass Valley (adult $1.50, 30 minutes) hourly from 6:30am to 5:30pm weekdays and 7:30am to 4:30pm Saturdays. Kids and bikes ride free. Check the website for connections to Auburn and schedule changes.

Amtrak (p340) bus connections are in Colfax, 15 miles south.

South Yuba River State Park

Brisk swimming holes are fed by rushing rapids in this 11,000-acre plot along the South Yuba River, a combination of state and federal lands. This area has a growing network of trails, including the wheelchair-accessible **Independence Trail**, which starts from the south side of the South Yuba River bridge on Hwy 49 and continues for a couple miles with canyon overlooks. June is the best time, when the rivers are rushing and the wildflowers are out.

The longest, single-span, wood-truss **covered bridge** in the USA, all 251ft of it, crosses the South Yuba River at Bridgeport (not to be confused with the Eastern Sierra town of the same name). It's easy to spend a whole day hiking and swimming in this wild area, where crowds can be left behind with little effort. The **Buttermilk Bend Trail** skirts the South Yuba for 1.4 miles, offering river access and bountiful wildflowers around April.

Maps and park information are available from the **state park headquarters** (☑530-432-2546; www.parks.ca.gov; 17660 Pleasant Valley Rd, Penn Valley; ⊙11am-4pm daily Mar-Nov, Thu-Sun Dec-Feb) in Bridgeport, or from the Tahoe National Forest Headquarters in Nevada City. The **South Yuba River Park Association** (www.southyubariverstatepark.org) is another great resource.

Malakoff Diggins State Historic Park

An otherworldly testament to the mechanical determination of the gold hunt, **Malakoff Diggins** (☑530-265-2740; 23579 North Bloomfield Rd; per car $8; ⊙sunrise-sunset) is a place to get lost on fern-lined trails and take in the raw beauty of a recovering landscape. The gold and crimson stratified cliffs and small mountains of tailings are curiously beautiful, and all part of the legacy of hydraulic mining.

In 1852, a French miner named Anthony Chabot channeled the Yuba through a canvas hose to blast away at the bedrock. To reach the veins of gold inside, miners eventually carved a canyon 600ft deep. To speed up the sorting process, they mixed

---

LOCAL KNOWLEDGE

SWIMMING HOLE 101

Gold Country's rivers carved out precious metals as well as emerald pools perfect for late-summer dips. Check out http://swimmingholes.org for spots.

On the South Yuba, 8 miles northeast of Nevada City on Bloomfield Rd, under the **Edwards Crossing** bridge is a lively, popular pool. Just a mile hike downstream is the scenic cascade of waterfalls known as **Mountain Dog**, perfect for a more secluded skinny dip.

For an even more remote spot, head to the Stanislaus River, to Parrots Ferry Rd 7 miles south of Murphys, and then turn north on Camp Nine Rd. Near the end, where the river splits, a half mile hike up the right fork will lead you to **Camp Nine**, a peaceful, limestone-bordered pool and beach.

Some keys to swimming hole usage: always test rope swings and currents before jumping in. Never dive. Pack in your supplies and pack out your trash. No glass. And always stay at least 100yd from the water when nature calls.

---

the slurry of gravel with quicksilver (mercury) to recover the gold, and then washed all the leftovers into the Yuba River. When a few decades later, 20ft high glaciers of tailings and toxic waste choked the rivers and caused deadly flooding, farmers and miners collided in the courtroom. In 1884, the Sawyer Decision set a critical precedent: a profitable industry can be stopped for the public good. No longer able to reap profits by dumping in the Yuba, most fortune hunters moved on. **North Bloomfield**, the mining community at the center of Malakoff's operation, still stands as an eerie ghost town within the park's limits.

The **Park Headquarters and Museum** (☑530-265-2740; ⊗9am-5pm, tour 1:30pm Fri-Sun May-Sep) offers a tour of the town and the chance to see some impressive gold nuggets. The one-mile **Diggins Loop Trail** is the quickest way to get a glimpse of the scarred moonscape. Reserve a **campsite** (☑800-444-7275; www.reserveamerica.com; tent sites $35, cabins $40; ⊗May-Sep) at Chute Hill or a miner's cabin for not much more.

Access Tyler-Foote Crossing Rd, the turnoff for the park, 10 miles northwest of Nevada City on Hwy 49.

North Yuba River

The northernmost segment of Hwy 49 follows the North Yuba River through some stunning, remote parts of the Sierra Nevada, known for a tough, short season of white water and great fly-fishing. An entire lifetime outdoors could hardly cover the trail network that hikers, mountain bikers and skiers blaze every season. In summer, snow remains at the highest elevations and many places have roaring fireplaces year-round.

The best source of trail and camping information is the **Yuba River Ranger Station** (☑530-288-3231; 15924 Hwy 49, Camptonville; ⊗8am-4:30pm Mon-Fri).

Downieville

Downieville, the biggest town in remote Sierra County, is located at the junction of the North Yuba and Downie rivers. With a reputation that quietly rivals Moab, Utah (before it got big), the town is one of the premier places for mountain-bike riding in the US, and a staging area for true wilderness adventures.

As with most Gold Rush towns, it wasn't always fun and games: the first justice of the peace was the local barkeep, and a placard tells the story of the racist mob that hanged a Chicana named Josefa on the town bridge in 1851, the only recorded lynching of a woman in California. The town retains a grisly affection for frontier justice and its ghosts; a reconstructed gallows is across the river, by the civic building.

Activities

The mountains and rivers in these parts beg to be explored. Favorite hikes include the **Sierra Buttes Fire Lookout**, a moderate 6 miler that joins the **Pacific Crest Trail** before a 1500ft elevation gain to epic views from the lookout tower, and **North Yuba Trail**, 12 miles along the canyon ridge, starting behind the courthouse in town. There are many more options. Pick up maps and a shuttle ride from the local outfitters. **Downieville Visitors' Center** (Main St), open seasonally next the mining equipment in Memorial Park, can also help.

Downieville Downhill   ADVENTURE SPORTS
(www.downievilleclassic.com) This world-class mountain-biking trail shoots riders over the Sierra Buttes and a molar-rattling 4000ft down into Downieville. There are plenty of other scenic biking trails to explore, including **Chimney Rock, Empire Creek** and **Rattlesnake Creek**, but this route is the reason why pro-riders arrive in August for the **Downieville Classic**, a mix of cross-country and downhill racing and general revelry.

Local outfitters run hourly shuttles to the start.

Yuba Expeditions   MOUNTAIN BIKING
(℡530-289-3010; www.yubaexpeditions.com; 208 Commercial St; bike rentals $65-85, shuttle $20; ◷shuttles 9am-5pm May-Oct, reserve Nov-Apr) Yuba Expeditions is run by Sierra Buttes Trail Stewardship, a nonprofit in the center of the trail-bike scene. Non-bikers will find them helpful with maps and general trail advice.

Downieville Outfitters   BICYCLE RENTAL
(℡530-289-0155; www.downievilleoutfitters.com; 114 Main St; bike rentals from $60, shuttle $20; ◷shuttles 8am-5pm May-Oct, reserve Nov-Apr) An option for bike rental and shuttles in Downieville.

🛏 Sleeping & Eating

In downtown Downieville, the soft roar of the rapids lull saddle-sore bikers to sleep in several small B&Bs. More secluded options are along Hwy 49 east of town. Find food at the intersection of Main and Commercial Sts. Most places are closed in winter.

Riverside Inn   HOTEL $
(℡530-289-1000; www.downieville.us; 206 Commercial St; r $90-120, ste incl breakfast $185; P🛉🛋🐾) There is a secluded, rustic charm to these 11 stove-warmed rooms overlooking the river. Five have kitchens and all have balconies for enjoying the river. Delightful innkeepers Nancy and Mike share excellent information about hiking and biking in the area, and in winter lend snowshoes.

Tahoe National Forest
Campgrounds   CAMPGROUND $
(℡518-885-3639, reservations 877-444-6777; www.recreation.gov; tent sites $24) West of town on Hwy 49 are a string of beautiful campsites. Most have vault toilets, running water

and unreserved sites along the Yuba River. Of these, the prettiest is **Fiddlecreek**, which has tent-only sites right on the river.

★Lure Resort   CABINS, CAMPGROUND $$
(℡800-671-4084; www.lureresort.com; camping cabins $80, housekeeping cabins $135-290; 🛉🛋) A great option if you want to come with biking buddies or a family, this circle of tidy, modernized cabins is along a sublime stretch of river open to fly fishing with big lawns for the kids to play. The basic camping cabins, which are BYO sleeping bag and have shared bathrooms, sleep four tightly.

Carriage House Inn   INN $$
(℡530-289-3573; www.downievillecarriagehouse. com; 110 Commercial St; r incl basic breakfast $85-175; 🛉🛋🐾) This renovated homey inn has country-style charms, which include rockers and river views. Two rooms share a shower.

Sierra Shangri-La   CABINS, HOTEL $$
(℡530-289-3455; www.sierrashangrila.com; r $115, cabins incl breakfast $168-273) Three miles east of Downieville on Hwy 49, in July and August these secluded, riverside cabins are usually booked with standing reservations, but rooms – each with a balcony overlooking the river – are often available.

★La Cocina de Oro Taqueria   MEXICAN $
(℡530-289-9584; 322 Main St; tacos from $3.75, burritos $10; ◷11am-9:30pm Apr-Dec; 🐾) Chef-owner Feather Ortiz uses herbs and peppers from her garden and sources everything else from local growers to make the freshest food around. The burritos are the size of chihuahuas. No credit cards.

Sierra City & the Lakes Basin

Sierra City is the primary supply station for people headed to the **Sierra Buttes**, a rugged, rocky shock of mountains that are probably the closest thing to the Alps you'll find in California without foisting a backpack. It's also the last supply point for people headed into the fishing paradise of the Lakes Basin. There's information about lodging and area activities at www.sierracity.com.

◉ Sights & Activities

There's a vast network of trails, including access to the famed **Pacific Crest Trail**. The **Sierra Country Store** (℡530-862-1560; 213 Main St/Hwy 49; ◷8am-8pm summer, 10am-6pm winter; 🛉) is about the only consistently open place in town, and it welcomes Pacific Crest Trail refugees with its laundromat and deli.

To reach the Buttes, and many lakes and streams nearby, take Gold Lake Hwy north from Hwy 49 at Bassetts, 9 miles northeast of Sierra City. An excellent hiking trail leads 1.1 miles to Haskell Peak (8107ft), where you can see from the Sierra Buttes right to Mt Shasta and beyond. To reach the trailhead, turn right from Gold Lake Hwy at Haskell Peak Rd (Forest Rd 9) and follow it for 8.5 miles to the marked parking lot.

🛏 Sleeping & Eating

There's just one main drag in town, and that's the Golden Chain Highway (Hwy 49). All commerce happens here. The hotels often have the best restaurants – when they're open. Winter time is quiet.

USFS Campgrounds   CAMPING $
(☑ 530-993-1410; tent sites $24) The cheapest way to stay the night are in the USFS campgrounds east from Sierra City along Hwy 49. Wild Plum, Sierra, Chapman Creek and Yuba Pass all have vault toilets and running water (Sierra has river water only), and first-come, first-served sites. Wild Plum

(47 sites) is the most scenic. North of Hwy 49, 2 miles north of Bassetts on Gold Lake Hwy, Salmon Creek is one of several great USFS campgrounds. It has vault toilets, running water and first-come, first-served sites for RVs and tents, but no hook-ups. This site offers the most dramatic view of the Sierra Buttes with no crowds. Sites 16 and 20 are separated from the rest by a creek.

Buttes Resort   CABIN $$
(☑ 530-862-1170; www.buttesresort.citymax.com; 230 Main St; cabins $90-155) In the heart of Sierra City, the small Buttes Resort occupies a lovely spot overlooking the river and is a favorite with hikers looking to recharge. Most cabins have a private deck and barbecue, some have full kitchens. You can borrow bikes and games from the wilderness-loving owners.

★ Big Springs Gardens   AMERICAN $$$
(☑ 530-862-1333; bigspringgardens.com; 32163 Hwy 49; adult/child $15/10, entry incl buffet $35-39; ☉ brunch noon Wed-Sun mid-Jun–Sep) Offers the perfect brunch of berries from the surrounding hills and trout fresh from the pond, served in an open-air dining area (reservations re-

---

GOING FOR THE GOLD

California's Gold Rush started in 1848 when James Marshall was inspecting the fatefully sited lumber mill he was building for John Sutter near present-day Coloma. He saw a sparkle in the mill's tailrace water and pulled out a nugget 'roughly half the size of a pea.' Marshall hightailed it to Sacramento and consulted Sutter, who tested the gold by methods described in an encyclopedia. Sutter still wanted to finish his mill so he made a deal with his laborers, allowing them to keep gold they found after hours if they kept working. Before long, word of the find leaked out.

Sam Brannan was among those who went to Coloma to investigate the rumors shortly after Marshall's find. After finding 6oz of gold in one afternoon, he paraded through San Francisco's streets proclaiming, 'Gold on the American River!' Then he snapped up every piece of mining equipment – from handkerchiefs to shovels – in the area. When gold seekers needed equipment for their adventure, Brannan sold them goods at a 100% markup and was a rich man before the gold seekers even reached the foothills.

The mill's construction was finished in the spring of 1848 when the first wave of miners arrived from San Francisco. Only a few months later, the cities were depleted of able-bodied men, while towns near the 'diggins,' as the mines were called, swelled to thousands. News of the Gold Rush spread around the world, and by 1849 more than 60,000 people (who became widely known as forty-niners) rushed into California. Everyone was looking for the Mother Lode: the mythical deposit believed to be the source of all the gold washing into the streams and riverbeds.

Most prospectors didn't stick around after the initial diggings petered out; gold-extraction processes became increasingly equipment-dependent, culminating in the practice of hydraulic mining, by which miners drained lakes and rivers to power their water cannons and blast away entire hillsides. People downstream were inundated by the muck and finally sued in 1884. The Sawyer court held the environmental cost was too great to justify staying in business.

quired). Friday BBQ dinners in July and August as well. There are hiking trails through the 'Wild Garden,' a waterfall-laced natural area with pretty views. You have to call ahead to do any of the above.

EL DORADO & AMADOR COUNTIES

In the heart of the pine- and oak-covered Sierra foothills, this is where gold was first discovered – Spanish-speaking settlers named El Dorado County after a mythical city of riches.

Today, SUVs en route to South Lake Tahoe pull off Hwy 50 to find a rolling hillside dotted with the historic towns, sun-soaked terraces and the fertile soil of one of California's burgeoning wine-growing regions. If you make the stop, don't leave without toasting a glass of regional Zinfandel, which, like the locals, is packed with earthy attitude and regional character. It's also worth the detour to pause at the shore where a glint of gold caught James Marshall's eye.

Traveling through much of the central part of Gold Country requires a car, as the public transportation is unreliable between the towns, but this stretch of Hwy 49 makes an excellent road trip.

Coloma-Lotus

Coloma-Lotus Valley surrounds Sutter's Mill (the site of California's first gold discovery) and Marshall Gold Discovery State Historic Park. It is also a great launching pad for rafting operations. The South Fork of the American River gets the most traffic, since it features exciting rapids but is still manageable. Adrenaline junkies who have never rafted before should try the Middle Fork.

🏃 Activities

Half-day rafting trips usually begin at **Chili Bar** and end close to the state park. Full-day trips put in at the **Coloma Bridge** and take out at **Salmon Falls**, near Folsom Lake. The half-day options start in class III rapids and are action-packed (full-day trips start out slowly, then build up to class IV as a climax). Full-day trips include a lavish lunch. The season usually runs from May to mid-October, depending on water levels. Prices are generally lower on weekdays.

Don't want to get wet? Watch people navigate the **Troublemaker Rapids**, upstream from the bridge near Sutter's Mill in the state park.

Whitewater Connection   RAFTING
(☑ 800-336-7238, 530-622-6446; www.whitewaterconnection.com; half-day trips $94-114, full-day $119-139; ☺ Apr-Oct) Whitewater Connection is typical of the area's operators, with knowledgeable guides and excellent food.

🛏 Sleeping & Eating

If you're looking for a basic hotel and don't mind the blandness of a highway motel, Auburn is a better bet. The food options around these parts pleasantly over-deliver.

American River Resort   CAMPGROUND, CABINS $
(☑ 530-622-6700; www.americanriverresort.com; 6019 New River Rd; tent & RV sites $35-55, cabins $180-280; 🛜🏊) Only a quarter mile off Hwy 49, just south of the Marshall Gold Discovery State Historic Park, this site is more built-up than other area campgrounds: there's a small convenience store, free wi-fi, a playground, fishing pond and pool. The sites are basic, but some are right on the river. The most spacious and pretty oak-shaded sites are 14 to 29.

Coloma Club Cafe & Saloon   BAR & GRILL $
(☑ 530-626-6390; colomaclub.com; 7171 Hwy 49, Coloma; mains from $9; ☺ restaurant 6:30am-9pm, bar 10am-2am) The patio at this rowdy old saloon comes alive with guides and river rats when the water is high.

Cafe Mahjaic   AMERICAN, GREEK $$
(Lotus Inn; ☑ 530-622-9587; www.cafemahjaic.com; 1006 Lotus Rd, Lotus; ☺ from 5pm Wed-Sun; 🛜) House-baked breads and organic meats with a sense a humor: the sophisticated menu includes a Moody Soup (which changes per chef's daily whims). The four-course prix fixe for $28 is a great deal. The owners also run the three-room **Lotus Inn** (rooms $109 to $139) tucked in the brick house behind the restaurant.

Marshall Gold Discovery State Historic Park

Compared to the stampede of gun-toting, hill-blasting, hell-raising settlers that populate tall tales along Hwy 49, the **Marshall Gold Discovery State Historic Park** (☑ 530-622-3470; marshallgold.org; per car $8;

☺park 8am-5pm, to 7pm late May-early Sep, museum 10am-5pm; ♿) is a place of bucolic tranquility, with two tragic protagonists in John Sutter and James Marshall.

Sutter, who had a fort in Sacramento, partnered with Marshall to build a sawmill on this swift stretch of the American River in 1847. It was Marshall who discovered gold here on January 24, 1848, and though the men tried to keep their findings secret, prospectors from around the world stampeded into town. In one of the tragic ironies of the Gold Rush, the men who made this discovery died nearly penniless. In another, many of the new immigrants who arrived seeking fortune were indentured, taxed and bamboozled out of anything they found.

In the rare moments there aren't a million school kids running around, the pastoral park by the river makes for a solemn stroll. Follow the trail to the bank where Marshall found gold and started the revolutionary birth of the 'Golden State.'

The park has been undergoing a restoration effort, which includes the mill itself and the **Visitor Information Center & Museum** (☎530-622-3470; 310 Back St, Coloma; tours adult/child $3/2; ☺10am-5pm Mar-Nov, to 4pm Dec-Feb, guided tours 11am & 1pm year-round), with historical dioramas and a shop with frontier-days trinkets.

On a hill overlooking the park is the **James Marshall Monument**, where he was buried in 1885, a ward of the state. You can drive the circuit but it's much better to meander the many trails around the park, past mining artifacts and pioneer cemeteries.

Panning for gold ($7, free if you have your own equipment) is popular. From 10am to 3pm in the summer, or by request, you get a quick training session and 45 minutes to pan.

🛏 Sleeping & Eating

Coloma Resort CAMPGROUND, CABINS $
(☎530-621-2267; www.colomaresort.com; 6921 Mt Murphy Rd; tent & RV sites $45-49, cabins & on-site RVs $100-295; 🛜🏊) Another long-established riverside campground, this is better for RVs. It comes with a full range of activities and wi-fi. With lots of family activities, this has the feel of a summer camp.

★ Argonaut Farm to Fork Cafe AMERICAN $
(www.argonautcafe.com; 331 Hwy 49, Coloma; sandwiches $8; ☺8am-4pm) Truly delicious soups, sandwiches and coffee from well-known Sacramento and Coloma purveyors

find their way to this little wooden house between Sutter's Mill and the blacksmith's shop in Marshall Gold Discovery State Historic Park. The crowds of school kids waiting for gelato can slow things down.

Placerville

Placerville has always been a travelers' town: it was originally a destination for fortune hunters who reached California by following the South Fork of the American River. In 1857 the first stagecoach to cross the Sierra Nevada linked Placerville to Nevada's Carson Valley, which eventually became part of the nation's first transcontinental stagecoach route.

Today, Placerville is a place to explore while traveling between Sacramento and Tahoe on Hwy 50. It has a thriving and well-preserved downtown with antique shops and bars, and local wags who cherish the wild reputation of 'Hangtown' – a name earned when a handful of men swung from the gallows in the mid-1800s. Among the many awesome local legends is 'Snowshoe' John A Thompson, a postal carrier who regularly delivered 80lbs of mail on skis from Placerville over the Sierras to Carson Valley during the winter.

◉ Sights

Main St is the heart of downtown Placerville and runs parallel to Hwy 50 between Canal St and Cedar Ravine Rd. Hwy 49 meets Main St at the west edge of downtown. Looking like a movie set, most buildings along Main St are false fronts and sturdy brick structures from the 1850s, dominated by the spindly **Bell Tower**, a relic from 1856 that once rallied volunteer firemen.

Gold Bug Park and Mine HISTORIC SITE
(www.goldbugpark.org; 2635 Goldbug Ln; adult/child $6/4; ☺10am-4pm Apr-Oct, noon-4pm Sat & Sun Nov-Mar) The best museum in Placerville, about 1 mile north of town on Bedford Ave. The park stands over the site of four mining claims that yielded gold from 1849 to 1888; you can descend into the self-guided Gold Bug Mine, do some gem panning ($2) and explore the grounds and picnic area for free. Guided tours cost $100 for up to 15 people.

El Dorado County
Historical Museum MUSEUM
(http://museum.edcgov.us; 104 Placerville Dr; entry by donation; ☺10am-4pm Wed-Sun) On the El Dorado County Fairgrounds west of

WORTH A TRIP

PLACERVILLE WINERIES

The Placerville region's high heat and rocky soil produces excellent wines, which frequently appear on California menus. Oenophiles could spend a long afternoon rambling through the welcoming vineyards of El Dorado County alone (though a full weekend of tasting could be had if it was coupled with adjoining Amador County). Details can be found at the **El Dorado Winery Association** (☑800-306-3956; www.eldoradowines.org) or **Wine Smith** (☑530-622-0516; www.thewinesmith.com; 346 Main St, Placerville; ☉11am-8pm Mon-Sat, from noon Sun), a local shop with just about everything grown in the area.

Some noteworthy wineries, all north of Hwy 50, include **Lava Cap Winery** (www.lavacap.com; 2221 Fruitridge Rd; ☉11am-5pm), which has an on-hand deli for picnic supplies, and **Boeger Winery** (www.boegerwinery.com; 1709 Carson Rd; ☉10am-5pm). Both have free tastings.

downtown (exit north on Placerville Dr from Hwy 50), is this complex of restored buildings, mining equipment and re-created businesses that tell the story of Old Hangtown.

🛏 Sleeping

Chain motels can be found at either end of the historic center of Placerville along Hwy 50.

National 9 Inn MOTEL $
(☑530-622-3884; www.national9inns.com; 1500 Broadway; r $50-89; ❋ 🛜) This mid-century motel, recently renovated by a young couple, is the best bargain in Placerville, even if it lies at the lonely north end of town. The building's exterior is ho-hum, but the rooms are sparkling with refrigerators, microwaves and remodeled baths. It's a great option for travelers who want a clean, no-frills stay and want to support independent businesses.

Cary House Hotel HISTORIC HOTEL $$
(☑530-622-4271; www.caryhouse.com; 300 Main St; r from $121; ❋@🛜) This historic hotel in the middle of downtown Placerville has a large, comfortable lobby with back-lit stained glass depicting scenes from the region's history. Once a bordello, it has up-

dated rooms (some with kitchenettes) with period decor. Ask for a room overlooking the courtyard to avoid street noise, or try room 212, a rumored supernatural haunt. Check online for deals.

Albert Shafsky House B&B B&B $$
(☑530-642-2776; www.shafsky.com; 2942 Coloma St; r $135-175; ❋🛜) Of all the Victorian bed-and-breakfast options in Placerville, Albert's proximity to downtown, ornate period furnishings and luxurious bedding make this cozy three-room option a favorite.

🍴 Eating

Z-Pie AMERICAN $
(www.z-pie.com; 3182 Center St; pies $7-8; ☉11am-9pm) With its whimsical take on the all-American comfort-food staple, this casual stop stuffs flaky, butter-crusted pot pies with a gourmet flourish (steak cabernet! Thai chicken! tomatillo stew!). California beers are on tap. The four-beer sampler ($8) is ideal for the indecisive.

Sweetie Pie's BREAKFAST $
(www.sweetiepies.biz; 577 Main St; mains $5-12; ☉6:30am-3pm Mon-Fri, 7am-3pm Sat, 7am-1pm Sun) Ski bunnies and bums fill this diner and bakery counter on the weekends en route to Lake Tahoe, filling up with egg dishes and top-notch homemade baked goods like heavenly cinnamon rolls. Breakfast is the specialty, but it also does a capable lunch.

Cozmic Café & Pub HEALTH FOOD $
(www.ourcoz.com; 594 Main St; items $4-10; ☉7am-6pm Tue, Wed & Sun, to midnight Thu-Sat; 🛜📶) In the historic Placerville Soda Works building, the menu is organic and boasts vegetarian and healthy fare backed by fresh smoothies. There's a good selection of microbrews and live music on weekends, when it stays open late.

Heyday Café CAFE $$
(www.heydaycafe.com; 325 Main St; mains $9-25; ☉11am-9pm Tue-Thu, to 10pm Fri & Sat, to 8pm Sun) Fresh and well-executed, the menu here leans toward simple Italian comfort food, made all the more comfortable by the wood-and-brick interior. The wine list is long on area vineyards. Locals rave about lunch.

🍷 Drinking & Nightlife

The profile of El Dorado County wines is rising, and several tasting rooms dot the main street offering earthy, elegant varietals of the region. Placerville's bars, on the other hand, are akin to the neighborhood watering holes in the Midwest: they open around 6am, get an annual cleaning at Christmas and are great for people who want to chew the fat with a colorful cast of locals.

Liar's Bench BAR
(☑530-622-0494; 255 Main St; ☺8am-1am) The Liar's Bench survives as the town's classic watering hole under a neon martini sign that beckons after dark.

🔒 Shopping

⭐**Gothic Rose Antiques** ANTIQUES
(www.gothicroseantiques.com; 484 Main St; ☺11am-5pm Thu-Sun) The most interesting antique and curiosity shop in Gold Country likely frightens the wigs off the other dealers in town with its collection of haute gothic house wares, antique occult goods and flawlessly macabre sensibility. Browsing the old medical instruments, taxidermy, 19th-century photos of corpses and the latest in latex and lace cemetery chic, is titillating.

Placerville Hardware HOMEWARES
(www.placervillehardware.com; 441 Main St; ☺8am-6pm Mon-Sat, to 5pm Sun) The 1852 building, an anchor of Placerville's main drag, is the oldest continuously operating hardware store west of the Mississippi and a place to pick up a brochure for a self-guided tour of the town. The store has a smattering of Gold Country bric-a-brac but most of what clutters the place are bona-fide dry goods, like hammers and buckets.

Placerville Antiques & Collectibles ANTIQUES
(☑530-626-3425; 448 Main St; ☺10am-6pm) Of Placerville's many antique shops, the collective of dealers in this brightly lit space is a favorite. Reasonably priced mid-century dishware is a particular strength.

Bookery BOOKS
(326 Main St; ☺10am-5:30pm Mon-Thu, to 7pm Fri & Sat, to 4pm Sun) A great used-book store to stock up on vacation pulp.

Placerville News Co BOOKS
(www.pvillenews.com; 409 Main St; ☺8am-6:30pm Mon-Thu, to 7pm Fri & Sat, to 5:30pm Sun) This plank-floored bookshop has a wealth of excellent maps, history and local-interest books.

ℹ️ Information

El Dorado County Visitors Authority (Chamber of Commerce; ☑530-621-5885; http://visit-el-dorado.com; 542 Main St; ☺9am-5pm Mon-Fri) Maps and local information on everything from farm trails to films, breweries and Tahoe.

ℹ️ Getting There & Away

Amtrak (☑877-974-3322; www.capitolcorridor.org) Runs several buses daily to Sacramento ($20, 1½ hours), though some require train connections to points further along the Capital Corridor route.

El Dorado Transit (☑530-642-5383; www.eldoradotransit.com; 6565 Commerce Way, Diamond Springs; adult/child $1.50/75¢) Operates hourly weekday commuter buses between 7am and 4pm to every corner of town out of the Placerville Station Transfer Center (2984 Mosquito Rd), a charming covered bus stop with benches and restrooms. It's about half a mile from downtown, on the north side of Hwy 50.

Plymouth & Amador City

Two small, sunny villages make equally good bases for exploring Amador County's wine region. The first, Plymouth, is where the region's Gold Rush history is evident in its original name, Pokerville. Few card sharks haunt the slumbering town today; it wakes late when the tiny main street fills with the smell of barbecue, a few strolling tourists and the odd rumble of a motorcycle posse. Amador City was once home to the Keystone Mine – one of the most prolific gold producers in California – but the town lay deserted from 1942 (when the mine closed) until the 1950s, when a family from Sacramento bought the dilapidated buildings and converted them into antique shops.

👁 Sights

Amador Whitney Museum MUSEUM
(☑209-267-5250; www.amador-city.com; Main St, Amador City; ☺noon-4pm Fri-Sun) **FREE** This is the main thing going in town. Housed in an old Wells Fargo outpost, it has a covered wagon and a replica school house scene and mineshaft. It's worth the 15-minute stop.

Chew Kee Store Museum MUSEUM
(www.fiddletown.info; Fiddletown; entry by donation; ☺noon-4pm Sat Apr-Oct) Remnants of the bygone era are just outside of Plymouth. The Chew Kee Store Museum, 6 miles east in Fiddletown, is an old herbal shop that once served railroad workers. The dusty collection of artifacts frozen in time are *objets d'art*.

DON'T MISS

AMADOR COUNTY WINE REGION

Amador County might be something of an underdog among California's winemaking regions, but a thriving circuit of family wineries, Gold Rush history and local characters make for excellent imbibing without a whiff of pretension. The region lays claim to the oldest Zinfandel vines in the United States and the surrounding country has a lot in common with this celebrated variety – bold and richly colored, earthy and constantly surprising.

The region has two tiny towns, Plymouth and Amador City (p351). Start in Amador and follow Hwy 49 north through the blip known as Drytown and on to Plymouth by Hwy 49, and then follow Shenandoah Rd northeast, which takes you past rolling hills of neatly pruned vines. Most hosts are exceedingly welcoming and helpful, offering free tastes and whatever you want to know about their operations. In July, 38 wineries throw an annual 10-day tasting extravaganza.

Maps are available at the wineries, and from the **Amador Vintners Association** (www.amadorwine.com).

Deaver Vineyards (www.deavervineyards.com; 12455 Steiner Rd, Plymouth; ⊙10:30am-5pm) A true family affair where nearly everyone pouring has the last name on the bottles.

Drytown Cellars (www.drytowncellars.com; 16030 Hwy 49, Drytown; ⊙11am-5pm) This is the most fun tasting room in Amador County, thanks to vintner Allen Kreutzer, a gregarious host, and his array of stunning reds.

Sobon Estate (www.sobonwine.com; 14430 Shenandoah Rd, Plymouth; ⊙9:30am-5pm Apr-Oct, to 4:30pm Nov-Mar) Founded in 1856, it's also home to the free Shenandoah Valley Museum featuring wine-making memorabilia.

Wilderotter (www.wilderottervineyard.com; 19890 Shenandoah School Rd, Plymouth; ⊙10:30am-5pm) As if the award-winning Sauvignon Blanc weren't enough, tastings here are paired with Cowgirl Creamery cheeses.

Amador 360 Wine Collective (amador360.com; 18950 Hwy 49, Plymouth; ⊙11am-6pm) Run by the couple that organizes Amador's annual Barbera extravaganza (http://barberafestival.com), this expansive shop reserves special billing to boutique vintners who otherwise would not offer tastings.

🛏 Sleeping & Eating

⭐ **Imperial Hotel**   B&B $$

(☑209-267-9172; www.imperialamador.com; 14202 Main St, Amador City; r $105-155, ste $125-195; ❄🛜) The nicest place to stay in these parts. Built in 1879, it's one of the area's most inventive updates to the typical antique-cluttered hotels, with sleek deco touches accenting the usual gingerbread flourish, a genteel bar and a very good, seasonally minded restaurant (mains $13 to $28). On weekends during the summer, expect a two-night minimum.

⭐ **Taste**   CALIFORNIAN $$$

(☑209-245-3463; www.restauranttaste.com; 9402 Main St, Plymouth; mains $23-40; ⊙11:30am-2pm Sat & Sun, from 5pm Mon-Thu, from 4:30pm Fri-Sun) Book a table at Taste, where excellent Amador wines are paired with a fine menu of California-style cooking.

🍷 Drinking & Nightlife

Drytown Club   BAR

(www.drytownclub.com; 15950 Hwy 49; ⊙noon-midnight Wed-Fri, to 2am Sat, to 9pm Sun) Tired of wine? Hit the Drytown Club, the kind of rowdy roadhouse where people start drinking a little too early and soak it up with weekend BBQ. The bands on the weekend are bluesy, boozy and sometimes brilliant.

Sutter Creek

Perch on the balcony of one of the gracefully restored buildings on this particularly scenic Main St and view Sutter Creek, a gem of a Gold Country town with raised, arcade sidewalks and high-balconied buildings with false fronts that are perfect examples of California's 19th-century architecture. This is another option for staying the night when visiting Amador and El Dorado County wineries.

Begin the visit at volunteer-operated Sutter Creek Visitor Center (☑800-400-0305, 209-267-1344; www.suttercreek.org; 71a Main St) to collect a walking-tour map of historic traces left by Cornish, Yugoslavian and Italian arrivals, or pick up the excellent, free driving-tour guide to local gold mines.

◉ Sights

Monteverde General Store HISTORIC BUILDING
(☑209-267-0493; 11a Randolph St; entry by donation; ◔by appointment) This building goes back in time to when the general store was the center of the town's social and economic life, represented by the chairs that circle the pot-belly stove and the detailed historic scale. Senior docents lead tours by appointment.

Knight Foundry MINE
(www.knightfoundry.org; 81 Eureka St) In its prime, Sutter Creek was Gold Country's main supply center for all things forged. Three foundries operating in 1873 made pans and rock crushers, but only this one operated until 1996 — the last water-powered foundry and machine shop in the US. At press time, the interior was closed to visitors, but plans to reopen were in the works.

🛏 Sleeping

Eureka Street Inn B&B $$
(☑209-267-5500; www.eurekastreetinn.com; 55 Eureka St; r incl breakfast $145; ❀🛜) Each of the four rooms in this 1914 Arts and Crafts–style home has unique decor and gas fireplaces. Once the home of a wealthy stagecoach operator, the inn is on a quiet side street.

Hotel Sutter HOTEL $$
(☑209-267-0242; www.hotelsutter.com; 53 Main St; r $115-175; P❀🛜) There was some controversy when they started gutting the beloved American Exchange, which had stood in repose for more than 150 years. The bricks and facade may be the only things left, but the modern rooms (some with en-suite bathrooms), and very fine restaurant (mains $14 to $25) and cool cellar bar seem to have quelled the protest.

Sutter Creek Inn B&B $$
(☑209-267-5606; www.suttercreekinn.com; 75 Main St; r $120-210; ❀) The 17 rooms and cottages here vary in decor and amenities (antiques, fireplaces, sunny patios). All have private bathrooms. Guests can snooze in the hammock by the gardens or curl up with a book on a comfy chair on the sprawling lawn.

✕ Eating

Sutter Creek Ice Cream Emporium SWEETS $
(☑209-267-0543; 51 Main St; ◔11am-6pm Thu-Sun) This sweet shop gets downright enchanting when town icon Stevens Price takes to the 1919 Milton piano and plays ragtime. The former proprietor still stops by in between organizing the **Sutter Creek Ragtime Festival** each August.

Pizza Plus PIZZA $
(www.suttercreekpizzaplus.com; 20 Eureka St; pizzas $14; ◔11am-9pm; ♿) Crisp, chewy thin-crust pizza and pitchers of beer make this a favorite; it's the perfect place to hang out and chat up locals. Combinations like the BBQ pizza put it over the top.

Thomi's Coffee & Eatery AMERICAN $
(www.thomissuttercreek.com; 40 Hanford St; mains $6-9; ◔8am-3pm Fri-Wed; 🛜) A real star in a galaxy of lunch spots, Thomi serves classic griddle breakfasts, huge salads and a pot-roast melt. The brick dining room is welcoming in winter; in summer there's a sunny little patio.

Sutter Creek Cheese Shoppe MARKET $
(☑209-267-5457; www.suttercreekcheese.com; 33b Main St; ◔10am-5pm) A stop for cheeses from California and beyond. Call ahead for a picnic box of cheese, a baguette and even a little cutting board and knife to enjoy on your winery hop.

☆ Entertainment

Sutter Creek Theatre PERFORMING ARTS
(www.suttercreektheater.com; 44 Main St) One of several excellent Gold Country arts groups, it has nearly a 100-year-long history of presenting live drama, films and other cultural events.

Volcano

One of the fading plaques in Volcano, 12 miles upstream from Sutter Creek, tellingly calls it a place of 'quiet history.' Even though the little L-shaped village on the bank of Sutter Creek yielded tons of gold and a Civil War battle, today it slumbers away in remote solitude. Only a smattering of patinated bronze monuments attest to Volcano's lively past.

Large sandstone rocks line Sutter Creek, which skirts the center of town. The rocks, now flanked by picnic tables, were blasted from surrounding hills by hydraulic mining before being scraped clean of their gold. The process had dire environmental consequences, but generated miners nearly $100 of booty a day.

◉ Sights & Activities

Daffodil Hill   FARM
(209-296-7048; 18310 Rams Horn Grade; donations accepted; ⏰10am-4pm mid-Mar–mid-Apr) This hilltop farm, 2 miles northeast of Volcano, is blanketed with more than 300,000 daffodil blooms in the spring. The McLaughlin and Ryan families have operated the farm since 1887 and keep hyacinths, tulips, violets, lilacs and the occasional peacock among the daffodils.

**Indian Grinding Rock
State Historic Park**   HISTORIC SITE
(209-296-7488; parks.ca.gov; 14881 Pine Grove-Volcano Rd; per car $8; ⏰museum 11am-2:30pm Fri-Sun) Two miles southwest of Volcano is a sacred area for the local Miwok. There's a village site and a limestone outcrop covered with petroglyphs – 363 originals and a few modern additions – and over 1000 mortar holes called *chaw'se*, used for grinding acorns and seeds into meal.

Black Chasm   CAVE
(888-762-2837; www.caverntours.com; 15701 Pioneer Volcano Rd; adult/child $14.95/7.95; ⏰10am-5pm) A quarter of a mile east of Volcano, this has the whiff of a tourist trap, but one look at the array of helictite crystals – rare, sparkling white snowflakes – makes the crowd more sufferable. The tour guides are all experienced cavers. Reservations required for the adventurous Labyrinth tour ($79).

🛏 Sleeping & Eating

**Indian Grinding Rock
State Historic Park**   CAMPGROUND $
(www.reserveamerica.com; tent & RV sites $30) The beautiful campground at Indian Grinding Rock State Historic Park has fresh water, plumbing and 22 unreserved sites set among the trees, with tent sites and hookups for RVs.

Volcano Union Inn   HISTORIC HOTEL $$
(209-296-7711; www.volcanounion.com; 21375 Consolation St; r incl breakfast $119-139; ❋🐾) The preferred of two historic hotels in Vol-

cano, there are four lovingly updated rooms with crooked floors: two have street-facing balconies. Flat-screen TVs and modern touches are a bit incongruous with the old building, but it's a comfortable place to stay. The on-site **Union Pub** has a superb menu and will host the occasional fiddler.

St George Hotel   HISTORIC HOTEL $$
(209-296-4458; www.stgeorgehotelvolcano.com; 16104 Main St; r $89-199) Up the crooked stairs of this charming, creaky hotel are 20 rooms that vary in size and amenity (most have shared bathrooms) and are free of clutter. The restaurant (open for dinner Thursday to Sunday, brunch Sunday) has a menu anchored by steak. Hang out in the saloon.

☆ Entertainment

Volcano Theatre Company   PERFORMING ARTS
(www.volcanotheatre.org; adult/child $16/11) On weekends between April and November, this highly regarded company produces live dramas in an outdoor amphitheater and the restored Cobblestone Theater.

Jackson

Jackson has some historic buildings and a small downtown, but it ain't much to look at. It stands at the junction of Hwy 49 and Hwy 88, which turns east from Hwy 49 here and heads over the Sierras near the Kirkwood ski resort.

◉ Sights

Kennedy Gold Mine   HISTORIC SITE
(209-223-9542; http://kennedygoldmine.com; 12594 Kennedy Mine Rd; adult/child $10/6) You can't miss the ominous steel headframe rising 125ft from the road. Its pulleys lifted ore and miners from the bowels of the earth. Once the deepest mine, this is now a peaceful park good for a stroll. Guided tours last about 1½ hours and take you past the stamp, gold recovery mill and massive tailing wheels. The parking lot is off of North Main St.

On-site **Kennedy Tailing Wheels Park** has marvelous examples of engineering and craftsmanship — four iron and wood wheels, 58ft in diameter, that transported tailings from neighboring Eureka Mine over two low hills. Be sure to climb to the top of the hill behind the wheels to see the impounding dam.

WORTH A TRIP

APPLE HILL

In 1860, a miner planted a Rhode Island Greening apple tree on a hill and with it established the foundation for bountiful Apple Hill, a 20-sq-mile area east of Placerville and north of Hwy 50 where there are more than 60 orchards. Apple growers sell directly to the public, usually from August to December, and some let you pick your own. Other fruits and Christmas trees are available during different seasons.

Maps of Apple Hill are available online through the **Apple Hill Association** (☑530-644-7692; www.applehill.com), or use the El Dorado **Farm Trails Guide** (www.visit-eldorado.com).

A great place to hunker down while touring the farms is the **Camino Hotel** (☑530-644-1800; www.caminohotel.com; 4103 Carson Rd, Camino; r incl breakfast $60-150), a former lumberjack bunkhouse – every bit as creaky as you'd hope – with rooms (some are very small) that have been recently redone. The rates are a steal (as low as $60 on weekdays) and room 4 is perfect for families with two rooms adjoined by a central sitting room. The breakfast is made to order.

Mokelumne Hill   HISTORIC SITE
(www.mokehill.org) The somewhat undiscovered settlement of Mokelumne Hill is 7 miles south of Jackson just off Hwy 49. Settled by French trappers in the early 1840s, it's a good place to see historic buildings without the common glut of antique stores and gift shops.

Sleeping & Eating

National Hotel   HISTORIC HOTEL **$$**
(☑209-223-0500; www.national-hotel.com; 2 Water St; r $125-165, ste $175-300) Jackson's historic hotel has had a serious upgrade from the Gold Rush era. While the restored building retains its historical details, all rooms are newly refurbished with luxurious details like gas fireplaces and heated floors. The top-notch steakhouse and bar downstairs complete the picture.

Mel's and Faye's Diner   AMERICAN **$$**
(www.melandfayesjackson.com; 31 N Hwy 49; meals $7-12; ☺10am-11pm Sun-Thu, to 2am Fri & Sat) A local institution near Hwy 88, there's a takeout window but it's not meant for quick stops. Take a seat for solid diner fare that includes huge breakfasts, classic burgers (try the chili-soaked 'Miner') and – to balance the grease binge – a decent salad bar.

❶ Information

Amador County Chamber of Commerce
(☑209-223-0350; www.amadorcountychamber.com; 115 Main St; ☺8am-4pm Mon-Fri, 10am-2pm Sat & Sun) Smack in the middle of Main St, has enough brochures to fill several recycling bins.

❶ Getting There & Away

The only way to easily travel through this area is with your own wheels. Placer County runs its bus system out of Jackson, but good luck catching it – the buses are few and far between. **Amador Transit** (☑209-267-9395; http://amadortransit.com; fares $1-2; ☺Mon-Fri) is a bit better. It makes a weekday connection through Sutter Creek to Sacramento ($1, one hour) and, if you have enough patience, you can connect to Calaveras County and southern Gold Country. By car, Jackson is 2½ hours from San Francisco and just over one hour to the ski resorts of South Lake Tahoe.

CALAVERAS COUNTY & SOUTH GOLD COUNTRY

The southern region of Gold Country is hot as blazes in the summer so cruising through its historic Gold Rush hubs will demand more than one stop for ice cream. The tall tales of yesteryear come alive here through the region's infamous former residents: author Mark Twain, who got his start writing about a jumping frog contest in Calaveras County, and Joaquin Murrieta, a controversial symbol of the lawlessness of the frontier era who somehow seems to have frequented every old bar and hotel in the area.

Angels Camp

On the southern stretch of Hwy 49 one figure looms over all others: literary giant Mark Twain, who got his first big break with the story of *The Celebrated Jumping Frog of Calaveras County*, written and set in Angels

Camp. There are differing claims as to when or where Twain heard this tale, but Angels Camp makes the most of it. There are gentlemanly Twain impersonators and statues, and bronze frogs on Main St honoring the champions of the past 80 years. Look for the plaque of Rosie the Ribeter, who set an impressive 21ft record in 1986. Today the town is an attractive mix of buildings from the Gold Rush to art-deco periods.

Calaveras County Visitors Bureau (209-736-0049; www.gocalaveras.com; 1192 S Main St; 9am-5pm Mon-Sat, 11am-4pm Sun;) has a walking and driving tour of Angels Camp, history books and lots more beta for your trip.

Activities

Moaning Cavern CAVE
(209-736-2708; www.caverntours.com; 5350 Moaning Cave Rd, Vallecito; adult/child $14.95/7.95; 10am-5pm) Perhaps not the greatest natural beauty, this cave does have the most thrills. Visitors can rappel 165ft to the bottom ($65). A pile of bones discovered here are some of the oldest human remains in the US. There's also above-ground zip lines and self-guided nature walk. Winter events like caroling utilize cave acoustics.

Festivals & Events

Angels Camp makes the most of the Twain connection; hosting the **Jumping Frog Jubilee** (www.frogtown.org) the third weekend in May (in conjunction with the county fair and something of a Harley rally) and Mark Twain impersonators make appearances at **Gold Rush Day** in the fall.

Eating

Strung out along Hwy 49 are a number of motels and diners to refill your gas tank or stomach.

Sidewinders CALIFORNIAN, MEXICAN $
(http://eatatsidewinders.com; 1252 S Main St; mains $6.50-8.50; 11am-8pm Tue-Sat;) Choose from beef, chicken, pork, fish and veggie fillings for these tacos, bowls and wraps. The guacamole-dressed, panko-breaded fish tacos are excellent with a local brew.

Crusco's ITALIAN $$
(www.cruscos.com; 1240 S Main St; mains $14-26; 11am-3pm & 5-9pm Thu-Mon) The class act in downtown Angels Camp puts out a serious, authentic northern Italian menu. The owners regularly hit Italy for more recipes,

like the Polenta Antonella (creamy cornmeal with chicken and mushroom sauce).

Getting There & Away

Calaveras Transit (209-754-4450; http://transit.calaverasgov.us; fare $2; office 6am-5pm Mon-Fri) operates the most reliable public transportation system in the region from the **Government Center** (891 Mountain Ranch Rd, San Andreas) in downtown San Andreas. You can use it to connect to Angels Camp ($2, 30 minutes, several times daily) and other surrounding towns. You can catch it mid-route, just flag it down. To connect via public transportation to the rest of California you have to catch Route 1 to San Andreas, switch to Route 3 to Mokelumne Hill, and finally transfer to Amador County Transit.

Murphys

With its white picket fences and old-world charm, Murphys is one of the more scenic towns along the southern stretch of Gold Country, befitting its nickname as 'Queen of the Sierra.' It lies 8 miles east of Hwy 49 on Murphys Grade Rd, and is named for Daniel and John Murphy, who founded a trading post and mining operation on Murphy Creek in 1848. They employed the struggling local Miwok and Yokut people as laborers. While some settlers continued to persecute the tribes, John eventually married Pokela, a chieftain's daughter.

The town's Main St is refined with tons of wine-tasting rooms, boutiques, galleries and good strolling. For information and a town overview, look to www.visitmurphys.com.

Sights & Activities

Even more than frogs, wine is a consistent draw in Calaveras County, and Murphys is at the center – a couple new tasting rooms seem to pop up downtown every summer.

Ironstone Vineyards WINERY
(www.ironstonevineyards.com; 1894 Six Mile Rd; 8:30am-5pm;) The unusually family-friendly atmosphere makes the wine feel secondary at Ironstone. There's a natural spring waterfall, a mechanical pipe organ, frequent exhibits by local artists, and blooming grounds. By the deli, the museum displays the world's largest crystalline gold leaf specimen (it weighs 44lb and was found in Jamestown in 1992). The enormous tasting room accommodates crowds.

CALAVERAS BIG TREES STATE PARK

From Angels Camp, Hwy 4 ascends into the High Sierra, eventually cresting at Ebbetts Pass (p440), at 8730ft, and then descending to junctions with Hwys 89 and 395. Along the way the road passes through the hardscrabble town of **Arnold**, which has a few cafes and motels strung along the roadside. But the real reason for taking Hwy 4 is 2 miles east of Arnold and 20 miles east of Murphys: a chance to commune with the largest living organisms on the planet.

Calaveras Big Trees State Park (p440) is home to giant sequoia redwood trees. Reaching as high as 325ft and with trunk diameters up to 33ft, these holdovers from the Mesozoic era are thought to weigh upwards of 3000 tons, or close to 20 blue whales.

The redwood giants are distributed in two large groves, one of which is easily viewed from the stroller-accessible **North Grove Trail**, a 1.7-mile self-guided loop, near the entrance, where the air is fresh with pine and rich soil. The **River Canyon Trail**, a challenging 8-mile hike out and back, climbs out of the North Grove, crosses a ridge and descends 1000ft to the Stanislaus River. Pack enough water for the return trip back up.

It's possible to find giant trees throughout the park's 6000 acres, though the largest are in fairly remote locations. The **visitor center** (☑209-795-7980; 1170 E Hwy 4, Arnold; ☉9am-5pm Sun-Thu, to 6pm Fri-Sat May-Sep, seasonal hrs Oct-Apr) has maps and good advice on the miles of trails. It's worth checking out the exhibits on sequoia biology and learning how a few dedicated individuals fought for decades to save them from becoming so many thousands of picnic tables.

Camping (☑800-444-7275; www.parks.ca.gov; off Hwy 4; tent & RV sites $35) is popular and reservations essential. **North Grove Campground** is near the park entrance; less crowded is **Oak Hollow Campground**, 4 miles farther on the park's main road. Most atmospheric are the hike-in **environmental sites**. Store food and toiletries in the provided bear lockers at all times.

Newsome-Harlow WINERY
(www.nhvino.com; 403 Main St; tasting $5; ☉noon-5pm Mon-Thu, 11am-5:30pm Fri-Sun; ⊞☻) This family-run winery pours the juicy red varietals that made them famous in their lively tasting lounge. At times, this place feels like the community social club. There's an on-site chef, fire pit, movie night, and kids and dogs are welcome.

Murphys Old Timers Museum MUSEUM
(www.murphysoldtimersmuseum.com; 470 Main St; donation requested; ☉noon-4pm Fri-Sun) The name is a good hint that this place approaches history with a humorous touch. Housed in an 1856 building, it has an inscrutable tin type of the outlaw Joaquin Murrieta and the entertaining 'Wall of Comparative Ovations.' Guided tours of town leave from the museum every Saturday at 10am.

California Cavern CAVE
(☑209-736-2708; www.caverntours.com; adult/child $14.95/7.95; ☉10am-5pm Apr-Oct; ⊞) In Cave City, 12 winding miles north of Murphys (take Main St to Sheep Ranch Rd to Cave City Rd), is a natural cavern, which John Muir described as 'graceful flowing folds deeply placketed like stiff silken drapery.' Regular tours take 60 to 90 minutes.

Ages 16 and up can try the Middle Earth Expedition ($130), which lasts four hours and involves serious spelunking. The Trail of Lakes walking tour, available only toward both ends of wet season, is magical. Conditions are unpredictable, so call to plan.

🛏 Sleeping

Most accommodations in Murphys are top-end B&Bs. For the same price, there is a cluster of picturesque **rental cottages** (☑209-736-9372; www.murphysvacationrentals.com; 549 S Algiers St; cottages $115-160) just off Main St, or check nearby Angels Camp or Arnold for cheaper alternatives.

★**Victoria Inn** B&B **$$**
(☑209-728-8933; www.victoriainn-murphys.com; 402 Main St; r $129-225, cottage $190-450; ☎) This newly built B&B has elegant rooms with claw-foot slipper tubs, sleigh beds and balconies. The common spaces, like the long verandah for enjoying tapas and wine from the restaurant and bar (p358), have a chic country-mod appeal. Opi's Cabin ($158) –

GOLD COUNTRY'S BEST CAVES

➡ California Cavern (p357) in Murphys offers a wide variety of tours, lengthy adventure trips and was marveled at by pioneering conservationist John Muir.

➡ Moaning Cavern (p356) in Angels Camp has the deepest cave rapelling in California and an above-ground zip line.

➡ Black Chasm (p354) in Volcano has a quiet self-guided Zen Garden walk above ground and rare helictite crystals below.

with its iron bed and exposed beams – is the most interesting of the basic rooms.

Murphys Historic Hotel & Lodge   B&B, LODGE **$$**
(☑ 800-532-7684, 209-728-3444; www.murphyshotel.com; 457 Main St; d $129-149) Since either 1855 or 1856 (you have your pick of plaques out front), this hotel has anchored Main St. A must-stop on the Twain-slept-here tour, the original structure is a little rough around the edges. The adjoining buildings have bland, modern rooms that cost more. Make your way down to the dining room for fried chicken ($17).

Murphys Inn Motel   MOTEL **$$**
(☑ 888-796-1800, 209-728-1818; www.centralsierralodging.com; 76 Main St; r $129-149, ste $180; ❄ @ 🛜 🐾) Just off Hwy 4, half a mile from the center of town, this option has clean and modern motel rooms with a small pool. Not so much personality but a solid choice.

✕ Eating

Alchemy Market & Café   MARKET **$$**
(www.alchemymarket.com; 191 Main St; meals $12-24; ⊘ market 11am-4:30pm Thu-Sun, cafe 11am-8pm Thu-Tue) For fancy picnic supplies. The cafe menu has many dishes great for sharing on the patio.

Firewood   CALIFORNIAN **$$**
(☑ 209-728-3248; www.firewoodeats.com; 420 Main St; mains $7-14; ⊘ 11am-9pm; 🐾) A rarity in a town with so much historical frill, Firewood's exposed concrete walls and corrugated metal offer a minimalist respite. When the weather's nice, they open the front wall for al-fresco dining. There are wines by the glass, half a dozen beers on tap and basic

pub fare, but the wood-fired pizzas are the hallmark.

Grounds   BISTRO **$$**
(☑ 209-728-8663; www.groundsrestaurant.com; 402 Main St; meals $10-29; ⊘ 7am-10:30pm Mon-Fri, to 11:15pm Sat, 8am-11:15pm Sun; 🐾) Casually elegant Grounds does everything competently – expert breakfast foods, a roster of light lunch mains and weekend dinners of steaks and fresh fish. The herbal ice tea and fresh vegetarian options are key when the temperatures rise.

V Restaurant & Bar   MEDITERRANEAN **$$**
(☑ 209-728-0107; http://vrestaurantandbar-murphys.com; 402 Main St; mains $10-25; ⊘ 11:30am-8:30pm Sun-Thu, to 9:30pm Fri & Sat) Attached to the Victoria Inn, Murphys' most classic dinner spot offers Mediterranean small and large plates and a creative cocktail list. Options start with tapas (deep-fried anchovy-stuffed olives!) and end with a commanding rib eye. The dining room and patio fill up on weekends, so reserve ahead.

Columbia State Historic Park

More than any other place in Gold Country, Columbia blurs the lines between present and past with a carefully preserved Gold Rush town – complete with volunteers in period dress – at the center of a modern community. In 1850 Columbia was founded over the 'Gem of the Southern Mines;' as much as $150 million in gold was found here, and the center of the town (which was taken over by the state parks system) looks almost exactly as it did in its heyday. The authenticity of the old Main St is only shaken a bit by the sugared fragrance of the fudge and the occasional play-acting forty-niner who forgets to remove his digital watch. On the fringe of these blocks are homes and businesses that blend in so well that it becomes hard to tell what's park and what's not.

The blacksmith's shop, theater, old hotels and authentic bar are carefully framed windows into history, completed by easy gold panning (from $5) and breezy picnic spots.

Docents lead free hour-long **tours** on weekends at 11am from the Columbia Museum. After most shops and attractions close around 5pm, you can have the atmospheric town to yourself, which makes staying overnight an attractive option.

👁 Sights

Columbia Museum HISTORIC SITE
(📋general info 209-588-9128, museum 209-532-3184; cnr Main & State Sts; ⏱9am-4:30pm spring & summer, 10am-4pm fall & winter) **FREE** Looking rather like dinosaur bones, limestone and granite boulders are noticeable around town. These were washed out of the surrounding hills by hydraulic mining and scraped clean by prospectors. There's a fascinating explanation of this technique at this renovated museum.

🛏 Sleeping & Eating

Fallon Hotel HOTEL $
(📋209-532-1470; parks.ca.gov; 11175 Washington St; r $50-115; ❄🐾) The historic Fallon Hotel hosts the most professional theater troupe in the region, the Sierra Repertory Theatre.

City Hotel HOTEL $$
(📋209-532-1479; parks.ca.gov/columbia; 22768 Main St; r $85-115; ❄🐾) Among the handful of restored Victorian hotels in the area, the City Hotel is the most elegant, with rooms that overlook a shady stretch of Main St and that open on lovely sitting rooms. The acclaimed restaurant (mains $15 to $30) is frequented by a Twain impersonator and the adjoining **What Cheer Saloon** is an atmospheric Gold Country joint with oil paintings of lusty ladies and stripped wallpaper.

Cottages COTTAGE $$
(📋209-532-1479; parks.ca.gov; 1-/2-/3-bedroom cottage $126.50/148.50/170.50) A cozy alternative to staying in a hotel are these cottages, two at the end of main street, and the largest with three bedrooms on Columbia St.

Columbia Mercantile MARKET $
(📋209-532-7511; cnr Main & Jackson Sts; ⏱9am-6pm) For town gossip and snacks, stop at the friendly Columbia Mercantile, which also has a wide variety of groceries.

⭐ Entertainment

Sierra Repertory Theatre THEATER
(📋209-532-3120; www.sierrarep.org; 11175 Washington St, Fallon Hotel) This theater mixes chestnuts of the stage (*Romeo & Juliet*, *South Pacific*) with popular reviews.

Sonora & Jamestown

Settled in 1848 by miners from Sonora, Mexico, this area was once a cosmopolitan center of commerce and culture with parks, elaborate saloons and the Southern Mines' largest concentration of gamblers and gold. Racial unrest drove the Mexican settlers out and their European immigrant usurpers got rich on the Big Bonanza Mine, where Sonora High School now stands. That single mine yielded 12 tons of gold in two years (including a 28lb nugget).

Today, people en route to Yosemite National Park use Sonora as a staging area, wandering through its pubs for refreshment or grabbing quick eats at the chain restaurants and stores that have cropped up on the periphery. Fortunately, the historic center is well preserved (so much so that it's a frequent backdrop in films).

The smaller **Jamestown** is 3 miles south of Sonora, just south of the Hwy 49/108 junction. Founded around the time of Tuolumne County's first gold strike in 1848, it has suffered the ups and downs of the region's roller-coaster development, and today it limps along on tourism and antiques. It has its charm but is only a few blocks long.

Two highways cross the Sierra Nevada east of Sonora and connect with Hwy 395 in the Eastern Sierra: Hwy 108 via Sonora Pass and Hwy 120 via Tioga Pass. Note that the section of Hwy 120 traveling through Yosemite National Park is only open in summer.

👁 Sights & Activities

The center of downtown Sonora is the T-shaped intersection of Washington and Stockton Sts, with Washington the main thoroughfare with boutiques, cafes and bars. If you're looking to get out of town, stroll the **Dragoon Gulch Trail**, a 2.5-mile loop through the oaks found just northwest of the main drag on Alpine Lane.

Sonora is also a base for white-water **rafting**: the Upper Tuolumne River is known for class IV and V rapids and its population of golden eagles and red-tailed hawks, while the Stanislaus River is more accessible with class III rapids. **Sierra Mac River Trips** (📋209-591-8027; www.sierramac.com; trips from $259) and **All-Outdoors** (📋800-247-2387; www.aorafting.com; from $164) both have good reputations and run trips of one day or more on multiple rivers.

Railtown 1897 State Historic Park HISTORIC SITE
(📋209-984-3953; www.railtown1897.org; 18115 5th Ave, Jamestown; adult/child $5/3, incl train ride $15/8; ⏱9:30am-4:30pm Apr-Oct, 10am-3pm

JOAQUIN MURRIETA: VILLAIN OR ANTIHERO?

In a land where tall tales tower, none casts a darker shadow than Joaquin Murrieta's, the infamous Mexican miner long known by some as the Robin Hood of the Gold Rush. Stories of the vengeful Murrieta are as ubiquitous as they are incongruous: he was born in either Sonora, Mexico or Quillota, Chile and, after immigrating to California in 1850 to find gold or maybe trade horses, he became a treacherous villain – or was it, a heroic vigilante? In the soft focus of historical hindsight, his fiery vengeance – real or not – forged Gold Country's most intriguing antihero.

Much of his legend is shaped by dime novels written at the time, but from what historians can gather, his life might have gone like this: Murrieta and his brother had a claim near Hangtown (now known as Placerville). They had some luck but were either forced off by a mob of Anglo miners who beat him and raped his wife, or the land was stolen after he refused to pay the Foreign Miners Tax levied by the state against resourceful non-Anglo prospectors. Either way, with no hope for justice, Murrieta formed a posse to kill his assaulters and began a life of banditry that left a trail of slashed throats and purloined gold. His band of highwaymen, known as the Five Joaquins, terrorized miners (ironically, mostly Chinese) in the countryside between 1850 and 1853.

Governor John Bigler put a large price on Murrieta's head, and in July of 1853 a Texas bounty hunter named Harry Love produced a jar containing the severed head of a man he claimed was Murrieta. Love toured cities of Northern California charging audiences $1 to see his trophy but, even in death, Murrieta's legend grew: a woman claiming to be Murrieta's sister disputed the kill and sightings of the bandit continued long after his supposed death. Joaquin Murrieta was celebrated as a peoples' hero by many Mexican and Chileno people who were enraged by the oppressive, racist laws of the Gold Rush, which are largely unmentioned today.

Nov-Mar, train rides 11am-3pm Sat & Sun Apr-Oct; ✈) Five blocks south of Jamestown's Main St, this 26-acre, state-operated collection of trains and railroad equipment is the photogenic sister to Sacramento's rail museum. It's served as backdrop for countless films and TV shows including *Back to the Future III*, *Unforgiven* and *High Noon*. On some weekends and holidays (hourly from 11am to 3pm) you can ride the narrow-gauge railroad that once transported ore, lumber and miners.

Though today it has been shortened to a quick 3-mile circuit, it's still the best train ride in Gold Country. Ask the passionate volunteers to show you the roundhouse and restored station, or just wander. There's a lyrical romance to the place, where an explosion of orange poppies grow among the rusting shells of steel goliaths, and the air is spiced with creosote, campfire and pine.

Tuolumne County Museum MUSEUM
(www.tchistory.org; 158 W Bradford St, Sonora; ⊙10am-4pm Mon-Fri, to 3:30pm Sat) FREE In the former 1857 Tuolumne County Jail, two blocks west of Washington St is this interesting museum with a fortune's worth of gold on display.

California Gold Panning Lessons OUTDOORS
(✆209-694-6768; www.gold-panning-california.com; 17712 Harvard Mine Rd, Jamestown; from $60; ⊙9am-3pm Jun-Oct, or by appointment) Miner John and his experienced crew provide boots and all needed equipment for a genuine experience panning at Woods Creek and beyond. Be warned, real prospecting involves lots of digging. A couple hours in, you'll have gold fever, a blister or both. Take a right onto Harvard Mine Rd and drive to the parking lot with a 'Gold Panning' sign. Best to call ahead.

🛏 Sleeping & Eating

Bradford Place Inn B&B $$
(✆209-536-6075; www.bradfordplaceinn.com; 56 W Bradford St, Sonora; r $145-265; ❄@🛈) Gorgeous gardens and inviting porch seats surround this four-room B&B, which emphasizes green living. With a two-person claw-foot tub, the Bradford Suite is the definitive, romantic B&B experience.

Gunn House Hotel HISTORIC HOTEL $$
(✆209-532-3421; www.gunnhousehotel.com; 286 S Washington St, Sonora; r incl breakfast $79-125; ❄🛈≋) For a lovable alternative to Gold Country's cookie-cut chains, this historic

hotel hits the sweet spot. Rooms feature period decor and guests take to rocking chairs on the wide porches in the evening. Teddy bears, a nice pool and a big breakfast also make it a hit with families.

Legends Books, Antiques & Old-Fashioned Soda Fountain ANTIQUES $
(209-532-8120; 131 S Washington, Sonora; ⊙11am-5pm) The place to sip sarsaparilla, snack on a polish dog, share a scoop of huckleberry ice cream, and then browse books downstairs in the old tunnel miners used to secret their stash directly into the former bank.

Lighthouse Deli & Ice Cream Shop DELI $
(www.thelighthousedeli.com; 28 S Washington, Sonora; sandwiches $8-9; ⊙8am-4pm Mon-Sat) The flavors of N'Awlins make this unassuming deli an unexpected delight. The muffeletta – a toasted piece of Cajun paradise that's stacked with ham, salami, cheese and olive tapenade – is the best sandwich within 100 miles.

Diamondback Grill AMERICAN $
(www.thediamondbackgrill.com; 93 S Washington St, Sonora; meals $6-11; ⊙11am-9:30pm Fri & Sat, to 8pm Sun) With exposed brick and modern fixtures, the fresh menu and contemporary details at this cafe are a reprieve from occasionally overbearing Victorian frill. Sandwiches dominate the menu (the salmon, and eggplant mozzarella are both great) and everything is homemade. For small bites, sample from the wine and cheese bar.

Drinking & Entertainment

The free and widely available weekend supplement of the *Union Democrat* comes out on Thursday and lists movies, music, performance art and events for Tuolumne County.

Iron Horse Lounge BAR
(209-532-4482; 97 S Washington St, Sonora; beer $3-6; ⊙8:30am-2am) Sonora's classic hangout in the center of town. Bottles glitter like gold on the backlit bar.

Sierra Repertory Theatre THEATER
(209-532-3120; www.sierrarep.com; 13891 Hwy 108, Sonora; adult $26-32, child $18) In East Sonora, close to the Junction Shopping Center. This critically acclaimed company

also performs in the Fallon Hotel (p359) in Columbia.

Shopping

Sierra Nevada dventure Company OUTDOOR EQUIPMENT
(www.snacattack.com; 173 S Washington St, Sonora; ⊙10am-6pm) This flagship is stocked with maps, equipment rental and sales, and offers friendly advice from guides with a passionate knowledge of ways to get outdoors in the area.

Information

Mi-Wok Ranger District Office (209-586-3234; 24695 State Hwy 108; ⊙8am-4:30pm Mon-Fri) For information and permits for the Stanislaus National Forest.

Tuolumne County Visitors Bureau (209-533-4420; www.yosemitegoldcountry.com; 542 Stockton St, Sonora; ⊙9am-6pm daily Jun-Sep, Mon-Sat Oct-May) More so than other brochure-jammed chamber of commerce joints, the staff here offers helpful trip planning advice throughout Gold Country as well as Yosemite National Park and Stanislaus National Forest up in the Sierras on Hwy 108.

Getting There & Away

Hwy 108 is the main access road here, and it links up with I-5, 55 miles west near Stockton. An entrance to Yosemite National Park is 60 scenic miles south on Hwy 120.

Navigating Southern Gold Country by public transportation can be tricky. Limited bus service is provided weekdays by **Tuolumne County Transit** (209-532-0404; www.tuolumnecountytransit.com; adult/child $1.50/free; ⊙Mon-Fri) buses, which make the Sonora loop hourly from 7am to 7:46pm, and stops in Columbia and Jamestown less frequently. On summer weekends, look for air-conditioned **green trolleys** (209-532-0404; www.historic49trolleyservice.com; adult/child $1.50/free; ⊙11am-9pm Sat, to 4pm Sun) that connect the historical sights in Columbia, Sonora and Jamestown hourly to Labor Day.

For Yosemite visitors staying in the Sonora area, **YARTS** (877-989-2878, 209-388-9589; www.yarts.com; adult/child return $25/18, one way $13/9) operates two round-trip buses connecting downtown Sonora, Jamestown's Main St and Yosemite from June 14 to September 1. There is just one round-trip bus in May and September. Ask nicely to be dropped off at unscheduled stops in Yosemite.

Lake Tahoe

Best Places to Eat

→ Moody's Bistro & Lounge (p391)

→ Cafe Fiore (p379)

→ Fire Sign Cafe (p384)

→ Rustic Lodge (p393)

→ Old Granite Street Eatery (p398)

Best Places to Stay

→ Cedar House Sport Hotel (p391)

→ Hostel Tahoe (p394)

→ PlumpJack Squaw Valley Inn (p388)

→ Deerfield Lodge at Heavenly (p377)

→ Clair Tappaan Lodge (p390)

Why Go?

Shimmering in myriad shades of blue and green, Lake Tahoe is the USA's second-deepest lake. Driving around the lake's spellbinding 72-mile scenic shoreline will give you quite a workout behind the wheel. Generally speaking, the north shore is quiet and upscale; the west shore, rugged and old-timey; the east shore, undeveloped; the south shore, busy and tacky, with aging motels and flashy casinos; and nearby Reno, the biggest little city in the region.

The horned peaks surrounding the lake, which straddles the California–Nevada state line, are year-round destinations. The sun shines on Tahoe three out of four days in the year. Swimming, boating, kayaking, windsurfing, stand-up paddleboarding and other water sports take over in summer, as do hiking, camping and wilderness backpacking adventures. Winter brings bundles of snow, perfect for those of all ages to hit the slopes at Tahoe's top-tier ski and snowboard resorts.

When to Go
South Lake Tahoe

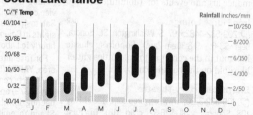

°C/°F Temp — Rainfall inches/mm

Jul & Aug Beach season; wildflowers bloom, and hiking and mountain-biking trails open.

Sep & Oct Cooler temperatures, colorful foliage and fewer tourists after Labor Day.

Dec–Mar Snow sports galore at resorts; storms bring hazardous roads.

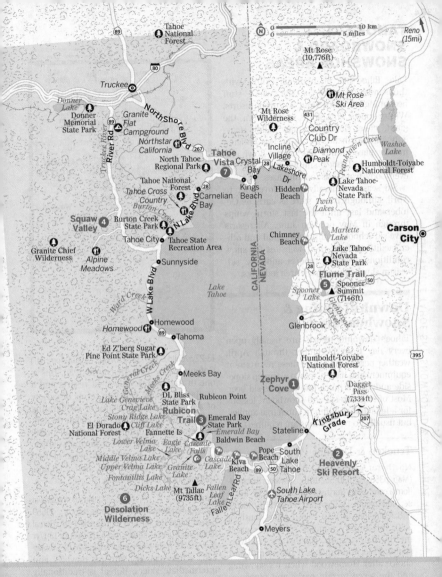

Lake Tahoe Highlights

❶ Survey the expanse of Lake Tahoe from aboard a kayak or from the sandy beach at **Zephyr Cove** (p371).

❷ Swoosh down the vertiginous double-black-diamond runs of **Heavenly ski resort** (p366).

❸ Trek the **Rubicon Trail** (p382) from Vikingsholm

Castle on sparkling Emerald Bay to DL Bliss State Park.

❹ Swim in an outdoor lagoon or ice-skate above 8000ft near the cable-car line in **Squaw Valley** (p387).

❺ Thunder down the **Flume Trail** (p396) on a mountain bike to tranquil Spooner Lake.

❻ Escape summer crowds with an overnight backpack to alpine lakes and high-country meadows in the **Desolation Wilderness** (p371).

❼ Cozy up with your family around a lakefront beach firepit or inside a comfortable cabin at **Tahoe Vista** (p392) on the no-fuss northern shore.

TAHOE SKI, SNOWBOARD & SNOWSHOE AREAS

Lake Tahoe has phenomenal skiing, with thousands of acres of the white stuff beckoning at more than a dozen resorts. Winter-sports complexes range from the giant, jet-set slopes of Squaw Valley, Heavenly and Northstar, to the no less enticing insider playgrounds like Sugar Bowl and Homewood. Tahoe's simply got a hill for everybody, from kids to kamikazes.

Ski season generally runs November to April, although it can start as early as October and last until the last storm whips through in May or even June. All resorts have ski schools, equipment rental and other facilities; check their websites for snow conditions, weather reports and free ski-season shuttle buses from area lodgings.

Downhill Skiing & Snowboarding

Tahoe's downhill resorts are usually open every day from December through April, weather permitting. All of these resorts rent equipment and have places to warm up slope-side and grab a quick bite or après-ski beer. Most offer group ski and snowboard lessons for adults and children (a surcharge applies, but usually no reservations are required).

Truckee & Donner Pass

Northstar California SKIING, SNOWBOARDING
(Map p368; ☑530-562-1010; www.northstarcalifornia.com; 5001 Northstar Dr, off Hwy 267, Truckee; adult/youth 13-22yr/child 5-12yr $116/96/69; ⊙8:30am-4pm; ▣) An easy 7 miles south of I-80, this hugely popular resort has great intermediate terrain. Northstar's relatively sheltered location makes it the second-best choice after Homewood when it's snowing, and the seven terrain parks and pipes are top-ranked. Advanced and expert skiers can look for tree-skiing challenges on the back of the mountain.

Recent additions to Northstar's 'Village' are making it look a lot more like amenity-rich Squaw. Weekends get superbusy. Stats: 20 lifts, 2280 vertical feet, 97 runs.

Sugar Bowl SKIING, SNOWBOARDING
(☑530-426-9000; www.sugarbowl.com; 629 Sugar Bowl Rd, off Donner Pass Rd, Norden; adult/youth

Tahoe Ski Areas

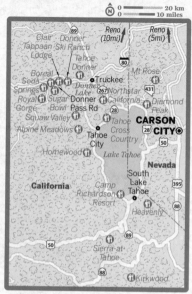

13-22yr/child 6-12yr $82/70/30; ⊙9am-4pm; ▣) Cofounded by Walt Disney in 1939, this is one of the Sierra's oldest ski resorts and a miniature Squaw Valley in terms of variety of terrain, including plenty of exhilarating gullies and chutes. Views are stellar on sunny days, but conditions go downhill pretty quickly, so to speak, during stormy weather.

The resort is 4 miles southeast of I-80 (exit Soda Springs/Norden). Stats: 13 lifts, 1500 vertical feet, 103 runs.

Boreal SKIING, SNOWBOARDING
(☑530-426-3666; www.rideboreal.com; 19659 Boreal Ridge Rd, off I-80 exit Castle Peak/Boreal Ridge Rd, Truckee; adult/child 5-12yr/youth 13-17yr $52/20/43, night-skiing adult/child $26/20, tubing $30; ⊙9am-9pm; ▣) Fun for newbies and intermediate skiers, Boreal is traditionally the first resort to open each year in the Tahoe area. For boarders, there are five terrain parks including a competition-level 450ft superpipe. Boreal is the only North Tahoe downhill resort besides Squaw that offers night skiing. Stats: seven lifts, 500 vertical feet, 33 runs.

Soda Springs SKIING, SNOWBOARDING
(☑530-426-3901; www.skisodasprings.com; 10244 Soda Springs Rd, off I-80 exit Soda Springs/Norden; Soda Springs; adult/child under 18yr $39/30, snow-

mobiling $12, tubing $30; ⊗10am-4pm Thu-Mon, daily during holidays; 🐾) This cute little resort is a winner with kids, who can snow-tube, ride around in pint-sized snowmobiles, or learn to ski and snowboard. Stats: two lifts, 650 vertical feet, 15 runs.

Donner Ski Ranch   SKIING, SNOWBOARDING

(☑530-426-3635;   www.donnerskiranch.com; 19320 Donner Pass Rd, Norden; adult/child 7-12yr/ youth 13-17yr $45/15/36; ⊗9am-4pm; 🐾) Generations of skiers have enjoyed this itty-bitty family-owned resort. It's a great place to teach your kids how to ski, or for beginners to build skills. Prices drop after 12:30pm. It's 3.5 miles southeast of I-80, exit Soda Springs/Norden. Stats: six lifts, 750 vertical feet, 52 runs.

Tahoe Donner   SKIING, SNOWBOARDING

(☑530-587-9444; www.tahoedonner.com; 11603 Snowpeak Way, off I-80 exit Donner Pass Rd, Truckee; adult/child 7-12yr/youth 13-17yr $45/21/40; ⊗9am-4pm; 🐾) Small, low-key and low-tech, Tahoe Donner is a darling resort with family-friendly beginner and intermediate runs only. Stats: five lifts, 600 vertical feet, 14 runs.

Tahoe City & Around

Squaw Valley   SKIING, SNOWBOARDING

(Map p368; ☑530-452-4331; www.squaw.com; 1960 Squaw Valley Rd, off Hwy 89, Olympic Valley; adult/youth 13-22yr/child under 13yr $114/94/66; 🐾) Few ski hounds can resist the siren call of this mega-sized, world-class, see-and-be-seen resort that hosted the 1960 Winter Olympic Games. Hardcore skiers thrill to white-knuckle cornices, chutes and bowls, while beginners practice their turns in a separate area on the upper mountain.

The valley turn-off is 5 miles northwest of Tahoe City. Stats: 29 lifts, 2850 vertical feet, over 170 runs.

Alpine Meadows   SKIING, SNOWBOARDING

(Map p368; ☑530-452-4356; www.skialpine. com; 2600 Alpine Meadows Rd, off Hwy 89, Tahoe City; adult/child under 13yr/youth 13-22yr $114/66/94; ⊗9am-4pm) Though now owned by neighboring Squaw (tickets are good at both resorts and a free shuttle connects them), Alpine remains a no-nonsense resort without the fancy village, attitude or crowds. It gets more snow than Squaw and its open-boundary policy makes it the most backcountry-friendly around. Boarders jib down the mountain in a terrain park designed by Eric Rosenwald. Also look for the supersmart and adorable ski patrol dogs.

The turn-off is 4 miles northwest of Tahoe City. Stats: 13 lifts, 1800 vertical feet, over 100 runs.

Homewood   SKIING, SNOWBOARDING

(Map p368; ☑530-525-2992; www.skihomewood. com; 5145 Westlake Blvd, off Hwy 89, Homewood; adult/child 5-12yr/youth 13-19yr $79/29/59; ⊗9am-4pm; 🐾) Larger than it looks from the road, this gem, 6 miles south of Tahoe City, proves that bigger isn't always better. Locals and in-the-know visitors cherish the awesome lake views, laid-back ambience,

LAKE TAHOE TAHOE SKI, SNOWBOARD & SNOWSHOE AREAS

ⓘ TOP WAYS TO SKI TAHOE FOR LESS MONEY

Midweek and half-day afternoon discounts on lift tickets are usually available, but expect higher prices on weekends and holidays. Lift-ticket rates go up incrementally almost every year, too. Parents should ask about the interchangeable 'Parent Predicament' lift tickets offered by some resorts, which let one parent ski while the other one hangs with the kids, then switch off later.

The **Bay Area Ski Bus** (☑925-680-4386; www.bayareaskibus.com) allows you to leave the headache of driving I-80 to others. Round-trips start at $109 including lift tickets, with various add-on packages available. Pick-up locations include San Francisco and Sacramento.

In San Francisco, **Sports Basement** (www.sportsbasement.com) sells deeply discounted lift tickets and has the best deals on multiday rental equipment because it doesn't charge for pick-up or drop-off days.

Handy money-saving websites:

Ski Lake Tahoe (www.skilaketahoe.com) Portal for the seven biggest Tahoe resorts, with deals covering all.

Sliding on the Cheap (www.slidingonthecheap.com) Homegrown website listing discounts and deals on lift tickets.

ⓘ WINTER DRIVING AROUND LAKE TAHOE

From late fall through early spring, always pack snow chains in case a storm rolls in. Chains can also be purchased and installed in towns along I-80 and Hwy 50. Also stash some emergency supplies (eg blankets, water, flashlights) in the trunk, just in case your car breaks down, traffic gets tied up or roads close completely due to snowfall or avalanche danger.

Before hopping in the car, check road closures and conditions:

California Department of Transportation (CalTrans; ☑ 800-427-7623; www.dot.ca.gov)

Nevada Department of Transportation (NDOT; ☑ 877-687-6237, within Nevada 511; www.nevadadot.com)

smaller crowds, tree-lined slopes, open bowls (including the excellent but expert 'Quail Face') and a high-speed quad that gets things moving.

Families love the wide, gentle slopes. It's also the best place to ski during stormy weather. Stats: eight lifts, 1650 vertical feet, 64 runs.

South Lake Tahoe

Heavenly   SKIING, SNOWBOARDING
(Map p372; ☑ 775-586-7000; www.skiheavenly.com; 3860 Saddle Rd, South Lake Tahoe; adult/youth 13-18yr/child 5-12yr $99/89/59; ⊘9am-4pm Mon-Fri, 8:30am-4pm Sat, Sun & holidays; 🌢) The 'mother' of all Tahoe mountains boasts the most acreage, the longest run (5.5 miles) and the biggest vertical drop around. Follow the sun by skiing on the Nevada side in the morning, moving to the California side in the afternoon. Views of the lake and the high desert are heavenly indeed.

Five terrain parks won't strand snowboarders of any skill level, with the High Roller for experts only. Stats: 29 lifts, 3500 vertical feet, 97 runs.

Kirkwood   SKIING, SNOWBOARDING
(☑ 209-258-6000; www.kirkwood.com; 1501 Kirkwood Meadows Dr, off Hwy 88, Kirkwood; adult/child 5-12yr/youth 13-18yr $89/61/76; ⊘9am-4pm) Off-the-beaten-path Kirkwood, set in a high-elevation valley, gets great snow and

holds it longer than almost any other Tahoe resort. It has stellar tree-skiing, gullies, chutes and terrain parks, and is the only Tahoe resort with backcountry runs accessible by snowcats. Novice out-of-bounds skiers should sign up in advance for backcountry safety-skills clinics.

It's 35 miles southwest of South Lake Tahoe via Hwy 89; ski-season shuttles are available (from $15). Stats: 15 lifts, 2000 vertical feet, 72 runs.

Sierra-at-Tahoe   SNOWBOARDING, SKIING
(☑ 530-659-7453; www.sierraattahoe.com; 1111 Sierra-at-Tahoe-Rd, off Hwy 50, Twin Bridges; adult/child 5-12yr/youth 13-22yr $84/25/74; ⊘9am-4pm Mon-Fri, 8:30am-4pm Sat, Sun & holidays; 🌢) About 18 miles southwest of South Lake Tahoe, this is snowboarding central, with five raging terrain parks and a 17ft-high superpipe. A great beginners' run meanders gently for 2.5 miles from the summit, but there are also gnarly steeps and chutes for speed demons.

Kids get four 'adventure zones', while adults-only Huckleberry Gates tempts with steep-and-deep backcountry terrain for experts. Stats: 14 lifts, 2200 vertical feet, 46 runs.

Nevada

Mt Rose   SKIING, SNOWBOARDING
(☑ 775-849-0704; www.mtrose.com; 22222 Mt Rose Hwy/Hwy 431, Reno; adult/child 6-12yr/youth 13-19yr $79/34/59; ⊘9am-4pm) Conveniently the closest ski resort to Reno, Mt Rose has Tahoe's highest base elevation (8260ft) and offers four terrain parks and good snow

DON'T MISS

SNOWSHOEING UNDER THE STARS

A crisp quiet night with a blazing glow across the lake. What could be more magical than a full-moon snowshoe tour? Reserve ahead, as ramblings at these places are very popular:

➥ Ed Z'Berg Sugar Pine Point State Park (p383)

➥ Squaw Valley (p387)

➥ Tahoe Donner (p365)

➥ Northstar California (p364)

➥ Kirkwood (p366)

SLEDDING, TUBING & SNOW PLAY FOR KIDS

Major ski resorts such as Heavenly and Kirkwood around South Lake Tahoe, and Squaw Valley and Northstar California near Truckee, offer sledding hills for the kiddos, some with tubing rentals and thrilling rope tows. Smaller ski mountains including Sierra-at-Tahoe outside South Lake Tahoe, and Boreal, Soda Springs and Tahoe Donner, all near Truckee, also offer child-friendly slopes.

To avoid the crowds, bring your own sleds to designated local snow-play areas at North Tahoe Regional Park in Tahoe Vista on the north shore, or to Nevada's Incline Village, Tahoe Meadows off the Mt Rose Hwy (Hwy 431) or Spooner Summit on Hwy 50, all along the east shore. Back in California, DIY **Sno-Parks** (☑916-324-1222; www.parks. ca.gov; pass per day/yr $5/25) are found along Hwy 89 at Blackwood Canyon (Map p368), 3 miles south of Tahoe City on the west shore, and Taylor Creek, just north of Camp Richardson at South Lake Tahoe. Coming from Sacramento or the San Francisco Bay Area, two Sno-Parks are along I-80 at Yuba Gap (exit 161) and Donner Summit (exit 176 Castle Peak/Boreal Ridge Rd); their parking lots often fill by 11am on winter weekends. Buy required Sno-Park parking passes online or at local shops.

For private groomed sledding and tubing hills, swing by **Hansen's Resort** (Map p372; ☑530-544-3361; www.hansensresort.com; 1360 Ski Run Blvd; per person incl rental per hr $15; ⊙9am-5pm) in South Lake Tahoe or **Adventure Mountain** (☑530-577-4352; www.adventuremountaintahoe.com; 21200 Hwy 50; per car $20, tube/2-person sled rental per day $20/10; ⊙10am-4:30pm Mon-Fri, 9am-4:30pm Sat, Sun & holidays), south of town at Echo Summit.

---

conditions well into spring. 'The Chutes' expert terrain delivers some screamers along its north-facing steeps. Crowds aren't too bad, but the mountain's exposure means it gets hammered in a storm and avalanche control may intermittently close runs.

Excellent weekday deals online; round-trip Reno shuttle $15. Stats: eight lifts, 1800 vertical feet, 60 runs.

Diamond Peak   SKIING, SNOWBOARDING
(Map p368; ☑775-832-1177; www.diamondpeak. com; 1210 Ski Way, off Tahoe Blvd/Hwy 28, Incline Village; adult/child 7-12yr/youth 13-23yr $59/120/49; ⊙9am-4pm;) This midsize mountain is a good place to learn, and boarders can romp around the terrain park, but experts get bored quickly. From the top you'll have a 360-degree panorama of desert, peaks and the lake. Free ski-season shuttle from Incline Village and Crystal Bay. Stats: six lifts, 1840 vertical feet, 30 runs.

Cross-Country Skiing & Snowshoeing

Tahoe's cross-country ski resorts are usually open daily from December through March, and sometimes into April. Most rent equipment and offer lessons; reservations typically aren't taken for either, so show up early in the morning for the best availability.

Truckee & Donner Pass

★**Royal Gorge**   SKIING, SNOWSHOEING
(☑530-426-3871; www.royalgorge.com; 9411 Pahatsi Rd, off I-80 exit Soda Springs/Norden, Soda Springs; adult/youth 13-22yr $29/22; ⊙9am-5pm;) Nordic skiing aficionados won't want to pass up a spin around North America's largest cross-country resort (now operated by Sugar Bowl) with its mind-boggling 125 miles of groomed track crisscrossing 6000 acres of terrain. It has great skating lanes and diagonal stride tracks and also welcomes telemark skiers and snowshoers.

Group lessons are offered a few times daily, with ski camps for kids ages five to 12 (reservations recommended). For a twist, catch some air at the new on-site **Sierra Snowkite Center** (www.sierrasnowkite.com).

Tahoe Donner   SKIING, SNOWSHOEING
(☑530-587-9484; www.tdxc.com; 15275 Alder Creek Rd, off I-80 exit Donner Pass Rd, Truckee; adult/child 7-12yr/youth 13-17yr $27/11/21; ⊙8:30am-5pm, night skiing 5-7pm Wed;) Occupying 4800 acres of thick forest north of Truckee, Tahoe Donner has lovely and varied terrain with over 62 miles of groomed tracks that cover three track systems and 51 trails. The most beautiful spot is secluded Euer Valley, where a warm hut serves food on weekends. A 1.5-mile loop stays open for night skiing, usually on Wednesdays.

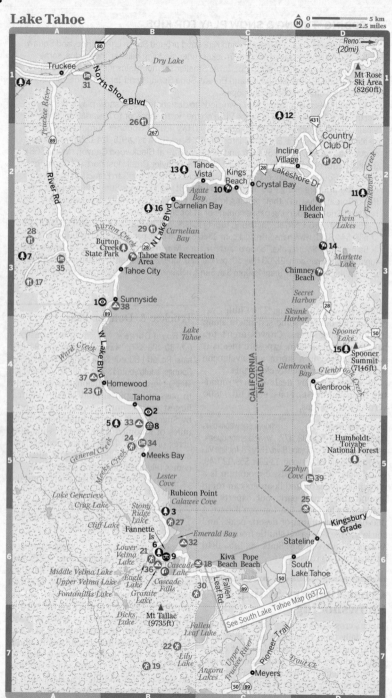

Lake Tahoe

Group lessons for beginners and 'Tiny Tracks', a supervised kids' ski and snow-play camp, are available; reserve ahead for intermediate skills clinics.

Northstar California SKIING, SNOWSHOEING
(Map p368; ☑ 530-562-3270; www.northstarcalifornia.com; 5001 Northstar Dr, off Hwy 267; adult/child 5-12yr $31/17; ⊙ 9am-3pm Mon-Thu, 8:30am-4pm Fri-Sun & holidays) Seven miles southeast of I-80, this mega ski resort has a highly regarded Nordic and telemark school, making it a great choice for novices. A package, which includes the trail fee, ski rental and a group lesson, costs $75. Afterwards you can explore the nearly 25 miles of groomed trails. Moonlight snowshoe tours take place a few times per month.

Clair Tappaan Lodge SKIING, SNOWSHOEING
(☑ 530-426-3632, hut reservations 800-679-6775; www.sierraclub.org/outings/lodges/ctl; adult/child under 12yr $7/3.50; ⊙ 9am-5pm; ♠) You can ski right out the door if you're staying at this rustic mountain lodge near Donner Summit. Its 7 miles of groomed and tracked trails are great for beginners and intermediate skiers, and connect to miles of backcountry skiing. Stop by the lodge for ski and snowshoe rent-

als, and value-priced ski lessons at all skill levels (sign-up starts at 9am daily).

Tahoe City & Around

Tahoe Cross Country SKIING, SNOWSHOEING
(Map p368; ☑ 530-583-5475; www.tahoexc.org; 925 Country Club Dr, off N Lake Blvd/Hwy 28, Tahoe City; adult/child under 12yr/youth 13-17yr $24/free/20; ⊙ 8:30am-5pm; ♠♥) Run by the nonprofit Tahoe Cross Country Ski Education Association, this center, about 3 miles north of Tahoe City, has 40 miles of groomed tracks (23 trails) that wind through lovely forest, suitable for all skill levels. Group lessons come with good-value equipment-rental packages; half-day and twilight trail-pass discounts are also available. Ask about free skate clinics and beginners' cross-country mid-week lessons.

Dogs are allowed on three trails.

Squaw Valley SKIING, SNOWSHOEING
(Map p368; ☑ 530-583-6300; www.squaw.com; 1960 Squaw Valley Rd, off Hwy 89; trail pass/with ski or snowshoe rental $18/32) Although downhill rules the roost at this ex-Olympic resort, 11 miles of groomed track winding around an alpine meadow will keep beginner-level Nordic skiers

LAKE TAHOE TAHOE SKI, SNOWBOARD & SNOWSHOE AREAS

busy, too. Book ahead for monthly moonlight snowshoe tours high atop the mountain.

To reach the trailheads at the Resort at Squaw Creek, which supplies cross-country ski, snowshoe and sled rentals, grab a free shuttle from the downhill ski area parking lot.

South Lake Tahoe

Kirkwood
SKIING, SNOWSHOEING

(☑ 209-258-7248; www.kirkwood.com; 1501 Kirkwood Meadows Dr, off Hwy 88, Kirkwood; adult/child 5-12yr/youth 13-18yr $24/12/18; ⏰ 9am-4pm; 🐕) Definitely not a jogging trail, this cross-country network has sections that are very challenging and where you can actually gain some elevation. Groomed track stretches for 50 miles with separate skating lanes and three trailside warming huts; the views from the higher slopes are phenomenal.

Rentals, lessons and tours are all available. Dogs are welcome on two trails. It's at least an hour's drive south of Lake Tahoe.

Camp Richardson Resort
SKIING, SNOWSHOEING

(☑ 530-542-6584; www.camprichardson.com; 1900 Jameson Beach Rd, off Emerald Bay Rd/Hwy 89, South Lake Tahoe; trail pass $12; ⏰ 9am-4pm) At this woodsy resort with 6 miles of groomed track, you can ski lakeside or head for the solitude of the Desolation Wilderness. Locals turn out in droves for full-moon ski and snowshoe parties, which kick off at the resort's Beacon Bar & Grill (p380).

SOUTH LAKE TAHOE & STATELINE

Highly congested and arguably overdeveloped, South Lake Tahoe is a chockablock commercial strip bordering the lake and framed by picture-perfect alpine mountains. At the foot of the world-class Heavenly mountain resort, and buzzing from the gambling tables in the casinos just across the border in Stateline, NV, Lake Tahoe's south shore draws visitors with a cornucopia of activities, lodging and restaurant options, especially for summer beach access and tons of powdery winter snow.

🅾 Sights

Heavenly Gondola
CABLE CAR

(Map p372; www.skiheavenly.com; Heavenly Village; adult/child 5-12yr/youth 13-18yr from $45/27/37; ⏰ 10am-5pm Jun-Aug, reduced off-season hours; 🐕) Soar to the top of the world as you ride this gondola, which sweeps you from Heavenly Village some 2.4 miles up the mountain in just 12 minutes. From the observation deck at 9123ft, get gobstopping panoramic views of the entire Tahoe Basin, the Desolation Wilderness and Carson Valley.

From here jump on the Tamarack Express chairlift to go to the mountain summit and the Tamarack Lodge restaurant and bar.

Tallac Historic Site
HISTORIC SITE

(Map p372; www.tahoeheritage.org; Tallac Rd; optional tour adult/child $10/5; ⏰ 10am-4pm daily mid-Jun–Sep, Fri & Sat late May–mid-Jun; 🐕) FREE Sheltered by a pine grove and bordering a wide, sandy beach, this national historic site sits on the archaeologically excavated grounds of the former Tallac Resort, a swish vacation retreat for San Francisco's high society around the turn of the 20th century. Feel free to amble or cycle around the forested grounds, today transformed into a community arts hub, where leashed dogs are allowed.

Inside the 1921 Baldwin Estate, the museum has exhibits on the history of the resort and its founder, Elias 'Lucky' Baldwin, who made a bundle off Nevada's Comstock Lode. Nearby is the 1894 Pope Estate, now used for art exhibits and open for guided tours (daily except Wednesday). The boathouse of the Valhalla Estate functions as a theater venue. The 1923 Grand Hall contains an art gallery and gift shop. In summer, concerts, plays and other cultural events happen here, most notably the three-decade-old Valhalla Festival of Arts, Music & Film (☑ 530-541-4975; www.valhallatahoe.com; ⏰ Jul-Aug).

The parking lot is about 3 miles north of the 'Y' junction of Hwys 89 and 50.

Lake Tahoe Historical Society Museum
MUSEUM

(Map p372; ☑ 530-541-5458; www.laketahoemuseum.org; 3058 Lake Tahoe Blvd; ⏰ usually 11am-3pm weekends) FREE A small but interesting museum displays artifacts from Tahoe's pioneer past, including Washoe tribal baskets, vintage black-and-white films, hoary mining memorabilia and a model of a classic Lake Tahoe steamship. On summer Saturday afternoons, join a volunteer-led tour of the restored 1930s cabin out back.

🏃 Activities

Hiking

Many miles of summer hiking trails start from the top of the Heavenly Gondola (p370), many with mesmerizing lake views. On the Nevada side of the state line, **Lam Watah Nature Trail** meanders for just over a mile each way across USFS land, winding underneath pine trees and beside meadows and ponds, on its way between Hwy 50 and Nevada Beach, starting from the community park off Kahle Dr.

Several easy kid- and dog-friendly hikes begin near the United States Forest Service (USFS) Taylor Creek Visitor Center (p380) off Hwy 89. The mile-long, mostly flat **Rainbow Trail** loops around a creekside meadow, with educational panels about ecology and wildlife along the way. On the opposite side of Hwy 89, the gentle, rolling one-mile **Moraine Trail** follows the shoreline of Fallen Leaf Lake; free trailhead parking is available near campsite No 75. Up at cooler elevations, the mile-long round-trip to **Angora Lakes** is another popular trek with kids, especially because it ends by a sandy swimming beach and a summer snack bar selling ice-cream treats. You'll find the trailhead on Angora Ridge Rd, off Tahoe Mountain Rd, accessed from Hwy 89.

For longer and more strenuous day hikes to alpine lakes and meadows, several major trailheads provide easy access to the evocatively named **Desolation Wilderness**: Echo Lakes (south of town); Glen Alpine (near Lily Lake, south of Fallen Leaf Lake), to visit a historic tourist resort and waterfall; and Tallac (opposite the entrance to Baldwin Beach). The latter two trailheads also lead to the peak of Mt Tallac (9735ft), a difficult 10- to 12-mile day hike. Self-serve wilderness permits for day hikers only are freely available at trailheads; overnight backpacking permits are subject to quotas.

Beaches & Swimming

On the California side, the nicest strands are **Pope Beach** (Map p372; per car $7), **Kiva Beach** (Map p372) and **Baldwin Beach** (Map p368; per car $7), each with picnic tables and barbecue grills; Kiva Beach offers free parking and allows leashed dogs, too. They're all found along Emerald Bay Rd (Hwy 89), running west and east of Tallac Historic Site. Nearby, **Fallen Leaf Lake**, where scenes from the Hollywood flicks *The Bodyguard* and *City of Angels* were filmed, is also good for summer swims. **El Dorado Beach** (Map p372) is a free public beach in town, just off Lake Tahoe Blvd.

Many folks prefer to head over to Stateline and keep driving north 2 miles to pretty **Nevada Beach** (Map p368; per car $7), where the wind really picks up in the afternoons, or always-busy **Zephyr Cove** (www.zephyrcove.com; 760 Hwy 50; per car $8), which has

---

DON'T MISS

HIKING & BACKPACKING THE DESOLATION WILDERNESS

Sculpted by powerful glaciers aeons ago, this relatively compact **wilderness area** (Map p368; www.fs.usda.gov/eldorado/specialplaces) spreads south and west of Lake Tahoe and is the most popular in the Sierra Nevada. It's a 100-sq-mile wonderland of polished granite peaks, deep-blue alpine lakes, glacier-carved valleys and pine forests that thin quickly at the higher elevations. In summer wildflowers nudge out from between the rocks.

All this splendor makes for some exquisite backcountry exploration. Six major trailheads provide access from the Lake Tahoe side: Glen Alpine (Map p368), Tallac (Map p368), Echo Lakes (near Echo Summit on Hwy 50), Bayview (Map p368), Eagle Falls (Map p368) and Meeks Bay (Map p368). Tallac and Eagle Falls get the most traffic, but solitude comes quickly once you've scampered past the day hikers.

Wilderness permits are required year-round for both day and overnight explorations. Day hikers can self-register at the trailheads, but overnight permits must be either reserved online (fee $6) at www.recreation.gov and printed at home, or picked up in person at one of the three USFS offices in South Lake Tahoe and Pollack Pines. Permits cost $5 per person for one night, $10 per person for two or more nights.

Quotas are in effect from late May through the end of September. Over half of the permits for the season may be reserved online, usually starting in late March or April; the other permits are available on a first-arrival basis on the day of entry only.

Bearproof canisters are strongly advised in all wilderness areas (hanging your food in trees will not work – these bears are too smart!). Borrow canisters for free from the USFS offices. Bring bug repellent as the mosquitoes can be merciless. Wood fires are a no-no, but portable stoves are OK. Dogs must be leashed at *all* times.

LAKE TAHOE SOUTH LAKE TAHOE & STATELINE

South Lake Tahoe

0 2 km
0 1 miles

STATELINE

Nevada Beach (1.5mi)
Zephyr Cove (3mi)
Nevada Pkwy
Lake Pkwy
Stateline Transit Center
State Line Ave
Lakeshore Blvd
Cedar Ave
Pine Blvd
Park Ave
Friday Ave
Explore Tahoe
Heavenly Village Way

HEAVENLY VILLAGE

Keller Rd
Wildwood Ave
Needle Peak Rd
Ski Run Blvd
Forest Ave
Spruce Ave
Pioneer Trail

NEVADA
CALIFORNIA

El Dorado National Park

Heavenly Valley Creek

Glenwood Way
Johnson Blvd
Fremont Ave
Rufus Allen Blvd
Bijou Community Park
Al Tahoe Blvd
College Dr
Black Bart Ave
Martin Ave
USDA Lake Tahoe Basin Management Unit
O'Malley Dr

South Lake Tahoe State Recreation Area
Lakeview Ave
Lake Tahoe Visitors Authority
Los Angeles Ave

Lake Tahoe
Trout Creek
Truckee Marsh

SOUTH LAKE TAHOE
Lake Tahoe Blvd

Upper Truckee River

Tahoe Keys Blvd
Venice Dr
15th St
13th St

TAHOE KEYS

Truckee Marsh

Pope Beach Rd
Jameson Beach Rd
Emerald Bay Rd

USFS Taylor Creek Visitor Center
Baldwin Beach (0.1mi)
Emerald Bay (3mi)

Fallen Leaf Lake Rd

El Dorado National Forest

TAHOE VALLEY
Dunlap Dr
The
Julie Ave
D St
10th St
11th St
Lake Tahoe Blvd
South Y Transit Center
Julie Ave

El Dorado National Forest

South Lake Tahoe

rustic resort and marina facilities along its sandy mile-long shoreline.

Boating & Water Sports

Ski Run Boat Company (Map p372; ☑530-544-0200; www.tahoesports.com; 900 Ski Run Blvd), at the Ski Run Marina (Map p372), and **Tahoe Keys Boat & Charter Rentals** (Map p372; ☑530-544-8888; www.tahoesports.com; 2435 Venice Dr), at the Tahoe Keys Marina (Map p372), both rent motorized powerboats, pontoons, sailboats and jet skis (rentals $110 to $235 per hour), as well as human-powered kayaks, canoes, hydro bikes, paddleboats and paddleboard sets (per hour $25 to $35). If you want to go parasailing up to 1200ft above Lake Tahoe's waves, the Ski Run Marina branch can hook you up (rides $55 to $80).

Kayak Tahoe KAYAKING, WATER SPORTS
(☑530-544-2011; www.kayaktahoe.com; kayak single/double 1hr $20/32, 1 day $65/85, lessons & tours from $40; ☺10am-5pm Sat & Sun Jun-Sep) Rent a kayak or stand-up paddleboard, take a lesson or sign up for a guided tour, including sunset cove paddles, trips to Emerald Bay and explorations of the Upper Truckee River estuary and the eastern shore. Five seasonal locations at Timber Cove Marina (Map p372), Vikingsholm (Emerald Bay) and Baldwin, Pope and Nevada Beaches.

Zephyr Cove Resort & Marina WATER SPORTS
(☑775-589-4901; www.zephyrcove.com; 760 Hwy 50, NV; ☺9am-5pm) Rents powerboats, pedal boats, waverunners, jet skis, canoes, kayaks and stand-up paddleboards; also offers single and tandem parasailing flights.

Camp Richardson
Resort Marina

WATER SPORTS

(Map p372; ☑ 530-542-6570; www.camprichardson.com; 1900 Jameson Beach Rd) Rents powerboats, paddleboats, water skis, kayaks and stand-up paddleboarding gear.

Mountain Biking

For expert mountain bikers, the classic **Mr Toad's Wild Ride**, with its steep downhill sections and banked turns reminiscent of a Disneyland theme-park ride, should prove sufficiently challenging. Usually open from June until October, the one-way trail along Saxon Creek starts off Hwy 89 south of town near Grass Lake and Luther Pass.

Intermediate mountain bikers should steer toward the mostly single-track **Powerline Trail**, which traverses ravines and creeks. You can pick up the trail off Ski Run Blvd near the Heavenly mountain resort, from the western end of Saddle Rd. For a more leisurely outing over mostly level terrain, you can pedal around scenic **Fallen Leaf Lake**. Anyone with good lungs might try the **Angora Lakes Trail**, which is steep but technically easy and rewards you with sweeping views of Mt Tallac and Fallen Leaf Lake. It starts further east, off Angora Ridge and Tahoe Mountain Ridge Rds.

For shuttle service and mountain-bike rentals for Mr Toad's Wild Ride, the Tahoe Rim Trail (p381) and other downhill adventures, as well as family-friendly tours, talk to **Wanna Ride** (☑ 775-588-5800; www.wannaridetahoe.com; ⊙ 8am-4pm Tue-Sat). For mountain-biking trail conditions, race schedules, volunteer days and other special events, contact the **Tahoe Area Mountain Biking Association** (www.mountainbiketahoe.org).

Cycling

The **South Lake Tahoe Bike Path** is a level, leisurely ride suitable for anyone. It heads west from El Dorado Beach, eventually connecting with the **Pope-Baldwin Bike Path** past Camp Richardson, Tallac Historic Site and the USFS Taylor Creek Visitor Center. Visitor centers carry the excellent Lake Tahoe bike route map, also available online from the **Lake Tahoe Bicycle Coalition** (www.tahoebike.org), which has an info-packed website for cycling enthusiasts. **Anderson's Bike Rental** (Map p372; ☑ 877-720-2121, 530-541-0500; www.laketahoebikerental.com; 645 Emerald Bay Rd/Hwy 89; per hr $10; ⊕) rents hybrid bikes with helmets.

Golf & Disc Golf

Edgewood Tahoe Golf Course

GOLF

(Map p372; ☑ 775-588-3566; www.edgewood-tahoe.com; 100 Lake Pkwy, Stateline; green fee $110-240) Stunning lakeside scenery is a major distraction at this challenging championship 18-hole course designed by George Fazio, a favorite for celebrity golf tournaments. Tee-time reservations are required; cart and club rentals available.

Bijou Golf Course

GOLF

(Map p372; ☑ 530-542-6097; www.cityofslt.us; 3464 Fairway Ave; green fee $17-28, club/cart rental

---

SOUTH LAKE TAHOE FOR CHILDREN

With oodles of outdoor activities, families will never run out of mountains to explore and beaches to dig. If the kids start to get fractious though, try one of these local favorites to mix things up a little.

Stream Profile Chamber (Map p372; ☑ 530-543-2674; www.tahoeheritage.org; trailhead at USFS Taylor Creek Visitor Center, off Hwy 89; ⊙ 8am-5pm late May-Sep, 8am-4pm Oct; ⊕) Along a family-friendly hiking trail, this submerged glass structure in a teeming creek lets you check out what plants and fish live below the waterline. The best time to visit is in October during the Kokanee salmon run, when the brilliant red beauties arrive to spawn. See the website for scheduled activities.

Tahoe Bowl (Map p372; ☑ 530-544-3700; www.tahoebowl.com; 1030 Fremont Ave; game per person $4.50, shoe rental $4; ⊕) For yucky-weather days or to tire out the tots by bedtime, this is a fun indoor haunt with 16 bowling lanes, a small diner and pizza joint, and an air hockey table. Call ahead for open-play schedules.

Shops at Heavenly Village (Map p372; www.theshopsatheavenly.com; 1001 Heavenly Village Way; ⊙ seasonal hr vary; ⊕) If you don't feel like wandering far, this downtown outdoor mall sets up a little putt-putt golf course in summer, and opens an outdoor ice-skating rink in winter. Check website for current schedules and prices.

ⓘ NAVIGATING SOUTH LAKE TAHOE TRAFFIC

South Lake Tahoe's main east–west thoroughfare is a 5-mile stretch of Hwy 50 called Lake Tahoe Blvd. Most hotels and businesses hover around the California–Nevada state line and Heavenly Village. Casinos are located in Stateline, which is officially a separate city.

West of town, Hwy 50 runs into Hwy 89 at the 'Y' junction. Heavy snowfall sometimes closes Hwy 89 north of the Tallac Historic Site. The section of Hwy 89 between South Lake Tahoe and Emerald Bay is also known as Emerald Bay Rd.

Traffic all along Hwy 50 between the 'Y' junction and Heavenly Village gets jammed around lunchtime and again by 5pm Monday to Friday in both summer and winter, but Sunday afternoons, when skiers head back down the mountain, are the worst.

An alternate, less-crowded route through town is Pioneer Trail, which branches east off the Hwy 89/50 junction (south of the 'Y') and reconnects with Hwy 50 at Stateline.

$15/5; ☉ mid-Apr–Oct) So you don't know your putter from your 9-iron? That's OK at this laid-back, no-reservations municipal course with views of Heavenly Mountain. Built in the 1920s, it's got just 9 holes, which you can play twice around.

Kirkwood Disc-Wood DISC GOLF
(☎ 209-258-7210; www.kirkwood.com; 1501 Kirkwood Meadows Dr, Kirkwood) **FREE** Crazy terrain, tons of distance and high-elevation Sierra Nevada views from an epic 18 holes. Call ahead for directions and to check opening hours before making the hour-long drive southwest of South Lake Tahoe.

Zephyr Cove Park DISC GOLF
(www.douglascountynv.gov; Hwy 50 at Warrior Way, NV) **FREE** PDGA-approved 18-hole course is scenically set on the eastern shore, with kick-ass uphill and downhill shoots.

Bijou Community Park DISC GOLF
(Map p372; www.cityofslt.us; 1201 Al Tahoe Blvd) **FREE** In town, these 27 holes will taunt even experts with loooong greens on a mostly flat, forested course (ahoy, trees!).

Horseback Riding
Both **Camp Richardson Corral & Pack Station** (Map p372; ☎ 877-541-3113, 530-541-3113; www.camprichardsoncorral.com; Emerald Bay Rd/Hwy 89; trail rides $43-164; ⊕) and **Zephyr Cove Stables** (☎ 775-588-5664; www.zephyrcovestable.com; Hwy 50, NV; trail rides $40-80; ⊕), about 4 miles north of Stateline casinos, offer daily horseback rides in summer, varying from one-hour kid-friendly trips through the forest, to extended treks with meadow and lake views (reservations required).

Zip-Lining
Zip Tahoe ZIP-LINING
(☎ 209-258-7330; www.ziptahoe.com; 1501 Kirkwood Meadows Dr, Kirkwood; 2hr tour $125; ☉ Dec–mid-Apr & mid-Jun–mid-Sep) At Kirkwood, careen through the tree canopy over six zip lines and two suspension bridges, checking out the snowboarders below in winter or the wildflowers in summer. Kids aged eight and up permitted.

☞ Tours

Lake Tahoe Cruises CRUISE
(Map p372; ☎ 800-238-2463; www.zephyrcove.com; adult/child from $49/15) Two paddle wheelers ply Lake Tahoe's 'big blue' year-round with a variety of sightseeing, drinking, dining and dancing cruises, including a narrated two-hour daytime trip to Emerald Bay. The *Tahoe Queen* leaves from Ski Run Marina (summer parking fee $8) in town, while the MS *Dixie II* is based at Zephyr Cove Marina on the eastern shore in Nevada.

Woodwind Cruises CRUISE
(☎ 775-588-3000; www.tahoecruises.com; Zephyr Cove Marina, 760 Hwy 50, NV; 1hr cruise adult/child 2-12yr from $42/15) Champagne and happy-hour floats aboard this sailing catamaran are the perfect way to chill after an afternoon lazing on the beach. Five daily departures during summer; reservations recommended.

Action Watersports BOAT TOUR
(Map p372; ☎ 530-544-5387; www.action-watersports.com; Timber Cove Marina, 3411 Lake Tahoe Blvd; adult/child under 13yr $59/30) In a hurry to get to Emerald Cove? Wanna avoid those near-constant traffic jams on Hwy 89? Jump on board the *Tahoe Thunder* speedboat, which zips across the lake – watch out,

though, you'll get wet! Also offers parasailing rides ($55 to $80).

Lake Tahoe Balloons
BALLOONING

(Map p372; ☑ 530-544-1221; www.laketahoeballoons.com; per person $295) From May through October (weather permitting), you can cruise on a catamaran launched from Tahoe Keys Marina, then clamber aboard a hot-air balloon launched right from the boat's upper deck. The lake and Sierra Nevada mountain views may take away what little breath you have left at 10,000ft. Reservations required.

🛏 Sleeping

🛏 South Lake Tahoe

South Lake Tahoe has a bazillion choices for all budgets. Lodging options line Lake Tahoe Blvd (Hwy 50) between Stateline and Ski Run Blvd. Further west, closer to the 'Y' at the intersection of Hwys 50 and 89 is a string of mostly budget motels ranging from barely adequate to inexcusable. Peak season is generally winter ski season from December to March and summer from June to August. Some properties may impose minimum stays, especially on weekends and holidays. For more ski condos and hotel rooms near the slopes, contact **Heavenly** (☑ 775-586-7000; www.skiheavenly.com).

Camp Richardson
Resort
CABINS, CAMPGROUND $

(Map p372; ☑ 530-541-1801; www.camprichardson.com; 1900 Jameson Beach Rd; tent sites from $35, RV sites with partial/full hookups from $40/45, r $95-215, cabins $125-263; ☎) Removed from downtown's strip-mall aesthetic, this sprawling family camp is a hectic place offering seasonal camping (expect marauding bears all night long!), forested cabins rented by the week in summer, and so-so beachside hotel rooms. Sports gear and bicycle rentals are available, and there's a popular ice-cream parlor across the road. Wi-fi in lobby only.

Fallen Leaf Campground
CAMPGROUND $

(Map p372; ☑ 530-544-0426, reservations 877-444-6777; www.recreation.gov; Fallen Leaf Lake Rd; tent & RV sites $32-34, yurts $84; ☺ mid-May–mid-Oct; ☀) Near the north shore of stunning Fallen Leaf Lake, this is one of the biggest and most popular campgrounds on the south shore, with pay showers and approximately 200 wooded sites and six canvas-sided yurts that can sleep a family of five (bring your own sleeping bags).

Big Pines Mountain House
MOTEL $

(Map p372; ☑ 530-541-5155; www.thebigpines.com; 4083 Cedar Ave; r incl breakfast $50-129; ✳@☎☀☀) Choose from over 70 comfortable rooms in various sizes – some with blissful mountain views – and in summertime, stroll to the private beach nearby or take a dip in the heated pool. Gas fireplaces cozy up the king kitchenette rooms. Pet fee $15.

Blue Lake Inn
MOTEL $

(Map p372; ☑ 530-544-6459; www.thebluelakeinn.com; 944 Friday Ave; r incl breakfast $89-104; ✳☎☀☀) A good value choice near the Heavenly Gondola, these ample motel rooms have the core amenities: microwave, fridge, coffeemaker and flat-screen TV, plus a hot tub and outdoor pool. Pet fee $15.

Campground by the Lake
CAMPGROUND $

(Map p372; ☑ 530-542-6096; www.cityofslt.us; 1150 Rufus Allen Blvd; tent & RV sites with/without hookups from $40/29, cabins $49-80; ☺ Apr-Oct; ☎☀) Highway noise can be an around-the-clock irritant, though proximity to the city pool and ice rink make this wooded in-town campground with an RV dump station a decent choice. Basic sleeping-platform cabins are available between Memorial Day (late May) and Labor Day (early September).

Alder Inn
INN $$

(Map p372; ☑ 530-544-4485; www.thealderinn.com; 1072 Ski Run Blvd; r $99-150; ☎☀) Even better than staying at your best friend's house by the lake, this hospitable inn on the Heavenly ski-shuttle route charms with color schemes that really pop, pillow-top mattresses, organic bath goodies, mini-fridges, microwaves and flat-screen TVs. Dip your toes in the kidney-shaped pool in summer. Continental breakfast included on weekends.

968 Park Hotel
BOUTIQUE HOTEL $$

(Map p372; ☑ 530-544-0968; www.968parkhotel.com; 968 Park Ave; r $109-309; @☎☀) 🌿 A refashioned motel with serious hipster edge, recycled, rescued and re-envisioned building materials have made this LEED-certified property an aesthetically pleasing ecohaven near the lake. A new lobby bar offers free wine tastings on Friday evenings, and in summer, unwind in a cabana by the sunny pool or in the zen garden before sinking into your dreamy Sterling bed.

Paradice Inn
MOTEL $$

(Map p372; ☑ 530-544-6800; www.paradice-moteltahoe.com; 953 Park Ave; r $148-218; ❄ ☎) Harried travelers will appreciate the fabulous hospitality (turndown service!) at this small two-story motel. Step outside your minimalist room bordered by flower baskets, then stroll across the street to the Heavenly Gondola. Families should ask about the two-bedroom suites.

Fireside Lodge
INN $$

(Map p372; ☑ 530-544-5515; www.tahoefiresidelodge.com; 515 Emerald Bay Rd/Hwy 89; d incl breakfast $149-219; ☎ ☎) This woodsy cabin B&B wholeheartedly welcomes families, with free bikes, kayaks and snow shoes to borrow and evening s'mores and wine and cheese. Kitchenette rooms and suites have river-rock gas fireplaces, cozy patchwork quilts and pioneer-themed touches like wagon wheels or vintage skis. Pet fee $25.

Heavenly Valley Lodge
B&B $$

(Map p372; ☑ 530-564-1500; www.heavenlyvalleylodge.com; 1261 Ski Run Blvd; d incl breakfast $145-255; ☎ ☎) Located along the Heavenly shuttle route, this family-run place perfects the balance of old Tahoe – all-fireplace rooms of knotty pine and river rock – and great amenities, like DVD players and a huge movie library, a fire-pit patio and afternoon happy hour. Some kitchenette units; pet fee $25.

Basecamp Hotel
BOUTIQUE HOTEL $$

(Map p372; ☑ 530-208-0180; www.basecamphotels.com; 4143 Cedar Ave; d $109-229, 8-person bunkroom $209-299, all incl breakfast; ☎ ☎) ✿ Recycled wood, original nature-themed canvases and artsy artifacts gussy up this stylish former motel. Lucky couples can rough it in the 'Great Indoors' room with a tented bed and faux campfire, and families can overnight in spacious bunk-bed rooms. A rooftop hot tub, beer and wine bar, and communal dinner nights sweeten the deal. Pet fee $40.

Spruce Grove Cabins
CABINS $$

(Map p372; ☑ 530-544-0549; www.sprucegrovetahoe.com; 3599-3605 Spruce Ave; 4-/6-person cabin $169/215; ☎ ☎) Away from the Heavenly hubbub, these tidy, private cabins are fenced off on a quiet residential street. The vintage look of the kitchen-equipped cabins, from knotty pine walls to the stone-bordered gas fireplaces, will make you feel like you're staying lakeside. Cleaning fee $30; refundable pet deposit $100.

Let your dogs cavort in the yard while you swing in the hammock or soak in outdoor hot tubs.

Inn by the Lake
HOTEL $$$

(Map p372; ☑ 530-542-0330; www.innbythelake.com; 3300 Lake Tahoe Blvd; r $180-300; ❄ @ ☎ ☎ ☎) Rooms here are rather nondescript, although a bilevel outdoor hot tub, spa suites with kitchens, and bicycles and snowshoes to borrow are nifty. Rooms out back are cheaper and quieter, but then you'll miss the lake views. Pet fee $20.

Deerfield Lodge at Heavenly
BOUTIQUE HOTEL $$$

(Map p372; ☑ 530-544-3337; www.tahoedeerfieldlodge.com; 1200 Ski Run Blvd; r/ste incl breakfast from $179/229; ❄ ☎) A small boutique hotel close to Heavenly ski resort, Deerfield has a dozen intimate rooms and spacious suites that each have a patio or balcony facing the green courtyard, along with a Jacuzzi, flickering gas fireplace and amusing coat racks crafted from skis and snowboards. Pet fee $25.

There's complimentary wine in the lobby, s'mores to be made over the fire pit, and barbecue grills appear in summer.

Timber Lodge
HOTEL $$$

(Map p372; ☑ 530-542-6600; www.marriott.com; 4100 Lake Tahoe Blvd; r $170-230, ste from $230; ❄ @ ☎ ☎) Don't let the Marriott chaingang brand put you off this modern ski lodge with an enviable position, where you can watch the Heavenly Gondola whoosh by outside your window. Cookie-cutter hotel rooms have kitchenettes, while apartment-style 'vacation villa' suites come with full kitchens, gas fireplaces and deep soaking tubs for après-ski warm-ups. Parking fee $26.

Landing
LUXURY HOTEL $$$

(Map p372; ☑ 855-700-5263; www.thelandingtahoe.com; 4104 Lakeshore Blvd; d/ste from $319/619; ❄ @ ☎ ☎ ☎) South Lake's newest and most luxurious lakeside resort dazzles with an in-house spa, marble bathrooms with toilet night lights and heated seats, Keurig coffeemakers, a private beach and the swank Jimmy's restaurant. Each room has a fireplace seating arrangement, and other perks include a complimentary town shuttle, a year-round outdoor pool and nightly wine tasting. Pet fee $100.

LAKE TAHOE SOUTH LAKE TAHOE & STATELINE

Stateline, NV

At Nevada's high-rise casino complexes, prices rise and fall like your luck at the slot machines. Season, day of the week and type of room are key. In winter ask about special ski-and-stay packages.

Nevada Beach Campground   CAMPGROUND $

(Map p368; 775-588-5562, reservations 877-444-6777; www.recreation.gov; off Hwy 50, NV; tent & RV sites $32-38; mid-May–mid-Oct;) Bed down on a carpet of pine needles at this tidy lakeside campground, about 3 miles north of Stateline, where 48 sites are nestled amid pines. Leashed dogs are allowed at campsites, but not the beach.

Zephyr Cove Resort   CABINS, CAMPGROUND $$

(Map p368; 775-589-4907; www.zephyrcove.com; 760 Hwy 50, NV; tent & RV sites with/without hookups from $73/41, cabins $160-389; camping May-Sep, cabins year-round;) In Nevada, about 4 miles north of Stateline, this family-oriented lakeside resort has historic cabins scattered among the pines and good facilities, including hot showers, barbecue grills and fire rings. Take your pick of 93 paved RV or 10 drive-in tent sites (some with lake views), or 47 walk-in tent sites tucked deeper into the shady forest.

Leashed dogs allowed, except on the main beach.

Harrah's   CASINO HOTEL $$

(Map p372; 775-588-6611; www.harrahslaketahoe.com; 15 Hwy 50, Stateline; r $80-369;) Clad in an oddly tasteful forest-green facade, this buzzing casino hotel is Stateline's top contender. Let yourself be swallowed up by even standard 'luxury' rooms, which each have two bathrooms with telephones, or spring for a luxury suite with panoramic lake-vista windows. For more eye-popping views, snag a window table at one of Harrah's upper-floor restaurants.

MontBleu   CASINO HOTEL $$

(Map p372; 775-588-3515; www.montbleuresort.com; 55 Hwy 50, Stateline; r $70-210, ste from $240;) The public areas may sport übercool modern boutique decor, but hallways are seriously dim. Recently remodeled rooms have fluffy duvets and art-deco-esque accents, and some of the marble-accented bathrooms sport hedonistic circular tubs. Rooms above the 5th floor are best, and the premier category have lake views. Unwind in the lavish indoor pool lagoon, accented by a rockscape and mini waterfalls.

Harvey's   CASINO HOTEL $$

(Map p372; 775-588-2411; www.harveys-stahoe.com; 18 Hwy 50, Stateline; r $80-229;) Harvey's was South Lake Tahoe's first casino, and with 740 rooms, is also its biggest. Mountain Tower rooms have fancy marble bathrooms and oodles of space, but renovated Lake Tower rooms are more chic and design-savvy. The heated outdoor pool is open year-round, for beach and snow bunnies alike. Pet fee $75; wi-fi $11 daily.

Eating

For late-night cravings, each of the big casinos in Stateline has a 24-hour coffee shop for hangover-helper and night-owl breakfasts. If you're just looking for filling pub grub or après-ski appetizers and cocktails, most bars and cafes also serve just-OK food, some with waterfront views and live music, too.

Sprouts   VEGETARIAN $

(Map p372; 3123 Harrison Ave; mains $7-10; 8am-9pm;) Cheerful chatter greets you at this energetic, mostly organic cafe that gets extra kudos for its smoothies. A healthy menu will have you noshing happily on satisfying soups, rice bowls, sandwiches, burrito wraps, tempeh burgers and fresh salads.

Sugar Pine Bakery   BAKERY $

(Map p372; 3564 Lake Tahoe Blvd; pastries $1-5; 8am-5pm Tue-Sat, to 4pm Sun) Crunchy baguettes, ooey-gooey cinnamon rolls, fruit tarts and choco-chunk cookies.

Cork & More   DELI $

(Map p372; www.thecorkandmore.com; 1032 Al Tahoe Blvd; sandwiches $5-10; 10am-7pm) Specialty foods, gourmet deli (sandwiches, soups, salads) and picnic baskets to go.

Ernie's Coffee Shop   DINER $

(Map p372; www.erniescoffeeshop.com; 1207 Hwy 50; mains $7.50-11; 6am-2pm;) A sun-filled local institution, Ernie's dishes out filling four-egg omelets, hearty biscuits with gravy, fruity and nutty waffles and bottomless cups of locally roasted coffee. Toddlers can happily munch the ears off the Mickey Mouse pancake.

Burger Lounge   FAST FOOD $

(Map p372; 530-542-2010; www.burgerlounge-intahoe.com; 717 Emerald Bay Rd; burgers $6-8; 10am-8pm daily Jun-Sep, 11am-7pm Wed-Sun

Oct-May; 🍺) You can't miss that giant beer mug standing outside a shingled cabin. Step inside for the south shore's tastiest burgers, including the crazy 'Jiffy burger' (with peanut butter and cheddar cheese), the zingy pesto fries or the knockout ice-cream shakes.

Freshie's
FUSION $$
(Map p372; ☎530-542-3630; www.freshiestahoe.com; 3330 Lake Tahoe Blvd; mains $14-28; ⏰11:30am-9pm; 🍴) From vegans to seafood lovers, everybody should be able to find a favorite on the extensive menu at this Hawaiian fusion joint with sunset upper-deck views. Most of the produce is local and organic, and the blackened fish tacos are South Lake Tahoe's best. Check the webcam to see if there's a wait.

Blue Angel Cafe
CALIFORNIAN $$
(Map p372; ☎530-544-6544; www.theblueangelcafe.com; 1132 Ski Run Blvd; lunch $11-16, dinner $12-25; ⏰11am-9pm; 🍴) Inside a cute wooden house on the way uphill to ski at Heavenly, this modern international-inspired kitchen churns out seafood, club sandwiches, elaborate salads, pastas and flank steaks to stuff your belly. Turn up for happy hour or the rotating lunch and dinner specials.

Off the Hook
SUSHI $$
(Map p372; www.offthehooksushi.com; 2660 Lake Tahoe Blvd; mains $14-23; ⏰5-10pm) Sushi, so far from the ocean? Yup. Locals keep on coming back to this dynamite little sushi shack, where you can feast on bento boxes and *nigiri* combos, or big steaming bowls of floury udon noodles and pan-fried halibut steaks off the Japanese, Hawaiian and Californian menu.

Latin Soul
LATIN AMERICAN $$
(Map p372; www.lakesideinn.com; 168 Hwy 50, Stateline; mains $9-28; ⏰8am-11pm) For something completely different, steal away to this little casino kitchen with a big, bold menu of spicy south-of-the-border flavors: Argentinean churrasco-grilled steak, Veracruz shrimp ceviche, goat *bírria* (stew) and outrageously mixed mojitos.

Getaway Cafe
AMERICAN $$
(www.getawaycafe.com; 3140 Hwy 50, Meyers; mains breakfast & lunch $8-13, dinner $10-19; ⏰7am-2:30pm Mon & Tue, to 9pm Wed-Sun Jun-Aug, reduced hours off-season; 🍺) On the outskirts of town, just south of the agriculture inspection checkpoint, this place really lives up to its name; avoid the weekend crowds here. Friendly wait staff sling heaped-up buffalo chicken salads, barbecue burgers, chile rellenos, coconut-encrusted French toast and more.

Lake Tahoe Pizza Co
PIZZA $$
(Map p372; ☎530-544-1919; www.laketahoepizzaco.com; 1168 Emerald Bay Rd/Hwy 89; pizzas $11-23; ⏰4-9:30pm; 🍴) Since the '70s, this classic pizza parlor has been hand rolling its housemade dough (cornmeal or whole wheat, anyone?), then piling the pizzas with crafty combos such as the meaty 'Barnyard Massacre' or vegan 'Green Giant.'

★ Cafe Fiore
ITALIAN $$$
(Map p372; ☎530-541-2908; www.cafefiore.com; 1169 Ski Run Blvd; mains $18-34; ⏰5:30-9pm) Upscale Italian without pretension, this tiny romantic eatery pairs succulent pasta, seafood and meats with an award-winning 300-vintage wine list. Swoon over the veal scaloppine, homemade white-chocolate ice cream and near-perfect garlic bread. With only seven tables (a baker's dozen in summer when the candle-lit outdoor patio opens), reservations are essential.

Self-Catering

Grass Roots Natural Foods
GROCERY
(Map p372; 2030 Dunlap Dr; ⏰9am-8pm; 🍴) Organic produce and home-baked muffins, sandwiches and fresh pizzas.

Safeway
SUPERMARKET
(Map p372; www.safeway.com; 1020 Johnson Blvd; ⏰24hr) Standard supermarket fare, with an in-house deli and bakery.

🍷 Drinking & Entertainment

The siren song of blackjack and slot machines calls the masses over to Stateline. It's no Vegas, but there are plenty of ways to help you part with a bankroll. Each of the major casinos has live entertainment and several bars and lounges for you to while away the night. Published on Thursdays, the free alt-weekly newspaper *Reno News & Review* (www.newsreview.com/reno) has comprehensive Stateline entertainment and events listings. For what's going on around South Lake Tahoe, pick up a copy of the free weekly *Lake Tahoe Action,* published by the *Tahoe Daily Tribune* (www.tahoedailytribune.com).

Beacon Bar & Grill   BAR
(Map p372; www.camprichardson.com; Camp Rich-ardson Resort, 1900 Jameson Beach Rd; ⏱11am-10pm) Imagine all of Lake Tahoe is your very own front yard when you and your buddies sprawl across this big wraparound wooden deck. If you want to get schnockered, order the signature Rum Runner cocktail. Bands rock here in summer.

Boathouse on the Pier   BAR
(Map p372; 3411 Lake Tahoe Blvd; ⏱11am-9pm, extended hours Jun-Sep) On the lake behind the Beach Retreat complex, this upstairs and upscale Timber Cove restaurant is the perfect spot for sunset cocktails, with outdoor tables to feel the summer breeze.

Brewery at Lake Tahoe   BREWERY
(Map p372; www.brewerylaketahoe.com; 3542 Lake Tahoe Blvd; ⏱11am-10:30pm) Crazy-popular brewpub pumps its signature Bad Ass Ale into grateful local patrons, who may sniff at bright-eyed out-of-towners. The barbecue is dynamite and a roadside patio opens in summer. Don't leave without a bumper sticker!

MacDuffs Pub   PUB
(Map p372; www.macduffspub.com; 1041 Fremont Ave; ⏱11:30am-10pm) With excellent beers rotating on tap, a dartboard on the wall, and fish-and-chips and shepherd's pie (as well as gourmet burgers and wood-fired pizzas) on the menu, this dark and bustling gastropub wouldn't look out of place in Edinburgh. Sports fans and beer drinkers, step right up.

Stateline Brewery   BREWERY
(Map p372; www.statelinebrewery.com; 4118 Lake Tahoe Blvd; ⏱11am-9pm Sun-Thu, to 10:30pm Fri & Sat) Seat yourself by the shiny industrial brewing vats at this subterranean eating and drinking spot. German and American-style ales taste mighty good after a day of sunning yourself on the lakeshore or skiing Heavenly (the gondola swings nearby).

Opal Ultra Lounge   CLUB
(Map p372; ☎775-586-2000; www.montbleuresort.com; MontBleu, 55 Hwy 50, Stateline; cover free-$10; ⏱10pm-4am Wed-Sat) With DJ booths and go-go dancers, this Top 40 and electro dance club draws a young party crowd that enjoys getting their bodies painted in-house. Ladies may get in free before midnight. On summer Sunday nights, hit up the casino's poolside DJ parties. Dress to impress.

Alpina Coffee Café   CAFE
(Map p372; 822 Emerald Bay Rd/Hwy 89; ⏱6am-5pm; ⏇) Internet-connected computers, plus locally roasted brews, toasted bagels and a summer garden patio.

Improv   COMEDY
(Map p372; www.harveystahoe.com; 18 Hwy 50, Stateline; tickets $25-30; ⏱usually 9pm Wed, Fri & Sun, 8:30pm & 10:30pm Sat) Catch up-and-coming stand-up comedians doing their funny shtick at the intimate cabaret theater inside Harvey's old-school casino.

❶ Information

Barton Memorial Hospital (☎530-541-3420; www.bartonhealth.org; 2170 South Ave; ⏱24hr) Around-the-clock emergency room. Barton's urgent-care clinic is inside the Stateline Medical Center at 155 Hwy 50, Stateline, NV.

Explore Tahoe (Map p372; ☎530-542-4637; www.cityofslt.us; Heavenly Village Transit Center, 4114 Lake Tahoe Blvd; ⏱9am-5pm) Interpretive exhibits and recreational and transportation information at a multipurpose 'urban trailhead.'

Lake Tahoe Visitors Authority (Map p372; ☎530-544-5255; www.tahoesouth.com; 3066 Lake Tahoe Blvd; ⏱9am-5pm) Tourist information, maps, brochures and money-saving coupons, with a second center in Stateline (☎800-288-2463; www.tahoesouth.com; 169 Hwy 50, Stateline, NV; ⏱9am-5pm Mon-Fri).

South Lake Tahoe Library (☎530-573-3185; www.eldoradolibrary.org/tahoe.htm; 1000 Rufus Allen Blvd; ⏱10am-8pm Tue & Wed, to 5pm Thu-Sat; ⏇) First-come, first-served free internet terminals.

Tahoe Urgent Care (☎530-553-4319; www.tahoeurgentcare.com; 2130 Lake Tahoe Blvd; ⏱8am-6pm) Walk-in medical clinic for nonemergencies.

USDA Lake Tahoe Basin Management Unit (Map p372; ☎530-543-2600; www.fs.usda.gov/ltbmu; 35 College Dr; ⏱8am-4:30pm Mon-Fri) Wilderness permits and camping and outdoor recreation information.

USFS Taylor Creek Visitor Center (Map p372; ☎530-543-2674; www.fs.usda.gov/ltbmu; Visitor Center Rd, off Hwy 89; ⏱8am-5:30pm late May-Oct) Outdoor information, wilderness permits and daily ranger-led walks and talks during July and August.

❶ Getting There & Away

From Reno-Tahoe International Airport, **South Tahoe Express** (☎866-898-2463, 775-325-8944; www.southtahoeexpress.com; adult/child 4-12yr one way $30/17) operates several daily shuttle buses to Stateline casinos; the journey takes 75 minutes up to two hours.

Amtrak (☑ 800-872-7245; www.amtrak.com) has a daily Thruway bus service between Sacramento and South Lake Tahoe ($34, 2½ hours), stopping at the South Y Transit Center.

❶ Getting Around

South Lake Tahoe's main transportation hubs are the **South Y Transit Center** (Map p372; 1000 Emerald Bay Rd/Hwy 89; just south of the 'Y' intersection of Hwys 50 and 89; and the more central **Stateline Transit Center** (Map p372; 4114 Lake Tahoe Blvd).

BlueGO (☑ 530-541-7149; www.tahoetransportation.org; fare/day pass $2/5) local buses operate year-round from 6am to 11pm daily, stopping all along Hwy 50 between the two transit centers.

On summer weekends, BlueGo's **Emerald Bay Trolley** (www.tahoetransportation.org; fare $2) heads north from the South Y Transit Center to the Vikingsholm and Eagle Falls parking lot at Emerald Bay, but confirm the schedule as it changes from year to year. During winter ski season, BlueGO provides free and frequent shuttle service from Stateline and South Lake Tahoe to all Heavenly base operations every 30 minutes from stops along Hwy 50, Ski Run Blvd and Pioneer Trail.

WESTERN SHORE

Lake Tahoe's densely forested western shore, between Emerald Bay and Tahoe City, is idyllic. Hwy 89 sinuously wends past gorgeous state parks with swimming beaches, hiking trails, pine-shaded campgrounds and historic mansions. Several trailheads also access the rugged splendor of the Desolation Wilderness.

All campgrounds and many businesses shut down between November and May. Hwy 89 often closes after snowfall for plowing or due to imminent avalanche danger. Once you drive its tortuous slopeside curves, you'll understand why. The further south you are, the more of a roller coaster it is, no matter the season – so grip that steering wheel!

Emerald Bay State Park

Sheer granite cliffs and a jagged shoreline hem in glacier-carved **Emerald Bay** (Map p368; ☑ 530-541-6498; www.parks.ca.gov; per car $10; ⊙ late May-Sep), a teardrop cove that

DON'T MISS

TAHOE RIM TRAIL

Partly paralleling the Pacific Crest Trail, the 165-mile **Tahoe Rim Trail** (www.tahoerimtrail.org) wraps around the lofty ridges and mountaintops of the Lake Tahoe Basin. Hikers, equestrians and – in some sections – mountain bikers can enjoy inspirational views of the lake and the snowcapped Sierra Nevada while tracing the footsteps of early pioneers, Basque shepherds and Washoe tribespeople. Dozens of marked trailheads all around the lakeshore provide easy access points for hikers, bikers and horseback riders.

Covering the entire basin, the **Lake Tahoe Basin Trail Map** (www.adventuremaps.net) is the best guide for hikers, bikers and cross-country skiers.

will have you digging for your camera. Its most captivating aspect is the water, which changes from cloverleaf green to light jade depending on the angle of the sun.

◉ Sights

You'll spy panoramic pullouts all along Hwy 89, including at **Inspiration Point** (Map p368), opposite USFS Bayview Campground. Just south, the road shoulder evaporates on both sides of a steep drop-off, revealing a postcard-perfect view of Emerald Bay to the north and Cascade Lake to the south.

The mesmerizing blue-green waters of the bay frame **Fannette Island**. This uninhabited granite speck, Lake Tahoe's only island, holds the vandalized remains of a tiny 1920s teahouse belonging to heiress Lora Knight, who would occasionally motorboat guests to the island from **Vikingsholm Castle** (Map p368; tour adult/child $10/8; ⊙ 11am-4pm late May–Sep), her Scandinavian-style mansion on the bay. The focal point of the state park, Vikingsholm Castle is a rare example of ancient Scandinavian-style architecture. Completed in 1929, it has trippy design elements aplenty, including sod-covered roofs that sprout wildflowers in late spring. The mansion is reached by a steep 1-mile trail, which also leads to a visitors center.

🏃 Activities & Tours

Hiking

Vikingsholm Castle is the southern terminus of the famous Rubicon Trail (p382).

Two popular trailheads lead into the Desolation Wilderness. From the Eagle Falls parking lot ($5), the **Eagle Falls Trail** (Map p368) travels one steep mile to Eagle Lake, crossing by Eagle Falls along the way. This scenic short hike often gets choked with visitors, but crowds disappear quickly as the trail continues up to the Tahoe Rim Trail and Velma, Dicks and Fontanillis Lakes (up to 10 miles round-trip).

From the back of USFS Bayview Campground, it's a steep 1-mile climb to glacial Granite Lake or a moderate 1.5-mile round-trip to Cascade Falls, which rushes with snowmelt in early summer.

Boating

Fannette Island is accessible by boat, except during Canada goose nesting season (typically February to mid-June). Rent boats at Meeks Bay or South Lake Tahoe; from the latter, you can also catch narrated bay cruises or speedboat tours.

Scuba Diving

Divers prepared for chilly high altitude plunges can explore sunken barges, a submerged rockslide and artifacts at a historic dumping ground at the unique Underwater State Parks of Emerald Bay and DL Bliss State Park. Reno-based **Sierra Diving Center** (*www.sierradive.com*) and *Adventure Scuba Center* (www.renoscuba.com) offer classes and trips.

🛏 Sleeping

Eagle Point Campground   CAMPGROUND $
(Map p368; ☎ 530-525-7277, reservations 800-444-7275; www.reserveamerica.com; Hwy 89; tent & RV sites $35; ☻ mid-Jun–early Sep) With over 90 sites perched on the tip of Eagle Point, this state-park campground provides flush toilets, hot pay-showers, beach access and bay views. Another 20 scattered sites are reserved for boat-in campers.

USFS Bayview Campground   CAMPGROUND $
(Map p368; Hwy 89; tent & RV sites $15; ☻ Jun-Sep; ☻) This rustic, nay, primitive forest-service campground has 13 no-reservation sites and vault toilets, but its potable water supplies are often exhausted sometime in July. It's opposite Inspiration Point.

DL Bliss State Park

Emerald Bay State Park spills over into **DL Bliss State Park** (Map p368; ☎ 530-525-7277;

www.parks.ca.gov; per car $10; ☻ late May–Sep; ♿), which has the western shore's most alluring beaches at **Lester Cove** and **Calawee Cove**. A half-mile round-trip nature trail leads to **Balancing Rock**, a 130-ton chunk of granite perched on a natural pedestal. Pick up an interpretive trail guide to park ecology and wildlife from the **visitor center** (☻ 8am-5pm) near the entrance.

Near Calawee Cove is the northern terminus of the scenic one-way **Rubicon Trail** (Map p368), which ribbons along the lakeshore for 4.5 mostly gentle miles from Vikingsholm Castle (add one mile for the downhill walk to the castle from Hwy 89) in Emerald Bay State Park. It leads past small coves perfect for taking a cooling dip, and treats you to great views along the way. Add an extra mile to loop around and visit the restored historic lighthouse, a square wood-enclosed beacon (that looks a lot like an outhouse) constructed by the Coast Guard in 1916. Poised above 6800ft, it's the USA's highest-elevation lighthouse.

The park's **campground** (Map p368; ☎ 800-444-7275; www.reserveamerica.com; tent & RV sites $35-45, hike-and-bike sites $7; ☻ mid-May–Sep; ☻) has 145 sites, including some coveted spots near the beach, along with flush toilets, hot pay-showers, picnic tables, fire rings and an RV dump station.

The small visitor parking lot at Calawee Cove usually fills up by 10am, in which case it's a 2-mile walk from the park entrance to the beach. Alternatively, ask park staff at the entrance station about closer access points to the Rubicon Trail.

Meeks Bay

With a wide sweep of shoreline, sleek and shallow **Meeks Bay** has warm water by Tahoe standards and is fringed by a beautiful, but busy, sandy beach. On the west side of the highway, a few hundred feet north of the fire station, is another **trailhead** for the Desolation Wilderness. A moderate, mostly level and nicely shaded path parallels Meeks Creek before kicking off more steeply uphill through the forest to **Lake Genevieve** (9 miles round-trip), **Crag Lake** (10 miles round-trip) and other backcountry ponds, all surrounded by scenic Sierra peaks.

🛏 Sleeping & Eating

USFS Meeks Bay Campground   CAMPGROUND $
(Map p368; ☎ 530-525-4733, reservations 877-444-6777; www.recreation.gov; tent & RV sites

$27-29; ⊗mid-May–mid-Oct) This developed campground offers 36 reservable sites along the beach, along with flush toilets, picnic tables and fire rings. For pay showers, head to Meeks Bay Resort next door.

Meeks Bay Resort CABINS, CAMPGROUND **$$**
(Map p368; ☑530-525-6946; www.meeksbayresort.com; 7941 Emerald Bay Rd/Hwy 89; tent/RV sites with full hookups $30/50, cabins $125-400; ⊗May-Oct) The Washoe tribe offers various lodging options (cabins require minimum stays) plus kayak, canoe and paddleboat rentals. If you're hungry, swing by the waterfront grill or small market, which stocks limited groceries and camping, fishing and beach gear, as well as Native American crafts and cultural books.

Ed Z'berg Sugar Pine Point State Park

About 10 miles south of Tahoe City, this woodsy state park (Map p368; ☑530-525-7982; www.parks.ca.gov; per car $10) occupies a promontory blanketed by a fragrant mix of pine, juniper, aspen and fir. It has a swimming beach, over a dozen miles of hiking trails and abundant fishing in General Creek. A paved cycling path travels north to Tahoe City. In winter, 12 miles of groomed cross-country trails await inside the park; book ahead for ranger-guided full-moon **snowshoe tours** (☑530-525-9920; adult/child under 12yr incl snowshoe rental $25/free). In summer, the park offers kayak and hiking tours through the **Sierra State Parks Foundation** (www.sierrastateparks.org).

Historic sights include the modest 1872 **cabin** (Map p368) of William 'General' Phipps, an early Tahoe settler, and the considerably grander 1903 Queen Anne–style **Hellman-Ehrman Mansion** (Map p368; tours adult/youth 7-17yr $10/8; ⊗10:30am-3:30pm mid-Jun–Sep), an elegant lakefront house also known as Pine Lodge. Guided tours take in the richly detailed interior, including marble fireplaces, leaded-glass windows and period furnishings.

The park's secluded **General Creek Campground** (Map p368; ☑800-444-7275; www.reserveamerica.com; tent & RV sites $25-35; ⊗late May–mid-Sep) has 120 fairly spacious, pine-shaded sites, plus flush toilets and hot pay-showers; a dozen sites stay open year-round (but without showers).

Tahoma

Another blink-and-you'll-miss-it lakeside outpost, Tahoma has a post office and a handful of places to stay and eat.

Cute but not too kitschy, the red cabins of **Tahoma Meadows Bed & Breakfast Cottages** (☑530-525-1553; www.tahomameadows.com; 6821 W Lake Blvd, Tahoma; cottages incl breakfast $99-389; ☞☜) dot a pine grove. Each has classy country decor, thick down comforters, a small TV, and bathrooms with clawfoot tubs. Pick up the in-room journal to record your impressions while you're toasting your feet by the gas-burning fireplace. Pet fee $20 per night.

Nearby, the **PDQ Market** (6890 W Lake Blvd; ⊗6:30am-10pm) has groceries and a deli. Laying claim to being Tahoe's oldest bar, lakeside **Chamber's Landing** (☑530-525-9190; 6400 W Lake Blvd; ⊗noon-8pm Jun-Sep) sees the biggest crowds descend for drinks and appetizers in the all-day bar, especially during happy hour. Do yourself a favor and skip the 'Chamber's Punch,' though.

Homewood

This quiet hamlet is popular with summertime boaters and, in winter, skiers and snowboarders. **West Shore Sports** (☑530-525-9920; www.westshoresports.com; 5395 W Lake Blvd; ⊗8am-5pm) rents bicycles, kayaks, stand-up paddleboarding gear and snowsports equipment including skis, snowboards and snowshoes.

🛏 Sleeping & Eating

USFS Kaspian Campground CAMPGROUND **$**
(Map p368; ☑877-444-6777; www.recreation.gov; tent sites $19-21; ⊗mid-May–mid-Oct) The closest campground is this nine-site, tent-only spot set among ponderosa and fir trees; amenities include flush toilets, picnic tables and fire rings.

West Shore Inn INN **$$$**
(☑530-525-5200; www.westshorecafe.com; 5160 W Lake Blvd; r/ste incl breakfast from $199/349; ☀☜) Oriental rugs and Arts and Crafts decor give this luxurious six-room inn a classic, aged ambience, and the lake's so close you feel like you could dive in. It's an upscale mountain lodge where crisp, modern suites feel decadent, and each has a fireplace and lake-view balcony. Rates include

complimentary use of bicycles, kayaks and stand-up paddleboards.

West Shore Café
CALIFORNIAN, AMERICAN $$$

(☑ 530-525-5200; www.westshorecafe.com; 5160 W Lake Blvd; mains $12-33; ⊙ 11am-9:30pm mid-Jun–Sep, 5-9:30pm Oct–mid-Jun) At the West Shore Inn's cozy destination restaurant, chef Mike Davis whips up worthy meals using fresh produce and ranched meats, from juicy burgers to Arctic char with spaghetti squash and hedgehog mushrooms. Dinner reservations recommended.

Sunnyside

Sunnyside is yet another lakeshore hamlet that may be just a dot on the map, but that has a couple of detour-worthy restaurants. To work off all that dang-good eating, rent a bicycle from another outpost of **West Shore Sports** (☑ 530-583-9920; www.westshoresports.com; 1785 W Lake Blvd), where you can get the scoop on all sorts of local outdoor information. You can pedal all the way north to Tahoe City along the paved bike path, or rent a stand-up paddleboarding set and hit the popular local beaches.

🛏 Sleeping & Eating

USFS William Kent Campground
CAMPGROUND $

(Map p368; ☑ 877-444-6777; www.recreation.gov; Hwy 89; tent & RV sites $27-29; ⊙ mid-May–mid-Oct) About 2 miles south of Tahoe City, this roadside campground offers over 85 nicely shaded, but cramped, sites that often fill up. Amenities include flush toilets, picnic tables and fire rings, along with swimming beach access.

Sunnyside Lodge
INN $$$

(☑ 530-583-7200; www.sunnysidetahoe.com; 1850 W Lake Blvd; d incl breakfast $150-380; ☏ 🐾) This recently upgraded lodge features modern rooms with new bathrooms, pillowtop mattresses and flat-screen TVs, afternoon tea and cookies, and a guests-only sitting room overlooking the lake. The less expensive 'garden view' rooms lack good lake views. Note that there's lots of activity from the restaurant and boat dock and the marina next door. Pet fee $35.

★ Fire Sign Cafe
AMERICAN $

(www.firesigncafe.com; 1785 W Lake Blvd; mains $7-13; ⊙ 7am-3pm; 🅿️🐾) For breakfast, everyone heads to the friendly Fire Sign for down-home omelets, blueberry pancakes, eggs Benedict with smoked salmon, fresh made-from-scratch pastries and other carbo-loading bombs, plus organic coffee. In summer, hit the outdoor patio. Lines are usually very long, so get there early.

Spoon
AMERICAN $$

(☑ 530-581-5400; www.spoontakeout.com; 1785 W Lake Blvd; mains $9.50-15; ⊙ 3-9pm, closed Tue & Wed Oct-May; 🅿️) Call ahead for takeout, or squeeze yourselves into the cozy upstairs dining room at this little slat-sided cabin by the side of the highway. Barbecue tri-tip beef sandwiches, roasted veggies, soups, baked pastas and chicken enchiladas are the comfort-food staples, with brownies and ice cream for dessert.

Sunnyside Restaurant
CALIFORNIAN $$

(☑ 530-583-7200; www.sunnysidetahoe.com; 1850 W Lake Blvd; mains lunch $9.50-13, dinner $16-35) Classic and innovative contemporary takes on steak and seafood – think porterhouse pork with cherry chutney or roasted chicken with braised fennel – pervade the lakeside dining room. In summer you'll probably have more fun doing lunch – or drinks with the signature zucchini sticks and a piece of hula pie – on the huge lakefront deck.

❶ Getting There & Around

From Tahoma, **Tahoe Area Rapid Transit** (TART; ☑ 530-550-1212; www.placer.ca.gov/tart; single/day pass $2/4; ⊙ 7am-6pm) buses stop hourly at Ed Z'berg Sugar Pine Point State Park, Homewood and Sunnyside year-round, continuing north to Tahoe City and the north shore.

Also, in summertime, the **North Lake Tahoe Water Shuttle** (☑ 530-581-8707; www.northlaketahoewatershuttle.com; one way adult/child under 11yr $10/7) operates a half dozen daily trips between Tahoe Vista and Homewood/West Shore Café (30 minutes). Reserve ahead; bikes permitted.

TAHOE CITY

The north shore's commercial hub, Tahoe City straddles the junction of Hwys 89 and 28, making it almost inevitable that you'll find yourself breezing through here at least once during your round-the-lake sojourn. The town is handy for grabbing food and supplies and renting sports gear. It's also the closest lake town to Squaw Valley. The main drag, N Lake Blvd, is chockablock with outdoor outfitters, touristy shops and cafes.

⊙ Sights

Gatekeeper's Museum & Marion Steinbach Indian Basket Museum   MUSEUM
(☏ 530-583-1762; www.northtahoemuseums.org; 130 W Lake Blvd/Hwy 89; adult/child under 13yr $5/ free; ⊙ 10am-5pm daily late May-Sep, 11am-4pm Fri & Sat Oct-Apr) In a reconstructed log cabin close to town, this museum has a small but fascinating collection of Tahoe memorabilia, including Olympics history and relics from the early steamboat era and tourism explosion around the lake. In the museum's newer wing, uncover an exquisite array of Native American baskets collected from over 85 indigenous California tribes.

Fanny Bridge   BRIDGE
Just south of the always-jammed Hwy 89/28 traffic stoplight junction, the Truckee River flows through dam floodgates and passes beneath this bridge, cutely named for the most prominent feature of people leaning over the railings to look at fish (in American slang, 'fanny' means your rear end). The side facing the lake displays historical photos and hydrological facts.

Watson Cabin   MUSEUM
(☏ 530-583-8717; www.northtahoemuseums.org; 560 N Lake Tahoe Blvd; adult/child under 13yr $2/ free; ⊙ noon-4pm Thu-Sun mid-Jun–early Sep) A few blocks east of the bridge over the Truckee River, this well-preserved 1908 settlers' cabin is one of the town's oldest buildings, built overlooking the beach.

🏃 Activities

Beaches & River Rafting
Though not an outstanding swimming area, **Commons Beach** is a small, attractive park with sandy and grassy areas, picnic tables, barbecue grills, a climbing rock and playground for kids, as well as free **summer concerts** (www.concertsatcommonsbeach.com) and outdoor movie nights. Leashed dogs welcome.

Truckee River Raft Rentals   RAFTING
(☏ 530-583-0123; www.truckeeriverraft.com; 185 River Rd; adult/child 6-12yr $30/25; ⊙ 8:30am-3:30pm Jun-Sep; 🖼) The Truckee River here is gentle and wide as it flows northwest from the lake – perfect for novice paddlers. This outfit rents rafts for the 5-mile float from Tahoe City to the River Ranch Lodge, including transportation back to town. Reservations strongly advised.

Hiking
Explore the fabulous trails of the **Granite Chief Wilderness** (Map p368) north and west of Tahoe City. For maps and trailhead directions, stop by the visitors center. Recommended day hikes include the moderately strenuous **Five Lakes Trail** (over 4 miles round-trip), which starts from Alpine Meadows Rd off Hwy 89 heading toward Squaw Valley, and the easy trek to **Paige Meadows**, leading onto the Tahoe Rim Trail. Paige Meadows is also good terrain for novice mountain bikers and for snowshoeing. Wilderness permits are not required, even for overnight trips, but free campfire permits are needed, even for gas stoves. Leashed dogs are allowed on these trails.

Cycling
The paved 4-mile **Truckee River Bike Trail** runs from Tahoe City toward Squaw Valley, while the multi-use **West Shore Bike Path** heads 9 miles south to Ed Z'berg Sugar Pine Point State Park, including highway shoulder and residential street sections. Both are fairly easy rides, but expect crowds on summer weekends. The whole family can rent bicycles from any of several shops along N Lake Blvd. Park and head out from the **64 Acres Park** trailhead behind the Tahoe City Transit Center. The excellent bike trail map of **Lake Tahoe Bicycle Coalition** (www.tahoebike.org) is also on its website.

Zip Lining
Tahoe Treetop Adventure Park   ZIP-LINING
(☏ 530-581-7563; www.tahoetreetop.com; 725 Granlibakken Rd, off Hwy 89; adult/child 5-12yr $45/35; ⊙ 10am-5:30pm Sat & Sun Jan-late May, 9am-7:30pm daily late May-Aug, reduced hours Sep-Dec; 🖼) At the Granlibakken resort, take a 2.5-hour monkey-like romp between tree platforms connected by zip lines and swinging bridges. Various courses are geared to everyone from little kids (no more than 10ft off the ground) to daredevils (two 100ft zip lines and one that's 300ft). Reserve ahead.

Winter Sports
Tahoe City is within easy reach of a half dozen downhill and cross-country skiing and snowboarding resorts.

Tahoe Dave's   OUTDOOR OUTFITTER
(☏ 530-583-0400, 530-583-6415; www.tahoedaves.com; 590 N Lake Tahoe Blvd; ski & snowboad rentals per day from $29) The main regional outfitter, with additional branches at Squaw Valley, Kings Beach and Truckee (rentals

can be returned to any shop); reservations accepted.

🛏 Sleeping

If you show up without reservations, dingy, last-resort budget motels are along N Lake Blvd. For camping, head north to USFS campgrounds off Hwy 89 or south along Hwy 89 to state parks and small towns along the lake's western shore.

Mother Nature's Inn
INN $$

(☑530-581-4278; www.mothernaturesinn.com; 551 N Lake Blvd; r $80-125; 🛜🐾) Right in town behind Cabin Fever knickknack boutique, this good-value option offers quiet motel-style rooms with a tidy country look, fridges and coffeemaker, eclectic furniture and comfy pillow-top mattresses. It's within walking distance of Commons Beach. Pet fee $15.

Pepper Tree Inn
MOTEL $$

(☑530-583-3711; www.peppertreetahoe.com; 645 N Lake Blvd; r incl breakfast $96-199; 🛜🐾) The tallest building in town, this somberly painted establishment redeems itself with some birds-eye lake views. Fairly comfortable modern rooms with that familiar log-cabin decor each have a microwave and mini fridge. Top-floor rooms with hot tubs are most in demand.

River Ranch Lodge
INN $$

(Map p368; ☑530-583-4264; www.riverranchlodge. com; Hwy 89 at Alpine Meadows Rd; r incl breakfast $115-190; 🛜🐾) Though there's some noise from traffic outside and the bar downstairs, request a river-facing room so you can drift off to dreamland as the Truckee River tumbles below your window. Rooms bulge with lodgepole-pine furniture; those upstairs have wistful balconies. Pet-friendly rooms available in summer only.

Granlibakken
LODGE $$

(☑530-583-4242; www.granlibakken.com; 725 Granlibakken Rd, off Hwy 89; r/ste from $150/242, 1-/2-/3-bedroom townhome from $330/409/516; 🛜🐾) Sleep old-school at this cross-country ski area and kitschy wedding and conference venue. Basic lodge rooms are spacious, but timeshare townhomes with kitchens, fireplaces and lofts can be a decent deal for families and groups. Amenities include tennis, a full spa, year-round outdoor pool and hot tub and winter shuttle service to Homewood.

✖ Eating & Drinking

Tahoe House Bakery
BAKERY $

(www.tahoe-house.com; 625 W Lake Blvd; items $2-10; ⊙6am-6pm; 🛜) Before you take off down the western shore for a bike ride or hike, drop by this mom-and-pop shop that opened in the 1970s. Their motto: 'While you sleep, we loaf.' Sweet cookies, European pastries, fresh-baked deli sandwiches and homemade salads and soups will keep you going all afternoon on the trail.

New Moon Natural Foods
DELI, GROCERY $

(505 W Lake Blvd; mains $6-12; ⊙9am-8pm Mon-Sat, 10am-7pm Sun; ☑) 🌱 A tiny but well-stocked natural-foods store, its gem of a deli concocts scrumptious ethnic food to go, all packaged in biodegradable and compostable containers. Try the Thai salad with organic greens and spicy peanut sauce.

Dam Cafe
CAFE $

(55 W Lake Blvd; mains $6-11; ⊙6am-3pm) Right by the Truckee River dam and the Fanny Bridge, stash your bikes in the racks outside this cute cottage and walk inside for a breakfast burrito, ice-cream fruit smoothie or pick-me-up espresso.

Syd's Bagelry and Espresso
CAFE $

(550 N Lake Blvd; items $2-8.50; ⊙7am-5pm; 🛜) A handy spot on the main drag serves bagels and locally roasted coffee, plus smoothies and breakfast burritos made with organic produce.

★Dockside 700 Wine Bar & Grill
AMERICAN $$

(☑530-581-0303; www.dockside700.com; 700 N Lake Blvd; lunch $10-17, dinner $14-32; ⊙11:30am-8pm Mon-Thu, to 9pm Fri-Sun; 👶🐾) On a lazy summer afternoon, grab a table on the back deck that overlooks the boats bobbing at Tahoe City Marina. Barbecue chicken, ribs and steak light a fire under dinner (reservations advised), alongside seafood pastas and pizzas.

Fat Cat
CALIFORNIAN $$

(www.fatcattahoe.com; 599 N Tahoe Blvd; mains $9-14; ⊙11am-9pm, bar to 2am; 👶) Hitting that happy Goldilocks median – not too expensive, but not too cheap – this casual, family-run restaurant with local art splashed on the walls does it all: from-scratch soups, heaped salads, sandwiches, pasta bowls and plenty of fried munchies for friends to share. Look for live indie music on Friday and Saturday nights.

Rosie's Cafe
DINER $$

(www.rosiescafe.com; 571 N Lake Blvd; breakfast & lunch $7-14, dinner $14-20; ⊙7:30am-9:30pm; 🍴) With antique skis, shiny bikes and lots of pointy antlers belonging to stuffed wildlife mounted on the walls, this quirky place serves breakfast until 2:30pm. The all-American hodge-podge menu is all right, but the convivial atmosphere is a winner.

River Ranch Lodge
NEW AMERICAN $$$

(☎530-583-4264; www.riverranchlodge.com; Hwy 89 at Alpine Meadows Rd; mains patio & cafe $8-13, restaurant $22-30; ⊙lunch Jun-Sep, dinner year-round, call for seasonal hours) This riverside dining room is a popular stop, drawing rafters and bikers to its patio for summer barbecue lunches.

Bridgetender Tavern
PUB

(www.tahoebridgetender.com; 65 W Lake Blvd; ⊙11am-11pm, to midnight Fri & Sat) Après-ski crowds gather for beer, burgers and chili-cheese or garlic waffle fries (mains $8 to $14) at this woodsy bar. In summer, grab a seat on the open-air patio.

Tahoe Mountain Brewing Co.
BREWERY

(www.tahoebrewing.com; 475 N Lake Blvd; ⊙11:30am-10pm) Brewed in nearby Truckee, the Sugar Pine Porter, barrel-aged sours and award-winning Paddleboard Pale Ale here pair splendidly with sweet potato fries, burgers and other pub grub on the outdoor lake-facing patio.

ℹ Information

Tahoe City Downtown Association (www.visittahoecity.org) Tourist information and online events calendar.

Tahoe City Library (☎530-583-3382; Boatworks Mall, 740 N Lake Blvd; ⊙10am-5pm Tue & Thu, 11am-6pm Wed & Fri, 10am-2pm Sat; 🛜) Free wi-fi and walk-in internet terminals.

Tahoe City Visitors Information Center (☎530-581-6900; www.gotahoenorth.com; 100 N Lake Blvd; ⊙9am-5pm) At the Hwy 89/28 split.

Truckee Tahoe Medical Group (☎ext 3 530-581-8864; www.ttmg.net; Trading Post Center, 925 N Lake Blvd; ⊙9am-6pm Mon-Sat year-round, also 10am-5pm Sun Jul-early Sep) Walk-in clinic for nonemergencies.

ℹ Getting There & Around

Just south of the Hwy 28/89 split, the modern new **Tahoe City Transit Center** (www.nextbus.com/tahoe; 870 Cabin Creek Rd, off Hwy 89) is the main bus terminal, with a comfy waiting room. Behind it you'll find trailhead parking for the Tahoe Rim Trail and various bike path routes.

With a saucy acronym and reliable service, bike rack-equipped **Tahoe Area Rapid Transit** (TART; ☎530-550-1212; www.laketahoetransit.com; single/day pass $1.75/3.50) runs buses along the north shore as far as Incline Village, down the western shore to Ed Z'berg Sugar Pine Point State Park, and north to Squaw Valley and Truckee via Hwy 89. The main routes typically depart hourly from about 6am until 6pm daily.

Between June and September, TART also operates the **Night Rider**, a free local bus service connecting Squaw Valley, Tahoe City, Carnelian Bay, Tahoe Vista, Kings Beach, Crystal Bay and Incline Village hourly from 7pm until about 1am. Two more free nighttime summer-only trolley routes loop between Tahoe City and Tahoma via Sunnyside and Homewood, and between Northstar, Kings Beach and Crystal Bay, every hour from 6:30pm until midnight or 1am daily.

SQUAW VALLEY

The nirvana of the north shore, Squaw Valley played host to the 1960 Olympic Winter Games and still ranks among the world's top ski resorts. The stunning setting amid granite peaks, though, makes it a superb destination in any season, and this deluxe family-friendly resort stays almost as busy in summer as in winter.

◉ Sights & Activities

Much of the summertime action centers on 8200ft **High Camp** (☎800-403-0206; www.squaw.com; cable-car adult/child 5-12yr/youth 13-22yr $39/15/25, all-access pass $46/19/38; ⊙11am-4:30pm; 📷), reached by a dizzying cable car (leashed dogs OK). At the top you'll find a heated seasonal outdoor swimming lagoon (adult/child $14/8), 18-hole disc-golf course (free), two high-altitude tennis courts (racquet rentals and ball purchase available), and a roller-skating rink (adult/child $14/8) that doubles as an ice-skating rink in winter. Cable-car tickets include admission to the **Olympic Museum**, which relives those magic moments from 1960.

Several hiking trails radiate out from High Camp, or try the lovely, moderate **Shirley Lake Trail** (round-trip 5 miles), which follows a sprightly creek to waterfalls, granite boulders and abundant wildflowers. It starts at the mountain base, near the end of Squaw Peak Rd, behind the cable-car building. Leashed dogs are allowed.

THE DOOMED DONNER PARTY

In the 19th century, tens of thousands of people migrated west along the Overland Trail with dreams of a better life in California. Among them was the ill-fated Donner Party.

When the families of George and Jacob Donner and their friend James Reed departed Springfield, IL, in April 1846 with six wagons and a herd of livestock, they intended to make the arduous journey as comfortable as possible. But the going was slow and, when other pioneers told them about a shortcut that would save 200 miles, they jumped at the chance.

However, there was no road for the wagons in the Wasatch Mountains, and most of the livestock succumbed under the merciless heat of the Great Salt Lake Desert. Arguments and fights broke out. James Reed killed a man, was kicked out of the group and left to trundle off to California alone. By the time the party reached the eastern foot of the Sierra Nevada, near present-day Reno, morale and food supplies ran dangerously low.

To restore their livestock's energy and reprovision, the emigrants decided to rest here for a few days. But an exceptionally fierce winter came early, quickly rendering what later came to be called Donner Pass impassable and forcing the pioneers to build basic shelter near today's Donner Lake. They had food to last a month and the fervent hope that the weather would clear by then. It didn't.

Snow fell for weeks, reaching a depth of 22ft. Hunting and fishing became impossible. In mid-December a small group of 15 made a desperate attempt to cross the pass. They quickly became disoriented and had to ride out a three-day storm that killed a number of them. One month later, less than half of the original group staggered into Sutter's Fort near Sacramento, having survived on one deer and their dead friends.

By the time the first rescue party arrived at Donner Lake in late February, the trapped pioneers were still surviving – barely – on boiled ox hides. But when the second rescue party, led by the banished James Reed, made it through in March, evidence of cannibalism was everywhere. Journals and reports tell of 'half-crazed people living in absolute filth, with naked, half-eaten bodies strewn about the cabins.' Many were too weak to travel.

When the last rescue party arrived in mid-April, only a sole survivor, Lewis Keseberg, was there to greet them. The rescuers found George Donner's body cleansed and wrapped in a sheet, but no sign of Tasmen Donner, George's wife. Keseberg admitted to surviving on the flesh of the dead, but denied charges that he had killed Tasmen for fresh meat. He spent the rest of his life trying to clear his name.

In the end, only 47 of the 89 members of the Donner Party survived. They settled in California, their lives forever changed by the harrowing winter at Donner Lake.

Other fun activities at the mountain base include a ropes course with zip lines, a climbing wall, mini golf and a Sky Jump (bungee trampoline), all operated by the **Squaw Valley Adventure Center** (☎530-583-7673; www.squawadventure.com). Golfers tee up at the 18-hole, par 71, Scottish-style links **Resort at Squaw Creek Golf Course** (☎530-583-6300; www.squawcreek.com; green fee incl cart $59-99); rental clubs are available.

🛏 Sleeping & Eating

For more resort hotel and condo lodging options, including ski-vacation packages, contact **Squaw Valley** (☎800-403-0206; www.squaw.com).

★ **PlumpJack Squaw Valley Inn** BOUTIQUE HOTEL $$$
(☎530-583-1576; www.plumpjacksquawvalleyinn.com; 1920 Squaw Valley Rd, Olympic Valley; r incl breakfast summer/winter $205-385/340-645; ❄@🖥❄🐕) Bed down at this artsy boutique hotel in the village, where every room has mountain views and extra-comfort factors like plush terry-cloth robes and slippers. Ski-in, ski-out access doesn't hurt either, but a $150 pet fee will. The chic **PlumpJack Cafe** (mains $24-45; ⏱7:30am-9:30pm), with its crisp linens and plush banquettes, serves seasonally inspired California cuisine with ace wines.

Wildflour Baking Company
BAKERY $

(www.wildfloursquaw.com; items $2-12; ⊘ 7am-5pm) Fresh-baked bread sandwiches and bagels make great breakfasts or afternoon snacks in the basement level of Squaw's Olympic House building. Baristas whip up Scharffenberger hot chocolate and brew Peet's coffee and teas.

Le Chamois & Loft Bar
PIZZERIA, PUB $$

(www.squawchamois.com; 1970 Squaw Valley Rd; mains $7-17; ⊘ 11am-6pm Mon-Fri, to 8pm Sat & Sun, bar open to 9pm or 10pm; 🖼 🖼) For a social bite after shedding your bindings, this slopeside favorite is handily positioned between the cable-car building and the rental shop. Slide on over to devour a hot sammy or pizza and a beer with eye-pleasing mountain views.

ⓘ Getting There & Away

The village at Squaw Valley, at the base of the mountain cable-car, is about a 20-minute drive from Tahoe City or Truckee via Hwy 89 (turn off at Squaw Valley Rd).

Tahoe Area Rapid Transit (TART; 📞 530-550-1212; www.laketahoetransit.com; single/day pass $1.75/3.50) buses between Truckee and Tahoe City, Kings Beach and Crystal Bay stop at Squaw Valley every hour or so between 6am and 5pm daily, with a free morning ski shuttle from December to April.

TRUCKEE & DONNER LAKE

Cradled by mountains and the Tahoe National Forest, Truckee is a thriving town steeped in Old West history. It was put on the map by the railroad, grew rich on logging and ice harvesting, and even had its brush with Hollywood during the 1924 filming of Charlie Chaplin's *The Gold Rush*. Today, tourism fills much of the city's coffers, thanks to a well-preserved historical downtown and its proximity to Lake Tahoe and no fewer than six downhill and four cross-country ski resorts.

◉ Sights

The aura of the Old West still lingers over Truckee's teensy one-horse downtown, where railroad workers and lumberjacks once milled about in raucous saloons, bawdy brothels and shady gambling halls. Most of the late-19th-century buildings now contain restaurants and upscale boutiques. Donner Memorial State Park and Donner Lake, a busy recreational hub, are another 3 miles further west.

Donner Memorial State Park
PARK

(Map p368; www.parks.ca.gov; Donner Pass Rd; per car $8; ⊘ museum 10am-5pm, closed Tue & Wed Sep-May; 🖼) At the eastern end of Donner Lake, this state-run park occupies one of the sites where the doomed Donner Party got trapped during the fateful winter of 1846–47. Though its history is gruesome, the park is gorgeous and has a sandy beach, picnic tables, hiking trails and wintertime cross-country skiing and snowshoeing. The entry fee includes admission to the excellent **Emigrant Trail Museum**, which has fascinating, if admittedly macabre historical exhibits and a 25-minute film re-enacting the Donner Party's horrific plight.

The new and more multicultural **High Sierra Crossing Museum** sits completed across the parking lot; it's scheduled to replace the other museum when funding becomes available. Outside, the **Pioneer Monument** has a 22ft pedestal – the exact depth of the snow piles that horrendous winter. A short trail leads to a memorial at one family's cabin site.

Old Jail
HISTORIC BUILDING

(www.truckeehistory.org; 10142 Jiboom St, cnr Spring St; suggested donation $2; ⊘ 11am-4pm Sat & Sun late May & mid-Jun–mid-Sep) Continuously in use until the 1960s, this 1875 red-brick building is filled with relics from the wild days of yore. George 'Machine Gun' Kelly was reportedly once held here for shoplifting at a local variety store, and 'Baby Face' Nelson and 'Ma' Spinelli and her gang did time here, too.

🏃 Activities

Northstar Mountain Bike Park
MOUNTAIN BIKING

(www.northstarcalifornia.com; 5001 Northstar Drive, off Hwy 267; lift ticket adult/child 9-12yr $50/31; ⊘ Jun-Sep) Sure, there's great cross-country here, but the downhill at this lift-serviced ski resort brings on the adrenaline with lots of intermediate and expert single-track and fire roads. Over 100 miles of trails; bikes and body armor rental available.

Back Country
OUTDOOR OUTFITTER

(📞 530-582-0909; www.thebackcountry.net; 11400 Donner Pass Rd; ⊘ 8am-6pm, call ahead in winter

& spring) Rents bicycles and snowshoes, and rents and sells new and used climbing gear, as well as backcountry ski gear.

Truckee Sports Exchange OUTDOOR OUTFITTER
(☑530-582-4510; www.truckeesportsexchange.com; 10095 W River St; ⊘8am-8pm) Rents bicycles, kayaks and stand-up paddleboard gear as well as skis and winter backcountry gear.

Beaches & Water Sports

Warmer than Lake Tahoe, tree-lined **Donner Lake** is great for swimming, boating, fishing (license required), waterskiing and windsurfing.

West End Beach SWIMMING
(www.tdrpd.com; adult/child $4/3; 🚸) This Donner Lake beach is popular with families for its roped-off swimming area, snack stand, volleyball nets, and kayak, paddleboat and stand-up paddleboard rentals.

Tributary Whitewater Tours RAFTING
(☑530-346-6812; www.whitewatertours.com; half-day trip per adult/child 7-17yr $69/62; 🚸) From roughly mid-May through September, this long-running outfitter operates a 7-mile, half-day rafting run on the Truckee River over Class III+ rapids that will thrill kids and their nervous parents alike.

Hiking & Climbing

Truckee is a great base for treks in the **Tahoe National Forest** (Map p368), especially around **Donner Summit**. One popular 5-mile hike reaches the summit of 8243ft **Mt Judah** for awesome views of Donner Lake and the surrounding peaks. A longer, more strenuous ridge-crest hike (part of the Pacific Crest Trail) links **Donner Pass** to Squaw Valley (15 miles each way) skirting the base of prominent peaks, but you'll need two cars for this shuttle hike.

Donner Summit is also a major rock-climbing mecca, with over 300 traditional and sport-climbing routes. To learn the ropes, so to speak, take a class with **Alpine Skills International** (☑530-582-9170; www.alpineskills.com; 11400 Donner Pass Rd).

☞ Tours

Tahoe Adventure Company ADVENTURE SPORTS
(☑530-913-9212; www.tahoeadventurecompany.com; tours per person from $55) A great option for guided Sierra adventures. Staff know the backcountry inside out and can customize any outing to your interest and skill level, from kayaking, hiking, mountain biking and rock climbing to any combination thereof. They also offer full-moon snowshoe tours, and stand-up paddleboarding lessons and guided lake paddles.

🛏 Sleeping

A few dependable midrange chain motels and hotels are found off I-80 exits. A new **hostel** (www.truckeehostel.com) is in the works behind the train station.

Clair Tappaan Lodge HOSTEL $
(☑530-426-3632; www.sierraclub.org; 19940 Donner Pass Rd, Norden; dm incl meals adult/child from $65/45) 🌿 About a mile west of Sugar Bowl, this cozy Sierra Club–owned rustic mountain lodge puts you near major ski resorts and sleeps up to 140 people in dorms and family rooms. Rates include family-style meals, but you're expected to do small chores and bring your own sleeping bag, towel and swimsuit (for the hot tub!).

In winter, go cross-country skiing or snowshoeing, or careen down the sledding hill out back.

Donner Memorial State Park Campground CAMPGROUND $
(Map p368; ☑530-582-7894, reservations 800-444-7275; www.reserveamerica.com; tent & RV sites $35, hike-and-bike sites $7; ⊘late May-late Sep) Near Donner Lake, this family-oriented campground has 138 campsites with flush toilets and hot pay-showers.

USFS Campgrounds CAMPGROUND $
(☑518-885-3639; www.recreation.gov; campsites $17-48; 🚸) Conveniently located along Hwy 89 (though with street noise) are three minimally developed riverside camping areas: Granite Flat, Goose Meadow and Silver Creek. All have potable water and vault toilets.

Truckee Hotel HISTORIC HOTEL $$
(☑530-587-4444; www.truckeehotel.com; 10007 Bridge St; r incl breakfast with shared bath $59-149, with private bath $129-179; 🐾) Tucked behind an atmospheric four-story red-brick street front arcade, Truckee's most historic abode has welcomed weary travelers since 1873. A recent remodel has updated the carpets and furniture to genteel Victorian-infused modern luxury. Parking available across the street. Expect some train noise and no elevator.

Truckee Donner Lodge HOTEL $$
(☑530-582-9999; www.truckeedonnerlodge.com; 10527 Cold Stream Rd, off I-80 exit Donner Pass

Rd; r incl breakfast $84-204; ❄❅⚏) Just west of Hwy 89, this ex–Holiday Inn property gives you easy driving access to area ski resorts, shaving time off your morning commute to the slopes. No-nonsense, spacious hotel rooms come with microwaves and mini-fridges, and some have gas fireplaces. The hot-and-cold continental breakfast bar is complimentary.

River Street Inn
B&B $$

(✆530-550-9290; www.riverstreetinntruckee.com; 10009 E River St; r incl breakfast $145-210; ☎) On the far side of the tracks, this sweet 1885 Victorian in Truckee's historic downtown has 11 rooms that blend nostalgic touches like clawfoot tubs with down comforters, but have few amenities other than TVs. Mingle with other guests over breakfast in the lounge. Bring earplugs to dull the occasional train noise.

★Cedar House Sport Hotel
BOUTIQUE HOTEL $$$

(Map p368; ✆530-582-5655; www.cedarhousesporthotel.com; 10918 Brockway Rd; r incl breakfast $180-280; @☎⚏) 🐾 This chic, environmentally conscious contemporary lodge aims at getting folks out into nature. It boasts countertops made from recycled paper, 'rain chains' that redistribute water from the green roof garden, low-flow plumbing and in-room recycling. However, it doesn't skimp on plush robes, sexy platform beds with pillow-top mattresses, flat-screen TVs or the outdoor hot tub. Pet fee $75.

Guided tours and multisport outdoor adventures can be arranged in-house.

Hotel Truckee-Tahoe
HOTEL $$$

(✆530-587-4525; www.hoteltruckeetahoe.com; 11331 Brockway Rd; r incl breakfast $189-229; ❄@☎⚏) Forget about retro ski-lodge kitsch as you cozy up inside these crisp, earth-toned and down-to-earth hotel rooms that abound in sunny, natural woods. Sink back onto the feather-topped mattresses, refresh yourself with spa-quality bath amenities or hit the seasonal outdoor heated pool by the hot tub. Pet fee $50.

✗ Eating & Drinking

Coffeebar
CAFE $

(www.coffeebartruckee.com; 10120 Jiboom St; items $3-9; ⏱6am-10pm; ☎) 🐾 This beatnik, bare-bones industrial coffee shop serves Italian gelato, delectable pastries and home-brewed kombucha. Go for tantalizing breakfast crepes and overstuffed panini on herbed focaccia bread, or for a jolt of organic espresso or specialty tea blends.

Squeeze In
DINER $$

(www.squeezein.com; 10060 Donner Pass Rd; mains $8-15; ⏱7am-2pm; 🖐) Across from the Amtrak station, this snug locals' favorite dishes up breakfasts big enough to feed a lumberjack. Over 60 varieties of humungous omelets – along with burgers, burritos and big salads – are dished up in this funky place crammed with silly tchotchkes and colorful handwritten notes plastered on the walls.

Burger Me
BURGERS $$

(www.burgermetruckee.com; 10418 Donner Pass Rd; burgers $6.50-12.50; ⏱11am-9pm; 🖐) Getting two thumbs up from Food Network punk Guy Fieri may have gone to these guys' heads, but this fresh take on a burger shop still stocks all-natural meats and farm-fresh vegetables in the kitchen. Try the 'Trainwreck' – a beef patty topped with cheddar cheese, onion rings, turkey chili and a fried egg – if you dare. Gluten-free buns available.

★Moody's Bistro & Lounge
CALIFORNIAN $$$

(✆530-587-8688; www.moodysbistro.com; 10007 Bridge St; lunch mains $12-18, dinner mains $13-32; ⏱11:30am-9:30pm) 🐾 With its sophisticated supper-club looks and live jazz (Thursday to Saturday evenings), this gourmet restaurant in the Truckee oozes urbane flair. Only fresh, organic and locally grown ingredients make it into the chef's perfectly pitched concoctions like pork loin with peach barbecue sauce, roasted beets with shaved fennel or pan-roasted Arctic char.

Stella
CALIFORNIAN $$$

(Map p368; ✆530-582-5665; www.cedarhousesporthotel.com; 10918 Brockway Rd; mains $28-59; ⏱5:30-8:30pm Wed-Sun) 🐾 Housed at the trendy Cedar House Sport Hotel, this modern mountain-lodge dining room elevates Truckee's dining scene with Californian flair, harmonizing Asian and Mediterranean influences on its seasonal menu of housemade pastas, grilled meats and pan-roasted seafood. Bonuses: veggies grown on-site, housemade artisan bread and a killer wine list.

Fifty Fifty Brewing Co
BREWERY

(www.fiftyfiftybrewing.com; 11197 Brockway Rd; ⏱11:30am-11:30pm) Inhale the aroma of toasting grains at this brewpub south of downtown, near the Hwy 267 intersection. Sip the popular Donner Party Porter or Eclipse barrel-aged imperial stout while noshing a huge plate of nachos or other pub grub.

ℹ Information

Tahoe Forest Hospital (☎ 530-587-6011; www.tfhd.com; 10121 Pine Ave, cnr Donner Pass Rd; ⊙ 24hr) Emergency room, specializing in sports injuries.

Truckee Donner Chamber of Commerce (☎ 530-587-2757; www.truckee.com; 10065 Donner Pass Rd; computer access per 15 min $3; ⊙ 9am-6pm; 🛜) Inside the Amtrak train depot; free walking-tour maps and wi-fi.

USFS Truckee District Ranger Station (☎ 530-587-3558; www.fs.usda.gov/tahoe; 10811 Stockrest Springs Rd, off I-80 exit 188; ⊙ 8am-5pm Mon-Sat, Mon-Fri in winter) Tahoe National Forest information.

ℹ Getting There & Around

Truckee straddles the I-80 and is connected to the lakeshore via Hwy 89 to Tahoe City or Hwy 267 to Kings Beach. The main drag through downtown Truckee is Donner Pass Rd, where you'll find the Amtrak train depot and metered on-street parking. Brockway Rd begins south of the river, connecting over to Hwy 267.

Though the Truckee Tahoe Airport has no commercial air service, **North Lake Tahoe Express** (☎ 866-216-5222; www.northlaketahoeexpress.com; one way/round-trip $45/85) shuttles to the closest airport at Reno. Buses make several runs daily from 3:30am to midnight, serving multiple northern and western shore towns and Northstar and Squaw Valley ski resorts. Make reservations in advance.

Greyhound (☎ 800-231-2222; www.greyhound.com) has twice-daily buses to Reno ($15, one hour), Sacramento ($40, 2½ hours) and San Francisco ($35, 5½ to six hours). Greyhound buses stop at the train depot, as do **Amtrak** (☎ 800-872-7245; www.amtrak.com) Thruway buses and the daily *California Zephyr* train to Reno ($16, 1½ hours), Sacramento ($41, 4½ hours) and Emeryville/San Francisco ($47, 6½ hours).

Truckee Transit (☎ 530-587-7451; www.laketahoetransit.com; single/day pass $2.50/5) links the Amtrak train depot with Donner Lake hourly from 9am to 5pm Monday through Saturday. For Tahoe City and other towns on the lake's north, west or east shores, hop on the TART bus at the train depot. Single-ride TART tickets cost $1.75 (day pass $3.50). During ski season, additional buses run to many area ski resorts.

NORTHERN SHORE

Northeast of Tahoe City, Hwy 28 cruises through a string of cute, low-key towns, many fronting superb sandy beaches, with reasonably priced roadside motels and hotels all crowded together along the lakeshore. Oozing old-fashioned charm, the north shore is a blissful escape from the teeming crowds of South Lake Tahoe, Tahoe City and Truckee, but still puts you within easy reach of winter ski resorts and snow parks, summertime swimming, kayaking, hiking trails and more.

The **North Lake Tahoe Visitors' Bureau** (☎ 888-434-1262; www.gotahoenorth.com) can help get you oriented, although their closest walk-in office is at Incline Village, NV.

Tahoe Vista

Pretty little Tahoe Vista has more **public beaches** (www.northtahoeparks.com) than any other lakeshore town. Sandy strands along Hwy 28 include small but popular **Moon Dunes Beach**, with picnic tables and firepits opposite the Rustic Cottages; **North Tahoe Beach** (7860 N Lake Blvd), near the Hwy 267 intersection, with picnic facilities, barbecue grills and beach volleyball courts; **Tahoe Vista Recreation Area** (7010 N Lake Blvd; parking $10), a locals' favorite with a small grassy area and marina; and the **Tahoe Adventure Company** (☎ 530-913-9212; www.tahoeadventurecompany.com) renting kayaks and stand-up paddleboarding gear ($15 to $80).

Away from all the maddening crowds, **North Tahoe Regional Park** (Map p368; www.northtahoeparks.com; 6600 Donner Rd, off National Ave; per car $3; 🖈) offers forested hiking and mountain-biking trails, an 18-hole disc-golf course, a children's playground and tennis courts lit-up for night play. In winter, a sledding hill (rentals available) and ungroomed cross-country ski and snowshoe tracks beckon. To find this hidden park, drive almost a mile uphill from Hwy 28 on National Ave, then go left on Donner Rd and follow signs.

🛏 Sleeping

Cedar Glen Lodge　　　　　CABINS, LODGE **$$**
(☎ 530-546-4281; www.tahoecedarglen.com; 6589 N Lake Blvd; r/ste/cottages incl breakfast $139-350; @ 🛜 🐾 🏊) Completely renovated and

upgraded, and boasting an excellent new upscale restaurant, these gorgeous cabins and rustic-themed lodge rooms opposite the beach have knotty pine paneling, new mattresses and kitchenettes or full kitchens. Kids go nuts over all the freebies, from ping-pong tables, horseshoe pit and volleyball to an outdoor swimming pool, putting green and toasty firepit. Pet fee $30.

Franciscan Lakeside Lodge
CABINS $$

(☎ 530-546-6300; www.franciscanlodge.com; 6944 N Lake Blvd; cabin $93-399; ☎ ⚹) Spend the day on a private sandy beach or in the outdoor pool, then light the barbecue grill after sunset – ah, now that's relaxation. All of the simple cabins, cottages and suites have kitchenettes. Lakeside lodgings have better beach access and views, but roomier cabins near the back of the complex tend to be quieter and will appeal to families with younger kids in tow.

Firelite Lodge
MOTEL $$

(☎ 530-546-7222; www.tahoelodge.com; 7035 N Lake Blvd; r incl breakfast $79-154; ☎ ⚹) Recently rebuilt with thick walls, sound-proofed windows, and kitchenettes and gas fireplaces in every room, the family-run Firelite is a good-value stay in a prime walkable location, with the Tahoe Vista Recreation Area right across the street. The upstairs king-bed rooms have perfect lakeview balconies. Outside amenities include bikes to rent and a hot tub.

Rustic Cottages
CABIN $$

(☎ 530-546-3523; www.rusticcottages.com; 7449 N Lake Blvd; cottage incl breakfast $109-244; ☎ ⚹) These cottages consist of a cluster of about 20 little storybook houses in the pines, with nametags fashioned from hand saws. They sport beautiful wrought-iron beds and a bevy of amenities. Most cabins have full kitchens, and some have gas or real wood-burning fireplaces.

Other perks: waffles and homemade muffins at breakfast, and free sleds and snowshoes to borrow in winter.

✖ Eating & Drinking

Old Post Office Cafe
AMERICAN $

(5245 N Lake Blvd, Tahoe Vista; mains $6-12; ⊙ 6:30am-2pm) Head west of town toward Carnelian Bay, where this always-packed, cheery wooden shack serves scrumptious breakfasts – buttery potatoes, crab-cake eggs Benedict, biscuits with gravy, fluffy omelets with lotsa fillings and fresh-fruit smoothies. Waits for a table get long on summer and winter weekends, so roll up early.

El Sancho's
MEXICAN, TAKEOUT $

(7019 N Lake Blvd; items $4-10; ⊙ 10am-9pm) Grab a big fat burrito or an order of *huaraches* – fried *masa* (cornmeal dough) topped with sauce, cheese and fried meat or beans – and a Mexican cane-sugar soda pop from this roadside *taqueria*.

★ Rustic Lodge
NEW AMERICAN $$$

(☎ 530-546-4281; www.tahoecedarglen.com/dining; 6589 N Lake Blvd; mains $19-36; ⊙ 5-9pm Wed-Sun; ⚹) ✆ Part of the va-va-va-vooming of Cedar Glen Lodge, this cozy wood-paneled restaurant and fireplace wine bar serve artisanal cheeses, locally-sourced produce and meats, free range chicken and hormone-free meats. Standouts include the truffle fries, roasted chicken breast, and absolutely anything made by the in-house pastry chef. Reservations recommended.

Gar Woods Grill & Pier
BAR

(☎ 530-546-3366; www.garwoods.com; 5000 N Lake Blvd; ⊙ 11:30am-11:30pm) A shoreline hot spot judging by the rowdy crowds, Gar Woods pays tribute to the era of classic wooden boats. Don't show up for the lackadaisical grill fare, but instead to slurp a Wet Woody cocktail while watching the sunset over the lake. Be prepared to duke it out for a table on the no-reservations side of the beachfront deck out back.

Kings Beach

The utilitarian character of fetchingly picturesque Kings Beach lies in its smattering of back-to-basics retro motels all lined up along the highway. But in summer all eyes are on **Kings Beach State Recreation Area** (Map p368; www.parks.ca.gov; ⊙ dawn-10pm; ⚹) ███ , a seductive 700ft-long beach that often gets deluged with sunseekers and leashed dogs. At the beach, you'll find picnic tables, barbecue grills and a fun kids' play structure, while nearby concessionaires rent kayaks, jet skis, paddleboats, stand-up paddleboarding (SUP) gear and more. **Adrift Tahoe** (☎ 530-546-1112; www.standuppaddletahoe.com; 8338 N Lake Blvd) is one of several local outfitters offering kayak, outrigger canoe and SUP rentals, private lessons and tours.

TIRED OF TAHOE?

To throw a few snowballs without blowing your family's budget or plodding along in weekend traffic, aim for some of California's 19 maintained **sno-parks** (☑916-324-1222; http://ohv.parks.ca.gov-/?page_id=1233; pass per day/year $5/25). Clustered along Sierra highways, these inexpensive winter activity parks offer opportunities for raucous sledding, serene cross-country ski touring or unhurried snowperson construction.

Or consider some of the smaller ski resorts. In addition to cheaper lift tickets, **Bear Valley** (www.bearvalley.com; Hwy 4) has its own snow play area, **Dodge Ridge** (www.dodgeridge.com; Hwy 108) has extensive get-to-know-the-snow lessons for kids, and **China Peak** (www.skichinapeak.com; Hwy 168) gets sparse crowds and is nowhere near the congested Tahoe-bound freeways.

Further inland, the nostalgic 1920s **Old Brockway Golf Course** (☑530-546-9909; www.oldbrockway.com; 400 Brassie Ave, nr cnr Hwy 267 & N Lake Blvd; greens fee $25-50, club/cart rental from $15/18) is a quick par-36, nine-hole diversion with peekaboo lake views from along pine tree-lined fairways where Hollywood celebs hobnobbed back in the day.

For drop-in yoga, Zumba and Jazzercise classes, check the schedule of the lakeside **North Tahoe Event Center** (www.northtahoeparks.com/ntec.php; 8318 N Lake Blvd).

🛌 Sleeping

★ Hostel Tahoe
HOSTEL $
(☑530-546-3266; www.hosteltahoe.com; 8931 N Lake Blvd; dm $35, d/f $80/90; @🖤) Minutes from Northstar and the beach, this former motel has private rooms and single-sex dorms with hand-painted murals and gauzy hanging textiles. A separate common building is the *pièce de résistance*, sunlight bathes the fireplace living room and a well-equipped honor kitchen stocks coffee, tea and food staples. Free loaner bikes, and breakfast included on Saturday and Sunday.

🍴 Eating & Drinking

Char-Pit
FAST FOOD $
(www.charpit.com; 8732 N Lake Blvd; items $3-11; ☺11am-9pm; 🐾) No gimmicks at this 1960s fast-food stand, which grills juicy burgers and St Louis–style baby back ribs, and also fries up crispy onion rings and breaded mozzarella sticks. Somebody call an ambulance!

Log Cabin Caffe
DINER $$
(☑530-546-7109; www.logcabinbreakfast.com; 8692 N Lake Blvd; mains $8-16; ☺7am-2pm) Come early (especially on weekends) to join the queue for the North Shore's best breakfast. Eggs Benedict, whole-wheat pancakes with hot fresh fruit and cranberry-orange waffles are just a few highlights from the huge menu. Tip: call ahead to put your name on the waitlist if you'd rather not wait an hour for a table.

Lanza's
ITALIAN $$
(www.lanzastahoe.com; 7739 N Lake Blvd; mains $12-23; ☺5-10pm, bar from 4:30pm) Next to the Safeway supermarket stands this beloved Italian trattoria where a tantalizing aroma of garlic, rosemary and 'secret' spices perfumes the air. Dinners, though undoubtedly not the tastiest you've ever had, are hugely filling and include salad and bread. Look for the owner's sepia-colored family photos in the entranceway.

Jason's Beachside Grille
BAR
(www.jasonsbeachsidegrille.com; 8338 N Lake Blvd; ☺11am-10pm) Looking for the party around sundown? Hit this waterfront deck with a schooner of microbrew. Never mind the unexciting American fare, like smoked chicken pasta, alongside an overflowing salad bar (dinner mains $13 to $25). On colder days, red-velvet sofas orbiting a sunken fireplace are the coziest, but in summer it's all about sunset views.

Grid Bar & Grill
PUB
(www.thegridbarandgrill.com; 8545 N Lake Blvd; ☺11am-2am) This locals' dive bar looks rough around the edges, but happy hours are super-cheap and you can catch live music, from bluegrass to punk, DJs, dancing or karaoke, or trivia nights.

ℹ️ Getting There & Around

Tahoe Area Rapid Transit (TART; ☑530-550-1212; www.laketahoetransit.com; single/day pass $1.75/3.50) buses between Tahoe City and Incline Village make stops in Tahoe Vista, Kings Beach and Crystal Bay hourly from approximately 6am until 6pm daily. Another TART route connects Crystal Bay and Kings Beach with the Northstar resort every hour or so from 8am until 5pm daily; in winter, this bus continues to Truckee (between May and November, you'll have to detour via Tahoe City first).

In summer, the North Lake Tahoe Water Shuttle (p384) operates a half dozen daily trips between Tahoe Vista and Tahoe City (30 minutes). Reserve ahead; bikes permitted.

EASTERN SHORE

Lake Tahoe's eastern shore lies entirely within Nevada. Much of it is relatively undeveloped thanks to George Whittell Jr, an eccentric San Franciscan playboy who once owned a lot of this land, including 27 miles of shoreline. Upon his death in 1969, it was sold off to a private investor, who later wheeled and dealed most of it to the US Forest Service and Nevada State Parks. And lucky it was, because today the eastern shore offers some of Tahoe's best scenery and outdoor diversion. Hwy 28 rolls into Nevada at Crystal Bay and runs past Incline Village, heading along the eastern shore to intersect with Hwy 50, which rolls south to Zephyr Cove and Stateline casinos.

Crystal Bay

Crossing into Nevada, the neon starts to flash and old-school gambling palaces pant after your hard-earned cash. Though closed at research time for a multimillion-dollar remodel, historic **Cal-Neva Resort** literally straddles the California–Nevada border and has a colorful history involving ghosts, mobsters and Frank Sinatra, who once owned the joint. Ask about the guided secret tunnel tours once it's reopened.

Also on the main drag, the **Tahoe Biltmore Lodge & Casino** (☑800-245-8667; www.tahoebiltmore.com; 5 Hwy 28; r $84-129; ☎❄), plays up its longevity with classic Tahoe photographs in the divey hotel rooms, though radiators give away the building's age. For greasy-spoon grill fare, duck under the mirrored ceilings into the artificial forest of the chintzy **Cafe Biltmore** (mains $8-15; ☉7am-4pm). Then catch a live-music show – often a tribute band – across the street at the **Crystal Bay Club Casino** (☑775-833-6333; www.crystalbaycasino.com; 14 Hwy 28).

For a breath of pine-scented air, flee the smoky casinos for the steep 1-mile hike up paved Forest Service Rd 1601 to **Stateline Lookout**. Sunset views over Lake Tahoe and the snowy mountains are all around.

A nature trail loops around the site of the former fire lookout tower – nowadays there's a split-level stone observation platform. To find the trailhead, drive up Reservoir Rd, just east of the Tahoe Biltmore parking lot, then take a quick right onto Lakeview Ave and follow it uphill just over a half-mile to the (usually locked) iron gate on your left.

Incline Village

One of Lake Tahoe's ritziest communities, Incline Village is the gateway to Diamond Peak and Mt Rose ski resorts. The latter is a 12-mile drive northeast via Hwy 431 (Mt Rose Hwy). During summer, the nearby **Mt Rose Wilderness** (Map p368; www.fs.usda.gov/ltbmu) offers miles of unspoiled terrain, including a strenuous 10-mile round-trip to the summit of majestic **Mt Rose** (10,776ft). The trail starts from the deceptively named Mt Rose Summit parking lot, 9 miles uphill from Incline Village. For a more mellow meadow stroll that even young kids can handle, pull over a mile or so earlier at wildflower-strewn **Tahoe Meadows** (🐾). Stay on the nature loop trails to avoid trampling the fragile meadows; leashed dogs are allowed.

In summer, you can also visit George Whittell's mansion, **Thunderbird Lodge** (☑800-468-2463; www.thunderbirdlodge.org; adult/child 6-12yr $39/19; ☉Tue-Sat May-Oct, reservations required), where he spent summers with his pet lion, Bill. Tours include a trip down a 600ft tunnel to the card house where George used to play poker with Howard Hughes and other famous recluses. The only way to get to the lodge is by shuttle bus, leaving from the helpful in-town **Incline Village/Crystal Bay Visitors Bureau** (☑775-832-1606; www.gotahoenorth.com; 969 Tahoe Blvd; ☉8am-5pm Mon-Fri, 10am-4pm Sat & Sun; 📶), or on a boat cruise or kayak tour ($120 to $135).

🛏 Sleeping

Hyatt Regency Lake Tahoe   RESORT $$$
(☑775-832-1234; www.laketahoe.hyatt.com; 111 Country Club Dr; r Sun-Thu/Fri & Sat from $199/379, ste & cottage Sun-Thu/Fri & Sat from $319/629; ❄@📶) Decorated like an Arts and Crafts-style mountain lodge, every room and lakeside cottage looks lavish, and the spa is even bigger than the casino. In summer you can sprawl on a private lakefront beach or in winter let the heated outdoor swimming lagoon warm you up after a day on the slopes.

🍴 Eating & Drinking

Bite
CALIFORNIAN $$

(☑ 775-831-1000; www.bitetahoe.com; 907 Tahoe Blvd; shared plates $8-19; ☺ 5-10pm, closed Wed Oct-May; ☑) Don't let the strip-mall location stop you from rocking this creative, eclectic tapas and wine bar. Mix light, seasonal, veggie-friendly dishes with modern takes on rib-sticking comfort food like honeyed baby back ribs or green-chili mac 'n' cheese. An après-ski crowd turns up for happy hour.

Austin's
AMERICAN $$

(www.austinstahoe.com; 120 Country Club Dr; mains $9-17; ☺ 11am-9pm; ☑🔥) A hearty welcome for the whole family is what you'll find at this wood-cabin diner with an outdoor deck. Buttermilk fries with jalapeño dipping sauce, chicken-fried steak, classic meatloaf, burgers, huge salad bowls and sandwiches will fill you up – and so will mountain-sized martinis.

Lone Eagle Grille
COCKTAIL BAR

(www.laketahoe.hyatt.com; 111 Country Club Dr; ☺ 11:30am-10pm Sun-Thu, to 11pm Fri & Sat) At the Hyatt's many-hearthed cocktail lounge, sip a divine orange-flavored margarita, then head outside for sunset and to flirt by the beach fire pit.

Lake Tahoe-Nevada State Park

Back on the lake, heading south, is **Lake Tahoe-Nevada State Park** (Map p368; www.parks.nv.gov; per car $7-12), which has beaches, lakes and miles of trails. Just 3 miles south of Incline Village is beautiful **Sand Harbor** (Map p368; ☑ 775-831-0494; www.parks.nv.gov/parks/sand-harbor; 2005 Hwy 28; per car $7-12), where two sand spits have formed a shallow bay with brilliant, warm turquoise water and white, boulder-strewn beaches. It gets very busy here, especially during July and August, when the **Lake Tahoe Shakespeare Festival** (☑ 800-747-4697; www.laketahoeshakespeare.com) is underway.

At the park's southern end, just north of the Hwy 50/Hwy 28 junction, **Spooner Lake** (Map p368; ☑ 775-749-5980; www.parks.nv.gov; per car $7-10) is popular for catch-and-release fishing, picnicking, nature walks, backcountry camping and cross-country skiing. Spooner Lake is also the start of the famous 13-mile **Flume Trail**, a holy grail for experienced mountain bikers. From the trail's end near Incline Village you can either backtrack 10 miles along the narrow, twisting shoulder of Hwy 28 or board a shuttle bus. Arrange shuttles and rent bikes by the trailhead inside the park at **Spooner Summit Bike Rental Shop** (☑ 775-749-1112; www.zephyrcove.com/flumetrail; mountain bike rental per day $40-60, shuttle $10-15; ☺ 8:30am-5pm May-Oct) or in town at **Flume Trail Bikes** (☑ 775-298-2501; www.theflumetrail.com; 1115 Tunnel Creek Rd, Incline Village; mountain bike rental per day $35-85, shuttle $10-15).

RENO (NEVADA)

A city of big-time gambling and top-notch outdoor adventures, Reno resists pigeonholing. 'The Biggest Little City in the World' has something to raise the pulse of adrenaline junkies, hardcore gamblers and city people craving easy access to wide open spaces. The formerly gritty **Midtown District** – bordered by Liberty St (south of the river) to the north and Plumb Lane to the south, with S Virginia St running through it – has recently revitalized downtown with loads of exceptional new bars, restaurants and arts spaces.

👁 Sights

National Automobile Museum
MUSEUM

(☑ 775-333-9300; www.automuseum.org; 10 S Lake St; adult/child 6-18yr $10/4; ☺ 9:30am-5:30pm Mon-Sat, 10am-4pm Sun; 🔥) Stylized street scenes illustrate a century's worth of automobile history at this engaging car museum. The collection is enormous and impressive, with one-of-a-kind vehicles – including James Dean's 1949 Mercury from *Rebel Without a Cause*, a 1938 Phantom Corsair and a 24-karat gold-plated DeLorean – and rotating exhibits bringing in all kinds of souped-up or fabulously retro rides.

Nevada Museum of Art
MUSEUM

(☑ 775-329-3333; www.nevadaart.org; 160 W Liberty St; adult/child 6-12yr $10/1; ☺ 10am-5pm Wed & Fri-Sun, to 8pm Thu) In a sparkling building inspired by the geological formations of the Black Rock Desert north of town, a floating staircase leads to galleries showcasing temporary exhibits and eclectic collections on the American West, labor and contemporary landscape photography.

Fleischmann Planetarium & Science Center
MUSEUM

(☑ 775-784-4811; http://planetarium.unr.nevada.edu; 1650 N Virginia St; planetarium adult/child under 12yr $7/5; ⊘ noon-7pm Mon-Thu, to 9pm Fri, 10am-9pm Sat, to 7pm Sun; 🖍) Pop into this flying-saucer-shaped building at the University of Nevada for a window on the universe during star shows and feature presentations.

Nevada Historical Society Museum MUSEUM
(📞775-688-1190; http://museums.nevadaculture.org; 1650 N Virginia St; adult/child under 17yr $4/free; ⊘10am-5pm Tue-Sat) Near the University of Nevada Science Center, this museum includes permanent exhibits on neon signs, local Native American culture and the presence of the federal government.

Circus Circus CASINO
(www.circusreno.com; 500 N Sierra St; ⊘24hr; 🖍) The most family-friendly of the bunch, Circus Circus has free circus acts to entertain kids beneath a giant big top, which also harbors a gazillion carnival and video games that look awfully similar to slot machines.

Silver Legacy CASINO
(www.silverlegacyreno.com; 407 N Virginia St; ⊘24hr) A Victorian-themed place, the Silver Legacy is easily recognized by its white landmark dome, where a giant mock mining rig periodically erupts into a fairly tame sound-and-light spectacle.

Eldorado CASINO
(www.eldoradoreno.com; 345 N Virginia St; ⊘24hr) The Eldorado has a kitschy Fountain of Fortune that probably has Italian sculptor Bernini spinning in his grave.

Harrah's CASINO
(www.harrahsreno.com; 219 N Center St; ⊘24hr) Founded by Nevada gambling pioneer William Harrah in 1946, it's still one of the biggest and most popular casinos in town.

Atlantis CASINO
(www.atlantiscasino.com; 3800 S Virginia St; ⊘24hr) Modeled on the legendary underwater city, with a mirrored ceiling and tropical flourishes like indoor waterfalls and palm trees.

🏃 Activities

Reno is a 30- to 60-minute drive from Lake Tahoe ski resorts, and many hotels and casinos offer special stay-and-ski packages.

For extensive information on regional hiking and mountain-biking trails, including the Mt Rose summit trail and the Tahoe-Pyramid Bikeway, download the **Truckee Meadows Trails guide** (www.washoecounty.us).

Mere steps from the casinos, the Class II and III rapids at the **Truckee River Whitewater Park** are gentle enough for kids riding inner tubes, yet sufficiently challenging for professional freestyle kayakers. Two courses wrap around Wingfield Park, a small island that hosts free concerts in summertime. **Tahoe Whitewater Tours** (📞775-787-5000; www.truckeewhitewaterrafting.com; 400 Island Ave; rafting adult/child $68/58) and **Sierra Adventures** (📞866-323-8928; www.wildsierra.com; 11 N Sierra St; tubing $29) offer kayak trips and lessons.

👉 Tours

Historic Reno Preservation Society WALKING TOUR
(📞775-747-4478; www.historicreno.org; tours $10) Dig deeper with a walking or biking tour of the city highlighting subjects including architecture, politics and literary history.

🎉 Festivals & Events

Reno River Festival SPORTS
(www.renoriverfestival.com; ⊘May) The world's top freestyle kayakers compete in a mad paddling dash through Whitewater Park in mid-May. Free music concerts as well.

Hot August Nights CULTURAL
(www.hotaugustnights.net; ⊘Aug) Catch the *American Graffiti* vibe during this seven-day celebration of hot rods and rock 'n' roll in early August. Hotel rates skyrocket to their peak.

🛏 Sleeping

Lodging rates vary widely depending on the day of the week and local events. Sunday through Thursday are generally the least

---

GREAT BALLS OF FIRE!

For one week at the end of August, **Burning Man** (www.burningman.com; admission $380-650) explodes onto the sunbaked Black Rock Desert, and Nevada sprouts a third major population center – Black Rock City. An experiential art party (and alternative universe) that climaxes in the immolation of a towering stick figure, Burning Man is a whirlwind of outlandish theme camps, dust-caked bicycles, bizarre bartering, costume-enhanced nudity and a general relinquishment of inhibitions.

WORTH A TRIP

PYRAMID LAKE

A piercingly blue expanse in an otherwise barren landscape, 25 miles north of Reno on the Paiute Indian Reservation, Pyramid Lake is popular for recreation. Permits for **camping** (primitive campsites per vehicle per night $9) on the beach on the west side of the lake and **fishing** (per person $9) are available online, at outdoor suppliers and CVS drugstore locations in Reno, and at the **ranger station** (775-476-1155; http://plpt.nsn.us/rangers; 2500 Lakeview Dr; 9am-1pm & 2-6pm Thu-Mon) east of SR 445 in Sutcliffe.

expensive; Friday is somewhat more expensive and Saturday can be as much as triple the midweek rate.

Mt Rose CAMPGROUND $
(877-444-6777; www.recreation.gov; Hwy 431; RV & tent sites $17-50; mid-Jun–Sep) In the summer months, there's gorgeous high-altitude camping here.

Sands Regency HOTEL $
(775-348-2200; www.sandsregency.com; 345 N Arlington Ave; r Sun-Thu from $39, Fri & Sat from $85;) With some of the largest standard digs in town, rooms here are decked out in a cheerful tropical palette of upbeat blues, reds and greens – a visual relief from standard-issue motel decor. The 17th-floor gym and Jacuzzi are perfectly positioned to capture your eyes with drop-dead panoramic mountain views. An outdoor pool opens in summer. Empress Tower rooms are best.

Wildflower Village MOTEL, B&B $
(775-747-8848; www.wildflowervillage.com; 4395 W 4th St; dm $34, motel $63, B&B $142;) Perhaps more of a state of mind than a motel, this artists colony on the west edge of town has a tumbledown yet creative vibe. Individual murals decorate the facade of each room, and you can hear the freight trains rumble on by. Frequent live music and poetry readings at its cafe and pub, and bike rentals available.

Peppermill CASINO HOTEL $$
(866-821-9996, 775-826-2121; www.peppermill-reno.com; 2707 S Virginia St; r Sun-Thu $59-129, Fri & Sat $79-209, resort fee $16;)

With a dash of Vegas-style opulence, the ever-popular Peppermill boasts Tuscan-themed suites in its newest 600-room tower, and plush remodeled rooms throughout the rest of the property. The three sparkling pools (one indoor) are dreamy, with a full spa on hand. Geothermal energy powers the resort's hot water and heat.

Eating

Reno's dining scene goes far beyond the casino buffets.

Pho 777 VIETNAMESE $
(201 E 2nd St; mains $6-8; 10am-9pm) A no-frills Vietnamese noodle shop just off the casino strip that serves up bowls and bowls of steamy soup.

Peg's Glorified Ham & Eggs DINER $
(www.eatatpegs.com; 420 S Sierra St; mains $7-14; 6:30am-2pm;) Locally regarded as the best breakfast in town, Peg's offers tasty grill food that's not too greasy.

★ Old Granite Street Eatery NEW AMERICAN $$
(775-622-3222; www.oldgranitestreeteatery.com; 243 S Sierra St; dinner mains $12-26; 11am-10pm Mon-Thu, to 11pm Fri, 10am-11pm Sat, to 3pm Sun) A lovely well-lit place for organic and local comfort food, old-school artisanal cocktails and seasonal craft beers, this antique-strewn hotspot enchants diners with its stately wooden bar, water served in old liquor bottles and lengthy seasonal menu. Forgot to make a reservation? Check out the iconic rooster and pig murals and wait at a communal table fashioned from a barn door.

Silver Peak Restaurant & Brewery BREWPUB $$
(www.silverpeakrestaurant.com; 124 Wonder St; lunch $8.50-11, dinner $10-23; restaurant 11am-10pm Sun-Thu, to 11pm Sat & Sun, pub open 1hr later) Casual and pretense-free, this place hums with the chatter of happy locals settling in for a night of microbrews and great eats, from pizza with barbecue chicken, to shrimp curry and filet mignon.

Drinking & Nightlife

Jungle CAFE, WINE BAR
(www.thejunglereno.com; 246 W 1st St; coffee 6am-midnight, wine 3pm-midnight Mon-Thu, 3pm-2am Fri, noon-2am Sat, noon-midnight Sun;) A side-by-side coffee shop and wine bar with a cool mosaic floor and riverside patio all rolled into one. The wine bar has weekly

tastings, while the cafe serves breakfast bagels and lunchtime sandwiches ($6 to $8), and puts on diverse music shows.

Chapel Tavern   COCKTAIL BAR
(www.chapeltavern.com; 1099 S Virgina St; ☺2pm-2am Mon-Wed, 2pm-4am Thu-Sun) Midtown's cocktail mecca makes its own infusions – try the bourbon with fig – and a seasonal drinks menu attracts year-round interest to its antler-adorned bar and outdoor patio. DJs keep it jamming on Friday and Saturdays, and patrons comprise a diverse age mix.

Edge   CLUB
(www.edgeofreno.com; 2707 S Virginia St, Peppermill; admission $20; ☺Thu & Sat from 10pm, Fri from 7pm) The Peppermill reels in the nighthounds with a big glitzy dance club, where go-go dancers, smoke machines and laser lights may cause sensory overload. If so, step outside to the lounge patio and relax in front of cozy fire pits.

☆ Entertainment

The free weekly *Reno News & Review* (www.newsreview.com) is your best source for listings.

Wedged between the I-80 and the Truckee River, downtown's N Virginia St is casino central. South of the river it continues as S Virginia St.

Knitting Factory   LIVE MUSIC
(☑775-323-5648; http://re.knittingfactory.com; 211 N Virginia St) This midsized music venue books mainstream and indie favorites.

ℹ Information

An information center sits near the baggage claim at Reno-Tahoe International Airport, which also has free wi-fi.
Reno-Sparks Convention & Visitors Authority (☑800-367-7366; www.visitrenotahoe.com; 135 N Sierra St, inside Reno Envy; ☺10am-6pm)

ℹ Getting There & Away

About 5 miles southeast of downtown, the **Reno-Tahoe International Airport** (RNO; www.renoairport.com; ☎) is served by most major airlines.

The **North Lake Tahoe Express** (☑866-216-5222; www.northlaketahoeexpress.com; one-way $45) operates a shuttle (five daily, 3:30am to midnight) to and from the airport to multiple North Shore Lake Tahoe locations including Truckee, Squaw Valley and Incline Village. Reserve in advance.

The **South Tahoe Express** (☑866-898-2463; www.southtahoeexpress.com; adult/child one way $29.75/16.75, round-trip $53/30.25) operates several daily shuttle buses from the airport to Stateline casinos; the journey takes from 75 minutes up to two hours.

To reach South Lake Tahoe (weekdays only), take the wi-fi-equipped **RTC Intercity bus** (www.rtcwashoe.com; intercity $5) to the Nevada DOT stop in Carson City ($5, one hour, six daily Monday to Friday) and then the **BlueGo** (www.tahoetransportation.org/southtahoe) 21X bus ($2 with RTC Intercity transfer, one hour, five to six daily) to the Stateline Transit Center.

Greyhound (☑775-322-2970; www.greyhound.com; 155 Stevenson St) buses run daily service to Truckee, Sacramento and San Francisco ($35, five to seven hours), as does the once-daily westbound *California Zephyr* route operated by **Amtrak** (☑800-872-7245, 775-329-8638; www.amtrak.com; 280 N Center St). The train is slower and more expensive, but also more scenic and comfortable, with a bus connection from Emeryville for passengers to San Francisco ($51, 7½ hours). Discount bus company **Megabus** (www.megabus.com; ☎) has two daily departures from the Silver Legacy casino to San Francisco (from $15, 4½ hours) via Sacramento.

ℹ Getting Around

Casino hotels offer frequent free airport shuttles for their guests (and don't ask to see reservations).

The local **RTC Ride buses** (☑775-348-7433; www.rtcwashoe.com; per ride $2) blanket the city, and most routes converge at the RTC 4th St station downtown (between Lake St and Evans Ave). Useful routes include the RTC Rapid line for S Virginia St, 11 for Sparks and 19 for the airport.

The **Sierra Spirit bus** (50¢) loops around all major downtown landmarks – including the casinos and the university – every 15 minutes from 7am to 7pm.

Yosemite & the Sierra Nevada

Best Places to Eat

➜ Evergreen Lodge (p416)

➜ Lakefront Restaurant (p447)

➜ Tioga Pass Resort (p441)

➜ Narrow Gauge Inn (p420)

➜ Mountain Room Restaurant (p416)

Best Places to Stay

➜ High Sierra Camps (p414)

➜ Ahwahnee Hotel (p413)

➜ Evergreen Lodge Resort (p415)

➜ Sierra Sky Ranch (p421)

➜ Benton Hot Springs (p452)

Why Go?

An outdoor adventurer's wonderland, the Sierra Nevada is a year-round pageant of snow sports, white-water rafting, hiking, cycling and rock climbing. Skiers and snowboarders blaze through hushed pine-tree slopes, and wilderness seekers come to escape the stresses of modern civilization.

The eastern spine of California is a formidable but exquisite topographical barrier enclosing magnificent natural landscapes. And interspersed between its river canyons and 14,000ft peaks are the decomposing ghost towns left behind by California's early settlers, bubbling natural hot springs and Native American tribes that still call it home.

In the majestic national parks of Yosemite and Sequoia & Kings Canyon, visitors will be humbled by the groves of solemn giant sequoias, ancient rock formations and valleys, and the ever-present opportunity to see bears and other wildlife.

When to Go
Yosemite National Park

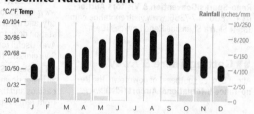

May & Jun The Yosemite waterfalls are gushing and spectacular in spring.

Jul & Aug Head for the mountains for wilderness adventures and glorious sunshine.

Dec–Mar Take a wintertime romp through snowy forests.

YOSEMITE NATIONAL PARK

The jaw-dropping head-turner of America's national parks, and a Unesco World Heritage Site, Yosemite (yo-*sem*-it-ee) garners the devotion of all who enter. From the waterfall-striped granite walls buttressing emerald-green Yosemite Valley to the skyscraping giant sequoias catapulting into the air at Mariposa Grove, the place inspires a sense of awe and reverence – four million visitors wend their way to the country's third-oldest national park annually. But lift your eyes above the crowds and you'll feel your heart instantly moved by unrivalled splendors: the haughty profile of Half Dome, the hulking presence of El Capitan, the drenching mists of Yosemite Falls, the gemstone lakes of the high country's subalpine wilderness and Hetch Hetchy's pristine pathways.

History

The Ahwahneechee, a group of Miwok and Paiute peoples, lived in the Yosemite area for around 4000 years before a group of pioneers, most likely led by legendary explorer Joseph Rutherford Walker, came through in 1833. During the Gold Rush era, conflict between the miners and native tribes escalated to the point where a military expedition (the Mariposa Battalion) was dispatched in 1851 to punish the Ahwahneechee, eventually forcing the capitulation of Chief Tenaya and his tribe.

Tales of thunderous waterfalls and towering stone columns followed the Mariposa Battalion out of Yosemite and soon spread into the public's awareness. In 1855 San Francisco entrepreneur James Mason Hutchings organized the first tourist party to the valley. Published accounts of his trip, in which he extolled the area's untarnished beauty, prompted others to follow, and it wasn't long before inns and roads began springing up. Alarmed by this development, conservationists petitioned Congress to protect the area – with success. In 1864 President Abraham Lincoln signed the Yosemite Grant, which eventually ceded Yosemite Valley and the Mariposa Grove of giant sequoias to California as a state park. This landmark decision paved the way for a national park system, of which Yosemite became a part in 1890, thanks to efforts led by pioneering conservationist John Muir.

Yosemite's popularity as a tourist destination continued to soar throughout the 20th century and, by the mid-1970s, traffic and congestion draped the valley in a smoggy haze. The General Management Plan (GMP), developed in 1980 to alleviate this and other problems, ran into numerous challenges and delays. Despite many improvements, and the need to preserve the natural beauty that draws visitors to Yosemite in the first place, the plan still hasn't been fully implemented.

⊙ Sights

There are four main entrances to the park: South Entrance (Hwy 41), Arch Rock (Hwy 140), Big Oak Flat (Hwy 120 W) and Tioga Pass (Hwy 120 E). Hwy 120 traverses the park as Tioga Rd, connecting Yosemite Valley with the Eastern Sierra.

Visitor activity is concentrated in Yosemite Valley, especially in Yosemite Village, which has the main visitor center, a post office, a museum, eateries and other services. Curry Village is another hub. Notably less busy, Tuolumne (too-*ahl*-uh-*mee*) Meadows, toward the eastern end of Tioga Rd, primarily draws hikers, backpackers and climbers. Wawona, the park's southern focal point, also has good infrastructure. In the northwestern corner, Hetch Hetchy, which has no services at all, receives the smallest number of visitors.

⊙ Yosemite Valley

The park's crown jewel, spectacular meadow-carpeted Yosemite Valley, stretches 7 miles long, bisected by the rippling Merced River and hemmed in by some of the most majestic chunks of granite anywhere on earth. The most famous are, of course, the monumental 7569ft **El Capitan** (El Cap), one of the world's largest monoliths and a magnet for rock climbers, and 8842ft **Half Dome**, the park's spiritual centerpiece – its rounded granite pate forms an unmistakable silhouette. You'll have great views of both from **Valley View** on the valley floor, but for the classic photo op head up Hwy 41 to **Tunnel View**, which boasts a new viewing area. With a little sweat you'll have even better postcard panoramas – sans the crowds – from **Inspiration Point**. The trail (2.6-mile round-trip) starts at the tunnel.

Yosemite's waterfalls mesmerize even the most jaded traveler, especially when the spring runoff turns them into thunderous

Yosemite & the Sierra Nevada Highlights

1 Marveling at the waterfall gush in spring at **Yosemite National Park** (p401).

2 Whooshing down the wintertime heights of snow-draped **Mammoth Mountain** (p443).

3 Gazing heavenward through the celestial sequoia canopies of **Sequoia & Kings Canyon National Parks** (p423).

4 Ambling around the evocative ghost town of **Bodie** (p439).

5 Canoeing or kayaking **Mono Lake** amid its haunting tufa (p441).

Reno (45mi)

CARSON CITY

NEVADA

Lake Tahoe

Incline Village

Tahoe City

South Lake Tahoe

El Dorado National Forest **4**

Walker Lake

Topaz Lake

Markleeville

Grover Hot Springs State Park **4**

Monitor Pass (8314ft)

Ebbetts Pass (8730ft)

Walker

Sonora Pass (9624ft)

Lake Alpine

Bear Valley

Calaveras Big Trees State Park **4**

Arnold

Murphys

Sonora

Stanislaus National Forest **4**

Groveland

El Portal

Briceburg

Midpines

Yosemite National Park **1**

Yosemite Village

Tioga Pass (9945ft) (closed in winter)

Humboldt-Toiyabe National Forest **4**

Bridgeport **7**

Bodie State Historic Park **4**

Mono Lake **5**

Lee Vining

Hoover Wilderness

Ansel Adams Wilderness **4**

June Lake

Mammoth Lakes

Devils Postpile National Monument **6**

Mammoth Mountain (11,053ft) **6**

Inyo National Forest **4**

Crowley Lake

Benton **7**

Inyo National Forest **4**

Humboldt-Toiyabe National Forest **4**

White Mountain (14,252ft)

Ancient Bristlecone Pine Forest **6**

Sierra

Dobbs Ridge

American River

Mokelumne River

Stanislaus River

Tuolumne River

Merced River

50 km
25 miles

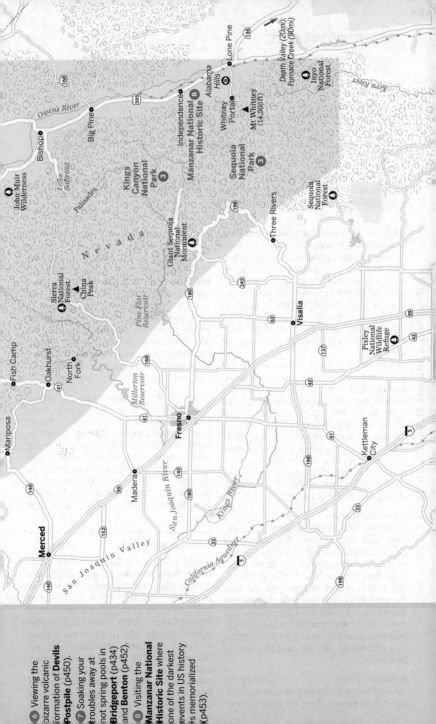

6 Viewing the bizarre volcanic formation of **Devils Postpile** (p450).

7 Soaking your troubles away at hot spring pools in **Bridgeport** (p434) and **Benton** (p452).

8 Visiting the **Manzanar National Historic Site** where one of the darkest events in US history is memorialized (p453).

ℹ️ VISITING YOSEMITE

From late June to September the entire park is accessible – all visitor facilities are open and everything from backcountry campgrounds to ice-cream stands are at maximum capacity. This is also when it's hardest – though not impossible – to evade the crush of humanity.

Crowds are smallest in winter but road closures (most notably of Tioga Rd but also of Glacier Point Rd beyond Badger Pass Ski Area) mean that activity is concentrated in the valley and on Badger Pass. Visitor facilities are scaled down to a bare minimum and most campgrounds are closed and other lodging options limited. Note that 'winter' in Yosemite starts with the first heavy snowfall, which can be as early as October, and often lasts until May.

Spring, when the waterfalls are at their best, is a particularly excellent time to visit. Fall brings fewer people, an enchanting rainbow of foliage and crisp, clear weather (although waterfalls have usually dried to a trickle by then).

cataracts. **Yosemite Falls** (west of Yosemite Village) is considered the tallest in North America, dropping 2425ft in three tiers. A slick wheelchair-accessible trail leads to the bottom of this cascade or, if you prefer solitude and different perspectives, you can also clamber up the **Yosemite Falls Trail**, which puts you atop the falls after a grueling 3.4 miles. No less impressive is nearby **Bridalveil Fall** and others scattered throughout the valley.

Any aspiring Ansel Adams should lug their camera gear along the 1-mile paved trail to **Mirror Lake** early or late in the day to catch the ever-shifting reflection of Half Dome in the still waters. The lake all but dries up by late summer.

South of here, where the Merced River courses around two small islands, lies **Happy Isles**, a popular area for picnics, swimming and strolls. It also marks the start of the **John Muir Trail** and **Mist Trail** to several waterfalls and Half Dome.

Yosemite Museum   MUSEUM
(📞 209-372-0200; 🕐 9am-5pm, often closed noon-1pm) **FREE** This museum has Miwok and Paiute artifacts, including woven baskets, beaded buckskin dresses and dance capes made from feathers. There's also an **art gallery** with paintings and photographs from the museum's permanent collection. Behind the museum, a self-guided interpretive trail winds past a reconstructed c 1870 **Indian village** with pounding stones, an acorn granary, a ceremonial roundhouse and a conical bark house.

Ahwahnee Hotel   HISTORIC BUILDING
About a quarter-mile east of Yosemite Village, the Ahwahnee Hotel is a graceful blend of rustic mountain retreat and elegant mansion dating back to 1927. You don't need to be a guest to have a gawk and a wander. Built from local granite, pine and cedar, the building is splendidly decorated with leaded glass, sculpted tiles, Native American rugs and Turkish kilims. You can enjoy a meal in the baronial dining room or a casual drink in the piano bar. Around Christmas, the Ahwahnee hosts the **Bracebridge Dinner** (📞 801-559-5000; www.bracebridgedinners.com; per person $389), sort of a combination banquet and Renaissance fair. Book early.

Nature Center at Happy Isles   MUSEUM
(🕐 9:30am-5pm late-May–Sep; ♿) A great hands-on nature museum, the Nature Center displays explain the differences between the park's various pinecones, rocks, animal tracks and (everyone's favorite subject) scat. Out back, don't miss an exhibit on the 1996 rock fall, when an 80,000-ton rock slab plunged 2000ft to the nearby valley floor, killing a man and felling about 1000 trees.

◎ Glacier Point

A lofty 3200ft above the valley floor, 7214ft Glacier Point presents one of the park's most eye-popping vistas and practically puts you at eye level with Half Dome. To the left of Half Dome lies U-shaped, glacially carved **Tenaya Canyon**, while below you'll see Vernal and Nevada Falls. Glacier Point is about an hour's drive from Yosemite Valley via Glacier Point Rd off Hwy 41. Along the road, hiking trails lead to other spectacular viewpoints, such as **Dewey Point** and **Sentinel Dome**. You can also hike up from the valley floor to Glacier Point via the thigh-burning

Four Mile Trail. If you've driven up to Glacier Point and want to get away from the madding crowd, hiking down the Four Mile Trail for a bit will net you comparative solitude and more breathtaking views. Another way to get here is on the Glacier Point Hikers' Bus. Many hikers take the bus one way and hike the other. Drivers should go in the morning to avoid the afternoon backup from the parking lot.

Tioga Road & Tuolumne Meadows

Tioga Rd (or Hwy 120 E), the only road through the park, travels through 56 miles of superb high country at elevations ranging from 6200ft at Crane Flat to 9945ft at Tioga Pass. Heavy snowfall keeps it closed from about November until May. Beautiful views await many after a bend in the road, the most impressive being **Olmsted Point**, where you can gawp all the way down Tenaya Canyon to Half Dome. Above the canyon's east side looms the aptly named 9926ft **Clouds Rest**. Continuing east on Tioga Rd soon drops you at **Tenaya Lake**, a placid blue basin framed by pines and granite cliffs.

Beyond here, about 55 miles from Yosemite Valley, 8600ft Tuolumne Meadows is the largest subalpine meadow in the Sierra. It provides a dazzling contrast to the valley, with its lush open fields, clear blue lakes, ragged granite peaks and domes, and cooler temperatures. If you come during July or August, you'll find a painter's palette of wildflowers decorating the shaggy meadows.

Tuolumne is far less crowded than the valley, though the area around the campground, lodge store and visitor center does get busy, especially on weekends. Some hiking trails, such as the one to **Dog Lake**, are also well traveled. Remember that the altitude makes breathing a lot harder than in the valley, and nights can get nippy, so pack warm clothes.

The main meadow is about 2.5 miles long and lies on the north side of Tioga Rd between **Lembert Dome** and **Pothole Dome**. The 200ft scramble to the top of the latter – preferably at sunset – gives you great views of the meadow. An interpretive trail leads from the stables to muddy **Soda Springs**, where carbonated water bubbles up in red-tinted pools. The nearby **Parsons Memorial Lodge** has a few displays.

Hikers and climbers will find a paradise of options around Tuolumne Meadows, which is also the gateway to the High Sierra Camps.

The Tuolumne Meadows Tour & Hikers' Bus makes the trip along Tioga Rd once daily in each direction, and can be used for one-way hikes. There's also a free Tuolumne Meadows Shuttle, which travels between the Tuolumne Meadows Lodge and Olmsted Point, including a stop at Tenaya Lake.

Wawona

Wawona, about 27 miles south of Yosemite Valley, is the park's historical center, home to the park's first headquarters (supervised by Captain AE Wood on the site of the Wawona Campground) and its first tourist facilities. The park will soon restore part of the Mariposa Grove by removing summertime parking and creating a new trail system with improved signage; visitors will be shuttled from parking areas at Wawona and a new lot outside the South Entrance.

★ Mariposa Grove   FOREST
The main lure here is the biggest, most impressive cluster of giant sequoias in Yosemite. The star of the show – and what everyone comes to see – is the **Grizzly Giant**, a behemoth that sprang to life some 1800 years ago. You can't miss it – it's a half-mile walk along a well-worn path starting near the parking lot. Beyond here, crowds thin out a

IMPASSABLE TIOGA PASS

Hwy 120, the main route into Yosemite National Park from the Eastern Sierra, climbs through Tioga Pass, the highest pass in the Sierra at 9945ft. On most maps of California, you'll find a parenthetical remark – 'closed in winter' – printed on the map. While true, this statement is also misleading. Tioga Rd is usually closed from the first heavy snowfall in October to May, June or even July! If you're planning a trip through Tioga Pass in spring, you're likely to be out of luck. According to official park policy, the earliest date the road will be plowed is April 15, yet the pass has been open in April only once since 1980. Other mountain roads further north, such as Hwys 108, 4 and 88/89, may also be closed due to heavy snow, albeit only temporarily. Call ☎ 800-427-7623 for road and weather conditions.

Yosemite National Park

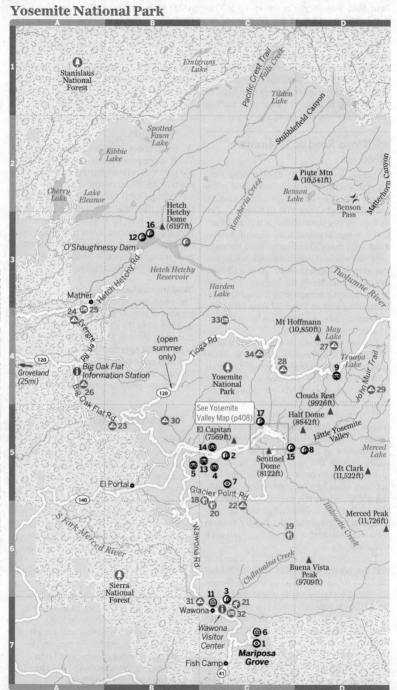

bit, although for more solitude, arrive early in the morning or after 6pm.

Also nearby is the walk-through **California Tunnel Tree**, which continues to survive despite having its heart hacked out in 1895.

In the upper grove you'll find the **Fallen Wawona Tunnel Tree**, the famous drive-through tree that toppled over in 1969. For scenic views, take a 1-mile (round-trip) amble from the fallen tree to Wawona Point.

Also in the upper grove, the **Mariposa Grove Museum** (⊙10am-4pm May-Sep) FREE has displays about sequoia ecology. The full hike from the parking lot to the upper grove is about 2.5 miles.

Parking can be very limited, so come early or late, or take the free shuttle bus from the Wawona Store or the South Entrance. The grove can also be explored on a one-hour guided **tour** (✆209-375-1621; adult/child $26.50/19; ⊙May-Sep) aboard a noisy open-air tram.

Pioneer Yosemite History Center MUSEUM (rides adult/child $5/4; ⊙24hr, rides Wed-Sun Jun-Sep) FREE In Wawona itself, about 6 miles north of the grove, take in the manicured grounds of the elegant Wawona Hotel and cross a covered bridge to this rustic center, where some of the park's oldest buildings were relocated. It also features stagecoaches that brought early tourists to Yosemite, and offers short rides.

⊙ Hetch Hetchy

In the park's northwestern corner, Hetch Hetchy, which is Miwok for 'place of tall grass,' gets the least amount of traffic yet sports waterfalls and granite cliffs that rival its famous counterparts in Yosemite Valley. The main difference is that Hetch Hetchy Valley is now filled with water, following a long political and environmental battle in the early 20th century. It's a lovely, quiet spot and well worth the 40-mile drive from Yosemite Valley, especially if you're tired of the avalanche of humanity rolling through that area. The 2013 Rim Fire charred a huge section of the forest in this region, but its beauty has not been significantly diminished.

The 8-mile long **Hetch Hetchy Reservoir**, its placid surface reflecting clouds and cliffs, stretches behind O'Shaughnessy Dam, the site of a parking lot and trailheads. An easy 5.4-mile (round-trip) trail leads to the

Yosemite Valley

spectacular **Tueeulala** (*twee*-lala) **Falls** and **Wapama Falls**, which each plummet more than 1000ft over fractured granite walls on the north shore of the reservoir. **Hetch Hetchy Dome** rises up in the distance. This hike is best in spring, when temperatures are moderate and wildflowers poke out everywhere. Keep an eye out for rattlesnakes and the occasional bear, especially in summer.

There are bathrooms, but no other visitor services at Hetch Hetchy. The road is only open during daylight hours; specifics are posted at the Evergreen Rd turnoff.

🏃 Activities

Hiking

Over 800 miles of hiking trails cater to hikers of all abilities. Take an easy half-mile stroll on the valley floor; venture out all day on a quest for viewpoints, waterfalls and lakes; or go camping in the remote outer reaches of the backcountry.

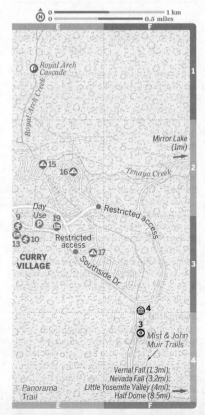

Some of the park's most popular hikes start right in Yosemite Valley, including to the top of Half Dome (17-mile round-trip), the most famous of all. It follows a section of the John Muir Trail and is strenuous, difficult and best tackled in two days with an overnight in Little Yosemite Valley. Reaching the top can only be done after rangers have installed fixed cables. Depending on snow conditions, this may occur as early as late May or as late as July, and the cables usually come down in mid-October. To whittle down the cables' notorious human logjams, the park now requires permits for day hikers, but the route is still nerve-wracking as hikers must 'share the road.' The less ambitious or physically fit will still have a ball following the same trail as far as **Vernal Fall** (2.6-mile round-trip), the top of **Nevada Fall** (6.5-mile round-trip) or idyllic **Little Yosemite Valley** (8-mile round-trip). The Four Mile Trail (9.2-mile round-trip) to Glacier Point is a strenuous but satisfying climb to a glorious viewpoint.

Along Glacier Point Rd, **Sentinel Dome** (2.2-mile round-trip) is an easy hike to the crown of a commanding granite dome. And one of the most scenic hikes in the park, the **Panorama Trail** (8.5-mile one-way) descends to the Valley (joining the John Muir and Mist Trails) with nonstop views, including Half Dome and Illilouette Fall.

If you've got the kids in tow, nice and easy destinations include **Mirror Lake** (2-mile round-trip, or 4.5 miles via the **Tenaya Canyon Loop**) in the valley, the **McGurk Meadow Trail** (1.6-mile round-trip) on Glacier Point Rd, which has a historic log cabin to romp around in, and the trails meandering beneath the big trees of the Mariposa Grove in Wawona.

Also in the Wawona area has one of the park's prettiest (and often overlooked) hikes to **Chilnualna Falls** (8.6-mile round-trip). Best done between April and June, it follows a cascading creek to the top of the dramatic overlook falls, starting gently, then hitting you with some grinding switchbacks before sort of leveling out again.

The highest concentration of hikes lies in the high country of **Tuolumne Meadows** (p, which is only accessible in summer. A popular choice here is the hike to **Dog Lake** (2.8-mile round-trip), but it gets busy. You can also hike along a relatively flat part of the John Muir Trail into lovely **Lyell Canyon**

Yosemite Valley

(17.6-mile round-trip), following the Lyell Fork of the Tuolumne River.

Backpacks, tents and other equipment can be rented from the **Yosemite Mountaineering School** (☎209-372-8344; www. yosemitepark.com; Curry Village; ☺Apr-Oct). The school also offers two-day Learn to Backpack trips for novices and all-inclusive three- and four-day guided backpacking trips ($375 to $500 per person), which are great for inexperienced and solo travelers. In summer the school operates a branch from Tuolumne Meadows.

Rock Climbing

With its sheer spires, polished domes and soaring monoliths, Yosemite is rock-climbing nirvana. The main climbing season runs from April to October. Most climbers, including some legendary stars, stay at Camp 4 (p413) near El Capitan, especially in spring and fall. In summer another base camp springs up at Tuolumne Meadows Campground (p414). Climbers looking for partners post notices on bulletin boards at either campground.

Yosemite Mountaineering School offers top-flight instruction for novice to advanced rock hounds, plus guided climbs and equipment rental. All-day group classes for beginners are $148 per person.

The meadow across from El Capitan and the northeastern end of Tenaya Lake (off Tioga Rd) are good for watching climbers dangle from granite (you need binoculars for a really good view). Look for the haul bags first – they're bigger, more colorful and move around more than the climbers, making them easier to spot. As part of the excellent **'Ask a Climber' program**, climbing rangers set up telescopes at El Capitan Bridge from 11am to 3pm (mid-May through mid-October) and answers visitors' questions.

Cycling

Mountain biking isn't permitted within the park, but cycling along the 12 miles of paved trails is a popular and environmentally friendly way of exploring the valley. It's also the fastest way to get around when valley traffic is at a standstill. Many families bring bicycles, and you'll often find kids doing laps through the campgrounds. Hardcore cyclists brave the skinny shoulders and serious altitude changes of the trans-Sierra Tioga Rd.

Swimming

On a hot summer day, nothing beats a dip in the gentle Merced River, though if chilly water doesn't float your boat, you can always pay to play in the scenic outdoor swimming pools at Curry Village and Yosemite Lodge at the Falls (adult/child $5/4). With a sandy beach, Tenaya Lake is a frigid but interesting option, though White Wolf's Harden Lake warms up to a balmy temperature by mid summer.

Horseback Riding

Yosemite Stables (www.yosemitepark.com; trips 2hr/half-day $64/88) runs guided trips to such scenic locales as Mirror Lake, Chilnualna Falls and the Tuolumne River from three bases: **Tuolumne Meadows** (☑209-372-8427), **Wawona** (☑209-375-6502) and **Yosemite Valley** (☑209-372-8348). The season runs from May to October, although this varies slightly by location. No experience is needed, but reservations are advised, especially at the Yosemite Valley stables. Some mounts are horses, but most likely you'll be riding a sure-footed mule.

Rafting

From around late May to July, floating the Merced River from Stoneman Meadow, near Curry Village, to Sentinel Bridge is a leisurely way to soak up Yosemite Valley views. Four-person **raft rentals** (☑209-372-4386; per person $31) for the 3-mile trip are available from the concessionaire in Curry Village and include equipment and a shuttle ride back to the rental kiosk. Children must be over 50 pounds. Or bring your own equipment and pay $5 to shuttle back.

River rats are also attracted to the fierce **Tuolumne River**, a classic class IV run that plunges and thunders through boulder gardens and cascades. Outfitters **OARS** (☑209-736-2597; www.oars.com) and

Groveland-based **Sierra Mac** (☑209-591-8027, www.sierramac.com) offer guided trips.

Winter Sports

The white coat of winter opens up a different set of things to do, as the valley becomes a quiet, frosty world of snow-draped evergreens, ice-coated lakes and vivid vistas of gleaming white mountains sparkling against blue skies. Winter tends to arrive in full force by mid-November and peter out in early April.

Cross-country skiers can explore 350 miles of skiable trails and roads, including 90 miles of marked trails and 25 miles of machine-groomed track near Badger Pass. The scenic but grueling trail to Glacier Point (21-mile round-trip) also starts from here. More trails are at Crane Flat and the Mariposa Grove. The nongroomed trails can also be explored with snowshoes.

A free shuttle bus connects the Yosemite Valley and Badger Pass. Roads in the valley are plowed, and Hwys 41, 120 and 140 are usually kept open, conditions permitting. The Tioga Rd (Hwy 120 E), however, closes with the first snowfall. Be sure to bring snow chains with you, as prices for them double once you hit the foothills.

Badger Pass　　　SKIING, SNOWBOARDING
(☑209-372-8430; www.badgerpass.com; lift ticket adult/child $49/25; ⊙9am-4pm mid-Dec–Mar) Most of the action converges on one of California's oldest ski resorts. The gentle slopes are perfect for families and beginner skiers and snowboarders. It's about 22 miles from

ⓘ MANDATORY HALF DOME PERMITS

To stem lengthy lines (and increasingly dangerous conditions) on the vertiginous cables of Half Dome, the park now requires that all-day hikers obtain an advance permit to climb the cables. There are currently three ways to do this, though check www.nps.gov/yose/planyourvisit/hdpermits.htm for the latest information. Rangers check permits at the base of the cables.

Preseason permit lottery (☑877-444-6777; www.recreation.gov; application fee online/by phone $4.50/6.50) Lottery applications for the 300 daily spots must be completed in March, with confirmation notification sent in mid-April; an additional $8 per person charge confirms the permit. Applications can include up to six people and seven alternate dates.

Daily lottery Approximately 50 additional permits are distributed by lottery two days before each hiking date. Apply online or by phone between midnight and 1pm Pacific Time; notification available late that same evening. It's easier to score weekday permits.

Backpackers Those with Yosemite-issued wilderness permits that *reasonably include* Half Dome can request Half Dome permits ($8 per person) without going through the lottery process. Backpackers with wilderness permits from a National Forest or another park can use that permit to climb the cables.

the valley on Glacier Point Rd. There are five chairlifts, 800 vertical feet and 10 runs, a full-service lodge, equipment rental ($27 to $37 for a full set of gear) and the excellent **Yosemite Ski School**, where generations of novices have learned how to get down a hill safely (group lessons from $47).

Badger Pass Cross-Country Center & Ski School
SKIING

(☎ 209-372-8444) Located in the Badger Pass Ski Area, this school offers beginner-lesson-plus-rental packages ($46), equipment rentals ($25), snow-camping rentals and guided tours. The center also runs overnight trips to **Glacier Point Ski Hut**, a rustic stone-and-log cabin. Rates, including meals, are $350/120 guided/self-guided for one night or $550/240 for two nights.

Ostrander Ski Hut
SKIING

(www.yosemiteconservancy.org) More experienced skiers can trek 10 miles out to the popular hut on **Ostrander Lake**, operated by Yosemite Conservancy. The hut is staffed all winter and open to backcountry skiers and snowshoers for $35 to $55 per person, per night on a lottery basis. See the website for details.

Curry Village Ice Rink
SKATING

(adult/child $10/9.50, skate rental $4) A delightful winter activity is taking a spin on the outdoor rink, where you'll be skating under the watchful eye of Half Dome.

Tours

The nonprofit **Yosemite Conservancy** (☎ 209-379-2317; www.yosemiteconservancy.org) has scheduled tours of all kinds, plus custom trips available.

First-timers often appreciate the year-round, two-hour **Valley Floor Tour** (per adult/child $25/13) run by **DNC Parks & Resorts** (www.yosemitepark.com), which covers the valley highlights.

For other tour options stop at the tour and activity desks at Yosemite Lodge at the Falls, Curry Village or Yosemite Village, call ☎ 209-372-4386 or check www.yosemitepark.com.

🛏 Sleeping

Competition for campsites is fierce from May to September, when arriving without a reservation and hoping for the best is tantamount to getting someone to lug your Barcalounger up Half Dome. Even first-come,

---

WILDERNESS PERMITS FOR OVERNIGHT CAMPING

Shedding the high-season crowds is easiest when you set foot into Yosemite's backcountry wilderness. Start by identifying a route that matches your schedule, skill and fitness level. Then secure a **wilderness permit** (☎ 209-372-0740; www.nps.gov/yose/planyourvisit/wpres.htm; advance reservation fee $5, plus $5 per person, free for walk-ins; ⊙ 8:30am-4:30pm Mon-Fri Dec-Sep, extended hours late-May–early Sep), which is mandatory for overnight trips. To prevent tent cities sprouting in the woods, a quota system limits the number of people leaving from each trailhead each day. For trips between mid-May and September, 60% of the quota may be reserved by fax, phone, or mail from 24 weeks to two days before your trip. Faxes received between 5pm (the previous day) and 7:30am (the first morning you can reserve) get first priority.

The remainder are distributed by the office closest to the trailhead on a first-come, first-served basis (beginning at 11am one day before your planned hike) at Yosemite Valley Wilderness Center, Tuolumne Meadows Wilderness Center, the information stations at Wawona and Big Oak Flat, and the Hetch Hetchy Entrance Station. Hikers who turn up at the wilderness center nearest the trailhead get priority over those at another wilderness centers. For example, if a person who's been waiting for hours in the valley wants the last permit left for Lyell Canyon, the Yosemite Valley Wilderness Center calls the Tuolumne Meadows Wilderness Center to see if any hikers in Tuolumne want it. If a hiker waltzing into the Tuolumne office says 'yes!', they get priority over the person in the valley.

Reservations are not available from October to April, but you'll still need to get a permit by self-registering at the park.

At night you must be sure to store all scented items in bear-resistant containers, which may be rented for $5 per week at the wilderness and visitor centers. For locations and details, check www.nps.gov/yose/planyourvisit/bearcanrentals.htm.

first-served campgrounds tend to fill by noon, especially on weekends and around holidays. Campsites can be reserved up to five months in advance. **Reservations** (☑877-444-6777, 518-885-3639; www.recreation. gov) become available from 7am PST on the 15th of every month in one-month blocks, and often sell out within minutes.

Without a booking, your only chance is to hightail it to an open **first-come, first-served campground** or proceed to one of four **campground reservation offices** (☑information only 209-372-8502; Curry Village parking lot; ☺8am-5pm) in **Yosemite Valley**, Wawona, Big Oak Flat and Tuolumne Meadows (the latter three are only open seasonally). Try to get there before they open at 8am (the valley office may open at 7:30am in summer), put your name on a waiting list and then hope for a cancellation or early departure. Return when the ranger tells you to (usually 3pm) and if you hear your name, consider yourself very lucky indeed.

All campgrounds have flush toilets, except for Tamarack Flat, Yosemite Creek and Porcupine Flat, which have vault toilets and no potable water. Those at higher elevations get chilly at night, even in summer, so pack accordingly. The Yosemite Mountaineering School (p410) rents camping gear.

If you hold a wilderness permit, you may spend the nights before and after your trip in the backpacker campgrounds at Tuolumne Meadows, Hetch Hetchy, White Wolf and behind North Pines in Yosemite Valley. The cost is $5 per person, per night and reservations aren't necessary.

Opening dates for seasonal campgrounds vary according to the weather.

All noncamping reservations within the park are handled by **DNC Parks & Resorts** (☑801-559-4884; www.yosemitepark.com) and can be made up to 366 days in advance; reservations are absolutely critical from May to early September. Rates – and demand – drop from October to April.

Yosemite Valley

Camp 4 CAMPGROUND $
(shared tent sites per person $5; ☺year-round) Walk-in campground at 4000ft, popular with climbers; sites are shared.

North Pines Campground CAMPGROUND $
(tent & RV sites $20; ☺Apr-Oct; 🐾) A bit off the beaten path (4000ft) with 81 sites near Mirror Lake; reservations required.

Upper Pines Campground CAMPGROUND $
(tent & RV sites $20; ☺year-round; 🐾) Busy, busy, busy – and big (238 sites, 4000ft); reservations required mid-March through November.

Lower Pines Campground CAMPGROUND $
(tent & RV sites $20; ☺Apr-Oct; 🐾) Crammed and noisy with 60 sites at 4000ft; reservations required.

Housekeeping Camp CABINS $
(q $98; ☺Apr-Oct) This cluster of 266 cabins, each walled in by concrete on three sides and lidded by a canvas roof, is crammed and noisy, but the setting along the Merced River has its merits. Each unit can sleep up to six and has electricity, light, a table and chairs, and a covered patio with picnic tables.

Curry Village CABINS $$
(tent cabin $123-128, cabin without/with bath $146/195; 🕿🖼) Founded in 1899 as a summer camp, Curry has hundreds of units squished tightly together beneath towering evergreens. The canvas cabins are basically glorified tents, so for more comfort, quiet and privacy get one of the cozy wood cabins, which have bedspreads, drapes and vintage posters. There are also 18 attractive motel-style rooms in the **Stoneman House** (r $198), including a loft suite sleeping up to six.

Yosemite Lodge at the Falls MOTEL $$$
(r from $199; @🕿🖼) ✈ Situated a short walk from Yosemite Falls, this multibuilding complex contains a wide range of eateries, a lively bar, big pool and other handy amenities. Delightful rooms, thanks to a recent eco conscious renovation, now feel properly lodge-like, with rustic wooden furniture and striking nature photography. All have cable TV, telephone, refrigerator and coffeemaker, and great patio or balcony panoramas.

Ahwahnee Hotel HISTORIC HOTEL $$$
(r from $470; @🕿🖼) The crème de la crème of Yosemite's lodging, this sumptuous historic property dazzles with soaring ceilings, Turkish kilims lining the hallways and atmospheric lounges with mammoth stone fireplaces. It's the gold standard for upscale lodges, though if you're not blessed with bullion, you can still soak up the ambience during afternoon tea, a drink in the bar or a gourmet meal.

HIGH SIERRA CAMPS

In the backcountry near Tuolumne Meadows, the exceptionally popular High Sierra Camps provide shelter and sustenance to hikers who'd rather not carry food or a tent. The camps – called **Vogelsang**, **Merced Lake**, **Sunrise**, **May Lake** and **Glen Aulin** – are set 6 to 10 miles apart along a loop trail. They consist of dormitory-style canvas tent cabins with beds, blankets or comforters, plus showers (at May Lake, Sunrise and Merced Lake – subject to water availability) and a central dining tent. Guests bring their own sheets and towels. The rate is $161 per adult ($102 for children seven to twelve) per night, including breakfast and dinner. Organized hiking or saddle trips led by ranger naturalists are also available (from $928).

A short season (roughly late June to September) and high demand mean that there's a lottery for reservations. **Applications** ([📞 559-253-5672; www.yosemitepark.com) are currently accepted in September and October only. If you don't have a reservation, call from February to check for cancellations. Dates vary year to year, so watch the website for updates.

🏕 Tioga Road

Tuolumne Meadows campers should note that the closest pay showers are located at Mono Vista RV Park (p441) in Lee Vining.

Tuolumne Meadows Campground　　　CAMPGROUND $
(tent & RV sites $20; ☉ mid-Jul–late-Sep; 🔋) Biggest campground in the park (8600ft) with 304 fairly well-spaced sites; half of these can be reserved.

Porcupine Flat Campground　　CAMPGROUND $
(tent & RV sites $10; ☉ Jul-Sep; 🔋) Primitive 52-site area, at 8100ft; some sites near the road.

Tamarack Flat Campground　　CAMPGROUND $
(tent sites $10; ☉ Jul-Sep) Quiet, secluded, primitive at 6315ft; the 52 tent sites are a rough 3-mile drive off Tioga Rd.

White Wolf Campground　　CAMPGROUND $
(tent & RV sites $14; ☉ Jul–mid-Sep; 🔋) Attractive setting at 8000ft, but the 74 sites are fairly boxed in.

Yosemite Creek Campground　　CAMPGROUND $
(tent sites $10; ☉ Jul–mid-Sep; 🔋) The most secluded and quiet campground (7659ft) in the park, reached via a rough 4.5-mile road. There are 75 primitive sites.

Tuolumne Meadows Lodge　　TENT CABINS $$
(tent cabin $123; ☉ mid-Jun–mid-Sep) In the high country, about 55 miles from the valley, this option attracts hikers to its 69 canvas tent cabins with four beds, a wood-burning stove and candles (no electricity). Breakfast and dinner are available.

White Wolf Lodge　　CABINS, TENT CABINS $$
(tent cabin $123, cabin with bath $156; ☉ Jul–mid-Sep) This complex enjoys its own little world a mile up a spur road, away from the hubbub and traffic of Hwy 120 and the valley. There are 24 spartan four-bedded tent cabins without electricity and four very-in-demand hard-walled cabins that feel like rustic motel rooms. The generator cuts out at 11pm, so you'll need a flashlight until early morning.

There's also a dining room and a tiny counter-service store.

🏕 Hetch Hetchy & Big Oak Flat Road

Crane Flat Campground　　CAMPGROUND $
(Big Oak Flat Rd; tent & RV sites $20; ☉ Jun-Sep) Large family campground at 6192ft, with 166 sites; reservations required.

Hodgdon Meadow Campground　　CAMPGROUND $
(Big Oak Flat Rd; tent & RV sites $14-20; ☉ year-round) Utilitarian and crowded 105-site campground at 4872ft; reservations required mid-April to mid-October.

Dimond O Campground　　CAMPGROUND $
([📞 877-444-6777; www.recreation.gov; Evergreen Rd; tent & RV sites $24; ☉ May–mid-Sep) Four miles off Hwy 120, this reservable United States Forest Service (USFS) campground has 35 forested sites adjacent to the Tuolumne River. Arriving from the west, it's the last campground before the Big Oak Flat entrance, and a good fallback if you can't get a campsite inside the park.

★**Evergreen Lodge Resort**   CABINS, CAMPGROUND $$$
(☑ 209-379-2606; www.evergreenlodge.com; 33160 Evergreen Rd; tents $85-120, cabins $180-415; @ 🛜 🛉) 🍽 Outside the park near the entrance to Hetch Hetchy, this classic 90-year-old resort lets roughing-it guests cheat with comfy, prefurnished tents and rustic to deluxe mountain cabins with private porches but no phone or TV. Outdoor recreational activities abound, many of them family-oriented, with equipment rentals available.

There's a general store, tavern with a pool table and a fantastic restaurant serving three hearty meals every day.

🛏 Wawona & Glacier Point Road

Bridalveil Creek Campground   CAMPGROUND $
(tent & RV sites $14; ⊙ Jul–early Sep; 🛉) Quieter than the valley campgrounds, with 110 sites at 7200ft.

Wawona Campground   CAMPGROUND $
(Wawona; tent & RV sites $14-20; ⊙ year-round; 🛉) Idyllic riverside setting at 4000ft with 93 well-spaced sites; reservations required April to September.

Wawona Hotel   HISTORIC HOTEL $$$
(r without/with bath incl breakfast $153/226; ⊙ mid-Mar–Dec; 🛜 🛉) This National Historic Landmark, dating from 1879, is a collection of six graceful, whitewashed New England-style buildings flanked by wide porches. The 104 rooms – with no phone or TV – come with Victorian-style furniture and other period items, and about half the rooms share bathrooms, with nice robes provided for the walk there.

The grounds are lovely, with a spacious lawn dotted with Adirondack chairs. Wi-fi available in annex building only.

🍴 Eating

You can find food options for all budgets and palates within the park, from greasy slabs of fast food to swanky cuts of top-notch steak. All carry good vegetarian options.

Bringing in or buying your own food saves money but remember that you *must* remove it all from your car (or backpack or bicycle) and store it overnight in a bear box or canister. The **Village Store** in Yosemite Village has the best selection (including toiletries, health-food items and some organic produce), while stores at Curry Village,

Wawona, Tuolumne Meadows, Housekeeping Camp and the Yosemite Lodge are more limited.

★**Yosemite Lodge Food Court**   CAFETERIA $
(Yosemite Lodge; mains $7-12; ⊙ 6:30am-8:30pm Sun-Thu, to 9pm Fri & Sat; ☑) This self-service restaurant has several tummy-filling stations serving a large choice of pastas, burgers, pizza and sandwiches, either made to order or served from beneath heat lamps. Proceed to the cashier and find a table inside or on the patio.

Degnan's Loft   PIZZA $
(mains $8-12; ⊙ 5-9pm Mon-Fri, noon-9pm Sat & Sun, late-May–Sep; ☑ 🛉) Head upstairs to this convivial place with high-beamed ceilings and a many-sided fireplace, and kick back under the dangling lift chair for decent salads, veggie lasagna and pizza.

Degnan's Deli   DELI $
(Yosemite Village; sandwiches $7-8; ⊙ 7am-5pm; ☑) Excellent made-to-order sandwiches, breakfast items and snack foods.

Curry Village Coffee Corner   CAFE $
(Curry Village; pastries $2-5; ⊙ 6am-10pm, shorter winter hours) For a coffee jolt or sugar fix.

Meadow Grill   FAST FOOD $
(Curry Village; mains $5-8; ⊙ 11am-5pm Apr-Oct) Hot dogs, burgers and a few salads on a deck near the parking area.

Tuolumne Meadows Grill   FAST FOOD $
(Tioga Rd; mains $5-9; ⊙ 8am-5pm mid-Jun–mid-Sep) Scarf down burgers and grill items at the outdoor picnic tables.

Village Grill   FAST FOOD $
(Yosemite Village; mains $5-11; ⊙ 11am-5pm Apr-Oct) Fight the chipmunks for burgers and tasty fries alfresco.

Curry Village Pizza Patio   PIZZA $
(Curry Village; pizzas from $9; ⊙ noon-10pm, shorter winter hours) Enjoy tasty pizza at this buzzing eatery that becomes a chatty après-hike hangout in the late afternoon.

Curry Village Dining Pavilion   CAFETERIA $$
(Curry Village; breakfast adult/child $10.50/6.50, dinner adult/child $15.50/8; ⊙ 7-10am & 5:30-8pm Apr-Nov) Although the cafeteria-style setting has all the charm of a train-station waiting room, the mediocre all-you-can-eat breakfast and dinner buffets are great for families, gluttons and the undecided.

★**Mountain Room Restaurant** AMERICAN $$$
(☏209-372-1403; www.yosemitepark.com; Yosemite Lodge; mains $21-35; ☺5:30-9:30pm; ☑️🅿️)
🍴 With a killer view of Yosemite Falls, the window tables at this casual and elegant contemporary steakhouse are a hot commodity. The chefs whip up the best meals in the park, with flat-iron steak and locally caught mountain trout wooing diners under a rotating display of nature photographs. Reservations accepted only for groups larger than eight; casual dress is OK.

★**Evergreen Lodge** CALIFORNIAN $$
(☏209-379-2606; www.evergreenlodge.com; 33160 Evergreen Rd; breakfast & lunch $11-18, dinner $12-28; ☺7-10:30am & noon-3pm & 5-9pm; ☑️🅿️) Creative and satisfying, the Evergreen's restaurant serves some of the best meals around, with big and delicious breakfasts, three types of burgers (Black Angus beef, buffalo, and veggie) and dinner choices including dishes like rib-eye steak, grilled venison and braised seitan. The homey wooden tavern is a perennial favorite for evening cocktails, beers on tap over a game of pool and live music on select weekends. A general store fills the gaps with to-go sandwiches, snacks and dreamy gelato.

Wawona Hotel Dining Room AMERICAN $$$
(Wawona Hotel; breakfast & lunch $11-15, dinner $22-30; ☺7:30-10am, 11:30am-1:30pm & 5:30-9pm Easter-Dec; ☑️🅿️) Beautiful sequoia-painted lamps light this old-fashioned white-tablecloth dining room, and the Victorian detail makes it an enchanting place to have an upscale (though somewhat overpriced) meal. 'Tasteful, casual attire' is the rule for dinner dress, and there's a barbecue on the lawn every Saturday during summer.

The Wawona's wide, white porch makes a snazzy destination for evening cocktails, and listen for veteran pianist Tom Bopp in the lobby.

Ahwahnee Dining Room CALIFORNIAN $$$
(☏209-372-1489; Ahwahnee Hotel; breakfast $7-22, lunch $16-22, dinner $28-46; ☺7-10am, 11:30am-3pm & 5:30-9pm; ☑️) 🍴 The formal ambience (mind your manners) may not be for everybody, but few would not be awed by the sumptuous decor, soaring beamed ceiling and palatial chandeliers. The menu is constantly in flux, but most dishes have perfect pitch and are beautifully presented. There's a dress code at dinner, but otherwise shorts and sneakers are OK.

Sunday brunch (adult/child $45/5; 7am to 3pm) is amazing. Reservations highly recommended for brunch and dinner.

🍷 **Drinking & Nightlife**

No one will mistake Yosemite for nightlife central, but there are some nice spots to relax with a Cabernet, cocktail or cold beer. Outside the park, the Yosemite Bug Rustic Mountain Resort (p422) and the Evergreen Lodge Resort (p415) both have lively lounges.

Mountain Room Lounge BAR
(Yosemite Lodge, Yosemite Valley; ☺noon-11pm Sat & Sun, 4:30-11pm Mon-Fri) Catch up on the latest sports news while knocking back draft brews at this large bar that buzzes in wintertime. Order a s'mores kit (graham crackers, chocolate squares and marshmallows) to roast in the open-pit fireplace. Kids welcome until 10pm.

Ahwahnee Bar BAR
(Ahwahnee Hotel, Yosemite Valley; ☺11:30am-11pm) The perfect way to experience the Ahwahnee without dipping too deep into your pockets; settle in for a drink at this cozy bar, complete with pianist. Appetizers and light meals ($10 to $25) provide sustenance.

⭐ **Entertainment**

In addition to the Yosemite Theater, other activities scheduled year-round include campfire programs, children's photo walks, twilight strolls, night-sky watching, ranger talks and slide shows, and the tavern at the Evergreen Lodge has live bands some weekends. Scan the *Yosemite Guide* for full details.

Yosemite Theater THEATER
(performances adult/child $8/4; ☺9am-7:30pm summer, shorter hours rest of year) Behind the visitor center, this theater screens two films: Ken Burns' *Yosemite: A Gathering of Spirit*, a celebration of the Yosemite Grant's 150th anniversary, and the painfully dramatic but beautifully photographed *Spirit of Yosemite*. The movies alternate, starting every half-hour between 9:30am and 4:30pm (from noon on Sundays), and offer a free, air-conditioned respite from the summer heat.

In the evening take your pick from a rotating cast of performers, including actor Lee Stetson, who portrays the fascinating life and philosophy of John Muir, and Park

Ranger Shelton Johnson, who re-creates the experiences of a Buffalo Soldier. There are also special children's shows.

ℹ Information

Yosemite's entrance fee is $20 per vehicle or $10 for those on bicycle or foot and is valid for seven consecutive days. Upon entering the park, you'll receive a National Park Service (NPS) map and a copy of the seasonal *Yosemite Guide* newspaper, which includes an activity schedule and current opening hours of all facilities.

For recorded park information, campground availability, and road and weather conditions, call ☎ 209-372-0200.

DANGERS & ANNOYANCES

Yosemite is prime black-bear habitat. Follow park rules on proper food storage and utilize bear-proof food lockers when parked overnight (see also p757). Mosquitoes can be pesky in summer, so bug spray's not a bad idea. And please don't feed those squirrels. They may look cute but they've got a nasty bite.

INTERNET ACCESS

Curry Village Lounge (Curry Village, behind registration office; ☎) Free wi-fi.

Degnan's Cafe (Yosemite Village; per 3 min $1; ⏰ 7am-6pm) Pay terminals in this cafe adjacent to Degnan's Deli.

Mariposa County Public Library (☎) Yosemite Valley (Girls Club Bldg, 58 Cedar Ct, Yosemite Valley; ⏰ 9am-noon Mon & Tue, 9am-1pm Wed & Thu); Bassett Memorial Library (Chilnualna Falls Rd, Wawona; ⏰ noon-5pm Mon, Wed & Fri, 10am-3pm Sat) Free internet terminals and wi-fi available.

Yosemite Lodge at the Falls (Yosemite Valley; per min 25¢; ⏰ 24hr) Pay terminals are in the lobby. Wi-fi costs $6 per day for nonguests.

INTERNET RESOURCES

Discussion forums with good local advice can be found at www.yosemite.ca.us/forum and www.yosemitenews.info.

Yosemite Conservancy (www.yosemiteconservancy.org) Information and educational programs offered by the nonprofit park-support organization.

Yosemite National Park (www.nps.gov/yose) Official Yosemite National Park Service site with the most comprehensive and current information. News and road closures/openings are often posted first on its Facebook page (www.facebook.com/YosemiteNPS).

Yosemite Park (www.yosemitepark.com) On-line home of DNC Parks & Resorts, Yosemite's main concessionaire. Has lots of practical information and a lodging reservations function.

MEDICAL SERVICES

Yosemite Medical Clinic (☎ 209-372-4637; 9000 Ahwahnee Dr, Yosemite Village; ⏰ 9am-7pm daily late-May–late Sep, 9am-5pm Mon-Fri late-Sep–late-May) Twenty-four-hour emergency service available. A dental clinic (☎ 209-372-4200) is also available next door.

MONEY

Stores in Yosemite Village, Curry Village and Wawona all have ATMs, as does the Yosemite Lodge at the Falls.

POST

The main **post office** is in Yosemite Village, but Wawona and Yosemite Lodge also have year-round services. A seasonal branch operates in Tuolumne Meadows.

TELEPHONE

There are pay phones at every developed location throughout the park. Cell-phone reception is sketchy, depending on your location; AT&T, Verizon and Sprint have the only coverage.

TOURIST INFORMATION

Extended summer hours may apply.

Big Oak Flat Information Station (☎ 209-379-1899; ⏰ 8am-5pm late-May–Sep) Also has a wilderness permit desk.

Tuolumne Meadows Visitor Center (☎ 209-372-0263; ⏰ 9am-5pm Jun-Sep)

Tuolumne Meadows Wilderness Center (☎ 209-372-0309; ⏰ approx 8:30am-4:30pm spring & fall, 7:30am-5pm Jul & Aug) Issues wilderness permits.

Yosemite Valley Wilderness Center (☎ 209-372-0745; Yosemite Village; ⏰ 7:30am-5pm May-Sep) Wilderness permits, maps and backcountry advice.

Wawona Visitor Center (☎ 209-375-9531; ⏰ 8:30am-5pm May-Sep) Issues wilderness permits.

Yosemite Valley Visitor Center (☎ 209-372-0299; Yosemite Village; ⏰ 9am-6pm summer, shorter hours year-round) The main office, with exhibits and free film screenings in the theater.

ℹ Getting There & Away

CAR

Yosemite is accessible year-round from the west (via Hwys 120 W and 140) and south (Hwy 41), and in summer also from the east (via Hwy 120 E). Roads are plowed in winter, but snow chains may be required at any time. In 2006 a mammoth rockslide buried part of Hwy 140, 6 miles west of the park; traffic there is restricted to vehicles under 45ft.

Gas up year-round at Wawona and Crane Flat inside the park or at El Portal on Hwy 140 just

California Wildlife

Unique creatures great and small inhabit the land, sky and waters of California's diverse ecosystems. Visit them at the ocean or in the forest, or just scan the skies.

1. Elephant seal
Equipped with a trunk-like nose, the enormous males noisily battle for dominance on the beach.

2. Black bear
The name is misleading, as bear fur can be shades of brown, black, cinnamon or tawny blonde.

3. California condor
A 10ft wingspan is the hallmark of these endangered carrion scavengers. Captive breeding has increased the population, though lead bullet poisoning remains its biggest threat.

4. Gray whale
Dramatic breaches and the puffs of water spouts mark the passage of these school-bus-sized mammals. Pods of whales migrate yearly between Mexico and Alaska, with peak viewing between December and April.

5. California sea lion
With dog-like faces and oversized flippers, vocal sea lions typically haul out in large social groups. The crowd-pleasing colony at San Francisco's Pier 39 mysteriously appeared soon after the 1989 Loma Prieta earthquake.

6. Mule deer
Ubiquitous throughout the state, mule deer are recognizable by their ample ears and black foreheads. Bucks wear forked antler racks.

7. Desert tortoise
Able to live for over half a century, these high desert reptiles burrow underground to survive extreme heat and cold.

8. Hawk
Frequently seen riding the thermal currents on windy ridges, a dozen types of hawks can be found in California. These speedy birds of prey are known for their keen eyesight and strong talons.

9. Mountain lion
Also known as cougars, panthers or pumas, these territorial big cats primarily stalk and feed on deer. They hunt from dusk to dawn, and can sprint at up to 50 miles per hour.

10. Banana slug
Tread carefully along the forest floor so you don't slip on these large and squishy bright yellow specimens.

11. Monarch butterfly
These orange and black beauties flutter thousands of miles to complete their annual migration.

12. Elk
Three subspecies of elk roam the state, with majestic males parading chandeliers of velvety antlers, and bugling dramatically during the fall rutting season.

2

3

5

6

8

9

11

12

outside its boundaries. In summer gas is also sold at Tuolumne Meadows. You'll pay dearly.

PUBLIC TRANSPORTATION

Yosemite is one of the few national parks that can be easily reached by public transportation. **Greyhound** (www.greyhound.com) buses and **Amtrak** (www.amtrak.com) trains serve Merced, west of the park, where they are met by buses operated by **Yosemite Area Regional Transportation System** (YARTS; ☎877-989-2787; www.yarts.com), and you can buy Amtrak tickets that include the YARTS segment all the way into the park. Buses travel to Yosemite Valley along Hwy 140 several times daily year-round, stopping along the way.

In summer (roughly June through September), another YARTS route runs from Mammoth Lakes along Hwy 395 to Yosemite Valley via Hwy 120. One-way tickets to Yosemite Valley are $13 ($9 child and senior, three hours) from Merced and $18 ($15 child and senior, 3½ hours) from Mammoth Lakes, less if boarding in between.

YARTS fares include the park-entrance fee, making them a super bargain, and drivers accept credit cards.

ⓘ Getting Around

BICYCLE

Bicycling is an ideal way to take in Yosemite Valley. You can rent a wide-handled cruiser (per hour/day $11.50/32) or a bike with an attached child trailer (per hour/day $19/59) at the Yosemite Lodge at the Falls or Curry Village. Strollers and wheelchairs are also rented here.

CAR

Roadside signs with red bears mark the many spots where bears have been hit by motorists, so think before you hit the accelerator, and follow the pokey posted speed limits. Valley visitors are advised to park and take advantage of the Yosemite Valley Shuttle Bus. Glacier Point and Tioga Rds are closed in winter.

PUBLIC TRANSPORTATION

The free, air-conditioned **Yosemite Valley Shuttle Bus** is a comfortable and efficient way of traveling around the park. Buses operate year-round at frequent intervals and stop at 21 numbered locations, including parking lots, campgrounds, trailheads and lodges. For a route map, see the *Yosemite Guide*.

Free buses also operate between Wawona and the Mariposa Grove (spring to fall), and Yosemite Valley and Badger Pass (winter only). The **Tuolumne Meadows Shuttle** runs between Tuolumne Lodge and Olmsted Point in Tuolumne Meadows (usually mid-June to early September), and the **El Capitan Shuttle** runs a summertime valley loop from Yosemite Village to El Capitan.

Two fee-based hikers' buses also travel from Yosemite Valley. For trailheads along Tioga Rd, catch the **Tuolumne Meadows Tour & Hikers' Bus** (☎209-372-4386; ☺Jul–early Sep), which runs once daily in each direction. Fares depend on distance traveled; the trip to Tuolumne Meadows costs $14.50/23 one way/round-trip. The **Glacier Point Hikers' Bus** (☎209-372-4386; one way/return $25/41; ☺mid-May–Oct) is good for hikers as well as for people reluctant to drive up the long, windy road themselves. Reservations are required.

YOSEMITE GATEWAYS

Fish Camp

Fish Camp, just south of the park on Hwy 41, is more of a bend in the road, but it does have some good lodging options as well as the ever-popular **Sugar Pine Railroad** (☎559-683-7273; www.ymsprr.com; rides adult/child $18/9; ☺Mar–Oct; ⛟), a historic steam train that chugs through the woods on a 4-mile loop.

🛏 Sleeping & Eating

Summerdale Campground CAMPGROUND $
(☎877-444-6677; www.recreation.gov; tent & RV sites $28; ☺May-Sep; ⛟) Has 28 well-dispersed United States Forest Service (USFS) sites along Big Creek.

White Chief Mountain Lodge MOTEL $$
(☎559-683-5444; www.whitechiefmountainlodge.com; 7776 White Chief Mountain Rd; r $145-155; ☺Apr-Oct; ⛟) The cheapest and most basic option in town, this 1950s-era motel has simple kitchenette rooms. New owners have upgraded the exterior and some furniture, but the rooms are still pretty blah. It's located a few hundred yards east of Hwy 41; watch for the sign and go up the wooded country road. The on-site **restaurant** (mains $10-21) serves breakfast and a small dinner menu.

★**Narrow Gauge Inn** INN $$$
(☎559-683-7720; www.narrowgaugeinn.com; 48571 Hwy 41; r incl breakfast Nov-Mar $89-134, Apr-Oct $229-369; ⛟⛟⛟) Next door to the Sugar Pine Railroad, this friendly, beautiful and supremely comfortable 26-room inn counts a hot tub, small bar, and the finest **restaurant** (☎559-683-6446; dinner mains $16-38; ☺5-9pm Apr-Oct) in the area. Each tastefully appointed room features unique decor and a pleasant deck facing the trees and mountains, and all have flat-screen TVs.

Big Creek Inn B&B
B&B $$$

(☎559-641-2828; www.bigcreekinn.com; 1221 Hwy 41; r incl full breakfast $239-299; ☎) Each of the three white-palette rooms has peaceful creek views and a private balcony, and two have gas fireplaces. From the comfortable rooms or the back patio, you can often spot deer and beavers, or hummingbirds lining up at the patio feeder. Amenities include in-room DVD/Blu-Ray players and a large movie library, kitchenette use and big soaking tubs with bath salts.

Oakhurst

At the junction of Hwys 41 and 49, about 15 miles south of the park entrance, Oakhurst functions primarily as a service town. This is your last chance to stock up on reasonably priced groceries, gasoline and camping supplies. The lodgings listed are outside the center of town, where ho-hum chain motels abound.

🛏 Sleeping & Eating

⭐ **Sierra Sky Ranch**
LODGE $$

(☎559-683-8040; www.sierraskyranch. com; 50552 Rd 632; r incl breakfast $145-225; ✳🕸🐾🐾) This former ranch dates back to 1875 and has numerous outdoor activities available on 14 attractive acres. The homespun rooms are phone-free and pet-friendly, with oversized wooden headboards and double doors that open onto shady verandahs. The rambling and beautiful old lodge features a **restaurant** (dinner mains $12-45) and a rustic saloon, and has loads of comfortable lounging areas.

With a storied history including previous uses as a TB hospital and a bordello, its past guests include Marilyn Monroe and John Wayne. Many swear that it's cheerfully haunted by former residents.

Hounds Tooth Inn
B&B $$

(☎559-642-6600; www.houndstoothinn.com; 42071 Hwy 41; r incl breakfast $118-199; ✳🕸) A few miles north of Oakhurst, this gorgeous B&B swims with rosebushes and Victorianesque charm. Its airy rooms and cottages, some with spas and fireplaces, feel like an English manor house. Complimentary wine and hot drinks are available in the afternoon.

Château du Sureau
BOUTIQUE HOTEL $$$

(☎559-683-6860; www.chateaudusureau.com; r incl breakfast $385-585, 2-bedroom villa $2950; ✳@🕸🐾) Never in a billion years would

SCENIC DRIVE: SIERRA VISTA SCENIC BYWAY

Set entirely within Sierra National Forest, this scenic **route** (www.sierravistascenicbyway.org) follows USFS roads in a 100-mile loop that takes you from 3000ft to nearly 7000ft. Along the way are dramatic vistas, excellent fishing, and camping almost anywhere you like (dispersed camping is allowed in most areas). It's a great way for car campers – and curious day trippers – to lose themselves within the mountains.

From its start in **North Fork**, the route takes a half-day to complete, emerging on Hwy 41 a few miles north of **Oakhurst**. Open from June to November, the road is paved most of the way, but narrow and laced with curves. See www.byways.org/explore/byways/2300 for a map and information on sights and the best overlooks.

you expect to find this in Oakhurst. A luxe and discreet full-service European-style hotel and world-class spa, this serene destination property boasts an exceptional level of service. With wall tapestries, oil paintings and ornate chandeliers, its **restaurant** (prix fixe dinner $108) could be a countryside castle.

Merced River Canyon

The approach to Yosemite via Hwy 140 is one of the most scenic, especially the section that meanders through Merced River Canyon. The springtime runoff makes this a spectacular spot for **river rafting**, with many miles of class III and IV rapids. Age minimums vary with water levels.

Outfitters include **Zephyr Whitewater Expeditions** (☎209-532-6249; www.zrafting.com; half-day/1-day trips per person from $109/135), a large, reputable outfitter with a seasonal office in El Portal, and **OARS** (☎209-736-2597; www.oars.com; 1-day trips per person $144-170), a worldwide rafting operator with a solid reputation.

Mariposa

About halfway between Merced and Yosemite Valley, Mariposa (Spanish for 'butterfly') is the largest and most interesting town near the park. Established as a mining and railroad town during the Gold Rush, it has the oldest courthouse in continuous use (since 1854) west of the Mississippi, loads of Old West pioneer character and a friendly feel.

Rock hounds should drive to the Mariposa County Fairgrounds, 2 miles south of town on Hwy 49, to see the 13-pound 'Fricot Nugget' – the largest crystallized gold specimen from the California Gold Rush era – and other gems and machinery at the **California State Mining & Mineral Museum** (☑20 9-742-7625; www.parks.ca.gov/?page_id=588; admission $4; ☺10am-5pm Thu-Sun May-Sep, to 4pm Oct-Apr). An exhibit on glow-in-the-dark minerals is also very cool.

🛏 Sleeping & Eating

★ River Rock Inn   MOTEL $$
(☑209-966-5793; www.riverrockmariposa.com; 4993 7th St; r incl breakfast $110-154; ✳🚻🐾🛁) A bold splash of psychedelic purple and dusty-orange paint spruces up what claims to be the oldest motel in town. Kitchenette rooms done up in artsy earth tones and have TVs but no phones, and calming ceiling fans resemble lily pads. A block removed from Hwy 140 on a quiet side street, it features a courtyard deck and deli cafe serving beer and wine, with live acoustic music some summer evenings.

Mariposa Historic Hotel   HISTORIC HOTEL $$
(☑209-966-7500; www.mariposahotelinn.com; 5029 Hwy 140; r incl breakfast $129-169; ✳🚻) This creaky 1901 building has six king or queen rooms with old-time quilts and period-style furniture, and a corridor crammed with old town photos and newspaper clippings. Room 6 has an original clawfoot tub. Hummingbirds love the flowery back patio where breakfast is served.

Happy Burger   DINER $
(www.happyburgerdiner.com; Hwy 140 at 12th St; mains $7-11; ☺5:30am-9pm; 🚻🐾♿) Boasting the largest menu in the Sierra, this buzzing roadside joint decorated with old LP album covers serves the cheapest meals in Mariposa. Its all-American cuisine means burgers, sandwiches, Mexican food and a ton of sinful ice-cream desserts. Free computer terminal, too.

Sugar Pine Cafe   AMERICAN $$
(www.sugarpinecafe.com; 5038 Hwy 140; breakfast $6-8, dinner $7-20; ☺7am-8:30pm Tue-Sat, to 3pm Sun & Mon) Gussied up with chrome

soda counter stools and red circular booths, this 1940s-era diner serves yummy breakfast items, hot or cold sandwiches and burgers on whole-wheat buns. Dinner fare is pure comfort food like spaghetti and meatballs, and pork chops.

Savoury's   NEW AMERICAN $$
(☑209-966-7677; www.savouryrestaurant.com; 5034 Hwy 140; mains $17-32; ☺5-9pm, closed Wed winter; 🐾) Upscale yet casual Savoury's is still the best restaurant in town. Black lacquered tables and contemporary art create a tranquil window dressing for dishes like chipotle-and-orange-glazed chicken, hearty pastas and steak Diane.

ℹ Information

At the junction of Hwy 49s and 140 is the info-laden **Mariposa County Visitor Center** (☑866-425-3366, 209-966-7081; www.yosemiteexperience.com; ☺9am-6pm), which has friendly staff and racks of brochures.

ℹ Getting There & Away

YARTS (☑877-989-2787, 209-388-9589; www.yarts.com) buses run year-round along Hwy 140 into Yosemite Valley (adult/child $12/8 round-trip, 1¾ hours one way) stopping at the Mariposa visitor center. Tickets include park admission.

Midpines

The highlight of this almost nonexistent town is the folksy **Yosemite Bug Rustic Mountain Resort** (☑866-826-7108, 209-966-6666; www.yosemitebug.com; 6979 Hwy 140, Midpines; dm $28, tent cabins $45-75, r without/with bath from $65/75; @🚻) 🐾, tucked away on a forested hillside about 25 miles from Yosemite National Park. It's more like a convivial mountain retreat than a hostel: at night, friendly folks of all ages and backgrounds share stories, music and delicious freshly prepared meals, and beer and wine in the woodsy **cafe** (mains $9-20; ☺7-10am, 11:30am-3pm & 6-9pm; 🐾) before retreating to their beds. Dorm dwellers have access to a communal kitchen, and the resort has a spa with a hot tub; yoga lessons and massages are also available. The YARTS bus stops a quarter mile up the driveway.

Briceburg

Some 20 miles outside the park, right where the Merced River meets Hwy 140, the town of Briceburg consists of a **visitors center** (☏ 209-379-9414; www.blm.gov/ca/st/en/fo/folsom/mercedriverrec.html; ⏱1-5pm Fri, from 9am Sat & Sun late-Apr–early-Sep) and three primitive **Bureau of Land Management campgrounds** (BLM; http://www.blm.gov/ca/st/en/fo/folsom/mercedriverrec.html; tent & RV sites $10; 🐾) with a to-die-for location right on the river. To reach them you cross a beautiful 1920s wooden suspension bridge, so long trailers and large RVs are not recommended.

El Portal

Right outside the Arch Rock Entrance, and primarily inhabited by park employees, El Portal makes a convenient Yosemite base. YARTS buses run to Yosemite Valley (adult/child round-trip $7/5, one hour).

🛏 Sleeping & Eating

Indian Flat RV Park CAMPGROUND, CABINS $
(☏ 209-379-2339; www.indianflatrvpark.com; 9988 Hwy 140; tent sites $30, RV sites $42-47, tent cabins $79, cottages $129; ⏱year-round; 🐾🐾) Primarily an inexpensive private campground, Indian Flat RV Park also has a number of interesting housing options, including two pretty stone cabin cottages with air-conditioning and roomy tent cabins with ceiling fans and private porches. Guests can use the pool and wi-fi at its sister property next door, and nonguests can pay to shower.

Cedar Lodge MOTEL $$
(☏ 888-742-4371, 209-379-2612; www.stayyosemitecedarlodge.com; 9966 Hwy 140; r $149-189; 🐾🐾🐾) Approximately 9 miles west of the Arch Rock Entrance, the Cedar is a sprawling establishment with more than 200 adequate rooms, an indoor pool, a seasonal outdoor pool and a couple of restaurants. Balcony rooms are the best of the bunch.

Yosemite View Lodge MOTEL $$$
(☏ 888-742-4371, 209-379-2681; www.stayyosemiteviewlodge.com; 11136 Hwy 140; r $189-269, ste $329-559; 🐾🐾🐾🐾🐾) Less than 2 miles from the park entrance, Yosemite View Lodge is a big, modern complex with hot tubs, two restaurants and four pools. All the 336 rooms feature kitchenettes, some have gas fireplaces and views of the Merced River, and the ground-floor rooms have big patios. Wi-fi is $10 per day.

The souped-up 'majestic suites' are massive, with opulent bathrooms featuring waterfall showers and plasma-TV entertainment centers.

Groveland

From the Big Oak Flat entrance, it's 22 miles to Groveland, an adorable town with restored Gold Rush-era buildings and lots of visitor services. About 15 miles east of town, **Rainbow Pool** (www.fs.usda.gov/stanislaus) is a popular swimming hole with a small cascade; it's signed on the south side of Hwy 120.

🛏 Sleeping & Eating

Groveland Hotel HOTEL $$
(☏ 800-273-3314, 209-962-4000; www.groveland.com; 18767 Main St; r incl breakfast $169-319; 🐾@🐾🐾) The historic Groveland Hotel dates from 1850 and now houses a small bar, an upscale **restaurant** (mains $15-27) and 17 bright, lovingly decorated rooms with wraparound verandahs and resident teddy bears. Breakfast included May through September only.

Hotel Charlotte HOTEL $$
(☏ 209-962-6455; www.hotelcharlotte.com; 18736 Main St; r incl breakfast $149-225; 🐾@🐾🐾) A friendly, 12-room 1918 confection with beds adorned in patchwork quilts, the Hotel Charlotte keeps the vintage flair alive but still has modern conveniences. A sophisticated **bistro** (mains $12-20; ⏱6-9pm May-Sep) and bar serves a creative small-plates menu.

Mountain Sage CAFE $
(www.mtsage.com; 18653 Main St; snacks $2-6; ⏱7am-3pm, to 5pm Jun-Aug; 🐾) 🍃 This popular cafe is also an art gallery, nursery and live-music venue all rolled into one, with organic and Fair Trade coffee, tasty baked treats and an excellent summer concert series (www.mountainsagemusic.org).

SEQUOIA & KINGS CANYON NATIONAL PARKS

The twin parks of Sequoia and Kings Canyon dazzle with superlatives, though they're often overshadowed by Yosemite, their smaller neighbor to the north (a three-hour drive away). With towering forests of giant sequoias containing some of the largest trees in the world, and the mighty Kings River

THE BUFFALO SOLDIERS

After the creation of the national parks in 1890, the US Army was called in to safeguard these natural resources. In the summer of 1903, troops from the 9th Cavalry – one of four well-respected (though segregated) African American regiments, known as the 'Buffalo Soldiers' – were sent to patrol here and in Yosemite. In Sequoia and what was then General Grant National Park, the troops had an impressively productive summer – building roads, creating a trail system and setting a high standard as stewards of the land.

The troops were commanded by Captain (later Colonel) Charles Young. At the time, Young was the only African American captain in the Army; his post as Acting Superintendent made him the first African American superintendent of a national park.

careening through the depths of Kings Canyon, one of the deepest chasms in the country, the parks are lesser-visited jewels where it's easier to find quiet and solitude. Throw in opportunities for caving, rock climbing and backcountry hiking through granite-carved Sierra landscapes, and backdoor access to Mt Whitney – the tallest peak in the lower 48 states – and you have all the ingredients for two of the best parks in the country.

The two **parks** (☑ 559-565-3341; www.nps.gov/seki; 7-day entry per car $20), though distinct, are operated as one unit with a single admission; for 24-hour recorded information, including road conditions, call the number listed or visit the parks' comprehensive website. At either entrance station (Big Stump or Ash Mountain), you'll receive an NPS map and a copy of the parks' *The Guide* newspaper, with information on seasonal activities, camping and special programs, including those in the surrounding national forests and the Giant Sequoia National Monument.

Cell-phone coverage is nonexistent except for limited reception at Grant Grove, and gas is available at Hume Lake and Stony Creek Lodge, both on USFS land.

History

In 1890 Sequoia became the second national park in the USA (after Yellowstone). A few days later, the 4 sq miles around Grant Grove were declared General Grant National Park and, in 1940, absorbed into the newly created Kings Canyon National Park. In 2000, to protect additional sequoia groves, vast tracts of land in the surrounding national forest became the Giant Sequoia National Monument.

❶ Dangers & Annoyances

Air pollution wafting up from the Sequoia Central Valley and Kings Canyon often thwarts long-range visibility, and people with respiratory problems should check with a visitor center about current pollution levels. Black bears are common and proper food storage is always required. Heed park instructions on wildlife procedures.

Kings Canyon National Park

With a dramatic cleft deeper than the Grand Canyon, Kings Canyon offers true adventure to those who crave seemingly endless trails, rushing streams and gargantuan rock formations. The camping, backcountry exploring and climbing here are all superb.

❍ Sights & Activities

Kings Canyon National Park has two developed areas with markets, lodging, showers and visitor information. Grant Grove Village is only 4 miles past the Big Stump entrance (in the park's west), while Cedar Grove Village is 31 miles east at the bottom of the canyon. The two are separated by the Giant Sequoia National Monument and are linked by Kings Canyon Scenic Byway/Hwy 180.

◉ Grant Grove

General Grant Grove FOREST
This sequoia grove is nothing short of magnificent. The paved half-mile **General Grant Tree Trail** is an interpretive walk that visits a number of mature sequoias, including the 27-story **General Grant Tree**. This giant holds triple honors as the world's third-largest living tree, a memorial to US soldiers killed in war, and as the nation's Christmas tree. The nearby **Fallen Monarch**, a massive, fire-hollowed trunk that you can walk through, has been a cabin, hotel, saloon and stables for US Cavalry horses.

Panoramic Point
LOOKOUT

For a breathtaking view of Kings Canyon, head 2.3 miles up narrow, steep and winding Panoramic Point Rd (trailers and RVs aren't recommended), which branches off Hwy 180. Follow a short paved trail uphill from the parking lot to the viewpoint, where precipitous canyons and the snowcapped peaks of the Great Western Divide unfold below you. Snow closes the road to vehicles during winter, when it becomes a cross-country ski and snowshoe route.

Redwood Canyon
CANYON

South of Grant Grove Village, more than 15,000 sequoias cluster in this secluded and pristine corner of the park, making it the world's largest such grove. Relatively inaccessible, this area lets you enjoy the majesty of the giants away from the crowds on several moderate-to-strenuous trails. The trailhead is at the end of an unsigned, 2-mile bumpy dirt road across from the Hume Lake/Quail Flat sign on Generals Hwy, about 6 miles south of the village.

Cedar Grove & Roads End

At Cedar Grove Village, a simple lodge and snack bar provide the last outpost of civilization before the rugged grandeur of the backcountry takes over. Pretty spots around here include Roaring River Falls, where water whips down a sculpted rock channel before tumbling into a churning pool, and the easy, 1.5-mile Zumwalt Meadow nature trail, which loops around a verdant green meadow bordered by river and granite canyon. A short walk from Roads End, Muir Rock is a large flat river boulder where John Muir often gave talks during Sierra Club field trips. The rock now bears his name, and the lazy river abounds with gleeful swimmers in summer.

The trail to Mist Falls (8-mile round-trip) is an easy to moderate hike to one of the park's larger waterfalls. The first 2 miles are fairly exposed, so start early to avoid the midday heat. Continuing past Mist Falls, the trail eventually connects with the John Muir/Pacific Crest Trail to form the 42-mile Rae Lakes Loop, the most popular long-distance hike in Kings Canyon National Park (a wilderness permit is required).

For guided horse trips, both day and overnight, check with Cedar Grove Pack Station (☑ 559-565-3464; Hwy 180, Cedar Grove; ☺ May–mid-Oct).

Sleeping & Eating

Unless noted, all campsites are first-come, first-served. Pay showers are available at Grant Grove Village and Cedar Grove Village.

Potential campers should also keep in mind that there are great free uncrowded and undeveloped campgrounds off Big Meadows Rd in the Sequoia National Forest. They're some of the only empty campsites in the Sierra Nevada during peak summer season. Free roadside camping is also allowed in the forest, but no campfires without a permit (available from the Grant Grove Visitor Center).

Markets in Grant Grove Village and Cedar Grove Village have a limited selection of groceries.

Grant Grove

Crystal Springs Campground CAMPGROUND $
(tent & RV sites $18; ☺ mid-May–mid-Sep; 🐾) Fifty wooded, well-spaced sites with flush toilets; the smallest campground in the Grant Grove area and generally very quiet.

Princess Campground CAMPGROUND $
(☑ 877-444-6777; www.recreation.gov; Giant Sequoia National Monument; tent & RV sites $18; ☺ mid-May–late-Sep; 🐾) About 6 miles north of Grant Grove, with vault toilets and 88 reservable sites.

Azalea Campground CAMPGROUND $
(tent & RV sites $18; ☺ year-round; 🐾) Flush toilets, 110 sites; the nicest sites border a

---

DON'T MISS

BUCK ROCK LOOKOUT

Built in 1923, this active fire lookout (www.buckrock.org; ☺ 9:30am-6pm Jul-Oct) is one of the finest restored watchtowers you could ever hope to visit. Staffed in fire season, its 172 stairs lead to a dollhouse-sized wooden cab on a dramatic 8500ft granite rise with panoramic forest views. To reach it from General Hwy, go about 1 mile north of the Montecito Sequoia Lodge and then east onto Big Meadows Rd (FS road 14S11). At approximately 2.5 miles, turn north on the signed dirt road (FS road 13S04) and follow signs another 3 miles to the lookout parking area.

Sequoia & Kings Canyon National Parks

Joaquin River

Mt Emerson
(13,225ft)

Bishop
(14 miles)

Lake
Sabrina

Mt Darwin
(13,829ft)

South
Lake

Mt Gilbert
(13,104ft)

Courtright
Reservoir

N Fork Kings River

North
Palisade
(14,242ft)

Mt Reinstein
(12,605ft)

Black Giant
(13,330ft)

John Muir &
Pacific Crest Trails

Wishon
Reservoir

John Muir
Wilderness
Area

Crown Creek

Middle Fork Kings River

Copper Crest Trail

S Fork Kings River

Kings Canyon
National Park

Woods Creek

Kings River

Paradise
Valley
Trail

Sequoia
National
Forest

Monarch
Wilderness
Area

11

Kings Canyon Scenic Byway

Roads End
Permit Station

Paradise Valley

Fresno
(53mi);
Hwy 99
(53mi)

3

180

30

36

Hume
Lake

1

(road open
summer only)

40 37

19

Cedar Grove
Village

27

26

18

12

14

Grant
Grove
Village

9

Zumwalt
Meadow

Giant
Sequoia
National
Monument

15

6

22

31

2

38

33

17

Bubbs Creek Trail

Bubbs Creek

43

Kings Canyon
Visitor Center

Cedar Grove
Visitor
Center

Roaring River

Big Stump
Entrance

245

20

42

Twin
Lakes

Silliman Crest

Mt Brewer
(13,570ft)

16

Lodgepole
Visitor
Center

Twin Lakes
Trail

29

Generals
Hwy

44

32

Lodgepole Village

45

34

5

Crystal
Cave Rd

7

Wolverton
Meadow

High Sierra
Trail

Mt Stewart
(12,025ft)

Black
Kaweah
(13,765ft)

Marble
Fork

8

Giant
Forest

4

23

Kaweah Gap
(10,700ft)

10 13

N Fork Kaweah River

Ash Mountain
Entrance

35

24

Sawtooth
Peak
(12,343ft)

Mt Kaweah
(13,802ft)

Little
Five
Lakes

39

Foothills Visitor Center

41

Mineral
King

46

25

(road open
summer only)

Mineral King Rd

Mineral King Ranger
Station

47

Three Rivers

28

Sequoia
National
Park

Lake
Kaweah

E Fork Kaweah River

21

Mineral King Rd

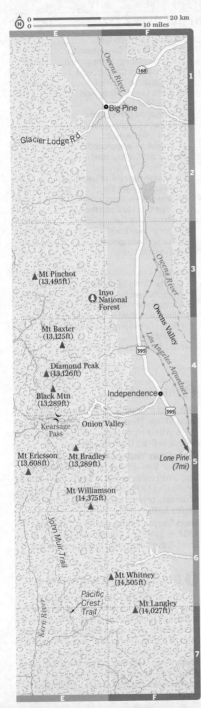

meadow. Close to Grant Grove Village (elevation 6500ft).

Sunset Campground
CAMPGROUND $

(tent & RV sites $18; ⊙late-May–early Sep; 🎾) Flush toilets, 157 sites, some overlooking the western foothills and the Central Valley. Close to Grant Grove Village.

Hume Lake Campground
CAMPGROUND $

(☑877-444-6777; www.recreation.gov; Hume Lake Rd, Giant Sequoia National Monument; tent & RV sites $20; ⊙late-May–early Sep; 🎾) Flush toilets, 74 reservable and uncrowded shady campsites, a handful with lake views; on the lake's northern shore about 10 miles northeast of Grant Grove.

Grant Grove Cabins
CABINS $$

(☑559-335-5500, 877-436-9615; www.visitsequoia.com; Hwy 180; cabins $63-140) Set amid towering sugar pines, around 50 cabins range from decrepit tent-top shacks (open from early June until early September) to rustic but comfortable heated duplexes (a few are wheelchair-accessible) with electricity, private bathrooms and double beds. For lovebirds, number 9 is the lone hard-sided, free-standing 'Honeymoon Cabin' with a queen bed, and books up fast.

John Muir Lodge
LODGE $$$

(☑877-436-9615, 559-335-5500; www.visitsequoia.com; Hwy 180; r $202-212; 🔊) An atmospheric wooden building hung with historical black-and-white photographs, this year-round hotel is a place to lay your head and still feel like you're in the forest. Wide porches have wooden rocking chairs, and homespun rooms contain rough-hewn wood furniture and patchwork bedspreads. Cozy up to the big stone fireplace on chilly nights with a board game.

Grant Grove Restaurant
AMERICAN $$

(Hwy 180; mains $9-18; ⊙7-10pm late-May–early Sep, reduced hours early Sep–late-May; 🔊🥗🚲) The only place to chow down in Grant Grove Village, its building will be torn down and rebuilt in 2015/2016, with plans for a temporary food area during construction. A new menu highlights seasonal dishes with rainbow trout or free-range chicken, but doesn't leave out comfort foods like pizza or fresh baked apple pie.

Cedar Grove

Cedar Grove's **Sentinel** campground, next to the village area, is open whenever Hwy

YOSEMITE & THE SIERRA NEVADA KINGS CANYON NATIONAL PARK

Sequoia & Kings Canyon National Parks

180 is open; **Sheep Creek**, **Canyon View** (tent only) and **Moraine** are opened as overflow when needed. These campgrounds are usually the last to fill up on busy summer weekends and are also good bets early and late in the season thanks to their comparatively low elevation (4600ft). All have flush toilets and $18 sites. Other facilities in the village don't start operating until mid-May.

Cedar Grove Lodge   LODGE $$
(☏866-522-6966, 559-335-5500; www.visitsequoia.com; Hwy 180; r $129-135; ⊙mid-May–early Oct; ❋) The only indoor sleeping option in the canyon, the riverside lodge offers 21 unexciting motel-style rooms, some with aircon. An in-progress remodel promises to dispel some of the frumpy decorations. Three ground-floor rooms have shady furnished patios have spiffy river views and kitchenettes. All rooms have phones and TVs.

Cedar Grove Restaurant   FAST FOOD $
(mains under $12; ⊙7am-8pm late-May–mid-Oct; ☎❖) A basic counter service grill with hot and greasy fare.

ⓘ Information

ATMs exist at Grant Grove Village and Cedar Grove Village. There's free wi-fi near the lodging check-in desk inside the Grant Grove Restaurant building in Grant Grove Village.

Cedar Grove Visitor Center (☏559-565-4307; ⊙8am or 9am-4:30pm or 5pm late-May–early Sep) Small visitor center in Cedar Grove Village. The Roads End Permit Station, which dispenses wilderness permits and rents bear canisters, is 6 miles further east.

Kings Canyon Visitor Center (☏559-565-4307; ⊙8am-5pm, shorter winter hours) In Grant Grove Village. Has exhibits, maps and wilderness permits.

ⓘ Getting There & Around

From the west, Kings Canyon Scenic Byway (Hwy 180) travels 53 miles east from Fresno to the Big Stump entrance. Coming from the south, you're in for a long 46-mile drive through Sequoia National Park along sinuous Generals Hwy. Budget about two hours' driving time from the Ash Mountain entrance to Grant Grove Village. The road to Cedar Grove Village is only open from around April or May until the first snowfall.

Sequoia National Park

Picture unzipping your tent flap and crawling out into a 'front yard' of trees as high as a 20-story building and as old as the Bible. Brew some coffee as you plan your day in this extraordinary park with its soul-sustaining forests and gigantic peaks soaring above 12,000ft.

◎ Sights & Activities

Nearly all of the park's star attractions are conveniently lined up along the Generals Hwy, which starts at the Ash Mountain entrance and continues north into Kings Canyon. Tourist activity concentrates in the Giant Forest area and in Lodgepole Village, which has the most facilities, including a visitor center and market. The road to remote Mineral King veers off Hwy 198 in the town of Three Rivers, just south of the park's Ash Mountain entrance.

◎ Giant Forest

Named by John Muir in 1875, this area is the top destination in the park, and about 2 miles south of Lodgepole Village. By volume the largest living tree on earth, the massive General Sherman Tree rockets 275ft to the sky. Pay your respects via a short descent from the Wolverton Rd parking lot, or join the Congress Trail, a paved 2-mile pathway that takes in General Sherman and other notable named trees, including the Washington Tree, the world's second-biggest sequoia, and the see-through Telescope Tree. To lose the crowds, set off on the 5-mile Trail of the Sequoias, which puts you into the heart of the forest.

Open in the warmer months, Crescent Meadow Rd heads east from the Giant Forest Museum for 3 miles to Crescent Meadow, a relaxing picnic spot, especially in spring when it's ablaze with wildflowers. Several short hikes start from here, including the 1-mile trail to Tharp's Log, where the area's first settler spent summers in a fallen tree. The road also passes Moro Rock, a landmark granite dome whose top can be reached via a quarter-mile carved staircase for breathtaking views of the Great Western Divide, a chain of mountains running north to south through the center of Sequoia National Park.

Giant Forest Museum MUSEUM
(☏ 559-565-4480; Generals Hwy; ☉ 9am-4:30pm or 6pm mid-May–mid-Oct; 🚻) **FREE** For a primer on the intriguing ecology, fire cycle and history of the 'big trees', drop in at this excellent museum, then follow up your visit with a spin around the paved (and

---

SCENIC DRIVE: KINGS CANYON SCENIC BYWAY (HIGHWAY 180)

The 31-mile rollercoaster road connecting Grant Grove and Cedar Grove ranks among the most dazzling in all of California. It winds past the Converse Basin Grove, which once contained the world's largest grove of mature sequoias until loggers turned it into a sequoia cemetery in the 1880s. A half-mile loop trail leads to the 20ft-high Chicago Stump, the remains of the 3200-year-old tree that was cut down, sectioned and reassembled for the 1893 World Columbian Exposition in Chicago. North of here, a second side road goes to Stump Meadow, where stumps and fallen logs make good picnic platforms, and to the Boole Tree Trail, a 2.5-mile loop to the only 'monarch' left to live.

The road then begins its jaw-dropping descent into the canyon, snaking past chiseled rock walls, some tinged by green moss and red iron minerals, others decorated by waterfalls. Turnouts provide superb views, especially at Junction View.

Eventually the road runs parallel with the gushing Kings River, its thunderous roar ricocheting off granite cliffs soaring as high as 8000ft, making Kings Canyon even deeper than the Grand Canyon. Stop at Boyden Cavern (www.caverntours.com/BoydenRt.htm; Hwy 180; tours adult/child from $14.50/8.50; ☉ May–Nov; 🚻) for a tour of its whimsical formations. While beautiful, they are smaller and less impressive than those in Crystal Cave in Sequoia National Park, but no advance tickets are required. Exciting canyoneering tours are also available by advance reservation. About 5 miles further east, Grizzly Falls can be torrential or drizzly, depending on the time of year.

On your return trip, consider a detour via Hume Lake, created in 1908 as a dam for logging operations and now offering boating, swimming and fishing. Facilities include a small market and a gas station.

wheelchair-accessible) 1.2-mile interpretive **Big Trees Trail**, which starts from the museum parking lot.

Foothills

From the Ash Mountain entrance in Three Rivers, the Generals Hwy ascends steeply through this southern section of Sequoia National Park. With an average elevation of about 2000ft, the Foothills are much drier and warmer than the rest of the park. Hiking here is best in spring when the air is still cool and wildflowers put on a colorful show. Summers are buggy and muggy, but fall again brings moderate temperatures and lush foliage.

The Potwisha people lived in this area until the early 1900s, relying primarily on acorn meal. Pictographs and grinding holes still grace the **Hospital Rock** picnic area, once a Potwisha village site. **Swimming holes** abound along the Marble Fork of the Kaweah River, especially near Potwisha Campground. Be careful, though – the currents can be deadly, especially when the river is swollen from the spring runoff.

Mineral King

A scenic, subalpine valley at 7500ft, Mineral King is Sequoia's backpacking mecca and a good place to find solitude. Gorgeous and gigantic, its glacially sculpted valley is ringed by massive mountains, including the jagged 12,343ft **Sawtooth Peak**. The area is reached via Mineral King Rd – a slinky, steep and narrow 25-mile road, not suitable for RVs or speed demons; the road is usually open from late May through October. Plan on spending the night unless you don't mind driving three hours round-trip.

Hiking anywhere from here involves a steep climb out of the valley along strenuous trails, so be aware of the altitude, even on short hikes. Enjoyable day hikes go to **Crystal, Monarch, Mosquito** and **Eagle Lakes**. For long trips, locals recommend the **Little Five Lakes** and, further along the High Sierra Trail, **Kaweah Gap**, surrounded by **Black Kaweah, Mt Stewart** and **Eagle Scout Peak** – all above 12,000ft.

In spring and early summer, hordes of hungry marmots terrorize parked cars at Mineral King, chewing on radiator hoses, belts and wiring of vehicles to get the salt they crave after their winter hibernation. If you're thinking of going hiking during that time, you'd be a fool not to protect your car by wrapping the underside with chicken wire or a diaper-like tarp.

From the 1860s to 1890s, Mineral King witnessed heavy silver mining and lumber activity. There are remnants of old shafts and stamp mills, though it takes some exploring to find them. A proposal by the Walt Disney Corporation to develop the area into a massive ski resort was thwarted when Congress annexed it to the national park in 1978. The website of the **Mineral King Preservation Society** (www.mineralking.org) has all kinds of info on the area, including its rustic and still-occupied historic mining cabins.

🛏 Sleeping & Eating

The market at Lodgepole Village is the best stocked in either park, but basic supplies are also available at the small store in Stony Creek Lodge (closed in winter).

🍽 Generals Highway

A handful of campgrounds line the highway and rarely fill up, although space may get tight on holiday weekends. Those in the Foothills area are best in spring and fall when the higher elevations are still chilly, but they get hot and buggy in summer. Unless noted, sites are available on a first-come, first-served basis. Free dispersed camping is possible in the Giant Sequoia National Monument. Stop by a visitor center or ranger station for details or a fire permit. Lodgepole Village and Stony Creek Lodge have pay showers.

Stony Creek Campground　　CAMPGROUND $
(☎877-444-6777; www.recreation.gov; tent & RV sites $24; ⊙mid-May–late-Sep; 🐾) USFS-operated with 49 comfortable wooded sites, including some right on the creek, and flush toilets. Smaller **Upper Stony Creek campground** is across the street and has vault toilets.

Lodgepole Campground　　CAMPGROUND $
(☎877-444-6777; www.recreation.gov; tent & RV sites $22; ⊙May-Nov) Closest to the Giant Forest area with over 200 closely packed sites and flush toilets; this place fills quickly because of proximity to Lodgepole Village amenities. A dozen or so walk-in sites are more private.

CRYSTAL CAVE

Discovered in 1918 by two fishermen, **Crystal Cave** (☎559-565-3759; www.sequoiahistory. org; Crystal Cave Rd; tours adult/child from $15/8; ☺mid-May–Nov; ♿) was carved by an underground river and has formations estimated to be 10,000 years old. Stalactites hang like daggers from the ceiling, and milky white marble formations take the shape of ethereal curtains, domes, columns and shields. The cave is also a unique biodiverse habitat for spiders, bats and tiny aquatic insects that are found nowhere else on earth. The 45-minute tour covers a half-mile of chambers, though adults can also sign up for more in-depth lantern-lit cave explorations and full-day spelunking adventures.

Tickets are *only* sold at the Lodgepole and Foothills visitor centers and *not* at the cave. Allow about one hour to get to the cave entrance, which is a half-mile walk from the parking lot (restroom available) at the end of a twisty 7-mile road; the turnoff is about 3 miles south of the Giant Forest. Bring a sweater or light jacket, as it's a huddle-for-warmth 48°F (9°C) inside.

Potwisha Campground   CAMPGROUND $
(tent & RV sites $22; ☺year-round; ☺) Also in the Foothills, and blazing in summertime, this campground has decent shade and swimming spots on the Kaweah River. It's 3 miles north of the Ash Mountain entrance, with 42 sites and flush toilets.

Dorst Creek Campground   CAMPGROUND $
(☎877-444-6777; www.recreation.gov; tent & RV sites $22; ☺late-Jun–early Sep; ☺) Big and busy campground with 204 sites and flush toilets; quieter back sites are tent-only.

Buckeye Flat Campground   CAMPGROUND $
(tent sites $22; ☺Apr–Sep; ☺) This campground is in the Foothills area, in an open stand of oaks about 6 miles north of the Ash Mountain entrance. There are 28 tent-only sites and flush toilets. Can be somewhat rowdy.

Stony Creek Lodge   LODGE $$
(☎559-565-3909; www.sequoia-kingscanyon.com; 65569 Generals Hwy; r $159-189; ☺mid-May–mid-Oct; ☺) About halfway between Grant Grove Village and Giant Forest, this lodge has a big river-rock fireplace in its lobby and 12 aging but folksy motel rooms with telephone and flat-screen TVs.

Sequoia High Sierra Camp   CABINS $$$
(☎877-591-8982; www.sequoiahighsierracamp. com; r without bath incl all meals per adult/child $250/150; ☺mid-Jun–early Oct) Accessed via a 1-mile hike deep into the Sequoia National Forest, off Generals Hwy, this off-the-grid, all-inclusive resort is nirvana for active, sociable people who don't think 'luxury camping' is an oxymoron. Canvas cabins are spiffed up by pillow-top mattresses, down pillows and

cozy wool rugs, with shared restrooms and a shower house. Reservations are required, with a two-night minimum stay.

Wuksachi Lodge   LODGE $$$
(☎866-807-3598, 559-565-4070; www.visitsequoia.com; 64740 Wuksachi Way, off Generals Hwy; r from $225; ☺) Built in 1999, the Wuksachi Lodge is the park's most upscale lodging and dining option. But don't get too excited – the wood-paneled atrium lobby has an inviting stone fireplace and forest views, but charmless motel-style kitchenette rooms with oak furniture and thin walls have an institutional feel. The lodge's location, however, just north of Lodgepole Village, can't be beat.

Lodgepole Village   MARKET $
(Generals Hwy; mains $6-10; ☺market & snack bar 9am-6pm mid-Apr–late-May & early Sep–mid-Oct, 8am-8pm late-May–early Sep, deli 11am-6pm mid-Apr–mid-Oct; ♿) The park's most extensive market sells all kinds of groceries, camping supplies and snacks. Inside, a fast-food snack bar slings burgers and grilled sandwiches and dishes up breakfast. The adjacent deli is a tad more upscale and healthy, with focaccia sandwiches, veggie wraps and picnic salads.

☞ Backcountry

Bearpaw High Sierra Camp   CABIN $$
(☎866-807-3598, 801-559-4930; www.visitsequoia.com; tent cabin incl breakfast & dinner $175; ☺mid-Jun–mid-Sep) About 11.5 miles east of Giant Forest on the High Sierra Trail, this tent hotel is ideal for exploring the backcountry without lugging your own camping gear. Rates include showers, dinner and breakfast, as well as bedding and towels.

Bookings start at 7am every January 2 and sell out almost immediately, though you should always check for cancellations.

Mineral King

Mineral King's two pretty campgrounds, **Atwell Mill** (tent sites $12; ⊙late-May–mid-Oct; 🍽) and **Cold Springs** (tent sites $12; ⊙late-May–mid-Oct; 🍽), often fill up on summer weekends. Pay showers are available at the Silver City Mountain Resort.

Silver City Mountain Resort CABINS $$
(📞559-561-3223; www.silvercityresort.com; Mineral King Rd; cabins with/without bath from $195/120, chalets $250-395; ⊙late-May–late-Oct; 🛜) The only food and lodging option anywhere near these parts, this rustic, old-fashioned and family-friendly place rents everything from cute and cozy 1950s-era cabins to modern chalets that sleep up to eight. Its **restaurant** (mains $10-18; ⊙8am-8pm Thu-Mon, pie & coffee only 9am-4pm Tue-Wed) serves delicious homemade pies and simple fare on wooden picnic tables under the trees. It's located 3.5 miles west of the ranger station.

There's a ping-pong table, outdoor swings, and nearby ponds to splash around in. All guests should bring their own sheets and towels (rentals $25 to $50 per cabin). Most cabins don't have electricity, and the property's generator usually shuts off around 10pm.

Three Rivers

Named for the nearby convergence of three Kaweah River forks, Three Rivers is a friendly small town populated mostly by retirees and artsy newcomers. The town's main drag, Sierra Dr (Hwy 198), is sparsely lined with motels, eateries and shops.

Sequoia Village Inn CABINS, COTTAGES $$
(📞559-561-3652; www.sequoiavillageinn.com; 45971 Sierra Dr; d $129-319; ❄🛜🍽🍴) These 10 pretty modern cottages, cabins and chalets (most with kitchens and the rest with kitchenettes), border the park and are great for families or groups. Most have outdoor woodsy decks and barbecues, and the largest can sleep 12.

Buckeye Tree Lodge MOTEL $$
(📞559-561-5900; www.buckeyetreelodge.com; 46000 Sierra Dr; d incl breakfast $134-159; ❄🛜🍽🍴) 🏊 Sit out on your grassy back patio or perch on the balcony and watch the river ease through a maze of boulders. Modern white-brick motel rooms, one with a kitchenette, feel airy and bright.

We Three Bakery & Restaurant BREAKFAST, BAKERY $
(43368 Sierra Dr; mains $7-15; ⊙7am-2:30pm, to 9pm Fri & Sat in summer; 🛜) Cinnamon French toast, biscuits with gravy and diner-style coffee lure in the breakfast crowd, while hot and cold sandwiches on blindingly bright Fiesta-ware make it a delish lunch spot. Chow down on the outdoor patio under a shady oak.

River View Restaurant & Lounge AMERICAN $$
(42323 Sierra Dr; lunch $9-12, dinner $16-24; ⊙11am-9pm, to 10pm Fri & Sat, bar open late) Colorful honky-tonk with a great back patio; live music Fridays through Sundays.

BACKPACKING IN SEQUOIA & KINGS CANYON NATIONAL PARKS

With over 850 miles of marked trails, the parks are a backpacker's dream. Cedar Grove and Mineral King offer the best backcountry access. Trails are usually open by mid to late May.

For overnight backcountry trips you'll need a wilderness permit (per group $15), which is subject to a quota system in summer; permits are free and available by self-registration outside the quota season. About 75% of spaces can be reserved, while the rest are available in person on a first-come, first-served basis. Reservations can be made from March 1 until two weeks before your trip. For details see www.nps.gov/seki/planyourvisit/wilderness_permits.htm. There's also a dedicated wilderness desk at the Lodgepole Visitor Center.

All ranger stations and visitor centers carry topo maps and hiking guides. Note that you need to store your food in park-approved bearproof canisters, which can be rented at markets and visitor centers (from $5 per trip).

WINTER FUN

In winter a thick blanket of snow drapes over trees and meadows, the pace of activity slows and a hush falls over the roads and trails. Note that snow often closes Generals Hwy between Grant Grove and Giant Forest and that tire chains may be required at any time. These can usually be rented near the parks' entrances, although you're not supposed to put them on rental cars. For up-to-date road conditions call ☎559-565-3341 or check www.nps.gov/seki.

Snowshoeing and cross-country skiing are both hugely popular activities, with 50 miles of marked but ungroomed trails crisscrossing the Grant Grove and Giant Forest areas. Winter road closures also make for excellent cross-country skiing and snowshoeing on Sequoia's Moro Rock–Crescent Meadow Rd, Kings Canyon's Panoramic Point Rd and the Sequoia National Forest's Big Meadows Rd. Trail maps are available at the visitor centers, and park rangers lead free snowshoe tours (equipment included). Tree-marked trails connect with those in the Giant Sequoia National Monument and the 30 miles of groomed terrain maintained by the private **Montecito Sequoia Lodge** (☎559-565-3388; www.montecitosequoia.com; 8000 Generals Hwy). Equipment rentals are available at Grant Grove Village, the Wuksachi Lodge and the Montecito Sequoia Lodge. There are also snow-play areas near Columbine and Big Stump in the Grant Grove region and at Wolverton Meadow in Sequoia.

In winter cross-country skiers with reservations can sleep in one of the 10 bunks at **Pear Lake Ski Hut** (☎559-565-3759; www.sequoiahistory.org; dm $38-42; ☺mid-Dec–late Apr), a 1940-era pine-and-granite building run by the Sequoia Natural History Association. You'll be glad to see it after the strenuous 6-mile cross-country ski or snowshoe trek from Wolverton Meadow. Reservations are assigned by lottery in November. Call or check the website for details.

ℹ Information

Lodgepole Village has an ATM, and there's free wi-fi at Wuksachi Lodge.

Foothills Visitor Center (☎559-565-4212; ☺8am-4:30pm) One mile north of the Ash Mountain entrance.

Lodgepole Visitor Center (☎559-565-4436; ☺9am-4:30pm or 6pm daily, shorter winter hours) Maps, information, exhibits, Crystal Cave tickets and wilderness permits.

Mineral King Ranger Station (☎559-565-3768; ☺8am-4pm late-May–early Sep) Twenty-four miles east of Generals Hwy; wilderness permits and campground availability info.

ℹ Getting There & Around

Coming from the south, Hwy 198 runs north from Visalia through Three Rivers past Mineral King Rd to the Ash Mountain entrance. Beyond here the road continues as the Generals Hwy, a narrow and windy road snaking all the way into Kings Canyon National Park, where it joins the Kings Canyon Scenic Byway (Hwy 180) near the western Big Stump entrance. Vehicles over 22ft long may have trouble negotiating the steep road with its many hairpin curves. Budget about one hour to drive from the entrance to the Giant Forest/Lodgepole area and another hour from there to Grant Grove Village in Kings Canyon.

Sequoia Shuttle (☎877-287-4453; www.sequoiashuttle.com; one way/round-trip $7.50/15; ☺late-May–early Sep) buses run five times daily between Visalia and the Giant Forest Museum (2½ hours) via Three Rivers; reservations required.

Shuttle buses run every 15 minutes from the Giant Forest Museum to Moro Rock and Crescent Meadow or to the General Sherman Tree parking areas and Lodgepole Village. Another route links Lodgepole, Wuksachi Lodge and Dorst Creek Campground every 30 minutes. All routes are free and currently operate 9am to about 6pm from late May to early September.

EASTERN SIERRA

Cloud-dappled hills and sun-streaked mountaintops dabbed with snow typify the landscape of the Eastern Sierra, where slashing peaks – many over 14,000ft – rush abruptly upward from the arid expanses of the Great Basin and Mojave deserts. It's a dramatic juxtaposition that makes for a potent cocktail of scenery. Pine forests, lush meadows, ice-blue lakes, simmering hot springs and glacier-gouged canyons are only some of the beautiful sights you'll find in this region.

The Eastern Sierra Scenic Byway, officially known as Hwy 395, runs the entire length of the range. Turnoffs dead-ending at the foot of the mountains deliver you to pristine wilderness and countless trails, including the famous Pacific Crest Trail, John Muir Trail and main Mt Whitney Trail. The most important portals are the towns of Bridgeport, Mammoth Lakes, Bishop and Lone Pine. Note that in winter, when traffic thins, many facilities are closed.

ⓘ Information

Locally produced and available throughout the region, Sierra Maps' *Eastern Sierra: Bridgeport to Lone Pine* recreation and road map shows hot springs, ghost towns, hiking trails and climbing areas. Check out www.thesierraweb.com for area events and links to visitor information, and *Sierra Wave* (www.sierrawave.net) for regional news.

ⓘ Getting There & Around

The Eastern Sierra is easiest to explore under your own steam, although it's possible to access the area by public transportation. Buses operated by **Eastern Sierra Transit Authority** (☑760-872-1901; www.estransit.com/) make a round-trip between Lone Pine and Reno ($59, six hours) on Monday, Tuesday, Thursday and Friday, stopping at all Hwy 395 towns in between. Fares depend on distance, and reservations are recommended. There's also an express bus between Mammoth Lakes and Bishop ($7, one hour, three times daily) that operates Monday through Friday.

In the summer connect to Yosemite via YARTS bus in Mammoth Lakes or Lee Vining.

Mono Lake Area

Bridgeport

Barely three blocks long, set amid open high valley and in view of the peaks of Sawtooth Ridge, Bridgeport flaunts classic western flair with charming old storefronts and a homey ambience. Most everything shuts down or cuts back hours for the brutal winters, but the rest of the year the town is a magnet for anglers, hikers, climbers and hot-spring devotees.

◉ Sights & Activities

Mono County Courthouse   HISTORIC BUILDING
(☉9am-5pm Mon-Fri) The gavel has been dropped since 1880 at the courthouse, an all-white Italianate dreamboat surrounded by a gracious lawn and a wrought-iron fence. On the street behind it, look for the **Old County Jail**, a spartan facility fashioned with iron latticework doors and stone walls 2ft thick. Unlucky inmates overnighted in its six cells from 1883 until 1964.

Mono County Museum   MUSEUM
(☑760-932-5281; www.monocomuseum.org; Emigrant St; adult/child $2/1; ☉9am-4pm Tue-Sat Jun-Sep) Two blocks away from the Mono County Courthouse, in a schoolhouse of the same age, this museum has mining artifacts on display from all the local ghost towns, plus a room of fine Paiute baskets.

★Travertine Hot Spring   HOT SPRING
A bit south of town, head here to watch a panoramic Sierra sunset from three hot pools set amid impressive rock formations. To get there, turn east on Jack Sawyer Rd just before the ranger station, then follow the dirt road uphill for about 1 mile.

Ken's Sporting Goods   FISHING
(☑760-932-7707; www.kenssport.com; 258 Main St; ☉7am-8pm Mon-Thu, to 9pm Fri & Sat mid-Apr–mid-Nov, 9am-4pm Tue-Sat mid-Nov–mid-Apr) Stop by Ken's for information and fishing gear. If you're trolling for trout, try the Bridgeport Reservoir and the East Walker River.

🛏 Sleeping & Eating

Redwood Motel   MOTEL $
(☑760-932-7060; www.redwoodmotel.net; 425 Main St; d from $88-99; ☉Apr-Nov; ✳🐾📶) A bucking bronco, an ox in a Hawaiian shirt and other wacky farm animal sculptures provide a cheerful welcome to this little kitchenette motel. Rooms are spotless and your dog-friendly host is super helpful in dispensing local area tips.

Bodie Victorian Hotel   HISTORIC HOTEL $
(☑760-932-7020; www.bodievictorianhotel.com; 85 Main St; r $60-125; ☉May-Oct) Go back to the 1800s in this curious building transplanted from Bodie that's completely furnished with antiques and rumored to be haunted. The bold Victorian wallpaper and striking bordello accoutrements more than make up for the slightly run-down feel. If no one's there, poke your head inside the Sportsmens Bar & Grill next door to rustle up an employee.

Hays Street Cafe   AMERICAN $
(www.haysstreetcafe.com; 21 Hays St; mains under $10; ☉6am-2pm May-Oct, 7am-1pm Nov-Apr) On

ℹ WILDERNESS PERMITS: EASTERN SIERRA

Free wilderness permits for overnight camping are required year-round in the Ansel Adams, John Muir, Golden Trout and Hoover Wilderness areas. For the first three, trailhead quotas are in effect frwilderom May through October and about 60% of the quota may be reserved online at www.recreation.gov for a $5 fee (per person). From November to April, you can pick up permits at most ranger stations. If you find the station closed, look for self-issue permits outside the office. Wilderness permits for the Inyo National Forest can be picked up in either Lone Pine, Bishop, Mammoth Lakes or its Mono Basin ranger stations. Yosemite's Tuolumne Meadows Wilderness Center can also issue permits for trips from Saddlebag Lake. For questions call the **Inyo National Forest Wilderness Permit Office** (☏ 760-873-2483; www.fs.usda.gov/inyo).

Permits for the Hoover Wilderness that depart from the Humboldt-Toiyabe National Forest (seasonal quotas on some trails) are issued at the Bridgeport Ranger Station & Visitor Center.

The forums on **High Sierra Topix** (www.highsierratopix.com) are an excellent resource for planning trips.

the south end of town, this country-style place prides itself on its many homemade items, including its biscuits and gravy, and cinnamon rolls as big as bricks.

J's on the Corner AMERICAN $
(247 Main St; mains $7-10; ⏰ 11am-9pm, variable hours Oct-Apr) Excellent hot and cold sandwiches and filling salads (no iceberg lettuce!) and great prices make this small grill a popular spot. Meat lovers should aim for the prime rib French dip.

Bridgeport Inn AMERICAN $$
(www.thebridgeportinn.com; 205 Main St; mains $10-22; ⏰ 8am-8:30pm Thu-Tue Apr-Oct; 🛜) Stop in at the country kitchen dining room of this whitewashed 1877 building for burgers, pot roast, steaks and seafood, and a dip into its modest wine list. Watch the world stream by from a classic soda fountain stool on the long front porch.

ℹ Information

Bridgeport Ranger Station & Visitor Center
(☏ 760-932-7070; www.fs.usda.gov/htnf; Hwy 395; ⏰ 8am-4:30pm daily Jun–mid-Sep, 8am-4:30pm Mon-Fri mid-Sep–May) Stop by this center for maps, information and Hoover Wilderness permits.

Twin Lakes

Eager anglers line the shoreline of Twin Lakes, a gorgeous duo of basins cradled by the fittingly named Sawtooth Ridge. The area's famous for its fishing – especially since some lucky guy bagged the state's largest ever brown trout here in 1987 (it weighed

in at a hefty 26lbs). Lower Twin is quieter, while Upper Twin allows boating and waterskiing. Other activities include mountain biking and, of course, hiking in the Hoover Wilderness Area and on into the eastern, lake-riddled reaches of Yosemite National Park.

⊙ Sights & Activities

A stroll down a loose hillside brings you to out-of-the-way **Buckeye Hot Spring**, though it can get crowded. Water emerges piping hot from a steep hillside and cools as it trickles down into several rock pools right by the side of lively Buckeye Creek, which is handy for taking a cooling dip. One pool is partially tucked into a small cave made from a rock overhang. Clothing is optional. To get there from Hwy 395 via Twin Lakes Rd, turn right at Doc & Al's Resort (7 miles from Hwy 395), driving 3 miles on a (momentarily paved and then) graded dirt road. Cross the bridge at Buckeye Creek (at 2.5 miles), and bear right at the Y-junction, following signs to the hot spring. Go uphill a half mile until you see a flattish parking area on your right. Follow a trail down to the pools.

For hikers the main trailhead is at the end of Twin Lakes Rd just past Annett's Mono Village; weekly overnight parking is $10 per vehicle. From here hikers can set off along Robinson Creek for adventures in the stunning **Hoover Wilderness** and overnight backpacking trips (wilderness permit required) into northeastern Yosemite. The day hike to lovely **Barney Lake** (8 miles round-trip) takes in magnificent views of jagged granite spires in **Little Slide Canyon**, where

MIMI DITCHIE PHOTOGRAPHY / GETTY IMAGES ©

1. Fall foliage, Lundy Canyon (p440) 2. May Lake, Yosemite National Park 3. Emerald Bay (p381) 4. John Muir Trail (p404)

KARSTEN MAY / GETTY IMAGES ©

Best Hikes of the Sierra Nevada

Packed with ancient granite peaks, icy blue lakes and serpentine stream meadows, the Sierra Nevada beckons mountain-worshippers. Though the sights may look lovely from the car, you need to stop, smell and touch to really experience the landscape. And once you witness its burning alpenglow, you'll understand why Sierra Club cofounder John Muir called it the 'Range of Light.'

Yosemite High Sierra Camps

Tour Yosemite's high country without a bulging backpack and share the sights with pudgy whistling marmots. Highlights include overnights at pristine May Lake, the waterfalls of Glen Aulin and lake-studded Vogelsang.

Lundy Canyon

In the Hoover Wilderness east of Yosemite, ambitious beavers gnaw and stack stands of leafy aspens, and frothy waterfalls draw you deeper and deeper into this stunning and solitary canyon.

John Muir Trail

Load up that pack and connect the dots from the heart of Yosemite to the pinnacle of Mt Whitney, the highest peak in the contiguous USA. This 200-plus mile trek goes step-by-step up and over six passes topping 11,000ft. Cross chilly rivers and streams between bumper-to-bumper Yosemite Valley, the roadless backcountry of Sequoia & Kings Canyon and the oxygen-scarce summit of Mt Whitney.

Little Lakes Valley

Marvel at this perfect chain of alpine lakes jostled between snow-tipped summits. With the Sierra's highest trailhead, there's no need to earn your elevation here.

Desolation Wilderness

West of Lake Tahoe, jaunt to Eagle Lake and points beyond from Emerald Bay, or do a longer day hike to scale the pinnacle of Mt Tallac. The glacially polished landscape of this easy-to-reach wilderness makes it well worth the crowds.

Mono Lake Area

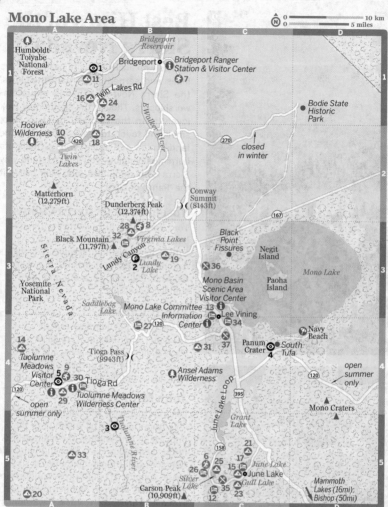

0 — 10 km
0 — 5 miles

rock climbers detour to scale a fierce wall called the **Incredible Hulk**, and steep boulder rockslides on the ridge to the north.

For a hike with great views of Twin Lakes, go south from Annett's on the **Horse Creek Trail**, which soon leads to the cascades of **Horsetail Falls**. It continues up to skirt the wilderness boundary and then descends back to Twin Lakes on the **Cattle Creek Trail**. Loop back along the lake for 7.5 miles in total. In *Dharma Bums*, Beat author Jack Kerouac describes an ascent he made from Horse Creek Canyon to nearby Matterhorn Peak (12,300ft) with poet Gary Snyder.

Twin Lakes Rd (Rte 420) runs through pastures and foothills for about 10 miles before reaching Lower Twin Lake. The road is a satisfying route for moderately fit cyclists, with mostly level terrain and heavenly scenery.

Sleeping & Eating

Past the bridge at Buckeye Creek, bear left at the signed Y-junction along a road for 2 miles to **Buckeye Campground** (tent & RV sites $15; ☉ May–mid-Oct), with tables, fire grates, potable water and toilets. You can also camp for free in undeveloped spots

Mono Lake Area

along Buckeye Creek on both sides of the creek bridge.

Honeymoon Flat, **Robinson Creek**, **Paha**, **Crags** and **Lower Twin Lakes** are all USFS campgrounds (☏ 800-444-7275; www.recreation.gov; tent & RV sites $17-20; ☉ mid-May– Sep) set among Jeffrey pine and sagebrush along Robinson Creek and Lower Twin Lake. All have flush toilets except for Honeymoon Flat, which has vault toilets.

Twin Lakes Rd dead-ends at **Annett's Mono Village** (☏ 760-932-7071; www.monovillage.com; tent sites $20, RV sites with hookups $30, r $75, cabin $85-205; ☉ late Apr-Oct; 🛜) a huge and rather chaotic tumbledown resort on Upper Twin Lake. It has cheap but cramped lodging, and a kitschy low-ceilinged **cafe** (mains $9-16) studded with taxidermied fish. Pay showers available.

Bodie State Historic Park

For a time warp back to the Gold Rush era, swing by **Bodie** (☏ 760-647-6445; www.parks.ca.gov/bodie; Hwy 270; adult/child $5/3; ☉ 9am-6pm mid-May–Oct, to 4pm Nov–mid-May), one of the West's most authentic and best-preserved ghost towns. Gold was first discovered here in 1859, and within 20 years the place grew from a rough mining camp

to an even rougher boomtown with a population of 10,000 and a reputation for unbridled lawlessness. Fights and murders took place almost daily, the violence no doubt fueled by liquor dispensed in the town's 65 saloons, some of which did double duty as brothels, gambling halls or opium dens. The hills disgorged some $35 million worth of gold and silver in the 1870s and '80s, but when production plummeted, so did the population, and eventually the town was abandoned to the elements.

About 200 weather-beaten buildings still sit frozen in time in this cold, barren and windswept valley heaped with tailing piles. Peering through dusty windows you'll see stocked stores, furnished homes, a schoolhouse with desks and books, and workshops filled with tools. The jail is still there, as are the fire station, churches, a bank vault and many other buildings.

The former Miners' Union Hall now houses a **museum** and **visitors center** (☉ 9am to one hour before park closes). Rangers conduct free general tours. In summertime they also offer tours of the landscape and the cemetery; call for details. The second Saturday of August is **Friends of Bodie Day** (www.bodiefoundation.org), with stagecoach rides,

SCENIC DRIVE: EBBETTS PASS SCENIC BYWAY

For outdoor fanatics, a scenic 61-mile section of Hwys 4 and 89 called the **Ebbetts Pass Scenic Byway** (www.scenic4.org) is a road trip through paradise. Heading northeast from Arnold, gaze up at the giant sequoias of **Calaveras Big Trees State Park** (☑209-795-2334; www.parks.ca.gov; per car $10; ☉sunrise-sunset) and in winter stop at the family-friendly ski resort of **Bear Valley** (☑209-753-2301; www.bearvalley.com; lift tickets adult/child $64/19; ☑). Continuing east the stunningly beautiful **Lake Alpine** is skirted by slabs of granite, several great beaches and a handful of campgrounds, and boasts excellent watersports, fishing and hiking.

The next stretch is the most dramatic, when the narrow highway continues past picturesque **Mosquito Lake** and the **Pacific Grade Summit** (8060ft) before slaloming through historic Hermit Valley and finally winding up and over the 8730ft summit of **Ebbetts Pass**. North on Hwy 89 and just west of **Markleeville**, visit the two developed pools and seasonal campground at **Grover Hot Springs State Park** (☑530-694-2249; www.parks.ca.gov/?page_id=508; per car $8, pool admission adult/child $7/5, tent & RV sites $35; ☉variable hours year-round).

From San Francisco it's a three-hour drive east to Arnold, via Hwy 108 and Hwy 49. Ebbetts Pass closes after the first major snowfall and doesn't reopen until June, but Hwy 4 is usually plowed from the west as far as Bear Valley.

history presentations and lots of devotees in period costumes.

ⓘ Getting There & Away

Bodie is about 13 miles east of Hwy 395 via Rte 270; the last 3 miles are unpaved. Although the park is open year-round, the road is usually closed in winter and early spring, so you'd have to don snowshoes or cross-country skis to get there.

Virginia Lakes

South of Bridgeport, Hwy 395 gradually arrives at its highest point, **Conway Summit** (8143ft), where you'll be whipping out your camera to capture the awe-inspiring panorama of Mono Lake, backed by the Mono Craters, and June and Mammoth Mountains.

Also at the top is the turnout for Virginia Lakes Rd, which parallels Virginia Creek for about 6 miles to a cluster of lakes flanked by **Dunderberg Peak** (12,374ft) and **Black Mountain** (11,797ft). A trailhead at the end of the road gives access to the Hoover Wilderness Area and the **Pacific Crest Trail**. The trail continues down Cold Canyon through to Yosemite National Park. With a car shuttle, the excellent 10.5-mile hike to **Green Creek** visits a bevy of perfect lakes; an extra mile (each way) takes you to windswept – check out the mammoth tree blowdown – Summit Lake at the Yosemite border. Check with the folks at the **Virginia Lakes Resort** (☑760-647-6484; www.virgin-

ialakesresort.com; cabins from $112; ☉mid-May–mid-Oct; ☑), opened in 1923, for maps and tips about specific trails. The resort itself has snug cabins, a cafe and a general store. Cabins sleep two to 12 people, and usually have a 3-day minimum stay.

There's also the option of camping at **Trumbull Lake Campground** (☑800-444-7275; www.recreation.gov; tent & RV sites $17; ☉mid-Jun–mid-Oct). The shady sites here are located among lodgepole pines.

Nearby, **Virginia Lakes Pack Station** (☑760-937-0326; www.virginialakes.com) offers horseback riding trips.

Lundy Lake

After Conway Summit, Hwy 395 twists down steeply into the Mono Basin. Before reaching Mono Lake, Lundy Lake Rd meanders west of the highway for about 5 miles to Lundy Lake. This is a gorgeous spot, especially in spring when wildflowers carpet the canyon along Mill Creek, or in fall when it is brightened by colorful foliage. Before reaching the lake, the road skirts first-come, first-served **Lundy Canyon Campground** (tent & RV sites $12; ☉mid-April–mid-Nov), with vault toilets; there's water available, but it must be boiled or treated. At the end of the lake, there's a ramshackle resort on the site of an 1880s mining town, plus a small store and boat rentals.

Past the resort a dirt road leads into **Lundy Canyon** where, in 2 miles, it dead-ends at the trailhead for the Hoover Wilderness Area. A fantastic 1.5-mile hike follows Mill Creek to the 200ft-high **Lundy Falls**. Industrious beavers define the landscape along the trail, with gnawed aspens scattered on the ground and a number of huge dams barricading the creek. Ambitious types can continue on via Lundy Pass to Saddlebag Lake and the Twenty Lakes Basin, though the final climb out of the canyon uses a very steep talus chute.

Lee Vining

Hwy 395 skirts the western bank of Mono Lake, rolling into the gateway town of Lee Vining where you can eat, sleep, gas up (for a pretty penny) and catch Hwy 120 to Yosemite National Park when the road's open. A superb base for exploring Mono Lake, Lee Vining is only 12 miles (about a 30-minute drive) from Yosemite's Tioga Pass entrance. **Lee Vining Canyon** is a popular location for **ice climbing**.

In town take a quick look at the **Upside-Down House**, a kooky tourist attraction created by silent film actress Nellie Bly O'Bryan. Originally situated along Tioga Rd, it now resides in a park in front of the tiny **Mono Basin Historical Society Museum** (www.monobasinhs.org; donation $2; ⏰10am-4pm Thu-Tue & noon-4pm Sun mid-May–early Oct). To find it, turn east on 1st St and go one block to Mattley Ave.

🛏 Sleeping

Lodging rates drop when Tioga Pass is closed. Psst, campers! **Mono Vista RV Park** (☏760-647-6401; www.monovistarvpark.net; Hwy 395; ⏰9am-6pm Apr-Oct) has the closest pay showers to Tuolumne Meadows.

El Mono Motel MOTEL $
(☏760-647-6310; www.elmonomotel.com; 51 Hwy 395; r $69-99; ⏰mid-May–Oct; 🛜) Grab a board game or soak up some mountain sunshine in this friendly flower-ringed place attached to an excellent cafe. In operation since 1927, and often booked solid, each of its 11 simple rooms (a few share bathrooms) is unique, decorated with vibrant and colorful art and fabrics.

USFS Campgrounds CAMPGROUND $
(www.fs.usda.gov/inyo; tent & RV sites $15-19; 🐾) Toward Yosemite, there are a handful of first-come, first-served campgrounds along Tioga Rd (Hwy 120) and Lee Vining Creek, most with vault toilets and about half with potable water.

★**Yosemite Gateway Motel** MOTEL $$
(☏760-647-6467; www.yosemitegatewaymotel.com; Hwy 395; r $119-159; 🛜) Think vistas. This is the only motel on the east side of the highway, and the views from some of the rooms are phenomenal. Recently remodeled, its boutique-style rooms have comfortable beds with thick duvets and swank new bathrooms.

Tioga Pass Resort CABINS $$
(www.tiogapassresort.com; Hwy 120; r $125, cabin $190-250; ⏰Jun-Sep) Founded in 1914 and located 2 miles east of Tioga Pass, this resort attracts a fiercely loyal clientele to its basic and cozy cabins beside Lee Vining Creek. The thimble-sized cafe (lunch $8 to $11, dinner $20) serves excellent fare all day at a few tables and a broken horseshoe counter, with a house pastry chef concocting dozens of freshly made desserts.

Murphey's Motel MOTEL $$
(☏760-647-6316; www.murpheysyosemite.com; Hwy 395; r $73-133; 🛜🐾) At the north end of town, this large and friendly motel offers comfy rooms with all mod cons.

🍴 Eating

Whoa Nellie Deli CALIFORNIAN $$
(☏760-647-1088; www.whoanelliedeli.com; Tioga Gas Mart, Hwys 120 & 395; mains $10-20; ⏰6:30am-9pm late-Apr–early Nov; 🛗) After putting this unexpected gas station restaurant on the map, its famed chef has moved on to Mammoth Lake, but locals think the food is still damn good. Stop in for delicious fish tacos, wild buffalo meatloaf and other tasty morsels, and live bands two nights a week.

Historic Mono Inn CALIFORNIAN $$
(☏760-647-6581; www.monoinn.com; 55620 Hwy 395; mains $10-28; ⏰5-9pm Apr–mid-Nov) A restored 1922 lodge owned by the family of photographer Ansel Adams, this is now an elegant lakefront restaurant with outstanding California comfort food, fabulous wine and views to match. Browse the 1000-volume cookbook collection upstairs, and stop in for the occasional live band on the creekside terrace. It's located about 5 miles north of Lee Vining. Reservations recommended.

Mono Lake

North America's second-oldest lake is a quiet and mysterious expanse of deep blue water, whose glassy surface reflects jagged Sierra peaks, young volcanic cones and the unearthly tufa (*too*-fah) towers that make the lake so distinctive. Jutting from the water like drip sand castles, tufas form when calcium bubbles up from subterranean springs and combines with carbonate in the alkaline lake waters.

In *Roughing It,* Mark Twain described Mono Lake as California's 'dead sea.' Hardly. The brackish water teems with buzzing alkali flies and brine shrimp, both considered delicacies by dozens of migratory bird species that return here year after year. So do about 85% of the state's nesting population of California gulls, which takes over the lake's volcanic islands from April to August. Mono Lake has also been at the heart of an environmental controversy.

Sights & Activities

South Tufa
NATURE RESERVE

(entry adult/child $3/free) Tufa spires ring the lake, but the biggest grove is on the south rim with a mile-long interpretive trail. Ask about ranger-led tours at the Mono Basin Scenic Area Visitor Center. To get to the reserve, head south from Lee Vining on Hwy 395 for 6 miles, then east on Hwy 120 for 5 miles to the dirt road leading to a parking lot.

Navy Beach
BEACH

The best place for swimming is at Navy Beach, just east of the South Tufa reserve. It's also the best place to put in canoes or kayaks. From late June to early September, the **Mono Lake Committee** (☑760-647-6595; www.monolake.org/visit/canoe; tours $25; ☺8am, 9:30am & 11am Sat & Sun) operates one-hour canoe tours around the tufas. Half-day kayak tours along the shore or out to Paoha Island are also offered by **Caldera Kayaks** (☑760-934-1691; www.calderakayak.com; tours $75; ☺mid-May–mid-Oct). Both require reservations.

Panum Crater
NATURAL FEATURE

Rising above the south shore, Panum Crater is the youngest (about 640 years old), smallest and most accessible of the craters that string south toward Mammoth Mountain. A panoramic trail circles the crater rim (about 30 to 45 minutes), and a short but steep 'plug trail' puts you at the crater's core. A dirt road leads to the trailhead from Hwy 120, about 3 miles east of the junction with Hwy 395.

Black Point Fissures
NATURAL FEATURE

On the north shore of Mono Lake are the Black Point Fissures, narrow crags that opened when lava mass cooled and contracted about 13,000 years ago. Access is from three places: east of Mono Lake County Park, from the west shore off Hwy 395, or south off Hwy 167. Check at the Mono Basin Scenic Area Visitor Center for specific directions.

ℹ Information

Mono Basin Scenic Area Visitor Center
(☑760-647-3044; www.fs.usda.gov/inyo; ☺8am-5pm Apr–Nov) Half a mile north of Lee Vining, this center has maps, interpretive displays, Inyo National Forest wilderness permits, bear-canister rentals, a bookstore and a 20-minute movie about Mono Lake.

Mono Lake Committee Information Center
(☑760-647-6595; www.monolake.org; cnr Hwy 395 & 3rd St; ☺9am-5pm late-Oct–mid-Jun, 8am-9pm mid-Jun–Sep) Internet access ($2 per 15 minutes), maps, books, free 30-minute video about Mono Lake and passionate, preservation-minded staff. Public restroom too.

June Lake Loop

Under the shadow of massive **Carson Peak** (10,909ft), the stunning 14-mile June Lake Loop (Hwy 158) meanders through a picture-perfect horseshoe canyon, past the relaxed resort town of **June Lake** and four sparkling, fish-rich lakes: Grant, Silver, Gull and June. It's especially scenic in fall when the basin is ablaze with golden aspens. Catch the loop a few miles south of Lee Vining.

🏃 Activities

June Lake is backed by the Ansel Adams Wilderness area, which runs into Yosemite National Park. **Rush Creek Trailhead** has a day-use parking lot, posted maps and self-registration permits. Gem and Agnew Lakes make stunning day hikes, while Thousand Island and Emerald Lake (both on the Pacific Crest/John Muir Trail) are stunning overnight destinations.

Boat and tackle rentals, as well as fishing licenses, are available at five marinas.

June Mountain Ski Area
SKIING

(☑888-586-3686, 24hr snow info 760-934-2224; www.junemountain.com; lift tickets adult/youth 13-18/child under 13 $72/48/free; ☺8:30am-4pm) Winter fun concentrates in this area, which is smaller and less crowded than nearby Mammoth Mountain and perfect for beginner and intermediate skiers. Some 35 trails crisscross 500 acres of terrain served by seven lifts, including two high-speed quads. Boarders can get their adrenaline flowing at three terrain parks with a kick-ass superpipe.

Ernie's Tackle & Ski Shop OUTDOOR EQUIPMENT
(☑760-648-7756; 2604 Hwy 158; ◷6am-7pm) One of the most established outfitters in June Lake village.

🛏 Sleeping & Eating

USFS Campgrounds CAMPGROUND $
(☑800-444-7275; www.recreation.gov; tent & RV sites $22; ◷mid-Apr–Oct) These include: June Lake, **Oh! Ridge**, **Silver Lake**, **Gull Lake** and **Reversed Creek**. The first three accept reservations; Silver Lake has gorgeous mountain views.

June Lake Motel MOTEL $$
(☑760-648-7547; www.junelakemotel.com; 2716 Hwy 158; r with/without kitchen $115/100; @ 🛜) Enormous rooms – most with full kitchens – catch delicious mountain breezes and sport attractive light-wood furniture. There's a fish-cleaning sink and barbecues, plus a book library.

Silver Lake Resort CABIN $$
(☑760-648-7525; www.silverlakeresort.net; Silver Lake; cabin $130-210; ◷late-Apr–mid-Oct) Across the road from Silver Lake and astride Alger Creek, this sweet cabin compound opened in 1916 and has a duck pond and boat rentals in addition to almost 20 rustic cabins with full kitchens. Its tiny old-time **cafe** (mains $8-11; ◷7am-2pm) displays antique winter sports equipment and serves diner fare like burgers, sandwiches and grilled chicken; it's most popular for excellent big breakfasts.

Double Eagle Resort & Spa RESORT $$$
(☑760-648-7004; www.doubleeagle.com; 5587 Hwy 158; r $229, cabins $349; 🛜 ⛱ 🐾) A swanky spot for these parts. The two-bedroom log cabins and balconied hotel rooms lack no comfort, while worries disappear at the elegant spa. Its **restaurant** (mains $15-25; ◷7:30am-9pm) exudes rustic elegance, with cozy booths, a high ceiling and a huge fireplace.

Tiger Bar AMERICAN $$
(www.thetigerbarcafe.com; 2620 Hwy 158; mains $8-19; ◷8am-10pm) After a day on slopes or trails, people gather at the long bar or around the pool table of this no-nonsense, no-attitude place. The kitchen feeds all appetites, with burgers, salads, tacos and other tasty grub, including homemade fries.

Carson Peak Inn AMERICAN $$$
(☑760-648-7575; Hwy 158 btwn Gull & Silver Lakes; meals $18-40; ◷5-10pm, shorter winter hours) Inside a cozy house with a fireplace, this restaurant is much beloved for its tasty old-time indulgences, such as fried chicken, pan-fried trout and chopped sirloin steak. Portion sizes can be ordered for regular or 'hearty' appetites.

Mammoth Lakes

This is a small mountain resort town endowed with larger-than-life scenery – active outdoorsy folks worship at the base of its dizzying 11,053ft **Mammoth Mountain**. Everlasting powder clings to these slopes, and when the snow finally fades, the area's an outdoor wonderland of mountain-bike trails, excellent fishing, endless alpine hiking and blissful hidden spots for hot-spring soaking. The Eastern Sierra's commercial hub and a four-season resort, outdoorsy Mammoth is backed by a ridgeline of jutting peaks, ringed by clusters of crystalline alpine lakes and enshrouded by the dense Inyo National Forest.

◉ Sights

★**Earthquake Fault** NATURAL FEATURE
(Map p444) On Minaret Rd, about 1 mile west of the Mammoth Scenic Loop, detour to gape at Earthquake Fault, a sinuous fissure half a mile long gouging a crevice up to 20ft deep into the earth. Ice and snow often linger at the bottom until late summer, and Native Americans and early settlers used it to store perishable food.

Mammoth Museum MUSEUM
(Map p446; ☑760-934-6918; www.mammothmuseum.org; 5489 Sherwin Creek Rd; suggested donation $3; ◷10am-6pm mid-May–Sep; 🐾) For a walk down memory lane, stop by this little museum inside the historic Hayden log cabin.

🏃 Activities

The excellent website of the **Mammoth Lakes Trail System** (www.mammothtrails.org) contains a comprehensive guide to local hiking, biking and cross-country ski trails, with maps and information on services available.

Skiing & Snowboarding

There's free cross-country skiing along the more than 300 miles of nongroomed trails in town and in the Inyo National Forest. Pick

Mammoth Lakes Area

N 0 ———————— 2 km
   0 ———————— 1 mile

Agnew Meadows Trailhead
Agnew Meadows Campground
Shadow Lake (3.5mi)
Middle Fork San Joaquin River
John Muir Trail & Pacific Crest Trail
Starkweather Lake
Inyo National Forest
Mammoth Scenic Loop
Ansel Adams Wilderness Area
Upper Soda Springs Campground
Minaret Vista (9265ft)
Reds Meadow/ Devils Postpile Shuttle Bus Stop
Earthquake Fault

See Mammoth Lakes Map (p446)

Main St 203
MAMMOTH LAKES

Pumice Flat Campground
closed in winter (Minaret Rd)
203
Minaret Falls Campground
Mammoth Mtn Ski Area & Bike Park
Devils Postpile Ranger Station
Inyo National Forest
▲ Mammoth Mtn (11,053ft)
Sotcher Lake
Reds Creek
OLD MAMMOTH
Tamarack Lodge; Tamarack Cross-Country Ski Center; Lakefront Restaurant
Reds Meadow Campground
Horseshoe Lake
Twin Lakes
Twin Lakes Campground
closed in winter
Devils Postpile National Monument
Ansel Adams Wilderness Area
Rainbow Falls
Inyo National Forest
Mammoth Lakes Basin
McLeod Lake
Lake Mary Campground
Lake Mary
Pokonobe Store and Marina
Lake Mamie
Pine City Campground
Lake George Campground
Lake George
Lake Mary
Coldwater Campground
Middle Fork San Joaquin River
John Muir Wilderness Area
Crystal Lake
Lake George
Lake Barrett
TJ Lake

YOSEMITE & THE SIERRA NEVADA MAMMOTH LAKES

up a free map at the Mammoth Lakes Welcome Center.

Tamarack Cross-Country Ski Center SKIING (Map p446; ☎760-934-2442; 163 Twin Lakes Rd; all-day trail pass adult/child/senior $28/16/22; ⏱8:30am-5pm) Let the town shuttle take you to the Tamarack Lodge, which has almost 20 miles of meticulously groomed track around Twin Lakes and the Lakes Basin. The terrain is also great for snowshoeing. Rentals and lessons are available.

Hiking

Mammoth Lakes rubs up against the Ansel Adams Wilderness (Map p446) and John Muir Wilderness (Map p446) areas, both laced with fabulous trails leading to shimmering lakes, rugged peaks and hidden canyons. Major trailheads leave from the Mammoth Lakes Basin, Reds Meadow and Agnew Meadows; the latter two are accessible only by shuttle. Shadow Lake is a stunning 7-mile

day hike from Agnew Meadows, and Crystal Lake makes a worthy 2.5-mile round-trip trek from Lake George in the Lakes Basin.

From various spots along the Reds Meadow area, long-distance backpackers with wilderness permits and bear canisters can easily jump onto the John Muir Trail (to Yosemite to the north and Mt Whitney to the south) and the Pacific Crest Trail (fancy walking to Mexico or Canada?).

Cycling & Mountain Biking

Stop at the Mammoth Lakes Welcome Center for a free biking map with area route descriptions.

Mammoth Mountain Bike Park MOUNTAIN BIKING (☎800-626-6684; www.mammothmountain.com; day pass adult/child 7-12 $49/23; ⏱9am-4:30pm Jun-Sep) Come summer, Mammoth Mountain morphs into the massive Mammoth Mountain Bike Park, with more than 80 miles of well-kept single-track trails. Several other trails traverse the surrounding forest. In general, Mammoth-style riding translates into plenty of hills and sandy shoulders, which are best navigated with big knobby tires.

But you don't need wheels (or a medic) to ride the vertiginous **Village Gondola** (Map p446) to the apex of the mountain, where there's a cafe and an interpretive center with scopes pointing toward the nearby peaks. And for kids 13 and under, a $39 Adventure Pass buys unlimited day access to a zip line, climbing wall, bungee trampoline and child's bike-park area.

When the park's open, it runs a free mountain-bike **shuttle** (⊘ 9am-5:30pm) from the Village area to the main lodge. Shuttles depart every 30 minutes, and mountain bikers with paid mountain passes get priority over pedestrians.

Lakes Basin Path   CYCLING

One of Mammoth's fantastic new multi-use paths, the 5.3-mile Lakes Basin Path begins at the southwest corner of Lake Mary and Minaret Rds and heads uphill (1000ft, at a 5% to 10% grade) to Horseshoe Lake, skirting lovely lakes and accessing open views of the Sherwin Range. For a one-way ride, use the free Lakes Basin Trolley, which tows a 12-bicycle trailer.

Fishing & Boating

From the last Saturday in April, the dozens of lakes that give the town its name lure in fly and trout fishers from near and far. California fishing licenses are available at sporting goods stores throughout town. For equipment and advice, head to **Troutfitter** (Map p446; ☑ 760-934-2517; cnr Main St & Old Mammoth Rd; ⊘ 8am-4pm) or **Rick's Sports Center** (Map p446; ☑ 760-934-3416; cnr Main & Center Sts; ⊘ 6am-8pm).

The **Pokonobe Store & Marina** (Map p444; ☑ 760-934-2437; www.pokonoberesort. com), on the north end of Lake Mary, rents motor boats ($20 per hour), rowboats ($10), canoes ($20) and kayaks ($20 to $25). **Caldera Kayaks** (☑ 760-935-1691; www.calderakayak.com) has single ($30 for a half-day) and double kayaks ($50) for use on Crowley Lake.

Bowling

★**Mammoth Rock 'n' Bowl**   BOWLING

(Map p446; ☑ 760-934-4200; www.mammothrocknbowl.com; 3029 Chateau Rd; per game adult $5-7/child under 13 $3-5, shoe rental adult/child $3/1; ⊘ 11am-midnight; 🏌) A psychedelic

mural of Devils Postpile crowns this stylish and modern new 12-lane complex that has the locals raving. The ground floor has foosball, ping-pong and darts, plus a casual TV-surrounded restaurant with outdoor patio and cocktail bar. Upstairs you'll find its more upscale eatery Mammoth Rock Brasserie (p448), and a bank of high-def golf simulators ($30 to $40 per hour) let you whack real golf balls across 30 virtual courses.

🛌 Sleeping

Mammoth B&Bs and inns rarely sell out midweek, when rates tend to be lower. During ski season, reservations are a good idea on weekends and essential during holidays. Many properties offer ski-and-stay packages. Condo rentals often work out cheaper for groups.

Stop by the Mammoth Lakes Welcome Center or check its website for a full list of campgrounds, dispersed free camping locations (don't forget to pick up a free but mandatory fire permit) and public showers.

USFS Campgrounds   CAMPGROUND $

(☑ 877-444-6777; www.recreation.gov; tent & RV sites $20-21; ⊘ approx mid-Jun–mid-Sep; 🐕) About 15 USFS campgrounds (see 'Recreation' at www.fs.usda.gov/inyo) are scattered in and around Mammoth Lakes, all with flush toilets but no showers. Many sites are available on a first-come, first-served basis, and some are reservable. Note that nights get chilly at these elevations, even in July. Campgrounds include New Shady Rest (Map p446), Old Shady Rest (Map p446), Twin Lakes (Map p444), Lake Mary (Map p444), Pine City (Map p444), Coldwater (Map p444), Lake George (Map p444), Reds Meadow (p450), Pumice Flat (Map p444), Minaret Falls (p449), Upper Soda Springs (Map p444) and Agnew Meadows (Map p444).

Davison Street Guest House   HOSTEL $

(Map p446; ☑ 760-924-2188, reservations 858-755-8648; www.mammoth-guest.com; 19 Davison St; dm $35-49, d $75-120; 🏠) A cute, five-room A-frame chalet hostel on a quiet residential street, this place has a stocked kitchen, plus mountain views from the living room with fireplace or sun deck. There's self-registration when the manager isn't around.

Tamarack Lodge   LODGE, CABINS $$

(Map p444; ☑ 760-934-2442; www.tamaracklodge.com; 163 Twin Lakes Rd; r incl breakfast with/

Mammoth Lakes

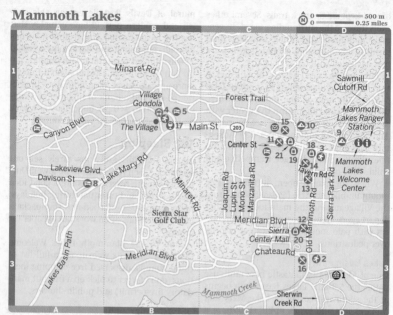

without bath $189/139, cabins from $229; @ 🛜)
🌿 In business since 1924, this charming year-round resort on Lower Twin Lake has a cozy fireplace lodge, a bar and excellent restaurant, 11 rustic-style rooms and 35 cabins. The cabins range from very simple to simply deluxe, and come with full kitchen, private bathroom, porch and wood-burning stove. Some can sleep up to 10 people. Daily resort fee $20.

Guests can use the pool and hot tub at the resort's Mammoth Mountain Inn.

Mammoth Creek Inn
INN $$
(Map p446; 📞760-934-6162; www.mammoth-creekinn.com; 663 Old Mammoth Rd; r $119-135, with kitchen $179-199; @ 🛜) It's amenities galore at this pretty inn at the end of a commercial strip, with down comforters and fluffy terry robes, as well as a sauna, a hot tub and a fun pool table loft. The best rooms overlook the majestic Sherwin Mountains, and some have full kitchens and can sleep up to six.

Austria Hof Lodge
LODGE $$
(Map p446; 📞760-934-2764; www.austriahof.com; 924 Canyon Blvd; r incl breakfast $109-215; 🛜) Close to Canyon Lodge, rooms here have modern knotty pine furniture, thick down duvets and DVD players. Ski lockers and a sundeck hot tub make winter stays here even

sweeter. The lodge restaurant (dinner mains $25 to $40) serves meaty gourmet German fare in a muraled cellar dining room.

Alpenhof Lodge
HOTEL $$
(Map p446; 📞760-934-6330; www.alpen-hof-lodge.com; 6080 Minaret Rd; r incl breakfast $149-189; @ 🛜 ≋ 🐾) A snowball's toss from the Village – and fresh from its star turn and teary Hollywood makeover in the TV reality show *Hotel Impossible* – this Euro-flavored inn has updated lodge rooms with tasteful accent walls and ski racks, plus more luxurious accommodations with gas fireplaces or kitchens.

Cinnamon Bear Inn
B&B $$
(Map p446; 📞760-934-2873; www.cinnamon-bearinn.com; 133 Center St; r incl breakfast $119-179; @ 🛜) At this down-to-earth inn you'll sleep like a log in four-poster beds, and most rooms have cozy gas fireplaces. Swap stories about the day's adventures with other guests over homemade refreshments in the afternoon, or soak away soreness in the small outdoor Jacuzzi.

🍴 Eating

Good Life Café
CALIFORNIAN $
(Map p446; www.mammothgoodlifecafe.com; 126 Old Mammoth Rd; mains $9-15; ⏰6:30am-3pm, to

Mammoth Lakes

9pm Thu-Mon in winter; 🎧) Healthy food, generously filled veggie wraps and big bowls of salad make this a perennially popular place. The front patio is blissful for a long brunch on a warm day.

Stellar Brew CAFE $
(Map p446; www.stellarbrewnaturalcafe.com; 3280b Main St; salads & sandwiches $5.50-10; ⊗5:30am-7pm, to 6pm Sep–mid-Jun; 🎧🖉🐾) Proudly locavore and mostly organic, settle into a comfy sofa here for your daily dose of locally roasted coffee, homemade granola, breakfast burritos and scrumptious vegan (and some gluten-free) pastries.

Base Camp Café AMERICAN $
(Map p446; www.basecampcafe.com; 3325 Main St; mains $7-15; ⊗7:30am-3pm Sun-Fri, to 9pm Sat; 🎧🖉) Fuel up with a bracing dose of organic tea or coffee and a filling breakfast, or comfort food like Tex-Mex jalapeño onion straws and pesto chicken fajitas. Decorated with various backpacking gear and beer mats, the bathroom has a hysterical photo display of backcountry outhouses.

Sierra Sundance Whole Foods HEALTH FOOD $
(Map p446; 26 Old Mammoth Rd; ⊗9am-7pm Mon-Sat, to 5pm Sun; 🖉) Self-catering vegetarians can stock up on organic produce, bulk foods and tofu at this large store and deli.

Toomey's NEW AMERICAN $$
(Map p446; www.toomeyscatering.com; 6085 Minaret Rd, The Village; mains $13-30; ⊗7am-9pm; 🖈) The legendary chef from Whoa Nellie Deli in Lee Vining has decamped here, along with his eclectic menu of wild-buffalo meatloaf, seafood jambalaya and lobster taquitos with mango salsa – plus a lifetime's worth of baseball paraphernalia. The central location's perfect for grabbing a to-go breakfast or a sit-down dinner near the Village Gondola or Mammoth Mountain bike-park shuttle.

Feeney's Starlight Cafe FUSION $$
(Map p446; www.facebook.com/StarlightCafe-Mammoth; 452 Old Mammoth Rd, Sierra Center Mall; mains $10-22; ⊗11am-9pm Mon-Sat, variable hours in fall & spring; 🖉🐾) Harvesting the best of Vietnamese, Korean and Italian cuisine, chef-owner James Feeney rocks the house with dishes like Korean burritos, kimchi burgers, shrimp po'boy sandwiches, housemade pasta and Creole fried chicken.

Stove AMERICAN $$
(Map p446; www.thestoverestaurantmammoth.com; 644 Old Mammoth Rd; breakfast $6-13, dinner $12-20; ⊗6:30am-2pm & 5-9pm) Great coffee and carbs; try the cinnamon-bread French toast. Dinner includes a choice of a dozen yummy side dishes.

★ Lakefront Restaurant NEW AMERICAN $$$
(☎760-934-3534; www.tamaracklodge.com/lakefront_restaurant; 163 Twin Lakes Rd; mains $24-38; ⊗5-9:30pm year-round, plus 11am-2pm summer, closed Tue & Wed in fall & spring) The most atmospheric and romantic restaurant in Mammoth, this intimate dining room at Tamarack Lodge overlooks lovely Twin Lakes. A new chef crafts specialties like pork belly, oxtail risotto and braised beef short ribs, and the staff are superbly friendly. Reservations recommended.

Petra's Bistro & Wine Bar CALIFORNIAN $$$
(Map p446; ☑760-934-3500; www.petrasbistro.com; 6080 Minaret Rd; mains $18-34; ◷5-9:30pm Tue-Sun) Settle in here for seasonal cuisine and wines recommended by the staff sommeliers. In wintertime the best seats in the house are the cozy fireside couches. Start the evening with a cheese course and choose from 36 wines available by the glass (250 vintages by the bottle), or the excellent cocktail menu. Reservations recommended.

Mammoth Rock Brasserie NEW AMERICAN $$$
(Map p446; 3029 Chateau Rd; mains $19-34; ◷5:30-9pm Mon-Thu, to 10pm Fri-Sun) This swanky brasserie at the Mammoth Rock 'n' Bowl serves tasty small plates and meaty main courses with breathtaking views of the Sherwin Range.

🍷 Drinking

Clocktower Cellar PUB
(Map p446; www.clocktowercellar.com; 6080 Minaret Rd; ◷4-11pm) In the winter especially, locals throng this half-hidden basement of the Alpenhof Lodge. The ceiling is tiled with a swirl of bottle caps, and the bar stocks 150 whiskies, 26 beers on tap and about 50 bottled varieties.

Mammoth Brewing Company Tasting Room BREWERY
(Map p446; www.mammothbrewingco.com; 18 Lake Mary Rd; ◷10am-6pm; 🐾) Now located in a large new space, try some of the dozen brews on tap (flights $5 to $7) – including special seasonal varieties not found elsewhere – then pick up some IPA 395 or Double Nut Brown to go.

🛍 Shopping

For outdoor equipment sales and rentals, in-town shops are usually cheaper than at Mammoth Mountain.

Footloose OUTDOOR EQUIPMENT
(Map p446; ☑760-934-2400; www.footloosesports.com; cnr Main St & Old Mammoth Rd; ◷8am-8pm) Full range of footwear and seasonal equipment; local biking info.

Mammoth Mountaineering Supply OUTDOOR EQUIPMENT
(Map p446; ☑760-934-4191; www.mammothgear.com; 3189 Main St; ◷8am-8pm) Offers friendly advice, topo maps and all-season equipment rentals.

Wave Rave OUTDOOR EQUIPMENT
(Map p446; ☑760-934-2471; www.waveravesnowboardshop.com; 3203 Main St; ◷7:30am-9pm Sun-Thu, 7:30am-10pm Fri & Sat, shorter hours off-season) Snowboarders worship here.

Mammoth Outdoor Sports OUTDOOR EQUIPMENT
(Map p446; ☑760-934-3239; www.mammothoutdoorsports.com; 452 Old Mammoth Rd, Sierra Center Mall; ◷8am-8pm Sun-Thu, to 9pm Fri & Sat) Bikes, boards and skis; across from Von's supermarket.

ⓘ Information

Mammoth Lakes Welcome Center (Map p446; ☑760-924-5500, 888-466-2666; www.visitmammoth.com; ◷8am-5pm) and the **Mammoth Lakes Ranger Station** (Map p446; ☑760-924-5500; www.fs.fed.us/r5/inyo; ◷8am-5pm) share a building on the north side of Hwy 203. This one-stop information center issues wilderness permits and rents bear canisters, helps find accommodations and campgrounds, and provides road and trail condition updates. From May through October, when trail quotas are in effect, walk-in wilderness permits are released at 11am the day before; permits are self-issue the rest of the year.

Two weekly newspapers, the *Mammoth Times* (www.mammothtimes.com) and the free *Sheet* (www.thesheetnews.com), carry local news and events listings.

Mammoth Hospital (☑760-934-3311; 85 Sierra Park Rd; ◷24hr) Emergency room.

ⓘ Getting There & Around

Mammoth's updated airport **Mammoth Yosemite** (MMH; www.visitmammoth.com/airport; 1300 Airport Rd, Mammoth Lakes) has a daily nonstop flight to San Francisco, operating winter through to spring on **United** (www.united.com). **Alaska Airlines** (www.alaskaair.com) runs year-round service to Los Angeles, and ski season service to San Diego. All flights are about an hour. Taxis meet incoming flights, and some lodgings provide free transfers. **Mammoth Taxi** (☑760-934-8294; www.mammoth-taxi.com) does airport runs as well as hiker shuttles throughout the Sierra Nevada.

Mammoth is a snap to navigate by public transportation year-round. In the summertime **YARTS** (☑877-989-2787; www.yarts.com) runs buses to and from Yosemite Valley, and the **Eastern Sierra Transit Authority** (☑800-922-1930; www.estransit.com) has year-round service along Hwy 395, north to Reno and south to Lone Pine.

Within Mammoth a year-round system of free and frequent **bus shuttles** connects the whole town with the Mammoth Mountain lodges; in summer, routes with bicycle trailers service the Lakes Basin and Mammoth Mountain Bike Park.

Around Mammoth Lakes

Reds Meadow

One of the beautiful and varied landscapes near Mammoth is the Reds Meadow Valley, west of Mammoth Mountain. Drive on Hwy 203 as far as Minaret Vista (Map p444) for eye-popping views (best at sunset) of the Ritter Range, the serrated Minarets and the remote reaches of Yosemite National Park.

The road to Reds Meadow is only accessible from about June until September, weather permitting. To minimize impact when it's open, the road is closed to private vehicles beyond Minaret Vista unless you are camping, have lodge reservations or are disabled, in which case you must pay a $10 per car fee. Otherwise you must use a mandatory shuttle bus (per adult/child $7/4). It leaves from a lot in front of the Adventure Center (next to the mammoth statue) approximately every 30 minutes between 7:15am and 7pm (last bus out leaves Reds Meadow at 7:45pm), and you must buy tickets inside before joining the queue. There are also three direct departures from the Village (on Canyon Blvd, under the gondola) before 9am, plus the option of using the free mountain-bike shuttle between the Village and the Adventure Center. The bus stops at trailheads, viewpoints and campgrounds before completing the one-way trip to Reds Meadow (45 minutes to an hour).

The valley road provides access to six campgrounds along the San Joaquin River. Tranquil willow-shaded Minaret Falls Campground (Map p444) is a popular fishing spot where the best riverside sites have views of its namesake cascade.

Hot Creek Geological Site

For a graphic view of the area's geothermal power, journey a few miles south of Mammoth to where chilly Mammoth Creek blends with hot springs and continues its journey as Hot Creek. It eventually enters a small gorge and forms a series of steaming, bubbling cauldrons, with water shimmering in shades of blue and green reminiscent of the tropics. Until recently, soakers reveled in the blissful but somewhat scary temperate zones where the hot springs mixed with frigid creek water. But in 2006 a significant increase in geothermal activity began sending violent geysers of boiling water into the air, and the site is off-limits for swimming until the danger has subsided.

To reach the site, turn off Hwy 395 about 5 miles south of town and follow signs to the Hot Creek Fish Hatchery. From here it's another 2 miles on gravel road to the parking area, and a short hike down into the canyon and creek.

For a soak that *won't* cook your goose, take Hwy 395 about 9 miles south of Mammoth to Benton Crossing Rd, which accesses a trove of primitive hot spring pools. Locals call this 'Green Church Rd,' because of the road's unmistakable marker. For detailed directions and maps, pick up the bible – Matt Bischoff's excellent *Touring California & Nevada Hot Springs*. And keep in mind these three golden rules: no glass, no additives to the water and, if you can, no bathing suit.

Convict Lake

Located just southeast of Mammoth, Convict Lake is one of the area's prettiest lakes, with emerald water embraced by massive peaks. A hike along the gentle trail skirting the lake, through aspen and cottonwood trees, is great if you're still adjusting to the altitude. A trailhead on the southeastern shore gives access to Genevieve, Edith, Dorothy and Mildred Lakes in the John Muir Wilderness. To reach the lake, turn south from Hwy 395 on Convict Lake Rd (across from the Mammoth airport) and go 2 miles.

In 1871 Convict Lake was the site of a bloody shoot-out between a band of escaped convicts and a posse that had given chase. Posse leader, Sheriff Robert Morrison, was killed during the gunfight and the taller peak, Mt Morrison (12,268ft), was later named in his honor. The bad guys got away only to be apprehended later near Bishop.

The campground (☎877-444-6777; www. recreation.gov; tent & RV sites $20; ☻mid-Apr–Oct) has flush toilets and nicely terraced sites. Otherwise your only option is Convict Lake Resort (☎760-934-3800; www. convictlake.com; 2000 Convict Lake Rd; cabins from $189; ☎☻☻), whose three houses and 28 cabins with kitchens sleep from two to 34 and range from rustic to ritzy. Foodies with deep pockets flock to the elegant restaurant (☎760-934-3803; lunch $10-15, dinner $24-38; ☻5:30-9pm daily, plus 11am-2:30pm Jul &

DEVILS POSTPILE

The most fascinating attraction in Reds Meadow is the surreal volcanic formation of **Devils Postpile National Monument** (Map p444; ☑ 760-934-2289; www.nps.gov/depo; shuttle day pass adult/child $7/4; ☺ late-May–Oct). The 60ft curtains of near-vertical, six-sided basalt columns formed when rivers of molten lava slowed, cooled and cracked with perplexing symmetry. This honeycomb design is best appreciated from atop the columns, reached by a short trail. The columns are an easy, half-mile hike from the Devils Postpile Ranger Station (Map p444).

From the monument, a 2.5-mile hike passing through fire-scarred forest leads to the spectacular **Rainbow Falls** (Map p444), where the San Joaquin River gushes over a 101ft basalt cliff. Chances of actually seeing a rainbow forming in the billowing mist are greatest at midday. The falls can also be reached via an easy 1.5-mile walk from the Reds Meadow area, which also has a cafe, store, the **Reds Meadow campground** (Map p444) and a pack station. Shuttle services run to the Reds Meadow area in season (p449).

Aug), which many consider the best within a 100-mile radius.

McGee Creek

Eight miles south of Mammoth Lakes, off Hwy 395, McGee Creek Rd rises into the mountains and dead-ends in a dramatic aspen-lined canyon, a particularly beautiful spot for autumn foliage. From here, the **McGee Pass Trail** enters the John Muir Wilderness, with day hikes to **Steelhead Lake** (10 miles round-trip) via an easy walk to subtle **Horsetail Falls** (four miles round-trip).

On the drive up, the **McGee Creek Pack Station** (☑ 760-935-4324; www.mcgeecreekpackstation.com) offers trail rides, and spacious **McGee Creek campground** (www.recreation.gov; McGee Creek Rd; tent & RV sites $20; ☺ late Apr–Oct; ☼) has 28 reservable sites at 7600ft with sun-shaded picnic tables along the creek and stunning mountain vistas.

At the intersection after you leave the highway, don't miss the coffee and home-baked goodies at the cute **East Side Bake Shop** (☑ 760-914-2696; www.facebook.com/EastSideBakeShop; 1561 Crowley Lake Dr; mains $8-15; ☺ 6:30am-3pm Wed-Sun, to 9pm Fri & Sat); check its calendar for fun local music on the weekends.

Rock Creek

South off Hwy 395 and roughly equidistant between Mammoth Lakes and Bishop, Rock Creek Rd travels 11 miles into some of the dreamiest landscapes in the Sierra. At roads' end, the Mosquito Flat trailhead into the **Little Lakes Valley** (part of the John Muir Wilderness) clocks in at a whopping

10,300ft of elevation. Mountaintops seem to be everywhere, with the 13,000ft peaks of Bear Creek Spire, Mt Dade, Mt Abbot and Mt Mills bursting out along the southwestern horizon and lush canyon meadows popping with scores of clear blue lakes. Ecstatic hikers and climbers fan out to explore, though most anglers and hikers just go as far as the first few lakes. An excellent day-hike destination is the second of the **Gem Lakes** (7 miles round-trip), a lovely aquamarine bowl and five-star lunch spot.

At the Rock Creek Lakes Resort, nine miles from the highway, don't put off a visit to tiny **Pie in the Sky Cafe** (☑ 760-935-4311; www.rockcreeklakesresort.com; pie $7; ☺ 7am-7pm late-May–mid-Oct, shorter hours early & late season). Its scratch-baked confections go on sale at 10:30am and usually sell out by 2pm. The slices of chocolate mud pie are gargantuan.

A dozen popular **USFS campgrounds** (☑ 877-444-6777; www.recreation.gov; tent & RV sites $20) line the road; most are along Rock Creek and a few are reservable. In wintertime there's a Sno-Park seven miles in, and during summer, the **Rock Creek Pack Station** (☑ 760-872-8331; www.rockcreekpackstation.com; Rock Creek Rd; trail rides from $45) offers trail rides from its location just before the trailhead.

The area is deservedly popular, and trailhead parking can be challenging; be prepared to trek an extra half mile from the overflow lot.

Bishop

The second-largest town in the Eastern Sierra, Bishop is about two hours from

Yosemite's Tioga Pass entrance. A major recreation hub, Bishop offers access to excellent fishing in nearby lakes, climbing in the Buttermilks just west of town, and hiking in the John Muir Wilderness via Bishop Creek Canyon and the Rock Creek drainage. The area is especially lovely in fall when dropping temperatures cloak aspen, willow and cottonwood in myriad glowing shades.

The earliest inhabitants of the Owens Valley were Paiute and Shoshone Native Americans, who today live on four reservations. White settlers came on the scene in the 1860s and began raising cattle to sell to nearby mining settlements.

◉ Sights

★ Laws Railroad Museum   MUSEUM
(☏ 760-873-5950; www.lawsmuseum.org; Silver Canyon Rd; donation $5; ☉ 10am-4pm; 🚗) Railroad and Old West aficionados should make the 6-mile detour north on Hwy 6 to this museum. It re-creates the village of Laws, an important stop on the route of the *Slim Princess,* a narrow-gauge train that hauled freight and passengers across the Owens Valley for nearly 80 years. You'll see the original 1883 train depot, a post office, a schoolhouse and other rickety old buildings. Many contain funky and eclectic displays (dolls, fire equipment, antique stoves etc) from the pioneer days.

Mountain Light Gallery   GALLERY
(☏ 760-873-7700; www.mountainlight.com; 106 S Main St; ☉ 10am-5pm Mon-Sat) FREE To see the Sierra on display in all its majesty, pop into this gallery, which features the stunning outdoor images of the late Galen Rowell. His work bursts with color, and the High Sierra photographs are some of the best in existence.

🏃 Activities

Fishing is good in the high-altitude lakes of Bishop Creek Canyon (west of town along Hwy 168). Other fine spots include the Owens River (northeast) and the Pleasant Valley Reservoir (Pleasant Valley Rd, north of town).

Eastside Sports   OUTFITTER
(☏ 760-873-7520; www.eastsidesports.com; 224 N Main St; ☉ 9am-9pm) Rents climbing and backpacking equipment and sells maps and guidebooks.

Mammoth Mountaineering Supply   OUTFITTER
(☏ 760-873-4300; www.mammothgear.com; 298 N Main St; ☉ 9am-7pm) Sells lots of used gear and clothing, including shoes.

Climbing
Bishop is prime bouldering and rock-climbing territory, with terrain to match any level of fitness, experience and climbing style. The main areas are the granite **Buttermilk Country**, west of town on Buttermilk Rd, and the stark **Volcanic Tablelands** and **Owens River Valley** to the north. The tablelands are also a wellspring of Native American petroglyphs – tread lightly.

Hiking
Hikers will want to head to the high country by following Line St (Hwy 168) west along Bishop Creek Canyon, past Buttermilk Country and on to several lakes, including Lake Sabrina and South Lake. Trailheads lead into the John Muir Wilderness and on into Kings Canyon National Park. Check with the White Mountain Ranger Station (p452) for suggestions, maps and wilderness permits for overnight stays.

Swimming
Keough's Hot Springs   SWIMMING
(☏ 760-872-4670; www.keoughshotsprings.com; 800 Keough Hot Springs Rd; adult/child 3-12 $10/6; ☉ 11am-7pm Wed-Fri & Mon, 9am-8pm Sat & Sun, longer summer hours) About 8 miles south of Bishop, this historic institutional-green outdoor pool (dating from 1919) is filled with bath-warm water from local mineral springs and doused with spray at one end. A smaller and sheltered 104°F (40°C) soaking pool sits beside it. Camping and tent cabins are also available.

🛏 Sleeping

Bishop has lots of economically priced motels, mostly chains.

USFS Campgrounds   CAMPGROUND $
(www.recreation.gov; tent & RV sites $21; ☉ May-Sep; 🐾) For a scenic night, stretch out your sleeping bag beneath the stars. The closest USFS campgrounds, all but one first-come, first-served, are between 9 miles and 15 miles west of town on Bishop Creek along Hwy 168, at elevations between 7500ft and 9000ft.

BENTON HOT SPRINGS

Soak in your own hot springs tub and snooze beneath the moonlight at **Benton Hot Springs** (☎866-466-2824, 760-933-2287; www.historicbentonhotsprings.com; Hwy 120, Benton; tent & RV sites for 2 people $40-50, d with/without bath incl breakfast $129/109; ☀), a small historic resort in a 150-year-old former silver-mining town nestled along the White Mountains. Choose from nine well-spaced campsites with private tubs or one of the themed antique-filled B&B rooms with semi-private tubs. Daytime dips ($10 hourly per person) are also available, and reservations are essential for all visits.

It's reachable from Mono Lake via Hwy 120 (in summer), Mammoth Lakes by way of Benton Crossing Rd, or Hwy 6 from Bishop; the first two options are undulating drives with sweeping red-rock vistas that glow at sunset, and all take approximately one hour. An **Eastern Sierra Transit Authority** (☎800-922-1930; www.estransit.com) bus connects Bishop and Benton ($6, one hour) on Tuesday and Friday, stopping right at the resort.

If you have time, ask for directions to the **Volcanic Tablelands petroglyphs** off Hwy 6, where ancient drawings decorate scenic rock walls.

Joseph House Inn Bed & Breakfast B&B $$
(☎760-872-3389; www.josephhouseinn.com; 376 W Yaney St; r incl breakfast $143-178; ❄☎☀) A beautiful restored ranch-style home, this place has a patio overlooking a tranquil 3-acre garden, and six nicely furnished rooms, some with fireplaces, all with TV and VCR. Guests enjoy a complimentary gourmet breakfast and afternoon wine.

Hostel California HOSTEL $
(☎760-399-6316; www.hostelbishop.com; 213 Academy Ave; dm $20, r $60-80; ❄@☎) A historic Victorian house located right in the center of town, this new hostel traded in the fussy doilies of the former B&B for climbing photos and gear displays. Hikers, anglers and climbers love the six-bed dorms, full kitchen and laundry-time loaner clothes, as well as the homey outdoors-loving atmosphere. Adults only.

🍴 Eating

Great Basin Bakery BAKERY, CAFE $
(www.greatbasinbakerybishop.com; 275-d S Main St, entrance on Lagoon St; salads & sandwiches $5-7; ⏱6am-4pm Mon-Sat, 6:30am-4pm Sun; ☀) 🍃 On a side street in the southern part of town, this excellent bakery serves locally roasted coffee, breakfast sandwiches on freshly baked bagels with local eggs, scratch-made soups and lots of delectable baked goods (with vegan and gluten-free options).

Erick Schat's Bakkerÿ BAKERY $
(☎760-873-7156; www.erickschatsbakery.com; 763 N Main St; sandwiches $5-8.50; ⏱6am-6pm Sun-Thu, to 7pm Fri) A much-hyped tourist mecca filled to the rafters with racks of fresh bread, it has been making its signature shepherd bread and other baked goodies since 1938. The bakery also features a popular sandwich bar.

Back Alley AMERICAN $$
(www.thebackalleybowlandgrill.com; 649 N Main St, behind Yamatani's Resturant; mains $13-23; ⏱11:30am-9pm) Tucked off the main drag, this busy bowling-alley bar and grill (with bowling pin carpeting!) earns the locals' love with huge portions of fresh fish, rib eye steak, burgers and homemade desserts. Tiki-meets-televisions surf decor.

ℹ️ Information

Public showers are available in town at **Wash Tub** (☎760-873-6627; 236 Warren St; ⏱approx 5pm & 8-10pm), and near South Lake at **Bishop Creek Lodge** (☎760-873-4484; www.bishop-creekresort.com; 2100 South Lake Rd; ⏱May-Oct) and **Parchers Resort** (☎760-873-4177; www.parchersresort.net; 5001 South Lake Rd; ⏱late-May–mid-Oct).

Bishop Area Visitors Bureau (☎760-873-8405; www.bishopvisitor.com; 690 N Main St; ⏱10am-5pm Mon-Fri, to 4pm Sat & Sun)

Inyo County Free Library (☎760-873-5115; 210 Academy Ave; ⏱10am-6pm Mon, Wed & Fri, noon-8pm Tue & Thu, 10am-4pm Sat; ☎) Free internet access.

Northern Inyo Hospital (☎760-873-5811; www.nih.org; 150 Pioneer Ln; ⏱24hr)

Spellbinder Books (☎760-873-4511; 124 S Main St; ⏱10am-5:30pm Mon-Sat; ☎) Great indie bookstore with attached cafe and wi-fi.

White Mountain Ranger Station (☎760-873-2500; www.fs.usda.gov/inyo; 798 N Main

St; ⊗8am-5pm daily May-Oct, Mon-Fri rest of year) Wilderness permits, trail and campground information for the entire area.

Big Pine

This blink-and-you-missed-it town has a few motels and basic eateries. It mainly functions as a launch pad for the Ancient Bristlecone Pine Forest and to the granite Palisades in the John Muir Wilderness, a rugged cluster of peaks including six above 14,000ft. Stretching beneath the pinnacles is Palisades Glacier, the southernmost in the USA and the largest in the Sierra.

To get to the trailhead, turn onto Glacier Lodge Rd (Crocker Ave in town), which follows trout-rich Big Pine Creek up Big Pine Canyon, 10 miles west into a bowl-shaped valley. The strenuous 9-mile hike to Palisades Glacier via the North Fork Trail skirts several lakes – turned a milky turquoise color by glacial runoff – and a stone cabin built by horror-film actor Lon Chaney in 1925.

An ear-popping ascent up Glacier Lodge Rd passes by a trio of USFS campgrounds (☑877-444-6777; www.recreation.gov; tent & RV sites $20; ⊗May–mid-Oct) – Big Pine Creek, Sage Flat and Upper Sage Flat. Showers are available for $5 at Glacier Lodge (☑760-938-2837; www.jewelofthesierra.com; tent sites $25, RV sites $35, d cabins $135; ⊗mid-Apr–mid-Nov; 🐾), a bunch of rustic cabins with kitchens, as well as a campground, with a two-night minimum stay; though the original building no longer exists, it was one of the earliest Sierra getaways when built in 1917.

Independence

This sleepy highway town has been a county seat since 1866 and is home to the Eastern California Museum (www.inyocounty.us/ecmuseum; 155 N Grant St; donation requested; ⊗10am-5pm). It contains one of the most complete collections of Paiute and Shoshone baskets in the country, as well as artifacts from the Manzanar relocation camp and historic photographs of primitively equipped local rock climbers scaling Sierra peaks, including Mt Whitney.

Fans of Mary Austin (1868–1934), renowned author of *The Land of Little Rain* and vocal foe of the desertification of the

Owens Valley, can follow signs leading to her former house at 253 Market St.

West of town via Onion Valley Rd (Market St in town), pretty Onion Valley harbors the trailhead for the Kearsage Pass (9.4 miles round-trip), an old Paiute trade route. This is also the quickest eastside access to the Pacific Crest Trail and Kings Canyon National Park.

In addition to a few small motels in town, Onion Valley has a couple of campgrounds (☑877-444-6777; www.recreation.gov; tent & RV sites $16; ⊗May-Sep) along Independence Creek. At 9200ft the Onion Valley campground is right at the Kearsage Pass trailhead and popular with backpackers.

Inexplicably located in a town otherwise inhabited by greasy spoon diners, Still Life Cafe (☑760-878-2555; 135 S Edward St; lunch $9-16, dinner $16-24; ⊗11am-3pm & 6-9:30pm Wed-Mon), a French gourmet bistro, pops out like an orchid in a salt flat. Escargot, duck-liver mousse, steak au poivre and other French delectables are served with Gallic charm in this bright, artistic dining room.

In the historic Masonic lodge next to the courthouse, bustling Jenny's Cafe (246 N Edwards St; mains $8-11; ⊗7am-2pm Sat-Tue, 7am-8pm Thu & Fri) serves rib-sticking fare like burgers, sandwiches and steaks in a country kitchen setting of rooster-print curtains and old teapots.

Manzanar National Historic Site

A stark wooden guard tower alerts drivers to one of the darkest chapters in US history, which unfolded on a barren and windy sweep of land some 5 miles south of Independence. Little remains of the infamous war concentration camp, a dusty square mile where more than 10,000 people of Japanese ancestry were corralled during WWII following the attack on Pearl Harbor. The camp's lone remaining building, the former high-school auditorium, houses a superb interpretive center (☑760-878-2194; www.nps.gov/manz; ⊗9am-4:30pm Nov-Mar, to 5:30pm Apr-Oct; 🚻) FREE. A visit here is one of the historical highlights of the state and should not be missed.

Watch the 20-minute documentary, then explore the thought-provoking exhibits chronicling the stories of the families that languished here yet built a vibrant community. Afterwards, take a self-guided 3.2-mile

HIKING MT WHITNEY

The mystique of Mt Whitney captures the imagination, and conquering its hulking bulk becomes a sort of obsession for many. The main **Mt Whitney Trail** (the easiest and busiest one) leaves from Whitney Portal, about 13 miles west of Lone Pine via the Whitney Portal Rd (closed in winter), and climbs about 6000ft over 11 miles. It's a super strenuous, really, *really* long walk that'll wear out even experienced mountaineers, but doesn't require technical skills if attempted in summer or early fall. Earlier or later in the season, you'll likely need an ice axe and crampons, and to overnight.

Many people in good physical condition make it to the top, although only superbly conditioned, previously acclimatized hikers should attempt this as a day hike. Breathing becomes difficult at these elevations and altitude sickness is a common problem. Rangers recommend spending a night camping at the trailhead and another at one of the two camps along the route: **Outpost Camp** at 3.5 miles or **Trail Camp** at 6 miles up the trail.

When you pick up your permit and pack-out kits (hikers must pack out their poop) at the Eastern Sierra Interagency Visitor Center in Lone Pine, get the latest info on weather and trail conditions. Near the trailhead, the **Whitney Portal Store** (www.whitneyportalstore.com) sells groceries and snacks. It also has public showers ($5) and a cafe with enormous burgers and pancakes. Its excellent website is a comprehensive starting point for Whitney research.

The biggest obstacle in getting to the peak may be to obtain a **wilderness permit** (per group $6 plus per person $15), which is required for all overnight trips and for day hikes past Lone Pine Lake (about 2.8 miles from the trailhead). A quota system limits daily access to 60 overnight and 100 day hikers from May through October. Because of the huge demand, permits are distributed via the online **Mt Whitney lottery** (www.fs.usda.gov/inyo), with applications accepted from February through mid-March.

Want to avoid the hassle of getting a permit for the main Mt Whitney Trail? Consider ascending this popular pinnacle from the west, using the backdoor route from Sequoia & Kings Canyon National Parks. It takes about six days from Crescent Meadow via the High Sierra Trail to the John Muir Trail – with no Whitney Zone permit required – and wilderness permits are much easier to secure.

driving tour around the grounds, which includes a re-created mess hall and barracks, vestiges of buildings and gardens, as well as the haunting camp cemetery.

Lone Pine

A tiny town, Lone Pine is the gateway to big things, most notably Mt Whitney (14,505ft), the loftiest peak in the contiguous USA, and Hollywood. In the 1920s cinematographers discovered that nearby Alabama Hills were a picture-perfect movie set for Westerns, and stars from Gary Cooper to Gregory Peck could often be spotted swaggering about town.

◎ Sights & Activities

A few basic motels, a supermarket, restaurants and stores (including gear and equipment shops) flank Hwy 395 (Main St in town). Whitney Portal Rd heads west at the lone stoplight, while Hwy 136 to Death Valley veers away about 2 miles south of town.

Mt Whitney   MOUNTAIN
(www.fs.usda.gov/inyo) West of Lone Pine, the jagged incisors of the Sierra surge skyward in all their raw and fierce glory. Cradled by scores of smaller pinnacles, Mt Whitney is a bit hard to pick out from Hwy 395, so for the best views, take a drive along Whitney Portal Rd through the Alabama Hills.

As you get a fix on this majestic megalith, remember that the country's lowest point is only 80 miles (as the crow flies) east of here: Badwater in Death Valley. Climbing to Mt Whitney's summit is among the most popular hikes in the entire country.

★ Alabama Hills   NATURAL FEATURE
Located on Whitney Portal Rd, the warm colors and rounded contours of the Alabama Hills stand in contrast to the jagged snowy Sierras just behind. The setting for count-

less ride-'em-out movies, the popular *Lone Ranger* TV series, and more recently, parts of Quentin Tarantino's *Django Unchained*, the stunning orange rock formations are a beautiful place to experience sunrise or sunset.

You can drive, walk or mountain bike along dirt roads rambling through the boulders, and along Tuttle and Lone Pine creeks. A number of graceful rock arches are within easy hiking distance of the roads. Head west on Whitney Portal Rd and either turn left at Tuttle Creek Rd, after a half-mile, or north on Movie Rd, after about 3 miles. The websites of the Lone Pine Chamber of Commerce and the Museum of Lone Pine Film History have excellent movie location maps.

Museum of Lone Pine Film History   MUSEUM

(☑ 760-876-9909; www.lonepinefilmhistorymuseum.org; 701 S Main St; adult/child $5/free; ☺ 10am-5pm Mon-Sat, to 4pm Sun, longer summer hours) Hundreds of movies have been shot in the area, and this museum contains exhibits of paraphernalia from locally set films. It hosts screenings in its theater twice a month.

🛏 Sleeping & Eating

Whitney Portal Hostel & Hotel   HOSTEL, MOTEL $

(☑ 760-876-0030; www.whitneyportalstore.com; 238 S Main St; dm/r $25/100; ❇ 🛜 🐾) A popular launching pad for Whitney trips and for post-hike wash-ups (public showers available), its hostel rooms are the cheapest beds in town – reserve them months ahead for July and August. There's no common space for the carpeted single-sex bunk-bed rooms, though amenities include towels, TVs, in-room kitchenettes and stocked coffeemakers. New management has converted most of the establishment into plush and modern new motel rooms, and many look out toward Whitney and its neighbors.

Lone Pine Campground   CAMPGROUND $

(☑ 877-444-6777, 518-885-3639; www.recreation.gov; Whitney Portal Rd; tent & RV sites $19; ☺ mid-Apr–Oct; 🐾) About midway between Lone Pine and Whitney Portal, this popular creekside USFS campground (elevation 6000ft) offers flush toilets and potable water.

Dow Hotel & Dow Villa Motel   HOTEL, MOTEL $$

(☑ 760-876-5521; www.dowvillamotel.com; 310 S Main St; hotel r with/without bath $87/69, motel r $113-155; ❇ @ 🛜 🐾 🐾) John Wayne and Errol Flynn are among the stars who have stayed at this venerable hotel. Built in 1922, the place has been restored but retains much of its rustic charm. The rooms in the newer motel section have air-con and are more comfortable and bright, but also more generic.

Alabama Hills Cafe   DINER $

(111 W Post St; mains $8-14; ☺ 7am-2pm; 🖉) Everyone's favorite breakfast joint, the portions here are big, the bread fresh-baked, and the hearty soups and scratch-made fruit pies make lunch an attractive option, too.

Seasons   NEW AMERICAN $$

(☑ 760-876-8927; 206 N Main St; mains $17-30; ☺ 5-9pm daily Apr-Oct, Tue-Sun Nov-Mar) Seasons has everything you fantasized about the last time you choked down freeze-dried rations. Sauteed trout, roasted duck, filet mignon and plates of carb-replenishing pasta will revitalize your appetite, and nice and naughty desserts will leave you purring. Reservations recommended.

🛈 Information

Eastern Sierra Interagency Visitor Center

(☑ 760-876-6222; www.fs.fed.us/r5/inyo; Hwys 395 & 136; ☺ 8am-5pm) USFS information central for the Sierra, Death Valley and Mt Whitney; about 1.5 miles south of town at the junction of Hwys 395 and 136.

Lone Pine Chamber of Commerce (☑ 760-876-4444; www.lonepinechamber.org; 120 S Main St; ☺ 8:30am-4:30pm Mon-Fri)

Central Coast

Includes →

Best Places to Eat

➡ Passionfish (p479)

➡ Ember (p513)

➡ Cracked Crab (p513)

➡ San Luis Obispo Farmers Market (p505)

➡ Penny Ice Creamery (p463)

Best Places to Stay

➡ Post Ranch Inn (p487)

➡ Dream Inn (p462)

➡ Cass House Inn (p494)

➡ HI Santa Cruz Hostel (p462)

➡ Pfeiffer Big Sur State Park Campground (p486)

Why Go?

Too often forgotten or dismissed as 'flyover' country between San Francisco and LA, this stretch of California coast is packed with wild beaches, misty redwood forests, and rolling golden hills of fertile vineyards and farm fields.

Coastal Hwy 1 pulls out all the stops, scenery-wise. Flower-power Santa Cruz and the historic port town of Monterey are gateways to the rugged wilderness of the bohemian Big Sur coast. It's an epic journey snaking down to vainglorious Hearst Castle, past lighthouses and edgy cliffs atop which endangered condors soar.

Get acquainted with California's agricultural heartland along inland Hwy 101, called El Camino Real (the King's Highway) by Spanish conquistadors and Franciscan friars. Colonial missions still line the route, which passes through Paso Robles' flourishing wine country. Then soothe your nature-loving soul in collegiate San Luis Obispo, ringed by sunny beach towns and volcanic peaks.

When to Go

Santa Cruz

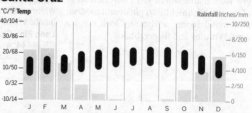

Apr–May Balmy temperatures, but fewer tourists than summer; wildflowers bloom.

Jul–Aug Fog disappears as ocean waters warm up for beach season.

Sep–Oct Sunny blue skies, smaller crowds and wine country harvest festivals.

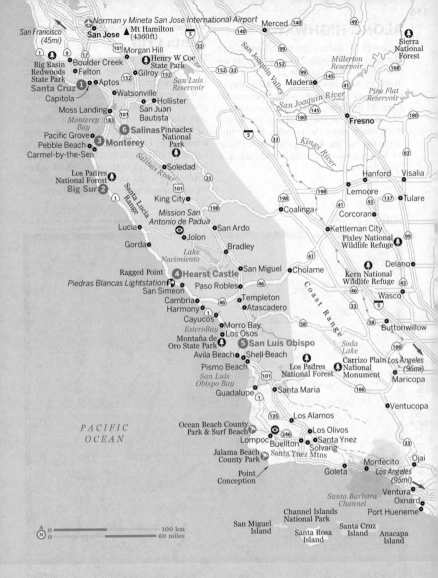

Central Coast Highlights

1 Screaming your head off aboard the Giant Dipper on the beach boardwalk, then learning to surf in **Santa Cruz** (p458).

2 Cruising Hwy 1, where the sky touches the sea, along the rocky coastline of mystical **Big Sur** (p481).

3 Being mesmerized by aquatic denizens of the 'indoor ocean' at the kid-friendly **aquarium** (p468) in Monterey.

4 Marveling in disbelief at the grandiosity of **Hearst Castle** (p490) after meeting the neighbors: ginormous elephant seals.

5 Hanging loose in college-town **San Luis Obispo** (p503), surrounded by beaches, vineyards and mountains.

6 Exploring down-to-earth novelist John Steinbeck's blue-collar world in the agricultural small town of **Salinas** (p498).

ALONG HIGHWAY 1

Anchored by Santa Cruz to the north and Monterey to the south, Monterey Bay teems with richly varied marine life and is bordered by wild beaches and seaside towns full of character and idiosyncratic charm all along its half-moon shore. On the 125-mile stretch south of the Monterey Peninsula, you'll snake along the unbelievably picturesque Big Sur coast and past Hearst Castle until Hwy 1 joins Hwy 101 in laid-back San Luis Obispo.

Santa Cruz

Santa Cruz has marched to its own beat since long before the Beat Generation. It's counterculture central, a touchy-feely, new-agey city famous for its leftie-liberal politics and live-and-let-live ideology – except when it comes to dogs (rarely allowed off-leash), parking (meters run seven days a week) and Republicans (allegedly shot on sight). It's still cool to be a hippie or a stoner here (or better yet, both), although some far-out-looking freaks are just slumming Silicon Valley millionaires and trust-fund babies.

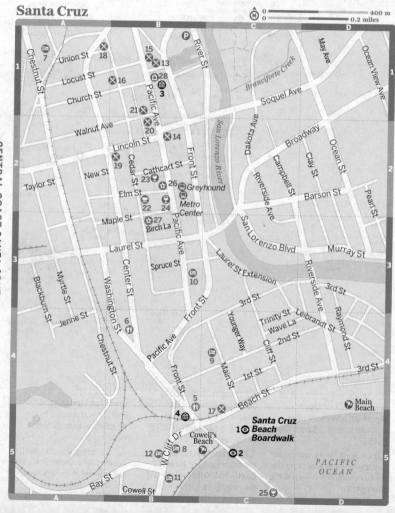

Santa Cruz

Santa Cruz is a city of madcap fun, with a vibrant but chaotic downtown. On the waterfront is the famous beach boardwalk, and in the hills redwood groves embrace the University of California, Santa Cruz (UCSC) campus. Plan to spend at least half a day here, but to appreciate the aesthetic of jangly skirts, crystal pendants and Rastafarian dreadlocks, stay longer and plunge headlong into the rich local brew of surfers, students, punks and eccentric characters.

⊙ Sights

One of the best things to do in Santa Cruz is simply stroll, shop and watch the sideshow along **Pacific Ave** downtown. A 15-minute walk away is the beach and **Municipal Wharf** (Map p458), where seafood restaurants, gift shops and barking sea lions compete for attention. Ocean-view **West Cliff Dr** follows the waterfront southwest of the wharf, paralleled by a paved recreational path.

★ Santa Cruz Beach Boardwalk
AMUSEMENT PARK

(Map p458; ☎831-423-5590; www.beachboardwalk.com; 400 Beach St; per ride $3-6, all-day pass $32-40; ☉ daily Apr-early Sep, seasonal hours vary; ⚑) The West Coast's oldest beachfront amusement park, this 1907 boardwalk has a glorious old-school Americana vibe. The smell of cotton candy mixes with the salt air, punctuated by the squeals of kids hanging upside down on carnival rides. Famous thrills include the Giant Dipper, a 1924 wooden roller coaster, and the 1911 Looff carousel, both National Historic Landmarks. During summer, catch free mid-week movies and Friday night concerts by rock veterans you may have thought were already dead.

Closing times and off-season hours vary. All-day parking costs $6 to $15.

★ Seymour Marine Discovery Center
MUSEUM

(Map p466; ☎831-459-3800; http://seymourcenter.ucsc.edu; 100 Shaffer Rd; adult/child 3-16yr $8/6; ☉10am-5pm Tue-Sun year-round, also 10am-5pm Mon Jul & Aug; ⚑) ✎ By Natural Bridges State Beach, this kids' educational center is part of UCSC's Long Marine Laboratory. Interactive natural-science exhibits include tidal touch pools and aquariums, while outside you can gawk at the world's largest blue-whale skeleton. Guided one-hour tours happen at 1pm, 2pm and 3pm daily, with a special 30-minute tour for families with younger children at 11am; sign up for tours in person an hour in advance (no reservations).

Sanctuary Exploration Center
MUSEUM

(Map p458; ☎831-421-9993; http://montereybay.noaa.gov; 35 Pacific Ave; ☉10am-5pm Wed-Sun; ⚑) ✎ FREE Operated by the Monterey Bay National Marine Sanctuary, this educational museum near the beach boardwalk is an interactive multimedia experience that teaches kids

CENTRAL COAST SANTA CRUZ

and adults about the bay's marine treasures, watershed conservation and high-tech underwater exploration for scientific research.

Santa Cruz Surfing Museum   MUSEUM
(Map p466; www.santacruzsurfingmuseum.org; 701 W Cliff Dr; admission by donation; ⏰ 10am-5pm Wed-Mon Jul 4-early Sep, noon-4pm Thu-Mon early Sep-Jul 3) A mile southwest of the wharf along the coast, this museum inside an old lighthouse is packed with memorabilia, including vintage redwood surfboards. Fittingly, Lighthouse Point overlooks two popular surf breaks.

University of California, Santa Cruz   UNIVERSITY
(Map p466; UCSC; www.ucsc.edu) Check it: the school mascot is a banana slug! Established in 1965 in the hills above town, UCSC is known for its creative, liberal bent. The rural campus has fine stands of redwoods and architecturally interesting buildings – some made with recycled materials – designed to blend in with rolling pastureland. Amble around the peaceful arboretum (http://arboretum.ucsc.edu; cnr High St & Arboretum Rd; adult/child 6-17yr $5/2, free 1st Tue of each month; ⏰ 9am-5pm) and picturesquely decaying 19th-century structures from Cowell Ranch, upon which the campus was built.

Santa Cruz Museum of Natural History   MUSEUM
(Map p466; ☎ 831-420-6115; www.santacruzmuseum.org; 1305 E Cliff Dr; adult/child under 18yr $4/free, free 1st Fri of each month; ⏰ 10am-5pm Tue-Sun; ♿) The collections at this pint-sized museum include stuffed animal mounts, Native Californian cultural artifacts and a touch-friendly tide pool that shows off sea critters living by the beach right across the street.

Museum of Art & History   MUSEUM
(Map p458; ☎ 831-429-1964; www.santacruzmah.org; McPherson Center, 705 Front St; adult/child 12-17yr $5/2, free 1st Fri of each month; ⏰ 11am-5pm Tue-Thu, Sat & Sun, to 9pm Fri) Rotating displays by contemporary California artists and exhibits on local history are worth a quick look.

🏃 Activities

DeLaveaga Disc Golf Club   GOLF
(Map p466; www.delaveagadiscgolf.com; Upper Park Rd) FREE Touring pros and families with kids toss discs across this challenging hillside layout that peaks at Hole No 27, nicknamed 'Top of the World.' It's a couple of miles northeast of downtown, off Branciforte Dr.

Surfing

Year-round, water temperatures average under 60°F, meaning that without a wetsuit, body parts quickly turn blue. Surfing is incredibly popular, especially at experts-only Steamer Lane and beginners' Cowell's, both off West Cliff Dr. Other favorite surf spots include Pleasure Point Beach, on East Cliff Dr toward Capitola, and Manresa State Beach off Hwy 1 southbound.

Santa Cruz Surf School   SURFING
(Map p458; ☎ 831-345-8875, 831-426-7072; www.santacruzsurfschool.com; 131 Center St; 2hr group/1hr private lesson $90/120; ♿) Wanna learn to surf? Near the wharf, friendly male and female instructors will have you standing and surfing on your first day out.

Richard Schmidt Surf School   SURFING
(Map p466; ☎ 831-423-0928; www.richardschmidt.com; 849 Almar Ave; 2hr group/1hr private lesson $90/120) Award-winning surf school can get you out there, all equipment included. Summer surf camps hook adults and kids alike.

O'Neill Surf Shop   SURFING
(Map p466; ☎ 831-475-4151; www.oneill.com; 1115 41st Ave; wetsuit/surfboard rental from $10/20; ⏰ 9am-8pm Mon-Fri, from 8am Sat & Sun) Head east toward Pleasure Point to worship at this internationally renowned surfboard maker's flagship store, with branches on the beach boardwalk and downtown.

Cowell's Beach Surf Shop   SURFING
(Map p458; ☎ 831-427-2355; www.cowellssurfshop.com; 30 Front St; 2hr group lesson $90; ⏰ 8am-6pm, to 5pm Nov-Mar; ♿) Rent surfboards, boogie boards, wetsuits and other beach gear near the wharf, where veteran staff offer local tips and lessons.

Kayaking

Kayaking lets you discover the craggy coastline and kelp beds where sea otters float.

Venture Quest   KAYAKING
(Map p458; ☎ 831-425-8445, 831-427-2267; www.kayaksantacruz.com; Municipal Wharf; kayak rental/tour from $30/55; ⏰ 10am-7pm Mon-Fri, from 9am Sat & Sun late-May–late-Sep, hours vary late-Sep–mid-May) Convenient rentals on the wharf, plus whale-watching and coastal sea-cave tours, moonlight paddles and kayak-sailing trips. Book ahead for kayak-surfing lessons.

Kayak Connection   WATER SPORTS
(Map p466; ☎ 831-479-1121; www.kayakconnection.com; Santa Cruz Harbor, 413 Lake Ave; kayak

TOP SANTA CRUZ BEACHES

Sun-kissed Santa Cruz has warmer beaches than San Francisco or Monterey. *Baywatch* it isn't, but 29 miles of coastline reveal a few Hawaii-worthy beaches, craggy coves, some primo surf spots and big sandy stretches where your kids will have a blast. Fog may ruin many a summer morning; it often burns off by the afternoon.

West Cliff Dr is lined with scramble-down-to coves and plentiful parking. If you don't want sand in your shoes, park yourself on a bench and watch enormous pelicans dive for fish. You'll find bathrooms and showers at the lighthouse parking lot.

Locals favor less-trampled **East Cliff Dr** beaches, which are bigger and more protected from the wind, meaning calmer waters. Except at a small metered lot at 26th Ave, parking is by permit only on weekends (buy a $8 per day permit at 9th Ave).

Main Beach *The* scene, with a huge sandy stretch, volleyball courts and swarms of people. Park on East Cliff Dr and walk across the Lost Boys trestle to the beach boardwalk.

Its Beach (Map p466; 🐾) The only official off-leash beach for dogs (before 10am and after 4pm) is just west of the lighthouse.

Natural Bridges State Beach (Map p466; www.parks.ca.gov; 2531 W Cliff Dr; per car $10; ⊘8am-sunset; ♿) Best for sunsets, this family favorite has lots of sand, tide pools and monarch butterflies from mid-October through mid-February. It's at the far end of W Cliff Dr.

Twin Lakes State Beach (Map p466; www.parks.ca.gov; E Cliff Dr & 9th Ave; ⊘8am-sunset; ♿) Big beach with bonfire pits and a lagoon, good for kids and often fairly empty. It's off E Cliff Dr.

Moran Lake County Park (Map p466; www.scparks.com; E Cliff Dr; ⊘8am-sunset) With a good surf break and bathrooms, this pretty all-around sandy spot is further east of 26th Ave off E Cliff Dr.

New Brighton State Beach (Map p466; ☑831-464-6330; www.parks.ca.gov; 500 Park Rd, Capitola; per car $10; ⊘8am-sunset) Heading east of Santa Cruz to Capitola, New Brighton State Beach is a quieter place for a swim, paddleboarding or camping on a forested bluff.

Seacliff State Beach (☑831-685-6442; www.parks.ca.gov; State Park Rd, Aptos; per car $10; ⊘8am-sunset) Seacliff State Beach harbors a 'cement boat,' a quixotic freighter built of concrete that floated OK, but ended up here as a coastal fishing pier.

Manresa State Beach (☑831-761-1975; www.parks.ca.gov; San Andreas Rd, Watsonville; per car $10; ⊘8am-sunset) Near Watsonville, the La Selva Beach exit off Hwy 1 leads here to this sparsely populated beach.

Sunset State Beach (☑831-763-7062; www.parks.ca.gov; San Andreas Rd, Watsonville; per car $10; ⊘8am-sunset) The La Selva Beach exit off Hwy 1, near Watsonville, brings you here, where you can have miles of sand and surf almost all to yourself.

rental/tour from $35/45; ♿) Rents kayaks and offers lessons and tours, including whale-watching, sunrise, sunset and full-moon trips. Also rents stand-up paddleboarding (SUP) sets (from $25), wetsuits ($10) and boogie boards ($10).

Whale-Watching & Fishing

Winter whale-watching trips run from December through April, though there's plenty of marine life to see on a summer bay cruise. Many fishing trips depart from the wharf, where a few shops rent fishing tackle and poles.

Stagnaro's BOAT TOUR
(Map p466; ☑info 831-427-0230, reservations 888-237-7084; www.stagnaros.com; 2896 Soquel Ave; adult/child under 14yr cruise from $20/13, whale-watching tour from $47/33) Longstanding tour operator offers scenic and sunset cruises around Monterey Bay and whale-watching tours year-round.

🎆 Festivals & Events

Woodies on the Wharf CULTURE
(www.santacruzwoodies.com) Classic car show features vintage surf-style station wagons on Santa Cruz's Municipal Wharf in late June.

MYSTERY SPOT

A kitschy, old-fashioned tourist trap, Santa Cruz's **Mystery Spot** (☑831-423-8897; www.mysteryspot.com; 465 Mystery Spot Rd; admission $6; ◷10am-4pm Mon-Fri, to 5pm Sat & Sun Sep-May, 10am-6pm Mon-Fri, 9am-7pm Sat & Sun Jun-Aug) has scarcely changed since it opened in 1940. On a steeply sloping hillside, compasses seem to point crazily, mysterious forces push you around and buildings lean at silly angles. Make reservations, or risk getting stuck waiting for a tour. It's about 4 miles northeast of downtown, up into the hills via Branciforte Dr. Parking costs $5. Don't forget your bumper sticker!

Wharf to Wharf Race   SPORTS
(www.wharftowharf.com) More than 15,000 runners cruise from Santa Cruz to Capitola accompanied by 50 different live-entertainment acts in late July.

Open Studio Art Tour   CULTURE
(www.ccscc.org) Step inside local artists' creative workshops over three weekends in October. The arts council also sponsors 'First Friday' art exhibitions on the first Friday of each month.

🛏 Sleeping

Santa Cruz does not have enough beds to satisfy demand: expect outrageous prices at peak times for nothing-special rooms. Places near the beach boardwalk run the gamut from friendly to frightening. If you're looking for a straightforward motel, cruise Ocean St inland or Mission St (Hwy 1) near the UCSC campus.

⭐**HI Santa Cruz Hostel**   HOSTEL $
(Map p458; ☑831-423-8304; www.hi-santacruz.org; 321 Main St; dm $26-29, r $60-110, all with shared bath; ◷check-in 5-10pm; @) Budget overnighters dig this hostel at the century-old Carmelita Cottages surrounded by flowering gardens, just two blocks from the beach. Cons: midnight curfew, daytime lockout (10am to 5pm) and three-night maximum stay. Reservations are essential. Street parking costs $2.

California State Park Campgrounds   CAMPGROUND $
(☑reservations 800-444-7275; www.reserveamerica.com; tent & RV sites $35-65; 🐾) Book well

ahead to camp at state beaches off Hwy 1 south of Santa Cruz or up in the foggy Santa Cruz Mountains off Hwy 9. Family-friendly campgrounds include Henry Cowell Redwoods State Park in Felton and New Brighton State Beach in Capitola.

⭐**Adobe on Green B&B**   B&B $$
(Map p458; ☑831-469-9866; www.adobeongreen.com; 103 Green St; r incl breakfast $169-219; 🛜) 🌿 Peace and quiet are the mantras at this place, a short walk from Pacific Ave. The hosts are practically invisible, but their thoughtful touches are everywhere, from boutique-hotel amenities in spacious, stylish and solar-powered rooms to breakfast spreads from their organic gardens.

Pelican Point Inn   INN $$
(Map p466; ☑831-475-3381; www.pelicanpointinn-santacruz.com; 21345 E Cliff Dr; ste $139-219; 🛜🐾) Ideal for families, these roomy apartments near a kid-friendly beach come with everything you'll need for a lazy vacation, including kitchenettes. Weekly rates available. Pet fee $20.

Mission Inn   MOTEL $$
(Map p466; ☑800-895-5455, 831-425-5455; www.mission-inn.com; 2250 Mission St; r incl breakfast $130-220; ✳🛜) Perfectly serviceable two-story motel with a garden courtyard, hot tub and complimentary continental breakfast. It's on busy Hwy 1 near the UCSC campus, away from the beach.

Sunny Cove Motel   MOTEL $$
(Map p466; ☑831-475-1741; www.sunnycovemotel.com; 21610 E Cliff Dr; r $90-250; ✳🐾) No-frills retro hideaway east of downtown is a staunch surfers' fave. The long-time Santa Cruzian owner rents well-worn rooms and kitchenette suites.

Dream Inn   HOTEL $$$
(Map p458; ☑866-774-7735, 831-426-4330; www.dreaminnsantacruz.com; 175 W Cliff Dr; r $249-479; ✳@🛜🐾) Overlooking the wharf from a spectacular hillside perch, this chic boutique hotel is as stylish as Santa Cruz gets. Rooms have all mod cons, while the beach is just steps away. Don't miss happy hour at Aquarius restaurant's ocean-view bar. Parking is $25.

Pacific Blue Inn   B&B $$$
(Map p458; ☑831-600-8880; www.pacificblueinn.com; 636 Pacific Ave; r incl breakfast $189-289; 🛜) 🌿 This downtown courtyard B&B is an eco-conscious gem, with water-saving fixtures

and renewable and recycled building materials. Refreshingly elemental rooms have pillowtop beds, electric fireplaces and flat-screen TVs with DVD players. Free loaner bikes.

West Cliff Inn
INN $$$

(Map p458; 800-979-0910, 831-457-2200; www. westcliffinn.com; 174 W Cliff Dr; r incl breakfast $195-325;) In a classy Victorian house west of the wharf, this boutique inn's quaint rooms mix sea-grass wicker, dark wood and jaunty striped curtains. The most romantic suites have gas fireplaces and let you spy on the breaking surf. Rates include a breakfast buffet and afternoon wine, tea and snacks.

Sea & Sand Inn
MOTEL $$$

(Map p458; 831-427-3400; www.santacruzmotels.com; 201 W Cliff Dr; r $199-419;) With a grassy lawn at the cliff's edge, this spiffy, if seriously overpriced motel overlooks Main Beach and the wharf. Fall asleep to braying sea lions! Rooms are smallish, but ocean views can be stellar. Rates include complimentary afternoon refreshments. Their contempo sister property, Carousel Beach Inn, is cheaper and closer to the beach boardwalk.

Babbling Brook Inn
B&B $$$

(Map p466; 831-427-2437, 800-866-1131; www. babblingbrookinn.com; 1025 Laurel St; r incl breakfast $229-309;) Built around a running stream with meandering gardens, the inn has cozy rooms decorated in French-provincial style. Most have gas fireplaces, some have whirlpool tubs and all have featherbeds. There's afternoon wine and hors d'oeuvres, plus a full breakfast.

Hotel Paradox
HOTEL $$$

(Map p466; 855-425-7200, 831-425-7100; www. thehotelparadox.com; 611 Ocean St; r from $189;) Downtown boutique hotel brings the great outdoors inside, with nature prints on the walls, textured wood panels and earth-toned furnishings. Relax in a cabana by the pool or next to an outdoor fire pit. Weekday rates can be reasonable, but summer weekends are high-priced. Parking is $10.

Eating

Downtown is chockablock with casual cafes. If you're looking for seafood, wander the wharf's takeout counter joints. Mission St, near UCSC, and 41st Ave offer cheaper eats.

Penny Ice Creamery
ICE CREAM $

(Map p458; www.thepennyicecreamery.com; 913 Cedar St; snacks $2-4; noon-11pm;) With a cult following, this artisan ice-cream shop crafts zany flavors like bourbon candied ginger, lemon verbena blueberry and ricotta apricot all from scratch using local, organic and wild-harvested ingredients. Even vanilla is special: it's made using Thomas Jefferson's original recipe. Also at a downtown kiosk (1520 Pacific Ave; noon-6pm Sun-Thu, to 9pm Fri & Sat;) and near Pleasure Point (820 41st Ave; noon-9pm Sun-Thu, to 11pm Fri & Sat;).

Picnic Basket
DELI $

(Map p458; http://thepicnicbasketsc.com; 125 Beach St; dishes $3-10; 7am-4pm Mon-Thu, to 9pm Fri-Sun;) Across the street from the beach boardwalk, this locavarian kitchen puts together creative sandwiches such as beet with lemony couscous or 'fancy pants' grilled cheese with fruit chutney, plus homemade soups, breakfast burritos and baked goods. Ice-cream treats are sweet.

Walnut Ave Cafe
BREAKFAST $

(Map p458; www.walnutavecafe.com; 106 Walnut Ave; mains $7-11; 7am-3pm Mon-Fri, 8am-4pm Sat & Sun;) Line up at this clean, well-lit breakfast spot for fluffy Belgian waffles, blackened ahi tuna eggs benny, Mexican huevos rancheros with pulled pork and all kinds of veggie scrambles. Lunch brings less-exciting sandwiches, salads and soups. Dogs are welcome on the outdoor patio.

Bagelry
DELI $

(Map p458; www.bagelrysantacruz.com; 320a Cedar St; dishes $1-9; 6:30am-5:30pm Mon-Fri, 7am-4:30pm Sat, 7:30am-4pm Sun;) The bagels here are twice-cooked (boiled, then baked), and come with fantastic spreads like crunchy 'Tofu del Fuego' or hummus with sprouts.

Tacos Moreno
MEXICAN $

(Map p466; www.tacosmoreno.com; 1053 Water St; dishes $2-6; 10am-10pm Mon-Fri, 11am-7pm Sat & Sun) Who cares how long the line is at lunchtime? Find taquería heaven with these marinated pork, chicken or beef soft tacos. Also on 41st Ave in Capitola.

New Leaf Community Market
SUPERMARKET $

(Map p458; www.newleaf.com; 1134 Pacific Ave; 8am-9pm;) Organic and local produce, natural-foods groceries and deli takeout meals downtown and also off Hwy 1 near the UCSC campus. The 41st Ave branch has a healthy-minded Beet Cafe.

Santa Cruz Farmers Market
MARKET $

(Map p458; www.santacruzfarmersmarket.org; cnr Lincoln & Center Sts; 1:30-6:30pm Wed;)

Organic produce, baked goods and arts-and-crafts and food booths all give you an authentic taste of the local vibe. Shorter fall and winter hours.

Pono Hawaiian Grill
FUSION $$

(Map p458; www.ponohawaiiangrill.com; 120 Union St; mains $7-15; ⏰11am-10pm Sun-Wed, to 11pm Thu-Sat) Inside the Reef bar, this kitchen runs on 'island time' as it mixes up your fresh ahi tuna, salmon, shellfish or veggie *poke* (cubed raw salad) in a bowl or ladled on a plate with two-scoop rice and creamy macaroni or tossed green salad. The *loco moco* burrito with spicy gravy is a huge hit.

Engfer Pizza Works
PIZZERIA $$

(Map p466; www.engferpizzaworks.com; 537 Seabright Ave; pizzas $8-23; ⏰usually 4-9:30pm Tue-Sun; ✏️🏠) Detour to find this old factory, where wood-fired oven pizzas are made from scratch – the no-name specialty is like a giant salad on roasted bread. Play ping-pong and down draft microbrews while you wait.

Soif
BISTRO $$$

(Map p458; ☎831-423-2020; www.soifwine.com; 105 Walnut Ave; small plates $5-17, mains $19-25; ⏰5-9pm Sun-Thu, to 10pm Fri & Sat) Bon vivants swoon over a heady selection of three dozen international wines by the glass, paired with a sophisticated, seasonally driven Euro-Cal menu. Expect tastebud-ticklers like roasted beet salad with fava beans and maple vinaigrette or squid-ink linguini with spicy chorizo.

Laili
AFGHANI $$$

(Map p458; ☎831-423-4545; www.lailirestaurant.com; 101b Cooper St; mains $13-28; ⏰11:30am-2:30pm Tue-Sun, 5-9pm Tue-Thu & Sun, to 10pm Fri & Sat) A chic downtown dining oasis, family-owned Laili invites diners in with an elegant high-ceilinged dining room and garden patio. Share apricot-chicken flatbread, tart pomegranate eggplant, roasted cauliflower with saffron, succulent lamb kebabs and more. Service is spotty. Reservations advised.

Drinking & Nightlife

Downtown overflows with bars, lounges and coffee shops. Heading west on Mission St (Hwy 1), several Santa Cruz Mountains winery tasting rooms hide out along Ingalls St.

★ Verve Coffee Roasters
CAFE

(Map p458; www.vervecoffeeroasters.com; 1540 Pacific Ave; ⏰6:30am-9pm; 🛜) To sip finely roasted artisan espresso or a cup of rich pour-over coffee, join the surfers and hipsters at this industrial-zen cafe. Single-origin brews and house blends rule.

Caffe Pergolesi
CAFE

(Map p458; www.theperg.com; 418 Cedar St; ⏰7am-11pm; 🛜) Discuss conspiracy theories over stalwart coffee, tea or beer at this landmark Victorian house with a big ol' tree-shaded verandah. There's live music some evenings.

Vino Prima
WINE BAR

(Map p458; www.vinoprimawines.com; 55 Municipal Wharf; ⏰2-8pm Mon-Tue, 2-10pm Wed-Fri, noon-

---

LOCAL KNOWLEDGE

TOP SANTA CRUZ COUNTY BREWERIES

We asked Derek Wolfgram, home brewer and local beer columnist, to share with us his favorite places for a pint:

Boulder Creek Brewery (p466) High up in the mountains, these guys brew amber 'Redwood Ale' and 'Dragon's Breath' American IPA.

Sante Adairius Rustic Ales (Map p466; www.rusticales.com; 103 Kennedy Dr; ⏰3-8pm Tue-Fri, from noon Sat & Sun) Off Hwy 1 east of Santa Cruz, Belgian-inspired and barrel-aged beers are a beer geek's dream.

Discretion Brewing (Map p466; www.discretionbrewing.com; 2703 41st Ave, Soquel; ⏰11:30am-9pm) Rye IPA, English ales and traditional Belgian and German brews are always on tap, off Hwy 1.

Santa Cruz Mountain Brewing (Map p466; www.scmbrew.com; 402 Ingalls St; ⏰11:30am-10pm) Bold organic beers make this tiny locals' tasting room crowded. Oddest flavor? Lavender IPA.

Santa Cruz Ale Works (Map p466; www.santacruzaleworks.com; 150 Dubois St; ⏰11am-6pm; 🏠🐾) Hefeweizen and 'Dark Night' oatmeal stout are commendable at this dog-friendly brewpub with a deli.

10pm Sat, noon-8pm Sun) With dreamy ocean views, this spot pours California boutique wines, including hard-to-find bottles from around Santa Cruz and Monterey Counties.

Surf City Billiards & Café   BAR
(Map p458; www.surfcitybilliardscafe.com; 931 Pacific Ave; ⊙5pm-midnight Sun-Thu, to 2am Fri & Sat) An escape from downtown's dives, this upstairs pool hall has Brunswick Gold Crown tables for shooting stick, darts, shuffleboard and big-screen sports TVs.

Hula's Island Grill   BAR
(Map p458; www.hulastiki.com; 221 Cathcart St; ⊙4:30-9:30pm Mon-Thu, 11:30am-11pm Fri & Sat, 11:30am-9:30pm Sun) Pull up a seat at this Hawaii-themed tiki bar for mai tais, *lilikoi* (passion fruit) margaritas, zombie cocktails and happy-hour *pupus* (appetizers).

☆ Entertainment

Free tabloid *Santa Cruz Weekly* (www.santacruzweekly.com) and *Good Times* (www.gtweekly.com) cover music, arts and nightlife scenes.

Catalyst   LIVE MUSIC
(Map p458; ☑831-423-1338; www.catalystclub.com; 1011 Pacific Ave) Over the years, this stage for local bands has seen big-time national acts perform, from Queens of the Stone Age to Snoop Dogg. Expect loads of punk attitude.

Kuumbwa Jazz Center   LIVE MUSIC
(Map p458; ☑831-427-2227; www.kuumbwajazz.org; 320 Cedar St) Hosting jazz luminaries since 1975, this nonprofit theater is for serious jazz cats snapping their fingers for famous-name performers in an intimate room.

Moe's Alley   LIVE MUSIC
(Map p466; ☑831-479-1854; www.moesalley.com; 1535 Commercial Way) In a way-out industrial wasteland, this joint puts on live sounds almost every night: jazz, blues, reggae, roots, salsa and acoustic world-music jams.

🛍 Shopping

Stroll Pacific Ave and downtown side streets to find one-of-a-kind, locally owned boutiques (not just smoke shops, dude). For vintage clothing and surf shops, amble 41st Ave around Portola Dr.

Annieglass   HOMEWARES
(Map p458; www.annieglass.com; 110 Cooper St; ⊙10:30am-6pm Mon-Sat, to 5pm Sun) Handcrafted sculptural glassware by an artist whose work is displayed at the Smithsonian American Art Museum is made right here in wackadoodle Santa Cruz.

Bookshop Santa Cruz   BOOKS
(Map p458; ☑831-423-0900; www.bookshopsantacruz.com; 1520 Pacific Ave; ⊙9am-10pm Sun-Thu, to 11pm Fri & Sat) Vast selection of new books, a few used ones, and 'Keep Santa Cruz Weird' bumper stickers.

Donnelly Fine Chocolates   FOOD
(Map p466; www.donnellychocolates.com; 1509 Mission St; ⊙10:30am-6pm Mon-Fri, from noon Sat & Sun) The Willy Wonka of Santa Cruz makes stratospherically priced chocolates on par with the big city. Try the cardamom or chipotle truffles.

ℹ Information

FedEx Office (www.fedex.com; 712 Front St; per min 30-40¢; ⊙6am-midnight Mon-Fri, 8am-9pm Sat, 9am-9pm Sun; 🛜) Pay-as-you-go internet workstations and photo-printing kiosks.

KPIG 107.5 FM (www.kpig.com) Streams the classic Santa Cruz soundtrack – think Bob Marley, Janis Joplin and Willie Nelson.

Public Library (www.santacruzpl.org; 224 Church St; ⊙10am-7pm Mon-Thu, 10am-5pm Fri & Sat, 1-5pm Sun; 🛜) Free wi-fi and public internet terminals for California public library cardholders (out-of-state visitors $10).

Santa Cruz Visitor Center (☑800-833-3494, 831-429-7281; www.santacruzca.org; 303 Water St; ⊙9am-noon & 1-4pm Mon-Fri, 11am-3pm Sat & Sun) Free public internet terminal, maps and brochures.

ℹ Getting There & Around

Santa Cruz is 75 miles south of San Francisco via coastal Hwy 1 or Hwy 17, a nail-bitingly narrow, winding mountain road. Monterey is about an hour's drive further south via Hwy 1.

Santa Cruz Airport Shuttles (☑831-421-9883; www.santacruzshuttles.com) runs shared shuttles to/from the airports at San Jose ($50), San Francisco ($80) and Oakland ($80), with a $5 cash discount; the second passenger pays $10.

Greyhound (☑800-231-2222; www.greyhound.com; Metro Center, 920 Pacific Ave) has a few daily buses to San Francisco ($16.50, three hours), Salinas ($14, one hour), Santa Barbara ($53, six hours) and Los Angeles ($59, nine hours).

Santa Cruz Metro (☑831-425-8600; www.scmtd.com; single-ride/day pass $2/6) operates local and countywide bus routes that converge on downtown's **Metro Center** (920 Pacific

Ave). Hwy 17 express buses link Santa Cruz with San Jose's Amtrak/CalTrain station ($5, 50 minutes, once or twice hourly).

From late May through early September, the **Santa Cruz Trolley** (www.santacruztrolley.com; per ride 25¢) shuttles between downtown and the beach from 11am until 9pm daily.

Around Santa Cruz

Santa Cruz Mountains

Winding between Santa Cruz and Silicon Valley, Hwy 9 is a 40-mile backwoods byway through the Santa Cruz Mountains, passing tiny towns, towering redwood forests and fog-kissed vineyards. Many wineries are only open for 'Passport Days' on the third Saturday of January, April, July and November. The **Santa Cruz Mountains Winegrowers Association** (www.scmwa.com) publishes a free winery map, available at tasting rooms, including those that have opened more convenient tasting rooms in Santa Cruz, mostly west of downtown off Hwy 1.

Heading north from Santa Cruz, it's 7 miles to Felton, passing **Henry Cowell Redwoods State Park** (info 831-335-4598, reservations 800-444-7275; www.parks.ca.gov; 101 N Big Trees Park Rd, Felton; entry per car $10, campsites $35; sun-rise-sunset;), which has miles of hiking trails through old-growth redwood groves along the San Lorenzo River and camping. In Felton, **Roaring Camp Railroads** (831-335-4484; www.roaringcamp.com; 5401 Graham Hill Rd, Felton; tours adult/child 2-12yr from $26/19, parking $8; call for schedules;)operates narrow-gauge steam trains up into the redwoods and a standard-gauge train down to the Santa Cruz Beach Boardwalk. Seven miles further north on Hwy 9, you'll drive through the rustic town of **Boulder Creek**, a decent place to grab a bite or a pint at **Boulder Creek Brewery & Cafe** (831-338-7882; www.bouldercreekbrew-ery.net; 13040 Hwy 9, Boulder Creek; mains $9-18; 11:30am-10pm Sun-Thu, to 10:30pm Fri & Sat).

Follow Hwy 236 northwest for nine miles to **Big Basin Redwoods State Park** (831-338-8860; www.bigbasin.org; 21600 Big Basin Way, Boulder Creek; entry per car $10, campsites $35; sunrise-sunset), where nature trails loop past giant old-growth redwoods and beside shady campgrounds. A 12.5-mile one-way section of the **Skyline to the Sea Trail** ends at Waddell Beach, almost 20 miles northwest of Santa Cruz on Hwy 1. On weekends between mid-March and mid-December, you can usually ride **Santa Cruz Metro** (831-425-8600; www.scmtd.com) bus 35A up to Big Basin in the morning and get picked up by bus 40 at the beach in the afternoon.

Around Santa Cruz

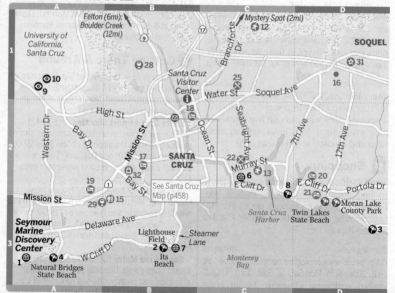

Capitola

Six miles east of Santa Cruz, the diminutive beach town of Capitola nestles quaintly between ocean bluffs. Show up for mid-September's **Capitola Art & Wine Festival**, or the famous **Begonia Festival** (www.begoniafestival.com), held over Labor Day weekend, with a flotilla of floral floats along Soquel Creek.

By the beach, downtown is laid out for strolling, where cutesy shops and touristy restaurants inhabit seaside houses. Drop by family-friendly **Capitola Beach Company** (Map p466; ☑831-462-5222; www.capitolabeach-company.com; 131 Monterey Ave; ⊙10am-6pm; ⚐) or **Capitola Surf & Paddle** (Map p466; ☑831-435-6503; www.capitolasurfandpaddle.com; 208 San Jose Ave; ⊙10am-6pm) to rent water-sports gear or, if you book ahead, take surfing and stand-up paddleboarding lessons.

Catch an organic, fair-trade java buzz at **Mr Toots Coffeehouse** (Map p466; www.tootscoffee.com; 2nd fl, 231 Esplanade; ⊙7am-10pm; ⚐), which has an art gallery, live music and ocean-view deck. Head inland to **Gayle's Bakery & Rosticceria** (Map p466; www.gaylesbakery.com; 504 Bay Ave; dishes $4-10; ⊙6:30am-8:30pm; ⚐), which has a deli for assembling beach picnics. A few miles farther east in Aptos, **Aptos St BBQ** (www.aptosstbbq.com; 8059

Aptos St, Aptos; mains $5-23; ⊙11:30am-9pm) pairs smoked tri-tip beef and pulled pork with California craft beers and live music.

The **Capitola Chamber of Commerce** (☑800-474-6522; www.capitolachamber.com; 716g Capitola Ave; ⊙10am-4pm) offers travel tips. Driving downtown can be a nightmare in summer and on weekends; use the parking lot behind City Hall, off Capitola Ave by Riverview Dr.

Moss Landing & Elkhorn Slough

Hwy 1 swings back toward the coast at Moss Landing, just south of the Santa Cruz County line, almost 20 miles north of Monterey. From the working fishing harbor, **Sanctuary Cruises** (☑831-917-1042; www.sanctuarycruises.com; 7881 Sandholdt Rd; adult/child 12yr & under $50/40; ⚐) ⚐ operates whale-watching and dolphin-spotting cruises year-round aboard biodiesel-fueled boats (reservations essential). Devour dock-fresh seafood at warehouse-sized **Phil's Fish Market** (☑831-633-2152; www.philsfishmarket.com; 7600 Sandholdt Rd; mains $11-21; ⊙10am-8pm Sun-Thu, to 9pm Fri & Sat; ⚐) or, after browsing the antiques shops, lunch at **Haute Enchilada** (☑831-633-5483; www.hauteenchilada.com; 7902 Moss Landing Rd; mains $13-26; ⊙11am-9pm Mon-Thu, from 9am Fri-Sun) ⚐, an inspired Mexican restaurant inside a Frida Kahlo–esque art gallery.

On the east side of Hwy 1, **Elkhorn Slough National Estuarine Research Reserve** (☑831-728-2822; www.elkhornslough.org; 1700 Elkhorn Rd, Watsonville; adult/child 16yr & under $4/free; ⊙9am-5pm Wed-Sun) is popular with bird-watchers and hikers. Docent-led tours typically depart at 10am and 1pm on Saturdays and Sundays, or sign up for an electric-boat cruise with **Whisper Charters** (☑800-979-3370; www.whispercharters.com; 2370 Hwy 1, Moss Landing; 2hr tour adult/child 12yr & under $49/39; ⚐) ⚐. Kayaking is a fantastic way to see the slough, though not on a windy day or when the tides are against you. Reserve ahead for kayak or SUP rentals, guided tours and paddling instruction with **Kayak Connection** (☑831-724-5692; www.kayakconnection.com; 2370 Hwy 1, Moss Landing; kayak rental $35-65, tours adult/child from $45/35; ⊙9am-5pm Mon-Fri, to 6pm Sat & Sun) or **Monterey Bay Kayaks** (☑800-649-5357, 831-373-5357; www.montereybaykayaks.com; 2390 Hwy 1, Moss Landing; kayak rental/tour from $30/55).

CAPITOLA

Soquel Dr

26

Bay Ave

Capitola Chamber of Commerce

30

Capitola Ave

Park Ave

New Brighton State Beach

23

11

5

Capitola Rd

41st Ave

27

24

14

Pleasure Point Beach

E Cliff Dr

Aptos (3mi);
Seacliff State Beach (2mi);
Manresa State Beach (6mi);
Sunset State Beach (11.5mi)

PACIFIC OCEAN

0 ___ 2 km
0 ___ 1 mile

CENTRAL COAST AROUND SANTA CRUZ

Around Santa Cruz

Monterey

Working-class Monterey is all about the sea. What draws many visitors is a world-class aquarium overlooking **Monterey Bay National Marine Sanctuary**, which protects dense kelp forests and a sublime variety of marine life, including seals and sea lions, dolphins and whales. The city itself possesses the best-preserved historical evidence of California's Spanish and Mexican periods, with many restored adobe buildings. An afternoon's wander through downtown's historic quarter promises to be more edifying than time spent in the tourist ghettos of Fisherman's Wharf and Cannery Row.

◎ Sights

★ **Monterey Bay Aquarium**　　AQUARIUM
(☑info 831-648-4800, tickets 866-963-9645; www.montereybayaquarium.org; 886 Cannery Row; adult/child 3-12yr/youth 13-17yr $40/25/30; ⊕9:30am-6pm daily Jun, 9:30am-6pm Mon-Fri, to 8pm Sat & Sun Jul-Aug, 10am-5pm or 6pm daily Sep-May; ⚓) ♪ Monterey's most mesmerizing experience is its enormous aquarium, built on the former site of the city's largest sardine cannery. All kinds of aquatic creatures are featured, from kid-tolerant sea stars and slimy sea slugs to animated sea otters and surprisingly nimble 800lb tuna.

The aquarium is much more than an impressive collection of glass tanks – thoughtful placards underscore the bay's cultural and historical contexts.

Every minute, up to 2000 gallons of seawater is pumped into the three-story **kelp forest**, re-creating as closely as possible the natural conditions you see out the windows to the east. The large fish of prey are at their charismatic best during mealtimes; divers hand-feed at 11:30am and 4pm. More entertaining are the sea otters, which may be seen basking in the **Great Tide Pool** outside the aquarium, where they are readied for reintroduction to the wild.

Even new-agey music and the occasional infinity-mirror illusion don't detract from the astounding beauty of jellyfish in the **Jellies Gallery**. To see marine creatures – including hammerhead sharks, ocean sunfish and green sea turtles – that outweigh kids many times over, ponder the awesome **Open Sea** tank. Upstairs and downstairs you'll find **touch pools**, where you can get close to sea cucumbers, bat rays and tidepool creatures. Younger kids love the interactive **Splash Zone**, with interactive bilingual exhibits and penguin feedings at 10:30am and 3pm.

To avoid long lines in summer and on weekends and holidays, buy tickets in advance. A visit can easily become a full-day affair, so get your hand stamped and break for lunch. Metered on-street parking is limited. Parking lots offering daily rates are plentiful just uphill from Cannery Row.

Cannery Row HISTORIC SITE

(🏛) John Steinbeck's novel *Cannery Row* immortalized the sardine-canning business that was Monterey's lifeblood for the first half of the 20th century. A bronze bust of the Pulitzer Prize–winning writer sits at the bottom of Prescott Ave, just steps from the unabashedly touristy experience that the famous row has devolved into. The historical **Cannery Workers Shacks** at the base of flowery Bruce Ariss Way provide a sobering reminder of the hard lives led by Filipino, Japanese, Spanish and other immigrant laborers.

Back in Steinbeck's day, Cannery Row was a stinky, hardscrabble, working-class melting pot, which the novelist described as 'a poem, a stink, a grating noise, a quality of light, a tone, a habit, a nostalgia, a dream.' Sadly, there's precious little evidence of that era now, as overfishing and climatic changes caused the sardine industry's collapse in the 1950s.

★ Monterey State Historic Park HISTORIC SITE

(🎧 audio tour 831-998-9458, info 831-649-7118; www.parks.ca.gov) 🅿 **FREE** Old Monterey is home to an extraordinary assemblage of 19th-century brick and adobe buildings, administered as Monterey State Historic Park, all found along a 2-mile self-guided walking tour portentously called the 'Path of History.' You can inspect dozens of buildings, many with charming gardens; expect some to be open while others aren't, according to a capricious schedule dictated by unfortunate state-park budget cutbacks.

➡ Pacific House

(📞 831-649-7118; www.parks.ca.gov; 20 Custom House Plaza; admission incl Custom House $3, incl walking tour $5; ⊙ 10am-4pm Fri-Sun) Find out what's currently open at Monterey State Historic Park, grab a free map and buy tickets for guided walking tours inside this 1847 adobe building, which has fascinatingly in-depth exhibits covering the state's early Spanish, Mexican and American eras.

Nearby are some of the state park's historical highlights, including an old whaling station and California's first theater. A 10-minute walk south is the old Monterey jail featured in John Steinbeck's novel *Tortilla Flat*.

➡ Custom House

(Custom House Plaza; admission incl Pacific House Museum $3, incl walking tour $5; ⊙ 10am-4pm Fri-Sun) In 1822, a newly independent Mexico ended the Spanish trade monopoly and stipulated that any traders bringing goods to Alta (Upper) California must first unload their cargoes here for duty to be assessed. In 1846 when the US flag was raised over the Custom House, *voilà!* California was formally annexed from Mexico. Restored to its 1840s appearance, today this adobe building displays an exotic selection of goods that traders once brought to exchange for California cowhides.

➡ Stevenson House

(www.parks.ca.gov; 530 Houston St; ⊙ 1-4pm Sat Apr-early Sep) **FREE** Scottish writer Robert Louis Stevenson came to Monterey in 1879 to court his wife-to-be, Fanny Osbourne. This building, then the French Hotel, was where he stayed while reputedly devising his novel *Treasure Island*. The boarding-house rooms were primitive and Stevenson was still a penniless unknown. Today the house displays a superb collection of the writer's memorabilia.

Cooper-Molera Adobe HISTORIC BUILDING

(📞 tour reservations 831-649-7172; 525 Polk St; ⊙ shop 10am-4pm, gardens from 9am, tours by appointment only) This stately early-19th-century adobe home was built by John Rogers Cooper, a New England sea captain, and three generations of his family resided here. Over time, the original adobe buildings were partitioned and expanded, gardens were added and later everything was willed to the National Trust for Historic Preservation. Worth a browse, the bookshop sells nostalgic toys and household goods.

Museum of Monterey MUSEUM

(📞 831-372-2608; www.museumofmonterey.org; 5 Custom House Plaza; adult/child under 13yr $8/free, free 1st Wed of each month; ⊙ 10am-7pm Tue-Sat & noon-5pm Sun late-May–early Sep, 10am-5pm Wed-Sat & noon-5pm Sun early Sep–late-May; 🏛) Near the waterfront, this voluminous modern exhibition hall illuminates Monterey's salty past, from early Spanish explorers to the roller-coaster-like rise and fall of the local sardine industry that brought Cannery Row to life in the mid-20th century. Highlights include a ship-in-a-bottle collection and the

Monterey

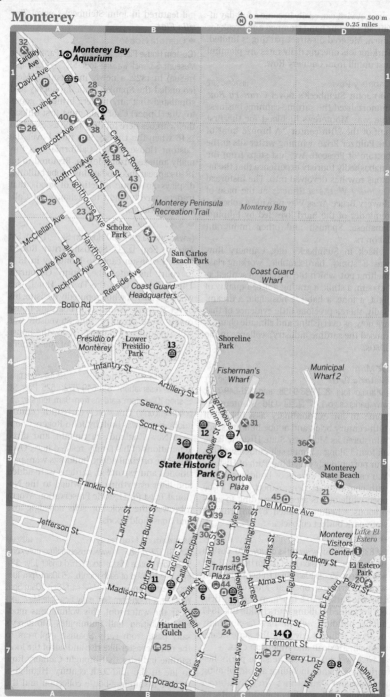

32 Eardley Ave

David Ave

1 ⊙ **Monterey Bay Aquarium**

Irving St

5 🏛

28

37

4 ⊚

26 🏛

40

Prescott Ave

38

Cannery Row

Hoffman Ave

Foam St

Wave St

18

43

42 🔒

Monterey Peninsula Recreation Trail

Monterey Bay

29 🏛

McClellan Ave

Lighthouse Ave

23

Hawthorne St

Drake Ave

Laine St

Dickman Ave

Reeside Ave

Scholze Park

17 ✚

San Carlos Beach Park

Coast Guard Wharf

Bolio Rd

Coast Guard Headquarters

Presidio of Monterey

Lower Presidio Park

13 🏛

Shoreline Park

Infantry St

Artillery St

Fisherman's Wharf

Municipal Wharf 2

Seeno St

Lighthouse Tunnel

22 ●

Scott St

12 🏛

Oliver St

7 🏛

31 ✕

3 🏛

2 ⊙

10

36 ✕

33 ✕

Monterey State Historic Park

16 ✚

Portola Plaza

Monterey State Beach

21 🏛

Franklin St

41 ★

39

45 🔒

Del Monte Ave

Jefferson St

Larkin St

Van Buren St

34 ✕

30

35

Tyler St

Washington St

Adams St

Figueroa St

Monterey Visitors Center

Lake El Estero

Anthony St

i

19

Transit Plaza

Calle Principal

Pacific St

Dutra St

11 🏛

9 🏛

Polk St

6

44

15 🔒

Houston St

Abrego St

Alma St

Camino El Estero

Pearl St

El Estero Park

20 🏛

Madison St

Church St

Hartnell St

Hartnell Gulch

24 🏛

14 🕮

Fremont St

27

Perry Ln

8 🏛

25 🏛

Cass St

Munras Ave

Abrego St

Mesa Rd

Fishnet Rd

El Dorado St

N 0 ——— 500 m
0 ——— 0.25 miles

Monterey

historic Fresnel lens from Point Sur's light-house.

Monterey Museum of Art MUSEUM
(MMA; www.montereyart.org; adult/child 18yr & under \$10/free; ⊙11am-5pm Thu-Mon) Downtown, **MMA Pacific Street** (🗺831-372-5477; 559 Pacific St) is particularly strong in California contemporary art and modern landscape painters and photographers, including Ansel Adams and Edward Weston. Temporary exhibits fill **MMA La Mirada** (🗺831-372-3689; 720 Via Mirada), a silent-film star's villa, whose humble adobe origins are exquisitely concealed. You can visit both locations on the same admission ticket.

Royal Presidio Chapel
& Heritage Center Museum CHURCH
(🗺831-373-2628; www.sancarloscathedral.org; 500 Church St; admission by donation; ⊙10am-noon Wed, to 3pm Fri, to 2pm Sat, 1-3pm Sun, also 10am-12pm 2nd & 4th Mon of each month) Built

of sandstone in 1794, this graceful chapel is California's oldest continuously functioning church and first stone building. The original 1770 mission church stood here before being moved to Carmel. As Monterey expanded under Mexican rule in the 1820s, older buildings were gradually destroyed, leaving behind this National Historic Landmark as the strongest reminder of the defeated Spanish colonial presence.

Presidio of Monterey Museum MUSEUM
(www.monterey.org/museums; Bldg 113, Corporal Ewing Rd; ⊙10am-1pm Mon, to 4pm Thu-Sat, 1-4pm Sun) **FREE** On the grounds of the original Spanish fort, this museum of interest only to history buffs looks at Monterey's history from a military perspective through the Native American, Mexican and American periods.

🏃 Activities

Like its larger namesake in San Francisco, Monterey's **Fisherman's Wharf** is a tacky tourist trap, but also a jumping-off point for deep-sea fishing trips and whale-watching cruises. A short walk east at workaday **Municipal Wharf 2**, fishing boats bob and sway in the bay.

Dennis the Menace Park — PLAYGROUND
(www.monterey.org; 777 Pearl St; ⊙10am-dusk, closed Tue Sep-May; ☻) FREE The brainchild of Hank Ketcham, the creator of the classic *Dennis the Menace* comic strip, this ain't your standard dumbed-down playground suffocated by Big Brother's safety regulations. With lightning-fast slides, a hedge maze, a suspension bridge and towering climbing walls, even some adults can't resist playing here.

Cycling & Mountain Biking
Along an old railway line, the **Monterey Peninsula Recreational Trail** travels for 18 car-free miles along the waterfront, passing Cannery Row en route to Lovers Point in Pacific Grove. Road-cycling enthusiasts can make the round trip to Carmel along the **17-Mile Drive**. Mountain bikers head to **Fort Ord National Monument** to pedal more than 80 miles of single-track and fire roads; the **Sea Otter Classic** (www.seaotterclassic. com) races there in mid-April.

Adventures by the Sea — CYCLING, KAYAKING
(☎831-372-1807; www.adventuresbythesea.com; 299 Cannery Row; rental per day kayak or bicycle $30, SUP set $50, tours from $60; ☻) Beach cruisers, electric bike and water-sports gear rentals and tours available at multiple locations on Cannery Row and **downtown** (☎831-372-1807; www.adventuresbythesea.com; 210 Alvarado St; ☻).

Bay Bikes — CYCLING
(☎831-655-2453; www.baybikes.com; 585 Cannery Row; bicycle rental per hour/day from $8/32) Cruiser, tandem, hybrid and road-bike rentals near the aquarium and also **downtown** (☎831-655-2453; www.baybikes.com; 486 Washington St).

Whale-Watching
You can spot whales off the coast of Monterey Bay year-round. The season for blue and humpback whales runs from April to early December, while gray whales pass by from mid-December through March. Tour boats depart from Fisherman's Wharf and Moss Landing (p467). Reserve trips at least a day in advance; be prepared for a bumpy, cold ride.

Monterey Whale Watching — BOAT TOUR
(☎831-205-2370, 888-223-9153; www.montereywhalewatching.com; 96 Fisherman's Wharf; 2½hr tour adult/child 5-11yr $45/35; ☻) Several daily departures; no children under age five or pregnant women allowed.

Monterey Bay Whale Watch — BOAT TOUR
(☎831-375-4658; www.montereybaywhalewatch.com; 84 Fisherman's Wharf; 3hr tour adult/child 4-12yr from $40/27; ☻) Morning and afternoon departures; young children are welcome on board.

Diving & Snorkeling
Monterey Bay offers world-renowned diving and snorkeling, including off **Lovers Point** in Pacific Grove and at Point Lobos State Natural Reserve (p479) south of Carmel-by-the-Sea. You'll want a wetsuit year-round. In summer upwelling currents carry cold water from the deep canyon below the bay, sending a rich supply of nutrients up toward the surface level to feed the bay's diverse marine life. These frigid currents also account for the bay's chilly water temperatures and the summer fog that blankets the peninsula.

Aquarius Dive Shop — DIVING
(☎831-375-1933; www.aquariusdivers.com; 2040 Del Monte Ave; snorkel/scuba-gear rental $35/65, dive tours from $65) Talk to this five-star PADI operation for gear rentals, classes and guided dives into Monterey Bay.

Monterey Bay Dive Charters — DIVING
(☎831-383-9276; www.mbdcscuba.com; scuba-gear rental $75, shore/boat dive from $65/85) Arrange shore or boat dives and rent a full scuba kit with wetsuit from this well-reviewed outfitter.

Kayaking & Surfing
Monterey Bay Kayaks — KAYAKING
(☎831-373-5357, 800-649-5357; www.montereybaykayaks.com; 693 Del Monte Ave; kayak or SUP set rental per day from $30, tours from $55) Rents kayaks and SUP equipment, offers paddling lessons and leads guided tours of Monterey Bay, including full-moon and sunrise trips.

Sunshine Freestyle Surf & Sport — SURFING
(☎831-375-5015; www.sunshinefreestyle.com; 443 Lighthouse Ave; rental surfboard/wetsuit/boogie board from $20/10/7) Monterey's oldest surf shop rents and sells all the surfing gear you'll need. Staff grudgingly dole out local tips.

★ Festivals & Events
Castroville Artichoke Festival — FOOD
(www.artichoke-festival.org) Head north of Monterey for 3D 'agro art' sculptures, cooking

demos, a farmers market and field tours in May or June.

Blues, Brews & BBQ FOOD, MUSIC
(www.bluesbrewsandbarbecue.com) Rockin' bands, California craft beers and barbecue-pit masters at the county fairgrounds in late July.

Strawberry Festival at Monterey Bay FOOD
(www.mbsf.com) Berry-licious pie-eating contests and live bands in Watsonville, north of Monterey, in early August.

Monterey County Fair CARNIVAL, FOOD
(www.montereycountyfair.com) Old-fashioned fun, carnival rides, horse-riding and livestock competitions, wine tasting and live music in late August and early September.

★**Monterey Jazz Festival** MUSIC
(www.montereyjazzfestival.org) One of the world's longest-running jazz festivals (since 1958) showcases big-name headliners over a long weekend in mid-September.

Monterey Bay Birding Festival OUTDOORS
(www.montereybaybirding.org) Enthusiastic birders and naturalists gather for field trips, workshops and lectures in Monterey and surrounding counties in late September.

🛏 Sleeping

Book ahead for special events, on weekends and in summer. To avoid the tourist congestion and jacked-up prices of Cannery Row, look to Pacific Grove. Cheaper motels line Munras Ave, south of downtown, and N Fremont St, east of Hwy 1.

HI Monterey Hostel HOSTEL $
(☏831-649-0375; www.montereyhostel.org; 778 Hawthorne St; dm with shared bath $26-35; ⊙check-in 4-10pm; @🛜) Four blocks from Cannery Row and the aquarium, this simple, clean hostel houses single-sex and mixed dorms, as well as private rooms (call for rates). Budget backpackers stuff themselves silly with make-your-own pancake breakfasts. Reservations strongly recommended. Take MST bus 1 from downtown's Transit Plaza.

Veterans Memorial Park Campground CAMPGROUND $
(☏831-646-3865; www.monterey.org; tent & RV sites $27) Tucked into the forest, this municipal campground has 40 grassy, nonreservable sites near a nature preserve's hiking trails. Amenities include coin-op hot showers, flush toilets, drinking water and barbecue fire pits. Three-night maximum stay.

Casa Munras BOUTIQUE HOTEL $$
(☏800-222-2446, 831-375-2411; www.hotelcasamunras.com; 700 Munras Ave; r from $120; @🛜🌊🐾) Built around an adobe hacienda once owned by a 19th-century Spanish colonial don, chic modern rooms come with lofty beds and some gas fireplaces, all inside two-story motel-esque buildings. Splash in a heated outdoor pool, unwind at the tapas bar or take a sea-salt scrub in the tiny spa. Pet fee $50.

Hotel Abrego BOUTIQUE HOTEL $$
(☏800-982-1986, 831-372-7551; www.hotelabrego.com; 755 Abrego St; r from $140; 🛜🌊🐾) At this downtown boutique hotel, most of the spacious, clean-lined contemporary rooms have gas fireplaces and chaise longues. Work out in the fitness studio, take a dip in the outdoor pool or warm up in the hot tub. Pet fee $30.

Monterey Hotel HISTORIC HOTEL $$
(☏800-966-6490, 831-375-3184; www.montereyhotel.com; 406 Alvarado St; r $80-220; 🛜) In the heart of downtown and a short walk from Fisherman's Wharf, this 1904 edifice harbors five-dozen small, somewhat noisy, but freshly renovated rooms with Victorian-styled furniture and plantation shutters. No elevator. Parking $17.

Colton Inn MOTEL $$
(☏800-848-7007, 831-649-6500; www.coltoninn.com; 707 Pacific St; r incl breakfast $119-209; 🛜) Downtown, this dated two-story motel prides itself on cleanliness and friendliness. There's no pool and zero view, but staff loan out DVDs, some rooms have real log-burning fireplaces, hot tubs or kitchenettes, and there's even a dry sauna.

★**InterContinental–Clement** HOTEL $$$
(☏866-781-2406, 831-375-4500; www.ictheclementmonterey.com; 750 Cannery Row; r from $200; 🌊@🛜🌊) Like an upscale version of a New England millionaire's seaside mansion, this all-encompassing resort presides over Cannery Row. For the utmost luxury and romance, book an ocean-view suite with a balcony and private fireplace, then breakfast in bayfront C Restaurant downstairs. Parking is $23.

Sanctuary Beach Resort HOTEL $$$
(☏877-944-3863, 831-883-9478; www.thesanctuarybeachresort.com; 3295 Dunes Dr, Marina;

r $179-329; 🌢 @ 🛜 📶 🐾) Be lulled to sleep by the surf at this low-lying retreat hidden in the sand dunes north of Monterey. Reached via golf carts, townhouses harbor petite rooms with gas fireplaces and binoculars for whale-watching. Sunset bonfires bring out s'mores. The beach is an off-limits nature preserve, but there are public beaches and walking trails nearby. Pet fee $40.

Jabberwock B&B $$$
(☎888-428-7253, 831-372-4777; www.jabberwockinn.com; 598 Laine St; r incl breakfast $169-309; @🛜) High atop a hill and barely visible through a shroud of foliage, this 1911 arts-and-crafts house hums a playful *Alice in Wonderland* tune through its seven immaculate rooms, a few with fireplaces and whirlpool tubs. Over afternoon tea and cookies or evening wine and hors d'oeuvres, ask the genial hosts about the house's many salvaged architectural elements.

Eating

Uphill from Cannery Row, Lighthouse Ave is chock-a-block with casual, budget-friendly eateries, from Hawaiian barbecue to Middle Eastern kebabs.

Old Monterey Marketplace MARKET $
(www.oldmonterey.org; Alvarado St, btwn Del Monte Ave & Pearl St; ⊙4-7pm Tue Sep-May, to 8pm Jun-Aug; 🖐) 🍃 Rain or shine, head downtown on Tuesdays for farm-fresh fruit and veggies, artisan cheeses, international food stalls and a scrumptious 'baker's alley.'

Crêpes of Brittany FRENCH $
(www.crepesofbrittany.com; 6 Fisherman's Wharf; crepes $5-10; ⊙8am-3pm Mon-Fri, to 4pm Sat & Sun Sep-May, 8am-6:30pm Mon-Fri, to 8pm Sat & Sun Jun-Aug; 🍴🖐) Authentic savory and sweet crepes are swirled by a French expat – the homemade caramel is a treat. Expect long lines on weekends. Cash only.

First Awakenings AMERICAN $$
(www.firstawakenings.net; American Tin Cannery, 125 Oceanview Blvd; mains $8-12; ⊙7am-2pm Mon-Fri, to 2:30pm Sat & Sun; 🖐) Sweet and savory, all-American breakfasts and lunches and bottomless pitchers of coffee merrily weigh down outdoor tables at this cafe uphill from the aquarium. Try the unusual 'bluegerm' pancakes or a spicy Sonoran frittata.

LouLou's Griddle in the Middle AMERICAN $$
(www.loulousgriddle.com; Municipal Wharf 2; mains $8-16; ⊙usually 7:30am-3pm & 5-8:30pm

Wed-Mon; 🖐🐾) Stroll down the municipal wharf to this zany diner, best for breakfasts of ginormous pancakes and omelets with Mexican pico de gallo salsa or fresh seafood for lunch. Breezy outdoor tables are dog-friendly.

Montrio Bistro CALIFORNIAN $$$
(☎831-648-8880; www.montrio.com; 414 Calle Principal; mains $17-29; ⊙5-10pm Sun-Thu, to 11pm Fri & Sat; 🖐) Inside a 1910 firehouse, Montrio looks dolled up with leather walls and iron trellises, but the tables have butcher paper and crayons for kids. The eclectic seasonal menu mixes local, organic fare with Californian, Asian and European flair, including tapas-style small bites and mini desserts.

Monterey's Fish House SEAFOOD $$$
(☎831-373-4647; 2114 Del Monte Ave; mains $9-28; ⊙11:30am-2:30pm Mon-Fri, 5-9:30pm daily; 🖐) Watched over by photos of Sicilian fishermen, dig into oak-grilled or blackened swordfish, barbecued oysters or, for those stout of heart, the Mexican squid steak. Reservations are essential (it's *so* crowded), but the vibe is island-casual: Hawaiian shirts seem to be de rigueur for men.

Sandbar & Grill SEAFOOD $$$
(☎831-373-2818; www.sandbarandgrillmonterey.com; Municipal Wharf 2; mains $18-30; ⊙11am-9pm; 🖐) Watch otters play outside the bay-view windows at this floating seafood kitchen on the wharf. Stick with the classics such as creamy clam chowder, grilled sand dabs and jumbo crab club sandwiches. Reservations strongly recommended. Ring the bell to let them know you've arrived.

🍸 Drinking & Nightlife

Prowl downtown's Alvarado St, touristy Cannery Row and locals-only Lighthouse Ave for more watering holes.

A Taste of Monterey WINE BAR
(www.atasteofmonterey.com; 700 Cannery Row; tasting fee $10-20; ⊙11am-7pm Sun-Wed, to 8pm Thu-Sat) Sample medal-winning Monterey County wines from as far away as the Santa Lucia Highlands while soaking up dreamy sea views, then peruse thoughtful exhibits on barrel-making and cork production.

East Village Coffee Lounge CAFE, LOUNGE
(www.eastvillagecoffeelounge.com; 498 Washington St; ⊙6am-late Mon-Fri, from 7am Sat & Sun; 🛜) Downtown coffee shop on a busy corner

brews with fair-trade, organic beans. At night, it pulls off a big-city lounge vibe with film, open-mic and live-music nights and an all-important booze license.

Crown & Anchor   PUB
(www.crownandanchor.net; 150 W Franklin St; ⊙11am-1:30am) At this basement British pub, the first thing you'll notice is the red plaid carpeting, then the plentiful draft beers and single-malt scotches, not to mention damn fine fish-and-chips.

Cannery Row Brewing Co   BAR
(www.canneryrowbrewingcompany.com; 95 Prescott Ave; ⊙11am-midnight Sun-Thu, to 2am Fri & Sat) Dozens of craft beers from around the world bring folks into this Cannery Row bar-and-grill, as does an outdoor deck with roaring fire pits.

Sardine Factory Lounge   LOUNGE
(www.sardinefactory.com; 701 Wave St; ⊙5pm-midnight) The legendary restaurant's fireplace lounge pours wines by the glass, delivers filling appetizers to your table and has a live piano player most nights.

☆ Entertainment

For comprehensive entertainment listings, browse the free tabloid *Monterey County Weekly* (www.montereycountyweekly.com).

Sly McFly's Fueling Station   LIVE MUSIC
(☑831-649-8050; www.slymcflys.net; 700 Cannery Row; ⊙11:30am-midnight Sun-Thu, to 2am Fri & Sat) Waterfront dive showcases live local blues, jazz and rock bands nightly after 8:30pm or 9pm. Skip the food, though.

Osio Cinemas   CINEMA
(☑831-644-8171; www.osiocinemas.com; 350 Alvarado St; adult $10, before 6pm $6.50) Downtown cinema screens indie dramas, cutting-edge documentaries and offbeat Hollywood films. Drop by its Cafe Lumiere for locally roasted coffee, loose-leaf tea, decadent cheesecake and wi-fi.

🛍 Shopping

Cannery Row is jammed with claptrap shops, while downtown's side streets hide more one-of-a-kind finds.

Wharf Marketplace   FOOD & DRINK
(www.thewharfmarketplace.com; 290 Figueroa St; ⊙7am-7pm Wed-Mon, to 2pm Tue) 🍴 Inside an old railway station, this gourmet-food emporium carries bountiful farm goodness and artisanal products from Monterey County and beyond.

Monterey Peninsula Art Foundation Gallery   ART
(www.mpaf.org; 425 Cannery Row; ⊙11am-5pm) Taking over a cozy sea-view house, more than 30 local artists sell plein-air paintings and sketches alongside contemporary works in all media.

Cannery Row Antique Mall   ANTIQUES
(www.canneryrowantiquemall.com; 471 Wave St; ⊙10am-5:30pm Mon-Fri, to 6pm Sat, to 5pm Sun) Inside a historic 1920s cannery building, two floors are stacked high with beguiling flotsam and jetsam from decades past.

Old Capitol Books   BOOKS
(559 Tyler St; ⊙10am-6pm Wed-Mon, to 7pm Tue) Tall shelves of new, used and antiquarian books, including rare first editions, California titles and John Steinbeck's works.

ℹ Information

Doctors on Duty (☑831-649-0770; www.doctorsonduty.com; 501 Lighthouse Ave; ⊙8am-8pm Mon-Sat, 8am-6pm Sun) Walk-in, nonemergency medical clinic.

FedEx Office (www.fedex.com; 799 Lighthouse Ave; per min 30-40¢; ⊙7am-10pm Mon-Fri, 8am-9pm Sat, 9am-9pm Sun; 🛜) Pay-as-you-go internet computer workstations.

Monterey Public Library (www.monterey.org; 625 Pacific St; ⊙noon-8pm Mon-Wed, 10am-6pm Thu-Sat, 1-5pm Sun; 🛜) Free wi-fi and public internet terminals.

Monterey Visitors Center (☑877-666-8373, 831-657-6400; www.seemonterey.com; 401 Camino El Estero; ⊙9am-6pm Mon-Sat, to 5pm Sun, closing 1hr earlier Nov-Mar) Free tourist brochures; ask for a *Monterey County Literary & Film Map*.

ℹ Getting There & Around

A few miles east of downtown off Hwy 68, Monterey Peninsula Airport (p761) has flights with United (LA, San Francisco and Denver), American (LA), Alaska (San Diego), Allegiant Air (Las Vegas) and US Airways (Phoenix).

Monterey Airbus (☑831-373-7777; www.montereyairbus.com; 🛜) links Monterey with international airports in San Jose ($40, 1½ hours) and San Francisco ($50, 2½ hours) almost a dozen times daily; book online for discounts.

To get here on public transportation, first take a Greyhound bus or Amtrak train to Salinas, then catch a Thruway bus (for Amtrak train passengers only) or MST bus 20 to Monterey ($3.50, one hour, every 30 to 60 minutes).

Monterey Peninsula

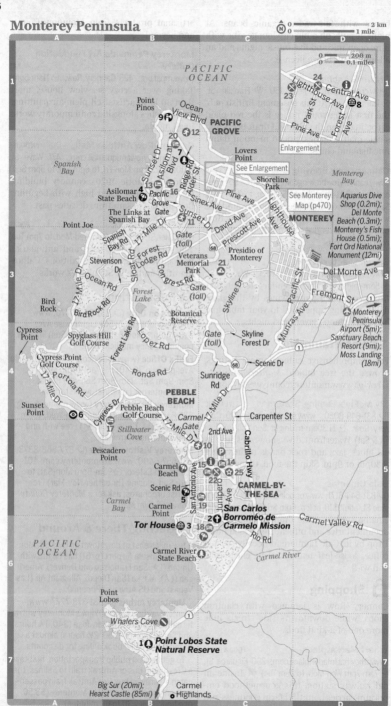

PACIFIC OCEAN

Point Pinos

Ocean View Blvd

PACIFIC GROVE

Spanish Bay

Point Joe

Asilomar State Beach

Pacific Grove

The Links at Spanish Bay

Spanish Bay Rd

Stevenson Dr

Ocean Rd

Bird Rock

Bird Rock Rd

Cypress Point

Spyglass Hill Golf Course

Cypress Point Golf Course

Sunset Point

Pescadero Point

Carmel Bay

PACIFIC OCEAN

Point Lobos

Sunset Dr

Asilomar Blvd

Ridge Rd

Alder St

Sinex Ave

Sunset Dr

David Ave

Pine Ave

Lovers Point

Shoreline Park

See Enlargement

Gate (toll)

Veterans Memorial Park

Forest Lake

Botanical Reserve

Gate (toll)

Skyline Forest Dr

Gate (toll)

Skyline Dr

Ronda Rd

PEBBLE BEACH

Sunridge Rd

Scenic Dr

Carpenter St

Carmel Gate

17-Mile Dr

2nd Ave

Pebble Beach Golf Course

Stillwater Cove

Carmel Beach

Scenic Rd

Carmel Point

Tor House

Carmel River State Beach

Carmel River

Cabrillo Hwy

San Antonio Ave

Juniper Ave

CARMEL-BY-THE-SEA

San Carlos Borroméo de Carmelo Mission

Carmel Valley Rd

Rio Rd

Whalers Cove

Point Lobos State Natural Reserve

Big Sur (20mi); Hearst Castle (85mi);

Carmel Highlands

See Monterey Map (p470)

MONTEREY

Monterey Bay

Aquarius Dive Shop (0.2mi); Del Monte Beach (0.3mi); Monterey's Fish House (0.5mi); Fort Ord National Monument (12mi)

Del Monte Ave

Fremont St

Monterey Peninsula Airport (5mi); Sanctuary Beach Resort (9mi); Moss Landing (18mi)

Presidio of Monterey

Pacific St

Munras Ave

Lighthouse Ave

Prescott Ave

Enlargement

Central Ave

Lighthouse Ave

Park St

Pine Ave

Forest Ave

CENTRAL COAST MONTEREY

Monterey-Salinas Transit (MST; ☎ 888-678-2871; www.mst.org; single-ride $1.50-3.50, day pass $10) operates local and regional buses; routes converge on downtown's **Transit Plaza** (cnr Pearl & Alvarado Sts). From late May until early September, MST's free **trolley** loops around downtown, Fisherman's Wharf and Cannery Row between 10am and 7pm or 8pm daily.

Pacific Grove

Founded as a tranquil Methodist summer retreat in 1875, PG maintained its quaint, holier-than-thou attitude well into the 20th century. The selling of liquor was illegal up until 1969, making it California's last 'dry' town. Today, leafy streets are lined by stately Victorian homes and a charming, compact downtown orbits Lighthouse Ave.

◎ Sights & Activities

Aptly named **Ocean View Blvd** affords views from Lovers Point Park west to Point Pinos, where it becomes **Sunset Dr**, offering tempting turnouts where you can stroll by pounding surf, rocky outcrops and teeming tide pools all the way to **Asilomar State Beach**. This seaside route is great for cycling too – some say it rivals the famous 17-Mile Drive for beauty, and even better, it's free.

Point Pinos Lighthouse   LIGHTHOUSE
(☎ 831-648-3176; www.pointpinos.org; 90 Asilomar Ave; suggested donation adult/child 6-17yr $2/1; ☺ 1-4pm Thu-Mon) The West Coast's oldest continuously operating lighthouse has been warning ships off the hazardous tip of the Monterey Peninsula since 1855. Inside are modest exhibits on the lighthouse's history and alas, its failures – local shipwrecks.

Monarch Grove Sanctuary   PARK
(www.ci.pg.ca.us; off Ridge Rd, btwn Lighthouse Ave & Short St; ☺ dawn-dusk; ⊞) ⊘ FREE Between October and February, more than 25,000 migratory monarch butterflies cluster in this thicket of tall eucalyptus trees, secreted inland. During peak season, volunteer guides answer all of your questions.

Pacific Grove Museum of Natural History   MUSEUM
(☎ 831-648-5716; www.pgmuseum.org; 165 Forest Ave; admission by donation; ☺ 10am-5pm Tue-Sat; ⊞) With a gray-whale sculpture out front, this small kid-oriented museum has old-fashioned exhibits about sea otters, coastal bird life, butterflies, the Big Sur coast and Native Californian tribes.

Pacific Grove Golf Links   GOLF
(☎ 831-648-5775; www.pggolflinks.com; 77 Asilomar Blvd; green fees $25-65) Can't afford to play at famous Pebble Beach? This historic

18-hole municipal course, where deer freely range, has impressive sea views, and it's a lot easier (not to mention cheaper) to book a tee time here.

🛏 Sleeping

Antique-filled B&Bs have taken over many stately Victorian homes around downtown and by the beach. Motels cluster at the peninsula's western end, off Lighthouse and Asilomar Aves.

Asilomar Conference Grounds   LODGE $$
(☏888-635-5310, 831-372-8016; www.visitasilomar.com; 800 Asilomar Ave; r incl breakfast from $145; @ 🛜 🏊) This state-park lodge sprawls by sand dunes in pine forest. Skip ho-hum motel rooms and opt for historic houses designed by early-20th-century architect Julia Morgan (of Hearst Castle fame) – the thin-walled, hardwood-floored rooms may be small, but share a fireplace lounge. Head to the lodge lobby for ping-pong and pool tables and wi-fi. Bike rentals available.

Sunset Inn   MOTEL $$
(☏831-375-3529; www.gosunsetinn.com; 133 Asilomar Blvd; r $90-235; 🛜) At this small motor lodge near the golf course and the beach, attentive staff hand out keys to crisply redesigned rooms that have hardwood floors, king-sized beds with cheery floral-print comforters and sometimes a hot tub and a fireplace.

Deer Haven Inn   MOTEL $$
(☏831-373-7784; www.deerhaveninn.com; 750 Crocker Ave; r incl breakfast $109-209; 🛜) Stylish renovations have brought this two-story motel into the modern age. Every room has a gas fireplace, and it's a quick walk to the beach.

🍴 Eating

Downtown PG teems with European-style bakeries, coffee shops and neighborhood cafes.

Red House Cafe   CAFE $$

(☏831-643-1060; www.redhousecafe.com; 662 Lighthouse Ave; mains breakfast & lunch $8-

---

SCENIC DRIVE: 17-MILE DRIVE

What to See

Pacific Grove and Carmel are linked by the spectacularly scenic, if overhyped, 17-Mile Drive, which meanders through Pebble Beach, a wealthy private resort. It's no chore staying within the 25mph limit – every curve in the road reveals another postcard vista, especially when wildflowers are in bloom. Cycling the drive is enormously popular: try to do it during the week, when traffic isn't as heavy, and ride with the flow of traffic from north to south.

Using the self-guided touring map you'll receive at the toll gate, you can easily pick out landmarks such as **Spanish Bay**, where explorer Gaspar de Portolá dropped anchor in 1769; treacherously rocky **Point Joe**, which was often mistaken for the entrance to Monterey Bay and thus became the site of shipwrecks; and **Bird Rock**, also a haven for harbor seals and sea lions. The ostensible pièce de résistance is the trademarked **Lone Cypress**, which has perched on a seaward rock for possibly more than 250 years.

Besides the coastal scenery, star attractions at Pebble Beach include world-famous **golf courses**, where a celebrity and pro tournament happens every February. The luxurious **Lodge at Pebble Beach** (☏800-654-9300, 831-624-3811; www.pebblebeach.com; 1700 17-Mile Drive; r from $765; ❄@🛜🏊) embraces a spa and designer shops where the most demanding of tastes are catered to. Even if you're not a trust-fund baby, you can still soak up the rich atmosphere in the resort's art-filled public spaces and bay views from the cocktail lounge.

The Route

Operated as a toll road by the Pebble Beach Company, the **17-Mile Drive** (www.pebblebeach.com; per car/bicycle $10/free) is open from sunrise to sunset. The toll can be refunded later as a discount on a $30 minimum food purchase at Pebble Beach restaurants.

Time & Mileage

There are five separate gates for the 17-Mile Drive; how far you drive and how long you take is up to you. To take advantage of the most scenery, enter off Sunset Dr in Pacific Grove and exit onto San Antonio Ave in Carmel-by-the-Sea.

14, dinner $12-23; ⊘8am-2:30pm daily, 5-9pm Tue-Sun;) Crowded with locals, this shingled late-19th-century house dishes up comfort food with haute touches, including cinnamon-brioche French toast, grilled eggplant-fontina sandwiches or spinach-cheese ravioli in lemon beurre blanc sauce. Oatmeal-apricot-pecan cookies are what's for dessert. Reservations helpful.

★**Passionfish** SEAFOOD $$$
(⌨831-655-3311; www.passionfish.net; 701 Lighthouse Ave; mains $16-32; ⊘5-9pm Sun-Thu, to 10pm Fri & Sat) ⬤ Fresh, sustainable seafood is artfully presented in any number of inventive ways, and a seasonally inspired menu also carries slow-cooked meats and vegetarian dishes spotlighting local farms. The earth-tone decor is spare, with tables squeezed conversationally close together. An ambitious world-ranging wine list is priced near retail, and there are twice as many Chinese teas as wines by the glass.

Reservations strongly recommended.

ⓘ Information

Pacific Grove Chamber of Commerce
(⌨800-656-6650, 831-373-3304; www.pacificgrove.org; 584 Central Ave; ⊘9:30am-5pm Mon-Fri, 10am-3pm Sat) Free maps and brochures.

ⓘ Getting There & Around

MST (⌨888-678-2871; www.mst.org) bus 1 connects downtown Monterey and Cannery Row with Pacific Grove, continuing to Asilomar ($2.50, every 30 to 60 minutes).

Carmel-by-the-Sea

With borderline fanatical devotion to its canine citizens, quaint Carmel has the well-manicured feel of a country club. Watch the parade of behatted ladies toting fancy-label shopping bags to lunch and dapper gents driving top-down convertibles along Ocean Ave, the village's slow-mo main drag.

Founded as a seaside resort in the 1880s – fairly odd, given that its beach is often blanketed in fog – Carmel quickly attracted famous artists and writers, such as Sinclair Lewis and Jack London, and their hangers-on. Artistic flavor survives in more than 100 galleries that line downtown's immaculate streets, but sky-high property values have long obliterated any salt-of-the-earth bohemia.

Dating from the 1920s, Comstock cottages, with their characteristic stone chimneys and pitched gable roofs, still dot the town, making it look vaguely reminiscent of the English countryside. Even payphones, garbage cans and newspaper vending boxes are quaintly shingled.

◉ Sights & Activities

Escape downtown's harried shopping streets and stroll tree-lined neighborhoods on the lookout for domiciles charming and peculiar. The Hansel and Gretel houses on Torres St, between 5th and 6th Avenues, are just how you'd imagine them. Another eye-catching house in the shape of a ship, made from local river rocks and salvaged ship parts, is on Guadalupe St near 6th Ave.

★**Point Lobos State Natural Reserve** PARK
(⌨831-624-4909; www.pointlobos.org; Hwy 1; per car $10; ⊘8am-7pm, closing 30min after sunset early Nov–mid-Mar;) They bark, they bathe and they're fun to watch – sea lions are the stars here at Punta de los Lobos Marinos (Point of the Sea Wolves), almost 4 miles south of Carmel, where a dramatically rocky coastline offers excellent tide-pooling. The full perimeter hike is 6 miles, but shorter walks take in wild scenery too, including Bird Island, shady cypress groves, the historical Whaler's Cabin and Devil's Cauldron, a whirlpool that gets splashy at high tide.

The kelp forest at **Whalers Cove** is popular with snorkelers and scuba divers; without donning a wetsuit, you can still get an idea of the underwater terrain with a 3D model located by the parking lot. Reserve snorkeling, scuba-diving, kayaking and SUP permits (per person $5 to $10) up to 60 days in advance online.

Arrive early on weekends; parking is limited. Don't skip paying the entry fee by parking outside the park gates on the highway shoulder – California's state parks are chronically underfunded and need your help.

★**San Carlos Borroméo de Carmelo Mission** CHURCH
(www.carmelmission.org; 3080 Rio Rd; adult/child 7-17yr $6.50/2; ⊘9:30am-7pm) Monterey's original mission was established by Franciscan friar Junípero Serra in 1770, but poor soil and the corrupting influence of Spanish soldiers forced the move to Carmel two years later. Today this is one of California's most strikingly beautiful missions, an oasis of solemnity bathed in flowering gardens. The

WORTH A TRIP

CARMEL VALLEY

Where sun-kissed vineyards rustle beside farm fields, Carmel Valley is a peaceful side trip, just a 20-minute drive east of Hwy 1 along eastbound Carmel Valley Rd. At organic **Earthbound Farm Stand** (☑ 805-625-6219; www.ebfarm.com; 7250 Carmel Valley Rd; ⊙ 8am-6:30pm Mon-Sat, 9am-6pm Sun; ⚑) ⚐, sample homemade soups and salads or harvest your own herbs from the garden. Several wineries further east offer tastings – don't miss the Pinot Noir bottled by **Boekenoogen** (www.boekenoogenwines.com; 24 W Carmel Valley Rd; tasting fee $8-10; ⊙ 11am-5pm). Afterwards, stretch your legs in the village of Carmel Valley, chock-a-block with genteel shops and bistros.

mission's adobe chapel was later replaced with an arched basilica made of stone quarried in the Santa Lucia Mountains. Museum exhibits are scattered throughout the meditative complex.

The spartan cell attributed to Serra looks like something out of *The Good, the Bad and the Ugly,* while a separate chapel houses his memorial tomb. Don't overlook the gravestone of 'Old Gabriel,' a Native American convert whom Serra baptized, and whose dates put him at 151 years old when he died. People say he smoked like a chimney and outlived seven wives. There's a lesson in there somewhere.

★ **Tor House**   HISTORIC BUILDING
(☑ 831-624-1813; www.torhouse.org; 26304 Ocean View Ave; adult/child 12-17yr $10/5; ⊙ tours hourly 10am-3pm Fri & Sat) Even if you've never heard of 20th-century poet Robinson Jeffers, a pilgrimage to this house built with his own hands offers fascinating insights into both the man and the bohemian ethos of Old Carmel. A porthole in the Celtic-inspired **Hawk Tower** reputedly came from the wrecked ship that carried Napoleon from Elba. The only way to visit the property is to reserve a tour (children under 12 years old not allowed), although the tower can be glimpsed from the street.

Carmel Beach City Park   BEACH
(off Scenic Rd; ⚑) **FREE** Not always sunny, Carmel Beach is a gorgeous blanket of white sand, where pampered pups excitedly run off-leash. South of 10th Ave, bonfires crackle after sunset.

⚑ Festivals & Events

Carmel Art Festival   CULTURE
(www.carmelartfestival.org) Meet plein-air painters and sculptors in Devendorf Park over a long weekend in mid-May.

Carmel Bach Festival   MUSIC
(www.bachfestival.org) Classical and chamber-music performances are staged around town in July.

Pebble Beach Concours d'Elegance PARADE
(www.pebblebeachconcours.net) Rare vintage and classic cars roll onto the fairways at Pebble Beach in mid-August.

Carmel Art & Film Festival   CULTURE, FILM
(www.carmelartandfilm.com) Contemporary fine art, live music and more than 100 independent film screenings in mid-October.

🛏 Sleeping

Shockingly overpriced boutique hotels, inns and B&Bs fill up quickly, especially in summer. Ask the chamber of commerce about last-minute deals. For better-value lodgings, head north to Monterey.

Carmel Village Inn   MOTEL $$
(☑ 800-346-3864, 831-624-3864; www.carmel-villageinn.com; cnr Ocean & Junípero Aves; d incl breakfast buffet from $129; ☎) With cheerful flowers decorating its exterior, this well-located motel across from Devendorf Park has cheapish rooms, some with gas fireplaces, and nightly quiet hours.

Cypress Inn   BOUTIQUE HOTEL $$$
(☑ 831-624-3871, 800-443-7443; www.cypress-inn.com; Lincoln St, at 7th Ave; r incl breakfast from $245; ☎🐾) Done up in Spanish Colonial style, this 1929 inn is co-owned by movie star Doris Day. Airy terra-cotta hallways with colorful tiles give it a Mediterranean feel, while sunny rooms face the courtyard. Pet fee $30.

Sea View Inn   B&B $$$
(☑ 831-624-8778; www.seaviewinncarmel.com; El Camino Real, btwn 11th & 12th Aves; r incl breakfast $145-295; ☎) Retreat from downtown's hustle to fireside nooks tailor-made for reading. The cheapest rooms with slanted ceilings are short on cat-swinging space. Rates in-

clude afternoon wine and noshes on the front porch.

Mission Ranch
INN $$$

(☑800-538-8221, 831-624-6436; www.mission-ranchcarmel.com; 26270 Dolores St; r incl breakfast $135-300; 🖥) If woolly sheep grazing on green fields by the beach doesn't convince you to stay here, maybe knowing Hollywood icon Clint Eastwood restored this historic ranch will. Accommodations are shabby-chic, even a tad rustic.

✖ Eating

Carmel's staid dining scene is more about old-world atmosphere than value.

Bruno's Market & Deli
DELI, MARKET $

(www.brunosmarket.com; cnr 6th & Junípero Aves; sandwiches $6-9; ⊙7am-8pm) Small supermarket deli counter makes a saucy sandwich of oakwood-grilled tri-tip beef and stocks all the accoutrements for a beach picnic, including Sparkys root beer from Pacific Grove.

Mundaka
SPANISH, TAPAS $$

(☑831-624-7400; www.mundakacarmel.com; San Carlos St, btwn Ocean & 7th Aves; small plates $6-25; ⊙5:30-10pm Sun-Wed, to 11pm Thu-Sat) This stone courtyard hideaway is a svelte escape from Carmel's stuffy 'newly wed and nearly dead' crowd. Taste Spanish tapas and house-made sangria while world beats spin.

Katy's Place
BREAKFAST $$

(www.katysplacecarmel.com; Mission St, btwn 5th & 6th Aves; mains $8-16; ⊙7am-2pm) It's pricey, but what isn't in Carmel? Start your day with an apple-cinnamon Belgian waffle, Swedish pancakes or one of 16 Californicized variations on eggs benedict.

♤ Drinking & Entertainment

Scheid Vineyards
WINE BAR

(www.scheidvineyards.com; San Carlos St, at 7th Ave; tasting fee $10-20; ⊙noon-6pm Sun-Thu, to 7pm Fri & Sat) Wine-tasting rooms abound downtown. Pop into Scheid Vineyards to sip a prodigious variety of grape varietals, all grown in Monterey County.

Forest Theater
THEATER

(☑831-626-1681; www.foresttheatercarmel.org; cnr Mountain View Ave & Santa Rita St) At this 1910 venue, community-theater musicals, dramas and comedies and film screenings take place under the stars by flickering fire pits.

ⓘ Information

Downtown buildings have no street numbers, so addresses specify the street and nearest intersection only.

Carmel Chamber of Commerce (☑800-550-4333, 831-624-2522; www.carmelcalifornia. org; San Carlos St, btwn 5th & 6th Aves; ⊙10am-5pm) Free maps and brochures, including local art gallery guides.

Carmel Pine Cone (www.pineconearchive.com) Free weekly newspaper packed with local personality and color – the police log is a comedy of manners.

ⓘ Getting There & Around

Carmel is about 5 miles south of Monterey via Hwy 1. There's free parking (no time limit) in a **municipal lot** (cnr 3rd & Junípero Aves) behind the Vista Lobos building.

MST (☑888-678-2871; www.mst.org) 'Grapevine Express' bus 24 ($2.50, hourly) connects Monterey's Transit Plaza with downtown Carmel, the mission and Carmel Valley. Bus 22 ($3.50) stops in downtown Carmel and at the mission en route to/from Point Lobos and Big Sur three times daily between late May and early September, and twice daily on Saturday and Sunday only the rest of the year.

Big Sur

Big Sur is more a state of mind than a place you can pinpoint on a map. There are no traffic lights, banks or strip malls, and when the sun goes down, the moon and the stars are the only streetlights – if summer's dense fog hasn't extinguished them, that is. Much ink has been spilled extolling the raw beauty and energy of this precious piece of land shoehorned between the Santa Lucia Range and the Pacific Ocean, but nothing quite prepares you for your first glimpse of the craggy, unspoiled coastline.

In the 1950s and '60s, Big Sur – so named by Spanish settlers living on the Monterey Peninsula, who referred to the wilderness as *el país grande del sur* ('the big country to the south') – became a retreat for artists and writers, including Henry Miller and Beat Generation visionaries such as Lawrence Ferlinghetti. Today Big Sur attracts self-proclaimed artists, new-age mystics, latter-day hippies and city slickers seeking to unplug and reflect more deeply on this emerald-green edge of the continent.

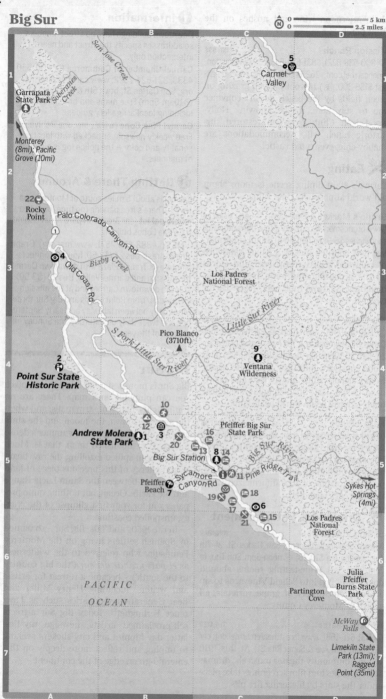

Big Sur

◉ Sights

At Big Sur's state parks, your parking fee ($10) receipt is valid for same-day entry to all except Limekiln. Please don't skip paying the entry fee by parking illegally outside the parks along Hwy 1 – California's state parks have suffered severe budget cutbacks, and every dollar helps.

Garrapata State Park PARK
(☏831-624-4909; www.parks.ca.gov; off Hwy 1; 🅿 FREE) Over 4 miles south of Point Lobos on Hwy 1, pull over to hike coastal headlands, where you might spot whales cruising by offshore during winter, or into canyons of wildflowers and redwood trees. *Garrapata* is Spanish for tick, of which there are many in the canyon and woods, so wearing long sleeves and pants is smart. Leashed dogs are allowed on the beach only.

Bixby Bridge LANDMARK
Less than 15 miles south of Carmel, this landmark spanning Rainbow Canyon is one of the world's highest single-span bridges. Completed in 1932, it was built by prisoners eager to lop time off their sentences. There's a perfect photo-op pull-off on the bridge's north side. Before Bixby Bridge was constructed, travelers had to trek inland on what's now called the **Old Coast Rd**, a rough

dirt route that reconnects after 11 miles with Hwy 1 near Andrew Molera State Park.

When the weather is dry enough, the old road is usually navigable by 4WD or a mountain bike.

★**Point Sur State Historic Park** LIGHTHOUSE
(☏831-625-4419; www.pointsur.org; off Hwy 1; adult/child 6-17yr from $12/5; ⊙tours usually at 1pm Wed, 10am Sat & Sun Nov-Mar, 10am & 2pm Wed & Sat, 10am Sun Apr-Oct, also 10am Thu Jul & Aug) A little more than 6 miles south of Bixby Bridge, Point Sur rises like a velvety green fortress out of the sea. It looks like an island, but is actually connected to land by a sandbar. Atop the volcanic rock sits an 1889 stone lightstation, which was staffed until 1974. During three-hour guided tours, ocean views and tales of the lighthouse keepers' family lives are engrossing. Meet your tour guide at the locked farm gate ¼-mile north of Point Sur Naval Facility.

Special monthly moonlight tours are given between April and October. Call ahead to confirm all tour schedules. Show up early because space is limited (no reservations, some credit cards accepted).

★**Andrew Molera State Park** PARK
(☏831-667-2315; www.parks.ca.gov; Hwy 1; per car $10; ⊙30min before sunrise-30min after

.., ⊕) Named after the farmer who first planted artichokes in California, this oft-overlooked park is a trail-laced pastiche of grassy meadows, ocean bluffs and rugged sandy beaches offering excellent wildlife watching. Look for the entrance just a little more than 8 miles south of Bixby Bridge.

South of the parking lot, you can learn all about endangered California condors inside the **Big Sur Discovery Center** (☑831-624-1202; www.ventanaws.org/discovery_center/; ⊙10am-4pm Sat & Sun late-May–early Sep; ⊕) 🖋 FREE. At the bird-banding lab inside a small shed, naturalists carry out long-term species monitoring programs.

From the main parking lot, a short walk along the beach-bound trail passes through a first-come, first-served campground, from where a gentle spur trail leads to the 1861 redwood **Cooper Cabin**, Big Sur's oldest building. Keep hiking on the main trail out toward a wild beach where the Big Sur River runs into the ocean; condors may be spotted circling overhead and migrating whales sometimes cruise by offshore.

Pfeiffer Big Sur State Park　PARK
(☑831-667-2315; www.parks.ca.gov; 47225 Hwy 1; per car $10; ⊙30min before sunrise-30min after sunset; ⊕) Named after Big Sur's first European settlers who arrived in 1869, this is Big Sur's largest state park, where hiking trails loop through stately redwood groves. The most popular hike – to 60ft-high **Pfeiffer Falls**, a delicate cascade hidden in the forest, which usually runs from December to May – is a 2-mile round-trip. Built in the 1930s by the Civilian Conservation Corps (CCC), rustic Big Sur Lodge stands near the park entrance, about 13 miles south of Bixby Bridge.

Pfeiffer Beach　BEACH
(www.fs.usda.gov/lpnf; end of Sycamore Canyon Rd; per car $10; ⊙9am-8pm; 🐾) This phenomenal, crescent-shaped and dog-friendly beach is known for its huge double rock formation, through which waves crash with life-affirming power. It's often windy, and the surf is too dangerous for swimming. But dig down into the wet sand – it's purple! That's because manganese garnet washes down from the craggy hillsides above. To get here from Hwy 1, make a sharp right onto Sycamore Canyon Rd, marked by a small yellow sign that says 'narrow road' at the top.

From the turnoff, which is a half-mile south of Big Sur Station on the ocean side of Hwy 1, it's two narrow, twisting miles down to the beach (RVs and trailers prohibited).

Henry Miller Memorial Library　ARTS CENTER
(☑831-667-2574; www.henrymiller.org; 48603 Hwy 1; ⊙11am-6pm) 'It was here in Big Sur I first learned to say Amen!' wrote novelist Henry Miller, a Big Sur denizen from 1944 to 1962. More of a beatnik memorial, alt-cultural venue and bookshop, this community gathering spot was never Miller's home. The house belonged to Miller's friend, painter Emil White, until his death and is now run by a nonprofit group. Stop by to browse and hang out on the front deck. It's about 0.4 miles south of Nepenthe restaurant.

Inside are copies of all of Miller's written works, many of his paintings and a collection of Big Sur and Beat Generation material, including copies of the top 100 books Miller said most influenced him. Check the online calendar for upcoming events.

Partington Cove　BEACH
(off Hwy 1) FREE It's a raw, breathtaking spot where crashing surf salts your skin. On the steep, half-mile dirt hike down to the cove, you'll cross a cool bridge and go through an even cooler tunnel. The cove's water is unbelievably aqua and within it grow tangled kelp forests. Look for the unmarked trailhead turnoff inside a hairpin turn on the ocean side of Hwy 1, about 6 miles south of Nepenthe restaurant and 2 miles north of Julia Pfeiffer Burns State Park.

The trail starts just beyond the locked vehicle gate. There's no real beach access and ocean swimming isn't safe, but some people scamper on the rocks and look for tide pools as waves splash ominously. Originally used for loading freight, Partington Cove allegedly became a landing spot for Prohibition-era bootleggers.

★ **Julia Pfeiffer Burns State Park**　PARK
(☑831-667-2315; www.parks.ca.gov; Hwy 1; per car $10; ⊙30min before sunrise-30min after sunset; ⊕) If you're chasing waterfalls, swing into this state park named for a Big Sur pioneer. From the parking lot, the 1.3-mile round-trip Overlook Trail rushes downhill toward the ocean, passing through a tunnel underneath Hwy 1. Everyone comes to photograph 80ft-high **McWay Falls**, which tumbles year-round over granite cliffs and freefalls into the sea – or the beach, depending on the tide. The park entrance is on the east side

of Hwy 1, about 8 miles south of Nepenthe restaurant.

McWay Falls is the classic Big Sur postcard shot, with tree-topped rocks jutting above a golden beach next to swirling blue pools and crashing white surf. From trailside benches, you might spot migrating whales during winter.

Limekiln State Park   PARK
(☑ 831-434-1996; www.parks.ca.gov; 63025 Hwy 1; per car $8; ☺ 8am-sunset) Two miles south of Lucia, this park gets its name from the four remaining wood-fired kilns originally built here in the 1880s to smelt quarried limestone into powder, a key ingredient in cement building construction from Monterey to San Francisco. Tragically, pioneers chopped down most of the steep canyon's old-growth redwoods to fuel the kilns' fires. A one-mile round-trip trail leads through a redwood grove to the historic site, passing a creekside spur trail to a delightful 100ft-high waterfall.

Los Padres National Forest   FOREST
(☑ 831-667-2315; www.fs.usda.gov/lpnf; ☒) The tortuously winding 40-mile stretch of Hwy 1 south of Lucia to Hearst Castle is even more sparsely populated, rugged and remote, mostly running through national forest lands. Around 5 miles south of Kirk Creek Campground and Nacimiento-Fergusson Rd, almost opposite Plaskett Creek Campground, is **Sand Dollar Beach** (http://campone.com; Hwy 1; per car $10, free with paid local USFS campground fee; ☺ 9am-8pm; ☒). From the picnic area, it's a five-minute walk to southern Big Sur's longest sandy beach, a crescent-shaped strip of sand protected from winds by high bluffs.

In 1971, in the waters of nearby **Jade Cove** (http://campone.com; Hwy 1; ☺ sunrise-sunset; ☒) FREE, local divers recovered a 9000lb jade boulder that measured 8ft long and was valued at $180,000. People still comb the beach today. The best time to find jade, which is black or blue-green and looks dull until you dip it in water, is during low tide or after a big storm. Keep an eye out for hang gliders flying in for a movie-worthy landing on the beach. Trails down to the water start from several mostly unmarked roadside pulloffs immediately south of Plaskett Creek Campground.

If you have any sunlight left, keep trucking down the highway to **Salmon Creek Falls** (www.fs.usda.gov/lpnf/; Hwy 1; ☒ ☒) FREE, which usually flows from December through May. Tucked up in a forested canyon, this double-drop waterfall can be glimpsed from the hairpin turn on Hwy 1, about 8 miles south of Gorda. Roadside parking gets very crowded, as everyone takes the 0.3-mile walk up to the falls to splash around in the pools, where kids shriek and dogs happily bark.

Before leaving Lucia, make sure you've got at least enough fuel in the tank to reach the expensive gas stations at Gorda, about 11 miles south of Limekiln State Park, or Ragged Point, another 12 miles further south.

Ragged Point   LANDMARK
(19019 Hwy 1) Your last – or first – taste of Big Sur's rocky grandeur comes at this craggy

CALIFORNIA'S COMEBACK CONDORS

When it comes to endangered species, one of the state's biggest success stories is the California condor. These gigantic, prehistoric birds weigh over 20lb with a wingspan of up to 10ft, letting them fly great distances in search of carrion. They're easily recognized by their naked pink head and large white patches on the underside of each wing.

This big bird became so rare that in 1987 there were only 27 left in the world, and all were removed from the wild to special captive-breeding facilities. Read the whole gripping story in journalist John Moir's book *Return of the Condor: The Race to Save Our Largest Bird from Extinction*.

There are more than 400 California condors alive today, with increasing numbers of captive birds being released back into the wild, where it's hoped they will begin breeding naturally, although it's an uphill battle. Wild condors are still dying of lead poisoning caused by hunter's bullets in the game carcasses that the birds feed on.

The Big Sur coast and Pinnacles National Park (p500) offer excellent opportunities to view this majestic bird. In Big Sur, the **Ventana Wildlife Society** (www.ventanaws.org) occasionally leads two-hour guided condor-watching tours ($50) using radio telemetry to track the birds; for sign-up details, check the website or ask inside the Big Sur Discovery Center.

VENTANA WILDERNESS

The 240,000-acre **Ventana Wilderness** is Big Sur's wild backcountry. It lies within the northern Los Padres National Forest, which straddles the Santa Lucia Range running parallel to the coast. Most of this wilderness is covered with oak and chaparral, though canyons cut by the Big Sur and Little Sur Rivers support virgin stands of coast redwoods and the rare endemic Santa Lucia fir, which grows on steep, rocky slopes too.

Partly reopened after devastating wildfires in 2008, Ventana Wilderness remains popular with adventurous backpackers. A much-trammeled overnight destination is **Sykes Hot Springs**, natural 100°F (35°C) mineral pools framed by redwoods. It's a moderately strenuous 10-mile one-way hike along the **Pine Ridge Trail**, starting from **Big Sur Station** (☑ 831-667-2315; www.parks.ca.gov; Hwy 1; ⊙ 8am-4pm, closed Mon & Tue Nov-Mar), where you can get free campfire permits and pay for overnight trailhead parking ($5). Don't expect solitude on weekends during peak season (April through September) and always follow **Leave No Trace** (www.lnt.org) principles.

cliff outcropping with fabulous views of the coastline in both directions, about 15 miles north of Hearst Castle. Once part of the Hearst empire, it's now taken over by a sprawling, ho-hum lodge with a pricey gas station. Heading south, the land grows increasingly wind-swept as Hwy 1 rolls gently down to the water's edge.

🏃 Activities

Molera Horseback Tours   HORSEBACK RIDING
(☑ 831-625-5486; www.molerahorsebacktours. com; Hwy 1; per person $48-74; 🐎) Across Hwy 1 from Andrew Molera State Park, Molera offers guided trail rides on the beach and through redwood forest. Walk-ins and novices are welcome; children must be at least six years old, with most rides recommended for ages 12 and up.

Esalen Institute   RETREAT CENTER
(☑ 888-837-2536; www.esalen.org; 55000 Hwy 1) Marked only by a lit sign reading 'Esalen Institute – By Reservation Only,' this spot is like a new-age hippie camp for adults. Esoteric workshops treat anything 'relating to our greater human capacity,' from shape-shifting to Thai massage. Esalen's famous **baths** (☑ 831-667-3047; per person $25, credit cards only; ⊙ public entry 1am-3am nightly, reservations accepted 8am-8pm Mon-Thu & Sat, 8am-noon Fri & Sun), fed by a natural hot spring, sit on a ledge above the ocean. The entrance is on the ocean side of Hwy 1, a little more than 11 miles south of Nepenthe restaurant and 10 miles north of Lucia.

Dollars to donuts you'll never take another dip that compares panorama-wise with the one here, especially on stormy winter nights. Only two small outdoor pools perch

directly over the waves, so once you've stripped down (bathing is clothing-optional) and taken a quick shower, head outside immediately to score the best views. Otherwise, you'll be stuck with a tepid, no-view pool or even worse, a rickety bathtub.

Things have sure changed a lot since Hunter S Thompson was the gun-toting caretaker here in the 1960s.

🛏 Sleeping

With few exceptions, Big Sur's lodgings do not have TVs and rarely have telephones. This is where you come to escape the world. There aren't a lot of rooms overall, so demand often exceeds supply and prices can be steep. Bigger price tags don't necessarily buy you more amenities either. In summer and on weekends, reservations are essential everywhere from campgrounds to deluxe resorts.

⭐ **Pfeiffer Big Sur State Park Campground**   CAMPGROUND $
(☑ reservations 800-444-7275; www.reserveamerica.com; 47225 Hwy 1; tent & RV sites $35-50; 🐎) Best for novice campers and families with young kids, here more than 200 campsites nestle in a redwood-shaded valley. Facilities include drinking water, fire pits and coin-op hot showers and laundry.

Andrew Molera State Park Campground   CAMPGROUND $
(www.parks.ca.gov; Hwy 1; tent sites $25) Two-dozen primitive tent sites (no reservations) in a grassy meadow come with fire pits and drinking water, but no ocean views. The campground is a 0.3-mile walk from the parking lot.

Limekiln State Park
Campground
CAMPGROUND **$**

(www.parks.ca.gov; 63025 Hwy 1; tent & RV sites $35; ▣) In southern Big Sur, this quiet state park has two-dozen campsites huddled under a bridge next to the ocean. Drinking water, fire pits and coin-op hot showers are available.

Julia Pfeiffer Burns State
Park Campground
CAMPGROUND **$**

(www.parks.ca.gov; Hwy 1; tent sites $30) Two small walk-in campsites sit up on a semi-shaded ocean bluff, with fire pits and vault toilets but no water. All campers must check in first at Pfeiffer Big Sur State Park, 11 miles north.

USFS Plaskett Creek
Campground
CAMPGROUND **$**

(☑ reservations 877-477-6777; www.recreation.gov; Hwy 1; tent & RV sites $25) Nearly 40 spacious, shady campsites with drinking water and vault toilets circle a forested meadow near Sand Dollar Beach in southern Big Sur.

USFS Kirk Creek Campground
CAMPGROUND **$**

(☑ reservations 877-444-6777; www.recreation.gov; Hwy 1; tent & RV sites $25) More than 30 exposed ocean-view blufftop campsites with drinking water and fire pits cluster close together, nearly 2 miles south of Limekiln State Park.

Big Sur Campground & Cabins
CABIN,
CAMPGROUND **$$**

(☑ 831-667-2322; www.bigsurcamp.com; 47000 Hwy 1; tent/RV sites from $50/60, cabins $120-345; ▣) On the Big Sur River and shaded by redwoods, cozy housekeeping cabins sport full kitchens and fireplaces, while canvas-sided tent cabins are dog-friendly (pet fee $20). The riverside campground, where neighboring sites have little privacy, is popular with RVs. There are hot showers, a coin-op laundry, playground and general store.

Ripplewood Resort
CABIN **$$**

(☑ 831-667-2242; www.ripplewoodresort.com; 47047 Hwy 1; cabins $105-225; ☎) North of Pfeiffer Big Sur State Park, Ripplewood has struck a blow for fiscal equality by charging the same rates year-round. Throwback Americana cabins mostly have kitchens and sometimes even wood-burning fireplaces. Quiet riverside cabins are surrounded by redwoods, but roadside cabins can be noisy. Wi-fi in restaurant only.

Deetjen's Big Sur Inn
LODGE **$$**

(☑ 831-667-2377; www.deetjens.com; 48865 Hwy 1; d $90-260) Nestled among redwoods and wisteria, this creekside conglomeration of rustic, thin-walled rooms and cottages was built by Norwegian immigrant Helmuth Deetjen in the 1930s. Some antiques-furnished rooms are warmed by wood-burning fireplaces, while cheaper ones share bathrooms. This timeless escape isn't for everyone.

Ragged Point Inn
MOTEL **$$**

(☑ 805-927-4502; www.raggedpointinn.net; 19019 Hwy 1; r $169-319; ☎▣) At Big Sur's southern edge, split-level motel rooms are nothing special, except for those with ocean horizon views. Pet fee $50.

★ Post Ranch Inn
RESORT **$$$**

(☑ 831-667-2200; www.postranchinn.com; 47900 Hwy 1; d incl breakfast from $675; ☎▣) The last word in luxurious coastal getaways, the exclusive Post Ranch pampers demanding guests with slate spa tubs, wood-burning fireplaces, private decks and walking sticks for coastal hikes. Ocean-view rooms celebrate the sea, while treehouses lack views and have a bit of sway. Paddle around the clifftop infinity pool after a shamanic-healing session or yoga class in the spa. No children allowed.

Panoramic sea-view Sierra Mar restaurant has mostly disappointing food, except for the gourmet breakfast buffet served to guests only.

Ventana Inn & Spa
RESORT **$$$**

(☑ 800-628-6500, 831-667-2331; www.ventanainn. com; 48123 Hwy 1; d incl breakfast from $510; ☎▣) ✎ Almost at odds with Big Sur's hippie-alternative vibe, Ventana injects a little soul into its deluxe digs. Honeymooning couples and paparazzi-fleeing celebs pad from tai chi class to the Japanese baths and outdoor pools (one is famously clothing-optional), or hole up all day next to the wood-burning fireplace in their own private villa, hot-tub suite or ocean-view cottage.

Treebones Resort
LODGE **$$$**

(☑ 877-424-4787, 805-927-2390; www.treebones-resort.com; 71895 Hwy 1; d with shared bath incl breakfast from $215; ☎▣) Don't let the word 'resort' throw you. Yes, they've got an ocean-view hot tub, heated pool and massage treatments. But a unique woven 'human nest' and canvas-sided yurts with polished pine floors, quilt-covered beds, sink vanities and redwood decks are more like glamping, with little privacy. Communal bathrooms and showers are a short stroll away. Wi-fi in main lodge only.

Children must be at least six years old. Look for the signposted turnoff a mile north of Gorda, at the southern end of Big Sur.

Glen Oaks Motel
MOTEL, CABIN $$$

(☎ 831-667-2105; www.glenoaksbigsur.com; 47080 Hwy 1; d $225-390; ☎) ✈ At this 1950s redwood-and-adobe motor lodge, rustic rooms and cabins seem effortlessly chic. Dramatically transformed by eco-conscious design, snug romantic hideaway rooms all have gas fireplaces. Woodsy cabins in a redwood grove have kitchenettes and share outdoor fire pits, or retreat to the one-bedroom house with a full kitchen.

Big Sur Lodge
LODGE $$$

(☎ 800-424-4787, 831-667-3100; www.bigsurlodge.com; 47225 Hwy 1; d $205-365; ☎) What you're really paying for is a peaceful location, right inside Pfeiffer Big Sur State Park. Fairly rustic duplexes each have a deck or balcony looking out into the redwood forest, while family-sized rooms may have a kitchenette or wood-burning fireplace. The outdoor swimming pool is closed in winter.

Lucia Lodge
MOTEL $$$

(☎ 831-667-2718, 866-424-4787; www.lucialodge.com; 62400 Hwy 1; d $195-275) Vertiginous clifftop views from an ocean-view deck, but tired 1930s cabin rooms.

✗ Eating

Like Big Sur's lodgings, restaurants and cafes alongside Hwy 1 are often overpriced, overcrowded and underwhelming.

Big Sur Deli & General Store
DELI, MARKET $

(www.bigsurdeli.com; 47520 Hwy 1; dishes $2-7; ◷ 7am-8pm) With the most reasonable prices in Big Sur, this family-owned deli slices custom-made deli sandwiches and piles up tortillas with carne asada, pork *carnitas*, veggies or beans and cheese. The small market carries camping food, snacks and beer and wine.

Big Sur Burrito Bar & General Store
DELI, MARKET $

(www.bigsurriverinn.com; 46840 Hwy 1; mains $8-10; ◷ 11am-7pm; ☀) Order a San Francisco-sized burrito or wrap sandwich with a fresh-fruit smoothie from the back of the Big Sur River Inn's well-stocked general store, which carries snacks, drinks and camping supplies.

Big Sur Lodge Restaurant & General Store
CALIFORNIAN $$

(☎ 831-667-3100; www.bigsurlodge.com/dining; 47225 Hwy 1; mains $10-30; ◷ 8am-9:30pm; ☀) Inside Pfeiffer Big Sur State Park, pull up a wooden table in the cabin-esque dining room or on an outdoor riverside deck to fill up on wild salmon, roasted veggie pasta and generous salads, all made with hungry hikers in mind. The lodge's small general store stocks camping groceries, snacks, drinks and ice-cream treats.

★ Restaurant at Ventana
CALIFORNIAN $$$

(☎ 831-667-4242; www.ventanainn.com; Ventana Inn & Spa, 48123 Hwy 1; lunch $16-26, 4-course dinner menu $75; ◷ 7-10:30am, 11:30am-4:30pm & 6-9pm; ☎) The old truism about the better the views, the worse the food just doesn't seem to apply here. The resort's clifftop terrace restaurant and cocktail bar are Big Sur's gathering spot for foodies and bon vivants. Feast on grilled swordfish with lemony couscous, a house-smoked pork sandwich or salads flavored with herbs grown in the garden right outside. Reservations essential.

Nepenthe
CALIFORNIAN $$$

(☎ 831-667-2345; www.nepenthebigsur.com; 48510 Hwy 1; mains $15-42; ◷ 11:30am-4:30pm & 5-10pm) Nepenthe comes from a Greek word meaning 'isle of no sorrow', and indeed, it's hard to feel blue while sitting by the fire pit on this aerial terrace. Just-okay California cuisine (try the renowned Ambrosia burger) takes a backseat to the views and Nepenthe's history – Orson Welles and Rita Hayworth briefly owned a cabin here in the 1940s. Reservations essential.

Downstairs, cheaper but still expensive Café Kevah delivers coffee, baked goods, light brunches and head-spinning ocean views on its outdoor deck (closed during winter and bad weather).

Big Sur Roadhouse
CALIFORNIAN, CAJUN $$$

(☎ 831-667-2370; www.bigsurroadhouse.com; 47080 Hwy 1; breakfast & lunch $6-12, dinner $19-30; ◷ 7:30am-9pm) This Southern-spiced roadhouse glows with color-splashed artwork and an outdoor fire pit. At riverside tables, fork into a New Orleans–born chef's hearty fried chicken, white grits with serrano peppers, po' boy sandwiches and blackened locally caught fish with a dollop of fresh herb aioli. Reservations advised for dinner, or just stop by for drinks and small bites such as buttermilk biscuits.

Big Sur Bakery & Restaurant CALIFORNIAN $$$

(☎831-667-0520; www.bigsurbakery.com; 47540 Hwy 1; bakery items $3-14, mains $14-36; ☺bakery from 8am daily, restaurant 9:30am-3:30pm Mon-Fri, 10:30am-2:30pm Sat & Sun, 5:30pm-close Tue-Sat) Behind the Shell station, this warmly lit, funky house has seasonally changing menus, on which wood-fired pizzas share space with more refined dishes such as butter-braised halibut. Fronted by a pretty patio, the bakery makes addictive fruit-and-ginger scones and super-stuffed sandwiches. Expect long waits and standoffish service. Dinner reservations essential.

Deetjen's Restaurant AMERICAN $$$

(☎831-667-2378; www.deetjens.com; Deetjen's Big Sur Inn, 48865 Hwy 1; mains $26-38; ☺breakfast 8am-noon Mon-Fri, to 12:30pm Sat & Sun, dinner 6-9pm daily) ✐ At a quaint yesteryear lodge, the cozy, candle-lit dining room has a daily changing menu of steaks, cassoulets and other hearty country fare, primarily sourced from organic local produce, hormone-free meat and sustainable seafood. Breakfast is a much better bet than dinner.

Big Sur River Inn AMERICAN $$$

(☎831-667-2700; www.bigsurriverinn.com; 46840 Hwy 1; breakfast & lunch $9-18, dinner $15-32; ☺8-11am, 11:30am-4:30pm & 5-9pm; ☎▣) Woodsy supper club with a deck overlooks a creek teeming with throaty frogs. The wedding-reception-quality food is mostly classic American seafood, grilled meats and pastas, but diner-style breakfasts and lunches – like berry pancakes and BLT sandwiches – satisfy.

🍷 Drinking & Entertainment

Big Sur Taphouse BAR

(www.bigsurtaphouse.com; 47520 Hwy 1; ☺noon-10pm Mon-Thu, to midnight Fri & Sat, 10am-10pm Sun; ☎) Down California craft beers and regional wines on the back deck or by the fireplace inside this high-ceilinged wooden bar with board games, sports TVs and pub grub from the next-door deli.

Maiden Publick House PUB

(☎831-667-2355; Village Center Shops, Hwy 1; ☺noon-2am) Just south of the Big Sur River Inn, this dive has an encyclopedic beer bible and motley local musicians jamming, mostly on weekends.

Rocky Point BAR

(www.rocky-point.com; 36700 Hwy 1; ☺11:30am-8pm) Come for the hillside ocean-view terrace, where cocktails are served all day long. It's about 2.5 miles north of Bixby Bridge.

Henry Miller Memorial Library PERFORMING ARTS

(☎831-667-2574; www.henrymiller.org; 48603 Hwy 1; ☎) Just south of Nepenthe, this nonprofit alternative space hosts a bohemian carnival of live-music concerts, author readings, open-mic nights and indie film screenings outdoors, especially during summer.

ⓘ Information

Visitors often wander into businesses along Hwy 1 and ask, 'How much further to Big Sur?' In fact, there is no town of Big Sur as such, though you may see the name on maps. Commercial activity is concentrated along the stretch north of Pfeiffer Big Sur State Park. Sometimes called 'the Village,' this is where you'll find most of the lodging, restaurants and shops, some of which offer free wi-fi. Cellphone reception is spotty to non-existent.

Big Sur Chamber of Commerce (☎831-667-2100; www.bigsurcalifornia.org; ☺9am-1pm Mon, Wed & Fri) Pick up the free *Big Sur Guide* newspaper at local businesses; it's also available online as a free PDF download.

Big Sur Station (☎831-667-2315; www.fs.usda.gov/lpnf; 47555 Hwy 1; ☺8am-4pm, closed Mon & Tue Nov-Mar) About 1.5 miles south of Pfeiffer Big Sur State Park, this multiagency ranger station has information and maps for state parks, the Los Padres National Forest and Ventana Wilderness.

Henry Miller Memorial Library (www.henrymiller.org; 48603 Hwy 1; ☺11am-6pm; ☎) Free wi-fi and public internet terminals (donation requested).

Post Office (☎800-275-8777; www.usps.com; 47500 Hwy 1; ☺8:30-11am & 1-4pm Mon-Fri) Just north of Big Sur Bakery.

ⓘ DRIVING HWY 1 IN BIG SUR

Driving this narrow two-lane highway through Big Sur and beyond is very slow going. Allow about three hours to cover the distance between the Monterey Peninsula and San Luis Obispo, much more if you want to explore the coast. Traveling after dark can be risky and more to the point, it's futile, because you'll miss out on the seascapes. Watch out for cyclists and make use of signposted roadside pullouts to let faster-moving traffic pass.

ℹ️ Getting There & Around

Big Sur is best explored by car, since you'll be itching to stop frequently and take in the rugged beauty and vistas that reveal themselves after every hairpin turn. Even if your driving skills are up to these narrow switchbacks, others' aren't: expect to average 35mph or less along the route. Parts of Hwy 1 are battle-scarred, evidence of a continual struggle to keep them open after landslides and washouts. Check current highway conditions with **CalTrans** (www.dot.ca.gov) and fill up your gas tank beforehand.

MST (☑ 888-678-2871; www.mst.org) bus 22 ($3.50, 1¼ hours) travels from Monterey via Carmel and Point Lobos as far south as Nepenthe restaurant, stopping en route at Andrew Molera State Park and the Big Sur River Inn. Buses run three times daily between late May and early September, and twice daily on Saturdays and Sundays only the rest of the year.

Point Piedras Blancas

Many lighthouses still stand along California's coast, but few offer such a historically evocative seascape. Federally designated an outstanding natural area, the jutting, wind-blown grounds of this 1875 **light station** (☑ 805-927-7361; www.piedrasblancas.gov; tours adult/child 6-17yr $10/5; ☺ tours usually 9:45am Mon-Sat mid-Jun–Aug, 9:45am Tue, Thu & Sat Sep–mid-Jun) have been laboriously replanted with native flora. Picturesquely, everything looks much the way it did when the first lighthouse keepers helped ships find safe harbor at the whaling station at San Simeon Bay. Guided tours meet at the old Piedras Blancas Motel, 1.5 miles north of the lighthouse gate on Hwy 1. No reservations are taken; call ahead to check tour schedules.

At a signposted vista point, around 4.5 miles north of Hearst Castle, you can observe a colony of northern elephant seals bigger than the one at Año Nuevo State Reserve near Santa Cruz. During peak winter season, about 18,000 seals seek shelter in the coves and beaches along this stretch of coast. On sunny days the seals usually 'lie around like banana slugs,' in the words of one volunteer. Interpretive panels along a beach boardwalk and blue-jacketed **Friends of the Elephant Seal** (www.elephantseal.org) guides demystify the behavior of these giant beasts.

Hearst Castle

The most important thing to know about William Randolph Hearst (1863–1951) is that he did not live like *Citizen Kane*. Not that Hearst wasn't bombastic, conniving and larger than life, but the moody recluse of Orson Welles' movie? Definitely not. Hearst also didn't call his 165-room estate a castle, preferring its official name, *La Cuesta Encantada* ('The Enchanted Hill'), or more often calling it simply 'the ranch.' From the 1920s into the '40s, Hearst and Marion Davies, his longtime mistress (Hearst's wife refused to grant him a divorce), entertained a steady stream of the era's biggest movers and shakers. Invitations were highly coveted, but Hearst had his quirks – he despised drunkenness, and guests were forbidden to speak of death.

Hearst Castle is a wondrous, historic (Winston Churchill penned anti-Nazi essays here in the 1930s), over-the-top homage to material excess, perched high on a hill. California's first licensed woman architect Julia Morgan based the main building, Casa Grande, on the design of a Spanish cathedral, and over the decades she catered to Hearst's every design whim, deftly integrating the spoils of his fabled European shopping sprees including artifacts from antiquity and pieces of medieval monasteries. The estate sprawls across acres of lushly landscaped gardens, accentuated by shimmering pools and fountains, statues from ancient Greece and Moorish Spain and the ruins of what was in Hearst's day the world's largest private zoo (drivers on Hwy 1 can sometimes spot the remnant zebra herd grazing on the hillsides of adjacent Hearst Ranch).

Much like Hearst's construction budget, the castle will devour as much of your time and money as you let it. To see anything of this **state historic monument** (☑ info 805-927-2020, reservations 800-444-4445; www.hearstcastle.org; 750 Hearst Castle Rd, San Simeon; tours adult/child 5-12yr from $25/12; ☺ from 9am daily except Thanksgiving, Christmas & New Year's Day, closing time varies), you must take a tour. In peak summer months, show up early enough and you might be able to get a same-day ticket. For holiday and evening tours, book at least two weeks in advance. Dress in plenty of layers: gloomy fog at the sea-level visitors center can turn into sunny skies at the castle's hilltop location, and vice versa.

Tours usually depart starting at 9am daily, with the last tour leaving the visitor center for the 10-minute ride to the hilltop by 4pm (later in summer). There are four main tours: the guided portion of each lasts about

EYEING ELEPHANT SEALS

The elephant seals that visit coastal California each year follow a precise calendar. In November and December, bulls (adult males) return to their colony's favorite California beaches and start the ritual struggles to assert superiority. Only the largest, strongest and most aggressive 'alpha' males gather a harem of nubile females. In January and February, adult females, already pregnant from last year's beach antics, give birth to pups and soon mate with the dominant males, who promptly depart on their next feeding migration. The bulls' motto is 'love 'em and leave 'em.'

At birth an elephant seal pup weighs about 75lb; while being fed by its mother, it puts on about 10lb a day. Female seals leave the beach in March, abandoning their offspring. For up to two months the young seals, now known as 'weaners,' lounge around in groups, gradually learning to swim, first in tidal pools, then in the ocean. The weaners depart by May, having lost 20% to 30% of their weight during a prolonged fast.

Between June and October, elephant seals of all ages and both sexes return in smaller numbers to the beaches to molt. Always observe elephant seals from a safe distance (minimum 25ft) and do not approach or otherwise harass these unpredictable wild animals, who surprisingly can move faster on the sand than you can!

---

45 minutes, after which you're free to wander the gardens and terraces, photograph the iconic Neptune Pool and soak up views. Best of all are Christmas holiday and springtime evening tours, featuring living-history reenactors who escort you back in time to the castle's 1930s heyday.

At the visitor center, a five-story-high **theater** shows a 40-minute historical film (free admission included with most tour tickets) about the castle and the Hearst family. Other visitor-center facilities are geared for industrial-sized mobs; it's better to grab lunch at Sebastian's General Store (p492) across Hwy 1. Before you leave, take a moment to visit the often-overlooked museum area at the back of the visitor center.

RTA (✆805-541-2228; www.slorta.org) bus 15 makes a few daily round-trips to Hearst Castle via Cambria and Cayucos from Morro Bay ($2, 55 minutes), where you can transfer to bus 12 to San Luis Obispo.

San Simeon

Little San Simeon Bay sprang to life as a whaling station in 1852, by which time California sea otters had been hunted almost to extinction by Russian fur traders. Shoreline whaling was practiced to catch gray whales migrating between Alaskan feeding grounds and birthing waters in Baja California. In 1865 Senator George Hearst purchased 45,000 acres of ranch land and established a small settlement beside the sea. Designed by architect Julia Morgan, the historic 19th-century houses today are rented to employees of the Hearst Corporation's 82,000-acre free-range cattle ranch.

⊙ Sights & Activities

William Randolph Hearst
Memorial State Beach   BEACH
(www.parks.ca.gov; Hwy 1; ⊙dawn-dusk) FREE
Across from Hearst Castle, this bayfront beach is a pleasantly sandy stretch punctuated by rock outcroppings, kelp forests, a wooden pier (fishing permitted) and picnic areas with barbecue grills.

Coastal Discovery Center   MUSEUM
(✆805-927-6575; www.montereybay.noaa.gov; Hwy 1; ⊙11am-5pm Fri-Sun mid-Mar–Oct, 10am-4pm Fri-Sun Nov–mid-Mar; ⊕) FREE Educational displays include a talking artificial tide pool that kids can touch and videos of deep-sea diving and a WWII-era shipwreck just offshore.

Kayak Outfitters   KAYAKING
(✆800-717-5225, 805-927-1787; www.kayakcambria.com; Hwy 1; single/double kayak rentals from $10/20, tours $50-110; ⊙10am-4pm or later mid-Jun–early Sep, call for off-season hours) Right on the beach, you can rent sea kayaks, wetsuits, stand-up paddleboarding (SUP) sets, bodyboards and surfboards, or take a kayak-fishing trip or a guided paddle around San Simeon Cove.

🛏 Sleeping & Eating

A few miles south of Hearst Castle, the modern town of San Simeon is nothing more than a strip of unexciting motels and lackluster restaurants. There are better-value places to stay and eat in Cambria and beach towns further south, such as Cayucos and Morro Bay.

**San Simeon State Park
Campground** CAMPGROUND $
(☑ reservations 800-444-7275; www.reserveamerica.com; Hwy 1; tent & RV sites $20-25) About 5 miles south of Hearst Castle are two state-park campgrounds: **San Simeon Creek**, with coin-op hot showers and flush toilets; and undeveloped **Washburn**, located along a dirt road. Drinking water is available at both.

Morgan MOTEL $$
(☑ 800-451-9900, 805-927-3828; www.hotel-morgan.com; 9135 Hearst Dr; r incl breakfast $139-235; 🛜😺🐾) Although rates are high for these revamped motel-style accommodations, the oceanfront setting makes up for a lot, as do gas fireplaces in deluxe rooms. Complimentary continental breakfast and board games to borrow. Pet fee $25.

Sebastian's General Store DELI, GROCERIES $
(442 SLO-San Simeon Rd; mains $7-12; ⏱ 11am-5pm, kitchen closes at 4pm) Down a side road across Hwy 1 from Hearst Castle, this tiny historic market sells cold drinks, Hearst Ranch beef burgers, giant deli sandwiches and salads for beach picnics at San Simeon Cove. Hearst Ranch Winery tastings are available at the copper-top bar.

Cambria

With a whopping dose of natural beauty, the coastal idyll of Cambria is a lone pearl cast along the coast. Built on lands that once belonged to Mission San Miguel, one of the village's first nicknames was Slabtown, after the rough pieces of wood that pioneer buildings were constructed from. Today, just like at neighboring Hearst Castle, money is no object in this wealthy community, whose motto 'Pines by the Sea' is affixed to the back of BMWs that toodle around town.

❂ Sights & Activities

Although its milky-white moonstones are long gone, **Moonstone Beach** still attracts romantics to its oceanfront boardwalk and truly picturesque rocky shoreline. For more solitude, take the Windsor Blvd exit off Hwy 1 and drive down to where the road dead-ends, then follow a 2-mile round-trip blufftop hiking trail across **East West Ranch**, where **Outback Trail Rides** (☑ 805-286-8772; www.outbacktrailrides.com; tours $65-95; ⏱ Wed-Mon May-Sep, by reservation only) offers horseback rides (reserve in advance).

A 10-minute drive south of Cambria, past the Hwy 46 turnoff to Paso Robles' wine country, tiny **Harmony** is a slice of rural Americana. An 1865 creamery now houses artists' workshops and a charming **cafe** (2177 Old Creamery Rd, Harmony; dishes $3-10; ⏱ usually 10am-4pm) run by an Italian chef, or visit the hillside winery, **Harmony Cellars** (www.harmonycellars.com; 3255 Harmony Valley Rd, Harmony; tasting fee $5; ⏱ 10am-5pm, to 5:30pm Jul & Aug). A few miles further south inside peaceful **Harmony Headlands State Park** (www.parks.ca.gov; Hwy 1; ⏱ 6am-sunset) **FREE**, a 4.5-mile round-trip hiking trail winds out to coastal bluffs with inspiring sea views.

🛏 Sleeping

Cambria's choicest motels and hotels line Moonstone Beach Dr, while quaint B&Bs cluster around the village.

HI Cambria Bridge Street Inn HOSTEL $
(☑ 805-927-7653; www.bridgestreetinncambria.com; 4314 Bridge St; dm from $28, r $49-84, all with shared bath; ⏱ check-in 5-9pm; 🛜) Inside a 19th-century parsonage, this tiny hostel seems more like a grandmotherly B&B. It has floral charm and a communal kitchen, but the shabby-chic rooms are thin-walled. Book ahead.

Bluebird Inn MOTEL $$
(☑ 805-927-5215, 800-552-5434; www.bluebirdmotel.com; 1880 Main St; r $80-180; 🛜) Surrounded by peaceful gardens, this friendly East Village motel offers basic, tidy rooms, some with fireplaces and private creekside patios or balconies. Wi-fi can be erratic.

Cambria Palms Motel MOTEL $$
(☑ 805-927-4485; www.cambriapalmsmotel.com; 2662 Main St; r $109-149; ⏱ check-in 3-9pm; 🛜) A 1950s motor lodge at the east edge of town, here simple wooden-floored rooms are spruced up by colorful wall art and above-average beds. The outdoor fire pit crackles after dark.

Blue Dolphin Inn MOTEL $$$
(☑ 800-222-9157, 805-927-3300; www.cambriainns.com; 6470 Moonstone Beach Dr; r incl breakfast from $199; 🛜😺) This sand-colored two-story, slat-sided building may not look

as upscale as other oceanfront motels, but rooms have romantic fireplaces, pillowtop mattresses and to-go breakfast picnics to take to the beach. If it's full, try its sister property, the Sand Pebbles Inn. Pet fee $25.

Fogcatcher Inn
HOTEL $$$

(☑ 800-425-4121, 805-927-1400; www.fogcatcher-inn.com; 6400 Moonstone Beach Dr; r incl breakfast from $220; 🛜 ❄ 🐾) Moonstone Beach Dr hotels are nearly identical, but this one stands out with its pool and hot tub. Faux English Tudor–style cottages harboring quietly luxurious modern rooms, some with fireplaces and ocean views. Pet fee $75.

Cambria Shores Inn
MOTEL $$$

(☑ 800-433-9179, 805-927-8644; www.cambri-ashores.com; 6276 Moonstone Beach Dr; r incl breakfast from $219; 🛜🐾) A stone's throw from Moonstone Beach, this ocean-view motel offers pampering amenities for pooches, including a welcome doggie basket. Rates include a breakfast basket delivered to your door. Pet fee $15.

✗ Eating & Drinking

It's a short walk between cutesy cafes in the East Village.

Linn's Easy as Pie Cafe
AMERICAN $

(www.linnsfruitbin.com; 4251 Bridge St; dishes $4-9; ☺ 10am-6pm Oct-Apr, to 7pm May-Sep; 🐾) If you don't have time to visit Linn's original farm stand out on Santa Rosa Creek Rd (a 20-minute drive east via Main St), you can fork into their famous olallieberry pie at this take-out counter that delivers soups, salads, sandwiches and comfort fare such as chicken pot pie to a sunny deck.

Boni's Tacos
MEXICAN $

(www.bonistacos.com; 2253 Main St; dishes $2-9; ☺ 10am-4pm Sat & Sun) Honest Mexican food is slung from this family-owned taco trailer parked in the East Village. Fiery tacos, taquitos, quesadillas and burritos all fly out of the busy window.

★ Indigo Moon
CALIFORNIAN $$$

(☑ 805-927-2911; www.indigomooncafe.com; 1980 Main St; lunch $9-14, dinner $14-33; ☺ 10am-9pm) Inside this artisan cheese-and-wine shop, breezy bistro tables complement superb salads and toasty sandwiches served with sweet-potato fries. Locals gossip over lunch on the back patio, where dinner dates order wild-mushroom risotto or crab-stuffed trout.

Cambria Pub & Steakhouse
AMERICAN $$$

(☑ 805-927-0782; www.thecambriapub.com; 4090 Burton Dr; pub mains $9-12, steakhouse mains $20-35; ☺ 11am-9pm Thu & Sun-Tue, to 10pm Fri & Sat; 🐾) Over in the East Village, pull up a barstool and order a burger while you watch big-screen sports TVs, or reserve a table in the contemporary-casual steakhouse to dig into Angus beef steaks (regrettably not from Hearst Ranch). The outdoor patio is dog-friendly.

ℹ Information

Cambria has three distinct parts. In the tourist-choked East Village, antiques shops, art galleries and cafes hug Main St. The newer West Village, along Main St closer to Hwy 1, is where you'll find the **chamber of commerce** (☑ 805-927-3624; www.cambriachamber.org; 767 Main St; ☺ 9am-5pm Mon-Fri, noon-4pm Sat & Sun). Hotel-lined Moonstone Beach Dr is west of Hwy 1.

ℹ Getting There & Around

From San Luis Obispo, **RTA** (☑ 805-541-2228; www.slorta.org) bus 15 makes a few daily trips from Morro Bay via Cayucos to Cambria ($2, 35 minutes), stopping along Main St and Moonstone Beach Dr. Most buses continue north to Hearst Castle.

Cayucos

With its historic storefronts housing antiques shops and eateries, the main drag of amiable, slow-paced Cayucos recalls an Old West frontier town. Just one block west of Ocean Ave, surf's up by the pier.

◉ Sights & Activities

Fronting a broad white-sand beach, Cayucos' long wooden pier is popular with fishers. It's also a sheltered spot for beginner surfers.

Estero Bluffs State Park
PARK

(www.parks.ca.gov; Hwy 1; ☺ sunrise-sunset) **FREE** Ramble along coastal grasslands and pocket beaches at this small state park, accessed from unmarked roadside pulloffs north of Cayucos. Look among the scenic sea stacks to spot harbor seals hauled out on tide-splashed rocks.

Good Clean Fun
WATER SPORTS

(☑ 805-995-1993; www.goodcleanfuncalifornia. com; 136 Ocean Front Ln; group surfing lesson or kayak tour from $75) By the beach, this friendly surf shop has all kinds of rental gear –

wetsuits, boogie boards, surfboards, SUP sets and kayaks. Book in advance for surfing lessons and kayak (or kayak-fishing) tours.

Cayucos Surf Company SURFING
(☑805-995-1000; www.cayucossurfcompany.com; 95 Cayucos Dr; 1hr private/2hr group lesson $90/100; ☺10am-5pm Sun-Thu, to 6pm Fri & Sat) Near the pier, this landmark local surf shop rents surfboards, boogie boards and wetsuits. Call ahead for learn-to-surf lessons.

🛏 Sleeping

Cayucos doesn't lack for motels or beachfront inns. If there's no vacancy or prices look too high, head 6 miles south to Morro Bay.

Shoreline Inn on the Beach HOTEL $$
(☑800-549-2244, 805-995-3681; www.cayucosshorelineinn.com; 1 N Ocean Ave; r $139-199; 🐾) There are few beachside lodgings on Hwy 1 where you can listen to the surf from your balcony for such a reasonable price tag. Standard-issue rooms are spacious, perked up by sea-foam painted walls, and also dog-friendly (pet fee $35).

Seaside Motel MOTEL $$
(☑800-549-0900, 805-995-3809; www.seasidemotel.com; 42 S Ocean Ave; d $80-160; 🐾) Expect a warm welcome from the hands-on owners of this vintage motel with a pretty garden. Country-kitsch rooms may be on the small side, though some have kitchenettes. Cross your fingers for quiet neighbors.

Cypress Tree Motel MOTEL $$
(☑805-995-3917; www.cypresstreemotel.com; 125 S Ocean Ave; d $80-120; 🐾🐾) Retro motor court has lovingly cared-for, but kinda hokey theme rooms, such as 'Nautical Nellie' with a net of seashells suspended behind the bed, plus a shared barbecue grill on the lawn. Pet fee $10.

Cayucos Beach Inn MOTEL $$
(☑800-482-0555, 805-995-2828; www.cayucosbeachinn.com; 333 S Ocean Ave; d incl breakfast $99-215; 🐾🐾🐾) At this remarkably dog-friendly motel, even the doors have special peepholes for canine companions. Big rooms look bland, but grassy picnic areas and barbecue grills await out front. Rates include continental breakfast. Pet fee $10.

Cass House Inn INN $$$
(☑805-995-3669; www.casshouseinn.com; 222 N Ocean Ave; d incl breakfast $195-365; 🐾) Inside a charmingly renovated 1867 Victorian inn, five boutique rooms beckon, some with ocean views, deep-soaking tubs and antique fireplaces to ward off chilly coastal fog. All rooms have plush beds, flat-screen TVs with DVD players and tasteful, romantic accents, while the beachy cottage comes with a full kitchen. Reservations essential.

🍴 Eating & Drinking

Ruddell's Smokehouse SEAFOOD $
(www.smokerjim.com; 101 D St; dishes $4-13; ☺11am-6pm; 🐾🐾) 'Smoker Jim' transforms fresh-off-the-boat seafood into succulently smoked slabs, sandwiches topped with spicy mustard and fish tacos slathered in a unique apple-celery relish. Squeeze yourself in the door to order. Dogs allowed at sidewalk tables.

Brown Butter Cookie Co BAKERY $
(www.brownbuttercookies.com; 98 N Ocean Ave; snacks from $2; ☺9am-6pm; 🐾) Seriously addictive, dearly priced cookies baked in all sorts of flavors – almond, citrus, cocoa, coconut-lime and original butter. Also in Paso Robles.

★Cass House Restaurant CALIFORNIAN, FRENCH $$$
(☑805-995-3669; www.casshouseinn.com; Cass House Inn, 222 N Ocean Ave; tasting menu without/with wine pairings $85/125; ☺5:30-7:30pm Thu-Mon) 🍴 The inn's chef-driven restaurant defies expectations. Linger over a locally sourced, seasonally inspired menu that ambitiously ranges from stone-fruit salad with whipped homemade ricotta and crispy abalone fritters to milk-and-honey almond cake, all paired with top-notch regional wines. Some diners lament portions are so modestly sized. Reservations essential.

Schooners Wharf BAR
(www.schoonerswharf.com; 171 N Ocean Ave; ☺11am-midnight) Come for drinks on the ocean-view deck, rather than the fried seafood.

ℹ Getting There & Away

RTA (☑805-541-2228; www.slorta.org) bus 15 travels three to five times daily from Morro Bay ($2, 15 minutes) to Cayucos, continuing north to Cambria ($2, 20 minutes) and Hearst Castle ($2, 35 minutes).

Morro Bay

Home to a commercial fishing fleet, Morro Bay's biggest claim to fame is Morro Rock, a volcanic peak jutting dramatically from the ocean floor. It's one of the Nine Sisters, a 21-million-year-old chain of rocks stretching all the way south to San Luis Obispo. The town's less boast-worthy landmark comes courtesy of the power plant, whose three cigarette-shaped smokestacks mar the bay views. Along this humble, working-class stretch of coast you'll find fantastic opportunities for kayaking, hiking and camping.

◉ Sights & Activities

This town harbors natural riches that are easily worth a half day's exploration. The bay itself is a deep inlet separated from the ocean by a 5-mile-long sand spit. South of Morro Rock is the **Embarcadero**, a small waterfront boulevard jam-packed with souvenir shops and eateries.

Morro Rock   LANDMARK
Chumash tribespeople are the only people legally allowed to climb this volcanic rock, now the protected nesting ground of peregrine falcons. You can laze at the small beach on the rock's north side, but you can't drive all the way around it. Instead, rent a kayak to paddle the giant estuary, inhabited by two-dozen threatened and endangered species, including brown pelicans, snowy plovers and sea otters.

Morro Bay State Park   PARK
(☑805-772-2694; www.parks.ca.gov; park entry free, museum admission adult/child under 17yr $3/free; ⊙museum 10am-5pm) This woodsy waterfront park is strewn with hillside hiking trails. A small **natural history museum** has interactive exhibits geared toward kids that demonstrate how the forces of nature affect us all. North of the museum, a eucalyptus grove harbors one of California's last remaining great blue heron rookeries.

Kayak Horizons   WATER SPORTS
(☑805-772-6444; www.kayakhorizons.com; 551 Embarcadero; kayak or SUP rental from $12, 3hr kayak tour $59; ⊙9am-5pm) One of several places on the Embarcadero offering kayak rentals and tours for novices, as well as SUP set and canoes rentals. When paddling out on your own, be aware of the tide schedules: ideally, you'll want to ride the tide out and then back in. Winds are generally calmest in the mornings.

Kayak Shack   WATER SPORTS
(☑805-772-8796; www.morrobaykayakshack.com; 10 State Park Rd; kayak or SUP rental from $12;

⊙usually 9am-4pm late-May–Jun, to 5pm Jul-early Sep, 9am-4pm Fri-Sun early-Sep–late-May) No one gets you out on the water faster than this laid-back kayak, canoe and SUP rental spot by the marina in Morro Bay State Park. A no-frills DIY operation, this is a calmer place to start paddling than the Embarcadero.

Cerro Alto   HIKING
(www.fs.usda.gov/lpnf; Cerro Alto Rd, Atascadero; per car $5; ⊛) A 7-mile drive inland from Morro Bay on Hwy 41, a USFS campground is the start of a challengingly steep 4-mile round-trip trail up Cerro Alto (2624ft). From the summit, 360° views sweep from mountains to the sea. With more gradual switchbacks, an alternative route (5.5 miles round trip) also begins near campsite No 18. Leashed dogs allowed.

Morro Bay Golf Course   GOLF
(☑805-782-8060; www.slocountyparks.com; 201 State Park Rd; green fees $13-49) South of the Embarcadero, adjacent to the state park, this 18-hole golf course boasts tree-lined fairways and ocean views. A driving range and rental clubs and carts are available.

☞ Tours

Sub-Sea Tours   BOAT TOUR
(☑805-772-9463; www.subseatours.com; 699 Embarcadero; 45min tour adult/child 3-12yr $14/7; ⊙hourly departures usually 11am-5pm; ⊛) For pint-sized views of kelp forests and schools of fish, take the kids on a spin around the bay in a yellow semi-submersible with underwater viewing windows.

Virg's Landing   FISHING
(☑800-762-5263, 805-772-1222; www.morrobay-sportfishing.com; 1169 Market Ave; tours from $59) Salty dogs ready for a little sportfishing can book half-day or all-day trips between May and December with this long-running local outfit.

Central Coast Outdoors   GUIDED TOUR
(☑888-873-5610, 805-528-1080; www.central-coastoutdoors.com; tours $65-150) Leads kayaking tours (including sunset and full-moon paddles), guided hikes and cycling trips along the coast and to Paso Robles and Edna Valley vineyards.

✺✦ Festivals & Events

Morro Bay Winter Bird Festival   OUTDOORS
(www.morrobaybirdfestival.org) Every January, bird-watchers flock here for guided hikes, kayaking tours and naturalist-led field trips,

during which more than 200 species can be spotted along the Pacific Flyway.

🛏 Sleeping

Dozens of motels cluster along Hwy 1 and around Harbor and Main Sts, between downtown and the Embarcadero.

California State Park Campgrounds
CAMPGROUND $

(🖊 reservations 800-444-7275; www.reserveamerica.com; tent & RV sites $35-50; 🐾) In **Morro Bay State Park**, more than 240 campsites are fringed by eucalyptus and cypress trees; amenities include coin-op hot showers and an RV dump station. At the north end of town off Hwy 1, **Morro Strand State Beach** has 75 simpler oceanfront campsites.

Pleasant Inn Motel
MOTEL $$

(📞 805-772-8521; www.pleasantinnmotel.com; 235 Harbor St; r $75-209; 🐾🐾) Two blocks uphill from the Embarcadero, this spiffy motel has nautical-esque rooms (some with full kitchens) sporting sailboat photos on the walls, open-beam wooden ceilings and blue-and-white rugs underfoot. Pet fee $20.

Beach Bungalow Inn & Suites
MOTEL $$

(📞 805-772-9700; www.morrobaybeachbungalow.com; 1050 Morro Ave; d $149-250; 🐾🐾) This motor court's chic, contemporary rooms are dressed up with hardwood floors, with rugs, pillowtop mattresses and down comforters for foggy nights. Pet fee $20.

Anderson Inn
INN $$$

(📞 866-950-3434, 805-772-3434; www.andersoninnmorrobay.com; 897 Embarcadero; d $239-299; 🐾) Like a small boutique hotel, this waterfront inn has just a handful of spacious, soothingly earth-toned rooms. If you're lucky, you'll get a gas fireplace, spa tub and harbor views.

Inn at Morro Bay
MOTEL $$$

(📞 800-321-9566, 805-772-5651; www.innatmorrobay.com; 60 State Park Rd; d $119-289; 🐾🐾) Dated two-story waterfront lodge with a kidney-shaped pool has an enviable waterfront setting inside the state park. Bicycle rentals available for guests.

🍴 Eating & Drinking

Predictably touristy seafood shacks line the Embarcadero.

Taco Temple
CALIFORNIAN, SEAFOOD $$

(2680 Main St; mains $8-20; ⏰ 11am-9pm Wed-Mon; 🐾) Overlook the Hwy 1 frontage-road location for huge helpings of Cal-Mex fusion flavor. At the next table, there might be fishers talking about the good ol' days or starving surfers. Try one of the specials – they deserve the name. Cash only.

Giovanni's Fish Market & Galley
SEAFOOD $$

(www.giovannisfishmarket.com; 1001 Front St; mains $6-15; ⏰ 9am-6pm; 🐾) At this family-run joint on the Embarcadero, folks line up for batter-fried fish and chips and killer garlic fries. You'll have to dodge beggar birds on the outdoor deck. Inside there's a market with all the fixin's for a beach campground fish-fry.

Stax Wine Bar
WINE BAR

(www.staxwine.com; 1099 Embarcadero; ⏰ noon-8pm Sun-Thu, to 10pm Fri & Sat) Perch on barstools in front of the harbor-view windows for a hand-selected tasting flight of California wines. Toasted panini, salads and artisan cheese and cured-meat plates keep sippers fueled.

Libertine Pub
PUB

(www.thelibertinepub.com; 801 Embarcadero; ⏰ noon-11pm Mon-Wed, to midnight Thu-Sun) Stroll down to the Embarcadero for barrel-aged house beer and sour cider or to try one of the almost 50 American craft beers on tap.

ℹ Information

Morro Bay Visitor Center (📞 805-225-1633, 800-231-0592; www.morrobay.org; 255 Morro Bay Blvd; ⏰ 9am-5pm) A few blocks uphill from the Embarcadero, in the less touristy downtown area.

ℹ Getting There & Around

From San Luis Obispo, **RTA** (📞 805-541-2228; www.slorta.org) bus 12 travels hourly on weekdays and a few times daily on weekends along Hwy 1 to Morro Bay ($2.50, 25 minutes). Three to five times daily, bus 15 heads north to Cayucos ($2, 15 minutes), Cambria ($2, 35 minutes) and Hearst Castle ($2, 55 minutes).

From late May through early October, a **trolley** (single-ride $1, day pass $3) loops around the waterfront, downtown and north Morro Bay, operating varying hours (no service Tuesday to Thursday).

Montaña de Oro State Park

In spring the hillsides are blanketed by bright California native poppies, wild mustard and other wildflowers, giving this **park** (☎805-772-7434; www.parks.ca.gov; 3550 Pecho Valley Rd, Los Osos; ⏰6am-10pm) **FREE** its Spanish name, meaning 'mountain of gold.' Wind-tossed coastal bluffs with wild, wide-open sea views make it a favorite spot with hikers, mountain bikers and horseback riders. The northern half of the park features sand dunes and an ancient marine terrace visible due to seismic uplifting.

Once used by smugglers, **Spooner's Cove** is now a postcard-perfect sandy beach and picnic area. If you go tidepooling, only touch the marine creatures such as sea stars, limpets and crabs with the back of one hand to avoid disturbing them, and never remove them from their aquatic homes. You can hike along the grassy ocean bluffs, or drive uphill past the **visitor center** inside a historic ranch house to the start of the exhilarating 7-mile loop trail tackling **Valencia Peak** (1346ft) and **Oats Peak** (1347ft).

🛏 Sleeping

Montaña de Oro State Park Campground CAMPGROUND $
(☎reservations 800-444-7275; www.reserveamerica.com; tent & RV sites $20-25) Tucked into a small canyon, this minimally developed campground has pleasantly cool drive-up and environmental walk-in sites. Limited amenities include vault toilets, drinking water and fire pits.

❶ Getting There & Away

From the north, exit Hwy 1 in Morro Bay at South Bay Blvd; after 4 miles, turn right onto Los Osos Valley Rd (which runs into Pecho Valley Rd) for 6 miles. From the south, exit Hwy 101 in San Luis Obispo at Los Osos Valley Rd, then drive northwest around 16 miles.

ALONG HIGHWAY 101

Driving inland along Hwy 101 is a quicker way to travel between the Bay Area and Southern California. Although it lacks the striking scenery of coastal Hwy 1, the historic El Camino Real (King's Highway), established by Spanish conquistadors and missionaries, has a beauty of its own, from the fertile fields of Salinas, immortalized by novelist John Steinbeck, to the oak-dappled golden hills of San Luis Obispo and beaches beyond. Along the way are ghostly missions,

jaw-dropping Pinnacles National Park and wineries worth stopping for.

Gilroy

About 30 miles south of San Jose, the self-proclaimed 'garlic capital of the world' hosts the jam-packed **Gilroy Garlic Festival** (www.gilroygarlicfestival.com) over the last full weekend in July. Show up for the chow – garlicky fries, garlic-flavored ice cream and more – and cooking contests under the blazing-hot sun.

Unusual **Gilroy Gardens** (☎408-840-7100; www.gilroygardens.org; 3050 Hecker Pass Hwy; adult/child 3-10yr $50/40; ⏰11am-5pm Mon-Fri early Jun–mid-Aug, plus 10am-6pm Sat & Sun late Mar-Nov; 🚗) is a nonprofit family-oriented theme park focused on food and plants rather than Disney-esque cartoon characters. You've got to really love flowers, fruit and veggies to get your money's worth, though. Most rides such as the 'Mushroom Swing' are tame. Buy tickets online to save. From Hwy 101, follow Hwy 152 west; parking is $12.

Heading east on Hwy 152 toward I-5, **Casa de Fruta** (☎408-842-7282; www.casadefruta.com; 10021 Pacheco Pass Hwy, Hollister; per ride $2.50-4; ⏰seasonal hours vary; 🚗) **FREE** is a commercialized farm stand with an old-fashioned carousel and choo-choo train rides for youngsters.

San Juan Bautista

In atmospheric old San Juan Bautista, where you can practically hear the whispers of the past, California's 15th mission is fronted by the state's only original Spanish plaza remaining. In 1876 the railroad bypassed the town, which has been a sleepy backwater ever since. Along 3rd St, evocative historic buildings mostly shelter antiques shops and petite garden restaurants. Hark! That cock you hear crowing is one of the town's roosters, which are allowed by tradition to stroll the streets at will.

⊙ Sights

Mission San Juan Bautista CHURCH
(☎831-623-4528; www.oldmissionsjb.org; 406 2nd St; adult/child 5-17yr $4/2; ⏰9:30am-4:30pm) Founded in 1797, this mission claims the largest church among California's original 21 missions. Unknowingly built directly atop the San Andreas Fault, the mission has been rocked by earthquakes. Bells hanging

in the tower today include chimes that were salvaged after the 1906 San Francisco earthquake toppled the original mission. Scenes from Alfred Hitchcock's thriller *Vertigo* were shot here, although the bell tower in the movie's climactic scene was just a special effect.

Below the mission cemetery, you can spy a section of El Camino Real, the Spanish colonial road built to link California's first missions.

San Juan Bautista State Historic Park
PARK

(☎831-623-4881; www.parks.ca.gov; 2nd St, btwn Mariposa & Washington Sts; museum entry adult/child $3/free; ⊙10am-4:30pm Tue-Sun) Buildings around the old Spanish plaza opposite the mission anchor this small historical park. Cavernous **stables** hint at San Juan Bautista in its 1860s heyday as a stagecoach stop. The 1859 **Plaza Hotel**, which started life as a single-story adobe building, now houses a little historical museum. Next door to the hotel, the **Castro-Breen Adobe** once belonged to Mexican general and governor José Castro. In 1848 it was bought by the Breen family, survivors of the Donner Party disaster.

Fremont Peak State Park
PARK

(☎observatory 831-623-2465; www.parks.ca.gov; San Juan Canyon Rd; per car $6; ☻) Equipped with a 30in telescope, Fremont Peak's **astronomical observatory** (www.fpoa.net) is usually open to the public on many Saturday nights between April and October, starting at 8pm or 8:30pm. Afternoon solar viewing happens monthly between March and October. It's about 11 miles south of town.

🛌 Sleeping

Fremont Peak State Park Campground
CAMPGROUND $

(☎reservations 800-444-7275; www.reserveamerica.com; San Juan Canyon Rd; tent & RV sites $25) A pretty, but primitive 25-site campground with vault toilets (no water) is shaded by oak trees on a hilltop with distant views of Monterey Bay.

🍴 Eating

On 3rd St, you'll find a long line-up of Mexican American restaurants; none are especially memorable.

San Juan Bakery
BAKERY $

(319 3rd St; snacks $2-4; ⊙usually 7am-5pm Wed-Mon) Get there early for fresh loaves of cinnamon bread, hot-cross buns and guava or apricot turnovers, as they often sell out.

Vertigo Coffee
CAFE $

(www.vertigocoffee.com; 81 4th St; dishes $3-10; ⊙7am-7pm Tue-Fri, from 8am Sat & Sun) Rich espresso and pour-over brews, wood-fired pizzas and garden salads make this coffee roaster's shop a find.

ℹ️ Getting There & Away

San Juan Bautista is on Hwy 156, a few miles east of Hwy 101, about a 20-minute drive south of Gilroy. Further south, Hwy 101 enters the sun-dappled eucalyptus grove that James Stewart and Kim Novak drove through in *Vertigo*.

Salinas

Best known as the birthplace of John Steinbeck and nicknamed the 'Salad Bowl of the World,' Salinas is a working-class agricultural center with down-and-out streets. It makes a thought-provoking contrast with the affluence of the Monterey Peninsula, a fact of life that helped shape Steinbeck's novel *East of Eden*. Historic downtown stretches along Main St, with the National Steinbeck Center capping off its northern end.

👁 Sights

National Steinbeck Center
MUSEUM

(☎831-775-4721; www.steinbeck.org; 1 Main St; adult/child 6-12yr/youth 13-17yr $15/6/8; ⊙10am-5pm; ☻) This museum will interest almost anyone, even if you don't know a lick about Salinas' Nobel Prize–winning native son, John Steinbeck (1902–68), a Stanford University dropout. Tough, funny and brash, he portrayed the troubled spirit of rural, working-class Americans in novels such as *The Grapes of Wrath*. Interactive, kid-accessible exhibits and short video clips chronicle the writer's life and works in an engaging way. Gems include Rocinante, the camper in which Steinbeck traveled around the USA while researching *Travels with Charley*.

Take a moment and listen to Steinbeck's Nobel acceptance speech – it's grace and power combined. Temporary exhibitions cover anything from agricultural history and political activism to California landscape photography.

Steinbeck House
HISTORIC BUILDING

(☎831-424-2735; www.steinbeckhouse.com; 132 Central Ave; tour $10; ⊙restaurant 11:30am-2pm

Tue-Sat, gift shop 11am-3pm Tue-Sat) Steinbeck was born and spent much of his boyhood in this house, four blocks west of the museum. It's now a twee lunch cafe, which we're not sure he'd approve of. Guided tours are given on select summer Sundays; check online for details.

Garden of Memories Memorial Park
CEMETERY

(850 Abbott St) Steinbeck is buried in the family plot at this cemetery, less than 2 miles southeast of downtown.

☞ Tours

Farm
GUIDED TOUR

(☎831-455-2575; www.thefarm-salinasvalley.com; 7 Foster Rd; call for tour prices; ⊙usually 10am-5pm or 6pm May-Dec, tours by reservation only) This family-owned organic fruit-and-veggie stand offers educational walking tours of its fields. On the drive in, watch for the giant sculptures of farm workers by local artist John Cerney, which also stand along Hwy 101. The farm is off Hwy 68 at Spreckels Blvd, about 3 miles southwest of downtown.

Ag Venture Tours
GUIDED TOUR

(☎831-761-8463; www.agventuretours.com; tours adult/child 5-16yr from $70/60) Take an in-depth look at commercial and organic farm fields around the Salinas Valley.

✦ Festivals & Events

California Rodeo Salinas
RODEO

(www.carodeo.com) Bull riding, calf roping, cowboy poetry and carnival rides in late July.

Steinbeck Festival
CULTURE

(www.steinbeck.org) Three-day festival in early May features films, lectures, live music and guided bus and walking tours.

California International Airshow
OUTDOORS

(www.salinasairshow.com) Professional stunt flying and vintage and military aircraft take wing in late September.

⊨ Sleeping

Salinas has plenty of motels off Hwy 101, including at the Market St exit.

Super 8 Salinas
MOTEL $

(☎800-454-3213,831-758-4693; www.super8.com; 131 Kern St; r incl breakfast from $79; ❈@🛜🏊) Revamped rooms have surprisingly stylish accents, from geometric patterned bed-

spreads to vanity mirrors. Complimentary breakfast buffet.

Laurel Inn
MOTEL $

(☎831-449-2474; www.laurelinnmotel.com; 801 W Laurel Dr; r from $80; ❈🛜🏊) If chain motels don't do it for you, this sprawling, family-owned cheapie has predictably worn rooms that are nevertheless spacious.

✖ Eating & Drinking

Bakery Station
BAKERY, DELI $

(www.thebakerystation.com; 202 Monterey St; dishes $3-9; ⊙6am-4pm Mon-Fri, 7am-2pm Sat; 🖐) Inside a converted gas station one block east of Main St, the breads, pastries and cookies are baked fresh daily. Tasty sandwiches are stuffed full of farm-fresh goodness.

Pica Fresh Mex
MEXICAN $$

(157 Main St; mains $6-12; ⊙11am-9pm Mon-Thu, to 10pm Fri & Sat, 2-9pm Sun; 🛜) Just south of the National Steinbeck Center, this storefront Mexican kitchen gets a stamp of approval for handmade tortillas, smoky chipotle salsa, carne asada tacos, burritos and *brochetas* (meat kebabs).

First Awakenings
AMERICAN $$

(www.firstawakenings.net; 171 Main St; mains $8-12; ⊙7am-2pm; 🖐) Fork into diner-style breakfasts of fruity pancakes, crepes and egg skillets, or turn up later in the day for hand-crafted sandwiches and market-fresh salads.

XL Public House
BAR

(www.facebook.com/XLPublichouse; 127 Main St; tasting fee $5; ⊙noon-10pm) Stumble into this brick-walled bottle shop for craft beers on tap, board games and retro video arcade consoles.

Monterey Coast Brewing Co
BREWERY

(165 Main St; ⊙11am-11pm Tue-Sun, to 4pm Mon) At this lively downtown microbrewery, an eight-beer tasting sampler costs just 10 bucks. The pub grub is bland.

ⓘ Information

Salinas 411 (☎831-435-4636; www.oldtown-salinas.com; 222 Main St; ⊙9am-7pm) Free information, maps and self-guided walking-tour brochures.

ⓘ Getting There & Away

Amtrak (☎800-872-7245; www.amtrak.com; 11 Station Pl) runs daily *Coast Starlight* trains north to Oakland ($16, three hours) and south to Paso

Robles ($19, two hours), San Luis Obispo ($27, 3¼ hours), Santa Barbara ($39, 6¼ hours) and LA ($56, 9¼ hours).

Greyhound (☑ 800-231-2222; www.grey-hound.com; 19 W Gabilan St) has a few daily buses north to Santa Cruz ($15, 65 minutes) and San Francisco ($27, 3½ to five hours) and south to San Luis Obispo ($32, 2½ hours) and Santa Barbara ($53, 4¾ hours). From the nearby **Salinas Transit Center** (110 Salinas St), **MST** (☑ 888-678-2871; www.mst.org) bus 20 goes to Monterey ($3.50, one hour, every 30 to 60 minutes).

Pinnacles National Park

Named for the towering spires that rise abruptly out of the chaparral-covered hills east of Salinas Valley, this off-the-beaten-path **park** (☑ 831-389-4486; www.nps.gov/pinn; per car $5) protects the remains of an ancient volcano. A study in geological drama, its craggy monoliths, sheer-walled canyons and twisting caves are the result of millions of years of erosion.

◉ Sights & Activities

Besides **rock climbing** (for route information, click to www.pinnacles.org), the park's biggest attractions are its two talus caves, formed by piles of boulders. **Balconies Cave** is almost always open for exploration. Scrambling through it is not an exercise recommended for claustrophobes, as it's pitch-black inside, making a flashlight essential. Be prepared to get lost a bit too. The cave is found along a 2.5-mile hiking loop from the west entrance. Nearer the east entrance, **Bear Gulch Cave** is closed seasonally, so as not to disturb a resident colony of Townsend's big-eared bats.

To really appreciate Pinnacles' stark beauty, you need to hike. Moderate loops of varying lengths and difficulty ascend into the **High Peaks** and include thrillingly narrow clifftop sections. In the early morning or late afternoon, you may spot endangered California condors soaring overhead. Get an early start to tackle the 9-mile round-trip trail to the top of **Chalone Peak**, granting panoramic views.

Rangers lead guided full-moon hikes and star-gazing programs on some weekend nights, usually in spring or fall. Reservations are required: call ☑ 831-389-4485 in advance or check for last-minute vacancies at the visitor center.

🛌 Sleeping

Pinnacles National Park Campground   CAMPGROUND $
(☑ 877-444-6777; www.recreation.gov; tent/RV sites $23/36; 🐾🐕) On the park's east side, this popular family-oriented campground has more than 130 sites (some with shade), drinking water, coin-op hot showers, fire pits and an outdoor pool (usually closed from October to March).

ℹ Information

The best time to visit Pinnacles National Park is during spring or fall; summer heat is extreme. Information, maps and books are available on the park's east side from the small **NPS visitor center** (☑ 831-389-4485; ⊙ 9:30am-5pm daily, to 8pm Fri late Mar-early Sep) inside the **campground store** (☑ 831-389-4538; ⊙ 3-4pm Mon-Thu, noon-6pm Fri, 9am-6pm Sat & Sun), which sells bottled water, snacks and sundries.

ℹ Getting There & Away

There is no road connecting the two sides of the park. To reach the less-developed **west entrance** (⊙ 7:30am-8pm), exit Hwy 101 at Soledad and follow Hwy 146 northeast for 14 miles. The **east entrance** (⊙ 24hr), where you'll find the visitor center and campground, is accessed via lonely Hwy 25 in San Benito County, southeast of Hollister and northeast of King City.

Mission San Antonio De Padua

Remote, tranquil and evocative, this historical **mission** (☑ 831-385-4478; www.missionsan-antonio.net; end of Mission Rd, Jolon; adult/child 12yr & under $5/3; ⊙ usually 10am-4pm) sits in the Valley of the Oaks, once part of Hearst Ranch's sprawling land holdings. Today it's inside the boundaries of the US Army's Fort Hunter Liggett.

The mission was founded in 1771 by Franciscan priest Junípero Serra. Built with Native American labor, the church has been restored to its early-19th-century appearance, with a wooden pulpit, canopied altar and decorative flourishes on whitewashed walls. A creaky door leads to a cloistered garden anchored by a fountain. The museum has a small collection of such utilitarian items as an olive press and a weaving loom once used in the mission's workshops. Around the grounds, you can inspect the remains of a mill and irrigation system with aqueducts.

It's seldom crowded here, and you may have the vast site all to yourself, except during **Mission Days** in early April and **La Fiesta** on the second Sunday of June. Pick up a visitor's pass from a military checkpoint on the way in; bring photo ID and proof of your vehicle's registration. From the north, take the Jolon Rd exit off Hwy 101 before King City and follow Jolon Rd (County Rte G14) about 18 miles south to Mission Rd. From the south, take the Jolon Rd (County Rte G18) exit off Hwy 101 and drive 22 miles northwest to Mission Rd.

San Miguel

San Miguel is a small farming town off Hwy 101, where life seems to have remained almost unchanged for decades. Founded in 1797, **Mission San Miguel Arcángel** (805-467-3256; www.missionsanmiguel.org; 775 Mission St; adult/child 5-17yr $3/2; 10am-4:30pm) suffered heart-breaking damage during a 2003 earthquake. Although repairs are still underway, the church, cemetery, museum and gardens are open. An enormous cactus out front was planted during the early days of the mission.

Hungry? Inside a converted retro gas station downtown, **San Miguel Coffee Station** (www.sanmiguelcoffeestation.com; 1199 Mission St; dishes $3-8; 6:30am-5pm Mon-Wed, to 8pm Thu-Sat) vends live-wire cups o' coffee, sweet baked goods, pulled-pork sandwiches and stuffed Cal-Mex burritos.

Paso Robles

In northern San Luis Obispo County, Paso Robles is the heart of a historic agricultural region where grapes are now the biggest money-making crop. Scores of wineries along Hwy 46 produce a brave new world of more-than-respectable bottles. The Mediterranean climate is yielding another bounty too: olive oil. Paso's historic downtown centers on Park and 12th Sts, where boutique shops and wine-tasting rooms await.

Sights & Activities

You could spend days wandering country back roads off Hwy 46, running east and west of Hwy 101. Most wineries have tasting rooms and a few offer vineyard tours. For dozens more wineries and olive-oil farms to visit, browse www.pasowine.com.

Eastside

J Lohr Vineyards & Wines WINERY
(www.jlohr.com; 6169 Airport Rd; tasting fee free-$10; 10am-5pm) A Central Coast wine pioneer, J Lohr owns vineyards in Napa Valley, Monterey's Santa Lucia Highlands and Paso's pastoral countryside. Knowledgeable staff guide you through a far-reaching wine list.

Tobin James Cellars WINERY
(www.tobinjames.com; 8950 Union Rd; 10am-6pm) Anti-serious Old West saloon pours bold reds, including an outlaw 'Ballistic' Zinfandel and 'Liquid Love' dessert wine. No tasting fee.

Eberle Winery WINERY
(www.eberlewinery.com; 3810 E Hwy 46; tasting fee free-$10; 10am-5pm Oct-Mar, 10am-6pm Apr-Sep) Offers lofty vineyard views and hourly tours of its wine caves. Sociable tastings run the gamut of white and red varietals and Rhône blends.

Cass Winery WINERY
(www.casswines.com; 7350 Linne Rd; tasting fee $10; 11am-5pm) All that rich Rhône varietal wine-tasting, from Roussanne to Syrah, going straight to your head? An epicurean market cafe here serves lunch until 5pm daily.

Westside

Tablas Creek Vineyard WINERY
(www.tablascreek.com; 9339 Adelaida Rd; tasting fee from $10; 10am-5pm) Breathe easy at this organic estate vineyard reached via a pretty winding drive up into the hills. Known for Rhône varietals, the signature blends also rate highly. Free tours at 10:30am and 2pm daily (reservations advised).

Castoro Cellars WINERY
(www.castorocellars.com; 1315 N Bethel Rd; tasting fee $5; 10am-5:30pm) Husband-and-wife team produces 'dam fine wine' (the mascot is a beaver, get it?), including from custom-crushed and organic grapes. Outdoor vineyard concerts happen during summer.

Chronic Cellars WINERY
(www.chroniccellars.com; 2020 Nacimiento Lake Dr; tasting fee $10; 11:30am-5:30pm) Everyone's favorite irreverent winery, where Día de Los Muertos designs cover bottles of bold blends. Play billiards in the tasting room or a game of horseshoes outside on the grass.

Re:Find Distillery & Villicana Winery WINERY
(www.villicanawinery.com; 2725 Adelaida Rd; tasting fee $10; 11am-5pm) Paso Robles' first

micro-distillery makes clean-tasting botanical brandy (read: gin), which you can taste along with dry rosé in the adjoining wine-tasting room.

Thacher Winery
WINERY

(www.thacherwinery.com; 8355 Vineyard Rd; tasting fee $10; 11am-5pm Thu-Mon) Breathe deeply as you drive up the dirt road to this historic ranch that makes memorable Rhône blends – 'Controlled Chaos' is a perennial fave.

Festivals & Events

Wine Festival
WINE, FOOD

(www.pasowine.com) Oenophiles come for Paso's premier Wine Festival in mid-May, but the Vintage Paso weekend, focusing on Zinfandel wines, in mid-March and the Harvest Wine Weekend in mid-October are just as fun.

California Mid-State Fair
CARNIVAL, MUSIC

(www.midstatefair.com) In mid-July, 12 days of live rock and country-and-western concerts, farm exhibits, carnival rides and a rodeo draw huge crowds.

Sleeping

Chain motels and hotels line Hwy 101. B&Bs and vacation rentals are scattered among the vineyards outside town.

Melody Ranch Motel
MOTEL $

(800-909-3911, 805-238-3911; 939 Spring St; r $70-100;) At this small, family-owned, 1950s motor court downtown, ultra-basic rooms mean prices that are almost as small as the outdoor pool.

Adelaide Inn
MOTEL $$

(800-549-7276, 805-238-2770; www.adelaideinn.com; 1215 Ysabel Ave; r incl breakfast $115-165;) Fresh-baked cookies, muffins for breakfast, mini golf and a fitness room keep families happy at this motel just off Hwy 101.

Summerwood Inn
B&B $$$

(www.summerwoodwine.com; 2175 Arbor Rd; d incl breakfast from $275) Along Hwy 46 within an easy drive of dozens of wineries, this gorgeously renovated inn mixes vintage and modern elements. Each room has a gas fireplace and balcony overlooking the vineyards. Indulge with the chef's gourmet breakfast, afternoon hors d'oeuvres and evening desserts.

Inn Paradiso
B&B $$$

(805-239-2800; www.innparadiso.com; 975 Mojave Ln; ste incl breakfast $350;) An intimate B&B pulls off no-fuss luxury with three suites decorated with art and antiques, and perhaps a fireplace, a deep soaking tub, a canopy king-sized bed or French balcony doors. Pet fee $50.

Zenaida Cellars
B&B $$$

(866-936-5638; www.zenaidacellars.com; 1550 W Hwy 46; ste $250-375;) Steal yourself away among the pastoral vineyards of Paso Robles' westside. The winemaker's loft above the tasting room sleeps four adults and has a full kitchen.

Eating & Drinking

Restaurants and wine-tasting rooms surround downtown's grassy central square, off Spring St between 11th and 12th Sts.

La Reyna Market
MEXICAN $

(www.lareynamarket.com; 532 24th St; dishes $2-8; 8am-9pm Mon-Thu, to 9:30pm Fri-Sun) Off Hwy 101, this authentic Mexican grocery store and butcher's deli makes savory *tortas* (sandwiches), wet burritos and street-food tacos (the *al pastor* edges out the carne asada) on hot, homemade tortillas.

Artisan
CALIFORNIAN $$$

(805-237-8084; www.artisanpasorobles.com; 843 12th St; shared plates $11-19, mains $30-38; 11:30am-9pm Mon-Thu, to 10pm Fri & Sat, 10am-9pm Sun) Chef Chris Kobayashi often ducks out of the kitchen just to make sure you're loving his impeccable contemporary renditions of modern American cuisine, featuring sustainably farmed meats, wild-caught seafood and artisan California cheeses. Impressive wine, beer and cocktail menus. Reservations essential.

Fish Gaucho
MEXICAN, SEAFOOD $$$

(www.fishgaucho.com; 1244 Spring St; mains $17-26; kitchen 3-9:30pm, from 11:30am Fri-Sun, bar till midnight daily) Hand-made furnishings, antiques and decor imported from Mexico fill this Baja-style seafood joint and tequila bar. Smoky, spicy and fruity cocktails wash down stuffed poblano chiles, braised short-rib tacos and oyster shooters with chorizo and cotija crumbles. Reservations recommended.

Firestone Walker Brewing Company
BREWERY

(805-225-5911; www.firestonebeer.com; 1400 Ramada Dr; noon-7pm) Bring your buddies to the taproom to sample the famous Double Barrel Ale or seasonal Velvet Merlin oatmeal stout, plus barrel-aged vintages and experimental brews. Book ahead for free brewery tours.

BarrelHouse Brewing Co BREWERY
(www.barrelhousebrewing.com; 3055 Limestone Way; ⏰ 2-8pm Wed-Thu, 11am-9pm Fri & Sat, 11am-8pm Sun) Detour south of downtown, where locals chill outside at picnic tables with pints of ales, stout and fruity Belgian-style beers, while live bands frequently play.

🛍 Shopping

Around the downtown square, side streets are full of wine-country boutiques.

Paso Robles General Store FOOD, GIFTS
(www.generalstorepr.com; 841 12th St; ⏰ 10am-7pm) Stock up on picnic provisions including California-made pistachio butter, fresh local baguettes, fruit jams and more, plus home goods such as lavender soap.

We Olive FOOD
(www.weolive.com/paso-robles; 1311 Park St; ⏰ 10am-6pm Mon-Sat, 11am-4pm Sun) Step right up to the tasting bar to sample local growers' olive oils and fruit-infused balsamic vinegars. Also in downtown San Luis Obispo.

ℹ Information

Paso Robles Chamber of Commerce (📞 805-238-0506; www.pasorobleschamber.com; 1225 Park St; ⏰ 8:30am-4:30pm, closed Sun Sep-May) Information and free winery maps.

ℹ Getting There & Away

From an unstaffed **Amtrak** (📞 800-872-7245; www.amtrak.com; 800 Pine St) station, daily *Coast Starlight* trains head north to Salinas ($19, two hours) and Oakland ($30, 4¾ hours) and south to Santa Barbara ($28, 4¼ hours) and LA ($41, 7½ hours). Several daily Thruway buses link to more-frequent regional trains, including the *Pacific Surfliner*.

From the train station, **Greyhound** (📞 800-231-2222; www.greyhound.com; 800 Pine St) runs a few daily buses along Hwy 101 south to Santa Barbara ($57, 2¾ hours) and LA ($81, six hours) and north to San Francisco ($74, six hours) via Santa Cruz ($57, 3¼ hours).

RTA (📞 805-541-2228; www.slorta.org) bus 9 travels between San Luis Obispo and Paso Robles ($2.50, 70 minutes) hourly Monday to Friday, and a few times daily on weekends.

San Luis Obispo

Almost midway between LA and San Francisco, at the junction of Hwys 101 and 1, San Luis Obispo is a popular overnight stop for road trippers. With no must-see attractions, SLO might not seem to warrant much of your time. Even so, this low-key town has an enviably high quality of life – in fact, it has been named America's happiest city. CalPoly university students inject a healthy dose of hubbub into the city's streets, bars and cafes throughout the school year. Nestled at the base of the Santa Lucia foothills, SLO is just a grape's throw from Edna Valley wineries too.

👁 Sights

San Luis Obispo Creek, once used to irrigate mission orchards, flows through downtown. Uphill from Higuera St, **Mission Plaza** is a shady oasis with restored adobe buildings and fountains overlooking the creek. Look for the **Moon Tree**, a coast redwood grown from a seed that journeyed on board Apollo 14's lunar mission.

Mission San Luis Obispo de Tolosa CHURCH
(📞 805-543-6850; www.missionsanluisobispo.org; 751 Palm St; donation $2; ⏰ 9am-5pm late Mar-Oct, to 4pm Nov–mid-Mar) Those satisfyingly reverberatory bells heard around downtown emanate from this active parish dating from 1772. The fifth California mission founded by Junípero Serra, it was named for a 13th-century French saint. The modest church has an unusual L-shape and whitewashed walls decorated with Stations of the Cross. An adjacent building contains an old-fashioned museum about daily life during the Chumash tribal and Spanish colonial periods.

San Luis Obispo Museum of Art MUSEUM
(www.sloma.org; 1010 Broad St; ⏰ 11am-5pm, closed Tue early Sep-early Jul) **FREE** By the creek, this small gallery showcases the work of local painters, sculptors, printmakers and fine-art photographers, as well as traveling California art exhibitions.

Bubblegum Alley STREET
(off 700 block of Higuera St) SLO's weirdest sight is colorfully plastered with thousands of wads of ABC ('already been chewed') gum. Watch where you step!

🏃 Activities

For more hiking with ocean views, head to Montaña de Oro State Park (p497), not far away.

Bishop Peak HIKING
SLO's most popular hike summits Bishop Peak (1546ft), the tallest of the Nine Sisters,

San Luis Obispo

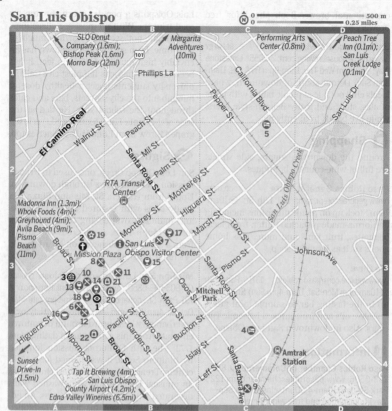

a chain of volcanic peaks that stretches north to Morro Bay. The 2.2-mile one-way trail starts in a grove of live oaks (watch out for poison oak) and heads uphill along rocky, mostly exposed switchbacks. Carefully scramble up boulders at the tippy-top for panoramic views.

To get to the trailhead, drive northwest from downtown on Santa Rosa St (Hwy 1), turn left onto Foothill Dr, then right onto Patricia Dr; after 0.8 miles, look for three black posts and a trailhead sign on your left.

Margarita Adventures ZIP LINING, KAYAKING
(☑ 805-438-3120; www.margarita-adventures.com; 22719 El Camino Real, Santa Margarita; adult/child zip-line tour $99/79, kayak tour $79/59; ⊙ closed Tue & Wed; ☻) Whoosh down five zip lines across the vineyards or paddle around a lake beneath the Santa Lucia Mountains at this historic ranch, about a 10-mile drive northeast of SLO via Hwy 101. Reservations required.

🎉 Festivals & Events

Concerts in the Plaza MUSIC, FOOD
(www.downtownslo.com) Every Friday night from early June through early September, downtown's Mission Plaza rocks out with local bands and food vendors.

Savor the Central Coast FOOD, WINE
(www.savorcentralcoast.com) Behind-the-scenes farm, aquaculture and ranch tours, wine-tasting competitions and celebrity chefs' dinners in late September or early October.

🛌 Sleeping

Motels cluster off Hwy 101, especially off Monterey St northeast of downtown and around Santa Rosa St (Hwy 1).

HI Hostel Obispo HOSTEL $
(☑ 805-544-4678; www.hostelobispo.com; 1617 Santa Rosa St; dm $27-31, r from $60, all with shared bath; ⊙ check-in 4:30-10pm; @ ☎) ☞ On a tree-lined street near the train station, this

San Luis Obispo

⦿ Sights
1	Bubblegum Alley	A3
2	Mission San Luis Obispo de Tolosa	A3
3	San Luis Obispo Museum of Art	A3

⌂ Sleeping
4	HI Hostel Obispo	C4
5	Petit Soleil	C2

✕ Eating
6	Big Sky Café	A3
7	Firestone Grill	B3
8	Luna Red	A3
9	Meze Wine Bar & Bistro	C4
10	Novo	A3
11	San Luis Obispo Farmers Market	B3
12	Sidecar	A3

⦿ Drinking & Nightlife
13	Creekside Brewing Co	A3
14	Downtown Brewing Co	A3
15	Granada Bistro	B3
16	Kreuzberg	A4
17	Luis Wine Bar	B3
18	Mother's Tavern	A3

⦿ Entertainment
19	Palm Theatre	A3

⦿ Shopping
20	Finders Keepers	B3
21	Hands Gallery	B3
22	Mountain Air Sports	A4

solar-empowered, avocado-colored hostel inhabits a converted Victorian, which gives it a bit of a B&B feel. Amenities include a kitchen, bike rentals (from $10 per day) and complimentary sourdough pancakes and coffee for breakfast. BYOT (bring your own towel).

Peach Tree Inn MOTEL $$
(☏800-227-6396, 805-543-3170; www.peachtree-inn.com; 2001 Monterey St; r incl breakfast $89-140; ☺office 7am-11pm; @☏) The folksy, nothing-fancy motel rooms here are inviting, especially those right by the creek or with rocking chairs on wooden porches overlooking grassy lawns, eucalyptus trees and rose gardens. Continental breakfast features homemade breads.

San Luis Creek Lodge HOTEL $$$
(☏800-593-0333, 805-541-1122; www.sanluis-creeklodge.com; 1941 Monterey St; r incl breakfast $149-269; ✳@☏) Rubbing shoulders with

neighboring motels, this boutique inn has fresh, spacious rooms with divine beds (and some have gas fireplaces and jetted tubs) inside three whimsically mismatched buildings built in Tudor, California arts-and-crafts and Southern plantation styles. DVDs, chess sets and board games are free to borrow.

Petit Soleil INN $$$
(☏800-676-1588, 805-549-0321; www.petitsoleils-lo.com; 1473 Monterey St; d incl breakfast $169-299; ☺office 7am-10pm; ☏✾) This French-themed, gay-friendly 'bed et breakfast' is a mostly charming retrofit of a courtyard motel. Each room is tastefully decorated with Provençal flair, and breakfast is a gourmet feast. The front rooms catch some street noise. Pet fee $25.

✕ Eating

★**San Luis Obispo Farmers Market** MARKET
(www.downtownslo.com; ☺6-9pm Thu) The county's biggest and best weekly farmers market turns downtown SLO's Higuera St into a giant street party, with smokin' barbecues, overflowing fruit and veggie stands, live music and free sidewalk entertainment, from salvation peddlers to wackadoodle political activists. Rain cancels it.

Firestone Grill BARBECUE $
(www.firestonegrill.com; 1001 Higuera St; dishes $4-10; ☺11am-10pm Sun-Wed, to 11pm Thu-Sat; 🍴) If you can stomach huge lines, long waits for a table, and sports-bar-style service, you'll get to sink your teeth into an authentic Santa Maria–style tri-tip steak sandwich on a toasted garlic roll and a basket of super-crispy fries.

SLO Donut Company SNACKS $
(www.slodoco.com; 793 E Foothill Blvd; snacks from $2; ☺24hr; ☏) Home of unusually good flavor combos like bacon-maple and mint-chip donuts, served with cups of organic, fair-trade, locally roasted coffee. It's northwest of downtown off Santa Rosa St (Hwy 1).

Whole Foods GROCERY, FAST FOOD $
(www.wholefoodsmarket.com; 1531 Froom Ranch Way; ☺8am-9pm) 🍃 For organic groceries, deli picnic meals and a hot-and-cold salad bar. It's 4 miles southwest of downtown via Hwy 101 (exit Los Osos Valley Rd).

Meze Wine Bar & Bistro MEDITERRANEAN $$
(www.mezewinebar.com; 1880 Santa Barbara Ave; mains $10-20; ☺11am-9pm Mon-Wed, to 10pm

MADONNA INN

'Oh, my!' is one of the more printable exclamations overheard from visitors at the **Madonna Inn** (805-543-3000, 800-543-9666; www.madonnainn.com; 100 Madonna Rd; r $189-309; ✳ @ 🛜 ⚽), a garish confection visible from Hwy 101. You'd expect outrageous kitsch like this in Las Vegas, not SLO, but here it is, in all its campy extravagance. Japanese tourists, vacationing Midwesterners and hipster, irony-loving urbanites all adore the 110 themed rooms – including Yosemite Rock, Caveman and hot-pink Floral Fantasy. Check out photos of the different rooms online, or wander the halls and spy into the ones being cleaned. The urinal in the men's room is a bizarre waterfall. But the most irresistible reason to stop here? Old-fashioned cookies from the storybook-esque bakery.

Thu-Sat) Hidden downhill from the Amtrak station, this tiny wine shop, gourmet market and tapas-style bar is an eclectic gem. Gather with friends around the cheese and charcuterie board, or stop in for a hand-crafted sandwich with a quinoa salad.

Big Sky Café
CALIFORNIAN $$
(www.bigskycafe.com; 1121 Broad St; dinner mains $11-22; ⊙7am-9pm Mon-Thu, to 10pm Fri, 8am-10pm Sat, to 9pm Sun; 🖉) 🌱 Big Sky is a big room, and still the wait can be long – its tagline is 'analog food for a digital world.' Vegetarians have almost as many options as carnivores, and many of the ingredients are sourced locally. Big-plate dinners can be a bit bland, but breakfast (served until 1pm daily) gets top marks.

★ Luna Red
FUSION $$$
(805-540-5243; www.lunaredslo.com; 1023 Chorro St; shared plates $6-20, mains $20-39; ⊙11am-9pm Mon-Wed, to 11:30pm Thu-Fri, 9:30am-11:30pm Sat, to 9pm Sun; 🖉) 🌱 Local bounty from the land and sea, artisan cheeses and farmers-market produce pervade the chef's Californian, Asian and Mediterranean small-plates menu. Cocktails and glowing lanterns enhance a sophisticated ambience indoors, or linger over brunch on the mission-view garden patio. Reservations recommended.

Novo
FUSION $$$
(805-543-3986; www.novorestaurant.com; 726 Higuera St; mains $15-34; ⊙11am-9pm Mon-Thu, to 1am Fri & Sat, 10am-9pm Sun) Novo spins out hit-and-miss European, Latin and Asian-inspired tapas, but with an artistic eye towards presentation. Pick from dozens of international beers, wines or sakes, then savor the view from tables on the creekside deck.

Sidecar
CALIFORNIAN $$$
(805-540-5340; www.sidecarslo.com; 1127 Broad St; mains $14-28; ⊙11am-10pm Mon-Fri, from 10am Sat & Sun) 🌱 A long saloon-style bar where locals mingle with serious cocktails, and a casual Californian menu – try the fried brussels sprouts or the signature house burger with smoked mozzarella – make this downtown eatery a social spot.

Drinking & Nightlife

Downtown, Higuera St is littered with college-student-jammed bars.

Downtown Brewing Co
BREWERY
(805-543-1843; www.slobrew.com; 1119 Garden St) Nicknamed SLO Brew, this study in rafters and exposed brick has plenty of craft beers to go, along with filling pub grub. Downstairs, you'll find DJs or live bands (including some surprisingly famous acts) on many nights.

Tap It Brewing
BREWERY
(805-545-7702; www.tapitbrewing.com; 675 Clarion St; ⊙noon-6pm Sun-Wed, to 8pm Thu-Sat) Head toward the airport to this brewery's tap room, where cacti grow inside an old Jeep and live bands sometimes rock on the patio.

Mother's Tavern
PUB
(www.motherstavern.com; 725 Higuera St; ⊙11am-1:30am; 🛜) Cavernous two-story 'MoTav' draws in writhing CalPoly student masses with a no-cover dance floor, DJ and karaoke nights, and big-screen sports TVs.

Kreuzberg
CAFE
(www.kreuzbergcalifornia.com; 685 Higuera St; ⊙7:30am-10pm; 🛜) Shabby-chic coffeehouse and roaster has earned a fervent following with its comfy couches, sprawling bookshelves, local art and occasional live music.

Granada Bistro
COCKTAIL BAR
(www.granadahotelandbistro.com; 1126 Morro St; ⊙5-10pm Sun-Thu, to 11pm Fri & Sat) A swank indoor/outdoor hotel cocktail lounge, adorned with wrought-iron candelabras and outdoor fire pits, classes up SLO's downtown scene.

Luis Wine Bar WINE BAR
(www.luiswinebar.com; 1021 Higuera St; ⊙ 3-11pm Mon-Thu, to midnight Fri, noon-midnight Sat, noon-11pm Sun) Evincing urbane style and unpretentious sophistication, this downtown wine bar has wide-open seating, a strong craft beer list and small noshes.

Creekside Brewing Co BREWERY
(www.creeksidebrewingcom.ipage.com; 1040 Broad St; ⊙ 4pm-close Mon-Thu, from noon Fri-Sun) On the tiny patio overhanging a bubbling creek, you can sample respectable homemade and imported craft beers and ciders.

☆ Entertainment

Palm Theatre CINEMA
(☏ 805-541-5161; www.thepalmtheatre.com; 817 Palm St; tickets $5-8) ✐ This small-scale movie house showing foreign and indie flicks just happens to be the USA's first solar-powered cinema. Look for the **SLO International Film Festival** (www.slofilmfest.org) in March.

Performing Arts Center PERFORMING ARTS
(PAC; ☏ 805-756-4849, 888-233-2787; www.pacslo.org; 1 Grand Ave) On the CalPoly campus, SLO's biggest cultural venue presents an internationally spiced variety of concerts, theater, dance recitals, stand-up comedy and other shows, including by big-name performers.

Sunset Drive-In CINEMA
(☏ 805-544-4475; www.facebook.com/sunset-drivein; 255 Elks Ln; ⊞) Recline your seat, put your feet up on the dash and munch on bottomless bags of popcorn at this classic Americana drive-in. Sticking around for the second feature (usually a B-list Hollywood blockbuster) doesn't cost extra. It's 2 miles southwest of downtown off Higuera St.

🔒 Shopping

Downtown Higuera and Marsh Sts, along with all of the arcades and cross streets in between, are full of unique boutiques. Just take a wander.

DON'T MISS

EDNA VALLEY WINERIES

A gorgeous bicycle ride into the rolling hills southeast of downtown SLO, Edna Valley wineries are best known for producing crisp Chardonnay and subtle Pinot Noir, as well as spicy and smoky Syrah. Annual events worth showing up for include 'Roll Out the Barrels' in mid-June and harvest celebrations in mid-November. For a winery map and more information, visit www.slowine.com.

Tolosa Winery (www.tolosawinery.com; 4910 Edna Rd; tasting fee $12-25; ⊙ 11am-4:45pm) No-oak Chardonnay, barrel-selected Pinot Noir and bold estate Syrah, with artisanal cheese, charcuterie and chocolate pairings on weekends.

Edna Valley Vineyard (www.ednavalleyvineyard.com; 2585 Biddle Ranch Rd; tasting fee $10-15; ⊙ 10am-5pm) Sip Paragon Vineyard estate Chardonnay by panoramic windows overlooking fields of grapes.

Baileyana (Niven Family Wine Estates; www.baileyana.com; 5828 Orcutt Rd; tasting fee $8-12; ⊙ 10am-5pm) Samples from six different labels inside an early-20th-century wooden schoolhouse, with a bocce ball court outside.

Talley Vineyards (www.talleyvineyards.com; 3031 Lopez Dr, Arroyo Grande; tasting fee $8-15; ⊙ 10:30am-4:30pm) Unpretentious, value-priced wines set among rolling hillsides, with vineyard tours ($10, including wine-tasting flight $15) by appointment.

Kynsi Winery (www.kynsi.com; 2212 Corbett Canyon Rd, Arroyo Grande; tasting fee $10; ⊙ 11am-5pm, closed Tue & Wed Nov-Jan) Small, family-run vineyard pours cult-worthy Pinot Noir inside a cozy brick tasting room.

Chamisal Vineyards (www.chamisalvineyards.com; 7525 Orcutt Rd; tasting fee $15; ⊙ 11am-5pm) In a rust-colored barn tasting room, tipple hand-crafted, small-lot wines grown mostly organically.

Sextant Wines (www.sextantwines.com; 1653 Old Price Canyon Rd; tasting fee $10; ⊙ 10am-4pm Mon-Fri, to 5pm Sat & Sun) Boisterous tasting room pours different varietals from Edna Valley and Paso Robles, with a tiny gourmet deli.

Hands Gallery
ARTS & CRAFTS

(www.handsgallery.com; 777 Higuera St; ☉10am-6pm Mon-Wed, to 9pm Thu, to 8pm Fri & Sat, 11am-5pm Sun) Brightly lit downtown shop sells vibrant contemporary pieces by California artisans, including jewelry, fiber arts, sculptures, ceramics and blown glass.

Mountain Air Sports
OUTDOOR EQUIPMENT

(www.mountainairsports.com; 667 Marsh St; ☉10am-6pm Mon-Sat, to 8pm Thu, 11am-4pm Sun) At this local outdoor outfitter, pick up anything from campstove fuel and tents to brand-name clothing and hiking boots.

Finders Keepers
CLOTHING

(www.finderskeepersconsignment.com; 1124 Garden St; ☉10am-5pm Mon-Sat) Seriously stylish secondhand women's fashions that match SLO's breezy, laid-back coastal lifestyle, plus hand-picked handbags, coats and jewelry.

ℹ️ Information

SLO's compact downtown is bisected by the parallel one-way arteries Higuera St and Marsh St. Banks with 24-hour ATMs are off Marsh St, near the post office. Most downtown coffee shops offer free wi-fi.

FedEx Office (www.fedex.com; 1127 Chorro St; per min 30-40¢; ☉7am-11pm Mon-Fri, 8am-9pm Sat, 9am-9pm Sun; 🛜) Pay-as-you-go internet workstations.

French Hospital (☏805-543-5353; www.frenchmedicalcenter.org; 1911 Johnson Ave; ☉24hr) Emergency-room services.

San Luis Obispo Library (☏805-781-5991; www.slolibrary.org; 995 Palm St; ☉10am-5pm Wed-Sat, to 8pm Tue; 🛜) Free wi-fi and public internet terminals.

San Luis Obispo Visitor Center (☏805-781-2777; www.visitslo.com; 895 Monterey St; ☉10am-5pm Sun-Wed, to 7pm Thu-Sat) Free maps and tourist brochures.

ℹ️ Getting There & Around

Off Broad St, a little more than 3 miles southeast of downtown, San Luis Obispo County Regional Airport (p761) has scheduled flights with United (San Francisco and LA) and US Airways (Phoenix).

Amtrak (☏800-872-7245; www.amtrak.com; 1011 Railroad Ave) runs daily Seattle–LA *Coast Starlight* and twice-daily SLO–San Diego *Pacific Surfliner* trains. Both routes head south to Santa Barbara ($27, 2¾ hours) and Los Angeles ($41, 5½ hours). The *Coast Starlight* connects north via Paso Robles to Salinas ($27, three hours) and Oakland ($39, six hours). Several daily Thruway buses link to more regional trains.

Inconveniently stopping off Hwy 101, nearly 4 miles southwest of downtown, **Greyhound** (☏800-231-2222; www.greyhound.com; 1460 Calle Joaquin) operates a few daily buses south to Los Angeles ($30, five hours) via Santa Barbara ($28, 2¼ hours) and north to San Francisco ($53, seven hours) via Santa Cruz ($42, four hours).

San Luis Obispo Regional Transit Authority (RTA; ☏805-541-2228; www.slorta.org; single-ride fares $1.50-3, day pass $5) operates daily county-wide buses with limited weekend services. All buses are equipped with bicycle racks. Lines converge on downtown's **transit center** (cnr Palm & Osos Sts).

SLO Transit (☏805-541-2877; www.slocity.org) runs local city buses ($1.25) and a trolley (50¢) that loops around downtown every 20 minutes between 5pm and 9pm on Thursdays year-round, on Fridays from June to early September and on Saturdays from April through October.

Avila Beach

Quaint, sunny Avila Beach lures crowds with its strand of golden sand and a shiny seafront commercial district of restaurants, cafes and shops. Two miles west of downtown, Port San Luis is a working fishing harbor with a rickety old pier.

👁 Sights & Activities

For a lazy summer day at the beach, you can rent beach chairs and umbrellas, surfboards, boogie boards and wetsuits underneath **Avila Pier**, off downtown's waterfront promenade. Over by the port, the beach has bonfire pits and the barking of sea lions accompanies your stroll atop **Harford Pier**, one of the Central Coast's most authentic fishing piers.

Point San Luis Lighthouse
LIGHTHOUSE

(☏guided hike reservations 805-541-8735, trolley tour reservations 855-533-7843; www.sanluislighthouse.org; lighthouse admission adult/child under 12yr $5/free, trolley tour incl admission per adult/child 3-12yr $20/15; ☉guided hikes usually 8:45am-1pm Wed & Sat, trolley tours usually noon & 2pm Wed & Sat, also 1pm Sat) Just getting to this scenic 1890 lighthouse, overshadowed by Diablo Canyon nuclear power plant, is an adventure. The cheapest way to reach the lighthouse is via a rocky, crumbling, 3.75-mile round-trip hiking trail, for which guided hike reservations are required. If you'd rather take it easy and ride out to the lighthouse, join an afternoon trolley tour, for which reservations are also required. Inside the lighthouse you can inspect an original Fresnel lens and authentic Victorian period furnishings.

The Pecho Coast Trail to the lighthouse is open only for guided hikes led by Pacific Gas & Electric (PG&E) docents, weather permitting. These guided hikes are free; children under nine years old are not allowed. Call for reservations at least two weeks in advance and bring plenty of water.

Avila Valley Barn
FARM
(www.avilavalleybarn.com; 560 Avila Beach Dr; ⊙ usually 9am-6pm mid-Mar–late Dec; ⊕) At this rural farmstand and pick-your-own berry farm, park alongside the sheep and goat pens, lick an ice-cream cone, then grab a basket and walk out into the fields to harvest jammy olallieberries in late spring and early summer, mid-summer peaches and nectarines, or autumn apples and pumpkins.

Sycamore Mineral Springs
SPA
(📞 805-595-7302; www.sycamoresprings.com; 1215 Avila Beach Dr; 1hr per person $13.50-17.50; ⊙ 8am-midnight, last reservation 10:45pm) Make time for a therapeutic soak in one of these private redwood hot tubs discreetly laddered up a woodsy hillside. Call in advance for reservations, especially during summer and after dark on weekends.

Central Coast Kayaks
KAYAKING
(📞 805-773-3500; www.centralcoastkayaks.com; 1879 Shell Beach Rd, Shell Beach; kayak or SUP set rental $20-60, classes $50-105, tours $60-120) Paddle out among sea otters and seals and through mesmerizing sea caves, rock grottos, arches and kelp forests. Wetsuits, paddle jackets and booties available (small surcharge applies) with kayak rentals.

Patriot Sportfishing
BOAT TOUR
(📞 805-595-7200; www.patriotsportfishing.com; Harford Pier, off Avila Beach Dr; 2hr whale-watching tour adult/child under 13yr $35/25) Long-running local biz organizes deep-sea fishing trips and tournaments, as well as whale-spotting cruises between December and April.

Avila Hot Springs
HOT SPRINGS
(📞 805-595-2359; www.avilahotsprings.com; 250 Avila Beach Dr; adult/child under 16yr $10/8; ⊙ usually 8am-9pm Sun-Tue & Thu, to 10pm Wed, Fri & Sat) Slightly sulfuric, lukewarm public swimming pool has kiddie waterslides that are usually open from noon to 5pm on Saturday and Sunday.

🛏 Sleeping

Port San Luis Campground
CAMPGROUND $
(📞 805-903-3395; www.portsanluis.com; RV sites without/with hookups from $40/65) First-come, first-served roadside parking spaces by the harbor have ocean views, but are for RVs only (no tents allowed).

Avila Lighthouse Suites
HOTEL $$$
(📞 800-372-8452, 805-627-1900; www.avilalighthousesuites.com; 550 Front St; ste incl breakfast from $289; ❄ @ 🛜 ⚊) Any closer to the ocean, and your bed would actually be sitting on the sand. With families in mind, this apartment-style hotel offers suites and villas with kitchenettes. But it's the giant heated outdoor pool, ping-pong tables, putting green and life-sized checkers board that keeps kids amused. Ask about steep off-season discounts.

Avila La Fonda
INN $$$
(📞 805-595-1700; www.avilalafonda.com; 101 San Miguel St; d from $329; @ 🛜) Downtown, this small boutique hotel is a harmonious mix of Mexican and Spanish colonial styles, with hand-painted tiles, stained-glass windows, wrought iron and rich wood. Gather around the fireplace for nightly wine and hors d'oeuvres. Complimentary beach gear to borrow for guests.

🍴 Eating

At Port San Luis, Harford Pier is home to shops that sell fresh catch right off the boats.

Avila Beach Farmers Market
MARKET $
(www.avilabeachpier.com; ⊙ 4-8pm Fri early Apr-late Sep) 🍃 With local farmers, food booths and rockin' live music, this outdoor street party takes over downtown's oceanfront promenade weekly from spring to fall.

Olde Port Inn
SEAFOOD $$$
(📞 805-595-2515; www.oldeportinn.com; Harford Pier, off Avila Beach Dr; mains $14-46; ⊙ 11:30am-9pm Sun-Thu, to 10pm Fri & Sat; ⊕) Clam chowder and cioppino are standouts at this seriously old-school seafood restaurant at the tip of Harford Pier. A few tables have see-through glass tops and floors, so lucky diners can peer down into the ocean. Reservations recommended.

ℹ Getting There & Around

Between 10am and 4pm on Saturdays and Sundays from late March until mid-October, a free **trolley** (SCT; 📞 805-781-4472; www.slorta.org) loops from Pismo Beach around downtown Avila

San Luis Obispo Bay

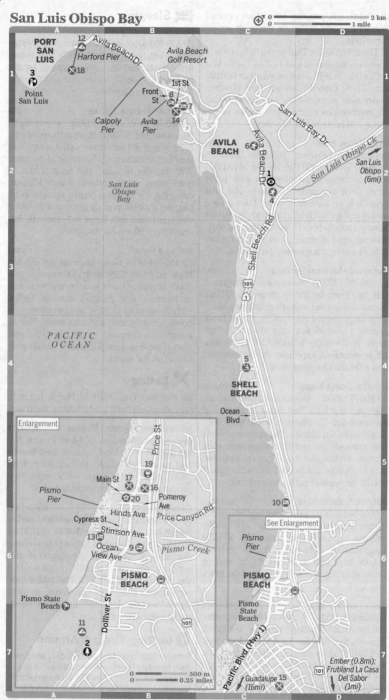

San Luis Obispo Bay

Beach to Port San Luis; from early June to early September, extended hours are 10am to 6pm Thursday through Sunday.

Pismo Beach

Backed by a wooden pier that stretches toward the setting sun, Pismo Beach is where James Dean once trysted with Pier Angeli. Fronted by an invitingly wide, sandy beach, this 1950s-retro town feels like somewhere straight out of *Rebel Without a Cause* or *American Graffiti*. If you're looking for a sand-and-surf respite from coastal road tripping, break your journey here.

◉ Sights & Activities

Pismo likes to call itself the 'Clam Capital of the World,' but these days the beach is pretty much clammed out. You'll have better luck catching something fishy off the pier, where you can rent rods. To rent a wetsuit, boogie board or surfboard, cruise nearby surf shops.

Pismo Beach Monarch
Butterfly Grove   PARK
(www.monarchbutterfly.org; ⏾ sunrise-sunset; 🚶) FREE From late October until February, more than 25,000 black-and-orange monarchs make their winter home here. Forming dense clusters in the tops of eucalyptus trees, they might easily be mistaken for leaves. Between 10am and 4pm during the roosting season, volunteers can tell you all about the insects' incredible journey, which outlasts any single generation of butterflies. Look for a gravel parking pull-out on the ocean side

of Pacific Blvd (Hwy 1), just south of Pismo State Beach's North Beach Campground.

✿ Festivals & Events

Wine, Waves & Beyond   CULTURE, FOOD
(www.winewavesandbeyond.com) Surfing competitions, surf-themed movies, wine tasting and a big bash on the beach with live music and food in late April or early May.

Classic at Pismo Beach   CULTURE
(www.theclassicatpismobeach.com) Show up in mid-June when hot rods and muscle cars roar off Hwy 1.

Clam Festival   FOOD
(www.pismochamber.com) In mid-October, celebrate the formerly abundant and still tasty mollusk with a clam dig, chowder cookoff, food vendors and live music.

⛺ Sleeping

Pismo Beach has dozens of motels, but rooms fill up quickly and prices skyrocket in summer, especially on weekends. Resorts and hotels roost on cliffs north of town via Price St and Shell Beach Rd, while motels cluster near the beach and along Hwy 101.

Pismo State Beach –
North Beach Campground   CAMPGROUND $
(🖉 reservations 800-444-7275; www.reserveamerica.com; 399 S Dolliver St; tent & RV sites $35; 🚼) About a mile south of downtown, off Hwy 1, the state park's North Beach Campground is shaded by eucalyptus trees and has more than 170 well-spaced, grassy sites with fire pits. The campground offers easy beach access, flush toilets and coin-op hot showers.

SCENIC DRIVE: HWY 1 SOUTH OF PISMO BEACH

What to See

Hwy 1 ends its fling with Hwy 101 at Pismo Beach, veering off toward the coast. Some truly wild, hidden beaches beckon along this back-door route to Santa Barbara.

Guadalupe Dunes

You almost expect to have to dodge tumbleweeds as you drive into the agricultural town of Guadalupe. Five miles further west at **Rancho Guadalupe Dunes Preserve** (www.countyofsb.org/parks; off Hwy 166; ⊙7am–sunset) **FREE**, enormous Egyptian-esque film sets from Cecil B DeMille's 1923 Hollywood epic *The Ten Commandments* still lie buried in the sand. Learn more about the 'Lost City of DeMille,' the ecology of North America's largest coastal dunes, and the mystical Dunites who lived here during the 1930s back at downtown's small **Dunes Center** (www.dunescenter.org; 1055 Guadalupe St; donation requested; ⊙10am–4pm Wed-Sun) museum.

Surf & Ocean Beaches

These wind-whipped beaches, one with a lonely Amtrak train whistlestop platform station, sidle up to Vandenberg Air Force Base. On the 10-mile drive west of Lompoc and Hwy 1 (take Hwy 246/W Ocean Ave), you'll pass odd-looking structures supporting spy and commerical satellite launches. Between March and September, **Ocean Beach County Park** (www.countyofsb.org/parks; Ocean Park Rd, off Hwy 246; ⊙8am–sunset, closed Mar-Sep) **FREE** is closed to the public and **Surf Beach** (www.vandenberg.af.mil/ploverupdate.asp; off Hwy 246; ⊙8am–6pm, subject to closure Mar-Oct) is also often closed to protect endangered snowy plovers during their nesting season.

Jalama Beach

Leaving Hwy 1 about 5 miles east of Lompoc, Jalama Rd follows 14 miles of twisting tarmac across ranch and farm lands before arriving at utterly isolated **Jalama Beach County Park** (☎ recorded info 805-736-3616; www.countyofsb.org/parks; 9999 Jalama Rd, Lompoc; per car $10). As you soak up the views, munch on a grilled seafood or beef burger from the **Jalama Beach Store** (www.jalamabeachstore.net; dishes $4-12; ⊙usually 8am–7pm in summer). To stay overnight, reserve a cabin in advance or arrive by 8am to get on the waiting list for a campsite in the crazily popular **campground** (www.sbparks.org/reservations; tent/RV sites from $23/38, cabins $110-210) – look for the 'campground full' sign back near Hwy 1 to avoid a wasted trip.

The Route

Heading south of Pismo Beach, Hwy 1 slowly winds along, passing through Guadalupe and Lompoc, where you can detour to La Purísima Mission State Historic Park (p538). Past Lompoc, Hwy 1 curves east to rejoin Hwy 101 south of Santa Barbara's wine country, near Gaviota.

Time & Mileage

With all of the detours described above, it's a 165-mile drive from Pismo Beach to Santa Barbara. The drive takes at least 3½ hours without any stops or traffic delays.

Beachwalker Inn & Suites MOTEL $$
(☎ 805-773-2725; www.pismobeachwalkerinn.com; 490 Dolliver St; r from $120; ☎ ⚟) Two blocks uphill from the beach, this renovated motel with a small outdoor heated pool lets you sleep peacefully atop deluxe mattresses. Suites have kitchenettes. Rates include morning coffee and pastries.

Pismo Lighthouse Suites HOTEL $$$
(☎ 800-245-2411, 805-773-2411; www.pismolighthousesuites.com; 2411 Price St; ste incl breakfast from $275; @ ⚟ ⚟ ⚟) With everything a vacationing family needs – from kitchenettes to a life-sized outdoor chessboard, a putting green, table tennis and badminton courts – this contemporary all-suites hotel right on the beach is hard to tear yourself away from. Ask about off-season discounts. Pet fee $30.

Sandcastle Inn
HOTEL $$$

(☎800-822-6606, 805-773-2422; www.sand-castleinn.com; 100 Stimson Ave; r incl breakfast $169-435; 🛜🐾) Many of these Eastern Sea-board–styled rooms are mere steps from the sand. The top-floor ocean-view patio is perfect for cracking open a bottle of wine at sunset or after dark by the fireplace. One-time pet fee $75.

✗ Eating

Doc Burnstein's Ice Cream Lab   ICE CREAM $
(www.docburnsteins.com; 114 W Branch St, Arroyo Grande; snacks $3-8; ⊙11am-9:30pm Sun-Thu, to 10:30pm Fri & Sat; 🚼) In neighboring Arroyo Grande, Doc's scoops up fantastical flavors such as Merlot raspberry truffle and the 'Elvis Special' (peanut butter with banana swirls). Live ice-cream lab shows start at 7pm sharp on Wednesday. From Hwy 101 southbound, exit at Grand Ave.

Old West Cinnamon Rolls   BAKERY $
(www.oldwestcinnamon.com; 861 Dolliver St; snacks $2-5; ⊙6:30am-5:30pm) The name says it all at this gobsmacking bakery by the beach.

Bunn Thai Bistro   THAI $$
(☎805-473-2824; www.bunnthaibistro.com; 968 W Grand Ave, Grover Beach; mains $10-18; ⊙11am-3pm & 4-9pm Thu-Tue; 🍴) In the next-door town of Grover Beach, this nouveau Thai restaurant is splashed with tropical colors. Making side trips into Asian fusion, it caters to omnivores, vegans, vegetarians and gluten-free folks. Lunch specials are a steal. Follow Hwy 1 south from Pismo Beach, turning left onto Grand Ave.

Frutiland La Casa Del Sabor   MEXICAN $$
(803 E Grand Ave, Arroyo Grande; mains $7-13; ⊙9:30am-7pm Mon & Wed, to 3:30pm Thu, to 8pm Fri & Sat, 10am-6pm Sun; 🚼) Oversized, overstuffed Mexican *tortas* (sandwiches) will feed two, and there are two dozen varieties to choose from. Or order a platter of blue-corn-tortilla fish tacos with a mango or papaya *agua fresca* (fruit drink). To find this taco shack in Arroyo Grande, exit Hwy 101 southbound at Halcyon Rd.

★Ember   CALIFORNIAN $$$
(☎805-474-7700; 1200 E Grand Ave, Arroyo Grande; shared dishes $8-20, mains $30; ⊙4-9pm Wed-Thu & Sun, to 10pm Fri & Sat; 🚼) 🍴 Chef Brian Collins, who once cooked at Alice Waters' revered Chez Panisse, has returned to his roots in SLO County. Out of this heart-warming restaurant's wood-burning oven come savory flatbreads, artfully charred squid and hearty red-wine-smoked short ribs. No reservations, so show up at 4pm or after 7:30pm, or be prepared for a very long wait for a table.

Sociable seating in the bar, where you can order off the full menu, is first-come, first-served. The restaurant is west of Hwy 101 (southbound exit Halcyon Rd) in Arroyo Grande.

★Cracked Crab   SEAFOOD $$$
(☎805-773-2722; www.crackedcrab.com; 751 Price St; mains $12-45; ⊙11am-9pm Sun-Thu, to 10pm Fri & Sat; 🚼) Fresh seafood and regional wines are the staples at this super-casual, family-owned grill. When the famous bucket o'seafood, full of flying bits of fish, Cajun sausage, red potatoes and cob corn, gets dumped on your butcher-paper-covered table, make sure you're wearing one of those silly-looking plastic bibs. No reservations, but the wait is worth it.

🍸 Drinking & Entertainment

Taste of the Valleys   WINE BAR
(www.pismowineshop.com; 911 Price St; ⊙noon-9pm Mon-Thu, to 10pm Fri & Sat, to 8pm Sun) Inside a wine shop stacked floor to ceiling with hand-picked vintages from around California and beyond, ask for a taste of anything they've got open, or sample from an astounding list of 500 wines poured by the glass.

Pismo Bowl   BOWLING ALLEY
(www.pismobeachbowl.com; 277 Pomeroy Ave; game per person $4, shoe rental $3; ⊙noon-10pm Sun-Thu, to midnight Fri & Sat; 🚼) Epitomizing Pismo Beach's retro vibe, this old-fashioned bowling alley is just a short walk uphill from the pier. Blacklight 'cosmic' and karaoke bowling rule Friday and Saturday nights.

ℹ Information

Pismo Beach Visitors Information Center
(☎800-443-7778, 805-773-4382; www.classiccalifornia.com; 581 Dolliver St; ⊙9am-5pm Mon-Fri, 11am-4pm Sat) Free maps and brochures. Smaller kiosk on the pier is open from 11am to 4pm on Sunday.

ℹ Getting There & Around

Hourly from Monday to Friday, and a few times daily on weekends, **RTA** (☎805-541-2228; www.slorta.org) bus 10 links San Luis Obispo with Pismo's Premium Outlets mall ($2, 30 minutes), a mile from the beach, before continuing to downtown Arroyo Grande ($1.50, 15 minutes).

Santa Barbara County

Includes ➜

Best Places to Eat

➜ Lark (p528)

➜ Lure Fish House (p550)

➜ Santa Barbara Shellfish Company (p527)

➜ Succulent Café (p541)

➜ Lucky Penny (p526)

Best Places to Stay

➜ El Encanto (p525)

➜ Inn of the Spanish Garden (p525)

➜ Santa Barbara Auto Camp (p524)

➜ Blue Iguana Inn (p548)

➜ Hamlet Inn (p541)

Why Go?

Frankly put, this area is damn pleasant to putter around. Low-slung between lofty mountains and the shimmering Pacific, chic Santa Barbara's red-tiled roofs, white stucco buildings and Mediterranean vibe give credence to its claim of being the 'American Riviera.' It's a surprisingly bewitching place to loll on the beach, eat and drink extraordinarily well, shop a bit and push all your cares off to another day. The city's car-free campaign has brought electric shuttle buses, urban bike trails and earth-friendly wine tours. Mother Nature returns the love with hiking, biking, surfing, kayaking, scuba diving and camping opportunities galore, from offshore Channel Islands National Park to arty Ojai, surrounded by hot springs. Meanwhile, winemaking is booming in the bucolic Santa Ynez Mountains, where over a hundred wineries vie for your attention. But if all you want to do is relax, no worries – plenty of sunny beaches await.

When to Go
Santa Barbara

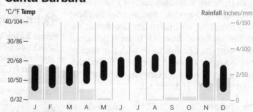

°C/°F Temp — Rainfall Inches/mm

Apr Balmy temperatures, fewer tourists than in summer. Wildflowers bloom on Channel Islands.

Jun Summer vacation and beach season begin. Summer Solstice Celebration parade.

Oct Sunny blue skies and smaller crowds. Wine Country harvest festivities.

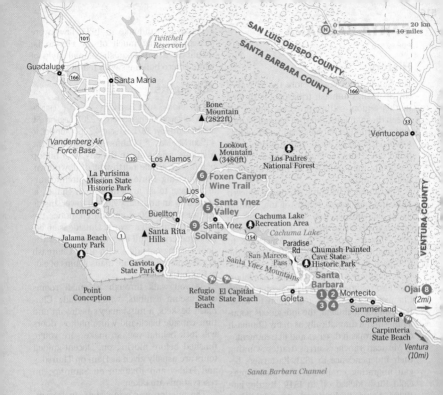

Santa Barbara County Highlights

1 Strolling **Stearns Wharf** (p517), then lazing on Santa Barbara's cinematic **beaches**.

2 Ambling between wine-tasting rooms, hip bars, art galleries and shops in Santa Barbara's **Funk Zone** (p528).

3 Exploring Spanish-colonial historic sites, such as **Mission Santa Barbara** (p516).

4 Eyeing panoramic views atop the *Vertigo*–esque clock tower of the **Santa Barbara County Courthouse** (p517).

5 Pedaling past vineyards and organic farms through the **Santa Ynez Valley** (p537).

6 Following the **Foxen Canyon Wine Trail** (p535) to taste top-rated pinot noir.

7 Kayaking sea caves and watching whales in **Channel Islands National Park** (p551).

8 Rejuvenating your body and soul in new-agey **Ojai** (p545).

9 Eating *ableskivers* (panacke popovers) by a kitschy windmill in the Danish village of **Solvang** (p539).

SANTA BARBARA

POP 89,640

History

For hundreds of years before the arrival of the Spanish, Chumash tribespeople thrived in this region, setting up trade routes between the mainland and the Channel Islands and constructing redwood canoes known as *tomols*. In 1542 explorer Juan Rodríguez Cabrillo sailed into the channel and claimed it for Spain, then quickly met his doom on a nearby island.

The Chumash had little reason for concern until the permanent return of the Spanish in the late 18th century. Catholic priests established missions up and down the coast, ostensibly to convert Native Americans to Christianity. Spanish soldiers often forced the Chumash to construct the missions and presidios (military forts) and provide farm labor; they also rounded up the tribespeople on the Channel Islands and forced them to leave. Back on the mainland, the indigenous population shrank dramatically, as many Chumash died of European diseases and ill treatment.

Mexican ranchers arrived after winning their independence in 1821. Easterners began migrating en masse after California's Gold Rush kicked off in 1849. By the late 1890s, Santa Barbara was an established SoCal vacation spot for the wealthy. After a massive earthquake in 1925, laws were passed requiring much of the city to be rebuilt in a faux-Spanish-colonial style of white-stucco buildings with red-tiled roofs.

⊙ Sights

★ Mission Santa Barbara   CHURCH
(www.santabarbaramission.org; 2201 Laguna St; adult/child 5-15yr $6/1; ⊙9am-4:30pm Apr-Oct, to 4:15pm Nov-Mar; ℗) California's 'Queen of the Missions' reigns above the city on a hilltop perch over a mile northwest of downtown. Its imposing Doric facade, an architectural homage to an ancient Roman chapel, is topped by an unusual twin bell tower. Inside the mission's 1820 stone church, notice the striking Chumash artwork. Outside is an eerie cemetery – skull carvings hang over the door leading outside – with 4000 Chumash graves and the elaborate mausoleums of early California settlers.

As you walk through 10 small rooms of museum exhibits, which include Chumash baskets, a missionary's bedroom and time-capsule black-and-white photos, doors will lock behind you, so make sure you're finished before moving on. Docent-guided tours are usually given at 11am on Thursday and Friday and 10:30am on Saturday; no reservations are taken.

The mission was established on December 4 (the feast day of St Barbara) in 1786, as the 10th California mission. Of California's

---

SANTA BARBARA COUNTY IN...

One Day

Spend your first morning soaking up rays at **East Beach**, walking out onto **Stearns Wharf** and down by the **harbor**. After lunch, visit downtown's museums, landmarks and shops along **State Street**, stopping at the **county courthouse** for 360-degree views from its clock tower. Finish up at the historic **mission**, then head down to the **Funk Zone** after dark.

Two Days

Cycle along the coast, go surfing or sea kayaking, or hike in the Santa Ynez foothills. In the afternoon, detour east to posh **Montecito** for shopping and people-watching or hang loose in **Carpinteria**, a retro beach town.

Three Days

Head up to Santa Barbara's Wine Country. Enjoy a do-it-yourself vineyards tour via car, motorcycle or bicycle along a scenic wine trail – **Foxen Canyon** and the **Santa Rita Hills** are exceptionally beautiful. Pack a picnic lunch or grab a bite in charming **Los Olivos** or Danish-esque **Solvang**.

Four Days

On your way back to LA, make time for a detour to arty **Ojai** up in the mountains for its hot springs and spas or book a day trip from **Ventura** by boat to **Anacapa Island** in rugged **Channel Islands National Park**.

original 21 Spanish-colonial missions, it's the only one that escaped secularization under Mexican rule. Continuously occupied by Catholic priests since its founding, the mission is still an active parish church.

From downtown, take MTD bus 22.

Santa Barbara County Courthouse
HISTORIC SITE

(☎805-962-6464; www.courthouselegacyfoundation.org; 1100 Anacapa St; ☉8:30am-4:45pm Mon-Fri, 10am-4:15pm Sat & Sun) FREE Built in Spanish-Moorish Revival style in 1929, the courthouse features hand-painted ceilings, wrought-iron chandeliers, and tiles from Tunisia and Spain. Step inside the hushed mural room depicting Spanish-colonial history on the 2nd floor, then climb El Mirador, the 85ft clock tower, for arch-framed panoramas of the city, ocean and mountains. You're free to explore on your own, but you'll get a lot more out of a free docent-guided tour, usually at 2pm daily and 10:30am on weekdays (except Thursday).

Stearns Wharf
HISTORIC SITE

(www.stearnswharf.org; P) FREE The southern end of State St gives way onto Stearns Wharf, a rough wooden pier lined with souvenir shops, snack stands and seafood shacks. Built in 1872, it's the oldest continuously operating wharf on the West Coast, although the actual structure has been rebuilt more than once. During the 1940s it was co-owned by tough-guy actor Jimmy Cagney and his brothers. If you've got kids, tow them inside the Ty Warner Sea Center (p520).

Parking on the wharf costs $2.50 per hour; the first 90 minutes are free with merchant validation. But trust us, you'd rather walk than drive over the wharf's bumpy wooden slats. The wharf entrance is a stop on MTD's downtown and waterfront shuttles.

Santa Barbara Museum of Art
MUSEUM

(☎805-963-4364; www.sbma.net; 1130 State St; adult/child 6-17yr $10/6, all free 5-8pm Thu; ☉11am-5pm Tue-Wed & Fri-Sun, to 8pm Thu) This thoughtfully curated, bite-sized art museum displays European and American masters – think Matisse and Diego Rivera – along with contemporary photography, classical antiquities and though-provoking temporary exhibits. Traipse up to the 2nd floor, where impressive Asian art collections include an intricate, colorful Tibetan sand mandala and the iron-and-leather armor of a Japanese warrior. Guided tours usually

DON'T MISS

MEETING MONARCHS

If you're here in late fall or winter, ask at the Outdoors Santa Barbara Visitors Center (p530) about the best places to see migratory monarch butterflies roosting in the trees – an extraordinary sight. See p467 for more information on roosting.

start at 1pm daily. There's also an interactive children's space, a museum shop and a cafe.

Santa Barbara Maritime Museum
MUSEUM

(☎805-962-8404; www.sbmm.org; 113 Harbor Way; adult/child 6-17yr $7/4, all free 3rd Thu of each month; ☉10am-5pm, to 6pm late May–early Sep; P♿) On the harborfront, this jam-packed, two-story exhibition hall celebrates the town's briny history with nautical artifacts, memorabilia and hands-on exhibits, including a big-game fishing chair from which you can 'reel in' a trophy marlin. Take a virtual trip through the Santa Barbara Channel, stand on a surfboard or watch deep-sea diving documentaries in the theater. There's 90 minutes of free parking in the public lot or take the Lil' Toot water taxi from Stearns Wharf.

Santa Barbara Historical Museum
MUSEUM

(☎805-966-1601; www.santabarbaramuseum.com; 136 E De La Guerra St; ☉10am-5pm Tue-Sat, from noon Sun) FREE Embracing a romantic cloistered adobe courtyard, this peaceful little museum has an endlessly fascinating collection of local memorabilia, ranging from the simply beautiful, such as Chumash woven baskets and Spanish-colonial-era textiles, to the intriguing, such as an intricately carved coffer that once belonged to Junípero Serra. Learn about the city's involvement in toppling the last Chinese monarchy, among other interesting footnotes in local history. Guided tours are usually offered at 2pm on Saturday and Sunday.

Santa Barbara Botanic Garden
GARDEN

(☎805-682-4726; www.sbbg.org; 1212 Mission Canyon Rd; adult/child 2-12yr/youth 13-17yr $10/6/8; ☉9am-6pm Mar-Oct, to 5pm Nov-Feb; P♿) Take a soul-satisfying jaunt around this 40-acre botanic garden, devoted to California's native flora. More than 5 miles of partly wheelchair-accessible trails meander past cacti, redwoods and wildflowers and by the old mission dam, originally built by Chumash tribespeople to irrigate the

Downtown Santa Barbara

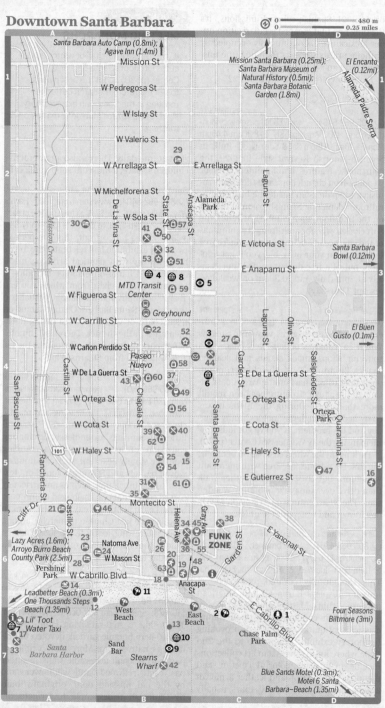

Downtown Santa Barbara

mission's fields. Leashed, well-behaved dogs are welcome. Guided tours typically depart at 11am and 2pm on Saturday and Sunday, and 2pm on Monday. On weekends, MTD bus 22 from the mission stops at the gardens upon request. If you're driving, head north from the mission to Foothill Blvd (Hwy 192), turn right and then left to continue on Mission Canyon Rd.

El Presidio de Santa Barbara State Historic Park HISTORIC SITE
(📞 805-965-0093; www.sbthp.org; 123 E Cañon Perdido St; adult/child under 17yr $5/free; ⊙ 10:30am-4:30pm) Founded in 1782 to defend the mission, this adobe-walled fort built by Chumash laborers was Spain's last military stronghold in Alta California. But its purpose wasn't solely to protect – the

presidio also served as a social and political hub, and as a stopping point for traveling Spanish military. Today this small urban park harbors some of the city's oldest structures. On a self-guided walking tour, be sure to stop at the chapel, its interior radiant with rich hues.

Admission also includes entry to nearby **Casa de La Guerra**, a 19th-century colonial adobe home displaying Spanish, Mexican and California heritage exhibits.

Karpeles Manuscript Library
Museum
MUSEUM
(☑805-962-5322; www.rain.org/~karpeles; 21 W Anapamu St; ⊙noon-4pm Wed-Sun) **FREE** Stuffed with a hodgepodge of historical written artifacts, this detour is for history nerds and book and music lovers. One of a dozen Karpeles manuscript museums nationwide, the rotating exhibits at this museum often spotlight literary masterworks, from Shakespeare to Sherlock Holmes.

🏃 Activities

Cycling

A paved **recreational path** stretches 3 miles along the waterfront in both directions from Stearns Wharf, west to Leadbetter Beach beyond the harbor and east just past East Beach. For more pedaling routes, **Bike Santa Barbara County** (www.bike-santabarbara.

org) offers free downloadable DIY cycling tours of the city, mountains and Wine Country, along with links to bicycle rentals and specialty shops.

Wheel Fun Rentals
CYCLING
(☑805-966-2282; www.wheelfunrentals.com) **Cabrillo Blvd** (www.wheelfunrentals.com; 23 E Cabrillo Blvd; ⊙8am-8pm Mar-Oct, to 6pm Nov-Feb; 👶); **State St** (www.wheelfunrentals.com; 22 State St; ⊙8am-8pm Mar-Oct, to 6pm Nov-Feb; 👶) Hourly rentals of beach cruisers ($10), mountain bikes ($11) and two-/four-person surreys ($29/39), with discounted half-day and full-day rates.

Santa Barbara Bikes To-Go
CYCLING
(☑805-628-2444; www.sbbikestogo.com; 812 E Gutierrez St) Delivers top-quality road and hybrid mountain bikes to your hotel. Rentals (per day $45 to $105) include helmets and emergency-kit saddle bags. Discounts for multiday, weekly and monthly rentals; reservations essential. Over-18s only.

Kayaking

Paddle the calm waters of Santa Barbara's harbor or the coves of the Gaviota coast, or hitch a ride to the Channel Islands for awesome sea caves.

Paddle Sports Center
KAYAKING
(☑805-617-3425; www.channelislandso.com; 117b Harbor Way; single/double kayak rental per

---

SANTA BARBARA FOR CHILDREN

Santa Barbara abounds with family-friendly fun for kids of all ages, from tots to tweens.

Ty Warner Sea Center (☑805-962-2526; www.sbnature.org; 211 Stearns Wharf; adult/child 2-12yr/youth 13-17yr $10/7/8; ⊙10am-5pm; P👶) From touch tanks full of tide-pool critters and crawl-through aquariums to whale sing-alongs, it's interactive and educational. Hourly parking on the wharf costs $2.50.

Santa Barbara Museum of Natural History (☑805-682-4711; www.sbnature.org; 2559 Puesta del Sol; adult/child 2-12yr/youth 13-17yr $11/7/8, incl planetarium show $15/11/12; ⊙10am-5pm; P👶) Giant skeletons, an insect wall and a pitch-dark planetarium captivate kids' imaginations. It's a half-mile drive uphill from the mission.

Santa Barbara Maritime Museum (p517) Peer through a periscope, reel in a virtual fish, watch underwater films or check out the model ships.

Santa Barbara Sailing Center Short, one-hour sails around the harbor ($15) let young 'uns spot sea lions up close.

Lil' Toot water taxi (p532) Take a joyride along the waterfront on this tiny yellow boat.

Chase Palm Park (323 E Cabrillo Blvd; 👶) Antique carousel rides ($2, cash only) plus a shipwreck-themed playground decked out with seashells and a miniature lighthouse.

Arroyo Burro Beach County Park (Hendry's; www.countyofsb.org/parks/; Cliff Dr at Las Positas Rd; ⊙8am-sunset; P👶) A wide, sandy beach, away from the tourists but not too far from downtown.

hr $25/40, per day $50/65; ⏱usually 8am-6pm) Long-established Channel Islands outfitter also guides harbor and coastal kayaking tours ($75 to $95) for beginner to advanced paddlers. Kayak rentals are available year-round at the harbor and Goleta Beach, and from late May through early September on West Beach. Book ahead online or by phone.

Santa Barbara Adventure Company
KAYAKING

(☎877-885-9283, 805-884-9283; www.sbadventureco.com; 32 E Haley St; kayak tours $49-209; 🖫) Leads all kinds of guided kayaking trips, from family-friendly harbor excursions and sunset floats to Gaviota coastal paddles and day and overnight trips to the Channel Islands. Some trips require a two- or four-person minimum.

Santa Barbara Sailing Center
KAYAKING

(☎805-962-2826; www.sbsail.com; off Harbor Way; single/double kayak rental per hr $10/15, 2hr kayak tour $50; 🖫) Just about the cheapest kayak rental and guided tours around, with paddling instruction available by prior arrangement. Call for seasonal hours.

Boating & Whale-Watching

Some tour companies offer year-round whale-watching boat trips, mostly to see grays in winter and spring, and humpbacks and blues in summer.

Condor Express
CRUISE

(☎888-779-4253, 805-882-0088; www.condorcruises.com; 301 W Cabrillo Blvd; adult/child 5-12yr 2½hr cruise $50/30, 4½hr cruise from $89/50; 🖫) Take a whale-watching excursion aboard the high-speed catamaran *Condor Express*. Whale sightings are guaranteed, so if you miss out the first time, you'll get a free voucher for another cruise.

Santa Barbara Sailing Center
CRUISE, SAILING

(☎805-962-2826; www.sbsail.com; off Harbor Way; cruises $15-65, sailing courses from $615; 🖫) Climb aboard the *Double Dolphin,* a 50ft sailing catamaran, for a two-hour coastal or sunset cruise. Seasonal whale-watching trips and quick one-hour spins around the harbor to view sea lions are also kid-friendly. If you want to learn to pilot your own sailboat, sign up for a 20-hour instructional course.

Sunset Kidd's Sailing Cruises
CRUISE

(☎805-962-8222; www.sunsetkidd.com; 125 Harbor Way; 2hr cruise $40-50) Float in an 18-passenger sailboat on a two-hour

ⓘ DIY WALKING TOURS

Santa Barbara's self-guided 12-block **Red Tile walking tour** is a convenient introduction to downtown's historical highlights. The tour's name comes from the half-moon-shaped red clay tiles covering the roofs of many Spanish Revival-style buildings. You can download a free map of this walking tour, as well as other paths along the waterfront and to the mission, from **Santa Barbara Car Free** (www.santabarbaracarfree.org) 🖉. For a lazy stroll between wine-tasting rooms, follow the city's Urban Wine Trail (p528).

whale-watching trip or a morning, afternoon, sunset cocktail or full-moon cruise. Reservations recommended.

Swimming

Los Baños del Mar
SWIMMING

(☎805-966-6110; www.friendsoflosbanos.org; 401 Shoreline Dr; admission $6; ⏱call for public swim schedules; 🖫) Beyond the beaches in and around Santa Barbara, you can also swim at this municipal outdoor pool near West Beach that's good for recreational and lap swimming. For kids under eight years old, there's a wading pool with a lifeguard that's open daily in summer, weather permitting.

Surfing

Unless you're a novice, conditions are too mellow in summer – come back in winter when ocean swells kick back up. Santa Barbara's **Leadbetter Point** is best for beginners. Experts-only **Rincon Point** awaits just outside Carpinteria.

Paddle Sports Center
SURFING

(☎805-617-3425; www.channelislandso.com; off Harbor Way; rental per 2hr/day wetsuit $5/15, boogie board or surfboard $10/30, SUP set $40/100; ⏱usually 8am-6pm) Rent a boogie board, surfboard or stand-up paddleboarding (SUP) set, along with a wetsuit, conveniently right at the harbor.

Santa Barbara Adventure Company
SURFING

(☎877-885-9283, 805-884-9283; www.sbadventureco.com; 32 E Haley St; 2hr surfing or SUP lesson $89, half-/two-day surfing lessons $109/199; 🖫) Learn the art of surfing or stand-up paddleboarding (SUP) from this family-friendly outfitter. Two-person minimum; children must be at least 7 years old.

TOP 10 BEACHES AROUND SANTA BARBARA

Although Santa Barbara's beaches are beauty-pageant prize winners, don't expect sunsets over the ocean because most of this coast faces south.

East Beach (E Cabrillo Blvd) Santa Barbara's largest and most popular beach is a long, sandy stretch sprawling east of Stearns Wharf, with volleyball nets for pick-up games, a children's play area and a snack bar. On Sunday afternoons, artists set up booths along the sidewalk, near the bike path.

Butterfly Beach (Channel Dr east of Butterfly Ln) Armani swimsuits and Gucci sunglasses abound at this narrow but chic swimming beach in front of the historic Biltmore hotel. Don't be surprised if you spot a celeb. The beach faces west, so you can catch a sunset here.

West Beach (W Cabrillo Blvd) Between Stearns Wharf and the harbor you'll find calm waters for kayaking, sailing and stand-up paddleboarding (SUP). It's most popular for sunbathing with tourists staying nearby. For lap swimming, head indoors to Los Baños del Mar (p521).

Leadbetter Beach (Shoreline Dr at Loma Alta Dr) Further west of the harbor, this is a fantastic spot for swimming or learning to surf or windsurf. A grassy picnic area atop the cliffs makes it just that much more family friendly.

One Thousand Steps Beach (foot of Santa Cruz Blvd at Shoreline Dr; ⊙ sunrise-10pm) Descend the cliffs on a historic staircase (don't worry, there aren't actually 1000 steps) for some windy beachcombing and tide-pooling (best at low tide), but no swimming. Neighboring **Shoreline Park** has a grassy area with picnic tables and a children's playground.

Arroyo Burro Beach County Park (p520) Near the junction of Cliff Dr and Las Positas Rd, this gem has a picnic area and the family-style Boathouse restaurant. The beach is flat, wide, away from tourists and great for kids, who can go tide-pooling. It's also a popular local surf spot. Look for an off-leash dog area at Douglas Family Preserve, on the cliffs above the beach.

Goleta Beach County Park (www.countyofsb.org/parks; Sandspit Rd, Goleta; ⊙ 8am-sunset) In the western suburbs near the University of California Santa Barbara (UCSB) campus, this beach is a locals' scene. There's a 1500ft-long fishing pier, a bike path and wide, sandy stretches for sunbathing after taking a dip or surfing easy waves. From Hwy 101, take Hwy 217 westbound.

Carpinteria State Beach (p544) About 12 miles east of Santa Barbara off Hwy 101, this mile-long beach has beautifully calm waters that are great for swimming, wading and tide-pooling, especially for younger kids.

El Capitán State Beach (www.parks.ca.gov; El Capitan State Beach Rd, Goleta; per car $10; ⊙ 8am-sunset; P ⓘ) & **Refugio State Beach** (www.parks.ca.gov; 10 Refugio Beach Rd, Goleta; per car $10; ⓘ) These twin beauties are worth the trip over 20 miles west of Santa Barbara via Hwy 101. Popular swimming and camping spots, they're connected by a bike path.

Surf-n-Wear's Beach House SURFING (☎ 805-963-1281; www.surfnwear.com; 10 State St; rental per hr/day wetsuit from $8/12, boogie board $10/16, surfboard $10/35, SUP set per day $50; ⊙ 9am-6pm Sun-Thu, to 7pm Fri & Sat) Not far from Stearns Wharf, rent soft (foam) boards, boogie boards, wetsuits and SUP sets from this 1960s surf shop that also sells collectible vintage boards.

Hiking

Gorgeous day hikes await in the foothills of the Santa Ynez Mountains and elsewhere in the Los Padres National Forest. Most trails cut through rugged chaparral and steep canyons – sweat it out and savor jaw-dropping coastal views. Spring and fall are the best seasons for hiking, when temperatures are moderate. Always carry plenty of extra water and watch out for poison oak.

To find even more local trails to explore, browse **Santa Barbara Hikes** (www.santabarbarahikes.com) online or visit the **Los Padres National Forest Headquarters** (☎805-968-6640; www.fs.usda.gov/lpnf; 6755 Hollister Ave, Goleta; ⏰8:30am-noon & 1-4:30pm Mon-Fri), west of the airport (from Hwy 101, exit Glen Annie Rd southbound onto Storke Rd).

Gliding

For condor's-eye ocean views, **Eagle Paragliding** (☎805-968-0980; www.eagleparagliding.com) and **Fly Above All** (☎805-965-3733; www.flyaboveall.com) offer paragliding lessons (from $200) and tandem flights ($100 to $200). For hang-gliding lessons and tandem flights, talk to Eagle Paragliding or **Fly Away** (☎805-403-8487; www.flyawayhanggliding.com).

☞ Tours

★ Architectural Foundation of Santa Barbara
WALKING TOUR

(☎805-965-6307; www.afsb.org; adult/child under 12yr $10/free; ⏰usually 10am Sat & Sun) Take time out for your weekend morning for a fascinating 90-minute guided walking tour of downtown's art, history and architecture. No reservations required; call or check the website for meet-up times and places.

Land & Sea Tours
GUIDED TOUR

(☎805-683-7600; www.out2seesb.com; adult/child 2-9yr $25/10; ⏰usually noon & 2pm daily year-round, also 4pm daily May-Oct; 👶) If you dig James Bond-style vehicles, take a narrated tour of the city on the *Land Shark*, an amphibious vehicle that drives right into the water. Trips depart from Stearns Wharf; buy tickets before boarding (no reservations).

Santa Barbara Trolley
BUS TOUR

(☎805-965-0353; www.sbtrolley.com; adult/child 3-12yr $18/9; 👶) ⚡ Biodiesel-fueled trolleys make a narrated 90-minute one-way loop around major tourist attractions, starting from Stearns Wharf (hourly departures 10am to 4pm). Hop-on, hop-off tickets are valid all day; pay the driver directly, or buy discounted tickets online in advance. One child under age 12 rides free with each paid adult ticket.

Santa Barbara Adventure Company
GUIDED TOUR

(☎805-884-9283, 877-885-9283; www.sbadventureco.com; 32 E Haley St) Maximize your outdoors time with a horseback ride on the beach or a Wine Country cycling tour, either costing around $150 per person (two-person minimum).

★★ Festivals & Events

To find out what's happening now, check the events calendars at www.santabarbaraca.com and www.independent.com online.

Santa Barbara International Film Festival
FILM

(http://sbiff.org) Film buffs and Hollywood A-list stars show up for screenings of more than 200 independent US and foreign films in late January and early February.

TOP DAY HIKES AROUND SANTA BARBARA

TRAIL NAME	ROUND-TRIP DISTANCE (MI)	DESCRIPTION	TRAILHEAD	DIRECTIONS
Inspiration Point	3.5	Popular with locals walking their dogs and for daily workouts	Tunnel Rd	Turn left off Mission Canyon Dr before reaching the Santa Barbara Botanic Garden
Rattlesnake Canyon	3.5	Offering shade and waterfalls as you ascend into the canyon; leashed dogs OK	Las Canoas Rd	Turn right off Mission Canyon Dr before reaching the Santa Barbara Botanic Garden
Cold Spring & Montecito Park	up to 9	Steady uphill hike past small cascades with a spur trail to a summit	Mountain Dr	From Montecito, follow Olive Mill Rd north of Hwy 101, continuing past Hwy 192 on Hot Springs Rd, then turn left

> ### ⓘ SANTA BARBARA ART WALKS
>
> Prime time for downtown gallery hopping is **First Thursday** (www.santabarbaradowntown.com), from 5pm to 8pm on the first Thursday of every month, when art galleries on and off State St throw open their doors for new exhibitions, artists' receptions, wine tastings and live music, all free. Closer to the beach, the **Funk Zone Art Walk** (http://funkzone.net) happens from 1pm to 5pm on the second Saturday of each month, featuring free events and entertainment at offbeat art galleries, bars and restaurants.

I Madonnari Italian Street Painting Festival   ART, FOOD

(www.imadonnarifestival.com; 🍴) Colorful chalk drawings adorn Mission Santa Barbara's sidewalks over Memorial Day weekend, with Italian food vendors and arts-and-crafts booths too.

⭐ Summer Solstice Celebration   FESTIVAL

(www.solsticeparade.com) Kicking off summer in late June, this wildly popular and wacky float parade down State St feels like something out of Burning Man. Live music, kids' activities, food stands, a wine-and-beer garden and an arts-and-craft show happen all weekend long.

French Festival   CULTURE, ART

(www.frenchfestival.com) In mid-July, California's biggest Francophile celebration has lots of food and wine, world music and dancing, a mock Eiffel Tower and Moulin Rouge, and even a poodle parade.

Santa Barbara County Fair   FAIR

(www.santamariafairpark.com; 🍴) In mid-July, this old-fashioned county fair combines agriculture exhibits, carnival rides, and lots of food and wine. The fairgrounds are in Santa Maria, over an hour's drive northwest of Santa Barbara via Hwy 101.

⭐ Old Spanish Days Fiesta   CULTURE, ART

(www.oldspanishdays-fiesta.org) The entire city fills up during late July and early August for this long-running – if slightly overblown – festival celebrating Santa Barbara's Spanish and Mexican colonial heritage. Festivities include outdoor bazaars and food markets, live music, flamenco dancing, horseback and rodeo events, and a big ol' parade.

🛏 Sleeping

Prepare for sticker shock: basic motel rooms by the beach command over $200 in summer. Don't show up at the last minute without reservations and expect to find any reasonably priced rooms, especially not on weekends. Cheaper motels cluster along upper State St and Hwy 101 northbound to Goleta and southbound to Carpinteria, Ventura and Camarillo.

⭐ Santa Barbara Auto Camp   CAMPGROUND $$

(✆888-405-7553; http://autocamp.com/sb; 2717 De La Vina St; d $175-215; P ❄ 🛜 🐾 🐕) 🚲 Bed down with vintage style in one of five shiny metal Airstream trailers parked near upper State St, north of downtown. All five architect-designed trailers have unique perks, such as a clawfoot tub or extra twin-size beds for kiddos, as well as a full kitchen and complimentary cruiser bikes to borrow. Book ahead; two-night minimum may apply. Pet fee $25.

Hotel Indigo   BOUTIQUE HOTEL $$

(✆805-966-6586, 877-270-1392; www.indigo-santabarbara.com; 121 State St; r from $170; P ❄ @ 🛜 🐕) 🚲 Poised between downtown and the beach, this petite Euro-chic boutique hotel has all the right touches: curated contemporary-art displays, rooftop patios and ecofriendly green-design elements like a living-plant wall. Peruse local-interest and art history books in the library nook, or retreat to your room and wrap yourself up in a plush bathrobe. Parking $14.

Agave Inn   MOTEL $$

(✆805-687-6009; http://agaveinnsb.com; 3222 State St; r incl breakfast from $119; P ❄ 🛜) While it's still just a motel at heart, this boutique-on-a-budget property's 'Mexican pop meets modern' motif livens things up with a color palette from a Frieda Kahlo painting. Flat-screen TVs, microwaves, minifridges and air-con make it a standout option. Family-sized rooms have kitchenettes and pull-out sofa beds. Continental breakfast included.

Harbor House Inn   MOTEL $$

(✆888-474-6789, 805-962-9745; www.harbor-houseinn.com; 104 Bath St; r from $180; P 🛜 🐕)

Down by the harbor, this converted motel offers brightly lit studios with hardwood floors and a beachy design scheme. A few have full kitchens and fireplaces, but there's no air-con. Rates include a welcome basket of breakfast goodies (with a two-night minimum stay) and beach towels, chairs and umbrellas and three-speed bicycles to borrow. Pet fee $20.

Marina Beach Motel MOTEL **$$**
(☑ 805-963-9311, 877-627-4621; www.marinabeachmotel.com; 21 Bath St; r incl breakfast from $155; P ✳ 🛜 🐾 🐕) Family-owned since 1942, this flower-festooned, one-story motor lodge that wraps around a grassy courtyard is worth a stay just for the location. Right by the beach, tidy remodeled rooms are comfy enough, and some have kitchenettes. Complimentary continental breakfast and beach-cruiser bikes to borrow. Small pets OK (fee $15).

Blue Sands Motel MOTEL **$$**
(☑ 805-965-1624; www.thebluesands.com; 421 S Milpas St; r from $120; P 🛜 🐾 🐕 🐕) With affable owners, this tiny two-story motel may be a bit kitschy, but who cares when you're just steps from East Beach? Book a remodeled room, or for a bigger splurge, one with a fireplace or a full kitchen and ocean views. No air-con. Two-night minimum stay on weekends. Pet fee $10.

Franciscan Inn MOTEL **$$**
(☑ 805-963-8845; www.franciscaninn.com; 109 Bath St; r incl breakfast $155-215; P 🛜 🐕) Settle into the relaxing charms of this Spanish-colonial two-story motel just over a block from the beach. Rooms differ in shape and decor, but many have kitchenettes and all evince French-country charm. Embrace the friendly vibe, afternoon cookies and outdoor pool and hot tub. Free continental breakfast. No air-con.

Holiday Inn Express Santa Barbara HOTEL **$$**
(☑ 877-834-3613, 805-963-9757; www.hotelvirginia.com; 17 W Haley St; r incl breakfast $185-250; P ✳ @ 🛜) ✈ Formerly the Hotel Virginia, this early-20th-century hotel has heaps of character, starting from the tile-filled lobby with a fountain. Upgraded rooms are serviceable, but its location just off downtown's State St merits a stay. Parking $12.

Motel 6 Santa Barbara–Beach MOTEL **$$**
(☑ 805-564-1392, 800-466-8356; www.motel6.com; 443 Corona del Mar; r $100-210; P ✳ 🛜 🐾 🐕) The very first Motel 6 to 'leave the light on for you' has been remodeled with IKEA-esque contemporary design, flat-screen TVs and multimedia stations. It fills nightly; book ahead. Wi-fi costs $3 extra every 24 hours. Pet fee $10.

★ **El Encanto** LUXURY HOTEL **$$$**
(☑ 805-845-5800, 800-393-5315; www.elencanto.com; 800 Alvarado Pl; d from $475; P ✳ @ 🛜 🐾 🐕 🐕) Triumphantly reborn, this 1920s icon of Santa Barbara style is a hilltop hideaway for travelers who demand the very best of everything. An infinity pool gazes out at the Pacific, while flower-filled gardens, fireplace lounges, a full-service spa and private bungalows with sun-drenched patios concoct the glamorous atmosphere perfectly fitted to SoCal socialites. Grab sunset drinks on the ocean-view terrace. Parking $35.

★ **Inn of the Spanish Garden** BOUTIQUE HOTEL **$$$**
(☑ 866-564-4700, 805-564-4700; www.spanishgardeninn.com; 915 Garden St; d incl breakfast from $309; P ✳ @ 🛜 🐾) At this Spanish-colonial-style inn, casual elegance, top-notch service and an impossibly romantic central courtyard will have you lording about like the don of your own private villa. Beds have

---

CAMPING & CABINS AROUND SANTA BARBARA

You won't find a campground anywhere near downtown Santa Barbara, but less than a half-hour drive west via Hwy 101, right on the ocean, are **El Capitán & Refugio State Beaches** (☑ reservations 800-444-7275; www.reserveamerica.com; off Hwy 101; tent & RV drive-up sites $35-55, hike-and-bike tent sites $10; P 🐕). Amenities include flush toilets, hot showers, picnic tables and convenience stores; parking costs an additional $10. You'll find family-friendly campgrounds with varying amenities in the mountainous Los Padres National Forest (p533) and at **Cachuma Lake Recreation Area** (☑ info 805-686-5054, reservations 805-686-5055; http://reservations.sbparks.org; 2225 Hwy 154; campsites $28-48, yurts $65-85, cabins $110-210; P 🐕 🐕) off Hwy 154, closer to Santa Barbara's Wine Country.

luxurious linens, bathrooms have oversized bathtubs and concierge service is top-notch. Palms surround a small outdoor pool, or unwind with a massage in your room.

El Capitan Canyon   CABIN, CAMPGROUND $$$
(☑ 805-685-3887, 866-352-2729; www.elcapitan-canyon.com; 11560 Calle Real; safari tent $155, yurt $205, cabins $225-795; ☐ 🛜 ⊠ 🐾) ✔ Inland from El Capitán State Beach, this 'glamping' resort is for those who hate to wake up with dirt under their nails. No cars are allowed up-canyon during peak season, making this woodsy resort more peaceful. Safari tents are rustic and share bathrooms, while creekside cabins are more deluxe, some with kitchenettes; all have their own outdoor firepit.

Borrow a bicycle to head over to the beach, or schedule a massage. The property is about 20 miles west of Santa Barbara, off Hwy 101.

Simpson House Inn   B&B $$$
(☑ 805-963-7067, 800-676-1280; www.simpsonhouseinn.com; 121 E Arrellaga St; d incl breakfast $255-610; ☐ ✳ 🛜) Whether you book an elegant suite with a clawfoot bathtub or a sweet cottage with a wood-burning fireplace, you'll be pampered at this Victorian-era estate ensconced in English gardens. From gourmet vegetarian breakfasts through evening wine, hors d'oeuvres and sweets, you'll be well fed. In-room mod cons include streaming internet radio and movies. Complimentary bicycles and beach gear to borrow.

Four Seasons Biltmore   RESORT $$$
(☑ info 805-969-2261, reservations 805-565-8299; www.fourseasons.com/santabarbara; 1260 Channel Dr; r from $425; ☐ ✳ @ 🛜 ⊠ 🐾) Wear white linen and live like Jay Gatsby at the oh-so-cushy 1927 Biltmore hotel on Butterfly Beach. Every detail is perfect, from bathrooms with Spanish tiles, French-milled soaps, deep soaking tubs and waterfall showers to bedrooms decked out with ultra-high-thread-count sheets. Indulge yourself at the spa or any of the oceanfront bars and restaurants.

Canary Hotel   BOUTIQUE HOTEL $$$
(☑ 805-884-0300, 877-468-3515; www.canary-santabarbara.com; 31 W Carrillo St; r $325-575; ☐ ✳ @ 🛜 🐾) ✔ On a busy block downtown, this haute multistory hotel has a rooftop pool and sunset-watching perch for cocktails. Stylish accommodations show off four-poster Spanish-framed beds and all mod cons. In-room spa services, yoga mats and bathroom goodies will soothe away stress, but ambient street noise may leave you sleepless. Complimentary fitness center access and cruiser bicycles. Parking $25.

Hungry? Taste local farm goodness at the hotel's downstairs restaurant, Finch & Fork.

White Jasmine Inn   B&B $$$
(☑ 805-966-0589; www.whitejasmineinnsantabarbara.com; 1327 Bath St; d $160-330; ☐ 🛜) Tucked behind a rose-entwined wooden fence, this cheery inn stitches together a California bungalow and two quaint cottages. Sound-insulated rooms all have private bathrooms and fireplaces, and some are air-conditioned and come with Jacuzzi tubs. Full breakfast basket delivered daily to your door. No children under 12 years old allowed.

Brisas del Mar   HOTEL $$$
(☑ 800-468-1988, 805-966-2219; www.sbhotels.com; 223 Castillo St; r incl breakfast from $230; ☐ ✳ @ 🛜 ⊠ 🐾) Kudos for all the freebies (DVDs, continental breakfast, afternoon wine and cheese, evening milk and cookies) and the newer Mediterranean-style front section, although some rooms are noisy. It's three blocks north of the beach. The hotel's sister properties, especially those further inland, may charge slightly less.

✖ Eating

Restaurants abound along downtown's State St and by the waterfront, where you'll find a few gems among the touristy claptrap. More creative kitchens are found down in the Funk Zone. East of downtown, Milpas St is lined with Mexicali taco shops.

★ Lucky Penny   PIZZERIA $
(www.luckypennysb.com; 127 Anacapa St; mains $7-10, pizzas $10-15; ⊙ 7am-9pm Mon-Sat, from 9am Sun; ✔) With shiny exterior walls covered in copper pennies, this pizzeria next to Lark restaurant is always jam-packed. It's worth the wait for a crispy pizza topped with smoked mozzarella and pork-and-fennel sausage or a wood oven-fired lamb meatball sandwich. Turn up before 11am for crazily inventive breakfast pizzas and farm-fresh egg skillets.

Lilly's Taquería   MEXICAN $
(http://lillystacos.com; 310 Chapala St; items from $1.60; ⊙ 10:30am-9pm Sun-Mon & Wed-Thu, to 10pm Fri & Sat) There's almost always a line roping around this downtown taco shack at lunchtime. But it goes fast, so you'd best be snappy with your order – the *adobada* (mar-

inated pork) and *lengua* (beef tongue) are stand-out choices. Second location in Goleta west of the airport, off Hwy 101.

Backyard Bowls
HEALTH FOOD **$**

(www.backyardbowls.com; 331 Motor Way; items $5-11; ⊙7am-5pm Mon-Fri, from 8am Sat & Sun) This eco-minded little shop serves up real-fruit smoothies and heaping açaí bowls with all kinds of health-conscious add-ons like fresh berries, granola, coconut milk, honey, bee pollen, almonds and loads of other locally sourced, sustainably harvested ingredients.

Metropulos
DELI **$**

(www.metrofinefoods.com; 216 E Yanonali St; dishes $2-10; ⊙8:30am-5:30pm or 6pm Mon-Fri, 10am-4pm Sat) Before a day at the beach, pick up custom-made sandwiches and fresh salads at this gourmet deli in the Funk Zone. Artisan breads, imported cheeses, cured meats, and California olives and wines will be bursting out of your picnic basket.

El Buen Gusto
MEXICAN **$**

(836 N Milpas St; dishes $2-8; ⊙8am-9pm; P) At this red-brick strip-mall joint, order authentic south-of-the-border tacos, tortas, quesadillas and burritos with an *agua fresca* (fruit drink) or cold Pacifico beer. Mexican music videos and soccer games blare from the TVs. *Menudo* (tripe soup) and *birria* (spicy meat stew) are weekend specials.

Silvergreens
CALIFORNIAN **$**

(www.silvergreens.com; 791 Chapala St; items $3-11; ⊙7:30am-10pm;) Who says fast food can't be fresh and tasty? With the tag line 'Eat smart, live well,' this sun-drenched corner cafe makes nutritionally sound salads, soups, sandwiches, burgers, breakfast burritos and more.

★Santa Barbara Shellfish Company
SEAFOOD **$$**

(www.sbfishhouse.com; 230 Stearns Wharf; dishes $4-19; ⊙11am-9pm; P) 'From sea to skillet to plate' sums up this end-of-the-wharf seafood shack that's more of a buzzing counter joint than a sit-down restaurant. Chase away the seagulls as you chow down on garlic-baked clams, crab cakes and coconut-fried shrimp at wooden picnic tables outside. Awesome lobster bisque, ocean views and the same location for over 25 years.

Olio Pizzeria
ITALIAN **$$**

(☏805-899-2699; www.oliopizzeria.com; 11 W Victoria St; shared plates $7-24, lunch mains $9-17; ⊙usually 11:30am-10pm) Just around the corner from State St, this high-ceilinged pizzeria with a happening wine bar proffers crispy, wood oven-baked pizzas, platters of imported cheeses and meats, garden-fresh *insalate* (salads), savory traditional Italian antipasti and sweet *dolci* (desserts). The entrance is off the parking lot alleyway.

Brophy Brothers
SEAFOOD **$$**

(☏805-966-4418; www.brophybros.com; 119 Harbor Way; mains $11-25; ⊙11am-10pm; P) A longtime favorite for its fresh-off-the-dock fish and seafood, rowdy atmosphere and salty harborside setting. Slightly less claustrophobic tables on the upstairs deck are worth the long wait – they're quieter and have the best ocean views. Or skip the long lines and start knocking back oyster shooters and Bloody Marys with convivial locals at the bar.

DIY DINING IN SANTA BARBARA

Stock up on fresh fruits and veggies, nuts and honey at the midweek **Santa Barbara Farmers Market** (www.sbfarmersmarket.org; 500 & 600 blocks of State St; ⊙4-7:30pm mid-Mar–early Nov, 3-6:30pm mid-Nov–mid-Mar;), which also happens on Saturday morning from 8:30am until 1pm at the corner of Santa Barbara and Cota Sts. Fill up a Wine Country picnic basket inside the **Santa Barbara Public Market** (http://sbpublicmarket.com; 38 W Victoria St; ⊙7am-10:30pm Mon-Thu, to 11pm Fri & Sat, 11am-8pm Sun) , where gourmet food purveyors and quick-fix food stalls are open every day of the week. The best place for healthy, organic groceries is **Lazy Acres** (www.lazyacres.com; 302 Meigs Rd; ⊙7am-11pm Mon-Sat, to 10pm Sun; P) , south of Hwy 101 via W Carrillo St. Downtown, **McConnell's Fine Ice Creams** (www.mcconnells.com; 728 State St; ⊙noon-9:30pm Sun-Wed, to 10:30pm Thu-Sat;) scoops up premium frozen treats. For more sweet endings, pop sea-salt or passion-fruit truffles from **Chocolate Maya** (www.chocolatemaya.com; 15 W Gutierrez St; ⊙10am-6pm Mon-Fri, to 5pm Sat, to 4pm Sun).

Sojourner Café   HEALTH FOOD **$$**
(www.sojournercafe.com; 134 E Cañon Perdido St; mains $8-13; ⊙ usually 11am-10pm; 🖊) 🍴 Vegetarians rejoice – the menu is extensive at this cozy, wholesome 1970s-era cafe. While supporting local farms, cooks get fairly creative with vegetables, tofu, tempeh, fish, seeds and other healthy ingredients. Daily desserts including vegan, dairy-free and wheat-free treats. Fair-trade coffee and local beers and wines are poured.

★**Lark**   CALIFORNIAN **$$$**
(📞805-284-0370; www.thelarksb.com; 131 Anacapa St; shared plates $5-32, mains $24-38; ⊙5-10pm Tue-Sun, bar till midnight) 🍴 There's no better place in Santa Barbara County to taste the bountiful farm and fishing goodness of this stretch of SoCal coast. Named after an antique Pullman railway car, this chef-run restaurant in the Funk Zone morphs its menu with the seasons, presenting unique flavor combinations like fried olives with chorizo aioli and chile-spiced mussels in lemongrass-lime broth. Make reservations.

Bouchon   CALIFORNIAN **$$$**
(📞805-730-1160; www.bouchonsantabarbara.com; 9 W Victoria Street; mains $25-36; ⊙5-9pm Sun-Thu, to 10pm Fri & Sat) 🍴 The perfect, unhurried follow-up to a day in the Wine Country is to feast on the bright, flavorful California cooking at pretty Bouchon (meaning 'wine cork'). A seasonally changing menu spotlights locally grown farm produce and ranched meats that marry beautifully with three dozen regional wines available by the glass. Lovebirds, book a table on the candle-lit patio.

Palace Grill   CAJUN, CREOLE **$$$**
(📞805-963-5000; http://palacegrill.com; 8 E Cota St; mains lunch $10-22, dinner $17-32; ⊙11:30am-3pm daily, 5:30-10pm Sun-Thu, to 11pm Fri & Sat; 🎤) With all the exuberance of Mardi Gras, this N'awlins-style grill makes totally addictive baskets of housemade muffins and breads, and ginormous (if so-so) plates of jambalaya, gumbo ya-ya, blackened catfish and pecan chicken. Stiff cocktails and indulgent desserts make the grade. Act unsurprised when the staff lead the crowd in a rousing sing-along.

🍷 Drinking & Nightlife

On lower State St, most of the meat-market watering holes have happy hours, tiny dance floors and rowdy college nights. Just south of Hwy 101, the arty Funk Zone's eclectic mix of bars and wine-tasting rooms is a trendy scene.

★**Figueroa Mountain Brewing Co**   BAR
(www.figmtnbrew.com; 137 Anacapa St; ⊙11am-11pm) Father and son brewers have brought their gold medal-winning hoppy IPA, Dan-

---

DON'T MISS

URBAN WINE TRAIL

No wheels to head up to Santa Barbara's Wine Country? No problem. Ramble between over a dozen wine-tasting rooms (and microbreweries, too) downtown and in the Funk Zone near the beach. Pick up the **Urban Wine Trail** (www.urbanwinetrailsb.com) anywhere along its route. Most tasting rooms are open every afternoon or sometimes into the early evening. On weekends, join the beautiful people rubbing shoulders as they sip outstanding glasses of regional wines and listen to free live music.

For a sociable scene, start at **Municipal Winemakers** (www.municipalwinemakers.com; 22 Anacapa St; tastings $12; ⊙11am-6pm; 🐾) or **Corks n' Crowns** (corksandcrowns.com; 32 Anacapa St; tastings $7-12; ⊙11am-7pm, last call for tastings 6pm) bottle shop. Then head up to Yanonali St, turning left for **Riverbench Winery Tasting Room** (📞805-324-4100; www.riverbench.com; 137 Anacapa St; tastings $10; ⊙11am-6pm); **Cutler's Artisan Spirits** (http://cutlersartisan.com; 137 Anacapa St; ⊙1-6pm Thu-Sun) distillery, a storefront where you can sample bourbon whiskey, vodka and apple liqueur; and Figueroa Mountain Brewing Co Walk further west to find more wine-tippling spots, one inside an old tire shop.

Or turn right on Yanonali St and stop at AVA Santa Barbara for a liquid education about Santa Barbara's five distinct wine-growing regions. It's less than a mile's detour to the refined **Carr Winery** (http://carrwinery.com; 414 N Salsipuedes St; tastings $10-12; ⊙11am-6pm Sun-Wed, to 7pm Thu-Sat) barrel room, next door to **Telegraph Brewing Company** (www.telegraphbrewing.com; 416 N Salsipuedes St; ⊙3-9pm Tue-Thu, 2-10pm Fri & Sat, 1-7pm Sun), which makes robust ales and a 'rhinoceros' rye wine.

ish red lager, and double IPA from Santa Barbara's Wine Country to the Funk Zone. Clink pint glasses on the taproom's open-air patio while acoustic acts play. Enter on Yanonali St.

AVA Santa Barbara
BAR

(www.avasantabarbara.com; 116 E Yanonali St; ⊙noon-7pm) From the sidewalk, passersby stop just to peek through the floor-to-ceiling glass windows at a wall-sized map of Santa Barbara's Wine Country, all hand-drawn in chalk. Inside, wine lovers lean on the tasting bar while sipping flights of cool-weather Chardonnay or pinot noir and sun-loving sauvignon blanc, grenache, Syrah and cabernet, all grown locally.

Handlebar Coffee Roasters
CAFE

(www.handlebarcoffee.com; 128 E Cañon Perdido St; ⊙7am-5pm Mon-Sat, from 8am Sun; 🐾) Bicycle-themed coffee shop brews rich coffee and espresso drinks from small-batch roasted beans. Sit and sip yours on the sunny patio.

Brewhouse
BREWERY

(sbbrewhouse.com; 229 W Montecito St; ⊙11am-11pm Sun-Thu, to midnight Fri & Sat; 🔊🐾) Down by the railroad tracks, the boisterous Brewhouse crafts its own unique small-batch beer (Saint Barb's Belgian-style ales rule), serves wines by the glass and has cool art and rock-in' live music Wednesday to Saturday nights.

Press Room
PUB

(http://pressroomsb.com; 15 E Ortega St; ⊙11am-2am) This tiny pub can barely contain the college students and European travelers who cram the place to its seams. Pop in to catch soccer games, stuff the jukebox with quarters and enjoy jovial banter with the British bartender.

Marquee
COCKTAIL BAR

(http://marqueesb.com; 1212 State St; ⊙4pm-2am) At downtown's Granada Theatre, flickering candles and glowing lights fill this bar mixing unusual cocktails, pouring wines by the glass and dishing up Mediterranean tapas. Look for jazz, open-mic and comedy nights.

Hollister Brewing Company
BREWERY

(www.hollisterbrewco.com; Camino Real Marketplace, 6980 Marketplace Dr, Goleta; ⊙11am-10pm) With over a dozen microbrews on tap, this place draws serious beer geeks out to Goleta, near the UCSB campus, off Hwy 101. IPAs are the permanent attractions, along with nitrogenated stout. Skip the food, though.

☆ Entertainment

Santa Barbara's appreciation of the arts is evidenced not only by the variety of performances available on any given night, but also its gorgeous, often historic venues. For a current calender of live music and special events, check www.independent.com online or pick up Friday's *Scene* guide in the *Santa Barbara News-Press*.

Santa Barbara Bowl
MUSIC

(☑805-962-7411; http://sbbowl.com; 1122 N Milpas St; most tickets $35-125) Built by Works Progress Administration (WPA) artisans during the Depression in the 1930s, this naturally beautiful outdoor stone amphitheater has ocean views from the highest cheap seats. Kick back in the sunshine or under the stars for live rock, jazz and folk concerts in summer. Big-name acts like Jack Johnson, Sarah McLachlan and The National have all taken the stage here.

Granada Theatre
THEATER, MUSIC

(☑805-899-2222; www.granadasb.org; 1216 State St) This beautifully restored 1930s Spanish Moorish-style theater is home to the city's symphony, ballet and opera, as well as touring Broadway shows and big-name musicians.

Lobero Theatre
THEATER, MUSIC

(☑888-456-2376, 805-963-0761; www.lobero.com; 33 E Cañon Perdido St) One of California's oldest theaters presents modern dance, chamber music, jazz and world-music touring acts and stand-up comedy nights.

Arlington Theatre
CINEMA

(☑805-963-4408; www.thearlingtontheatre.com; 1317 State St) Harking back to 1931, this Mission Revival–style movie palace has a Spanish courtyard and a star-spangled ceiling. It's a drop-dead gorgeous place to attend a film festival screening.

Soho
MUSIC

(☑805-962-7776; www.sohosb.com; ste 205, 1221 State St; most tickets $8-25) One unpretentious brick room plus live music almost nightly equals Soho, upstairs inside a downtown office complex behind McDonald's. Lineups range from indie rock, jazz, folk and funk to world beats. Some all-ages shows.

Velvet Jones
MUSIC, COMEDY

(☑805-965-8676; http://velvet-jones.com; 423 State St; most tickets $10-15) Long-running downtown punk and indie dive for rock, hip-hop, comedy and 18-plus DJ nights for the city's college crowd. Many bands stop here between gigs in LA and San Francisco.

Zodo's Bowling & Beyond
BOWLING

(☎805-967-0128; www.zodos.com; 5925 Calle Real, Goleta; bowling per game $4-8, shoe rental $4; ⊙8:30am-2am Tue-Sat, to midnight Sun & Mon;) With over 40 beers on tap, pool tables and a video arcade (Skee-Ball!), this bowling alley near UCSB is good ol' family fun. Call ahead to get on the wait list and 'Glow Bowling' blacklight nights with DJs. From Hwy 101 west of downtown, exit Fairview Ave north.

🛍 Shopping

Downtown's **State St** is packed with shops of all kinds, and even chain stores conform to the red-roofed architectural style. Cheapskates stick to lower State St, while trust-fund babies should head uptown. For more local art galleries and indie shops, dive into the **Funk Zone**, south of Hwy 101, spreading east of State St.

Paseo Nuevo
MALL

(www.paseonuevoshopping.com; 651 Paseo Nuevo; ⊙10am-9pm Mon-Fri, to 8pm Sat, 11am-6pm Sun) This busy open-air mall is anchored by Macy's and Nordstrom department stores and clothing chains. Browse Kitson for cutting-edge styles from LA, Bettie Page Clothing's retro pin-up fashions and the eco-green goddesses' bath, body and beauty shop Lush. First 75 minutes of parking free in the underground garage.

Surf-n-Wear's Beach House
CLOTHING

(www.surfnwear.com; 10 State St; ⊙9am-6pm Sun-Thu, to 7pm Fri & Sat) Modern and vintage surfboards dangle from the ceiling at this beach-minded emporium where unique T-shirts and hoodies, colorful bikinis, shades, beachbags and flip-flops jostle for your attention. This shop has been around since before 1967's Summer of Love.

REI
OUTDOOR EQUIPMENT

(www.rei.com; 321 Anacapa St; ⊙10am-9pm Mon-Fri, to 7pm Sat, to 6pm Sun) If you forgot your tent or rock-climbing carabiners at home, the West Coast's most popular independent co-op outdoor retailer is the place to pick up outdoor recreation gear, active clothing, sport shoes and topographic maps.

Channel Islands Surfboards
OUTDOOR EQUIPMENT

(www.cisurfboards.com; 36 Anacapa St; ⊙10am-7pm Mon-Sat, 11am-5pm Sun) Are you ready to take home a handcrafted, Southern California-born surfboard? Down in the Funk Zone, this surf shack is the place for innovative pro-worthy board designs, as well as surfer threads and beanie hats.

CRSVR Sneaker Boutique
SHOES, CLOTHING

(www.crsvr.com; 632 State St; ⊙10am-8pm) Check out this sneaker boutique run by DJs, not just for limited-editions Nikes and other athletic-shoe brands, but also T-shirts, jackets, hats and more urban styles for men.

La Arcada
MALL

(www.laarcadasantabarbara.com; 1114 State St; ⊙individual shop hr vary) Filled with specialty boutiques, restaurants and whimsical art galleries, this historic red-tile-roofed passageway was designed by Myron Hunt (builder of Pasadena's Rose Bowl) in the 1920s. Savor handmade French candies from Chocolats du Calibressan as you wander around.

Diani
CLOTHING, SHOES

(www.dianiboutique.com; 1324 State St, Arlington Plaza; ⊙10am-6pm Mon, 10am-7pm Tue-Sat, noon-6pm Sun) Carries high-fashion, Euro-inspired designs, with a touch of funky California soul thrown in for good measure. Think Humanoid dresses, Rag & Bone skinny jeans, Stella McCartney sunglasses and Chloé shoes.

El Paseo
MALL

(800 block of State St; ⊙individual shop hr vary) A smattering of locally owned boutiques surround a tiny, flower-festooned courtyard, constructed in Spanish-colonial style in the 1920s. It cameoed in the romantic comedy *It's Complicated*.

ℹ Information

FedEx Office (www.fedex.com; 1030 State St; per min 30-40¢; ⊙7am-11pm Mon-Fri, 8am-9pm Sat, 9am-9pm Sun) Self-service online computer workstations.

Outdoors Santa Barbara Visitors Center (☎805-884-1475; 4th fl, 113 Harbor Way; ⊙11am-4pm) Inside the same building as the maritime museum, this volunteer-staffed visitor center offers info on Channel Islands National Park and a harbor-view deck.

Santa Barbara Central Library (☎805-962-7653; www.sbplibrary.org; 40 E Anapamu St; ⊙10am-7pm Mon-Thu, to 5:30pm Fri & Sat, 1-5pm Sun;) Free walk-in internet terminals (photo ID required).

Santa Barbara Cottage Hospital (☎805-682-7111; www.cottagehealthsystem.org; 400 W Pueblo St; ⊙24hr) Emergency room (ER) open 24 hours.

Santa Barbara Independent (www.independent.com) Free alternative weekly tabloid with eating and entertainment listings and reviews, plus an events calendar.

Santa Barbara News-Press (www.newspress.com) Daily newspaper offers an events calendar and Friday's arts-and-entertainment supplement *Scene*.

Santa Barbara Visitors Center (☎805-568-1811, 805-965-3021; www.santabarbaraca.com; 1 Garden St; ⊙9am-5pm Mon-Sat & 10am-5pm Sun Feb-Oct; 9am-4pm Mon-Sat Nov-Jan) Pick up maps and brochures while consulting the helpful but busy staff. The website offers free downloadable DIY touring maps and itineraries, from famous movie locations to wine trails, art galleries and outdoors fun. Self-pay metered parking lot nearby.

❶ Getting There & Away

The small Santa Barbara Airport (p761), less than 10 miles west of downtown via Hwy 101, has scheduled flights to/from LA, Las Vegas, San Francisco and other western US cities. A taxi to downtown or the waterfront costs about $30

to $35 plus tip. Car-rental agencies with airport lots include Alamo, Avis, Budget, Enterprise, Hertz and National; reserve in advance.

Santa Barbara Airbus (☎800-423-1618, 805-964-7759; www.sbairbus.com) shuttles between Los Angeles International Airport (LAX) and Santa Barbara ($46/88 one way/round-trip, 2½ hours, eight departures daily). The more people in your party, the cheaper the fare. For more discounts, prepay online.

Amtrak (☎800-872-7245; www.amtrak.com; 209 State St) trains run south to LA ($31, three hours) via Carpinteria, Ventura and Burbank's airport, and north to San Luis Obispo ($27, 2¾ hours) and Oakland ($82, 8¾ hours), with stops in Paso Robles, Salinas and San Jose.

Greyhound (☎800-231-2222, 805-965-7551; www.greyhound.com; 224 Chapala St) operates a few buses daily to LA ($15, three hours), San Luis Obispo ($28, 2¼ hours), Santa Cruz ($53, six hours) and San Francisco ($57, nine hours).

Vista (☎800-438-1112; www.goventura.org) runs frequent daily 'Coastal Express' buses to Carpinteria ($3, 20 to 30 minutes) and Ventura ($3, 40 to 70 minutes); check online or call for schedules.

If you're driving on Hwy 101, take the Garden St or Carrillo St exits for downtown.

GO GREEN IN SANTA BARBARA

Santa Barbara's biggest eco-travel initiative is Santa Barbara Car Free (www.santabarbaracarfree.org). Browse the website for tips on seeing the city without your car, plus valuable discounts on accommodations, vacation packages, rail travel and more. Still don't believe it's possible to tour Santa Barbara without a car? Let us show you how to do it.

From LA, hop aboard the *Pacific Surfliner* for a memorably scenic three-hour coastal ride to Santa Barbara's Amtrak station, a few blocks from the beach and downtown. Then hoof it or catch one of the electric shuttles that zips north-south along State St and east-west along the waterfront. Take MTD bus line 22 to reach the famous mission and the botanic gardens. For a DIY cycling tour, Wheel Fun Rentals (p520) is a short walk from the train station.

Even Santa Barbara's Wine Country is getting into the sustainable swing of things. More and more vineyards are implementing biodynamic farming techniques and following organic guidelines. Many vintners and oenophiles are starting to think that the more natural the growing process, the better the wine, too. Sustainable Vine Wine Tours (p538) whisks you around family-owned sustainable vineyards. Minimize your carbon footprint even further by following Santa Barbara's Urban Wine Trail (p528) on foot. If you love both wine and food, Edible Santa Barbara (http://ediblecommunities.com/santabarbara/) magazine publishes insightful articles about vineyards and restaurants that are going green. It's available free at many local markets, restaurants and wineries.

Santa Barbara County abounds with ecofriendly outdoor activities, too. Take your pick of hiking trails, cycling routes, ocean kayaking, swimming, surfing or stand-up paddleboarding (SUP). If you're going whale-watching, ask around to see if there are any alternative-fueled tour boats with trained onboard naturalists.

❶ Getting Around

Local buses operated by the **Metropolitan Transit District** (MTD; ☎805-963-3366; www.sbmtd.gov) cost $1.75 per ride (exact change, cash only). Equipped with front-loading bike racks, these buses travel all over town and to adjacent communities; ask for a free transfer upon boarding. **MTD Transit Center** (1020 Chapala St) has details about routes and schedules.

BUS	DESTINATION	FREQUENCY
5	Arroyo Burro Beach	hourly
11	State St, UCSB campus	every 30 minutes
20	Montecito, Summerland, Carpinteria	hourly
22	Mission, Museum of Natural History and (weekends only) Botanic Garden	seven or eight buses daily

MTD's electric **Downtown Shuttle** buses run along State St down to Stearns Wharf every 10 to 30 minutes from 9am to 6pm daily. A second **Waterfront Shuttle** travels from Stearns Wharf west to the harbor and east to the zoo every 15 to 30 minutes from 9am or 10am to 6pm daily. Between late May and early September, both routes also run every 15 minutes from 6pm to 9pm on Fridays and Saturdays. The fare is 50¢ per ride; transfers between routes are free.

Lil' Toot water taxi (☎888-316-9363; www.sbwatertaxi.com; 113 Harbor Way; one-way fare adult/child 2-12yr $4/1; ☺usually noon-6pm Apr-Oct, hr vary Nov-Mar; 🚼) provides an eco-friendly, biodiesel-fueled ride between Stearns Wharf and the harbor, docking in front of the maritime museum. Look for ticket booths on the waterfront. Trips run every half-hour, weather permitting.

For bicycle rentals, Wheel Fun Rentals (p520) has two locations by Stearns Wharf. Downtown, **Pedego** (☎805-963-8885; http://pedegosb.com; 436 State St; ☺9:30am-6:30pm Tue-Sun) rents electric bicycles (per hour/day from $16/70) and pedal-it-yourself models (from $10/40).

Taxis are metered around $3 at flagfall, with an additional $3 to $4 for each mile. Call **Yellow Cab** (☎805-965-5111, 800-549-8294; www.santabarbarayellowcab.com).

Downtown street parking or in any of a dozen municipal lots is free for the first 75 minutes; each additional hour costs $1.50.

SANTA BARBARA WINE COUNTRY

Oak-dotted hillsides, winding country lanes, rows of sweetly heavy grapevines stretching as far as the eye can see – it's hard not to gush about the Santa Ynez and Santa Maria Valleys and the Santa Rita Hills wine regions. From fancy convertibles and Harleys to ecofriendly touring vans and road bikes, you'll find an eclectic, friendly mix of travelers sharing these bucolic back roads.

You may be inspired to visit by the Oscar-winning film *Sideways,* which is like real life in at least one respect: this Wine Country is ideal for do-it-yourself-exploring with friends. Locals here are friendly, from longtime landowners and farmers displaying small-town graciousness to vineyard owners who've fled big cities to follow their passion. Ever more winemakers are showing their passion for the vine in earth-conscious ways, implementing organic practices and biodynamic farming techniques. Many happily share their knowledge and intriguing personal histories, as well as their love of the land, in intimate vineyard tasting rooms.

With more than 100 wineries spread out across the landscape, it can seem daunting at first. But the Santa Ynez Valley's five small towns – Los Olivos, Solvang, Buellton, Santa Ynez and Ballard – are all clustered within 10 miles of one another, so it's easy to stop, shop and eat whenever and wherever you feel like it. Don't worry about sticking to a regimented plan or following prescriptive wine guides. Instead, let yourself be captivated by the scenery and pull over wherever signs looks welcoming.

Wineries

The big-name appellations for Santa Barbara's Wine Country are the Santa Ynez Valley, Santa Maria Valley and Santa Rita Hills, plus smaller Happy Canyon and upstart Ballard Canyon. Wine-tasting rooms abound in Los Olivos and Solvang, handy for anyone with limited time.

The Santa Ynez Valley, where you'll find most of the wineries, lies south of the Santa Maria Valley. Hwy 246 runs east–west, via Solvang, across the bottom of the Santa Ynez Valley, connecting Hwy 101 with Hwy 154.

SCENIC DRIVE: HIGHWAY 154 (SAN MARCOS PASS RD)

What to See

As Hwy 154 climbs from the coast, you'll leave oh-so civilized Santa Barbara behind and enter the rugged Santa Ynez Mountains. You'll notice places where the hillsides have been scarred by wildfires, but don't be alarmed: wildfires are part of the natural process of forest birth and regrowth.

Chumash Painted Cave State Historic Park

This tiny, off-the-beaten path historic site (www.parks.ca.gov; ☉ dawn-dusk) FREE shelters pictographs painted by Chumash tribespeople over 400 years ago. The sandstone cave is now protected from graffiti and vandalism by a metal screen, so bring a flashlight to get a good look. The turnoff to Painted Cave Rd is off Hwy 154 below San Marcos Summit, about 6 miles from Hwy 101. The two-mile twisting side road to the site is extremely narrow, rough and steep (no RVs). Look for a small signposted pull-off on your left.

Cold Spring Tavern

Cold Spring Tavern (☏ 805-967-0066; www.coldspringtavern.com; 5995 Stagecoach Rd; mains breakfast & lunch $9-14, dinner $22-31; ☉ 11am-8:30pm Mon-Fri, from 8am Sat & Sun) is an 1860s stagecoach stop that's still a popular watering hole. A rough-hewn plank floor connects a warren of dimly lit rooms decorated with an odd assortment of Western memorabilia. Call ahead to check if the barbecue grill is open, then order the Santa Maria-style tri-tip barbecue sandwich. The tavern's signposted turnoff from Hwy 154 is about a mile downhill beyond the mountain summit, then follow the signs for another 1.5 miles around the loop road.

Los Padres National Forest

The Los Padres National Forest (☏ 805-967-3481; www.fs.usda.gov/lpnf) stretches over 200 miles from the Carmel Valley to the western edge of LA County. It's a giant playground for hiking, camping, horseback riding and mountain biking.

Several scenic hiking trails lead off Paradise Rd, which crosses Hwy 154 north of San Marcos Pass, over 10 miles from Hwy 101. On the 1-mile round-trip Red Rock Pools Trail, the Santa Ynez River deeply pools among rocks and waterfalls, creating a swimming and sunbathing spot; the trailhead is at the end of Paradise Rd.

Stop at the ranger station (☏ 805-967-3481; 3505 Paradise Rd; ☉ 8am-4:30pm Mon-Fri, also 8am-4:30pm Sat late May-early Sep) for posted trail maps and information and a National Forest Adventure Pass (per day $5), which is required for parking (unless you have an 'America the Beautiful' Annual Pass (p472)). Family-friendly campgrounds (☏ 877-444-6777; www.recreation.gov; campsites $19-35) with drinking water, flush toilets and both first-come, first-served and reservable sites are along Paradise Rd.

Cachuma Lake Recreation Area

This county-run park (☏ cruise reservations 805-686-5050/5055; www.countyofsb.org/parks; admission per vehicle $10, 2hr cruise adult/4-12yr $15/7; ☉ open daily, seasonal hr vary; ☷) is a haven for anglers and boaters, with wildlife-watching cruises offered year-round. There's also a child-friendly nature center (☏ 805-693-0691; www.clnaturecenter.org; ☉ 10am-4pm Tue-Sat, to 2pm Sun; ☷) and a large campground (p525) with hot showers. First-come, first-served sites fill quickly; book ahead on weekends or for ecofriendly yurts.

The Route

From Hwy 101 west of downtown Santa Barbara, Hwy 154 (San Marcos Pass Rd) heads northwest, winding up through the Los Padres National Forest and passing Cachuma Lake. Beyond the Hwy 246 turnoff west to Solvang, Hwy 154 bisects the Santa Ynez Valley before rejoining Hwy 101 past Los Olivos.

Time & Mileage

It's 35 miles from downtown Santa Barbara to Los Olivos, taking 40 minutes without stops or traffic jams. Returning to Santa Barbara, it's under an hour's trip via Hwy 101.

Santa Barbara Wine Country

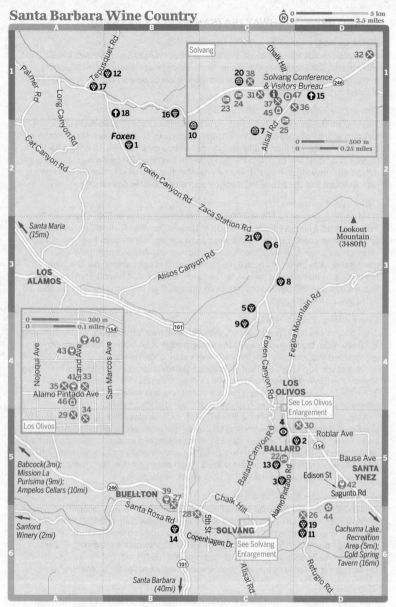

North–south secondary roads bordered by vineyards include Alamo Pintado Rd from Hwy 246 to Los Olivos, and Refugio Rd between Santa Ynez and Ballard.

A half-day trip will allow you to see one winery or tasting room, have lunch and return to Santa Barbara. Otherwise make it a full day and plan to have lunch and possibly dinner before returning to the city.

Santa Barbara Wine Country

Foxen Canyon Wine Trail

The scenic **Foxen Canyon Wine Trail** (www.foxencanyonwinetrail.com) runs north from Hwy 154, just west of Los Olivos, deep into the heart of the rural Santa Maria Valley. It's a must-see for oenophiles or anyone wanting to get off the beaten path. For the most part, it follows Foxen Canyon Rd.

★ **Foxen** WINERY
(📞 805-937-4251; www.foxenvineyard.com; 7200 & 7600 Foxen Canyon Rd, Santa Maria; tastings $10; ⊙ 11am-4pm) On what was once a working cattle ranch, Foxen crafts warm Syrah, steel-cut Chardonnay, full-fruited pinot noir and rich Rhône-style wines, all sourced from standout vineyards. The newer tasting room is solar-powered, while the old 'shack' – a dressed-down space with a corrugated-metal roof, funky-cool decor and leafy patio – pours Bordeaux-style and Cal-Ital varietals under the 'Foxen 7200' label.

Demetria Estate WINERY
(📞 805-686-2345; www.demetriaestate.com; 6701 Foxen Canyon Rd, Los Olivos; tastings $20; ⊙ by appt only) 🍃 This hilltop retreat has the curving arches and thick wooden doors of your hospitable Greek uncle's country house, with epic views of vineyards and rolling hillsides. Tastings are by appointment only, but worth it just to sample the biodynamically farmed Chardonnay, Syrah and viognier, plus rave-worthy Rhône-style red blends.

Zaca Mesa Winery WINERY
(www.zacamesa.com; 6905 Foxen Canyon Rd, Los Olivos; tastings $10; ⊙ 10am-4pm daily year-round, to 5pm Fri & Sat late May–early Sep) Stop by this barn-style tasting room for a rustic, sipping-on-the-farm ambience. Santa Barbara's highest-elevation winery, Zaca Mesa is known not only for its estate-grown Rhône varietals and signature Z Cuvée red blend and Z Blanc white blend, but also a life-sized outdoor chessboard, a tree-shaded picnic

> ### ⓘ WINE COUNTRY CELEBRATIONS
>
> **Santa Barbara Vintners** (☎805-668-0881; www.sbcountywines.com) publishes a free touring map brochure of the county's vineyards and wine trails, which you can pick up at just about any winery or visitors center, or download their free mobile app. Special events worth planning your trip around include the **Spring Weekend** (www.sbvintnersweekend.com) in mid-April and mid-October's **Celebration of Harvest** (www.celebrationofharvest.com).

area that's dog-friendly and a short, scenic trail overlooking the vineyards.

Firestone Vineyards WINERY
(☎805-688-3940; www.firestonewine.com; 5017 Zaca Station Rd, Los Olivos; tastings $15, incl tour $20; ☉10am-5pm) Founded in the 1970s, Firestone is Santa Barbara's oldest estate winery. Sweeping views of the vineyard from the sleek, wood-paneled tasting room are nearly as satisfying as the value-priced Chardonnay, sauvignon blanc, merlot and Bordeaux-style blends. Arrive in time for a winery tour, usually offered at 11:15am, 1:15pm and 3:15pm daily (no reservations).

Curtis Winery WINERY
(www.curtiswinery.com; 5249 Foxen Canyon Rd, Los Olivos; tastings $10; ☉10:30am-5:30pm) Just up the road from Firestone Vineyards, artisan winemaker Andrew Murray specializes in Rhône-style wines, including estate-grown Syrah, Mourvèdre, viognier, grenache blanc and Roussanne. The same wines are poured at Andrew Murray Vineyards' tasting room in downtown Los Olivos.

Kenneth Volk Vineyards WINERY
(☎805-938-7896; www.volkwines.com; 5230 Tepusquet Rd, Santa Maria; tastings $10; ☉10:30am-4:30pm) Only an established cult winemaker could convince oenophiles to drive so far out of their way to taste rare heritage varietals like floral-scented Malvasia and inky Negrette, as well as standard-bearing pinot noir, Chardonnay, cabernet sauvignon and merlot.

Riverbench Vineyard & Winery WINERY
(www.riverbench.com; 6020 Foxen Canyon Rd, Santa Maria; tastings $10; ☉10am-4pm) Riverbench has been growing prized pinot noir and Chardonnay grapes since the early 1970s. The rural tasting room is inside a butter-yellow Arts and Crafts farmhouse with panoramic views across the Santa Maria Valley. Out back is a picnic ground and bocce ball court. You can also sample their wines on Santa Barbara's Urban Wine Trail.

Fess Parker Winery & Vineyard WINERY
(www.fessparkerwines.com; 6200 Foxen Canyon Rd; tastings $12; ☉10am-5pm) Besides its on-screen appearance as Frass Canyon in the movie *Sideways,* the winery's other claim to fame is its late founder Fess Parker, best known for playing Davy Crockett on TV. Even though Fess has now passed on, his winery still gives away coonskin-cap-etched souvenir glasses. Savor the pricey, award-winning Chardonnay and pinot noir.

Rancho Sisquoc Winery WINERY
(www.ranchosisquoc.com; 6600 Foxen Canyon Rd, Santa Maria; tastings $10; ☉10am-4pm Mon-Thu, to 5pm Fri-Sun) This tranquil gem is worth the extra mileage, not necessarily for its hit-and-miss wines, but for the charmingly rustic tasting room surrounded by pastoral views. Turn off Foxen Canyon Rd when you spot **San Ramon Chapel** (www.sanramonchapel.org), a little white church built in 1875. Incidentally, *sisquoc* is the Chumash term for 'gathering place.'

Santa Rita Hills Wine Trail

When it comes to country-road scenery, eco-conscious farming practices and top-notch pinot noir, the less-traveled **Santa Rita Hills** (www.staritahills.com) region holds its own. Almost a dozen tasting rooms line an easy driving loop west of Hwy 101 via Santa Rosa Rd and Hwy 246. Be prepared to share the roads with cyclists and an occasional John Deere tractor. More artisan winemakers hide out in the industrial warehouses of Buellton near Hwy 101 and farther afield in Lompoc's 'Wine Ghetto' (www.lompoctrail.com).

Alma Rosa Winery & Vineyards WINERY
(☎805-688-9090; www.almarosawinery.com; tastings $5-15; ☉11am-4:30pm) ✦ Richard Sanford left the powerhouse winery bearing his name to start this new winery with his wife, Thekla, using sustainable, organic farming techniques. Cacti and cobblestones welcome you to the ranch, reached via a long, winding gravel driveway. Vineyard-designated pinot noir and

fine pinot blanc and pinot gris are what's poured. Call ahead for directions to the new tasting room.

Sanford Winery WINERY
(www.sanfordwinery.com; 5010 Santa Rosa Rd, Lompoc; tastings $15-20, incl tour $25; ⏰ 11am-4pm Sun-Thu, to 5pm Fri & Sat Mar-Oct, 11am-4pm daily Nov-Feb) Be enchanted by this romantic tasting room built of stone and handmade adobe bricks, all embraced by estate vineyards on the historic Rancho La Rinconda property. Watch the sun sink over the vineyards from the back patio with a glass of silky pinot noir or citrusy Chardonnay in hand. Winery tours are typically given at 11:30am daily (no reservations).

Babcock WINERY
(www.babcockwinery.com; 5175 E Hwy 146, Lompoc; tastings $12-15; ⏰ 10:30am-5pm) Family-owned vineyards overflow with different grape varietals – Chardonnay, Sauvignon Blanc, Pinot Gris, pinot noir, Syrah, Cabernet Sauvignon, merlot and more – that let innovative small-lot winemaker Bryan Babcock be the star. 'Slice of Heaven' pinot noir alone is worthy of a pilgrimage to this eclectically furnished tasting room with elevated views.

Ampelos Cellars TASTING ROOM
(☎805-736-9957; www.ampeloscellars.com; 312 N 9th Ave, Lompoc; tastings $10; ⏰ 11am-5pm Thu-Sat, to 4pm Mon) 🌿 Danish grower Peter Work and wife Rebecca display their passion for the vine through biodynamic farming techniques and encyclopedic knowledge of their lots. Their pinot noir, Syrah and grenache shine. Sample them in Lompoc's Wine Ghetto, an industrial area far from the vineyards, where most of the family-run tasting rooms (Flying Goat Cellars is a fave) are open only on weekends.

Mosby Winery WINERY
(☎805-688-2415; www.mosbywines.com; 9496 Santa Rosa Rd, Buellton; tastings $10; ⏰ 10am-4pm Mon-Thu, to 4:30pm Fri-Sun) Just west of Hwy 101, by a hillside olive orchard, this casual red carriage house pours unusual Cal-Italian varietals, including a lip-puckering, fruit-forward Dolcetto and a crisp, citrusy estate-grown Cortese. Be forewarned: the 80-proof grappa distilled from estate-grown Traminer grapes is a knock-out punch.

Santa Ynez Valley
Popular wineries cluster between Los Olivos and Solvang along Alamo Pintado Rd and Refugio Rd, south of Roblar Ave and west of Hwy 154. Noisy tour groups, harried staff and stingy pours often disappoint, but thankfully that's not the case at better wine-tasting rooms.

Beckmen Vineyards WINERY
(www.beckmenvineyards.com; 2670 Ontiveros Rd, Solvang; tastings $10-15; ⏰ 11am-5pm) 🌿 Bring a picnic to the pondside gazebo at this tranquil winery, where estate-grown Rhône varieties flourish on the unique terroir of Purisima Mountain. Using biodynamic farming principles, natural (not chemical), means are used to prevent pests. To sample superb Syrah and a rare cuvée blend with grenache, Mourvèdre and Counoise, follow Roblar Ave west of Hwy 154 to Ontiveros Rd.

Lincourt Vineyard WINERY
(www.lincourtwines.com; 1711 Alamo Pintado Rd, Solvang; tastings from $10; ⏰ 10am-5pm) Respected winemaker Bill Foley, who runs Firestone Vineyard on the Foxen Canyon Wine Trail, founded this vineyard first in the late 1990s on a former dairy farm. Today you can still see the original 1926 farmhouse built from a Sears catalog kit. Inside

---

SANTA BARBARA WINE COUNTRY 101

Although large-scale winemaking has only been happening here since the 1980s, the climate of Santa Barbara's Wine Country has always been perfect for growing grapes. Two parallel, transverse mountain ranges – Santa Ynez and San Rafael – cradle the region and funnel coastal fog eastward off the Pacific into the valleys between. The farther inland you go, the warmer it gets.

To the west, fog and low clouds may hover all day, keeping the weather crisp even in summer, while only a few miles inland, temperatures approach 100°F in July. These delicately balanced microclimates support two major types of grapes. Nearer the coast in the cooler Santa Maria Valley, pinot noir – a particularly fragile grape – and other Burgundian varietals such as Chardonnay thrive. Inland in the hotter Santa Ynez Valley, Rhône-style grapes do best, including Syrah and viognier.

the yellow cottage's tasting room, sip finely crafted Syrah, pinot noir and a dry French-style rosé, all made from grapes grown in the Santa Maria Valley and Santa Rita Hills.

Kalyra Winery   WINERY
(www.kalyrawinery.com; 343 N Refugio Rd, Santa Ynez; tastings $10-12; ⏰11am-5pm Mon-Fri, from 10am Sat & Sun) Australian Mike Brown has traveled halfway around the world to combine his two loves: surfing and winemaking. Try one of his full-bodied red blends, unusual white varietals or sweet dessert wines (the orange muscat is a crowd-pleaser), all in bottles with Aboriginal art-inspired labels. Kalyra also pours at a smaller tasting room on Santa Barbara's Urban Wine Trail.

Sunstone Vineyards & Winery   WINERY
(www.sunstonewinery.com; 125 N Refugio Rd, Santa Ynez; tastings $10-15; ⏰11am-5pm) 🐾 Wander inside what looks like an 18th-century stone farmhouse from Provence and into a cool hillside cave housing wine barrels. Sunstone crafts Bordeaux-style wines made from 100% organically grown grapes. Bring a picnic to eat in the courtyard beneath gnarled oaks.

Buttonwood Farm Winery & Vineyard   WINERY
(www.buttonwoodwinery.com; 1500 Alamo Pintado Rd, Solvang; tastings $10-15; ⏰11am-5pm; 🧒) 🐾 Bordeaux and Rhône varieties do well in the sun-dappled limestone soil at this friendly winery, best for wine-tasting neophytes and dog owners. The trellised back patio, bordering a fruit-tree orchard, is a pleasant spot to relax with a bottle of zingy sauvignon blanc.

🚗 Tours

Full-day wine-tasting tours average $105 to $160 per person; most leave from Santa Barbara, and some require a minimum number of participants.

Santa Barbara Wine Country Cycling Tours   CYCLING
(☎888-557-8687, 805-686-9490; www.wine-countrycycling.com; 3630 Sagunto St, Santa Ynez; ⏰8:30am-4:30pm Mon-Sat, by appt Sun) Guided and DIY cycling tours start from the Santa Ynez storefront, which also rents road and hybrid mountain bikes (from $35/45 per half/full day).

Wine Edventures   GUIDED TOUR
(☎805-965-9463; www.welovewines.com) Serves up a fun-lovin' side dish of local history and wine education on its shuttle-driven wine-tasting tours, one of which visits a microbrewery, too.

Sustainable Vine Wine Tours   GUIDED TOUR
(☎805-698-3911; www.sustainablevine.com) 🐾 Biodiesel-van tours of wineries implementing organic and sustainable agricultural practices include a local picnic lunch in the vineyards.

Los Olivos
POP 1130

The posh ranching town of Los Olivos is many visitors' first stop when exploring Santa Barbara's Wine Country. Its four-block-long main street is lined with rustic wine-tasting rooms, bistros and boutiques seemingly airlifted straight out of Napa.

⊙ Sights

Clairmont Farms   FARM
(☎805-688-7505; www.clairmontfarms.com; 2480 Roblar Ave; ⏰usually 10am-6pm Mon-Sat, to 5pm Sun) 🐾 Natural beauty awaits just outside town at this organic family-owned farm, where purple lavender fields bloom like a Monet masterpiece, usually peaking from mid-June to late July. Peruse lavender honey and sea salt and aromatherapy, bath and body products in the small shop.

WORTH A TRIP

MISSION LA PURÍSIMA

One of the most evocative of Southern California's missions, **La Purísima Mission State Historic Park** (☎805-733-3713; www.lapurisimamission.org; 2295 Purísima Rd, Lompoc; per car $6; ⏰9am-5pm; 🚻) 🐾 was completely restored in the 1930s by the Civilian Conservation Corps (CCC). Today its buildings are furnished just as they were during Spanish-colonial times. The mission's fields still support livestock, while outdoor gardens are planted with medicinal plants and trees once used by Chumash tribespeople. Surrounding the mission are miles of peaceful hiking trails. One-hour guided tours begin at 1pm daily. The mission is about 16 miles west of Hwy 101, via Hwy 146 from Buellton.

🛏 Sleeping & Eating

Ballard Inn & Restaurant　　　B&B $$$
(☎805-688-7770, 800-638-2466; www.ballardinn.
com; 2436 Baseline Ave, Ballard; r incl breakfast
$265-345; 🛜) For romantics, this quaint inn
awaits in the 19th-century stagecoach town
of Ballard, south of Los Olivos heading to-
ward Solvang. Wood-burning fireplaces
make en-suite rooms feel even more cozy,
though some are dearly in need of updat-
ing. Rates include a full hot breakfast and
weekend wine tastings. Reservations are es-
sential for rooms and also dinner at the inn's
chef-driven Eurasian restaurant.

Los Olivos Grocery　　　MARKET, DELI $
(http://losolivosgrocery.com; 2621 W Hwy 154, San-
ta Ynez; ⊙7am-9pm) This tiny local market
heaps barbecue tri-tip sandwiches, artisan
breads, specialty cheeses and everything
you'll need for a vineyard picnic, or grab a
table on the front porch.

Panino　　　SANDWICHES $$
(http://paninorestaurants.com; 2900 Grand Ave;
sandwiches $10-12; ⊙10am-4pm; 🍴) Take your
pick of gourmet deli sandwiches and salads: curry chicken is a perennial fave, but
there are robust vegetarian options too.
Order at the counter, then eat outside at an
umbrella-covered table.

**Los Olivos Café & Wine
Merchant**　　　CALIFORNIAN, MEDITERRANEAN $$$
(☎805-688-7265; www.losolivoscafe.com; 2879
Grand Ave; mains breakfast $9-12, lunch & dinner
$12-29; ⊙11:30am-8:30pm daily, also 8-10:30am
Sat & Sun) With white canopies and a
wisteria-covered trellis, this wine-country
landmark (as seen in *Sideways*) swirls up
a casual-chic SoCal ambience. It stays open
between lunch and dinner for antipasto
platters, hearty salads and crispy pizzas and
wine flights at the bar.

Sides Hardware & Shoes　　　AMERICAN $$$
(☎805-688-4820; http://brothersrestaurant.com;
2375 Alamo Pintado Ave; mains lunch $14-18, dinner
$26-34; ⊙11am-2:30pm daily, 5-8:30pm Sun-Thu,
to 9pm Fri & Sat) Inside a historic storefront,
this bistro delivers haute country cooking
like 'hammered pig' sandwiches topped with
apple slaw, fried chicken with garlicky kale
and Colorado lamb sirloin alongside goat-
cheese gnocchi. Book ahead for dinner.

Petros　　　GREEK $$$
(☎805-686-5455; www.petrosrestaurant.com;
Fess Parker Wine Country Inn & Spa, 2860 Grand
Ave; mains lunch $13-20, dinner $16-32; ⊙7am-
10pm Sun-Thu, to 11pm Fri & Sat) In a sunny
dining room, sophisticated Greek cuisine
makes a refreshing change from Italianate
wine-country kitsch. Housemade *meze* (ap-
petizers) will satisfy even picky foodies.

🍷 Drinking

Grand Ave and Alamo Pintado Rd are lined
with wine and beer tasting rooms, which
you can amble between all afternoon long.

Los Olivos Tasting Room　　　WINE BAR
(☎805-688-7406; http://site.thelosolivostasting-
room.com; 2905 Grand Ave; tastings $10; ⊙11am-
5pm) Inside a rickety 19th-century general
store, this tasting room stocks rare vintag-
es you won't find anywhere else. Well-oiled
servers are by turns loquacious and gruff,
but refreshingly blunt in their opinions
about local wines, and pours are generous.

Sarloos + Sons　　　WINE BAR
(☎805-688-1200; http://saarloosandsons.com;
2971 Grand Ave; tastings $10; ⊙11am-5pm
Wed-Fri & Sun, to 6pm Sat, last pour 30min be-
fore closing) Wine snobs are given the boot
at this shabby-chic tasting room pouring
estate-grown, small-lot Syrah, grenache noir,
pinot noir and sauvignon blanc. Pair your
wine flight with a 'cupcake flight' ($10, avail-
able Thursday through Sunday).

Carhartt Vineyard Tasting Room　　　WINE BAR
(☎805-693-5100; www.carharttvineyard.com;
2990A Grand Ave; tastings $10; ⊙11am-6pm) An
unpretentious tasting room inside a red-
trimmed wooden shack leads onto a shady
garden patio out back, where a fun-loving
younger crowd sips unfussy Syrah, sauvi-
gnon blanc and 'Chase the Blues Away' rosé.

🛍 Shopping

Jedlicka's Western Wear　　　CLOTHING, SHOES
(www.jedlickas.com; 2883 Grand Ave; ⊙9am-
5:30pm Mon-Sat, 10am-4:30pm Sun) Wranglers
and prairie babes should mosey over to
Jedlicka's for name-brand boots – Lucchese,
Justin and Tony Lama – as well as genuine
cowboy hats, jeans and jackets.

Solvang

POP 5345
My God, cap'n, we've hit a windmill! Which
can only mean one thing in Wine Coun-
try: Solvang, a Danish village founded
in 1911 on what was once a 19th-century

LOCAL KNOWLEDGE

CHRIS BURROUGHS: TASTING ROOM MANAGER

Alma Rosa Winery's tasting-room manager is already familiar to moviegoers for his appearance in the 2004 indie hit *Sideways* as – what else? – a cowboy-hat-wearing tasting-room manager. He shared a few smart wine-tasting tips with us.

Novices Never Fear

Don't let a lack of wine savvy keep you away. Winemakers enjoy sharing their passion and knowledge, and beginners are often their favorite guests.

Travel Light

Most tasting rooms aren't equipped for large crowds. Traveling in small groups means you'll have more time to chat with the staff.

Less is More

Don't keep a scorecard on the number of wineries visited. Spend time at only a handful of tasting rooms on any given day. Wine drinking is a social vehicle (not a mobile party crawl).

Be Open-Minded

At most tasting rooms you'll sample six wines: three whites and three reds. Don't tell the staff you never drink Chardonnay – who knows, the wine you try that day may change your mind.

Nice Guys Finish First

Smoking and heavy perfume? Not so considerate of others, and smoking dulls your wine-tasting senses besides. Be friendly, too. I'd rather drink a mediocre bottle of wine with a cool person than special wine with a jerk.

Spanish-colonial mission and later a Mexican *rancho* land grant. This Santa Ynez Valley town holds tight to its Danish heritage, or at least stereotypical images thereof. With its knickknack stores and cutesy motels, the town is almost as sticky-sweet as the Scandinavian pastries foisted upon the wandering crowds of day trippers. Solvang's kitschy charms make it worth visiting if only to gawk.

⊙ Sights

Old Mission Santa Ínes CHURCH
(☏805-688-4815; www.missionsantaines.org; 1760 Mission Dr; adult/child under 12yr $5/free; ⊙9am-4:30pm) Off Hwy 246 just east of downtown's Alisal Rd, this historic Catholic mission set the stage for a Chumash revolt against Spanish-colonial cruelty in 1824. Ask for a free (albeit historically biased) audioguide tour of the gardens, small museum and restored church, still an active parish today.

Elverhøj Museum MUSEUM
(www.elverhoj.org; 1624 Elverhoy Way; suggested donation adult/child under 12yr $5/free; ⊙11am-4pm Wed-Sun) South of downtown, tucked away on residential side streets, the delightful little museum has modest but thoughtful exhibits on Solvang's Danish heritage, as well as Danish culture, art and history.

Wildling Museum MUSEUM
(☏805-688-1802; www.wildlingmuseum.org; 1511 Mission Dr; adult/child 6-17yr $5/3; ⊙11am-5pm Mon & Wed-Fri, from 10am Sat & Sun) Need a break from boozing? This petite art museum exhibits wilderness-themed paintings and photography that may inspire you to go hiking in the mountains outside town.

Hans Christian Andersen Museum MUSEUM
(2nd fl, 1680 Mission Dr; ⊙10am-5pm) **FREE** If you remember childhood fairy tales with fondness, stop by this tiny two-room museum where original letters and first-edition copies of the Danish storyteller's illustrated books are on display.

🏃 Activities

Solvang is best known by cyclists for the **Solvang Century** (www.bikescor.com) races in March. For self-guided cycling tours, visit www.solvangusa.com and www.bike-santabarbara.org online and drop by Wheel Fun Rentals (p520), which has a second location in town at 1465 Copenhagen Dr.

🛏 Sleeping

Sleeping in Solvang isn't cheap, not even at older motels with faux-Danish exteriors. On weekends, rates skyrocket and rooms fill fast, so book ahead or make it a day trip.

⭐ Hamlet Inn
MOTEL $$
(☏ 805-688-4413; http://thehamletinn.com; 1532 Mission Dr; r $90-230; ❄ 🐾) This remodeled motel is to wine-country lodging what IKEA is to interior design: a budget-friendly, trendy alternative. Crisp, modern rooms have bright Danish flag bedspreads and iPod docking stations. Free loaner bicycles and a bocce ball court for guests.

Hadsten House
BOUTIQUE HOTEL $$
(☏ 800-457-5373, 805-688-3210; www.hadstenhouse.com; 1450 Mission Dr; r incl breakfast $165-215; ❄ 🐾 🏊) This revamped motel has luxuriously updated just about everything, except for its routine exterior. Inside, rooms are surprisingly plush, with flat-screen TVs, comfy duvets and high-end bath products. Spa suites come with jetted tubs. Rates include a breakfast buffet.

Hotel Corque
HOTEL $$$
(☏ 805-688-8000, 800-624-5572; www.hotelcorque.com; 400 Alisal Rd; r $169-350; ❄ @ 🐾 🏊) Downtown, this clean-lined hotel is a relief from all things Danish. Overpriced rooms may look anonymous, but they're quite spacious. Amenities include an outdoor swimming pool and hot tub, plus access to the next-door fitness center, where you can work off all those Danish butter rings.

🍴 Eating

El Rancho Market
SUPERMARKET $
(http://elranchomarket.com; 2886 Mission Dr; ⏰ 6am-11pm) East of downtown, this upscale supermarket – with a full deli, smokin' barbecued meats and an espresso bar – is the best place to fill your picnic basket before heading out to the wineries.

Solvang Restaurant
BAKERY $
(www.solvangrestaurant.com; 1672 Copenhagen Dr; items from $4; ⏰ 6am-3pm or 4pm Mon-Fri, to 5pm Sat & Sun; 🐾) Duck around the Danish-inscribed beams with decorative borders to order *ableskivers* – round pancake popovers covered in powdered sugar and raspberry jam. They're so popular, there's even a special take-out window.

Solvang Bakery
BAKERY $
(www.solvangbakery.com; 438 Alisal Rd; items from $2; ⏰ 7am-6pm Sun-Thu, to 7pm Fri & Sat; 🐾) Tubs of Danish butter cookies and rich almond kringles are popular takeaway treats.

Mortensen's Danish Bakery
BAKERY $
(www.mortensensbakery.com; 1588 Mission Dr; ⏰ 7:30am-5:30pm, to 8pm Jun-Aug) Gobble a custardy Danish butter ring, fruit-filled Danish pastry or apple strudel for breakfast.

New Frontiers Natural Marketplace
SUPERMARKET $
(https://newfrontiersmarket.com; 1984 Old Mission Dr; ⏰ 8am-8pm Mon-Sat, to 7pm Sun; 🐾) To keep things healthy, organic and local, pick up a tasty variety of deli sandwiches, salads and take-out dishes for picnicking.

⭐ Succulent Café
CALIFORNIAN $$
(☏ 805-691-9235; www.succulentcafe.com; 1555 Mission Dr; mains breakfast & lunch $9-13, dinner $19-29; ⏰ breakfast 8:30am-noon Sat & Sun; lunch 11am-3pm Mon & Wed-Fri, to 4pm Sat & Sun; dinner 5:30-9pm Mon & Wed-Sun) An inspired menu allows farm-fresh ingredients to speak for themselves at this family-owned gourmet cafe and market. Fuel up on breakfast biscuits stuffed with cinnamon-cumin pork tenderloin and pineapple chutney with bacon gravy, buttermilk-fried chicken salad and artisan grilled-cheese sandwiches for lunch, or pumpkin seed-crusted lamb for dinner. On sunny days, eat outside on the patio.

Root 246
AMERICAN $$$
(☏ 805-686-8681; www.root-246.com; 420 Alisal Rd; dinner mains $19-35, brunch buffet per adult/child 6-12yr $27/11; ⏰ 5-9pm Tue-Thu, 5-10pm

---

ℹ BEST SANTA BARBARA WINERIES FOR PICNICS

You won't have any problem finding picnic fare in Santa Barbara's Wine Country. The region is chock-full of local markets, delis and bakeries serving up portable sandwiches and salads. When picnicking at a winery, remember it's polite to buy a bottle of wine before spreading out your feast.

➡ Beckmen Vineyards (p537)

➡ Sunstone Vineyards & Winery (p538)

➡ Zaca Mesa Winery (p535)

➡ Lincourt Vineyard (p537)

➡ Rancho Sisquoc (p536)

Fri & Sat, 10am-2pm & 5-9pm Sun) Next to the Hotel Corque, chef Bradley Ogden's creative farm-to-table cuisine shows an artful touch. It's hard to beat the pastrami short ribs or Sunday brunch buffet. Make reservations or seat yourself in the sleek fireplace lounge to sip California wines by the glass after 4pm.

Drinking & Entertainment

Sorry, but after dinner this town is deader than an ancient Viking.

Chumash Casino Resort   CASINO, LIVE MUSIC
(☑ 800-248-6274; www.chumashcasino.com; 3400 E Hwy 246; ⊙24hr) Drive east on Hwy 246 to cutesy Solvang's vice-minded doppelganger, where the slots are plentiful, the cocktails watered-down and the cigarette smoke so thick you could cut it with a Danish butter knife. Get last-minute tickets for concerts by yesterday's pop and rock superstars.

Maverick Saloon   BAR
(☑ 805-686-4785; www.mavericksaloon.org; 3687 Sagunto St, Santa Ynez; ⊙noon-2am Mon-Fri, from 10am Sat & Sun) Off Hwy 246 east of Solvang, the one-horse town of Santa Ynez is home to this Harley-friendly honky-tonk dive bar with live country-and-western and rock bands, dancing and DJs.

Shopping

Downtown Solvang's notoriously kitschy shops cover a half dozen blocks south of Mission Dr (Hwy 246) between Atterdag Rd and Alisal Rd. For Danish cookbooks, handcrafted quilts and other homespun items, visit the Elverhøj Museum (p540).

Gaveasken   GIFTS
(433 Alisal Rd; ⊙9:30am-5pm Mon-Sat, from 10am Sun) If decorative Danish plates, elegant silver trays and heart-warming, handmade Christmas ornaments top your shopping list, you'll be crossing off items like mad at 'The Gift Box,' which stocks a primo mix of authentic Scandinavian wares.

Solvang Antique Center   ANTIQUES
(http://solvangantiques.com; 1693 Copenhagen Dr; ⊙10am-6pm) For truly fine furnishings, antique clocks and music boxes, decorative art and jewelry from around Europe and America, step inside this museum-like emporium.

Book Loft   BOOKS
(www.bookloftsolvang.com; 1680 Mission Dr; ⊙9am-8pm Tue-Thu, to 9pm Fri & Sat, to 6pm Sun & Mon) Downstairs from the Hans Christian Anderson Museum, this independent bookshop carries antiquarian and Scandinavian titles and children's storybooks.

ⓘ Information

Solvang is the busiest hub for wine-country visitors.

Solvang Coffee Company (1680 Mission Dr, Solvang; ⊙6am-6pm Sun-Tue, to 7pm Wed-Sat; 🖤) Enjoy wi-fi with your espresso next to the Book Loft and Hans Christian Anderson Museum.

Solvang Conference & Visitors Bureau (☑ 805-688-6144, 800-468-6765; www.solvangusa.com; 1639 Copenhagen Dr, Solvang; ⊙9am-5pm) Pick up free tourist brochures and winery maps at this kiosk in the town center, by the municipal parking lot and public restrooms.

Buellton

POP 4905

A mostly humdrum gateway to Santa Barbara's Wine Country, tiny Buellton is best known for the cartoonish landmark towering over the intersection of Hwys 101 and 246: Anderson's Pea Soup Restaurant, where you can get heaping bowls of the green stuff (though we would advise against it).

🛏 Sleeping & Eating

Buellton has slightly less expensive, but more well-worn chain motels and hotels than Solvang, 3 miles further east along Hwy 246.

Ellen's Danish Pancake House   BREAKFAST $$
(☑ 805-688-5312; www.ellensdanishpancakehouse.com; 272 Ave of Flags; mains $7-12; ⊙6am-8pm Mon-Sat, to 2pm Sun) West of Hwy 101, this old-fashioned, always-busy diner is where locals congregate for the Wine Country's best Danish pancakes, Danish sausages and not-so-Danish Belgian waffles. Breakfast served all day.

Hitching Post II   STEAKHOUSE $$$
(☑ 805-688-0676; www.hitchingpost2.com; 406 E Hwy 246; mains $23-50; ⊙5-9:30pm; 🚸) As seen in the movie *Sideways*, this dark-paneled chophouse offers oak-grilled steaks, pork ribs, smoked duck breast and rack of lamb. Every old-school meal comes with a veggie tray, garlic bread, shrimp cocktail or soup, salad and potatoes. The Hitching Post makes its own pinot noir, and it's damn good (wine tastings at the bar start at 4pm).

🍷 Drinking & Nightlife

Avant Tapas & Wine WINE BAR
(☑805-686-4742; www.avantwines.com; 35 Industrial Way; ⊙11am-9pm) Hidden upstairs in an industrial-chic space, Avant's Enomatic dispensing system pours tastes of over 30 boutique wines barreled in the warehouse – just walk out onto the catwalk and take a look. Happy hour runs 3pm to 5pm on weekdays.

Figueroa Mountain Brewing Co BREWPUB
(☑805-694-2252; www.figmtnbrew.com; 45 Industrial Way; ⊙4-9pm Mon-Thu, from 11am Fri-Sun) Fig Mountain's original brewpub hosts live-music, comedy and quiz nights. Across the valley in Los Olivos, their cottage taproom also pours tasting samplers of their award-winning brews such as Danish Red Lager and Hoppy Poppy IPA.

ⓘ Getting There & Around

From Santa Barbara, you can drive to Wine Country in under an hour. Via Hwy 101, it's 45 miles from Santa Barbara to Buellton. Hwy 246 runs east–west from Buellton to Solvang, then across the bottom of the Santa Ynez Valley to Hwy 154. From Santa Barbara, Hwy 154 is a more scenic route; it's fewer miles than taking Hwy 101, but takes longer because the road is often only two lanes wide, with slow-moving traffic. North of Hwy 246, Hwy 154 leads to Los Olivos.

Central Coast Shuttle (☑805-928-1977, 800-470-8818; www.cclax.com) will bus you from LAX to Buellton for $75/138 one way/round-trip, slightly less if you prepay 24 hours in advance. **Amtrak** (☑800-872-7245; www.amtrak.com) provides a couple of daily connecting Thruway buses to and from Solvang, but only if you're catching a train (or arriving on one) in Santa Barbara.

Santa Ynez Valley Transit (☑805-688-5452; www.syvt.com) runs local buses equipped with bike racks on a loop around Buellton, Solvang, Santa Ynez, Ballard and Los Olivos. Buses operate roughly between 7am and 7pm Monday through Saturday; one-way rides cost $1.50 (exact change only).

AROUND SANTA BARBARA

Can't quit your day job to follow your bliss? Don't despair: a long weekend in the mountains, valleys and beaches between Santa Barbara and LA will keep you inspired until you can. In this land of daydreams, perfect waves beckon off Ventura's coast, shady trails wind skyward in the Los Padres National Forest and spiritual Zen awaits you in Ojai Valley. Surf, stroll, seek – if outdoor rejuvenation is your goal, this is the place.

And then there's Channel Islands National Park, a biodiverse chain of islands shimmering just off the coast where you can kayak majestic sea caves, scuba dive in wavy kelp forests, wander fields of wildflower blooms or simply disappear from civilization at a remote wilderness campsite.

Montecito

POP 8965

The well-heeled community of Montecito, just east of Santa Barbara, is like a hitherto-unknown cousin who just inherited the family fortune. This leafy village in the Santa Ynez foothills is not just home to the rich and famous but to the obscenely rich and the uber-famous: it's the type of guarded enclave that would have incited revolutions in eras past.

Though many homes hide behind manicured hedges, a taste of the Montecito lifestyle of yesteryear can be experienced by taking a tour of **Casa del Herrero** (☑805-565-5653; http://casadelherrero.com; 1387 E Valley

---

WORTH A TRIP

LOTUSLAND

In 1941 the eccentric opera singer and socialite Madame Ganna Walka bought the 37 acres that make up **Lotusland** (☑info 805-969-3767, reservations 805-969-9990; www.lotusland.org; 695 Ashley Rd; adult/child 3-18yr $45/20; ⊙tours by appt 10am & 1:30pm Wed-Sat mid-Feb–mid-Nov; 🅿) with money from the fortunes she inherited after marrying – and then divorcing – a string of wealthy men. She spent the next four decades tending and expanding this incredible collection of rare and exotic plants from around the world; there are over 120 varieties of aloe alone. Come in summer when the lotuses bloom, typically during July and August. Reservations are required for tours, but the phone is only attended from 9am to 5pm weekdays, 9am to 1pm Saturday.

Rd; 90min tour $20; ⊙10am & 2pm Wed & Sat; Ⓟ), a gorgeously well-preserved 1920s estate built in Spanish-colonial style and bordered by strolling gardens.

Montecito's cafe and boutique-filled main drag is Coast Village Rd (exit Hwy 101 at Olive Mill Rd). **Dressed & Ready** (☑805-565-1253; www.dressedonline.com; 1253 Coast Village Rd; ⊙10am-5pm Mon-Sat, 11am-4pm Sun) are twin couture shops that cater to a star-quality crowd with flirty women's fashions by hand-picked designers. For breakfast or weekend brunch, nab a table on the patio at **Jeannine's** (http://jeannines.com; 1253 Coast Village Rd; mains $9-14; ⊙7am-3pm; 🖫) bakery and cafe, where from-scratch kitchen goodness includes challah French toast with caramelized bananas in Kahlua sauce.

From Santa Barbara, MTD buses 14 and 20 run to and from Montecito ($1.75, 20 minutes, hourly); bus 20 also connects Montecito with Summerland and Carpinteria.

Summerland

POP 1450

This drowsy seaside community was founded in the 1880s by HL Williams, a real-estate speculator. Williams was also a spiritualist, whose followers believed in the power of mediums to connect the living with the dead. Spiritualists were rumored to keep hidden rooms in their homes for séances with the dearly departed – a practice that earned the town the indelicate nickname of 'Spookville.'

Today, those wanting to connect to the past wander the town's antique shops, where you won't find any bargains, but you can ooh and ahh over beautiful furniture, jewelry and art from decades or even centuries gone by. From Hwy 101 southbound, take exit 91 and turn north, then right onto Lillie Ave. To find the beach, turn south off exit 91 instead and cross the railroad tracks to cliffside **Lookout Park** (www.countyofsb.org/parks; Lookout Park Rd; ⊙8am-sunset; 🖫) **FREE**, with a kids' playground, picnic tables, barbecue grills and access to a wide, relatively quiet stretch of sand (leashed dogs OK).

Grab breakfast or brunch at the Victorian seaside-style **Summerland Beach Café** (☑805-969-1019; www.summerlandbeachcafe.com; 2294 Lillie Ave; mains $7-14; ⊙7am-3pm Mon-Fri, to 4pm Sat & Sun; 🖫🖫), known for its fluffy omelets, and enjoy the ocean breezes

on the patio. Or walk over to **Tinker's** (2275 Ortega Hill Rd; items $5-10; ⊙11am-8pm; 🖫), an eat-out-of-a-basket burger shack that delivers seasoned curly fries and old-fashioned milkshakes.

From Santa Barbara, MTD bus 20 runs to Summerland ($1.75, 25 minutes, hourly) via Montecito, continuing to Carpinteria.

Carpinteria

POP 13,230

Lying 11 miles east of Santa Barbara, the time-warped beach of Carpinteria – so named because Chumash tribespeople once built seafaring canoes here – is a laid-back place. You could easily spend an hour or two wandering in and out of antiques shops and beachy boutiques along Linden Ave, downtown's main street. To gawk at the world's largest vat of guacamole, show up for the **California Avocado Festival** (www.avofest.com) in early October.

⊙ Sights & Activities

If you're an expert surfer, **Rincon Point** has long, glassy, right point-break waves. It's about 3 miles southeast of downtown, off Hwy 101 (exit Bates Rd)

Carpinteria State Beach   BEACH
(☑805-968-1033; www.parks.ca.gov; end of Linden Ave; per car $10; ⊙7am-sunset; 🖫) It's an idyllic, mile-long strand where kids splash around in calm waters and go tide-pooling along the shoreline. In winter, you may spot harbor seals and sea lions hauled out on the sand, especially if you hike over a mile south along the coast to a blufftop overlook.

Surf Happens   SURFING
(☑805-966-3613; http://surfhappens.com; 2hr group/private lesson from $110/160; 🖫) Welcoming families, beginners and 'Aloha Surf Sisters,' these highly reviewed classes and weekend camps led by expert staff incorporate the Zen of surfing. In summer, you'll begin your spiritual wave-riding journey off Hwy 101 (exit Santa Claus Ln). Make reservations in advance.

🛏 Sleeping

Carpinteria's cookie-cutter chain motels and hotels are unexciting, but usually less expensive than those just up the road in Santa Barbara.

Carpinteria State Beach Campground

CAMPGROUND $

(800-444-7275; www.reserveamerica.com; tent & RV drive-up sites $35-80, hike-and-bike tent sites $10;) Often crowded, this oceanfront campground offers lots of family-friendly amenities including flush toilets, hot showers, picnic tables and barbecue grills. Book ahead.

Eating & Drinking

Padaro Beach Grill

AMERICAN $

(3766 Santa Claus Ln; items $3-11; usually 10:30am-8pm Mon-Sat, from 11am Sun;) Off Hwy 101 west of downtown, this oceanfront grill makes darn good burgers, grilled fish tacos, sweet-potato fries and thick, hand-mixed milkshakes.

Tacos Don Roge

MEXICAN $

(751 Linden Ave; items from $1.50; 10am-9pm) This Mexican taquería stakes its reputation on a rainbow-colored salsa bar with up to a dozen different sauces to drizzle on piquant meat-stuffed, double-rolled corn tortillas – try the jalapeño or pineapple versions.

Corktree Cellars

CALIFORNIAN $$

(805-684-1400; www.corktreecellars.com; 910 Linden Ave; small plates $5-15; usually 11:30am-9pm Tue-Thu, to 10pm Fri & Sat, 10am-9pm Sun) Downtown's contemporary wine bar and bistro offers tasty California-style tapas, charcuterie and cheese plates, and a dizzying number of wine flights. Neglectful service can try diners' patience.

Island Brewing Co

BREWERY

(www.islandbrewingcompany.com; 5049 6th St, off Linden Ave; 2-9pm Mon-Fri, from 11am Sat & Sun;) Wanna hang loose with beach bums and drink bourbon barrel-aged brews? Find this locals-only, industrial space with an outdoor, dog-friendly patio by the railroad tracks.

Getting There & Away

Carpinteria is 11 miles east of Santa Barbara via Hwy 101 (southbound exit Linden Ave, northbound Casitas Pass Rd). From Santa Barbara, take MTD bus 20 ($1.75, 45 minutes, hourly) via Montecito and Summerland. **Amtrak** (800-872-7245; www.amtrak.com; 475 Linden Ave) has an unstaffed platform downtown; buy tickets online or by phone before catching one of five daily *Pacific Surfliner* trains south to Ventura ($11, 25 minutes) or LA ($29, 2¾ hours).

Ojai

POP 7560 / ELEV 745FT

Hollywood director Frank Capra chose the Ojai Valley to represent a mythical Shangri-la in his 1937 movie *Lost Horizon*. Today Ojai ('oh-hi', from the Chumash word for 'moon') attracts artists, organic farmers, spiritual seekers and anyone ready to indulge in day-spa pampering. Bring shorts and flip-flops: Shangri-la sure gets hot in summer.

Sights & Activities

Inside downtown's historic firehouse, **Ojai Vineyard** (805-798-3947; www.ojaivineyard.com; 109 S Montgomery St; tastings $15; noon-5pm) pours tastes of its delicate, small-batch wines. It's best known for standard-bearing Chardonnay, pinot noir and Syrah, but the crisp sauvignon blanc, dry Reisling and zippy rosé are also worth sampling. Outside town, take a free guided tour of the olive orchards and sample fruity and herb-infused oils at family-owned **Ojai Olive Oil Company** (805-646-5964; www.ojaioliveoil.com; 1811 Ladera Rd; usually hourly tours 1-4pm Wed & 10am-3pm Sat) FREE.

For the ultimate in relaxation, book a day at top-tier **Spa Ojai** (877-597-3731; www.ojairesort.com/spa-ojai/; Ojai Valley Inn & Spa, 905 Country Club Rd), where non-resort guests pay an extra $20 to access two swimming pools, a workout gym and mind/body fitness classes. Or unwind with an aromatherapy or hot-rock massage in a hobbitlike cottage at **Day Spa of Ojai** (805-640-1100; www.thedayspa.com; 1434 E Ojai Ave), about a mile east of downtown.

Running beside the highway, the 9-mile **Ojai Valley Trail**, converted from defunct railway tracks, is popular with walkers, runners, cyclists and equestrians. Pick it up downtown two blocks south of Ojai Ave, then pedal west through the valley. Rent bikes downtown at the **Mob Shop** (805-272-8102; www.themobshop.com; 110 W Ojai Ave; bicycle rental per day $25-50; 1-6pm Mon, 10am-5pm Tue-Fri, 9am-5pm Sat, 9am-4pm Sun).

Gather camping tips and trail maps for hiking to hot springs, waterfalls and mountaintop viewpoints in the **Los Padres National Forest** at the **Ojai Ranger Station** (805-646-4348; http://www.fs.usda.gov/lpnf; 1190 E Ojai Ave; 8am-4:30pm Mon-Fri) or on weekends at **Wheeler Gorge Visitors Center** (http://lpforest.org/wheeler; 17017

HAL BERGMAN / GETTY IMAGES ©

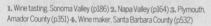

1. Wine tasting, Sonoma Valley (p186) 2. Napa Valley (p164) 3. Plymouth, Amador County (p351) 4. Wine maker, Santa Barbara County (p532)

SEAN BOGGS / GETTY IMAGES ©

California's Best Wine Countries

Vineyards never feel very far away in California, where world-beating wines wait to be tasted. The pleasures of California's many wine-producing regions hark back to nature: touring biodynamic farms and olive orchards, cycling along sunny back roads to tasting rooms, and dining at high-flying chefs' seasonally inspired kitchens.

Napa & Sonoma Valleys

In this premier wine-growing region, you can still unearth the uniqueness of terroir, where famed winemakers offer barrel tastings in sun-dappled vineyards. Chardonnay and Cabernet Sauvignon are especially esteemed in Napa.

Russian River Valley

In western Sonoma County, the Russian River's woodsy vineyards are revered for producing velvety, ruby-red Pinot Noir and bright Chardonnay, best sampled at intimate tasting rooms down winding country lanes.

Santa Barbara County

In the Santa Ynez and Santa Maria Valleys, follow rural wine trails and chat with winemakers while tippling biodynamic Pinot Noir.

Paso Robles

Renowned for its spicy and fruity Zinfandel, this hot, sunny wine country on the Central Coast hides dozens of wineries beside horse ranches, rural farmstands and boutique olive-oil makers.

Anderson Valley

In western Mendocino County, take a scenic drive through this pastoral valley, where apple orchards abound and delicate Alsatian-style whites, sparkling wines and soft Pinot Noir are poured.

Amador County

Up in the Sierra Nevada foothills, old Zinfandel vines absorb their uniquely bold, brambly character from the mineral-rich soil.

WORTH A TRIP

OJAI'S PINK MOMENT

Ojai is famous for the rosy glow that emanates from its mountains at sunset, the so-called 'Pink Moment.' The ideal vantage point for catching the show is the peaceful lookout atop **Meditation Mount** (https://meditationmount.org; 10340 Reeves Rd; ⊙10am-sunset Wed-Sun) FREE. Head east of downtown on Ojai Ave (Hwy 150) for about 2 miles, turn left at Boccali's farm-stand restaurant and drive another 2.5 miles on Reeves Rd until it dead-ends.

Maricopa Hwy; ⊙9am-3pm Sat & Sun), 8 miles north of Hwy 150 via Hwy 33.

🛏 Sleeping

★Blue Iguana Inn   INN $$
(☏805-646-5277; www.blueiguanainn.com; 11794 N Ventura Ave; r $129-199, ste from $159, all incl breakfast; 🐾🏊🐕) Artsy iguanas lurk everywhere at this funky architect-designed inn – on adobe walls around Mediterranean-tiled fountains and anywhere else that reptilian style could bring out a smile. Roomy bungalow and cottage suites are unique, and the pool is a social scene for LA denizens. Rates include continental breakfast; two-night minimum stay on weekends. Some pets allowed with prior approval only.

For a more romantic atmosphere, try the sister Emerald Iguana Inn, just north of downtown.

Ojai Retreat   B&B $$
(☏805-646-2536; www.ojairetreat.com; 160 Besant Rd; d incl breakfast $99-299; 🏊@🐾) On a hilltop on the outskirts of town, this peaceful nonprofit inn has a back-to-nature collection of remodeled, country Arts and Crafts–style guest rooms and cottage suites, all perfect for unplugging. Find a quiet nook for reading or writing, ramble through the woods or practice your downward dog in a yoga class. Rates include a healthy breakfast buffet.

Ojai Rancho Inn   MOTEL $$
(☏805-646-1434; http://ojairanchoinn.com; 615 W Ojai Ave; r $120-200; 🏊🐾🏊🐕) At this low-slung motel next to the highway, pine-paneled rooms each have a king bed. Cottage rooms come with fireplaces, and some have Jacuzzi tubs and kitchenettes. Besides competitive rates, the biggest bonuses of staying here are a small pool and sauna, shuffleboard, fire pit and bicycles to borrow for the half-mile ride to downtown. Pet fee $20.

Ojai Valley Inn & Spa   RESORT $$$
(☏855-697-8780, 805-646-1111; www.ojairesort.com; 905 Country Club Rd; r from $329; 🐾@🏊🐕) At the west end of town, this pampering resort has landscaped gardens, tennis courts, swimming pools, a championship golf course and a fabulous spa. Luxurious rooms are outfitted with all mod cons, and some sport a fireplace and balcony. Recreational activities run the gamut from kids' camps and bike rentals to full-moon yoga and astrological readings. Nightly 'service' surcharge $25.

🍴 Eating

Ojai Certified Farmers Market   MARKET $
(www.ojaicertifiedfarmersmarket.com; 300 E Matilija St; ⊙9am-1pm Sun; 🐾🍴) 🌿 Mingle with Ojai's bohemians at this rain-or-shine farmers market, where you'll find eggs, oils, jams, homemade bread and locally grown, organic-certified fruit, nuts and vegetables.

Farmer & the Cook   MEXICAN, VEGETARIAN $$
(http://farmerandcook.com; 339 W Roblar Ave; mains $7-14; ⊙8am-8:30pm; 🐾🍴) 🌿 The flavorful goodness of organic, homemade Mexican cooking bursts out of this tiny roadside market, which has its own farm nearby. Come for the squash and goat cheese tacos with fresh corn tortillas, saucy huevos rancheros or at dinner on weekends, creative pizzas and a salad bar.

Boccali's   ITALIAN $$
(☏805-646-6116; http://boccalis.com; 3277 Ojai-Santa Paula Rd; mains $10-18; ⊙4-9pm Mon & Tue, from noon Wed-Sun; 🍴) This roadside farm stand with red-and-white-checkered tablecloths does simple Italian cooking. Much of the produce is grown behind the restaurant, and the fresh tomato salad is often still warm from the garden. The real draw is wood oven-baked pizzas, which take time to make. No credit cards. It's over 2 miles east of downtown via Ojai Ave.

Hip Vegan VEGETARIAN $$
(www.hipvegancafe.com; 928 E Ojai Ave; mains $9-13; ⏰11am-5pm; 🅿🚲) 🍴 Tucked back from the street in a tiny garden, this locals' kitchen stays true to Ojai's granola-crunchy hippie roots with sprout-filled wraps, raw salads, fake-meat Reuben sandwiches and classic SoCal date shakes.

Knead BAKERY, CAFE $$
(http://kneadbakingcompany.com; 469 E Ojai Ave; items $3-16; ⏰8am-4pm Wed-Sun) Family-run artisan bakery mixes batters with the best of Ojai's fresh fruit, herbs, honey and nuts. Get a slice of a sweet tart or savory quiche, or a made-to-order breakfast sandwich. No credit cards.

🛍 Shopping

Arcade Plaza, a maze of Mission Revival-style buildings on Ojai Ave (downtown's main drag), is stuffed with gifty boutiques.

Bart's Books BOOKS
(www.bartsbooksojai.com; 302 W Matilija St; ⏰9:30am-sunset) One block north of Ojai Ave, this unique indoor-outdoor space sells new and well-loved tomes. It demands at least a half-hour's browse – just don't step on the lurking but surprisingly nimble cat.

Ojai Clothing CLOTHING
(http://ojaiclothing.com; 325 E Ojai Ave; ⏰noon-5pm Mon & Wed-Thu, noon-5:30pm Fri, 10am-5:30pm Sat, 11am-5pm Sun) Equally comfy for doing an interpretive dance or just hanging out, these earth-toned and vibrantly patterned casual pieces for women and men are made from soft cotton knits and woven fabrics.

Human Arts Gallery ARTS & CRAFTS
(www.humanartsgallery.com; 246 E Ojai Ave; ⏰11am-5pm Mon-Fri, to 6pm Sat, noon-5pm Sun) Browse the colorful handmade jewelry, sculpture, woodcarvings, glassworks, folk-art furnishings and more.

Soul Centered GIFTS, BOOKS
(www.soulcentered.com; 311 N Montgomery St; ⏰10:30am-6pm) A 'metaphysical shoppe' echoes Ojai's hippie-dippie vibe with healing crystals, dream therapy and magic books.

ℹ Information

Ojai Valley Chamber of Commerce (📞805-646-8126; www.ojaichamber.org; 206 N Signal St; ⏰9am-4pm Mon-Fri) Pick up free tourist maps and brochures here.
Ojai Library (111 E Ojai Ave; ⏰10am-8pm Mon-Thu, noon-5pm Fri-Sun) Free online computer terminals for public use.

ℹ Getting There & Away

Ojai is 33 miles east of Santa Barbara via scenic Hwy 150, or 15 miles inland (north) from Ventura via Hwy 33. On Main St at Ventura Ave in downtown Ventura, catch **Gold Coast Transit** (📞805-487-4222; www.goldcoasttransit.org) bus 16 to downtown Ojai ($1.50, 40 minutes, hourly).

Ventura

POP 107,735
The primary pushing-off point for Channel Island boat trips, the beach town of San Buenaventura may not look to be the most enchanting coastal city, but it has seaside charms, especially on the historic pier and

SANTA PAULA

Now calling itself 'the citrus capital of the world,' the small town of Santa Paula once found its treasure in black gold. If you've seen the movie *There Will Be Blood*, loosely based on the Upton Sinclair novel *Oil!*, then you already know that SoCal's early oil boom was a bloodthirsty business. Today the **California Oil Museum** (📞805-933-0076; www.oilmuseum.net; 1001 E Main St; adult/child 6-17yr $4/1; ⏰10am-4pm Wed-Sun) tells the story of Santa Paula's 'black bonanza' with modest historical exhibits that include an authentic 1890s drilling rig and a collection of vintage gas pumps. Afterward take a walk around downtown Santa Paula's historic district, painted with interesting outdoor murals. Pick up a free self-guided walking tour map inside the museum or one block north at the **chamber of commerce** (📞805-525-5561; www.discoversantapaula.com; 200 N 10th St, Santa Paula; ⏰10am-2pm Mon-Fri, gift shop 10am-noon & 1-4pm Mon-Fri, noon-4pm Sat & Sun). Santa Paula is a 16-mile drive east of Ventura or Ojai, at the intersection of Hwys 126 and 150.

downtown along Main St, north of Hwy 101 via California St.

⊙ Sights & Activities

South of Hwy 101 via Harbor Blvd, **Ventura Harbor** is the main departure point for boats to Channel Islands National Park.

San Buenaventura State Beach   BEACH
(☑ 805-968-1033; www.parks.ca.gov; enter off San Pedro St; per car $10; ⊙ dawn-dusk; ⊕) Along the waterfront off Hwy 101, this long white-sand beach is ideal for swimming, surfing or just lazing on the sand. A recreational cycling path connects to nearby **Emma Wood State Beach**, another popular spot for swimming, surfing and fishing.

Mission San Buenaventura   CHURCH
(☑ 805-643-4318; www.sanbuenaventuramission.org; 211 E Main St; adult/child under 18yr $4/1; ⊙ 10am-5pm Mon-Fri, 9am-5pm Sat, 10am-4pm Sun) Ventura's Spanish-colonial roots go back to this last mission founded by Junípero Serra in California. A stroll around the mellow parish church leads you through a garden courtyard and a small museum, past statues of saints, centuries-old religious paintings and unusual wooden bells.

Limoneira   FARM
(☑ 805-525-5541; www.limoneira.com; 1131 Cummings Rd, Santa Paula; tours $20-40; ⊙ call for hrs) ⚲ A 20-minute drive from downtown, this working farm lets you get up close to sniff the fruit Ventura is most famous for growing: lemons. Drop by the historical ranch store and play bocce outside, or book ahead for a guided tour of the modern packing house and sea-view orchards.

Museum of Ventura County   MUSEUM
(☑ 805-653-0323; http://venturamuseum.org; 100 E Main St; adult/child 6-17yr $5/1; ⊙ 11am-5pm Tue-Sun) This tiny downtown museum has a mishmash of displays including Chumash baskets, vintage wooden surfboards and a massive stuffed California condor with wings outspread. Temporary exhibits usually spotlight local history and art.

🛏 Sleeping & Eating

Midrange motels and high-rise beachfront hotels cluster off Hwy 101 in Ventura. For better deals, keep driving on Hwy 101 southbound about 15 miles to Camarillo, where chain lodgings abound.

In downtown Ventura, Main St is chocka-block with Mexicali taco shops, casual cafes and globally flavored kitchens.

Ventura Certified Farmers Market   MARKET $
(http://vccfarmersmarkets.com; cnr Santa Clara & Palm Sts; ⊙ 8:30am-noon Sat; 🚗 ⊕) ⚲ Over 45 farmers and food vendors show up each week, offering fresh fruits and vegetables, homebaked bread and ready-made meals – Mediterranean, Mexican and more. Another farmers market sets up at midtown's Pacific View Mall from 9am to 1pm on Wednesdays.

Jolly Oyster   SEAFOOD $$
(911 San Pedro St; items $5-16; ⊙ noon-7pm Fri, from 11am Sat & Sun; ⊕) ⚲ At San Buenaventura State Beach, this happy-go-lucky seafood shack vends its own farm-raised Kumamoto and Pacific oysters and Manila clams. Seat yourself at picnic tables to shuck 'em raw or cook 'em yourself on barbecue grills. A short menu of tacos, tostadas, ceviche and salads changes weekly. One-hour parking free.

★ Lure Fish House   SEAFOOD $$$
(☑ 805-567-4400; www.lurefishhouse.com; 60 S California St; mains lunch $10-22, dinner $15-33; ⊙ 11:30am-9pm Sun-Tue, to 10pm Wed-Thu, to 11pm Fri & Sat; ⊕) ⚲ For seafood any fresher, you'd have to catch it yourself off Ventura pier. Go nuts ordering off a stalwart menu of sustainably caught seafood, organic regional farm produce and California wines. Make reservations or turn up at the bar during happy hour (4pm to 6pm Monday to Friday, 11:30am to 6pm Sunday) for strong cocktails, fried calamari and charbroiled oysters.

🍷 Drinking & Nightlife

You'll find plenty of rowdy dives down by the harbor.

Surf Brewery   BREWERY
(☑ 805-644-2739; http://surfbrewery.com; suite A, 4561 Market St; ⊙ 4-9pm Tue-Thu, from 1pm Fri, noon-9pm Sat, noon-7pm Sun) Ventura's newest microbrewery makes big waves with its hoppy and black IPAs and rye American pale ale. Beer geeks and food trucks gather at the sociable taproom in an industrial area, about 5 miles from downtown (take Hwy 101 southbound, exit Donlon St).

Wine Rack   WINE BAR
(☑ 805-653-9463; http://thewineracklounge.com; 14 S California St; ⊙ 2-10pm Tue-Thu, to midnight Fri, noon-midnight Sat, noon-6pm Sun) At this upbeat wine shop, novices can sidle up to

the bar for a wine flight, loiter over a cheese plate, flatbread pizza or fondue and listen to live music Thursday to Saturday nights.

🛍 Shopping

B on Main   GIFTS
(www.bonmain.com; 337 E Main St; ⊘10:30am-6pm Mon-Fri, 10am-8pm Sat, 11am-5pm Sun) For coastal living, B sells nifty reproductions of vintage surf posters, shabby-chic furnishings, SoCal landscape art, locally made jewelry and beachy clothing for women.

Ormachea   JEWELRY
(www.ormacheajewelry.com; 451 E Main St) Run by a third-generation Peruvian jewelry craftsman, Ormachea skillfullly hammers out one-of-a-kind, handmade rings, pendants and bangles in a downtown studio.

ARC Foundation Thrift Store   VINTAGE
(www.arcvc.org; 265 E Main St; ⊘9am-6pm Mon-Sat, 10am-5pm Sun) Loads of thrift stores, antiques malls and secondhand and vintage shops cluster downtown. Most are on Main St, west of California St, where ARC is always jam-packed with bargain hunters.

Rocket Fizz   FOOD & DRINK
(www.rocketfizz.com; 105 S Oak St; ⊘10:30am-7pm Sun-Thu, to 9pm Fri & Sat) Retro-style soda pop and old-fashioned candy store is genius for stocking your cooler before a day at the beach.

Camarillo Premium Outlets   MALL
(www.premiumoutlets.com/camarillo; 740 E Ventura Blvd, Camarillo; ⊘10am-9pm Mon-Sat, to 8pm Sun) For steeply discounted designer duds, from LA's Kitson to Nike, Neiman Marcus and North Face, drive about 20 minutes from Ventura on Hwy 101 southbound.

ℹ Information

Ventura Visitors & Convention Bureau
(☑805-648-2075, 800-483-6214; www.ventura-usa.com; 101 S California St; ⊘9-5pm Mon-Sat, 10am-4pm Sun Mar-Oct, till 4pm daily Nov-Feb) Downtown visitor center hands out free maps and tourist brochures.

ℹ Getting There & Away

Ventura is about 30 miles southeast of Santa Barbara via Hwy 101. **Amtrak** (☑800-872-7245; www.amtrak.com; Harbor Blvd at Figueroa St) operates five daily trains north to Santa Barbara ($15, 45 minutes) via Carpinteria and south to LA ($24, 2¼ hours). Amtrak's platform station is unstaffed; buy tickets in advance online or by phone. **Vista** (☑800-438-1112; www.goventura.org) runs several daily 'Coastal Express' buses between downtown Ventura and Santa Barbara ($3, 40 to 70 minutes) via Carpinteria; check online or call for schedules.

Channel Islands National Park

Don't let this off-the-beaten-path **national park** (www.nps.gov/chis) FREE loiter for too long on your lifetime to-do list. It's easier to access than you might think, and the payoff is immense. Imagine hiking, kayaking, scuba diving, camping and whale-watching, and doing it all amid a raw, end-of-the-world landscape. Rich in unique species of flora and fauna, tide pools and kelp forests, the islands are home to 145 plant and animal species found nowhere else in the world, earning them the nickname 'California's Galapagos.'

Geographically, the Channel Islands are an eight-island chain off the Southern California coast, stretching from Santa Barbara

---

CALIFORNIA'S CHANNEL ISLANDS: PARADISE LOST & FOUND

Human beings have left a heavy footprint on the Channel Islands. Livestock overgrazed, causing erosion, and rabbits fed on native plants. The US military even used San Miguel as a practice bombing range. In 1969 an offshore oil spill engulfed the northern islands in an 800-sq-mile slick, killing off uncountable seabirds and mammals. Meanwhile, deep-sea fishing has caused the destruction of three-quarters of the islands' kelp forests, which are key to the marine ecosystem.

Despite past abuses, the future isn't all bleak. Brown pelicans – decimated by the effects of DDT and reduced to one surviving chick on Anacapa Island in 1970 – have rebounded. On San Miguel Island, native vegetation has returned a half century after overgrazing sheep were removed. On Santa Cruz Island, the National Park Service and the Nature Conservancy have implemented multiyear plans to eliminate invasive plants and feral pigs, and hopefully their recovery efforts will meet with success.

ISLAND OF THE BLUE DOLPHINS

For bedtime reading aloud around the campfire, pick up Scott O'Dell's Newberry Medal–winning *Island of the Blue Dolphins*. This children's novel was inspired by the true life story of a Native American girl left behind on San Nicolas Island during the early 19th century, when indigenous people were forced off the Channel Islands. Incredibly the girl survived mostly alone on the island for 18 years, living in a whale-bone hut and sourcing water from a spring, before being rescued in 1853. However, fate was still not on her side: she died just seven weeks after being brought to the mainland. Today her body lies buried in the graveyard at Mission Santa Barbara, where a commemorative plaque is inscribed with her Christian baptismal name, Juana María.

to San Diego. Five of them – San Miguel, Santa Rosa, Santa Cruz, Anacapa and tiny Santa Barbara – comprise Channel Islands National Park. Originally the islands were inhabited by Chumash tribespeople, who were forced to move to mainland Catholic missions by Spanish military forces in the early 1800s. The islands were subsequently taken over by Mexican and American ranchers during the 19th century and the US military in the 20th, until conservation efforts began in the 1970s and '80s.

Sights & Activities

Anacapa and Santa Cruz, the park's most popular islands, are within an hour's boat ride of Ventura. Anacapa is a doable day trip, while Santa Cruz is better suited for overnight camping. Bring plenty of water, because none is available on either island except at Scorpion Ranch Campground on Santa Cruz.

Most visitors arrive during summer, when island conditions are hot, dusty and bone-dry. Better times to visit are during the spring wildflower bloom or in early fall, when the fog clears. Winter can be stormy, but it's also great for wildlife-watching, especially whales.

Before you shove off from the mainland, stop by Ventura Harbor's NPS Visitor Center (p554) for educational natural history exhibits, a free 25-minute nature film and on weekends and holidays, family-friendly activities and ranger talks.

Anacapa Island

Actually three separate islets totaling just over 1 sq mi, Anacapa gives a memorable introduction to the islands' ecology. It's the best option if you're short on time. Boats dock year-round on the East Island and after a short climb, you'll find 2 miles of trails offering fantastic views of island flora, a historic lighthouse, and rocky Middle and West Islands. Kayaking, diving, tide-pooling and watching seals and sea lions are popular activities here. Inside the small museum at the island's visitors center, scuba divers with video cameras occasionally broadcast images to a TV monitor you can watch during spring and summer.

Santa Cruz Island

Santa Cruz, the largest island at 96 sq miles, claims two mountain ranges and the park's tallest peak, Mt Diablo (2450ft). The western three-quarters of Santa Cruz is mostly wilderness owned and managed by the Nature Conservancy (www.nature.org) and it can only be accessed with a permit (apply online at www.nature.org/cruzpermit). However, the remaining eastern quarter, managed by the National Park Service (NPS), packs a wallop – ideal for those wanting an action-packed day trip or a more laid-back overnight trip. You can swim, snorkel, scuba dive and kayak. Rangers meet incoming boats at Scorpion Anchorage, a short walk from historic Scorpion Ranch.

There are rugged hikes too, which are best not attempted at midday as there's little shade. It's a 1-mile climb to captivating Cavern Point. Views don't get much better than from this windy spot. For a longer jaunt, continue 1.5 miles west mostly along scenic bluffs to Potato Harbor. From Scorpion Anchorage, the 4.5-mile Scorpion Canyon Loop heads uphill to an old oil well for fantastic views, then drops through Scorpion Canyon to the campground. Alternatively, follow Smugglers Rd all the way to the cobblestone beach at Smugglers Cove, a strenuous 7.5-mile round-trip from Scorpion Anchorage.

Other Islands

The Chumash called **Santa Rosa** 'Wima' (driftwood) because of the redwood logs that often came ashore here, with which they built plank canoes called *tomols*. This 84-sq-mile island has rare Torrey pines, sandy beaches and hundreds of plant and bird species. Beach, canyon and grasslands hiking trails abound, but high winds can make swimming, diving and kayaking tough for anyone but experts.

While 14-sq-mile **San Miguel** can guarantee solitude and a remote wilderness experience, it's often windy and shrouded in fog. Some sections are off-limits to prevent disruption of the island's fragile ecosystem, which includes a caliche forest (containing hardened calcium-carbonate castings of trees and vegetation) and seasonal colonies of seals and sea lions.

Santa Barbara, only 1 sq mile in size and the smallest of the islands, is a jewel-box for nature lovers. Big, blooming coreopsis, cream cups and chicory are just a few of the island's memorable plant species. You'll also find the humongous northern elephant seal here as well as Scripps's murrelets, a bird that nests in cliff crevices. Get more information from the island's small visitor center.

Tours

Most trips require a minimum number of participants, and may be canceled due to high surf or weather conditions.

Island Packers CRUISE
(☑ 805-642-1393; www.islandpackers.com; 1691 Spinnaker Dr, Ventura; 3hr cruise adult/child 3-12yr from $36/26) Offers wildlife cruises year-round, including seasonal whale-watching excursions from late December to mid-April (gray whales) and mid-May through mid-September (blue and humpback whales).

> **MOVING ON?**
>
> For tips, recommendations and reviews, head to shop.lonelyplanet.com to purchase a downloadable PDF of the Central Coast chapter from Lonely Planet's *California* guide.

Santa Barbara Adventure Company KAYAKING
(☑ 805-884-9283, 877-885-9283; www.sbadventureco.com; 32 E Haley St, Santa Barbara; ☑) This family-friendly outfitter runs a variety of guided paddling tours, from the sea caves of Santa Cruz to the sea arches of Anacapa. Choose from day trips ($180 to $210) or overnight camping expeditions (from $329).

Channel Islands Outfitters KAYAKING, SNORKELING
(☑ 805-899-4925; www.channelislandso.com; 117b Harbor Way, Santa Barbara) Expertly guided kayaking and snorkeling trips visit Anacapa, Santa Cruz or Santa Barbara ($99 to $225, plus ferry tickets); wetsuits are included.

Truth Aquatics DIVING, KAYAKING
(☑ 805-962-1127; www.truthaquatics.com; 301 W Cabrillo Blvd, Santa Barbara) Based in Santa Barbara, this long-running outfitter organizes diving, kayaking and hiking day trips and multiday excursions aboard specially designed dive boats. See website for prices.

Raptor Dive Charters DIVING
(☑ 805-650-7700; www.raptordive.com; 1559 Spinnaker Dr, Ventura) For certified and experienced divers, boat trips to Anacapa and Santa Cruz, including night dives, cost $110 to $125; equipment rentals available for a surcharge.

Aquasports KAYAKING
(☑ 800-773-2309, 805-968-7231; www.islandkayaking.com) Led by naturalist guides, day and

CHANNEL ISLANDS NATIONAL PARK CAMPGROUNDS

CAMPGROUND	NUMBER OF SITES	ACCESS FROM BOAT LANDING	DESCRIPTION
Anacapa	7	0.5-mile walk with over 150 stairs	High, rocky, sun-exposed and isolated
Santa Cruz (Scorpion Ranch)	31	Flat 0.5-mile walk	Popular with groups; often crowded and partly shady
Santa Barbara	10	Steep 0.25-mile walk uphill	Large, grassy and surrounded by trails
San Miguel	9	Steep 1-mile walk uphill	Windy, often foggy with volatile weather
Santa Rosa	15	Flat 1.5-mile walk	Eucalyptus grove in a windy canyon

❶ CHANNEL CROSSINGS

The open seas on the boat ride out to the Channel Islands may feel choppy to landlubbers. To avoid seasickness, sit outside on the upper deck, away from the diesel fumes in back. The outbound trip is typically against the wind and a bit bumpier than the return. Over-the-counter motion-sickness pills (eg Dramamine) can make you drowsy. Staring at the horizon may help. Boats usually brake when dolphins or whales are spotted – always a welcome distraction from any nausea.

overnight kayaking trips to Santa Cruz, Anacapa and Santa Barbara ($125 to $245, plus ferry tickets) leave from Ventura Harbor.

Channel Islands Kayak Center KAYAKING (☎ 805-984-5995; www.cikayak.com; 1691 Spinnaker Dr, Ventura; ⊙ by appt only) Book ahead to rent kayaks (single/double per day $35/55) or arrange a private guided kayaking tour of Santa Cruz or Anacapa (from $200 per person, two-person minimum).

🛏 Sleeping

Each island has a primitive year-round **campground** (☎ reservations 877-444-6777; www.recreation.gov; tent sites $15) with pit toilets and picnic tables. Water is only available on Santa Rosa and Santa Cruz Islands. You must pack everything in and out, including trash. Due to fire danger, campfires aren't allowed, but enclosed gas campstoves are OK. Advance reservations are required for all island campsites.

❶ Information

NPS Visitor Center (☎ 805-658-5730; www.nps.gov/chis; 1901 Spinnaker Dr, Ventura; ⊙ 8:30am-5pm; 🚻) Trip-planning information, books and maps are available on the mainland at the far end of Ventura Harbor.

❶ Getting There & Away

You can access the national park by taking a boat from Ventura or Oxnard or a plane from Camarillo. Trips may be canceled anytime due to high surf or weather conditions. Reservations are essential for weekends, holidays and summer trips.

Island Packers (☎ 805-642-1393; www.islandpackers.com; 1691 Spinnaker Dr, Ventura; round-trip fare adult/child 3-12yr from $59/41) From Ventura Harbor and Oxnard, Island Packers offers regularly scheduled boat service to all islands. Day trips to Anacapa and Santa Rosa are less expensive than visiting other islands; campers pay an additional surcharge. Be forewarned: if you camp overnight and seas are rough the following day, you could get stuck for an extra night or more.

Channel Islands Aviation (☎ 805-987-1301; www.flightstothechannelislands.com; 305 Durley Ave, Camarillo) If you're prone to seasickness, you can take a 25-minute scenic flight to Santa Rosa Island from Camarillo. Half-day packages (per person $160 to $220) include hiking or a guided 4WD tour, while overnight camping excursions (per person $300) are more DIY. Ask about surf-fishing charter trips.

Los Angeles

Best Places to Eat

➡ Bestia (p578)
➡ Sushi Gen (p578)
➡ Fishing with Dynamite (p563)
➡ Bar Ama' (p579)
➡ Elf Cafe (p580)

Best Places to Stay

➡ Palihouse (p577)
➡ Chateau Marmont (p572)
➡ Terranea (p563)
➡ Ace Hotel (p571)
➡ Vibe Hotel (p571)

Why Go?

LA runs deeper than her blonde beaches, bosomy hills and ubiquitous beemers would have you believe. She's a myth. A beacon for countless small-town dreamers, rockers and risk-takers, an open-minded angel who encourages her people to live and let live without judgment or shame. She has given us Quentin Tarantino, Jim Morrison and Serena and Venus Williams, spawned skateboarding and gangsta rap, popularized implants, electrolysis and Spandex, and has nurtured not just great writers, performers and directors, but also the ground-breaking yogis who first brought Eastern wisdom to the Western world.

LA is best defined by those simple life-affirming moments. A cracked-ice, jazz-age cocktail on Beverly Blvd, a hike high into the Hollywood Hills sagebrush, a swirling pod of dolphins off Point Dume, a pink-washed sunset over a thundering Venice Beach drum circle, the perfect taco. And her night music. There is always night music.

When to Go
Los Angeles

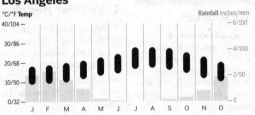

Feb The red carpet is rolled out for the Academy Awards. Prime time for celeb-spotting.	**Apr & Sep** Most tourists visit when the sun shines the brightest on LA's golden sands.
	Oct–Nov & Jan–Mar The region's two distinct (not that) wet seasons.

DON'T MISS

On a balmy summer evening, there are few better places to find yourself than at art deco Dodger Stadium (p586), where the sunsets are stunning, the beer cold, the crowd passionate and the ball club a consistent winner.

Fast Facts: LA County

➡ **Population** 9,963,000

➡ **Area** 4,060 sq miles

➡ **Major movie studios** six

➡ **Unsold screenplays** countless

Planning your Trip

Think about what you want to see and where you want to hang out, and book accommodation accordingly. We suggest moving around the city, staying for a few nights each in different neighborhoods.

Book your accommodation at http://hotels.lonelyplanet.com.

Resources

➡ **www.laobserved.com** Offers a high-brow, independent and incisive perspective on the inner workings of the city – from arts to fashion to politics to dining.

LA Now

Now is an exciting time to visit LA. Downtown is booming, tech money has turned Santa Monica and Venice into Silicon Beach, and Echo Park and Highland Park bring the Eastside cool. The economy is thriving, and an open and experimental climate energizes the art, architecture, music and fashion scenes, while LA's eclectic palate is challenged and sated by progressive chefs who source from local growers, who flaunt their earthy goods at hundreds of weekly outdoor farmers markets throughout the city.

DON'T MISS

The sheer abundance of world-class musicians within LA's orbit, paired with spectacular and historic venues, make it a minor tragedy to leave town without a concert in the memory files. The Hollywood Bowl, which aside from being the summer home of the LA Philharmonic, has hosted countless legends from Ella to Radiohead. Sitting beneath and among the stars, in a natural bowl tucked into the Hollywood Hills, while music washes over you will make you feel all kinds of glamorous. A second, and only slightly less tasty, summertime venue is the Greek Theatre (p584) – another nature-cupped outdoor amphitheater, which hosts rock and pop acts from MGMT to Gary Clark Jr to Wilco.

The music doesn't stop when the weather turns. The Walt Disney Concert Hall, the winter base for the LA Phil, is an architectural masterwork and also hosts jazz giants.

Acoustic troubadours hold pre-tour residencies at the **Bootleg Theater** (www.bootlegtheater.org; 2220 Beverly Blvd) in Silver Lake, and the recently renovated United Artists Theatre (p584) (adjacent to uber-cool Ace Hotel (p571) downtown), launched with a stirring show by Spiritualized.

LA's Best Beaches

➡ Westward Beach is often overshadowed by Zuma to the north, but this wide sweep of sand rambles all the way to Point Dume. Seals, sea lions and dolphins are frequently glimpsed beyond the break.

➡ El Matador State Beach is defined by sandstone rock spires that rise from the swirling azure sea, and its top-optional ethos.

➡ Venice Beach offers boardwalk, body builders, street ballers, skate rats and hippies old and new peddling goods bizarre, bland and beautiful. The Sunday drum circle is an institution.

⊙ Sights & Activities

⊙ Downtown Los Angeles

Downtown Los Angeles is historical, multi-layered and fascinating. It's a city within a city, blessed with landmark architecture and superb kitchens for all budgets. It's a power nexus with City Hall, the courts and the hall of records, and an ethnic mosaic. Yet just 15 years ago it was still a relative ghost town at night when it was abandoned to the skid-row tramps and addicts, and the ravers who braved the scene for a warehouse or loft party in rickety relics. But today its streets are alive with young professionals, designers and artists who have snapped up stylish lofts in rehabbed art-deco buildings, and the growing gallery district along Main and Spring Sts draws thousands to its monthly art walks. And speaking of art, street art is everywhere. It's as if an entire city has something to say in just a few blocks. Start at **Olvera Street** (Map p560; www.calleolvera.com; 🚇), where the original Mexican city was founded, then stroll from **Little Tokyo** to **Chinatown** (www.chinatown-la.com) to the **Fashion District** (Map p560; www.fashiondistrict.org). Don't miss the molten blend of steel music and psychedelic architecture that is Frank Gehry's **Walt Disney Concert Hall** (Map p560; ☑ info 213-972-7211, tickets 323-850-2000; www.laphil.org; 111 S Grand Ave; ⊙ guided tours usually noon & 1pm Tue-Sat; 🅿) FREE. **Union Station** (Map p560; ⊙ 6am-6:30pm Mon-Fri) is an architectural classic from a bygone era. **Museum of Contemporary Art** (MOCA; Map p560; ☑ 213-626-6222; www.moca.org; 250 S Grand Ave; adult/child $12/free, 5-8pm Thu free; ⊙ 11am-5pm Mon & Fri, to 8pm Thu, to 6pm Sat & Sun) is downtown's best museum, followed closely by the **Grammy Museum** (Map p560; www.grammymuseum.org; 800 W Olympic Blvd; adult/child $13/11, after 6pm $8; ⊙ 11:30am-7:30pm Mon-Fri, from 10am Sat & Sun; 🚇) in the **LA Live** (Map p560; www.lalive.com; 800 W Olympic Blvd) complex.

⊙ Hollywood

Dear sweet Hollywood, the vortex of a global entertainment industry, has some backstory. First, there was the Golden Age, the dawn of motion pictures, when industry strongmen ruled and owned it all. Then the '70s happened, which brought edgy productions even while studios fled in search of more space in Burbank and Studio City. Soon the only 'stars' left were embedded in the sidewalk. Worse, you had to hopscotch around runaways and addicts to see them. In the late '90s the momentum began to shift, and over the next 10 years, big, intelligent dollars, along with a touch of smart design flooded the area and transformed it into what it is today. A gleaming, bustling, gritty, dazzling mosh pit of fun, food and questionable behavior.

⭐**Hollywood Bowl** LANDMARK
(www.hollywoodbowl.com; 2301 Highland Ave; rehearsals free, performance costs vary; ⊙ Apr-Sep; 🅿) Summers in LA wouldn't be the same without this chill spot for symphonies under the stars, and big-name acts from Baaba Maal and Sigur Rós to Radiohead and Paul McCartney. A huge natural amphitheater, the Hollywood Bowl has been around since 1922 and has great sound.

Hollywood Walk of Fame LANDMARK
(Map p564; www.walkoffame.com; Hollywood Blvd) Big Bird, Bob Hope, Marilyn Monroe and Aretha Franklin are among the stars being sought out, worshiped, photographed and stepped on along the Hollywood Walk of Fame. Since 1960 more than 2400 performers – from legends to bit-part players – have been honored with a pink-marble sidewalk star.

Grauman's Chinese Theatre LANDMARK
(Map p564; ☑ 323-463-9576; www.tclchinesetheatres.com; 6925 Hollywood Blvd; tours & movie tickets adult/child/senior $13.50/6.50/11.50) Ever wondered what it's like to be in George Clooney's shoes? Just find his footprints in the forecourt of this world-famous movie palace. The exotic pagoda theater – complete with temple bells and stone heaven dogs from China – has shown movies since 1927 when Cecil B DeMille's *The King of Kings* first flickered across the screen.

Hollywood Sign LANDMARK
(Map p566) LA's most famous landmark first appeared in the hills in 1923 as an advertising gimmick for a real-estate development called 'Hollywoodland'. Each letter is 50ft tall and made of sheet metal. Once aglow with 4000 light bulbs, the sign even had its own caretaker who lived behind the 'L' until 1939.

Hollywood Museum MUSEUM
(Map p564; ☑ 323-464-7776; www.thehollywoodmuseum.com; 1660 N Highland Ave; adult/child $15/5; ⊙ 10am-5pm Wed-Sun) We quite like this musty temple to the stars, crammed with

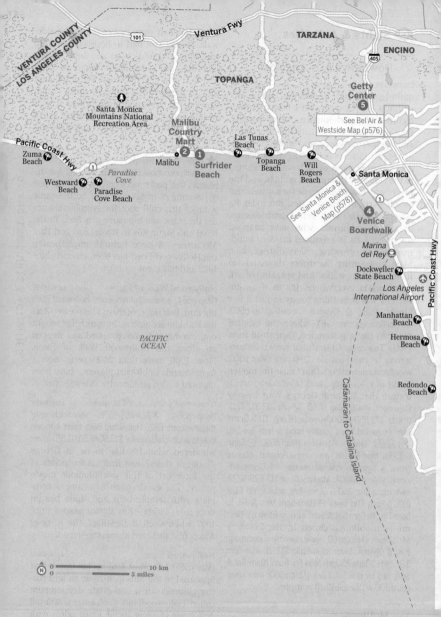

Los Angeles Highlights

1 Watching surfers carve waves at **Surfrider Beach** (p565) in Malibu.

2 Shopping like a star at **Malibu Country Mart** (p588).

3 Swerving along breathtaking Palos Verdes Drive, then hunting for starfish and anemones in the tide pools of **Abalone Cove Shoreline Park** (p563).

4 Getting your freak on while milling with snake charmers, tarot readers and athletes on the **Venice Boardwalk** (p566).

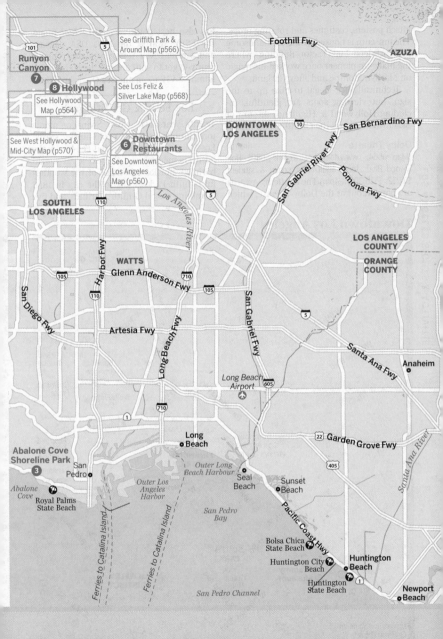

5 Feeling your spirits soar surrounded by the fantastic art, architecture, views and gardens of the **Getty Center** (p563).

6 Getting gourmet at one of several outstanding **downtown restaurants** (p578).

7 Joining the buff, the famous and their canine companions on a hike through **Runyon Canyon** (p563).

8 Hitting the bars and clubs of **Hollywood** (p583) for a night of tabloid-worthy decadence and debauchery.

kitsch posters, costumes and rotating props. The museum is housed inside the handsome 1914 art-deco Max Factor Building, where the make-up pioneer once worked his magic on Marilyn Monroe and Judy Garland.

Technically, it's illegal to hike up to the sign, but viewing spots are plentiful, including Hollywood & Highland, the top of Beachwood Dr and the Griffith Observatory.

Dolby Theatre   THEATER
(Map p564; www.dolbytheatre.com; 6801 Hollywood Blvd; tours adult/child, senior & student $17/12; ⊙10:30am-4pm) The Academy Awards are handed out at the Dolby Theatre, which

has also hosted the *American Idol* finale, the ESPY awards, the Miss USA pageant and a recent Neil Young residency. On the tour you get to sniff around the auditorium, admire a VIP room and see Oscar up close.

Los Feliz & Griffith Park

Twenty years ago, when Swingers mania tore through LA like a proto-hipster storm, Los Feliz, (mis-) pronounced Fee-lez by the hordes, emerged as LA's next great neighborhood, not least because of the wonderful Griffith Park. A gift to the city in 1896 by mining mogul Griffith J Griffith, and five

Downtown Los Angeles

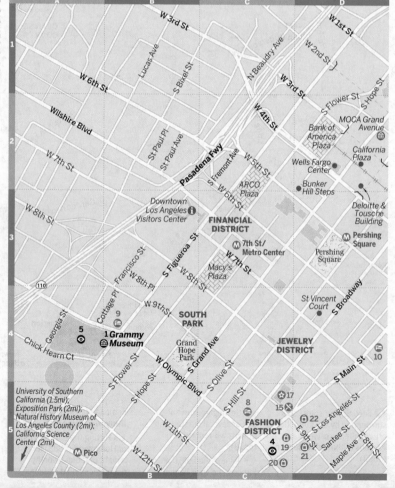

times the size of New York's Central Park, **Griffith Park** (Map p566; 323-913-4688; www.laparks.org/dos/parks/griffithpk; 4730 Crystal Springs Dr; 5am-10:30pm, trails sunrise-sunset; P) FREE is one of the country's largest urban green spaces. There you'll find a major outdoor theater, the city zoo, two museums, golf courses, playgrounds, 53 miles of **hiking trails**, Batman's caves and the Hollywood sign. It's crowned by the iconic 1935 **Observatory** (Map p566; 213-473-0800; www.griffithobservatory.org; 2800 E Observatory Rd; admission free, planetarium shows adult/child $7/3; noon-10pm Tue-Fri, from 10am Sat & Sun; P)

FREE, a first-class planetarium and wonderful Instagram photo-op. Don't miss it.

Silver Lake & Echo Park

Behold the Silver Lake ideal – revitalized modernist homes, groovy bistros, coffee-houses and boutiques patronized by a real community of upwardly mobile, progressive creatives. Which is to say, Silver Lake, a once-gritty Eastside hub has long since gentrified. Rents have soared, working-class Latino families were pushed out and yuppie babies came along with gaggles of East-side soccer moms pushing jogger strollers

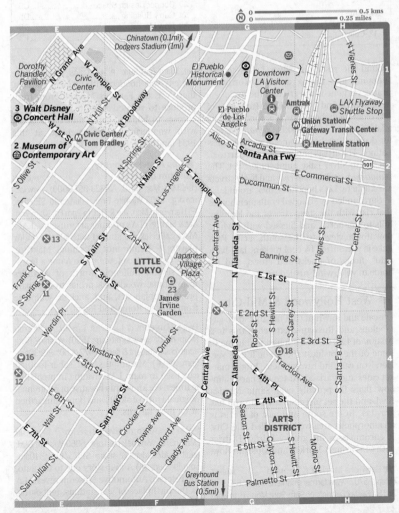

Downtown Los Angeles

around the reservoir. Silver Lake's terrific shopping and dining are still worthy of praise, yet gone is the grit and the funk.

But you'll find both in Echo Park. One of LA's oldest neighborhoods, it is punctuated by a lake featured in Polanski's *Chinatown,* and for decades has been home to working-class Latinos. The artists and hipsters have arrived, but not in Silver Lake numbers just yet. The *panaderias* and *cevicherias* and lively streets are still here. Let's hope they stick around.

Surrounded by shingled craftsmen homes that rise with the steep streets and looming hills to the north, and blessed with keyhole downtown views to the south, Echo Park Lake is patronized by cool rockers, laid-back vatos, flocks of ducks and crows, and it's home to wild, wind-rustled palms.

◎ West Hollywood & Mid-City

Upscale and low-rent (but not that low), gay fabulous and Russian-ghetto chic, this is a bastion of LA's fashionista best and home to some of the trashiest shops you'll ever see. Here you can find raw kitchens, bright market cafes and dark-edged tequila bars. Rainbow flags fly proudly over Santa Monica Blvd, and the set piece Sunset Strip still has gravitas. To the south and east of WeHo is an amorphous area we have called Mid-City. It encompasses the groovy Fairfax District with the Farmers Market, and Museum Row.

★ **Farmers Market & Around** MARKET
(Map p570; www.farmersmarketla.com; 6333 W 3rd St, Fairfax District; ⊘ 9am-9pm Mon-Fri, to 8pm Sat, 10am-7pm Sun; P ☉) FREE Long before the city was flooded with farmers markets, there was the Farmers Market. From fresh produce to roasted nuts, to doughnuts to cheeses to blinis – you'll find them, along with wonderful people-watching, at this 1934 landmark. Perfect for families.

★ **Los Angeles County Museum of Art** MUSEUM
(LACMA; Map p570; ☎ 323-857-6000; www.lacma.org; 5905 Wilshire Blvd; adult/child $15/free; ⊘ 11am-5pm Mon, Tue & Thu, to 9pm Fri, 10am-7pm Sat & Sun; P) LA's premier art museum, LACMA's galleries are stuffed with all the major players – Rembrandt, Cézanne, Magritte, Mary Cassat, Ansel Adams, to name a few – plus several millennia worth of ceramics from China, woodblock prints from Japan, pre-Columbian art, and ancient sculpture from Greece, Rome and Egypt.

Page Museum & La Brea Tar Pits MUSEUM
(Map p570; www.tarpits.org; 5801 Wilshire Blvd; adult/child/student & senior $7/2/4.50; ⊘ 9:30am-5pm; P ☉) Mammoths and saber-toothed cats used to roam LA's savanna in prehistoric times. We know this because of an archaeological trove of skulls and bones unearthed at La Brea Tar Pits.

Petersen Automotive Museum MUSEUM
(Map p570; www.petersen.org; 6060 Wilshire Blvd; adult/child/student & senior $15/5/10; ⊘ 10am-6pm Tue-Sun; P) A four-story ode to the auto, the Petersen Automotive Museum reveals LA as the birthplace of gas stations, billboards, drive-in restaurants and drive-in movie

theaters. Glimpse hot rods, movie cars and celebrity-owned rarities.

Ace Gallery
GALLERY

(Map p570; www.acegallery.net; 5514 Wilshire Blvd; ☺10am-6pm Tue-Sat) An amazing gallery sprawls the entire 2nd floor of the Desmond building (c 1927). The art is all modern-edged works from the likes of Bernar Venet, Gary Lang, Gisele Colon and Peter Alexander.

Sunset Strip
STREET

(Map p570; Sunset Blvd) A visual cacophony of billboards, giant ad banners and neon signs, the sinuous stretch of Sunset Blvd running between Laurel Canyon and Doheny Dr has been nightlife central since the 1920s.

These days, it seems to be coasting on its legacy. The young, hip and fickle have moved west to Abbot Kinney and east to Downtown, leaving the Strip to the cashed-up suburbanites, though midweek and during awards season the celebs still appear.

Runyon Canyon
HIKING

(www.lamountains.com; 2000 N Fuller Ave; ☺dawn-dusk) A chaparral-draped cut in the Hollywood Hills, this 130-acre public park is as famous for its beautiful, bronzed and buff runners, as it is for the panoramic views from the upper ridge. Follow the wide, partially paved fire road up, then take the smaller track down the canyon where you'll pass the remains of the Runyon estate.

◉ Beverly Hills & the Westside

With its reputation for old-Hollywood glamour, top-end couture and posh dining still circulating in the collective consciousness, Beverly Hills remains impressive to those who stroll Beverly Blvd and Rodeo Drive for the first time.

West and south of Beverly Hills are a string of well-to-do 'hoods that make up LA's Westside, including Westwood, Bel Air, Brentwood and Culver City.

The chief sight in the area is Richard Meier's wonderfully designed **Getty Center** (☎310-440-7300; www.getty.edu; 1200 Getty Center Dr, off I-405 Fwy; ☺10am-5:30pm Tue-Fri & Sun, to 9pm Sat; **P**) **FREE**, whose five buildings hold collections of manuscripts, drawings,

LOS ANGELES SIGHTS & ACTIVITIES

DON'T MISS

SOUTH BAY BEACHES

This string of beach towns will soothe the big city mess from your psyche in one sunset. It all starts just 15 minutes from the airport with **Manhattan Beach**, a tony town with high-end shopping and dining, and homes stacked high on steep streets because of the sublime stretch of sand and sea out front. USC frat boys and sorority girls, financially challenged surfers and the beautiful boys and girls who love them call **Hermosa Beach** home. The rents are lower here, and the scene trashier, but that's part of the charm. As the coast winds to the south end of Santa Monica Bay you can follow it to diverse **Redondo Beach**, with its signature **pier**, and onto the stunning **Palos Verdes Peninsula**, where you'll find Lloyd Wright's spectacular, glass-walled **Wayfarers Chapel** (☎310-377-1650; www.wayfarerschapel.org; 5755 Palos Verdes Dr S; ☺10am-5pm; **P**) and the swanky seaside resort, **Terranea** (☎310-265-2800; www.terranea.com; 100 Terranea Way, Palos Verdes; r $350-500, ste $655-2150; **P @ 🕸 🕱**). Also on the peninsula is **Abalone Cove Shoreline Park** (www.palosverdes.com; Palos Verdes Dr; entry per vehicle $5; ☺9am-4pm; **P 🚼**). The best place to hunt for starfish, anemones and other tidepool critters is in and around this rock-strewn eco-preserve. The walk down to the beach gets pretty steep in some sections, so watch your footing.

South Bay gastropubs are a staple. We enjoy **Simmzy's** (www.simmzys.com; 229 Manhattan Beach Blvd; mains $10-14; ☺11am-1am) in Manhattan Beach and **Abigaile** (☎310-798-8227; www.abigailerestaurant.com; 1301 Manhattan Ave; mains $10-30; ☺5pm-late Mon-Fri, from 11am Sat & Sun) in Hermosa, but our favorite place to eat is Manhattan Beach's wonderful raw bar, **Fishing with Dynamite** (☎310-893-6299; www.eatfwd.com; 1148 Manhattan Ave; oysters from $2.25, dishes $9-19; ☺11:30am-10pm Sun-Wed, to 10:30pm Thu-Sat), and the most inventive is **Standing Room** (☎310-374-7575; www.facebook.com/thestandingroomRB; 144 N Catalina Ave, Redondo Beach; burgers & sandwiches $7-14, plates $13-20; ☺11am-9:30pm Mon-Sat, noon-8pm Sun), a fusion greasy spoon tucked into the back of a Redondo Beach liquor store. Find it.

Hollywood

500 m
0.25 miles

Runyon Canyon Park

Runyon Canyon Park Entrance (0.25mi)

Foothill Dr

Tamarind Ave
12

Cheremoya Ave

N Beachwood Dr

Primrose Ave

Vista Del Mar Ave

N Gower St

Yucca St

Carlos Ave

Carlos Ave

Carlton Way

Harold Way

Gordon St

8

N Gower St

CBS Studios

N El Centro Ave

Argyle Ave

Hollywood/Vine

Franklin Ave

Vine St

Longview Ave

Vedanta Tce

Holly Dr

Hollywood Fwy

Yucca St

N Cahuenga Blvd

Ivar Ave

Ivar Ave

N Vine St

13

Whitley Tce

Grace Ave

Whitley Ave

Cherokee Ave

Las Palmas Ave

Greyhound

Hollywood Blvd

10

11

LA Gay & Lesbian Center

7

Schrader Blvd

Selma Ave

9

W Sunset Blvd

Hollywood Bowl (0.4mi)

Camrose Dr

Milner Rd

Bonair Pl

Emmett Tce

Hollywood Visitor Information Center

Hollywood Tourist Information

Hollywood/Highland

3

Hillcrest Rd

Sycamore Ave

Franklin Ave

N Orange Dr

1

2

5

4

Hawthorn Ave

Lanewood Ave

Pizzeria & Osteria Mozza (1mi)

Scenic Gardens

Hollywood Franklin Park

N Sycamore Ave

6

Outpost Dr

El Cerrito Pl

N La Brea Ave

Hawthorn Ave

Detroit St

Marshfield Way

N Formosa Ave

N Formosa Ave

Formosa Cafe (1mi)

Hollywood

photographs, furniture, decorative arts and a strong assortment of pre-20th-century European paintings. Must-sees include Van Gogh's *Irises*, Monet's *Wheatstacks*, Rembrandt's *The Abduction of Europa* and Titian's *Venus and Adonis*. Don't miss the lovely Cactus Garden on the remote South Promontory for amazing city views.

Art lovers should also find **Blum & Poe** (www.blumandpoe.com; 2727 S La Cienega Blvd; ◎10am-6pm Tue-Sat) gallery in Culver City and the **Hammer Museum** (Map p576; http://hammer.ucla.edu; 10899 Wilshire Blvd; ◎11am-8pm Tue-Fri, to 5pm Sat & Sun) FREE has one of the great gift shops and is set in Westwood near the **University of California, Los Angeles** (UCLA; Map p576; www.ucla.edu; P) campus.

◎ Malibu

Malibu enjoys near-mythical status thanks to its large celebrity population and the incredible beauty of its coastal mountains, pristine coves, wide sweeps of golden sand and epic waves. Stretched out for 27 miles, there are several small commercial strips, but the heart of town is at the foot of Pepper-

dine, where you'll find the Malibu Country Mart and the Malibu Civic Center.

The beach is king, of course, and whether you find a sliver of sand among the sandstone rock towers and topless sunbathers at **El Matador** (32215 Pacific Coast Hwy; parking $8; P) or enjoy the wide loamy blonde beaches of **Zuma & Westward**, you'll have a special afternoon. **Topanga Canyon State Park** (www.parks.ca.gov; Entrada Rd; per vehicle $10; ◎8am-dusk) offers 36 miles of hiking trails and the **Getty Villa** (☑310-430-7300; www.getty.edu; 17985 Pacific Coast Hwy; ◎10am-5pm Wed-Mon; P) FREE, a replica of a 1st-century Roman villa, is stocked with Greek and Roman antiquities.

Surfrider Beach   BEACH
(26000 Pacific Coast Hwy; P) Surf punks descend on this cove that shapes some of the best waves in Southern California. There are several breaks here: the first is well formed for beginners and long boarders, the second and third breaks demand short boards and advanced-level skills. Whichever way you ride, know your etiquette before paddling out.

**★ Mishe Mokwa Trail
& Sandstone Peak**   HIKING
(www.nps.gov/samo; 12896 Yerba Buena Rd) On warm spring mornings when the snowy blue *ceonothus* perfumes the air with honeysuckle, there's no better place to be than this 6-mile loop trail that winds through a redrock canyon, through the oak oasis at **Split Rock** and up to the tallest mountain in the Santa Monica Mountains, Mount Allen, aka Sandstone Peak.

Malibu Surf Shack   SURFING
(www.malibusurfshack.com; 22935 Pacific Coast Hwy; kayaks per day $30, surf boards per day $20-35, SUP per hour/day $45/75, wetsuits per day $10-15, surf/stand-up paddleboard lessons per person $125/100; ◎10am-6pm) This barefoot surf shop rents (and sells) kayaks, SUP (stand-up paddleboard) kits and surfboards. Surf and SUP lessons take place on Surfrider beach, last 90 minutes and include a full day's rental of the board and wetsuit. The paddling between here and Point Dume is excellent, with frequent dolphin and sea-lion sightings.

◎ Santa Monica

Here's a place where real-life Lebowskis sip white Russians next to martini-swilling Hollywood producers, and celebrity chefs and soccer mom's shop shoulder to shoulder at

Griffith Park & Around

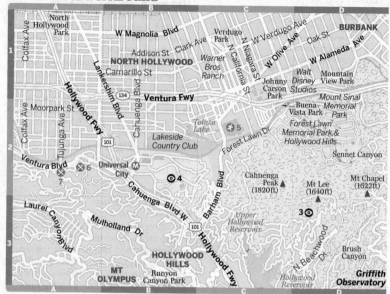

abundant farmers markets. It's a small city with forward-thinking social and environmental ideals (and fascist parking codes) alive with surf rats, skate punks, string bikinis, yoga freaks, psychics, street performers and a prodigious homeless population. Most, if not all, of which can be found along a stretch of sublime coastline that cradles the city to the west, and laps at the heels of an undulating mountain range that defines the entire LA area to the north. This is Santa Monica – LA's hippie-chic little sister, its karmic counterbalance and, to many, its salvation.

Once the very end of the mythical Route 66, and still a tourist love affair, the **Santa Monica Pier** (Map p578; ☎ 310-458-8900; www.santamonicapier.org; 👪) dates back to 1908, is stocked with rides and arcade games and blessed with spectacular views, and is the city's most compelling landmark. After a stroll on the pier, hit the **beach** (Map p578; ☎ 310-458-8411; http://www.smgov.net/portals/beach/; ☐ BBB 1). We like the stretch just north of Ocean Park Blvd. Or rent a bike or some skates from **Perry's Cafe** (Map p578; ☎ 310-939-0000; www.perryscafe.com; Ocean Front Walk; mountain bikes & Rollerblades per hr/day $10/30, bodyboards per hr/day $7/17; ☺9:30am-5:30pm) and explore the 22-mile **South Bay Bicycle Trail**.

◉ Venice

If you were born too late, and have always been jealous of the hippie heyday, come down to the Boardwalk and inhale an incense-scented whiff of Venice, a boho beach town and longtime haven for artists, New Agers, road-weary tramps, freaks and free spirits. This is where Jim Morrison and the Doors lit their fire, where Arnold Schwarzenegger pumped himself to stardom and where the late Dennis Hopper once lived.

The **Venice Boardwalk** (Ocean Front Walk; Map p578; Venice Pier to Rose Ave; ☺24hr), officially known as Ocean Front Walk, is a wacky carnival alive with altered-states hoola-hoop acrobats, old-timey jazz combos, solo distorted garage rockers and artists – good and bad, but as far as LA experiences go, it's a must. Rent a **bike** (Map p578; ☎ 310-396-2453; 517 Ocean Front Walk; per hr/2hr/day bikes $7/12/20, surfboards $10/20/30, skates $7/12/20) and join the parade, glimpse **Muscle Beach** (Map p578; www.musclebeach.net; 1800 Ocean Front Walk; per day $10; ☺8am-7pm May-Sep, to 6pm Oct-Apr) or hit the **Skate Park** (Map p578; 1800 Ocean Front Walk; ☺dawn-dusk). The Sunday afternoon **drum circle** is always wild.

Just a couple of blocks away from the Boardwalk madness is an idyllic neighbor-

high-tech indoor ocean where sharks dart, jellyfish dance and sea lions frolic. The **Queen Mary** (www.queenmary.com; 1126 Queens Hwy, Long Beach; tours adult/child from $26/15; ⊙10am-6:30pm; P), a supposedly haunted British luxury liner from yesteryear, is another flagship attraction. The special **Museum of Latin American Art** (www.molaa.org; 628 Alamitos Ave, Long Beach; adult/child /student & senior $9/free/6, Sun free; ⊙11am-5pm Wed, Thu, Sat & Sun, to 9pm Fri; P) is worth seeking out.

◉ San Fernando Valley

Home to most of LA's major movie studios – including Warner Bros, Disney and Universal – 'the Valley' is an exercise in sprawl. Attractions are few and scattered about; Burbank has Disney and **Warner Bros** (Map p566; ☎818-972-8687, 877-492-8687; www.wbstudiotour.com; 3400 W Riverside Dr, Burbank; tours from $54; ⊙8:15am-4pm Mon-Sat, hours vary Sun), and North Hollywood, west of here, is home to a growing arts scene. Studio City has some superb sushi on Ventura Blvd. At last count there were 21 sushi bars within a six-block radius, which is why some call it LA's Sushi Row. But the chief attraction is the **Universal Studios Hollywood** (Map p566; www.universalstudioshollywood.com; 100 Universal City Plaza, Universal City; admission from $87, under 3yr free; ⊙open daily, hours vary; P) theme park. Here are stage shows, thrill rides, back lot tours and major family fun.

◉ Pasadena

One could argue that there is more blue-blood, meat-eating, robust Americana in

hood of eclectic homes laced with 3 miles of the original **canals** (Map p578), built as an homage to the late Abbot Kinney's beloved Venezia. Hence the name.

◉ Long Beach & San Pedro

Over the past two decades, LA's southernmost seaside enclave has reinvented its gritty downtown making it an attractive place to live and party. On any Saturday night the restaurants, clubs and bars along lower Pine Ave and the Promenade, a new upscale loft district, are abuzz with everyone from buttoned-down conventioneers to hipsters to the testosterone-fuelled frat pack. Additional eateries line Shoreline Village, the departure point for boat cruises.

'San Pedro is real quiet,' Bukowski once observed. That's still true today, except for the distant clanging of containers being hoisted on and off gigantic cargo vessels. LA's own 'Golden Gate', the 1500ft-long suspended Vincent Thomas Bridge, links San Pedro with Terminal Island.

Long Beach's most mesmerizing experience, the **Aquarium of the Pacific** (☎tickets 562-590-3100; www.aquariumofpacific. org; 100 Aquarium Way, Long Beach; adult/child/senior$29/15/26; ⊙9am-6pm; ▣) is a vast,

Los Feliz & Silver Lake

Los Feliz & Silver Lake

Pasadena than in all other LA neighborhoods combined. Here is a community with a preppy old soul, a historical perspective, an appreciation for art and jazz and a slightly progressive undercurrent.

The Rose Parade and **Rose Bowl** (☎ 626-577-3100; www.rosebowlstadium.com; 1001 Rose Bowl Dr, Pasadena) football game may have given Pasadena its long-lasting fame, but it's the spirit of this genteel city and its location beneath the lofty San Gabriel Mountains

that make it a charming and attractive place year-round. Don't miss the **Huntington Library** (☎ 626-405-2100; www.huntington.org; 1151 Oxford Rd, San Marino; adult weekday/weekend & holidays $20/23, child $8, 1st Thu each month free; ⊙ 10:30am-4:30pm Wed-Mon Jun-Aug, noon-4:30pm Mon & Wed-Fri, from 10:30am Sat, Sun & holidays Sep-May; P), with it's tranquil Zen gardens, **Norton Simon Museum** (www.nortonsimon.org; 411 W Colorado Blvd, Pasadena; adult/child $10/free; ⊙ noon-6pm Wed-Mon, to 9pm Fri; P), home to many a masterpiece, and when the **Descanso Gardens** (www.descansogardens.org; 1418 Descanso Dr, La Cañada Flintridge; adult/5-12yr/student & senior $9/4/6; ⊙ 9am-5pm; P) bloom in January and February, they're magic.

The two-lane **Angeles Crest Scenic Byway** (www.byways.org/explore/byways/10245/travel.html; Hwy 2) treats you to fabulous views of big-shouldered mountains, the Mojave Desert and deep valleys on its 55-mile meander from La Cañada to the resort town of

Wrightwood. The road skirts LA County's tallest mountain, officially called Mt San Antonio (10,064ft), but better known as Old Baldy for its treeless top.

◉ South Central & Exposition Park

South Central LA burst into global consciousness with the rat-a-tat-tat rhythm and rhyme of some of hip-hop's greatest pioneers in the 1980s, and was suddenly defined by its gangs, drugs, poverty, crime and drive-by shootings, which never told the whole story.

After WWII more than five million African Americans left what at the time was a violently racist South and moved to northern cities in the Second Great Migration. Some of those families moved west, from Mississippi, Louisiana and Texas to Los Angeles. They found manufacturing jobs, bought property and built working-class communities south of downtown. Life wasn't perfect, but it was a step up. Fast-forward 30 years and suddenly the high-wage manufacturing jobs dried up, drug addiction soared, families fell apart, guns became accessible, gang violence bloomed, and South Central began to earn its reputation. But recent investment and expanded rail service has helped turn the tide somewhat.

Most folks come for the excellent **Natural History Museum** (☏213-763-3466; www.nhm.org; 900 Exposition Blvd; adult/child /student & senior $12/5/9; ⊗9:30am-5pm; ⓘ) and **California Science Center** (☏film schedule 213-744-2109, info 323-724-3623; www.californiasciencecenter.org; 700 Exposition Park Dr; IMAX movie adult/child $8.25/5; ⊗10am-5pm; ⓘ) **FREE**, home to the recently decommisioned **Space Shuttle Endeavor**. Both are located at **Exposition Park** (www.expositionpark.org; 700 Exposition Park Dr) next door to the **University of Southern California** (USC; ☏213-740-6605; www.usc.edu; Exposition Blvd & Figueroa St) **FREE**, where the Trojans play football, George Lucas studied film, and Will Ferrell became, well, Will Ferrell.

For a blast of African American culture find **Leimert Park** (Degnan Blvd & 43rd St). A fun time to visit South Central is during the annual **Pan African Film Festival** (www.paff.org; ⊗February) when filmmakers from across the African diaspora congregate for two weeks each February, and show their films at the **Rave Theaters** (www.baldwinhillscrenshawplaza.com; 3650 W Martin Luther King Jr Blvd; adult/child $14/7). A wonderful arts and handicrafts bazaar takes over both floors of the attached shopping center as well.

And don't miss the wonderful **Watts Towers** (www.wattstowers.us; 1761-1765 E 107th St; adult/under 12yr/teen & senior $7/free/$3; ⊗11am-3pm Fri, 10:30am-3pm Sat, 12:30-3pm Sun; ⓟ), one of the world's great folk-art monuments.

☞ Tours

★ Esotouric BUS TOUR
(☏323-223-2767; www.esotouric.com; tours $58) Discover LA's lurid and fascinating underbelly on these offbeat, insightful and entertaining walking and bus tours themed around famous crime sites (Black Dahlia anyone?), literary lions (Chandler to Bukowski) and more.

Melting Pot Tours WALKING TOUR
(☏424-247-9666; www.meltingpottours.com; adult/child from $59/45) Duck into aromatic alleyways, stroll through fashionable shopping districts, and explore LA landmarks while tasting some of the city's best ethnic eats in Pasadena, Mid-City and East LA.

Dearly Departed BUS TOUR
(☏1-855-600-3323; www.dearlydepartedtours.com; tours $48-75) This long-running, occasionally creepy, frequently hilarious tour will clue you in on where celebs kicked the bucket, George Michael dropped his trousers, Hugh Grant received certain services and the Charles Manson gang murdered Sharon Tate. Not for kids.

TMZ Tours HOLLYWOOD TOUR
(Map p564; ☏855-4TMZ-TOUR; www.tmz.com/tour; 6925 Hollywood Blvd; adult/child $55/45; ⊗approx 10 tours daily) Cut the shame, do you really want to spot celebrities, glimpse their homes, and gawk and laugh at their dirt? Join this branded tour devised by paparazzi who have themselves become famous.

✵ Festivals & Events

From the Rose Parade to the Hollywood Christmas Parade, from the Oscars to the *LA Times* Festival of Books, from the progressive, hard-rocking Sunset Junction street fair to the candy-colored mayhem of Halloween in WeHo, LA has its share of annual festivities.

Rose Parade PARADE
(www.tournamentofroses.com) A cavalcade of flower-festooned floats snakes through Pasadena on New Year's Day. Get close-ups during post-parade viewing at Victory Park. Avoid traffic and take the Metro Rail Gold Line to Memorial Park.

West Hollywood & Mid-City

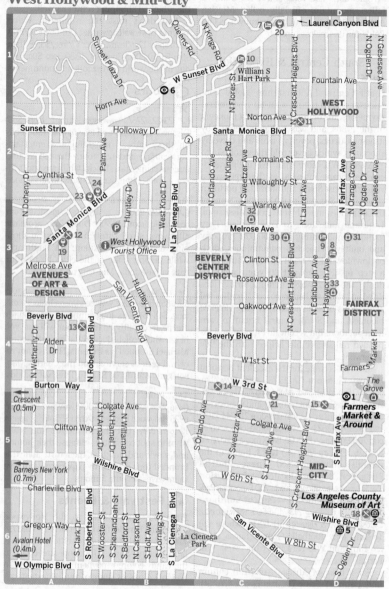

Toyota Grand Prix of Long Beach SPORTS (www.gplb.com) World-class drivers tear up city streets at this week-long racing spectacle by the sea.

Fiesta Broadway CARNIVAL (http://fiestabroadway.la) One of the world's largest Cinco de Mayo parties brings half a million folks to Downtown LA; in 2014 it was held in late April. See website for details.

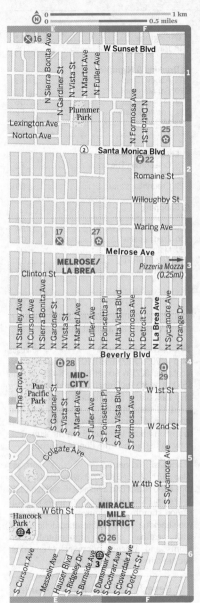

🛏 Sleeping

🛏 Downtown Los Angeles

Stay
HOTEL, HOSTEL **$**

(Map p560; ☑ 213-213-7829; www.stayhotels.com; 640 S Main St; dm $39, r $89; P @ 🛜 🐾) Formerly the Hotel Cecil, Stay has marble floors and shared baths, retro furnishings and bedspreads, iPod docks and accent walls. Gleaming shared baths serve just two dorm rooms each and include showers hewn from marble. Rooms all have private baths.

Figueroa Hotel
HISTORIC HOTEL **$$**

(Map p560; ☑ 800-421-9092, 213-627-8971; www.figueroahotel.com; 939 S Figueroa St; r $148-184, ste $225-265; P ✳ @ 🛜 🐾 🐾) It's hard not to be charmed by this rambling owner-operated oasis. Global-chic rooms blend Moroccan mirrors, Iraqi quilts and Kurdish grain-sack floor cushions, with paper lanterns from Chinatown.

Ace Hotel
HOTEL **$$$**

(Map p560; ☑ 213-623-3233; www.acehotel.com/losangeles; 929 S Broadway Ave; r from $250, stes from $400) Either lovably cool, a bit too hip or a touch self-conscious depending upon your purview, there is no denying that the minds behind Downtown's newest sleep care deeply about their product. Some rooms are cubby-box small, but the 'medium' rooms are doable.

🛏 Hollywood

Vibe Hotel
HOSTEL **$**

(Map p564; ☑ 323-469-8600; www.vibehotel.com; 5920 Hollywood Blvd; dm $22-25, r $85-95; P @ 🛜) A funky motel-turned-hostel with both co-ed and female-only dorms – each with a flat screen and kitchenette – and several recently re-done private rooms that sleep three. You'll share space with a happening international crowd.

USA Hostels Hollywood
HOSTEL **$**

(Map p564; ☑ 800-524-6783, 323-462-3777; www.usahostels.com; 1624 Schrader Blvd; dm $30-40, r with shared bath $81-104; ✳ @ 🛜) This sociable hostel puts you within steps of the Hollywood party circuit. Private rooms are a bit cramped, but making new friends is easy during staff-organized barbecues, comedy nights and $25 all-you-can-drink limo tours. Freebies include a cook-your-own-pancake breakfast. They have cushy lounge seating on the front porch and free beach shuttles.

West Hollywood
Halloween Carnaval
CARNIVAL

(www.visitwesthollywood.com) This street fair brings 350,000 revelers – many in over-the-top and/or X-rated costumes – out for a day of dancing, dishing and dating on Halloween.

West Hollywood & Mid-City

★**Magic Castle Hotel**   HOTEL $$
(Map p564; ☏323-851-0800; http://magiccastle-hotel.com; 7025 Franklin Ave; r incl breakfast from $174; P✳@🖥🏊) Walls at this perennial pleaser are a bit thin, but otherwise it's a charming base of operation with large, modern rooms, exceptional staff and a petite courtyard pool where days start with fresh pastries and gourmet coffee. Enquire about access to the Magic Castle, a fabled members-only magic club in an adjacent Victorian mansion. Parking costs $10.

⬛ **West Hollywood & Mid-City**

Orbit   HOSTEL $
(Banana Bungalow; Map p570; ☏323-655-1510; www.orbithotels.com; 603 N Fairfax Ave; dm $22-25, r $69-79) This popular, well-run hostel occupies a converted art-deco-styled nursing home. The local bubbies are gone and the young nomads have moved in to private rooms that have their own baths, TV and mini-fridge or into one of the six 12-bed dorms.

★**Pali Hotel**   BOUTIQUE HOTEL $$
(Map p570; ☏323-272-4588; www.pali-hotel.com; 7950 Melrose Ave; r from $179; P@🖥) We love the rustic wood-paneled exterior, the polished concrete floor in the lobby, the Thai massage spa (just $35 for 30 minutes), and the 32 contemporary rooms with two-tone paint jobs, wall-mounted flat screen and enough room for a sofa too. Some have terraces. A terrific all-around value.

★**Chateau Marmont**   HOTEL $$$
(Map p570; ☏323-656-1010; www.chateaumarmont.com; 8221 W Sunset Blvd; r $435, ste from $550; P🖥🏊) Its French-flavored indulgence may look dated, but this faux castle has long lured A-listers with its five-star mystique and legendary discretion. Howard Hughes used to spy on bikini beauties from the same balcony suite that became Bono's favorite.

Standard Hollywood   HOTEL $$$
(Map p570; ☏323-650-9090; www.standardhotel.com; 8300 Sunset Blvd; r from $235, ste from $335; ✳@🖥🏊) Kind of yesterday's news but still a good standby, this Sunset Strip haunt has you shacking up in sizable shagadelic rooms with beanbag chairs, orange-tiled bathrooms and Warhol poppy-print curtains. South-facing rooms have the views.

⬛ **Beverly Hills & the Westside**

★**Mr C**   HOTEL $$$
(☏877-334-5623; www.mrhotels.com; 1224 Beverwil Dr; r from $320) A long-standing tower hotel has been re-imagined by the Ciprioni brothers, who have been so involved in their passion project that they've designed everything right down to the furniture. North-facing rooms have spectacular views.

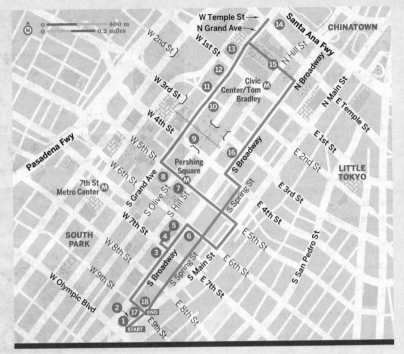

🏃 City Walk
Downtown Revealed

START UNITED ARTISTS THEATRE
END WOODSPOON
LENGTH 2.5 MILES; THREE HOURS

Start at the **1 United Artists Theatre** (p584), grab a coffee at the **2 Ace Hotel** (p571) next door, then head north on Broadway through the old theater district. This heady mixture of beaux-arts architecture, discount jewelers and new bars, restaurants and shops sums up the Downtown renaissance in just a few short blocks. Take note of the **3 State Theatre** and **4 St Vincent Court**, **5 Los Angeles Theatre** and the **6 Palace Theatre**.

Turn right at 6th St, continue along for two blocks, then turn left onto Main, where you'll see a flowering of new restaurants and bars at nearly every turn. Turn left on 5th St and continue for several blocks, passing **7 Pershing Square** and glimpsing the **8 Biltmore Hotel**. At Grand Ave turn right

and walk past the **9 Deloitte & Tousche** building, then bisect **10 MOCA** (p557) on one side and the **11 Broad** on the other, continuing until you reach the stunning **12 Walt Disney Concert Hall** (p557) and the **13 Music Center**. You'll see the **14 Cathedral of Our Lady of Angels** beckoning. Duck inside, then follow the traffic down the steps of **15 Grand Park** until you reach Broadway once more.

Make a right on Broadway, and grab lunch at the **16 Grand Central Market**. Afterward, walk another block south, turn left on 4th St, and then right on lively Spring St, which is dotted with still more cafes and bars. Enjoy the street life and the people-watching until Spring dead ends at Main St, just above 9th St. Say hello to the Cheri Rae at **17 Peace Yoga** (you kind of have to meet her), and hang a right on 9th to Broadway. If you're hungry for dinner by now, grab a table at **18 Woodspoon** (p578).

Southern California's Best Beaches

Hundreds of miles of Pacific beaches edge SoCal's golden coast – which makes choosing just one to visit almost impossible. Take your pick depending on what you prefer doing: launching your surfboard onto a world-famous break; snapping on a snorkel mask and peeking at colorful marine life; or just lazing on the sand.

1. Santa Monica (p565)

A carnival pier with a solar-powered Ferris wheel and a tiny aquarium for the kiddos sits atop this idyllic, 3-mile long strand, where LA comes to play.

2. Malibu (p565)

Celebrity residents aren't keen to share their paradisaical pocket beaches, but with persistence and some insider tips, you too can share these million-dollar views.

3. Huntington Beach (p609)

Officially 'Surf City, USA,' Huntington Beach is everything you imagined SoCal beach life to be, from surfing by the pier to sunset bonfires on the sand.

4. Mission Beach (p633)

A day trip to San Diego's most fun-crazed beach should begin with a ride on the Giant Dipper wooden roller coaster and end with sunset along Ocean Front Walk.

5. Crystal Cove State Park (p617)

Tired of manicured beaches filled with bikini babes? Escape instead to this wilder, undeveloped Orange County gem for beachcombing and scuba diving.

6. Coronado (p633)

Pedal a beach cruiser along the Silver Strand, or frolic like Marilyn Monroe did on the golden sand fronting San Diego's landmark Hotel Del.

7. East Beach (p522)

Next to historic Stearns Wharf, where Santa Barbara meets the sea, this easy-access beach fills in summer with swimmers, volleyball players and even sea kayakers.

8. Carpinteria State Beach (p544)

Even tots can get their feet wet or poke around the tide pools at this Santa Barbara County classic, where palm trees wave above soft sands.

N
0   500 m
0   0.25 miles

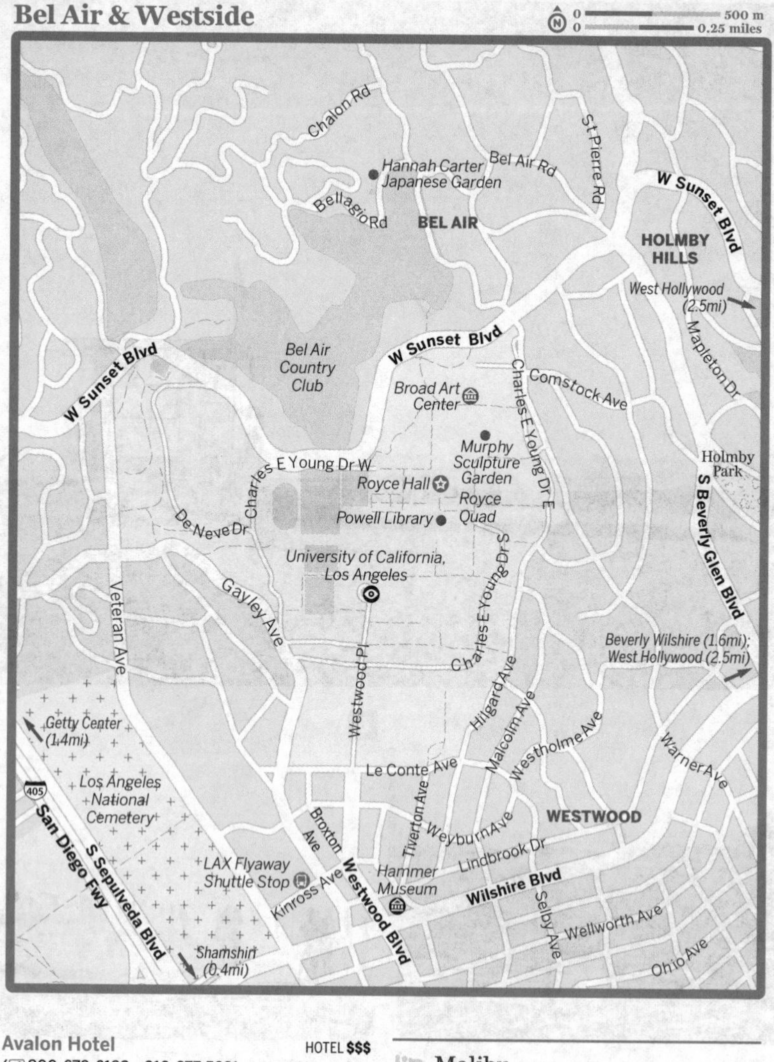

Avalon Hotel   HOTEL **$$$**
(☏800-670-6183, 310-277-5221; www.viceroyho-telgroup.com/avalon; 9400 W Olympic Blvd; r from $200; ✳@🖥✳🏊) Mid-century modern gets a 21st-century spin at this fashion-crowd fave, which was Marilyn Monroe's old pad in its days as an apartment building. Funky retro rooms are all unique.

Crescent   HOTEL **$$$**
(☏310-247-0505; www.crescentbh.com; 403 N Crescent Dr; r from $217; ℗@🖥) Single rooms are a tight squeeze, but Queen rooms are spacious and good value. There's jazz in the lounge every Thursday night.

🛏 Malibu

Leo Carrillo State Park Campground   CAMPGROUND **$**
(☏800-444-7275; www.reserveamerica.com; 35000 W Pacific Coast Hwy; tent sites $45, per vehicle $12; 🖥) This kid-friendly campground sits on a famous 1.5-mile stretch of beach. Offshore kelp beds, caves, tide pools, plus the wilderness of the Santa Monica Mountains create a natural playground. There are 140 flat, tree-shaded sites, flush toilets and coin-operated hot showers. Bookings for summer weekends should be made months in advance.

★ **Malibu Country Inn**   INN $$
(☑ 310-457-9622; www.malibucountryinn.com; 6506 Westward Beach Rd; r $160-275; P 🛜)
Overlooking Westward Beach is this humble shingled inn with an array of fairly large rooms drenched in corny florals. They all have sun patios and some have sea views.

Santa Monica

HI Los Angeles-Santa Monica   HOSTEL $
(Map p578; ☑ 310-393-9913; www.hilosangeles.org; 1436 2nd St; dm $38-49, r $99-159; ✻ @ 🛜) Near the beach and promenade, this hostel has an enviable location on the cheap. Its 200 beds in single-sex dorms and bed-in-a-box doubles with shared bathrooms are clean and safe, and there are plenty of public spaces to lounge and surf, but those looking to party are better off in Venice or Hollywood.

★ **Palihouse**   BOUTIQUE HOTEL $$$
(Map p578; ☑ 310-394-1279; www.palihousesantamonica.com; 1001 3rd St; r $279-319, studios $319-379; P ✻ @ 🛜) LA's grooviest new hotel brand (not named Ace) has taken over the 36 rooms, studios and one-bedroom apartments of the historic Embassy Hotel (c 1927). Expect a lobby with terra-cotta floors, beamed ceilings and coffee bar, plus booths and leather sofas on which you can canoodle and surf.

Shore Hotel   HOTEL $$$
(Map p578; ☑ 310-458-1515; www.shorehotel.com; 1515 Ocean Ave; r from $309) Massive, clean-lined and modern, featuring wood and glass rooms each with private terraces, this is one of the newest hotels on Ocean Ave, and the only gold LEED-certified hotel in Santa Monica, which means it has a reasonably light footprint. Case in point: the lovely back garden is seeded with drought-tolerant plants.

Venice

Venice Beach Inn & Suites   BOUTIQUE HOTEL $$
(Map p578; ☑ 310-396-4559; www.venicebeachsuites.com; 1305 Ocean Front Walk; r from $159; P 🛜) This place right on the Boardwalk scores big for its bend-over-backwards staff, and its bevy of beach toys for rent. There are exposed-brick walls, kitchenettes, wood floors and built-in closets. It's ideal for long stays. Kitchen suites are big enough for dinner parties.

Hotel Erwin   BOUTIQUE HOTEL $$$
(Map p578; ☑ 800-786-7789; www.hotelerwin.com; 1697 Pacific Ave; r from $263; P ✻ @ 🛜)

An old motor inn has been dressed up and otherwise funkified in retro style. Think: eye-popping oranges, yellows and greens, framed photos of graffiti art, flat screens, and ergo sofas in the spacious rooms. Book online for the best deals. That rooftop lounge is a wonderful place for a sundowner.

Long Beach & San Pedro

Queen Mary Hotel   SHIP $$
(☑ 562-435-3511; www.queenmary.com; 1126 Queens Hwy, Long Beach; r from $99; ✻ @ 🛜) There's an irresistible romance to ocean liners such as the *Queen Mary,* a nostalgic retreat that time-warps you back to a long-gone, slower-paced era. Yes, the rooms are small, but the 1st-class staterooms are nicely refurbished with original art-deco details. Avoid the cheapest cabins on the inside – claustrophobic!

Hotel Maya   BOUTIQUE HOTEL $$
(☑ 562-435-7676; www.hotelmayalongbeach.com; 700 Queens Way, Long Beach; r from $179; P ✻ @ 🛜 ≋) This once boutique property hits you with hip immediately upon entering the rusted-steel and glass lobby, and continues in the rooms (think: coral tile, river-rock headboards), which are set in four 1970s-era hexagons with views of downtown Long Beach. The poolside cabanas aren't bad either.

Pasadena

★ **Bissell House B&B**   B&B $$
(☑ 626-441-3535626-441-3535; www.bissellhouse.com; 201 S Orange Grove Blvd, Pasadena; r $159-259; P 🛜 ≋) Antiques, hardwood floors and a crackling fireplace make this secluded Victorian B&B on 'Millionaire's Row' a bastion of warmth and romance. The hedge-framed garden feels like a sanctuary, and there's a pool for cooling off on hot summer days. The Prince Albert room has gorgeous wallpaper and a claw-foot tub. All seven rooms have private baths.

Langham   RESORT $$$
(☑ 626-568-3900; www.pasadena.langhamhotels.com; 1401 S Oak Knoll Ave, Pasadena; r from $230; P @ 🛜 ≋) Opened as the Huntington Hotel in 1906, this place spent the last several decades as the Ritz Carlton before recently donning the robes of Langham. But some things don't change: this incredible 23-acre, palm-dappled, beaux-arts country estate – complete with rambling gardens, giant swimming pool and covered picture bridge – has still got it. Rates are reasonable.

✕ Eating

✕ Downtown Los Angeles

Cole's
SANDWICHES $

(Map p560; www.213nightlife.com/colesfrench-dip; 118 E 6th St; sandwiches $6-9; ⊙11am-10pm Sun-Wed, to 11pm Thu, to 1am Fri & Sat) A funky old basement tavern known for originating the French Dip sandwich way back in 1908, when those things cost a nickel. You know the drill – french bread piled with sliced lamb, beef, turkey, pork or pastrami, dipped once or twice in *au jus*.

★ Sushi Gen
JAPANESE $$

(Map p560; ✆213-617-0552; www.sushigen.org; 422 E 2nd St; sushi $11-21; ⊙11:15am-2pm & 5:30-9:45pm) Seven chefs stand behind the blond-wood bar, carving thick slabs of melt-in-your-mouth salmon, buttery toro, and a wonderful Japanese snapper, among other staples. The sashimi special at lunch ($18) is a steal. Sushi Gen doesn't do jazzy rolls, and you best come early to grab a seat.

Woodspoon
BRAZILIAN $$

(Map p560; ✆213-629-1765; www.woodspoonla.com; 107 W 9th St; mains $11-20; ⊙11am-2:45pm & 5-10pm Tue-Fri, noon-3pm & 6-11pm Sat, closed Sun) We love it all: the hand-picked china, the vintage Pyrex pots of black beans and rice, and the Brazilian owner-operator who still chefs it up in the back. Her pork ribs fall off the bone, in a bath of grits and gravy. Her take on steak frites substitutes wedges of fried yucca for fries, and her pot pie put this place on the map.

Maccheroni Republic
ITALIAN $$

(Map p560; ✆213-346-9725213-346-9725; 332 S Broadway Ave; mains $10-14; ⊙11:30am-3pm & 5:30-10pm Mon-Fri, 5:30-10pm Sat, 4:30-9pm Sun) Tucked away on a still ungentrified corner is this gem with a lovely heated patio and tremendous Italian slow food. Don't miss the *polpettine di gamberi*, flattened ground shrimp cakes fried in olive oil. It serves a range of delicious housemade pastas, but doesn't have beer or wine. Bring your own.

★ Bestia
ITALIAN $$$

(✆213-514-5724; www.bestia.com; 2121 7th Pl; dishes $10-29; ⊙6-11pm Sun-Thu, to midnight Fri & Sat) The most sought-after reservation in town can be found at this new and splashy Italian kitchen in the Arts District. The antipasti ranges from crispy lamb pancetta to sea urchin crudo to veal tartare crostino. Did

Santa Monica & Venice Beach

Santa Monica & Venice Beach

we mention the lamb's heart? Yeah, you may have to leave the vegan at home.

There are tasty pizzas and pastas, squid-ink risotto stuffed with chunks of lobster, mussels, clams and calamari, and roast chops and whole fish. A worthy splurge indeed.

★ Bar Ama'   MEXICAN, FUSION $$$
(Map p560; ☑213-687-8002; www.bar-ama. com; 118 W 4th St; dishes $8-25, dinners $32-36; ⊙11:30am-2:30pm & 5:30-11pm Mon-Thu, 11:30am-3pm & 5:30pm-midnight Fri, 11:30am-midnight Sat, to 10pm Sun) One of three exquisite downtown restaurants with profound Mexican influences offered by Josef Centeno. This one fries pig ears, braises short rib and smothers enchiladas with mole sauce. Brussels sprouts are garnished with pickled red onions, and the roasted cauliflower and cilantro pesto, served with cashew and pine nuts, is a tremendous veggie choice.

✕ Hollywood

Jitlada   THAI $$
(☑323-667-9809; jitladala.com; 5233 W Sunset Blvd; appetizers $5-10, mains $11-30; ⊙lunch & dinner; ℙ) A transporting taste of southern Thailand. Its crab curry and fried *som tum* (papaya salad) are fantastic, as is its Thai-style burger. The vivacious owner operator counts Ryan Gosling and Natalie Portman among her loyal, mostly *farang* (European American) customers. Look for the wall of fame near the bathrooms.

Pikey   PUB $$
(Map p570; ☑323-850-5400; www.thepikeyla. com; 7617 W Sunset Blvd; dishes $12-28; ⊙noon-2am Mon-Fri, from 11am Sat & Sun) A tasteful kitchen that began life as Coach & Horses, one of Hollywood's favorite dives before it was reimagined into a place where you can get broccoli roasted with bacon, Arctic char crudo with grapefruit and jalapenos, seared squid with curried chickpeas, and a slow-roasted duck leg. The cocktails rock.

★ Pizzeria & Osteria Mozza   ITALIAN $$$
(☑323-297-0100; www.mozza-la.com; 6602 Melrose Ave; pizzas $11-19, dinner mains $27-38; ⊙pizzeria noon-midnight daily, osteria 5:30-11pm Mon-Fri, 5-11pm Sat, 5-10pm Sun) Osteria Mozza is all about fine dining crafted from market fresh, seasonal ingredients, but being a Mario Batali joint you can expect adventure (think: squid-ink chitarra freddi with Dungeness crab, sea urchin and jalapeno) and consistent excellence. Reservations are recommended.

★ Little Fork   SOUTHERN $$$
(Map p564; ☑323-465-3675; www.littleforkla. com; 1600 Wilcox Ave; dishes $9-28; ⊙11am-3pm Sat & Sun, 5-10pm Sun-Thu, to midnight Fri & Sat; ℙ) The stucco exterior of this converted studio is a horror show, but inside all is dark and moody. More importantly, the kitchen churns out plates of house-smoked trout, brick-roasted chicken, potato gnocchi cooked in bacon lard, tarragon and cream, and a 1lb lobster roll!

Los Feliz & Griffith Park

Yuca's
MEXICAN $

(Map p568; ☎323-662-1214; www.yucasla.com; 2056 Hillhurst Ave; items $4-10; ☺11am-6pm Mon-Sat) The tacos, *tortas,* burritos and other Mexi faves at this snack shack earned the Herrera family the coveted James Beard Award in 2005.

★Mess Hall
PUB $$

(☎323-660-6377; www.messhallkitchen.com; 4500 Los Feliz Blvd; mains $15-31; ☺11:30am-3pm & 4-11pm Mon-Thu, to midnight Fri, 10am-3pm & 5pm-midnight Sat, 10am-3pm & 4-11pm Sun) On Tuesdays there are $1 oysters and $5 beers. It's been written up for having one of the best burgers in LA, and it does a nice pulled-pork sandwich and a kale caesar.

Alcove
CAFE $$

(Map p568; ☎323-644-0100; www.thealcovecafe.com; 1929 Hillhurst Ave; mains $10-17; ☺6am-midnight; P✿) Hillhurst's choice breakfast hangout, this sunny cafe spills onto a multi-level, streetside brick patio. It's housed in a restored 1897 Spanish-style duplex, and the food is quite good.

Silver Lake & Echo Park

★Elf Cafe
VEGETARIAN $$

(☎213-484-6829; www.elfcafe.com; 2135 Sunset Blvd; mains $12-20; ✿) Simply one of the best vegetarian (not vegan) restaurants in LA, if not the very best. Start with feta wrapped in grape leaves and some spiced olives and almonds, move onto a kale salad dressed with citrus, wild-mushroom risotto and a kebab of seared oyster mushrooms that is fantastic.

Sage
VEGAN $$

(☎310-456-1492; www.sageveganbistro.com; 1700 W Sunset Blvd; mains $10-14; ☺11am-10pm Mon-Wed, to 11pm Thu & Fri, 9am-4pm & 5-11pm Sat, to 10pm Sun; ✿✿) An organic vegan kitchen with sandwiches and veggie burgers, and tacos stuffed with jackfruit or butternut squash. All served in heaping portions. And the menu is the second-best thing here. The best? That would be Kind Kreme's good-for-you, raw ice cream. Taste to believe.

★L&E Oyster Bar
SEAFOOD $$$

(Map p568; ☎323-660-2255; www.leoysterbar.com; 1637 Silver Lake Blvd; mains $17-28; ☺5-10pm Mon-Thu, to 11pm Fri & Sat) Silver Lake's seafood house opened to rave reviews in 2012, and is still a neighborhood darling

where locals and celebs claim tables in the intimate dining room and heated porch to feast on raw and grilled oysters, smoked mussels and whole roasted fish dressed in miso, pickled ginger, chili and garlic.

West Hollywood & Mid-City

Pingtung
ASIAN $

(Map p570; ☎323-866-1866; www.pingtungla.com; 7455 Melrose Ave; dishes $6-12; ☺11:30am-10:30pm; ☎) Our new favorite place to eat on Melrose is this Pan-Asian market cafe where the dim sum seaweed and green papaya salads, and rice bowls piled with curried chicken and BBQ beef are all worthy of praise. It has an inviting back patio with ample seating, wi-fi and good beer on tap.

Mercado
MEXICAN $$

(Map p570; ☎323-944-0947; www.mercadorestaurant.com; 7910 W 3rd St; dishes $9-26; ☺5-10pm Mon-Wed, to 11pm Thu & Fri, 4-11pm Sat, 10am-3pm & 4-10pm Sun) Terrific *nuevo* Mexican food served in a dining room that is beneath dangling bird-cage chandeliers and anchored by a terrific marble tequila bar. The slow-cooked *carnitas* (pork cubes) melt in your mouth. Mercado also does spit-roast beef and grilled sweet corn, and folds tasty tacos and enchiladas. The Hora Feliz (happy hour) is among the best in the city.

Joan's on Third
CAFE $$

(Map p570; ☎323-655-2285; www.joansonthird.com; 8350 W 3rd St; mains $10-16; ☺8am-8pm Mon-Sat, to 7pm Sun; ✿✿) One of the first market cafes in the LA area is still one of the best. The coffee and pastries are absurdly good and the deli churns out tasty gourmet sandwiches and salads. Hence all the happy people eating alfresco on buzzy 3rd St.

★Ray's
MODERN AMERICAN $$$

(Map p570; ☎323-857-6180; www.raysandstarkbar.com; 5905 Wilshire Blvd; dishes $11-27; ☺11:30am-3pm & 5-10pm Mon-Fri, from 10am Sat & Sun; ✿MTA 20) Ray's changes the menu twice daily, but if it's offered order the shrimp and grits: it's rich and buttery, afloat with chunks of andouille sausage, okra and two king prawns. The *burrata* (fresh Italian cheese made from mozzarella and cream) melts with tang, the yellow tail collar is crisp and moist, and the bacon-wrapped rabbit sausage will wow you.

★Connie & Ted's
SEAFOOD $$$

(Map p570; ☎323-848-2722; www.connieandteds.com; 8171 Santa Monica Blvd; mains $12-26;

⊙5-11pm Mon & Tue, noon-11pm Wed-Sun) The design is instant classic, there are always up to a dozen oyster varieties on the stocked raw bar. Fresh fish is pan fried or grilled to order. The lobster roll can be served cold with mayo and hot with drawn butter, and the shellfish marinara is a sacred thing.

Beverly Hills & the Westside

Still hungry? **Little Osaka**, West LA's Asian bloom, which runs along Sawtelle for about two blocks north from Olympic Blvd to La Grange Ave, is not exclusively Japanese. Among the karaoke bars, grocers, cafes and boutiques are restaurants devoted to ramen and Korean-style tofu, shabu-shabu, macaroons, dim sum, *pho* and *yakitori*.

Shamshiri   PERSIAN **$$**
(www.shamshiri.com; 1712 Westwood Blvd, Westwood; appetizers $4-16, mains $13-22; ⊙11:30am-10pm Mon-Thu, to 11pm Fri & Sat, noon-10pm Sun; P ♿) One of a string of Persian kitchens, this place bakes its own pita, which is then used to wrap chicken, beef and lamb shwarma, kebabs and falafel served with a green, *shirazi* or tabouli salad. It also does broiled lamb and seafood platters, and vegan stews. Come for one of its great-value lunch specials ($8 to $10).

Nate 'n Al   DELI **$$**
(☎310-274-0101; www.natenal.com; 414 N Beverly Dr; dishes $6.50-13; ⊙7am-9pm; ♿) Dapper seniors, chatty girlfriends, busy execs and even Larry King have kept this New York–style nosh spot busy since 1945. The huge menu brims with corned beef, lox and other old-school favorites, but we're partial to the pastrami, made fresh on-site.

Picca   SOUTH AMERICAN **$$$**
(☎310-277-0133; www.piccaperu.com; 9575 W Pico Blvd; dishes $8-28; ⊙6-11pm) Start with a crispy chicken tail, move onto a skirt steak topped with a fried egg and served with fried bananas and chickpeas and finish with a vanilla-bean pisco flan. Or better yet, dive deep and wide into the spectacular raw bar – filled with a variety of ceviche, sashimi and other succulent seafood concoctions.

Bouchon   FRENCH **$$$**
(☎310-279-9910; www.bouchonbistro.com; 235 N Cañon Dr; mains $17-59; ⊙11:30am-9pm Mon, to 10:30pm Tue-Fri, 11am-10:30pm Sat, to 9pm Sun; P) Quiche and salad, oysters on the half-shell or mussels steamed opened in white-wine sauce, steak frittes or roast leg of lamb with artichoke, Thomas Keller's Bouchon empire brings you classic French bistro cuisine in classy environs. Taste the goods at a discount at **Bar Bouchon** downstairs.

Ivy   CALIFORNIAN **$$$**
(Map p570; ☎310-274-8303; www.theivyrestaurants.com; 113 N Robertson Blvd; mains $22-97; ⊙8am-11pm) With a long history of celebrity power-lunches, this is where Southern comfort food (like fried chicken and crab cakes) have been elevated to haute cuisine. Service is refined and impeccable, and paparazzi etiquette (among one another and their prey) is a fluid, dynamic beast.

Malibu

Café Habana   MEXICAN, CUBAN **$$**
(☎310-317-0300; www.habana-malibu.com; 3939 Cross Creek Rd; mains $14-22; ⊙11am-11pm Sun-Wed, to 1am Thu-Sat; P ♿) A Mexican joint disguised as a Cuban joint with terrific margaritas, sumptuous booths on the heated patio, salsa on the sound system and two dishes that prevail above all else: the shrimp and carne asada tacos. Both come piled with either chili- and lime-sautéed rock shrimp, or cubes of ancho-rubbed and grilled steak.

Duck Dive   PUB **$$**
(☎310-589-2200; www.duckdivegastropub.com; 29169 Heathercliff Rd; small plates $5-13, mains $9-32; ⊙11:30am-10pm Sun-Thu, to late Fri & Sat) A fantastic little concrete-floor pub with stainless-steel bar and patio seating. It pours craftsman draught brews, and serves hand-cut fries sizzled in duck fat. The smoked mac 'n' cheese can be ramped up with jalapeños and pork belly. It also offers a housemade veggie burger and hearty meat ones too.

Nobu Malibu   JAPANESE **$$$**
(☎310-317-9140; www.noburestaurants.com; 22706 Pacific Coast Hwy; dishes $8-46; ⊙11am-3pm & 5:30pm-late; P) South of the pier and born again in landmark quality digs, here's a cavernous, modern-wood chalet with a long sushi bar on the back wall and a dining room that spills onto a patio that overlooks the swirling sea. Remember, it's the cooked food that built the brand.

Santa Monica

⭐ **Santa Monica Farmers Markets** MARKET **$**
(Map p578; www.smgov.net/portals/farmersmarket; Arizona Ave, btwn 2nd & 3rd Sts; ⊙8:30am-1:30pm

Wed, to 1pm Sat; 🖮) 🍴 You haven't really experienced Santa Monica until you've explored one of its weekly outdoor farmers markets stocked with organic fruits, vegetables, flowers, baked goods and fresh-shucked oysters.

Bay Cities
DELI, ITALIAN $

(Map p578; www.baycitiesitaliandeli.com; 1517 Lincoln Blvd; sandwiches $5-9; ⊙9am-7pm Tue-Sat, to 6pm Sun) Not just the best Italian deli in LA, this is arguably the best deli, period. With sloppy, spicy godmothers (piled with salami, mortadella, coppacola, ham, prosciutto, provolone, and pepper salad), house-roasted tri-tip, tangy salads, imported meats, cheeses, breads, oils and extras. Get your sandwich with the works. And, yes, it's worth the wait.

★ Milo and Olive
ITALIAN $$

(☎310-453-6776; www.miloandolive.com; 2723 Wilshire Blvd; dishes $7-20; ⊙7am-11pm) We love it for its small-batch wines, incredible pizzas and terrific breakfasts (creamy polenta and poached eggs anyone?), breads and pastries, all of which you may enjoy at the marble bar or shoulder to shoulder with new friends at one of two common tables. It's a cozy, neighborhoody kind of joint; no reservations.

★ Bar Pintxo
SPANISH $

(Map p578; ☎310-458-2012; www.barpintxo.com; 109 Santa Monica Blvd; tapas $4-16, paella $30; ⊙4-10pm Mon-Wed, to 11pm Thu, to midnight Fri, noon-midnight Sat, to 10pm Sun) A Barcelona-inspired tapas bar. It's small, it's cramped, it's a bit loud and a lot of fun. Tapas include pork belly braised in duck fat, filet mignon skewers, lamb meatballs and a tremendous seared calamari.

🍴 Venice

Wurstkuche
GERMAN $

(www.wurstkuche.com; 625 Lincoln Blvd; dishes $4-8; ⊙11am-midnight, bar to 2am) Set in a brick-house loft, but sealed off from the on-rushing madness of Lincoln Blvd, this German sausage and beer *haus* specializes in three things: gourmet and classic grilled sausages; fine Belgian, German and North American beers; and Belgian fries with ample dipping sauces.

★ Gjelina
ITALIAN $$$

(Map p578; ☎310-450-1429; www.gjelina.com; 1429 Abbot Kinney Blvd; dishes $8-26; ⊙11:30am-midnight Mon-Fri, from 9am Sat & Sun; 🖮) Carve out a slip on the communal table between the hipsters and yuppies, or get your own slab of wood on the elegant, tented stone ter-

race, and dine on imaginative small plates (think raw yellowtail spiced with chili and mint and drenched in olive oil and blood orange), and sensational thin crust, wood-fired pizza. It serves until midnight.

Tasting Kitchen
ITALIAN $$$

(Map p578; ☎310-392-6644; www.thetastingkitchen.com; 1633 Abbot Kinney Blvd; mains $16-40; ⊙10:30am-2pm Sat & Sun, 6pm-late daily) From the salt-roasted branzino to the procini-crusted hangar steak to the burger and the quail, it's all very good here. Especially the pastas (that bucatini is a gift from the gods), and the cocktails, of course. Which is why it's almost always packed. Book ahead.

Scopa
ITALIAN $$$

(☎310-821-1100; www.scopaitalianroots.com; 2905 Washington Blvd; dishes $6-49; ⊙5pm-2am) Spacious and open with polished concrete floors and an expansive marble L-shaped bar. The crudo bar serves scallops and steak tartare, four varieties of oysters, uni and mussels, while mains include a whole roasted branzino and a 24oz T-bone.

Long Beach & San Pedro

Pier 76
SEAFOOD $$

(☎562-983-1776; www.pier76fishgrill.com; 95 Pine Ave, Long Beach; mains $8-19; ⊙11am-9pm) A terrific, affordable seafood house in downtown Long Beach. Step to the counter and order yellowtail, salmon, trout, mahi mahi or halibut glazed and grilled, and served with two sides. The fries and kale salad are both good. It does fish tacos and sandwiches, poke and ceviche too, and a $19 lobster.

James Republic
MODERN AMERICAN $$

(☎562-901-0235; www.jamesrepublic.com; 500 E 1st St, Long Beach; mains $11-26; ⊙7-10:30am & 11:30am-2:30pm Mon-Fri, 10:30am-3pm Sat & Sun, 6-10pm Mon-Sat, 6-9pm Sun) The best new restaurant in Long Beach offers farm-to-table Modern American eating, though some dishes have a South Asian twist. It grills cauliflower and hangar steaks, spoons a rabbit bucatini, and makes grass-fed burgers, a pastrami sandwich with gruyere and beer mustard, and a wonderful roast chicken.

San Pedro Fish Market & Restaurant
SEAFOOD $$

(www.sanpedrofishmarket.com; 1190 Nagoya Way, San Pedro; meals $13-18; ⊙8am-8pm; 🅿🖮) Seafood feasts don't get more decadent than at this family-run, harbor-view institution.

Pick from the day's catch, have it spiced and cooked to order with potatoes, tomatoes and peppers, lug your tray to a picnic table, fold up your sleeves and devour meaty crabs, plump shrimp, melty yellowtail and tender halibut.

San Fernando Valley

★Daichan   JAPANESE $$
(Map p566; 11288 Ventura Blvd, Studio City; mains $8.50-19; ⊙11:30am-3pm & 5:30-9pm Mon-Sat; P) Stuffed with knickknacks, pasted with posters, and staffed by the sunny and sweet owner-operator, this offbeat Japanese diner offers the best (and one of the tastiest) deals on sushi row. The fried seaweed tofu *gyoza* are divine and so are the bowls – especially the *negitoro* bowl, where fatty tuna is served over rice, lettuce and seaweed.

Kazu Sushi   JAPANESE $$$
(Map p566; ☑818-763-4836; 11440 Ventura Blvd, Studio City; dishes $10-19; ⊙noon-2pm & 6-10pm Mon-Sat; P) Stuck in a cramped and otherwise nondescript, split-level minimall that's easy to miss is one of the best-kept secrets among LA's sushi aficionados. It's Michelin-rated, very high-end, has a terrific sake selection, and is worth the splurge.

Pasadena

★Little Flower   CAFE $
(☑626-304-4800; www.littleflowercandyco.com; 1424 W Colorado Blvd, Pasadena; mains $8-15; ⊙7am-7pm Mon-Sat, 9am-4pm Sun) Locally loved cafe set just a mile over the Colorado Bridge from Old Town. It does exquisite pastries, *bánh mì* sandwiches with chicken, roast beef or tempeh, and bowls stuffed with such things as dahl, raita, curried eggplant and steamed spinach, or salmon, shredded carrots and daikon, micro greens and ponzu.

🍷 Drinking & Nightlife

Downtown Los Angeles

Las Perlas   BAR
(Map p560; 107 E 6th St; ⊙7pm-2am Mon-Sat, 8pm-2am Sun) With Old Mexico whimsy, a chalkboard menu of more than 80 tequilas and mescals, and friendly barkeeps who mix things such as egg whites, blackberries and port syrup into new-school takes on the margarita, there's a reason we love downtown's best tequila bar. But if you truly want to dig tequila, select a highland variety and sip it neat.

Varnish   BAR
(Map p560; ☑213-622-9999; www.213nightlife.com/thevarnish; 118 E 6th St; ⊙7pm-2am) Tucked into the back of Cole's, is this cubbyhole-sized speakeasy, where good live jazz burns Sunday to Tuesday.

Hollywood

La Descarga   LOUNGE
(☑323-466-1324; www.ladescargala.com; 1159 N Western Ave; ⊙8pm-2am Wed-Sat) This tastefully frayed, sublimely sweaty rum and cigar lounge is a revelation. Behind the marble bar are more than 100 types of rum from Haiti and Guyana, Guatemala and Venezuela.

★No Vacancy   BAR
(Map p564; ☑323-465-1902; www.novacancyla.com; 1727 N Hudson Ave; ⊙8pm-2am) An old, shingled Victorian has been converted into LA's hottest night out at research time. Even the entrance is theatrical. You'll follow a rickety staircase into a narrow hall and enter the room of a would-be Madame (dressed in fishnet), who will press a button to reveal another staircase down into the living room and out into a courtyard of mayhem.

Dirty Laundry   BAR
(Map p564; ☑323-462-6531; dirtylaundrybarla.com; 1725 N Hudson Ave; ⊙10pm-2am) Under a cotton-candy-pink apartment block of no particular import is a funky den of musty odor and great times, low ceilings, exposed pipes, good whiskey, groovy funk on the turntables and plenty of uninhibited pretty people. There are velvet-rope politics at work here, so reserve a table to make sure you slip through.

Sayers Club   CLUB
(Map p564; ☑323-871-8416; www.sbe.com/nightlife/locations/thesayersclub-hollywood; 1645 Wilcox Ave; cover varies; ⊙8pm-2am Tue, Thu & Fri) When rock royalty such as Prince, established stars like the Black Keys and even movie stars like Joseph Gordon Levitt decide to play secret shows in intimate environs, they find the back room at this brick-house Hollywood nightspot, where the booths are leather, the lighting moody and the music – whether live, or spun by DJs – satisfies.

Silver Lake & Echo Park

Short Stop   CLUB
(☑213-482-4942; 1455 W Sunset Blvd; ⊙5pm-2am Mon-Fri, from 2pm Sat & Sun) Echo Park's beloved and deceptively sprawling dive has a

dance floor in one room, a bar strobing ball-games on flat screens in another, and a pool table and pinball machines in still another section. Echo Park locals and hipsters bump shoulders, especially on Motown Mondays, when vintage jams fill the room with joy.

West Hollywood & Mid-City

El Carmen
BAR

(Map p570; 8138 W 3rd St; ⏰5pm-2am Mon-Fri, from 7pm Sat & Sun) A pair of mounted bull heads and *lucha libre* (Mexican wrestling) masks create a 'Tijuana North' look and pull in an industry-heavy crowd at LA's ultimate tequila and mescal tavern.

Bar Marmont
BAR

(Map p570; ☎323-650-0575; www.chateaumarmont.com/barmarmont.php; 8171 Sunset Blvd; ⏰6pm-2am) Elegant, but not stuck up. Been around, yet still cherished. With high ceilings, molded walls and terrific martinis, the famous, and the wish-they-weres, still flock here. If you time it right, you might see Thom Yorke, or perhaps Lindsey Lohan? Come midweek. Weekends are for amateurs.

Formosa Cafe
BAR

(Map p570; ☎323-850-9050; 7156 Santa Monica Blvd; ⏰4pm-2am Mon-Fri, 6pm-2am Sat & Sun) Humphrey Bogart and Clark Gable used to knock 'em back at this dark railcar of a watering hole so authentically noir that scenes from *LA Confidential* were filmed here.

Malibu

Sunset
BAR

(www.thesunsetrestaurant.com; 6800 Westward Rd; ⏰noon-10pm; 🖵) A perfectly strange oasis after a day at the beach. Mostly because the Happy Hour crowd gets weird. Like rich, celebrity, plastic surgery, comb-over weird.

Santa Monica

★ Basement Tavern
BAR

(Map p578; www.basementtavern.com; 2640 Main St; ⏰5pm-2am) This creative speakeasy is our favorite well in Santa Monica. We love it for its cocktails, cozy booths and nightly live-music calendar that features blues, jazz, bluegrass and rock. It gets too busy on weekends, but weeknights can be special.

Misfit
LOUNGE

(Map p578; ☎310-656-9800; www.themisfitbar.com; 225 Santa Monica Blvd; ⏰noon-late Mon-Fri, from 11am Sat & Sun) This darkly lit emporium of food, drink and fun is notable for the decent – not great – menu, and phenomenal cocktails made from craftsman spirits. Set in a historic building decked out with a retro interior, it's busy from brunch to last call.

Venice

Townhouse & Delmonte Speakeasy
BAR

(Map p578; www.townhousevenice.com; 52 Windward Ave; ⏰5pm-2am Mon-Thu, noon-2am Fri-Sun) Upstairs is a cool, dark and perfectly dingy bar with pool tables, booths and good booze. Downstairs is the speakeasy, where DJs spin pop, funk and electronic music, comics take the mic and jazz players set up and jam. It's a reliably good time almost any night.

☆ Entertainment

Live Music

Orpheum Theatre
LIVE MUSIC

(Map p560; ☎877-677-4386; www.laorpheum.com; 842 S Broadway) In the early 20th century, cacophonous Broadway was a glamorous shopping and theater strip, where mega-stars such as Charlie Chaplin leapt from limos to attend premieres at lavish movie palaces like this one. The Orpheum was the first to be fully restored. Jam band Gods, Widespread Panic, and younger phenoms, MGMT, played here recently.

United Artists Theatre
LIVE MUSIC, DANCE

(Map p560; ☎213-623-3233; www.acehotel.com/losangeles/theatre; 929 S Broadway) A historic gem of a theater, restored by Ace Hotel, which curates the calendar as well. It's homebase for LA's best modern-dance company and stages indie and up-and-coming bands.

★ Greek Theatre
LIVE MUSIC

(Map p566; ☎323-665-5857; www.greektheatrela.com; 2700 N Vermont Ave; ⏰May-Oct) A more intimate version of the Hollywood Bowl, this 5800-seat outdoor amphitheater tucked into a woodsy hillside of Griffith Park is much beloved for its vibe and variety – Los Lobos to MGMT to Willie Nelson. Parking is stacked, so plan on a post-show wait.

Royce Hall
LIVE MUSIC

(Map p576; www.uclalive.org; UCLA; tickets from $22) An exceptional theater housed in UCLA's historic heart. The brick building reeks of academia, but UCLA Live has been known

GAY & LESBIAN LOS ANGELES

LA is one of the country's gayest cities (the city has made a number of contributions to gay culture), and the rainbow flag flies especially proudly in Boystown, along Santa Monica Blvd in West Hollywood (WeHo). Thursday through Sunday nights are prime time.

If nightlife isn't your scene, there are plenty of other ways to meet, greet and engage. Outdoor activities include the **Frontrunners** (www.lafrontrunners.com) running club and the **Great Outdoors** (www.greatoutdoorsla.org) hiking club. There's gay theater all over town, but the **Celebration Theatre** (Map p570; www.celebrationtheatre.com; 7051 Santa Monica Blvd, West Hollywood) ranks among the nation's leading stages for LGBT plays.

The **LA Gay & Lesbian Center** (Map p564; ☎ 323-993-7400; www.laglc.org; 1625 Schrader Blvd, Hollywood; ⊙9am-8pm Mon-Fri, to 1pm Sat) is a one-stop service, and its affiliated **Village at Ed Gould Plaza** (www.laglc.org; 1125 N McCadden Pl, Hollywood; ⊙6-10pm Mon-Fri, 9am-5pm Sat) offers art exhibits and theater programs around a leafy courtyard.

The festival season kicks off in mid- to late May with the **Long Beach Pride Celebration** (www.longbeachpride.com) and continues with the three-day **LA Pride** (www.lapride.org) in early June with a parade down Santa Monica Blvd. On **Halloween** (October 31), the same street brings out 350,000 outrageously costumed revelers of all persuasions.

WeHo

Abbey (Map p570; www.abbeyfoodandbar.com; 692 N Robertson Blvd; mains $9-13; ⊙11am-2am Mon-Thu, from 10am Fri, from 9am Sat & Sun) Once a humble coffeehouse, the Abbey has developed into WeHo's bar/club/restaurant of record. Always cool and fun, it has so many different-flavored martinis and mojitos that you'd think they were invented here. It also has a full menu. Match your mood to the many different spaces, from outdoor patio to goth lounge to chill room. On weekends they're all busy.

Micky's (Map p570; www.mickys.com; 8857 Santa Monica Blvd; ⊙5pm-2am Sun-Thu, to 4am Fri & Sat) A two-story, quintessential WeHo dance club, with go-go boys, expensive drinks, attitude and plenty of eye candy. There is a marble circle bar, exposed steel girders and doors that open all the way to the street. Check online for special events.

Trunks (Map p570; www.trunksbar.com; 8809 Santa Monica Blvd; ⊙1pm-2am) With pool tables and sports on the flat screens, this brick house, low-lit dive is a long-running boulevard staple that is less fabulous and more down-to-earth than most in WeHo.

Hamburger Habit (Map p570; ☎ 310-659-8774; 8954 Santa Monica Blvd; mains $5-8; ⊙10am-midnight) The greasy burgers are middling, but the evening scene, which may include sing-alongs and topless men dancing on tables, is as unique as it is wonderful.

Beyond WeHo

Akbar (Map p568; www.akbarsilverlake.com; 4356 W Sunset Blvd; ⊙4pm-2am) Best jukebox in town, Casbah-style atmosphere, and a great mix of people that's been known to change from hour to hour – gay, straight, on the fence or just hip, but not too hip for you.

Casita del Campo (Map p568; www.casitadelcampo.net; 1920 Hyperion Ave; mains lunch $8, dinner $14-17; ⊙11am-11pm Sun-Wed, to midnight Thu, to 2am Fri & Sat; P) What's not to love about this Mexican cantina? It's cozy, it's fun, and you might even catch a drag show in the tiny Cavern Club Theater.

Faultline (Map p568; www.faultlinebar.com; 4216 Melrose Ave; ⊙5pm-2am Wed-Fri, 2pm-2am Sat & Sun) Indoor-outdoor venue that's party central for manly men, with nary a twink in sight. Take off your shirt and join the Sunday-afternoon beer bust (it's an institution), but get there early or expect a long wait.

to bring in authors such as David Sedaris and Anthony Bourdain for lively readings, and spectacular musicians like piano man Chick Corea, and the Philip Glass ensemble.

El Rey LIVE MUSIC
(Map p570; www.theelrey.com; 5515 Wilshire Blvd; cover varies) An old art-deco dance hall decked out in red velvet and chandeliers and flaunting an awesome sound

system with excellent sightlines. Although it can hold 800 people, it feels quite small. Performance-wise, it's popular with indie acts and the rockers who love them.

★Echo
LIVE MUSIC

(www.attheecho.com; 1822 W Sunset Blvd; cover varies) Eastsiders hungry for an eclectic alchemy of sounds pack this funky-town dive that's basically a sweaty bar with a stage and a smoking patio. It books indie bands, and also has regular club nights. The Funky Sole party every Saturday is always a blast.

Comedy & Theater

★Upright Citizens Brigade Theatre
COMEDY

(Map p564; ☑323-908-8702; www.losangeles. ucbtheatre.com; 5919 Franklin Ave; tickets $5-10) Founded in New York by *SNL* alums Amy Poehler and Ian Roberts along with Matt Besser and Matt Walsh, this sketch-comedy group cloned itself in Hollywood in 2005 and is arguably the best improv theater in town. Most shows are $5 or $8, but Sunday's 'Asssscat' is freeeee.

Groundlings
COMEDY

(Map p570; ☑323-934-4747; www.groundlings. com; 7307 Melrose Ave; tickets $10-20) This improv school and company has launched Lisa Kudrow, Will Ferrell, Maya Rudolph and other top talent. Their sketch comedy and improv can bring on belly-laughs, especially on Thursdays when the main company, alumni and surprise guests get to riff together in 'Cookin' with Gas.'

Anateus Company
THEATER, COMEDY

(☑818-506-5436; www.antaeus.org; 5112 Lankershim Blvd, North Hollywood; tickets $30-34) A theater, among the better reviewed in LA, offering plays and stand-up comedy.

Noho Arts Center Ensemble
THEATER

(www.thenohoartscenter.com; 11136 Magnolia Blvd, North Hollywood; tickets $25; ☉shows 8pm Fri & Sat, 3pm Sun) The crown jewel of North Hollywood's budding theater scene offers reimagined classic and new cutting-edge theater.

Sports

Dodger Stadium
BASEBALL

(☑866-363-4377; www.dodgers.com; 1000 Elysian Park Ave; ☉Apr-Sep) Few clubs can match the Dodgers organization when it comes to history (Jackie Robinson, Sandy Koufax, Kirk Gibson, and Vin Scully), winning and fan loyalty. The club's current owners bought the organization for roughly two billion dollars, an American team sports record at the time.

🔒 Shopping

🔒 Downtown Los Angeles

★Raggedy Threads
VINTAGE

(Map p560; ☑213-620-1188; www.raggedythreads. com; 330 E 2nd St; ☉noon-8pm Mon-Sat, to 6pm Sun) A vintage Americana store just off the main Little Tokyo strip. You'll find plenty of beautifully raggedy denim and overalls, soft T-shirts, a few Victorian dresses, and a wonderful turquoise collection at great prices. Sensational glasses frames and watches too.

Apolis
FASHION

(Map p560; ☑213-613-9626; www.apolisglobal.com; 806 E 3rd St) A tremendous, not cheap, men's wear brand that does tailored chinos, jeans and T-shirts, and blazers too. Owned by two Santa Barbarian brothers, the line fits comfortably between J Crew and James Perse. It's all about fair trade, and proves it with development projects in American inner cities and Peruvian, Bangladeshi and Ugandan villages.

🔒 Hollywood

Amoeba Music
MUSIC

(Map p564; ☑323-245-6400; www.amoeba. com; 6400 W Sunset Blvd; ☉10:30am-11pm Mon-Sat, 11am-9pm Sun) When a record store not only survives but thrives in this techno age, you know it's doing something right. Flip through half-a-million new and used LPs, CDs, DVDs, videos and vinyl at this granddaddy of music stores. Handy listening stations and its outstanding *Music We Like* booklet keep you from buying lemons.

🔒 West Hollywood & Mid-City

This is by far the best and most diverse shopping territory in a city that often feels like it's built by, and for, shopoholics.

★Reformation
FASHION

(Map p570; www.thereformation.com; 8253 Melrose Ave; ☉11am-7pm) Here's classic, retro-inspired, fashionable outer wear that's eco-conscious without the granola. The tagline is 'change the world without changing your style.' Products use only pre-existing materials, which means no additional dying of fabrics and half the water use of other fashion brands. Everything is made downtown.

LA'S FASHION DISTRICT DEMYSTIFIED

Bargain hunters love this frantic, 90-block warren of fashion in southwestern downtown. Deals can be amazing, but first-timers are often bewildered by the district's size and immense selection. For orientation, check out www.fashiondistrict.org, where you can download a free app and a map to the area.

Basically, the area is subdivided into several distinct retail areas:

➡ Women – Los Angeles St between Olympic and Pico Blvds; 11th St between Los Angeles and San Julian Sts

➡ Children – Wall St between 12th St and Pico Blvd

➡ Men and bridal – Los Angeles St between 7th and 9th Sts

➡ Textiles – 9th St between Santee and Wall Sts

➡ Jewelry and accessories – Santee St between Olympic Blvd and 13th St

➡ Designer knockoffs – Santee Alley and New Alley (enter on 11th St between Maple and Santee Aves)

Shops are generally open from 10am to 5pm daily, with Saturday being the busiest because that's when many wholesalers open up to the public. Cash is king and haggling may get you 10% or 20% off, especially when buying multiple items. Refunds or exchanges are a no-no, so choose carefully and make sure items are in good condition. Most stores don't have dressing rooms.

Sample Sales

Every last Friday of the month, clued-in fashionistas descend upon the corner of 9th St and Los Angeles St armed with cash and attitude to catfight it out for designer clothes priced below wholesale. Their destination: the hip showrooms at the **Gerry Building** (Map p560; www.gerrybuilding.com; 910 S Los Angeles St), **Cooper Design Space** (Map p560; ☏213-627-3754; www.cooperdesignspace.com; 860 S Los Angeles St) and the **New Mart** (Map p560; ☏213-627-0671; www.newmart.net; 127 E 9th St). They each specialize in contemporary and young fashions – though the Cooper and the Gerry are considered the hippest of the bunch. The **California Market Center** (Map p560; ☏213-630-3600; www.californiamarketcenter.com; 110 E 9th St) has a great fashion bookstore on the ground floor, among make-up and fragrance retailers, and houses both clothing and home-furnishing wholesalers. Open from 9am to 3pm, this is the only time the general public is allowed in these trade-only buildings. Come early and leave your modesty at home, as you'll either be trying things on in front of others or not at all. During Christmas season there are often several sales each week. Check the websites for dates and participating showrooms.

Fahey/Klein Gallery   GALLERY
(Map p570; www.faheykleingallery.com; 148 S La Brea Ave; ⊙10am-6pm Tue-Sat) The best in vintage and contemporary fine-art photography by icons such as Annie Leibovitz, Bruce Weber and the late, great rock-and-roll shutterbug, Jim Marshall. It even has his lesser-known civil rights catalog in its vast archives.

Espionage   VINTAGE
(Map p570; ☏323-272-4942; www.espionagela. com; 7456 Beverly Blvd; ⊙11am-6pm Mon, to 7pm Tue-Fri, 10:30am-7pm Sat, to 6pm Sun) A fabulous boutique blessed with a tasteful mélange of new and vintage goods. Their jewelry is fantastic, so are the chunky vin-

tage perfume bottles and ash trays. Those leather chairs work perfectly with their brass and glass end tables and they offer a collection of vintage couture clothing sold on consignment.

Supreme   FASHION
(Map p570; ☏323-655-6205; supremenewyork. com; 439 N Fairfax Ave) When we rolled by, this beloved skate punk hip-hop mashup of a label had just re-opened its doors, and the heads lined up for half a block to get a taste of the new line. So, yes, it's a *thing*. Also, it has a half pipe in the store, and that's maybe the best of things.

Melrose Trading Post   MARKET
(Map p570; http://melrosetradingpost.org; Fairfax High School, 7850 Melrose Ave; admission $2; ⊙ 9am-5pm Sun) Threads, jewelry, housewares and other offbeat items proffered by more than 100 purveyors. Held in the Fairfax High parking lot; proceeds help fund school programs.

Fred Segal   FASHION
(Map p570; ☑ 323-651-4129; www.fredsegal.com; 8100 Melrose Ave; ⊙ 10am-7pm Mon-Sat, noon-6pm Sun) Celebs and beautiful people circle for the very latest from Babakul, Aviator Nation and Robbi & Nikki at this warren of high-end boutiques under one impossibly chic but slightly snooty roof. The only time you'll see bargains (sort of) is during the two-week blowout sale in September.

Beverly Hills & the Westside

While Beverly Hills and **Rodeo Drive** (btwn Wilshire & Santa Monica Blvds) get most of the hype, the best boutiques are on Robertson, between Beverly Blvd and Burton Way.

Barneys New York   DEPARTMENT STORE
(☑ 310-276-4400; www.barneys.com; 9570 Wilshire Blvd; ⊙ 10am-7pm Mon-Wed, Fri & Sat, to 8pm Thu, noon-6pm Sun) Four floors of straight-up chic. Prices are steep, so keep any eye out for one of its twice-annual warehouse sales. There's a special deli on the top floor worth trying too.

Scoop   FASHION
(☑ 310-362-6100; www.scoopnyc.com; 265 N Beverly Dr; ⊙ 10am-7pm Mon-Sat, 11am-6pm Sun) A grab bag of designer denim and limited-edition sneakers, funky belts and designer camo jackets. The women's line is more chic than sporty, sprinkled with dresses, handbags, and heels. It's set in the ground floor of the fabulous blue-glass MGM building.

Malibu

Malibu Country Mart   MALL
(www.malibucountrymart.com; 3835 Cross Creek Rd) Across from Surfrider Beach, this mall spans both sides of Cross Creek Rd. Which is why it's affectionately known as Cross Creek by the sun-kissed local beach girls and boys who gather at this high-end outdoor shopping mall to flirt, grub and shop.

Santa Monica

For big chains such as Anthropologie, the flagship Apple, Guess and Converse make your way to the **Third Street Promenade** (Map p578). **Santa Monica Place** (Map p578; www.santamonicaplace.com; 395 Santa Monica Pl; ⊙ 10am-9pm Mon-Thu, to 10pm Fri & Sat, 11am-8pm Sun) offers more upscale corporate consumption. For indie-minded boutiques, such as **Planet Blue** (Map p578; www.shopplanetblue.com; 2940 Main St; ⊙ 10am-6pm), head to **Montana Ave** and **Main St**.

🏠 Venice

Boho-chic **Abbot Kinney Blvd** (www.abbotkinneyonline.com) has become one of LA's top shopping destinations. Come see it on the monthly **First Friday** (www.abbotkinney-1stfridays.com) gathering, when galleries stay open late.

Alexis Bittar   JEWELRY
(Map p578; ☑ 310-452-6901; www.alexisbittar.com; 1612 Abbot Kinney Blvd; ⊙ 11am-7pm Mon-Sat, noon-6pm Sun) High-end jewelry known for Bittar's use of lucite, which is hand carved and painted in his Brooklyn studio. Some of it looks like stone. He started by selling it on the streets in Manhattan where he was picked up by the MOMA store. Now, he's kind of a big deal.

Will   LEATHER GOODS
(Map p578; www.willleathergoods.com; 1360 Abbot Kinney Blvd; ⊙ 10am-8pm) A terrific leather-goods store out of Portland, and one of just three nationwide. It does fine leather bags, briefcases, backpacks, belts, wallets and sandals for men and women. Our favorite was the bike messenger bag inlaid with colorful remnant Oaxacan wool.

🛈 Information

EMERGENCY

Police, Fire, Ambulance (☑ 911)
Police (☑ 877-275-5273; www.lapdonline.org) For nonemergencies within the city of LA.
Rape & Battering Hotline (☑ 310-392-8381, 213-626-3393; ⊙ 24hr)

INTERNET ACCESS

Internet cafes in LA seem to have the lifespan of a fruit fly, but dozens of cafes and restaurants around town offer free wi-fi.

MEDIA

KCRW 89.9 FM (www.kcrw.com) LA's cultural pulse and the best station in the city. Beams National Public Radio (NPR), eclectic and indie music, intelligent talk, and hosts shows and events throughout Southern California.

La Opinión (www.laopinion.com) Spanish-language daily.

LA Weekly (www.laweekly.com) Free alternative news, live music and entertainment listings.

Los Angeles Downtown News (www.downtownnews.com) The finger on the cultural, political and economic pulse of the booming downtown district.

Los Angeles Times (www.latimes.com) Major daily newspaper.

MEDICAL SERVICES

Cedars-Sinai Medical Center (☑ 310-423-3277; http://cedars-sinai.edu; 8700 Beverly Blvd, West Hollywood; ☺ 24hr) Emergency room.

Rite Aid Pharmacies (☑ 800-748-3243; www.riteaid.com)

MONEY

Travelex Santa Monica (☑ 310-260-9219; www.travelex.com; 201 Santa Monica Blvd, Suite 101, Santa Monica; ☺ 9am-5pm Mon-Thu, to 6pm Fri); West Hollywood (☑ 310-659-6093; www.travelex.com; US Bank, 8901 Santa Monica Blvd, West Hollywood; ☺ 9:30am-5pm Mon-Thu, 9am-6pm Fri, 9am-1pm Sat).

POST

Call ☑ 800-275-8777 for the nearest post office branch.

TOURIST INFORMATION

Downtown LA Visitor Center (Map p560; www.discoverlosangeles.com; 800 N Alameda St, Downtown; ☺ 8:30am-5pm Mon-Fri)

Hollywood Visitor Information Center (Map p564; ☑ 323-467-6412; http://discoverlosangeles.com; Hollywood & Highland complex, 6801 Hollywood Blvd, Hollywood; ☺ 10am-10pm Mon-Sat, to 7pm Sun) In the Dolby Theatre walkway.

Long Beach Area Convention & Tourism Bureau (☑ 562-628-8850; www.visitlongbeach.com; 3rd fl, One World Trade Center, 301 E Ocean Blvd, Long Beach; ☺ 11am-7pm Sun-Thu, 11:30am-7:30pm Fri & Sat Jun-Sep, 10am-4pm Fri-Sun Oct-May)

Santa Monica (Map p578; ☑ 800-544-5319; www.santamonica.com; 2427 Main St, Santa Monica) Roving information officers patrol on and around the promenade (on Segways!).

ⓘ Getting There & Away

AIR

The main LA gateway is **Los Angeles International Airport** (LAX; ☑ 310-646-5252; www.lawa.org/lax; 1 World Way; ☏), a U-shaped, bilevel complex with nine terminals linked by the free **Shuttle A** leaving from the lower (arrival) level.

Cabs and hotel and car-rental shuttles stop here as well. A free minibus for travelers with a disability can be ordered by calling ☑ 310-646-6402. Ticketing and check-in are on the upper (departure) level. The hub for most international airlines is the Tom Bradley International Terminal.

Domestic flights operated by Alaska, American, Southwest, United and other major US airlines also arrive at Bob Hope/Burbank Airport (p761), which is handy if you're headed for Hollywood, downtown or Pasadena.

To the south, on the border with Orange County, the small Long Beach Airport (p761) is convenient for Disneyland and is served by Alaska, US Airways and Jet Blue.

BUS

The main bus terminal for **Greyhound** (☑ 213-629-8401; www.greyhound.com; 1716 E 7th St) is in a grimy part of downtown, so avoid arriving after dark. Take bus 18 to the 7th St subway station or bus 66 to Pershing Square Station, then hop on the Metro Rail Red Line to Hollywood or Union Station with onward service around town. Some Greyhound buses go directly to the terminal in **Hollywood** (1715 N Cahuenga Blvd).

CAR & MOTORCYCLE

All the major car-rental agencies have branches at area airports. **Eagle Rider** (☑ 888-600-6020; www.eaglerider.com; 11860 S La Cienega Blvd, Hawthorne; per day from $99; ☺ 9am-5pm) and Route 66 (p766) rent Harleys.

TRAIN

Amtrak trains roll into downtown's historic **Union Station** (☑ 800-872-7245; www.amtrak.com; 800 N Alameda St). The *Pacific Surfliner* travels daily between San Diego, Santa Barbara and San Luis Obispo via LA.

ⓘ Getting Around

TO/FROM THE AIRPORT

All services mentioned below leave from the lower terminal level of LAX. Door-to-door shuttles, such as those operated by **Prime Time** (☑ 800-733-8267; www.primetimeshuttle.com) and Super Shuttle (www.supershuttle.com) charge $21, $27 and $16 for trips to Santa Monica, Hollywood or downtown, respectively.

Curbside dispatchers will be on hand to summon a taxi. The flat rate to downtown LA is $47, while going to Santa Monica costs $30 to $35, to West Hollywood around $40, to Hollywood $50 and to Disneyland $90.

LAX FlyAway (☑ 866-435-9529; www.lawa.org; one-way $8) buses travel nonstop to downtown's Union Station ($8, 45 minutes), Van Nuys ($8, 45 minutes), Westwood Village near UCLA ($10, 30 minutes), and to the Expo Line Light Rail station at La Brea and Exposition Blvd ($7,

1¼ hours) for connections to South Central, Hollywood and Union Station.

For Santa Monica or Venice, catch the free Shuttle C bus to the **LAX Transit Center** (96th St & Sepulveda Blvd), then change to the Santa Monica Rapid 3 ($1, one hour). The center is the hub for buses serving all of LA. If you're headed for Culver City, catch Culver City bus 6 ($1, 20 minutes). For Manhattan or Hermosa Beach, hop aboard Beach Cities Transit 109 ($1), which also stops at Lot G. For Redondo Beach head to Lot C and hop aboard the Metro Local 232 ($1.50).

BICYCLE

Most buses have bike racks, and bikes ride for free, although you must load and unload them yourself. Bicycles are allowed on Metro Rail trains except during rush hour (6:30am to 8:30am and 4:30pm to 6:30pm Monday to Friday).

CAR & MOTORCYCLE

Unless time is no factor – or money is extremely tight – you're going to want to spend some time behind the wheel, although this means contending with some of the worst traffic in the country. Avoid crossing town at rush hour (7am to 9am and 3:30pm to 7pm).

Parking at motels and cheaper hotels is usually free, while fancier ones charge anywhere from $8 to $40 for the privilege. Valet parking at nicer restaurants and hotels is commonplace with rates ranging from $5 to $10.

PUBLIC TRANSPORTATION

Most public transportation is handled by **Metro** (☑ 323-466-3876; www.metro.net), which offers trip-planning help through its website.

The regular base fare is $1.75 per boarding or $7 for a day pass with unlimited rides. Weekly passes are $25 and valid from Sunday to Saturday. Monthly passes are $100 and valid for 30 days.

Single tickets and day passes are available from bus drivers and vending machines at each train station. Weekly and monthly passes must be bought at one of 650 locations around town.

Metro operates about 200 bus lines, most of them local routes stopping every few blocks. Metro Rapid buses stop less frequently.

Metro Rail is a network of six light-rail lines and two subway lines, with five of them converging in downtown. The Expo Line linking Exposition Park and downtown LA with Culver City is expected to reach Santa Monica by 2015.

Red Line The most useful for visitors, it links downtown's Union Station to North Hollywood (San Fernando Valley) via central Hollywood and Universal City.

Blue Line Downtown to Long Beach; connects with the Red Line at 7th St/Metro Center station and the Green Line at the Imperial/Wilmington stop.

Gold Line East LA to Little Tokyo, Chinatown and Pasadena via Union Station, Mt Washington and Highland Park; connects with the Red Line at Union Station.

Green Line Norwalk to Redondo Beach; connects with the Blue Line at Imperial/Wilmington.

Purple Line Subway between downtown LA and Koreatown; shares six stations with the Red Line.

Orange Line Links downtown and Hollywood with the west San Fernando Valley; connects with the Red Line in North Hollywood.

Expo Line Links USC and Exposition Park with Culver City to the west and downtown LA to the northeast, where it connects with the Red Line at Union Station. The Santa Monica extension is scheduled to open in 2015.

Santa Monica–based **Big Blue Bus** (☑ 310-451-5444; www.bigbluebus.com; fares from $1) burns clean fuel and serves Santa Monica, Venice, Westwood and LAX ($1). Its express bus 10 runs from Santa Monica to downtown ($2, one hour).

The **Culver CityBus** (www.culvercity.org) provides service throughout Culver City and the Westside, including LAX ($1). **Long Beach Transit** (www.lbtransit.com) serves Long Beach and surrounding communities.

DASH Buses, operated by the **LA Department of Transportation** (LADOT; www.ladottransit.com), offer 33 routes serving local communities (50¢ per boarding) until 7pm.

TAXI

Getting around by cab will cost you. Cabs are best organized over the phone, though some prowl the streets late at night. In the city of LA, taxi rates are $2.85 at flagfall plus about $2.70 per mile. Cabs leaving from LAX charge a $4 airport fee. For details, check www.taxicabsla.org. In Santa Monica, call **Taxi Taxi** (☑ 310-444-4444; www.santamonicataxi.com).

Uber and UberX (www.uber.com) are extremely popular for cheap and more luxurious rides in LA.

AROUND LOS ANGELES

Ditch the congestion, crowds and smog, and use LA as a hub to all the natural glory of California. Get an early start to beat the traffic (or catch a ferry, Greyhound bus or ride the Amtrack rails), point the compass across the ocean or up into the mountains.

Catalina Island

Mediterranean-flavored Catalina Island is a popular getaway for harried Angelenos, but sinks under the weight of day-trippers in summer. Stay overnight, though, and feel the ambience go from frantic to romantic.

It's a nice stroll along the Avalon waterfront to the art-deco **Casino** (1 Casino Way), which has murals, a movie theater and a fabulous upstairs ballroom; the last can only be seen on guided one-hour tours ($23). There's good snorkeling at **Lovers' Cove** and at **Casino Point Marine Park**, a marine reserve that's also the best shore dive. **Descanso Beach Ocean Sports** (www.kayakcatalinaisland.com; kayak rentals per hr/day from $22/52, SUP rentals per hr/day $24/60) rents snorkeling gear, stand up paddleboard kits and kayaks.

About 1.5 miles inland from Avalon harbor is the peaceful **Wrigley Memorial & Botanical Gardens** (☑310-510-2595; 1400 Avalon Canyon Rd; adult/child /senior $7/free/5; ☺8am-5pm), where you'll enjoy sweeping garden views from a monument awash in colorful local tile.

To get into the protected backcountry, hop on the **Safari Bus** (☑310-510-2800; tickets $10-32; ☺mid-Jun–early Sep), which goes all the way to Two Harbors. You must book in advance and get a permit (and maps) from the **Catalina Conservancy** (☑310-510-2595; www.catalinaconservancy.org; 125 Claressa Ave, Avalon; biking/hiking $35/free) if you're going to be hiking or mountain biking.

Certified scuba divers should find **Catalina Dive Shop** (www.catalinadiveshop.com; Lovers Cove; per trip $99-129) to glimpse local shipwrecks and kelp forests. It rents snorkel gear here too. **Two Harbors Dive and Recreation Center** (www.visitcatalinaisland.com; guided dive trips $100-140) accesses pristine dive sites off the island's less-developed coast.

In Avalon nest at the laid-back **Pavilion Hotel** (☑877-778-8322; www.visitcatalinaisland.com/hotels-packages/avalon/pavilion-hotel; 513 Crescent Ave; r from $185) or splashier **Hotel Metropole** (☑800-300-8528; www.hotel-metropole.com; 205 Crescent Ave; r from $175). In Two Harbors, it's all about the **Banning House Lodge** (☑877-778-8322; www.visitcatalinaisland.com/hotels-packages/two-harbors/banning-house-lodge; 1 Banning House Rd; r from $129), a 1910 California Craftsman classic. For camping information, see www.visitcatalinaisland.com/avalon/camping.php.

Bluewater Grill (☑310-510-3474; www.bluewatergrill.com; 306 Crescent Ave; mains $19-39; ☺11am-10pm) offers sumptuous seafood dinners and **CC Gallagher** (www.ccgallagher.com; 523 Crescent Ave; ☺7am-midnight Sun-Thu, to 1am Fri & Sat), part wine shop, part cafe, part sushi bar, does it all quite well.

❶ Getting There & Away

Reservations are recommended in the summer for ferries to Avalon and Two Harbors.

Catalina Express (www.catalinaexpress.com; round-trip adult/child $75/60) Ferries to Avalon from San Pedro, Long Beach and Dana Point (Orange County), and to Two Harbors from San Pedro. It takes one to 1½ hours, with up to three ferries daily. Ride free on your birthday!

Catalina Flyer (☑800-830-7744; www.catalinaferries.com; round-trip adult/under 12yr/senior $70/53/65) Catamaran to Avalon and Two Harbors from Balboa Harbor in Newport Beach (one to 1½ hours).

Big Bear Lake

Big Bear Lake is a low-key and family-friendly mountain resort (elevation 6750ft) about 110 miles northeast of LA. Snowy winters lure scores of skiers and boarders to its two mountains; summers bring hikers, mountain bikers and water-sports enthusiasts wishing to escape the stifling heat down in the basin. Blessed with postcard canyon views, the **Rim of the World Scenic Byway** (Hwy 18) is one of America's great drives. We suggest diverging from the trodden path early, and visiting the sculpted sandstone of **Mormon Rocks**. From there take Hwy 138 past **Silverwood Lake** and **Lake Gregory**, then climb Hwy 18 into quaint **Blue Jay** and **Lake Arrowhead**. This is where the vistas get serious and the hairpins exciting. Lake Arrowhead's fashionable mall and ski resort makes a nice respite from the road. Once back on the highway, the most jaw-dropping stretch of road takes you into Big Bear Lake.

🏃 Activities

Big Bear's two ski mountains are jointly managed by **Big Bear Mountain Resorts** (www.bigbearmountainresorts.com; adult/child lift ticket $56/46). The higher of the two, **Bear Mountain** (8805ft) is nirvana for freestyle freaks with more than 150 jumps, 80 jibs, and two pipes including a 580ft in-ground superpipe. **Snow Summit** (8200ft) is more about traditional downhill and has trails for everyone. Altogether the mountains are served by 26 lifts and crisscrossed by more than 55 runs. Ski and boot rentals are about $30.

In summer Snow Summit issues its siren call to mountain bikers. Several pro and amateur races take place here each year. The 9-mile **Grandview Loop** is great for getting your feet in gear. The **Scenic Sky**

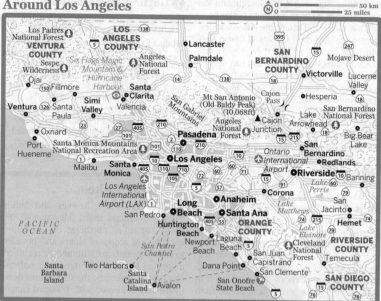

Chair (one-way/day $12/25; ⊙ May–start of ski season) provides easy access to the top. Maps, tickets and bike rentals are available from **Bear Valley Bikes** (www.bvbikes.com; 40298 Big Bear Blvd; bikes per hr incl helmet $10-20, per day $40-70). It charges higher rates for full suspension, and has fat bikes too.

To get off the beaten track, take your car for an off-road spin along the **Gold Fever Trail**, a 20-mile self-guided romp on a graded dirt road around an old gold-mining area.

🛏 Sleeping & Eating

For cheap sleeps tuck into the clean and friendly **Big Bear Hostel** (☎ 909-866-8900; www.adventurehostel.com; 527 Knickerbocker Rd; r $20-40; P@🖤). **Switzerland Haus** (☎ 800-335-3729, 909-866-3729; www.switzerlandhaus.com; 41829 Switzerland Dr; r incl breakfast $125-249; @🖤) offers comfy rooms with mountain-view patios and a Nordic sauna. **Himalayan** (www.himalayanbigbear.com; 672 Pine Knot Ave; mains $8-17; ⊙ 11am-9pm Sun-Tue, to 10pm Fri & Sat; 🌿🖤) is a popular Nepali and Indian kitchen with speedy service. **North Shore Cafe** (☎ 909-866-5879; www.dininginbigbear.com; 39226 North Shore Dr/Hwy 38, Fawnskin; breakfast & lunch mains $6-12; ⊙ 8am-4pm Wed-Thu, 8am-9pm Fri, 7am-9pm Sat, 7am-6pm Sun Oct-Apr, also 8am-4pm Mon May-Sep; 🖤🖤) is a dear

sweet diner set in a cabin with tasty breakfasts. Hit **Peppercorn Grille** (☎ 909-866-5405; www.peppercorngrille.com; 553 Pine Knot Ave; mains $8.95-15.95; ⊙ 11am-9pm Sun-Thu, to 10pm Fri & Sat) for candlelight and tablecloths.

ℹ Information

Big Bear Blvd (Hwy 18), the main road, runs south of the lake, skirting the pedestrian-friendly village with cutesy shops, galleries, restaurants and the **visitors center** (www.bigbear.com; 630 Bartlett Rd; ⊙ 8am-5pm Mon-Fri, 9am-5pm Sat & Sun). The ski resorts are east of the village. Quiet N Shore Dr (Hwy 38) provides access to campgrounds and trails.

If you're driving, pick up a National Forest Adventure Pass, available at the **Big Bear Discovery Center** (☎ 909-382-2790; www.bigbeardiscoverycenter.com; 40971 N Shore Dr, Fawnskin; ⊙ 8am-4:30pm, closed Wed & Thu mid-Sep–mid-May) on the North Shore.

ℹ Getting There & Away

Big Bear is on Hwy 18, an offshoot of Hwy 30 in San Bernardino. A quicker approach is via Hwy 330, which starts in Highland and intersects with Hwy 18 in Running Springs. **Mountain Area Regional Transit Authority** (Marta; ☎ 909-878-5200; www.marta.cc) buses connect Big Bear with the Greyhound and Metrolink stations in San Bernardino ($2.50, 1¼ hours).

Disneyland & Orange County

Best Places to Eat

➡ Walt's Wharf (p608)

➡ Napa Rose (p603)

➡ 242 Cafe Fusion Sushi (p621)

➡ Bear Flag Fish Company (p615)

➡ Ramos House Café (p623)

Best Places to Stay

➡ Shorebreak Hotel (p610)

➡ Disney's Grand Californian Hotel & Spa (p601)

➡ The Tides Inn (p620)

➡ Crystal Cove Beach Cottages (p617)

➡ Resort at Pelican Hill (p614)

Why Go?

Chances are that Orange County, that stretch between Los Angeles and San Diego, has seeped into your consciousness even if you've never been here.

No doubt Mickey Mouse and friends have been a part of that (Disneyland is California's biggest attraction). So too have TV series from *Real Housewives* to MTV's *Laguna Beach,* from *The OC* to *Arrested Development,* which have all been set here, taking the county's image from humdrum to hip, a place of mythically (gl)amorous teens, gorgeous beaches and socialite catfights.

While there's a whiff of truth to those stereotypes of life behind the 'Orange Curtain' – big, boxy mansions, fortress-like shopping malls, the overly entitled tossing Happy Meals out of their Humvees – this diverse county's 789 sq miles, 34 cities and three million people create deep pockets of individuality, beauty and different ways of thinking, keepin' the OC 'real,' no matter one's reality.

When to Go
Anaheim

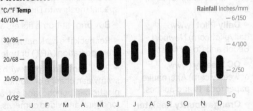

May Visitation dips after spring break until Memorial Day. Mostly sunny days, balmy temperatures.

Jul & Aug Summer vacation and beach season peak. Surfing and art festivals by the coast.

Sep Blue skies, cooler temperatures inland, fewer crowds. Tall Ships Festival at Dana Point.

SURFING WALK OF FAME

The OC's answer to Hollywood Boulevard immortalizes surf legends steps from the Huntington Beach Pier.

Top Shows & Parades at Disney Resort

➡ **World of Color** (DCA)

➡ **Fantasmic!** (Disneyland)

➡ **Mickey's Soundsational Parade** (Disneyland)

➡ **Pixar Play Parade** (DCA)

California Culture

Culture vultures: don't miss some of California's best-known cultural institutions: Segerstrom Center for the Arts (p616), South Coast Repertory (p616), Bowers Museum (p606) and Laguna Beach's Festival of Arts (p619) and Pageant of the Masters (p620).

For Local News

➡ **Coastline Pilot** (www.coastlinepilot.com) Laguna Beach.

➡ **Daily Pilot** (www.dailypilot.com) Newport Beach and Costa Mesa.

➡ **OC Weekly** (www.ocweekly.com) Alternative paper for arts and politics.

➡ **Orange County Register** (www.ocregister.com) National and regional news, culture and sports.

Theme-Park Passes

Visiting a lot of SoCal theme parks? The **Southern California CityPass** (www.citypass.com/southern-california; adult/child 3-9yr from $328/284) covers three-day 'Park Hopper' admission to Disneyland Resort, plus one-day admission to SeaWorld San Diego (p633) and Universal Studios Hollywood (p567). The CityPass price is at least $100 less than the combined regular ticket prices. Otherwise, look online for specials (eg five-day Park Hopper passes for the three-day price) or seasonal discounts on annual passports for Southern California residents and their guests.

FEELING THE HEAT AT DISNEYLAND

When Walt Disney opened Disneyland on July 17, 1955, he declared it the 'Happiest Place on Earth.' However, its opening day was a disaster. Temperatures over 100°F (38°C) melted asphalt underfoot, leaving women's high heels stuck in the tar. There were plumbing problems: all of the drinking fountains quit working. Hollywood stars didn't show up on time, and more than twice the number of expected guests – some 28,000 by day's end – crowded through the gates, some holding counterfeit tickets. None of this kept eager Disney fans away for long; more than 50 million tourists visited in its first decade alone. Nowadays, more than 14 million kids, grandparents, honeymooners and international tourists come to Walt's playground every year.

Disneyland To-Do List

➡ Make hotel reservations or book a Disneyland package.

➡ Sign up online for Disney Fans Insider e-newsletters and resort updates.

➡ Check the parks' opening hours and live show and entertainment schedules online.

➡ Make dining reservations for sit-down restaurants or special meals with Disney characters.

➡ Buy print-at-home tickets and passes online.

➡ Recheck the park opening hours and Anaheim Resort Transportation (ART) or hotel-shuttle schedules.

➡ Pack a small day pack with sunscreen, hat, sunglasses, swimwear, change of clothes, jacket or hoodie, lightweight plastic rain poncho, and extra batteries and memory cards for digital and video cameras.

➡ Fully charge your electronic devices, including cameras and phones.

➡ Download a Disneyland app to your smartphone.

Map labels:

Barstow (80mi)

Ontario

SAN BERNADINO COUNTY

RIVERSIDE COUNTY

Diamond Bar

Los Angeles

Whittier

LOS ANGELES COUNTY

Downey

Chino Hills State Park

Prado Flood Control Basin

Corona

Brea

Norwalk

Buena Park

Fullerton

Glen Ivy Hot Springs

Long Beach Airport

San Vicente (22mi)

Anaheim

Disneyland

Old Towne Orange

Santa Ana Mountains

Los Alamitos Reserve Center

Discovery Science Center

ORANGE COUNTY

Long Beach

Seal Beach

US Naval Weapons Station

Westminster

Santa Ana

Escondido (60mi); San Diego (90mi)

Seal Beach Pier

Sunset Beach

Bolsa Chica State Beach & Ecological Reserve

Dog Beach

Huntington Beach

Huntington Beach Pier

Huntington State Beach

Santa Ana River

Costa Mesa

John Wayne Airport

Irvine

UC Irvine

Cleveland National Forest

Newport Beach

Balboa Island

Mission Viejo

Balboa Peninsula

Corona del Mar

Crystal Cove State Park

Laguna Beach

Mission San Juan Capistrano

Crystal Cove State Beach

Aliso Beach

San Juan Capistrano

Dana Point

Capistrano Beach

SAN DIEGO COUNTY

Ferry to Catalina Island

Doheny State Beach

San Clemente

Camp Pendleton (US Marine Corps)

PACIFIC OCEAN

San Onofre State Beach

N 0 — 20 km
0 — 10 miles

Oceanside (12mi); San Diego (50mi)

Disneyland & Orange County Highlights

❶ Screaming your head off on Space Mountain at **Disneyland** (p596).

❷ Experiencing the eye of a hurricane at the **Discovery Science Center** (p606).

❸ Shopping for vintage treasures and slurping milkshakes in **Old Towne Orange** (p606).

❹ Building a beach bonfire after a day of surfing at **Huntington Beach** (p609).

❺ Cycling the as-seen-on-TV sands of Newport Beach's **Balboa Peninsula** (p612).

❻ Discovering Orange County's alternative side at the Lab and the Camp 'anti-malls' in **Costa Mesa** (p616).

❼ Falling asleep to the sound of the surf at **Crystal Cove State Beach** (p617).

❽ Watching the sun dip below the horizon at **Laguna Beach** (p618).

❾ Being awed by the Spanish colonial history and the beauty of **Mission San Juan Capistrano** (p622).

DISNEYLAND & ANAHEIM

Mickey is one lucky mouse. Created by animator Walt Disney in 1928, this irrepressible mouse caught a ride on a multimedia juggernaut (film, TV, publishing, music, merchandising and theme parks) that rocketed him into a global stratosphere of recognition, money and influence. Plus, he lives in the 'Happiest Place on Earth,' an 'imagineered' hyper-reality where the streets are always clean, the employees – called 'cast members' – are always upbeat and there are parades every day of the year.

Since opening his Disneyland home in 1955, he has been a pretty thoughtful host. For the more than 14 million kids, grandparents, honeymooners and international tourists who visit every year, Disneyland remains a magical experience.

Sights & Activities

The Disneyland Resort is open 365 days a year, though hours vary; check the website. One-day admission to *either* Disneyland or Disney California Adventure (DCA) currently costs $96 for adults and $90 for children aged three to nine. To visit *both* parks in one day costs $135/129 per adult/child on a 'Park Hopper' ticket. A variety of multiday Park Hopper tickets cost up to $305/289 for five days of admission within a two-week period.

Tickets cover all attractions and rides and a variety of parades and shows throughout the day and fireworks most nights in summer and selected times year-round.

Disneyland Park

It's hard to deny the change in atmosphere as you're whisked by tram from the parking lot into the heart of the resort and wide-eyed children lean forward with anticipation. This is their park, but adults who can willingly suspend disbelief may well also give in to the 'magic of Disney'; Uncle Walt's taken care of every detail.

Main Street, U.S.A.   RIDES, ATTRACTIONS
Fashioned after Walt's hometown of Marceline, Missouri, bustling Main Street, U.S.A. resembles the classic turn-of-the-20th-century all-American town. It's an idyllic, relentlessly upbeat representation, complete with barbershop quartet, penny arcades, ice-cream shops and a steam train. The music playing in the background is from American musicals, and there's a flag-retreat ceremony every afternoon.

Great Moments with Mr. Lincoln, a 15-minute Audio-Animatronics presentation on Honest Abe, sits inside the fascinating Disneyland Story exhibit. Nearby, kids love seeing old-school Disney cartoons like *Steamboat Willie* inside **Main Street Cinema**.

Lording it over Main Street is the iconic **Sleeping Beauty Castle**, featured on the Disney logo.

Tomorrowland   RIDES, ATTRACTIONS
This 'land' honors three timeless futurists – Jules Verne, HG Wells, and Leonardo da Vinci – while major corporations like Microsoft, Honda, Siemens and HP sponsor futur-

---

DISNEYLAND RESORT IN...

One Day
Get to **Disneyland** early. Stroll Main Street, U.S.A. toward **Sleeping Beauty Castle**. Enter Tomorrowland to ride **Space Mountain**. In Fantasyland (p597) don't miss the classic **"it's a small world"** ride. Race down the **Matterhorn Bobsleds** or take tots to **Mickey's Toontown**. Grab a FASTPASS for the **Indiana Jones™ Adventure** or **Pirates of the Caribbean** (p598) before lunching in **New Orleans Square** (p598). Plummet down **Splash Mountain** (p598), then visit the **Haunted Mansion** (p598) before the **fireworks** and **Fantasmic!** shows begin.

Two Days
At **Disney California Adventure** (p602), take a virtual hang-gliding ride on **Soarin' Over California** (p600) and let kids tackle the **Redwood Creek Challenge Trail** (p600) before having fun at **Paradise Pier** (p600), with its roller coaster, Ferris wheel and carnival games. Watch the **Pixar Play Parade**, then explore **Cars Land** (p600) or cool off on the **Grizzly River Run** (p600). After dark, drop by **The Twilight Zone Tower of Terror** (p599) and **World of Color** show.

ℹ FASTPASS

Disneyland and DCA's FASTPASS system can significantly cut your wait times on many of the most popular rides and attractions.

➜ At FASTPASS ticket machines – located near entrances to select rides – insert your park entrance ticket. You'll receive an additional ticket showing a return time.

➜ Show up within the window of time on the ticket and join the ride's FASTPASS line. There'll still be a wait, but it's shorter (typically 15 minutes or less). Hang on to your FASTPASS ticket until you board the ride.

➜ If you miss the time window printed on your FASTPASS ticket, you can still try joining the FASTPASS line.

istic robot shows and interactive exhibits in the **Innovations** pavilion.

The retro high-tech **monorail** glides to a stop in Tomorrowland, its rubber tires traveling a 13-minute, 2.5-mile round-trip route to Downtown Disney. Kiddies will want to shoot laser beams on **Buzz Lightyear's Astro Blaster** and drive their own miniature cars in the classic **Autopia** ride (don't worry, they're on tracks).

Then jump aboard the **Finding Nemo Submarine Voyage** to look for the world's most famous clownfish from within a refurbished submarine and rumble through an underwater volcanic eruption.

Star Tours – The Adventure Continues clamps you into a Starspeeder shuttle for a wild and bumpy 3D ride through the desert canyons of Tatooine on a space mission with several alternate storylines, so you can ride it again and again. **Space Mountain**, Tomorrowland's signature attraction and one of the USA's best roller coasters, hurtles you into complete darkness at frightening speed. Another classic is Captain EO, a special-effects tribute film starring Michael Jackson.

Fantasyland
RIDES, ATTRACTIONS

Fantasyland is home to **"it's a small world,"** a boat ride past hundreds of creepy Audio-Animatronics children from different cultures all singing the annoying theme song in an astounding variety of languages, joined by Disney characters. Another classic, the **Matterhorn Bobsleds**, mimics a ride down a mountain. The old-school, *Wind in the Willows*–inspired **Mr. Toad's Wild Ride** is a loopy jaunt in an open-air jalopy through London.

Younger kids love whirling around the **Mad Tea Party** teacup ride and **King Arthur Carrousel**, then cavorting with characters in **Mickey's Toontown**, a topsy-turvy mini-metropolis where kiddos can traipse through Mickey and Minnie's houses and dozens of storefronts.

Frontierland
RIDES, ATTRACTIONS

Frontierland's Tom Sawyer Island – the only attraction in the park personally designed by Uncle Walt – has been reimagined as **Pirate's Lair on Tom Sawyer Island**, and now honors Tom in name only. After a raft ride to the island, wander among roving Jack Sparrow-inspired pirates, cannibal cages, ghostly apparitions and buried treasure.

Cruise around the island on the **Mark Twain Riverboat**, a Mississippi-style paddle-wheel boat, or the 18th-century replica sailing ship **Columbia**. The rest of Frontierland gives a nod to the rip-roarin' Old West with a shooting gallery and **Big Thunder Mountain Railroad**, a mining-themed roller coaster.

Adventureland
RIDES, ATTRACTIONS

The hands-down highlight of jungle-themed Adventureland is the safari-style **Indiana Jones™ Adventure**. Enormous Humvee-type vehicles lurch and jerk their way through the wild for spine-tingling re-creations of stunts from the famous film trilogy. Nearby, little ones love climbing the stairways of **Tarzan's Treehouse™**.

Cool down with a **Jungle Cruise** featuring exotic Audio-Animatronics animals from the Amazon, Ganges, Nile and Irrawaddy Rivers. Drop by the **Enchanted Tiki Room** to look at the carvings of Hawaiian gods and goddesses, and animatronic birds singing a

ℹ SINGLE-RIDER LINES

If you're here alone, look for a separate, shorter single-rider line. Availability may depend on the size of the crowd – and also on how that particular cast member is feeling that day, so be nice!

Disneyland Resort

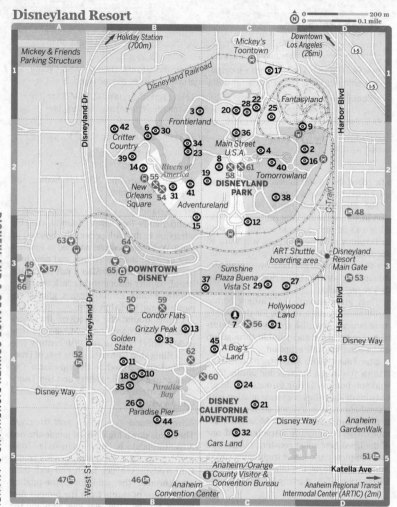

New 0 ——————— 200 m
0 ——————— 0.1 mile

corny song so good natured it's hard not to love.

New Orleans Square
RIDES, ATTRACTIONS

New Orleans was Walt's and his wife Lillian's favorite city, and this stunning square has all the charm of the French Quarter minus the marauding drunks. **Pirates of the Caribbean** is the longest ride in Disneyland (17 minutes) and inspired the popular movies. Tawdry pirates and dead buccaneers perch atop their mounds of booty and Jack Sparrow pops up occasionally.

At the **Haunted Mansion**, 999 happy spirits, goblins and ghosts appear while

you ride in a cocoonlike 'Doom Buggy' through web-covered graveyards of dancing skeletons.

Critter Country
RIDES, ATTRACTIONS

Critter Country's main attraction is **Splash Mountain**, a flume ride that transports you through the story of Brer Rabbit and Brer Bear, based on the controversial 1946 film *Song of the South*. Your picture is taken at the top, and occasionally guests will lift their shirts, leading to the ride's sometime nickname 'Flash Mountain' (naughty photos are deleted!). Just past Splash Mountain, hop in a mobile beehive on **The Many Ad-**

Disneyland Resort

⦿ Sights

1	Animation Building	C4
2	Autopia	D2
3	Big Thunder Mountain Railroad	B1
4	Buzz Lightyear's Astro Blaster	C2
5	California Screamin'	B5
6	Davy Crockett's Explorer Canoes	B2
7	Disney California Adventure	C4
8	Enchanted Tiki Room	C2
9	Finding Nemo Submarine Voyage	D2
10	Golden Zephyr	B4
11	Goofy's Sky School	B4
12	Great Moments with Mr. Lincoln	C3
13	Grizzly River Run	B4
14	Haunted Mansion	B2
15	Indiana Jones™ Adventure	B3
16	Innoventions	D2
17	"it's a small world"	C1
18	Jumpin' Jellyfish	B4
19	Jungle Cruise	C2
20	King Arthur Carrousel	C1
21	Luigi's Flying Tires	C4
22	Mad Tea Party	C1
23	Mark Twain Riverboat	B2
24	Mater's Junkyard Jamboree	C4
25	Matterhorn Bobsleds	C1
26	Mickey's Fun Wheel	B4
27	Monsters, Inc: Mike & Sulley to the Rescue!	C3
28	Mr. Toad's Wild Ride	C1
29	Muppet Vision 3D theater	C3
30	Pirate's Lair on Tom Sawyer Island	B2
31	Pirates of the Caribbean	B2
32	Radiator Springs Racers	C5
33	Redwood Creek Challenge Trail	B4
34	Sailing Ship Columbia	B2
35	Silly Symphony Swings	B4
36	Sleeping Beauty Castle	C2
37	Soarin' Over California	C3
38	Space Mountain	C2
39	Splash Mountain	B2
40	Star Tours – The Adventure Continues	C2
41	Tarzan's Treehouse™	B2
42	The Many Adventures of Winnie the Pooh	B2
43	The Twilight Zone Tower of Terror	C4
44	Toy Story Midway Mania!	B5
45	Walt Disney Imagineering Blue Sky Cellar	C4

🛏 Sleeping

46	Anabella	B5
47	Best Western Plus Stovall's Inn	A5
48	Camelot Inn & Suites	D2
49	Disneyland Hotel	A3
50	Disney's Grand Californian Hotel & Spa	B3
51	Hotel Indigo Anaheim Main Gate	D5
52	Paradise Pier Hotel	A4
53	Park Vue Inn	D3

✕ Eating

54	Blue Bayou	B2
55	Café Orleans	B2
56	Carthay Circle	C4
57	Earl of Sandwich	A3
58	Jolly Holiday Bakery & Cafe	C2
59	Napa Rose	B3
60	Pacific Wharf Cafe	C4
61	Plaza Inn	C2
	Steakhouse 55	(see 49)
62	Wine Country Terrace	B4

☕ Drinking & Nightlife

63	ESPN Zone	A3
64	House of Blues	B3
65	Ralph Brennan's New Orleans Jazz Kitchen	B3
66	Trader Sam's Enchanted Tiki Lounge	A3

🛍 Shopping

	D Street	(see 65)
67	Disney Vault 28	B3

ventures of **Winnie the Pooh**. Nearby on the Rivers of America, you can paddle **Davy Crockett's Explorer Canoes** on summer weekends.

⦿ Disney California Adventure

Across the plaza from Disneyland, Disney California Adventure (DCA) is a G-rated ode to California. Opened in 2001, it covers more acres than Disneyland and feels less crowded, and it has more modern rides and attractions.

Hollywood Land   RIDES, ATTRACTIONS
California's biggest factory of dreams is presented here in miniature, with soundstages, movable props and – of course – a studio store. **The Twilight Zone Tower of Terror** is a 13-story drop down an elevator chute situated in a haunted hotel eerily resembling the historic **Hollywood Roosevelt Hotel** (www.hollywoodroosevelt.com; 7000 Hollywood Blvd; ⊙24hr; ℗) **FREE**. From the upper floors of the tower, you'll have views of the Santa Ana mountains, if only for a few heart-pounding seconds.

TOP 10 RIDES FOR TEENS

For the adventure seekers in your brood, try the following;

→ Indiana Jones™ Adventure (p597); Adventureland

→ Space Mountain (p597); Tomorrowland

→ Twilight Zone Tower of Terror (p599); Hollywood Land, DCA

→ Splash Mountain (p598); Critter Country

→ California Screamin'; Paradise Pier, DCA

→ Soarin' Over California; Golden State, DCA

→ Big Thunder Mountain Railroad (p597); Frontierland

→ Grizzly River Run; Golden State, DCA

→ Matterhorn Bobsleds (p597); Fantasyland

→ Radiator Springs Racers; Cars Land, DCA

Less brave children can navigate a taxicab through 'Monstropolis' on the **Monsters, Inc: Mike & Sulley to the Rescue!** ride heading back toward the street's beginning.

The air-conditioned **Muppet Vision 3D** theater shows a special-effects film. Learn how to draw like Disney in the Animation Academy, discover how cartoon artwork becomes 3D at the Character Close-Up or simply be amazed by the interactive Sorcerer's Workshop, all housed inside the **Animation Building.**

Golden State   RIDES, ATTRACTIONS

Golden State highlights California's natural and human achievements. **Soarin' Over California** is a virtual hang-gliding ride using Omnimax technology that 'flies' you over the Golden Gate Bridge, Yosemite Falls, Lake Tahoe, Malibu and, of course, Disneyland. Keep your senses open for breezes and aromas of the sea, orange groves and pine forests.

Grizzly River Run takes you 'rafting' down a faux Sierra Nevada river – you will get wet, so come when it's warm. Kids can tackle the **Redwood Creek Challenge Trail**, with its 'Big Sir' redwoods, wooden towers and lookouts, and rock slide and climbing traverses. Get a behind-the-scenes looks at what's in the works next for Disneyland's theme parks inside **Walt Disney Imagineering Blue Sky Cellar.**

Paradise Pier   RIDES, ATTRACTIONS

Paradise Pier, which looks like a combination of all the beachside amusement piers in California, presents carnival rides like **California Screamin'**; this state-of-the-art roller coaster resembles an old wooden coaster, but it's got a smooth-as-silk steel track.

At **Toy Story Midway Mania!**, a 4D ride, earn points by shooting at targets while your carnival car swivels and careens through an oversize, old-fashioned game arcade. **Mickey's Fun Wheel** is a 15-story Ferris wheel where gondolas pitch and yaw in little loops as well as the big one. **Silly Symphony Swings** is a hybrid carousel with tornado-like chair swings, the pre-school set can ride a more sedate version on the **Golden Zephyr** and bounce along on the **Jumpin' Jellyfish**. **Goofy's Sky School** is a cute and relatively tame cartoon-themed coaster ride.

Cars Land   RIDES, ATTRACTIONS

Based on Disney·Pixar's popular *Cars* movies, this place gives top billing to the wacky **Radiator Springs Racers**, a race-car ride that bumps and jumps around a track painstakingly decked out like the Great American West. Tractor-towed trailers swing their way around the 'dance floor' at **Mater's Junkyard Jamboree**. Steer your bumper car (well, bumper tire, to be exact) through **Luigi's Flying Tires** (enter via the Casa Della Tires shop) or ride along with Route 66–themed gift shops and diners like the tepee-style Cozy Cone Motel.

🛏 Sleeping

🛏 Disneyland Resort

Each of the resort's **hotels** (☎ 800-225-2024, reservations 714-956-6425; www.disneyland. com) has a swimming pool with waterslide, kids' activity programs, fitness center, restaurants and bars, business center, and valet or complimentary self-parking for registered guests. Every standard room can accommodate up to five guests and has a mini-refrigerator and a coffeemaker. Look for discounted lodging-and-admission packages and early park entry times for resort guests.

★ Disney's Grand Californian
Hotel & Spa
LUXURY HOTEL **$$$**

(☑ info 714-635-2300, reservations 714-956-6425; disneyland.disney.go.com/grand-californian-hotel; 1600 S Disneyland Dr; d from $360; [P][✿][@][🛜][🛋]) Soaring timber beams rise above the cathedral-like lobby of this six-story homage to the Arts and Crafts architectural movement. Cushy rooms have triple-sheeted beds, down pillows, bathrobes and all-custom furnishings. Outside there's a faux-redwood waterslide into the pool. At night, kids wind down with bedtime stories by the lobby's giant stone hearth. For a little adult pampering, your coconut rub and milk ritual wrap awaits at the Mandara Spa.

Paradise Pier Hotel
HOTEL **$$$**

(☑ info 714-999-0990, reservations 714-956-6425; http://disneyland.disney.go.com/paradise-pier-hotel; 1717 S Disneyland Dr; d from $240; [P][✿][🛜][🛋]) Sunbursts, surfboards and a giant superslide are all on deck at the Paradise Pier Hotel, the smallest (472 rooms), cheapest and maybe the most fun of the Disney hotel trio. Kids will love the beachy decor and game arcade, not to mention the roof-deck pool and the tiny-tot video room filled with mini Adirondack chairs.

Disneyland Hotel
HOTEL **$$$**

(☑ 714-778-6600; www.disneyland.com; 1150 Magic Way; r $210-395; [P][@][🛜][🛋]) Built in 1955, the park's original hotel has expanded to three towers with themed lobbies (adventure, fantasy and frontier), and good-sized rooms boasting Mickey-hand wall sconces and headboards lit like the fireworks over Sleeping Beauty Castle. This 972-room hotel also has the best swimming pool of the three Disney hotels, plus cartoon character-themed Signature Suites.

🛏 Anaheim

Apart from Disneyland, Anaheim is a year-round convention destination. Room rates spike accordingly. Look for packages including tickets to Disneyland or other local attractions, or free Disneyland shuttles, or modestly priced shuttles operated by Anaheim Resort Transportation (p605).

Hotel Indigo Anaheim
Main Gate
BOUTIQUE HOTEL **$$**

(☑ 714-772-7755; F; 435 W Katella Ave; $159-279; [P][@][🛜][🛋][🛋]) New in 2013, this 104-room hotel has a clean, mid-century-modernist look and a dancing fountain out front. It also has a fitness center, pool and guest laundry. Mosaic murals are modeled after the walnut trees that once bloomed here. It's about 20 minutes' walk or a quick drive from Disneyland's main gate. Free parking.

★ Anabella
HOTEL **$$**

(☑ 800-863-4888, 714-905-1050; www.anabellahotel.com; 1030 W Katella Ave; r $89-199, ste $109-199; [P][✿][🛜][🛋]) This 7-acre complex has the feel of a laid-back country club, complete with golf carts that ferry guests from the lobby to their buildings. Large rooms have wooden floors and a whisper of Spanish Colonial style, with extras like minifridges and TV entertainment systems. Bunk-bedded kids' suites have Disney-inspired decor.

Best Western Plus Stovall's Inn
MOTEL **$$**

(☑ 800-854-8175, ext 3, 714-778-1880; www.bestwestern.com; 1110 W Katella Ave; r incl breakfast $90-170; [P][✿][@][🛜][🛋]) The 290 remodeled, sleek and sophisticated motel rooms sparkle; all have a microwave and minifridge, and there's a hot breakfast included. Walk to Disneyland in 15 minutes. Parking $10.

Camelot Inn & Suites
MOTEL **$$**

(☑ 714-635-7275, 800-828-4898; www.camelotanaheim.com; 1520 S Harbor Blvd; r $99-179, ste $190-269; [P][@][🛋]) This five-story, 200-room motel with accents of English Tudor style has minifridges and microwaves in every room, plus on-site laundry, a pool and hot tub. You can walk to Disneyland in 10 minutes. The pool deck and some top-floor rooms have fireworks views. Parking is $9.

Park Vue Inn
MOTEL **$$**

(☑ 714-772-3691, 800-334-7021; www.parkvueinn.com; 1570 S Harbor Blvd; r $105-163; [P][✿][@][🛋]) This two-story, 86 room motel gets rotating hordes of families, but well-scrubbed, contemporary-style rooms come with microwaves and minifridges, and downstairs it has an outdoor pool and hot tub. It's almost opposite Disneyland's main gate.

TOP FIVE THEME-PARK AREAS FOR YOUNG KIDS

➡ Fantasyland (p597), Disneyland

➡ Mickey's Toontown, Disneyland

➡ Critter Country (p598), Disneyland

➡ Paradise Pier, DCA

➡ Cars Land, DCA

Eating

From Mickey-shaped pretzels ($4) and jumbo turkey legs ($10) to deluxe, gourmet dinners (sky's the limit), there's no shortage of eating options inside the Disney parks, though they're mostly pretty expensive and mainstream. Phone **Disney Dining** (☎714-781-3463) to make reservations up to 60 days in advance.

Driving just a couple miles into Anaheim will expand the offerings and price points considerably.

✗ Disneyland Park

Jolly Holiday Bakery & Cafe　　　RESTAURANT, BAKERY $
(Main Street, U.S.A.; mains $7-10; ⊙breakfast, lunch & dinner) At this *Mary Poppins*–themed restaurant, the Jolly Holiday combo (grilled cheese sandwich and tomato basil soup for $9) is a decent deal. The cafe does other sandwiches on the sophisticated side, like the mozzarella *caprese* or turkey on ciabatta. Great people-watching from outdoor seating.

Café Orleans　　　CAJUN, CREOLE $$
(New Orleans Square; mains $16-20; ⊙seasonal hours vary; ☷) The next best thing to Blue Bayou is this Southern-flavored restaurant, famous for its Monte Cristo sandwiches at lunch.

Plaza Inn　　　AMERICAN $$
(Main Street, U.S.A.; mains $12-17, breakfast buffet adult/child 3-9yr $27/13; ⊙breakfast, lunch & dinner) Finger-lickin'-good fried chicken platter and pot roast come with mashed potatoes, buttermilk biscuits and veggies at this 1950s original. There's a fun breakfast buffet with Disney characters. The rest of the day, if you can snag an outdoor table, you'll also get great people-watching here.

Blue Bayou　　　SOUTHERN $$$
(☎714-781-3463; New Orleans Sq; lunch $26-40, dinner $30-46; ⊙lunch & dinner) Surrounded by the 'bayou' inside the Pirates of the Caribbean attraction, this is the top choice for sit-down dining in Disneyland, serving Creole and Cajun specialties at dinner.

✗ Disney California Adventure

★ Carthay Circle　　　AMERICAN $$
(Buena Vista St; lunch $20-30, dinner $25-44; ⊙lunch & dinner) Decked out like a Hollywood country club, new Carthay Circle is the best dining in either park, with steaks, seafood, pasta, smart service and a good wine list. Your table needs at least one order of fried biscuits, stuffed with white cheddar, bacon, and jalapeño and served with apricot honey butter. Inquire about special packages including dinner and the *World of Color* show.

Wine Country Terrace　　　CALIFORNIAN $$
(Golden State; mains $13-17; ⊙lunch & dinner) This sunny Cal-Italian terrace restaurant is a fine spot. Fork into Italian pastas, salads or veggie paninis. Decent wine list.

WORTH A TRIP

ANAHEIM PACKING DISTRICT & CENTER STREET

To paraphrase *Aladdin*, there's a whole new Anaheim outside Disneyland's gates. Case in point: the **Anaheim Packing District** (anaheimpackingdistrict.com; S Anaheim Bl), around a long-shuttered 1925 car dealership and 1919 orange-packing house a couple miles away, near the city's actual downtown. It relaunched in 2013-14 with chic new restaurants like Umami Burger, the **Anaheim Brewery** (www.anaheimbrew.com; 336 S Anaheim Blvd; ⊙5-9pm Tue-Thu, 4-9pm Fri, 11am-9pm Sat, 11am-6pm Sun), an evolving collection of shops and a park for events.

About a quarter-mile from here is **Center Street** (www.centerstreetanaheim.com; W Center St), a quietly splashy redeveloped neighborhood with an ice rink designed by starchitect Frank Gehry, and a couple of blocks of hipster-friendly shops like the **Good** (161 W Center St Promenade) for men's clothing, the **Look** (201 Center St Promenade) for women's, **Barbeer** (165 Center St Promenade) for a shave, haircut and brewski, and the writerly **Ink & Bean** (www.inkandbeancoffee.com; 115 W Center St Promenade) coffee saloon. Dining offerings include **118 Degrees** (185 W Center St; ☷), dedicated to the raw diet, and **Good Food**, a mini food court where you might indulge in healthy junk at **Healthy Junk** (www.healthyjunk.com; 201 Center St Promenade).

Pacific Wharf Cafe AMERICAN $$
(Golden State; mains $9-12; ⊘breakfast, lunch & dinner) Hearty soups in sourdough bread bowls, farmers-market salads and deli sandwiches are pretty filling.

Downtown Disney & Hotels

Downtown Disney is often packed, but the restaurant selection is better than inside the parks.

Earl of Sandwich SANDWICHES $
(☑714-817-7476; Downtown Disney; mains $4-7; ⊘8am-11pm Sun-Thu, 8am-midnight Fri & Sat) This counter-service spot near the Disneyland Hotel serves grilled sandwiches that are both kid- and adult-friendly. The 'original 1762' is roast beef, cheddar and horseradish, or look for chipotle chicken with avocado, or holiday turkey. There are also pizza, salad and breakfast options.

★Napa Rose CALIFORNIAN $$$
(☑714-300-7170; Grand Californian Hotel & Spa; mains $39-45, 4-course prix-fixe dinner from $90; ⊘5:30-10pm; 🖘) Soaring windows, high-back Arts and Crafts–style chairs, leaded-glass windows and towering ceilings befit the Disneyland Resort's top-drawer restaurant. On the plate, impeccably crafted, seasonal 'California Wine Country' cuisine. Kids' menu available. Reservations essential.

Steakhouse 55 AMERICAN $$$
(☑714-781-3463; 1150 Magic Way, Disneyland Hotel; breakfast $8-12, dinner $30-40, 3-course prix-fixe menu $40; ⊘breakfast & dinner) Dry-rubbed bone-in rib eye, Australian lobster tail, heirloom potatoes and green beans with applewood-smoked bacon uphold a respectable chophouse menu. Kids' menu available. Good wine list.

Anaheim

Most restaurants immediately surrounding Disneyland are chains, although **Anaheim Garden Walk** (☑714-635-7400; www.anaheimgardenwalk.com; 321 W Katella Ave) has some upscale ones (California Pizza Kitchen, McCormick & Schmick's, Johnny Rocket's, etc).

Umami Burger HAMURGERS $$
(☑714-991-8626; www.umamiburger.com; 338 S Anaheim Blvd; mains $11-15; ⊘11am-11pm Sun-Thu, to midnight Fri & Sat) In the Anaheim Packing District. Burgers span classic to truffled and the Hatch burger with roasted green chilies.

Get 'em with deep-fried 'smushed' potatoes with housemade ketchup, and top it off with a salted-chocolate-ice-cream sandwich. Good beer selection too.

★Olive Tree MIDDLE EASTERN $$
(☑714-535-2878; 512 S Brookhurst St; mains $8-16; ⊘9am-9pm) In Anaheim's Little Arabia, this simple restaurant in a nondescript strip mall flying flags of Arab nations has earned accolades from local papers and from *Saveur* magazine. You *could* get standards like falafel and kebabs, but daily specials are where it's at; Saturday's *kabseh* is righteous, fall-off-the-bone lamb shank over spiced rice with currants and onions.

🍷 Drinking & Entertainment

🍸 Disneyland Resort

It's tiki to the max and good, clean fun at **Trader Sam's Enchanted Tiki Lounge** (1150 Magic Way, Disneyland Hotel). Score a personal leather recliner and watch the game on 175-plus screens at **ESPN Zone** (www.espnzone.com; Downtown Disney), or hear big-name acts at **House of Blues** (☑714-778-2583; www.houseofblues.com; Downtown Disney) or jazz at **Ralph Brennan's New Orleans Jazz Kitchen** (http://rbjazzkitchen.com; Downtown Disney). There's also a 12-screen cinema in Downtown Disney.

🍺 Anaheim

As one of California's largest cities, Anaheim has a variety of entertainment options, from the tasting room of Anaheim Brewery in the Anaheim Packing District to professional sports at the **Honda Center** (☑800-745-3000; www.hondacenter.com; 2695 E Katella Ave) for hockey and **Angel Stadium** (☑714-940-2000, 888-796-4256; www.angelsbaseball.com; 2000 Gene Autry Way) for baseball, and rock concerts at the **City National Grove of Anaheim** (☑714-712-2700; www.thegroveofanaheim.com; 2200 E Katella Ave). At the **Block at Orange** (☑714-769-4001; www.simon.com; 20 City Blvd W, Orange; 🖘) are a video game arcade, a skate park and a bowling and billiards establishment.

🔒 Shopping

Each 'land' has its own shopping, appropriate to its particular theme, a mind-boggling variety of souvenirs, clothing and Disneyana, from T-shirts to mouse ears.

Downtown Disney, too, is a triumph of marketing – once inside the dozens of shops here (not just Disney stuff either), it may be hard to extract yourself. **Disney Vault 28** (Downtown Disney) traffics in a hipster inventory of distressed Cinderella-print T-shirts, familiar brands like Betsey Johnson and Disney-only boutique lines like Disney Couture. **D Street** (Downtown Disney) gives the same treatment to wannabe gangstas, skate rats and surfers. Shop hours are timed to the theme park hours.

ℹ Information

Before you arrive, visit **Disneyland Resort** (☑ live assistance 714-781-7290, recorded info 714-781-4565 ; www.disneyland.com) website for up-to-date information.

INTERNET RESOURCES & MOBILE APPS
Disneyland Explorer Official Disney-released app for iPhone and iPad.
Lonely Planet (www.lonelyplanet.com/usa/california/disneyland-and-anaheim) For planning advice, author recommendations, traveler reviews and insider tips.
MousePlanet (www.mouseplanet.com) One-stop fansite for all things Disney, with news updates, podcasts, trip reports, reviews and discussion boards.
MouseWait (www.mousewait.com) Free iPhone app offers up-to-the-minute updates on ride wait times and what's happening in the parks.

LOCKERS
Self-service lockers with in-and-out privileges cost $7 to $15 per day. You'll find them near entry gates to Disneyland and DCA and at the picnic area just outside.

MEDICAL SERVICES
You'll find first-aid facilities at Disneyland (Main Street, U.S.A.), DCA (Pacific Wharf) and Downtown Disney (next to Ralph Brennan's Jazz Kitchen).
Western Medical Center (WMC; ☑ 714-533-6220; 1025 S Anaheim Blvd, Anaheim; ⊙24hr) Hospital emergency room.

MONEY
Disneyland's City Hall offers foreign-currency exchange. In DCA, head to the guest relations lobby. Multiple ATMs are found in both theme parks and at Downtown Disney.
Travelex (☑ 714-502-0811; Downtown Disney; ⊙10am-4pm Mon-Fri) Foreign exchange.

POST
Holiday Station (www.usps.com; 1180 W Ball Rd, Anaheim; ⊙9am-5pm Mon-Fri) Full-service post office.

TOURIST INFORMATION
Inside the parks, visit Disneyland's City Hall or DCA's guest relations lobby, or just ask any cast member.
Anaheim/Orange County Visitor & Convention Bureau (☑ 855-405-5020; www.anaheimoc.org; Anaheim Convention Center) Offers information on countywide lodging, dining and transportation. Convention Center parking is $15.

ℹ Getting There & Away

AIR
Most international travelers arrive at Los Angeles International Airport (LAX), but for easy-in, easy-out domestic travel, the manageable John Wayne Airport (p761) in Santa Ana is served by all major US airlines and Canada's WestJet. It's near the junction of Hwy 55 and I-405 (San Diego Fwy).

From LAX, Super Shuttle (www.supershuttle.com) offers one-way fares of $16 per person to Disneyland-area hotels.

BUS
Southern California Gray Line/Coach America (☑ 714-978-8855, 800-828-6699; www.graylineanaheim.com) runs Disneyland Resort Express buses from LAX and SNA to Disneyland-area hotels every 30 minutes to one hour from 7:30am until 10pm.

Greyhound (☑ 714-999-1256, 800-231-222; www.greyhound.com; 100 W Winston Rd, Anaheim) has several daily buses to/from Downtown LA ($12, 40 minutes) and San Diego ($18, 2¼ hours). The bus station is a half mile east of the Disneyland Resort, accessible via taxi or the ART shuttle.

The **Orange County Transportation Authority** (☑ 714-560-6282; www.octa.net; ride/day pass $2/5) operates buses throughout the county. Fares and passes are sold on board (cash only, exact change).

CAR & MOTORCYCLE
Disneyland Resort is just off I-5 (Santa Ana Fwy), about 30 miles southeast of Downtown LA.

TRAIN
Trains stop at the newly opened **Anaheim Regional Transit Intermodal Center** (ARTIC) next to Angel Stadium, a quick ART shuttle or taxi ride east of Disneyland. **Amtrak** (☑ 714-385-1448; www.amtrak.com; 2150 E Katella Ave) has almost a dozen daily trains to/from LA's Union Station ($15, 40 minutes) and San Diego ($28, two hours). Less frequent **Metrolink** (☑ 800-371-5465; www.metrolinktrains.com; 2150 E Katella Ave) commuter trains connect Anaheim to LA's Union Station ($9, 50 minutes), Orange

($5.25, five minutes) and San Juan Capistrano ($8.75, 40 minutes).

❶ Getting Around

CAR & MOTORCYCLE

All-day parking costs $16 ($20 for oversize vehicles). Enter the 'Mickey & Friends' parking structure from southbound Disneyland Dr, off Ball Rd, and board the free tram to the parks.

Downtown Disney parking, reserved for diners, shoppers and movie-goers, offers the first three hours free.

SHUTTLE

Anaheim Resort Transportation (ART; ☎714-563-5287; www.rideart.org; single ride $3, day pass adult/child $5/2) operates some 20 shuttle routes between Disneyland and area hotels, transit center, convention center and other points of interest, saving traffic and parking headaches. Departures are typically two to three times per hour. Purchase single or multiday ART passes at kiosks near ART shuttle stops or online in advance.

TRAM & MONORAIL

With a ticket to Disneyland, you can ride the monorail between Tomorrowland and the far end of Downtown Disney, near the Disneyland Hotel.

AROUND DISNEYLAND

Within 10 easy miles of the Mouse House you'll find a big scoopful of sights and attractions that are worth a visit in their own right.

Knott's Berry Farm

America's oldest theme park (☎714-220-5200; www.knotts.com; 8039 Beach Blvd, Buena Park; adult/child $62/33; ☺from 10am, closing time varies 6-11pm; ◪), Knott's is smaller and less frenetic than Disneyland, but it can be more fun, especially for thrill-seeking teens, roller coaster fanatics and younger kids.

The park opened in 1932, when Walter Knott's boysenberries (a blackberry-raspberry hybrid) and his wife Cordelia's fried-chicken dinners attracted crowds of local farmhands. Mr Knott built an imitation ghost town to keep them entertained, and eventually hired local carnival rides and charged admission.

Today Knott's keeps the Old West theme alive and thriving with shows and demonstrations at Ghost Town, but it's the thrill

KNOTT'S SCARY FARM

Every year, Knott's Berry Farm puts on SoCal's scariest Halloween party. On select days from late September through October 31, the park closes and reopens at night as Knott's Scary Farm. Horror-minded thrills include a dozen creepy mazes, monster-themed shows and a thousand employees trying to scare the bejeezus out of you in 'scare zones'. Boo!

rides that draw the big crowds. The **Sierra Sidewinder** roller coaster rips through banks and turns while rotating on its axis. The suspended, inverted **Silver Bullet** screams through a corkscrew, a double spiral and an outside loop. **Xcelerator** is a 1950s-themed roller coaster that blasts you from 0mph to 82mph in under 2½ seconds with a hair-raising twist at the top. **Perilous Plunge** whooshes at 75mph down a 75-degree angled water chute that's almost as tall as Niagara Falls.

Minimum height restrictions apply for many rides and attractions. For the little(st) ones, **Camp Snoopy** is a kiddy wonderland populated by the *Peanuts* characters.

Opening hours vary seasonally, and online savings can be substantial (eg $10 off adult admission for buying print-at-home tickets).

Next door to Knott's Berry Farm is the affiliated water park **Soak City Orange County** (☎714-220-5200; www.soakcityoc.com; 8039 Beach Blvd, Buena Park; adult/child 3-11yr $36/26; ☺10am-5pm, 6pm or 7pm mid-May–mid-Sep), boasting a 750,000-gallon wave pool and dozens of high-speed slides, tubes and flumes. You must have a bathing suit without rivets or metal pieces to go on some slides. Bring a beach towel and a change of dry clothes.

🛏 Sleeping & Eating

Knott's Berry Farm Resort Hotel (☎714-995-1111, 866-752-2444; www.knottshotel.com; 7675 Crescent Ave, Buena Park; r $79-169; @ 🛜 🏊) is a high-rise with bland rooms, outdoor pool, fitness center and tennis and basketball courts. For young Charlie Brown fans, ask about Camp Snoopy rooms, where kids are treated to *Peanuts*-themed decor (dog house headboards? Awesome!), telephone bedtime stories and a goodnight 'tuck-in' visit from Snoopy himself. Overnight parking costs $7.

The park has plenty of carnival-quality fast food, but the classic meal is the button-busting fried chicken and mashed potato dinner at the nuthin'-fancy **Mrs Knott's Chicken Dinner Restaurant** (☑ 714-220-5055; 8039 Beach Blvd, Buena Park; mains $7-17, chicken dinner $17; ⊙ 8am-8:30pm Mon-Thu, 7am-9pm Fri, 7am-9:30pm Sat, 7am-8:30pm Sun). It and other eateries are in the California Marketplace, a shopping center outside the park's main gate.

❶ Getting There & Away

Knott's Berry Farm is about 6 miles northwest of Disneyland, off the I-5 Fwy or Hwy 91 (Artesia Fwy). All-day parking costs $12. There's free three-hour parking for California Marketplace visitors only.

Discovery Science Center

Follow the giant 10-story cube – balanced on one of its points – to the doors of the best educational kiddie attraction in town, the **Discovery Science Center** (☑ 714-542-2823; www.discoverycube.org; 2500 N Main St, Santa Ana; adult/child 3-14yr & senior $16/13, 4D movies $2 extra; ⊙ 10am-5pm; ♿), about 5 miles southeast of Disneyland via the I-5. More than 100 interactive displays await in exhibit areas with names such as Discovery Theater (playing 4D movies), Dino Quest and more. Step into the eye of a hurricane – your hair will get mussed – or grab a seat in the Shake Shack to virtually experience a magnitude 6.4 quake.

Bowers Museum & Kidseum

The under-the-radar **Bowers Museum** (☑ 714-567-3600, 877-250-8999; www.bowers.org; 2002 N Main St, Santa Ana; Tue-Fri adult/child 6-17yr & senior $13/10, Sat & Sun $15/12, special-exhibit surcharge varies; ⊙ 10am-4pm Tue-Sun) explodes onto the scene every year or two with a remarkable exhibit that reminds LA-centric museum-goers not to get too smug. The museum's permanent exhibits are impressive, too, a rich collection of pre-Columbian, African, Oceanic and Native American art.

General admission tickets to the Bowers Museum include entry to the family-focused **Kidseum** (☑ 714-480-1520; 1802 N Main St, Santa Ana; admission $3, child under 3yr free; ⊙ 10am-3pm Tue-Fri, 11am-3pm Sat & Sun; ♿), two blocks south.

The museums are 6 miles southeast of Disneyland, off I-5 in Santa Ana. Admission is free on the first Sunday of each month. Public parking in nearby lots costs $2.

Old Towne Orange

Settlers began arriving en masse in Orange County after the Civil War, lured by cheap land and fertile fields. Today the city of Orange, 7 miles southeast of Disneyland, retains its charming historical center. Locals, antique hounds, SoCal nostalgia buffs and foodies continue to flock here.

✘ Eating

Browse Old Towne Orange's traffic circle and Glassell St for more than a dozen cafes, restaurants, wine bars and brewpubs.

★**Filling Station** DINER $
(www.fillingstationcafe.com; 201 N Glassell St; mains $7-14; ⊙ 6:30am-9pm, to 10pm Fri & Sat; ♿) For breakfast, nothing beats this former vintage gas station now serving haute pancakes, chorizo eggs, Cobb salads and patty melts, instead of unleaded. Check out the vintage SoCal photographs on the walls. Sit on the outdoor patio (which is dog-friendly), or grab a shiny counter stool or booth inside. Breakfast is served all day, lunch from 11am.

Watson Drug DINER $$
(www.watsonsdrugs.com; 116 E Chapman Ave; mains $6-15; ⊙ 7am-9pm Mon-Sat, 8am-6pm Sun) Old-fashioned soda-fountain treats such as malts, milkshakes and sundaes, as well as burgers and all-day breakfast burritos, set inside an 1899 pharmacy with a vintage lunch counter and a contemporary ice-pop stand next door.

Felix Continental Cafe LATIN AMERICAN $$$
(☑ 714-633-5842; www.felixcontinentalcafe.com; 36 Plaza Sq; mains $8-17; ⊙ 11am-10pm Mon-Fri, 8am-10pm Sat & Sun) Longtime downtown favorite serves spiced-just-right Caribbean, Cuban, and Spanish dishes, most accompanied by a hefty serving of plantains, black beans and rice. Paella is the house specialty, and the roast pork is popular too. Scope out a patio table if you can. Lunch served until 5pm.

LITTLE SAIGON

Vietnamese immigrants began arriving in Orange County after the end of the Vietnam War in the early 1970s, carving out their own vibrant commercial district (largely of strip malls) about 7 miles from Disneyland, south of Hwy 22 (Garden Grove Fwy) and east of the I-405 (San Diego Fwy).

Start at **Asian Garden Mall** (9200 Bolsa Ave; 🛜), a behemoth packed with scores of food shops, boutiques, herbalists, silver jewelers and anime-inspired clothing and goods. Newbies can chow at the mall's **Lee's Sandwiches** (www.leessandwiches.com; 9200 Bolsa Ave, Suite 305; sandwiches from $4; ⊗8am-7pm; 🛜) or just west of the mall at **Ba Le** (9152 Bolsa Ave; sandwiches from $3; ⊗6am-6pm Mon-Sat, 7am-6pm Sun), both fast-growing chains serving budget-friendly Vietnamese sandwiches on French baguette rolls. The traditional toppings on these belly-fillers provide a delish, not-too-spicy kick – try the pork. Another classic, inexpensive, casual eatery in the mall is **Pho 79** (9200 Bolsa Ave, Suite 117; mains from $6; ⊗8am-7:30pm), which dishes up a variety of noodle and vegetable dishes. The *pho ga* (chicken noodle soup) has a hearty broth.

🔒 Shopping

Old Towne has the OC's most concentrated collection of antiques, collectibles, and vintage and consignment shops.

Woody's Antiques   ANTIQUES
(173 N Glassell St) Woody's Antiques feels like walking on to a *Mad Men* set, with mid-century modern and art-deco furnishings and accent pieces.

Elsewhere Vintage   VINTAGE CLOTHING
(www.elsewhere vintage.com; 131 W Chapman Ave) A hipsters' love affair, this store hangs sundresses next to hats, leather handbags and fabulous costume jewelry.

Joy Ride   VINTAGE CLOTHING
(133 W Chapman Ave) Sells men's clothing such as 1950s bowling shirts and immaculately maintained wool blazers.

ℹ️ Getting There & Away

The drive from Anaheim takes under 20 minutes: take I-5 south to Hwy 22 east, then drive north on Grand Ave, which becomes Glassell St. Both **Amtrak** (📞800-872-7245; www.amtrak. com) and **Metrolink** (📞800-371-5465; www. metrolinktrains.com) commuter trains stop at Orange's **train station** (191 N Atchison St), a few blocks west of the plaza.

Richard Nixon Library & Museum

About 10 miles northeast of Anaheim, the **Richard Nixon Presidential Library & Museum** (📞714-993-5075; www.nixonfoundation. org; 18001 Yorba Linda Blvd, Yorba Linda; adult/child 7-11yr/student/senior $12/5/7/8.50; ⊗10am-5pm Mon-Sat, 11am-5pm Sun) offers a fascinating walk though America's modern history and that of this controversial native son of Orange County. Noteworthy exhibits include excerpts from the Nixon and Kennedy debates, a full-size replica of the White House's East Room, audiotapes of conversations with Apollo 11 astronauts while on the moon and access to the ex-presidential helicopter, complete with wet bar and ashtrays.

That said, it's the exhibits about Watergate, the infamous scandal that ultimately brought down Nixon's administration, that rightfully garner the most attention. The museum's original Watergate exhibit called it a 'coup' instigated by Nixon's rivals and provided favorably edited White House tapes. That changed when the library was transferred to federal control in 2007, with oversight by the National Archives. The old exhibit was completely torn out, and now the story unfolds from many perspectives, like a spy thriller. It was a bold move, considering that 'Tricky Dick' and First Lady Pat Nixon lie buried just outside.

To get here, take Hwy 57 north and exit east on Yorba Linda Blvd, then continue straight and follow the signs.

ORANGE COUNTY BEACHES

Orange County's 42 miles of beaches are a land of gorgeous sunsets, prime surfing, just-off-the-boat seafood and serendipitous discoveries. Whether you're learning to surf

> ### ⓘ CHEAP(ER) SLEEPS
>
> In summer the OC's beach accommodations get booked out far in advance, room rates rise, and some places require minimum two- or three-night stays. You can often save money by staying multiple nights in one beach town and taking day trips to the others. Otherwise, look inland to chain motels and hotels inland, closer to I-405 and I-5 Fwys.

the waves in Seal Beach, playing Frisbee oceanside with your pooch, piloting a boat around Newport Harbor, wandering around eclectic art displays in Laguna Beach, or spotting whales on a cruise out of yacht-filled Dana Point harbor, you'll discover that each beach town has its own brand of quirky charm.

Seal Beach

The first enclave over the LA County line is one of the last great California beach towns and a refreshing alternative to the more-crowded coast further south. Look for 1.5 miles of pristine beach and Main St, a stoplight-free zone bustling with mom-and-pop restaurants and indie shops that are low on 'tude and high on charisma.

◉ Sights & Activities

Amble Main St and check out the laid-back local scene – barefoot surfers, friendly shopkeepers and silver-haired foxes scoping the way-too-young beach bunnies. Where Main St ends, walk out onto Seal Beach Pier, extending 1865ft over the ocean.

M&M Surfing School SURFING
(☑714-846-7873; www.surfingschool.com; 802 Ocean Ave; 3hr group lesson from $72, wetsuit/surfboard rental $15/25; 🐾) Learn to surf.

✖ Eating

Crema Café BAKERY, CAFE $
(☑562-493-2501; cremacafe.com; 322 Main St; mains $5-13; ☉6:30am-3pm Mon-Fri, 7am-4pm Sat & Sun) The specialty at this breezy, open-air cafe is crepes, from the 'simple' French crepe covered with cinnamon sugar, whipped cream and caramel sauce to savory and fruit-filled varieties. In a hurry? Made-from-scratch pastries and muffins are fab, as

are garden-fresh salads and toasted panini sandwiches.

★**Walt's Wharf** SEAFOOD, STEAKHOUSE $$$
(☑562-598-4433; www.waltswharf.com; 201 Main St; lunch $11-23, dinner $20-45; ☉11am-3:30pm & 4-9pm) Everybody's favorite for fresh fish (some drive in from LA), Walt's packs them in on weekends. You can't make reservations for dinner (though they're accepted for lunch), but it's worth the wait for the oak fire–grilled seafood and steaks in the many-windowed ground floor or upstairs in captain's chairs. Otherwise, eat at the bar.

🍷 Drinking

Bogart's Coffee House CAFE
(www.bogartscoffee.com; 905 Ocean Ave; ☉6am-9pm Mon-Thu, to 10pm Fri, 7am-10pm Sat, 7am-9pm Sun; 🛜) Sip espresso on the leopard-print sofa and play Scrabble by the beach view as you watch the surf roll in. Bogart's sometimes hosts live music, psychic readings, book clubs and morning meditations by the sea.

☆ Entertainment

Jazz, folk and bluegrass bands play by the pier at the foot of Main St from 6pm to 8pm every Wednesday during July and August for the annual Summer Concerts in the Park.

🛍 Shopping

Walk the full three blocks of Main St and browse the eclectic shops, including for surf gear and clothing at Harbour Surfboards (www.harboursurfboards.com; 329 Main St) and Endless Summer (124 Main St), toys at Knock Knock (www.knockknocktoystore.com; 219½ Main St) and even kites at Up, Up & Away (http://upupandawaykites.com; 139½ Main St), plus plenty of cafes and watering holes.

ⓘ Getting There & Around

OCTA (☑714-560-6282; www.octa.net) bus 1 connects Seal Beach with the OC's other beach towns and LA's Long Beach every hour; the one-way fare is $2 (exact change).

There's two-hour free parking along Main St between downtown Seal Beach and the pier – if you can snag a spot. Public parking lots by the pier cost $3 per two hours, $6 all day. Free parking along residential side streets is subject to posted restrictions.

Huntington Beach

With consistently good waves, surf shops, a surf museum, beach bonfires, a canine-friendly beach and a sprinkling of hotels and restaurants with killer views, HB is an awesome place for sun, surf and sand.

Hawaiian-Irish surfing star George Freeth gave demonstrations here in 1914, and the city has been a surf destination ever since, with the trademarked nickname 'Surf City, USA' (Santa Cruz lost that fight, sorry). The sport is big business, with a **Surfing Walk of Fame** (www.hsssurf.com/shof) and test-marketing for surf products and clothing.

⊙ Sights

Huntington Pier HISTORIC SITE
(⊙5am-midnight) The 1853ft-long Huntington Pier has been here – in one form or another – since 1904. On the pier, rent a fishing pole from **Let's Go Fishin'** bait and tackle shop.

International Surfing Museum MUSEUM
(www.surfingmuseum.org; 411 Olive Ave; donations welcome; ⊙noon-5pm Mon-Fri, 11am-6pm Sat & Sun) This small museum is an entertaining stop for surf-culture enthusiasts, chock-ablock with photos, vintage surfboards, movie memorabilia, surf music and knowledgeable, all-volunteer staff.

Huntington City Beach BEACH
(⊙5am-midnight) One of SoCal's best beaches. Surrounding the pier at the foot of Main St, it gets packed on summer weekends with surfers, volleyball players, swimmers and families. Check at the visitor center for dog-friendly beaches and parks.

By night, volleyball games give way to beach bonfires. Stake out one of the 1000 cement fire rings early in the day, and you can buy firewood from concessionaires.

🏃 Activities

If you forgot to pack beach gear, you can rent umbrellas, beach chairs, volleyballs, bikes and other essentials from Zack's Pier Plaza. Just south of the pier on the Strand, friendly **Dwight's Beach Concession** (201 Pacific Coast Hwy), around since 1932, rents bikes, boogies boards, umbrellas and chairs.

Surfing

Surfing in HB is competitive. If you're a novice, take lessons, or risk annoying the locals.

Zack's SURF GEAR
(☏714-536-0215; www.zackshb.com; 405 Pacific Coast Hwy) Offers one-hour lessons ($75 to $100) at the beach that include all-day board and wetsuit rental. For board rentals, you'll pay $12/35 per hour/day, plus $5/15 each for bodyboards and wetsuits.

Huntington Surf & Sport SURF GEAR
(☏714-841-4000; www.hsssurf.com; 300 Pacific Coast Hwy) Megastore at the corner of Pacific Coast Hwy and Main St rents surfboards for $10/30 per hour/day (wetsuit $8/15).

Cycling & Skating

Explore the coast while zipping along the 8.5-mile **paved recreational path** from Huntington State Beach north to Bolsa Chica State Beach. Rent beach cruisers ($10/30 per hour/day) or tandem bikes ($18/50) at Zack's Pier Plaza.

Frisbee

Throw a disc back and forth for hours on the beach, or test your skills at the **Huntington Beach Disc Golf Course** (Huntington Central Park, 18381 Goldenwest St; admission $1-2). Aim for baskets at this scenic 18-hole course, downhill from the sports complex. The on-site pro shop sells discs.

🎉 Festivals & Events

Every Tuesday brings Surf City Nights, a street fair on the first three blocks of Main St, with live music, farmers market goodies, a petting zoo and bounce house for kids, and crafts and sidewalk sales for grownups.

Car buffs, get up early on Saturday mornings for the **Donut Derelicts Car Show** (www.donutderelicts.com), a weekly gathering of woodies, beach cruisers and pimped-out street rods at the corner of Magnolia St and Adams Ave, 2.5 miles inland from Pacific Coast Hwy.

US Open of Surfing SURFING
(www.usopenofsurfing.com; ⊙late Jul & early Aug) In late July and early August, this six-day competition lasts several days and draws more than 600 world-class surfers. Festivities include beach concerts, motocross shows and skateboard jams.

Huntington Harbor Cruise of Lights CHRISTMAS
(www.cruiseoflights.org; ⊙Dec) If you're here for the Christmas holidays, don't miss the evening boat tour past harborside homes twinkling with holiday lights.

BOLSA CHICA STATE BEACH

A 3-mile-long strip of sand favored by surfers, volleyball players and fishers, **Bolsa Chica State Beach** (www.parks.ca.gov; Pacific Coast Hwy, btwn Seapoint & Warner Aves; parking $15; 6am-10pm; P) stretches alongside the Pacific Coast Hwy north of Huntington Dog Beach. Even though it faces a monstrous offshore oil rig, Bolsa Chica (meaning 'little pocket' in Spanish) gets mobbed on summer weekends. All-day parking costs $15. You'll find picnic tables, fire rings and beach showers, plus a bike path.

Across Pacific Coast Hwy, **Bolsa Chica Ecological Reserve** (http://bolsachica.org; sunrise-sunset) may look desolate, but its restored salt marsh is an environmental success story and teems with more than 200 species of birds on over 1200 acres, which were saved by a band of determined locals.

Sleeping

Huntington Surf Inn　　　MOTEL $$
(714-536-2444; www.huntingtonsurfinn.com; 720 Pacific Coast Hwy; r $159-209; P) You're paying for location at this two-story motel just south of Main St and across from the beach. Nine of its rooms were recently redesigned by surf company Hurley in conjunction with surfers – cool, brah. There's a small common deck area with a beach view.

★ Shorebreak Hotel　　　BOUTIQUE HOTEL $$$
(714-861-4470; www.shorebreakhotel.com; 500 Pacific Coast Hwy, Huntington Beach; r $189-495; P) Stow your surfboard (lockers provided) as you head inside HB's hippest hotel, a stone's throw from the pier. The Shorebreak has a surf concierge, a fitness center and yoga studio, beanbag chairs in the lobby, and rattan and hardwood furniture in geometric-patterned rooms. Have sunset cocktails on the upstairs deck at Zimzala restaurant. Parking is $27.

Hilton Waterfront Beach Resort　RESORT $$$
(714-845-8000, 800-445-8667; www.waterfrontbeachresort.hilton.com; 21100 Pacific Coast Hwy; r $279-390; P) The backdrop: miles and miles of gorgeous deep-blue sea. This 100% nonsmoking hotel has a giant tower from which every room has an angled balcony for ocean view. Rooms are plush but tempered with earth tones. Bicycle rentals available. Parking $30.

Eating

Sancho's Tacos　　　MEXICAN $
(714-536-8226; www.sanchostacos.com; 602 Pacific Coast Hwy; mains $3-10; 8am-9pm Mon-Sat, to 8pm Sun) There's no shortage of taco stands in HB, but locals are fiercely dedicated to Sancho's, across from the beach. This two-room shack with patio grills flounder, shrimp and tri-tip to order. Trippy Mexican-meets-skater art.

Sugar Shack　　　CAFE $
(www.hbsugarshack.com; 213½ Main St; mains $4-10; 6am-4pm Mon-Tue & Thu, to 8pm Wed, to 5pm Fri-Sun) Expect a wait at this HB institution, or get here early to see surfer dudes don their wetsuits. Breakfast is served all day on the bustling Main St patio and inside, where you can grab a spot at the counter or a two-top. Photos of surf legends plastering the walls raise this place almost to shrine status.

Duke's　　　SEAFOOD, HAWAIIAN $$
(714-374-6446; www.dukeshuntington.com; 317 Pacific Coast Hwy; lunch $7-16, dinner $19-32; 11:30am-2:30pm Tue-Fri, 10am-2pm Sun, 5-9pm Tue-Sun) It may be touristy, but this Hawaiian-themed restaurant – named after surfing legend Duke Kahanamoku – is a kick. With unbeatable views of the beach, a long list of fresh fish and a healthy selection of sassy cocktails, it's a primo spot to relax and show off your tan.

Sandy's　　　CALIFORNIAN $$
(714-374-7273; www.sandyshb.com; 315 Pacific Coast Hwy; lunch $10-17, dinner $11-32; 11:30am-8:30pm Mon, to 9:30pm Tue-Fri, 9am-9:30pm Sat, 9am-8:30pm Sun) At beach-volleyball level with a generous beachside deck and an easy breezy dining room. Features dishes ranging from breakfast pizza and short rib breakfast burrito for weekend brunch, to pecan-crusted seabass with shrimp couscous, or the jalapeño-date burger.

Drinking

It's easy to find a bar in HB. Walk up Main St and you'll spot them all.

Hurricanes Bar & Grill　　　BAR
(www.hurricanesbargrill.com; 2nd fl, 200 Main St) Two words: meat market. But then again,

any strip of beach bars worth its margarita salt needs at least one. DJs nightly, ocean-view patios, a laser-light dance floor, 22 beer taps and loads of special cocktails.

Huntington Beach Beer Co BAR
(www.hbbeerco.com; 2nd fl, 201 Main St; ⊙from 11am; 🕏) Two-decade-old, cavernous brew-pub with a big balcony, specializing in ales brewed in a half dozen giant, stainless-steel kettles on site, like the HB Blonde, Brickshot Red and seasonal beers flavored with sage to cherry. Try the sampler. DJs and dancing Thursday to Saturday nights.

🛍 Shopping

Huntington Surf & Sport SPORTS, CLOTHING
(www.hsssurf.com; 300 Pacific Coast Hwy) This massive store supports the Surf City way of life with rows of surfboards, beachwear, surfing accessories and test-marketing for OC-based Hurley.

❶ Information

Huntington Beach Hospital (📞714-843-5000; www.hbhospital.com; 17772 Beach Blvd; ⊙24hr) 24-hour emergency room.

Main St Library (www.hbpl.org; 525 Main St; internet per hr $5; ⊙10am-7pm Tue-Fri, 9am-5pm Sat; 🕏) Small but just five blocks from the beach; free wi-fi.

Visitors Bureau (📞800-729-6232; www.surfcityusa.com) Main St (📞714-969-3492; www.surfcityusa.com; 2nd fl, 301 Main St; ⊙9am-5pm); Pier Plaza (www.surfcityusa.com; Pier Plaza; ⊙11am-7pm) Hard-to-spot upstairs office on Main St provides maps and information, but the Pier Plaza booth is more convenient.

❶ Getting There & Around

Public parking lots by the pier and beach – when you can even get a spot – are $1.50 per hour, $15 daily maximum. On-street parking meters cost $1 per 40 minutes.

OCTA (📞714-560-6282; www.octa.net) bus 1 connects HB with the rest of OC's beach towns every hour; one-way/day pass $2/5, payable on board (exact change). At press time, a free **Surf City Downtown Shuttle** (📞714-536-5542) operates from 10am until 8pm on weekends during summer, making a 3.5-mile loop around downtown to the pier, starting from the free public parking lot at **City Hall** (2000 N Main St).

Newport Beach

There are really three Newport Beaches demographics: wealthy Bentley- and Porsche-driving yachtsmen and their trophy wives; surfers and stoners who populate the beachside dives and live for the perfect wave; and everyone else trying to live day-to-day, chow on seafood and enjoy glorious sunsets. Somehow, these diverse communities all seem to live – mostly – harmoniously.

For visitors, the pleasures are many: just-off-the-boat seafood, boogie-boarding the human-eating waves at the Wedge, and the ballet of yachts in the harbor. Inland is posh Fashion Island, one of the OC's biggest shopping centers.

👁 Sights

Balboa Fun Zone AMUSEMENT PARK
(www.thebalboafunzone.com; 600 E Bay Ave; ⊙Ferris wheel 11am-8pm Sun-Thu, to 9pm Fri, to 10pm Sat) On the harbor side of Balboa Peninsula, the Fun Zone has delighted locals

---

DON'T MISS

BALBOA ISLAND

For a quick pleasure trip across Newport Harbor, the **Balboa Island Ferry** (www.balboaislandferry.com; 410 S Bay Front; adult/child $1/50¢, car incl driver $2; ⊙6:30am-midnight Sun-Thu, to 2am Fri & Sat) leaves from the Balboa Fun Zone about every 10 minutes. It's tiny, holding just three cars packed single file between open-air seats for the 800ft, sub-five-minute trip.

The ferry lands a half mile west of Marine Ave, the main drag on **Balboa Island** (www.balboa-island.net). It's lined with beachy boutique shops, cafes and restaurants, and old-fashioned ice-cream shops vending Balboa bars (vanilla ice cream dipped in chocolate, peanuts, sprinkles and crushed Oreo cookies on a stick).

For close-ups of the island's beautiful, well-maintained homes, take a stroll along its shoreline. It's only about 1.5 miles around. Then catch the ferry back.

You can also reach Balboa Island by driving south of Pacific Coast Hwy along Jamboree Rd to Marine Ave. But what fun is that?

Newport Beach

and visitors since 1936. There's a small Ferris wheel ($4 per ride, where Ryan and Marissa shared their first kiss on *The OC*), arcade games, touristy shops and restaurants, and frozen banana stands (just like the one in the TV sit-com *Arrested Development*). The landmark 1905 **Balboa Pavilion** is beautifully illuminated at night.

ExplorOcean MUSEUM
(☏949-675-8915; www.explorocean.org; 600 E Bay Ave, Balboa Fun Zone; adult/child 4-12yr $5/3; ☉11am-3:30pm Mon-Thu, to 6pm Fri & Sat, to 5pm Sun) In the Balboa Fun Zone, this newly refurbished museum calls itself an 'ocean literacy center' with critter-filled touch tanks, remotely operated vehicles, the rowboat used by adventurer Roz Savage on her five-year, round-the-world solo voyage, and an innovation lab.

★**Orange County Museum of Art** MUSEUM
(☏949-759-1122; www.ocma.net; 850 San Clemente Dr; adult/student/child under 12yr $10/8/free; ☉11am-5pm Wed-Sun, to 8pm Thu) This engaging museum highlights California art and cutting-edge contemporary artists, with exhibitions rotating through two large spaces. There's also a sculpture garden, eclectic gift shop and theater screening classic, foreign and art-related films.

🏃 Activities

Balboa Peninsula BEACHES
Four miles long but less than a half mile wide, the Balboa Peninsula has a white-sand beach on its ocean side, great people-watching and countless stylish homes.

Hotels, restaurants and bars cluster around the peninsula's two famous piers: **Newport Pier** near the western end and **Balboa Pier** at the eastern end. Near Newport Pier, several shops rent umbrellas, beach chairs, volleyballs and other necessities. For swimming, families will find a more relaxed atmosphere and calmer waves at **Mothers Beach** (10th St & 18th St).

Surfing

Surfers flock to the breaks at the small jetties surrounding the Newport Pier. At the tip of Balboa Peninsula, by the West Jetty, the **Wedge** is a bodysurfing, bodyboarding and knee-boarding spot famous for its perfectly hollow waves that can swell up to 30ft high. Warning: locals can be territorial, and newcomers should head a few blocks west.

Rent surf, body surfing and stand-up paddleboard equipment and gear at **15th Street Surf Shop** (☏949-673-5810; www.15thstreetsurfshop.com; 103 15th St; boogie

Newport Beach

boards per hr/day $2.50/8, surfboards $6/20) or **Paddle Power** (☏949-675-1215; www.paddle-powerh2o.com; 1500 W Balboa Blvd).

Boating

Take a boat tour or rent your own kayak, sailboat or outboard motorboat. Even better, rent a flat-bottomed electric boat that you pilot yourself and cruise with up to 12 friends. Find boats at **Duffy Electric Boat Rentals** (☏949-645-6812; www.duffyofnewportbeach.com; 2001 W Pacific Coast Hwy; per hr weekday/weekend $85/100; ◎10am-8pm) or **Balboa Boat Rentals** (☏949-673-7200; http://boats4rent.com; 510 E Edgewater Pl; kayaks

per hr from $15, sailboats $45, powerboats from $70, electric boats from $75).

Cycling & Skating

For fabulous ocean views, ride along the paved **recreational path** that encircles almost the entire Balboa Peninsula. Inland, cyclists like the paved **scenic loop** around Newport Bay Ecological Reserve (p614).

There are many places to rent bikes near Newport and Balboa Piers. **Easyride's Back Alley Bicycles** (☏949-566-9850; www.easyridebackalleybikes.com; 204 Washington St; beach cruisers per day $20, tandem bicycles per hr/day $15/30, surreys per hr from $25) even rents surreys (you know, with the fringe on top), but think twice because locals are known to pelt them with water balloons.

Diving

There's terrific diving just south of Newport Beach at the underwater park at Crystal Cove State Park (p617), where divers can check out reefs, anchors and an old military plane crash site. For dive-boat trips, stop by **Beach Cities Scuba Center** (☏949-650-5440; www.beachcitiesscuba.com; 4537 W Coast Hwy), where full equipment rental costs $60 per day.

☞ Tours

Fun Zone Boat Co   BOAT TOUR
(☏949-673-0240; www.funzoneboats.com; 600 Edgewater Pl; 45min cruise per adult/senior/child 5-11yr from $14/7/11) Sea lion–watching and celebrity home tours depart beneath the Ferris wheel in the Fun Zone.

Davey's Locker   BOAT TOUR
(☏949-673-1434; www.daveyslocker.com; 400 Main St; 2½hr whale-watching cruise per adult/child 3-12yr & senior from $32/26, half-day sportfishing $41.50/34) At Balboa Pavilion; offers whale-watching and sportfishing trips.

Gondola Adventures   BOAT TOUR
(☏949-646-2067, 888-446-6365; www.gondola.com; 3101 W Coast Hwy; 1hr cruise per couple from $135) Totally cheesy Venetian-esque gondola rides with chocolates and sparkling cider for your sweetie.

☆☆ Festivals & Events

Newport Beach Wine & Food Festival   FOOD, WINE
(newportwineandfood.com; ◎mid-Sep) Flashy food-and-wine fest shows off local restaurateurs, top chefs, prestigious winemakers and

brewmasters, with live rock concerts staged near Fashion Island.

Christmas Boat Parade CHRISTMAS
(www.christmasboatparade.com; ☺Dec) The week before Christmas brings thousands of spectators to Newport Harbor to watch a tradition dating back over a century. The 2½-hour parade of up to 150 boats, which includes some fancy multimillion-dollar yachts all decked out with Christmas lights and holiday cheer, begins at 6:30pm. You can watch for free from the Fun Zone or Balboa Island, or book ahead for a harbor boat tour.

🛏 Sleeping

A Newport stay ain't cheap, but outside peak season, rates listed here often drop 40% or more.

Newport Channel Inn MOTEL $$
(☎800-255-8614, 949-642-3030; www.newportchannelinn.com; 6030 W Coast Hwy; r $129-199; P❈🐾) The ocean is just across Pacific Coast Hwy from this spotless 30-room, two-story 1960s-era motel. Other perks include large rooms with microwaves and mini-fridges, a big common sundeck, beach equipment for loan and genuinely friendly owners with lots of local knowledge. Enjoy a vacation-lodge vibe under the A-frame roof of Room 219, which sleeps up to seven.

WORTH A TRIP

NEWPORT BAY ECOLOGICAL RESERVE

Inland from the harbor, where runoff from the San Bernardino Mountains meets the sea, the brackish water of 752-acre **Newport Bay Ecological Reserve** (from $20 per person) 🚶 supports nearly 200 bird species. It's one of SoCal's few preserved estuaries and an important stopover on the migratory Pacific Flyway. It's also under the flyway for planes taking off from John Wayne Airport, but this annoyance doesn't overly detract from the wildlife viewing. Stop by the **Muth Interpretive Center** (☎949-923-2290; www.ocparks.com/unbic; 2301 University Dr, off Irvine Ave; ☺10am-4pm Tue-Sun; 🚻), made from sustainable and renewable materials and home to kid-friendly exhibits.

Newport Dunes Waterfront RV Resort & Marina CABINS, CAMPING $$
(☎949-729-3863, 800-765-7661; www.newportdunes.com; 1131 Back Bay Dr; campsites from $55, studios/cottages from $150/200; P❈🐾🌊❄🐾) RVs and tents aren't required for a stay at this upscale campground: two dozen tiny A-frame studios and one-bedroom cottages are available, all within view of Newport Bay. A fitness center and walking trails, kayak rentals, board games, family bingo, ice-cream socials, horseshoe and volleyball tournaments, an outdoor pool and playground, and summertime movies on the beach await.

Resort at Pelican Hill RESORT $$$
(☎949-467-6800, 800-315-8214; www.pelicanhill.com; 22701 Pelican Hill Rd S; r from $495; P@🐾🌊) At this Tuscan-themed resort, secluded in the Newport Coast hills, mature trees and Palladian columns line the way to over 300 deluxe air-con bungalows and villas. Pleasures include a circular mosaic-inlaid swimming pool (diameter: 136ft), two 18-hole championship golf courses, a soothing spa, top-notch Northern Italian fare at Andrea restaurant and multilingual concierge staff who define solicitous. Rates: sky high. Pampering: priceless.

🍴 Eating

Newport has some of the county's best restaurants.

Eat Chow CALIFORNIAN $$
(☎949-423-7080; www.eatchownow.com; 211 62nd St; mains $8-15; ☺8am-9pm Mon-Thu, to 10pm Fri, 7am-10pm Sat, 7am-9pm Sun) Hidden a block off W Coast Hwy, the crowd is equal parts tatted hipsters and ladies who lunch, which makes it very Newport indeed. They all queue happily for dishes like ribeye Thai beef salad, grilled salmon tacos with curry slaw, and bodacious burgers like the Chow BBQ burger with home-made barbecue sauce, smoked gouda, crispy onions and more.

Crab Cooker SEAFOOD $$
(☎949-673-0100; www.crabcooker.com; 2200 Newport Blvd; mains $12-23, lobster $40; ☺11am-9pm Sun-Thu, to 10pm Fri & Sat; 🚻) Expect a wait at this always-busy joint, a landmark since 1951. It serves great seafood and fresh crab on paper plates to an appreciative crowd wearing flip-flops and jeans. Don't miss the

delish chowder. If you're in a hurry, there's a to-go counter.

★ Bear Flag Fish Company SEAFOOD $$
(☎949-673-3434; www.bearflagfishco.com; 407 31st St, Newport Beach; mains $8-15; ☉11am-9pm Tue-Sat, to 8pm Sun & Mon;) This squat glass box is *the* place for generously sized, grilled and panko-breaded fish tacos, ahi burritos, spankin' fresh ceviche and oysters. Pick out what you want from the ice-cold display cases, then grab a picnic-table seat.

Bluewater Grill SEAFOOD $$
(☎949-675-3474; www.bluewatergrill.com; 630 Lido Park Dr; mains $10-39; ☉11am-10pm Mon-Thu, to 11pm Fri & Sat, 10am-10pm Sun) Sit on the wooden deck and watch the boats at this polished harborside restaurant and oyster bar, which serves incredibly fresh fish. Great for Bloody Marys and a leisurely lunch – maybe swordfish tacos and coleslaw, beer-battered fish and chips or seared ahi with white-bean hummus.

☕ Drinking

Alta Coffee Warehouse COFFEEHOUSE
(www.altacoffeeshop.com; 506 31st St; ☉6am-10:30pm Mon-Thu, 7am-11pm Fri & Sat, 7am-10:30pm Sun) Hidden on a side street, this cozy coffeehouse in a beach bungalow with a covered patio lures locals with live music and poetry readings, art on the brick walls, tasty vittles and honest baristas.

Newport Beach Brewing Company BREWPUB
(www.newportbeachbrewingcompany.com; 2920 Newport Blvd; ☉11:30am-11pm Sun-Thu, to 1am Fri & Sat; ☎) The town's only microbrewery (try the signature Newport Beach Blonde or Bisbee's ESB), 'Brewco' is a laid-back place to catch the big game or just kick it over burgers, pizzas and fried fare with your buds after a day at the beach.

Mutt Lynch BEACH BAR
(www.muttlynchs.com; 2301 W Oceanfront; ☉7am-midnight) Rowdy dive by the beach offers pool tables, schooners filled with dozens of beers on tap and martinis made with soju (Korean vodka). Food is large portions, especially at breakfast. Best on 'Sunday Fundays.'

🛍 Shopping

On Balboa Island, **Marine Ave** is lined with darling shops in an old-fashioned village atmosphere, a good place to pick up something for the kids, unique gifts, beachy souvenirs, jewelry, art or antiques. At the other end of the scale and of town, chic, outdoor mall **Fashion Island** (☎949 721 2000; 550 Newport Center Dr; ☉10am-9pm Mon-Fri, 11am-7pm Sat, 11am-6pm Sun) sits inland with more than 400 specialty stores and department stores Bloomingdale's, Macy's and Neiman Marcus.

ℹ Information

Balboa Branch Library (www.city.newport-beach.ca.us/nbpl; 100 E Balboa Blvd; ☉9am-6pm Tue & Thu-Sat, to 9pm Mon & Wed; ☎) Near the beach; ask for a free internet-terminal guest pass.

Hoag Memorial Hospital Presbyterian (☎949-764-4624; www.hoaghospital.org; 1 Hoag Dr; ☉24hr) With 24-hour emergency room.

Explore Newport Beach (www.visitnewportbeach.com; 401 Newport Center Dr, Fashion Island, Atrium Court, 2nd fl; ☉10am-9pm Mon-Fri, to 7pm Sat, to 6pm Sun) The city's official visitor center.

ℹ Getting There & Around

BUS
OCTA (☎714-560-6282; www.octa.net) bus 1 connects Newport Beach with the OC's other beach towns, including Corona del Mar just east, every 30 minutes to one hour. From the intersection of Newport Blvd and Pacific Coast Hwy, bus 71 heads south along the Balboa Peninsula to Main Ave around every hour or so. On all routes, the one-way fare is $2 (make sure you have exact change).

BOAT
The West Coast's largest passenger catamaran, the **Catalina Flyer** (☎800-830-7744; www.catalinainfo.com; 400 Main St; round-trip adult/child 3-12yr/senior $70/53/65, per bicycle $7), makes a daily round-trip to Catalina Island (p590), taking 75 minutes each way. It leaves Balboa Pavilion around 9am and returns before 6pm; check online for discounts.

CAR & MOTORCYCLE
The municipal lot beside Balboa Pier costs 50¢ per 20 minutes, or $15 per day. Street parking meters on the Balboa Peninsula cost 50¢ to $1 per hour. Free parking on residential streets, a block or two from the sand, is time-limited and subject to other restrictions. In summer, expect to circle like a hawk for a space.

Around Newport Beach

Costa Mesa

At first glance the Costa Mesa looks like just another landlocked suburb transected by the I-405, but three top venues attract some 24 million visitors each year. South Coast Plaza is SoCal's largest mall, and steps away are Orange County's prime performing-arts venues: Segerstrom Center for the Arts and South Coast Repertory, one of the nation's most-acclaimed theater companies. A pair of 'anti-malls' (the Lab and the Camp) brings hipster cool to the shopping scene, while strip malls reveal surprisingly tasty cafes and ethnic-food holes-in-the-wall.

✗ Eating

Avanti Natural Kitchen   VEGETARIAN $
(www.avantinatural.com; 259 E 17th St; mains $8-11; ⊘11am-10pm Mon-Fri, 10:30am-10pm Sat, 10:30am-8pm Sun; 🖉) 🍴 A mom-and-pop vegetarian cafe so good, even carnivores will leave feeling sated. It looks like just another strip-mall storefront, but step inside for the creative chef duo's magic with pizzas, roasted stuffed portobello mushrooms and the hot taco brunch. The menu features organic produce from local farms.

Plums Café   CALIFORNIAN $$
(📞949-722-7586; www.plumscafe.com; 369 E 17th St; mains $10-25; ⊘8am-3pm, dinner from 5pm) Raise your breakfast game at this gourmet caterer's bistro tucked in the corner of a cookie-cutter strip mall. With its exposed brick walls and sleek designs, Plums will have you feeling oh-so-chic as you nibble Dutch baby pancakes with Oregon pepper bacon, or alderwood smoked salmon hash. Breakfast served until 11:30am weekdays, brunch till 3pm on weekends.

Habana   LATIN AMERICAN $$
(📞714-556-0176; the Lab, 2930 Bristol St; lunch $6-13, dinner $15-36; ⊘11:30am-4pm & 5-11pm Sun-Thu, to midnight Fri & Sat) With flickering votive candles, ivy-covered courtyard and spicy Cuban, Mexican and Jamaican specialties, this sultry cantina whispers rendezvous. Paella, *ropa vieja* (shredded flank steak in tomato sauce) and salmon *al parilla* (grilled) come with plantains and black beans on the side. On weekends, the bar gets jumpin' late-night.

Memphis Café Bar   SOUTHERN $$
(📞714-432-7685; memphiscafe.com; 2920 Bristol St; mains lunch $7-12, dinner $12-22; ⊘8am-10pm Mon-Wed, to 10:30pm Thu-Sat, 8am-3pm & 5-9:30pm Sun) Inside a vintage mid-century modern building, this fashionable eatery is all about down-home flavor – think pulled-pork sandwiches, popcorn shrimp, gumbo and buttermilk-battered fried chicken. Happy hour at the bar is best.

🍷 Drinking

Milk + Honey   CAFE
(the Camp, 2981 Bristol St; ⊘8am-10pm Mon-Thu, to 11pm Fri & Sat, 10am-10pm Sun; 🛜) Fair-trade, shade-grown and organic coffee, chai tea and strong espresso drinks, plus fruit smoothies, seasonal frozen-yogurt flavors and Japanese-style shaved ice with flavors like strawberry, red bean and almond.

Wine Lab   WINE BAR
(www.winelabcamp.com; the Camp, 2937 Bristol St, Suite A101B; ⊘noon-10pm Tue-Thu, to 11pm Fri & Sat, to 9pm Sun, 4-9pm Mon) This friendly wine shop offers New World wine and craft-beer tasting flights, plus small plates of artisan cheeses and charcuterie.

☆ Entertainment

Segerstrom Center for the Arts   THEATER, CONCERT HALL
(📞714-556-2787; www.scfta.org; 600 Town Center Dr) Orchestral and dance performances.

South Coast Repertory   THEATER
(📞714-708-5555; www.scr.org; 655 Town Center Dr) One of the nation's most-acclaimed theater companies.

🛍 Shopping

South Coast Plaza   MALL
(www.southcoastplaza.com; 3333 Bristol St; ⊘10am-9pm Mon-Fri, to 8pm Sat, 11am-6:30pm Sun) The stats at SoCal's premier luxury shopping destination speak for themselves. About $2 billion in annual sales, nearly 300 luxury brand and chain shops, five department stores, five valet stations and 12,750 parking spaces. Grab a map from a concierge booth. South Coast Plaza offers thrice-daily shuttles (📞888-288-5823) from Anaheim hotels.

Lab   MALL
(www.thelab.com; 2930 Bristol St) This outdoor, ivy-covered 'anti-mall' is an in-your-face alternative to South Coast Plaza. Indie-

minded shoppers can sift through vintage clothing, unique sneakers, art galleries in trailers, and trendy duds for teens, tweens and 20-somethings.

Camp MALL
(www.thecampsite.com; 2937 Bristol St) 🌿
Vegans, tree-huggers and rock climbers, lend me your ears. The Camp offers one-stop shopping for all your outdoor and natural-living needs. Active Ride Shop, fair-trade Seed People's Market and the toxin-free nail salon Lollipop are among the stores clustered along a leafy outdoor walkway. The parking lot is painted with inspirational quotes like 'Show Up for Life.'

ℹ Information

Travelex (South Coast Plaza, 1st fl, 3333 Bristol St; ⊙10am-9pm Mon-Fri, to 8pm Sat, 11am-6:30pm Sun) Foreign-currency exchange inside the mall, between Sears and Bloomingdale's.

ℹ Getting There & Around

Costa Mesa is inland from Newport Beach via Hwy 55.

Several **OCTA** (☑714-560-6282; www.octa.net) routes converge on South Coast Plaza, including bus 57 running along Bristol Ave south to Newport Beach's Fashion Island ($2, 20 minutes, every half hour).

Corona del Mar

Savor some of SoCal's most celebrated ocean views from the bluffs of Corona del Mar, a chichi community stretching along Pacific Coast Hwy and hugging the eastern flank of Newport Channel. In addition to stellar lookouts, several postcard-perfect beach-

es, rocky coves and child-friendly tidepools beckon along this idyllic stretch of coast.

A half mile long, **Main Beach** (Map p612; ☑949-644-3151; ⊙6am-10pm; 🅿), aka Corona del Mar State Beach lies at the foot of rocky cliffs. There are restrooms, fire rings (arrive early to snag one) and volleyball courts. All-day parking costs $15, but spaces fill by 9am on weekends. Scenes from the classic TV show *Gilligan's Island* were shot at waveless, family-friendly **Pirates Cove**; take the nearby stairs off the north end of the Main Beach parking lot.

Crystal Cove State Park

With 3.5 miles of open beach and over 2300 acres of undeveloped woodland, this is both a **state beach** (☑949-494-3539; www.parks.ca.gov; 8471 N Coast Hwy; per car $15, campsites $25-75) and an underwater park. Scuba enthusiasts can check out two historic anchors dating from the 1800s as well as the crash site of a Navy plane that went down in the 1940s. Alternatively just go tide pooling, fishing, kayaking and surfing along the undeveloped shoreline.

🛏 Sleeping & Eating

⭐ **Crystal Cove Beach Cottages** CABIN $$
(☑reservations 800-444-7275; www.crystalcovebeachcottages.com; 35 Crystal Cove, Newport Beach; r with shared bath $42-127, cottages $162-249; ⊙check-in 4-9pm) Snag these historic oceanfront cottages in the park's historic district. Book on the first day of the month six months before your intended stay – or pray for last-minute cancellations.

Ruby's Crystal Cove Shake Shack DINER $
(www.rubys.com; 7703 E Coast Hwy; shakes $5; ⊙6:30am-9pm, to 10pm Fri & Sat) A SoCal institution, this been-here-forever wooden shake stand is now part of a chain, but the ocean views are as good as ever. Try the date shake.

Beachcomber Café AMERICAN $$
(☑949-376-6900; www.thebeachbercafe.com; 15 Crystal Cove; breakfast $9-18, lunch $13-21, dinner $23-36; ⊙7am-9:30pm; 🅿) This atmospheric cafe lets you soak up the vintage 1950s beach vibe as you tuck into macadamia-nut pancakes, roasted turkey club sandwiches or more serious surf-and-turf. Sunset is the magic hour for Polynesian tiki drinks. Validated parking with purchase over $15.

Laguna Beach

It's easy to love Laguna: secluded coves, romantic cliffs, azure waves and waterfront parks imbue the city with a Riviera-like feel.

But nature isn't the only draw. Laguna has a strong tradition in the arts, starting with the 'plein air' impressionists who lived and worked here in the early 1900s. Today it's the home of renowned arts festivals, several dozen galleries, a well-known museum and exquisitely preserved Arts and Crafts cottages and bungalows.

⊙ Sights

With 30 public beaches sprawling along 7 miles of coastline, there's always another stunning view or hidden cove just around the bend. Just look for 'beach access' signs, and be prepared to pass through people's backyards to reach the sand. Rent beach equipment from **Main Beach Toys** (�949-494-8808; 150 Laguna Ave; chairs/umbrellas/boards per day $10/10/15; ⊙9am-9pm).

★**Laguna Art Museum**　　　　　MUSEUM
(⊘949-494-8971; www.lagunaartmuseum.org; 307 Cliff Dr; adult/student & senior/child $7/5/free, 1st Thu of month free; ⊙11am-5pm Fri-Tue, to 9pm Thu) This breezy museum has changing exhibitions featuring contemporary Californian artists, and a permanent collection heavy on Californian landscapes, vintage photographs and works by early Laguna bohemians.

Pacific Marine Mammal Center　ANIMAL PARK
(⊘949-494-3050; www.pacificmmc.org; 20612 Laguna Canyon Rd; admission by donation; ⊙10am-4pm) 🏊 A nonprofit organization dedicated to rescuing and rehabilitating injured or ill marine mammals, this center northeast of town has a small staff and many volunteers who help nurse rescued pinnipeds – mostly sea lions and seals – before releasing them back into the wild. There are several outside pools and holding pens – but remember, this is a rescue center, not SeaWorld.

🏃 Activities

Central Beaches　　　　　　BEACHES
Near downtown's village, **Main Beach** has volleyball and basketball courts, a playground and restrooms. It's Laguna's best beach for swimming. Just north at **Picnic Beach**, it's too rocky to surf; tide pooling is best. Pick up a tide table at the visitors bureau. (Tide pool etiquette: tread lightly on dry rocks only and don't pick anything up that you find living in the water or on the rocks.)

Above Picnic Beach, the grassy, bluff-top **Heisler Park** offers vistas of craggy coves and deep-blue sea. Bring your camera – with its palm trees and bougainvillea-dotted bluffs, the scene is definitely one for posterity. A scenic walkway also connects Heisler Park to Main Beach.

North of downtown, Crescent Bay has big hollow waves good for bodysurfing, but parking is difficult; try the bluffs atop the beach; the views here are reminiscent of the Amalfi Coast.

Southern Beaches　　　　　　BEACHES
About 1 mile south of downtown, secluded **Victoria Beach** has volleyball courts and **La Tour**, a Rapunzel's-tower-like structure from 1926. Skimboarding (at the south end) and scuba diving are popular here. Take the stairs down Victoria Dr; there's limited parking along Pacific Coast Hwy.

Further south, **Aliso Beach County Park** (www.ocparks.com/alisobeach; 31131 S Pacific Coast Hwy; parking per hr $1; ⊙6am-10pm) is popular with surfers, boogie boarders and skimboarders. With picnic tables, fire pits and a play area, it's also good for families. Pay-and-display parking costs $1 per hour, or drive south and park on Pacific Coast Hwy for free.

Jealously guarded by locals, **Thousand Steps Beach** is hidden about 1 mile south of Aliso Beach. Just past Mission Hospital, park along Pacific Coast Hwy or residential side streets. At the south end of 9th St, more than 200 steps (OK, so it's not 1000) lead down to the sand. Though rocky, the beach is great for sunbathing, surfing and bodysurfing.

Diving & Snorkeling
With its coves, reefs and rocky outcroppings, Laguna is one of the best SoCal beaches for diving and snorkeling. **Divers Cove** just below Heisler Park is part of the **Glenn E Vedder Ecological Reserve**, an underwater park stretching to the northern border of Main Beach. Check weather and surf conditions (⊘949-494-6573) beforehand. **Laguna Sea Sports** (⊘949-494-6965; www.beachcitiesscuba.com; 925 N Coast Hwy; ⊙10am-6pm Mon-Thu, to 7pm Fri, 7am-7pm Sat, 8am-5pm Sun) rents gear and offers classes.

Laguna Beach

Kayaking

Take a guided kayaking tour of the craggy coves of Laguna's coast – and you might just see a colony of sea lions – with **La Vida Laguna** (☑ 949-275-7544; www.lavidalaguna.com; 1257 S Coast Hwy; 2hr guided tour $95). Make reservations at least a day in advance.

Hiking

Surrounded by a green belt – a rarity in SoCal – Laguna has great nature trails for hikes. At **Alta Laguna Park**, a locals-only park up-canyon from town, the moderate 1.25-mile **Park Avenue Nature Trail** takes you through fields of spring wildflowers and past panoramic views. Open to hikers and mountain bikers, the 2.5-mile **West Ridge Trail** follows the ridgeline of the hills above Laguna. To reach the trailheads, take Park Ave to Alta Laguna Blvd then turn left.

☞ Tours

Stop by the visitors bureau for brochures about self-guided tours on foot and by public bus, including heritage walks and public art.

✸ Festivals & Events

Festival of Arts   ART SHOW
(www.foapom.com; 650 Laguna Canyon Rd; admission $7-10; ⏱ usually 10am-11:30pm Jul & Aug) A two-month celebration of original artwork in almost all its forms. About 140 exhibitors display works ranging from paintings and handcrafted furniture to scrimshaw, plus kid-friendly art workshops and live music and entertainment daily.

Laguna Beach

◉ Top Sights
1 Laguna Art Museum B2

◎ Sights
2 Heisler Park A2
3 Main Beach C2

◉ Activities, Courses & Tours
4 Divers Cove..A2
5 Worldwide Opportunities on
   Organic Farms D1

⌖ Sleeping
6 Inn at Laguna Beach B2
7 Laguna Cliffs Inn A2
8 The Tides Inn B2

✖ Eating
9 242 Cafe Fusion Sushi C2
10 Zinc Cafe & Market...........................C2

⛃ Drinking & Nightlife
11 Ocean Brewing Company...................C2

✪ Entertainment
12 Laguna Playhouse C1

⛒ Shopping
13 Hobie Surf Shop.................................C2

Sawdust Festival   ART SHOW
(☑ 949-494-3030; www.sawdustartfestival.org; 935 Laguna Canyon Rd; adult/child 6-12yr/senior $8.50/4/7; ⏱ 10am-10pm late Jun-early Aug, to 6pm Sat & Sun late Nov–mid-Dec) Independent-minded festival that takes place in late autumn.

DISNEYLAND & ORANGE COUNTY LAGUNA BEACH

🛈 FIRE!

Forest fires are an ever-present danger all over Southern California, a truth Laguna Beach knows too well, due to fires large and small over the years. The canyons act like chimneys and small grass fires can quickly become infernos. Use extreme caution when lighting matches and don't just toss your cigarette butts – extinguish them with water or dirt, and once they're completely out, dispose of them properly.

Pageant of the Masters PERFORMANCE ART
(☏800-487-3378; www.foapom.com; 650 Laguna Canyon Rd; tickets from $15; ⌚8:30pm daily mid-Jul–Aug) The most thrilling part of the main festival, an experience that will leave you rubbing your eyes in disbelief, is the Pageant of the Masters performance, where human models blend seamlessly into re-creations of famous paintings. Tickets are hard to get unless you order them more than six months in advance, but you may be able to snag last-minute cancellations.

🛏 Sleeping

Most lodging in Laguna is on busy Pacific Coast Hwy (called Coast Hwy here), so expect traffic noise; bring earplugs or ask for a room away from the road.

★ The Tides Inn MOTEL $$
(☏888-777-2107, 949-494-2494; www.tideslaguna.com; 460 N Coast Hwy; r $175-285; P❄🕸🐾🐕) A bargain for Laguna, especially considering its convenient location just three long blocks north of the village. It feels rather upscale, with plush bedding, beachy-keen decor and inspirational quotes painted into each room. Each room is different; some have kitchenettes. Shared facilities include saltwater pool, barbecue grill and a fireplace for toasting marshmallows. Pet fee $25 to $40.

Inn at Laguna Beach HOTEL $$$
(☏949-497-9722, 800-544-4479; www.innatlagunabeach.com; 211 N Coast Hwy; r $210-600; P❄🕸🐾🐕) Pride of place goes to this three-story white concrete hotel, at the north end of Main Beach. Its 70 rooms were recently renovated with rattan furniture, blond woods, marble, French blinds and thick featherbeds. Some have balconies overlooking the water. Extras include DVD and CD players, bathrobes, beach gear to borrow and a nightly ocean-view wine and beer reception.

Casa Laguna Inn & Spa B&B $$$
(☏949-494-2996, 800-233-0449; www.casalaguna.com; 2510 S Coast Hwy; r $159-389, ste from $279; P❄@🕸🐕) Laguna's most romantic B&B is built around a historic 1920s Mission Revival house surrounded by flowering gardens. Smallish rooms include those inside former artists' bungalows from the 1930s and '40s. All have fluffy beds and some have Jacuzzis. There's also a full chef-prepared breakfast made with local, organic ingredients and evening wine-and-cheese reception. Some pets OK (fee $25).

Laguna Cliffs Inn HOTEL $$$
(☏800-297-0007, 949-497-6645; www.lagunacliffsinn.com; 475 N Coast Hwy; r $165-325; P❄@🐕) Be it good feng shui, friendly staff or proximity to the beach, something just feels right at this renovated 36-room courtyard inn. From the big earth-tone pillows and hardwood floors to air-con and flat-screen TVs, the decor is contemporary, comfy and clean. Settle into the outdoor heated Jacuzzi with a glass of wine as the sun drops over the ocean.

🍴 Eating

Taco Loco MEXICAN $
(http://tacoloco.net; 640 S Coast Hwy; mains $3-14; ⌚11am-midnight Sun-Thu, to 2am Fri & Sat; 🌱) Throw back Coronas with the surfers while watching the passersby at this Mexican sidewalk cafe. Taco, quesadilla and nacho options seem endless: blackened calamari or tofu, swordfish, veggie (potato, mushroom, tofu) and shrimp to name a few. For dessert: hemp brownies. Order at the counter, dude.

Zinc Cafe & Market CAFE $
(www.zinccafe.com; 350 Ocean Ave, Laguna Beach; mains $6-11; ⌚market 7am-6pm, cafe to 4pm; 🌱) Ground zero for see-and-be-seen vegetarians, this gourmet market has a hedge-enclosed patio where you can munch on tasty vegetarian and vegan meals such as garden-fresh salads and pizzas. Strong espresso too.

Orange Inn DINER $
(☏949-494-6085; www.orangeinnlagunabeach.com; 703 S Coast Hwy; mains $5-10; ⌚6:30am-5pm, to 7pm Sat & Sun) Surfers fuel up, at this little shop from 1931, found in the *Guinness Book of Records* for inventing the smoothie. Also look for date shakes, big

breakfasts, homemade muffins and deli sandwiches on whole-wheat or sourdough bread.

House of Big Fish & Cold Beer　SEAFOOD $$
(☏949-715-4500; www.houseofbigfish.com; 540 S Coast Hwy; mains $7-15; ☉11:30am-10:30pm) The name says it all (what else do you need?): Hawaii-style *poke* (marinated raw fish), Baja-style fish tacos, coconut shrimp and the fresh catch o' the day. Fish are sustainably raised, and there are dozens of beers with about one-third from California. Make reservations, or wait, like, forever.

★242 Cafe Fusion Sushi　JAPANESE $$$
(www.fusionart.us; 242 N Coast Hwy; mains $18-45; ☉4:30-10pm Sun-Thu, to 10:30pm Fri & Sat) One of the only female sushi chefs in Orange County, Miki Izumisawa slices and rolls organic rice into Laguna's best sushi, artfully presented. The place seats maybe two dozen people at a time, so expect a wait or come early. The 'sexy' handroll – spicy ahi and scallops with mint, cilantro, avocado and crispy potato – is date-enhancing.

Mozambique　AFRICAN FUSION $$$
(☏949-715-7777; www.mozambiqueoc.com; 1740 S Coast Hwy; dinner $14-69; ☉11am-11pm Sun-Thu, to midnight Fri & Sat) Macaws and toucans welcome guests to this trendy, sophisticated, three-level ode to exotically spiced dishes from southern Africa – peri-peri prawns, chicken pops, grilled pineapple, soaring steaks and seafood, ranging from small plates to pricey surf and turf. Who knows? You might see a *Real Housewife* hiding out in the rooftop bar, where there's live music on weekends.

🍷 Drinking

There are almost as many watering holes in downtown's village as there are art galleries. Most cluster along S Coast Hwy and Ocean Ave, making for an easy pub crawl. If you drink, don't drive; local cops take DUI's very seriously.

Ocean Brewing Company　PUB
(www.oceanbrewing.com; 237 Ocean Ave) Does pub grub and microbrews, excellent after a day of surfing, or look for music and karaoke at night.

Rooftop Lounge　BAR
(www.rooftoplagunabeach.com; 1289 S Coast Hwy) Perched atop **La Casa del Camino** (☏855-634-5736, 949-497-2446; www.lacasadelcamino.

FIRST THURSDAYS

On the first Thursday of the month, downtown Laguna Beach gets festive during the **First Thursdays Gallery Art Walk** (☏949-683-6871; www.first-thursdaysartwalk.com; ☉6pm-9pm 1st Thu of month) FREE. You can make the rounds of 40 local galleries and the Laguna Art Museum via free shuttles circling Laguna's art-gallery districts.

com; 1289 S Coast Hwy; r from $159; P✳@🛜), this bar, has 270-degree coastal views, mango and wild berry mojitos and tasty plates like meatballs in guava BBQ sauce.

Koffee Klatsch　COFFEEHOUSE
(1440 S Coast Hwy; ☉7am-11pm Sun-Thu, to midnight Fri & Sat) A low-key coffee shop that draws a mixed gay/straight/hipster crowd for coffees, breakfasts, salads and ginormous cakes.

☆ Entertainment

Laguna Playhouse　THEATER
(☏949-497-2787; www.lagunaplayhouse.com; 606 Laguna Canyon Rd) Orange County's oldest continuously operating community theater stages lighter plays in summer, more serious works in winter.

🔒 Shopping

Downtown's village is awash with shops in hidden courtyards and eclectic little bungalows. Forest Ave has the highest concentration of chic boutiques from sleek beachwear to **Hobie Surf Shop** (www.hobie.com; 294 Forest Ave) – Hobie Alter started his internationally known surf line in his parents' Laguna Beach garage in 1950. South of downtown, Pacific Coast Hwy teems with fashionable, eclectic and arty shops where you can shop for goddess clothing, balance your chakras or find vintage rock albums and posters.

For a DIY **art gallery walk**, Laguna has three distinct districts: Gallery Row, along the 300 to 500 blocks of N Coast Hwy; in downtown's village, along Forest Ave and Pacific Coast Hwy; and further south on S Coast Hwy between Oak St and Bluebird Canyon Dr. Pick up an art-walk map at the visitors bureau.

ⓘ Information

INTERNET ACCESS

Visit Laguna Beach's Visitor Center for free wi-fi and internet terminal access.

Laguna Beach Library (www.ocpl.org/libloc/lbch; 363 Glenneyre St; ⊙10am-8pm Mon-Wed, to 6pm Thu, to 5pm Fri & Sat; ☏) Free wi-fi and walk-in online computer access.

MEDICAL SERVICES

Mission Hospital Laguna Beach (☏949-499-1311; www.missionforhealth.com; 31872 Coast Hwy; ⊙24hr) 24-hour emergency room, 4 miles south of downtown along PCH.

TOURIST INFORMATION

Visit Laguna Beach Visitors Center (☏949-497-9229; www.lagunabeachinfo.com; 381 Forest Ave; ⊙10am-5pm; ☏) Helpful staff, bus schedules, restaurant menus and free brochures on everything from hiking trails to self-guided walking tours.

ⓘ Getting There & Away

From I-405, take Hwy 133 (Laguna Canyon Rd) southwest. Hwy 1 goes by several names in Laguna Beach: south of Broadway, downtown's main street, it's called South Coast Hwy; north of Broadway it's North Coast Hwy. Locals also call it Pacific Coast Hwy or just PCH.

OCTA (☏714-560-6282; www.octa.net) bus 1 heading along the coast connects Laguna Beach with Orange County's other beach towns, including Dana Point heading south, every 30 to 60 minutes. The one-way fare is $2 (exact change).

ⓘ Getting Around

Laguna Beach Transit (www.lagunabeachcity.net; 375 Broadway) has its central bus depot in downtown's village, served by three routes including to festival sites. Rides cost 75¢ (exact change) or are free during July and August.

Through town, Pacific Coast Hwy moves slowly in summer, especially on weekends.

Parking lots in downtown's village charge between $10 and $20 per entry; they fill up early in the day during summer. Street parking can be

---

TOP FIVE OC SURF SPOTS

➜ Huntington Pier (p609), Huntington Beach

➜ Newport Pier (p612), Newport Beach

➜ Trestles (p623), Dana Point

➜ San Onofre State Beach

➜ Doheny State Beach, Dana Point

---

hard to find near the beaches during summer, especially in the afternoons and on weekends – arrive early. Coin- and credit-card-operated meters cost from $1 per hour and pay-and-display lots cost $2 per hour. Alternatively, park for free in residential areas, but obey time limits and posted restrictions, otherwise your car will be towed.

Around Laguna Beach

San Juan Capistrano

Famous for the swallows that fly back to town every March, San Juan Capistrano is also home to the 'jewel of the California missions.' It's a little town, about 11 miles south and inland of Laguna Beach, but there's enough history and charm here to make almost a day of it.

⊙ Sights & Activities

★ **Mission San Juan Capistrano** CHURCH
(☏949-234-1300; www.missionsjc.com; 26801 Ortega Hwy, San Juan Capistrano; adult/child $9/6; ⊙9am-5pm) Padre Junipero Serra founded the mission on November 1, 1776, and tended it personally for many years. Particularly moving are the towering remains of the Great Stone Church, almost completely destroyed by a powerful earthquake on December 8, 1812. The **Serra Chapel** – whitewashed outside with restored frescoes inside – is believed to be the oldest existing building in California (1778). Plan on spending at least an hour poking around the sprawling mission's tiled roofs, covered arches, lush gardens, fountains and courtyards – including the padre's quarters, soldiers' barracks and the cemetery.

Admission includes a worthwhile free audio tour with interesting stories narrated by locals.

Los Rios Historic District HISTORIC BUILDINGS
One block southwest of the Mission, next to the Capistrano train depot, this peaceful assemblage of a few dozen historic cottages and adobes now mostly houses cafes and gift shops. Pick up a free walking-tour guide at the information kiosk off Verdugo St, by the railroad tracks.

✗ Eating & Drinking

★ **El Campeon** MEXICAN $
(31921 Camino Capistrano; mains $2-9; ⊙6:30am-9pm; ⚑) Real-deal Mexican food, in a strip

FIESTA DE LA GOLONDRINAS

Swallows return to nest in the walls of Mission San Juan Capistrano every year around March 19, the feast of St Joseph, after wintering in South America. Their flight covers about 7500 miles each way. The highlight of the town's month-long **Festival of the Swallows** (www.swallowsparade.com) is the big parade and outdoor *mercado* (market), held on a Saturday in mid-March.

mall south of the Mission. There's a simple counter-service restaurant, *panadería* (bakery) and *mercado* (grocery store). Look for tacos, tostadas and burritos in freshly made tortillas, *aguas frescas* (fruit drinks) in flavors like watermelon and grapefruit, and breads and pastries starting at 59¢.

★ **Ramos House Café**   CALIFORNIAN **$$**
(www.ramoshouse.com; 31752 Los Rios St; mains $15-20; ⊗8:30am-3pm Tue-Sun) The best spot for breakfast or lunch near the Mission, this Old West–flavored wood-built house from 1881 is famous for organically raised comfort food flavored with herbs grown on-site.

El Adobe de Capistrano   MEXICAN **$$**
(www.eladobedecapistrano.com; 31891 Camino Capistrano; lunch $11-21, dinner $11-34; ⊗11am-9pm Mon-Thu, to 10pm Fri & Sat, 10am-9pm Sun) In a building that traces its origins to 1797, this sprawling, beamed-ceilinged restaurant and bar does big business, from the standards (enchiladas, fajitas) to blackened fish or lobster tacos and grilled steaks. It was a favorite of President Nixon, who lived in nearby San Clemente, which might be good or bad depending on your outlook.

Coach House   CLUB
(☑949-496-8930; www.thecoachhouse.com; 33157 Camino Capistrano) Long-running live-music venue features a roster of local and national rock, indie, alternative and retro bands; expect a cover charge of $15 to $40. Recent performers include classic rockers like Marshall Tucker and Johnny Winter, tribute bands and comedy shows like the *Funniest Housewives of Orange County*.

❶ Getting There & Away

From Laguna Beach, ride **OCTA** (☑714-560-6282; www.octa.net) bus 1 south to Dana Point.

At the intersection of Pacific Coast Hwy and Del Obispo St, catch bus 91 northbound toward Mission Viejo, which drops you near the Mission. Buses run every 30 to 60 minutes. The trip takes about an hour. You'll have to pay the one-way fare ($2, exact change) twice.

Drivers should take I-5 exit 82 (Ortega Hwy), then head west about 0.25 miles. There's free three-hour parking on streets and in municipal lots.

The **Amtrak** (☑800-872-7245; www.amtrak.com; 26701 Verdugo St) depot is one block south and west of the Mission. You could arrive by train from LA ($21, 75 minutes) or San Diego ($22, 90 minutes). A few daily **Metrolink** (☑800-371-5465; www.metrolinktrains.com) commuter trains link San Juan Capistrano to Orange ($8, 45 minutes), with limited connections to Anaheim.

Dana Point

Dana Point's built-up, parking-lotted harbor detracts from its charm, but it still gets lots of visitors its lovely beaches and port and for whale watching and sport fishing.

TRESTLES

World-renowned **Trestles**, southeast of Dana Point and next to San Diego County, is famous for its natural surf break, which consistently churns out perfect waves, even in summer. It's also endangered; for years surfers and environmentalists have been fighting the extension of a nearby toll road that they contend would negatively affect the waves. Visit http://savetrestles.surfrider.org to learn more.

Trestles lies inside protected **San Onofre State Beach** (www.parks.ca.gov; parking $15 per day), which has rugged bluff-top walking trails, swimming beaches and a developed inland **campground** (☑800-444-7275; www.reserveamerica.com; sites $35-60) with flush toilets, indoor hot showers, picnic tables and fire pits. To get here, exit I-5 at Basilone Rd or Los Christianos Rd (for the campground), then hoof to Trestles along the nature trail.

◉ Sights & Activities

Doheny State Beach   BEACH
(☑949-496-6172; www.dohenystatebeach.org; entry per vehicle $15; ⊗6am-10pm, to 8pm Nov-Feb; ℙ ☸) This mile-long beach is great for swimmers, surfers, surf fishers and tidepoolers. You'll also find picnic tables with grills, volleyball courts and a butterfly exhibit.

Rent bicycles at **Wheel Fun Rentals** (☑949-496-7433; www.wheelfunrentals.com; 25300

Dana Point Harbor Dr; cruiser rental per hr/day $10/28; ⊙9am-sunset daily late May-early Sep, Sat & Sun early Sep-late May), just south of the picnic area at Doheny State Beach. Off Dana Point Harbor Dr, **Capo Beach Watercraft Rentals** (☑949-661-1690; www.capobeachwatercraft.com; 34512 Embarcadero Pl) and **Dana Point Jet Ski & Kayak Center** (☑949-661-4947; www.danapointjetski.com; 34671 Puerto Pl) both rent kayaks for harbor paddling. For scuba rentals and dive-boat trips (from $115), try **Beach Cities Scuba** (☑949-443-3858; www.beachcitiescsuba.com; 34283 Pacific Coast Hwy).

Ocean Institute
MUSEUM

(☑949-496-2274; www.ocean-institute.org; 24200 Dana Pt Harbor Dr; adult/child $6.50/4.50; ⊙10am-3pm Sat & Sun; ☖) On Sundays, admission to this child-friendly eco-center includes the guided tours aboard a replica of an early 19th-century tall ship, the brig **Pilgrim**, sailed by Richard Dana during his journey around Cape Horn to California.

Make reservations for the **R/V Sea Explorer** (adult/child 4 to 12 years from $35/22), a 70ft-long floating lab, for a science-focused snorkeling cruise or blue whale safari, or join a 'pyrate' adventure or gray-whale-watching cruise on the **Spirit of Dana Point** (adult/child 4 to 12 years $40/23), a replica of an American Revolution-era ship.

☞ Tours

In Mariner's Village off Dana Point Harbor Dr, Dana Wharf is the starting point for most boat tours and trips to Catalina Island. Contact **Capt Dave's Dolphin and Whale Safari** (☑949-488-2828; www.dolphin-safari.com; 34451 Ensenada Pl; adult/child 3-12yr from $59/39) or **Dana Wharf Sportfishing** (☑949-496-5794, 888-224-0603; www.danawharf.com; 34675 Golden Lantern St; sportfishing trips adult/child 3-12yr from $46/29, whale-watching tours from $45/25). For more kid-friendly whale-watching tours and coastal cruises, book ahead with the **Ocean Institute**.

✹ Festivals & Events

Festival of Whales
SEA FESTIVAL

(www.dpfestivalofwhales.com; ⊙early–mid-Mar) A parade, street fair, nature walks and talks, canoe races, surfing clinics, art exhibitions, live music, and surf 'woody' wagon and hot-rod show make up the merriment.

Doheny Blues Festival
MUSIC FESTIVAL

(www.omegaevents.com/dohenyblues; ⊙mid-May) Blues legends such as Buddy Guy and Keb Mo perform alongside up-and-comers over a weekend of funky live-music performances and family fun at Doheny State Beach.

Tall Ships Festival
SEA FESTIVAL

(www.tallshipsfestival.com; ⊙early Sep) The Ocean Institute hosts the West Coast's largest gathering of tall ships, with living-history encampments, scrimshaw carving demonstrations and lots more family-friendly marine-themed activities.

🍴 Sleeping & Eating

Mostly chain midrange motels and luxury resorts are what you'll find along Pacific Coast Hwy. The latter include the oceanfront **Ritz-Carlton Laguna Niguel** (☑949-240-2000; www.ritzcarlton.com; 1 Ritz-Carlton Dr; r from $420; @🐾🔊🏊), well-positioned for catching sunsets at Salt Creek Beach. **Doheny State Beach** (☑800-444-7275; www.reserveamerica.com; 25300 Dana Point Harbor Dr; inland/beachfront campsites $35/60) is regularly voted the county's best campground.

Restaurants around Dana Point Harbor serve straight-off-the-boat seafood. At Dana Wharf, **Turk's** (☑949-496-9028; 34683 Golden Lantern St; mains $5-16; ⊙8am-2am, shorter hours winter) dive bar is so dark it feels like you're drinking while jailed in the brig of a ship, but never mind. There's plenty of good pub grub (including burgers and fish-and-chips), Bloody Marys and beers, a mellow crowd and a groovy jukebox.

ℹ Information

Visitors Center (☑949-248-3501; www.danapoint.org; ⊙9am-4pm Fri-Sun late May-early Sep) Stop at this tiny booth at the corner of Golden Lantern St and Dana Point Harbor Dr for tourist brochures and maps. Gung-ho volunteers sure love their city.

ℹ Getting There & Around

From the harbor, **Catalina Express** (☑800-481-3470; www.catalinaexpress.com; 34675 Golden Lantern St; round-trip adult/child 2-11yr/senior $76.50/70/61) makes daily round-trips to Catalina Island, taking 90 minutes each way.

OCTA (☑714-560-6282; www.octa.net) bus 1 connects Dana Point with the OC's other beach towns every 30 to 60 minutes. The one-way fare is $2 (exact change).

Four-hour public parking at the harbor is free, or pay $5 per day (overnight $10).

San Diego & Around

Why Go?

New York has its cabbie, Chicago its bluesman and Seattle its coffee-drinking boho. San Diego, meanwhile, has the valet guy in a polo shirt, khaki shorts and crisp new sneakers. With his perfectly tousled hair, great tan and gentle enthusiasm, he looks like he's on a perennial spring break, and when he wishes you welcome, he really means it.

This may sound pejorative, but our intention is the opposite. San Diego calls itself 'America's Finest City' and its breezy confidence and sunny countenance filter down even to folks you encounter every day on the street.

What's not to love? San Diego bursts with world-famous attractions for the entire family, including the zoo, Legoland, the museums of Balboa Park and SeaWorld, plus a bubbling downtown and beaches ranging from ritzy to raucous, and America's most perfect weather.

Best Places to Eat

➜ Cucina Urbana (p641)

➜ Puesto at the Headquarters (p643)

➜ Urban Solace (p642)

➜ Fish 101 (p657)

Best Places to Stay

➜ Hotel del Coronado (p639)

➜ Legoland Hotel (p659)

➜ La Pensione Hotel (p638)

➜ Hotel Solamar (p638)

When to Go
San Diego

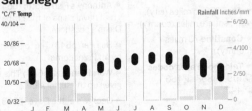

Jun–Aug High season. Temperatures and hotel rates are highest.

Sep–Oct, Mar–May Shoulder seasons; moderate rates.

Nov–Feb Hotel rates fall while most of America is hard at work.

MISSION SAN DIEGO DE ALCALÁ

Although the first California mission was on Presidio Hill by present-day Old Town, in 1774 Padre Junípero Serra moved it about 7 miles upriver, closer to water and more arable land. Now the Mission Basilica San Diego de Alcalá (p632) has been lovingly restored into a pretty white church and ancillary buildings (including California's oldest) and welcomes visitors.

Up-and-Coming Neighborhoods

➡ East Village
➡ Little Italy
➡ North Park

Population

With a population of 1,322,553, San Diego is the USA's eighth largest city. San Diego County, at 3,095,313, is fifth largest.

Fast Facts

➡ **Area** 372 sq miles (city); 4526 square miles (county)

➡ **Coastline** 70 miles (county)

➡ **Telephone area codes**
☑ 619, ☑ 858, ☑ 760, ☑ 442

Balboa Park

San Diego's best-known attraction, the zoo, is ensconced in Balboa Park, one of America's great urban spaces. Balboa Park rose to fame with a world's fair about 100 years ago, the Panama-California Exposition of 1915-16. Grand Spanish-colonial revival-style pavilions were constructed, which dominated the California design sense for generations. Here's the thing, though: they were temporary, made largely of stucco, chicken wire, plaster, hemp and horsehair like Hollywood movie sets, but they proved so popular that many were later replaced with the durable concrete structures that you see today. And among the park's many stages and amphitheaters, the jewel is the 600-seat Old Globe, modeled after the London theater where Shakespeare's works were performed. At 1200 acres, Balboa Park is more than 50% bigger than Central Park in New York City (778 acres).

GAY & LESBIAN SAN DIEGO

Historians trace the roots of San Diego's thriving gay community to WWII. Amid the enforced intimacy of military life, gay men from around the US were suddenly able to create strong if clandestine social networks. Postwar, many of these new friends stayed, and by the late 1960s, a newly politicized gay community made its unofficial headquarters in the Hillcrest neighborhood, which still has the highest concentration of LGBT bars, restaurants, cafes and shops, though the center is gradually branching out to other neighborhoods including nearby North Park. Visitors and locals alike find San Diego's gay scene generally more casual and friendly than in San Francisco or LA.

San Diego County's Best Water-View Dining

➡ Anthony's Fish Grotto (p643) Seafood classic next to the great naval ships of the Embarcadero, by Downtown San Diego's seashore.

➡ Bali Hai (p643) Tiki to the max, baby; watch the sailboats go by off Point Loma.

➡ World Famous (p644) This spot in Pacific Beach has never given up the surfer vibe.

➡ George's at the Cove (p653) Consistently rated one of America's top restaurants, with three venues for your dining pleasure. The rooftop lounge has awesome views.

➡ Jake's Del Mar (p656) After a day at the races, stop for a cocktail and an awesome happy hour.

CENTRAL & COASTAL SAN DIEGO

Whoosh – here comes a skateboarder. And there goes a wet-suited surfer toting his board to the break, while a Chanel-clad lady lifts a coffee cup off a porcelain saucer. Downtown San Diego and its nearby coastal communities offer all that and more.

◉ Sights

◉ San Diego Zoo & Balboa Park

San Diego's Zoo is a highlight of any trip to California and should be a high priority for first-time visitors. It's in Balboa Park, which itself is packed with museums and gardens.

To visit the zoo, all 14 museums, half-dozen botanical gardens and more would take days;

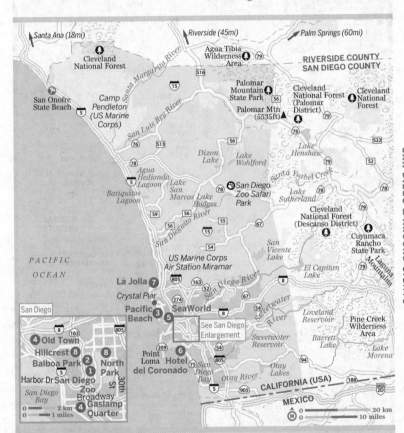

SAN DIEGO & AROUND SIGHTS

San Diego & Around Highlights

❶ Cooing at koalas and pandering to pandas at the **San Diego Zoo** (p629).

❷ Museum-hopping in **Balboa Park** (p629).

❸ Sunning and skating seaside in **Pacific Beach** (p633).

❹ Swilling margaritas in **Old Town** (p631) and pub-crawling downtown's **Gaslamp Quarter** (p644).

❺ Cheering for Shamu at **SeaWorld** (p633).

❻ Marveling at the history and architecture of the **Hotel del Coronado** (p633).

❼ Hang gliding, kayaking or giving your credit card a workout in **La Jolla** (p650).

❽ Sampling fish tacos or the next great taste in **Hillcrest and North Park** (p641).

❾ Mingling with the hoi polloi at **Del Mar Racetrack** (p653).

Metropolitan San Diego

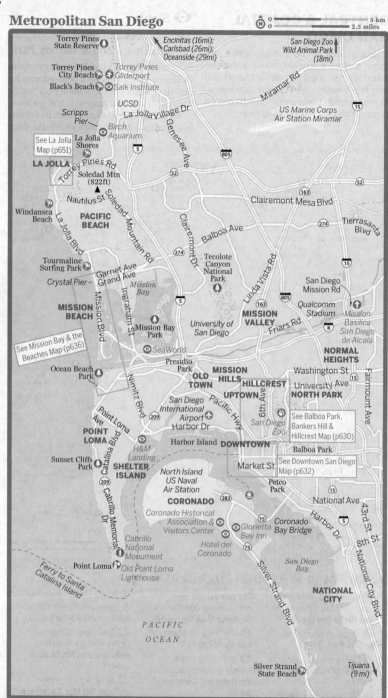

0 — 5 km
0 — 2.5 miles

Torrey Pines State Reserve

Encinitas (16mi);
Carlsbad (26mi);
Oceanside (29mi)

San Diego Zoo
Wild Animal Park
(18mi)

Torrey Pines City Beach
Torrey Pines Gliderport
Black's Beach
Salk Institute

Miramar Rd

UCSD
La Jolla Village Dr

US Marine Corps
Air Station Miramar

Scripps Pier
Birch Aquarium

See La Jolla Map (p651)
La Jolla Shores

LA JOLLA

Torrey Pines Rd
Soledad Mtn
(822ft)

Clairemont Mesa Blvd

Nautilus St

Windansea Beach

PACIFIC BEACH

Soledad Mountain Rd

Balboa Ave

Tierrasanta Blvd

Tourmaline Surfing Park
Garnet Ave
Grand Ave
Crystal Pier

Mission Bay

Tecolote Canyon National Park

Linda Vista Rd

San Diego Mission Rd

MISSION BEACH

Ingraham St

Mission Blvd

Mission Bay Park

University of San Diego

MISSION VALLEY

Friars Rd

Qualcomm Stadium

Mission Basilica San Diego de Alcalá

See Mission Bay & the Beaches Map (p636)

SeaWorld

Presidio Park

OLD TOWN

MISSION HILLS

NORMAL HEIGHTS

Ocean Beach Park

Nimitz Blvd

HILLCREST

UPTOWN

Washington St
University Ave

NORTH PARK

Fairmount Ave

Point Loma Ave

San Diego International Airport
Pacific Hwy
Harbor Dr

6th Ave

San Diego Zoo

See Balboa Park, Bankers Hill & Hillcrest Map (p630)

POINT LOMA

Cabrillo Memorial Dr

Harbor Island

DOWNTOWN

Balboa Park

Sunset Cliffs Park

H&M Landing

SHELTER ISLAND

North Island US Naval Air Station

Market St

See Downtown San Diego Map (p632)

Petco Park

National Ave

Cabrillo National Monument

CORONADO

Coronado Historical Association & Visitors Center

Glorietta Bay Inn

Coronado Bay Bridge

Harbor Dr

43rd St

8th St

National City Blvd

Point Loma

Old Point Loma Lighthouse

Hotel del Coronado

San Diego Bay

Ferry to Santa Catalina Island

Silver Strand Blvd

NATIONAL CITY

PACIFIC OCEAN

Silver Strand State Beach

Tijuana (9 mi)

plan your trip at the **Balboa Park Visitors Center** (Map p630; ☎619-239-0512; www.balboapark.org; House of Hospitality, 1549 El Prado; ⊙9:30am-4:30pm). Pick up a map (suggested donation $1) and the opening schedule.

★San Diego Zoo ZOO

(Map p630; ☎619-231-1515; www.sandiegozoo.org; 2920 Zoo Dr; 1-day pass adult/child from $46/36; 2-visit pass to Zoo and/or Safari Park adult/child $82/64; ⊙9am-9pm mid-Jun–early Sep, to 5pm or 6pm early Sep–mid-Jun; P⊕) ◢ This justifiably famous zoo is one of SoCal's biggest attractions, showing more than 3000 animals representing over 800 species in a beautifully landscaped setting, typically in enclosures that replicate their natural habitats. Its sister park is San Diego Zoo Safari Park (p658) in northern San Diego County.

Arrive early, as many of the animals are most active in the morning – though many perk up again in the afternoon. Pick up a map at the entrance to the zoo to find your own favorite exhibits.

Balboa Park Museums MUSEUM

(www.balboapark.org; Balboa Park; Passport (s entry to each museum within 1 week) adult/child $53/29, Stay for the Day (5 museums in 1 day) $43; Combo Pass (Passport plus zoo) adult/child $89/52) Among the park's museums, standouts are the **Reuben H Fleet Science Center** (Map p630; ☎619-238-1233; www.rhfleet.org; 1875 El Prado; adult/child $13/11, incl Giant Dome Theater $17/14; ⊙10am-5pm Mon-Thu, to 6pm Fri-Sun; ⊕), with its Giant Dome movie presentations; the **San Diego Natural History Museum** (Map p630; ☎619-232-3821; www.sdnhm.org; 1788 El Prado; adult/child $17/11; ⊙10am-5pm; ⊕); the **San Diego Museum of Art** (SDMA; Map p630; ☎619-232-7931; www.sdmart.org; 1450 El Prado; adult/child $12/4.50; ⊙10am-5pm Mon-Tue & Thu-Sat, from noon Sun, also 5-9pm Thu Jun-Sep), the city's largest; the **Timken Museum of Art** (Map p630; ☎619-239-5548; www.timkenmuseum.org; 1500 El Prado; ⊙10am-4:30pm Tue-Sat, from 1:30pm Sun) FREE, with works by masters such as Rembrandt, Rubens, El Greco, Cézanne and Pissarro; and the **Mingei International Museum** (Map p630; ☎619-239-0003; www.mingei.org; 1439 El Prado; adult/child $8/5; ⊙10am-5pm Tue-Sun; ⊕), featuring folk crafts from around the world.

Other, museums include the **San Diego Model Railroad Museum** (Map p630; ☎619-696-0199; www.sdmrm.org; Casa de Balboa, 1649 El Prado; adult/child under 6yr $8/free; ⊙11am-4pm Tue-Fri, to 5pm Sat & Sun; ⊕), the **Museum of Photographic Arts** (Map p630; ☎619-238-7559; www.mopa.org; Casa de Balboa, 1649 El Prado; adult/student/child $8/6/free; ⊙10am-5pm Tue-Sun, to 9pm Thu late May–Aug), the **Spanish Village Art Center Artist Colony** (Map p630; ⊙11am-4pm) FREE and the **Marie Hitchcock Puppet Theater** (Map p630; ☎619-685-5990; www.balboaparkpuppets.com; Balboa Park; admission $5.50; ⊙11am, 1pm

SAN DIEGO IN...

It's easy to spend most of a week in San Diego, but if your time is limited, here's a whirlwind itinerary. Things will go more smoothly if you've got access to a car.

One Day

Rub elbows with the locals over breakfast in the **Gaslamp Quarter** then ramble around **Old Town State Historic Park** (p631) for a bit of history before a Mexican lunch. Devote the afternoon to the **San Diego Zoo**, which is among the world's best, and if time permits visit some of the museums or gardens in graceful **Balboa Park** (Map p630). For dinner and a night out on the town, head to the hip **East Village** or back to the Gaslamp Quarter, where many restaurants have terrace seating for people-watching, and the partying ranges from posh to raucous.

Two Days

Take the ferry to Coronado for a sea-view breakfast at the Hotel del Coronado (p633), then enjoy the California beach scene at **Mission and Pacific Beaches. La Jolla** beckons this afternoon: explore **Torrey Pines State Reserve** (p650), **Birch Aquarium at Scripps** (p650), kayak the **sea caves**, try a **glider ride** or head to **La Jolla Village** to browse the 1920s Spanish Revival landmarks and boutiques. As the sun begins its descent over the ocean, head to **Del Mar**, where you can cheer from, or snuggle at, one of the restaurants on the roof of **Del Mar Plaza** (1555 Camino Del Mar) while the sky turns brilliant orange and fades to black.

Balboa Park, Bankers Hill & Hillcrest

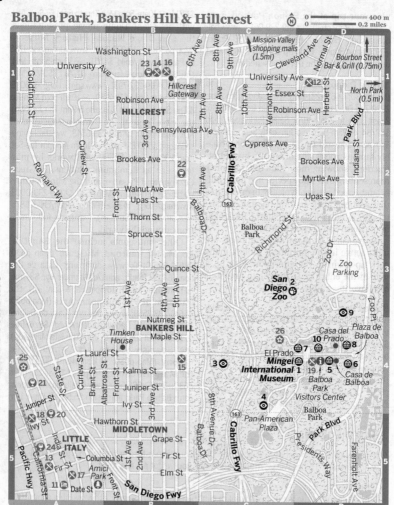

& 2:30pm Wed-Sun late May-early Sep, shorter hours early Sep-late May; 🎦).

◉ Downtown San Diego

Downtown San Diego was a rough place in the 19th century, full of saloons, gambling joints, bordellos and opium dens. By the 1960s it had declined to a skid row of flophouses and bars.

But thanks to strong bones and a local preservation and restoration movement, historic buildings have been restored and collectively renamed the **Gaslamp Quarter**,

now full of restaurants, nightspots and theaters amid 19th-century-style street lamps, trees and brick sidewalks. A few 'adult entertainment' shops, and a fair number of homeless folks serve as reminders of the old days.

See the Gaslamp's early history at the **Gaslamp Museum & William Heath Davis House** (www.gaslampquarter.org; 410 Island Ave; adult/senior & student $5/4, walking tour $10/8; ⊙10am-6pm Tue-Sat, 9am-3pm Sun, walking tour 11am Sat), **San Diego Chinese Historical Museum** (404 3rd Ave; ⊙10:30am-4pm Tue-Sun) **FREE** and **US Grant Hotel** (☎619-232-3121; 326 Broadway).

Balboa Park, Bankers Hill & Hillcrest

Next door, the East Village is a hub of exciting contemporary architecture like the baseball stadium **Petco Park** (☏ 619-795-5011; www.padres.com; 100 Park Blvd; tours adult/child/senior $12/8/9; ☉ tours 10:30am & 12:30pm Sun-Fri, 10:30am, 12:30pm & 3pm off season; ⧗) and the stunning new **Main Library** (www.sandiego.gov/public-library; 330 Park Blvd; ☉ noon-8pm Mon, Wed & Fri, 9:30am-5:30pm Tue & Thu, 9:30am-2:30pm Sat, 1-5pm Sun), both open for visitors.

Museum of Contemporary Art MUSEUM
(MCASD Downtown; ☏ 858-454-3541; www.mcasd.org; 1001 Kettner Blvd; adult/child under 25yr/senior $10/free/5, 5-7pm 3rd Thu each month free; ☉ 11am-5pm Thu-Tue, to 7pm 3rd Thu each month) This museum brings an ever-changing variety of innovative artwork to San Diegans, in the downtown location and the La Jolla branch (p650). Across from the main building, a slickly renovated section of San Diego's train station houses permanent works by Jenny Holzer and Richard Serra. Tickets are valid for seven days in all locations.

★ New Children's Museum MUSEUM
(www.thinkplaycreate.org; 200 W Island Ave; admission $10; ☉ noon-4pm Sun, 1am-4pm Mon & Wed-Sat; ⧗) This interactive children's museum opened in 2008. Artists have designed installations so that tykes can learn principles of movement and physics while simultaneously being exposed to art and working out the ants in their pants. Exhibits change roughly every 18 months, so there's always something new.

◉ Little Italy

Little Italy was settled in the mid-19th century by Italian immigrants, mostly fishermen and their families, who lived off a booming fish industry and whiskey trade.

Over the last few years, the Italian community has been joined by exciting contemporary architecture, galleries, gourmet restaurants and design and architecture businesses. Fun bars and restaurants have made this one of San Diego's hippest neighborhoods.

◉ Old Town

In 1821, when California was under Mexican rule, the area below the Presidio (fort) became the first official civilian Mexican settlement in California: the **Pueblo de San Diego**.

In 1968 the area was named **Old Town State Historic Park** (☏ 619-220-5422; www.parks.ca.gov; 4002 Wallace St; ☉ visitor center & museums 10am-4pm Oct-Apr, to 5pm May-Sep; ℗ ⧗) **FREE**, archaeological work began, and the few surviving original buildings were restored.

There's the **park visitor center** and an excellent **history museum** in the Robinson-Rose House at the southern end of the plaza. The **Whaley House** (☏ 619-297-7511; www.whaleyhouse.org; 2476 San Diego Ave; adult/child before 5pm $6/4, after 5pm $10/5; ☉ 10am-10pm late May-early Sep, 10am-5pm Mon-Tue, to 10pm Thu-Sat early Sep-late May) is the city's

Downtown San Diego

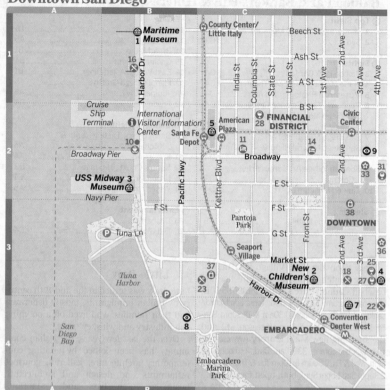

oldest brick building and nearby is **El Campo Santo** (San Diego Ave btwn Arista & Conde Sts), an 1849 cemetery for some 20 souls with their biographies on signage. The **Junipero Serra Museum** (☎ 619-297-3258; www.sandiegohistory.org; 2727 Presidio Dr; adult/child $6/3; ⊙ 10am-4pm Sat & Sun mid-Sep–mid-May, to 5pm Sat & Sun mid-May–mid-Sep; ᴾ⚑) is named for the Spanish *padre* who established the first Spanish settlement in California, in 1769, and has artifacts of the city's Mission and Rancho Periods. The **Mission Basilica San Diego de Alcalá** (☎ 619-281-8449; www.missionsandiego.com; 10818 San Diego Mission Rd; adult/child $3/1; ⊙ 9am-4:30pm; ᴾ) eventually moved 7 miles away and is worth a visit.

◉ Embarcadero & the Waterfront

South and west of the Gaslamp Quarter, San Diego's well-manicured waterfront prom-

enades stretch along Harbor Dr, home to excellent museums of naval and sea life, and are perfect for strolling or jogging (or watching well-built members of the US Navy doing same, if that's your thing!).

★ USS Midway Museum
MUSEUM
(☎ 619-544-9600; www.midway.org; 910 N Harbor Dr; adult/child $20/10; ⊙ 10am-5pm, last entry 4pm; ᴾ⚑) The permanent home of this giant aircraft carrier (1945–91). On the flight deck, walk right up to some 25 restored aircraft. Admission includes an audio tour to admiral's war room, brig and primary flight control.

★ Maritime Museum
MUSEUM
(☎ 619-234-9153; www.sdmaritime.org; 1492 N Harbor Dr; adult/child $16/8; ⊙ 9am-9pm late May-early Sep, to 8pm early Sep-late May; ⚑) Look for the 100ft-high masts of the iron-hulled square-rigger *Star of India*, a tall ship that plied the England–India trade route.

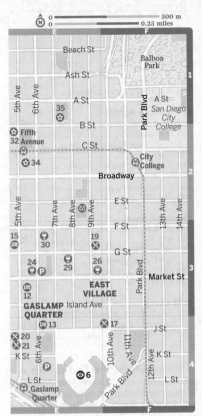

as easily recognized or as much loved as the 'The Del'. The world's largest resort when it was built in 1888, the all-timber, whitewashed main building offers conical towers, cupolas, turrets, balconies and dormer windows, but its biggest fame came as the backdrop to the 1959 Marilyn Monroe classic *Some Like It Hot*. Acres of polished wood give the interior a warm feel that conjures up daydreams of Panama hats and linen suits.

Point Loma

On maps Point Loma looks like an elephant's trunk guarding the entrance to San Diego Bay. Highlights are the Cabrillo National Monument (at the end of the trunk), the shopping and dining of Liberty Station (p647; at its base) and harborside seafood meals.

Cabrillo National Monument MONUMENT
(☑ 619-557-5450; www.nps.gov/cabr; 1800 Cabrillo Memorial Dr; per car/person walk-in $5/3, good for 7 days; ☺ 9am-5pm; ☑) Atop a hill at the tip of the peninsula, this is San Diego's finest locale for history, views and nature walks. It's also the best place in town to see the gray-whale migration (January to March) from land.

The **visitors center** has a comprehensive, old-school presentation on Portuguese explorer Juan Rodríguez Cabrillo's 1542 voyage up the California coast, plus exhibits on native inhabitants and the area's natural history.

Ocean Beach

San Diego's most bohemian seaside community is a place of seriously scruffy haircuts, facial hair and body art. You can get tattooed, shop for antiques and walk into a restaurant barefoot and shirtless without anyone batting an eye. Newport Ave, the main drag, is a compact business district of bars, surf shops, music stores, used-clothing stores and antiques consignment stores.

Mission Bay & Mission & Pacific Beaches

The big ticket attraction around Mission Bay is SeaWorld, while the nearby Mission, Ocean and Pacific Beaches are the SoCal of the movies.

SeaWorld San Diego THEME PARK
(☑ 800-257-4268; www.seaworldsandiego.com; 500 SeaWorld Dr; adult/child 3-9yr $84/78; ☺ daily; ☑ ⚐) SeaWorld opened in San Diego in 1964

Coronado

Across the bay from Downtown San Diego, Coronado is an escape from the jumble of the city. The story of Coronado is in many ways the story of the Hotel del Coronado, opened in 1888 and the centerpiece of one of the West Coast's most fashionable getaways. Coronado's visitors center (p648) doubles as the **Coronado Museum of History and Art** and offers 90-minute historical walking tours. **Coronado Municipal Beach** (parking up to $8; ⚐) is consistently ranked in America's top 10. Four-and-a-half miles south of Coronado Village is **Silver Strand State Beach** (☑ 619-435-5184; www.parks.ca.gov; 5000 Hwy 75; per car $10-15; ⚐). Both have warm, calm water, perfect for swimming and good for families.

★ **Hotel del Coronado** HOTEL
(☑ 800-582-2595, 619-435-6611; www.hoteldel.com; 1500 Orange Ave; ⚐) Few hotels in the world are

Downtown San Diego

and remains one of California's most popular theme parks. Many visitors spend the whole day here, shuttling between shows, rides and exhibits – you can pick up a map to plan your day around scheduled events.

The attraction is best known for live shows featuring trained dolphins, sea lions and killer whales. **One Ocean** is the most visually impressive, a 30-minute show featuring the famous Shamu and other killer whales gliding through the water while interacting with each other, their trainers and the audience.

There are numerous other installations where you can see and learn about aquatic life: in **Penguin Encounter** several penguin species share a habitat that simulates Antarctic living conditions; while **Shark Encounter** offers the chance to see different species of shark as you walk through a 57ft acrylic tunnel. Several amusement-park-style rides are also available. The new **Manta Ray** roller coaster swoops across the park at up to 43mph; **Journey to Atlantis** is a combination flume ride and roller coaster; and **Wild Arctic** is a simulated helicopter flight followed by a walk past beluga whales and polar bears. Expect long waits for rides, shows and exhibits during peak seasons.

Theme parks like SeaWorld have begun to attract controversy in recent years. While the park maintains that it does its share of animal conservation, rescue, rehabilitation, breeding and research, animal welfare groups disagree, questioning the whole idea of places like SeaWorld and criticizing them for keeping the marine life in captivity, arguing that the conditions and treatment of the animals are harmful and stressful, and that all of this is exacerbated further by human interaction. A bill in the California state legislature in 2014 proposed to do away with killer whale shows; it was sent back for further study.

SeaWorld can also be an expensive day out, what with loud advertisements as you wait in line and omnipresent corporate logos and gift shops encouraging additional souvenir spending. That said, good deals are often available for multiday or combination tickets with other parks, including San Diego Zoo and Wild Animal Park, Universal Studios Hollywood and/or Disneyland. Inquire at tourist offices and hotels. To save on food, all-you-can-eat passes to multiple SeaWorld restaurants are available seasonally, or keep a cooler in the car and picnic at tables outside the gates – get a hand-stamp for re-entry.

To get here by car, take SeaWorld Dr off I-5 less than a mile north of where it intersects with I-8. Parking costs $15. Check with Metropolitan Transit System (p649) for public transit. Some hotels offer shuttles.

Mission Bay   OUTDOOR ACTIVITIES

Just east of Mission and Pacific Beaches is this 7-sq-mile playground, with 27 miles of shoreline and 90 acres of parks on islands, coves and peninsulas. Sailing, windsurfing and kayaking dominate northwest Mission Bay, while waterskiers zip around Fiesta Island. Kite flying is popular in Mission Bay Park, beach volleyball on Fiesta Island, and there's delightful cycling and inline skating on bike paths.

Belmont Park   AMUSEMENT PARK

(Map p636; ☑858-458-1549; www.belmontpark. com; 3146 Mission Blvd; per ride $2-6, all-day pass adult/child $27/16; ⊙from 11am daily, closing time varies; P) At the southern end of Mission Beach, this old-style family amusement park (built 1925), has a large indoor pool, known as the **Plunge**, and the **Giant Dipper**, a classic wooden roller coaster that'll shake the teeth right outta your mouth, plus bumper cars, a tilt-a-whirl, carousel and other classics.

Activities

Surfing

A good number of San Diegans moved here for the surfing (p638), and boy is it good. Even beginners will understand why it's so popular.

For the latest beach, weather and surf reports, call San Diego County Lifeguard Services at ☑619-221-8824.

Rental rates vary, but figure on soft boards from $15/45 per hour/day; wetsuits cost $7/28. Equipment and/or lessons are available from outfits including **Pacific Beach Surf School** (Map p636; ☑858-373-1138; www.pbsurfshop.com; 4150 Mission Blvd; ⊙store 9am-7pm, lessons hourly until 4pm) and **Bob's Mission Surf** (Map p636; ☑858-483-8837; www.missionsurf.com; 4320 Mission Blvd, Pacific Beach).

Diving & Snorkeling

Off the coast, divers will find kelp beds, shipwrecks (including the *Yukon*, a WWII destroyer sunk off Mission Beach in 2000) and canyons deep enough to host bat rays, octopuses and squid. Check for hazardous conditions before you set out via San Diego County Lifeguard Services at ☑619-221-8824.

Fishing

The most popular public fishing piers are Imperial Beach Pier, Embarcadero Fishing Pier, Shelter Island Fishing Pier, Ocean Beach Pier and Crystal Pier at Pacific Beach. Generally the best pier fishing is from April to October. For offshore fishing, catches can include barracuda, bass and yellowtail and, in summer, albacore. A state fishing license (one day/two day/calendar year $15/23/46) is required for people over 16 for offshore fishing, available from fishing-trip operators in

---

SAN DIEGO FOR KIDS

Tiny hands down, San Diego is one of America's best destinations for family travel. Here are some highlights to jump start your vacation.

Do the Zoo (p629); it's everything they say and more, and while you're there, spend another day enjoying the rest of Balboa Park (p629), one of the nation's best collections of museums. The Reuben H Fleet Science Center (p629), Model Railroad Museum (p629) and Natural History Museum (p629) are all tailor-made for kids, and the plazas, fountains and gardens offer plenty of space for them to let off steam.

Kids elementary-school age and older will appreciate Old Town State Historic Park (p631) and the Mexican restaurants nearby.

Along the coast, SeaWorld (p633) is another landmark (look for specials and combo tickets to keep costs down). Coronado is a calming getaway for the Hotel Del Coronado (p633) and the kid-friendly public library. Views from Cabrillo National Monument (p633) inspire awe, and a museum tells of the Spanish explorers key to local history.

Teens will be in their element among the surfers, bikers and bladers in Mission and Pacific Beaches, while up the coast in La Jolla the Birch Aquarium at Scripps (p650) entertains as it teaches. More active kids can go snorkeling off La Jolla Cove (p650).

In northern San Diego County, Legoland (p657) is the place for the 12-and-under set (and their parents will thrill at the workmanship of the millions of little bricks). Inland, the San Diego Zoo Safari Park (p658) will have the kids roaring.

addition to tour fees (from $46/36 per adult/child per half-day), including **H&M Landing** (☎619-222-1144; www.hmlanding.com; 2803 Emerson St, Point Loma), **Point Loma Sport Fishing** (☎619-223-1627; www.pointlomasportfishing.com; 1403 Scott St, Point Loma) and **Seaforth Sportfishing** (☎619-224-3383; www.seaforthlanding.com; 1717 Quivira Rd, Mission Bay).

Boating

You can rent powerboats (from $125 per hour), sailboats (from $24 per hour), and kayaks (from $13 per hour) and canoes on Mission Bay, from **Mission Bay Sportcenter** (Map p636; ☎858-488-1004; www.missionbaysportcenter.com; 1010 Santa Clara Pl) and **Resort Watersports** (Map p636; ☎858-488-2582; www.resortwatersports.com).

Kayaking

Ocean kayaking is a good way to observe sea life, and explore cliffs and caves inaccessible from land. Guided tours and lessons are available from **Family Kayak** (☎619-282-3520; www.familykayak.com; adult/child from $44/18; ☑).

Sailing

Experienced sailors may charter boats ranging from catamarans to yachts. Prices start at about $135 for four hours and rise steeply. Charter operators around Harbor Island (on the west side of San Diego Bay near the airport) include **Harbor Sailboat** (☎619-291-9568, 800-854-6625; www.harborsailboats.com; Suite 104, 2040 Harbor Island Dr) and **Harbor Yacht Clubs** (☎800-553-7245; www.harboryc.com; 1880 Harbor Island Dr).

Whale-Watching

Gray whales pass San Diego from mid-December to late February on their way south to Baja California, and again in mid-March on their way back up to Alaskan waters. Visit Cabrillo National Monument (p633) to spy whales from land, or go on a tour.

☞ Tours

Old Town Trolley Tours & Seal Tours   TROLLEY TOUR
(☎888-910-8687; www.trolleytours.com; adult/child $39/19) Hop-on-hop-off open-air buses loop around the main attractions of Downtown and Coronado. The same company operates 90-minute amphibious Seal Tours, which depart from **Seaport Village** (☎619-235-4014; www.seaportvillage.com; ⏱10am-10pm summer).

Mission Bay & the Beaches

Mission Bay & the Beaches

San Diego Scenic Tours BUS TOUR
(www.sandiegoscenictours.com; adult/child from $38/19) Half- and full-day bus tours around San Diego and Tijuana, Mexico, some of which allow time to shop and dine. You can combine some tours with a harbor cruise.

Flagship Cruises BOAT TOUR
(☏619-234-4111; www.flagshipsd.com; 990 N Harbor Dr; tours adult/child from $23/11.50; ⏩) Harbor tours and seasonal whale-watching cruises from the Embarcadero, from one to several hours long.

★ Festivals & Events

March/April

San Diego Crew Classic SPORTING EVENT
(www.crewclassic.org; ⊘late Mar/early Apr) The national college rowing regatta takes places at Mission Bay.

June

Rock 'n' Roll Marathon SPORTING EVENT
(www.runrocknroll.competitor.com; ⊘early Jun) Live bands perform at each mile mark of this 26.2-mile race, with a big concert at the finish line.

San Diego County Fair COUNTY FAIR
(www.sdfair.com; Del Mar Fairgrounds; ⊘early Jun-early Jul) Well over a million people watch headline acts, enjoy hundreds of carnival rides and shows, and pig out on 'fair fare' (plus some healthier options).

July

Opening Day at Del Mar Racetrack SPORTING EVENT
(www.dmtc.com; ⊘mid-late Jul) Outrageous hats, cocktails and general merriment kicks off the horseracing season, 'where the turf meets the surf.' Racing through early September.

San Diego LGBT Pride COMMUNITY FESTIVAL
(www.sdpride.org; ⊘late Jul) The city's gay community celebrates in Hillcrest and Balboa Park at the month's end, with parades, parties, performances, art shows and more.

Comic-Con International CONVENTION
(www.comic-con.org; San Diego Convention Center; ⊘late Jul) America's largest event for collectors of comic, pop culture and movie memorabilia has gone from geek chic to trendmaker.

September

Fleet Week MILITARY
(www.fleetweeksandiego.org; ⊘mid-Sep–early Oct) More like 'Fleet Month.' The US military shows its pride at events such as a sea and air parade, special tours of ships, the Miramar Air Show (the world's largest) and the Coronado Speed Festival featuring vintage cars.

October

Little Italy Festa FOOD, CULTURE
(www.littleitalysd.com; ⊘mid-Oct) Come for the tastes and aromas of old Italia, and stay for Gesso Italiano, chalk-art drawn directly onto the streets.

TOP BEACHES IN SAN DIEGO

Choosing San Diego's best beaches is like comparing jewels at Tiffany. Coronado Municipal Beach (p633) has appeared on just about every Top 10 list; others depend on what you're looking for.

Bodysurfing: Pacific Beach and La Jolla Shores. Experienced bodysurfers can head to La Jolla for the big swells of Boomer Beach near La Jolla Cove, or the *whomp* (forceful tubes that break directly onshore) at Windansea or the beach at the end of Sea Lane.

Family friendly: Shell Beach (La Jolla), 15th St Beach (Del Mar), Moonlight Beach (Encinitas).

Nude beach: Black's Beach.

Surf breaks, from south to north: Imperial Beach (best in winter); Point Loma (reef breaks, less accessible but less crowded; best during winter); Sunset Cliffs (Ocean Beach); Pacific Beach. In La Jolla: Big Rock (California's Pipeline), Windansea (hot reef break, best at medium to low tide), La Jolla Shores (beach break, best in winter) and Black's Beach (a fast, powerful wave). Cardiff State Beach; San Elijo State Beach (Cardiff); Swami's (Encinitas); Carlsbad State Beach and Oceanside.

Teen scene: Mission Beach, Pacific Beach.

December

December Nights
HOLIDAY FESTIVAL
(www.balboapark.org/decembernights; ⊙early Dec) This festival in Balboa Park includes crafts, carols and a candlelight parade.

🛏 Sleeping

San Diego Tourism runs a **room-reservation line** (☑800-350-6205; www.sandiego.org).

🛏 Downtown San Diego

500 West Hotel
HOTEL $
(☑619-234-5252, 866-500-7533; www.500westhotelsd.com; 500 W Broadway; s/d with shared bath from $59/79; @🛜) Rooms are shoebox-sized and many bathrooms are down the hallway in this 1920s YMCA building, but hipsters on a budget love the bright decor, tiny TVs, communal kitchen (or diner-style restaurant), gym at the Y ($10) and easy access to trolleys and long-distance buses. No air-con.

HI San Diego Downtown Hostel
HOSTEL $
(☑619-525-1531; www.sandiegohostels.org; 521 Market St; 10-/4-bed dm with shared bath incl breakfast from $22/30, d from $75; ✱@🛜) Location, location, location. This Gaslamp Quarter HI facility is steps from public transportation, restaurants and big-city fun, and it has a wide range of rooms, including some with private bath. If the local nightlife doesn't suffice, there are movie nights and group dinners to join. Access is 24-hour.

★USA Hostels San Diego
HOSTEL $
(☑619-232-3100, 800-438-8622; www.usahostels.com; 726 5th Ave; dm/r with shared bath incl breakfast from $33/79; @🛜) Lots of charm and color at this convivial hostel in a former Victorian-era hotel. Look for cheerful rooms, a full kitchen, a communal lounge for chilling and in-house parties and beach barbecues. Rates include linens, lockers and pancakes for breakfast. And it's smack-dab in the middle of Gaslamp nightlife. No aircon.

★Hotel Solamar
BOUTIQUE, CONTEMPORARY $$
(☑877-230-0300, 619-531-8740; www.hotelsolamar.com; 435 6th Ave; r $169-299; 🅿✱@🛜🛀) A great compromise in the Gaslamp: hip style that needn't break the bank. Lounge beats play in the background as you gaze at the Downtown skyscrapers from the pool deck and bar, and rooms have sleek lines and nautical blue and neo-rococo accents for a touch of fun. It has a fitness center, in-room yoga kit, loaner bikes and a nightly complimentary wine hour. Parking costs $41.

★La Pensione Hotel
BOUTIQUE HOTEL $$
(Map p630; www.lapensionehotel.com; 606 W Date St; r $110-159; 🅿✱🛜; ◻5, 🚇Pacific Hwy & W Cedar St) Despite the name, Little Italy's La Pensione isn't a pension but an intimate, friendly, recently renovated hotel of 68 rooms – around a frescoed courtyard – with queen-size beds and private bathrooms. It's only steps from the neighborhood's dining, cafes and galleries, and is within walking dis-

tance of most Downtown attractions. There's an attractive cafe downstairs. Parking is $15.

Sofia Hotel BOUTIQUE HOTEL $$
(☏800-826-0009, 619-234-9200; www.the-sofiahotel.com; 150 W Broadway; r from $159; ▣➀◉ⓢ☀) Across from Westfield Horton Plaza, the historic Sofia has 211 rooms with fashionable dark wood furniture and sprightly printed fabrics. There are also in-room spa services, concierge, complimentary guided walks around the Gaslamp Quarter (Saturday and Sunday) and a fitness and yoga studio. There are three restaurants, including branches of So-Cal chains Coffee Bean and Tender Greens. Parking costs $30.

★US Grant Hotel LUXURY $$$
(☏619-232-3121, 800-237-5029; www.starwood.com; 326 Broadway; r from $249; ▣✳◉ⓢ) This 1910 hotel was built as the fancy city counterpart to the Hotel del Coronado and has hosted everyone from Albert Einstein to Harry Truman. Today's quietly flashy lobby combines chocolate-brown and ocean-blue accents, and rooms boast original artwork on the headboards. Parking costs $39.

🛏 Old Town

Cosmopolitan Hotel HISTORIC B&B $$
(☏619-297-1874; www.oldtowncosmopolitan.com; 2660 Calhoun St; r incl breakfast $150-250; ☉front desk 9am-9pm; ▣ⓢ) Right in Old Town State Park, this creaky, 10-room hotel from 1870 has oodles of charm, antique furnishings, and a restaurant downstairs for lunch and dinner. Don't go expecting modern conveniences like phones and TV, though there's free wi-fi. Breakfast is a simple affair based on coffee and scones. Free parking.

🛏 Coronado

Glorietta Bay Inn HISTORIC B&B $$
(☏619-435-3101, 800-283-9383; www.glorietta-bayinn.com; 1630 Glorietta Blvd; r incl breakfast from $219; ▣✳◉ⓢ☀) Overshadowed by the neighboring Hotel del Coronado, the Glorietta is built in and around a neoclassical 1908 mansion (11 rooms in the mansion, 89 in boxier two-story buildings). Rooms have handsome furnishings and extras such as triple-sheeted beds and high-end bath products. Mansion rooms are more expensive and have even more luxe amenities.

El Cordova Hotel HISTORIC HOTEL $$
(☏619-435-4131, 800-229-2032; www.elcor-dovahotel.com; 1351 Orange Ave; r from $199; ✳◉ⓢ☀) This exceedingly cozy Spanish-style former mansion from 1902 has rooms and suites around an outdoor courtyard of shops, restaurants, pool, hot tub and barbecue grills. Rooms are charming in an antiquey sort of way, though nothing fancy.

★Hotel del Coronado LUXURY HOTEL $$$
(Hotel Del; ☏619-435-6611, 800-468-3533; www.hoteldel.com; 1500 Orange Ave; r from $289; ▣➀◉ⓢ☀🐾) San Diego's iconic hotel provides the essential Coronado experience: over a century of history, a pool, a full-service spa, shops, restaurants, manicured grounds, a white-sand beach and an ice-skating rink in winter. Even the basic rooms have luxurious marbled bathrooms. For a sense of place, book a room in the original hotel, not in the adjacent 1970s building. Parking is $37.

🛏 Point Loma Area

HI San Diego Point Loma Hostel HOSTEL $
(☏619-223-4778; www.sandiegohostels.org; 3790 Udall St; dm/r per person with shared bath incl breakfast from $19/33; ◉ⓢ) It's a 20-minute walk from central Ocean Beach to this hostel, in a largely residential area close to a market and library. Cheery private rooms are a great deal. There are often cheap dinners, movie nights and free excursions. Bus 923 runs along nearby Voltaire St. No lock-out times. No air-con.

Pearl MOTEL $$
(☏619-226-6100, 877-732-7574; www.thepearlsd.com; 1410 Rosecrans St; r $129-169; ▣✳ⓢ☀) The mid-century-modern Pearl feels more Palm Springs than San Diego. The 23 rooms in its 1959 shell have soothing blue hues, trippy surf motifs and betas in fishbowls. There's a lively pool scene (including 'dive-in' movies on Wednesday nights), or you can play Jenga or Parcheesi in the groovy, shag-carpeted lobby. Light sleepers: request a room away from busy street traffic.

🛏 Ocean Beach

Ocean Beach (OB) is under the outbound flight path of San Diego airport. Light sleepers should stay elsewhere or bring earplugs.

Ocean Beach International Hostel HOSTEL $
(Map p636; ☏619-223-7873, 800-339-7263; www.sandiegohostel.us; 4961 Newport Ave; dm $15-40) Central OB's cheapest option is only a couple

of blocks from the ocean; it's a simple but friendly and fun place reserved for international travelers and educators, with barbecues, music nights, bonfires and more. Free transfer from airport, bus or train station on arrival. No air-con.

Inn at Sunset Cliffs BEACHSIDE INN $$$
(☎619-222-7901, 866-786-2453; www.innatsunsetcliffs.com; 1370 Sunset Cliffs Blvd; r/ste from $175/289; P ❄ @ ☎ ≋) At the south end of Ocean Beach, wake up to the sound of surf crashing onto the rocky shore. This low-key 1965 charmer wraps around a flower-bedecked courtyard with small heated pool. Its 24 breezy rooms are compact, but most have attractive stone and tile bathrooms, and some suites have full kitchens. Even if the ocean air occasionally takes its toll on exterior surfaces, it's hard not to love. Free parking.

Pacific Beach & Mission Beach

Banana Bungalow HOSTEL $
(Map p636; ☎858-273-3060; www.bananabungalowsandiego.com; 707 Reed Ave, Pacific Beach; dm/d $35/100; ☎; 30) Right on Pacific Beach, the Bungalow has a top location, a beach-party atmosphere and is reasonably clean, but it's very basic and gets crowded. Shared rooms are mixed-gender. The communal patio fronts right on the boardwalk; it's a great place for people-watching and beer drinking. No air-con.

Campland on the Bay CAMPING $
(☎858-581-4260, 800-422-9386; www.campland.com; 2211 Pacific Beach Dr, Mission Bay; RV & campsites $45-238, beachfront from $194; P ☎ ≋) On more than 40 acres fronting Mission Bay, amenities include a restaurant, two pools, boat rentals, full RV hookups and outdoor activities from skateboarding to singalongs. Price varies depending on proximity to the water; reservations are recommended. Off-season discounts.

Catamaran Resort Hotel RESORT $$
(Map p636; ☎858-488-1081, 800-422-8386; www.catamaranresort.com; 3999 Mission Blvd; r from $159; P @ ☎ ≋) Tropical landscaping and tiki decor fill this resort backing onto Mission Bay (there's a luau on some summer evenings!). A plethora of activities make it a perfect place for families (sailing, kayaking, tennis, biking, skating, spa-ing, etc) or board the *Bahia Belle* paddleboat from here. Rooms are in low-rise buildings or in a 14-story tower; some have views and full kitchens.

Tower 23 BOUTIQUE HOTEL $$$
(Map p636; ☎858-270-2323, 866-869-3723; www.t23hotel.com; 723 Felspar St, Pacific Beach; r from $249; P ❄ @ ☎ 🐾) If you like your oceanfront stay to come with contemporary cool, this modernist place has an awesome location, minimalist decor, lots of teals and mint blues, water features and a sense of humor. There's no pool, but dude, you're right on the beach. The hotel's **JRDN** (Jordan; Map p636; ☎858-270-5736; Tower 23 Hotel, 723 Felspar St; mains breakfast & lunch $9-14, dinner $26-46; ⏰9am-9pm Sun-Thu, to 9:30pm Sat & Sun) restaurant is expensive but worth it. Parking is $20.

Crystal Pier Hotel & Cottages COTTAGE $$$
(Map p636; ☎858-483-6983, 800-748-5894; www.crystalpier.com; 4500 Ocean Blvd; d $185-525; P ☎) Charming, wonderful and unlike anyplace else in San Diego, Crystal Pier has cottages built right on the pier above the water. Almost all 29 cottages have full ocean views and kitchens; most date from 1936. Newer, larger cottages sleep up to six. Book eight to 11 months in advance for summer reservations. Minimum-stay requirements vary by season. No air-con. Rates include parking.

Eating

Despite its border location, San Diego's food scene doesn't have the ethnic breadth of LA's, but there's a growing locavore and gourmet scene. Reservations are recommended, especially on weekends.

Balboa Park

★Prado CALIFORNIAN $$$
(Map p630; ☎619-557-9441; www.pradobalboa.com; House of Hospitality, 1549 El Prado; mains lunch $12-21, dinner $22-35; ⏰11:30am-3pm Mon-Fri, from 11am Sat & Sun, 5-9pm Sun & Tue-Thu, to 10pm Fri & Sat) In one of San Diego's most beautiful dining rooms, feast on Cal-eclectic cooking by one of San Diego's most renowned chefs: bakery sandwiches, chicken and orecchiette pasta, and pork prime rib. Go for a civilized lunch on the verandah or for afternoon cocktails and appetizers in the bar.

Gaslamp Quarter

Café 222 BREAKFAST $
(☎619-236-9902; www.cafe222.com; 222 Island Ave; mains $7-11; ⏰7am-1:30pm) Downtown's favorite breakfast place serves renowned peanut butter and banana French toast; buttermilk, orange-pecan or granola pancakes; and

TOP FIVE CHEAP EATS

➡ Bread & Cie (p642)

➡ Café 222 (p640)

➡ Porkyland (p652)

➡ Saffron (p642)

➡ East Village Asian Diner (p642)

eggs in scrambles or Benedicts. It also sells lunchtime sandwiches and salads, but we always go for breakfast (available until closing).

Gaslamp Strip Club STEAK $$
(☑ 619-231-3140; www.gaslampsteak.com; 340 5th Ave; mains $14-24; ⊙ 5-10pm Sun-Thu, to midnight Fri & Sat) Pull your own bottle from the wine vault, then char your own favorite cut of steak, chicken or fish on the open grills in the retro-Vegas dining room at Downtown's best bargain for steak, salad and grill-your-own garlic bread. No bottle costs more than $36, no steak more than $25. Fab, creative martinis and 'pin-up' art by Alberto Vargas. Tons of fun. No one under 21 allowed.

Dick's Last Resort PUB FOOD $$
(☑ 619-231-9100; www.dickslastresort.com; 345 5th Ave; lunch $9-20, dinner $12-24; ⊙ 11am-1:30am) At Dick's, a legendary indoor-outdoor bar and grill with a riotously fun atmosphere, you can carry on in full voice while guzzling beer and chowing down on burgers, pork ribs, fried chicken and fish, while the staff makes you a giant dunce cap out of table paper.

Oceanaire SEAFOOD $$$
(☑ 619-858-2277; www.theoceanaire.com; 400 J St; mains $23-52; ⊙ 5-10pm Sun-Thu, to 11pm Fri & Sat) The look is art-deco ocean liner, and the service is just as elegant, with an oyster bar and creations like Maryland blue-crab cakes and horseradish-crusted Alaskan halibut. If you don't feel like a total splurge, happy hour features bargain-priced oysters and fish tacos in the bar (times vary).

⁂ East Village

Basic PIZZA $
(☑ 619-531-8869; www.barbasic.com; 410 10th Ave; small/large pizzas from $9/14; ⊙ 11:30am-2am) Savvy East Villagers feast on fragrant New Haven–style, thin-crust, brick-oven-baked pizzas under Basic's high-ceilinged roof (it's in a former warehouse). Toppings range from the usual to the newfangled, like

mashed potatoes. Wash them down with beers (craft, naturally) or one of several mule cocktails.

Café Chloe FRENCH $$
(☑ 619-232-3242; www.cafechloe.com; 721 9th Ave; breakfast $7-12, lunch $11-17, dinner $20-29; ⊙ 7:30am-10pm Mon-Fri, 8:30am-10:30pm Sat, 8:30am-9:30pm Sun) This delightful corner French bistro has a simple style and gets the standards perfect, and everything else as well. Mac 'n' cheese transforms into macaroni, pancetta and French blue gratin, and the *steak frites* is served with herb butter and salad. Wonderful egg dishes for weekend brunch.

⁂ Bankers Hill & Old Town

At the giant Mexican eateries all along San Diego Ave, hard-working ladies churn out an estimated 210,000 fresh tortillas per month and most have great bar scenes too.

★Cucina Urbana CALIFORNIAN, ITALIAN $$
(Map p630; ☑ 619-239-2222; 505 Laurel St, Bankers Hill; lunch $10-23, dinner $12-28; ⊙ 11:30am-2pm Tue-Fri, 5-9pm Sun & Mon, 5-10pm Tue-Thu, 5pm-midnight Fri & Sat) In this corner place with modern rustic ambience, business gets done, celebrations get celebrated and friends hug and kiss over refined yet affordable Cal Ital cooking. Look for short rib pappardelle, pizzas like foraged mushroom with taleggio cheese and braised leeks, and smart cocktails and local 'brewskies.'

Fred's MEXICAN $$
(☑ 619-858-8226; 2470 San Diego Ave; mains $9-15; ⊙ 11am-11pm Sun, Mon, Wed & Thu, to midnight Tue, Fri & Sat) Every night, party people on a budget crowd into raucous Fred's.

Old Town Mexican Café MEXICAN $$
(☑ 619-297-4330; www.oldtownmexcafe.com; 2489 San Diego Ave; mains $4-16; ⊙ 7am-2am; ♠) Rowdy and always crowded.

El Agave MEXICAN $$$
(☑ 619-220-0692; www.elagave.com; 2304 San Diego Ave; lunch $12-20, dinner $22-40; ⊙ 11am-10pm; Ⓟ) Subdued, sophisticated El Agave has superb mole and a whopping 1500 different tequila varieties.

⁂ North Park & Hillcrest

San Diego's restaurant scene is booming in these neighborhoods north of downtown.

Bread & Cie
BAKERY, CAFE $

(Map p630; www.breadandcie.com; 350 University Ave, Hillcrest; mains $6-11; ⊙7am-7pm Mon-Fri, to 6pm Sat, 8am-6pm Sun; P) Aside from crafting some of San Diego's best breads (including anise and fig, kalamata black olive and three-raisin), this wide-open bakery-deli makes fabulous sandwiches with fillings such as curried-chicken salad and Black Forest ham. Boxed lunches cost $11. Great pastries.

★Urban Solace
CALIFORNIAN $$

(☑619-295-6464; www.urbansolace.net; 3823 30th St, North Park; mains lunch $10-23, dinner $17-27; ⊙11:30am-10pm Mon-Thu, to 11pm Fri, 5-11pm Sat, 5-9pm Sun) North Park's young hip gourmets revel in creative comfort food here: bluegrass burger; 'not your mama's' meatloaf of ground lamb, fig, pine nuts and feta; 'duckaroni' (mac 'n' cheese with duck confit); and chicken and dumplings. The setting is surprisingly chill for such great eats; maybe it's the cocktails like mojitos made with bourbon.

Waypoint Public
GASTROPUB $$

(☑619-255-8778; www.waypointpublic.com; 3794 30th St, North Park; mains $9-21; ⊙4pm-1am Mon-Fri, from 10am Sat & Sun) The comfort-food menu at chef-driven Waypoint is meant to pair craft beers with its dishes, which range from smoked tomato minestrone with grilled cheese to a burger with mozzarella, pulled pork, tomatillo salsa, fried egg and spicy pickled vegetables. Glass garage doors roll up to the outside, all the better for people-watching in busy North Park.

East Village Asian Diner
ASIAN FUSION $$

(Map p630; ☑619-220-4900; www.eateastvillage. com; 406 University Ave, Hillcrest; mains $9-14; ⊙11:30am-2:30pm Mon-Fri, 5-10pm Mon-Wed, to midnight Fri, 11:30am-midnight Sat, 11:30am-10pm Sun) This den of modernist cool fuses mostly Korean cooking with Western and other Asian influences (witness the 'super awesome' beef and kimchi burrito). Try noodle dishes (thai peanut, beef and broccoli, etc), or build your own 'monk's stone pot,' a super-heated rice bowl to which you can add ingredients ranging from pulled pork to salmon. Sauces are made in-house.

Baja Betty's
MEXICAN $$

(Map p630; ☑619-269-8510; bajabettyssd. com; 1421 University Ave, Hillcrest; mains $6-15; ⊙11am-midnight Mon-Fri, 10am-1am Sat, 10am-midnight Sun) Gay-owned and straight-friendly, this restaurant-bar is always a party

with a just-back-from-Margaritaville vibe (and dozens of tequilas to take you back there) alongside dishes like Mexi Queen queso dip, You Go Grill swordfish tacos and Fire in the Hole fajitas. Daily specials.

Little Italy

Little Italy is – surprise! – a happy hunting ground for Italian cooking and cafes, and some non-Italian newcomers round out the scene, like Ballast Point Tasting Room (p645).

Bencotto
ITALIAN $$

(Map p630; ☑619-450-4786; www.lovebencotto. com; 750 W Fir St; mains $14-26; ⊙11:30am-9:30pm Sun-Thu, to 10:30pm Fri & Sat; P) Bencotto melds the old with the new of Little Italy – contemporary, angular, architect-designed, arty and green – and the food is great, too, from fresh-sliced prosciutto to pasta *a modo tuo* (your way), with a over 100 potential combos of fresh pasta and sauce.

Filippi's Pizza Grotto
PIZZA, DELI $$

(Map p630; ☑619-232-5094; 1747 India St; dishes $6-20; ⊙9am-10pm Sun & Mon, to 10:30pm Tue-Thu, to 11:30pm Fri & Sat; ⊕) There are often lines out the door for Filippi's old-school Italian cooking (pizza, spaghetti and ravioli) served on red-and-white-checked tablecloths in the dining room festooned with murals of *la bella Italia*. The front of the shop is an excellent Italian deli.

★Juniper & Ivy
CONTEMPORARY CALIFORNIAN $$$

(Map p630; ☑619-269-9036; www.juniperandivy. com; 2228 Kettner Bl; small plates $9-17, mains $19-36; ⊙4-10pm Sun-Thu, to 11pm Fri & Sat) Chef Richard Blais has opened San Diego's restaurant of the moment. The menu changes daily, but if we mention molecular gastronomic takes on prawn and pork rigatoni; artisan-farmed strip steak with smoked potato, porcini onion rings and kimchi ketchup; and homemade yodel snack cakes for dessert, do you get the idea?

Mission Hills

Mission Hills is the neighborhood north of Little Italy and west of Hillcrest. On India St, where it meets Washington St, there's a block of well-regarded eateries.

Saffron
THAI $

(☑619-574-0177; www.saffronsandiego.com; 3731 India St; mains $7-10; ⊙10:30am-9pm Mon-Sat, 11am-8pm Sun) This multi-award-winning hole-in-the-wall is actually two shops – Saffron Thai Grilled Chicken and Noodles & Saté, but you can get both at either shop and enjoy it in the noodle shop. Chicken is cooked over a charcoal-grill and comes with a choice of sauces, salad, jasmine rice and a menu of finger foods.

El Indio   MEXICAN $

(☎619-299-0333; www.el-indio.com; 3695 India St; dishes $3-9; ☺8am-9pm; Ⓟ⚹) Counter-service shop famous since 1940 for its *taquitos*, *mordiditas* (tiny *taquitos*), tamales and excellent breakfast burritos. Eat in a rudimentary dining room or at picnic tables under metal umbrellas across the street.

Shakespeare Pub & Grille   PUB FOOD $$

(☎619-299-0230; www.shakespearepub.com; 3701 India St; dishes $5-15; ☺10:30am-midnight Mon-Thu, to 1am Fri, 8am-1am Sat, 8am-midnight Sun) One of San Diego's most authentic English ale houses, Shakespeare is the place for darts, soccer by satellite, beer on tap and pub grub, including fish and chips, and bangers and mash. On weekends, load up with a British breakfast: bacon, mushrooms, black and white pudding and more. One thing they don't have in Britain: a great sundeck.

✘ Embarcadero & the Waterfront

★**Puesto at the Headquarters**   MEXICAN $$

(☎610-233-8800; www.eatpuesto.com; 789 W Harbor Dr, The Headquarters; mains $11-19; ☺11am-10pm) This upscale eatery serves Mexican street food that knocked our *zapatos* off: innovative takes on traditional tacos like chicken (with hibiscus, chipotle, pineapple and avocado) and some out-there fillings like potato soy chorizo. Other highlights: crab guacamole, *barbacoa* short ribs (braised in chili sauce) and Mexican street bowl, ie tropical fruits with chili, sea salt and lime.

Anthony's Fish Grotto & Fishette   SEAFOOD $

(www.gofishanthonys.com; 1360 N Harbor Dr; dinner $14-29, lunch specials $10-15; ⚹) Fishette (☎619-232-2175; Fishette; mains $10-15; ☺10am-9pm Mon-Fri, 8am-9pm Sat & Sun); Grotto (☎619-232-5105; Grotto; lunch $8-15, dinner $12-25; ☺11am-9:30pm Sun-Thu, to 10pm Sat & Sun) This pair of restaurants serves seafood and chowders with views of the tall ships on the harbor. The sit-down Grotto has an old-style nautical theme (ahoy, mateys!), while the counter at the Fishette serves a more limited menu (think fish and chips or sandwiches) that you eat out on the deck.

✘ Coronado

Clayton's Coffee Shop   DINER $

(☎619-435-5425; 979 Orange Ave; mains $8-12; ☺6am-9pm Sun-Thu, to 10pm Fri & Sat; ⚹) Some diners are old-fashioned. This one is the real deal from the 1940s, with red leatherette swivel stools and booths with mini-jukeboxes. It does famous all-American breakfasts and some Mexican specialties like *machaca* (Mexican-style marinated beef) with eggs and cheese, and it's not above panini and croque monsieur sandwiches. For dessert: mile-high pie from the counter.

★**1500 Ocean**   CALIFORNIAN $$$

(☎619-435-6611; www.hoteldel.com/1500-ocean; Hotel del Coronado, 1500 Orange Ave; mains $33-45; ☺5:30-10pm Tue-Sat, plus Sun summer; Ⓟ) It's hard to beat the romance of supping at the Hotel del Coronado, especially at a table overlooking the sea from the verandah of its 1st-class dining room, where silver service and coastal cuisine with local ingredients set the perfect tone for popping the question or fêting an important anniversary.

Boney's Bayside Market   MARKET $

(155 Orange Ave; sandwiches $5-7; ☺8:30am-9pm) For picnics, stop by this market near the ferry for (mostly) healthy sandwiches and an assortment of salads and organic products.

✘ Point Loma Area

★**Stone Brewing World Bistro & Gardens**   BEER HALL $$

(www.stonelibertystation.com; Liberty Station, 2816 Historic Decatur Rd #116; lunch $14-21, dinner $15-29; ☺11:30am-10pm Mon-Sat, 11am-9pm Sun; Ⓟ) Local brewer Stone has transformed the former mess hall of the naval training center at Liberty Station into a temple to local craft beer. Tuck into standard-setting span-the-globe dishes (yellowfin *poke* tacos, chicken schnitzel, beef *ssambap* – Korean-style lettuce cups – etc) at long tables or comfy booths under the tall beamed ceiling, or beneath twinkling lights in its courtyard.

Bali Hai   POLYNESIAN $$

(☎619-222-1181; www.balihairestaurant.com; 2230 Shelter Island Dr; lunch $13-19, dinner $17-31, Sun brunch adult/child $35/17; ☺11:30am-9pm Mon-Thu, to 10pm Fri & Sat, 9:30am-2pm & 4-9pm Sun; Ⓟ) Near the tiki-themed hotels of Point

Loma, this long-time special occasion restaurant serves Hawaiian-themed meals like tuna *poke, pupus* (small plates), chicken of the gods (with tangy orange and cream sauces) and a massive Sunday champagne brunch buffet. Views are clear across San Diego Bay through its circular wall of windows.

★**Point Loma Seafoods**   SEAFOOD $$
(www.pointlomaseafoods.com; 2805 Emerson St; mains $7-16; ⏰9am-7pm Mon-Sat, 10am-7pm Sun; 🅿🚻) For off-the-boat-fresh seafood sandwiches, salads, fried dishes and icy cold beer, order at the counter at this fish-market-cum-deli and grab a seat at a picnic table on the upstairs, harbor-view deck. In the Shelter Island Marina, it's a San Diego institution dating back to Portuguese fishermen days. It also does great sushi and takeout dishes from ceviche to clam chowder.

🍴 Ocean Beach

★**Hodad's**   BURGERS $
(Map p636; 🕿619-224-4623; www.hodadies.com; 5010 Newport Ave, Ocean Beach; dishes $4-13; ⏰11am-9pm Sun-Thu, to 10pm Fri & Sat) Since the Flower Power days of 1969, OB's legendary burger joint has served great shakes, massive baskets of onion rings and succulent hamburgers. The walls are covered in license plates, grunge/surf-rock plays (loud!) and your bearded, tattooed server might sidle in to your booth to take your order.

Ortega's Cocina   CAFE $
(Map p636; 🕿619-222-4205; 4888 Newport Ave; mains $4-15; ⏰8am-10pm Mon-Sat, to 9pm Sun) Tiny, family-run Ortega's is so popular that people often queue for a spot at the counter (there are indoor and sidewalk tables too). Seafood, *moles, tortas* (sandwiches) and handmade tamales are the specialties, but all its dishes are soulful and classic.

Ocean Beach People's Market   VEGETARIAN $
(Map p636; 🕿619-224-1387; 4765 Voltaire St; dishes $8, per pound from $7.50; ⏰8am-9pm; 🍴) 🌱
For strictly vegetarian groceries and fabulous prepared meals and salads north of central Ocean Beach, this organic cooperative does bulk foods, and excellent counter-service soups, sandwiches, salads and wraps.

🍴 Pacific Beach

World Famous   SEAFOOD $$$
(Map p636; 🕿858-272-3100; www.worldfamouspb.com; 711 Pacific Beach Dr; breakfast & lunch $9-16,

dinner $15-25; ⏰7am-midnight) Watch the surf while enjoying 'California coastal cuisine,' an ever-changing all-day menu of inventive dishes from the sea (lobster Benedict for breakfast or lunch; banana rum mahi-mahi), plus steaks, salads and lunchtime sandwiches and burgers, and occasional specials like fish or lobster taco night.

Kono's Surf Club   CAFE, BREAKFAST $
(Map p636; 🕿858-483-1669; 704 Garnet Ave; mains $3-6; ⏰7am-3pm Mon-Fri, to 4pm Sat & Sun; 🚻) This place makes four kinds of breakfast burritos that you eat out of a basket in view of Crystal Pier as well as pancakes, eggs and Kono potatoes. It's always crowded but well worth the wait. Cash only.

Green Flash   CAFE $$
(Map p636; 🕿619-270-7715; www.greenflashrestaurant.com; 701 Thomas Ave; breakfast & lunch $5-15, dinner $11-29; ⏰8am-10pm) A terrific casual, beach-view breakfast or lunch spot for eggs, meaty burgers, big salads and triple-decker clubs, the Flash also has weekday sunset special meals ($11; 4:30pm to 6pm Sunday to Thursday), with happy hour until 7pm Monday through Friday. Score a table outside on the patio.

🍷 Drinking & Nightlife

San Diego may not have the breadth of LA's nightlife, but the Gaslamp Quarter makes up for it in enthusiasm.

Gay and lesbian nightlife tends to concentrate around Hillcrest and North Park. Try **Urban Mo's** (Map p630; 🕿619-491-0400; www.urbanmos.com; 308 University Ave, Hillcrest; ⏰9am-2am) and **Bourbon Street** (🕿619-291-4043; www.bourbonstreetsd.com; 4612 Park Blvd, North Park; ⏰4pm-2am Tue-Sun, from 11am Sun).

🍸 Gaslamp Quarter

★**Bang Bang**   BAR
(www.bangbangsd.com; 526 Market St; ⏰closed Mon) Beneath lantern-light, the Gaslamp's hottest new spot hosts local and world-known DJs, and serves sushi and Asian small plates to accompany imaginative cocktails (some in giant goblets meant for sharing with your posse). Bathrooms are shrines to Ryan Gosling and Hello Kitty: in a word, awesome.

Fluxx   CLUB
(www.fluxxsd.com; 500 4th Ave; ⏰Thu-Sat) Think Vegas in the Gaslamp. San Diego's hottest dance club has amazing design with rotating

SURF & SUDS

'The beer that made San Diego famous' may not quite roll off the tongue, but never mind: America's Finest City is home to some of America's finest brew pubs. The **San Diego Brewers Guild** (www.sandiegobrewersguild.org) counts some 40 member establishments. Here are some pubs to get you started. See also **Stone Brewing Company** (☑760-471-4999; www.stonebrew.com; 1999 Citracado Pkwy, Escondido; ☉tours noon-6pm daily), Ballast Point Tasting Room & Kitchen and **Karl Strauss Brewery & Grill** (☑619-234-2739, 858-551-2739; 1157 Columbia St, cnr Wall St & Herschel Ave; ☉hours vary).

Coronado Brewing Co (www.coronadobrewingcompany.com; 170 Orange Ave, Coronado; ☉from 11am) Delicious Coronado Golden house brew goes well with pizzas, pastas, sandwiches and fries; near the ferry terminal.

Pacific Beach Ale House (Map p636; www.pbalehouse.com; 721 Grand Ave, Pacific Beach; mains $9-25; ☉11am-2am) Contempo-cool setting and a huge menu including lobster mac 'n' cheese, steamed clams and bistro meatloaf.

Pizza Port (☑760-720-7007; www.pizzaport.com; 571 Carlsbad Village Dr; mains $8-20; ☉11am-10pm Sun-Thu, to midnight Fri & Sat; ⊞) Rockin' and raucous local pizza chain with surf art, rock music and 'anti-wimpy' pizzas to go with the signature 'sharkbite red' brew. Multiple locations.

To leave the driving to someone else, **Brewery Tours of San Diego** (☑619-961-7999; www.brewerytoursofsandiego.com; per person $65-95) offers bus tours to different breweries for a variety of tastes. Tour price varies by timing and whether a meal is served.

themes (jellyfish and mermaids, anyone?), DJs spinning electronic dance music and the occasional celeb sighting. Even a crowded dance floor, expensive cocktails and sometimes steep cover charges can't stop this place from being jam-packed.

Dublin Square   IRISH PUB
(www.dublinsquareirishpub.com; 544 4th Ave) Guinness? Check. Corned beef? Check. But what sets this pub apart is its selection of nightly music. Try to go when the band Fooks is playing – check website for schedule.

Quality Social   DIVE BAR
(www.qualitysocial.com; 789 6th Ave) It sounds like an oxymoron: an upscale dive bar. This concrete box has big windows out to the street, loud music and lots of beers, but you can snack on charcuterie and artisanal cheeses. Look also for $6 shots and cocktails like 'Not Your Grandma's Gin & Tonic.'

Star Bar   BAR
(423 E St) When you're looking for a historic dive bar, head to this bar decorated year-round with Christmas lights for the cheapest drinks in the Gaslamp.

East Village

While out-of-towners frolic happily in the Gaslamp Quarter, locals and hipsters instead head east.

East Village Tavern & Bowl   BOWLING
(930 Market St, East Village; ☉11:30am-1am, from 10am Sat & Sun) This large sports bar a few blocks from Petco Park has six bowling lanes (thankfully, behind a wall for effective soundproofing). Pub menu (dishes $6 to $11) is served all day.

Noble Experiment   BAR
(☑619-888-4713; http://nobleexperimentsd.com; 777 G St; ☉7pm-2am Tue-Sun) This speakeasy is literally a find. Text for a reservation, and they'll tell you if your requested time is available and how to get there. Once inside, it's a treasure trove with miniature gold skulls on the walls, classical paintings on the ceilings and some 400 cocktails on the list.

Little Italy

Ballast Point Tasting Room & Kitchen   PUB
(Map p630; ☑619-255-7213; www.ballastpoint.com; 2215 India St; dishes $7-14; ☉11am-11pm Mon-Sat, to 9pm Sun) The brew pub of this San Diego–based brewery does R&D for the rest of the company. Three four-ounce tasters for just $5 is the best craft-beer deal in town. Enjoy them with a full menu, including housemade pretzels, beer-steamed mussels, salads and grilled dishes.

El Camino   LOUNGE
(Map p630; 2400 India St) We're not sure what it means that this buzzy watering hole has

a Día de los Muertos (Mexican Day of the Dead holiday) theme in the flight path of San Diego Airport – watch planes land from the outdoor patio – but whatever, dude. The clientele is cool, the design mod, the drinks strong and the Mexican vittles *fabuloso*.

Waterfront   BAR
(Map p630; 2044 Kettner Blvd) San Diego's first liquor license was granted to this place in the 1930s (it was on the waterfront until the harbor was filled and the airport built). A room full of historic bric-a-brac, big windows looking onto the street and the spirits of those who went before make this a wonderful place to spend the afternoon or evening.

 Bankers Hill & Old Town

Harney Sushi   BAR
(3964 Harney St) If you're staying in Old Town and are done with tequila, Harney Sushi is a sushi bar where a DJ takes over at night.

Nunu's Cocktail Lounge   COCKTAIL BAR
(Map p630; www.nunuscocktails.com; 3537 5th Ave, Hillcrest) In Bankers Hill, hipster haven Nunu's Cocktail Lounge started pouring when JFK was president and still looks the part.

 North Park

Two spots nicely encapsulate North Park's hipster vibe.

Coin-Op Game Room   BAR, GAME ROOM
(☑619-255-8523; www.coinopsd.com; 3926 30th St, North Park; ☺4pm-1am) The walls of this place are lined with dozens of classic arcade games – from pinball and the Claw to Mortal Kombat – to go along with craft beers, creative cocktails and slider burgers.

★ **Polite Provisions**   COCKTAIL BAR
(www.politeprovisions.com; 4696 30th St, North Park; ☺11:30am-1:30am) A mile north of central North Park, this cocktail bar custom crafts syrups, sodas and infusions and serves many on tap, with a 'sodas and swine' menu.

 Coronado to Pacific Beach

Pacific Beach (PB) is party central on the coast, with mostly 20-somethings on a beach bar bender (drivers: watch for tipsy pedestrians). If you've been there/done that, you might prefer one of the quieter coffee houses or restaurant bars, or head to Ocean Beach or Coronado.

Mc P's Irish Pub   PUB
(www.mcpspub.com; 1107 Orange Ave, Coronado) Dyed-in-the-wool Irish pub that's been there for a generation. Pints o' Guinness complement down-home Irish fare – corned beef, stew, meatloaf – as you listen to nightly live music from rock to Irish folk. Indoor and patio seating.

Jungle Java   CAFE
(Map p636; 5047 Newport Ave, Ocean Beach; ☺7am-6pm Mon, Tue & Thu, to 8pm Wed & Fri-Sun) Funky-dunky, canopy-covered cafe and plant shop, also crammed with crafts and art treasures.

Coaster Saloon   DIVE BAR
(Map p636; ☑858-488-4438; 744 Ventura Pl, Mission Beach) Old-fashioned neighborhood dive bar with front-row views of the Belmont Park roller coaster. It draws an unpretentious crowd for events like Wii-bowling. Good margaritas too.

Society Billiard Cafe   BAR
(Map p636; 1051 Garnet Ave, Pacific Beach; ☺noon-2pm) Why settle for a beat-up pool table in the back of a dark bar when you can visit San Diego's plushest pool hall? The billiard room has about a dozen full-sized tables, snacks and a bar.

Café 976   CAFE
(Map p636; 976 Felspar St, Pacific Beach; ☺7am-11pm) Not everyone in PB spends the days surfing or the nights partying; some drink coffee and read books at this delightful side-street cafe in a converted old wooden house ensconced in rose bushes and flowering trees.

☆ Entertainment

Check out the San Diego *City Beat* or *UT San Diego* for the latest movies, theater, galleries and music gigs around town. **Arts Tix** (☑858-381-5595; www.sdartstix.com; Lyceum Theatre, 79 Horton Plaza), in a kiosk near Westfield Horton Plaza, has half-price tickets for many shows.

Live Music

4th & B   LIVE MUSIC
(www.4thandB.com; 345 B St) A mid-sized venue with a mix of unsigned artists to Snoop Dogg and the Last Comic Standing tour.

Casbah   LIVE MUSIC
(Map p630; ☑619-232-4355; www.casbahmusic.com; 2501 Kettner Blvd; tickets $5-45) Bands from Smashing Pumpkins to Death Cab for

Cutie all rocked the Casbah on their way up the charts and it's still a good place to catch tomorrow's headliners.

House of Blues
BLUES, R&B
(www.hob.com; 1055 5th Ave) You know what this is.

Shout House
LIVE MUSIC
(☎ 619-231-6700; 655 4th Ave; cover free-$10) Good, clean fun for everyone from college kids to conventioneers around the dueling pianos at Shout House.

Winston's
LIVE MUSIC
(Map p636; www.winstonsob.com; 1921 Bacon St, Ocean Beach) A different happening every night: open mic, karaoke, comedy, cover bands, etc.

710 Beach Club
LIVE MUSIC
(Map p636; www.710beachclub.com; 710 Garnet Ave, Pacific Beach) PB's main venue for live music books a solid lineup of rock, karaoke and comedy.

Classical Music

San Diego Symphony
CLASSICAL
(www.sandiegosymphony.com; 750 B St, Jacobs Music Center) This accomplished orchestra presents classical and family concerts and Summer Pops concerts at Embarcadero Marina Park South.

Theater

Theater is one of the city's greatest cultural assets. The main stage of the **Old Globe Theaters** (Map p630; www.theoldglobe.org; Balboa Park) is modeled after the 17th-century Globe in England, where Shakespeare's works were originally performed. See also La Jolla Playhouse (p653). Pick up San Diego *CityBeat* (www.sdcitybeat.com) for current listings.

Spectator Sports

San Diego's two big-league sports teams, the **Padres** (www.padres.com; Petco Park, 100 Park Blvd; tickets $11-91; ☉ season Apr-early Oct) baseball team and **Chargers** (www.chargers.com; Qualcomm Stadium, 9449 Friars Rd; tickets from $52; ☉ season Aug-Jan) football team, play in the East Village and Mission Valley, respectively.

Shopping

Souvenir hunters will find stuffed Shamus at SeaWorld, realistic-looking rubber snakes at the zoo and all manner of beachy souvenirs all over.

On Newport Ave in Ocean Beach are a dozen antiques consignment shops such as **Newport Avenue Antique Center** (Map p636; 4864 Newport Ave). **Cow** (Map p636; 5040 Newport Ave) gives the same treatment to music, and **Galactic** (Map p636; 4981 Newport Ave) to comics and video. Thrift shoppers should head to Garnet Ave in Pacific Beach for vintage and recycled clothing at shops including **Pangaea Outpost** (Map p636; 909 Garnet Ave, Pacific Beach) and **Buffalo Exchange** (Map p636; 1007 Garnet Ave, Pacific Beach). Most stores buy, sell and trade.

Westfield Horton Plaza downtown and **Westfield Mission Valley** (www.westfield.com/missionvalley; 1640 Camino del Rio N; ☉ 10am-9pm Mon-Sat, 11am-6pm Sun), **Fashion Valley** (www.simon.com; 7007 Friars Rd; ☉ 10am-9pm Mon-Sat, 11am-7pm Sun) and **Hazard Center** (www.hazardcenter.com; 7510-7610 Hazard Center Dr) in Mission Valley offer a feast for mall shoppers.

Central San Diego

Headquarters at Seaport District
MALL
(www.theheadquarters.com; 789 W Harbor Dr) San Diego's newest shopping center (opened 2013) is also one of its oldest buildings, the 1939 former police headquarters now turned into some 30 mostly swanky shopping, dining and entertainment options. The old jail cells are still there, for photo ops.

Liberty Station
MALL
(www.libertystation.com; 2640 Historic Decatur Rd) Between downtown and Point Loma, one-time offices and barracks of the decommissioned Naval Training Center are gradually being converted to shopping and dining venues. Look for fishing and outdoor gear and top restaurants including **Corvette Diner** (☎ 619-542-1476; 2965 Historic Decatur Rd; mains $8-11.50; ☉ 11:30am-9pm Sun-Thu, to 11pm Fri & Sat;) and Stone Brewing Co (p645).

Westfield Horton Plaza
MALL
(www.westfield.com/hortonplaza) At the edge of the Gaslamp, this five-story, seven-block shopping mall features shops big and small, including Nordstrom, Bebe and Coach. Colorful arches and postmodernist balconies make it feel slightly like an MC Escher drawing. Free three-hour parking with validation.

Seaport Village
SHOPPING DISTRICT
(www.seaportvillage.com; ☉ 10am-10pm;) Neither seaport nor village, this 14-acre collection of novelty shops and restaurants has a

TRAVELING TO TIJUANA

Just beyond the most-crossed border in the world, Tijuana, Mexico (population around two million), had fallen on hard times in the last decade, but locals have been reclaiming their city.

Avenida Revolución ('La Revo') is the main tourist drag, its charm marred by cheap clothing and souvenir stores, strip joints and pharmacies selling bargain-priced meds. It's much more appealing around Avenida Constitución: **Catedral de Nuestra Seño-ra de Guadalupe** (Cathedral of our Lady of Guadalupe; cnr Av Niños Héroes & Calle 2a) is Tijuana's oldest church, the atmospheric market hall **Mercado El Popo** (cnr Calle 2a & Av Constitución) sells needs from tamarind pods to religious iconography, and the arcade **Pasaje Rodríguez** (btwn Avenida Revolución & Avenida Constitución, Calles 3 & 4) is filled with youthful art galleries, bars and trendsetters.

A short ride away, **Museo de las Californias** (Museum of the Californias; ☑ from US 011-52-664-687-9600; www.cecut.gob.mx; cnr Paseo de los Héroes & Av Independencia; adult/child under 12yr M$20/free; ☉10am-6pm Tue-Sun; ☒) offers an excellent history of the border region from prehistory to the present; there's signage in English. Friday nights, check out **lucha libre** (☑ from US 011-52-664-250-9015; Blvd Díaz Ordaz 12421, Auditorio Municipal Fausto Gutierrez Moreno; admission US$8-35), Mexican wrestling by oversized men in gaudy masks.

The Caesar salad was invented at **Hotel Caesar** (☑ from US 011-52-664-685-1606; Av Revolución 827; Caesar salad $6; ☉9am-midnight), prepared tableside in the elegant dining room. Contemporary superstar chef Javier Plascencia runs the fun storefront **Erizo** (☑ from US 011-52-686-3895; 3808 Avenida Sonora; tacos M$18-45, ceviche $62-180, ramen $90-120) for innovative takes on tacos, ceviche and even ramen, worth the 10-minute taxi ride from La Revo.

Turista Libre (www.turistalibre.com) runs public and private tours in English.

A passport is required for the border crossing. The **San Diego Trolley** (www.sdmts.com) runs to the border at San Ysidro. By car, take I-5 south and park on the US side (around $8 for up to 24 hours). Cross the border on foot, and follow signs reading 'Centro Downtown,' a 20-minute walk. If traveling by taxi within Mexico, be sure the car has a meter. Driving into Mexico is not recommended.

faux New England theme. It's touristy but good for souvenir shopping and casual eats.

ℹ Information

INTERNET ACCESS

All public libraries and most coffeehouses and hotel lobbies offer free wi-fi. Libraries also offer computer terminals for access.

MEDIA

KPBS 89.5 FM (www.kpbs.org) National Public Radio station.

San Diego Magazine (www.sandiegomagazine.com) Glossy monthly.

UT San Diego (www.utsandiego.com) The city's major daily.

Free listings magazines Tabloid-sized magazines, **CityBeat** (www.sdcitybeat.com) and **San Diego Reader** (www.sdreader.com), cover the active music, art and theater scenes. Find them in shops and cafes.

MEDICAL SERVICES

Scripps Mercy Hospital (☑ 619-294-8111; www.scripps.org; 4077 5th Ave) Has a 24-hour emergency room.

POST

For post-office locations, call ☑ 800-275-8777 or log on to www.usps.com.

Downtown Post Office (815 E St; ☉9am-5pm Mon-Fri)

Coronado Post Office (1320 Ynez Pl; ☉8:30am-5pm Mon-Fri, 9am-noon Sat)

TOURIST INFORMATION

International Visitor Information Center (☑ 619-236-1212; www.sandiego.org; 1140 N Harbor Dr; ☉9am-5pm Jun-Sep, to 4pm Oct-May) Across from the B St Cruise Ship Terminal, helpful staff offer detailed neighborhood maps, sell discounted tickets to attractions and maintain a hotel reservation hotline.

Coronado Visitors Center (☑ 619-437-8788, 866-599-7242; www.coronadovisitorcenter.

com; 1100 Orange Ave; ⊙9am-5pm Mon-Fri, 10am-5pm Sat & Sun)

WEBSITES

Lonely Planet (www.lonelyplanet.com/usa/san-diego)

San Diego Tourism (www.sandiego.org) Search hotels, sights, dining, rental cars and more, and make reservations.

🛈 Getting There & Away

AIR

San Diego International Airport-Lindbergh Field (p761) sits just 3 miles west of downtown. All major US airlines serve San Diego, plus Air Canada, British Airways, Japan Airlines, Mexico's Volaris and the Canadian carrier WestJet.

BUS

Greyhound (☑619-515-1100, 800-231-2222; www.greyhound.com; 1313 National Ave) serves San Diego from cities across North America from its new location in East Village. Many discounts and special fares are available only online.

Buses depart frequently for LA (one-way/round-trip $18/36, 2½ to four hours) and several daily to Anaheim ($18/36, about 2¼ hours).

CAR & MOTORCYCLE

Allow two hours from LA in non-peak traffic. With traffic, it's anybody's guess.

TRAIN

Amtrak (☑800-872-7245; www.amtrak.com) runs the *Pacific Surfliner* several times daily to Anaheim ($28, two hours), Los Angeles ($37, 2¾ hours) and Santa Barbara ($42, 6½ hours) from the historic **Union Station** (Santa Fe Depot; 1055 Kettner Blvd).

🛈 Getting Around

While most people get around by car, municipal buses and trolleys run by the **Metropolitan Transit System** (MTS; ☑619-557-4555; www.sdmts.com) can get you most places. The Transit Store dispenses route maps and tickets. Transfers are not available, so purchase a day pass if you're going to be taking more than two rides in a day; one-/two-/three-/four-day passes ($5/9/12/15). A refillable **Compass Card** ($2 one-time purchase) will save hassles.

TO/FROM THE AIRPORT

Bus 992 (the Flyer, $2.25) operates at 10- to 15-minute intervals between the airport and downtown. Taxis between downtown and the airport typically cost between $10 and $16. Airport shuttle services, including **Super Shuttle** (☑800-258-3826; www.supershuttle.com), run from about $13 per person to downtown, more to other destinations.

BICYCLE

A few outfits like **Bikes & Beyond** (☑619-435-7180; www.bikes-and-beyond.com; 1201 1st St, Coronado; per hr/day from $8/30; ⊙9am-sunset), **Holland's Bicycles** (☑619-435-3153; www.hollandsbicycles.com; 977 Orange Ave, Coronado) and **Cheap Rentals** (Map p636; ☑858-488-9070, 800-941-7761; 3689 Mission Blvd, Pacific Beach; ⊙9am-7pm, shorter hours autumn-spring) rent bicycles, from mountain and road bikes to kids' bikes and cruisers. Expect to pay from about $8 per hour, $15 to $22 per half-day (four hours) and $25 to $30 per day.

BOAT

Flagship Cruises (p637) operates the hourly **Coronado Ferry** (☑619-234-4111; www.flagshipsd.com; tickets $4.25; ⊙9am-10pm) shuttling between the **Broadway Pier** (1050 N Harbor Dr) on the Embarcadero and the ferry landing at the foot of B Ave in Coronado, two blocks south of Orange Ave (15 minutes). Bikes are permitted on board at no extra charge.

BUS

MTS (www.sdmts.com) covers most of the metropolitan area. It's most convenient if you're based downtown and not staying out late. Useful routes to/from downtown:

No 3 Balboa Park, Hillcrest, UCSD Medical Center

No 7 Balboa Park, Zoo, Hillcrest, North Park

No 8/9 Old Town to Pacific Beach, SeaWorld

No 30 Old Town, Pacific Beach, La Jolla, University Towne Centre

No 35 Old Town to Ocean Beach

No 901 Coronado

CAR

All the big-name car-rental companies have desks at the airport, and lesser-known ones may be cheaper. Shop around – prices vary widely, even from day to day within the same company.

TAXI & RIDE SHARE

Plan on about $2.40 to start, plus $2.60 for each additional mile. Established companies include **Orange Cab** (☑619-223-5555; www.orange-cabsandiego.com) and **Yellow Cab** (☑619-444-4444; www.driveu.com). Recently app-based ride-share companies such as Uber and Sidecar have entered the market with lower fares.

TROLLEY

MTS trolleys operate on three main lines. Most useful for visitors, from the transit center across from the Santa Fe Depot, **Blue Line** trolleys go south to San Ysidro (Mexico border) and north to Old Town Transit Center. The **Green Line** runs from Old Town east through Mission Valley.

LA JOLLA & NORTH COUNTY COAST

Immaculately landscaped parks, white-sand coves, upscale boutiques, top restaurants, and cliffs above deep, clear blue waters make it easy to understand why 'La Jolla' translates from Spanish as 'the jewel' – say la-*hoy*-yah, if you please. The name may actually date from Native Americans who inhabited the area from 10,000 years ago to the mid-19th century, who called the place 'mut la hoya, la hoya' – the place of many caves. Whether your interest is jewels or caves, you'll feel at home in this lovely enclave.

Northward from La Jolla, small beach towns extend like pearls on a strand. 'North County,' as locals call it, begins with pretty Del Mar and continues through Encinitas and Carlsbad (home of Legoland), before hitting Oceanside, largely a bedroom community for Camp Pendleton Marine Base.

La Jolla

◎ Sights

◎ La Jolla Village

★ **Museum of Contemporary Art San Diego – La Jolla**   ART MUSEUM
(MCASD; ☑ 858-454-3541; www.mcasd.org; 700 Prospect St, La Jolla; adult/child $10/free, 5-7pm 3rd Thu each month free; ☉ 11am-5pm Thu-Tue, to 7pm 3rd Thu each month) La Jolla's branch of this museum gets changing, world-class exhibitions. The original 1916 building renovated by Philadelphia's postmodern architect Robert Venturi and has an Andy Goldsworthy sculpture out the front. Tickets are good for one week at all three of the museum's locations (p631).

Athenaeum   LIBRARY
(☑ 858-454-5872; www.ljathenaeum.org; 1008 Wall St; ☉ 10am-5:30pm Tue-Sat, to 8:30pm Wed) Housed in a graceful Spanish renaissance structure, this space is devoted exclusively to art and music. Its reading room is a lovely place to relax and read, and it hosts a series of concerts from chamber music to jazz.

◎ La Jolla Coast

A wonderful walking path skirts the shoreline for half a mile. At the west it begins at Children's Pool, where a jetty protects the beach from big waves. Originally intended to give La Jolla's youth a safe place to frolic, this beach is now given over to sea lions, which you can view up close as they lounge on the shore.

Atop Point La Jolla, at the path's eastern end, **Ellen Browning Scripps Park** is a tidy expanse of green lawns and palm trees, with **La Jolla Cove** to the north. The cove's gem of a beach provides access to some of the best snorkeling around.

White buoys offshore mark the **San Diego-La Jolla Underwater Park Ecological Reserve**, with a variety of marine life, kelp forests, reefs and canyons.

★ **Cave Store**   CAVES
(☑ 858-459-0746; www.cavestore.com; 1325 Coast Rd; adult/child $4/3; ☉ 10am-5pm; ♿) Waves have carved a series of caves into the sandstone cliffs east of La Jolla Cove. The largest is called Sunny Jim Cave, which you can access via this store. Taller visitors, watch your head as you descend the 145 steps.

Birch Aquarium at Scripps   AQUARIUM
(☑ 858-534-3474; www.aquarium.ucsd.edu; 2300 Exhibition Way, La Jolla; adult/child $17/12.50; ☉ 9am-5pm; 🅿 ♿) 🖉 Marine scientists were working at the Birch Aquarium at Scripps Institution of Oceanography (SIO) as early as 1910 and, helped by donations from the ever-generous Scripps family, the institute has grown to be one of the world's largest marine research institutions. It is now a part of the University of California San Diego. Off N Torrey Pines Rd, the aquarium has brilliant displays. The **Hall of Fishes** has more than 30 fish tanks, simulating marine environments from the Pacific Northwest to tropical seas.

Salk Institute   ARCHITECTURE
(☑ 858-453-4100, ext 1287; www.salk.edu; 10010 N Torrey Pines Rd; tours $15; ☉ tours by reservation 11:45am Mon-Fri; 🅿) In 1960 Jonas Salk, the polio-prevention pioneer, founded the Salk Institute for biological and biomedical research, and this building by renowned architect Louis Kahn was completed in 1965. It is regarded as a modern masterpiece, with its classically proportioned travertine marble plaza and cubist, mirror-glass laboratory blocks framing a perfect view of the Pacific. The original buildings were expanded with new laboratories designed by Jack McAllister, a follower of Kahn's work.

Torrey Pines State Natural Reserve   PARK
(☑ 858-755-2063; www.torreypine.org; 12600 N Torrey Pines Rd, La Jolla; ☉ 7:15am-dusk, visitor

La Jolla

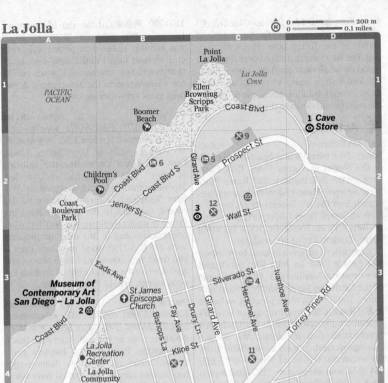

La Jolla

center 10am-4pm Oct-Apr, 9am-6pm May-Sep; [P])

🦋 This reserve preserves the last mainland stands of the Torrey pine (*Pinus torreyana*). The views north and out over the ocean (good for whale-watching) are superb. Rangers lead nature walks weekends and holidays. Several walking trails wind through the reserve and down to the beach.

🏃 Activities

La Jolla Beaches
BEACHES

Some of the county's best beaches are north of the Shores in **Torrey Pines City Park**, between the Salk Institute and Torrey Pines State Reserve. Hang-gliders and paragliders launch into the sea breezes rising over the cliffs at Torrey Pines Gliderport, at the end of Torrey Pines Scenic Dr. It's a beautiful sight – tandem flights are available.

Experienced surfers can head to **Windansea Beach** (take La Jolla Blvd south and turn west on Nautilus St). However, some of the locals can be unfriendly toward outsiders. You'll find a more pleasant welcome at **Big Rock**, California's version of Hawaii's Pipeline, immediately south of Windansea Beach, at the foot of Palomar Ave. For the less experienced, lessons are available from the wonderful women of **Surf Diva** (☎858-454-8273; www.surfdiva.com; 2160 Avenida de la Playa; ⊙ store 8:30am-6pm, varies seasonally).

San Diego-La Jolla Underwater Park
SNORKELING, DIVING

Some of California's best and most accessible diving is in this reserve, accessible from La Jolla Cove. With an average depth of 20ft, the 6000 acres of look-but-don't-touch underwater real estate is great for snorkeling, too. Ever-present are the spectacular, bright orange Garibaldi fish – California's official state fish and a protected species (there's a $500 fine for poaching one). Further out you'll see forests of giant California kelp (which can increase its length by up to 3ft per day) and the 100ft-deep La Jolla Canyon.

A number of commercial outfits conduct scuba-diving courses, sell or rent equipment, fill tanks, and conduct boat trips to nearby wrecks and islands. The Cave Store (p650) and other outfitters rent snorkel and fin sets (about $20 for two hours).

🛏️ Sleeping

La Jolla Village Lodge
MOTEL $$

(☎858-551-2001, 877-551-2001; www.lajollavillagelodge.com; 1141 Silverado St; r incl breakfast $100-200; [P]🛜📶) At the edge of downtown La Jolla, this 30-room 1950s-era motel was recently restored in period style with custom-built tables and chairs, teak headboards and new mattresses. Flat-screen TVs are a concession to the 21st century. A roof deck gives long-distance views.

La Valencia
HISTORIC HOTEL $$$

(☎800-451-0772, 858-454-0771; www.lavalencia.com; 1132 Prospect St; r from $385; [P]✳@📶🏊📶) 🦋 Publicity stills of Lon Cheney, Lillian Gish and Greta Garbo line the hallways of this 1926 landmark: pink-walled, Mediterranean-style and designed by William Templeton Johnson. Among its 112 rooms, the ones in the main building are rather compact (befitting the era), but villas are spacious and in any case the property wins for Old Hollywood romance. Even if you don't stay, consider lifting a toast – and a pinkie – to the sunset from its Spanish Revival lounge, la Sala. Parking is $29.

Pantai Inn
BOUTIQUE HOTEL $$$

(☎858-224-7600, 855-287-2682; www.pantaiinn.com; 1003 Coast Blvd; r from $295; [P]✳@📶) About as close as you can stay to the beach and Scripps Park, colorful banners mark the perimeter of this new, Balinese-style inn. Rooms vary in size, but all have kitchens and sitting areas, and suites are filled wtih Balinese art and antiques. Continental breakfast is served in the Gathering Room; enjoy it on multiple ocean-view decks.

🍴 Eating

Harry's Coffee Shop
DINER $

(☎858-454-7381; 7545 Girard Ave; dishes $5-13; ⊙6am-3pm; 🚼) This classic 1960s coffee shop has a posse of regulars from blue-haired socialites to sports celebs. The food is standard-issue American – pancakes, tuna melts, burgers and breakfast burritos – but it's the aura of the place that makes it special.

Porkyland
MEXICAN $

(☎858-459-1708; 1030 Torrey Pines Rd; dishes $4-9; ⊙9am-7pm) This tiny Mexican joint in a corner shopping center on the edge of La Jolla Village has only simple indoor-outdoor seating, but the burritos and fish tacos have a devoted following. The *verde carnitas* burrito ($6) will make your taste buds roar (in a good way) and still leave you money for beer.

Whisknladle
CALIFORNIAN $$

(☎858-551-7575; www.wnlhosp.com; 1044 Wall St; lunch $14-21, dinner $15.36; ⊙11:30am-9pm Mon-

Thu, to 10pm Fri, 10am-10pm Sat, 10am-9:30pm Sun) Gourmets and gourmands alike love Whisknladle's 'slow food' preparations of local, farm-fresh ingredients, served on a breezy covered patio and meant for sharing. Every minute preparation from curing to pickling and macerating is done in house. The menu changes daily, but it's always clever. So are the cocktails (the London's Burning mixes gin and jalapeño water).

El Pescador SEAFOOD $$
(☑858-456-2526; www.elpescadorfishmarket.com; 634 Pearl St; mains $7-20; ⊙10am-8pm) You could pay three times as much for seafood at fancier restaurants in town while locals will be at this fish market and restaurant, just moved to spanking new digs on the edge of La Jolla Village. Your catch will be prepared into a sandwich, salad or plate.

Cottage MODERN AMERICAN $$
(☑858-454-8409; 7702 Fay Ave; breakfast $9-12, lunch $10-19, dinner $11-26; ⊙7:30am-9pm) Shhh! Don't tell anybody that the stuffed French toast, eggs La Jolla (with bacon, mushrooms, spinach and garlic and balsamic vinegar) and fish tacos make this place a local favorite. It's crowded enough as it is, especially on weekends for brunch. Expect a wait if you arrive much after 8:30am.

★George's at the Cove CALIFORNIAN $$$
(☑858-454-4244; www.georgesatthecove.com; 1250 Prospect St, La Jolla; mains $13-50; ⊙11am-10pm Mon-Thu, to 11pm Fri-Sun) The Euro-Cal cooking here is as dramatic as the oceanfront location thanks to the imagination of chef Trey Foshée. George's has graced just about every list of top restaurants in California and the USA. Three venues allow you to enjoy it at different price points: Ocean Terrace, George's Bar and George's California Modern.

🍷 Drinking & Entertainment

Pannikin CAFE
(pannikincoffeeandtea.com; 7467 Girard Ave; ⊙6am-6pm Mon-Fri, 6:30am-6pm Sat & Sun; 🛜) A few blocks from the water, this clapboard shack with a generous balcony is popular for its organic coffees, Italian espresso and Mexican chocolate, and occasional live music. Like all the Pannikins, it's a North County institution.

Comedy Store COMEDY
(☑858-454-9176; www.comedystorelajolla.com; 916 Pearl St) One of the area's most established comedy venues, the Comedy Store also serves meals, drinks and barrels of laughs. Expect a cover charge ($15 to $20 on weekends with a two-drink minimum), and some of tomorrow's big names.

La Jolla Symphony & Chorus CLASSICAL MUSIC
(☑858-534-4637; www.lajollasymphony.com; UCSD) Quality concerts at UCSD's Mandeville Auditorium running from October to June.

La Jolla Playhouse THEATER
(☑858-550-1010; www.lajollaplayhouse.org; 2910 La Jolla Village Dr, Mandell Weiss Center for the Performing Arts) This nationally recognized theater has sent dozens of productions to Broadway, including *Jersey Boys* and 2010 Tony winner *Memphis*.

🛍 Shopping

La Jolla's skirt-and-sweater crowd pays retail for cashmere sweaters and expensive art and tchotchkes downtown. Mall shoppers make a bee-line for **Westfield UTC** (UTC; 4545 La Jolla Village Dr).

ℹ️ Getting There & Away

Via I-5 from downtown San Diego, take the La Jolla Pkwy exit and head west toward Torrey Pines Rd, from where it's a right turn onto Prospect St.

Del Mar

The ritziest of North County's seaside suburbs, with a Tudor aesthetic that somehow doesn't feel out of place, Del Mar boasts good (if pricey) restaurants, unique galleries, high-end boutiques and, north of town, the West Coast's most renowned horse-racing track, also the site of the annual county fair.

👁 Sights & Activities

Del Mar Racetrack & Fairgrounds RACETRACK
(☑858-755-1141; www.dmtc.com; admission from $6; ⊙race season mid-Jul–early Sep) Del Mar's biggest draw was founded in 1937 by a prestigious group including Bing Crosby and Jimmy Durante, and is still worth a visit for its lush gardens and Mediterranean architecture. Go on opening day for the spectacle of ladies wearing over-the-top hats.

Seagrove Park PARK
At the end of 15th St, this park overlooks the ocean. Perfect for a picnic.

California Dreamin' BALLOONING
(☑800-373-3359; www.californiadreamin.com; per person from $288) Brightly colored hot-air balloons are a trademark of the skies above Del Mar.

North County Coast

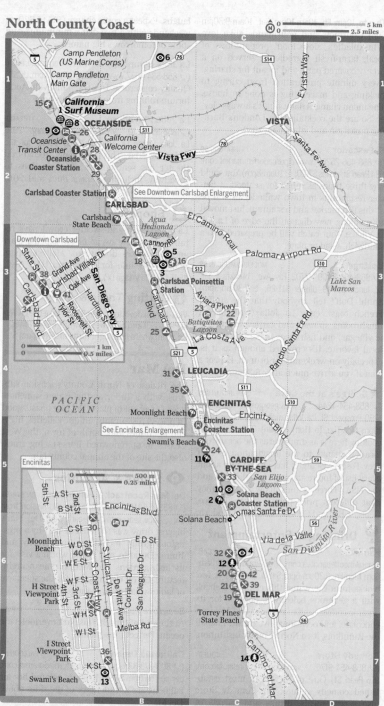

SAN DIEGO & AROUND DEL MAR

North County Coast

SAN DIEGO & AROUND DEL MAR

🛌 Sleeping

Les Artistes Inn
BOUTIQUE HOTEL **$$**

(📞858-755-4646; www.lesartistesinn.com; 944 Camino Del Mar; r $165-250; 🅿️❄️@🛜🏊) Behind the eclectic Craftsman-style facade of this inn set back from Camino del Mar, each of the 12 spacious rooms is meticulously furnished in the style of an artist or art movement: Botero through O'Keefe to van Gogh, even Zen.

L'Auberge Del Mar Resort & Spa
LUXURY **$$$**

(📞800-553-1336, 858-259-1515; www.laubergedelmar.com; 1540 Camino Del Mar; r $350-540; 🅿️❄️@🛜🏊🏊) Rebuilt in the 1990s on the grounds of the historic Hotel del Mar, where 1920s Hollywood celebrities once frolicked, L'Auberge continues a tradition of European-style elegance with luxurious linens, a spa and lovely grounds. It feels so intimate and the service is so individual, you'd never know there are 120 rooms. Parking $25.

Hotel Indigo San Diego Del Mar
BOUTIQUE HOTEL **$$$**

(📞858-755-1501; www.hotelindigosddelmar.com; 710 Camino Del Mar; r from $199; 🅿️➗❄️@🛜🏊🏊) This collection of white-washed buildings with gray clay-tiled roofs, two pools, a spa and new fitness and business centers received a tip-to-toe renovation for 2014. Rooms boast hardwood floors, mosaic tile accents and horserace- and beach-inspired motifs. Some units have kitchenettes and distant ocean views, and Ocean View Bar & Grill serves breakfast, lunch and dinner.

🍴 Eating

En Fuego
MEXICAN **$$**

(📞858-792-6551; www.enfuegocantina.com; 1342 Camino Del Mar; mains $6-16; ⏰11:30am-midnight Sun-Thu, to 1am Fri & Sat) On the site of Del Mar's first restaurant, this airy, multilevel Nuevo Mexicano spot is both restaurant and bar. Specialties on the forward-thinking menu include borracho shrimp (sautéed in tequila), filet mignon rancheros and honey habanero chicken (in a sweet spicy glaze), with lots of indoor-outdoor space to enjoy them.

Zel's
CALIFORNIAN $$

(☑858-755-0076; www.zelsdelmar.com; 1247 Camino Del Mar; mains lunch $9-15, dinner $9-24; ⊙11am-10pm Mon-Thu, 9am-midnight Sat, 9am-10pm Sun) Zel was a longstanding local merchant, and his grandson continues the family tradition of welcoming locals and visitors, with excellent flatbread pizzas (like chicken with asparagus, truffle oil, arugula and avocado), burgers of bison, quinoa or locally raised beef, and lots of craft beers. Live music Thursday to Sunday.

Americana
MODERN AMERICAN $$

(☑858-794-6838; 1454 Camino del Mar; mains breakfast & lunch $7-14, dinner $14-21; ⊙7am-3pm Sun & Mon, to 10pm Tue-Sat) This quietly chichi and much-loved local landmark serves a diverse lineup of regional American cuisine: cheese grits to chicken Reubens, sesame salmon on succotash to seared duck breast with Israeli couscous, plus artisan cocktails, all amid checkerboard linoleum floors, giant windows and homey wainscoting.

Jake's Del Mar
SEAFOOD $$$

(☑858-755-2002; www.jakesdelmar.com; 1660 Coast Blvd; mains lunch $11-26, dinner $16-36; ⊙4-9pm Mon, 11:30am-9pm Tue-Fri, 11:30am-9:30pm Sat, 8am-9pm Sun) Head to this beachside classic for ocean-view drinks and half-price appetizers from 4pm to 6pm weekdays and from 2:30pm to 4:30pm on Saturday. The view's great, the atmosphere chic and the food imaginative, like burrata and heirloom tomato salad, ahi tartare tacos and 'surfing steak' with herb-grilled jumbo shrimp, sweet corn cream, sautéed spinach, truffle mash potatoes.

🛍 Shopping

Del Mar Plaza
MALL

(www.delmarplaza.com; 555 Camino del Mar) Where 15th St crosses Camino del Mar, the tastefully designed Del Mar Plaza shopping center has restaurants, boutiques and upper-level terraces that look out to sea.

ℹ Getting There & Away

N Torrey Pines Rd from La Jolla is the most scenic approach from the south. Heading north, the road (S21) changes its name from Camino del Mar to Coast Hwy 101 to Old Hwy 101.

Cardiff-by-the-Sea

Beachy Cardiff is good for surfing and popular with a laid-back crowd for the miles of restaurants and surf shops along Hwy 101 by Cardiff (www.parks.ca.gov; ⊙7am-sunset; ℙ) and San Elijo State Beaches. The other main draw is the 1000-acre San Elijo Lagoon (☑760-623-3026; www.sanelijo.org; 2710 Manchester Ave; ⊙nature center 9am-5pm) FREE ecological preserve, popular with bird-watchers for its herons, coots, terns, ducks, egrets and more than 250 other species.

San Elijo State Beach (☑760-753-5091, reservations 800-444-7275; www.parks.ca.gov; 2050 S Coast Hwy 101; summer tent/RV sites from $35/55) has a campground, while Las Olas (mains $9-19; ⊙11am-9pm Mon-Thu, to 9:30pm Fri, 10am-9:30pm Sat, 10am-9pm Sun; ℙ🚻) serves fish tacos with a sea view; it's so popular that it has its own traffic light. Also across from the beach, Ki's (☑760-436-5236; 2591 S Coast Hwy 101; breakfast $5-9, lunch $7-14, dinner $13-22; ⊙8am-8:30pm Sun-Thu, to 10pm Fri, 9pm Sat; ℙ🍴) is an organic cafe/restaurant and a hub of local activity; there are inspiring beach views from the 2nd-floor bar and dining areas.

Encinitas

Peaceful Encinitas has a decidedly down-to-earth vibe and a laid-back beach-town main street, perfect for a relaxing day trip or weekend escape. North of central Encinitas, yet still part of the city, is Leucadia, a leafy stretch of N Hwy 101 with a hippie vibe of used-clothing stores and taco shops.

◉ Sights

Self-Realization Fellowship Retreat
RETREAT

(☑760-753-1811; www.yogananda-srf.org; 215 K St; ⊙meditation garden 9am-5pm Tue-Sat, 11am-5pm Sun) FREE Yogi Paramahansa Yogananda founded his center here in 1937, and the town has been a magnet for holistic healers and natural-lifestyle seekers ever since. The gold lotus domes of the hermitage – conspicuous on South Coast Hwy 101 – mark the southern end of Encinitas and the turn-out for Swami's Beach, a powerful reef break surfed by territorial locals. The fellowship's compact but lovely Meditation Garden has wonderful ocean vistas, a stream and a koi pond. If you're interested in more detailed exploration of meditation and the religion's principles, visit the website.

🛌 Sleeping

Best Western Encinitas Inn & Suites
MOTEL **$$**

(☏760-942-7455, 866-236-4648; www.bwencinitas.com; 85 Encinitas Blvd; r incl breakfast from $169; P@🛜🐾🏊🐕) Atop a hill between the freeway, shopping center and Coast Hwy is this hexagonal hotel, a few minutes on foot from the sand. Design is nothing fancy, but it's well kept, all rooms have balconies and suites have kitchenettes and sleep sofas. Some rooms have ocean or park views.

🍴 Eating

🍴 Central Encinitas

Swami's Café
CAFE **$**

(☏760-944-0612; 1163 S Coast Hwy 101; mains $5-10; ⏱7am-5pm; 🖊👶) This local institution can't be beat for breakfast burritos, multigrain pancakes, stir-fries, salads, smoothies and three-egg *ohm*-lettes (sorry, we couldn't resist). Vegetarians will be satisfied, too. Most of the seating is out on an umbrella-covered patio.

★ Trattoria I Trulli
ITALIAN **$$**

(☏760-943-6800; www.trattoriaitrullisd.com; 830 S Coast Hwy 101; mains lunch $13-21, dinner $14-26; ⏱11:30am-2:30pm daily, 5-10pm Sun-Thu, to 10:30pm Fri & Sat) Country-style seating indoors and great people-watching on the sidewalk. Just one taste of the homemade gnocchi, ravioli or lasagne, salmon in brandy mustard sauce or *pollo uno zero uno* (101; chicken stuffed with cheese, spinach and artichokes in mushroom sauce) and you'll know why this mom-and-pop Italian trattoria is always packed. Reservations are recommended.

El Callejon
MEXICAN **$$**

(☏760-634-2793; www.el-callejon.com; 345 S Coast Hwy 101; mains $9-22; ⏱11am-9pm Mon-Thu, to 11pm Fri, 10am-11pm Sat, 10am-9pm Sun; 🖊👶) A raucous, fun, local favorite, this indoor-outdoor candy-colored cantina is at the north end of the town center. The menu is as long as the phone book of a small village, and it would take you over two years of trying a different tequila every day to go through the tequila list.

🍴 North Encinitas/Leucadia

Pannikin Coffee & Tea
CAFE **$**

(☏760-436-0033; mains $4-8; ⏱6am-6pm) In a sunny, yellow wooden building that used to be the Encinitas train station (transported from its original site), Pannikin is an adorable sprawl of nooks, crannies, balconies and lawns. Muffins and coffees are wonderful, natch, and bagel and lox with steamed scrambled eggs is very attractive indeed.

★ Fish 101
SEAFOOD **$$**

(☏760-634-6221; www.fish101restaurant.com; 1468 N. Coast Hwy 101; mains $10-19) In this roadside shack all growed up, order at the counter, sidle into a butcher block or picnic table, sip craft beer, wine or Mexican Coke from a Mason jar and use paper towels to wipe your face. Simple grilling techniques allow the natural flavors of the fresh catch to show through, and healthy rice bran oil is used for deep frying.

🍷 Drinking

Daley Double
DIVE BAR

(546 S Coast Hwy 101) Once Encinitas' most notorious dive bar, it's now Encinitas' hippest dive bar. Fantastic Old West saloon-style murals make a great backdrop for good old-fashioned sipping and flirting. Expect a line out the door on weekends.

ℹ Getting There & Away

By car, the Encinitas Blvd exit off I-5 is about a quarter mile east of central Encinitas. Encinitas is served by Coaster trains and Breeze buses (www.gonctd.com) connecting San Diego, Oceanside and points between.

Carlsbad

Legoland is by far North County's biggest attraction, but a few miles away sits a quaint downtown enclave and long, sandy beaches great for walking and searching for seashells. Carlsbad has a number of other worthwhile attractions outside the village and Legoland areas – from flowers to musical instruments and go-karts. You pretty much need a car to reach them.

◉ Sights & Activities

Legoland
AMUSEMENT PARK

(☏760-918-5346; http://california.legoland.com; 1 Legoland Dr, Carlsbad; adult/child from $83/73; ⏱daily mid-Mar–Aug, Wed-Sun Sep–mid-Mar;

SAN DIEGO ZOO SAFARI PARK

Since the early 1960s, the San Diego Zoological Society has been developing this 1800-acre, **open-range zoo** (☑760-747-8702; www.sdzsafaripark.org; 15500 San Pasqual Valley Rd, Escondido; admission adult/child $45/36, 2-day pass incl San Diego Zoo $82/64; ☉mid-Jun–mid-Aug 9am-7pm, other hours vary seasonally; ⬤) where herds of giraffes, zebras, rhinos and other animals roam the open valley floor. For an instant safari feel, board the **Africa Tram** ride, which tours you around the second-largest continent in under half an hour.

Elsewhere, animals are in enclosures so naturalistic it's as if the humans are guests, and there's a petting krall and animal shows; pick up a map and schedule. Additional 'safaris,' like zip-lining, a chance to observe a cheetah whizz by while chasing a mechanical rabbit, and even sleepovers (yowza!) are available with reservations and additional payment (from $45).

The park's just north of Hwy 78, 5 miles east of I-15 from the Via Rancho Parkway exit. Parking is $10. Plan on 45 minutes transit by car from San Diego, except in rush hour when that figure can double. For bus information contact **North San Diego County Transit District** (☑619-233-3004, from North County 800-266-6883; www.gonctd.com).

(Ⓟ⬤) A fantasy environment built largely of those little colored plastic blocks from Denmark. Many rides and attractions are targeted to elementary schoolers: a junior 'driving school,' a jungle cruise lined with Lego animals, wacky 'sky cruiser' pedal cars on a track, and fairytale, princess, pirate, adventurer and dino-themed escapades. If you have budding scientists (aged 10 and over) with you, sign them up on arrival at the park for an appointment with **Mindstorms**, where they can make computerized Lego robots.

There are also lots of low-thrill activities like face-painting and princess-meeting.

Carlsbad Ranch Flower Fields   GARDENS
(☑760-431-0352; www.theflowerfields.com; 5704 Paseo del Norte; adult/child $12/6; ☉usually 9am-6pm Mar–mid-May; Ⓟ) The 50-acre flower fields of Carlsbad Ranch are ablaze in a sea of the carmine, saffron and snow-white blossoms of ranunculuses. Take the Palomar Airport Rd exit off of I-5, head east and turn left on Paseo del Norte.

Batiquitos Lagoon   PARK
(☑760-931-0800; www.batiquitosfoundation.org; 7380 Gabbiano Ln; ☉nature center 9am-12:30pm Mon-Fri, to 3pm Sat & Sun) One of the last remaining tidal wetlands in California, Batiquitos Lagoon separates Carlsbad from Encinitas. A self-guided tour lets you explore area plants, including the prickly pear cactus, coastal sage scrub and eucalyptus trees, as well as lagoon birds such as the great heron and the snowy egret.

Museum of Making Music   MUSEUM
(www.museumofmakingmusic.com; 5790 Armada Dr; adult/child & senior $8/5; ☉10am-5pm Tue-Sun) Historical exhibits and listening stations of 450 instruments from the 1890s to the present, from manufacturing to the distribution of popular music.

Chopra Center   MIND-BODY CENTER
(www.chopra.com; 2013 Costa del Mar Rd, Omni La Costa Resort & Spa) Slow down with alternative-health guru Deepak Chopra, who leads seminars on mind-body medicine, complemented by specialized spa treatments.

K1 Speed   ADVENTURE SPORTS
(www.k1speed.com; Corte Del Abeto; 14-lap race $20; ☉noon-10pm Mon-Thu, 11am-11pm Fri, 10am-11pm Sat, 10am-8pm Sun) To pick up the pace, this place fills your need for speed with indoor karting (electric drag racing). It supplies all the necessary equipment, including helmet and 'head socks'; first-timers must purchase a special license, $6 extra. Inquire about midweek discounts.

🛏 Sleeping

Below are some of Carlsbad's standout lodgings. Numerous chain motels near the freeway cater to budget travelers.

On Batiquitos Lagoon, two large and luxurious resorts boast golf and extensive fitness and kids' programs: **Omni La Costa Resort & Spa** (☑760-438-9111, 800-854-5000; www.lacosta.com; 2100 Costa Del Mar Rd; r from $300; Ⓟ⬤⬤⬤⬤) ⬤ has the Chopra Center and a touch of Hollywood history, while the

Park Hyatt Aviara (☑760-603-6800; www.parkhyattaviara.com; 7100 Aviara Resort Dr; r from $249; ℗@☎☂☒) is done up in acres of marble and has a 15,000-sq-ft spa.

South Carlsbad State Park Campground   CAMPGROUND $
(☑760-438-3143, reservations 800-444-7275; www.reserveamerica.com; 7201 Carlsbad Blvd; ocean-/street-side campsites $50/35; ℗) Three miles south of town and sandwiched between Carlsbad Blvd and the beach, this campground has over 200 tent and RV sites.

★Legoland Hotel   HOTEL $$$
(☑877-534-6526, 760-918-5346; california.legoland.com/legoland-hotel; 5885 the Crossings Dr; r incl breakfast from $369; ℗✿@☎☂☒) To quote the *Lego Movie,* 'everything is awesome' at this new hotel just outside Legoland's main gate, where Lego designers were let loose. There are 3500 Lego models (dragons to surfers) populating the property, and the elevator turns into a disco between floors. Each floor has its own theme (pirate, adventure, kingdom) down to the rooms' wallpaper, props (Lego cannonballs!) even the shower curtains.

Hilton Carlsbad Oceanfront Resort & Spa   RESORT HOTEL $$$
(☑760-602-0800; www.carlsbadoceanfrontresortandspa.hilton.com; 1 Ponto Rd; r from $249; ℗✿@☎☂☒) Most of Carlsbad's top lodgings are inland, but this swanky new spot (opened 2012) is an easy walk to the ocean across Hwy 101. Pools, spa and business and fitness centers will keep you busy on land. Chandler's restaurant serves three squares, including creative dinners like falafel crabcakes and diver scallops with artichokes and smoked almonds. Parking costs $19.

West Inn & Suites   HOTEL $$$
(☑866-431-9378, 760-448-4500; www.westinnandsuites.com; 4970 Avenida Encinas; r incl breakfast $159-359; ℗✿@☎☂☒) About halfway between Legoland and Carlsbad Village, this hyperfriendly, independently run 86-room inn caters to both business travelers (note business and fitness centers) and vacationing families (note the sparkling pool, beach and Legoland shuttle service and nightly milk and cookies). Free parking.

✕ Eating & Drinking

All the hotels mentioned have quite decent restaurants. In town, State St is Carlsbad's most charming stretch, with a number of restaurants worth browsing. Nearby are branches of the brew pub Pizza Port (p645) and Mexican fave **Las Olas** (☑760-434-5850; 2939 Carlsbad Blvd).

Vigilucci's Cucina Italiana   ITALIAN $$
(☑760-434-2500; 2943 State St; lunch $8-18, dinner $15-32; ☉11am-10pm) Enjoy the white-tablecloth service and the lovely sidewalk terrace at this State St institution. For lunch try pastas or panini (the one with parma ham and portobello mushrooms is a fave), while dinner might be pappardelle with field mushrooms and seared diver scallops in white truffle and brandy cream sauce.

Relm   WINE BAR
(☑760-434-9463; www.thewinerelm.com; 2917 State St; ☉from 4pm Tue-Sun) This cozy, modernist storefront pours from over 60 bottles (wine flights $12) and serves cheeseboards and flatbreads to go with them. When it has live music, it's irresistible.

ⓘ Information

Carlsbad Visitors Center (☑760-434-6093; www.visitcarlsbad.com; 400 Carlsbad Village Dr) Housed in the town's original 1887 Santa Fe train depot.

ⓘ Getting There & Away

Carlsbad is a stop on Coaster trains and Breeze buses (www.gonctd.com). By car, take the Cannon Dr exit from I-5 for Legoland, the outlet mall and other sights and lodgings. For Carlsbad Village, take the Carlsbad Village Dr exit.

Oceanside

The largest North County town, Oceanside is home to many who work at giant Camp Pendleton Marine Base just to the north. The huge military presence mixes with an attractive natural setting, surf shops and head shops.

◉ Sights & Activities

Oceanside Pier   PIER
(per hr/day $5/15) This wooden pier extends more than 1900ft out to sea. Bait-and-tackle shops rent poles to the many anglers who line its wooden fences. Two major surf competitions – the West Coast Pro-Am and the National Scholastic Surf Association (NSSA) – take place near the pier each June.

Surfers and would-be surfers can rent equipment from **Asylum Surf** (www.asylumboardshop.com; 310 Mission Ave; surfboards 3hr/full day $20/30, wetsuits $10/15) and take lessons from **Surfcamps USA** (www.surfcampsusa.com; 1202 N Pacific St; lessons per person from $55; 🚺).

★ **California Surf Museum**　　MUSEUM
(www.surfmuseum.org; 312 Pier View Way; adult/student/child $5/3/free, Tue free; ⏲10am-4pm Fri-Wed, to 8pm Thu) It's easy to spend an hour in this heartfelt museum of surf artifacts, ranging from a timeline of surfing history to surf-themed art and a radical collection of boards, including the one chomped by a shark when it ate the arm of surfer Bethany Hamilton. Special exhibits change frequently along different themes (eg women of surfing).

Oceanside Museum of Art　　MUSEUM
(www.oma-online.org; 704 Pier View Way; adult/senior/student $8/5/3; ⏲10am-4pm Tue-Sat, 1-4pm Sun) This museum also underwent a recent revamp and it now stands at an impressive 16,000 sq ft in a modernist, white shell. There are about 10 rotating exhibits a year, with an emphasis on SoCal artists and local cultures.

Mission San Luis Rey de Francia　　MISSION
(www.sanluisrey.org; 4050 Mission Ave; adult/child & senior $5/4; ⏲10am-4pm) About 4.5 miles inland from central Oceanside, this was the largest California mission and the most successful in recruiting Native American converts. At one point some 3000 neophytes lived and worked here. After the Mexican government secularized the missions, San Luis fell into ruin; the adobe walls of the church, from 1811, are the only original parts left. Inside are displays on work and life in the mission, with some original religious art and artifacts.

Helgren's　　BOAT CHARTERS
(☎760-722-2133; www.helgrensportfishing.com; 315 Harbor Dr S) This outfit leads a variety of charter trips for sportfishing (from $55 per half-day) and whale-watching (adult/child $35/20). Phone for details and reservations.

🛏 Sleeping & Eating

★ **Springhill Suites Oceanside Downtown**　　HOTEL **$$**
(☎760-722-1003; www.shsoceanside.com; 110 N Myers St; r incl breakfast $219-279; 🅿@🛜🌊) Brand new for 2014, this modern, six-story, ocean-view hotel is awash in summery yellows and sea blues in the lobby. Rooms have crisp lines and distressed-wood headboards, and ocean- and pier-view rooms have balconies or patios. Best views are from the pool and hot tub on the top floor, where there's also a fitness center.

Beach Break Café　　DINER **$**
(☎760-439-6355; 1802 S Coast Hwy; mains $7-12; ⏲7am-2pm; 🅿🚺) Fuel up before surfing on omelets, scrambles and pancakes, or afterwards on sandwiches, tacos and salads at this surfers' diner on the east side of the road. A second location by the **harbor** (280 Harbor Dr) serves the same menu in a stellar setting.

101 Café　　DINER **$**
(☎760-722-5220; 631 S Coast Hwy; mains $6-10; ⏲7am-2pm; 🅿🚺) This tiny 1928 streamline moderne diner serves the classics: omelets, burgers etc. If you're lucky, you'll catch the owner and can quiz him about local history.

Hello Betty Fish House　　SEAFOOD **$$**
(☎760-722-1008; www.hellobettyoceanside.com; 211 Mission Ave; mains $10-24; ⏲11am-10pm Sun-Thu, to 11pm Fri & Sat) This new beachfront spot opened in 2014 and locals already love its Baja stone crab and cheese dip, fried and grilled tacos (from $4.50) and salmon burger with Asian slaw and wasabi aioli. Grilled fish platters and other large plates run up to $24. Plus O'side's best views from the bar and deck.

That Boy Good　　BARBECUE **$$**
(TBG; ☎760-433-4227; www.tbgbbq.com; 207 N Coast Hwy; mains $9-25; ⏲from 4pm Mon, 11am Tue-Sun) This new shrine to the Mississippi Delta serves belly-busting portions of fried chicken and waffles, pork ribs and the Crossroads Cup (baked beans, mac 'n' cheese, cole slaw topped with your choice of meat). Wash it all down with a craft or canned beer or the BBQ Bloody Mary, topped with a rib.

ⓘ Information

California Welcome Center (☎760-721-1101, 800-350-7873; www.visitoceanside.org; 928 N Coast Hwy; ⏲9am-5pm)

ⓘ Getting There & Away

Oceanside Transit Center (235 S Tremont St) Buses and trains all stop here. North County Transit District (NCTD; ☎760-966-6500; www.gonctd.com) Breeze Bus 101 departs from UTC in La Jolla (p653) and follows the coastal road to Oceanside. NCTD also operates the Coaster commuter train from San Diego, stopping in Encinitas, Carlsbad and Oceanside. A few Amtrak (p649) Pacific Surfliner trains stop here daily.

Greyhound buses stop at Oceanside and San Diego.

Palm Springs & the Deserts

Why Go?

There's something undeniably artistic in the way the landscape unfolds in the California desert. Weathered volcanic peaks stand sentinel over singing sand dunes and mountains shimmering in hues from mustard yellow to vibrant pink. Hot mineral water spurts from the earth's belly to feed palm oases and soothe aching muscles in stylish spas. Tiny wildflowers push up from the hard-baked soil to celebrate springtime.

The riches of the desert soil have lured prospectors and miners, while its beauty and spirituality have tugged at the hearts of artists, visionaries and wanderers. Eccentrics, misfits and the military are drawn by its vastness and solitude. Hipsters and celebs come for the climate and retro flair. Through it all threads iconic Route 66, lined with moodily rusting roadside relics. No matter what your trail, the desert will creep into your consciousness and never fully leave.

Best Places to Eat

➡ Trio (p671)

➡ Cheeky's (p671)

➡ Inn at Furnace Creek (p699)

➡ Pastels Bistro (p702)

Best Places to Stay

➡ Riviera Palm Springs (p670)

➡ El Morocco Inn & Spa (p670)

➡ La Casa del Zorro (p686)

➡ Sacred Sands (p680)

➡ Mandalay Bay (p709)

When to Go
Palm Springs

°C/°F Temp

40/104 —

30/86 —

20/68 —

10/50 —

0/32 —

J F M A M J J A S O N D

Rainfall Inches/mm

— 6/150

— 4/100

— 2/50

— 0

Dec–Apr Moderate temperatures lure in 'snowbirds' and LA weekend trippers.

May–mid-Jun, mid-Sep–Nov Crowds thin out as temperatures arc during shoulder season.

Jun–Sep Some inns and restaurants close in summer's heat; many of the rest offer great deals.

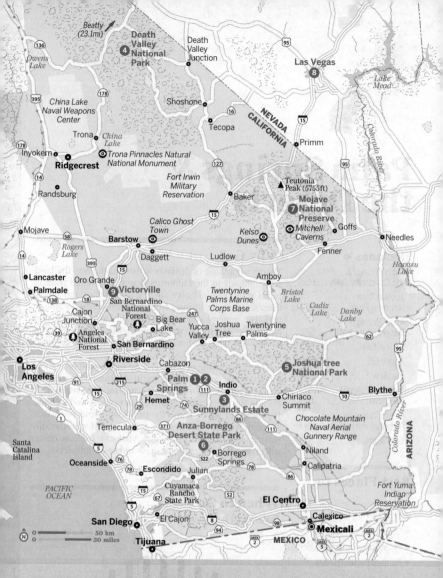

Palm Springs & the Deserts Highlights

1 Ascend through five zones in less than 15 minutes aboard the **Palm Springs Aerial Tramway** (p663).

2 Stretch out next to a kidney-shaped pool in a mid-century modern hotel in **Palm Springs**.

3 Walk in the footsteps of presidents and royalty at **Sunnylands Estate** (p671).

4 Traverse to the lowest point in the Western Hemisphere in **Death Valley National Park** (p693)

5 Navigate smooth boulders in the **Hidden Valley** (p675) at **Joshua Tree National Park**.

6 Scramble around the wind caves of vast **Anza-Borrego Desert State Park** (p682).

7 Hide out at **Hole-in-the-Wall** (p692) in the forgotten **Mojave National Preserve**.

8 Lose yourself (but hopefully not your money) on the **Las Vegas Strip** (p704).

9 Revel in the mythology of the Mother Road at the **California Route 66 Museum** (p689) in **Victorville**.

PALM SPRINGS & THE COACHELLA VALLEY

The Rat Pack is back, baby, or at least its hangout is. In the 1950s and '60s, Palm Springs, some 100 miles east of LA, was the swinging getaway of Sinatra, Elvis and dozens of other stars, partying the night away in fancy modernist homes. Once the Rat Pack packed it in, though, the 300-sq-mile Coachella Valley surrendered to retirees in golf clothing. That is, until the mid-1990s, when a new generation fell in love with the city's retro-chic charms: steel-and-glass bungalows designed by famous architects, boutique hotels with vintage decor and kidney-shaped pools, and hushed piano bars serving the perfect martini. In today's Palm Springs, retirees and snowbirds mix comfortably with hipsters, hikers and a significant gay and lesbian contingent, on weekend getaways from LA or from clear across the globe.

Palm Springs is the principal city of the Coachella Valley, a string of desert towns ranging from ho-hum Cathedral City to glamtastic Palm Desert and America's date capital of Indio, all linked by Hwy 111. North of Palm Springs, Desert Hot Springs is garnering its share of visitors thanks to a slew of chic boutique hotels built on top of those soothing springs.

History

Cahuilla (ka-*wee*-ya) tribespeople have lived in the canyons on the southwest edge of the Coachella Valley for over 1000 years. Early Spanish explorers called the hot springs beneath Palm Springs *agua caliente* (hot water), which later became the name of the local Cahuilla band.

In 1876 the federal government carved the valley into a checkerboard of various interests. The Southern Pacific Railroad received odd-numbered sections, while the Agua Caliente were given even-numbered sections as their reservation. Casinos have made the tribes actually quite wealthy today.

In the town of Indio, about 20 miles southeast of Palm Springs, date palms were imported from French-held Algeria in 1890 and have become the valley's major crop, along with citrus and table grapes.

◎ Sights

In Palm Springs' compact downtown, Hwy 111 runs south as Palm Canyon Dr, paralleled by northbound Indian Canyon Dr. Tahquitz

Canyon Way, dividing addresses north from south, heads east to Palm Springs' airport.

Some of the area's attractions are spread out across the Coachella Valley, also called 'Down Valley', as you head southeast from Palm Springs. Travel on Hwy 111 links the towns, but can be extremely slow thanks to dozens of traffic lights. Depending on where in the valley you're headed, it may be quicker to take I-10.

Notable buildings around town include the **1884 McCallum Adobe**, 1946 international-style **Kaufmann House**, and the E Stewart Williams–designed **Chase Bank**.

◎ Palm Springs

★ **Palm Springs Aerial Tramway** CABLE CAR (☑ 888-515-8726; www.pstramway.com; 1 Tram Way; adult/child $24/17; ☺ from 10am Mon-Fri, 8am Sat & Sun, last tram up 8pm, last tram down 9:45pm daily) North of downtown, this rotating cable car is a highlight of any Palm Springs trip. It climbs nearly 6000 vertical feet through five different vegetation zones, from the Sonoran desert floor to the San Jacinto Mountains, in less than 15 minutes. The 2.5-mile ascent is said to be the temperature equivalent of driving from Mexico to Canada. It's 30°F to 40°F (up to 22°C) cooler as you step out into pine forests at the top, so bring warm clothing.

Snow is not uncommon, even in the spring and fall.

The **Mountain Station** (8516ft), at the top of the tramway, has a bar, restaurant, observation area and theater showing documentary films. Beyond here sprawls the wilderness of **Mt San Jacinto State Park**, which is criss-crossed by hiking trails.

The turnoff for the tram is about 3 miles north of downtown Palm Springs.

Coachella Valley

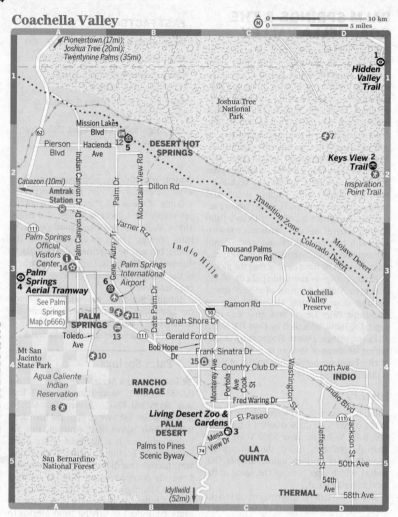

Coachella Valley

★ Palm Springs Art Museum   MUSEUM

(📞 760-322-4800; www.psmuseum.org; 101 Museum Dr; adult/child $12.50/free, 4-8pm Thu free; ⏰10am-5pm Tue-Wed & Fri-Sun, noon-8pm Thu) See the evolution of American painting, sculpture, photography and glass art over the past century. Alongside well-curated temporary exhibitions, the permanent collection is especially strong in modern painting and sculpture, with works by Henry Moore, Ed Ruscha, Mark di Suvero and other heavy hitters. There's also stunning glass art by Dale Chihuly and William Morris and a collection of pre-Columbian figurines.

The museum recently renovated an iconic 1961 mid-century modern bank building into its **Architecture and Design Center** (300 S Palm Canyon Dr), at the southern edge of downtown. Designed to pay tribute to the region's signature style, it opened in late 2014 and is the first free-standing architecture and design museum housed in a modern building.

Agua Caliente Cultural Museum   MUSEUM

(📞 760-323-0151; www.accmuseum.org; 219 S Palm Canyon Dr, Village Green Heritage Center; ⏰10am-5pm Wed-Sat, noon-5pm Sun) **FREE** The largest of the museums in the Village Green Heritage Center, this museum showcases the history and culture of the Agua Caliente band of Cahuilla peoples through permanent and changing exhibits and special events.

Palm Springs Historical Society   MUSEUM

(www.pshistoricalsociety.org; 221 S Palm Canyon Dr; adult/child $1/free; ⏰10am-4pm Wed-Sat, noon-3pm Sun Oct-May) Palm Springs Historical Society delves into a rich past in a small, but classy exhibit of photos and memorabilia in the town's oldest building, the 1884 McCallum Adobe.

Ruddy's General Store   HISTORIC SITE

(www.palmsprings.com/points/heritage/ruddy. html; 221 S Palm Canyon Dr; adult/child 95¢/free; ⏰10am-4pm Thu-Sun Oct-Jun, 10am-4pm Sat & Sun Jul-Sep) This reproduction of a 1930s general store shows amazingly preserved original products from groceries to medicines, beauty aids to clothing and hardware, with period showcases and signage.

Moorten Botanical Gardens   GARDENS

(📞 760-327-6555; www.moortenbotanicalgarden. com; 1701 S Palm Canyon Dr; adult/child $4/2; ⏰10am-4pm Thu-Tue, Fri-Sun only in summer) Chester 'Cactus Slim' Moorten, one of the original Keystone Cops, and his wife Patri-

cia channeled their passion for plants into this compact garden founded in 1938. Today, it's an enchanting symphony of cacti, succulents and other desert flora.

Palm Springs Air Museum   MUSEUM

(📞 760-778-6262; www.palmspringsairmuseum. org; 745 N Gene Autry Trail; adult/child $15/8; ⏰10am-5pm) Adjacent to the airport, this museum has an exceptional collection of WWII aircraft and flight memorabilia, a movie theater and occasional flight demonstrations.

⊙ Around Palm Springs

★ Living Desert Zoo & Gardens   ZOO

(📞 760-346-5694; www.livingdesert.org; 47900 Portola Ave, Palm Desert, off Hwy 111; adult/child $17.25/8.75; ⏰9am-5pm Oct-May, 8am-1:30pm Jun-Sep; 🚻) 🌱 This amazing zoo exhibits a variety of desert plants and animals, alongside exhibits on desert geology and Native American culture. Highlights include a walk-through wildlife hospital and an African-themed village with a fair-trade market and storytelling grove. Camel rides, a spin on the endangered species carousel, and a hop-on, hop-off shuttle cost extra. It's educational fun and worth the 30-minute (15 mile) drive down-valley.

Cabot's Pueblo Museum   MUSEUM

(📞 760-329-7610; www.cabotsmuseum.org; 67616 E Desert Ave, Desert Hot Springs; tour adult/child $11/9; ⏰tours 9:30am, 10:30am, 11:30am, 1:30pm & 2:30pm Tue-Sun Oct-May, 9:30am, 10:30am & 11:30am Wed-Sun Jun-Sep) Cabot Yerxa, a wealthy East Coaster who traded high society for desert solitude, hand built this rambling 1913 adobe from reclaimed and found objects, including telephone poles and wagon parts. Today it's a quirky museum displaying Native American basketry and pottery, as well as a photo collection from Cabot's turn-of-the-century travels to Alaska. Call ahead to confirm tour availability. It's about 13 miles north of central Palm Springs.

🏃 Activities

Tahquitz Canyon   HIKING

(📞 760-416-7044; www.tahquitzcanyon.com; 500 W Mesquite Ave; adult/child $12.50/6; ⏰7:30am-5pm Oct-Jun, Fri-Sun only Jul-Sep) A historic and sacred centerpiece for the Agua Caliente people, this canyon featured in the 1937 Frank Capra movie *Lost Horizon*. In the 1960s it was taken over by teenage squatters and soon

Palm Springs

○ 4

Toucan's Tiki Lounge (0.2mi);
Palm Springs Official
Visitors Center (1mi)

W Vista Chino

Palm Springs
Air Museum
(1.9mi)

🍴 21

N Av Caballeros

Tachevah Dr

N Sunrise Way

N Indian Canyon Dr

N Palm Canyon Dr

41
40

Tamarisk Rd

28
25
12

Granvia
Valmonte

Alejo Rd

32

39

36

37

Amado Rd

Andreas Rd

Palm Springs
Art Museum

1 Museum

Tahquitz Canyon Way

S Av Caballeros

9

19

29

Arenas Rd

8 38
31

S Tahquiz Dr

35 34

2

Baristo Rd

16
23

W Baristo Rd

30

S Patencio Rd

S Cahuilla Rd

6

Calle Encilia

Palm Springs
International ✈
(2.9mi)

S Indian Canyon Dr

3

33

7

Ramon Rd

Belardo
Rd

17
15

18

Grenfall
Rd

Sunny Dunes Dr

San Lorenzo Rd

Mesquite Rd

10

Jensen's Finest
Foods (0.25mi);
Parker Palm
Springs (1.6mi)

22

S Palm Canyon Dr

26

14

5

13

11 24

E Palm Canyon Dr

20

27

PALM SPRINGS & THE DESERTS

Palm Springs

became a point of contention between tribes-people, law-enforcement agencies and squatters in its rock alcoves and caves. After the squatters were booted out, it took the tribe years to haul out trash, erase graffiti and restore the canyon to its natural state.

The visitors center has natural and cultural history exhibits and shows a video about the legend of Tahquitz, a shaman of the Cahuilla people. Rangers lead educational 2-mile, 2½-hour hikes; reserve in advance. Self-guided hiking is available until 3:25pm.

Indian Canyons HIKING
(☑760-323-6018; www.indian-canyons.com; 38520 S Palm Canyon Dr; adult/child $9/5, 90min guided hike $3/2; ☺8am-5pm Oct-Jun, Fri-Sun only Jul-Sep) Streams flowing from the San Jacinto Mountains sustain a rich variety of plants in oases around Palm Springs. Home to Native American communities for hundreds of years and now part of the Agua Caliente Indian Reservation, these canyons, shaded

by fan palms and surrounded by towering cliffs, are a delight for hikers.

Ask for directions to canyons with picnic areas, bird watching, Native American mortar holes, and possibly a bighorn sheep sighting.

From downtown Palm Springs, head south on Palm Canyon Dr (continue straight when the main road turns east) for about 2 miles to the reservation entrance. From here, it's 3 miles up to the Trading Post, which sells hats, maps, water and knickknacks.

Mt San Jacinto State Park HIKING
(☑951-659-2607; www.parks.ca.gov) The wilderness beyond the Palm Springs Aerial Tramway mountain station is criss-crossed by 54 miles of hiking trails, including a nontechnical route up Mt San Jacinto (10,834ft). If you're heading into the backcountry (even just for a few hours of hiking), you must self-register for a wilderness permit at the ranger station.

PALM SPRINGS & THE DESERTS

Winter Adventure Center SKIING, SNOWSHOEING

(general info 760-325-1449; www.pstramway.com/winter-adventure-center.html; snowshoe/skis rental per day $18/21; ⊙open seasonally 10am-4pm Thu-Fri & Mon, from 9am Sat & Sun, last rentals 2:30pm) Outside the Palm Springs Aerial Tramway mountain station, this outfit gets you into the snowy backcountry on snowshoes and cross-country skis, available on a first-come, first-served basis.

Smoke Tree Stables HORSEBACK RIDING

(✆760-327-1372; www.smoketreestables.com; 2500 S Toledo Ave; 1-/2hr guided ride $50/100) Near the Indian Canyons, this outfit arranges trail rides ranging from one-hour outings to all-day treks, for both novice and experienced riders. Reservations required.

Wet 'n' Wild Palm Springs WATER PARK

(✆760-327-0499; www.wetnwildpalmsprings.com; 1500 S Gene Autry Trail; adult/child & senior $37/27; ⊙mid-Mar–mid-Oct) To keep cool on hot days, Wet 'n' Wild boasts a massive wave pool, thunderous water slides and tube rides, and 'dive-in' movies on Fridays in midsummer. Parking costs $14. Call or check the website for current opening hours.

Stand By Golf GOLF

(✆760-321-2665; www.standbygolf.com) Golf is huge here, with more than 100 public, semi-private, private and resort golf courses scattered around the valley. This outfit books tee times for discounted same-day or next-day play at a few dozen local courses.

☞ Tours

Pick up self-guided tour brochures at the visitors center (p674): public art and historic sites (free), modernism ($5) and stars' homes ($5). For guided tours, reservations are a must.

Best of the Best Tours GENERAL INTEREST

(✆760-320-1365; www.thebestofthebesttours.com; 490 S Indian Canyon Dr; tours from $35) Extensive program includes windmill tours and bus tours of celebrity homes.

Desert Adventures 4WD

(✆760-340-2345; www.red-jeep.com; tours $59-135) Four-wheel-drive tours cover a diverse lineup from gay icons of Palm Springs to an eco-tour to canyons of the San Andreas Fault.

Historic Walking Tours WALKING

(✆760-323-8297; www.pshistoricalsociety.org; tours $15) Just what it says: a variety of tours covering architecture, Hollywood stars and more. Organized by the Palm Springs Historical Society.

Palm Springs Modern Tours DESIGN

(✆760-318-6118; www.palmspringsmoderntours.com; tours $75) Three-hour minivan tour of mid-century modern architectural jewels by such masters as Albert Frey, Richard Neutra and John Lautner.

☆ Festivals & Events

During festivals, especially the Coachella Music & Arts Festival, expect hotel rooms to be scarce and costly. Book early.

Every Thursday night locals and visitors alike flock to Palm Canyon Dr in downtown Palm Springs for **Villagefest**, with a farmers market, food stalls, craft vendors and street performers.

Palm Springs International Film Festival FILM

(www.psfilmfest.org) Early January brings a Hollywood-star-studded film festival, showing more than 200 films from over 60 countries. A short-film festival follows in June.

TOP FIVE SPAS

Get your stressed-out self to these pampering shrines to work out the kinks and turn your body into a glowing lump of tranquility. Reservations are de rigueur.

Estrella Spa at Viceroy Palm Springs (p670) Stylish boutique-hotel spa for massages in poolside cabanas.

Feel Good Spa at Ace Hotel & Swim Club (p669) At Palm Springs' newest hipster spa you can get a treatment inside a yurt.

Spa Resort Casino (✆760-778-1772; www.sparesortcasino.com; 100 N Indian Canyon Dr) Try a five-step 'taking of the waters' course through the valley's original hot springs.

Spa Terre at Riviera Palm Springs (p670) The ultimate in swanky pampering, with Watsu pool and exotic spa rituals.

Palm Springs Yacht Club (p670) This newly renovated spa is again the ritzy, glitzy fave of celebs and society ladies.

Modernism Week CULTURAL
(www.modernismweek.com) Ten-day celebration of all things mid-century modern: architecture and home tours, films, lectures, design show and lots of parties. Held in mid-February.

Coachella Music & Arts Festival MUSIC
(www.coachella.com; 1-/3-day pass around $100/300) Held at Indio's Empire Polo Club over two weekends in April, this is one of the hottest indie-music festivals of its kind. Get tickets early or forget about it.

Stagecoach Festival MUSIC
(www.stagecoachfestival.com; 1-/3-day pass from $100/250) The weekend after Coachella, also held at Indio's Empire Polo Club, this festival celebrates new and established country-music artists.

Restaurant Week FOOD
(www.palmspringsrestaurantweek.com) Discounted prix-fixe menus at top restaurants throughout the valley. Held in June.

🛏 Sleeping

Palm Springs and the Coachella Valley offer an astonishing variety of lodging options, including fine vintage-flair boutique hotels, full-on luxury resorts, and chain motels. We quote high-season (November to April) rack rates; summer savings can be significant. Campers should head to Joshua Tree National Park or Mt San Jacinto State Park.

🛏 Palm Springs

Caliente Tropics MOTEL $
(📞 760-327-1391, 800-658-6034; www.caliente-tropics.com; 411 E Palm Canyon Dr; r weekday/weekend from $54/109; P🅿❄🛜🏊) Elvis once frolicked poolside at this premier budget pick, a nicely kept 1964 tiki-style motor lodge. Drift off to dreamland on quality mattresses in rooms that are spacious and dressed in warm colors.

★ Orbit In BOUTIQUE HOTEL $$
(📞 760-323-3585, 877-966-7248; www.orbitin.com; 562 W Arenas Rd; r incl breakfast from $149; P❄🛜🏊) Swing back to the '50s – pinkie raised and all – during the 'Orbitini' happy hour at this fabulously retro property, with high-end mid-century modern furniture (Eames, Noguchi et al) in rooms set around a quiet saline pool with a Jacuzzi and fire pit. The long list of freebies includes bike rentals and daytime sodas and snacks.

ELVIS' LOVE NEST

One of the most spectacular mid-century modern houses in Palm Springs was designed in the early 1960s by local developer Robert Alexander for his wife, Helene. It consists of four circular rooms built on three levels, accented with glass and stone. *Look* magazine called it the 'House of Tomorrow' and featured it in an eight-page spread, making the Alexanders national celebrities. Sadly the entire family died in a plane crash in 1965, but the estate gained even greater fame a year later when Elvis Presley moved in. On May 1, 1967 he carried his new bride Priscilla over the threshold to begin their honeymoon. The **Elvis Honeymoon Hideaway** (📞 760-322-1192; www.elvis-honeymoon.com; 1350 Ladera Circle; per person $30; ⊙ tours 1pm & 3:30pm daily or by appointment) has been authentically restored and can be visited on daily tours (reservations recommended).

★ Ace Hotel & Swim Club HOTEL $$
(📞 760-325-9900; www.acehotel.com/palmsprings; 701 E Palm Canyon Dr; r from $200; P❄@🛜🏊🐕) Palm Springs goes Hollywood – with all the sass, but sans the attitude – at this former Howard Johnson motel turned hipster hangout. Rooms (many with patio) sport a glorified tent-cabin look and are crammed with lifestyle essentials (big flat-screen TVs, MP3 plugs). Happening pool scene and the **Feel Good Spa** (📞 760-329-8791; www.acehotel.com/palmsprings/spa; 701 E Palm Canyon Dr), onsite restaurant and bar to boot.

Saguaro HOTEL $$
(📞 760-323-1711, 877-808-2439; www.thesaguaro.com; 1800 E Palm Canyon Dr; r from $159; P❄@🛜🏊🐕) The hot colors of a desert blooming with wildflowers animate this newly updated mid-century hotel. Three stories of rooms look over a generous pool deck. The main restaurant, Tinto, serves tapas and Spanish-inspired cooking by Iron Chef Jose Garces, and his El Jefe bar does great tacos and tequilas.

Del Marcos Hotel BOUTIQUE HOTEL $$
(📞 760-325-6902, 800-676-1214; www.delmarcoshotel.com; 225 W Baristo Rd; r incl breakfast $139-269; ❄🛜🏊🐕) At this 1947 gem, designed by William F Cody, groovy lobby tunes usher

you to a saltwater pool and ineffably chic rooms. And it's steps from the shops and eats of downtown Palm Springs' village.

Alcazar BOUTIQUE HOTEL **$$**
(760-318-9850; www.alcazarpalmsprings.com; 622 N Palm Canyon Dr; r incl breakfast from $149; P ❄ @ ≈ ☒) At the edge of Uptown, a fashionable (but not party) crowd makes new friends poolside before retiring to one of the 34 rooms around a pool. Some have Jacuzzi tubs, patios, fireplaces or all three. Gleaming white floors lead to equally minimalist walls and bed linens. Look for loaner bikes and pastries from Cheeky's (p671).

★ **Riviera Palm Springs** LUXURY HOTEL **$$$**
(760-327-8311; www.psriviera.com; 1600 Indian Canyon Dr; r $240-260, ste $290-540; P ⊖ ❄ @ ≈ ☒ 🐾) This Rat Pack playground now sparkles brighter than ever. Expect the full range of fancy mod-cons amid luscious gardens, three amoeba-shaped pools, 17 (count 'em) fire pits, the **Spa Terre** (760-778-6690; www.psriviera.com; 1600 N Indian Canyon Dr), and '60s accents such as shag rugs, classy-campy crystal chandeliers and Warhol art. **Circa 59** indoor-outdoor restaurant and lounge makes you and your sweetie look good.

It's about a mile to downtown Palm Springs; shuttle service available.

★ **Parker Palm Springs** RESORT **$$$**
(760-770-5000; www.theparkerpalmsprings.com; 4200 E Palm Canyon Dr; r from $300; P ❄ @ ≈ ☒ 🐾) Featured in the Bravo TV series *Welcome to the Parker*, this posh resort highlights whimsical decor by Jonathan Adler. Drop by for a cocktail at Mister Parker's or a posh brunch at Norma's five-star coffee shop. The grounds boast hammocks, *boules* (lawn bowling) and a fabulous spa. The $30 resort charge covers parking, wi-fi, and access to the **Palm Springs Yacht Club spa** (760-770-5000; www.theparkerpalmsprings.com/spa; Parker Palm Springs, 4200 E Palm Canyon Dr).

Viceroy BOUTIQUE HOTEL **$$$**
(760-320-4117; www.viceroypalmsprings.com; 415 S Belardo Rd; r from $300; ❄ ≈ ☒) Wear a Pucci dress and blend right in at *Top Design*'s Kelly Wearstler's 1960s-chic miniresort done up in black, white and lemon-yellow (think Austin Powers meets Givenchy). There's the **Estrella** (760-320-4117; www.viceroypalmsprings.com; 415 S Belardo Rd) spa, a fab but pricey Cal-French restaurant for a white-linen luncheon or swanky supper, and free town-cruiser bikes to borrow.

Desert Hot Springs

★ **El Morocco Inn & Spa** BOUTIQUE HOTEL **$$**
(888-288-9905, 760-288-2527; www.elmoroccoinn.com; 66814 4th St, Desert Hot Springs; r incl breakfast $179-219; ❄ ≈ ☒) Heed the call of the casbah at this drop-dead gorgeous hideaway where the scene is set for romance. Twelve exotically furnished rooms wrap around a pool deck where your enthusiastic host serves free 'Moroccotinis' during happy hour. Other perks: on-site spa, huge DVD library and delicious homemade mint iced tea.

Spring BOUTIQUE HOTEL **$$**
(760-251-6700; www.the-spring.com; 12699 Reposo Way; r incl breakfast $179-279; P ❄ ≈ ☒) Splash out in this humble 1950s motel that's morphed into a chic, whisper-quiet spa retreat where natural hot mineral water feeds three pools. The 13 rooms are minimalist in design but not in amenities (rich duvets, fluffy robes, small kitchens). Achieve a state of bliss while enjoying a treatment or simply calming valley and mountain views.

Eating

Tyler's Burgers BURGERS **$**
(www.tylersburgers.com; 149 S Indian Canyon Dr; dishes $3-9; ⌚11am-4pm Mon-Sat; 👪) This tiny shack in the center of downtown Palm Springs serves the best burgers in town, bar none. Waits are practically inevitable, which is presumably why there's an amazingly well-stocked magazine rack. Cash only.

WHAT THE...?

West of Palm Springs, you may do a double take when you see the **World's Biggest Dinosaurs** (951-922-0076; www.cabazondinosaurs.com; 50770 Seminole Dr, Cabazon; adult/child $8/7; ⌚10am-5:30pm Mon-Fri, 10am-6:30pm Sat & Sun). Claude K Bell, a sculptor for Knott's Berry Farm, spent over a decade crafting these concrete behemoths, now owned by Christian creationists who contend that God created the original dinosaurs in one day, along with the other animals. In the gift shop, alongside the sort of dino-swag you might find at science museums, you can read about the alleged hoaxes and fallacies of evolution and Darwinism.

SUNNY LIVING AT SUNNYLANDS

Sunnylands (☏760-328-2829; www.sunnylands.org; 37977 Bob Hope Dr, Rancho Mirage; admission free, house tour $35; ⊙9am-4pm Thu-Sun, closed Jul & Aug) is the retro-glam, mid-century modern estate of Walter and Leonore Annenberg, one of America's 'first families'. Walter (1908–2002) was an American publisher, ambassador and philanthropist, and 'Lee' (1918–2009) was Chief of Protocol under President Ronald Reagan. At their winter estate in Rancho Mirage, designed by A Quincy Jones and surrounded by grounds incorporating a nine-hole golf course, the Annenbergs entertained seven US presidents, royalty, and Hollywood and international celebrities. These days Sunnylands is nicknamed the 'West Coast Camp David' for summits between President Obama and world leaders including Chinese president Xi Jinping and King Abdullah of Jordan.

Now the rest of us can visit too. A new visitor center and museum screen a film and show changing exhibits about the estate. Just beyond is a magnificent desert garden. Reserve as early as possible for tours of the stunning house with its art collection, architecture and furniture. Tickets go on sale online on the 1st and 15th of each month for the period beginning two weeks onward.

Native Foods
VEGAN $

(☏760-416-0070; www.nativefoods.com; Smoke Tree Village, 1775 E Palm Canyon Dr; mains $8-11; ⊙11am-9:30pm Mon-Sat; ⚙️♿) Vegan cooking guru Tanya Petrovna does an amazing job at injecting complex flavors into meat and dairy substitutes. The creative sandwiches, southwestern salads, sizzling-hot rice bowls, and tasty pizzas and burgers feed both body and soul.

★Cheeky's
CALIFORNIAN $$

(☏760-327-7595; www.cheekysps.com; 622 N Palm Canyon Dr; mains $8-13; ⊙8am-2pm Wed-Mon, last seating 1:30pm) 🌿 Waits can be long and service only so-so, but the farm-to-table menu dazzles with witty inventiveness. Dishes change weekly, but custardy scrambled eggs, arugula pesto frittata and bacon bar 'flights' keep making appearances.

El Mirasol
MEXICAN $$

(☏760-323-0721; www.elmirasolrestaurants.com; 140 E Palm Canyon Dr; mains $10-19; ⊙11am-10pm) There are showier Mexican places around town, but everyone ends up back at El Mirasol, with its earthy decor, generous margaritas and snappy dishes. The chicken in mole or in *pipián* sauce (made from ground pumpkin seeds and chilis) are menu stars.

King's Highway
AMERICAN $$

(☏760-325-9900; www.acehotel.com; Ace Hotel & Swim Club, 701 E Palm Canyon Dr; mains $8-30; ⊙7am-11pm Sun-Thu, to 3am Fri & Sat; 🛜) A fine case of creative recycling, this former Denny's is now a diner for the 21st century where the tagliatelle is handmade, the sea bass wild-caught, the beef grass-fed, the veg-

etables organic and the cheeses artisanal. Great breakfast, too.

Wang's in the Desert
CHINESE $$

(☏760-325-9264; www.wangsinthedesert.com; 424 S Indian Canyon Dr; mains $12-20; ⊙5-9:30pm Sun-Thu, to 10:30 Fri & Sat) This mood-lit local fave with indoor koi pond delivers creatively crafted Chinese classics and has a busy daily happy hour – it's a huge gay scene on Fridays.

Appetito
ITALIAN, DELI $$

(☏760-327-1929; www.appetitodeli.com; 1700 S Camino Real; mains $8-20; ⊙11am-10pm Sun-Thu, until 11pm Fri & Sat) This newcomer dishes up paninis such as porchetta, broccoli rabe, provolone and chili aioli; pastas like pillowy ricotta gnocchi with kale pesto, walnuts and lemon; and tiramisu profiteroles, to spirited crowds hanging out in the tall, minimalist room or on the enclosed terrace.

★Trio
CALIFORNIAN $$$

(☏760-864-8746; www.triopalmsprings.com; 707 N Palm Canyon Dr; mains lunch $11-26, dinner $14-29; ⊙11am-10pm Sun-Thu, until 11pm Fri & Sat) The winning formula in this '60s modernist space: updated American comfort food (awesome Yankee pot roast!), eye-catching artwork and picture windows. The $19 prix-fixe three-course dinner (served until 6pm) is a steal.

🍷 Drinking & Nightlife

Many restaurants have hugely popular happy hours, and there are happening hotel bars at the Parker, Riviera, Ace and Saguaro.

GAY & LESBIAN PALM SPRINGS

Nicknamed 'Provincetown in the Desert' and 'Key West of the West,' Palm Springs is one of America's great gay destinations.

In early April, **Dinah Shore Weekend** (www.thedinah.com) hosts lesbian comedy, pool parties, mixers and more during the Kraft Nabisco (ex-Dinah Shore) LPGA golf tournament. Over Easter weekend, the **White Party** (www.jeffreysanker.com) is one of the USA's biggest gay dance events. Show up in early November for **Palm Springs Pride** (www.pspride.org).

Accommodations

Most men's hotels are concentrated in the Warm Sands neighborhood, just southeast of downtown Palm Springs, and are clothing-optional. Lesbian resorts (fewer in number) are scattered throughout town. As with other lodging in the desert, rates fall steeply in summer (roughly mid-June to mid-September) and shoulder seasons.

Hacienda at Warm Sands (☎760-327-8111; www.thehacienda.com; 586 Warm Sands Dr; r incl breakfast & lunch $250-400; P🅿️❄️@🛜🏊) With Indonesian teak and bamboo furnishings, the Hacienda raises the bar for luxury gay men's lodging and has genial innkeepers who are never intrusive but always available.

Inndulge (☎760 327 1408, 800 833 5675; www.inndulge.com; 601 Grenfall Rd; r incl breakfast from $195; P❄️@🛜) Don't let the randy name fool you; this is a solid midrange choice for gay men. It gets plenty of repeat customers for its 1950s shell and variety of up-to-date rooms and suites (some have kitchens). The nightly social hour, pool and hot tub encourage mingling.

Century Palm Springs (☎760-323-9966; www.centurypalmsprings.com; 598 Grenfall Rd; r incl breakfast $180-300; P❄️@🛜🏊🐾) At the small gay-oriented Century, designed by William Alexander in 1955, rooms are hued in cheerful orange and olive and are furnished with plush bedding and pieces by Starck, Eames and Noguchi. Soak up cocktails and serene mountain views from the minimalist pool deck.

Casitas Laquita (☎760-416-9999; www.casitaslaquita.com; 450 E Palm Canyon Dr; r $155-195; P❄️🛜🏊) This newly made-over, southwest-flavored compound for lesbians has rooms and suites with kitchens; some even have kiva-style fireplaces. Afternoon tapas and drinks are complimentary, as is continental breakfast.

Queen of Hearts (☎760-322-5793; www.queenofheartsps.com; 435 Avenida Olancha; r incl breakfast $120-145; P❄️🛜🏊🐾) Palm Springs' original lesbian hotel counts many regulars among its guests, thanks, in large part, to its super-friendly owner, Michelle. It's in a quiet neighborhood with nine rooms encircling a swimming pool and patios framed by fruit trees.

Drinking & Entertainment

The city's main 'gayborhood' is the block of Arenas Rd east of S Indian Canyon Dr, with about a dozen gay-themed bars, cafes and shops. Other venues are scattered throughout town. The bars at Azul (p673) and Wang's in the Desert (p671) are also buzzy stops on the gay party circuit.

Hunters (www.huntersnightclubs.com; 302 E Arenas Rd; ⏰10am-2am) Wildly diverse male clientele, lots of TV screens, a cruisy dance scene and pool tables.

Streetbar (www.psstreetbar.com; 224 E Arenas Rd) Congenial mix of locals, long-time visitors and occasional drag performers. There's a cozy streetside patio for watching the crowds saunter by.

Toucan's Tiki Lounge (www.toucanstikilounge.com; 2100 N Palm Canyon Dr; ⏰noon-2am) North of town, this locals' hangout has something for everyone: tropical froufrou, trivia, karaoke, drag revues, smoking patio and dance floor. Packed on weekends.

Birba BAR
(www.birbaps.com; 622 N Palm Canyon Dr; ⏰5-11pm Sun & Wed-Thu, to midnight Fri & Sat) It's cocktails and pizza at this fabulous indoor-outdoor space where floor-to-ceiling sliding glass doors separate the long marble bar from a hedge-fringed patio with sunken fire pits.

Shanghai Red's   BAR
(www.fishermans.com; 235 S Indian Canyon Dr; ⊙4pm-late Mon-Sat, from noon Sun) This bar has a busy courtyard, an inter-generational crowd and live blues on Friday and Saturday nights.

Melvyn's   BAR
(www.inglesideinn.com; Ingleside Inn, 200 W Ramon Rd) Join the Bentley pack for stiff martinis and quiet jazz at this former Sinatra haunt at the Ingleside Inn. Sunday afternoon jazz is a long-standing tradition. Shine your shoes.

Koffi   COFFEE SHOP
(www.kofficoffee.com; 515 N Palm Canyon Dr; snacks & drinks $3-6; ⊙5:30am-7pm; 🛜) Tucked among the art galleries on N Palm Canyon Dr, this coolly minimalist, indie java bar serves strong organic coffee. There's a second Palm Springs location at 1700 S Camino Real, near the Ace Hotel.

Village Pub   PUB
(www.palmspringsvillagepub.com; 266 S Palm Canyon Dr; 🛜) This casual dive is perfect for kicking back with your posse over beers, darts, loud music and the occasional live band.

☆ Entertainment

Azul   MUSIC
(☑760-325-5533; www.azultapaslounge.com; 369 N Palm Canyon Dr; mains $11-24, Judy Show incl dinner $35; ⊙11am-late) Popular with gays and their friends, the Azul restaurant has almost nightly entertainment in its piano bar, plus the wickedly funny **Judy Show** (www.thejudyshow.com) on Sundays, starring impersonator Michael Holmes as Judy Garland, Mae West and other campy legends of yore.

Annenberg Theater   PERFORMING ARTS
(☑760-325-4490; www.psmuseum.org; 101 Museum Dr) This intimate theater at the Palm Springs Art Museum presents an eclectic schedule of films, lectures, theater, ballet and music performances.

Spa Resort Casino   CASINO
(www.sparesortcasino.com; 401 E Amado Rd; ⊙24hr) There's this perfectly legal Native American–owned den of vice right in the heart of downtown Palm Springs, as well as other gambling halls off I-10. Vegas they ain't.

🛍 Shopping

Central Palm Springs has two main shopping districts along N Palm Canyon Dr, divided by Alejo Rd. North of Alejo, Uptown is more for art and design(-inspired) shops, while Downtown (south of Alejo) is ground zero for souvenirs and fun clothing. Given the city's demographic, vintage clothing stores flourish here like few other places. West of town is a destination outlet mall.

Trina Turk   CLOTHING, HOMEWARES
(☑760-416-2856; www.trinaturk.com; 891 N Palm Canyon Dr; ⊙10am-5pm Mon-Fri, to 6pm Sat, noon-5pm Sun) Trina makes form-flattering 'California-chic' fashions that are beautifully presented amid shag carpeting and floral foil wallpaper in her original boutique in a 1960s Albert Frey building. Her Mr Turk menswear line is also available here.

Modern Way   FURNITURE
(www.psmodernway.com; 745 N Palm Canyon Dr) The oldest and most stylin' consignment shop for collectors of modern furniture.

Angel View   THRIFT SHOP
(☑760-320-1733; www.angelview.org; 462 N Indian Canyon Dr; ⊙9am-6pm Mon-Sat, 10am-5pm Sun) At this well-established thrift store, today's hipsters can shop for clothes and accessories as cool as when they were first worn a generation or two ago.

Collectors Corner   VINTAGE
(71280 Hwy 111, Rancho Mirage; ⊙9:30am-4:15pm Mon-Sat) It's a trek from central Palm Springs (about 12 miles), but this two-story shop is oh so worth it for large collections of antiques, vintage clothing, jewelry and furniture.

El Paseo   MALL
(www.elpaseo.com; El Paseo, Palm Desert) For serious shopping, head to Palm Desert where the elegant El Paseo shopping strip has been dubbed the 'Rodeo Drive of the Desert'. It's one block south of and parallel to Hwy 111, 14 miles southeast of Palm Springs.

Desert Hills Premium Outlets   MALL
(www.premiumoutlets.com; 48400 Seminole Dr, Cabazon; ⊙10am-8pm Sun-Thu, to 9pm Fri, 9am-9pm Sat) Bargain hunters, make a beeline for dozens of outlet stores: Gap to Gucci, Polo to Prada, Off 5th to Barneys New York. Wear comfortable shoes – this mall is huge! It's off I-10 (exit at Fields Rd), 20 minutes west of Palm Springs. If you've got energy to spare, the smaller Cabazon Outlets mall is next door.

ℹ Information

High season is October to April, but Palm Springs (elevation 487ft) stays reasonably busy even in summer, when hotel rates drop and temperatures spike above 100°F (37°C). Between June and August many businesses keep shorter hours or even close, so call ahead to check.

Palm Springs Official Visitors Center (☑760-778-8418; www.visitpalmsprings.com; 2901 N Palm Canyon Dr; ⊙9am-5pm) Well-stocked and well-staffed visitors center 3 miles north of downtown, in a 1965 Albert Frey–designed gas station at the tramway turnoff.

Desert Regional Medical Center (☑760-323-6511; www.desertregional.com; 1150 N Indian Canyon Dr; ⊙24hr) Emergency room and physician referral.

Palm Springs Police (☑760-323-8116) For nonemergency situations. In case of emergency, dial 911.

Post Office (333 E Amado Rd; ⊙8am-5pm Mon-Fri, 9am-3pm Sat)

Palm Springs Library (www.palmspringsca.gov; 300 S Sunrise Way; ⊙10am-5pm Wed-Sat, to 7pm Tue; ☎) Free wi-fi and internet terminals.

❶ Getting There & Away

AIR

A 10-minute drive northeast of downtown, Palm Springs International Airport (p761) is served year-round by Alaska, Allegiant, American, Delta, Horizon, United, US Airways and Westjet, and seasonally by Frontier, Sun Country and Virgin America.

BUS

Greyhound (www.greyhound.com) operates a few daily buses to/from LA ($28, three hours). The terminus is at Palm Springs train station.

CAR & MOTORCYCLE

From LA, the trip to Palm Springs and the Coachella Valley takes about two to three hours via I-10 with no traffic. With traffic, it's anybody's guess.

TRAIN

Amtrak (www.amtrak.com) serves the unstaffed and kinda-creepy – it's deserted and in the middle of nowhere – North Palm Springs station, 5 miles north of downtown Palm Springs. Trains run to/from LA ($41, 2½ hours) a few days per week and are often late.

❶ Getting Around

TO/FROM THE AIRPORT

Many downtown Palm Springs hotels provide free airport transfers. Otherwise, a taxi to downtown Palm Springs costs about $12 to $15. If you're staying in another Coachella Valley town, rides on shared shuttle vans, such as **Skycap Shuttle** (☑760-272-5988; www.skycapshuttle.com), will likely be more economical. Fares de-

pend on distance and reservations are advised. SunLine bus 24 stops by the airport and goes most of (though, frustratingly, not all of) the way to downtown Palm Springs.

BICYCLE

Central Palm Springs is pancake-flat, and more bike lanes are being built all the time. Many hotels have loaner bicycles.

Bike Palm Springs (☑760-832-8912; bikepsrentals.com; 194 S Indian Canyon Dr; standard/kids/electric/tandem bikes half-day from $20/12/30/40, full day $25/15/50/50) Great for tooling around central Palm Springs.

Funseekers (☑760-340-3861; www.palmdesertbikerentals.com; 73-865 Hwy 111, Palm Desert; bicycles per 24hr/3 day/week from $25/50/65, delivery & pick up $30) Outside of central Palm Springs, this outlet rents and sells bikes, mopeds and Segways for city and nature excursions.

BUS

Alternative-fuel–powered **SunLine** (www.sunline.org; fare/day pass $1/3; ⊙ around 5am-10pm) buses travel around the valley, albeit slowly. Bus 111 links Palm Springs with Palm Desert (one hour) and Indio (1½ hours) via Hwy 111. Buses have air-con, wheelchair lifts and a bicycle rack. Cash only (bring exact change).

CAR & MOTORCYCLE

Though you can walk to most sights in downtown Palm Springs, you'll need a car to get around the valley. Major rental-car companies have airport desks. **Scoot Palm Springs** (☑760-413-2883; www.scootpalmsprings.com; 701 East Palm Canyon Dr; half day scooter rentals from $65) rents scooters. For motorcycles try **Eaglerider** (☑877-736-8243; www.eaglerider.com), whose rates start at $99 per day.

JOSHUA TREE NATIONAL PARK

Taking a page from a Dr Seuss book, the whimsical Joshua trees (actually tree-sized yuccas) welcome visitors to this 794,000-acre **park** (☑760-367-5500; www.nps.gov/jotr; 7-day entry per car $15) at the convergence of the Colorado and Mojave Deserts. It was Mormon settlers who named the trees because the branches stretching up toward heaven reminded them of the Biblical prophet Joshua pointing the way to the promised land.

Rock climbers know 'JT' as the best place to climb in California, but kids and the young at heart also welcome the chance to scramble up, down and around the giant boulders. Hikers seek out hidden, shady, desert-fan-palm oases fed by natural springs and small streams, while mountain bikers are hypnotized by the desert vistas.

In springtime, the Joshua trees send up a huge single cream-colored flower, and the octopus-like tentacles of the ocotillo cactus shoot out crimson flowers. The mystical quality of this stark, boulder-strewn landscape has inspired many artists, most famously the band U2, who named their 1987 album *The Joshua Tree*.

Unless you plan on day-tripping from Palm Springs, base yourself in the desert communities linked by Twentynine Palms Hwy (Hwy 62) along the park's northern perimeter.

◎ Sights & Activities

Joshua Tree has three park entrances. Access the west entrance from the town of Joshua Tree, the north entrance from Twentynine Palms and the south entrance from I-10. The park's northern half harbors most of the attractions, including all of the Joshua trees.

★ **Hidden Valley Trail** NATURAL LANDSCAPE
Some 8 miles south of the West Entrance, this whimsically dramatic cluster of rocks is a rock climbers' mecca, but just about anyone can enjoy a clamber on the giant boul-

ders. An easy 1-mile trail loops through it and back to the parking lot and picnic area.

★ **Keys View Trail** LOOKOUT
From Park Blvd, it's an easy 20-minute drive up to Keys View (5185ft), where breathtaking views take in the entire Coachella Valley and extend as far as the Salton Sea and – on a good day – Mexico. Looming in front of you are Mt San Jacinto (10,834ft) and Mt San Gorgonio (11,500ft), two of Southern California's highest peaks, while down below you can spot a section of the San Andreas Fault.

Desert Queen Ranch HISTORIC SITE
(☑ reservations 760-367-5555; tour adult/child $5/2.50; ☉ tours 10am & 1pm daily year-round, 7pm Tue & Thu-Sat Oct-May) Anyone interested in local history and lore should take the 90-minute guided tour of this ranch that's also known as Keys Ranch after its builder, Russian immigrant William Keys. He built a homestead here on 160 acres in 1917 and over the next 60 years turned it into a full working ranch, school, store and workshop. The buildings stand much as they did when Keys died in 1969.

Tour reservations are highly recommended; remaining tickets may be available one day in advance at the Cottonwood, Joshua Tree and Oasis park visitors centers.

The ranch is about 2 miles northeast of Hidden Valley Campground, up a dirt road.

THE PERFECT DATE

The Coachella Valley is the ideal place to find the date of your dreams – the kind that grows on trees, that is. Some 90% of US date production happens here, with dozens of permutations of shape, size and juiciness, and species with exotic-sounding names such as halawy, deglet noor and golden zahidi.

Date orchards let you sample different varieties for free, an act of shameless but delicious self-promotion. Another signature taste is the date shake: crushed dates mixed into a vanilla milkshake (about $4). They're much richer than they look!

Shields Date Gardens (www.shieldsdategarden.com; 80-225 Hwy 111, Indio; ☉9am-5pm) In business since 1924 this is where you can watch *The Romance and Sex Life of the Date*, with the chirpy feel of a 1950s educational film.

Oasis Date Gardens (www.oasisdate.com; 59-111 Grapefruit Blvd, Thermal; ☉9am-4pm) En route to the Salton Sea, this certified-organic date garden is handy for picking up gift boxes and yummy date shakes.

Hadley Fruit Orchards (☑ 888-854-5655; www.hadleyfruitorchards.com; 48980 Seminole Dr, Cabazon; ☉9am-7pm Mon-Thu, 8am-8pm Fri-Sun) This landmark claims to have invented trail mix and makes a good grab-and-go stop on your way to or from LA.

National Date Festival (www.datefest.org; Riverside County Fairgrounds, 82-503 Hwy 111, Indio; adult/child $8/6; ⊞) For old-fashioned carnival fun, come in February for outrageous camel and ostrich races. From I-10, exit at Monroe St.

Joshua Tree National Park

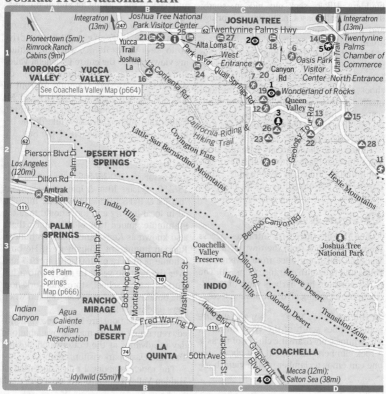

Joshua Tree National Park

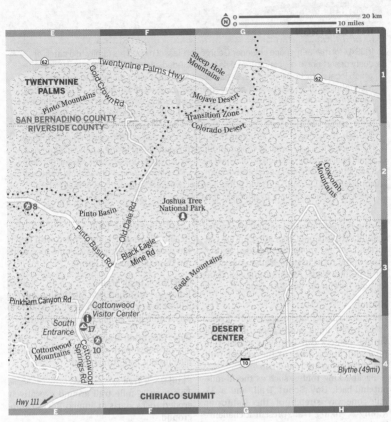

Drive as far as the locked gate where your guide will meet you.

Oasis of Mara
OASIS

Behind the Oasis visitors center in Twentynine Palms, this natural oasis encompasses the original 29 palm trees for which the town is named. They were planted by members of the Serrano tribe, who named this 'the place of little springs and much grass.' The Pinto Mountain Fault, a small branch of the San Andreas, runs through the oasis, as does a 0.5-mile, wheelchair-accessible nature trail with labeled desert plants.

Geology Tour Road
DRIVING TOUR

East of Hidden Valley, travelers with 4WD vehicles or mountain bikes can take this 18-mile field trip into and around Pleasant Valley, where the forces of erosion, earthquakes and ancient volcanoes have played out in stunning splendor. Before setting out, pick up a self-guided tour brochure and an up-

date on road conditions at any park visitors center.

Covington Flats
DRIVING TOUR

Joshua trees grow throughout the northern section of the park, including right along Park Blvd, but some of the biggest trees are found in this area accessed via La Contenta Rd, which runs south off Hwy 62 between the towns of Yucca Valley and Joshua Tree. For photogenic views, follow the dirt road 3.8 miles up Eureka Peak (5516ft) from the picnic area.

Pinto Basin Road
DRIVING TOUR

To see the natural transition from the high Mojave Desert to the low Colorado Desert, wind down to Cottonwood Spring, a 30-mile drive from Hidden Valley. Stop at **Cholla Cactus Garden**, where a 0.25-mile loop leads around waving ocotillo plants and jumping 'teddy bear' cholla. Near the Cottonwood visitors center, **Cottonwood**

INTEGRATRON

In 1947 former aerospace engineer George van Tassel moved his family to a patch of dusty desert north of Joshua Tree. The land included a free-standing boulder, beneath which local desert rat Frank Critzer had excavated a series of rooms. Van Tassel started meditating in these rooms and, as the story goes, was visited in August 1953 by a flying saucer from Venus. The aliens invited him aboard and taught him the technique for rejuvenating living cells. Van Tassel used his otherworldly knowledge to build the **Integratron** (☎ 760-364-3126; www.integratron.com; 2477 Belfield Boulevard, Landers; sound baths $20-80), a wooden domed structure that he variously called a time machine, an antigravity device and a rejuvenation chamber. Judge for yourself by taking a personal tour or a sonic healing bath, in which crystal bowls are struck under the acoustically perfect dome. Check the website for special events such as UFO symposiums. Public sound baths are conducted at 11:45am, 1pm and 2:15pm on two weekends a month (the website has dates). All other visits are by appointment only.

Spring is an oasis with a natural spring that Cahuilla tribespeople depended on for centuries. Look for *morteros,* rounded depressions in the rocks used by Native Americans for grinding seeds. Miners came searching for gold here in the late 19th century.

Hiking

Leave the car behind to appreciate Joshua Tree's trippy lunar landscapes. Staff at the visitors centers can help you match your time and fitness level to the perfect trail. Distances given are round-trip.

Backpacking routes, such as the 16-mile, out-and-back **Boy Scout Trail**, and a 35-mile one-way stretch of the **California Riding & Hiking Trail**, present a challenge because of the need to carry gallons of water per person per day. No open fires are allowed in the park, so you'll also have to bring a camping stove and fuel. Overnight backcountry hikers must register (to aid in census-taking, fire safety and rescue efforts) at one of 13 backcountry boards located at trailhead parking lots throughout the park. Unregistered vehicles left overnight may be cited or towed.

49 Palms Oasis Trail HIKING
Escape the crowds on this 3-mile, up-and-down trail starting near **Indian Cove**.

Barker Dam Trail HIKING
A 1.1-mile loop that passes a little lake and a rock incised with Native American petroglyphs; starts at Barker Dam parking lot.

Lost Horse Mine Trail HIKING
A strenuous 4-mile climb that visits the remains of an authentic Old West silver and gold mine, in operation until 1931.

Lost Palms Oasis Trail HIKING
Reach this remote canyon filled with desert fan palms on a fairly flat 7.2-mile hike starting from Cottonwood Spring.

Mastodon Peak Trail HIKING
Enjoy views of the Eagle Mountains and the Salton Sea from an elevation of 3371ft on this 3-mile hike from Cottonwood Spring.

Ryan Mountain Trail HIKING
For bird's-eye park views, tackle the 3-mile hike up this 5458ft-high peak.

Skull Rock Trail HIKING
This easy 1.7-mile trail around evocatively eroded rocks starts at Jumbo Rocks campground.

Cycling

Popular riding routes include challenging **Pinkham Canyon Rd**, starting from the Cottonwood visitors center, and the long-distance **Black Eagle Mine Rd**, which starts 6.5 miles further north. **Queen Valley** has a gentler set of trails with bike racks found along the way, so people can lock up their bikes and go hiking, but it's busy with cars, as is the bumpy, sandy and steep Geology Tour Rd (p677). There's a wide-open network of dirt roads at Covington Flats (p677).

Cycling is only permitted on paved and dirt public roads; bikes are not allowed on hiking trails.

Rock Climbing

JT's rocks are famous for their rough, high-friction surfaces; from boulders to cracks to multipitch faces, there are more than 8000 established routes. Some of the most popular climbs are in the Hidden Valley area.

Shops catering to climbers with quality gear, advice and tours include **Joshua Tree Outfitters** (☑760-366-1848; www.joshuatreeoutfitters.com; 61707 Hwy 62), **Nomad Ventures** (☑760-366-4684; www.nomadventures.com; 61795 Twentynine Palms Hwy, Joshua Tree; ☺8am-6pm Mon-Thu, to 8pm Fri & Sat, to 7pm Sun Oct-Apr, 9am-7pm daily May-Sep) and **Coyote Corner** (☑760-366-9683; www.joshuatreevillage.com/546/546.htm; 6535 Park Blvd, Joshua Tree; ☺9am-7pm).

Joshua Tree Rock Climbing School (☑760-366-4745; www.joshuatreerockclimbing.com), **Vertical Adventures** (☑949-854-6250; www.verticaladventures.com) and **Uprising Adventure** (☑888-254-6266; www.uprising.com) offer guided climbs and climbing instruction starting at $135 for a one-day introduction.

★☆ Festivals & Events

National Park Art Festival   ART
(www.joshuatree.org/art-festival) This nonprofit festival shows desert-themed paintings, sculpture, photography, ceramics and jewelry in early April.

Joshua Tree Music Festival   MUSIC
(www.joshuatreemusicfestival.com; day pass $20-80, weekend pass $140) Over a long weekend in May, this family-friendly, indie-music fest grooves out at Joshua Tree Lake Campground. It's followed by a soulful roots celebration in mid-October. No dogs.

Pioneer Days   CULTURAL
(www.visit29.org) Twentynine Palms' Old West-themed carnival on the third October weekend has a parade, an arm-wrestling competition and a chili dinner.

Hwy 62 Art Tours   ART
(www.hwy62art.org) Tour artists' studios, galleries and workshops over two weekends in October and/or November.

🛏 Sleeping

Inside the park there are only campgrounds, but there are plenty of lodging options along Hwy 62. Twentynine Palms has the biggest selection of accommodations, including national chain motels. Pads in Joshua Tree have more character and charm.

Joshua Tree Inn   MOTEL $
(☑760-366-1188; www.joshuatreeinn.com; 61259 Twentynine Palms Hwy, Joshua Tree; r/ste incl breakfast from $89/159; ☺reception 3pm to 8pm; ✳🛜🏊) This funky-cool, rock 'n' roll–infused, wisteria-strewn motel has 11 spacious rooms behind turquoise doors leading off from a desert-garden courtyard with great views. It gained notoriety in 1973 when rock legend Gram Parsons overdosed in Room 8, now decorated in tribute. Other famous guests have included John Wayne, Donovan and Emmylou Harris.

The communal area features a rock fireplace, where coffee, tea and granola bars are served.

Safari Motor Inn   MOTEL $
(☑760-366-1113; www.joshuatreemotel.com; 61959 Twentynine Palms Hwy, Joshua Tree; r from $49; 🅿♨✳🛜🏊) This basic, 12-room motel around a simple courtyard is a good option for modern nomads not keen on dropping bunches of cash for a roof over their heads. Most of the well-worn rooms have microwaves and mini refrigerators. It's a short walk to eateries and outdoor outfitters. Pool opens in summer only.

Harmony Motel   MOTEL $
(☑760-367-3351; www.harmonymotel.com; 71161 Twentynine Palms Hwy, Twentynine Palms; r $75-85; 🅿✳@🛜🏊) This 1950s motel, where U2 stayed while working on the *Joshua Tree* album, has a small pool and large, cheerfully painted rooms; some have kitchenettes.

Hicksville Trailer Palace   MOTEL $$
(☑310-584-1086; www.hicksville.com; d $100-250; ✳🛜🏊) Fancy sleeping among glowing wigs, in a haunted house, or in a horse stall? Check in at Hicksville, where 'rooms' are eight outlandishly decorated vintage trailers set around a kidney-shaped, saltwater swimming pool. The vision of LA writer and director Morgan Higby Night, each offers a journey into a unique, surreal and slightly wicked world. All but two share facilities. To keep out looky-loos, you'll only be given directions after making reservations.

Spin & Margie's Desert Hide-a-Way   INN $$
(☑760-366-9124; www.deserthideaway.com; 64491 Hwy 62; ste $145-175; ✳🛜) This handsome hacienda-style inn is perfect for restoring calm after a long day on the road. The five boldly colored suites are an eccentric symphony of corrugated tin, old license plates and cartoon art. Each has its own kitchen and flat-screen TV with DVD and CD player. Knowledgeable, gregarious owners ensure a relaxed visit. It's down the dirt Sunkist Rd, about 3 miles east of downtown Joshua Tree.

★ **Sacred Sands** B&B $$$

(📞760-424-6407; www.sacredsands.com; 63155 Quail Springs Rd, Joshua Tree; d incl breakfast $299-329; ❋🗖) In an isolated, pin-drop-quiet spot, these two desert-chic suites, each with a private outdoor shower, hot tub, sundeck, 2ft-thick walls and sleeping terrace under the stars, are the ultimate romantic retreat. There are astounding views across the desert hills and into the National Park. Owners Scott and Steve are gracious hosts and killer breakfast cooks.

It's four miles south of Twentynine Palms Hwy (via Park Bl), one mile west of the park entrance.

29 Palms Inn HOTEL $$$

(📞760-367-3505; www.29palmsinn.com; 73950 Inn Ave, Twentynine Palms; r & cottages incl breakfast $100-300; 🅿🌀❋@🗖🛇🐾) ✈ History oozes from every nook and cranny in these old-timey adobe- and wood-built cabins dotted around a palm oasis.

Camping

Of the park's nine **campgrounds** (www.nps.gov/jotr; camping & RV sites $10-15; 🛇), only **Cottonwood** and **Black Rock** have potable water, flush toilets and dump stations. **Indian Cove** and Black Rock accept **reservations** (📞877-444-6777, 518-885-3639; www.recreation.gov). The others are first-come, first-served and have pit toilets, picnic tables and fire grates. None have showers, but there are some at Coyote Corner in Joshua Tree, which charges $4. During the springtime wildflower bloom, campsites fill by noon, if not earlier.

Backcountry camping (no campfires) is allowed 1 mile from any trailhead or road and 100ft from water sources; free self-registration is required at the park's 13 staging areas. Joshua Tree Outfitters (p679) rents and sells quality camping gear.

Along Park Blvd, **Jumbo Rocks** has sheltered rock alcoves that act as perfect sunset- and sunrise-viewing platforms. **Belle** and **White Tank** also have boulder-embracing views. **Hidden Valley** is always busy. **Sheep Pass** and **Ryan** are also centrally located campgrounds.

Family-friendly Black Rock is good for camping novices; more remote Indian Cove also has 100-plus sites. Cottonwood, near the park's southern entrance, is popular with RVs.

🍴 Eating & Drinking

Yucca Valley has several large supermarkets, as well as the tiny **Earth Wise Organic Farms**, a co-op that sells produce grown by local farmers; it's at the turnoff to Pioneertown Rd. On Saturday mornings, locals gather for gossip and groceries at the **farmers market** in a parking lot just west of Park Blvd in Joshua Tree. For drinking, check out Pappy & Harriet's (p681) in Pioneertown.

JT's Country Kitchen BREAKFAST, ASIAN $

(📞760-366-8988; 61768 Twentynine Palms Hwy, Joshua Tree; mains $4-10; ⏱6:30am-3pm Wed-Mon) This roadside shack serves all-day breakfasts of down-home cookin': eggs, pancakes, biscuits with gravy, sandwiches and... what's this? Cambodian noodles and salads? Delish.

Crossroads Cafe AMERICAN $

(📞760-366-5414; 61715 Twentynine Palms Hwy, Joshua Tree; mains $5-12; ⏱7am-9pm daily; 🗖) The much-loved Crossroads is the go-to place for carbo-loaded breakfasts, fresh sandwiches and dragged-through-the-garden salads that make both omnivores (burgers, Reuben sandwich) and vegans (spinach salad) happy.

Restaurant at 29 Palms Inn AMERICAN, ORGANIC $$

(📞760-367-3505; www.29spalmsinn.com; 73950 Inn Ave, Twentynine Palms; mains lunch $7-15, dinner $12-28; ⏱11am-2pm Mon-Sat, 9am-2pm Sun, 5-9pm Sun-Thu, 5pm-9:30pm Fri & Sat; 🗖) ✈ This well-respected restaurant has its own organic garden and does burgers and salads at lunchtime, and grilled meats and toothsome pastas for dinner.

Pie for the People PIZZERIA $$

(📞760-366-0400; www.pieforthepeople.com; 61740 Hwy 62, Joshua Tree; pizzas $11-25; ⏱11am-9pm Mon-Thu, to 10pm Fri & Sat, to 8pm Sun; 🍴) Thin-crust pizzas for takeout and delivery. Flavors span standards to the David Bowie: white pizza with mozzarella, Guinness caramelized onions, jalapenos, pineapple, bacon, and sweet plum sauce. Enjoy yours under the exposed rafters in the wood and corrugated metal dining room, or under the tree on the back patio.

Joshua Tree Saloon BAR

(www.thejoshuatreesaloon.com; 61835 Twentynine Palms Hwy; ⏱8am-2am; 🗖) This watering hole with jukebox, pool tables and cowboy flair serves bar food along with rib-sticking burgers and steaks. Most people come here for the nightly entertainment, such as open-mic Tuesdays, karaoke Wednesdays and DJ Fridays. Over 21 only.

🔒 Shopping

In arty Joshua Tree, look for a cluster of galleries on Twentynine Palms Hwy within a couple blocks of the park entrance. Opening hours and works vary.

Wind Walkers CRAFTS
(http://windwalkershoppe.com; 61731 Twentynine Palms Hwy, Joshua Tree; ⊙ 9am-4pm Thu-Tue) This neat place has an entire courtyard with pottery large and small, as well as a hand-picked selection of Native American crafts, silver jewelry, blankets and knickknacks.

Ricochet Vintage Wears VINTAGE
(61705 Twentynine Palms Hwy, Joshua Tree; ⊙ 11am-3pm Fri & Mon, 10am-3pm Sat & Sun) Great assortment of recycled clothing and accessories, including cowboy shirts and boots, along with some neat old aprons, housewares and vinyl records.

Funky & Darn Near New VINTAGE
(55812 Twentynine Palms Hwy, Yucca Valley) This store just west of the Pioneertown Rd turnoff sells immaculate hand-picked vintage dresses and hand-tailored new clothing at fair prices. It's in a funky block of specialty stores for art and antiques (plus a cool coffee bar).

ℹ️ Information

Joshua Tree National Park (p674) is flanked by I-10 in the south and by Hwy 62 (Twentynine Palms Hwy) in the north. Entry permits ($15 per vehicle) are valid for seven days and come with a map and the seasonally updated Joshua Tree Guide.

There are no facilities inside the park other than restrooms, so gas up and bring drinking water and whatever food you need. Potable water is available at the Oasis of Mara, the Black Rock and Cottonwood campgrounds, the West Entrance and the Indian Cove ranger station.

Cell phones don't work in the park, but there's an emergency-only telephone at the Intersection Rock parking lot near the Hidden Valley Campground. Shops around the intersection of Twentynine Palms Hwy and Park Blvd offer internet access.

Pets must be kept on leash and are prohibited on trails.

MEDICAL SERVICES
Hi-Desert Medical Center (☑ 760-366-3711; 6601 Whitefeather Rd, Joshua Tree; ⊙ 24hr)

TOURIST INFORMATION
Joshua Tree National Park Visitor Center (6554 Park Blvd, Joshua Tree; ⊙ 8am-5pm) Just south of Hwy 62.

Black Rock Nature Center (9800 Black Rock Canyon Rd; ⊙ 8am-4pm Sat-Thu, noon-8pm Fri Oct-May; ♿) National Park visitor center, at the Black Rock Campground.

Cottonwood Visitor Center (Cottonwood Springs, 8 miles north of I-10 Fwy; ⊙ 9am-3pm)

TURN BACK THE CLOCK AT PIONEERTOWN

Turn north off Hwy 62 onto Pioneertown Rd in Yucca Valley and drive 5 miles straight into the past. Looking like an 1870s frontier town, **Pioneertown** (www.pioneertown.com; admission free; ♿) was actually built in 1946 as a Hollywood Western outdoor movie set. Gene Autry and Roy Rogers were among the original investors, and more than 50 movies and several TV shows were filmed here in the 1940s and '50s. These days the Pioneertown Posse stages mock gunfights on 'Mane St' at 2:30pm on Saturdays and Sundays from April to October.

For local color, toothsome BBQ, cheap beer and kick-ass live music, drop in at **Pappy & Harriet's Pioneertown Palace** (☑ 760-365-5956; www.pappyandharriets.com; 53688 Pioneertown Rd, Pioneertown; mains $8-29; ⊙ 11am-2am Thu-Sun, from 5pm Mon), a textbook honky-tonk. Monday's open-mic nights are legendary and often bring out astounding talent.

Within staggering distance is the atmospheric **Pioneertown Motel** (☑ 760-365-7001; www.pioneertown-motel.com; 5040 Curtis Rd, Pioneertown; r $70-120; ❄ 🛜 🐾), where yesteryear's silver-screen stars once slept during filming, and whose rooms are now filled with eccentric Western-themed memorabilia; some have kitchenettes.

About 4.5 miles north of here, **Rimrock Ranch Cabins** (☑ 760-228-1297; www.rimrockranchcabins.com; 50857 Burns Canyon Rd, Pioneertown; cabins $90-140; ❄ 🐾) is a cluster of vintage 1940s cabins with kitchens and private patios perfect for stargazing.

National Park visitor center, just inside the park's south entrance.

Joshua Tree Chamber of Commerce (☑760-366-3723; www.joshuatreechamber.org; 6448 Hallee Rd; ☺10am-4pm Tue, Thu & Sat) Info about hotels, restaurants and shops in the town of Joshua Tree, just north of Hwy 62.

Oasis Park Visitor Center (National Park Blvd, at Utah Trail, Twentynine Palms; ☺8am-5pm) Outside the north entrance.

Twentynine Palms Chamber of Commerce (☑760-367-3445; www.visit29.org; 73484 Twentynine Palms, Twentynine Palms; ☺9am-5pm Mon-Fri, 10am-4pm Sat & Sun)

❶ Getting There & Around

Rent a car in Palm Springs or LA. From LA, the trip takes about 2½ to three hours via I-10 and Hwy 62 (Twentynine Palms Hwy). From Palm Springs it takes about an hour to reach the park's west (preferable) or south entrances.

Bus 1, operated by **Morongo Basin Transit Authority** (www.mbtabus.com; one way $2.50, day pass $3.75), runs frequently along Twentynine Palms Hwy. Bus 12 to Palm Springs from Joshua Tree and Yucca Valley (one way/round-trip $10/15) has fewer departures. Many buses are equipped with bicycle racks.

ANZA-BORREGO DESERT STATE PARK

Shaped by an ancient sea and tectonic forces, enormous and little-developed **Anza-Borrego** (☑760-767-4205; www.parks.ca.gov; visitors center 200 Palm Canyon Dr; ☺park 24hr, visitors center 9am-5pm daily Oct-Apr, Sat, Sun & hol only May-Sep; ♿) covers 640,000 acres, making it the largest state park in the USA outside Alaska. Human history here goes back more than 10,000 years, as recorded by Native American pictographs and petroglyphs. The park is named for Spanish explorer Juan Bautista de Anza, who arrived in 1774, pioneering a colonial trail from Mexico and no doubt running into countless *borregos,* the wild peninsular bighorn sheep that once ranged as far south as Baja California. (Today only a few hundred of these animals survive due to drought, disease, poaching and off-highway driving.) In the 1850s Anza-Borrego became a stop along the Butterfield stagecoach line, which delivered mail between St Louis and San Francisco.

Winter and spring are high seasons. Depending on winter rains, wildflowers bloom brilliantly, albeit briefly, starting in late February. Summers are extremely hot; the daily average temperature in July is 107°F (41°C), but it can reach 125°F (51°C).

❍ Sights & Activities

The park's main town, **Borrego Springs** (population 3429), has a handful of restaurants and lodgings. Nearby are the park visitors center and easy-to-reach sights, such as Borrego Palm Canyon and Fonts Point, that are fairly representative of the park as a whole. The Split Mountain area, east of Ocotillo Wells, is popular with off-highway vehicles (OHVs), but also contains interesting geology and spectacular wind caves. The desert's southernmost region is the least visited and, aside from Blair Valley, has few developed trails and facilities.

Many of the sights are accessible only by dirt roads. To find out which roads require 4WD vehicles, or are currently impassable, check the signboard inside the park visitors center.

Peg Leg Smith Monument   MONUMENT
The pile of rocks by the road northeast of Borrego Springs, where County Rte S22 takes a 90-degree turn east, is actually a monument to Thomas Long 'Peg Leg' Smith – mountain man, fur trapper, horse thief, con artist and Wild West legend. He passed through Borrego Springs in 1829 and allegedly picked up some rocks that were later found to be pure gold. Strangely, when he returned during the Gold Rush era, he was unable to locate the lode. Nevertheless, he told lots of prospectors about it (often in exchange for a few drinks) and many came to search for the 'lost' gold and add to the myths.

Fonts Point   LOOKOUT
East of Borrego Springs, a 4-mile dirt road, sometimes passable without 4WD, diverges south from County Rte S22 out to Fonts Point (1249ft). From up here a spectacular panorama unfolds over the Borrego Valley to the west and the Borrego Badlands to the south. You'll be amazed when the desert seemingly drops from beneath your feet.

Vallecito County Park   HISTORIC SITE
(☑760-765-1188; www.co.san-diego.ca.us/parks; 37349 County Rte S2; admission per car $3; ☺Sep-May) This pretty little park in a refreshing valley in the southern part of the Anza-Borrego park centers on a replica of a histor-

ic **Butterfield Stage Station**. It's 36 miles south of Borrego Springs via County Rte S2.

Agua Caliente County Park   SWIMMING

(☎760-765-1188; www.sdcounty.ca.gov/parks/; 39555 Rte S2; entry per car $5; ☺9:30am-5pm Sep-May) In a lovely park 4 miles from Vallecito, you can take a dip in indoor and outdoor pools fed by hot natural mineral springs.

Hiking

Borrego Palm Canyon Trail   HIKING

This popular 3-mile loop trail starts at the top of Borrego Palm Canyon Campground, 1 mile north of the visitors center, and goes past a palm grove and waterfall, a delightful oasis in the dry, rocky countryside. Keep an eye out for bighorn sheep.

Maidenhair Falls Trail   HIKING

This plucky trail starts from the Hellhole Canyon Trailhead, 2 miles west of the visitors center on County Rte S22, and climbs for 3 miles past several palm oases to a seasonal waterfall that supports bird life and a variety of plants.

Ghost Mountain Trail   HIKING

A steep 2-mile round-trip trail climbs to the remains of the 1930s adobe homestead built by desert recluse Marshall South and his family. Pick it up in Blair Valley, at the Little Pass primitive campground.

Pictograph/Smuggler's Canyon Trail   HIKING

In Blair Valley, this 2-mile round-trip trail skirts boulders covered in Native American pictographs and also offers a nice view of the Vallecito Valley. Take the Blair Valley turnoff on County Rte S2, and continue on the dirt road for about 3.8 miles to the turnoff for a parking area reached in another 1.5 miles.

Elephant Tree Trail   HIKING

The rare elephant trees get their name from their stubby trunks, which are thought to resemble elephant legs. Unfortunately only one living elephant tree remains along this 1.5-mile loop trail but it's still a nice, easy hike through a rock wash. The turnoff is on Split Mountain Rd, about 6 miles south of Hwy 78 and Ocotillo Wells.

Split Mountain Wind Caves   HIKING

Four miles south of the Elephant Tree Trail, on Split Mountain Rd, is the dirt-road turnoff for Fish Creek primitive campground; another 4 miles brings you to Split Mountain, where a popular 4WD road goes right between 600ft-high walls created by earthquakes and erosion. At the southern end of this 2-mile-long gorge, a steep 1-mile trail leads up to delicate **wind caves** carved into sandstone outcrops.

Blair Valley   HIKING

In the west of the park, about 5 miles southeast of Scissors Crossing (where County Rte S2 crosses Hwy 78), is Blair Valley, known for its Native American pictographs and *morteros* (hollows in rocks used for grinding seeds). The valley and its hiking trailheads lie a few miles east of County Rte S2, along a dirt road. Over on the north side of the valley, a **monument** at Foot and Walker Pass marks a difficult spot on the Butterfield Overland Stage Route. In **Box Canyon** you can see the marks where wagons had to hack through the rocks to widen the Emigrant Trail.

Cycling

Over 500 miles of the park's dirt and paved roads (but never hiking trails) are open to bikes. Popular routes are Grapevine Canyon off Hwy 78 and Canyon Sin Nombre in the Carrizo Badlands. Flatter areas include Blair

---

EASY HIKES IN ANZA-BORREGO

Bill Kenyon Overlook This 1-mile loop from Yaqui Pass primitive campground rolls out to a viewpoint over the San Felipe Wash, the Pinyon Mountains and, on clear days, the Salton Sea.

Yaqui Well Trail A 2-mile trail that leads past labeled desert plants and a natural water hole that attracts a rich variety of birds; starts opposite Tamarisk Grove campground.

Narrows Earth Trail Some 4.5 miles east of Tamarisk Grove along Hwy 78, this 0.5-mile path is an amateur geologist's dream walk through a fault zone. Look for low-lying, brilliant-red chuparosa shrubs, which attract hummingbirds.

Cactus Loop Trail A self-guided, 1-mile round-trip past a great variety of cacti; starts across from Tamarisk campground and delivers nice views of San Felipe Wash.

Anza-Borrego State Park

N

0 ——————— 10 km
0 ——————— 5 miles

A | **B** | **C** | **D**

Torres
Martinez Indian
Reservation

Colorado Desert

Anza-Borrego
Desert State Park
Visitor Center

Hoberg Rd

Borrego Desert
Nature Center

Chamber of
Commerce

21 25
26

23

Palm Canyon Dr

27 Christmas
Circle

20

Borrego
Springs
Rd

0 ——————— 1 km

**BORREGO
SPRINGS**

53

Coyote Creek

4

522

Peg Leg Rd

19 24

San Ysidro
Peak
(6147ft)

9

See Enlargement

Palm Canyon
Dr

Salton Sea
(20mi)

2

Borrego Badlands

Borrego Palm
Canyon

14

Borrego
Springs Rd

522

Pinyon Ridge
Grapevine Canyon

22 Borrego
Sink

53

Anza Trail

Ocotillo Wells
State Vehicular
Recreation Area

Buttes Pass
Rd

Pacific Crest Trail

San Felipe Creek

78

Ocotillo
Wells

52

Julian (8mi)

78

18

11

Yaqui Pass Rd

7

15

Old Kane Springs Rd

Split Mountain Rd

12

Vallecito
Mountains

Pinyon Mtn Rd

Blair Valley

Granite Mtn
(5633ft)

3 8
13

16 Whale Peak
(5320ft)

1

52

10

Split Mtn
(14,058ft)

17

5

Carrizo
Badlands

6

Garnet Peak
(5905ft)

Vallecito Creek

Pacific Crest Trail

51

Carrizo Creek

S2

Canyon Sin
Nombre

Jacumba
Mountains

I-8 (8mi)

San Diego (50mi)

8

Anza-Borrego State Park

Sights

1 Anza-Borrego Desert State Park C5
2 Fonts Point C2
3 Foot and Walker Pass Monument B5
4 Peg Leg Smith Monument B2
5 Vallecito County Park B5

Activities, Courses & Tours

6 Agua Caliente County Park C6
7 Bill Kenyon Overlook B3
8 Blair Valley B5
9 Borrego Palm Canyon Trail A2
10 Box Canyon A5
11 Cactus Loop Trail B3
12 Elephant Tree Trail D4
13 Ghost Mountain Trail B5
14 Maidenhair Falls Trail A2
15 Narrows Earth Trail C4
16 Pictograph/Smuggler's Canyon Trail B5
17 Split Mountain Wind Caves D5
18 Yaqui Well Trail B3

Sleeping

Agua Caliente County Park Campground ..... (see 6)
19 Borrego Palm Canyon Campground A2
20 Borrego Valley Inn B1
21 Hacienda del Sol B1
22 La Casa del Zorro B3
23 Palm Canyon Hotel & RV Resort A1
24 Palms at Indian Head A2
Vallecito County Park Campground ..... (see 5)

Eating

25 Borrego Springs Center Market B1
26 Carlee's Place C1
Carmelita's Bar & Grill ..... (see 27)
27 Kendall's Café B1

Valley and Split Mountain. Get details at the visitors center.

Festivals & Events

Peg Leg Smith Liars Contest CULTURAL
In this hilarious event on the first Saturday of April, amateur liars compete in the Western tradition of telling tall tales. Anyone can enter, so long as the story is about gold and mining in the Southwest, is less than five minutes long and is anything but the truth.

Sleeping

Free backcountry camping is permitted anywhere that's off-road and at least 100ft from water. There are also several free primitive campgrounds with pit toilets but no water in the park. All campfires must be in metal containers. Gathering vegetation (dead or alive) is strictly prohibited.

Room rates drop significantly in summer; some places close altogether.

Hacienda del Sol HOTEL $
(760-767-5442; www.haciendadelsol-borrego.com; 610 Palm Canyon Dr; r/duplex/cottages $80/135/165;) Bask in the retro glow of this small hotel that's been put through some upgrades and now sports new beds and DVD players (free DVD rentals). Choose from hotel rooms, cottages and duplex units. The pool is great for relaxing or socializing.

Borrego Palm Canyon Campground CAMPGROUND $
(800-444-7275; www.reserveamerica.com; tent/RV sites $25/35;) Near the visitors center, this campground has award-winning toilets, close-together campsites and an amphitheater with ranger programs.

Agua Caliente County Park Campground CAMPGROUND $
(reservations 858-565-3600; www.co.san-diego.ca.us/parks; 39555 County Rte S2; tent sites $19, RV sites with partial/full hookups $24/28; Sep-May;) A good choice for sociable RVers, with natural hot-spring pools.

Vallecito County Park Campground CAMPGROUND $
(reservations 858-565-3600; www.co.san-diego.ca.us/parks; 37349 County Rte S2; tent & RV sites $19; Sep-May;) Has tent-friendly sites in a cool, green valley refuge.

Palm Canyon Hotel & RV Resort MOTEL $$
(760-767-5341; www.palmcanyonresort.com; 221 Palm Canyon Dr, Borrego Springs; r $99-179;) For that Old West flair, check into this welcoming motel, but don't be fooled: the place was only built in the '80s! It's about a mile from the park's visitors center and has two pools for unwinding, and a restaurant and saloon for sustenance.

Palms at Indian Head
BOUTIQUE HOTEL $$

(☑ 760-767-7788; www.thepalmsatindianhead.com; 2200 Hoberg Rd; r $139-229; ℙ❋☷) This former haunt of Cary Grant, Marilyn Monroe and other old-time celebs has been reborn as a chic mid-century modern retreat. Connect with the era over martinis and chicken cordon bleu at the on-site bar and grill (called Red Ocotillo during the day and Krazy Coyote at night) while enjoying mesmerizing desert views.

La Casa del Zorro
RESORT $$$

(☑ 760-767-0100; www.lacasadelzorro.com; 3845 Yaqui Pass Rd; r Sun-Thu from $189, from Fri & Sat $289; ℙ❋☎☷☷) About 5 miles south of central Borrego Springs, San Diego families have been coming to this resort for generations. It had seen hard times and was closed earlier this decade, but it's reopened and is again the region's grandest stay. It has 67 rooms and casitas on 42 landscaped acres with tennis, 26 swimming pools, bocce and croquet courts, as well as a spa and gourmet restaurant.

Borrego Valley Inn
INN $$$

(☑ 800-333-5810, 760-767-0311; www.borregovalleyinn.com; 405 Palm Canyon Dr; r incl breakfast $215-295; ℙ☺❋☎☷) This petite, immaculately kept inn, filled with Southwestern knickknacks and Native American weavings, is an intimate spa-resort, perfect for adults. There's 15 rooms on 10 acres. One pool is clothing-optional. Most rooms have kitchenettes. The grounds are entirely nonsmoking.

✕ Eating & Drinking

In summer many places keep shorter hours or close additional days. Self-caterers can stock up at the **Center Market** (590 Palm Canyon Dr; ☺8:30am-6:30pm Mon-Sat, to 5pm Sun) in Borrego Springs.

Kendall's Café
DINER $

(☑ 760-767-3491; 587 Palm Canyon Dr, the Mall; mains breakfast $4-12, lunch $6-12, dinner $9-17; ☺6am-8pm) This coffee shop is a hometown favorite for blueberry pancakes at breakfast and a combination of Mexican (enchiladas, fajitas etc) and straight-down-the-middle American standards the rest of the day.

Carmelita's Bar & Grill
MEXICAN $$

(☑ 760-767-5666; 575 Palm Canyon Dr, the Mall; breakfast $5-9, lunch & dinner $9.50-14; ☺10am-9pm Mon-Fri, 8am-9pm Sat & Sun; ☷) This lively joint with its cheerful decor serves the best Mexican food in town, including delicious huevos rancheros. The bar staff knows how to whip up a good margarita.

Carlee's Place
AMERICAN $$

(☑ 760-767-3262; 660 Palm Canyon Dr; mains lunch $8-14, dinner $12-27; ☺11am-9pm) Even though the decor feels like it hasn't been updated since the 1970s, locals pick Carlee's for its burgers, pastas and steak dinners. The pool table, live music and karaoke are big draws, too.

❶ Information

Driving through the park is free but if you camp, hike or picnic, a day fee of $8 per car applies. You'll need a 4WD to tackle the 500 miles of backcountry dirt road.

Borrego Springs has stores, ATMs, banks, gas stations, a post office and a public library with free internet access and wi-fi. Cell phones may work in Borrego Springs but nowhere else.

Borrego Desert Nature Center (☑ 760-767-3098; www.california-desert.org; 652 Palm Canyon Dr, Borrego Springs; ☺9am-5pm daily Sep-Jun, 9am-3pm Fri & Sat Jul & Aug) Excellent bookshop run by the Anza-Borrego Desert Natural History Association, which also organizes tours, lectures, guided hikes and outdoor-skills courses.

Chamber of Commerce (☑ 760-767-5555; www.borregospringschamber.com; 786 Palm Canyon Dr, Borrego Springs; ☺9am-4pm Mon-Sat) Tourist information.

Anza-Borrego Desert State Park Visitor Center (☑ 760-767-4205; www.parks.ca.gov; 200 Palm Canyon Dr, Borrego Springs; ☺9am-5pm Oct-May, Sat & Sun only Jun-Sep) Built partly underground, the stone walls of the park visitors center blend beautifully with the mountain backdrop, while inside are top-notch displays and audiovisual presentations. Two miles west of Borrego Springs.

Wildflower Hotline (☑ 760-767-4684).

❶ Getting There & Around

There is no public transport to Anza-Borrego Desert State Park. From Palm Springs (1½ hours) take I-10 to Indio, then Hwy 86 south along the Salton Sea and west onto S22. From LA (three hours) and Orange County (via Temecula) take I-15 south to Hwy 79 to County Rtes S2 and S22. From San Diego (two hours), I-8 to County Rte S2 is easiest, but if you want a more scenic ride, take twisty Hwy 79 from I-8 north through Cuyamaca Rancho State Park and into Julian, then head east on Hwy 78.

AROUND ANZA-BORREGO

Salton Sea

Driving along Hwy 111 southeast of Indio, it's a most unexpected sight: California's largest lake in the middle of its largest desert. The Salton Sea has a fascinating past, complicated present and uncertain future.

Geologists say that the Gulf of California once extended 150 miles north of the present-day Coachella Valley, but millions of years' worth of rich silt flowing through the Colorado River gradually cut it off, leaving a sink behind. By the mid-1800s the sink was the site of salt mines and geologists realized that the mineral-rich soil would make excellent farmland. Colorado River water was diverted into irrigation canals.

In 1905 the Colorado River breached, giving birth to the Salton Sea. It took 18 months, 1500 workers and 500,000 tons of rock to put the river back on course, but with no natural outlet, the water was here to stay. Today, the Salton Sea is about 35 miles long and 15 miles wide and has water that is 30% saltier than the Pacific Ocean.

By mid-century the Salton Sea was stocked with fish and marketed as the 'California Riviera'; vacation homes lined its shores. The fish, in turn, attracted birds, and the sea remains a prime spot for bird-watching, including 400 species of migratory and endangered species such as snow geese, eared grebes, ruddy ducks, white and brown pelicans, bald eagles and peregrine falcons.

These days, if you've heard of the Salton Sea at all, it's probably due to annual fish die-offs, which are caused by phosphorous and nitrogen in agricultural runoff from nearby farmland. The minerals cause algal blooms, and when the algae die they deprive the water – and fish – of oxygen. Even if farming were to stop tomorrow, there are still generations' worth of minerals in the soil, waiting to reach the sink.

One solution would seem to be to cut off the water to the sea and let it die, but that carries its own dilemma. A dry Salton Sea would leave a dust bowl with a potential dust cloud that could widely devastate the local air quality. The debate rages on.

Stop by the visitor center of the **Salton Sea State Recreation Area** (☑760-393-3810; www.parks.ca.gov; ☺ visitor center 10am-

OFF THE BEATEN TRACK

SALVATION MOUNTAIN

Southeast of the Salton Sea, **Salvation Mountain** (www.salvationmountain.us) is a mighty strange sight indeed: a 100ft-high hill of concrete and hand-mixed adobe slathered in colorful paint and found objects (hay bales, tires, telephone poles) and inscribed with religious messages, surrounded by chapel-like grottoes. The work of Leonard Knight (1931–2014) was 28 years in the making and has become one of the great works of American folk art that's even been recognized as a national treasure in the US Senate. It's in Niland, about 3 miles off Hwy 111, via Main St/Beal Rd and past train tracks and trailer parks.

4pm Nov-Mar), on the north shore. Further south, **Sonny Bono Salton Sea National Wildlife Refuge** (www.fws.gov/saltonsea; 906 W Sinclair Rd, Calipatria; ☺ sunrise-sunset, visitors center 7am-3:15pm Mon-Fri year-round) is a major migratory stopover along the Pacific Flyway and has a visitors center, a short self-guided trail, an observation tower and a picnic area. It's about 4 miles west of Hwy 111, between Niland and Calipatria.

Julian

The mountain hamlet of Julian, with its three-block main street, is a favorite getaway for city folk who love its quaint 1870s streetscape, gold-mining lore and famous apple pies. Prospectors, including many Confederate veterans, arrived here after the Civil War, but the population did not explode until the discovery of flecks of gold in 1869. Today, apples are the new gold. There are nearly 17,000 trees in the orchards flanking Hwy 178 outside town. The harvest takes place in early fall when some farmers may let you pick your own apples. At any time, at least taste a slice of delicious apple pie, sold at bakeries all over town.

Julian sits at the junction of Hwys 78 and 79. It's about 1¼ hours from San Diego (via I-8 east to Hwy 79 north) and 40 minutes from Borrego Springs Head (south over Yaqui Pass on County Rte S3, then Hwy 78 west).

For more information, contact the **Chamber of Commerce** (☑760-765-1857; www.julianca.com; 2129 Main St; ☺10am-4pm).

⊙ Sights

Eagle and High Peak Mine   HISTORIC SITE
(☎760-765-0036; end of C St; adult/child $10/5;
⊙10am-2pm Mon-Fri, to 3pm Sat & Sun; ⛟) Be
regaled with tales of the hardscrabble life
of the town's early pioneers during an hour-
long underground tour through these former gold mines.

🛏 Sleeping & Eating

Julian Gold Rush Hotel   B&B $$
(☎760-765-0201, 800-734-5854; www.julianhotel.
com; 2032 Main St; d incl breakfast $135-210; 🕸)
At this 1897 antique-filled B&B, lace cur-
tains, claw-foot tubs and other parapherna-
lia painstakingly evoke a bygone era.

Orchard Hill Country Inn   B&B $$$
(☎760-765-1700; www.orchardhill.com; 2502
Washington St; incl breakfast r $195-250, cottage
$295-375; @🕸) Turn back the clock at this
romantic B&B where rooms are spread
across a craftsman lodge and a dozen cozy
cottages, all furnished with impeccable
taste. Each is decorated differently but all
feature a fireplace or patio; some also have
Jacuzzi tubs.

Julian Pie Company   BAKERY $
(www.julianpie.com; 2225 Main St; snacks & pies
$3-15; ⊙9am-5pm; ⛟) This popular joint
churns out apple cider, cinnamon-dusted
cider donuts and classic apple-filled pies
and pastries.

ROUTE 66

Completed in 1926, iconic Route 66 connected Chicago and Los Angeles across the
heartland of America. What novelist John
Steinbeck called the 'Mother Road' came
into its own during the Depression, when
thousands of migrants escaped the Dust
Bowl by slogging westward in beat-up old
jalopies painted with 'California or Bust'
signs, *Grapes of Wrath*–style. After WWII
Americans took their newfound wealth and
convertible cars on the road to get their
kicks on Route 66.

As traffic along the USA's post-WWII
interstate highway system boomed, many
small towns along Route 66, with their neon-
signed motor courts, diners and drive-ins,
eventually went out of business.

In California Route 66 mostly follows the
National Trails Hwy, prone to potholes and

dangerous bumps. From the beach in Santa
Monica, it rumbles through the LA basin,
crosses over the Cajon Pass to the railroad
towns of Barstow and Victorville and runs
a gauntlet of Mojave Desert ghost towns, arriving in Needles near the Nevada stateline.

In larger towns, Mother Road relics may
require a careful eye amid more contemporary architecture, but as you head toward
Nevada, wide open vistas and the occasional
landmark remain barely changed from the
days of road trippers.

Los Angeles to Barstow

Route 66 kicks off in Santa Monica, at the
intersection of Ocean Ave and Santa Monica
Blvd. Follow the latter through Beverly Hills
and West Hollywood, turn right on Sunset
Blvd and pick up the 110 Fwy north to Pasadena. Take exit 31B and drive south on Fair
Oaks Ave for an egg cream at the **Fair Oaks
Pharmacy** (☎626-799-1414; www.fairoaksphar-
macy.net; 1526 Mission St; mains $4-8; ⊙9am-
9pm Mon-Fri, to 10pm Sat, 10am-7pm Sun; ⛟),
a nostalgic soda fountain from 1915. Turn
around and follow Fair Oaks Ave north, then
turn right on Colorado Blvd, where the vintage Saga Motor Hotel (p198) still hands out
quaint metal room keys to its guests.

Continue east on Colorado Blvd to Colorado Pl and Santa Anita Park (p197), where
the Marx Brothers' *A Day at the Races* was
filmed and legendary thoroughbred Seabis-
cuit ran. During the live-racing season, free
tram tours take you behind the scenes into
the jockeys' room and training areas; weekends only, reservations required.

Colorado Pl turns into Huntington Dr E,
which you'll follow to 2nd Ave, where you
turn north, then east on Foothill Blvd. This
older alignment of Route 66 follows Foothill
Blvd through Monrovia, home of the 1925
Mayan Revival–style architecture of the
allegedly haunted Aztec Hotel (☎626-358-
3231; 311 W Foothill Blvd, Monrovia).

Continue east on W Foothill Blvd, then
jog south on S Myrtle Ave and hook a left
on E Huntington Dr through Duarte, which
puts on a **Route 66 parade** (http://duarter-
oute66parade.com; ⊙September), with boisterous marching bands, old-fashioned carnival
games and a classic-car show. In Azusa, Huntington turns into E Foothill Blvd, which becomes Alosta Blvd in Glendora where **The
Hat** (☎626-857-0017; www.thehat.com; 611 W
Route 66, Glendora; mains $4-8; ⊙10am-11pm Sun-

Wed, to 1am Thu-Sat; [icon]) has made piled-high pastrami sandwiches since 1951.

Continue east on Foothill Blvd, where two campily retro steakhouses await in Rancho Cucamonga. First up is the 1955 **Magic Lamp Inn** ([icon]909-981-8659; www.themagiclamp-inn.com; 8189 Foothill Blvd, Rancho Cucamonga; mains lunch $11-17, dinner $15-42; [clock]11:30am-2:30pm Tue-Fri, 5-11pm Tue-Thu, 5-10:30pm Fri & Sat, 4-9pm Sun), easily recognized by its fabulous neon sign. There's dancing Wednesday through Saturday nights. Up the road, the rustic **Sycamore Inn** ([icon]909-982-1104; www.thesycamoreinn.com; 8318 Foothill Blvd, Rancho Cucamonga; mains $22-49; [clock]5-9pm Mon-Thu, to 10pm Fri & Sat, 4-8:30pm Sun) has been dishing up juicy steaks since 1848.

Cruising on through Fontana, birthplace of the notorious Hells Angels biker club, you'll see the now-boarded-up **Giant Orange** (15395 Foothill Blvd, Fontana; [clock]no public entry), a 1920s juice stand of the kind that was once a fixture alongside SoCal's citrus groves.

Foothill Blvd continues on to Rialto where you'll find the **Wigwam Motel** ([icon]909-875-3005; www.wigwammotel.com; 2728 W Foothill Blvd, Rialto; r $65-80; [icon]), whose kooky concrete faux-tepees date from 1949. Continue east, then head north on N East St to the unofficial **First McDonald's Museum** ([icon]909-885-6324; 1398 N E St, San Bernardino; admission by donation; [clock]10am-5pm), which has interesting historic Route 66 exhibits. Continue north, then turn left on W Highland Ave and pick up the I-215 Fwy to I-15 and exit at Cleghorn for Cajon Blvd to trundle north on an ancient section of the Mother Road. Get back onto I-15 and drive up to the Cajon Pass. At the top, take the Oak Hill Rd exit (No 138) to the **Summit Inn Cafe** ([icon]760-949-8688; 5960 Mariposa Rd, Hesperia; mains $5-10; [clock]6am-8pm Mon-Thu, to 9pm Fri & Sat), a 1950s roadside diner with antique gas pumps, a retro jukebox and a lunch counter that serves ostrich burgers and date shakes.

Get back on I-15 and drive downhill to Victorville, exiting at 7th St and driving past the San Bernardino County Fairgrounds, home of the Route 66 Raceway. Along 7th St in Old Town Victorville, look for landmarks including the bucking bronco sign of the **New Corral Motel**. At D St, turn left for the excellent **California Route 66 Museum** ([icon]760-951-0436; www.califrt66museum. org; 16825 D St, Victorville; donations welcome; [clock]10am-4pm Thu-Sat & Mon, 11am-3pm Sun), opposite the Greyhound bus station. Inside a

NAVIGATING THE MOTHER ROAD

For Route 66 enthusiasts who want to drive every mile of the old highway, free turn-by-turn driving directions are available online at www.historic66.com. Other useful sites are www.cart66pf.org and www.route66ca.org.

former cafe is a wonderfully eclectic collection including a 1930s teardrop trailer, sparkling red naughahyde booth with tabletop mini-jukebox, advertising signage, vintage photos, and bits and pieces from the Roy Rogers Museum that used to be in Victorville before moving to Branson, Missouri (where it closed in 2010).

Follow South D St north under I-15 where it turns into the National Trails Hwy. Beloved by Harley bikers, this stretch of rolling hills and vast expanses of high desert to Barstow is like a scavenger hunt for Mother Road ruins, such as antique filling stations and tumbledown motor courts.

In Oro Grande, the **Iron Hog Saloon** (20848 National Trails Hwy, Oro Grande; [clock]8am-10pm Mon-Thu & Sun, to 2am Fri & Sat) is an old-time honky-tonk dripping with memorabilia and character(s). It's hugely popular with bikers and serves large portions of rib-stickers, including rattlesnake and ostrich. About 5 miles further north, **Bottle Tree Ranch** (Elmer's Place; 24266 National Trails Hwy, Oro Grande) is a colorful roadside folk-art collection of glass bottles artfully arranged on telephone poles along with weathered railroad signs.

Barstow

At the junction of I-40 and I-15, nearly halfway between LA and Las Vegas, down-and-out Barstow (population 23,000) has been a desert travelers' crossroads for centuries. In 1776 Spanish colonial priest Francisco Garcés caravanned through, and in the mid-19th century the Old Spanish Trail passed nearby, with pioneer settlers on the Mojave River selling supplies to California immigrants. Meanwhile, mines were founded in the hills outside town. Barstow, named after a railway executive, got going as a railroad junction after 1886. After 1926 it became a major rest stop for motorists along Route

66 (Main St). Today it exists to serve nearby military bases and is still a busy pit stop for travelers.

◉ Sights

Barstow is well known for its history-themed **murals** that spruce up often empty and boarded-up downtown buildings, mostly along Main St between 1st and 6th Sts. Pick up a map at the Chamber of Commerce (p691).

Route 66 'Mother Road' Museum   MUSEUM
(📞760-255-1890; www.route66museum.org; 681 N 1st St; ⊙10am-4pm Fri & Sat, 11am-4pm Sun, or by appointment) FREE Inside the beautifully restored **Casa del Desierto**, a 1911 Harvey House (architecturally significant railway inns named for their originator Fred Harvey), this museum documents life along the historic highway with some great old black-and-white photographs alongside eclectic relics, including a 1915 Ford Model T, a 1913 telephone switchboard and products made from locally mined minerals. The excellent gift shop stocks Route 66 driving guides, maps and books.

Western America Railroad Museum   MUSEUM
(www.barstowrailmuseum.org; 685 N 1st St; ⊙11am-4pm Fri-Sun) FREE Rail buffs make a beeline to the Casa del Desierto to marvel at a century's worth of railroad artifacts, including old timetables, uniforms, china and the Dog Tooth Mountain model railroad. Even when the building's closed, outside you can see historic locomotives, bright-red cabooses and even a car used to ship racehorses.

Desert Discovery Center   MUSEUM
(📞760-252-6060; www.desertdiscoverycenter.com; 831 Barstow Rd; ⊙11am-4pm Tue-Sat; 🏤) FREE The US Bureau of Land Management operates this kid-oriented, educational center in an adobe building near I-15. Activities include animal-feeding, art club and monthly programs from drums to composting, and you can get info on exploring the local deserts. The star exhibit is the Old Woman Meteorite, the second-largest ever found in the USA, weighing in at a hefty 6070lbs.

Calico Ghost Town   THEME PARK
(📞800-862-2542; www.calicotown.com; 36600 Ghost Town Rd, Yermo; adult/child $8/5; ⊙9am-5pm; 🏤) This endearingly hokey Old West attraction is a cluster of pioneer-era buildings amid the ruins of a circa 1881 silver mining town, reconstructed nearly a century later by Walter Knott of Knott's Berry Farm (p605). Admission is cheap, but you'll pay extra to go gold panning, tour the Maggie Mine, ride a narrow-gauge railway or see the 'mystery shack.' Old-timey heritage celebrations include Civil War re-enactments and a bluegrass 'hootenanny.' Take the Ghost Town Rd exit off I-15; it's about 3.5 miles uphill. There's also a campground (tent/RV sites with full hookup $30/35).

🛏 Sleeping & Eating

Only when the Mojave freezes over will there be no rooms left in Barstow. Just drive along E Main St and take your pick from the string of national chain motels, many with doubles from $40.

Oak Tree Inn   MOTEL $
(📞760-254-1148; www.oaktreeinn.com; 35450 Yermo Rd, Yermo; r incl breakfast $53-74; P⟦⟧🐾⟦⟧🅿⟦⟧) For class and comfort, steer towards this three-story, 65-room motel near the freeway, where rooms have blackout draperies and triple-paned windows. It's 11 miles east of town (exit Ghost Town Rd off I-15). Breakfast is served at the adjacent 1950s-style diner.

Lola's Kitchen   MEXICAN $
(1244 E Main St; mains $5-12; ⊙4am-7:30pm Mon-Fri, to 4:30pm Sat; 🏤) Interstate truckers, blue-collar workers and Vegas-bound hipsters all gather at this simple, colorful Mexican *cocina*, tucked away inside a strip mall and run by two sisters who make succulent *carne asada* burritos, *chile verde* enchiladas and more.

Idle Spurs Steakhouse   STEAKHOUSE $$
(📞760-256-8888; www.idlespurssteakhouse.com; 690 Hwy 58; mains lunch $10-24, dinner $14-28; ⊙11am-9pm Mon-Fri, from 4pm Sat & Sun; 🏤) In the saddle since 1950, this Western-themed spot, ringed around an atrium and a full bar, is a fave with locals and RVers. Surrender to your inner carnivore with slow-roasted prime rib, hand-cut steaks and succulent lobster tail. Kids menu available. It's a couple miles off Rte 66.

Peggy Sue's   DINER $$
(📞760-254-3370; www.peggysuesdiner.com; Ghost Town Rd, Yermo; mains $8-13; ⊙6am-10pm; 🏤) Built in 1954 as a simple, ninestool, three-booth diner, Peggy Sue's has since grown into a mini-empire with ice-cream shop, pizza parlor, a park out back with metal sculptures of 'diner-saurs' and a kitschy-awesome gift shop. It's down the street from Oak Tree Inn (p690).

⭐ Entertainment

Skyline Drive-In   CINEMA
(📞760-256-3333; 31175 Old Hwy 58; adult/child
$7/2; 🚗) One of the few drive-ins left in California, this 1960s movie theater shows one
or two flicks nightly.

ℹ Information

Barstow Area Chamber of Commerce
(📞760-256-8617; www.barstowchamber.com;
681 N 1st Ave; ⏱8:30am-5:30pm Mon-Fri,
10am-2pm Sat; 📶) At the train station, just
north of downtown.

Barstow Community Hospital (📞760-256-
1761; 820 E Mountain View St; ⏱emergency
room 24hr)

ℹ Getting There & Around

You'll need a car to get around Barstow and drive
Route 66. A few major car-rental agencies have
in-town offices.

Frequent Greyhound buses from LA ($37, 2½
to 5¼ hours), Las Vegas ($32, 2¾ hours) and
Palm Springs ($44, 4½ hours) arrive at the main
bus station (1611 E Main St) east of downtown,
near I-15.

Amtrak's *Southwest Chief* runs to/from LA
(www.amtrak.com, from $30, 3¾ hours, advance reservations suggested) daily but is often
late. There's no staffed ticket office at Barstow's
historic **train station** (685 N 1st Ave).

Barstow to Needles

Leave Barstow on I-40 east and exit at Daggett (exit 7), site of the California inspection
station once dreaded by Dust Bowl refugees.
Drive north on A St, cross the railroad tracks
and turn right on Santa Fe St. On your left,
just past the general store, you'll see the
moodily crumbling, late-19th-century **Daggett Stone Hotel**, where desert adventurers
such as Death Valley Scotty (p696) used to stay.

Continue on Santa Fe, take your first
right, then turn left to pick up the National
Trails Hwy going east.

Shortly after the highway ducks under
I-40, you're in Newberry Springs, where
the grizzled, 1950s **Bagdad Cafe** (📞760-
257-3101; www.bagdadcafethereal.com; 46548
National Trails Hwy, Newberry Springs; mains $6-12;
⏱7am-7pm) was the main filming location
of the eponymous 1987 indie flick starring
CCH Pounder and Jack Palance, a cult hit
in Europe. The interior is chockablock with
posters, movie stills and momentos left by
fans, while outside, the old water tower and
airstream trailer are slowly rusting away.

The National Trails Hwy runs south along
the freeway, crosses it at Lavic and continues east along the northern side of I-40. This
potholed, crumbling backcountry stretch
of Route 66 crawls through ghostly desert
towns. In Ludlow turn right on Crucero Rd,
cross I-40 again and pick up the highway by
turning left.

Beyond Ludlow, Route 66 veers away
from the freeway and bumps along past
haunting ruins spliced into the majestic
landscape. Only a few landmarks interrupt
the limitless horizon, most famously the
sign of the well-preserved but defunct, 1950s
Roy's Motel & Cafe (there's a working gas
station and small shop). It's east of **Amboy
Crater**, an almost perfectly symmetrical volcanic cinder cone that went dormant 600
years ago. You can scramble up its west side
(don't attempt it in high winds or summer
heat).

Past Essex the Mother Road leaves National Trails Hwy and heads north on Goffs
Rd through Fenner, where it once more
crosses I-40. In Goffs the one-room, 1914
Mission-style **Goffs Schoolhouse** (📞760-
733-4482; www.mdhca.org; 37198 Lanfair Rd; donations welcome; ⏱usually 9am-4pm Sat & Sun)
remains part of the best-preserved historic
settlement in the Mojave Desert.

Continue on Goffs Rd (US Hwy 95) to I-40
East and follow it to **Needles**. Named after
nearby mountain spires, it's the last Route
66 stop before the Arizona border, where the
Old Trails Arch Bridge carried the Joad family across the Colorado River in *The Grapes
of Wrath.*

Exit at J St and turn left, follow J St to W
Broadway, turn right and then left on F St,
which runs into Front St, paralleling the railway track. Go past the old mule-train wagon
and 1920s Palm Motel to **El Garces**, a 1908
Harvey House that's been undergoing restorations for years.

MOJAVE NATIONAL PRESERVE

If you're on a quest for the 'middle of nowhere,' you'll find it in the wilderness of the
Mojave National Preserve (📞760-252-6100;
www.nps.gov/moja; **FREE**), a 1.6-million-acre
jumble of sand dunes, Joshua trees, volcanic cinder cones, and habitats for bighorn
sheep, desert tortoises, jackrabbits and coyotes. Solitude and serenity are the big draws.

SLOW: DESERT TORTOISE X-ING

The Mojave is the home of the desert tortoise, which can live for up to 80 years, munching on wildflowers and grasses. Its canteen-like bladder allows it to go for up to a year without drinking. Using its strong hind legs, it burrows to escape the summer heat and freezing winter temperatures, and also to lay eggs. The sex of the hatchlings is determined by temperature: cooler for males, hotter for females.

Disease and shrinking habitat have decimated the desert tortoise population. They do like to rest in the shade under parked cars (take a quick look around before just driving away), and are often hit by off-road drivers. If you see a tortoise in trouble (eg stranded in the middle of a road), call a ranger.

It's illegal to pick one up or even approach too closely, and for good reason: a frightened tortoise may urinate on a perceived attacker, possibly dying of dehydration before the next rains come.

Daytime temperatures hover above 100°F (37°C) during summer, then hang around 50°F (10°C) in winter, when snowstorms are not unheard of. Strong winds will practically knock you over in spring and fall. No gas is available within the preserve.

◉ Sights & Activities

You can spend an entire day or just a few hours driving around the preserve, taking in its sights and exploring some of them on foot.

Cima Dome   MOUNTAIN
Visible to the south from I-15, Cima Dome is a 1500ft hunk of granite spiked with volcanic cinder cones and crusty outcrops of basalt left by lava. Its slopes are smothered in Joshua trees that collectively make up the largest such forest in the world. For close-ups, tackle the 3-mile round-trip hike up **Teutonia Peak** (5755ft), starting on Cima Rd, 6 miles northwest of Cima.

Kelso Dunes   DUNES
Rising up to 600ft high, these beautiful 'singing' dunes are the country's third-tallest sand dunes. Under the right conditions they emanate low humming sounds that are caused by shifting sands. Running downhill sometimes jump-starts the effect. The dunes are 3 miles along a graded dirt road west of Kelbaker Rd, 7.5 miles south of Kelso Depot.

Hole-in-the-Wall   HIKING, DRIVING
These vertical walls of rhyolite tuff (pronounced toof), which look like Swiss-cheese cliffs made of unpolished marble, are the result of a powerful prehistoric volcanic eruption that blasted rocks across the landscape. On the 0.5-mile **Rings Trail**, metal rings lead down through a narrow slot canyon, once used by Native Americans to escape 19th-century ranchers. **Wild Horse Canyon Rd**, an incredibly scenic 9.5-mile backcountry drive up to Mid Hills, also starts at Hole-in-the-Wall. Ask at the visitors center if it's currently passable. Hole-in-the-Wall is on Black Canyon Rd, east of Kelso-Cima Rd via unpaved Cedar Canyon Rd. Coming from I-40, exit at Essex Rd.

🍴 Sleeping & Eating

Baker, north of the Mojave National Preserve along I-15, has plenty of cheap, largely charmless motels and takeout restaurants. Southeast of the preserve, along Route 66, Needles has slightly better options.

Camping
First-come, first-served sites with pit toilets and potable water are available at two small, developed **campgrounds** (tent & RV sites $12): Hole-in-the-Wall, surrounded by rocky desert landscape; and Mid Hills (no RVs), set among pine and juniper trees. Free backcountry and roadside camping is permitted throughout the preserve in areas already used for the purpose, such as the Rainy Day Mine Site and Granite Pass off the Kelbaker Rd, and Sunrise Rock off the Cima Rd. Ask for details and directions at the visitors centers. There's no camping along paved roads, in day-use areas or within 200yd of any water source.

❶ Information

Hole-in-the-Wall Visitor Center (☑760-252-6104; ⊙9am-4pm Wed-Sun Oct-Apr, 10am-4pm Sat May-Sep) Seasonal ranger programs, backcountry information and road-condition updates. It's about 20 miles north of I-40 via Essex Rd.

Kelso Depot Visitor Center (☏760-252-6108; ⊗9am-5pm Fri-Tue) The preserve's main visitors center is in a gracefully restored, 1920s Spanish-Mission-revival railway depot. It is staffed with knowledgeable rangers who can help you plan your day. There are also excellent natural and cultural history exhibits, as well as an old-fashioned **lunch counter** (dishes $3.50 to $8.50).

❶ Getting There & Away

Mojave National Preserve is hemmed in by I-15 in the north and I-40 in the south. The main entrance off I-15 is at Baker, from where it's about 30 miles south to the central Kelso Depot visitors center via Kelbaker Rd, which links up with I-40 after another 23 miles. Cima Rd and Morning Star Mine Rd near Nipton are two other northern access roads. From I-40, Essex Rd leads to the Black Canyon Rd and Hole-in-the-Wall.

AROUND MOJAVE NATIONAL PRESERVE

Nipton

On the northeastern edge of the preserve, the teensy, remote outpost of **Nipton** (www.nipton.com) got its start in 1900 as a camp for workers in a nearby gold mine. The railway has passed through here since 1905 en route from Salt Lake City to Los Angeles. In 2010 the settlement made news when it opened a solar plant that generates 85% of its electrical needs.

The charismatic **Hotel Nipton** (☏760-856-2335; http://nipton.com; 107355 Nipton Rd; cabins/r with shared bath from $65/80; ⊗reception 8am-6pm; 🛜) dates to the first decade of the 20th century. There are five rooms sharing two baths in an adobe hotel with wraparound porch, as well as 'eco-lodges' (tented cabins) equipped with electricity, fans, woodstoves and platform beds. All guests may unwind in the two outdoor hot tubs.

Check-in is at the well-stocked **trading post** (open 8am to 6pm), which has maps, books, groceries, beverages and souvenirs. Next door is the **Whistle Stop Oasis** (☏760-856-1045; dishes $7-10; ⊗11am-6pm, dinner by reservation; 🛜). No alcohol is served, but you're welcome to purchase beer or wine at the trading post and bring it with you.

There's also an **RV park** (sites $25).

Primm

At the Nevada state line, next to an outlet shopping mall off I-15, **Terrible's Primm Valley Casino Resorts** (☏888-774-6668, 702-386-7867; www.primmvalleyresorts.com; 31900 Las Vegas Blvd S; r from $30; ❇@🛜🏊) is a trio of casino hotels linked by a tram. Rooms are basic and long in the tooth, but fine for a night. Family-friendly Buffalo Bill's is best and has its own amusement park, including a white-knuckle roller coaster and a log flume ride, as well as a buffalo-shaped swimming pool. Whiskey Pete's accepts pets ($15 fee). Primm Valley Hotel & Casino, across the freeway, has a spa and updated fitness center. Each has the gamut of casino-style dining options, including fast-food courts, all-you-can-eat buffets and 24-hour coffee shops.

DEATH VALLEY NATIONAL PARK

The very name evokes all that is harsh, hot and hellish – a punishing, barren and lifeless place of Old Testament severity. Yet closer inspection reveals that in **Death Valley** (☏760-786-3200; www.nps.gov/deva; 7-day entry per car $20) nature is putting on a truly spectacular show: singing sand dunes, water-sculpted canyons, boulders moving across the desert floor, extinct volcanic craters, palm-shaded oases and plenty of endemic wildlife. This is a land of superlatives, holding the US records for hottest temperature (134°F/57°C), lowest point (Badwater, 282ft below sea level) and largest national park outside Alaska (over 5000 sq miles).

Peak seasons are winter and the springtime wildflower bloom. From late February until early April, lodging within a 100-mile radius is usually booked solid and campgrounds fill before noon, especially on weekends. In summer, when the mercury climbs above 120°F (49°C), a car with reliable aircon is essential and outdoor explorations in the valley should be limited to the early morning and late afternoon. Spend the hottest part of the day by a pool or drive up to the higher – and cooler – elevations. Most of the park is served by paved roads, but if your plans include dirt roads, a high clearance vehicle and off-road tires are essential.

Death Valley & Around

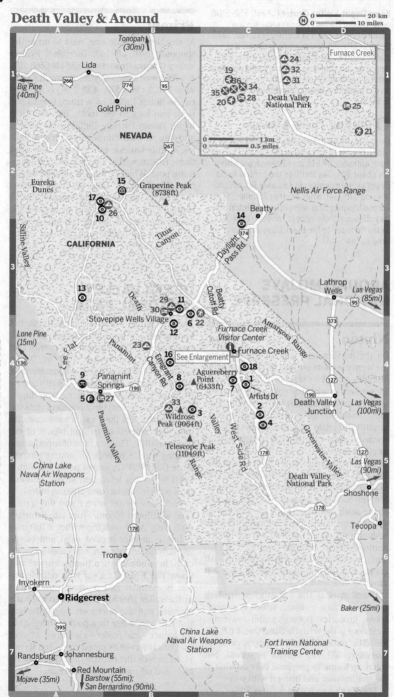

Death Valley & Around

Sights

Furnace Creek

At 190ft (58m) below sea level, Furnace Creek is Death Valley's commercial hub, with the park's main visitors center, a general store, gas station (super expensive!), post office, ATM, internet access, golf course, lodging and restaurants. Cleverly concealed by a date palm grove is a solar power plant that currently generates one-third of Furnace Creek's energy needs.

Borax Museum   MUSEUM
(📞760-786-2345; ⏰9am-9pm Oct-May, variable in summer) FREE On the grounds of the Ranch at Furnace Creek (p698), this museum explains what all the fuss about borax was about, with alluring samples of local borate minerals and their uses; it's in the 1883 miners' bunkhouse. Out back there's a large collection of pioneer-era stagecoaches and wagons. A short drive north, an interpretive trail follows in the footsteps of late-19th-century Chinese laborers and through the adobe ruins of **Harmony Borax Works**, where you can take a side trip through twisting **Mustard Canyon**.

South of Furnace Creek

If possible start out early in the morning to drive up to **Zabriskie Point** for spectacular valley views across golden badlands eroded into waves, pleats and gullies. Escape the heat by continuing on to **Dante's View** at 5475ft, where you can simultaneously see the highest (Mt Whitney) and lowest (Badwater) points in the contiguous USA. The drive there takes about 1½ to two hours round-trip.

Badwater itself, a foreboding landscape of crinkly salt flats, is a 17-mile drive south of Furnace Creek. Here you can walk out onto a constantly evaporating bed of salty, mineralized water that's otherworldly in its beauty. Along the way, you may want to check out narrow **Golden Canyon**, easily explored on a 2-mile round-trip walk, and **Devil's Golf Course**, where salt has piled up into saw-toothed miniature mountains. About 9 miles south of Furnace Creek, the 9-mile, one-way **Artists Drive** scenic loop offers 'wow' moments around every turn; it's best done in the late afternoon when exposed minerals and volcanic ash make the hills erupt in fireworks of color.

PALM SPRINGS & THE DESERTS DEATH VALLEY NATIONAL PARK

Stovepipe Wells & Around

Stovepipe Wells, about 26 miles northwest of Furnace Creek, was Death Valley's original 1920s tourist resort. Today it has a small store, gas station, ATM, motel, campground and bar. En route, look for the roadside pull-off where you can walk out onto the powdery, Sahara-like **Mesquite Flat sand dunes**. The dunes are at their most photogenic when the sun is low in the sky and are especially magical during a full moon. Across the road, look for the **Devil's Cornfield**, full of arrow weed clumps. Just southwest of Stovepipe Wells, a 3-mile gravel side road leads to **Mosaic Canyon**, where you can hike and scramble along the smooth multihued rock walls. Colors are sharpest at midday.

Along Emigrant Canyon Rd

Some 6 miles southwest of Stovepipe Wells, Emigrant Canyon Rd veers off Hwy 190 and travels south to the park's higher elevations. En route you'll pass the turnoff to **Skidoo**, a mining ghost town where the silent movie *Greed* was filmed in 1923. It's an 8-mile trip on a graded gravel road suitable for high-clearance vehicles only to get to the ruins and jaw-dropping Sierra Nevada views.

Further south, Emigrant Canyon Rd passes the turnoff for the 7-mile dirt road leading past the **Eureka Mines** to the vertiginous **Aguereberry Point** (high-clearance vehicles only), where you'll have fantastic views into the valley and out to the colorful Funeral Mountains from a lofty 6433ft. The best time to visit is in the late afternoon.

Emigrant Canyon Rd now climbs steeply over Emigrant Pass and through Wildrose Canyon to reach the **charcoal kilns**, a line-up of large, stone, beehive-shaped structures historically used by miners to make fuel for smelting silver and lead ore. The landscape is subalpine, with forests of piñon pine and juniper; it can be covered with snow, even in spring.

Panamint Springs

About 30 miles west of Stovepipe Wells, on the edge of the park, Panamint Springs is a tiny enclave with a motel, campground, pricey gas station and small store. Several often overlooked, but wonderful hidden gems are easily accessed from here. **Father Crowley Point**, for instance, peers deep into Rainbow Canyon, created by lava flows and scattered with colorful volcanic cinders. In spring DIY adventurers attempt the 2-mile graded gravel road, followed by a mile-long cross-country hike out to **Darwin Falls**, a spring-fed cascade that plunges into a gorge, embraced by willows that attract migratory birds. You could also take roughshod Saline Valley Rd out to **Lee Flat**, where Joshua trees thrive.

Scotty's Castle & Around

About 55 miles north of Furnace Creek, **Scotty's Castle** (☎877-444-6777; www.recreation.gov; tours adult/child from $15/7.50; ⊙grounds 7am-4:15pm, tour schedules vary) is named for Walter E Scott, alias 'Death Valley Scotty,' a gifted tall-tale teller who captivated people with his fanciful stories of gold. His most lucrative friendship was with Albert and Bessie Johnson, insurance magnates from Chicago. Despite knowing that Scotty was a freeloading liar, they bankrolled the construction of this elaborate Spanish-inspired villa, complete with red-tiled roofs, bell towers and swimming pool (now empty). Restored to its 1930s glory, the historic house has sheepskin drapes, carved California redwood, handmade tiles, elaborately wrought iron, woven Shoshone baskets and a bellowing pipe organ.

There's no charge to enter the grounds, but entrance to the house is by tour only. Costumed guides recount Scotty's apocryphal story in colorful detail on the **Living History Tour** (⊙10am-3pm) and the more technically minded **Underground Tours** (⊙Nov-Apr, as staffing permits). Ranger-guided hiking tours to Scotty's cabin at **Lower Vine Ranch** (adult/child $20/10; ⊙as staffing permits) operate on a more limited schedule.

Advance tickets are recommended at least one day before your visit. On tour days, tickets are sold on a first-come, first-served basis at the Scotty's Castle visitors center. Waits of two hours or more for the next available tour are common on high-traffic weekends and holidays.

Three miles west of Scotty's pad, a rough 5-mile road leads to 770ft-deep **Ubehebe Crater,** formed by the explosive meeting of fiery magma and cool groundwater. Hikers can loop around its half-mile-wide rim and over to younger **Little Hebe Crater**.

It's slow going for another 27 miles on a tire-shredding dirt road to the eerie **Racetrack**, where you can ponder the mystery of faint tracks that slow-moving rocks have etched into the dry lakebed. Despite the name, the Racetrack can be accessed only on foot; it's completely off limits when the ground is wet. High-clearance vehicle and off-road tires are required to reach the Racetrack; without them, in the likely event of a flat tire, towing will set you back $1100.

There's a snack bar, but no gas station at Scotty's.

◉ Towards Beatty

Driving north from Furnace Creek, Hwy 374 veers off Hwy 190 and runs 22 miles east to Beatty, across the Nevada state line. About 2 miles outside the park boundary is the turnoff to one-way **Titus Canyon Rd**, one of the most spectacular backcountry roads, leading back toward Scotty's Castle in about 27 miles of unpaved track. The road climbs, dips and winds to a crest in the Grapevine Mountains then slowly descends back to the desert floor past a ghost town, petroglyphs and dramatic canyon narrows. The best light conditions are in the morning. High-clearance vehicles are required. Check road conditions at the visitors center.

Rhyolite (www.rhyolitesite.com; off Hwy 374; ⊙sunrise-sunset) FREE, a ghost town a few miles beyond the Titus Canyon turnoff, epitomizes the hurly-burly, boom-and-bust story of Western gold-rush mining towns at the turn of the last century. Amid the skeletal remains of houses, municipal buildings and a three-story bank is the 1906 'bottle house' (built of beer bottles salvaged from town saloons). Also here is the bizarre **Goldwell Open Air Museum** (www.goldwellmuseum.org; off Hwy 374; ⊙24hr) FREE, a trippy art installation conceived by Belgian artist Albert Szukalski.

🏃 Activities

Families can pick up fun-for-all-ages **junior ranger program** activity books at the Furnace Creek visitors center, which has info-packed handouts on all kinds of activities, including hiking trails and mountain-biking routes.

Farabee's Jeep Rentals   DRIVING TOUR
(☎760-786-9872; www.farrabeesjeeprentals.com; 2-/4-door Jeep incl 200 miles $195/235; ⊙mid-Sep–late May) If you don't have a 4WD but would like to explore the park's backcountry, rent a Jeep from this outfit. You must be over 25 years old, have a valid driver's license, credit card and proof of insurance.

Rates include water and supplies such as GPS in case of emergency. It's next to Inn at Furnace Creek (p698).

Furnace Creek Bike Rentals   MOUNTAIN BIKING
(☎760-786-3371; bike hire 1/24hr $15/49, Hells Gate Downhill Bike Tour $49; ⊙year-round, Hells Gate Downhill Bike Tour 10am & 2pm) The general store at the Ranch at Furnace Creek (p698) rents mountain bikes. Cycling is allowed on all established paved and dirt roads, but never on hiking trails. On demand, staff also organize the 2½-hour **Hells Gate Downhill Bike Tour**, which transports you up to a 2200ft elevation for a 10-mile downhill ride back to the valley floor.

Furnace Creek Golf Course   GOLF
(☎760-786-3373; www.furnacecreekresort.com/activities/golfing; Hwy 190, Furnace Creek; green fees summer/winter $30/60; ⊙year-round) For novelty's sake, play a round at the world's lowest-elevation golf course (214ft below sea level, 18 holes, par 70), redesigned by Perry Dye in 1997. It's also been certified by the Audubon Society for its environment-friendly management.

Furnace Creek Stables   HORSEBACK RIDING
(☎760-614-1018; www.furnacecreekstables.net; Hwy 190, Furnace Creek; 1/2hr rides $55/70; ⊙mid-Oct–mid-May) Saddle up to see what Death Valley looks like from the back of a horse on these guided rides. The monthly full-moon rides are the most memorable.

Ranch at Furnace Creek Swimming Pool

SWIMMING

This huge spring-fed pool is kept at a steady 84°F (29°C) and cleaned with a nifty flow-through system that uses minimal chlorine. It's primarily for Ranch at Furnace Creek (p698) guests, but a limited number of visitor passes are available ($5).

Hiking

Avoid hiking in summer, except on higher-elevation mountain trails, which may be snowed in during winter.

On Hwy 190, just north of Beatty Cutoff Rd, is the half-mile **Salt Creek Interpretive Trail**; in late winter or early spring, rare pupfish splash in the stream alongside the boardwalk. A few miles south of Furnace Creek is Golden Canyon (p695), where a self-guided interpretive trail winds for a mile up to the now-oxidized iron cliffs of **Red Cathedral**. With a good sense of orientation, you can keep going up to Zabriskie Point (p695) for a hardy 4-mile round-trip. Before reaching Badwater, stretch your legs with a 1-mile round-trip walk to the **Natural Bridge**.

Off Wildrose Canyon Rd, starting by the charcoal kilns, **Wildrose Peak** (9064ft) is an 8.4-mile round-trip trail. The elevation gain is 2200ft, but great views start about halfway up.

The park's most demanding summit is **Telescope Peak** (11,049ft), with views that plummet down to the desert floor – which is as far below as two Grand Canyons deep! The 14-mile round-trip climbs 3000ft above Mahogany Flat, off upper Wildrose Canyon Rd. Get full details from the visitors center before setting out.

✹ Festivals & Events

Death Valley '49ers

CULTURAL

(www.deathvalley49ers.org) In early or mid-November, Furnace Creek hosts this historical encampment, featuring cowboy poetry, campfire sing-alongs, a gold-panning contest and a Western art show. Show up early to watch the pioneer wagons come thunderin' in.

🛏 Sleeping

In-park lodging is pricey and often booked solid in springtime, but there are several gateway towns with cheaper lodging.

Panamint Springs Resort

MOTEL, CAMPGROUND $

(☎775-482-7680; www.panamintsprings.com; 40440 Hwy 190, Panamint Springs; tent site $10, RV partial/full hookup $20/35, r $79-129; 🅿❋🛜🐾) Elsewhere 'off the grid' is a state of mind, but it's a statement of fact at this low-key, family-run village of cabins and campgrounds on the park's western border. A generator creates electricity, limited internet access comes via satellite, and phone service is dicey at best (reserve via email or website). At these prices it ain't the Ritz, but rooms, while simple and aging, are clean and decent-sized.

Stovepipe Wells Village

MOTEL $$

(☎760-786-2387; www.escapetodeathvalley.com; Hwy 190, Stovepipe Wells; RV sites $33, r $117-176; 🅿❋@🛜🐾) The 83 rooms at this sea-level tourist village are newly spruced-up and have quality linens beneath Death Valley-themed artwork, cheerful Native American–patterned bedspreads, coffee-makers and TVs. The small pool is cool and the cowboy-style Toll Road restaurant (p699) serves three squares a day.

Ranch at Furnace Creek

RESORT $$

(☎760-786-2345; www.furnacecreekresort.com; Hwy 190, Furnace Creek; cabins $130-162, r $162-213; 🅿➸❋🛜🐾) Tailor-made for families, this rambling resort with multiple, motel-style buildings has received a vigorous facelift, resulting in spiffy rooms swathed in desert colors, updated bathrooms and French doors leading to porches with comfortable patio furniture. The grounds encompass a playground, spring-fed swimming pool, tennis courts, restaurants, shops and the Borax Museum (p695).

Inn at Furnace Creek

HOTEL $$$

(☎800-236-7916, 760-786-2345; www.furnacecreekresort.com; Hwy 190; r/ste from $345/450; ⊙mid-Oct–mid-May; 🅿➸❋@🛜) Roll out of bed and count the colors of the desert as you pull back the curtains in your room at this elegant 1927 Mission-style hotel. After a day of sweaty touring, enjoy languid valley views while lounging by the spring-fed swimming pool, cocktail in hand. The lobby has a 1930s retro look.

🍴 Eating & Drinking

Furnace Creek and Stovepipe Wells have general stores stocking basic groceries and camping supplies. Scotty's Castle has a snack bar.

Stovepipe Wells

Toll Road Restaurant & Badwater Saloon
AMERICAN $$

(Stovepipe Wells Village, Hwy 190; breakfast buffet $13, lunch $10-17, dinner $13-26; ⏱ 7am-10am, 11:30am-2pm & 6-10pm; 🛜🔌) Above-par cowboy cooking happens at this ranch house, which gets Old West flair from a rustic fireplace and rickety wooden chairs and tables. Many of the mostly meaty mains are made with local ingredients, such as mesquite honey, prickly pear and piñons. Lunch, mid-afternoon drinks and late-night snacks are served next door at **Badwater Saloon** (⏱ from 11am), along with cold draft beer and Skynyrd on the jukebox.

Furnace Creek

49'er Cafe
AMERICAN $$

(www.furnacecreekresort.com; Ranch at Furnace Creek, Hwy 190; mains breakfast $9-16, lunch $13-20, dinner $10-25; ⏱ 6am-10am & 11am-9pm Oct-May, 4-9pm only Jun-Sep; 🛜🔌) The smallest of the Ranch's main restaurants, this family-friendly stop serves giant omelets, Benedicts and pancakes for breakfast, plus fish and chips, sandwiches and burgers for lunch. It's always crowded. Portions are huge.

Corkscrew Saloon
AMERICAN $$

(Ranch at Furnace Creek, Hwy 190, Furnace Creek; mains $9-19, barbecue $28-36; ⏱ 11:30am-midnight) This gregarious joint has darts, draft beer and a dynamite barbecue at dinner time, as well as pretty good, but pricey pizzas and pub grub such as onion rings and burgers.

★ Inn at Furnace Creek
INTERNATIONAL $$$

(☎ 760-786-2345; mains lunch $13-17, dinner $18-45; ⏱ 7:30-10:30am, noon-2:30pm & 5:30-9:30pm mid-Oct–mid-May) Views of the Panamint Mountains are stellar from this formal dining room with a dress code (no shorts or T-shirts, jeans ok), where the menu draws inspiration from Continental, Southwestern and Mexican cuisine. Afternoon tea in the lobby lounge and Sunday brunch are hoity-toity affairs. At least have a cocktail on the stone terrace as the sun sets beyond the mountains (and the parking lot, but who's complaining?).

Wrangler Restaurant
STEAKHOUSE $$$

(Ranch at Furnace Creek, Hwy 190, Furnace Creek; breakfast/lunch buffet $11/15, dinner mains $27-39; ⏱ 6-9am, 11am-2pm & 5:30-9pm Oct-May, 6-10am & 6-9:30pm May-Oct) The Ranch at Furnace Creek's main restaurant serves pretty standard but belly-busting buffets at breakfast and lunchtime (when tour bus groups invade) and turns into a pricey steakhouse at night.

CAMPING IN DEATH VALLEY

Of the park's nine campgrounds, only **Furnace Creek** (☎ 877-444-6777; www.recreation.gov) accepts reservations and only from mid-April to mid-October. All other campgrounds are first-come, first-served. At peak times, such as weekends during the spring wildflower bloom, campsites fill by mid-morning.

Backcountry camping (no campfires) is allowed 2 miles off paved roads and away from developed and day-use areas, and 100yd from any water source; pick up free permits at visitors centers.

Furnace Creek Ranch and Stovepipe Wells Village offer public showers ($5, including swimming-pool access).

CAMPGROUND	SEASON	LOCATION	FEE	CHARACTERISTICS
Furnace Creek	year-round	valley floor	$18	pleasant grounds, some shady sites
Sunset	Oct-Apr	valley floor	$12	huge, RV-oriented
Texas Spring	Oct-Apr	valley floor	$14	good for tents
Stovepipe Wells	Oct-Apr	valley floor	$12	parking-lot style, close to dunes
Mesquite Springs	year-round	1800ft	$12	close to Scotty's Castle
Emigrant	year-round	2100ft	free	tents only
Wildrose	year-round	4100ft	free	seasonal water
Thorndike	Mar-Nov	7400ft	free	may need 4WD, no water
Mahogany Flat	Mar-Nov	8200ft	free	may need 4WD, no water

✕ Panamint

Panamint Springs Resort AMERICAN $$
(Hwy 190, Panamint Springs; dishes from $10;
☺breakfast, lunch & dinner; ☎) Friendly out-
back cafe serving pizzas, burgers, salads,
steaks and other standards. Toast the pano-
ramic views from the front porch with one of
its 100 bottled beers from around the world.

❶ Information

Entry permits ($20 per vehicle) are valid for sev-
en days and are sold at self-service pay stations
throughout the park. For a free map and newspa-
per, show your receipt at the visitors center.

Cell-phone reception is poor to nonexistent
in the park; you'll have better luck at Furnace
Creek, Stovepipe Wells and Scotty's Castle; get
phone cards at general stores in Stovepipe Wells
and Furnace Creek.

Furnace Creek Visitor Center (☎760-786-
3200; www.nps.gov/deva; ☺8am-5pm) The
park's recently renovated main visitors center
has fabulous exhibits on the local ecosystem
and the native Timbasha and Shoshone peo-
ples. The gorgeously shot movie *Seeing Death
Valley* screens here. Fill up water bottles, and
check schedules for ranger-led activities.

Scotty's Castle Visitors Center (☎760-786-
2392, ext 231; North Hwy; ☺8:45am-4:30pm
May-Oct, 8:30am-5:30pm Nov-Apr) Has exhib-
its from the castle's museum-worthy collection.

❶ Getting There & Away

Gas is expensive in the park, so fill up your tank
beforehand.

Furnace Creek can be reached via Baker
(115 miles, two to 2½ hours), Beatty (45 miles,
one to 1½ hours), Las Vegas (via Hwy 160, 120
miles, 2½ to three hours), Lone Pine (105 miles,
two hours), Los Angeles (300 miles, five to 5½
hours) and Ridgecrest (via Trona, 120 miles, 2½
to three hours).

AROUND DEATH VALLEY NATIONAL PARK

Beatty, Nevada

Around 45 miles north of Furnace Creek,
this historic mining town (population 1154)
has certainly seen better days but makes a
reasonably inexpensive launch pad for visit-
ing Death Valley. There's an ATM, gas station
and library with internet access all along
Hwy 95 (Main St).

🛏 Sleeping

★ Atomic Inn MOTEL $
(☎775-553-2250; www.atomic-inn.com; 350 S
1st St; r incl breakfast from $57; ❄☎) ✿ At
this nicely updated, mid-century motel, get
a deluxe room to enjoy (somewhat) more
contemporary design, flat-screen TVs and
DVD players; there's a movie library. Classic
movies play in the lobby nightly. Kudos for
the solar water-heating system, xeriscaped
grounds and little green men out front.

LIFE AT DEATH VALLEY JUNCTION

The spot where Hwys 127 and 190 collide, about 30 miles east of Furnace Creek, is known
as Death Valley Junction (population 2, plus a few resident ghosts) and is home to one of
California's kookiest roadside attractions: the **Amargosa Opera House** (www.amargo-
saoperahouse.com; ☺9am-8pm). Built by the Pacific Borax Company, this 1920s Mexican
colonial-style courtyard building was the social hub of Death Valley Junction but fell into
disrepair after 1948. In 1967 New York dancer Marta Becket's car broke down nearby. Mar-
ta fell in love with the place and decided to inject new life into it by opening an opera house.
She entertained the curious with heartbreakingly corny dance-and-mime shows in an
auditorium whose walls she personally adorned with fanciful murals showing an audience
she imagined attending an opera in the 16th century, including nuns, gypsies and royalty.
In 2010 she starred in a 70-minute documentary, *The Ghosts of Death Valley Junction*.

Now in her 80s, Marta's high-stepping days are over, but she still occasionally re-
gales fans with narratives of old times. Tours of the opera house cost $5; enquire at the
reception of the attached **motel** (☎775-852-4441; r $70-85). To complete the eccentric
experience, spend the night in one of its seriously faded rooms with boudoir lamps and
Marta's murals but no TVs or phones. A newer **art gallery** and **train museum** open
sporadically, and a **cafe** (mains $9-19, pie per slice $5; ☺10am-6pm Mon-Thu, 8am-8pm Fri &
Sat, 8am-3pm Sun) has delicious homemade pies.

Stagecoach Hotel & Casino   CASINO MOTEL **$**
(☎775-553-2419, 800-424-4946; www.bestdeath-
valleyhotels.com; 900 E Hwy 95 N; r $60-108;
❄☎✉🐾) At the edge of town, rooms are
pretty bland but large and comfy, while the
pool is a nice place to lounge away a dusty
day in Death Valley. There's also a small,
smoky casino – hello, Nevada! – for slots,
blackjack and roulette, and a kids' arcade.

Exchange Club Motel   MOTEL **$**
(☎775-553-2333; 119 W Main St; s/d $57/62;
❄☎) The 44 rooms here have had a recent
makeover, resulting in new carpets and neu-
trally hued furniture.

🍴 Eating & Drinking

KC's Outpost Eatery & Saloon   AMERICAN **$**
(☎775-553-9175; 100 Main St; mains $8-9;
⊙10am-10pm Sun-Thu, to 11pm Fri & Sat; 🌐) The
simple, cinder-block building and formica
tables and chairs aren't much to look at, but
KC's bulging sandwiches – on homemade
bread, no less! – garner raves. The T-bird
sandwich is like a mini-Thanksgiving dinner. Potato salad makes a delish side dish.
Pizza menu too.

Sourdough Saloon   DIVE BAR
(☎775-553-2266; 106 Main St; ⊙10am-midnight)
At the crossroads of town, this classic serves
up Jaeger shots, a few American beers on
tap, a country-western–heavy jukebox, and
locals to mingle with. Every last bit of wall
and ceiling space is covered with signed
dollar bills. Look for billiards, darts, slot
machines and decent pub grub. Downside:
main bar is smoky.

Shoshone

Just a blip on the desert map, Shoshone
(population 30) is 55 miles from Furnace
Creek via Death Valley Junction, though
most folks follow the 20-mile-longer, but
more scenic, Hwy 178 through Badwater Basin instead. It has a gas station, store, lodging and free public wi-fi access.

Look for a rusted old Chevy parked outside the **Shoshone Museum** (admission by
donation; ⊙9am-3pm), which houses quirky
and well-meaning exhibits as well the local
visitors center (☎760-852-4524; www.death-
valleychamber.org; ⊙10am-4pm; 🛜).

Across the street the 1950s **Shoshone
Inn** (☎760-852-4335; www.shoshonevillage.com/
shoshone-inn; Hwy 127; d $94-102, cabins $113;
❄🛜✉) has updated cabins and a dozen

basic rooms set around a pine-shaded courtyard, all with satellite TV, that were getting
a sprucing up during our visit. Some have
a refrigerator and microwave. Bonus: small,
warm-springs pool. **Shoshone RV Park**
(☎760-852-4569; RV site with full hookup $25) is
just north of town.

Shoshone's only restaurant is **Crow Bar**
(☎760-852-4123; www.shoshonevillage.com/sho-
shone-crowbar-cafe-saloon; Hwy 127; mains $6-25;
⊙8am-9:30pm), a 1920 road house next to
the visitors center. It continues to charm
with Mexican dishes with cactus salsa and
all-American burgers, sandwiches, steaks
and 'rattlesnake' chili (sorry, no actual rattlesnake in it).

Tecopa

Some 8 miles south of Shoshone, the old
mining town of Tecopa (population 150) was
named after a peace-making Paiute chief
and is home to some wonderfully soothing,
hot natural mineral springs.

🏃 Activities

Delight's Hot Springs Resort   HOT SPRINGS
(☎760-852-4343; www.delightshotspringsresort.
com; 368 Tecopa Hot Springs Rd; hot springs 10am-
5pm $10, 10am-10pm $15) There are four private hot-springs tubs for splashing around
in as well as a handful of 1930s cabins with
kitchenette ($89 to $125) and newer motel
rooms ($79), in case you want to spend the
night.

Tecopa Hot Springs Resort   HOT SPRINGS
(☎760-852-4420; www.tecopahotsprings.org; 860
Tecopa Hot Springs Rd; bathing $8, incl towel $10;
⊙call ahead Jun-Sep) Motel lodging ($75 to
$95), cabins and campsites (tent/RV $25/35)
with spa-pool access included in overnight
rates – plus a rock labyrinth and art gallery.

Next door, **Tecopa Hot Springs Campground & Pools** (☎760-852-4481; ⊙hrs vary)
has two simple, but clean men's and wom-
en's bathhouses (entry $7), where tribal el-
ders, snowbird RVers and curious tourists
soak together, plus a private pool for $25 for
up to six people.

China Ranch Date Farm   FARM
(www.chinaranch.com; ⊙9am-5pm) Just outside
Tecopa, this family-run, organic date farm is
a lush oasis in the middle of the blistering
desert. You can go hiking or bird-watching
and, of course, stock up on luscious dates or
try their yummy date nut bread. To get here,

follow the Old Spanish Trail Hwy east of Tecopa Hot Springs Rd, turn right on Furnace Creek Rd and look for the signs.

Sleeping & Eating

Cynthia's
HOSTEL, INN $$

(☑760-852-4580; www.discovercynthias.com; 2001 Old Spanish Trail Hwy; dm $22-25, r $75-118, tepee $165-225; ⊙check-in 3-8pm; P🐾) Match your budget to the bed at this congenial inn helmed by the friendly Cynthia, about three miles from central Tecopa. Your choices: a colorful and eclectically decorated private room in a vintage trailer, a bed in a dorm, or a Native American–style tepee (a short drive away) with thick rugs, fire pits and comfy king-size beds.

Pre-made and freezer-to-grill meals are available with pre-order. Reservations are essential, even if that means just calling ahead from the road.

★Pastels Bistro
CALIFORNIAN $$

(860 Tecopa Hot Springs Rd; mains $13-22; ⊙noon-9pm Fri-Mon; 🐾) This artsy road house sure looks funky-dunky, but the chow is seriously gourmet with lots of healthy, veggie-friendly options (Mediterranean plate, Moroccan eggplant curry, etc.) and charming staff. The California fusion menu, often made with organic ingredients, is always changing. No phone, internet or credit cards.

UPPER MOJAVE DESERT

The Mojave Desert covers a vast region, from urban areas on the northern edge of LA County to the remote, sparsely populated country of the Mojave National Preserve. The upper Mojave is a harsh land, with sporadic mining settlements and vast areas set aside for weapons and aerospace testing. But there are a few things out here worth stopping for, too.

Lancaster-Palmdale

The Antelope Valley is dead flat. It's difficult to see a valley, much less an antelope. But in spring, bright-orange fields of California poppies create a spectacular carpet, like a vision out of The Wizard of Oz.

West of Lancaster the **Antelope Valley California Poppy Reserve** (☑661-724-1180; www.parks.ca.gov; 15101 Lancaster Rd, at 170th St W; per vehicle $10; ⊙sunrise-sunset) offers hillside walks among the wildflowers. To get there take Hwy 14 south of Mojave for about 25 miles, exit at Ave I in Lancaster and drive 15 miles west. **Arthur B Ripley Desert Woodland State Park** (Lancaster Rd, at 210th St W; ⊙sunrise-sunset), 5 miles west, has an untrammeled interpretive trail leading through precious stands of Joshua trees.

East of Lancaster, **Antelope Valley Indian Museum** (☑661-942-0662; www.avim. parks.ca.gov; Ave M, btwn 150th & 170th Sts; adult/child under 12yr $3/free; ⊙11am-4pm Sat & Sun) displays Native-American artifacts from around California and the Southwest. There is first-come, first-served camping among Joshua trees and desert-tortoise habitat at nearby **Saddleback Butte State Park** (☑661-942-0662; www.parks.ca.gov; 170th St E, south of Ave J; tent & RV sites $20), about 17 miles east of Lancaster.

Budget motels line Sierra Hwy, east of downtown Lancaster and Hwy 14. The retro 1950s **Town House Motel** (☑661-942-1195; www.townhouselancaster.com; 44125 Sierra Hwy; r $60-70; P🌸@🐾🐾) has clean, simple rooms.

Downtown Lancaster has a quaint, tree-lined main street along Lancaster Ave, lined with plaques commemorating test pilots. **Lemon Leaf Cafe** (☑661-942-6500; www.lemonleaf.com; 653 W Lancaster Blvd; mains $10-20; ⊙7am-9pm Mon-Thu & Sat, to 10pm Fri) dishes generous portions of market-fresh Mediterranean salads such as the cranberry turkey cobb, grilled panini sandwiches, pastas and pizzas, plus a nicely tangy lemon tart. **Bex** (☑661-945-2399; www.bexgrill.com; 706 W Lancaster Bl) is a cavernous, all-purpose bar and grill with burgers, pizzas, a music hall and bowling alley.

Mojave

Driving north on Hwy 14, Mojave (population 4238) is the first stop on the 'Aerospace Triangle' that also includes Boron and Ridgecrest. The modest town is home to a huge air-force base as well as the country's first commercial space port, and has witnessed major moments in air- and space-flight history.

The storied **Edwards Air Force Base** (☑661-277-3511; www.edwards.af.mil) is a flight-test facility for the US Air Force, NASA and civilian aircraft, and a training school for test pilots with the 'right stuff'. It was from here that Chuck Yeager piloted the world's first supersonic flight, and where the first space shuttles glided in after their missions. Free five-hour tours of the on-base flight museum and NASA flight research center are usually given on the first and third Fridays of the month. Reservations are essential and must be made at least 14 days in advance (30 days for non-US citizens).

The **Mojave Air & Space Port** (www.mojaveairport.com) made history in 2003 with the launch of **SpaceShipOne**, the first privately funded human space flight, thus laying the groundwork for commercial space tourism. Dozens of aerospace companies are hard at work here developing the latest aeronautical technologies, including SpaceShipTwo for Richard Branson's Virgin Galactic.

A replica of SpaceShipOne is on display in the airport's small **Legacy Park**, along with a huge Rotary Rocket, which was an early reusable civilian space vehicle developed here in the late '90s. The **Voyager Cafe** has some great old photographs.

The Air & Space Port is also home to a huge **airplane graveyard** (off-limits to visitors) where retired commercial airplanes roost in the dry desert air waiting to be scavenged for spare parts.

There are national chain motels along Rte 14 in Mojave, but locally owned **Mariah Country Inn & Suites** (☑ 661-824-4980; www.mariahhotel.com; 1385 Hwy 58, Mojave; r incl breakfast from $89; P✳☎🐾🐕) is by the entrance to the Air & Space Port. Immaculately kept rooms have early American-style furniture, and there's a pool, small hot tub and a few fitness machines.

Boron

Off Hwy 58, about midway between Mojave and Barstow, this tiny town (population 2253) catapulted onto the map in 1927 with the discovery of one of the world's richest borax deposits. Today, it is home to California's **largest open-pit mine**, operated by the global mining concern Rio Tinto. At 1 mile wide, 2.5 miles long and up to 650ft deep, the mine looks like a man-made Grand Canyon and supplies 40% of the world's demand for this versatile mineral (used in everything from glass to detergents). Historically, Boron was where Death Valley's famous 20-mule teams deposited their huge loads of borax at a dusty desert railway station, hauled from over 165 miles away.

◉ Sights

Borax Visitors Center　　　　　　　MUSEUM
(☑ 760-762-7588; www.borax.com; Borax Rd, off Hwy 58; per car $3; ☉9am-5pm) On a hilltop on the grounds of the mining complex, this museum reeks 'corporate promo' but also has some fine exhibits and a film explaining the history and process of borax mining, processing, distribution and uses. Views of the mine from up here are stupendous.

Saxon Aerospace Museum　　　　　MUSEUM
(☑ 760-762-6600; www.saxonaerospacemuseum.com; 26922 Twenty Mule Team Rd; admission by donation; ☉10am-4pm) This modest, volunteer-run museum recounts milestones in experimental flight testing in the surrounding desert, including the first breaking of the sound barrier, the first hypersonic flight and the first space-shuttle landing. It has one of America's largest collections of rocket engines, from the X-1 and X-15 to the latest composites

Twenty Mule Team Museum　　　　MUSEUM
(☑ 760-762-5810; www.20muleteammuseum.com; 26962 Twenty Mule Team Rd; admission by donation; ☉10am-4pm) Next door to Saxon Aerospace Museum, this low-budget museum is a haphazardly organized treasure trove of historic knickknacks: a 1930s beauty shop, products made with locally mined borax, watch fobs, belt buckles and memorabilia of the 2000 movie *Erin Brockovich*, which was filmed nearby and employed many locals as extras; Julia Roberts won an Oscar for the title role.

✖ Eating

Domingo's　　　　　　　　　　MEXICAN $$
(☑ 760-762-6266; 27075 Twenty Mule Team Rd; mains $6-13; ☉11am-10pm Mon-Sat, 10am-10pm Sun; 🐾) Autographed photos of astronauts and air-force test pilots hang on the walls of this festive roadside cantina. Lunchtime crowds from the nearby military base feast on killer homemade salsa with roasted chiles and famous fajitas.

Ridgecrest

Ridgecrest (population 28,325) is a service town where you can find gas, supplies, information and cheap lodging en route to Death Valley or the Eastern Sierra Nevada. Its main raison d'être is the China Lake US Naval Air Weapons Station that sprawls for a million acres (one third the size of Delaware!) north of the town.

US Naval Museum of Armament & Technology (☑ 760-939-3530; www.chinalakemuseum.org; ⊙ 10am-4pm Mon-Sat) FREE, right on the base, is an unapologetic celebration of US military might that is likely to fascinate technology, flight, history and military buffs – and perhaps even utter pacifists.

Many of the rockets, guided missiles, torpedoes, guns, bombs, cluster weapons etc on display were developed or tested on this very base before seeing action in wars from WWII to Afghanistan. If you ever wanted to touch a **Tomahawk missile** or have your picture taken with a 'Fat Man' (the atomic bomb that was dropped on Japan, that is), this is the place to do it. A documentary takes you on a helicopter flight of the base for bird's-eye views of the 4-mile-long **supersonic research track** and the antimissile testing grounds.

To get to the museum, you need to stop at the base's visitors center on China Lake Blvd (near Inyokern Rd), fill out a form and present your driver's license, car registration and vehicle insurance. Foreign visitors must also show their passport.

Trona Pinnacles

What do the movies *Battlestar Galactica, Star Trek V: The Final Frontier* and *Planet of the Apes* have in common? Answer: they were all filmed at Trona Pinnacles, an awesome natural landmark where tufa spires rise out of an ancient lakebed in alien fashion. You'll want an off-road vehicle for this trip. Look for the turnoff from Rte 178, about 18 miles east of Ridgecrest. From there it's another 5 miles south along a rutted dirt road to the scenic driving loop and short walking trails. Free primitive campsites are available.

Randsburg

About 20 miles south of Ridgecrest, off US Hwy 395, Randsburg is a 'living ghost town', an abandoned and now (somewhat) reinhabited mining town circa 1895. You can visit a tiny historical museum, antiques shops, a saloon, general store with lunch counter, and an opera house cafe (where old-timey melodramas are occasionally performed).

LAS VEGAS

It's three in the morning in a smoky casino when you spot an Elvis lookalike sauntering by arm in arm with a glittering showgirl just as a bride in a short white dress shrieks 'Blackjack!'

Vegas, baby: It's the only place in the world you can see ancient hieroglyphics, the Eiffel Tower, the Brooklyn Bridge and the canals of Venice in a few short hours. Sure, they're all reproductions, but in a desert metropolis that has transformed itself into one of the most lavish getaway destinations on the planet, nothing is executed halfway – not even the illusions.

Las Vegas is the ultimate escape. Time is irrelevant here. There are no clocks, just never-ending buffets and ever-flowing drinks. This city has been constantly reinventing herself since the days of the Rat Pack. Today its pull is all-inclusive: Hollywood bigwigs gyrate at A-list ultralounges, while college kids seek cheap debauchery and grandparents whoop it up at the hot, hot penny slots.

Welcome to the dream factory.

⊙ Sights

Four miles long, the **Strip** (Las Vegas Blvd) is the center of all the action. The Stratosphere caps the north end of the Strip and Mandalay Bay the south end. Don't be fooled: a walk to what looks like a nearby casino usually takes longer than expected.

Downtown is home to the city's oldest hotels and casinos: expect a retro feel, cheaper drinks and lower table limits. Its main drag is the fun-loving **Fremont Street Experience** (www.vegasexperience.com; Fremont St, btwn Main St & Las Vegas Blvd; ⊙ hourly dusk-midnight; ▣ Deuce, SDX) FREE, a five-block covered pedestrian mall featuring a zip line and a trippy light show hourly after dark.

Major tourist areas are safe. Las Vegas Blvd between downtown and the Strip gets shabby, as does much of downtown off Fremont St.

◎ The Strip

⭐ **Bellagio** CASINO
(☑ 702-693-7111; www.bellagio.com; 3600 Las Vegas Blvd S; ⊙ 24hr) Bellagio dazzles with Tuscan architecture and an 8-acre artificial lake, complete with don't-miss choreographed dancing **fountains** (www.bellagio.com; Bellagio; ⊙ sh ows every 30min 3-7pm Mon-Fri, noon-7pm Sat & Sun, every 15min 7pm-midnight daily; ▣).

Look up as you enter the lobby: the ceiling is adorned with a backlit glass sculpture composed of 2000 handblown flowers by artist Dale Chihuly. Although small, the **Bellagio Gallery of Fine Art** (☑877-957-9777, 702-693-7871; adult/child under 12yr $16/free; ⊙10am-7pm, last entry 6:30pm) showcases museum-quality paintings. Inside the **Bellagio Conservatory** (Bellagio; ⊙24hr; 🏛) **FREE**, impressive floral exhibits change throughout the year.

★**CityCenter**   LANDMARK
(www.citycenter.com; 3780 Las Vegas Blvd S) This futuristic-feeling complex is a small galaxy of hyper-modern hotels in orbit around glitzy **Crystals** (www.crystalsatcitycenter.com; 3720 Las Vegas Blvd S, CityCenter; ⊙10am-11pm Sun-Thu, to midnight Fri & Sat) shopping mall. The dramatic architectural showpiece is **Aria** (☑702-590-7111; www.aria.com; 3730 Las Vegas Blvd S, CityCenter; ⊙24hr), whose sophisticated casino provides a fitting backdrop for a $40 million public contemporary-art collection. Step inside the hush-hush opulent **Mandarin Oriental** (www.mandarinoriental.com; 3752 Las Vegas Blvd S) hotel for afternoon tea or evening cocktails in the 23-floor 'sky lobby' lounge, which has panoramic Strip views.

★**Venetian**   CASINO
(☑702-414-1000; www.venetian.com; 3355 Las Vegas Blvd S; ⊙24hr) Hand-painted ceiling frescoes, roaming mimes and operatic singers, **gondola rides** (shared ride per person $19, child under 3yr free, private 2-passenger ride $76; ⊙indoor 10am-10:45pm Sun-Thu, 10am-11:45pm Fri & Sat, outdoor rides noon-9:45pm, weather permitting; 🏛) and full-scale reproductions of Venice's most famous landmarks are found at this romantic casino hotel. Next door, its sister resort **Palazzo** (☑702-607-7777; www.palazzo.com; 3325 Las Vegas Blvd S; ⊙24hr) puts a more chichi spin on the Italian theme, with even more culinary heavyweights and high-end shopping.

LINQ & High Roller   LANDMARK
(☑800-223-7277; www.thelinq.com; 3545 Las Vegas Blvd S; High Roller ride before/after 5:50pm $25/35; ⊙High Roller noon-2am daily) Eclectic shops, buzzing bars and restaurants, live-music venues, a groovy bowling alley and a unique Polaroid photo museum line this new center-Strip pedestrian promenade. Towering above it all and lit by 2000 colorful glowing LEDs, High Roller is the world's tallest observation wheel.

Cosmopolitan   CASINO
(☑702-698-7000; www.cosmopolitanlasvegas.com; 3708 Las Vegas Blvd S; ⊙24hr) Hipsters once too cool for Vegas finally have a place to go, with a bevy of eclectic eateries and boutiques. Thankfully, Cosmo avoids utter pretension, despite wink-wink flourishes like Art-o-Mats (vintage cigarette machines hawking original art) and larger-than-life stiletto heel sculptures you can climb into for a photo op.

Stratosphere   CASINO
(☑702-380-7777; www.stratospherehotel.com; 2000 Las Vegas Blvd S; tower entry adult/child $18/10, all-day pass incl unlimited thrill rides $34, SkyJump from $110; ⊙casino 24hr, tower & thrill rides 10am-1am Sun-Thu, to 2am Fri & Sat, weather permitting; 🏛) Atop the 1149ft-high tapered tripod tower, vertiginous indoor and outdoor viewing decks afford Vegas' best 360-degree panoramas. To get to the top, ride one of America's fastest elevators, lifting you 108 floors in a mere 37 ear-popping seconds,

---

LAS VEGAS FOR CHILDREN

State law prohibits people under 21 years of age from loitering in casino gaming areas.
Circus Circus (☑702-734-0410; www.circuscircus.com; 2880 Las Vegas Blvd S; ⊙24hr; 🏛) casino hotel is all about families. Acrobats, contortionists and magicians perform on a **stage** (⊙shows every 30min, 11am-midnight) suspended above the casino. The **Adventuredome** (www.adventuredome.com; Circus Circus; day pass over/under 48in tall $30/17, per ride $5-8; ⊙10am-6pm daily, later on weekends & May-Sep; 🏛) indoor theme park is loaded with more family fun.

Also on the Strip, New York–New York (p708) casino hotel offers a roller coaster, a video-game arcade and Greenwich Village, where cobblestone streets are packed with family-friendly eateries.

East of the Strip, the **Pinball Hall of Fame** (www.pinballmuseum.org; 1610 E Tropicana Ave; per game 25¢-$1; ⊙11am-11pm Sun-Thu, to midnight Fri & Sat; 🏛; 🚌201) is an interactive mini museum that's better than any slot machines.

Las Vegas Strip

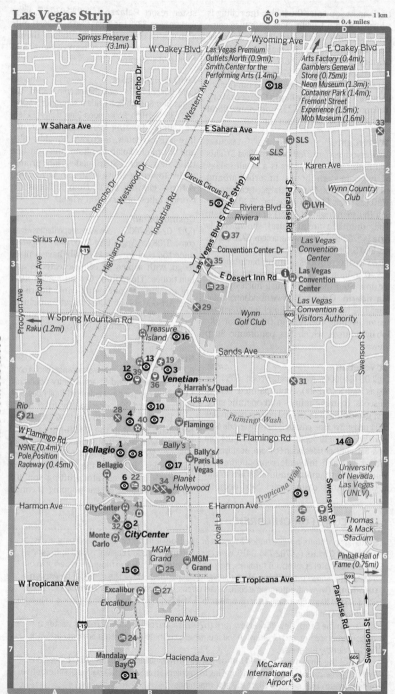

Las Vegas Strip

then queue for high-altitude thrill rides or a 'SkyJump' over the side of the tower.

Paris Las Vegas   CASINO
(☏ 702-946-7000; www.parislasvegas.com; 3655 Las Vegas Blvd S; ☺ 24hr) Evoking the gaiety of the City of Light, this pint-sized version of the French capital may not exude the true charm of Paris – it feels like a themed section of Disney World's Epcot – but efforts to emulate famous landmarks, including the Arc de Triomphe and **Eiffel Tower** (☏ 888-727-4758; adult/child 12yr & under/family $10.50/7.50/32,

after 7:15pm $15.50/10.50/47; ☺ 9:30am-12:30am Mon-Fri, to 1am Sat & Sun, weather permitting), make it an entertaining stop.

Mirage   CASINO
(☏ 702-791-7111; www.mirage.com; 3400 Las Vegas Blvd S; ☺ 24hr) Circling the rainforest atrium is a vast Polynesian-themed casino, including a pro-worthy poker room. In the hotel lobby's 20,000-gallon saltwater **aquarium**, 60 species of critters hailing from Fiji to the Red Sea swim. Out front in a lagoon, a fiery faux **volcano** (☺ shows hourly 6pm, 7pm or

8-11pm or midnight; (♿) **FREE** erupts after dark, halting Strip traffic.

Caesars Palace
CASINO

(☎702-731-7110; www.caesarspalace.com; 3570 Las Vegas Blvd S; ⊗24hr) Quintessentially kitschy Vegas, Caesars is a Greco-Roman fantasyland featuring marble reproductions of classical statuary, towering fountains, costumed cocktail waitresses, not one but two giant casinos and the fashionable Forum Shops (p713).

Flamingo
CASINO

(☎702-733-3111; www.flamingolasvegas.com; 3555 Las Vegas Blvd S; ⊗24hr) Opened by gangster Bugsy Siegel in 1946, the Flamingo is vintage Vegas. Weave through the slot machines out back to the **wildlife habitat** (☎702-733-3349; 3555 Las Vegas Blvd S; ⊗8am-dusk, pelican feedings 8am & 2:30pm; ♿) **FREE** to see Chilean flamingos, African penguins and brown pelicans.

New York–New York
CASINO

(☎702-740-6969; www.newyorknewyork.com; 3790 Las Vegas Blvd S; ⊗24hr) This mini metropolis shows off scaled-down replicas of the Empire State Building, the Statue of Liberty and the Brooklyn Bridge. Wrapping around the flashy facade is the **Big Apple roller coaster** (1 ride/day pass $14/25; ⊗11am-11pm Sun-Thu, 10:30am-midnight Fri & Sat; ♿), with NYC taxi-style cars.

Mandalay Bay
CASINO

(☎702-632-7777; www.mandalaybay.com; 3950 Las Vegas Blvd S; ⊗24hr) Besides its private beach, tropically themed M-Bay has only one standout attraction: the **Shark Reef** (☎702-632-4555; www.sharkreef.com; adult/child 5-12yr $18/12; ⊗10am-10pm daily late May–early Sep, 10am-8pm Sun-Thu, to 10pm Fri & Sat early Sep–late May, last admission 1hr before closing; ♿), an aquarium home to thousands of submarine beasties, with a shallow pool where kids can pet pint-sized sharks.

◎ Downtown & Off-Strip

★ Neon Museum
MUSEUM

(☎702-387-6366; www.neonmuseum.org; 770 Las Vegas Blvd N; 1hr tour adult/child 7-17yr daytime $18/12, after dark $25/22; ⊗tours daily, schedules vary) Take a fascinating historical walking tour of the Neon Museum's 'boneyard,' where irreplaceable vintage neon signs – Vegas' original art form – are salvaged. If tours

are sold out (book at least a few days ahead), you can stroll the museum's free al-fresco **Urban Gallery** of restored neon signs, including a sparkling genie lamp and retro motel marquees, at the Neonopolis on the Fremont Street Experience and the N 3rd St cul-de-sac just off Fremont St.

★ Mob Museum
MUSEUM

(☎702-229-2734; www.themobmuseum.org; 300 Stewart Ave; adult/child 11-17yr $20/14; ⊗10am-7pm Sun-Thu, to 8pm Fri & Sat; ☒Deuce) Inside the historic federal courthouse where mobsters sat for hearings in 1950–51, thoughtfully curated exhibits tell the story of organized crime in America with hands-on FBI equipment, mob-related artifacts and multimedia exhibits featuring interviews with real-life Tony Sopranos. Parking is $5.

Springs Preserve
MUSEUM, PARK

(☎702-822-7700; www.springspreserve.org; 333 S Valley View Blvd; adult/child 5-17yr $19/11; ⊗10am-6pm; ♿; ☒104) ✎ On the site of the natural springs that fed *las vegas* ('the meadows'), where southern Paiutes and Spanish Trail traders camped, and later Western pioneers settled the valley, this educational museum and gardens complex is an incredible trip through historical, cultural and biological time. The **Desert Living Center** demonstrates sustainable architectural design and everyday eco-conscious living.

Golden Nugget
CASINO

(☎702-385-7111; www.goldennugget.com; 129 E Fremont St; ⊗24hr; ☒Deuce, SDX) Looking like a million bucks, the Nugget has set the downtown benchmark since opening in 1946. No brass or cut glass was spared inside the swanky casino, with a nonsmoking poker room. The 61lb Hand of Faith, the world's largest gold nugget, is displayed around the corner from the hotel lobby.

Hard Rock
CASINO

(☎702-693-5000; www.hardrockhotel.com; 4455 Paradise Rd; ⊗24hr; ☒108) The original rock 'n' roll casino hotel is home to one of the world's most impressive collections of rock memorabilia, including Jim Morrison's handwritten lyrics to one of the Door's greatest hits, and leather jackets from a who's who of famous rock stars. The **Joint** (☎888-929-7849; most tickets $40-200; ☒108) concert hall, **Vinyl** music lounge and **Rehab** pool parties attract a sex-charged crowd.

National Atomic Testing Museum MUSEUM
(☎702-794-5151; www.nationalatomictestingmuseum.org; 755 E Flamingo Rd, Desert Research Institute; adult/child 7-17yr $14/12; ☉10am-5pm Mon-Sat, noon-5pm Sun; ⬚202) Recalling an era when the word 'atomic' conjured modernity and mystery, this Smithsonian afilliate writes an intriguing testament to the period when nuclear bombs were tested just outside Las Vegas. The deafening **Ground Zero Theater** mimics a concrete test bunker.

Downtown Arts District ARTS CENTER
On the **First Friday** (www.firstfridaylasvegas.com; ☉5-11pm) of each month, a carnival of 10,000 art-lovers, hipsters, indie musicians and hangers-on descend on Las Vegas' downtown arts district. These giant monthly block parties feature gallery openings, performance art, live bands and food trucks. The action revolves around the **Arts Factory** (☎702-383-3133; www.theartsfactory.com; 107 E Charleston Blvd; ☉9am-6pm daily, to 10pm 1st Fri of month; ⬚Deuce, SDX).

🏃 Activities

Qua Baths & Spa SPA
(☎866-782-0655; Caesars Palace; fitness center day pass $25, incl spa facilities $45; ☉6am-8pm) Social spa going is encouraged in the tea lounge, herbal steam room and arctic ice room, where dry-ice snowflakes fall.

VooDoo Zipline OUTDOORS
(☎702-777-7776; www.voodoozipline.com; 3700 W flamingo Blvd, Rio; day/night ride $25/37; ☉noon-midnight Mon-Thu, from 10am Fri-Sun, weather permitting) Suspended between the Rio's two casino-hotel towers, this rooftop zip line slingshots tandem riders over 30mph.

Stripper 101 DANCE
(☎866-932-1818, 702-260-7200; www.stripper101.com; 3663 Las Vegas Blvd S, Miracle Mile Shops, V Theater; tickets from $40; ☉schedules vary) Ladies, take a (non-nude) pole-dancing class in a cabaret setting completed with strobe lights, cocktails and feather boas.

Pole Position Raceway RACING
(☎702-227-7223; www.polepositionraceway.com; 4175 S Arville St; 1-week membership $6, per race $22-26; ☉11am-10pm Sun-Thu, to midnight Fri & Sat; ⬚202) Modeled on F1 road courses, this indoor racetrack lets you drive the USA's fastest indoor go-karts (up to 45mph!).

🛏 Sleeping

Rates rise and fall dramatically, depending on the season, special events, conventions etc, but weekday rates (Sunday through Thursday nights) are generally lower than weekend rates (Friday and Saturday nights). Check hotel websites, which usually feature calendars listing day-by-day room rates. Book ahead and beware of mandatory resort fees (up to $25 plus tax per night).

🛏 The Strip

Luxor CASINO HOTEL $
(☎888-386-4658, 702-262-4000; www.luxor.com; 3900 Las Vegas Blvd S; weekday/weekend r from $45/85; P❄✳@⚛) As long as you steer clear of noisier, older Pyramid rooms, this less-expensive Strip casino resort is functional enough for a few nights.

★ Mandalay Bay CASINO HOTEL $$
(☎877-632-7800, 702-632-7777; www.mandalaybay.com; 3950 Las Vegas Blvd S; weekday/weekend r from $105/130; P❄✳@🛜⚛) Ornately appointed rooms have a South Seas theme, with floor-to-ceiling windows and luxurious

---

VEGAS' COOLEST HOTEL POOLS

Mandalay Bay Splash around an artificial surf beach made of California sand, with a wave pool, lazy-river ride and casino games.

Hard Rock (p710) Seasonal swim-up blackjack, wild Rehab weekend pool parties and celeb-spotting at the über-hip Beach Club.

Mirage (p707) Lushly landscaped pools with waterfalls tumbling off cliffs, deep grottoes and palm-tree-studded islands for sunbathing.

Caesars Palace Corinthian columns, fountains, marble-inlaid pools and the topless Venus pool lounge make the Garden of the Gods Oasis divine.

Golden Nugget (p710) At this petite downtown pool, play blackjack or take the waterslide that corkscrews through a shark aquarium.

marble bathrooms. For more luxury, book a room at the Four Seasons or Delano boutique hotels, also at M-Bay. Swimmers will swoon over the sprawling pool complex, which has its own sandy beach.

MGM Grand
CASINO HOTEL $$

(☎877-880-0880, 702-891-1111; www.mgmgrand.com; 3799 Las Vegas Blvd S; weekday/weekend r from $70/140; P❋@🗟⛱) Vegas' biggest hotel is a gargantuan place, with over a dozen restaurants and bars and the Strip's most mammoth pool complex. For more space and quiet, nab a condo-style suite next door at the Signature towers.

Tropicana
CASINO HOTEL $$

(☎800-462-8767, 702-739-2222; www.troplv.com; 3801 Las Vegas Blvd S; weekday/weekend r from $75/120; P❋@🗟⛱) Keeping the Strip's tropical vibe going since 1953, the Trop's recent multimillion-dollar renovations have brought sunset colors and South Beach–style digs. Tropical gardens and lagoon pools await out back.

★ Encore
CASINO HOTEL $$$

(☎877-321-9966, 702-770-7100; www.wynnlasvegas.com; 3131 Las Vegas Blvd S; weekday/weekend ste from $199/249; P❋@🗟⛱) Newer than its sister resort Wynn Las Vegas, Encore offers equally opulent, but even more spacious suites amid gorgeous surrounds. Encore's glam nightclubs and DJ-driven pool club are envied hangouts.

Cosmopolitan
CASINO HOTEL $$$

(☎855-435-0005, 702-698-7000; www.cosmopolitanlasvegas.com; 3708 Las Vegas Blvd S; r/ste from $160/220; P❋@🗟⛱🞅) Are the luxuriously hip rooms worth the price tag? Style-conscious jetsetters seem to think so. Stumble out of your room at 1am to play some pool in the upper hotel lobby before going on a mission to find the 'secret' pizza joint.

🛏 Downtown & Off-Strip

Downtown hotels are generally less expensive than those on the Strip.

Hard Rock
CASINO HOTEL $

(☎800-473-7625, 702-693-5000; www.hardrockhotel.com; 4455 Paradise Rd; weekday/weekend r from $45/89; P❋@🗟⛱) Everything about this boutique hotel spells stardom. Brightly colored Euro-minimalist rooms feature souped-up stereos and plasma-screen TVs.

Golden Nugget
CASINO HOTEL $

(☎800-634-3454, 702-385-7111; www.goldennugget.com; 129 E Fremont St; weekday/weekend r from $49/89; P❋@🗟⛱) Pretend to relive the fabulous heyday of Vegas in the 1950s at this swank Fremont St address, where upgrades to the Rush Tower are worth every penny.

El Cortez Cabana Suites
HOTEL $

(☎800-634-6703, 702-385-5200; http://elcortezhotelcasino.com; 651 E Ogden Ave; weekday/weekend r from $40/80; P❋@🗟) Overhauled since its cameo in Scorcese's *Casino*, this downtown hotel has vintage-style suites painted in chartreuse with retro black-and-white tiled bathrooms.

Rumor
BOUTIQUE HOTEL $$

(☎877-997-8667, 702-369-5400; www.rumorvegas.com; 455 E Harmon Ave; weekday/weekend ste from $60/120; P❋@🗟⛱🞅) Opposite the Hard Rock, a sultry, nightclub atmosphere infuses these bachelor/ette pad suites, some with Jacuzzi tubs and white leather sofas.

🍴 Eating

Sin City is an unmatched eating adventure. Reservations are a must for upscale restaurants, especially on weekends.

🍴 The Strip

Along the Strip, cheap eats beyond fast-food joints are tough to find.

Tacos El Gordo
MEXICAN $

(☎702-641-8228; http://tacoselgordobc.com; 3049 Las Vegas Blvd S; items $2-10; ⊙9pm-3am Sun-Thu, to 5am Fri & Sat; 🚌Deuce, SDX) This Tijuana-style taco shop from SoCal is just the ticket when it's way late, you're almost broke and have a desperate craving for meaty tacos in handmade corn tortillas.

Earl of Sandwich
DELI $

(www.earlofsandwichusa.com; Planet Hollywood; items $2-7; ⊙24hr; 🖐) Pennypinchers sing the praises of this popular deli next to the casino that pops out toasted sandwiches, wraps and tossed salads, all with quick service.

Holsteins
BURGERS $$

(☎702-698-7940; www.holsteinslv.com; Cosmopolitan; items $6-18; ⊙11am-midnight, to 2am Fri & Sat; 🖐) Hand-crafted burgers are championship-worthy, as are all-American classic side dishes with unusual twists – deep-fried pickles, truffled mac 'n' cheese and milkshakes spiked with chocolate vodka.

Five50
PIZZERIA $$

(Aria, CityCenter; shared plates $9-18, pizzas $22-29; ⊙11am-midnight) At this chef-owned pizza bar, be bewildered by an extra-large menu of artisanal meat and cheese platters, garden-fresh salads, antipasti and more.

★ Joël Robuchon
FRENCH $$$

(☏702-891-7925; www.joel-robuchon.com/en; MGM Grand; tasting menu per person $120-425; ⊙5:30-10pm Sun-Thu, to 10:30pm Fri & Sat) A once-in-a-lifetime culinary experience; block off a solid three hours and get ready to eat your way through a multicourse seasonal French menu inside what feels like a 1930s Parisian mansion. Step next door to **L'Atelier de Joël Robuchon** for a marginally more economical meal. Book well in advance.

Jaleo
SPANISH, TAPAS $$$

(☏702-698-7950; www.jaleo.com; Cosmopolitan; shared plates $5-35; ⊙noon-midnight; ⚲) Pioneering Spanish chef José Andrés' restaurant serves creative modern tapas in a rustic contemporary dining room: recycled wooden tables have mismatched chairs and whimsical glassware. Reservations essential.

Todd English's Olives
MEDITERRANEAN $$$

(www.toddenglish.com; Bellagio; mains lunch $17-29, dinner $25-49; ⊙restaurant 11am-2:45pm & 5-10:30pm, bar 3-5pm; ⚲) East Coast chef Todd English crafts an homage to the life-giving fruit. Flatbread pizzas and housemade pastas get top billing, but the real selling point is patio tables overlooking Lake Como. Book ahead, even for lunch.

✕ Downtown & Off-Strip

Restaurants downtown offer better value than on the Strip. West of the Strip, the pan-Asian restaurants on Chinatown's Spring Mountain Rd are budget-saving options.

★ Container Park
FAST FOOD $

(☏702-637-4244; http://downtowncontainerpark.com; 707 E Fremont St; most items $3-9; ⊙11am-11pm Sun-Thu, to 1am Fri & Sat) With food truck menus, outdoor seating and late-night hours, vendors inside downtown's Container Park satisfy all appetites. Over-21s only after 9pm.

★ Raku
JAPANESE $

(☏702-367-3511; www.raku-grill.com; 5030 W Spring Mountain Rd; shared dishes $2-12; ⊙6pm-3am Mon-Sat; ☐203) LA chefs come to dine

when they're in town on this Japanese owner-chef's small plates of *robata*-grilled meats, homemade tofu and more. Book ahead.

Culinary Dropout
AMERICAN, FUSION $$

(☏702-522-8100; www.hardrockhotel.com; 4455 Paradise Rd, Hard Rock; mains brunch $8-14, lunch & dinner $14-32; ⊙11am-11pm Mon-Thu, 11am-midnight Fri, 10am-midnight Sat, 10am-11pm Sun; ☐108) With nouveau comfort food, a pool-view patio and rockin' live bands, there's no funkier gastropub around. Weekend brunch brings out bacon Bloody Marys.

Lotus of Siam
THAI $$

(☏702-735-3033; www.saipinchutima.com; 953 E Sahara Ave; mains $9-30; ⊙11:30am-2:30pm Mon-Fri, 5:30-10pm daily; ⚲; ☐SDX) It may look like just a strip-mall hole-in-the-wall, but the authentic northern Thai cooking has won almost as many awards as the wine cellar. Make reservations.

Firefly
TAPAS $$

(☏702-369-3971; www.fireflylv.com; 3824 Paradise Rd; shared plates $5-12, mains $15-20; ⊙11:30am-midnight; ☐108) Twice as fun as an overdone Strip restaurant, but at half the price, is that why it's always hopping? Nosh on traditional Spanish tapas and sip housemade sangria.

★ N9NE
STEAKHOUSE $$$

(☏702-933-9900; www.palms.com; 4321 W Flamingo Rd, Palms; mains $28-72; ⊙5:30-10pm Sun-Thu, to 11pm Fri & Sat; ☐202) At this hip steakhouse heavy with celebs, a dramatically lit dining room serves up beautifully aged steaks and chops, along with everything else from oysters Rockefeller to Pacific sashimi.

🍷 Drinking & Nightlife

Dress to impress at nightclubs, where cover charges vary depending on the door staff, male-to-female ratio, special guests and how crowded it is that night.

🍸 The Strip

★ XS
CLUB

(☎702-770-0097; www.xslasvegas.com; Encore; cover $20-50; ⏰9:30pm-4am Fri & Sat, from 10:30pm Sun & Mon) XS is *the* hottest nightclub in Vegas – at least for now. Surrounded by extravagantly gold-drenched decor, electronica DJs make the dance floor writhe. High rollers opt for VIP bottle service at poolside cabanas.

Marquee
CLUB

(☎702-333-9000; www.marqueelasvegas.com; Cosmopolitan; ⏰10pm-5am Thu-Sat & Mon) A-list celebrities, famous-name DJs, an outdoor beach club (open seasonally) and an alluring *je ne sais quoi* all make this top-tier club worth waiting in line for.

Hyde Bellagio
LOUNGE, NIGHTCLUB

(☎702-693-8700; www.hydebellagio.com; Bellagio; cover $20-40, usually free before 10pm; ⏰lounge 5-11pm daily, nightclub 10pm-4am Tue, Fri & Sat) Sink into a plush loveseat next to an oversized mirror or just stand on the balcony, awestruck, as the Bellagio's fountains dance outside this chic ultralounge.

Mix Lounge
LOUNGE

(64th fl, Mandalay Bay; cover after 10pm $20-25; ⏰5pm-midnight Sun-Tue, to 3am Wed-Sat) A posh place to grab sunset cocktails. The glass elevator has amazing views, and that's before you even glimpse the Strip panoramas from the soaring balcony.

Chandelier Bar
COCKTAIL BAR

(Cosmopolitan; ⏰24hr) In a city full of lavish casino bars, this triple-decker one pulls out all the stops. Mingle with hipsters and cocktail mixologists in spaces draped with colorful glowing beads.

Rhumbar
COCKTAIL BAR

(☎702-792-7615; www.rhumbarlv.com; Mirage; ⏰usually 1pm-midnight Sun-Thu, to 2am Fri & Sat, weather permitting) Caribbean-inspired bar's mojitos and daiquiris are a big step up from the sugary, yard-long frozen drinks sold along the Strip. Cool off on the outdoor patio.

Carnaval Court
BAR

(☎702-369-5000; www.harrahslasvegas.com; 3475 Las Vegas Blvd S, Harrah's; cover charge varies; ⏰11am-3am) Flair bartenders juggling fire and live cover bands keep this open-air bar packed with the kind of party people for whom spring break never ends.

Fireside Lounge
LOUNGE

(www.peppermilllasvegas.com; 2985 Las Vegas Blvd S, Peppermill; ⏰24hr) At the Strip's most unlikely romantic hideaway next to a casino coffee shop, couples canoodle with low lighting by a sunken fire pit. Sip a Scorpion with a straw.

🍸 Downtown & Off-Strip

Want to chill out with the locals? Head to one of these offbeat favorites.

Beauty Bar
BAR

(☎702-598-3757; www.thebeautybar.com; 517 Fremont St; cover free-$10; ⏰10pm-4am; 🚌Deuce) At the salvaged innards of a 1950s New Jersey beauty salon, swill a cocktail or chill out with DJs and live bands in the edgy Fremont East Entertainment District.

★ Frankie's Tiki Room
BAR

(☎702-385-3110; www.frankiestikiroom.com; 1712 W Charleston Blvd; ⏰24hr; 🚌206) At the city's only round-the-clock tiki bar, cocktails are rated in strength by skulls and famous tiki designers, sculptors and painters have their work on display all around.

Hofbräuhaus
BAR

(www.hofbrauhauslasvegas.com; 4510 Paradise Rd; ⏰11am-11pm Sun-Thu, to midnight Fri & Sat) At this replica Bavarian beer hall and garden, celebrate Oktoberfest year-round with imported suds, fair *fräuleins* and live oompah bands nightly.

☆ Entertainment

Las Vegas has no shortage of entertainment on any given night, with hundreds of production shows to choose from.

Tix 4 Tonight
BOOKING SERVICE

(☎877-849-4868; www.tix4tonight.com; 3200 Las Vegas Blvd S, Fashion Show; ⏰10am-8pm) Offers half-price tix for a limited lineup of same-day shows and small discounts on 'always sold-out' shows. Multiple locations.

★ **Beatles LOVE** THEATER

(☑702-792-7777, 800-963-9634; www.cirquedusoleil.com; Mirage; tickets $79-180; ☺7pm & 9:30pm Thu-Mon; ♿) Those who have seen every acrobatic Cirque production on the Strip say this kaleidoscopic music-and-dance homage to the Fab Four is the best yet.

Smith Center for the Performing Arts PERFORMING ARTS

(☑702-749-2000; www.thesmithcenter.com; 361 Symphony Park Ave, Symphony Park; tickets from $20; ☺schedule varies; ▣SDX) 🎵 Cabaret jazz, classical and contemporary music, dance troupes and comedians all perform at this art deco–inspired center downtown.

Absinthe THEATER

(☑800-745-3000; www.absinthevegas.com; Roman Plaza, Caesars Palace; tickets $99-125; ☺7:30pm & 9:30pm Wed-Sun) Raucous variety show mixes bawdy and surreal comedy with burlesque, cabaret and acrobatics under a big-top tent. No under-18s allowed.

🛍 Shopping

Gamblers General Store SOUVENIRS

(☑702-382-9903; www.gamblersgeneralstore.com; 800 S Main St; ☺9am-6pm Mon-Sat, to 5pm Sun; ▣108, Deuce) Authentic gaming supply shop sells collectible decks of cards used in Vegas casinos.

Grand Canal Shoppes at the Venetian MALL

(www.grandcanalshoppes.com; Venetian; ☺10am-11pm Sun-Thu, to midnight Fri & Sat) Italianate luxury with gondolas and international designers, including in the next-door Palazzo.

Forum Shops MALL

(www.simon.com; Caesars Palace; ☺10am-11pm Sun-Thu, to midnight Fri & Sat) Fashionista shop in an air-conditioned version of an ancient Roman marketplace.

Container Park MALL

(☑702-637-4244; http://downtowncontainerpark.com; 719 E Fremont St; ☺10am-9pm Mon-Sat, to 8pm Sun) An incubator for up-and-coming local art, clothing and jewelry designers.

Las Vegas Premium Outlets North MALL

(☑702-474-7500; www.premiumoutlets.com/vegasnorth; 875 S Grand Central Pkwy; ☺9am-9pm Mon-Sat, to 8pm Sun; ♿; ▣SDX) Vegas' biggest-ticket outlet mall features 120 high-end and casual brands.

ℹ Information

Wi-fi is available in most hotel rooms ($12 to $15 per 24 hours, sometimes included in the 'resort fee'). Cheaper cybercafes are inside souvenir shops on the Strip. Every casino, shopping mall and bank and most convenience stores have ATMs; casino transaction fees are highest (around $5).

Harmon Medical Center (☑702-796-1116; www.harmonmedicalcenter.com; 150 E Harmon Ave; ☺8am-8pm Mon-Fri) Discounts for uninsured patients; limited translation services.

Las Vegas Convention & Visitors Authority (LVCVA; ☑702-892-7575, 877-847-4858; www.lasvegas.com; 3150 Paradise Rd; ☺8am-5:30pm Mon-Fri; monorail Las Vegas Convention Center) Small walk-in office near the city's convention center.

Las Vegas Review-Journal (www.lvrj.com) Daily newspaper with Friday's arts-and-entertainment guide, *Neon*.

Las Vegas Weekly (http://lasvegasweekly.com) Free alt-weekly with entertainment, event and restaurant listings.

Lonely Planet (www.lonelyplanet.com/usa/las-vegas) Planning advice, author recommendations, traveler reviews and insider tips.

Police (☑702-828-3111; www.lvmpd.com).

University Medical Center (UMC; ☑702-383-2000; www.umcsn.com; 1800 W Charleston Blvd; ☺24hr) Nevada's advanced trauma center.

Vegas.com (www.vegas.com) Travel info and booking service.

ℹ Getting There & Around

Just southeast of the Strip and easily accessible from I-15, **McCarran International Airport** (LAS; ☑702-261-5211; www.mccarran.com; 5757 Wayne Newton Blvd; 🚕) has direct flights from most US cities, and some from Canada and Europe. **Bell Trans** (☑800-274-7433; www.bell-trans.com) offers airport shuttles to the Strip (one way/round trip $7/13); fares to downtown and off-Strip destinations are slightly higher.

A fast, wheelchair-accessible **monorail** (☑702-699-8299; www.lvmonorail.com; single-ride $5, 24/48/72hr pass $12/22/28; ☺7am-midnight Mon, to 2am Tue-Thu, to 3am Fri-Sun) connects the MGM Grand and SLS casino hotels, stopping at some Strip casinos and the city's convention center. **Deuce & SDX** (☑702-228-7433; www.rtcsnv.com; 2hr/24hr/3-day pass $6/8/20) buses run frequently between the Strip and downtown; double-decker Deuce buses run 24 hours, but SDX buses are faster.

All Strip casinos have taxi stands, free self-parking and also free valet parking (tip at least $2). Many downtown casinos charge a self-parking fee; it's usually refundable with ticket validation inside the casino (no gambling required).

Understand California

California Today

California is not a finished work. The nightmares faced by the region in the 1990s – race riots, the Northridge earthquake – already belong to a different age. Today's issues revolve around growth. In a state that has an economy bigger than Canada's and is the headquarters for cutting-edge industries, from space probes to Silicon Valley, how to manage a burgeoning human population – with accompanying traffic gridlock, housing shortages and a sky-high cost of living – is challenging.

Best on Film

The Maltese Falcon (1941) Humphrey Bogart as a San Francisco private eye.
Sunset Boulevard (1950) A classic bonfire of Hollywood vanities.
Vertigo (1958) Alfred Hitchcock's noir thriller, set in SF.
The Graduate (1967) Surviving life in 1960s SoCal suburbia.
Chinatown (1974) LA's brutal 20th-century water wars.
Bladerunner (1982) Ridley Scott's futuristic cyberpunk vision of LA.
Pulp Fiction (1994) Quentin Tarantino's outrageous interlocking LA stories.
LA Confidential (1997) Neo-noir tale of corruption and murder in 1950s LA.
The Big Lebowski (1998) Coen brothers' zany LA farce starring 'The Dude.'
Crash (2004) Racial tensions play out in contemporary LA.

Best in Print

The Tortilla Curtain (TC Boyle) Mexican-American culture clash and chasing the Californian dream.
My California: Journeys by Great Writers (Angel City Press) Insightful stories by talented chroniclers.
Where I Was From (Joan Didion) California-born essayist shatters palm-fringed fantasies.

California Dreams vs Reality

Even if you've seen it in movies or on TV, California still comes as a shock to the system. Venice Beach skateboarders, Santa Cruz hippies, Rodeo Drive–pillaging trophy wives and Silicon Valley millionaires aren't on different channels; they all live here, where tolerance for other people's beliefs, be they conservative, liberal or just plain wacky, is the social glue. Yet as LA police beating victim Rodney King famously asked, 'Can we all get along?' Sometimes yes, sometimes no.

Until recently, the most divisive political hot-potato topic was same-sex marriage, until a state constitutional amendment to ban it was struck down for good in 2013. Still controversial elsewhere in the USA, medical marijuana is not a big deal for most Californians, who approved a state proposition allowing its use back in 1996 – although the proliferation of marijuana clubs and raids by federal agents have raised eyebrows.

Environmental Roots

There's no denying California's culture of conspicuous consumption, exported via Hollywood flicks and reality TV (hello, *Real Housewives of Orange County*). But since the 1960s, Californians have trailblazed another 'greener' way by choosing more sustainable foods and low-impact lifestyles, preserving old-growth forests with tree-sitting activism, declaring nuclear-free zones, pushing for environmentally progressive legislation and establishing the USA's biggest market for hybrid vehicles. Over 60% of Californians admit that, yes, they've actually hugged a tree.

That shouldn't come as a surprise. It was Californians who helped kick-start the world's conservation movement in the midst of the 19th-century industrial revolution, with laws curbing industrial dumping, setting aside swaths of prime real estate as urban greenspace, and protecting wilderness inside national, state and county parks. Even conservative California politicians may prioritize environmental issues. That said, the state's long-term drought has resulted in a suspension of some key environmental legal protections, as well as more intense, prolonged and ultimately costly wildfire seasons.

Fast Companies, Slow Food

California's technological innovations need no introduction by anyone. Perhaps you've heard of PCs, iPods, Google and the internet? The home of Silicon Valley and a burgeoning biotech industry, Northern California is giving Southern California's gargantuan movie, TV and entertainment industry a run for its money as the state's main economic engine.

Meanwhile, although less than 10% of Californians live in rural areas, they're still responsible for one of the state's other powerhouse industries: agriculture. With over 80,000 farms statewide raising $42 billion worth of food for the rest of the country and the world each year, it's obvious why climate change and ongoing drought are of such concern to many Californians.

You may notice Californians tend to proselytize about their food and idolize homegrown chefs like rock stars. After a few bites, you may begin to understand their obsession. Reading restaurant menus means taking a stand on issues close to many Californians' hearts: organic and non-GMO crops, veganism, grass-fed versus grain-fed meat, biodynamic vineyards, fair-trade coffee and the importance of buying local. It's no accident that the term 'locavore' – people who eat food grown locally – was born here.

New World Religions

Despite their proportionately small numbers, California's alternative religions and utopian communities dominate the popular imagination, from modern-day pagans to New Age healers. California made national headlines in the 1960s with gurus from India, in the 1970s with Jim Jones' People's Temple and Erhard Seminars Training (EST), in the 1990s with the Heaven's Gate doomsday UFO cult in San Diego, and in 2011 when Oakland radio minister Harold Camping proselytized that the Rapture was about to happen. Around since 1954, the controversial Church of Scientology is still seeking acceptance with celebrity proponents from movie-star Tom Cruise to musician Beck.

POPULATION: **38.3 MILLION**

AREA: **155,780 SQ MILES**

PROPORTION OF US GDP:
12% ($1.96 TRILLION)

MEDIAN HOUSEHOLD
INCOME: **$61,400**

UNEMPLOYMENT: **8%**

if California were 100 people

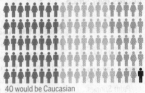

40 would be Caucasian
38 would be Latino
14 would be Asian American
7 would be African American
1 would be other

belief systems
(% of population)

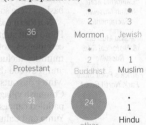

36 Protestant
2 Mormon
3 Jewish
2 Buddhist
1 Muslim
31 Catholic
24 other
1 Hindu

population per sq mile

USA   California   Los Angeles

👤 ≈ 80 people

History

When European explorers first arrived in the 16th century, more than 100,000 Native Americans called this land home. Spanish conquistadors and priests marched through in search of a fabled 'city of gold' before establishing Catholic missions and presidios (military forts). After winning independence from Spain, Mexico briefly ruled California, but then got trounced by the fledgling USA just before gold was discovered here in 1848. Immigrant waves of star-struck California dreamers have washed up on these Pacific shores ever since.

Learn About Native Californians

Indian Canyons & Tahquitz Canyon, Palm Springs

Autry National Center, Griffith Park, LA

Indian Grinding Rock State Historic Park, Gold Country

California State Indian Museum, Sacramento

Maidu Museum & Historical Site, Roseville

Patrick's Point State Park, North Coast

Native Californians

Immigration is hardly a new phenomenon here, since people have been migrating to California for millennia. Archaeological sites have yielded evidence – from large middens of seashells along the beaches to campfire sites on the Channel Islands – of humans making their homes in California as early as 13,000 years ago.

Speaking some 100 distinct languages, Native Californians mostly lived in small communities and a few migrated with the seasons. Their diet was largely dependent on acorn meal, supplemented by small game such as rabbits and deer, and fish and shellfish. They were skilled craftspeople, making earthenware pots, fishing nets, bows, arrows and spears with chipped stone points. Many tribes developed a knack for weaving baskets made from local grasses and plant fibers, decorating them with geometric designs – some baskets were so tightly woven that they could even hold water.

Northern coastal fishing communities such as the Ohlone, Miwok and Pomo built subterranean roundhouses and sweat lodges, where they held ceremonies, told stories and gambled for fun. Northern hunting communities including the Hupa, Karok and Wiyot constructed big houses and redwood dugout canoes, while the Modoc lived in summer tipis and winter dugouts; all chased salmon during seasonal runs. Kumeyaay and Chumash villages dotted the central coast, where tribespeople fished and paddled canoes, including out to the Channel Islands. Southern Mojave, Yuma and Cahuilla tribes made sophisticated pottery and developed irrigation systems for farming in the desert.

TIMELINE

13,000 BC	AD 1542–43	1769
Native American communities get settled across the state, from the Yurok in redwood plank houses in the north to the Kumeyaay's thatched domed dwellings in the south.	Portuguese navigator Juan Rodríguez Cabrillo and his Spanish crew are the first Europeans to sail California's coast. His journey ends in the Channel Islands when a gangrenous wound kills him.	Franciscan friar Junípero Serra and Captain Gaspar de Portolá lead a Spanish expedition to establish missions, rounding up Native Californians as converts and conscripted labor.

HISTORY THE SPANISH MISSION PERIOD

HOW CALIFORNIA (MAYBE) GOT ITS NAME

Gold is the usual reason given for the madcap course of Californian history, but it all actu-ally started with a dazzling pack of lies. Have you heard the one about the sunny island of Amazon women armed with gold weapons, who flew griffins fed with their own sons? No, this isn't a twisted Hollywood Wonder Woman remake. It's the plot of Garcí Rodríguez de Montalvo's 16th-century Spanish novel *Las Sergas de Esplandián* that inspired Spanish adventurers, including Hernán Cortés, who said in a 1524 letter from Mexico he hoped to find the island a couple of days' sail to the northwest.

Apart from the mythical bird-beasts and filicidal wonder women, Montalvo and Cortés weren't entirely wrong. Across the water from mainland Mexico was a peninsula that Spanish colonists called Baja (Lower) California, after Queen Calafía, Montalvo's legend-ary queen of the Amazons. Above it was Alta (Upper) California – not exactly an island, though certainly rich in gold. But in Montalvo's tale, the warrior Queen Calafía willingly changed her wild ways, settled down and converted to Christianity – which is not quite how it really happened in California.

When English sea captain Sir Francis Drake harbored briefly on Mi-wok land north of San Francisco in 1579, the English were taken to be the dead returned from the afterworld, and shamans saw the arrival as a warning of apocalypse. The omens weren't far wrong: within a century after the arrival of Spanish colonists in 1769, California's indigenous pop-ulation would be decimated by 80 percent to just 20,000 due to foreign diseases, conscripted labor, violence, hunger and culture shock.

The Spanish Mission Period

In the 18th century, when Russian and English trappers began trading valuable pelts from Alta California, Spain concocted a plan for coloniza-tion. For the glory of God and the tax coffers of Spain, missions would be built across California, and within 10 years these would be going concerns run by local converts. This was approved by quixotic Spanish colonial official José de Gálvez of Mexico, who was full of grand schemes – including controlling Baja California with a trained army of apes.

Almost immediately after Spain's missionizing plan was approved in 1769, it began to fail. When Franciscan friar Junípero Serra and Cap-tain Gaspar de Portolá made the overland journey to establish Mission San Diego de Alcalá in 1769, only half the sailors on their supply ships survived. Portolá had heard of a fabled cove to the north, but failing to recognize Monterey Bay in the fog, he gave up and turned back.

Portolá reported to Gálvez that if the Russians or English wanted Cal-ifornia, they were welcome to it. But Serra wouldn't give up, and secured

The distance between each of California's Spanish colonial missions equaled a day's journey by horseback. Learn more about the missions' histor-ical significance and cultural influence at www.missionscalifor-nia.com.

1781	1821	1835	1846
Spanish governor Felipe de Neve sets out from Mission San Gabriel with a tiny band of settlers, trekking west just 9 miles to establish the future Los Angeles.	Mexican independence ends Spanish coloni-zation of California. Mexico inherits 21 mis-sions, along with unruly Californio cowboys and a radically reduced Native Californian population.	An emissary of US President Andrew Jackson makes a formal offer to buy Alta California, but Mexico tries to unsuccessfully sell it off to England instead.	Sierra Nevada blizzards strand the Donner Par-ty of settlers, some of whom avoid starvation by eating their dead companions. Five wom-en and two men survive by snowshoeing 100 miles for help.

support to set up presidios (military posts) alongside missions. When soldiers weren't paid regularly, they looted and pillaged local communities. Clergy objected to this treatment of potential converts, but still relied on soldiers to round up conscripts to build missions. In exchange for their forced labor, Native Californians were allowed one meal a day and a place in God's kingdom – which came much sooner than expected, due to diseases like smallpox and syphilis that the Spanish brought.

It's no surprise that California's indigenous tribes often rebelled against the Spanish colonists. The missions did achieve modest success at farming and just barely managed to become self-sufficient, however. But as a way of colonizing California and converting the indigenous people to Christianity, they were an abject failure. The Spanish population remained small, foreign intruders were not greatly deterred, and ultimately, more Native Californians died than were converted.

> Find out more about the traditions and lifestyles of indigenous tribes with *California Indians and Their Environment*, a readable natural history guide by Kent Lightfoot and Otis Parrish.

California Under Mexican Rule

Spain wasn't sorry to lose California to Mexico in the 1810–21 Mexican War of Independence. As long as missions had the best grazing land, *rancheros* (ranchers) couldn't compete in the growing market for cowhides and tallow (for use in soap). Yet Spanish, Mexican and American settlers who had intermarried with Native Californians were now a sizable constituency, and together these 'Californios' convinced Mexico to secularize the missions beginning in 1834.

Californios quickly snapped up deeds to privatized mission property. Only a few dozen Californios were literate in the entire state, so boundary disputes that arose were settled with muscle, not paper. By law, half the lands were supposed to go to Native Californians who worked at the missions, but few actually received their entitlements.

Through marriage and other mergers, most of the land and wealth in California was held by just 46 *ranchero* families by 1846. The average *rancho* (ranch) was now 16,000 acres, having grown from cramped shanties to elegant haciendas where women were supposedly confined to quarters at night. But *rancheras* (ranch women) weren't so easily bossed around: women owned some Californian ranches, rode horses as hard as men and caused romantic scandals worthy of *telenovelas* (soap operas).

Meanwhile, Americans were arriving in the trading post of Los Angeles via the Old Spanish Trail. Northern passes through the Sierra Nevada were trickier, as the Donner Party tragically discovered in 1846 – stranded by snow near Lake Tahoe, some survivors resorted to cannibalism.

Still, the US saw potential in California. When US president Andrew Jackson offered the financially strapped Mexican government $500,000 for the territory in 1835, the offer was tersely rejected. After the US annexed the Mexican territory of Texas in 1845, Mexico broke off diplomatic

1848	1850	1851	1869
Gold is discovered near present-day Placerville by mill employees. San Francisco newspaper publisher, vigilante and bigmouth Sam Brannan lets the secret out, and the Gold Rush is on.	With hopes of solid-gold tax revenues, the US declares California the 31st state. When miners find tax loopholes, SoCal ranchers are left carrying the tax burden, creating early north–south rivalries.	The discovery of gold in Australia means cheering in the streets of Melbourne and panic in the streets of San Francisco, as the price for California gold plummets.	On May 10, the 'golden spike' is nailed in place at Promontory, Utah, completing the first transcontinental railroad, which connects California with the East Coast.

THE BEAR FLAG REPUBLIC

In June 1846, American settlers tanked up on liquid courage declared independence in the northern town of Sonoma. Not a shot was fired – instead, they captured the nearest Mexican official and hoisted a hastily made flag. Locals awoke to discover they were living in the independent 'Bear Republic,' under a flag painted with a grizzly that looked like a drunken dog. The Bear Flag Republic lasted only a month before US orders telling settlers to stand down arrived.

relations and ordered all foreigners without proper papers deported from California. The Mexican–American War was declared in 1846, lasting two years with very little fighting in California. Hostilities ended with the Treaty of Guadalupe Hidalgo, in which Mexico ceded much of its northern territory (including Alta California) to the US. The timing was fortuitous: a few weeks after the US took possession of California, gold was discovered.

California's Gold Rush

The Gold Rush era in California began with a bluff. Real-estate speculator, lapsed Mormon and tabloid publisher Sam Brannan was looking to unload some California swampland in 1848 when he heard rumors of gold flakes found near Sutter's Mill in the Sierra Nevada foothills. Figuring this news should sell some newspapers and raise real-estate values, Brannan published the rumor as fact.

Initially Brannan's story didn't generate excitement – gold flake had surfaced in southern California as far back as 1775. So he ran another story, this time verified by Mormon employees at Sutter's Mill who had sworn him to secrecy. Brannan reportedly kept his word by running through San Francisco's streets, brandishing gold entrusted to him as tithes for the Mormon church, shouting, 'Gold on the American River!'

Other newspapers around the world weren't scrupulous about getting their facts straight either, hastily publishing stories of gold near San Francisco. By 1850, the year California was fast-tracked for admission as the 31st US state, California's foreign population had ballooned from 15,000 to 93,000. Early arrivals from across the country and around the world panned for gold side by side, slept in close quarters, drank locally made wine and ate wok-fired Chinese food, and when they struck it rich, ordered the 'Hangtown Fry' (an omelet with bacon and oysters).

With each wave of new arrivals, profits dropped and gold became harder to find. In 1848 each prospector earned an average of about $300,000 in today's terms; by 1849, earnings were less than half that, and by 1865 they had dipped to $35,000. When surface gold became

The Oscar-winning film *There Will Be Blood* (2007), adapted from Upton Sinclair's book *Oil!*, depicts a Californian oil magnate based on real-life SoCal tycoon Edward Doheny.

1882	1906	1927	1927
The US Chinese Exclusion Act suspends new immigration from China, denies citizenship to those already in the country and sanctions racially discriminatory laws that stay on the books until 1943.	An earthquake levels entire blocks of San Francisco in 42 seconds flat, setting off fires that rage for three days. Survivors start rebuilding immediately.	After a year of tinkering, San Francisco inventor Philo Farnsworth transmits the first successful TV broadcast of...a straight line.	*The Jazz Singer*, about a Jewish singer who rebels against his father and performs in blackface, is the first feature-length 'talkie' movie. Hollywood's Golden Age kicks off.

scarce, miners picked, shoveled and dynamited through mountains. The work was grueling and dangerous; the cost of living in cold, filthy mining camps was sky-high; and with few doctors around, injuries often proved lethal. With only one woman for every 400 men in some camps, many turned to paid company, booze and opium for consolation.

Vigilantes, Robber Barons & Railroads

Gold prospectors who did best arrived early and got out quick, while those who stayed too long either lost fortunes searching for the next nugget or became targets of resentment. Successful Peruvians and Chileans were harassed and denied renewals to their mining claims, and most left California by 1855. Native Californian laborers who helped miners strike it rich were denied the right to hold claims. Also frozen out of mining claims, many Chinese opened service-based businesses that survived when mining ventures went bust. Meanwhile, criminal wrongdoing was sometimes hastily pinned on Australians – starting in 1851, San Francisco's self-appointed Committee of Vigilance tried, convicted, lynched and deported the 'Sydney Ducks' gang, so when another gold rush began in Australia that same year, many were ready to head home.

The classic flick *Chinatown* (1974) is a fictionalized yet surprisingly accurate account of the brutal water wars that were waged to build Los Angeles.

Inter-ethnic rivalries obscured the real competitive threat posed not by fellow workers, but by those who controlled the means of production: California's 'robber barons.' These Californian speculators hoarded the capital and industrial machinery necessary for deep-mining operations. As mining became industrialized, fewer miners were needed, and jobless prospectors turned anger toward a convenient target: Chinese workers, who by 1860 had become the second-most populous group in California after Mexicans. Discriminatory Californian laws restricting housing, employment and citizenship for anyone born in China were reinforced in the 1882 US Chinese Exclusion Act, which remained law until 1943.

Laws limiting work options for Chinese arrivals served the needs of robber barons, who needed cheap labor to build railroads to their mining claims and reach East Coast markets. To blast tunnels through the Sierra Nevada, workers were lowered down sheer mountain faces in wicker baskets, planted lit dynamite sticks in rock crevices, then urgently tugged the rope to be hoisted out of harm's way. Those who survived the day's work were confined to bunkhouses under armed guard in cold, remote mountain regions. With little other choice of legitimate employment, an estimated 12,000 Chinese laborers blasted through the Sierra Nevada, meeting the westbound end of the transcontinental railroad in 1869.

Fighting for Oil & Water

During the US Civil War (1861–65), California couldn't count on food shipments from the East Coast, and started growing its own. California

1934	1942	1955	1965
A longshoremen's strike ends with 34 shot and 40 gassed or beaten by police in San Francisco. After mass funeral processions and citywide strikes, shipping magnates meet union demands.	Executive Order 9066 sends nearly 120,000 Japanese Americans to internment camps. Lawsuits filed by the Japanese American Citizens League help lay the groundwork for the 1964 Civil Rights Act.	Disneyland opens in Anaheim on July 17. As crowds swarm the park, plumbing breaks and Fantasyland springs a gas leak. Walt Disney calls a do-over, relaunching successfully the next day.	It takes 20,000 National Guards to quell the six-day Watts Riots in LA, which cause death, devastation and over $40 million in property damage. That same year, Rodney King is born.

recruited Midwestern homesteaders to farm the Central Valley with shameless propaganda. 'Acres of Untaken Government Land...for a Million Farmers...Health & Wealth without Cyclones or Blizzards,' trumpeted one California-boosting poster, neglecting to mention earthquakes or ongoing land disputes with *rancheros* and Native Californians. Over 120,000 homesteaders came to California in the 1870s and '80s.

These homesteaders soon discovered that California's Gold Rush had left the state badly tarnished. Hills were stripped bare, vegetation wiped out, streams silted up and mercury washed into water supplies. Cholera spread through open sewers of poorly drained camps claiming many lives, and smaller mineral finds in southern California mountains diverted streams essential to the dry valleys below. Because mining claims leased by the US government were granted significant tax exemptions, there were insufficient public funds for clean-up programs or public water works.

Frustrated farmers south of Big Sur voted to secede from California in 1859, but appeals for secession were shelved by the Civil War. In 1884 Southern Californians passed a pioneering law preventing dumping into rivers and, with the support of budding agribusiness and real-estate concerns, passed bond measures to build aqueducts and dams that made large-scale farming and real-estate development possible. By the 20th century, the lower one-third of the state took two-thirds of available water supplies, inspiring Northern California's own calls for secession.

Meanwhile, another equally precious natural resource – oil – was discovered by flat-broke mining prospector and failed real-estate speculator Edward Doheny in Downtown LA, near where Dodger Stadium stands today, sparking a major oil boom in California. Inside of a year, his oil well was yielding 40 barrels daily, and within five years, 500 wells were operational in Southern California. By the end of the decade, the state was producing four million barrels of 'black gold' annually. Downtown LA sprang up around Doheny's well, becoming a hub of industry with over 100,000 inhabitants by 1900.

While pastoral Southern California was urbanizing, Northern Californians who had witnessed the environmental devastation of mining and logging firsthand were jump-starting the nation's first conservation movement. Sierra Nevada naturalist, lyrical writer and San Francisco Bay Area farmer John Muir founded the Sierra Club in 1892. Dams and pipelines to support communities in California's deserts and coastal cities were built over Muir's strenuous objections – including Hetch Hetchy Reservoir in Yosemite, which supplies Bay Area water today. In drought-prone California, tensions still regularly come to a boil between land developers and conservationists.

Top California History Books

California: A History (Kevin Starr)

City of Quartz (Mike Davis)

Slouching Towards Bethlehem (Joan Didion)

Journey to the Sun (Gregory Orfalea)

1966	1967	1968	1969
Ronald Reagan is elected governor of California, setting a career precedent for fading film stars. He served until 1975, then in 1981 became the 40th US President.	The Summer of Love kicks off on January 14 at the Human Be-In in Golden Gate Park with blown conch shells and brain cells, and draft cards used as rolling papers.	Presidential candidate, former US attorney-general and civil-rights ally Robert Kennedy is fatally shot in Los Angeles after winning the critical California presidential primary.	UCLA sends data from one of its computers to another at Stanford University, typing just two characters before the system crashes. The internet is born.

Reforming the Wild West

When the great earthquake and fire hit San Francisco in 1906, it signaled change for California. With public funds for citywide water mains and fire hydrants siphoned off by corrupt political bosses, there was only one functioning water source in all of San Francisco. When the smoke lifted, one thing was clear: it was time for the Wild West to change its ways.

While San Francisco was rebuilt at a rate of 15 buildings a day, political reformers set to work on city, state and national policies, one plank at a time. Californians concerned about public health and trafficking in women pushed for the passage of the 1914 Red Light Abatement Act, which shut down brothels statewide. Mexico's revolution from 1910 to 1921 brought a new wave of migrants and revolutionary ideas, including ethnic pride and worker solidarity. As California's ports grew, longshoremen's unions coordinated a historic 83-day strike in 1934 along the entire West Coast that forced concessions for safer working conditions and fair pay.

At the height of the Depression in 1935, some 200,000 farming families fleeing the drought-struck Dust Bowl on the Great Plains arrived in California, where they found scant pay and deplorable working conditions. California's artists alerted middle America to the migrants' plight, and the nation rallied around Dorothea Lange's haunting documentary photos of famine-struck families and John Steinbeck's harrowing fictionalized account in his Pulitzer Prize–winning novel *The Grapes of Wrath*. The book was widely banned, while the 1940 movie version, its star Henry Fonda and Steinbeck himself were accused of harboring communist sympathies. Even so, the public support it won for farm workers set the stage later for launching the United Farm Workers union.

California's workforce permanently changed during WWII, when women and African Americans were recruited for wartime industries and Mexican workers were brought in to fill labor shortages. Contracts in military communications and aviation attracted an international elite of engineers, who would birth California's high-tech industry. Within a decade after WWII, California's population had grown by almost 40%, surpassing 13 million.

Erin Brockovich (2000) is based on the true story of a Southern Californian mom who discovered a small town being poisoned by industrial waste, and helped win a class-action lawsuit that raised the standard for corporate accountability.

Hollywood & California Counterculture

In the early 20th century, California's greatest export was the sunny, wholesome image it projected to the world through its homegrown film and TV industry. Southern California became a convenient movie location because of its consistent sunlight and versatile locations, although its role was limited to doubling for more exotic locales and providing backdrops for period-piece productions like Charlie Chaplin's *The Gold Rush* (1925). Gradually, California began stealing the scene in movies and

1969	1977	1989	1992
Native American activists symbolically reclaim Alcatraz until ousted by the FBI in 1971. Public support for protesters strengthens self-rule concessions for Native American tribes.	San Francisco Supervisor Harvey Milk becomes the first openly gay man elected to California public office. Milk sponsors a gay-rights bill before being murdered by political opponent Dan White.	On October 17, the Loma Prieta Earthquake hits 6.9 on the Richter scale near Santa Cruz, collapsing a two-level section of Interstate 880 and resulting in 63 deaths and almost 4000 injuries.	Four white police officers charged with assaulting African American Rodney King are acquitted by a predominantly white jury. Following the trial, Los Angeles endures six days of riots.

CALIFORNIA'S CIVIL RIGHTS MOVEMENT

Before the 1963 march on Washington, DC, the civil rights movement was well under way in California.

When almost 120,000 Japanese Americans living along the West Coast were ordered into internment camps by President Roosevelt in 1942, the Japanese American Citizens League immediately filed suits that advanced all the way to the US Supreme Court. These lawsuits established groundbreaking civil rights legal precedents, and in 1992 internees received reparations and an official letter of apology signed by President George HW Bush.

Adopting the non-violent resistance practices of Mahatma Gandhi and Martin Luther King Jr, labor leaders Cesar Chavez and Dolores Huerta formed United Farm Workers in 1962 to champion the rights of under-represented immigrant laborers. Four years later, Chavez and Californian grape pickers marched on Sacramento, bringing the issue of fair wages and the health risks of pesticides to the nation's attention. When Bobby Kennedy was sent to investigate, he sided with Chavez, bringing Latinos into the US political fold.

iconic TV shows with its palm trees and sunny beaches. Through the power of Hollywood, California tamed its Wild West veneer and adopted a more marketable image of beach boys and bikini-clad blondes.

Northern Californians didn't imagine themselves as extras in *Beach Blanket Bingo* (1965), however. WWII sailors discharged for insubordination and homosexuality in San Francisco found themselves at home in North Beach's bebop jazz clubs, bohemian coffeehouses and City Lights Bookstore. San Francisco was home to free speech and free spirits, and soon everyone who was anyone was getting arrested: Beat poet Lawrence Ferlinghetti for publishing Allen Ginsberg's epic poem 'Howl' and comedian Lenny Bruce for uttering the F-word onstage. When the CIA made the mistake of using writer and willing test-subject Ken Kesey to test psychoactive drugs intended to create the ultimate soldier, it inadvertently kicked off the psychedelic era. At the January 14, 1967 Human Be-In in Golden Gate Park, trip-master Timothy Leary urged a crowd of 20,000 hippies to dream a new American dream and 'turn on, tune in, drop out.' When hippy 'flower power' faded, other Bay Area rebellions grew in its place, such as Black Power and gay pride.

While Northern California had the more attention-grabbing counterculture in the 1940s to '60s, nonconformity in sunny SoCal still shook the country to the core. In 1947, when Senator Joseph McCarthy attempted to root out suspected communists in the film industry, 10 writers and directors who refused to admit to communist alliances or to name names were charged with contempt of Congress and barred from working in Hollywood.

1994	1994	2000	2003
Orange County, one of the wealthiest municipalities in the US, declares bankruptcy after the county treasurer loses $1.7 billion investing in risky derivatives and pleads guilty to felony charges.	The 6.7-magnitude Northridge earthquake strikes LA on January 17, killing 72 and causing $20 billion in property damage – one of the costliest natural disasters in US history.	The NASDAQ crashes, ending the dot-com boom. Traditional industries gloat over the burst bubble, until knock-on effects lead to a devalued dollar and NYSE slide starting in 2002.	Republican Arnold Schwarzenegger (aka 'The Governator') is elected governor of California. Schwarzenegger breaks party ranks on environmental issues and wins re-election in 2007.

But the Hollywood Ten's impassioned defenses of the US Constitution were heard nationwide, and major Hollywood players voiced dissent and hired blacklisted talent until lawsuits put a stop to McCarthyism in the late 1950s.

Ultimately, California's beach-paradise image – and its oil-industry dealings – would be permanently changed not by Hollywood directors, but Santa Barbara beachgoers. On January 28, 1969, an oil rig dumped 100,000 barrels of crude oil into the Santa Barbara Channel, killing dolphins, seals and thousands of birds. Playing against type, the laid-back SoCal beach community organized a highly effective protest, spurring the establishment of the US Environmental Protection Agency and the California Coastal Commission, as well as the passage of important state and national legislation against environmental pollution.

To read more about the garage-workshop culture of Silicon Valley go to www.folklore.org, which covers the crashes and personality clashes that made geek history.

Geeking Out in California

When Silicon Valley introduced the first personal computer in 1968, advertisements gushed that Hewlett-Packard's 'light' (40lb) machine could 'take on roots of a fifth-degree polynomial, Bessel functions, elliptic integrals and regression analysis' – all for just $4900 (over $33,000 today). Consumers didn't know quite what to do with computers, but in his 1969 *Whole Earth Catalog*, author Stewart Brand explained that the technology governments used to run countries could empower ordinary people. Hoping to bring computer power to the people, 21-year-old Steve Jobs and Steve Wozniak introduced the Apple II at the 1977 West Coast Computer Faire with unfathomable memory (4KB of RAM) and microprocessor speed (1MHz). But the question remained: what would people do with all that computing power?

By the mid-1990s an entire dot-com industry boomed in Silicon Valley with online start-ups, and suddenly people were getting everything – their mail, news, politics, pet food and, yes, sex – online. But when dot-com profits weren't forthcoming, venture-capital funding dried up and fortunes in stock-options disappeared when the dot-com bubble burst and the NASDAQ plummeted on March 10, 2000. Overnight, 26-year-old vice-presidents and Bay Area service-sector employees alike found themselves jobless. But as online users continued to look for useful information – and one another – in those billions of web pages, search engines and social media boomed.

Meanwhile, California's biotech industry started to take off. In 1976 an upstart company called Genentech was founded in the San Francisco Bay Area, and quickly got to work cloning human insulin and introducing the Hepatitis B vaccine. In 2004 California voters approved a $3 billion bond measure for stem-cell research, and by 2008 California had become the USA's biggest funder of stem-cell research, as well as the focus of NASDAQ's new Biotechnology Index. Now all that's missing is another biotech boom – but if history is any indication, California will make good on its big talk, no matter how outlandish it might sound at first.

2004	2005	2007	2008
Google's IPO raises a historic $1.67 billion at $85 per share. Since then share prices have increased over 900% and the company's market value now exceeds $350 billion.	Antonio Villaraigosa is elected mayor of LA, the first Latino to hold that office since 1872. Born poor in East LA, he says in his victory speech, 'I will never forget where I came from.'	Wildfires sweep drought-stricken Southern California forcing one million people to evacuate their homes. Migrant workers, state prisoners and Tijuana firefighters help curb the blazes.	California voters pass Proposition 8, defining legal marriage as between a man and a woman. Courts eventually rule the law unconstitutional, and same-sex marriages resume in 2013.

The Way of Life

In the California of the dream world you wake up, have your shot of wheatgrass and roll down to the beach while the surf's up. Lifeguards wave to you as they go jogging by in their bathing suits. You skateboard down the boardwalk to your yoga class where everyone admires your downward dog. A food truck pulls up with your favorite: low-carb, sustainable fish tacos with organic mango chipotle salsa. Wait, can anyone honestly make this dream come true here?

Living the Dream

Let's keep dreaming. Napping on the beach after yoga class, you awake to find a casting agent hovering over you, blocking your sunlight, imploring you to star in a movie based on a best-selling graphic novel. You say you'll have your lawyer look over the papers, and by your lawyer you mean your roommate who plays one on TV. The conversation is cut short when you get a text to meet up with some friends at a bar.

That casting agent was a stress case – she wanted an answer in, like, a month – so you swing by your medical marijuana dispensary and a tattoo parlor to get 'Peace' inscribed on your bicep in Tibetan as a reminder to yourself to stay chill. At the bar you're called onstage to play a set with the band, and afterwards you tell the drummer how the casting agent harshed your mellow. She recommends a wine country getaway, but you're already doing that Big Sur primal scream chakra-cleansing retreat this weekend.

You head back to your beach house to update your status on your social-networking profile, alerting your one million online friends to the major events of the day: 'Killer taco, solid downward dog, peace tattoo, movie offer.' Then you repeat your nightly self-affirmations: 'I am a child of the universe...I am blessed, or at least not a New Yorker...tomorrow will bring sunshine and possibility...om.'

Riptionary (www.riptionary.com), the world's most definitive online lexicon of surfer slang, will help you translate stuff like 'The big mama is fully mackin' some gnarly grinders!'

Regional Identity

Now for the reality check. Any Northern Californian hearing your California dream is bound to get huffy. What, political protests and Silicon Valley start-ups don't factor in your dreams? But Southern Californians will also roll their eyes at these stereotypes: they didn't create NASA's Jet Propulsion Lab and almost half of the world's movies by slacking off.

Still there is some truth to your California dreamscape. Some 80% of Californians live near the coast rather than inland, even though California beaches aren't always sunny or swimmable (the odds of that increase the further south you go, thus Southern California's inescapable associations with surf, sun and prime-time TV soaps like *Baywatch* and *The OC*). And there's truth in at least one other outdoorsy stereotype: over 60% of Californians admit to having hugged a tree.

Self-help, fitness and body modification are major industries throughout California, successfully marketed since the 1970s as 'lite' versions of religious experience – all the agony and ecstasy of the major religions, without all those heavy commandments. Exercise and healthy food help

SoCal inventions include the space shuttle, Mickey Mouse, whitening toothpaste, the hula hoop (or at least its trademark), Barbie, skateboard and surfboard technology, the Cobb salad and the fortune cookie.

keep Californians among the fittest in the nation. Yet more than half a million Californians are apparently ill enough to merit prescriptions for medical marijuana. Ahem.

At least Northern and Southern Californians do have one thing in common: they are all baffled by New Yorkers' delusion that the world revolves around the Big Apple. We all know it totally doesn't, dude.

Lifestyle

The charmed existence you dreamed about is a stretch, even in California. Few Californians can afford to spend entire days tanning and networking, what with the aging effects of UVA rays and the sky-high rent to consider. According to a recent Cambridge University study, creativity, imagination, intellectualism and mellowness are all defining characteristics of Californians, compared with inhabitants of other US states.

If you're like most Californians, you effectively live in your car. Californians commute an average of 30 minutes each way to work and spend at least $1 out of every $5 earned on car-related expenses. But Californians have zoomed ahead of the national energy-use curve in their smog-checked cars, buying more hybrid and fuel-efficient cars than any other state. Despite California's reputation for smog, two of the 25 US cities with the cleanest air are in California (kudos, Redding and Salinas!).

Few Californians could afford a beach dream home anyway, and most rent rather than own on a median household income of $61,400 per year. Eight of the 10 most expensive US housing markets are in California, and in the two most expensive areas, Newport Beach and Palo Alto, the average house price is over $1.5 million. Almost half of all Californians reside in cities, but most of the other half live in the suburbs, where the cost of living is just as high, if not higher: San Jose near Silicon Valley has been ranked the most overpriced city in America. Yet Californian cities (especially San Francisco and San Diego) consistently top national quality-of-life indexes.

As for those roommates you dreamed about: if you're a Californian aged 18 to 24, there's a 50/50 possibility that your roomies are your parents. Among adult Californians, one in four live alone, and almost 50% are unmarried. Of those who are currently married, 33% won't be in 10 years. Increasingly, Californians are shacking up: the number of unmarried cohabiting couples has increased 40% since 1990.

Homelessness is not part of the California dream, but it's a reality for at least 135,000 Californians, representing over 20% of the total US homeless population. Some are teens who have run away or been kicked out by their families, but the largest contingent of homeless Californians are US military veterans – estimated at 31,000 people. What's more, in the 1970s mental-health programs were cut, and state-funded drug treatment programs were dropped in the 1980s, leaving many Californians with mental illnesses and substance-abuse problems no place to go.

Also standing in line at homeless shelters are the working poor, unable to afford to rent even a small apartment on minimum-wage salaries. Rather than addressing the underlying causes of homelessness, some California cities have criminalized loitering, panhandling, even sitting on sidewalks. More than three out of every 1000 Californians already sit in the state's notoriously overcrowded jails, mostly for drug-related crimes.

Population & Multiculturalism

With more than 38 million residents, California is the most populous US state: one in every nine Americans lives here. It's also one of the fastest growing states, with three of America's 10 biggest cities (Los Angeles, San Diego and San Jose) and over 300,000 newcomers every year. You

Southern California has thousands of believers in Santeria, a fusion of Catholicism and Yoruba beliefs practiced by West African slaves in the Caribbean and South America. Drop by a *botànica* (herbal folk medicine shop) for charms and candles.

still don't believe it's crowded here? California's population density is 239 people per sq mile – almost triple the national average.

If you were the average Californian, you'd be statistically likely to be Latina, aged about 35, living in densely populated LA, Orange or San Diego Counties, and you'd speak more than one language. There's a one in four chance you were born outside the US, and if you were born in the US the odds are 50/50 you moved here recently from another state.

One of every four immigrants to the US lands in California, with the largest segment coming from Mexico, followed by Central America. Most legal immigrants to California are sponsored by family members who already live here. In addition, nearly three million undocumented immigrants are estimated to currently live in California. But this is not a radical new development: before California became a US state in 1850 it was a territory of Mexico and Spain, and historically most of the state's growth has come from immigration, legal or otherwise.

Most Californians see their state as a laid-back, open-minded multicultural society that gives everyone a chance to live the American dream. No one is expected to give up their cultural or personal identity to become Californian: Chicano pride, Black Power and gay pride all built political bases here. But historically, California's Chinatowns, Japantowns and other ethnic enclaves were often the result of segregationist sentiment, not created by choice. While equal opportunity may be a shared goal, in practice it's very much a work in progress. Even racially integrated areas can be quite segregated by ethnicity in terms of income, language, education and, perhaps most surprisingly, internet access (never mind that this is the home of Silicon Valley).

Californian culture reflects the composite identity of the state. California's Latino and Asian populations are steadily increasing. Over one third of the nation's Asian American population lives in California, while Latinos became the state's majority ethnic group in 2014. Latino culture is deeply enmeshed with Californian culture, from J.Lo and Tejano tunes to burritos and margaritas, and ex-Governor Arnold Schwarzenegger's catchphrase in *Terminator II:* 'Hasta la vista, baby.' Despite being just over 6% of the population, and relatively late arrivals during the WWII shipping boom, African Americans have also defined West Coast popular culture, from jazz and hip-hop to fashion and beyond.

The bond holding the Golden State together isn't a shared ethnic background or common language: it's choosing to be Californian. Despite high-profile media exposure given to race-related incidents (such as LA's 20th-century riots), day-to-day civility between races is the norm, and interracial couples and families barely raise an eyebrow.

Likewise, religious tolerance is usually the rule. Although Californians are less church-going than the American mainstream, and one in five

In his column '¡Ask a Mexican!', *OC Weekly* columnist Gustavo Arellano tackles such questions as why Mexicans swim with their clothes on, alongside weighty social issues involving immigrants' rights. Read it at www. ocweekly.com.

THE WAY OF LIFE POPULATION & MULTICULTURALISM

CALIFORNIA'S BATTLES OVER MARRIAGE EQUALITY

In 2004, San Francisco Mayor Gavin Newsom issued marriage licenses to same-sex couples in defiance of a statewide ban, and 4000 same-sex couples promptly got hitched. Four years later, the same-sex marriage ban was nixed by California courts, but then Proposition 8 was narrowly passed by voters to amend the state's constitution to limit marriage to between one man and one woman.

Civil-rights activists challenged the constitutionality of Proposition 8 as discriminatory. The case eventually wound its way to the US Supreme Court, which decided in 2013 to uphold a lower court's ruling that Prop 8 was unconstitutional. Same-sex marriages quickly resumed in California, one of a growing number of US states to legalize marriage equality for all.

professes no religion at all, California is one of the most religiously diverse US states. About a third of residents are Catholic, in part due to a large Latino population, while another third are Protestants. There are almost two million Muslims and four million Hindus statewide. LA has one of the 10 biggest Jewish communities in the nation, and California has the largest number of Buddhists anywhere outside Asia. Controversially, the state has long been a breeding ground for radical offshoots of mainstream religions and religious cults, especially in SoCal.

Sports

Over 200 different languages are spoken in California, with Spanish, Chinese, Tagalog, Persian and German in the top 10. Almost 40% of state residents speak a language other than English at home.

California has more professional sports teams than any other state, and loyalties to NFL football, NBA basketball and major-league baseball teams run deep. If you doubt that Californians get excited about pro sports, go ahead and just try to find tickets before they sell out for an Oakland Raiders or San Diego Chargers football, San Francisco Giants or LA Dodgers baseball, LA Lakers basketball or LA Kings hockey game.

According to a recent study, Californians are less likely to be couch potatoes than other Americans. Nevertheless, when Californian teams play against one another, the streets are deserted and all eyes glued to the tube. The biggest grudge matches are between the San Diego Chargers and Oakland Raiders football teams, the San Francisco Giants and LA Dodgers baseball teams, and the LA Lakers and LA Clippers basketball teams. California college sports rivalries are equally fierce, especially UC Berkeley's Cal Bears versus the Stanford University Cardinals and the USC Trojans versus UCLA Bruins.

Tickets are easier to get for San Diego Padres and Anaheim Angels major-league baseball games. To see small but dedicated crowds of hometown fans (and score cheaper tickets too), watch women's pro basketball in LA, men's pro basketball in Sacramento, pro hockey in Anaheim and San Jose or pro soccer in San Jose and LA. Or catch minor-league baseball teams up and down the state, especially the Sacramento River Cats.

Except for championship play-offs, the regular season for major-league baseball runs from April to September, NFL football from September to January, NBA basketball from October to April, WNBA basketball from May to August, NHL ice hockey from October to April, and major-league soccer from April to October.

The roaring Grand Prix, a Formula 1 race, takes over the streets of Long Beach, just south of LA, every April. Inland at Bakersfield, NASCAR and other auto-racing events take place year-round. In San Diego County, Del Mar boasts the state's ritziest horse-racing track, while LA County's historic Santa Anita Racetrack featured in the classic Marx Brothers movie *A Day at the Races* and the short-lived HBO series *Luck*.

Surfing first hit California in 1914, when Irish-Hawaiian surfer George Freeth gave demonstrations at Huntington Beach in Orange County. Extreme sports date back to the 1970s when skateboarders on LA's Santa Monica–Venice border honed their craft by breaking into dry swimming pools in the backyards of mansions, as chronicled in the 2005 film *Lords of Dogtown*.

On Location: Film & TV

Imagine living in a world without Orson Welles whispering 'Rosebud,' Judy Garland clicking her sparkly red heels three times or the Terminator threatening 'I'll be back.' California is where all of these iconic film images hatched. Shakespeare claimed 'all the world's a stage,' but in California, it's actually more of a filming location set. With over 40 TV shows and scores of movies shot here annually, every palm-lined boulevard or beach seems to come with its own IMDB.com resume.

The Industry

You might know it as TV and movie-making entertainment, but to Southern Californians it's simply 'The Industry'. It all began in the humble orchards of Hollywoodland, a residential suburb of Los Angeles, where entrepreneurial moviemakers established studios in the early 20th century. German-born Carl Laemmle opened Universal Studios in 1915, selling lunch to curious guests who came to watch the magic of moviemaking. One year earlier, Polish immigrant Samuel Goldwyn joined with Cecil B DeMille to form Paramount Studios. Jack Warner and his brothers, born to Polish parents, arrived a few years later from Canada.

SoCal's perpetually balmy weather (over 315 days of sunshine per year) meant that most outdoor scenes could be easily shot here, and moviemaking flourished in Los Angeles. What's more, the proximity of the Mexican border enabled filmmakers to rush their equipment to safety when challenged by the collection agents of patent holders such as Thomas Edison. Palm Springs became a favorite weekend getaway for Hollywood stars, partly because its distance from LA (just under 100 miles) was as far as they could travel then under restrictive studio contracts.

Fans loved early silent-film stars like Charlie Chaplin and Harold Lloyd, and the first big Hollywood wedding occurred in 1920 when Douglas Fairbanks wed Mary Pickford, becoming Hollywood's defacto royal couple. The silent-movie era gave way to 'talkies' after 1927's *The Jazz Singer,* a Warner Bros musical starring Al Jolson, was screened in downtown LA, where the first big movie palaces stood on Broadway.

MILESTONES IN CALIFORNIA FILM HISTORY

1914
The first full-length Hollywood feature movie, a silent Western drama called *The Squaw Man,* is shot by director Cecil B DeMille.

1927
The first talkie, *The Jazz Singer,* ends the silent-film era. Sid Grauman opens his Chinese Theatre in Hollywood, where stars have been leaving their handprints ever since.

1939
The Wizard of Oz is the first wide-release movie shown in full color. Nonetheless, it loses the Oscar for Best Picture to *Gone with the Wind.* Both were filmed in Culver City.

1950s
On a witch hunt for communists, the federal House Un-American Activities Committee investigates and blacklists many Hollywood actors, directors and screenwriters, some of whom leave for Europe.

1975
The age of the modern blockbuster begins with the thriller *Jaws,* by a young filmmaker named Steven Spielberg, whose later blockbusters include *ET* and *Jurassic Park.*

2001
In the Hollywood & Highland Complex on Hollywood Blvd, the new Kodak (now Dolby) Theatre becomes the permanent home of the Academy Awards ceremony.

CALIFORNIA ON CELLULOID

Images of California are distributed far beyond its borders, ultimately reflecting back upon the state itself. Hollywood films often feature California not only as a setting but as a topic and, in some cases, almost as a character. LA especially loves to turn the camera on itself, often with a dark film-noir angle. For classic 20th-century California flicks, here are our top picks:

The Maltese Falcon (1941) John Huston directs Humphrey Bogart as Sam Spade, the classic San Francisco private eye.

Sunset Boulevard (1950) Billy Wilder's classic stars Gloria Swanson and William Holden in a bonfire of Hollywood vanities.

Vertigo (1958) The Golden Gate Bridge dazzles and dizzies in Alfred Hitchcock's noir thriller starring Jimmy Stewart and Kim Novak.

The Graduate (1967) Dustin Hoffman flees status-obsessed California suburbia to search for meaning, heading across the Bay Bridge to Berkeley (in the wrong direction).

Chinatown (1974) Roman Polanski's gripping version of the early 20th-century water wars that made and nearly broke LA.

Blade Runner (1982) Ridley Scott's sci-fi cyberpunk thriller projects a future LA of high-rise corporate fortresses and chaotic streets.

The Player (1992) Directed by Robert Altman and starring Tim Robbins, this satire on the Industry features dozens of cameos by actors spoofing themselves.

LA Confidential (1997) James Ellroy's neo-noir story deftly portrays the violent world of deals, sexual betrayal and double-crossing by cops in the crime-ridden 1950s.

Hollywood & Beyond

By the 1920s, Hollywood became the Industry's social and financial hub, but it's a myth that most movie production took place there. Of the major studios, only Paramount Pictures is in Hollywood proper, albeit surrounded by block after block of production-related businesses like lighting and post-production. Most movies have long been shot elsewhere around LA, for example, in Culver City (at MGM, now Sony Pictures), Studio City (at Universal Studios) and Burbank (at Warner Bros and later at Disney).

Moviemaking hasn't been limited to LA either. Founded in 1910, the American Film Manufacturing Company (aka Flying 'A' Studios) made box-office hits for years, first in San Diego and then Santa Barbara. Balboa Studios in Long Beach was another major silent-era dream factory. Well-known contemporary movie production companies based in the San Francisco Bay Area include Francis Ford Coppola's American Zoetrope, George Lucas' Industrial Light & Magic, and Pixar. Both San Francisco and LA remain creative hubs for emerging independent filmmakers.

During the 1930s, '40s and '50s, many famous US writers – including F Scott Fitzgerald, Dorothy Parker, Truman Capote, William Faulkner and Tennessee Williams – did stints as Hollywood screenwriters.

The Los Angeles Economic Development Council reports that only 1.6% of people living in LA County today are employed directly in film, TV and radio production. The high cost of filming has sent location scouts far beyond LA's San Fernando Valley (where most of California's movie and TV studios are found) all the way across the country and north of the border to Canada, where film production crews are welcomed with open arms (and pocketbooks) in 'Hollywood North,' especially in Vancouver, Toronto and Montreal.

For stargazers or movie buffs, however, LA is still *the* place for a pilgrimage. There you can tour major movie studios, be part of a live TV studio audience, line up alongside the red carpet before an awards ceremony, attend a high-wattage film festival, shop at boutiques favored by today's hottest stars and see where celebrities live, dine out, drink and go clubbing in real life.

Animated Magic

A young cartoonist named Walt Disney arrived in LA in 1923. Five years later he had his first breakout hit, *Steamboat Willie,* starring a mouse named Mickey. That film spawned the entire Disney empire, and dozens of other animation studios have followed with films, TV programs and special effects. Among the most beloved are Warner Bros (Bugs Bunny et al in *Looney Tunes*), Hanna-Barbera (*The Flintstones, The Jetsons,* Yogi Bear and Scooby-Doo), DreamWorks (*Shrek, Madagascar, Kung-Fu Panda*) and Film Roman (*The Simpsons*). Even if much of the hands-on work takes place overseas (in places such as South Korea), concept and supervision is still done in LA.

In San Francisco, George Lucas's Industrial Light & Magic is made up of a team of high-tech wizards who produce computer-generated special effects for such blockbuster series as Star Wars, Terminator, Jurassic Park, Indiana Jones and Harry Potter. Pixar Animation Studios, located in Emeryville in the East Bay, has produced an unbroken string of animated hits, including *Toy Story, Finding Nemo, Cars* and *Brave.*

The Small Screen

Ever since the first TV station began broadcasting in Los Angeles in 1931, iconic images of the city have been beamed into living rooms across America and around the world in shows such as *Dragnet* (1950s), *The Beverly Hillbillies* (1960s), *The Brady Bunch* and *Charlie's Angels* (1970s), *LA Law* (1980s) and *Baywatch, Melrose Place* and *The Fresh Prince of Bel-Air* (1990s). Teen 'dramedy' (drama-comedy) *Beverly Hills 90210* (1990s) made that LA zip code into a status symbol, while *The OC* (2000s) glamorized Newport Beach, Orange County. If you're a fan of reality TV, you'll spot Southern California starring in everything from *Top Chef* to the *Real Housewives of Orange County* and MTV's hybrid drama-reality series *Laguna Beach* and *The Hills.*

More recently, Southern California has been a versatile backdrop for edgy cable TV dramas, starting with HBO's *Six Feet Under,* which examined modern LA through the eyes of an eccentric family running a funeral home. With dark humor, Showtime's *Weeds* depicted the life of a pot-growing SoCal widow with ties to Mexican drug cartels, while FX's *The Shield* riffed on police corruption in the City of Angels. HBO's *Entourage* portrayed the highs, the lows and the intrigues of the Industry through the eyes of a rising star and his posse, loosely based on the life of Mark Wahlberg. With no holds barred, Showtime's *Californication* shows what happens when a successful New York novelist goes Hollywood. For more biting social satire about the Industry, check out the early LA-based seasons of HBO's *Curb Your Enthusiasm,* by *Seinfeld* co-creator Larry David and often guest starring Hollywood celebrities playing themselves.

Top California Film Festivals

AFI Fest (www.afi.com/afifest)

LA Film Fest (www.lafilmfest.com)

Outfest (www.outfest.org)

Palm Springs International Film Festival (www.psfilmfest.org)

San Francisco International Film Festival (www.sffs.org)

Sonoma International Film Festival (www.sonomafilmfest.org)

ON LOCATION: FILM & TV ANIMATED MAGIC

Music & the Arts

Go ahead and mock. But when Californians thank their lucky stars – or good karma, or the goddess – they don't live in New York, they're not just talking about beach weather. This place has long supported thriving music and arts scenes that aren't afraid to be completely independent, even outlandish at times. Given that this is the USA's most racially and ethnically diverse state, unlimited creativity makes perfect sense.

Music

In the 1950s, the hard-edged, honky-tonk Bakersfield Sound emerged inland in California's Central Valley, where Buck Owens and the Buckaroos and Merle Haggard performed their own twist on Nashville country hits for hard-drinkin' audiences of Dust Bowl migrants and cowboy ranchers.

In your California dreamin', you jam with a band – so what kind of music do you play? Beach Boys covers, West Coast rap, bluegrass, off-key punk, classic soul, hard bop, heavy-metal riffs on opera or DJ mashups of all of the above? No problem: a walk down a city street here can sound like the world's most eclectic iPod set to shuffle.

Much of the recording industry is based in LA, and SoCal's film and TV industries have proven powerful talent incubators. But today's troubled pop princesses and airbrushed boy bands are only here thanks to the tuneful revolutions of all of the decades of innovation that came before.

Early Eclectic Sounds

Chronologically speaking, Mexican folk music arrived in California first, during the rancho era. Later in the 19th century, Gold Rush immigrants introduced bluegrass, bawdy dancehall ragtime and Chinese classical music.

By the turn of the 20th century, opera had become California's favorite sound. The city of San Francisco alone had 20 concert and opera halls before the 1906 earthquake literally brought down the houses. Soon afterward, talented opera performers converged on the shattered city for free public performances that turned arias into anthems for the city's rebirth. San Francisco's War Memorial Opera House today is home to North America's second-largest opera company, after NYC's Metropolitan Opera.

Swing Jazz, Blues & Soul

Swing was the next big thing to hit California. In the 1930s and '40s, big bands sparked a lindy-hopping craze in LA and sailors on shore leave hit San Francisco's underground, integrated jazz clubs.

California's African American community grew with the 'Great Migration' during the WWII shipping and manufacturing boom, and from this thriving scene emerged the West Coast blues sound. Texas-born bluesman T-Bone Walker worked in LA's Central Ave clubs before making hit records of his electric guitar stylings for Capitol Records. Throughout the 1940s and '50s, West Coast blues were nurtured in San Francisco and Oakland by guitarists like Pee Wee Crayton from Texas and Oklahoma-born Lowell Fulson.

With Beat poets riffing over improvised bass lines and audiences finger-snapping their approval, the cool West Coast jazz of Chet Baker and Bay Area–born Dave Brubeck emerged from San Francisco's North

Beach neighborhood in the 1950s. At the same time, in the African American cultural hub along LA's Central Ave, the hard bop of Charlie Parker and Charles Mingus kept SoCal's jazz scene alive and swinging.

In the 1950s and '60s, doo-wop, rhythm and blues, and soul music were all in steady rotation at nightclubs in South Central LA, considered the 'Harlem of the West.' Soulful singer Sam Cooke ran his own hit-making record label, attracting soul and gospel talent to LA.

Rockin' Out

The first homegrown rock-and-roll talent to make it big in the 1950s was Ritchie Valens, born in the San Fernando Valley, whose 'La Bamba' was a rockified version of a Mexican folk song. Dick Dale (aka 'the King of the Surf Guitar'), whose recording of 'Miserlou' featured in the movie *Pulp Fiction*, started experimenting with reverb effects in Orange County in the 1950s, then topped the charts with his band the Del-Tones in the early '60s, influencing everyone from the Beach Boys to Jimi Hendrix.

Waiting for the Sun: A Rock 'n' Roll History of Los Angeles, by Barney Hoskyns, follows the twists and turns of the SoCal music scene from the Beach Boys to Black Flag.

When Joan Baez and Bob Dylan had their Northern California fling in the early 1960s, Dylan plugged in his guitar and played folk rock. Janis Joplin and Big Brother & the Holding Company developed their shambling musical stylings in San Francisco, splintering folk rock into psychedelia. Emerging from that same San Francisco mélange, Jefferson Airplane remade Lewis Carroll's children's classic *Alice's Adventures in Wonderland* into the psychedelic hit 'White Rabbit.'

Meanwhile, LA bands the Byrds and the Doors, the latter with vocalist Jim Morrison as front man, blew minds on LA's famous Sunset Strip. The epicenter of LA's psychedelic rock scene was the Laurel Canyon neighborhood, just uphill from the Sunset Strip and the legendary Whisky a Go Go nightclub. Sooner or later, many of these 1960s rock-and-roll headliners wound up overdosing on drugs. Those that survived cleaned up and cashed out – though for the original jam band, the Grateful Dead, the song remained the same until guitarist Jerry Garcia's passing in a Marin County rehabilitation clinic in 1995.

The country-influenced pop of the Eagles, Jackson Browne and Linda Ronstadt became America's soundtrack for the early 1970s, joined by the Mexican fusion sounds of Santana from San Francisco and iconic funk bands War from Long Beach, and Sly and the Family Stone, who got their groove on in San Francisco before moving to LA.

PUNK'S NOT DEAD IN CALIFORNIA

In the 1970s, American airwaves were jammed with commercial arena rock that record companies paid DJs to shill like laundry soap, much to the articulate ire of California rock critics Lester Bangs and Greil Marcus. California teens bored with prepackaged anthems started making their own with secondhand guitars, three chords and crappy amps that added a loud buzz to their unleashed fury.

LA punk paralleled the scrappy local skate scene with the hardcore grind of Black Flag from Hermosa Beach and the Germs from LA. LA band X bridged punk and new wave from 1977 to 1987 with John Doe's rockabilly guitar, Exene Cervenka's angsty wail, and disappointed-romantic lyrics inspired by Charles Bukowski and Raymond Chandler. Local LA radio station KROQ rebelled against the tyranny of playlists, putting local punk on the airwaves and launching punk-funk sensation the Red Hot Chili Peppers.

San Francisco's punk scene was arty and absurdist, in rare form with Dead Kennedys singer (and future San Francisco mayoral candidate) Jello Biafra howling 'Holiday in Cambodia.' That was suitably anarchic for a city where local band the Avengers opened for the Sex Pistols' 1978 San Francisco show.

Post-Punk to Pop

The 1980s saw the rise of such influential LA crossover bands as Bad Religion (punk) and Suicidal Tendencies (hardcore/thrash), while more mainstream all-female bands the Bangles and the Go-Gos, new wavers Oingo Boingo, and rockers Jane's Addiction and Red Hot Chili Peppers took the world by storm. Bangin' out of Hollywood, Guns N' Roses was the '80s hard-rock band of choice. On avant-garde rocker Frank Zappa's 1982 single *Valley Girl*, his 14-year-old daughter Moon Unit taught the rest of America to say 'Omigo-o-od!' like an LA teenager.

By the 1990s alternative rock acts like Beck and Weezer had gained national presence. Hailing from East LA, Los Lobos was king of the Chicano (Mexican American) bands, an honor that has since passed to Ozomatli. Another key '90s band was Orange County's ska-punk-alt-rock No Doubt, which later launched the solo career of lead singer Gwen Stefani. Berkeley's 924 Gilman Street club revived punk in the '90s, including with Grammy Award–winning Green Day.

SoCal rock stars of the new millennium include the approachable hip-hop of LA's Black Eyed Peas, anchored by Fergie and will.i.am., San Diego-based pop-punksters Blink 182, Orange County's punk band the Offspring, and for better or for worse, whoever wins the finals of this year's *American Idol*, staged at Downtown LA's Nokia Theatre.

Rap & Hip-Hop Rhythms

Since the 1980s, LA has been a hotbed for West Coast rap and hip-hop. Eazy E, Ice Cube and Dr Dre released the seminal NWA (Niggaz With Attitude) album, *Straight Outta Compton*, in 1989. Death Row Records, cofounded by Dr Dre, has launched megawatt rap talents including Long Beach bad boys Snoop Dogg, Warren G and the late Tupac Shakur, who began his rap career in Marin County of all places and was fatally shot in 1996 in Las Vegas in a suspected East Coast/West Coast rap feud. Feuds also once checkered the musical career of LA rapper Game, whose 2009 *R.E.D Album* featured an all-star line-up of Diddy, Dr Dre, Snoop Dogg and more.

Throughout the 1980s and '90s, California maintained a grassroots hip-hop scene closer to the streets in LA and in the heart of the Black Power movement in Oakland. In the late 1990s, the Bay Area birthed 'hyphy' (short for hyperactive), a reaction against the increasing commercialization of hip-hop, and underground artists like E-40. Oakland-based Michael Franti & Spearhead blend hip-hop with funk, reggae, folk, jazz and rock stylings into messages for social justice and peace. Elsewhere, Korn from Bakersfield and Linkin Park from LA County combined hiphop with rap and metal to popularize 'nu metal.'

Architecture

There's more to California than beach houses and boardwalks. Californians have adapted imported styles to the climate and available materials, building cool, adobe-inspired houses in San Diego and fog-resistant redwood-shingle houses in Mendocino. After a century and a half of Californians grafting on inspired influences and eccentric details as the mood strikes them, the element of the unexpected is everywhere: tiled Maya deco facades in Oakland, Shinto-inspired archways in LA, English thatched roofs in Carmel and Chinoiserie streetlamps in San Francisco. California's architecture was postmodern before the word even existed.

Spanish Missions & Victorian Queens

The first Spanish missions were built around courtyards, using materials that Native Californians and Spaniards found on hand: adobe, limestone and grass. Many missions crumbled into disrepair as the church's

---

Tune into the 'Morning Becomes Eclectic' show on Southern California's KCRW radio station (www.kcrw.com) for live in-studio performances and musician interviews.

Oddball California Architecture

Hearst Castle

Winchester Mystery House

Tor House

Theme Building, LAX Airport

Wigwam Motel

Integratron

CALIFORNIA'S NAKED ARCHITECTURE

Clothing-optional California has never been shy about showcasing its assets. Starting in the 1960s, California embraced the stripped-down, glass-wall aesthetics of the International Style championed by Bauhaus architects Walter Gropius, Ludwig Mies van der Rohe and Le Corbusier. Open floor-plans and floor-to-ceiling windows were especially suited to the see-and-be-seen culture of Southern California.

Austrian-born Rudolph Schindler and Richard Neutra brought early modernism to LA and Palm Springs. PS's signature style is still celebrated every February during Modernism Week. Neutra and Schindler were also influenced by Frank Lloyd Wright, who designed LA's Hollyhock House in a style he dubbed 'California Romanza.'

With LA-based designers Charles and Ray Eames, Neutra contributed to the experimental open-plan Case Study Houses, several of which jut out of the LA landscape and are used as filming locations, for example, in *LA Confidential*.

influence waned, but the style remained practical for the climate. Early California settlers later adapted it into the rancho adobe style, as seen in Downtown LA's El Pueblo de Los Angeles and San Diego's Old Town.

Once the mid-19th-century Gold Rush was on, California's nouveau riche imported materials to construct grand mansions matching European fashions, and raised the stakes with ornamental excess. Many millionaires favored the gilded Queen Anne style. Outrageous examples of Victorian architecture, including 'Painted Ladies' and 'gingerbread' houses, can be found in such NorCal towns as San Francisco, Ferndale and Eureka.

But Californian architecture has always had its contrarian streak. Many turn-of-the-20th-century architects rejected frilly Victorian styles in favor of the simpler, classical lines of Spanish designs. Spanish Colonial Revival architecture, also known as Mission Revival style, hearkened back to early California missions with restrained and functional details: arched doors and windows, long covered porches, fountain courtyards, solid walls and red-tile roofs. Downtown Santa Barbara showcases this revival style, as do stately buildings in San Diego's Balboa Park, Scotty's Castle in Death Valley and several SoCal train depots, including in Downtown LA, San Diego, San Juan Capistrano and Santa Barbara, as well as Kelso Depot in the Mojave National Preserve.

In 1919, newspaper magnate William Randolph Hearst commissioned California's first licensed female architect Julia Morgan to build Hearst Castle. It would take her decades to finish.

Arts and Crafts & Art Deco

Simplicity and harmony were hallmarks of California's early-20th-century Arts and Crafts style. Influenced by both Japanese design principles and England's Arts and Crafts movement, its woodwork and handmade touches marked a deliberate departure from the Industrial Revolution's mechanization. SoCal architects Charles and Henry Greene and Bernard Maybeck and Julia Morgan in Northern California popularized the versatile one-story bungalow. Today you'll spot them in Pasadena and Berkeley with their overhanging eaves, airy terraces and sleeping porches harmonizing warm, livable interiors with the natural environment outdoors.

California was cosmopolitan from the start, and couldn't be limited to any one set of international influences. In the 1920s, the international art-deco style took elements from the ancient world – Mayan glyphs, Egyptian pillars, Babylonian ziggurats – and flattened them into modern motifs to cap stark facades and outline streamlined skyscrapers, notably in LA and Oakland. Streamline moderne kept decoration to a minimum and mimicked the aerodynamic look of ocean liners and airplanes.

Post-Modern Evolutions

True to its mythic nature, California couldn't help wanting to embellish the facts a little, veering away from strict high modernism to add unlikely postmodern shapes to the local landscape.

In 1997 Richard Meier made his mark on West LA with the Getty Center, a cresting white wave of a building on a sunburned hilltop. Canadian-born Frank Gehry relocated to Santa Monica, and his billowing, sculptural style for LA's Walt Disney Concert Hall winks cheekily at shipshape streamline moderne. Also in Downtown LA, the Cathedral of Our Lady of the Angels, designed by Spanish architect Rafael Moneo, echoes the grand churches of Mexico and Europe from a controversial deconstructivist angle. Renzo Piano's signature inside-out industrial style can be glimpsed in the sawtooth roof and red-steel veins of the Broad Contemporary Art Museum at the Los Angeles County Museum of Art.

The Bay Area's most iconic postmodern building is the San Francisco Museum of Modern Art, which Swiss architect Mario Botta made stand out with a black-and-white striped, marble-clad atrium in 1995. Lately SF has championed a brand of postmodernism by Pritzker Prize–winning architects that magnify and mimic the great outdoors, especially in Golden Gate Park. Swiss architects Herzog & de Meuron clad the MH de Young Memorial Museum in copper, which will eventually oxidize green to match its park setting. Nearby, Renzo Piano literally raised the roof on sustainable design at the LEED platinum-certified California Academy of Sciences, capped by a living-roof garden.

Visual Arts

To find museums, art galleries, fine-art exhibition spaces and calendars of upcoming shows throughout SoCal, check out *ArtScene* (www. artscenecal.com) and *Artweek LA* (www.artweek.la) magazines.

Although the earliest European artists were trained cartographers accompanying Western explorers, their images of California as an island show more imagination than scientific rigor. This mythologizing tendency continued throughout the Gold Rush era, as Western artists alternated between caricatures of Wild West debauchery and manifest-destiny propaganda urging pioneers to settle the golden West. The completion of the Transcontinental Railroad in 1869 brought an influx of romantic painters, who produced epic California wilderness landscapes. After the 20th century arrived, homegrown colonies of California Impressionist plein-air painters emerged at Laguna Beach and Carmel-by-the-Sea.

With the invention of photography, the improbable truth of California's landscape and its inhabitants was revealed. Pirkle Jones saw expressive potential in California landscape photography after WWII, while San Francisco–born Ansel Adams' sublime photographs had already started doing justice to Yosemite. Adams founded Group f/64 with Edward Weston and Imogen Cunningham in San Francisco. Berkeley-based Dorothea Lange turned her unflinching lens on the plight of Californian migrant workers in the Great Depression and Japanese Americans forced to enter internment camps during WWII, producing poignant documentary photos.

As the postwar American West became crisscrossed with freeways and divided into planned communities, Californian painters captured the abstract forms of manufactured landscapes on canvas. In San Francisco, Richard Diebenkorn and David Park became leading proponents of Bay Area Figurative Art, while San Francisco–born sculptor Richard Serra captured urban aesthetics in massive, rusting monoliths resembling ship prows and industrial Stonehenges. Meanwhile, pop artists captured the ethos of conspicuous consumerism, through Wayne Thiebaud's gumball machines, British émigré David Hockney's LA pools, and above all, Ed Ruscha's studies of SoCal pop culture. In the Bay Area, artists showed their love for rough-and-readymade 1950s Beat collage, '60s psychedelic

LATINO MURALS: TAKING IT TO THE STREETS

Beginning in the 1930s, when the federal Works Progress Administration sponsored schemes to uplift and beautify cities across the country, murals came to define California cityscapes. Mexican muralists Diego Rivera, David Alfaro Siqueiros and José Clemente Orozco sparked an outpouring of murals across LA that today number in the thousands. Rivera was also brought to San Francisco to paint murals at the San Francisco Art Institute, and his influence is reflected in the interior of San Francisco's Coit Tower and scores of murals lining the Mission District. Murals gave voice to Chicano pride and protests over US Central American policies in the 1970s, notably in San Diego's Chicano Park and East LA murals by collectives such as East Los Streetscapers.

rock posters from Fillmore concerts, earthy '70s funk and beautiful-mess punk, and '80s graffiti art.

Today's California contemporary art scene brings all these influences together with muralist-led social commentary, an obsessive dedication to craft and a new-media milieu pierced by cutting-edge technology. LA's Museum of Contemporary Art puts on provocative and avant-garde shows, as does LACMA's Broad Contemporary Art Museum, San Francisco's Museum of Modern Art, and the Museum of Contemporary Art San Diego, which specializes in post-1950s pop and conceptual art. To see California-made art at its most experimental, browse the SoCal gallery scenes in Downtown LA and Culver City, then check out independent NorCal art spaces in San Francisco's Mission District and the laboratory-like galleries around SoMa's Yerba Buena Center for the Arts.

Theater

In your California dream you're discovered by a movie talent scout, but most Californian actors actually get their start in theater. Home to about 25% of the nation's professional actors, LA is the USA's second-most influential city for theater after NYC. Meanwhile San Francisco has been a national hub for experimental theater since the 1960s.

Spaces to watch around LA include the Geffen Playhouse close to UCLA, the Ahmanson Theatre and Mark Taper Forum in Downtown LA, and the Actors' Gang Theatre, cofounded by actor Tim Robbins. Small theaters flourish in West Hollywood (WeHo) and North Hollywood (NoHo), the West Coast's versions of off- and off-off-Broadway. Influential multicultural theaters include Little Tokyo's East West Players, while critically acclaimed outlying companies include the innovative Long Beach Opera and Orange County's South Coast Repertory in Costa Mesa.

San Francisco's priorities have been obvious since the great earthquake of 1906, when survivors were entertained in tents set up amid the smoldering ruins, and its famous theaters were rebuilt well before City Hall. Major productions destined for the lights of Broadway and London premiere at the American Conservatory Theater, and San Francisco's answer to Edinburgh is the annual SF Fringe Festival at the EXIT Theatre. The Magic Theatre gained a national reputation in the 1970s, when Sam Shepard was the theater's resident playwright, and it still premieres innovative California playwrights today. An audience-interactive troupe, We Players stages classic plays including Shakespearean dramas at unusual locations like Alcatraz. Across the Bay, the Berkeley Repertory Theatre has launched acclaimed productions based on such unlikely subjects as the rise and fall of Jim Jones's Peoples Temple.

Timeless, rare Ansel Adams photographs are paired with excerpts from canonical Californian writers such as John Steinbeck and Joan Didion in *California: With Classic California Writings*, edited by Andrea Gray Stillman.

By the Book

Californians make up the largest market for books in the US, and read much more than the national average. Skewing the curve is bookish San Francisco, with more writers, playwrights and book purchases per capita than any other US city. The West Coast has long attracted novelists, poets and storytellers from across the country and around the planet, and California's multicultural literary community today is stronger than ever.

Early Voices of Social Realism

Get a slice of the state's heartland by reading *Highway 99: A Literary Journey Through California's Great Central Valley*, edited by Oakland-based writer Stan Yogi. It's full of multicultural perspectives, from early European settlers to 20th-century Mexican and Asian immigrant farmers.

Arguably the most influential author to emerge from California was John Steinbeck, born in Salinas in 1902. Steinbeck focused attention on Central Valley farming communities. Published during the 1930s, his first California novel, *Tortilla Flat*, takes place in Monterey's Mexican American community, while his masterpiece, *The Grapes of Wrath*, tells of the struggles of migrant farm workers during the Depression. Another social realist, Eugene O'Neill took his 1936 Nobel Prize money and transplanted himself near San Francisco, where he wrote the autobiographical play *Long Day's Journey into Night*.

Beginning in the 1920s, many novelists looked at LA in political terms, often viewing it unfavorably as the ultimate metaphor for capitalism. Classics in this vein include Upton Sinclair's *Oil!*, a muckraking work of historical fiction with socialist overtones. Aldous Huxley's *After Many a Summer* is based on the life of publisher William Randolph Hearst (also an inspiration for Orson Welles' film *Citizen Kane*). F Scott Fitzgerald's final novel, *The Last Tycoon*, makes scathing observations about the early years of Hollywood by following the life of a 1930s movie producer who is slowly working himself to death.

In Northern California, professional hell-raiser Jack London grew up and cut his teeth in Oakland. He turned out a massive volume of influential fiction, including tales of the late-19th-century Klondike Gold Rush. Oakland was famously scorned by 'Lost Generation' literary luminary Gertrude Stein (who lived there briefly) when she quipped, 'There is no there there,' although, to be fair, she was really only saying that she couldn't find her old house when she returned from Europe in the 1930s.

Pulp Noir & Science Fiction

California Poetry: From the Gold Rush to the Present, edited by Dana Gioia, Chryss Yost and Jack Hicks, is a ground-breaking anthology. Enlightening introductions give each poet a deserved context.

In the 1930s, San Francisco and Los Angeles became the capitals of the pulp detective novel, examples of which were often made into noir crime films. Dashiell Hammett (*The Maltese Falcon*) made San Francisco's fog a sinister character. The king of hard-boiled crime writers was Raymond Chandler, who thinly disguised his hometown of Santa Monica as Bay City. Starting in the 1990s, a neo-noir renaissance of California crime fiction was masterminded by James Ellroy (*LA Confidential*), the late Elmore Leonard (*Get Shorty*) and Walter Mosley (*Devil in a Blue Dress*), whose Easy Rawlins detective novels are set in South Central LA.

California has also proved fertile ground for the imaginations of sci-fi writers. Raised in Berkeley, Philip K Dick is chiefly remembered for his science fiction, notably *Do Androids Dream of Electric Sheep?*, later

> ### READING CALIFORNIA
>
> Crack open these classics from some of California's less likely literary locations:
>
> **Central Coast** *The Selected Poetry of Robinson Jeffers* – In the looming, windswept pines surrounding his Tor House, Jeffers found inspiration for staggeringly beautiful poems.
>
> **Central Valley** *The Woman Warrior: Memoirs of a Girlhood Among Ghosts* (Maxine Hong Kingston) – A chronicle of growing up Chinese American, reflecting the shattered mirror of Californian identity.
>
> **Gold Country** *Roughing It* (Mark Twain) – The master of sardonic observation tells of earthquakes, silver booms and busts, and getting by for a month on a dime in the Wild West.
>
> **Sierra Nevada** *Riprap and Cold Mountain Poems* (Gary Snyder) – Influenced by Japanese and Chinese spirituality and classical literature, a Beat poet captures the meditative openness of wild landscapes.

adapted into the 1982 dystopian sci-fi movie *Blade Runner*. Dick's novel *The Man in the High Castle* presents the ultimate what-if scenario: imagine San Francisco circa 1962 if Japan, fascist Italy and Nazi Germany had won WWII. Berkeley-born Ursula K Le Guin (*The Left Hand of Darkness, A Wizard of Earthsea*) is a lauded fantasy writer, feminist and essayist.

Social Movers & Shakers

After the chaos of WWII, the Beat Generation brought about a provocative new style of writing: short, sharp, spontaneous and alive. Based in San Francisco, the scene revolved around Jack Kerouac (*On the Road*), Allen Ginsberg (*Howl*) and Lawrence Ferlinghetti, the Beats' patron publisher who co-founded City Lights Bookstore. Poet-painter-playwright Kenneth Rexroth was instrumental in advancing the careers of several Bay Area writers and artists of that era, and he shared an interest in Japanese culture with Buddhist Gary Snyder, another Beat poet.

Few writers have nailed contemporary California culture as well as Joan Didion. She's best known for her collection of literary nonfiction essays, *Slouching Towards Bethlehem,* which take a caustic look at 1960s flower power. Tom Wolfe also put '60s San Francisco in perspective with *The Electric Kool-Aid Acid Test,* which follows Ken Kesey's band of Merry Pranksters and their LSD-laced 'magic bus' journey starting near Santa Cruz.

In the 1970s, Charles Bukowski's semiautobiographical novel *Post Office* captured down-and-out downtown LA, while Richard Vasquez's *Chicano* took a dramatic look at LA's Latino barrio. For a frothy taste of 1970s San Francisco, the serial-style *Tales of the City,* by Armistead Maupin, collars the reader as the author follows the lives of several colorful, fictional characters, gay and straight. Zooming ahead, the mid-1980s brought the startling revelations of Bret Easton Ellis' *Less Than Zero,* about the cocaine-addled lives of wealthy Beverly Hills teenagers.

You've probably already read famous novels by Californians without knowing it, as some of the best-known titles by resident writers aren't set in their adopted home state. Take for example Ray Bradbury's 1950s dystopian classic *Fahrenheit 451;* Alice Walker's Pulitzer Prize–winning *The Color Purple;* Ken Kesey's quintessential 1960s novel *One Flew Over the Cuckoo's Nest;* Isabel Allende's best-selling *The House of the Spirits;* feminist poetry by the late Adrienne Rich; and Michael Chabon's Pulitzer Prize–winning *The Amazing Adventures of Kavalier and Clay.*

For a memorable romp through California, join contemporary authors, including Pico Iyer and Michael Chabon, in *My California: Journeys by Great Writers.* Proceeds from purchases via Angel City Press (www.angelcitypress.com) support the California Arts Council.

The Land & Wildlife

From snowy peaks to scorching deserts, and golden-sand beaches to misty redwood forests, California is home to a bewildering variety of ecosystems, flora and fauna. Its Mediterranean climate, characterized by dry summers and mild wet winters, is favored by scores of unique plants and animals, giving it the distinction of being North America's most biodiverse spot. At the same time, California has the largest human population of any US state, which puts a tremendous strain on its many precious natural resources.

Lay of the Land

According to the US Geological Survey, the odds of a magnitude 6.7 or greater earthquake hitting California in the next 30 years is 99.7%.

The third-biggest state after Alaska and Texas, California covers over 155,000 sq miles, making it larger than 85 of the world's smallest nations. It's bordered to the north by Oregon, to the south by Mexico, to the east by Nevada and Arizona, and by 840 miles of Pacific shoreline to the west.

Geology & Earthquakes

California is a complex geologic landscape formed from fragments of rock and earth crust scraped together as the North American continent drifted westward over hundreds of millions of years. Crumpled coast ranges, the downward-bowing Central Valley and the still-rising Sierra Nevada all provide evidence of gigantic forces exerted as the continental and ocean plates crushed together.

Everything changed about 25 million years ago, when the ocean plates stopped colliding and instead started sliding against each other, creating the massive San Andreas Fault. Because this contact zone doesn't slide smoothly, but catches and slips irregularly, it rattles California with an ongoing succession of tremors and earthquakes.

In 1906 the state's most famous earthquake measured 7.8 on the Richter scale and demolished San Francisco, leaving more than 3000 people dead. The Bay Area made headlines again in 1989 when the Loma Prieta earthquake (6.9) caused a section of the Bay Bridge to collapse. Los Angeles' last 'big one' was in 1994, when the Northridge quake (6.7) caused parts of the Santa Monica Fwy to fall down, making it the most costly quake in US history – so far, that is.

Browse through more than 1200 aerial photos covering almost every mile of California's gorgeously rugged coastline, stretching from Oregon to Mexico, at www.california-coastline.org.

From the Coast to the Central Valley

Much of California's coast is fronted by rugged mountains that capture winter's water-laden storms. San Francisco divides the Coast Ranges roughly in half, leaving the foggy North Coast sparsely populated. The Central and Southern California coasts have a balmier climate and many more people.

The northernmost reaches of the Coast Ranges get 120in of rain in a typical year, and in some places, persistent summer fog contributes another 12in of precipitation. Nutrient-rich soils and abundant moisture foster stands of towering coast redwoods, growing (where they haven't been cut down) as far south as Big Sur and all the way north to Oregon.

On their eastern flanks, the Coast Ranges subside into gently rolling hills that give way to the sprawling Central Valley. Once an inland sea, this flat inland basin is now an agricultural powerhouse producing about half of America's fruits, nuts and vegetables. Stretching about 450 miles long and 50 miles wide, the valley sees about as much rainfall as a desert, but gets huge volumes of water run-off from the Sierra Nevada.

Before the arrival of Europeans, the Central Valley was a natural wonderland – a region of vast marshes and home to flocks of geese that blackened the sky, not to mention grasslands carpeted with countless flowers and populated by millions of antelopes, elk and grizzly bears. Virtually this entire landscape has been plowed under and replaced with alien weeds (including agricultural crops) and livestock ranches.

Mountain Ranges

On the eastern side of the Central Valley looms California's most prominent topographic feature, the Sierra Nevada, nicknamed the 'Range of Light' by conservationist John Muir. At 400 miles long and 70 miles wide, this is one of the world's largest mountain ranges and is home to 13 peaks over 14,000ft high. The vast wilderness of the High Sierra (mostly above 9000ft) is an astounding landscape of shrinking glaciers, sculpted granite peaks and remote canyons, beautiful to look at but difficult to access, and one of the greatest challenges for 19th-century settlers attempting to reach California.

The soaring Sierra Nevada captures storm systems and drains them of their water, with most of the precipitation above 3000ft falling as snow, creating a premier winter-sports destination. Melting snow flows down into a half-dozen major river systems on the range's western and eastern slopes, providing the vast majority of water needed for agriculture in the Central Valley and for the metro areas of San Francisco and LA.

At its northern end, the Sierra Nevada merges imperceptibly into the volcanic Cascade Mountains, which continue north into Oregon and Washington. At its southern end, the Sierra Nevada makes a funny westward hook and connects via the Transverse Ranges (one of the USA's few east–west mountain ranges) to the southern Coast Ranges.

California claims both the highest point in contiguous US (Mt Whitney, 14,505ft) and the lowest elevation in North America (Badwater, Death Valley, 282ft below sea level) – and they're only 90 miles apart, as the condor flies.

The Deserts & Beyond

With the west slope of the Sierra Nevada capturing the lion's share of water, most lands east of the Sierra crest are dry and desertlike, receiving less than 10in of rain a year. Surprisingly, some valleys at the eastern foot of the Sierra Nevada are well watered by creeks and support a vigorous economy of livestock and agriculture.

At the western edge of the Great Basin, the elevated Modoc Plateau in far northeastern California is a cold desert blanketed by hardy sagebrush shrubs and juniper trees. Temperatures increase as you head south, with a prominent transition on the descent from Mono Lake into the Owens Valley east of the Sierra Nevada. This southern hot desert (part of the Mojave Desert) includes Death Valley, one of the hottest places on the planet. Further south, the Mojave Desert morphs into the Colorado Desert (part of Mexico's greater Sonoran Desert) around the Salton Sea.

CALIFORNIA: ALMOST AN ISLAND

Much of California is a biological island cut off from the rest of North America by the soaring peaks of the Sierra Nevada. As on other 'islands' in the world, evolution has created unique plants and animals under these biologically isolated conditions. California ranks first in the nation for its number of endemic plants, amphibians, reptiles, freshwater fish and mammals. Even more impressive is the fact that 30% of all plant species, 50% of all bird species and 50% of all mammal species in the USA can be found here.

Geography of California

California's Flora & Fauna

Although the staggering numbers of animals that greeted the first foreign settlers are now a thing of the past, it's easy to see wildlife thriving in California in the right places and at the right times of year. You're likely to spot at least a few charismatic species during your sojourn. Unfortunately, some are but shadow populations, hovering at the edge of survival, pushed up against California's burgeoning human population.

Marine Mammals

Spend even one day along California's coast and you may spot pods of bottle-nosed dolphins and porpoises swimming and doing acrobatics in the ocean. Playful sea otters and harbor seals typically stick closer to shore, especially around public piers and protected bays. Since the 1989 earthquake, loudly barking sea lions have been piling up on San

Francisco's Pier 39, where delighted tourists ogle them. To see more wild pinnipeds, visit Point Lobos State Natural Reserve near Monterey or Channel Islands National Park in Southern California.

Once threatened by extinction, gray whales now migrate in growing numbers along California's coast between December and April. Adult whales live up to 60 years, are longer than a city bus and can weigh up to 40 tons, making quite a splash when they dive below or leap out of the water. Every year they travel from summertime feeding grounds in the arctic Bering Sea, down to southern breeding grounds off Baja California – and then all the way back up again, making a 6000-mile round trip.

Also almost hunted to extinction by the late 19th century for their oil-rich blubber, northern elephant seals have made a remarkable comeback along California's coast. Año Nuevo State Reserve, north of Santa Cruz, is a major breeding ground for northern elephant seals. California's biggest elephant seal colony is found at Piedras Blancas, south of Big Sur. There's a smaller rookery at Point Reyes National Seashore in Marin County.

> Peak mating season for northern elephants seals along California's coast just happens to coincide with Valentine's Day (February 14).

Land Mammals

California's most symbolic land animal – it graces the state flag – is the grizzly bear. Extirpated in the 1920s after relentless persecution, grizzlies once roamed California's beaches and grasslands in large numbers, eating everything from acorns to whale carcasses. Grizzlies were particularly abundant in the Central Valley, but retreated upslope into the Sierra Nevada as they were hunted out.

California's mountain forests are still home to an estimated 25,000 to 30,000 black bears, the grizzlies' smaller cousins. Despite their name, their fur ranges in color from black to dark brown, cinnamon or even blond. These burly omnivores feed on berries, nuts, roots, grasses, insects, eggs, small mammals and fish, but can become a nuisance around campgrounds and cabins where food and trash are not secured.

As foreign settlers moved into California in the 19th century, many other large mammals fared almost as poorly as grizzlies. Immense herds of tule elk and antelope in the Central Valley were particularly hard hit, with antelope retreating in small numbers to the northeastern corner of the state, and tule elk hunted into near-extinction (a small remnant herd was moved to Point Reyes, where it has since rebounded).

Mountain lions (also called cougars) hunt throughout California's mountains and forests, especially in areas teeming with deer. Solitary lions, which can grow 8ft in length and weigh 175lb, are formidable predators. Few attacks on humans have occurred, mostly where encroachment has pushed hungry lions to their limits – for example, at the boundaries between wilderness and rapidly developing suburbs.

> The Audubon Society's California chapter website (www.ca.audu-bon.org) offers helpful birding checklists, photos and descriptions of key species, conservation news and a Pacific Flyway blog (www.audublog.org).

Birds & Butterflies

California is an essential stop on the migratory Pacific Flyway between Alaska and Mexico. Almost half the bird species in North America use

---

CALIFORNIA'S DESERT CRITTERS

California's deserts are far from deserted, but most animals are too smart to hang out in the daytime heat, coming out only at night like bats do. Roadrunners, those black-and-white mottled ground cuckoos with long tails and punk-style mohawks, can often be spotted on roadsides. Other desert inhabitants include burrowing kit foxes, tree-climbing grey foxes, hopping jackrabbits and kangaroo rats, slow-moving (and endangered) desert tortoises and a variety of snakes, lizards and spiders. Desert bighorn sheep and myriad birds flock to watering holes, often around seasonal springs and native fan-palm oases – spy them in Joshua Tree National Park and Anza-Borrego Desert State Park.

the state's wildlife refuges and nature preserves for rest and refueling. Migration peaks during the wetter winter season. Witness, for example, the congregation of two million ducks and geese at the Klamath Basin National Wildlife Refuges during October and November.

Year-round you can see birds at California's beaches, estuaries and bays, where herons, cormorants, shorebirds and gulls gather, including at Point Reyes National Seashore and in the Channel Islands. Monarch butterflies are gorgeous orange creatures that follow long-distance migration patterns in search of milkweed, their only source of food. They winter in California by the tens of thousands, mostly on the Central Coast, for example, in Santa Cruz, Pacific Grove, Pismo Beach and Santa Barbara County.

As you drive along the Big Sur coastline, look skyward to spot endangered California condors, which also soar inland over Pinnacles National Park and Los Padres National Forest. Also keep an eye out for regal bald eagles, which have regained a foothold on the Channel Islands, and some spend their winters at Big Bear Lake in the mountains near LA.

The California condor is the largest flying bird in North America. In 1987 there were only two dozen or so birds left in the wild. Thanks to captive breeding and release programs, there are about 240 flying free today.

Wildflowers & Trees

California's 6000 kinds of plants are both flamboyant and subtle. Many species are so obscure and similar that only a dedicated botanist could tell them apart, but add them all together in the spring and you end up with riotous carpets of wildflowers that can take your breath away. The state flower is the orange-yellow native California poppy.

California is also a region of superlative trees: the oldest (bristlecone pines of the White Mountains that are nearly 5000 years old), the tallest (coast redwoods approaching 380ft) and the largest (giant sequoias of the Sierra Nevada exceeding 36ft across at the base). The latter, which are unique to California, survive in isolated groves scattered on the Sierra Nevada's western slopes, including in Yosemite, Sequoia & Kings Canyon National Parks.

An astounding 20 native species of oak grow in California, including live (evergreen) oaks with holly-like leaves and scaly acorns. Other common trees include the aromatic California bay laurel, whose long slender leaves turn purple. Rare native trees include Monterey pines and Torrey pines, both gnarly species that have adapted to harsh coastal conditions such as high winds, sparse rainfall and sandy, stony soils; the latter only grows at Torrey Pines State Reserve near San Diego and in the Channel Islands, home to dozens more endemic plant species.

Heading inland, the Sierra Nevada has three distinct ecozones: the dry western foothills covered with oak and chaparral; conifer forests starting from an elevation of 2000ft; and an alpine zone above 8000ft.

GOING WILD FOR CALIFORNIA'S WILDFLOWERS

The famous 'golden hills' of California are actually the result of plants drying up in preparation for the long hot summer. Many plants have adapted to long periods of almost no rain by growing prolifically during California's mild wet winters, springing to life with the first rains of autumn and blooming as early as February.

In Southern California's desert areas, wildflower blooms usually peak in March, with other lowland areas of the state producing abundant wildflowers into April. Visit Anza-Borrego Desert State Park, Death Valley National Park, the Antelope Valley California Poppy Reserve and Carrizo Plain National Monument for some of the most spectacular and predictable wildflower displays.

As snows melt later at higher elevations in the Sierra Nevada, Yosemite National Park's Tuolumne Meadows is another prime spot for wildflower walks and photography, with blooms usually peaking in late June or early July.

Almost two dozen species of conifer grow in the Sierra Nevada, with mid-elevation forests home to massive Douglas firs, ponderosa pines and, biggest of all, the giant sequoia. Deciduous trees include quaking aspen, a white-trunked tree whose shimmering leaves turn pale yellow in the fall, creating spectacular scenery, notably in the Eastern Sierra.

Cacti & Other Desert Flora

In Southern California's deserts, cacti and other plants have adapted to the arid climate with thin, spiny leaves that resist moisture loss (and deter grazing animals), and seed and flowering mechanisms that kick into gear during brief winter rains. With enough winter rainfall, desert flora can bloom spectacularly in spring, carpeting valleys and drawing thousands of onlookers and shutterbugs.

Among the most common and easy to identify is cholla, which appears so furry that it is nicknamed 'teddy-bear cactus.' But it's far from cuddly and instead will bury extremely sharp, barbed spines in your skin at the slightest touch. Also watch out for catclaw acacia, nicknamed 'wait-a-minute bush' because its small, sharp, hooked thorny spikes can snatch clothing or skin as you brush past.

Almost as widespread is prickly pear, a flat, fleshy-padded cacti whose juice is traditionally used as medicine by Native Americans. Then there's cactuslike creosote (actually, a small evergreen bush with a distinctive smell) and spiky ocotillo, which grows up to 20ft tall and has canelike branches that sprout blood-red flowers in spring.

Like whimsical figments from a Dr Seuss book, Joshua trees are the largest type of yucca, with heavy, creamy greenish-white flowers in spring. Allegedly, they were named by emigrant Mormons, who thought the crooked branches resembled the outstretched arms of a biblical prophet. Joshua trees grow throughout the Mojave Desert, although their habitat and long-term survival is severely threatened by climate change.

> In 2006 the world's tallest known living tree was discovered in a remote area of Redwood National Park (its location is kept secret to protect it). It's named Hyperion and stands a whopping 379ft tall.

California's National & State Parklands

Most Californians rank outdoor recreation as vital to their quality of life, and the amount of preserved public lands has steadily grown due to important pieces of legislation passed since the 1960s. The landmark 1976 California Coastal Act saved the coastline from further development, while the controversial 1994 California Desert Protection Act angered many ranchers, miners and off-highway vehicle (OHV) enthusiasts.

Today, **California State Parks** (www.parks.ca.gov) protect nearly a third of the state's coastline, along with redwood forests, mountain lakes, desert canyons, waterfalls, wildlife preserves and historical sites. In recent decades, state budget shortfalls and chronic underfunding of California's parks have been partly responsible for widespread closures, limited visitor services and increased park entry and outdoor recreation fees. Even so, it's in California's economic best interests to protect its wilderness, since revenues from recreational tourism consistently outpace competing 'resource extraction' industries like mining.

Some of California's parklands are being loved to death. Too many visitors stress the natural environment, and it's increasingly difficult to balance public access with conservation. To avoid the biggest crowds and shrink your environmental footprint, visit popular parks like Yosemite outside of peak season. Alternatively, less-famous natural areas managed by the **National Park Service** (www.nps.gov/state/CA) may go relatively untouched most of the year, which means you won't have to reserve permits, campsites or lodging many months in advance.

There are 18 national forests in California managed by the **US Forest Service** (USFS; www.fs.usda.gov/r5), comprising lands around Mt

> Marc Reisner's must-read *Cadillac Desert: The American West and Its Disappearing Water* examines the contentious, sometimes violent, water wars that gave rise to modern California.

Whitney, Mt Shasta, Lake Tahoe, Big Bear Lake and Big Sur. Beloved by birders, national wildlife refuges (NWR) including the Salton Sea and Klamath Basin are managed by the **US Fish & Wildlife Service** (USF-WS; www.fws.gov/refuges). More wilderness tracts in California, including the Lost Coast and Carrizo Plain, are overseen by the **Bureau of Land Management** (BLM; www.blm.gov/ca/st/en.html).

Top National Parks

....

Yosemite National Park

....

Sequoia & Kings Canyon National Parks

....

Death Valley National Park

....

Joshua Tree National Park

....

Lassen Volcanic National Park

....

Redwood National & State Parks

Conserving California

In California, rapid development and uncontrolled growth have often come at great environmental cost. Starting in 1849, Gold Rush miners tore apart the land in their frenzied quest for a lucky strike, ultimately sending more than 1.5 billion tons of debris and uncalculated amounts of poisonous mercury downstream into the Central Valley, where rivers and streams became clogged and polluted.

Water, or the lack thereof, has long been at the heart of California's epic environmental struggles and catastrophes. Despite campaigning by John Muir, California's greatest environmental champion, in the 1920s the Tuolumne River was dammed at Hetch Hetchy in Yosemite National Park, so that San Francisco could have drinking water. Likewise, the diversion of water to LA has contributed to the destruction of Owens Lake and its fertile wetlands, and the degradation of Mono Lake in the Eastern Sierra. Statewide, the damming of rivers and capture of water for houses and farms has destroyed countless salmon runs and drained marshlands. The Central Valley today resembles a dust bowl; its underground aquifer is in poor shape, with some land sinking as much as a foot each year.

Altered and compromised habitats, both on land and in the water, make easy targets for invasive species, including highly aggressive species that wreak havoc on California's ecosystems and economy. In San Francisco Bay, one of the most important estuaries in the world, there are now over 230 alien species choking the aquatic ecosystem; in some areas they already comprise as much as 95% of the total biomass.

Co-founded by naturalist John Muir in 1892, the Sierra Club (www.sierraclub.org) was the USA's first conservation group. It remains the nation's most active, offering educational programs, group hikes, organized trips and volunteer vacations.

Although air quality in California has improved markedly in past decades, it's still among the worst in the country. Auto exhaust and fine particulates generated by the wearing down of vehicle tires, along with industrial emissions, are the chief culprits. An even greater health hazard is ozone, the principal ingredient in smog, which makes sunny days around LA, Sacramento, the Central Valley and the western Sierra Nevada look hazy.

But there's hope. Low-emission vehicles are becoming one of the most sought-after types of car in the state, and rapidly rising fuel costs are keeping more gas-guzzling SUVs off the road. Californians recently voted to fund construction of solar-power plants. There's even talk of harnessing the tremendous tidal flows of the Pacific to generate more clean energy. By law California's utilities must get 33% of their energy from renewable resources by 2020, the most ambitious target yet set by any US state.

Survival Guide

Directory A–Z

Accommodations

Amenities

➡ Budget-conscious accommodations include campgrounds, hostels and motels. Because midrange properties generally offer better value for money, most of our accommodations fall into this category.

➡ At midrange motels and hotels, expect clean, comfortable and decent-sized rooms with at least a private bathroom, and standard amenities such as cable TV, direct-dial telephone, a coffeemaker, and perhaps a microwave and mini-fridge.

➡ Top-end lodgings offer top-notch amenities and perhaps a scenic location, high design or historical ambience. Pools, fitness rooms, business centers, full-service restaurants and bars and other convenient facilities are all standard.

➡ In Southern California, nearly all lodgings have air-conditioning, but in Northern California, where it rarely gets hot the opposite is true. In coastal areas as far south as Santa Barbara, only fans may be provided.

➡ Accommodations offering online computer terminals for guests are designated with the internet icon (@). A fee may apply (eg at full-service business centers inside hotels).

➡ There may be a fee for wireless internet (🛜), especially for in-room access. Look for free wi-fi hot spots in hotel public areas (eg lobby, poolside).

➡ Many lodgings are now exclusively nonsmoking. Where they still exist, smoking rooms are often left unrenovated and in less desirable locations. Expect a hefty 'cleaning fee' ($100 or more) if you light up in designated nonsmoking rooms.

Rates & Reservations

➡ Generally, midweek rates are lower except at urban hotels geared toward business travelers, which lure leisure travelers with weekend deals.

➡ Discount membership cards (eg AAA, AARP) may get you about 10% off standard rates at participating hotels and motels.

➡ Look for freebie ad magazines packed with hotel and motel discount coupons at gas stations, highway rest areas, tourist offices and online at **HotelCoupons** (http://hotelcoupons.com).

➡ High season is from June to August everywhere, except the deserts and mountain ski areas, where December through April are the busiest months.

➡ Demand and prices spike higher around major holidays and for festivals, when some properties may impose multiday minimum stays.

➡ Reservations are recommended for weekend and holiday travel year-round, and every day of the week during high season.

➡ Bargaining may be possible for walk-in guests without reservations, especially at off-peak times.

B&Bs & Vacation Rentals

If you want an atmospheric or perhaps romantic alternative to impersonal motels and hotels, bed-and-breakfast inns typically inhabit fine old Victorian houses or other heritage buildings, bedecked with floral wallpaper and antique furnishings. Travelers

BOOK YOUR STAY ONLINE

For more accommodation reviews by Lonely Planet authors, check out http://lonelyplanet.com/hotels/. You'll find independent reviews, as well as recommendations on the best places to stay. Best of all, you can book online.

SLEEPING PRICE RANGES

The following price ranges refer to a private room with bath during high season, unless otherwise specified. Taxes and breakfast are not normally included in the price.

➡ **$** less than $100

➡ **$$** $100 to $200

➡ **$$$** more than $200

who prefer privacy may find B&Bs too intimate.

Rates often include breakfast, but occasionally do not (never mind what the name 'B&B' suggests). Amenities vary widely, but rooms with TV and telephone are the exception; the cheapest units share bathrooms. Standards are high at places certified by the **California Association of Boutique & Breakfast Inns** (www.cabbi.com). Quality varies wildly at hosted and DIY-style vacation rental properties listed with **Airbnb** (www.airbnb.com) and **Vacation Rentals By Owner** (www.vrbo.com).

Most B&Bs require advance reservations; only a few will accommodate drop-in guests. Smoking is generally prohibited and children are usually not welcome. Multiple-night minimum stays may be required, especially on weekends and during high season.

Camping

In California, camping is much more than just a cheap way to spend the night. The best campsites will have you bedding down with ocean views by the beach, underneath pine trees next to an alpine lake or beside sand dunes in the desert.

Hostels

California has 19 hostels affiliated with **Hostelling International USA** (HI-USA; ☏888-464-4872; www.hiusa. org). Dorms in HI hostels are typically gender-segregated and alcohol and smoking are prohibited. HI membership cards (adult/senior $28/18 per year, free for under-18s) get you $3 off per night.

California also has many independent hostels, particularly in coastal cities. They generally have more relaxed rules, with frequent guest parties and activities. Some hostels include a light breakfast in their rates, arrange local tours or offer pick-ups at transportation hubs. No two hostels are alike, but facilities typically include mixed dorms, semi-private rooms with shared bathrooms, communal kitchens, lockers, internet access, coin-op laundry and TV lounges.

Some hostels say they accept only international visitors, but Americans who look like travelers (eg you're in possession of an international plane ticket) may be admitted, especially during slow periods.

Dorm-bed rates range from $25 to $55 per night, including tax. Reservations are always a good idea, especially in high season. Most hostels take reservations online or by phone. Booking services like www.hostels. com, www.hostelz.com and www.hostelworld.com sometimes offer lower rates than the hostels directly.

Hotels & Motels

Rooms are often priced by the size and number of beds, rather than the number of occupants. A room with one double or queen-size bed usually costs the same for one or two people, while a room with a king-size bed or two double beds costs more.

There is often a small surcharge for the third and fourth person, but children under a certain age (this varies) may stay free. Cribs or rollaway cots usually incur an additional fee. Beware that suites or 'junior suites' may simply be oversized rooms; ask about the layout when booking.

Recently renovated or larger rooms, or those with a view, are likely to cost more. Descriptors like 'oceanfront' and 'oceanview' are often too liberally used, and you may require a periscope to spot the surf.

You can make reservations at chains by calling their central reservation lines, but to learn about specific amenities and local promotions, call the property directly. If you arrive without reservations, ask to see a room before paying for it, especially at motels.

Rates may include breakfast, which could be just a stale doughnut and wimpy coffee, an all-you-can-eat hot and cold buffet, or anything in between.

GREEN HOTELS & MOTELS

Surprisingly, many of California's hotels and motels haven't yet jumped on the environmental bandwagon. Apart from offering you the option of reusing your towels and sheets, even such simple eco-initiatives as providing recycling bins, switching to bulk soap dispensers or replacing plastic and Styrofoam cups and dropping prepackaged breakfast items are pretty rare. The **California Green Lodging Program** (www.calrecycle.ca.gov/epp/greenlodging/) is a voluntary state-run certification program – in the online directory, look for properties that have achieved the 'Environmentalist Level,' denoted by three palm trees.

Customs Regulations

Currently, non-US citizens and permanent residents may import:

➡ 1L of alcohol (if you're over 21 years old)

➡ 200 cigarettes (one carton) or 100 non-Cuban cigars (if you're over 18 years old)

➡ $100 worth of gifts

➡ Amounts higher than $10,000 in cash, traveler's checks, money orders and other cash equivalents must be declared. Don't even think about bringing in illegal drugs.

For more complete, up-to-date information, check the **US Customs and Border Protection website** (www.cbp.gov).

Discount Cards

'America the Beautiful' Annual Pass (http://store.usgs.gov/pass; 12-month pass $80) Admits four adults and all children under 16 years for free to all national parks and federal recreational lands (eg USFS, BLM) for 12 months from the date of purchase. US citizens and permanent residents 62 years and older are eligible for a lifetime Senior Pass ($10) that grants free entry and 50% off some recreational-use fees such as camping.

American Association of Retired Persons (AARP; ☏800-566-0242; www.aarp.org; annual membership $16) Advocacy group for Americans 50 years and older offers member discounts (usually 10%) on hotels, car rentals and more.

American Automobile Association (AAA; ☏877-428-2277; www.aaa.com; annual membership from $57) Members of AAA and its foreign affiliates (eg CAA) qualify for small discounts (usually 10%) on Amtrak trains, car rentals, motels and hotels, chain restaurants and shopping, tours and theme parks.

Go Los Angeles, San Diego & San Francisco Cards (www.smarterdestinations.com; 1-day pass adult/child 3-12yr from $58/50) The Go LA Card and pricier Go San Diego Card include admission to major SoCal theme parks (but not Disneyland). The cheaper Go San Francisco Card covers museums, bicycle rental and a Bay cruise. You've got to do a lot of sightseeing over multiple days to make passes even come close to paying off. For discounts, buy online.

International Student Identity & Youth Travel Cards (www.isic.org; 1-year card $25) Offers savings on airline fares, travel insurance and local attractions for full-time students (ISIC) and for nonstudents under 26 years of age (IYTC). Cards are issued by student unions, hosteling organizations and youth-oriented budget travel agencies.

Senior Discounts People over the age of 65 (sometimes 55, 60 or 62) often qualify for the same discounts as students; any ID showing your birth date should suffice as proof.

Southern California CityPass (www.citypass.com/southern-california; adult/child 3-9yr from $328/284) If you're visiting SoCal theme parks, CityPass covers three-day admission to Disneyland and Disney California Adventure and one-day admission each to Universal Studios and SeaWorld, with add-ons available for Legoland and the San Diego Zoo or Safari Park. Passes are valid for 14 days from the first day of use. It's cheapest to buy them online in advance.

Student Advantage Card (☏800-333-2920; www.studentadvantage.com; 1-year card $22.50) For international and US students, offers 15% savings on Amtrak trains and 20% on Greyhound buses, plus discounts of 10% to 20% on some rental cars and shopping.

Electricity

120V/60Hz

Food

➡ Lunch is generally served between 11:30am and 2:30pm, and dinner between 5pm and 9pm daily, though some restaurants stay open later, especially on Friday and Saturday nights.

➡ If breakfast is served, it's usually between 7:30am and 10:30am. Some diners and cafes keep serving breakfast into the afternoon, or all day. Weekend brunch is a laid-back affair, usually available from 11am until 3pm on Saturdays and Sundays.

➡ Like all things Californian, restaurant etiquette tends to be informal. Only a handful of restaurants require more than a dressy shirt, slacks and a decent pair of shoes; most places require far less.

➡ Tipping 18% to 20% is expected anywhere you receive table service.

➡ Smoking is illegal indoors. Some restaurants have patios or sidewalk tables where smoking is tolerated (ask first, or look around for ashtrays), but don't expect your neighbors to be happy about secondhand smoke.

➡ You can bring your own wine to most restaurants; a 'corkage' fee of $15 to $30 usually applies. Lunches rarely include booze, though a glass of wine or beer, while not common everywhere, is socially acceptable.

➡ If you ask the kitchen to divide a plate between two (or more) people, there may be a small split-plate surcharge.

➡ Vegetarians, vegans and travelers with food allergies or restrictions are in luck – many restaurants are used to catering to specific dietary needs.

Gay & Lesbian Travelers

California is a magnet for LGBTQ travelers. Hot spots include the Castro in San Francisco, West Hollywood (WeHo), Silver Lake and Long Beach in LA, San Diego's Hillcrest neighborhood, the desert resort of Palm Springs, Guerneville in the Russian River Valley and Calistoga in Napa Valley. Some scenes are predominantly male-oriented, but women usually won't feel too left out.

Same-sex marriage is legal in California. Despite widespread tolerance, homophobic bigotry still exists. In small towns, especially away from the coast, tolerance often comes down to a 'don't ask, don't tell' policy.

Helpful Resources

Advocate (www.advocate.com/travel) Online news, gay travel features and destination guides.

Damron (www.damron.com) Classic, advertiser-driven gay travel guides and 'Gay Scout' mobile app.

GayCities (www.gaycities.com) Local events, activities, tours, lodging, shopping, restaurants, bars and nightlife in a dozen California cities.

Gay.net Travel (www.gay.net/travel) City guides, travel news and pride events coverage.

Gay & Lesbian National Hotline (☏888-843-4564; www.glnh.org; ⊙1-9pm Mon-Fri, 9am-2pm Sat) For counseling and referrals of any kind.

Out Traveler (www.outtraveler.com) Free online magazine with travel tips, destination guides and hotel reviews.

Purple Roofs (www.purpleroofs.com) Online directory of LGBTQ accommodations.

Health

Healthcare & Insurance

➡ Medical treatment in the USA is of the highest caliber, but the expense could kill you. Many healthcare professionals demand payment at the time of service, especially from out-of-towners or international visitors.

➡ Except for medical emergencies (in which case call ☏911 or go to the nearest 24-hour hospital emergency room, or ER), phone around to find a doctor who will accept your insurance.

➡ Keep all receipts and documentation for billing and insurance claims, and reimbursement purposes.

➡ Some health-insurance policies require you to get pre-authorization for medical treatment before seeking help.

➡ Overseas visitors with travel-health-insurance policies may need to contact a call center for an assessment by phone before getting medical treatment.

Dehydration, Heat Exhaustion & Heatstroke

➡ Take it easy as you acclimatize, especially on hot summer days and in Southern California's deserts. Drink plenty of water. A minimum of 3L per person per day is recommended when you're active outdoors. Be sure to eat a salty snack too, as sodium is necessary for rehydration.

➡ Dehydration (lack of water) or salt deficiency can cause heat exhaustion, often characterized by heavy sweating, fatigue, lethargy, headaches, nausea, vomiting, dizziness and muscle cramps.

➡ Long, continuous exposure to high temperatures can lead to possibly fatal heatstroke, when body temperatures rise to dangerous levels. Warning signs include altered mental status, hyperventilation and flushed, hot and dry skin (ie sweating stops).

➡ For heatstroke, immediate hospitalization is essential. Meanwhile, get out of the sun, remove clothing that retains heat (cotton is OK), douse the body with water and fan continuously; ice packs can be applied to the neck, armpits and groin.

Hypothermia

➡ Skiers and hikers will find that temperatures in the

mountains and desert can quickly drop below freezing, especially during winter. Even a sudden spring shower or high winds can lower your body temperature dangerously fast.

➜ Instead of cotton, wear synthetic or woolen clothing that retains warmth even when wet. Carry waterproof layers (eg Gore-Tex jacket, poncho, rain pants) and high-energy, easily digestible snacks like chocolate, nuts and dried fruit.

➜ Symptoms include exhaustion, numbness, shivering, stumbling, slurred speech, dizzy spells, muscle cramps and irrational or violent behavior.

➜ To treat mild hypothermia, get out of bad weather and change into dry, warm clothing. Drink hot liquids (no caffeine or alcohol) and snack on high-calorie food.

➜ For more advanced hypothermia, seek immediate medical attention. Do not rub victims, who must be handled gently.

Insurance

Travel Insurance

Getting travel insurance to cover theft, loss and medical problems is highly recommended. Some policies do not cover 'risky' activities such as scuba diving, motorcycling and skiing so read the fine print. Make sure the policy at least covers hospital stays and an emergency flight home.

Paying for your airline ticket or rental car with a credit card may provide limited travel accident insurance. If you already have private US health insurance or a homeowners or renters policy, find out what those policies cover and only get supplemental insurance. If you have prepaid a large portion of your vacation, trip cancellation insurance may be a worthwhile expense.

Worldwide travel insurance is available at www.lonelyplanet.com/travel-insurance. You can buy, extend and claim online anytime – even if you're already on the road.

Internet Access

➜ Cybercafes typically charge $6 to $12 per hour for online access.

➜ With branches in most cities and towns, **FedEx Office** (☎800-463-3339; www.fedex.com/us/office/) offers internet access at self-service computer workstations (30¢ to 40¢ per minute) and sometimes free wi-fi, plus digital-photo printing and CD-burning stations.

➜ Accommodations, cafes, restaurants, bars etc that provide guest computer terminals for going online are identified by the internet icon (@); the wi-fi icon (🛜) indicates that wireless access is available. There may be a charge for either service.

➜ Free or fee-based wi-fi can be found at major airports; many hotels, motels and coffee shops (eg Starbucks); and some tourist information centers, campgrounds (eg KOA), stores (eg Apple), bars and restaurants (including fast-food chains such as McDonald's).

➜ Free public wi-fi is proliferating (for a list, visit http://ca.gov/WiFi/) and even some state parks are now wi-fi–enabled (get details at www.parks.ca.gov).

➜ Public libraries have internet terminals (online time may be limited, advance sign-up required and a nominal fee charged for out-of-network visitors) and, increasingly, free wi-fi.

Legal Matters

Drugs & Alcohol

➜ Possession of less than 1oz of marijuana is a

misdemeanor in California. Possession of any other drug or an ounce or more of weed is a felony punishable by lengthy jail time. For foreigners, conviction of any drug offense is grounds for deportation.

➜ Police can give roadside sobriety checks to assess if you've been drinking or using drugs. If you fail, they'll require you to take a breath, urine or blood test to determine if your blood-alcohol level is over the legal limit (0.08%). Refusing to be tested is treated the same as if you had taken and failed the test.

➜ Penalties for driving under the influence (DUI) of drugs or alcohol range from license suspension and fines to jail time.

➜ It's illegal to carry open containers of alcohol inside a vehicle, even if they're empty. Unless they're full and still sealed, store them in the trunk.

➜ Consuming alcohol anywhere other than at a private residence or licensed premises is a no-no, which puts most parks and beaches off-limits (although many campgrounds allow it).

➜ Bars, clubs and liquor stores often ask for photo ID to prove you are of legal drinking age (21 years old). Being 'carded' is standard practice, so don't take it personally.

Police & Security

➜ For police, fire and ambulance emergencies, dial ☎911. For nonemergency police assistance, contact the nearest police station (directory assistance ☎411).

➜ If you are stopped by the police, be courteous. Don't get out of the car unless asked. Keep your hands where the officer can see them (eg on the steering wheel) at all times.

➜ There is no system of paying fines on the spot.

Attempting to pay the fine to the officer may lead to a charge of attempted bribery.

➜ For traffic violations the ticketing officer will explain your options. There is usually a 30-day period to pay a fine; most matters can be handled by mail or online.

➜ If you are arrested, you have the right to remain silent and are presumed innocent until proven guilty. Everyone has the right to make one phone call. If you don't have a lawyer, one will be appointed to you free of charge. Foreign travelers who don't have a lawyer, friends or family to help should call their embassy or consulate; the police can provide the number upon request.

➜ Due to security concerns about terrorism, never leave your bags unattended, especially not at airports or bus and train stations.

➜ Carrying mace or cayenne-pepper spray is legal in California, as long as the spray bottle contains no more than 2.5oz of active product. Federal law prohibits it from being carried on planes.

➜ In cases of sexual assault, rape crisis center and hospital staff can advocate on your behalf and act as a liaison to community services, including the police. Telephone books have listings of local crisis centers, or call the 24-hour **National Sexual Assault Hotline** (☑800-656-4673; www.rainn.org).

Smoking

➜ Smoking is generally prohibited inside all public buildings, including airports, shopping malls and train and bus stations.

➜ There is no smoking allowed inside restaurants, although lighting up may be tolerated at outdoor patio or sidewalk tables (ask first).

➜ At hotels, you must specifically request a

PRACTICALITIES

DVDs coded for region 1 (USA and Canada only)

Electricity 110/120V AC, 50/60Hz

Newspapers *Los Angeles Times* (www.latimes.com), *San Francisco Chronicle* (www.sfchronicle.com), *San Jose Mercury News* (www.mercurynews.com), *Sacramento Bee* (www.sacbee.com)

Radio National Public Radio (NPR), lower end of FM dial

Time California is on Pacific Standard Time (UTC-8). Clocks are set one hour ahead during Daylight Saving Time (DST), from the second Sunday in March until the first Sunday in November.

TV PBS (public broadcasting); cable: CNN (news), ESPN (sports), HBO (movies), Weather Channel

Weights & Measures Imperial (except 1 US gallon = 0.83 gallons)

---

smoking room, but note some properties are entirely nonsmoking by law.

➜ In some cities and towns, smoking outdoors within a certain distance of any public business is illegal.

Maps

➜ GPS navigation is handy, but cannot be relied upon 100% of the time, especially in remote wilderness and rural areas.

➜ Visitor centers distribute free (but often very basic) maps. If you're doing a lot of driving around California, you'll need a more detailed road map or map atlas.

➜ Members of the **American Automobile Association** (AAA; ☑800-874-7532; www.aaa.com) or its international affiliates (bring your membership card from home) can get free driving maps from local AAA offices.

➜ DeLorme's comprehensive *California Atlas* & *Gazetteer* ($25) shows campgrounds, hiking trails, recreational areas and topographical land features, although it's less useful for navigating urban areas.

Money

ATMs

➜ ATMs are available 24/7 at most banks, shopping malls, airports and grocery and convenience stores.

➜ Expect a minimum surcharge of around $3 per transaction, in addition to any fees charged by your home bank.

➜ Most ATMs are connected to international networks and offer decent foreign-exchange rates.

➜ Withdrawing cash from an ATM using a credit card usually incurs a hefty fee and high interest rates; contact your credit-card company for details and a PIN number.

Cash

➜ Most people do not carry large amounts of cash for everyday use, relying instead on credit and debit cards. Some businesses refuse to accept bills over $20.

Credit Cards

➜ Major credit cards are almost universally accepted. In fact, it's almost impossible to rent a car, book a hotel room or buy tickets over the

TIPPING

Tipping is *not* optional. Only withhold tips in cases of outrageously bad service.

Airport skycaps & hotel bellhops	$2 per bag, minimum $5 per cart
Bartenders	15% per round, minimum $1 per drink
Concierges	Nothing for simple information, up to $10 for securing last-minute restaurant reservations, sold-out show tickets etc
Housekeeping staff	$2 to $4 daily, left under the card provided; more if you're messy
Parking valets	At least $2 when car keys handed back
Restaurant servers & room service	18% to 20%, unless a gratuity is already charged (common for groups of six or more)
Taxi drivers	10% to 15% of metered fare, rounded up to the next dollar

phone without one. A credit card may also be vital in emergencies.

→ Visa, MasterCard and American Express are the most widely accepted.

Moneychangers

→ You can exchange money at major airports, banks and all currency-exchange offices such as **American Express** (www.americanexpress.com) or **Travelex** (www.travelex.com). Enquire about rates and fees.

→ Outside big cities, exchanging money may be a problem, so make sure you have a credit card and sufficient cash on hand.

Taxes

→ California state sales tax (7.5%) is added to the retail price of most goods and services (gasoline is an exception).

→ Local and city sales taxes may tack on up to an additional 2.5%.

→ Tourist lodging taxes vary statewide, but currently average 12% or more.

Traveler's Checks

→ Traveler's checks have pretty much fallen out of use.

→ Big-city restaurants, hotels and department stores will often accept traveler's checks (in US dollars only), but small businesses, markets and fast-food chains may refuse them.

→ Visa and American Express are the most widely accepted issuers of traveler's checks.

Opening Hours

Standard opening hours are as follows.

Banks 9am–5pm Monday–Friday, to 6pm Friday, some 9am–1:30pm Saturday

Bars 5pm–2am daily

Business hours (general) 9am–5pm Monday–Friday

Nightclubs 10pm–4am Thursday–Saturday

Pharmacies 8am–9pm Monday–Friday, 9am–5pm Saturday & Sunday, some 24 hour

Post offices 8:30am–4:30pm Monday–Friday, some 9am–noon Saturday

Restaurants 7:30am–10:30am, 11:30am–2:30pm & 5.30–9pm daily, some later Friday & Saturday

Shops 10am–6pm Monday–Saturday, noon–5pm Sunday (malls open later)

Supermarkets 8am–9pm or 10pm daily, some 24 hour

Post

→ The **US Postal Service** (USPS; ☎800-275-8777; www.usps.com) is inexpensive and reliable. Postal rates increase by a few pennies every couple of years.

→ For sending important documents or packages internationally, try **Federal Express** (FedEx; ☎800-463-3339; www.fedex.com) or **United Parcel Service** (UPS; ☎800-742-5877; www.ups.com).

Public Holidays

On the following national holidays, banks, schools and government offices (including post offices) are closed, and transportation, museums and other services operate on a Sunday schedule. Holidays falling on a weekend are usually observed the following Monday.

New Year's Day January 1

Martin Luther King Jr Day Third Monday in January

Presidents' Day Third Monday in February

Good Friday Friday before Easter in March/April

Memorial Day Last Monday in May

Independence Day July 4

Labor Day First Monday in September

Columbus Day Second Monday in October

Veterans Day November 11

Thanksgiving Day Fourth Thursday in November

Christmas Day December 25

School Holidays

➡ Colleges take a one- or two-week 'spring break' around Easter, sometime in March or April. Some hotels and resorts, especially along the coast, in SoCal's theme parks and in the deserts, raise their rates during this time.

➡ School summer vacations run from mid-June until mid-August; July and August are the busiest travel months.

Safe Travel

Despite its seemingly apocalyptic list of dangers – guns, violent crime, riots, earthquakes – California is a reasonably safe place to visit. The greatest danger is posed by car accidents (buckle up – it's the law), while the biggest annoyances are metro-area traffic and crowds. Wildlife poses some small threats, and of course there is the dramatic, albeit unlikely, possibility of a natural disaster.

Earthquakes

Earthquakes happen all the time but most are so tiny they are detectable only by sensitive seismological instruments. If you're caught in a serious shaker:

➡ If indoors, get under a desk or table or stand in a doorway.

➡ Protect your head and stay clear of windows, mirrors or anything that might fall.

➡ Don't head for elevators or go running into the street.

➡ If you're in a shopping mall or large public building, expect the alarm and/or sprinkler systems to come on.

➡ If outdoors, get away from buildings, trees and power lines.

➡ If you're driving, pull over to the side of the road away from bridges, overpasses and power lines. Stay inside the car until the shaking stops.

➡ If you're on a sidewalk near buildings, duck into a doorway to protect yourself from falling bricks, glass and debris.

➡ Prepare for aftershocks.

➡ Turn on the radio and listen for bulletins.

➡ Use the telephone only if absolutely necessary.

Wildlife

➡ Never feed or approach any wild animal, not even harmless-looking critters – it causes them to lose their innate fear of humans, which in turn makes them dangerously aggressive. Many birds and mammals, including deer and rodents such as squirrels, carry serious diseases that can be transmitted to humans through biting.

➡ Disturbing or harassing protected species, including many marine mammals such as whales, dolphins and seals, is a crime, subject to enormous fines.

➡ Black bears are often attracted to campgrounds, where they may find food, trash and any other scented items left out on picnic tables or stashed in tents and cars. Always use bear-proof containers where they are provided. For more bear-country travel tips, visit the **SierraWild website** (http://sierrawild.gov/bears).

➡ If you encounter a black bear in the wild, don't run. Stay together, keeping small children next to you and picking up little ones. Keep back at least 100yds. If the bear starts moving toward you, back away slowly off-trail and let it pass by, being careful not to block any of the bear's escape routes or to get caught between a mother and her cubs. Sometimes a black bear will 'bluff charge' to test your dominance. Stand your ground by making yourself look as big as possible (eg waving your arms above your head) and shouting menacingly.

➡ Mountain lion attacks on humans are rare, but can be deadly. If you encounter a mountain lion stay calm, pick up small children, face the animal and retreat slowly. Make yourself appear larger by raising your arms or grabbing a stick. If the lion becomes menacing, shout or throw rocks at it. If attacked, fight back aggressively.

➡ Snakes and spiders are common throughout California, not just in wilderness areas. Always look inside your shoes before putting them back on outdoors, especially when camping. Snake bites are rare, but occur most often when a snake is stepped on or provoked (eg picked up or poked with a stick). Antivenom is available at most hospitals.

Telephone

Cell (Mobile) Phones

➡ You'll need a multiband GSM phone to make calls in the USA. Popping in a US prepaid rechargeable SIM card is usually cheaper than using your network.

➡ SIM cards are sold at telecommunications and electronics stores. These stores also sell inexpensive prepaid phones, including some airtime.

➡ You can rent a cell phone at Los Angeles (LAX) and San Francisco (SFO) International Airports from **TripTel** (☎877-874-7835; www.triptel.com); pricing plans vary, but typically are expensive.

Dialing Codes

➡ US phone numbers consist of a three-letter area code followed by a seven-digit local number.

➡ When dialing a number within the same area code, use the seven-digit number (if that doesn't work, try all 10 digits).

➞ For long-distance calls, dial 1 plus the area code plus the local number.

➞ Toll-free numbers begin with 800, 855, 866, 877 or 888 and must be preceded by 1.

➞ For direct international calls, dial 011 plus the country code plus the area code (usually without the initial '0') plus the local phone number.

➞ If you're calling from abroad, the country code for the US is 1 (which is the same as for Canada, but do be be aware that international rates apply between the two countries).

Payphones & Phonecards

Where payphones still exist, they are usually coin-operated, although some may only accept credit cards (eg in national parks). Local calls usually cost 50¢ minimum. For long-distance calls, you're usually better off buying a prepaid phone-card, sold at supermarkets, pharmacies, newsstands and electronics and convenience stores.

Tourist Information

➞ For pretrip planning, peruse the information-packed website of the **California Travel and Tourism Commission** (www.visitcalifornia.com).

➞ The same government agency operates nearly 20 statewide **California Welcome Centers** (www.visitcwc.com), which have maps and brochures, and staff may be able to help find accommodations.

➞ Almost every city and town in the state has a local visitor center or a chamber of commerce where visitors can pick up maps, brochures and other tourism-related information.

Travelers with Disabilities

Much of California is reasonably well-equipped for travelers with disabilities, especially in metro areas and popular tourist spots.

Accessibility

➞ Most traffic intersections have dropped curbs and sometimes audible signals.

➞ The Americans with Disabilities Act (ADA) requires public buildings built after 1993 to be accessible, including restrooms.

➞ Motels and hotels built after 1993 must have at least one ADA–compliant accessible room; state your specific needs when making reservations.

➞ For nonpublic buildings built prior to 1993, including hotels, restaurants, museums and theaters, there are no accessibility guarantees; call ahead to find out what to expect.

➞ Most national and many state parks and some other outdoor recreation areas offer paved or boardwalk-style nature trails accessible by wheelchairs.

➞ Many theme parks go out of their way to be accessible to wheelchairs and guests with mobility limitations and various disabilities.

➞ US citizens and permanent residents with a permanent disability quality for a free lifetime **'America the Beautiful' Access Pass** (http://store.usgs.gov/pass/access.html), which waives entry fees to all national parks and federal recreational lands and offers 50% discounts on some recreation fees (eg camping).

➞ California State Parks' disabled pass ($3.50) entitles those with permanent disabilities to 50% off day-use parking and camping fees; see www.parks.ca.gov.

Communications

➞ Telephone companies provide relay operators (dial 🖅711) for the hearing impaired.

➞ Many banks provide ATM instructions in Braille.

Helpful Resources

A Wheelchair Rider's Guide to the California Coast (www.wheeling-calscoast.org) Free accessibility information covering beaches, parks and trails, plus downloadable PDF guides to the San Francisco Bay Area and Los Angeles and Orange County coasts.

Access Northern California (www.accessnca.com) Extensive links to accessible-travel resources, publications, tours and transportation, including outdoor recreation opportunities, plus a searchable lodgings database and an events calendar.

Accessible San Diego (http://access-sandiego.org) Free online city guide (downloadable/print version $4/5) that's updated annually.

California State Parks (http://access.parks.ca.gov) Searchable online map and database of accessible features at state parks.

Disabled Sports Eastern Sierra (http://disabledsport-seasternsierra.org) Offers summer and winter outdoor activity programs around Mammoth Lakes (annual membership $40).

Disabled Sports USA Far West (www.dsusafw.org) Organizes summer and winter sports, 4WD adventures and adaptive-ski rental around Lake Tahoe in the Sierra Nevada (annual membership $30).

Flying Wheels Travel (www.flyingwheelstravel.com) Full-service travel agency for travelers with disabilities, mobility issues and chronic illness.

Los Angeles for Disabled Visitors (www.discover-losangeles.com/search/site/disabled) Tips for accessible sightseeing, entertainment, museums and transportation.

MossRehab Resource Net (www.mossresourcenet.org/travel.htm) Useful links and general advice for accessible travel.

San Francisco Access Guide (www.sanfrancisco.travel/accessibility/San-Francisco-Access-Guide.html) Free downloadable accessible travel info – dated, but useful.

Santa Cruz County Access Guide (www.scaccessguide.com) Dated but still-handy English/Spanish accessible travel guide (US shipping $3).

Theme Park Access Guide (www.mouseplanet.com/tag) An insider's view of Disneyland and other theme parks 'on wheels.'

Yosemite National Park Accessibility (www.nps.gov/yose/planyourvisit/accessibility.htm) Detailed, downloadable accessibility information for Yosemite National Park, including American Sign Language (ASL) interpretation.

Wheelchair Traveling (www.wheelchairtraveling.com) Travel tips, lodging and helpful California destination info.

Transportation

➡ All major airlines, Greyhound buses and Amtrak trains can accommodate people with disabilities, usually with 48 hours of notice required.

➡ Major car-rental agencies offer hand-controlled vehicles and vans with wheelchair lifts at no extra charge, but you must reserve these well in advance.

➡ For wheelchair-accessible van rentals, try **Wheelchair Getaways** (☎800-642-2042; www.wheelchairgetaways.com) in LA and San Francisco or **Mobility Works** (☎877-275-4915; www.mobilityworks.com) in LA, San Francisco, Oakland, San Jose, Sacramento, Fresno and Chico.

➡ Local buses, trains and subway lines usually have wheelchair lifts.

➡ Seeing-eye dogs are permitted to accompany passengers on public transportation.

➡ Taxi companies have at least one wheelchair-accessible van, but you'll usually need to call and then wait for one.

Visas

➡ Visa information is highly subject to change. Depending on your country of origin, the rules for entering the USA keep changing. Double-check current visa requirements *before* coming to the USA.

➡ Currently, under the US Visa Waiver Program (VWP), visas are not required for citizens of 38 countries for stays up to 90 days (no extensions) as long as you have a machine-readable passport (MRP) that meets current US standards and is valid for six months beyond your intended stay.

➡ Citizens of VWP countries must still register with the Electronic System for Travel Authorization (ESTA) online (https://esta.cbp.dhs.gov) at least 72 hours before travel. Once approved, ESTA registration ($14) is valid for up to two years or until your passport expires, whichever comes first.

➡ For most Canadian citizens traveling with Canadian passports that meet current US standards, a visa for short-term visits (usually up to six months) and ESTA registration aren't required.

➡ Citizens from all other countries or whose passports don't meet US standards need to apply for a visa in their home country. The process costs a nonrefundable fee (minimum $160), involves a personal interview and can take several weeks, so apply as early as possible.

➡ For up-to-date information about entry requirements and eligibility, check the visa section of the **US Department of State website** (http://travel.state.gov) or contact the nearest USA embassy or consulate in your home country (for a complete list, visit www.usembassy.gov).

Volunteering

Casual drop-in volunteer opportunities, where you can socialize with locals while helping out nonprofit organizations, are most common in cities. Browse upcoming projects and activities and sign up online with local organizations such as **One Brick** (www.onebrick.org) in San Francisco, Silicon Valley and LA; **HandsOn Bay Area** (www.handsonbayarea.org); **LA Works** (www.laworks.com) and Orange County's **OneOC** (www.oneoc.org). For more opportunities, check local alternative weekly tabloids and **Craigslist** (www.craiglist.org) online.

Helpful Resources

California Volunteers (www.californiavolunteers.org) State-run volunteer directory and matching service, with links to national service days and long-term programs.

Habitat for Humanity (www.habitat.org) Nonprofit organization helps build homes for impoverished families across California, including day, weekend and week-long projects.

Idealist.org (www.idealist.org) Free searchable database includes both short- and long-term volunteer opportunities.

Wilderness Volunteers (www.wildernessvolunteers.org) Week-long trips help maintain national parks, preserves, forests, seashores and other wilderness conservation and outdoor recreation areas.

Worldwide Opportunities on Organic Farms (Map p619; www.wwoofusa.org) Long-term volunteering opportunities on local organic farms (annual membership from $30).

Transportation

GETTING THERE & AWAY

Getting to California by air or overland by bus, car or train is easy, although it's not always cheap. Flights, cars and tours can be booked online at www.lonelyplanet. com/bookings.

Entering the Region

Under the US Department of Homeland Security's Orwellian-sounding Office of Biometric Identity Management, almost all visitors to the USA (excluding, for now, many Canadians, some Mexican citizens, children under age 14 and seniors over age 79) will be digitally photographed and have their electronic (inkless) fingerprints scanned upon arrival.

Regardless of your visa status, immigration officers have absolute authority to refuse entry to the USA. They may ask about your plans and whether you have sufficient funds; it's a good idea to list an itinerary, produce an onward or round-trip ticket and have at least one major credit card. Don't make too much of having friends, relatives or business contacts in the US, because officers may think this makes you more likely to overstay. For more information about entering the USA, visit the **US Customs and Border Protection website** (www. cbp.gov).

California is an important agricultural state. To prevent the spread of pests and diseases, certain food items (including meats, fresh fruit and vegetables) may not be brought into the state. Bakery items, chocolates and hard-cured cheeses are admissible. If you drive into California across the border from Mexico or from the neighboring states of Oregon, Nevada or Arizona, you may have to stop for a quick questioning and inspection by **California Department of Food and Agriculture** (www.cdfa.ca.gov) agents.

Passports

➡ Under the Western Hemisphere Travel Initiative (WHTI), all travelers must have a valid machine-readable passport (MRP) when entering the USA by air, land or sea.

➡ The only exceptions are for some US, Canadian and Mexican citizens traveling *by land* who can present other WHTI-compliant documents (eg preapproved 'trusted traveler' cards). A regular driver's license is *not* sufficient.

➡ All foreign passports must meet current US standards and be valid for at least six months longer than your intended stay.

CLIMATE CHANGE & TRAVEL

Every form of transport that relies on carbon-based fuel generates CO_2, the main cause of human-induced climate change. Modern travel is dependent on aeroplanes, which might use less fuel per kilometre per person than most cars but travel much greater distances. The altitude at which aircraft emit gases (including CO_2) and particles also contributes to their climate change impact. Many websites offer 'carbon calculators' that allow people to estimate the carbon emissions generated by their journey and, for those who wish to do so, to offset the impact of the greenhouse gases emitted with contributions to portfolios of climate-friendly initiatives throughout the world. Lonely Planet offsets the carbon footprint of all staff and author travel.

➡ MRPs issued or renewed after October 26, 2006, must be e-passports (ie have a digital photo and integrated chip with biometric data).

➡ For more information, consult www.cbp.gov/travel.

Air

➡ To get through airport security checkpoints (30-minute wait times are standard), you'll need a boarding pass and photo ID.

➡ Some travelers may be required to undergo a secondary screening, involving hand pat-downs and carry-on bag searches.

➡ Airport security measures restrict many common items (eg pocket knives, scissors) from being carried on planes. Check current restrictions with the **Transportation Security Administration** (TSA; ☑866-289-9673; www.tsa.gov).

➡ Currently, TSA requires that all carry-on liquids and gels be stored in 3oz or smaller bottles placed inside a quart-sized clear plastic zip-top bag. Exceptions, which must be declared to checkpoint security officers, include medications.

➡ All checked luggage is screened for explosives. TSA may open your suitcase for visual confirmation, breaking the lock if necessary. Leave your bags unlocked or use a TSA-approved lock.

Airports

California's major international airports are in Los Angeles and San Francisco. Smaller regional airports are served primarily by domestic US carriers.

Arcata/Eureka Airport (ACV; www.co.humboldt.ca.us/aviation; 3561 Boeing Ave, McKinleyville) On the North Coast.

Bob Hope Airport (BUR; www.burbankairport.com; 2627 N Hollywood Way, Burbank) About 14 miles northwest of Downtown LA, close to Universal Studios.

Fresno Yosemite International Airport (FAT; www.flyfresno.com; 5175 E Clinton Way) In Fresno, about 70 miles south of Yosemite National Park.

John Wayne Airport (SNA; www.ocair.com; 18601 Airport Way, Santa Ana) Off the I-405 Fwy in inland Orange County.

Long Beach Airport (LGB; www.lgb.org; 4100 Donald Douglas Dr, Long Beach) Easy access to LA and Orange County.

Los Angeles International Airport (LAX; www.lawa.org/lax; 1 World Way) California's largest and busiest airport, 20 miles southwest of Downtown LA, near the beaches.

Mineta San José International Airport (SJC; www.flysanjose.com; 1701 Airport Blvd, San Jose) Forty-five miles south of San Francisco, near Silicon Valley.

Monterey Regional Airport (MRY; www.montereyairport.com; 200 Fred Kane Dr, Monterey) On the Central Coast, south of Santa Cruz.

Oakland International Airport (OAK; www.oaklandairport.com; 1 Airport Dr) In San Francisco's East Bay.

Ontario International Airport (ONT; www.lawa.org/ont; 2500 & 2900 E Airport Dr, Ontario) In Riverside County, east of LA.

Palm Springs International Airport (PSP; www.palmspringsairport.com; 3400 E Tahquitz Canyon Way) In the desert, east of LA.

Sacramento International Airport (SMF; www.sacairports.org; 6900 Airport Blvd) Midway between the San Francisco Bay Area and Lake Tahoe

San Diego International Airport (SAN; www.san.org; 3325 N Harbor Dr) Just 4 miles from downtown San Diego.

San Francisco International Airport (SFO; www.flysfo.com; S McDonnell Rd) Northern California's major hub,

14 miles south of downtown San Francisco.

San Luis Obispo County Regional Airport (SBP; www.sloairport.com; 903 Airport Dr, San Luis Obispo) On the Central Coast, north of Santa Barbara.

Santa Barbara Airport (SBA; www.flysba.com; 500 Fowler Rd, Goleta; ☎) Nine miles west of downtown Santa Barbara, off Hwy 101.

Land

Border Crossings

It's relatively easy crossing from the USA into Canada or Mexico; it's crossing back into the USA that can pose problems if you haven't brought all of the required documents. Check the ever-changing passport and visa requirements with the **US Department of State** (http://travel.state.gov) beforehand.

The **US Customs & Border Protection** (http://bwt.cbp.gov) tracks current wait times at every US border crossing. On the US–Mexico border between San Diego and Tijuana, San Ysidro is the world's busiest border crossing, with average wait times of an hour or more.

US citizens do not require a visa for stays of 72 hours or less within the Mexican border zone (ie as far south as Ensenada). But to re-enter the USA, they need to present a US passport or other WHTI-compliant document; a regular US driver's license is no longer enough.

BUS

➡ US-based **Greyhound** (☑800-231-2222; www.greyhound.com) and **Greyhound México** (☑800-710-8819; www.greyhound.com.mx) have cooperative service; that is, buses run direct between main towns in Mexico and California.

➡ Northbound buses from Mexico can take some time

to cross the US border, as US immigration may insist on checking every person on board.

➜ **Greyhound Canada** (☎800-661-8747; www.greyhound.ca) routes between Canada and the US usually require transferring buses at the border.

CAR & MOTORCYCLE

➜ If you're driving into the USA from Canada or Mexico, bring your vehicle's registration papers, liability insurance and driver's license; an International Driving Permit (IDP) is a good supplement but is not required.

➜ If you're renting a car or a motorcycle, ask if the agency allows its vehicles to be taken across the Mexican or Canadian border – chances are it doesn't.

TO/FROM MEXICO

➜ Unless you're planning an extended stay in Mexico, taking a car across the Mexican border is more trouble than it's worth. Instead take the trolley from San Diego or park your car on the US side and walk across instead.

➜ If you do decide to drive across, you must buy Mexican car insurance either beforehand or at the border crossing.

➜ Expect long border-crossing waits, especially on weekends and holidays and during weekday commuter rush hours.

TO/FROM CANADA

➜ Canadian auto insurance is typically valid in the USA and vice versa.

➜ If your papers are in order, taking your own car across the US–Canada border is usually quick and easy.

➜ On weekends and holidays, especially in summer, border-crossing traffic can be heavy and waits long.

➜ Occasionally the authorities of either country decide to search a car *thoroughly*. Remain calm and be polite.

TRAIN

➜ **Amtrak** (☎800-872-7245; www.amtrak.com) operates twice-daily *Cascades* trains (with on-board wi-fi) and several daily Thruway buses from Vancouver, British Columbia in Canada to Seattle, Washington.

➜ US or Canadian customs and immigration inspections happen at the border, not upon boarding.

➜ From Seattle, Amtrak's daily *Coast Starlight* rail service connects south to several destinations in California, including Sacramento and the San Francisco Bay Area, en route to Los Angeles.

➜ Currently, no trains connect California and Mexico.

Bus

Greyhound (☎800-231-2222; www.greyhound.com) is the major long-distance bus company, with routes throughout the USA, including to/from California. It has recently stopped service to many small towns; routes trace major highways and may only stop at larger population centers.

Train

Amtrak (☎800-872-7245; www.amtrak.com) operates a fairly extensive rail system throughout the USA. Trains are comfortable, if a bit slow, and are equipped with dining and lounge cars on long-distance routes. Fares vary according to the type of train and seating (eg coach or business class, sleeping compartments).

Amtrak's major long-distance routes to/from California:

California Zephyr Daily service between Chicago and Emeryville (from $163, 52 hours), near San Francisco, via Denver, Salt Lake City, Reno, Truckee and Sacramento.

Coast Starlight Travels the West Coast daily from Seattle to LA (from $92, 35 hours) via Portland, Sacramento, Oakland and Santa Barbara.

Southwest Chief Daily departures from Chicago and LA (from $135, 43 hours) via Kansas City, Albuquerque, Flagstaff and Barstow.

Sunset Limited Thrice-weekly service between New Orleans and LA (from $130, 47 hours) via Houston, San Antonio, El Paso, Tucson and Palm Springs.

TRAIN PASSES

Amtrak's USA Rail Pass is valid for coach-class train travel only (and not Thruway buses) for 15 ($449), 30 ($679) or 45 ($879) days; children aged two to 15 pay half-price. Travel is limited to eight, 12 or 18 one-way 'segments,' respectively. A segment is not the same as a one-way trip; if reaching your destination requires riding more than one train, you'll use multiple pass segments. Purchase passes online, then make advance reservations for each trip segment.

GETTING AROUND

Most people drive around California, although you can also fly (if time is limited, but your budget isn't) or save money by taking buses or often scenic trains.

Air

Several major US carriers fly within California. Flights are often operated by their regional subsidiaries, such as American Eagle, Delta Connection and United Express. Alaska Airlines, Frontier Airlines and Horizon Air serve many regional airports, as do low-cost airlines Southwest and Spirit. Virgin America currently flies out of Los Angeles, San Francisco, San Diego and Palm Springs. JetBlue serves LA County, the San Francisco Bay Area, San Diego and Sacramento.

Bicycle

Although cycling around California is a nonpolluting 'green' way to travel, the distances involved demand a high level of fitness and make it hard to cover much ground. Forget about the deserts in summer and the mountains in winter.

Adventure Cycling Association (www.adventurecycling.org) Online resource for purchasing bicycle-friendly maps and long-distance route guides.

California Bicycle Coalition (http://calbike.org) Links to cycling route maps and events, safety tips and laws, bike-sharing programs and community nonprofit bicycle shops.

Better World Club (866-238-1137; www.betterworldclub.com) Annual membership (from $40) gets you two 24-hour emergency roadside pickups

and transport within a 30-mile radius.

Road Rules

➜ Cycling is allowed on all roads and highways – even along freeways if there's no suitable alternative, such as a smaller parallel road; all mandatory exits are marked.

➜ Some cities have designated bicycle lanes, but make sure you have your wits about you in traffic.

➜ Cyclists must follow the same rules of the road as vehicles. Don't expect drivers to always respect your right of way.

➜ Wearing a bicycle helmet is mandatory for riders under 18 years old.

➜ Ensure you have proper lights and reflective gear, especially if you're pedaling at night or in fog.

Rental & Purchase

➜ You can rent bikes by the hour, day or week in most cities and tourist towns.

➜ Rentals start around $10 per day for beach cruisers up to $45 or more for mountain bikes; ask about multiday and weekly discounts.

➜ Most rental companies require a large security deposit using a credit card.

➜ Buy new models from specialty bike shops and sporting-goods stores, or used from notice boards at hostels, cafes etc.

➜ To buy or sell used bikes online, check **Craigslist** (www.craigslist.org).

Transporting Bicycles

➜ Greyhound transports bicycles as luggage (surcharge typically $30 to $40), provided the bicycle is disassembled and placed in a rigid container ($10 box available at some terminals).

➜ Amtrak's *Cascades, Pacific Surfliner,* and *San Joaquin* trains have onboard racks where you can secure your

bike unboxed; try to reserve a spot when making your ticket reservation ($5 surcharge may apply).

➜ On Amtrak trains without racks, bikes must be put in a box ($15 at most staffed terminals) then checked as luggage (fee $10). Not all stations or trains offer checked-baggage service.

Boat

Boats won't get you around California, although there are a few offshore routes, notably to Catalina Island off the coast of Los Angeles and Orange County, and to Channel Islands National Park from Ventura or Oxnard, north of LA toward Santa Barbara. On San Francisco Bay, regular ferries operate between San Francisco and Sausalito, Larkspur, Tiburon, Angel Island, Oakland, Alameda and Vallejo.

Bus

Greyhound (800-231-2222; www.greyhound.com) buses are an economical way to travel between major cities and to points along the coast, but won't get you off the beaten path or to national parks or small towns. Frequency of service varies from 'rarely' to 'constantly,' but the main routes have service several times daily.

Greyhound buses are usually clean, comfortable and reliable. The best seats are typically near the front, away from the bathroom. Limited on-board amenities include freezing air-con (bring a sweater) and slightly reclining seats; select buses have electrical outlets and wi-fi. Smoking on board is prohibited. Long-distance buses stop for meal breaks and driver changes.

Bus stations are typically dreary, often in dodgy areas; if you arrive at night, take a taxi into town or directly to your lodgings. In small towns where there is no station, know exactly where and when the bus arrives, be obvious as you flag it down and pay the driver with exact change.

Costs

You may save money by purchasing tickets at least seven days in advance and by traveling between Monday and Thursday.

Discounts (on unrestricted fares only) are offered to seniors over 62 (5% off), students with a Student Advantage Card (20%) and children aged two to 11 (25%). Tots under two years old ride for free.

Special promotional discounts, such as 50% off companion fares, are often available, though they may come with restrictions or blackout periods. Check the website for current fare specials or ask when buying tickets.

Sample Greyhound fares and times:

LA–Anaheim ($10 to $16, 45 minutes to 1¼ hours, seven daily)

LA–San Francisco ($55, 7½ to 12¼ hours, 14 daily)

LA–San Diego ($11 to $22, 2½ to 3¼ hours, 20 daily)

LA–Santa Barbara ($9 to $19, 2¼ to 2¾ hours, four daily)

San Francisco–Sacramento ($5 to $22, two to 2½ hours, seven daily)

San Francisco–Santa Cruz ($14 to $21, three hours, three daily)

San Francisco–San Luis Obispo ($32 to $61, 6½ to seven hours, three daily)

Tickets & Reservations

It's easy to buy tickets online with a credit card, then pick them up (bring photo ID) at the terminal. You can also buy tickets over the phone or in person from a ticket agent. Greyhound terminal ticket agents also accept debit cards, traveler's checks (in US dollars) and cash.

Most boarding is done on a first-come, first-served basis. Buying tickets in advance does not guarantee you a seat on any particular bus unless you also purchase priority boarding (fee $5), available only at some terminals. Otherwise, arrive at least one hour before the scheduled departure to secure a seat; allow extra time on weekends and around holidays.

Travelers with disabilities who need special assistance should call ☎800-752-4841 (TDD/TTY ☎800-345-3109) at least 48 hours before traveling. Wheelchairs are accepted as checked baggage (or carry-on, if space allows) and service animals are allowed on board.

Car, Motorcycle & RV

California's love affair with cars runs deep for at least one practical reason: the state is so big, public transportation can't cover it. For flexibility and convenience, you'll probably want a car, but rental rates and gas prices can eat up a good chunk of your trip budget.

Automobile Associations

For 24-hour emergency roadside assistance, free maps and discounts on lodging, attractions, entertainment, car rentals and more, consider joining an auto club.

American Automobile Association (AAA; ☎877-428-2277; www.aaa.com) Walk-in offices throughout California, add-on coverage for RVs and motorcycles, and reciprocal agreements with some international auto clubs (eg CAA in Canada, AA in the UK) – bring your membership card from home.

Better World Club (☎866-238-1137; www.betterworldclub.com) Ecofriendly alternative auto club supports environmental causes and offers optional

emergency roadside assistance for cyclists.

Driver's Licenses

➡ Visitors may legally drive a car in California for up to 12 months with their home driver's license.

➡ If you're from overseas, an International Driving Permit (IDP) will have more credibility with traffic police and simplify the car-rental process, especially if your license doesn't have a photo or isn't written in English.

➡ To drive a motorcycle, you'll need a valid US state motorcycle license or a specially endorsed IDP.

➡ International automobile associations can issue IDPs, valid for one year, for a fee. Always carry your home license together with the IDP.

Fuel

➡ Gas stations in California, nearly all of which are self-service, are ubiquitous, except in national parks and some sparsely populated desert and mountain areas.

➡ Gas is sold in gallons (one US gallon equals 3.78L). At press time, the average cost for mid-grade fuel was more than $4.

Insurance

California law requires liability insurance for all vehicles. When renting a car, check your auto-insurance policy from home or your travel insurance policy to see if you're already covered. If not, expect to pay about $20 per day.

Insurance against damage to the car itself, called Collision Damage Waiver (CDW) or Loss Damage Waiver (LDW), costs another $10 to $20 or more per day. The deductible may require you to pay the first $100 to $500 for any repairs.

Some credit cards will cover CDW/LDW, provided you charge the entire cost of the car rental to the card. If there's an accident you may have to pay the rental-car company first, then seek reimbursement from the credit-card company.

Parking

➡ Parking is usually plentiful and free in small towns and rural areas, but often scarce and/or expensive in cities.

➡ When parking on the street, read all posted regulations and restrictions (eg street-cleaning hours, permit-only residential areas) and pay attention to colored curbs, or you may be ticketed and towed.

➡ You can pay municipal parking meters and sidewalk pay stations with coins (eg quarters) and sometimes credit or debit cards.

➡ Expect to pay $30 to $50 for overnight parking in a city lot or garage.

➡ Flat-fee valet parking at hotels, restaurants, nightclubs etc is common in major cities, especially LA and Las Vegas, NV.

Rental

CARS

To rent your own wheels, you'll typically need to be at least 25 years old, hold a valid driver's license and have a major credit card, *not* a check or debit card. A few companies may rent to drivers under 25 but over 21 for a hefty surcharge. If you don't have a credit card, occasionally you may be able to make a large cash deposit instead.

With advance reservations, you can often get an economy-size vehicle from around $30 per day, plus insurance, taxes and fees. Weekend and weekly rates are usually the most economical. Airport rental locations may offer lower rates, but have higher fees; if you buy a fly-drive package, local taxes may be extra. City-center branches sometimes offer free pickups and drop-offs.

Rates generally include unlimited mileage, but expect surcharges for additional drivers and one-way rentals. Some rental companies let you pre-pay for your last tank of gas; this is rarely a good deal, as prices are higher than at gas stations and you'd need to bring the car back almost on empty. Child or infant safety seats are legally required; reserve them when booking for about $10 per day.

If you'd like to minimize your contribution to California's polluted air, some major car-rental companies now offer 'green' fleets of hybrid or bio-fueled rental cars, but they're in short supply. Expect to pay significantly more for these models and reserve them well in advance.

To find and compare independent car-rental companies, as well as to search for cheaper long-term rentals, try **Car Rental Express** (www.carrentalexpress.com).

Alamo (☑877-222-9075; www.alamo.com)

Avis (☑800-633-3469; www.avis.com)

Budget (☑800-218-7992; www.budget.com)

Dollar (☑800-800-4000; www.dollar.com)

Enterprise (☑800-261-7331; www.enterprise.com)

Fox (☑800-225-4369; www.foxrentacar.com) Locations near LA, Burbank, San Diego, Orange County and San Francisco Bay Area airports.

Hertz (☑800-654-3131; www.hertz.com)

National (☑877-222-9058; www.nationalcar.com)

Rent-a-Wreck (☑877-877-0700; www.rentawreck.com) Minimum rental age and under-25 driver surcharges vary at a dozen locations, mostly around LA and the San Francisco Bay Area.

Simply Hybrid (☑888-359-0055, 323-653-0011; www.simplyhybrid.com) Rents hybrid, electric and flex-fuel vehicles in LA; ask about free delivery and pickup.

Super Cheap! Car Rental (www.supercheapcar.com) No surcharge for drivers aged 21 to 24; nominal daily fee applies for drivers aged 18 to 21 (full-coverage insurance required). Locations in the San Francisco Bay Area, LA and Orange County.

Thrifty (☑800-847-4389; www.thrifty.com)

Zipcar (☑866-494-7227; www.zipcar.com) Currently available in the San Francisco Bay Area, LA, San Diego, Sacramento, Santa Barbara and Santa Cruz; this car-sharing club charges usage fees (per hour or day), including free gas, insurance (a damage fee of up to $750 may apply) and limited mileage. Apply online (foreign drivers OK); application fee $25, annual membership from $60.

MOTORCYCLES

Motorcycle rentals and insurance are not cheap, especially if you've got your eye on a Harley. Depending on the model, renting a motorcycle costs $100 to $250 per day plus taxes and fees, including helmets, unlimited miles and liability insurance; one-way rentals and collision insurance (CDW) cost extra. Discounts may be available for multiday and weekly rentals. Security deposits range up to $2000 (credit card required).

California Motorcycle Adventures (☑800-601-5370, 650-969-6198; http://californiamotorcycleadventures.com; 2554 W Middlefield Rd, Mountain View; ⊙9am-6pm Mon-Fri, to 5pm Sat, 10am-5pm Sun) Harley-Davidson rentals in Silicon Valley.

Dubbelju (☑866-495-2774, 415-495-2774; www.dubbelju.com; 689a Bryant St, San Francisco; ⊙9am-6pm Mon-Sat) Rents Harley-Davidson, BMW and Japanese and Italian imported motorcycles, as well as scooters.

Eagle Rider (☑888-900-9901, 310-536-6777; www.eaglerider.com) Nationwide company with 10 locations in California, as well as Las Vegas, NV.

Route 66 Riders (☎888-434-4473, 310-578-0112; www.route66riders.com; 4161 Lincoln Blvd, Marina del Rey; ⏰10am-6pm Tue-Sat, 11am-5pm Sun) Harley-Davidson rentals in LA's South Bay.

RECREATIONAL VEHICLES

It's easy to find campgrounds throughout California with electricity and water hookups for RVs, but in big cities RVs are a nuisance, since there are few places to park or plug them in. RVs are cumbersome to drive and they burn fuel at an alarming rate. That said, they do solve transportation, accommodation and cooking needs in one fell swoop. Even so, there are many places in national and state parks and in the mountains that RVs can't go.

Book RV rentals as far in advance as possible. Rental costs vary by size and model, but you can expect to pay over $100 per day. Rates often don't include mileage, taxes, vehicle prep fees and bedding or kitchen kits. If pets are even allowed, a surcharge may apply.

Cruise America (☎800-671-8042, 480-464-7300; www.cruiseamerica.com) Nationwide RV rental company with almost two-dozen locations statewide.

El Monte (☎888-337-2214, 562-483-4956; www.elmonterv.com) With 15 locations across California, this national RV rental agency offers AAA discounts.

Escape Campervans (☎877-270-8267, 310-672-9909; www.escapecampervans.com) Awesomely painted campervans at economical rates in LA and San Francisco.

Happy Travel Campers (☎310-929-5666, 855-754-6555; www.camperusa.com) Campervan rentals in the San Francisco Bay Area and LA.

Jucy Rentals (☎800-650-4180; www.jucyrentals.com) Campervan rentals in San Francisco, LA and Las Vegas, NV.

Vintage Surfari Wagons (☎714-585-7565, 949-716-3135; www.vwsurfari.com) VW campervan rentals in Orange County.

Road Conditions & Hazards

For up-to-date highway conditions in California, including road closures and construction updates, dial ☎800-427-7623 or visit www.dot.ca.gov. For Nevada highways, call ☎877-687-6237 or check www.nvroads.com.

In places where winter driving is an issue, snow tires and tire chains may be required in mountain areas. Ideally, carry your own chains and learn how to use them before you hit the road. Otherwise, chains can usually be bought (but not cheaply) on the highway, at gas stations or in the nearest town. Most car-rental companies don't permit the use of chains and also prohibit driving off-road or on dirt roads.

In rural areas, livestock sometimes graze next to unfenced roads. These areas are typically signed as 'Open Range,' with the silhouette of a steer. Where deer and other wild animals frequently appear roadside, you'll see signs with the silhouette of a leaping deer. Take these signs seriously, particularly at night.

In coastal areas thick fog may impede driving – slow down and if it's too soupy, get off the road. Along coastal cliffs and in the mountains, watch out for falling rocks, mudslides and avalanches that could damage or disable your car if struck.

Road Rules

➡ Drive on the right-hand side of the road.

➡ Talking or texting on a cell phone without a hands-free device while driving is illegal.

➡ The use of seat belts is required for drivers, front-seat passengers and children under age 16.

➡ Infant and child safety seats are required for children under six years old or weighing less than 60lb.

➡ All motorcyclists must wear a helmet. Scooters are not allowed on freeways.

➡ High-occupancy (HOV) lanes marked with a diamond symbol are reserved for cars with multiple occupants, sometimes only during signposted hours.

➡ Unless otherwise posted, the speed limit is 65mph on freeways, 55mph on two-lane undivided highways, 35mph on major city streets and 25mph in business and residential districts and near schools.

➡ Except where indicated, turning right at a red stoplight after coming to a full stop is permitted, although intersecting traffic still has the right of way.

➡ At four-way stop signs, cars proceed in the order in which they arrived. If two cars arrive simultaneously, the one on the right has the right of way. When in doubt, politely wave the other driver ahead.

➡ When emergency vehicles (ie police, fire or ambulance) approach from either direction, carefully pull over to the side of the road.

➡ California has strict anti-littering laws; throwing trash from a vehicle may incur a $1000 fine.

➡ Driving under the influence of alcohol or drugs is illegal. It's also illegal to carry open containers of alcohol, even empty ones, inside a vehicle. Store them in the trunk.

Local Transportation

Except in cities, public transit is rarely the most convenient option, and coverage to outlying towns and suburbs can be sparse. However, it's usually cheap, safe and reliable.

Bicycle

➜ Cycling is a feasible way of getting around smaller cities and towns, but it's not much fun in traffic-dense areas like LA.

➜ San Francisco, Calistoga, Arcata, Sacramento, Santa Cruz, San Luis Obispo, Santa Barbara, Santa Monica and Coronado are among California's most bike-friendly communities, as rated by the **League of American Bicyclists** (www.bikeleague.org).

➜ Bicycles may be transported on many local buses and trains, sometimes during off-peak, non-commuter hours only.

Bus, Cable Car, Streetcar & Trolley

➜ Almost all cities and larger towns have reliable local bus systems (average $1 to $3 per ride). Outside of major metro areas, they may provide only limited evening and weekend service.

➜ San Francisco's extensive Municipal Railway (MUNI) network includes not only buses and trains, but also historic streetcars and those famous cable cars.

➜ San Diego runs trolleys around some neighborhoods and to the Mexican border.

Train

➜ LA's Metro is a combined, ever-expanding network of subway and light-rail. Metrolink commuter trains connect LA with surrounding counties.

➜ San Diego's *Coaster* commuter trains run from downtown and Old Town to Carlsbad, Encinitas, Solana Beach and Oceanside in the North County.

➜ To get around the San Francisco Bay Area, hop aboard Bay Area Rapid Transit (BART) or Caltrain.

Taxi

➜ Taxis are metered, with flag-fall fees of $2.50 to

> ### CALIFORNIA'S SCENIC RAILWAYS
>
> **Railtown 1897 State Historic Park** (p359)
>
> **Roaring Camp Railroads** (p466)
>
> **Skunk Train** (p234)
>
> **California State Railroad Museum** (p311)
>
> **Napa Valley Wine Train** (p168)
>
> **Yosemite Mountain Sugar Pine Railroad** (p420)

$3.50 to start, plus around $2 to $3 per mile. Credit cards may be accepted, but bring cash just in case.

➜ Taxis may charge extra for baggage and airport pickups.

➜ Drivers expect a 10% to 15% tip, rounded up to the next dollar.

➜ Taxis cruise the streets of the busiest areas in large cities, but elsewhere you may need to call a cab company.

Tours

Green Tortoise (☏800-867-8647, 415-956-7500; www.greentortoise.com) Youthful budget-backpacker trips utilize converted sleeping-bunk buses for adventure tours of California's national parks, northern redwood forests, southern deserts and Pacific Coast.

Road Scholar (☏800-454-5768; www.roadscholar.org) Formerly Elderhostel, this nonprofit organization offers educational trips – including bus and walking tours and outdoor activities like hiking and birding – for older adults.

Train

Amtrak (☏800-872-7245; www.amtrak.com) runs comfortable, if occasionally tardy, trains to major California cities and limited towns. At some stations Thruway buses provide onward connections. Smoking is prohibited on board trains and buses.

Amtrak routes within California:

California Zephyr Daily service from Emeryville (near San Francisco) via Davis and Sacramento to Truckee (near Lake Tahoe) and Reno, NV.

Capitol Corridor Links San Francisco's East Bay (including Oakland, Emeryville and Berkeley) and San Jose with Davis and Sacramento several times daily; on-board wi-fi available. Thruway buses connect to San Francisco, Auburn in the Gold Country, Truckee and Reno, NV.

Coast Starlight Chugs roughly north–south almost the entire length of the state. Daily stops include LA, Burbank, Santa Barbara, San Luis Obispo, Paso Robles, Salinas, San Jose, Oakland, Emeryville, Davis, Sacramento, Chico, Redding and Dunsmuir.

Pacific Surfliner Eight daily trains ply the San Diego–LA route, stopping at San Diego's North County beach towns and San Juan Capistrano and Anaheim in Orange County. Five trains continue north to Santa Barbara via Burbank, Ventura and Carpinteria, with three going all the way to San Luis Obispo. The trip itself, which hugs the coastline for much of the route, is a visual treat. On-board wi-fi may be available.

San Joaquin Several daily trains with on-board wi-fi run between Bakersfield and Oakland or Sacramento. Thruway bus connections include San Francisco, LA, Palm Springs, Yosemite National Park and Visalia (for Sequoia National Park).

Costs

Purchase tickets at train stations, by phone or online

(in advance for the cheapest prices). Fares depend on the day of travel, the route, the type of seating etc. Fares may be slightly higher during peak travel times (eg summer). Round-trip tickets typically cost the same as two one-way tickets.

Usually seniors over 62 years and students with an ISIC or Student Advantage Card receive a 15% discount, while up to two children aged two to 15 who are accompanied by an adult get 50% off. AAA members save 10%. Special promotions can become available anytime, so check the website or ask when making reservations.

Sample Amtrak coach-class fares and times:

Los Angeles–Oakland ($62, 12½ hours)

Los Angeles–San Diego ($37, 2¾ hours)

Los Angeles–Santa Barbara ($32, 2¾ hours)

San Diego–Anaheim ($28, 2¼ hours)

Emeryville–Sacramento ($29, 1¾ hours)

Emeryville–Truckee ($44, 6½ hours)

Reservations

Amtrak reservations can be made up to 11 months prior to departure. In summer and around holidays, trains sell out quickly, so book tickets as early as possible. The cheapest coach fares are usually for unreserved seats;

business-class fares come with guaranteed seats.

Travelers with disabilities who need special assistance, wheelchair space, transfer seats or accessible accommodations should call ☎800-872-7245 (TDD/TTY ☎800-523-6590), and also inquire about discounted fares when booking.

Train Passes

Amtrak's California Rail Pass costs $159 ($80 for children aged two to 15) and is valid on all trains (except certain long-distance routes) and most connecting Thruway buses for seven days of travel within a 21-day period. Passholders must reserve each leg of travel in advance and obtain hard-copy tickets prior to boarding.

Behind the Scenes

SEND US YOUR FEEDBACK

We love to hear from travelers – your comments keep us on our toes and help make our books better. Our well-traveled team reads every word on what you loved or loathed about this book. Although we cannot reply individually to your submissions, we always guarantee that your feedback goes straight to the appropriate authors, in time for the next edition. Each person who sends us information is thanked in the next edition – the most useful submissions are rewarded with a selection of digital PDF chapters.

Visit **lonelyplanet.com/contact** to submit your updates and suggestions or to ask for help. Our award-winning website also features inspirational travel stories, news and discussions.

Note: We may edit, reproduce and incorporate your comments in Lonely Planet products such as guidebooks, websites and digital products, so let us know if you don't want your comments reproduced or your name acknowledged. For a copy of our privacy policy visit lonelyplanet.com/privacy.

OUR READERS

Many thanks to the travelers who used the last edition and wrote to us with helpful hints, useful advice and interesting anecdotes:
Buzz Berridge, Tony Brett, Guillaume Croussette, Taryn Dickinson, Stephan Haagensen, Janet Noonan, Anne-Marie Tremblay, Margareta Troein Töllborn

AUTHOR THANKS

Sara Benson

Thanks to Suki Gear, Cliff Wilkinson, Alison Lyall and the entire Lonely Planet team, including my co-authors. Family and friends all over California generously gave me insider tips, good company on road trips and most importantly, spare rooms to crash in. Special thanks to my Golden Gate Bridge running partners Beth Kohn (also my Sierra Nevada trail guru) and Derek Wolfgram (home brewer and an expert advisor on Bay Area craft beer).

Andrew Bender

Thanks to Suki Gear, Cliff Wilkinson, Alison Lyall, Hilary Angel, Juan Flores, Joe Timko, Sarah Weinberg, Suzi Dennett and the good folks at the SPP Help Desk.

Alison Bing

Thanks to Suki Gear, Rana Freedman, Cliff Wilkinson, Katie O'Connell, Melissa Wong, and above all, Marco Flavio Marinucci, for making a Muni bus ride into the adventure of a lifetime.

Celeste Brash

Thanks first to my road trip buddies on this trip, Heather Griggs and Tevai Humbert (who is also my son). On the road I was given all the scoop by local heroes Grant Roden, Audie Theole, Freda Moon, John Vlahides, Kem Pence and Ken Pence. Thanks to Sara Benson for being so passionate about the region and the great Suki Gear for getting me on her last book.

Tienlon Ho

Thanks to Cliff Wilkinson, Suki Gear, Dianne and the SPP team, and Sara Benson for the opportunity and support along the way. Thanks to Ken Ho, Wenhuei Ho, Tienchin Ho, Richard Winters, Anli Winters, Mayli Winters, Alison Shinsato and, of course, Jon Adams for inspiration and everything else. Most importantly, thanks to the truly weary travelers who came before me, recorded or forgotten, who built the Central Valley, Gold Country and so, California.

Beth Kohn

Brava to Suki Gear for all her years of work on so many fantastic editions of this guide, and to Sara B, my running, hiking, baking and writing heroine! Thanks to Visit Oakland, Lisa Cesaro of DNC, Kari Cobb in Yosemite National Park and Lara Kaylor at Mammoth Lakes Tourism for their excellent on-the-ground assistance.

Jen and Dillon provided worthy campfire s'mores and Claude kept me (reasonably) sane throughout.

Adam Skolnick

Los Angeles is a city I love, full of people I love. LA is home. Still, it's never easy to dissect your own backyard, mostly because you usually know what you're missing. So thanks to Alma Lauer, Trisha Cole, Jessica Ritz, Nina Gregory, Burton Breznick, Tchaiko Omawale, Dan Cohn, Angel Payne, Christine Lazzaro, Liebe Geft, the folks at the Wende Museum, Michael McDowell, Alex Capriotti, and John Moore. Thanks also to all those wild seals, sea lions, dolphins and whales that keep us entertained in the water, and to the LP staff and my cohorts Sara Benson and Andy Bender.

John A Vlahides

I owe great thanks to my commissioning editor, Suki Gear, whom I miss; to my co-author, Sara Benson, for her always-sunny disposition; and to my editor Clifton Wilkinson for giving me free reign – I'm grateful. And to you, dear readers: please accept my most heartfelt gratitude for letting me be your guide to Wine Country. Have fun. I know you will!

ACKNOWLEDGEMENTS

Climate map data adapted from Peel MC, Finlayson BL & McMahon TA (2007) 'Updated World Map of the Köppen-Geiger Climate Classification', Hydrology and Earth System Sciences, 11, 1633¬44.

Illustration pp76-7 by Michael Weldon.

Cover photograph: Tunnel View, Yosemite Valley, Eddie Lluisma/Getty.

THIS BOOK

This 7th edition of *California* was researched and written by Sara Benson, Andrew Bender, Alison Bing, Celeste Brash, Tienlon Ho, Beth Kohn, Adam Skolnick and John A Vlahides. Sara, Andrew, Alison, Beth and John also wrote the previous edition, alongside Nate Cavalieri, Bridget Gleeson and Andrea Schulte-Peevers. This guidebook was commissioned in Lonely Planet's Oakland office, and produced by the following:

Commissioning Editor Suki Gear

Destination Editor Clifton Wilkinson

Coordinating Editor Simon Williamson

Product Editor Katie O'Connell

Assisting Editors Katie Connolly, Melanie Dankel, Jenna Myers, Rosie Nicholson, Monique Perrin, Saralinda Turner

Senior Cartographer Alison Lyall

Assisting Cartographers Julie Dodkins, Mick Garrett

Book Designer Wibowo Rusli

Cover Image Researcher Naomi Parker

Thanks to Imogen Bannister, Kate Chapman, Penny Cordner, Indra Kilfoyle, Claire Naylor, Karyn Noble, John Taufa, Samantha Tyson, Juan Wanita

Index

NOTES

Map Legend

Sights

- Beach
- Bird Sanctuary
- Buddhist
- Castle/Palace
- Christian
- Confucian
- Hindu
- Islamic
- Jain
- Jewish
- Monument
- Museum/Gallery/Historic Building
- Ruin
- Sento Hot Baths/Onsen
- Shinto
- Sikh
- Taoist
- Winery/Vineyard
- Zoo/Wildlife Sanctuary
- Other Sight

Activities, Courses & Tours

- Bodysurfing
- Diving
- Canoeing/Kayaking
- Course/Tour
- Skiing
- Snorkeling
- Surfing
- Swimming/Pool
- Walking
- Windsurfing
- Other Activity

Sleeping

- Sleeping
- Camping

Eating

- Eating

Drinking & Nightlife

- Drinking & Nightlife
- Cafe

Entertainment

- Entertainment

Shopping

- Shopping

Information

- Bank
- Embassy/Consulate
- Hospital/Medical
- Internet
- Police
- Post Office
- Telephone
- Toilet
- Tourist Information
- Other Information

Geographic

- Beach
- Hut/Shelter
- Lighthouse
- Lookout
- Mountain/Volcano
- Oasis
- Park
- Pass
- Picnic Area
- Waterfall

Population

- Capital (National)
- Capital (State/Province)
- City/Large Town
- Town/Village

Transport

- Airport
- BART station
- Border crossing
- Boston T station
- Bus
- Cable car/Funicular
- Cycling
- Ferry
- Metro/Muni station
- Monorail
- Parking
- Petrol station
- Subway/SkyTrain station
- Taxi
- Train station/Railway
- Tram
- Underground station
- Other Transport

Note: Not all symbols displayed above appear on the maps in this book

Routes

- Tollway
- Freeway
- Primary
- Secondary
- Tertiary
- Lane
- Unsealed road
- Road under construction
- Plaza/Mall
- Steps
- Tunnel
- Pedestrian overpass
- Walking Tour
- Walking Tour detour
- Path/Walking Trail

Boundaries

- International
- State/Province
- Disputed
- Regional/Suburb
- Marine Park
- Cliff
- Wall

Hydrography

- River, Creek
- Intermittent River
- Canal
- Water
- Dry/Salt/Intermittent Lake
- Reef

Areas

- Airport/Runway
- Beach/Desert
- Cemetery (Christian)
- Cemetery (Other)
- Glacier
- Mudflat
- Park/Forest
- Sight (Building)
- Sportsground
- Swamp/Mangrove

Tienlon Ho

Sacramento & Central Valley, Gold Country An Ohioan by birth but a Californian at stomach, Tienlon Ho has walked, run, climbed, crawled, tumbled, fished, swam, and eaten her way around the state enough times to say California is huge: and spectacular. Besides writing guides and books for Lonely Planet, she writes about food, environment, and technology for a number of publications. Follow her travels and more at tienlon.com and @tienlonho.

Beth Kohn

Marin County & the Bay Area, Lake Tahoe, Yosemite & the Sierra Nevada, California Wildlife, Best Hikes of the Sierra Nevada A lucky long-time resident of San Francisco, Beth lives to be playing outside or splashing in big puddles of water. For this guide, she hiked and biked Bay Area byways, backpacked Yosemite and Lake Tahoe in winter and soaked in myriad mountain view hot springs. An author of Lonely Planet's *Yosemite, Sequoia & Kings Canyon National Parks* and *Mexico* guides, you can see more of her work at www.bethkohn.com.

Adam Skolnick

Los Angeles Adam Skolnick has written about travel, culture, health, sports, human rights and the environment for Lonely Planet, *New York Times*, *Outside*, *Men's Health*, *Travel & Leisure*, Salon.com, BBC.com and ESPN.com. He has authored or co-authored 25 Lonely Planet guidebooks. Find him on Twitter and Instagram (@adamskolnick).

John A Vlahides

Napa & Sonoma Wine Country John A Vlahides co-hosts the TV series *Lonely Planet: Roads Less Travelled*, screening on National Geographic Channels International. John studied cooking in Paris, with the same chefs who trained Julia Child, and is also a former luxury-hotel concierge and member of Les Clefs d'Or, the international union of the world's elite concierges. He lives in San Francisco, sings tenor with the Grammy-winning San Francisco Symphony, and spends free time biking SF and skiing the Sierra. For more, see JohnVlahides.com, twitter.com/JohnVlahides.

Read more about John at:
lonelyplanet.com/members/johnvlahides

OUR STORY

A beat-up old car, a few dollars in the pocket and a sense of adventure. In 1972 that's all Tony and Maureen Wheeler needed for the trip of a lifetime – across Europe and Asia overland to Australia. It took several months, and at the end – broke but inspired – they sat at their kitchen table writing and stapling together their first travel guide, *Across Asia on the Cheap*. Within a week they'd sold 1500 copies. Lonely Planet was born. Today, Lonely Planet has offices in Franklin, London, Melbourne, Oakland, Beijing and Delhi, with more than 600 staff and writers. We share Tony's belief that 'a great guidebook should do three things: inform, educate and amuse'.

OUR WRITERS

Sara Benson

Coordinating Author, Santa Barbara County, Central Coast, California's Best Wine Countries, Southern California's Best Beaches After graduating from college, Sara jumped on a plane to California with just one suitcase and $100 in her pocket. After driving tens of thousands of miles to every corner of this state, she settled in a little beach town halfway between San Francisco and LA. She's an avid hiker, backpacker, cyclist and all-seasons outdoor enthusiast who has worked for the National Park Service in the Sierra Nevada Mountains. The author of more than 65 travel and nonfiction books, Sara is the lead writer for Lonely Planet's *California*, *California's Best Trips*, *Coastal California* and *Los Angeles, San Diego & Southern California* guides. Follow her latest adventures online at www.indietraveler.blogspot.com, www.indietraveler.net, @indie_traveler on Twitter and indietraveler on Instagram.

Read more about Sara at:
lonelyplanet.com/members/Sara_Benson

Andrew Bender

Disneyland & Orange County, San Diego & Around, Palm Springs & the Deserts Andy is a true Angeleno, not because he was born in Los Angeles but because he's made it his own. This native New Englander drove cross-country to work in film production, and eventually realized that the joy was in the journey (and writing about it). He writes the Seat 1A travel site for Forbes, and his writing has also appeared in the *Los Angeles Times*, in-flight magazines and over three dozen LP titles. Current obsessions: discovering SoCal's next great ethnic enclave, and photographing winter sunsets over the Pacific.

Alison Bing

San Francisco Over 10 guidebooks and 20 years in San Francisco, author Alison Bing has spent more time on Alcatraz than some inmates, become an aficionado of drag and burritos, and willfully ignored Muni signs warning that "safety requires avoiding unnecessary conversation."

Celeste Brash

North Coast & Redwoods, Northern Mountains Celeste's ancestors moved to Northern California in 1906 and this is the region she will always consider home. After 15 years in French Polynesia she now lives in the Pacific Northwest and was thrilled to head south to explore and imbibe the treasures of her old stomping grounds, hike snowy peaks, find petroglyphs in caves, be awed by redwoods and seduced by the wild coast. Find out more about Celeste at www.celestebrash.com.

OVER PAGE | MORE WRITERS

Published by Lonely Planet Publications Pty Ltd
ABN 36 005 607 983
7th edition – February 2015
ISBN 978 1 74220 619 6
© Lonely Planet 2015 Photographs © as indicated 2015
10 9 8 7 6 5 4 3 2 1
Printed in China

Although the authors and Lonely Planet have taken all reasonable care in preparing this book, we make no warranty about the accuracy or completeness of its content and, to the maximum extent permitted, disclaim all liability arising from its use.